THE PRINCIPLES OF LAND LAW

THE PRINCIPLES OF LAND LAW

First Edition

EMMA LEES

*Lecturer in Environmental and Property Law,
University of Cambridge*

Great Clarendon Street, Oxford, OX2 6DP,
United Kingdom

Oxford University Press is a department of the University of Oxford.
It furthers the University's objective of excellence in research, scholarship,
and education by publishing worldwide. Oxford is a registered trade mark of
Oxford University Press in the UK and in certain other countries

© Oxford University Press 2020

The moral rights of the author have been asserted

Impression: 1

All rights reserved. No part of this publication may be reproduced, stored in
a retrieval system, or transmitted, in any form or by any means, without the
prior permission in writing of Oxford University Press, or as expressly permitted
by law, by licence or under terms agreed with the appropriate reprographics
rights organization. Enquiries concerning reproduction outside the scope of the
above should be sent to the Rights Department, Oxford University Press, at the
address above

You must not circulate this work in any other form
and you must impose this same condition on any acquirer

Public sector information reproduced under Open Government Licence v3.0
(http://www.nationalarchives.gov.uk/doc/open-government-licence/open-government-licence.htm)

Published in the United States of America by Oxford University Press
198 Madison Avenue, New York, NY 10016, United States of America

British Library Cataloguing in Publication Data
Data available

Library of Congress Control Number: 2019952617

ISBN 978-0-19-881099-5

Printed in Great Britain by
Ashford Colour Press Ltd, Gosport, Hampshire

Links to third party websites are provided by Oxford in good faith and
for information only. Oxford disclaims any responsibility for the materials
contained in any third party website referenced in this work.

To Felicity and Edward

OUTLINE CONTENTS

Table of Cases — xvii
Table of Statutes — xxv
Table of International and EU Sources — xxviii

1. INTRODUCTION—PRINCIPLES AND THEMES OF LAND LAW — 1
2. PERSONAL AND PROPERTY RIGHTS IN LAND — 25
3. REGISTERED AND UNREGISTERED LAND — 57
4. FORMALITIES AND THE CREATION OF RIGHTS IN LAND — 81
5. LAND REGISTRATION — 115
6. ADVERSE POSSESSION — 162
7. IMPLIED TRUSTS — 191
8. PROPRIETARY ESTOPPEL — 233
9. FREEHOLD ESTATE — 273
10. LEASES — 290
11. MORTGAGES — 331
12. EASEMENTS AND PROFITS — 376
13. FREEHOLD COVENANTS — 417
14. ESTATE CONTRACTS, OPTIONS TO PURCHASE, AND RIGHTS OF PRE-EMPTION — 446
15. PRIORITIES — 462
16. CO-OWNERSHIP — 496
17. PROPERTY LAW AND HUMAN RIGHTS — 545
18. TORTS — 582

Index — 607

DETAILED CONTENTS

Table of Cases — xvii
Table of Statutes — xxv
Table of International and EU Sources — xxviii

1 INTRODUCTION—PRINCIPLES AND THEMES OF LAND LAW — 1

1.1 Introduction — 1
1.2 The Land Law System—A Brief Review — 3
    1.2.1 What are the legal rights which can exist in relation to land, and what do they allow a person to do? — 3
    1.2.2 How are these rights created and transferred? — 4
    1.2.3 How do such rights interact when there is a conflict in relation to land? — 5
1.3 The Principles of Land Law — 6
    1.3.1 Principle 1: Certainty — 6
    1.3.2 Principle 2: Sensitivity to context — 9
    1.3.3 Principle 3: Transactability — 11
    1.3.4 Principle 4: Systemic and individual effects — 13
    1.3.5 Principle 5: Recognition of the social effects of rules — 14
1.4 The Logic of Land Law — 17
    1.4.1 Legal and equitable rights — 17
    1.4.2 Interests under a trust — 19
    1.4.3 Estates in land — 20
1.5 Conclusion — 21
    1.5.1 How to navigate this book — 22
    Table of Definitions — 23
    Further Reading — 24

2 PERSONAL AND PROPERTY RIGHTS IN LAND — 25

2.1 Introduction — 25
2.2 Interests in Land — 26
    2.2.1 Nature of property rights — 26
    2.2.2 Licences — 33
    2.2.3 Property rights and third party effects — 42
2.3 What is Land? — 46
    2.3.1 Land—corporeal — 46
    2.3.2 Land—incorporeal, and use, occupation, and possession — 51
2.4 Relativity of Title — 52
2.5 Conclusion — 53
    Principles — 54
    Table of Definitions — 55
    Further Reading — 56

3 REGISTERED AND UNREGISTERED LAND — 57

- 3.1 Introduction — 57
- 3.2 Land Law in the 20th and 21st Centuries — 59
- 3.3 Registered Land — 60
  - 3.3.1 Ambition in the Land Registration Act 2002 — 61
  - 3.3.2 Mirror principle — 64
  - 3.3.3 Insurance principle — 66
  - 3.3.4 Curtain principle — 67
- 3.4 Unregistered Land — 70
  - 3.4.1 Legal interests—universal application — 71
  - 3.4.2 Registration in unregistered land—the Land Charges Act 1972 — 71
  - 3.4.3 Purchaser for value without notice — 73
  - 3.4.4 Problems of proof in unregistered land — 78
- 3.5 Conclusion — 79
  - Principles — 79
  - Table of Definitions — 80
  - Further Reading — 80

4 FORMALITIES AND THE CREATION OF RIGHTS IN LAND — 81

- 4.1 Introduction — 81
- 4.2 Purposes of Formality Rules — 82
- 4.3 The Rules — 86
  - 4.3.1 Contracts — 87
  - 4.3.2 Deeds — 106
  - 4.3.3 Interests under a trust — 111
  - 4.3.4 Dispositions of equitable interests — 112
- 4.4 Conclusion — 112
  - Principles — 112
  - Table of Definitions — 114
  - Further Reading — 114

5 LAND REGISTRATION — 115

- 5.1 Introduction — 115
- 5.2 Registration and Rights-Creation — 116
  - 5.2.1 Interests which much be registered — 117
  - 5.2.2 Owner's powers and guarantee of title — 124
  - 5.2.3 Boundaries — 126
- 5.3 Errors on the Register — 127
  - 5.3.1 The system of alteration and rectification in outline — 127
  - 5.3.2 Types of registration error — 129
  - 5.3.3 The statutory framework — 131
  - 5.3.4 The framework in practice — 134
  - 5.3.5 Conclusions on land registration—title by registration or registration of title — 154
  - 5.3.6 Availability of indemnities — 155
- 5.4 Reform of the Rectification and Indemnity Provisions — 157
  - 5.4.1 Law Commission proposals — 157
  - 5.4.2 The advent of E-conveyancing? — 158

	5.5 Conclusion	159
	Principles	160
	Table of Definitions	161
	Further Reading	161

6 ADVERSE POSSESSION — 162

6.1 Introduction	162
6.2 Adverse Possession and Unregistered Land	163
6.2.1 Possession	163
6.2.2 Adverse	170
6.2.3 Consequences of adverse possession	172
6.3 Adverse Possession and Registered Land	174
6.4 Adverse Possession and Leases	181
6.4.1 Adverse possession against a tenant	182
6.4.2 Adverse possession by a tenant against his landlord	182
6.4.3 Adverse possession by a tenant against a third party	183
6.5 Adverse Possession and Criminal Law	184
6.6 Explanations for Adverse Possession	185
6.7 Conclusion	188
Principles	189
Table of Definitions	190
Further Reading	190

7 IMPLIED TRUSTS — 191

7.1 Introduction	191
7.2 Express Trusts	192
7.3 Statutory Trusts	194
7.4 Constructive Trusts	195
7.4.1 The history of the constructive trust	195
7.4.2 *Stack v Dowden* and *Jones v Kernott*	200
7.4.3 Post-*Stack* case law—the rules in practice	208
7.4.4 The 'rules'	214
7.5 Resulting Trusts	220
7.5.1 Explanation for resulting trusts	221
7.5.2 When will a resulting trust arise?	223
7.6 Reform	228
7.7 Conclusion	230
Principles	231
Table of Definitions	232
Further Reading	232

8 PROPRIETARY ESTOPPEL — 233

8.1 Introduction	233
8.2 Requirements of Estoppel	234
8.2.1 Estoppel by acquiescence	235
8.2.2 Estoppel by representation	236
8.2.3 Promise or assurance-based estoppel	237

	8.2.4 Unconscionability	252
8.3	Consequences of Estoppel	257
	8.3.1 The equity arising by estoppel	257
	8.3.2 Remedy	258
8.4	Effect of the Estoppel on Third Parties	262
	8.4.1 Burden of an estoppel	262
	8.4.2 Benefit of the estoppel	264
8.5	Relationship between Estoppel and Formalities	265
8.6	Relationship between Estoppel and Constructive Trusts	266
8.7	Conclusion	270
	Principles	271
	Table of Definitions	272
	Further Reading	272

9 FREEHOLD ESTATE 273

9.1	Introduction	273
9.2	The Content of the Freehold Estate	274
	9.2.1 Limitations on use	275
	9.2.2 Geographical scope	276
	9.2.3 The right of reversion and rights of re-entry	278
9.3	Multiple Freeholds and Relativity of Title	279
9.4	The Transfer and Registration of Freehold Interests in Land	282
9.5	Flying Freehold	283
9.6	Commonhold	284
9.7	Termination of the Freehold Estate	285
9.8	Conclusion	287
	Principles	288
	Table of Definitions	289
	Further Reading	289

10 LEASES 290

10.1	Introduction	290
10.2	The Nature of the Lease	291
	10.2.1 Exclusive possession	292
	10.2.2 Term	299
	10.2.3 Rent	302
	10.2.4 Intention to create a legal relationship	302
10.3	Creation of Leases	303
10.4	Forms of Leases	305
	10.4.1 Periodic tenancies	305
	10.4.2 Tenancies at will	307
	10.4.3 The '*Bruton* lease'	308
10.5	Relationship Between Landlord and Tenant and Bringing a Lease to an End	311
	10.5.1 Covenants between landlord and tenant	311
	10.5.2 Terminating leases—effluxion of time	318

10.5.3 Terminating leases—forfeiture and notices		319
10.5.4 Terminating leases—surrender		321
10.5.5 Security of tenure		322
10.5.6 Tenants' fixtures at the end of a lease		327
10.6 Sub-Leases, Concurrent Leases, and Reversionary Interests		327
10.7 Conclusion		328
Principles		328
Table of Definitions		329
Further Reading		330

11 MORTGAGES — 331

11.1 Introduction	331
11.2 Nature of Mortgages	332
11.3 Formalities for the Creation of a Mortgage	333
11.4 Remedies of the Legal Mortgagee	336
11.4.1 Action on the contract debt	336
11.4.2 Foreclosure	337
11.4.3 Right to possession	338
11.4.4 Power of sale	350
11.4.5 Power to appoint a receiver	355
11.5 Remedies—Equitable Mortgages and Charges	356
11.6 Position of the Mortgagor	358
11.6.1 Clogs, fetters, and other limitations on rights to redeem	359
11.6.2 Interest rates	363
11.6.3 Consumer protection legislation	364
11.6.4 Undue influence	364
11.7 Mortgages and Third Parties	368
11.7.1 Multiple mortgages	368
11.7.2 Subrogation	369
11.7.3 Mortgages and trust interests	370
11.7.4 Mortgages and tenants	372
11.7.5 Mortgages and purchasers	373
11.8 Conclusion	373
Principles	373
Table of Definitions	375
Further Reading	375

12 EASEMENTS AND PROFITS — 376

12.1 Introduction	376
12.2 The Nature of Easements and Profits	377
12.2.1 What rights can be easements?	377
12.2.2 What rights can be profits?	392
12.3 The Creation of Easements	394
12.3.1 Express easements	394
12.3.2 Implied easements	395
12.3.3 By prescription	404

xiv Detailed Contents

12.4 The Use of Easements	405
12.5 Extinction of Easements	410
12.6 Transfers, Priorities, and Third Parties	410
12.6.1 Express legal easements	410
12.6.2 Implied legal easements	411
12.6.3 Express equitable easements	412
12.6.4 Implied equitable easements	414
12.7 Reform of the Law of Easements	414
12.8 Conclusion	415
Principles	415
Table of Definitions	416
Further Reading	416

13 FREEHOLD COVENANTS   417

13.1 Introduction	417
13.2 The Nature of Freehold Covenants	418
13.3 Creation and Interpretation of Freehold Covenants	421
13.4 Transmissibility of Freehold Covenants	422
13.4.1 Liability and remedies of original covenantor and original covenantee	422
13.4.2 Running of the benefit—successor in title to original covenantee sues original covenantor	427
13.4.3 Running of the benefit—person deriving title from the original covenantee sues original covenantor	432
13.4.4 Running of the burden—restrictive covenants	435
13.5 Positive Covenants	438
13.6 Modification and Discharge of Covenants—Section 84 LPA 1925	441
13.7 Reform of Freehold Covenants	442
13.8 Conclusion	444
Principles	444
Table of Definitions	445
Further Reading	445

14 ESTATE CONTRACTS, OPTIONS TO PURCHASE, AND RIGHTS OF PRE-EMPTION   446

14.1 Introduction	446
14.2 Estate Contracts	447
14.2.1 Interests other than freehold and leasehold estate	447
14.2.2 Nature of the right which arises	448
14.3 Options to Purchase	455
14.4 Rights of Pre-Emption	458
14.5 Conclusion	460
Principles	460
Table of Definitions	461
Further Reading	461

15 PRIORITIES — 462

- 15.1 Introduction — 462
- 15.2 First in Time—The Basic Priority Rule — 464
- 15.3 Purchaser of a Legal Estate who Later Becomes Registered—The Special Priority Rule — 465
  - 15.3.1 Short legal leases of a duration of 7 years or less — 466
  - 15.3.2 Relevant social housing leases — 467
  - 15.3.3 The interests of a person in actual occupation — 468
  - 15.3.4 Implied legal easements and profits — 478
  - 15.3.5 Other unregistered interests which may override — 478
- 15.4 Priorities on First Registration — 479
- 15.5 Rules Applicable to Registered Charges — 480
- 15.6 Exceptional Cases of Priority — 480
  - 15.6.1 Official searches — 480
  - 15.6.2 Waiver and consent — 480
  - 15.6.3 Implied consent—the acquisition mortgage — 482
  - 15.6.4 Overreaching — 487
  - 15.6.5 Subrogation — 488
- 15.7 Consequences of a Loss of Priority — 488
- 15.8 Conclusion — 491
  - Principles — 493
  - Table of Definitions — 494
  - Further Reading — 495

16 CO-OWNERSHIP — 496

- 16.1 Introduction — 496
- 16.2 Interests Under a Trust of Land — 497
  - 16.2.1 The nature of a trust of land — 497
  - 16.2.2 Creation of trusts of land — 500
  - 16.2.3 Rights and powers of trustees — 501
  - 16.2.4 Registered land and the use of restrictions — 503
- 16.3 Forms of Co-Ownership — 503
  - 16.3.1 Legal title — 503
  - 16.3.2 Equitable title — 506
  - 16.3.3 Severance — 507
- 16.4 Disputes Relating to Co-Owned Land — 517
  - 16.4.1 Applications under section 14 TOLATA 1996 — 517
  - 16.4.2 Rights of occupation and occupation rent — 529
  - 16.4.3 Priority disputes between co-owners and third parties — 531
- 16.5 Conclusion — 541
  - Principles — 541
  - Table of Definitions — 544
  - Further Reading — 544

17 PROPERTY LAW AND HUMAN RIGHTS 545

17.1 Introduction 545
17.2 Modes of Influence—Property and Human Rights 547
   17.2.1 Sources 547
   17.2.2 Human Rights 'bolstering' property law 548
   17.2.3 Human rights and property law—conflicts 551
   17.2.4 Mechanics 553
   17.2.5 Understanding horizontal effect 557
17.3 Areas of Influence 559
   17.3.1 Adverse possession 559
   17.3.2 Possession actions against public authority tenants and licensees 560
   17.3.3 Actions for possession by private landowners in the context of leases and licences 573
   17.3.4 Actions for possession against trespassers 574
   17.3.5 Mortgagee's remedies 575
17.4 Conclusion 579
   Principles 579
   Table of Definitions 581
   Further Reading 581

18 TORTS 582

18.1 Introduction 582
18.2 Trespass 583
   18.2.1 What constitutes a trespass? 583
   18.2.2 Who can sue in trespass? 583
   18.2.3 Defences to an action in trespass 584
   18.2.4 Remedies 584
18.3 Nuisance 587
   18.3.1 The role of nuisance 587
   18.3.2 Categories of nuisance 591
   18.3.3 Locality principle and planning permission 597
   18.3.4 Who can sue? 600
   18.3.5 Who can be sued in nuisance? 602
   18.3.6 Defences to nuisance 602
   18.3.7 Remedies 603
18.4 *Rylands v Fletcher* 604
18.5 Conclusion 604
   Principles 605
   Table of Definitions 606
   Further Reading 606

Index 607

TABLE OF CASES

Abbahall Ltd v Smee [2002] EWCA Civ 1831, [2003] 1 WLR 1472 . . . **283–4**

Abbey National v Cann [1991] 1 AC 56 (HL) . . . 371, 449, 450, 451, 472, 476, **482–483**, 484, 485, 486, 493

Adams v Lindsell 106 ER 250, (1818) 1 B & Ald 681 (KBD) . . . 510

AG Securities v Vaughan and Antoniades v Villiers [1990] 1 AC 417 (HL) . . . **295–6**, 297, 298, 504

Agarwala v Agarwala [2013] EWCA Civ 1763, [2014] 2 FLR 1069 . . . 208, **209–10**

Ajibade v Bank of Scotland & Endeavor Personal Finance HM Land Adjudicator, REF/2006/0163/0174 . . . 137

Alliance & Leicester v Slayford [2001] 1 All ER (Comm) 1 (CA) . . . **336–7**, 345, 346

Amsprop Trading Ltd v Harris Distribution Ltd [1997] 1 WLR 1025 (ChD) . . . 426

Annetts v Adeleye [2018] EWCA Civ 555, [2018] 2 P & CR DG9 . . . 410

Antoine v Barclays Bank [2018] EWHC 395 (Ch) . . . 152, **153**

Ashburn Anstalt v Arnold [1989] Ch. 1 (CA) . . . 33, **40–1**, 302

Ashe v Mumford (2001) 33 HLR 67 . . . 223

Asher v Whitlock (1865–66) LR 1 QB 1 (QBD) . . . 172

Aslan v Murphy [1990] 1 WLR 766 (CA) . . . 295, 297

Aspden v Elvy [2012] EWHC 1387 (Ch), [2012] 2 FLR 807 . . . 219

Austerberry v Oldham Corp (1885) 29 Ch D 750 (CA) . . . 435, 439

Aveling v Knipe 34 ER 580, (1815) 19 Ves Jr 441 . . . 223

Bailey v Stephens 142 ER 1077, (1862) 12 CB NS 91 (Court of Common Pleas) . . . 381

Baker v Craggs [2016] EWHC 3250 (Ch), [2017] 2 WLR 1483; [2018] EWCA Civ 1126 . . . 449–50, 451, 453

Bank of Ireland v Bell [2001] 2 All ER (Comm) 920 (CA) . . . 511, 524, 526, 540

Bankers Trust Co v Namdar [1995] NPC 139 (ChD) . . . 511

Bannister v Bannister [1948] 2 All ER 133 . . . 192

Barca v Mears [2004] EWHC 2170 (Ch), [2004] All ER (D) 153 . . . 528, 577

Barclays Bank Plc v Zaroovabli [1997] Ch. 321, ChD . . . 477

Barclays Bank v Guy (no 1) [2008] EWCA Civ 452, [2008] 2 EGLR 74 . . . 134, 135–6, 152, 160

Barclays Bank v Guy (no 2), [2010] EWCA Civ 1396, [2011] 1 WLR 681 . . . 136–7

Barclays Bank v O'Brien [1994] 1 AC 180 (HL) . . . 365, 366–7

Barnes v Philips [2015] EWCA Civ 1056, [2016] 2 FLR 1292 . . . 211

Barr v Biffa Waste Services Ltd [2012] EWCA Civ 312, [2013] QB 455 . . . 15, 587

Batchelor v Marlow [2001] EWCA Civ 1051, [2003] 1 WLR 764 . . . 386, 389, 390, 391

Batt v Adams (2001) 82 P & CR 32 . . . 166

Baxter v Mannion [2011] EWCA Civ 120, [2011] 1 WLR 1594 . . . 150, 176–7

Begum v Issa, unreported, recorded on westlaw as 2014 WL 5833780 . . . 478

Bernstein of Leigh v Skyviews [1978] QB 479 (QBD) . . . 46, 47, 277, 278

Berrisford v Mexfield Housing Co-operative Ltd [2011] UKSC 52, [2012] 1 AC 955 . . . 300, 301, 306

Best v Chief Land Registrar [2015] EWCA Civ 17; [2016] QB 23 . . . 185

Beswick v Beswick [1966] Ch 538 (CA) . . . 424–5

Beswick v Beswick [1968] AC 58 (HL) . . . 424, 425

BHP Petroleum Great Britain Ltd v Chesterfield Properties Ltd [2001] EWCA Civ 1797, [2002] Ch 194 . . . 316

Binions v Evans [1972] Ch 359 (CA) . . . 39–40

Birmingham Citizens Permanent Building Society v Caunt [1962] Ch 883 (ChD) . . . 348

Birmingham City Council v Lloyd [2012] EWCA Civ 969, [2012] HLR 44 . . . 566, 574

Birmingham Midshires Mortgage Services Ltd v Sabherwal (2000) 80 P & CR 256 . . . 264, 305, 488

Bishop v Blake [2006] EWHC 831 (Ch), [2006] 17 EG 113 (CS) . . . 353–4

Bocardo SA v Star Energy UK [2010] UKSC 35, [2011] 1 AC 380 . . . 46, 47, 277, 278

Bradbury v Taylor [2012] EWCA Civ 1208, [2013] WTLR 29 . . . 251

Bridges v Mees (1957) Ch . . . 451

Brocklesby v Temperance Permanent Building Society [1895] AC 173 (HL) . . . 535, 536

Bruton v London & Quadrant Housing Trust [2001] 1 AC 406 (HL) . . . 293, 308, 309–11
Buckinghamshire County Council v Moran [1990] Ch 623 (CA) . . . 169, 170
Burgess v Rawnsley [1975] Ch 429 (CA) . . . 506, 512–13, 514
Butler v Standard Telephones & Cables Ltd [1940] 1 KB 399 (KB) . . . 591

Cambridge Water Co Ltd v Eastern Counties Leather Plc [1994] 2 AC 264 (HL) . . . 596
Campbell v Griffin [2001] EWCA Civ 990, (2001) 82 P & CR DG23 . . . 246, 248, 252, 262
Canadian Pacific Railway v The King [1931] AC 414 . . . 34, 35
Chandler v Kerley [1978] 1 WLR 693 (CA) . . . 37, 43, 54
Chaudhary v Yavuz [2011] EWCA Civ 1314, [2013] Ch 249 . . . 261, 264, 413, 474
Chelsea Yacht and Boat v Pope [2000] 1 WLR 1941 (CA) . . . 48
Cheltenham & Gloucester v Appleyard [2004] EWCA Civ 291, [2004] 13 EG 127 (CS) . . . 369, 370
Cheltenham & Gloucester v Krausz [1997] 1 WLR 1558 (CA) . . . 344–5, 346, 347
Cheltenham & Gloucester v Norgan [1996] 1 WLR 343 (CA) . . . 342–3
Cherry Tree Investments v Landmain [2012] EWCA Civ 736, [2013] Ch. 305 . . . 154
Chun v Ho [2002] EWCA Civ 1075, [2003] 1 P & CR DG2 . . . 248, 249
Church of England Building Society v Piskor [1954] Ch 553 (CA) . . . 483
Church of Jesus Christ of the Latter-Day Saints v Price [2004] EWHC 3245 (QB) . . . 588
City of London Building Society v Flegg [1988] AC 54 (HL) . . . 533, 534
City Permanent Building Society v Miller [1952] Ch 840 (CA) . . . 467
Cityland and Property (Holdings) Ltd v Dabrah [1968] Ch 166 (ChD) . . . 361
Clarke v Meadus [2010] EWHC 3117 (Ch), [2011] 1 P & CR DG18 . . . 193, 215, 219
Claughton v Charalambous [1999] 1 FLR 740 (ChD) . . . 529
Cobbe v Yeoman's Row Management Ltd [2008] UKHL 55; [2008] 1 WLR 1752 . . . 5, 9, 105, 238–9, 240, 241, 242, 243, 250, 256, 266, 268, 269, 271
Cocking v Eacott [2016] EWCA Civ 140, [2016] QB 1080 . . . 602
Collie v Marr [2017] UKPC 17, [2017] 3 WLR 1507 . . . 10, 205, 212, 213–14, 215, 216, 220, 222, 226
Colls v Home and Colonial Stores Ltd [1904] AC 179 (HL) . . . 385
Coombes v Smith [1986] 1 WLR 808 (Ch) . . . 251
Copeland v Greenhalf [1952] Ch 488 (ChD) . . . 388, 390, 391
Corbett v Halifax [2002] EWCA Civ 1849, [2003] 1 WLR 964 . . . 352–3
Cousens v Rose (1871) LR 12 Eq 366 (Chancery) . . . 385
Coventry (t/a RDC Promotions) v Lawrence [2014] UKSC 13, [2014] AC 822 . . . 15, 387, 388, 594, 598–600, 603, 605
Cowan v Scargill [1985] Ch. 270 (ChD) . . . 502
Crabb v Arun DC [1976] Ch 179 (CA) . . . 261, 264, 395
Crago v Julian [1992] 1 WLR 372 . . . 98
Crest Nicholson Residential (South) Ltd v McAllister [2004] EWCA Civ 410, [2004] 1 WLR 2409 . . . 430, 431
Crow v Wood [1971] 1 QB 77 (CA) . . . 386
Cuckmere Brick Co v Mutual Finance [1971] Ch 949 (CA) . . . 353
Cumberland Consolidated Holdings Ltd v Ireland [1946] KB 264 (CA) . . . 450

D'eyncourt v Gregory (No.1) (1866–67) LR 3 Eq 382 (Ch) . . . 50
Dalton v Henry Angus & Co (1881) 6 App Cas 740 . . . 386
Davies v Davies [2016] EWCA Civ 463, [2016] 2 P & CR 10 . . . 259–60
Dear v Reeves [2001] EWCA Civ 277, [2002] Ch 1 . . . 459
DHN Food Distributors v Tower Hamlets LBC [1976] 1 WLR 852 (CA) . . . 40
Dillwyn v Llewelyn 45 ER 1285, (1862) 4 De GF & J 517 . . . 267
Doberman v Watson Ref. HC–2017–000370 . . . 430, 431
Drewell v Towler 110 ER 268, (1832) 3 B & Ad 735 (King's Bench) . . . 382, 386
Dyer v Dyer 30 ER 42 (1788) 2 Cox Eq Cas 92 . . . 223

Earl of Sefton v Tophams Ltd (No.2) [1967] 1 AC 50 (HL) . . . 437
Eaton Mansions (Westminster) Ltd v Stinger Compania De Inversion SA [2013] EWCA Civ 1308, [2014] HLR 4 . . . 585–6
Edwards v Fashion 24 ER 156, (1712) Prec Ch 332 . . . 223
Edwards v Lloyds TSB [2004] EWHC 1745 (Ch), [2005] 1 FCR 139 (ChD) . . . 523, 524–5, 527
Elitestone v Morris [1997] 1 WLR 687 (HL) . . . 48, 49–50

Elliston v Reacher [1908] 2 Ch 665 . . . 432
Entick v Carrington (1765) 2 Wilson, KB 275, 95 ER 807; 19 Howell's State Trials 1029 (1765) . . . 288, 547, 548–9
Errington v Errington [1952] 1 KB 290 (CA); Chandler v Kerley [1978] 1 WLR 693 (CA) . . . 36, 38–9, 41, 54, 267
Everitt v Budhram [2009] EWHC 1219 (Ch), [2010] Ch 170 . . . 528
Eves v Eves [1975] 1 WLR 1338 . . . 196, 199

Fairclough v Swan Brewery Co Ltd [1912] AC 565 (PC) . . . 359
Fairweather v St Marylebone [1963] AC 510 (HL) . . . 279
Federated Homes Ltd v Mill Lodge Properties Ltd [1980] 1 WLR 594 (CA) . . . 420, 428, 429, 430, 433
First National Bank v Achampong [2003] EWCA Civ 487, [2004] 1 FCR 18 . . . 523, 524, 525
Firstpost Homes v Johnson [1995] 1 WLR 1567 . . . 92, 93, 94
Fitzkriston LLP v Panayi [2008] EWCA Civ 283, [2008] L & TR 26 (CA (Civ Div)) . . . 97
Fitzpatrick v Sterling Housing Association Ltd [2001] 1 AC 27 . . . 554
Fitzwilliam v Richall Holdings [2013] EWHC 86 (Ch), [2013] 1 P & CR 19 . . . 142, 143–4, 145, 227
Foskett v McKeown [2001] 1 AC 102 (HL) . . . 499
Four Maids v Dudley Marshall [1957] Ch 317 . . . 349
Fowkes v Pascoe (1874–75) LR 10 Ch App 343 . . . 223
Fowler v Barron [2008] EWCA Civ 377, [2008] 2 FLR 831 . . . 211–12

G&C Kreglinger v New Patagonia Meat & Cold Storage Co Ltd [1914] AC 25 (HL) . . . 360
Gardner v Davis [1999] EHLR 13 (CA) . . . 394
Geary v Rankine [2012] EWCA Civ 555, [2012] 2 FLR 1409 . . . 208–9, 501
Generator Developments Ltd v Lidl UK GmbH, [2018] EWCA Civ 396, [2018] 2 P & CR 7 . . . 244
Ghaidan v Godin–Mendoza [2004] UKHL 30, [2004] 2 AC 557 . . . 554–5, 558, 574
Giles v Tarry [2012] EWCA Civ 837, [2012] 2 P & CR 15 . . . 408, 409
Gillett v Holt [2001] Ch 210 (CA) . . . 238, 240, 243, 244, 249, 250, 251, 252, 255, 256, 261, 266
Gissing v Gissing [1971] AC 886 (HL) . . . 192, 196, 197, 198–9, 203, 204, 219, 481

Gold Harp Properties Ltd v MacLeod [2014] EWCA Civ 1084, [2015] 1 WLR 1249 . . . 132, 133, 138, 150, 151, 152, 158
Golden Ocean Group Ltd v Salgaocar Mining Industries Pvt Ltd [2012] EWCA Civ 265; [2012] 1 WLR 3674 . . . 93, 94
Goldman v Hargrave [1967] 1 AC 645 (PC) . . . 597
Good Harvest Partnership LLP v Centaur Services Ltd [2010] EWHC 330 (Ch), [2010] Ch 426 . . . 317
Goodhart v Hyett (1883) 25 ChD 182 (ChD) . . . 386
Goodman v Gallant [1986] Fam 106 . . . 193, 214
Gott v Lawrence, [2016] EWHC 68 (Ch) . . . 166
Gould v Kemp 39 ER 959, (1834) 2 My & K 304 (Ch) . . . 506, 511, 515
Governing Body of Henrietta Barnett School v Hampstead Garden Suburb Institute (1995) 93 LGR 470 . . . 34, 35
Grant v Edwards [1986] Ch. 638 (CA) . . . 199, 203
Graysim Holdings Ltd v P&O Property Holdings Ltd [1996] AC 329 (HL) . . . 324
Greasley v Cooke [1980] 1 WLR 1306 (CA) . . . 247
Gregory v Piper (1929) 8 BC 591 . . . 583

Habberfield v Habberfield [2019] EWCA Civ 890 . . . 260
Halifax Plc v Curry Popeck (A Firm) [2008] EWHC 1692 (Ch), [2009] 1 P & CR DG3 . . . 490–1, 492, 493, 538
Halsall v Brizell [1957] Ch 169 (ChD) . . . 438, 439, 440
Halsey v Esso Petroleum Co Ltd [1961] 1 WLR 683 (QB) . . . 587, 592
Hammersmith & Fulham v Monk [1992] 1 AC 478, 24 HLR 206 HL . . . 306–307, 562, 571
Harris v Flower (1904) 91 LT 816 . . . 393, 408, 409
Harris v Goddard [1983] 1 WLR 1203 (CA) . . . 507
Heaney v Kirkby [2015] UKUT 0178 (TCC) . . . 166
Helby v Matthews [1895] AC 471 (HL) . . . 457
Helden v Strathmore Ltd [2011] EWCA Civ 452, [2011] HLR 41 . . . 89, 90
Henry v Henry (St Lucia) [2010] UKPC 3, [2010] 1 All ER 98 . . . 251, 252, 258, 259, 263
Henthorn v Fraser [1892] 2 Ch. 27 (CA) . . . 510
Herbert v Doyle [2010] EWCA Civ 1095, [2011] 1 EGLR 119 . . . 268
Hervey v Smith 69 ER 510, (1855) 1 Kay & J 389 (ChD) . . . 386

Heywood v Mallalieu (1883) 25 ChD 357 (ChD) . . . 386
Hill v Tupper 159 ER 51, (1863) 2 Hurl & C 121 . . . 382, 383, 385
Hilton v Plustitle [1989] 1 WLR 149 (CA) . . . 297
Holland v Hodgson (1871–72) LR 7 CP 328 (Court of Exchequer) . . . 48
Horsham Properties v Beech [2008] EWHC 2327 (Ch), [2009] 1 WLR 1255 . . . 348–9, 576
Hounslow LBC v Powell [2011] UKSC 8, [2011] 2 AC 186 . . . 563, 564, 565, 566, 570, 571
Hounslow LBC v Powell [2011] UKSC 8, [2011] 2 AC 186 . . . 15
Hounslow v Twickenham Garden Developments [1971] Ch 233 (Ch) . . . 36–7
HSBC v Dyche [2009] EWHC 2954 (Ch), [2010] 2 P & CR 4 . . . 537, 538
Hunt v Luck [1901] 1 Ch 45 (Chd) . . . 75
Hunt v Soady [2007] EWCA Civ 366 . . . 251
Hunter v Canary Wharf [1997] AC 655 (HL) . . . 387, 600–2

IAM Group v Chowdery [2012] EWCA Civ 505, [2012] 2 P & CR 13 . . . 180–1
IDC Group Ltd v Clark (1993) 65 P & CR 179 (CA) . . . 41, 299
In re Connolly Brothers (no 2) [1912] 2 Ch 25 (CA) . . . 483
Inglewood v Baker [2002] EWCA Civ 1733, [2003] 2 P & CR 23 . . . 170
International Tea Stores v Hobbs [1903] 2 Ch 165 . . . 387, 400, 402
Investor Compensation Scheme v West Bromwich Building Society [1998] 1 WLR 896 . . . 421
Inwards v Baker [1965] 2 QB 29 (CA) . . . 267

J Pereira Fernandes SA v Mehta [2006] EWHC 813 (Ch); [2006] 1 WLR 1543 . . . 94
JA Pye (Oxford) Ltd v Graham [2002] UKHL 30, [2003] 1 AC 419 . . . 168, 169, 170, 171, 182, 187, 190, 559–60
Javad v Aqil [1991] 1 WLR 1007 (CA) . . . 308
Jennings v Rice [2002] EWCA Civ 159, [2003] 1 P & CR 8 . . . 252, 259, 261, 264
Jones v Kernott [2011] UKSC 53, [2012] 1 AC 776 . . . 10, 195, 196, 200, 202, 204–6, 207, 211, 212, 215, 218, 220, 232, 481, 501, 515
Jones v Morgan [2001] EWCA Civ 995, [2002] 1 EGLR 125 . . . 359–60, 361
Jones v Smith (1841) 1 Hare 43, 66 ER 943 . . . 75–6
Joyce v Rigolli [2004] EWCA Civ 79, [2004] 1 P & CR DG22 . . . 91, 100–2

Kay v Lambeth LBC [2006] UKHL 10, [2006] 2 AC 465 . . . 309, 310
Kaye v Massbetter (1992) 24 HLR 28 (CA) . . . 297
Keay v Morris Homes Ltd [2012] EWCA Civ 900, [2012] 1 WLR 2855 . . . 103, 104
Kent v Kavanagh [2006] EWCA Civ 162, [2007] Ch. 1 . . . 402
Keppell v Bailey 39 ER 1042, (1834) 2 My & K 517 . . . 443
Kinane v Mackie-Conteh [2005] EWCA Civ 45, [2005] 2 P & CR DG3 . . . 269
Kinch v Bullard [1999] 1 WLR 423 (ChD) . . . 508–9
King v David Allen & Sons Billposting Ltd [1916] 2 AC 54 (HL) . . . 38, 39
King v Suffolk County Council FTT Ref No 2015/0867, 13 October 2016 . . . 166
Kingsnorth Finance v Tizard [1986] 1 WLR 783 (Chd) . . . 76–7, 78
Kling v Keston Properties (1985) 49 P & CR 212 (Ch) . . . 459
Knights Construction v Roberto Mac REF/2009/1459, [2011] 2 EGLR 123 . . . 138–9, 140, 146, 152
Knightsbridge Estates v Byrne [1940] AC 613 (HL) . . . 359
Knightsbridge Property Development Corp (UK) Ltd v South Chelsea Properties Ltd [2017] EWHC 2730 (Ch) . . . 150

Lace v Chantler [1944] KB 368 (CA) . . . 299, 300
Lambeth LBC v Blackburn [2001] EWCA Civ 912, (2001) 33 HLR 74 . . . 283
Laskar v Laskar [2008] EWCA Civ 347, [2008] 1 WLR 2695 . . . 10, 212, 213, 215, 223
Law v Haider [2017] UKUT 212 (TCC) . . . 459
Laws v Florinplace Ltd [1981] 1 All ER 659 . . . 588
Lemaitre v Davis (1881) 19 Ch D 281 . . . 386
Lester v Woodgate [2010] EWCA Civ 199, [2010] 2 P & CR 21 . . . 265
Link Lending Ltd v Hussein [2010] EWCA Civ 424, [2010] 2 EGLR 55 . . . 470, 471, 472, 473, 476
Lippiatt v South Gloucestershire Council [2000] QB 51 (CA) . . . 602
Lloyd v Dugdale [2001] EWCA Civ 1754, [2002] 2 P & CR 13 . . . 41
Lloyds Bank v Carrick [1996] 4 All ER 630 (CA) . . . 450, 451, 454
Lloyds Bank v Rosset [1991] 1 AC 107 (HL) . . . 9, 196, 197, 199–200, 203, 204, 211, 219

London & Blenheim Estates Ltd v Ladbroke Retail Parks Ltd [1994] 1 WLR 3 . . . 379, 380, 386, 389
London and South Western Railway Company v Gomm (1882) 20 ChD 562 . . . 457
London Borough of Hounslow v Minchinton (1997) 74 P & CR 221 (CA) . . . 170
London CC v Allen [1914] 3 KB 642 (CA) . . . 435
London Diocesan Fund v Avonridge Property Co Ltd [2005] UKHL 70, [2005] 1 WLR 3956 . . . 315, 316, 318, 329
Looe Fuels Ltd v Looe Harbour Commissioners [2008] EWCA Civ 414, [2007] All ER (D) 263 . . . 97

Macepark (Whittlebury) Ltd v Sargeant [2003] EWHC 427 (Ch), [2003] 1 WLR 2284 . . . 408
Malayan Credit v Jack Chia [1986] AC 549 . . . 223
Maleverer v Spinke (1583) Dyer 53b . . . 584
Malik v Fassenfelt [2013] EWCA Civ 798, [2013] 3 EGLR 99 . . . 574, 575
Malory v Cheshire Homes [2002] EWCA Civ 151, [2002] Ch 216 . . . 142–3, 144, 145, 227
Manchester Airport v Dutton [2000] QB 133 (CA) . . . 42, 43–4, 46, 53, 54, 583, 586, 606
Manchester City Council v Pinnock [2011] UKSC 6, [2011] 2 WLR 220 . . . 15, 563, 564, 565, 570, 571, 573
Manchester Ship Canal v Vauxhall [2018] EWCA Civ 1100 . . . 42, 45–6
Manjang v Drammeh (1991) 61 P & CR 194 (PC) . . . 385, 398
Marten v Flights Refuelling Ltd [1962] Ch 115. . . . 436
Mason v Shrewsbury & Hereford Railway Company (1870–71) LR 6 QB 578 . . . 386
Matchmove v Dowding [2016] EWCA Civ 1233 . . . 106, 268–9
Mayor of London v Hall [2010] EWCA Civ 817, [2011] 1 WLR 504 . . . 42, 44–5
McAdams Homes Ltd v Robinson [2004] EWCA Civ 214 . . . 407
McDonald v McDonald [2016] UKSC 28, [2017] AC 273 . . . 554, 558, 573, 574, 575
Medforth v Blake [2000] Ch 86 (CA) . . . 356
Meretz Investments NV v ACP Ltd (No 3) (2006) . . . 354
Metropolitan Asylum District Managers v Hill (No.2) (1881) 6 App Cas 193 (HL) . . . 588, 592
Mew v Tristmire [2011] EWCA Civ 912, [2012] 1 WLR 852 . . . 48
Midland Bank Plc v Farmpride Hatcheries Ltd (1980) 260 EG 493 (CA) . . . 40

Midland Bank v Cooke [1995] 4 All ER 562 (CA) . . . 203
Mikeover v Brady [1989] 3 All ER 618 (CA) . . . 297
Miller v Emcer Products Ltd [1956] Ch 304 (CA) . . . 382, 386
Miller v Jackson [1977] QB 966 (CA) . . . 594–5
Mirza v Mirza [2009] EWHC 3 (Ch), [2009] 2 FLR 115 . . . 103, 104, 335
Mitchell v Potter [2005] EWCA Civ 88 . . . 393
Moncrieff v Jamieson [2007] UKHL 42, [2007] 1 WLR 2620 (HL) . . . 386, 389–90, 391
Moody v Steggles (1879) 12 ChD 261 (ChD) . . . 382, 383, 385, 386
Moore v British Waterways Board [2013] EWCA Civ 73; [2013] Ch 488 . . . 167
Moore v Moore [2018] EWCA Civ 2669, [2019] 1 FLR 1277 . . . 261
Morrells of Oxford Ltd v Oxford United Football Club Ltd [2001] Ch 459 (CA) . . . 437
Morris–Garner v One Step (Support) Ltd [2018] UKSC 20 . . . 586
Mortgage Corporation v Shaire [2001] Ch 743 . . . 519–20, 526
Mortgage Express v Lambert [2016] EWCA Civ 555, [2017] Ch 93 . . . 264, 304, 305, 487–8
MRA Engineering v Trimster (1988) 56 P & CR 1 (CA) . . . 385, 398
Multiservice Bookbinding Ltd v Marden [1979] Ch 84 (ChD) . . . 361–2
Mulvaney v Gough [2002] EWCA Civ 1078, [2003] 1 WLR 360 . . . 381, 386, 387

Nash v Paragon Finance [2001] EWCA Civ 1466, [2002] 1 WLR 685 . . . 363
National Provincial Bank v Ainsworth [1965] AC 1175 . . . 4, 27–8, 33, 39, 90, 392
Newton Abbott Cooperative Society Ltd v Williamson & Treadgold Ltd [1952] Ch 286 (ChD) . . . 434, 436
Nicholls v Lan [2006] EWHC 1255 (Ch), [2007] 1 FLR 744 . . . 577, 578
Nickerson v Barraclough [1981] Ch 426 (CA) . . . 385, 398
NRAM v Evans [2017] EWCA Civ 1013, [2018] 1 WLR 639 . . . 149–50, 152, 153

Odogwu v Vastguide [2009] EWHC 3565 (Ch) . . . 137
Ofulue v Bossert [2008] EWCA Civ 7, [2009] Ch 1 . . . 560
Ottey v Grundy [2003] EWCA Civ 1176; [2003] WTLR 1253 . . . 245, 247, 248, 261, 264
Oxley v Hiscock [2004] EWCA Civ 546, [2005] Fam 211 . . . 200, 201, 202, 203

P & A Swift Investments v Combined English Stores Group [1989] AC 632 . . . 428, 436
P&S Platt Ltd v Crouch [2003] EWCA Civ 1110, [2004] 1 P & CR 18 . . . 383, 402, 403
Paddington Building Society v Mendelsohn (1985) 50 P & CR 244 (CA) . . . 372, 480, 481
Palk v Mortgage Services Funding [1993] Ch 330 (CA) . . . 344, 345–6, 347
Paragon Finance v Pender [2005] EWCA Civ 760, [2005] 1 WLR 3412 . . . 363–4
Parshall v Hackney [2013] EWCA Civ 240, [2013] Ch 568 . . . 140, 141, 157, 279, 280–1
Pascoe v Turner [1979] 1 WLR 431 (CA) . . . 261, 267
Patel v K&J Restaurants Ltd [2010] EWCA Civ 1211, [2011] L & TR 6 (CA (Civ Div)) . . . 320–1
Paton v Todd [2012] EWHC 1248 (Ch) . . . 137
Pettitt v Pettitt [1970] AC 777 (HL) . . . 196, 197–8, 203, 204, 219
Phipps v Pears [1965] 1 QB 76 (CA) . . . 384, 387
Pilcher v Rawlins (1872) 7 Ch App 259 . . . 73
Pole v Peake [1998] EG 125 (CS) (CA) . . . 394
Port of London Authority v Ashmore [2010] EWCA Civ 30; [2010] 1 All ER 1139 . . . 167
Powell v McFarlane (1979) 38 P & CR 452 . . . 164, 165, 166, 168, 170
Pritchard v Briggs [1980] Ch 338 (CA) . . . 459
Prudential Assurance v London Residuary Body [1992] 2 AC 386 (HL) . . . 299–300, 301, 306
Pwllbach Colliery Co Ltd v Woodman [1915] AC 634 (HL) . . . 592

Qazi v Harrow LBC [2003] UKHL 43, [2004] 1 AC 983 . . . 561, 562, 565, 576
Quigley v Masterson [2011] EWHC 2529 (Ch), [2012] 1 All ER 1224 . . . 509

R (Best) v Chief Land Registrar [2015] EWCA Civ 17, [2016] QB 23 . . . 15
R (Gloucester CC) v Secretary of State for the Environment, Transport and the Regions (2001) 82 P & CR 15 (QBD) . . . 406
R v Oxfordshire CC Ex p Sunningwell PC [2000] 1 A.C. 335 . . . 404
R v Williams (1735) Bunb 342 . . . 506
Raby v Ridehalgh 44 ER 41, (1855) 7 De GM & G 104 (QBD) . . . 502
Ramnarace v Lutchman [2001] UKPC 25, [2001] 1 WLR 1651 . . . 171
Ramsden v Dyson (1866) LR 1 HL 129 (HL) . . . 256
Ramsey v Love [2015] EWHC 65 (Ch) . . . 94
Re Basham [1986] 1 WLR 1498 (Ch) . . . 238
Re Citro [1991] Ch 142 (CA) . . . 517, 518

Re Ellenborough Park [1956] Ch 131 (CA) . . . 31, 378, 379, 380, 381, 385
Re Gorman [1990] 1 WLR 616 (DC) . . . 511
Re North East Property Buyers Litigation (Scott v Southern Pacific Mortgages Ltd) [2014] UKSC 52, [2015] AC 38 . . . 371, 449, 451, 460, 472, 482, 483–4, 485, 486
Re Potters Oils (No 2) [1986] All ER 890 . . . 355
Re Union of London and Smith's Bank Ltd's Conveyance [1933] Ch 611 (CA) . . . 433
Re White Rose Cottage [1965] Ch. 940 . . . 357
Re Wilks [1891] 3 Ch. 59, 61 (ChD) . . . 511
Red House Farms (Thorndon) Ltd v Catchpole (1976) 121 Sol Jo 136, [1977] 2 EGLR 125 . . . 166
Regency Villas Title Ltd v Diamond Resorts (Europe) Ltd [2018] UKSC 57 . . . 21, 378, 381–2, 384, 386, 387, 389, 391, 392, 415
Rhone v Stephens [1994] 2 AC 310 (HL) . . . 439–40, 441
Roake v Chadha [1984] 1 WLR 40 (ChD) . . . 430
Robinson v Kilvert (1889) 41 ChD 88 (CA) . . . 593
Ropaigealach v Barclays Bank [2000] QB 263 (CA) . . . 339, 343
Rosefair v Butler REF/2013/0046, 49, 50, 51, 52, 53 . . . 490, 491, 493
Roy v Roy [1996] 1 FLR 541 . . . 193, 214
Royal Bank of Scotland Plc v Etridge (No.2) [2001] UKHL 44, [2002] 2 AC 773 . . . 367–8
Rylands v Fletcher (1868) LR 3 HL 330 . . . 582, 587, 604

Saeed v Plustrade [2001] EWCA Civ 2011, [2002] 2 P & CR 19 . . . 413, 474
Samuel v Jarrah Timber & Wood Paving Corp Ltd [1904] AC 323 (HL) . . . 359
Santander UK Plc v Fletcher [2018] EWHC 2778 (Ch), [2019] 2 P & CR 4 . . . 368
Saunders v Vautier 49 ER 282, (1841) 4 Beav 115 . . . 224
Scandinavian Trading Tanker Co AB v Flota Petrolera Ecuatoriana (The Scaptrade), [1983] 2 AC 694 (HL) . . . 45
Scmlla Properties Ltd v Gesso Properties (BVI) Ltd [1995] BCC 793 . . . 286, 287
Scott v Corby BC & West Kent Housing Association v Haycraft [2012] EWCA Civ 969, [2012] HLR 44 . . . 566–7
Security Trust Co v Royal Bank of Canada [1976] AC 503 (PC) . . . 483
Seddon v Smith (1877) 36 LT 168 (CA) . . . 167, 170
Shelfer v City of London Electric Lighting Co (No.1) [1895] 1 Ch 287 (CA) . . . 592, 603

Silven Properties Ltd v Royal Bank of Scotland Plc [2003] EWCA Civ 1409, [2004] 1 WLR 997 . . . 353

Sims v Dacorum BC [2014] UKSC 63, [2015] AC 1336 . . . 306–7, 348, 571, 572, 580

Sledmore v Dalby (1996) 72 P & CR 196 (CA) . . . 258, 261

Smith v Davies [2011] EWCA Civ 1603, [2012] 1 FLR 1177 (CA) . . . 514

Smith v Giddy [1904] 2 KB 448 (KB) . . . 591

Smith v River Douglas Catchment Board [1949] 2 KB 500 (CA) . . . 423, 424–5, 429

Sookraj v Samaroo [2004] UKPC 50, [2005] 1 P&CR DG11 . . . 448, 450, 454

Sovmots Investments Ltd v Secretary of State for the Environment [1979] AC 144 (HL) . . . 402

Spiro v Glencrown [1991] Ch 537 (ChD) . . . 456–7

Springette v Defoe [1992] 2 FLR 388 . . . 199, 223

St Helens Smelting Co v Tipping 11 ER 1483, (1865) 11 HL Cas 642 (HL) . . . 591, 592

Stack v Dowden [2007] UKHL 17, [2007] AC 432 . . . 10, 192, 194, 195, 196, 197, 200–3, 204, 205, 207, 208, 210, 211, 212, 213, 214, 215, 217, 218, 219, 222, 224, 228, 230, 232, 267, 474, 501

Stewart v Lancashire Mortgage Corp HM Land Adjudicator, REF/2009/0086 and 1556 . . . 137

Stone v Bolton [1949] 1 All ER 237 (HC) . . . 593

Street v Mountford [1985] 1 AC 809 . . . 30, 292, 294, 298, 299

Sturges v Bridgman (1879) 11 ChD 852 (CA) . . . 597

Suggitt v Suggitt [2012] EWCA Civ 1140, [2012] WTLR 1607 . . . 253–4, 261

Swift 1st v Chief Land Registrar [2015] EWCA Civ 330, [2015] Ch 602 . . . 143, 144, 145, 146, 148, 155, 156, 157, 227

Swift 1st v Colin [2011] EWHC 2410 (Ch), [2012] Ch 206 . . . 334, 357–8

Tailby v Official Receiver (1888) 13 AppCas 523 . . . 486

Taylor Fashions v Liverpool Victoria Trustees [1982] QB 133 (Ch) . . . 252

Thamesmead Town v Allotey (1998) 30 HLR 1052 (CA) . . . 440

Thompson v Foy [2009] EWHC 1076 (Ch), [2010] 1 P & CR 16 . . . 471–2, 475–6, 477, 493

Thompson v Hurst [2012] EWCA Civ 1752, [2014] 1 FLR 238 . . . 208, 209

Thompson–Schwab v Costaki [1956] 1 WLR 335 (CA) . . . 588

Thorner v Major [2009] UKHL 18; [2009] 1 WLR 776 . . . 5, 9, 10, 236, 238, 240–1, 242, 243, 252, 253, 256, 260, 261, 266, 268, 270

Thurrock BC v West [2012] EWCA Civ 1435, [2013] HLR 5 . . . 566, 567–8, 569

Tichborne v Weir (1891) 94 All Er Rep 449 (CA) . . . 172

Toff v McDowell (1993) 25 HLR 650 . . . 285

Tootal Clothing Ltd v Guinea Properties Management Ltd (1992) 64 P & CR 452 . . . 103, 104

Tower Bridge Yacht and Boat Company v London Port Authority [2013] EWHC 3084 (Ch) . . . 167

Tower Hamlets London Borough Council v Barrett 2006 1 P&CR 9 . . . 167, 169

Tulk v Moxhay 41 ER 1143, (1848) 2 Ph 774 (ChD) . . . 312, 420, 435

UBS Estate ManagementUBS Asset Management Ltd v Crown Estate Commissioners [2011] EWHC 3368 (Ch) v Crown Estate Commissioners . . . 286, 287

Umma v Appu [1939] AC 136 . . . 166

United Bank of Kuwait v Sahib [1997] Ch. 107. . . . 103

Uratemp Ventures Ltd v Collins [2001] UKHL 43, [2002] 1 AC 301 . . . 325, 341, 473

Vincent v Premo Enterprises [1969] 2 QB 609 . . . 108

Virdi v Chana [2008] EWHC 2901 (Ch), [2008] NPC 130 . . . 386, 391, 392

Walker v Burton [2013] EWCA Civ 1228, [2014] 1 P & CR 9 . . . 150, 151

Walsh v Lonsdale (1882) 21 ChD 9 . . . 106, 283, 334, 357, 421, 447

Walter v Selfe 64 ER 849, (1851) 4 De G & Sm 315 . . . 595

Ward v Kirkland [1967] Ch 194 (ChD) . . . 386

Wayling v Jones (1995) 69 P & CR 170 (CA) . . . 245, 247

Wheeldon v Burrows (1879) 12 ChD 31 . . . 396, 403, 404, 416

White v City of London Brewery Company (1889) 42 Ch D 237 . . . 350

White v White [2003] EWCA Civ 924, [2004] 2 FLR 231 . . . 521

Williams & Glyn's Bank Ltd v Boland [1981] AC 487 (HL) . . . 143, 481, 533, 534, 535, 536

Williams v Hensman 70 ER 862, (1861) 1 John & H 546 (QBD) . . . 507, 515, 516

Williams v Wellingborough BC 73 LGR 33 (ChD) . . . 352

Willmott v Barber (1880) 15 ChD 96 (ChD) . . . 235

Winter Garden Theatre v Millennium Productions [1948] AC 173 (HL) . . . 34, 35

Wishart v Credit and Mercantile Plc [2015] EWCA Civ 655, [2015] 2 P & CR 15 . . . 533, 534, 535, 536
Wong v Beaumont Property Trust [1965] 1 QB 173 (CA) . . . 386, 399
Wood v Waddington [2015] EWCA Civ 538, [2015] 2 P & CR 11 . . . 401, 402, 403
Wood v Watkin [2019] EWHC 1311 (Ch) . . . 225
Wright v Macadam [1949] 2 KB 744 (CA) . . . 386, 390, 400
Wrotham Park Estates Co v Parkside Homes [1974] 1 WLR 798 . . . 436

Yaxley v Gotts [2000] Ch 162 (CA) . . . 257, 268, 269
Yeates v Line [2012] EWHC 3085 (Ch), [2013] Ch 363 . . . 100–2
York v Stone 91 ER 146, (1709) 1 Salk 158 (KBD) . . . 511

Zarb v Parry [2011] EWCA Civ 1306, [2012] 1 WLR 1240 . . . 180

TABLE OF STATUTES

Administration of Justice Act 1970, section 36 . . . 339, 340, 341, 342, 343, 346, 347, 348, 349, 350, 375, 576
   section 36(1) . . . **340**
   section 36(2) . . . **341**
Administration of Justice Act 1973 . . . 343
   section 8 . . . 343

Coal Industry Act 1994 . . . 479
Commonhold and Leasehold Reform Act 2002 . . . 284, 319
Commons Act 2006, part I . . . 120
Companies Act 2006, section 1012 . . . 286
Consumer Credit Act 1974 . . . 364
Consumer Credit Act 2006 . . . 356
   section 64 . . . 364
Consumer Rights Act 2015 . . . 364
Contracts (Rights of Third Parties) Act 1999 . . . 422, **426**
   section 7(3) . . . 426
Conveyancing Act 1882 . . . 74
Criminal Damage Act 1971 . . . 184
Criminal Law Act 1977 . . . 339, 340
   section 6 . . . 184, 340, 350, 375
   section 6(1) . . . **340**
   section 6(4)(a) . . . 340
   section 7 . . . 184

Deregulation Act 2015 . . . 326

Equality Act 2010, section 199 . . . 225

Financial Services and Markets Act 1986 . . . 98
Financial Services and Markets Act 2000 . . . 95, 98, 113, 340, 364

Housing Act 1985
   schedule 2 . . . 326
   section 80 . . . 326
   section 81 . . . 326
Housing Act 1988 . . . 309
   schedule 2 . . . 325
   section 21 . . . 326
Housing Act 1996 . . . 299
Housing and Planning Act 2016 . . . 325, 326
Human Rights Act 1998 . . . 187, 306, 349, 529, 547, 548, 553, 557, 558, 559, 560, 580
   section 3 . . . 187, 348, 553, 554, 555, 556, 558, 560, 561, 563
   section 3(1) . . . **553**, 554
   section 4 . . . **555**, 556, 558, 560, 561, 563
   section 6 . . . 187, 348, **556**, 557, 558, 559, 561, 563, 573, 574, 575
   section 6(3)(a) . . . 556

Infrastructure Act 2015 . . . 277
Insolvency Act 1986, section 178 . . . 286
   section 335A . . . 336, 518, 523, 528, 558, 562, 577, 578

Land Charges Act 1972 . . . 70, 71, 72, 73, 75, 438
   section 2 . . . 72
   section 3(1) . . . 73
   section 4(6) . . . 454
Land Registration Act 1925 . . . 227
Land Registration Act 2002, schedule 1 . . . 118, 119, 120, 263, 479, 492
   schedule 1, paragraph 1 . . . 122
   schedule 1, paragraph 2 . . . 401, 413, 480, 493, 539
   schedule 1, paragraph 3 . . . 411, 480
   schedule 3 . . . 65, 123, 263, 476, 477, **478–479**, 480, 492
   schedule 3, paragraph 1 . . . 122, **466**
   schedule 3, paragraph 1A . . . **467**
   schedule 3, paragraph 2 . . . 263. 371, 373, 401, 413, 438, 458, 459, 466, 474, 475, 476, 477, 539
   schedule 3, paragraph 3 . . . 411, 478
   schedule 4 . . . 65, 124, **131–2**, 139, 146, 149, 159, 469
   schedule 4, paragraph 1 . . . 127, 128, **131**, 132
   schedule 4, paragraph 2 . . . 127, 128, **132**, 136, 139, 153
   schedule 4, paragraph 3 . . . 128, **132**
   schedule 4, paragraph 6 . . . 138
   schedule 4, paragraph 8 . . . **132**, 152
   schedule 6 . . . **175–6**, 177, 181, 183, 185
   schedule 6, paragraph 1 . . . 176
   schedule 6, paragraph 11 . . . 181
   schedule 6, paragraph 2 . . . 176
   schedule 6, paragraph 3 . . . 176
   schedule 6, paragraph 4 . . . 176
   schedule 6, paragraph 5 . . . 127, **178–9**, 180, 181, 189
   schedule 6, paragraph 6 . . . 177
   schedule 6, paragraph 9 . . . 177
   schedule 8 . . . 65, 131, **133–4**, 138, 139, 146, 156, 159

schedule 8, paragraph 1 . . . 128, **133**, 145
schedule 8, paragraph 10 . . . 128, **134**
schedule 8, paragraph 5 . . . 128, **133**
schedule 8, paragraph 6 . . . **134**
section 4 . . . **117**, 118, 282, 287, 335, **466**, 479
section 4(1)(g) . . . 333
section 11 . . . 118
section 12 . . . 118
section 19 . . . 119
section 23 . . . 65, 118, 121, 124, **125**, 126, 131, 159, 501, 503, 517, 540
section 24 . . . 65, 118, 121, 124, **125**, 126, 131, 159, 501, 503
section 27 . . . 117, **120**, 282, 335, 395, 400, 475
section 27(1) . . . 477, 492
section 27(2) . . . 110
section 27(2)(f) . . . 333, 475
section 28 . . . 159, 263, 368, 435, 438, 464, 480, 485, 490, 491, 492, 539, 540
section 29 . . . 158, 159, 263, 368, 412, 435, 438, **465**, 468, 475, 476, 480, 485, 488, 489, 490, 491, 492, 493, 539
section 29(1) . . . 475, 477
section 30 . . . 263, 368, 369, 371, 435, 438, 480, 492
section 32(1) . . . 438
section 40 . . . 503
section 48 . . . 368, 369
section 58 . . . 65, 69, 121, **124**, 125, 126, 129, 131, 135, 136, 138, 146, 159, 227, 281
section 60 . . . 126, 179
section 90 . . . 467
section 115 . . . 91, 458
section 116 . . . 257, 262, 263, 395
Land Registration Act, section 34 . . . 122
    section 95 . . . 175
    section 96 . . . 175
Land Registration Rules 2003, rule 189 . . . 176
    rule 190 . . . 176
Landlord and Tenant Act 1954 . . . 308, 318, 323
Landlord and Tenant Covenants Act 1995 . . . 311, 315, 316, 317, 329
    section 2 . . . **312**
    section 3 . . . **313**
    section 3(6) . . . 316
    section 5 . . . **314**
    section 6 . . . **314**
    section 8 . . . 314, 315
    section 16 . . . **317**
Law of Property (Miscellaneous Provisions) Act 1989, section 1 . . . 87, 114, 282, 333, 335, 421
    section 1(2) . . . 107
    section 1(2)(b) . . . 120, 121
    section 1(2)(e) . . . 120, 121

section 1(3) . . . 107, 109
section 2 . . . 87, 90, 91, 92, 93, 97, 101, 102, 105, 112, 114, 234, 239, 265, 268, 269, 271, 282, 303, 333, 334, 335, 356, 357, 395, 421, 448, 450, 456, 457, 458, 510
section 2(1) . . . 89, 90, 91, 93, 94, 95, 97, 98, 99, 100, 101, 102, 103, 104
section 2(3) . . . 94
section 2(5) . . . 95, 96, 98, 265
Law of Property Act 1925, section 1 . . . 60, 71, 121, 123, 392, 395
section 1(2) . . . 105, 109, 110, 279, 421, 456
section 1(8) . . . 487
section 2 . . . 68, 264, **487**, **532**, 538
section 2(1)(ii) . . . 537
section 2(3) . . . 487, 488
section 24 . . . 501
section 27 . . . **68**, **532**
section 27(1) . . . 532
section 27(2) . . . **532**
section 30 . . . 517, 518, 519, 526
section 32 . . . 121
section 34 . . . 221, 503, 504
section 34(2) . . . 194, 504
section 36 . . . 500, 507, 509, 516
section 36(2) . . . **507**, 508, 515
section 40 . . . 266, 457, 501
section 52 . . . 87, 109, 110, 303, 395
section 53 . . . 87, 111, 193, 268, 356, 357
section 53(1) . . . 111, 199, 335
section 53(1)(a) . . . 448
section 53(1)(b) . . . 112, 192, 501
section 53(1)(c) . . . 112, 335
section 53(2) . . . 193
section 5 . . . 495, 97, 109, 110, 466
section 56 . . . 422, **423–6**, 427
section 62 . . . 264, 380, 396, 397, 399, 400, 401, 402, 403, 404, 411, 414, 416
section 78 . . . **429**, 430, 431, 432, 433, 437
section 79 . . . 429, 437
section 84 . . . 414, 417, **441–2**
section 84(1) . . . **442**
section 87 . . . 333
section 91 . . . 338, 345, 346, 347, 350, 356
section 91(1) . . . 540
section 91(2) . . . 346, 347
section 101 . . . 335, 349, 351, 356, 357, 576
section 101(1) . . . 350
section 101(1)(iii) . . . **355**
section 101(4) . . . 351
section 103 . . . **351**, 356
section 104 . . . 353
section 104(2) . . . **354**
section 105 . . . 355

section 109 . . . **355–6**
section 136 . . . 427
section 141 . . . 312
section 146 . . . **319–20**, 321
section 149(6) . . . 300, 301
section 196 . . . 509, 510
section 196(3) . . . 509
section 20 . . . 590, 537, 538
section 205(1)(ii) . . . 89
section 205(1)(xxvii) . . . 302
Law of Property Act 1969 . . . 77
Legal Aid, Sentencing, and Punishment
 of Offenders Act 2012, section 144 . . . 184, 185
Limitation Act 1980 . . . 175, 182, 187, 559, 560, 578
section 15 . . . 172
section 17 . . . 172
Localism Act 2011 . . . 326, 467
Localism Act 2011, section 134 . . . 467, **468**

Mortgage Repossessions (Protection of Tenants) Act 2010 . . . 372

Perpetuities and Accumulations Act 2009 . . . 456
Prescription Act 1832 . . . 404, **405**
Proceeds of Crime Act 2000 . . . 185

Rent Act 1977 . . . 292, 296, 298, 325, 554

schedule 1, paragraph 2 . . . 554

Settled Land Act . . . 123, 479, 492
Statute of Frauds . . . 108

Trustee Act 2000, section 1(1) . . . 502
Trusts of Land and Appointment of Trustees Act 1996 . . . 356, 497, 499, 501, 526, 529, 543
section 6 . . . 501, 540
section 6(2) . . . 521
section 6(5) . . . 503
section 8 . . . 502
section 11 . . . 503
section 11(1) . . . 502
section 12 . . . **529**, 531
section 13 . . . **529–30**
section 14 . . . 68, **368**, **517**, 518, 519, 520, 521, 523, 524, 525, 526, 527, 528, 529, 530, 540, 577, 578
section 15 . . . 336, 519, **521**, 522, 523, 524, 525, 526, 528, 530, 540, 544
section 15(1) . . . 521
section 15(1)(a) . . . 521
section 15(1)(b) . . . 522
section 15(1)(c) . . . 523, 524
section 15(1)(d) . . . 525, 543
section 15(3) . . . 521, 527
section 19 . . . 505

TABLE OF INTERNATIONAL AND EU SOURCES

Mackay v Wilson (1947) 47 SR (NSW) 3 . . . 456

Kay v UK [2010] ECHR 1322, 37341/06 . . . 562, 565

Paulic v Croatia 3572/06, [2009] ECHR 1614 . . . 565

Pye v UK (2006) 43 EHRR 3, [2005] ECHR 921 . . . **559–60**

Sporring and Lönnroth v Sweden [1983] 5 EHRR 35, [1982] ECHR 5, 7151/75 . . . 550

Stubbings v UK (1996) 23 EHRR 213, [1996] ECHR 44 . . . 188

European Convention on Human Rights . . . 547, 548, 551, 552, 553, 555, 556, 558, 559, 560, 572, 573

article 1 protocol 1 . . . 138, 187, 307, 549, 550, 551, 553, 554, 558, 559, 571, 572, 573, 574, 575, 576, 577, 579

article 8 . . . 307, 348, 529, 550, **551**, 552, 554, 558, 562, 564, 565, 566, 567, 568, 569, 571, 573, 574, 575, 576, 577, 578

article 10 . . . 551, **552**, 574

article 11 . . . 551, **552**, 574

article 14 . . . 554, 561, 565

Mortgage Credit Directive 2015 . . . 84, 364

European Charter of Fundamental Rights . . . 547, 548

Universal Declaration of Human Rights . . . 548

1

INTRODUCTION—PRINCIPLES AND THEMES OF LAND LAW

1.1	Introduction	1	1.5	Conclusion	21
1.2	The Land Law System—A Brief Review	3		Table of Definitions	23
1.3	The Principles of Land Law	6		Further Reading	24
1.4	The Logic of Land Law	17			

1.1 INTRODUCTION

Land law is not the dry, unappealing subject it sometimes appears. A mandatory part of the law degree, but perceived, by many, as something to be endured, it is occasionally presented as highly technical and without interesting debates. Partly this is because the rules are complicated. There is a preponderance for 'exceptions to exceptions', and a wide range of statutes which are nothing if not unreadable. Partly, however, it is because the logic underpinning land law and the 'jigsaw' like nature of the rules, often only fall into place at the end of the course. By this time any potential interest in it has waned. The goal of this book, therefore, is to give a sense of the picture that emerges upon completion of the jigsaw, right from the outset.

The tensions and pressures which rest on a land law system, and which have enormous implications for the day-to-day functioning of the economy, of our social systems, and of family life, are often underplayed in doctrinal textbooks which seek clearly to elucidate the rules, leaving the policy-based analysis for other more specialist works considering housing law, for example. But this approach, despite its merits in terms of explaining the law as it stands in a clear, comprehensible and accessible way, does not allow for the integration of analytical thinking into approaches to those rules. The essence of this book is that it attempts to do both. It highlights how the rules interact with these wider concerns, but also explains the rules clearly and accurately. With that in mind, this first chapter is concerned to draw out some of the principles that underpin the logic of the land law system, to give a sense of the overall picture that emerges. The subsequent chapters consider this in more detail. These principles are at once legal, and social and economic, just as the law is more than mere machinery. Throughout this book, at the end of each chapter, we will return to the relevant principles to consider how the rules as explained and analysed in each topic affect the overall picture emerging from the land law puzzle. The structure of these chapters is explained further here.

What, then, is land law all about? The land law system, at its heart, does two things. First, it operates to provide a system of rules within which individuals—both persons and commercial entities—are able to design for themselves a mode of living, of transacting, of borrowing, and of investing in land which suits their individual needs. It is, in this sense, a system of law which is designed to facilitate autonomy by being flexible yet comprehensive. Second, the system aims to protect those who may be vulnerable in the face of the autonomy and power of others. It is therefore constantly seeking to strike a balance between these two overriding goals. Furthermore, this balance is one which must be struck in an enormous variety of contexts. Land law rules operate to explain the basis on which a family occupies their first home together, and to facilitate large-scale investments by pension trusts in billions of pounds of real estate in central London. Yet the rules are, with some exceptions in the details, largely the same for these two ends of the spectrum. This means that three further concerns arise. First, the land law rules must be operable within both domestic and commercial contexts whilst being able to distinguish and work within the concerns individual to each. Second, given the scope and scale of the system, there is a continual desire to ensure that a decision which produces the 'right' outcome in a very specific or particular context does not have detrimental impacts across the system as a whole. In this sense there is a tension between the individual and the systemic. Finally, the law strives to ensure sufficient certainty to facilitate easy and cheap transactions which can be carried out by experienced and inexperienced parties alike, without allowing this simplification to produce an over-simplification, leaving the system unable to account for the importance of context.

In modern land law too there is an additional set of pressures, which have emerged more recently and which have had, and continue to have, an influence on how the law operates. The first is a question of public resources. Cuts to public funding twinned with increasing pressures on services can be felt across the range of land law topics. Rules are designed with court time and availability in mind, and the system of land registration, for example, has made deliberate choices *not* to require the public recording of certain types of rights as it would over-burden the land registry. Similarly, the law relating to the provision of public housing has been adapted in recent years to give public authorities more flexibility in the face of increasing demands for housing against the background of diminishing housing stock. The second more recent set of developments relates to the increasingly important role of technology in land law. From the potential to move to an online e-conveyancing system, to the emerging role which blockchain may play in relation to real estate investments, such technologies provide significant opportunities for land lawyers to reach those goals expressed earlier.

However, new challenges also thereby emerge. Primarily these challenges relate to the possibilities of fraud and identify theft. Until the 20th century, the context of transactions in relation to land law (between a very small percentage of the population, all of whom were essentially already known to one another, either first hand or through other acquaintances) meant that identity and fraud were less important to the system than, say, the difficulties in finding and understanding a broken chain of documentation stretching back centuries. In modern law, however, the potential for impersonation and for the forging of documents is ever present, and the rules have adapted to face these challenges. The modern law too has come to recognise that the justice system as a whole, thanks to its path to development, has the potential to prioritise the rights of certain kinds of persons, leaving others on the outside of the system, at its mercy, but unable to access the benefit of its rules.[1] Because of this, legal protections from human rights—both political and civil, and economic and social—have begun to shape the land law rules. The internal rules too have begun to change to recognise that the idea of equality of power between individuals, despite the ostensibly equal footing of all people in a modern state, is a myth in modern economic conditions.

Keeping all these concerns in mind, we can say that the modern land law system has a number of principles that underpin it, but which, in different ways, are challenged, changed, manipulated and breached by some of the rules within the system. These principles are not often made explicit in the case law, and indeed many academics would disagree with the characterisation of the principles expressed here. However, what matters for this book is not so much that these principles represent a *definitive* explanation of what underpins land law, but that understanding these principles as *part of* the legal system provides an excellent starting point for learning, applying, and analysing the legal framework, and provides an insight into the concerns of those researching and working within the land law system.

Finally, a brief note on terminology. In this book, we refer regularly to 'English land law' and 'English law'. Strictly speaking, this is English and Welsh law, but continually repeating this seems unecessarily cumbersome. Unless specifically mentioned, therefore, English land law should be taken to include the rules operating in Wales.

1.2 THE LAND LAW SYSTEM—A BRIEF REVIEW

Before we move onto explain these principles, and to look briefly at some examples where these principles may be more or less apparent within the system in practice, it is useful to attempt to give a sense of the picture of the system as a whole. This is difficult, primarily because of the unfamiliar nature of much of the terminology, but also because the system is not easily condensed without losing accuracy. Nevertheless, we can say that the operation of the land law rules can be split into three questions:

1. What are the legal rights which can exist in relation to land, and what do they allow a person to do in relation to land?
2. How are these rights created and transferred?
3. How do such rights interact when there is a conflict in relation to land?

1.2.1 WHAT ARE THE LEGAL RIGHTS WHICH CAN EXIST IN RELATION TO LAND, AND WHAT DO THEY ALLOW A PERSON TO DO?

We explore the nature of rights in land in detail in chapter 2. Rights in land are divided into two categories—licences, which are personal rights, and property rights. A property right is a right which has potential legal effects in respect of all people in the world. Its binding nature is not

---

[1] For more, see S Gardner, 'The Land Registration Act 2002—the show on the road' (2013) 77 MLR 763; L Fox O'Mahony, 'Property outsiders and the hidden politics of doctrinalism' (2014) 62 Current Legal Problems 409; and more generally, and from further afield, the excellent A van der Walt, *Property in the Margins* (Hart, Oxford, 2009).

premised upon the consent or actions of other individuals, but instead operates automatically whenever a property right is created. Because of the significance that such rights have, they are limited in number and type. This produces a system where individuals are able to predict whether such rights exist, and can know how this will affect them. This list of rights can be broken down into two categories: rights which a person has in 'their own land'—in simple language, ownership rights—and rights which a person might have in relation to another's land. In the first category sit the 'estates in land'—freehold rights (the closest which English and Welsh law has to ownership) and leasehold rights ('ownership' rights fixed for a certain duration, be that one week, or 999 years). In the second category there is a wide range of rights, generally referred to as 'interests in land'. These span from rights that allow a person to do a defined activity in relation to another's land, such as easements which, amongst much else, give rise to private rights of way, allow storage and parking on another's land, and even create a property right to use and enjoy leisure facilities such as a tennis court and landscaped garden; to very nebulous rights which exist in a sort of shadow form before the court provides a fixed remedy in the case of their breach, such as proprietary estoppel. The language of all these rights at this point is likely to feel daunting. Rest assured, this is normal. It is useful however to have a reference point for some very basic definitions. As a result, at the end of every chapter you will find a table of some very basic definitions summarising some of the terms used in this chapter. This table of definitions is available in full in the online resources. Please keep in mind however that such definitions are a necessary simplification. We place the tables of definitions at the end of each chapter to encourage a contextual and nuanced approach to their content. These definitions are definitely not statutory tests!

In theory, it is not possible to create a definitive list of property rights. This book presents only a snapshot of the *current* list of rights in land. The courts and the legislature always have the option of creating new rights in accordance with the principles of precedent and statute. In practice though we do operate with effectively a closed list.[2] We go into detail in what is included in this list in chapter 2. For now we can say that the possible interests in another's land are, essentially: leases; mortgages; easements; rights of re-entry; rights of reversion; restrictive covenants; rights to rectify documents and the register; rights to set aside transactions; mere equities; equities arising by estoppel; options to purchase and rights of pre-emotion; and interests under a trust. For those reading about land law for the first time, this is an intimidating and unfamiliar list. The rest of this book is devoted to explaining the operation of these rights. But suffice to say here, this list, unfamiliar as it may be, is not really all that long. These rights represent essentially the totality of the land law rules. These rights, therefore, be they the 'ownership' type rights—known as estates in land—or the rights against another's land—known as interests in land—form the fundamental building blocks of the system.

1.2.2 HOW ARE THESE RIGHTS CREATED AND TRANSFERRED?

The second question, ie how are these rights created and transferred, is essential to the operation of land law rules within the market. It is the transmissibility of these rights which gives them value. This value has had an enormous influence on how we treat these rights in practice. However, simplifying the rules, the question of mode of creation can be split into different categories.

---

[2] See *National Provincial Bank v Ainsworth* [1965] AC 1175.

On the one hand are so-called 'legal rights'. These are the most important commercial rights in land law. As such, their mode of creation requires the completion of a number of formal steps, culminating in registration of these rights at the public record of the land registry.[3] On the other hand, there are 'equitable rights'. These rights, although enormously important to individuals and in practice, do not lie at the heart of the *value* of land. The law has therefore decided that these require less formality and publicity in their creation and transfer.[4] For these kinds of rights, it is necessary only to enter into a written contract or other form of written documentation where appropriate. Finally, there is a small residual category of rights which are created informally, often without the volition of the parties, in response to unfairness; to one person taking advantage of another; or making promises which are never fulfilled. Since the creation of such rights is usually not deliberate, the possibility of formalities falls away. Instead the law has to respond to the behaviour of the parties. Thus there are three sets of rules: one for legal rights (most importantly, freehold, leasehold, easement and profits, and mortgages); one for equitable rights (all of these, plus some others as explained in chapter 2); and informal rights, which are equitable in nature, but which do not require formalities (implied trusts,[5] and equities arising by estoppel[6]).

1.2.3 HOW DO SUCH RIGHTS INTERACT WHEN THERE IS A CONFLICT IN RELATION TO LAND?

The third question, ie how do these rights interact, is a question for what is known as the 'priority rules'. These rules are concerned not with the contents of individual rights, nor with their mode of creation. They are concerned with what happens when the property right of one person interacts with the property rights of another. The priority rules, at least in relation to registered land, as we explain in chapter 3, are established by the registration system itself. Again, to simplify, the rules essentially mean that priority between rights is a question, first, for the order in which rights are created. Thus, older rights will take priority over newer ones.[7] However, when a person *buys* an estate in land—the freehold and leasehold 'ownership' rights mentioned earlier—they *may* be able to avoid certain rights which pre-dated this transfer.[8] In such a case, only those rights which appear on the public record of the land register or certain other kinds of rights which have been given special protection in this regard because of their social importance, will be binding on the new owner of the land.[9] Such rights are often referred to as 'overriding interests'. You will encounter mention

---

[3] A written contract will usually be created, in accordance with section 2 Law of Property (Miscellaneous Provisions) Act 1989, followed by a deed, as result of section 52 Law of Property Act 1925, in line with section 1 Law of Property (Miscellaneous Provisions) Act 1989, and then registration of title under section 4 and 27 Land Registration Act 2002.

[4] A written contract may be required, complying with section 2 Law of Property (Miscellaneous Provisions) Act 1989, or it may be enough simply to use a written document, in line with section 53 Law of Property Act 1925.

[5] See section 53(2) Law of Property Act 1925.

[6] For discussion of the interaction between estoppel and formalities, see *Cobbe v Yeoman's Row* [2008] UKHL 55, [2008] 1 WLR 1752 and *Thorner v Major* [2009] UKHL 18, [2009] 1 WLR 776.

[7] Section 28 Land Registration Act 2002.

[8] Under section 29 Land Registration Act 2002, and in accordance with the principles of unregistered land as explained in chapter 3.

[9] This rule is explained in section 29 Land Registration Act 2002, and the rights given special protection are listed in either schedule 1 or 3 of the Land Registration Act 2002 depending upon the circumstances of the case.

of overriding interests at a number of places in this book, and it is useful to keep this concept of 'unregistered but binding' in mind. They are explained in full in chapter 15 at 15.3.1–15.3.5.

The operation of all of these rules is then tempered by allowances which are made to reflect the fact that land law is not the province only of the commercially experienced, but rather also control the rights of an individual in respect of their home. This means that land law makes special provision for those who have been the victim of fraud, of undue pressure from a close family member or other influential person, and in respect of the actions of other persons with rights in the relevant land who have behaved in such a way as to potentially deprive a person of their home. These considerations are particularly influential in respect of the law of mortgages and in relation to rights created in relation to family homes.

Summary: The land law system

In summary, there are three central questions: first, the content and nature of individual rights in land—both ownership-estates, and interests in another's land; second, the method of creation and transfer of these individual rights; and third, the interaction between these rights and the rights of others. The law's answer to these questions is shaped by the social context within which the rules operate, and by the principles of land law with which this book is concerned.

These principles are:

1. certainty;
2. sensitivity to context;
3. transactability;
4. systemic and individual effects; and
5. the importance of recognising social effects.

1.3 THE PRINCIPLES OF LAND LAW

1.3.1 PRINCIPLE 1: CERTAINTY

The effective operation of the land law system demands certainty.[10] To some extent, uncertainty in law is and always will be a problem, whatever the context. We can say that it is particularly problematic in two situations. When an individual's life and livelihood depend upon the law's protection, certainty is needed so that they are able to plan their life around these rules. When a person will suffer serious detriment, penalty, or even prison sentence if rules are broken, they need to be

---

[10] The meaning and importance of certainty in land law is only a small part of a much wider debate regarding certainty in general, and the rule of law as a fundamental part of a democratic society. However, there is quite some scepticism about whether such can ever be achieved. For discussion of these issues, see: H W R Wade, 'The concept of legal certainty: a preliminary skirmish' (1941) 4 Modern Law Review 183; O Raban, 'The fallacy of legal certainty: why vague legal standards may be better for capitalism and liberalism' (2010) 19 Public Interest Law Journal 175; D McBarnet and C Whelan, 'The elusive spirit of the law: formalism and the struggle for legal control' (1991) 54 Modern Law Review 848; K Kress, 'Legal indeterminacy' (1989) 77 California Law Review 283. For consideration of the relationship between property and the rule of law, see L M Austin, 'Property and the rule of law' (2014) 20 Legal Theory 79.

able to know how to comply with these rules. The first concern here is largely a concern of private law. The second is the concern of criminal law. It is therefore with the first characterisation of certainty that land law is primarily concerned. The rules need to be clear and predictable, so that people know how the rules work.

Why is such certainty important? At its most basic, certainty in law allows for planning. For commercial parties this planning is a corollary of risk assessment and valuation. So, where a commercial lender seeks to lend money on a property in the form of a mortgage, they need to make a number of assessments. Is the land worth the amount that I am lending so that if the person does not pay me back, I can recover my loan by selling the land? Is it going to be possible for me to sell the land easily, so that I do not have to waste money to achieve that sale? Can I pass the responsibility of conducting the sale onto a third party so that I do not have to do it myself? What happens to the proceeds of the sale? What happens if there is another person living in the house? The actual answer to these questions is obviously important to the lender, but really they simply want to be sure what the answer is, then they can calculate a price for the risks they take on and build that into the amount of interest charged on the loan or into their fees. If the operation of the rules is not predictable, then the commercial party cannot accurately calculate the risks they are undertaking, and will become more cautious as a result. Given the critical importance of the mortgage market to the real estate market as a whole, it is easily to see why ensuring this certainty may be a central concern of the property law system.

For individuals certainty is also critical. Imagine a scenario in which a person has bought a plot of land and spent a large amount of their personal savings on the construction of a beautiful home there for themselves and their family. With so much of their personal wealth at stake, as well as the well-being of their family, such a person will want to be absolutely certain that the access way from the round to the building plot will always be usable; that the fence marking the boundary of their land is in the right place; and that the person previously occupying the property no longer has any claim to that property so that they can be certain of being able to live in that home for as long as they like. To take another example, for a person who has just started to rent their first flat in London, beginning a new life and a new job perhaps, they want to know that they will not be thrown out of that flat and can start to form roots there, or save up money to provide a deposit for alternative accommodation, without always being worried about the security of their accommodation for now. Certainty in land law is not only about risk, value, and investment. It is also about allowing people to plan their lives and make long-term decisions on the basis of the provision of safe, secure, long-term housing.

What do these concerns mean that land law strives to do? Certainty is not a simple concept. There are many different kinds of certainty. As we shall see as this book progresses, the law responds at different times to these alternative forms. The first kind of certainty is what is sometimes referred to as 'formal certainty'. This is simply a requirement that rules be clear, and predictable. In land law, there are many rules which meet this kind of requirement. For example, there are different rules depending upon the length of leases (the 'ownership' right which is limited in length, as explained earlier). A rule which says: you must do *x, y, and z* if you want to create a lease of more than three years in duration, is a clear and simple rule. Three years in duration is not a concept which is susceptible to interpretation or to variation. The 'must' is not susceptible to the discretionary implementation of the courts. But few rules will be perfectly clear, not least because the rules must always be expressed in words, and virtually no words are totally free from interpretive difficulties.[11] But this kind of certainty is also potentially very blunt. Yes, it may produce clear outcomes, but where, for example, the interaction between two very clear rules produces a completely absurd outcome, we may say that the absurdity will produce a form of uncertainty in that people may assume that the law would 'never let that happen'.

This points to another form of certainty: so called, moral certainty. This concept is explained by Gardner:

> 'Moral clarity is secured, not by the use of straightforward and unornamented language in legal texts, but by the adequate replication in the law of clear distinctions and significances which apply outside the law, together with reasonably clear indication (in the titles of Acts, the common names and classifications of offences, etc.) of which cluster of distinctions and significances people can expect to find replicated in which legal contexts'.[12]

Where a rule is closely calibrated to what people expect, to common sense, and to an intuitive moral sense of what is and what is not fair, then the operation of that rule is likely to be more predictable and certain in practice.

In this respect, it is critical to keep in mind how we learn legal rules. We look at statutes, and at case law. Statutes are not, by their nature, designed to be 'easy reads', but rather to produce comprehensive rules (even if they fail). In learning the rules, the focus in teaching, in academic analysis, and in problem questions and essays, is often where certainty falls away. We focus on what is unclear. Furthermore, in many situations where a case comes before a court, particularly if the case reaches the Court of Appeal or Supreme Court, there will be no statutory rule or directly applicable case law rule covering the precise dispute between the parties (or it would have been resolved by an earlier court, or more likely settled out of court). Rather, the court will have to look at previous case law for similar questions, and reason by analogy. Thus, the law may appear less clear and predictable in its learning than it is in practice.

However, this practice of how law develops also gives us a clue as to how courts will often go about filling these 'gaps' in the system. The closer the outcome to both the rule and the *spirit* of the rule in earlier cases and in the land law system as a whole, the more predictable that outcome is likely to be. A simple example of how this has played out in land law relates to the register. There is a long-running dispute regarding the possibility of changes to the land register in cases where there has been a fraud. This is discussed at length in chapter 5. This dispute has been about whether appearing as the 'owner'[13] of land on the land register is conclusive proof that someone *is* 'owner' of that land, or whether they can be taken off the register if, for example, three 'owners' previously there was a forged transfer. Most people would assume that if they pay good money for a property, and created a proper transaction with the vendor, dealing with lawyers, that they would be certain of keeping their title to that land unless they themselves chose to sell it. The fact that land law has created certain situations in which that will not be the case undermines the 'moral certainty' present in the system. In undermining people's expectations, this can make it difficult for such persons to plan their lives.

---

[11] Ibid.
[12] J Gardner, 'Rationality and the rule of law in offences against the person' (1994) 53 CLJ 502, 513.
[13] See later in this chapter, chapter 2, and chapter 9 for consideration of the concept of ownership in English land law.

Finally, there is the certainty in the legal system which comes from the straightforward and easy accessibility of rules and of the system as a whole. If rules are contained in statutes then those statutes should be easy to access and in expressed in language which is not unnecessarily complex and which is clear to those who are not experienced in the law. The way in which one set of rules interacts with another should also be comprehensible, so that a person can read about the rules and understand what their legal rights and responsibilities are, not just in relation to a specific narrow question, but more generally, in relation to the land 'as a whole'. However, this is tempered by the need to ensure that the rules are precise and not so vague as to require an enormous amount of judicial interpretation, for that too would undermine certainty. In this respect, sometimes technical language is required: this language is unclear to the layman, but contains a necessary clarity for practising lawyer.

Certainty as a principle underpinning the system does not therefore always point in one direction. Many of the disputes we will see represent conflicts between different forms of certainty, particularly the clash between formal and moral certainty. Nevertheless, there are regular appeals to the need for certainty both in the case law and in the academic literature, and it is without doubt a central concern of the land law system.

Summary: Principle 1—Certainty

Certainty in land law takes different forms: clarity, predictability in the operation of rules, and a close alignment between what people 'expect', and what actually occurs. Often these forms of certainty work together, but sometimes they conflict. Certainty is important because it allows for planning of lives, livelihoods, risks and investments.

1.3.2 PRINCIPLE 2: SENSITIVITY TO CONTEXT

The importance of context to the operation of land law rules is central to many areas considered in this book. Context, as with certainty, can mean different things. First, it is an appeal to take account of the nature of the land in question when assessing how land law rules apply to it. This can be as simple as a recognition that where land is undergoing major construction works, it may not be possible for a person to live there.[14] It could also be a reflection of the fact that changes in the natural environment may mean that a fence or wall is not in quite the place as was intended 500 years previously when land was divided. It could be an understanding that the precise route of a right of way may have hugely significant implications for the possibility of a development on sites. It can also be a reflection of the nature of the relationship between the parties to a transaction and of the relative experience between those parties. So, where a person makes a promise to another that they will share a property, the law may change its attitude to how it deals with such a promise depending upon whether the parties are close family members or in a romantic relationship, or whether they are commercial parties dealing at arm's length in a transaction which has been negotiated with the help of professional lawyers.[15]

---

[14] As in *Lloyds Bank v Rosset* [1991] 1 AC 107 (HL).
[15] Contrast *Cobbe v Yeoman's Row* [2008] UKHL 55, [2008] 1 WLR 1752 and *Thorner v Major* [2009] UKHL 18, [2009] 1 WLR 776.

By its very nature, it is not possible to create blanket rules for such context. There is no such thing as a purely domestic situation where the commercial value of the land is irrelevant to the parties.[16] So too, there is no property in existence where no human being will suffer personal consequences should something have gone wrong in the transaction leading to purchase of that land. In this respect, sensitivity to context is, in part, a question of flexibility. Flexibility can however be the opposite of certainty. This is an important lesson about the principles expressed here. They will sometimes operate together, sometimes conflict. This is how principles work, and indeed a principle will never dictate a single right answer to a question. Instead, principles act as advocates in favour of a solution to a problem.[17]

How does land law currently respond to the principle of sensitivity to context? The primary way in which we see the need for sensitivity to context playing out is in the rough distinction which is drawn in some areas of land law between the domestic and the commercial context. This distinction is apparent in a number of different places. There are different rules in relation to lender remedies in mortgages in cases involving dwellings (homes).[18] Some rules relating to leases vary as to whether the lease in question is a business commercial lease or a residential lease.[19] The law relating to implied trusts (the mechanism which allows for multiple owners of land) responds differently depending upon the nature of the property in question and the relationship between the parties.[20] The rules regarding estoppel (essentially concerned with attempts to go back on certain kinds of promise) too are more generous in domestic cases.[21] These slight variations in the operation of the rules in the different contexts are designed to capture the fact that in domestic cases not only are the parties unlikely to be dealing at arms' length, or if they are dealing at arms' length, are very unlikely to be an in an equal position as far as bargaining power is concerned (eg the lender/borrower relationship), but domestic cases are also likely to involve a property being used as a person's home.

This brings us to a critical point, one which is sometimes underplayed in the literature concerning land law.[22] Land is not only a valuable asset, it is also potentially someone's home, and someone's family's home. This is a trite, but enormously important consideration, in how the law should and does operate. For some observers, the land law principle of certainty and the desire to maintain commercial value in land has gone so far that we have forgotten that at the heart of the land law system are individuals seeking to live in safety and security. The courts have not forgotten it however, and the influence of this consideration is apparent in the way the rules are applied. Throughout this work, we seek to keep this role of the land law system in mind throughout.

Furthermore, context is also relevant as part of the question of how the different principles of land law should interact. We can prioritise different principles within different contexts, and indeed, to a large extent, this is already happening in English and Welsh land law. As Etherton

---

[16] See N Hopkins, 'The relevance of context in property law: a case for judicial restraint?' (2011) 31 Legal Studies 175.
[17] R Dworkin, *Taking Rights Seriously* (Duckworth, London, 1977), 26.
[18] See section 36 Administration of Justice Act 1970 as amended.
[19] Contrast the Landlord and Tenant Act 1954, Part II; Housing Act 1980; and Housing Act 1985.
[20] See discussion in *Stack v Dowden* [2007] UKHL 17, [2007] 2 AC 432, *Jones v Kernott* [2011] UKSC 53, [2012] 1 AC 776, *Laskar v Laskar* [2008] EWCA Civ 347, [2008] 1 WLR 2695 and the recent decision of the Privy Council in *Collie v Marr* [2017] UKPC 17, [2017] 3 WLR 1507.
[21] *Thorner v Major* [2009] UKHL 18, [2009] 1 WLR 776.
[22] See the criticisms of this in N Cobb et al, *Great Debates in Land Law* (Palgrave, London, 2016).

explains in the context of constructive trusts (co-ownership situations which are managed or established by a court):

> 'A case by case approach, in the context of an adversarial system of increasingly specialist advocates, where they and busy courts have concentrated on the facts and outcome of the case in hand, has not worked well so far in this field. Nor has the ability of the law to provide practical justice been assisted ... by a mantra type invocation of the need for certainty. The tension between the desirability of providing a remedy and the need for certainty in the law has always been a critical feature of judicial decision-making in the common law and equity. The tension is resolved in different ways and with different results according to the context'.[23]

The resolution of the conflict between certainty and sensitivity to context manifested in flexibility therefore varies across the legal landscape.

> **Summary: Principle 2—Sensitivity to context**
>
> Sensitivity to context in land law demands, primarily, a recognition of the type of land, the nature of the parties dealing with that land, the purpose of their transaction, and the consequences for those parties of any particular rule. In this sense, given the unique nature of each piece of land and each legal relationship, sensitivity to context demands flexibility and responsiveness.

1.3.3 PRINCIPLE 3: TRANSACTABILITY

For those who have considered the way in which markets operate in an economics course, for example, you will be aware that the value of a transaction is determined by a number of features: the levels of supply of the item being traded, the demand for that item, and the transaction costs involved in moving that asset from one person to another. In land law, the transaction costs come from a number of different sources. One is the direct cost of the actual transaction steps, such as the fee which the land registry charges individuals to register a transfer with them, or the cost of stamp duty which must be paid on the purchase of most properties. Another cost is the cost of legal advice as part of this process. Professional conveyancing, compared to the cost of the property in question, or indeed often compared to the fees charged by a commercial lender to lend on the property, is often a relatively small part of the overall expense. But it is an expense which many people resent. Furthermore, the cost of involving a conveyancing solicitor will enormously increase in complicated transactions, where more legal research is required. The less clear the law, the more expensive this process will be.

There is an additional 'hidden' cost factor in the need to engage professional legal help, and that lies in the time which it takes to transact in land. This time is not only costly in itself—due, for example, to the need to rent property for longer—but is also risky because transactions regularly fall apart because one party needs to move quickly, and the other side cannot cajole their conveyancing solicitor into expediting the sale. But conveyancing practice is not slow merely because it is slow. It is slow because there are a number of steps which must be undertaken, a wide-range of

---

[23] T Etherton, 'Constructive trusts and proprietary estoppel: the search for clarity and principle' [2009] Conv 104, 125–6.

duties resting on a conveyancing solicitor's shoulders regarding money laundering, identity verification, and duties to commercial lenders, which are a result of the conveyancing system being used to achieve other social goals beyond merely the transaction of the land. These concerns are not central to this book but are hugely important in how the law actually works in the practice of conveyancing. We will refer to them at appropriate junctures.

There is another aspect to transactability which is central to the issues considered here. This is the substantive question of how easy it is to transfer rights in land, and how much will the law 'defend' those rights. This question is sometimes expressed as being about ensuring static and dynamic security (the distinction between the person who originally held a right, and the person who now holds it).[24] In common with the other principles we have considered, this principle does not always pull in one single direction, but different aspects of the principle can in fact conflict with each other. The fundamental issue is this: How can a system of land law ensure that those who purchase land in good faith are able to keep the value of that land, safe in the knowledge that their investment is protected by the law whilst at the same time protecting those who may be victims of a fraud, or the behaviour of a family member or friend which has deprived them of their home, and their own security?

This effect is explained by Gardner:

'That is, to assure (putative) disponees [those to whom property has been transferred] that they can safely enter into transactions regarding land on the faith of what they can, easily and cheaply, discover from the register—at the expense of those whose interests would otherwise subsist in the land, but must be sacrificed if dynamic security is to be achieved'.[25]

This substantive question is concerned with the protection of innocent individuals. A dispute is rarely between one innocent party and one fraudster or perpetrator of undue pressure, but rather between two innocent parties both of whom are victims of the act of a third party. When keeping the idea of transactability in mind, the law is concerned to strike a balance between these two innocent parties which makes sense in terms of ensuring that a transaction involving a right in land is, as far as possible, a secure one. However, we must acknowledge that both cannot be achieved simultaneously. The 'instinct' of many is to prefer static security. This is explained by Cooke, who argues that, '[i]t may be that a deep-seated preference for solutions that secure A's [the original owner's] title, in line with our instinct... makes any form of dynamic security (protecting a purchaser in preference while leaving a defrauded proprietor to the indemnity) a source of disquiet'.[26]

Transactability is also about practicalities. It is here that we see the potential influence of technology shaping the substantive land law rules. The land registry has, for a number of years, been considering the possibility of implementing a so-called 'e-conveyancing' system.[27] This is a system whereby rights in land are created or transferred directly 'through' the land registry using electronic

---

[24] See E Cooke, *Land Law* (OUP, Oxford, 2006) 8.
[25] S Gardner, 'Alteration of the register: an alternative view', [2013] Conv 530, 533.
[26] E Cooke, 'Chickens coming home to roost', [2014] Conv 444, 448. See also E Cooke, The register's guarantee of title [2013] Conv 344.
[27] See Law Commission Report no. 271, section 93 Land Registration Act 2002, and the recent Land Registry press release regarding its intentions in relation to e-conveyancing at https://www.gov.uk/government/news/hm-land-registry-moves-forward-with-digital-conveyancing.

systems, rather than the land registry recording transactions which take place on paper in the offices of conveyancing specialists across the country. The advantages of such a system are said to be cost, time and security. But of course if ownership of land is transferred in this way, rather than remotely across different locations 'offline', then the whole system becomes much more vulnerable to hacking and identity theft. For this reason, conversations are now emerging about the potential role which blockchain can play in ensuring safety in e-conveyancing.[28] The same technology that underpins bitcoin and other crypto-currencies, blockchain allows the record of transactions in assets to be recorded remotely on hundreds or thousands of different servers, making hacking of the transaction chain extremely difficult if not impossible. Certainly if these technological innovations emerge as feasible, there is clear appetite amongst the various 'concerned' parties (land registry, Law Commission, and Parliament) to move towards a new electronic system. Whether this will happen in the near future, and quite what such a system would actually look like are less clear.

> **Summary: Principle 3—Transactability**
>
> Transactibility is the source of value in land law rights—it allows them to be freely and easily transferred. However, in allowing rights to be transferred, we must be aware of the risks to those 'left behind'.

1.3.4 PRINCIPLE 4: SYSTEMIC AND INDIVIDUAL EFFECTS

The fourth principle of the system which we consider here is a desire to ensure that all rules and cases as decided strike a good balance between what might be seen as justice or fairness in an individual decision, and a wider systemic justice which creates an appropriate balance between different competing policy goals in the system in general. This concern is particularly important when dealing with the common law system of case law precedent. Any court which seeks to change the law too far, when faced with a hard case in front of it, will potentially skew the system as a whole creating potentially serious social and economic effects.

To give a simple example, considered in more detail in chapter 11 concerning mortgages, it is easy to imagine circumstances where an individual is unable to pay their mortgage, entirely due to factors wholly without their control and in circumstances in which they are not in the least to be blamed. In such a case, a court, when asked to deprive that person of their home and to sell that property without their consent by a 'faceless' commercial lender, is likely to feel an enormous amount of sympathy for the borrower. It may perhaps even be tempted to stretch a particular term within relevant legislation, or to depart from or distinguish earlier case law, to provide an outcome which seems fair to that individual. However, in so-doing, the court will produce knock-on effects within the lending system as a whole. The precedent value of the decision will mean that in future similar cases the lender will also be prevented from realising their security. There is nothing here to say that this may not be 100 per cent the right decision for the court to reach, but the collective consequences of that decision must also be taken into account. In this respect, the principle of taking both into account pushes in favour of a balanced outcome.

---

[28] See R Thomas and C Huang, 'Blockchain, the Borg collective and digitalisation of land registries' [2017] Conv 14.

Similarly, in relation to the dispute considered earlier regarding the guarantees provided by registering title to land, the courts will be concerned about setting precedents that upset the whole land registration system when faced with a particularly hard case of a vulnerable individual losing or being faced with the loss of their ownership right in land when they had no power to prevent the circumstances which have given rise to the flaw in their title. Any proposed solution to these problems inevitably has knock on consequences within the system, and may, further down the line, produce severe hardship for a similarly vulnerable individual in a slightly different position.

We shall see as we progress through this book that the courts are acutely aware of these issues. So too is the Law Commission and other bodies responsible for some of the reforms which we consider here. We examine proposed reforms to the system relating to co-ownership of homes where individuals co-habit but are not married,[29] to the rules relating to easements and restrictive covenants,[30] and to land registration (amongst others).[31] In all of these areas there is a pressure to keep the system the same due to the amount of experience, knowledge, and investment that has been made on the basis of the rules as they currently stand, and to change these rules to better reflect the needs of modern society. In part, this desire for conservatism in reform of land law rules is based on a recognition of the fact that any change will have systemic, potentially unforeseen, consequences, as well as individual consequences in specific situations envisaged by the drafters of the new rules.

> **Summary: Principle 4—Systemic and individual effects**
>
> Changes to rules, and new interpretations, will always create two forms of effects: individual effects for parties involved in the instant dispute, and wider effects across the land law system. The recognition of both individual and systemic effects as a principle requires that both be considered.

1.3.5 PRINCIPLE 5: RECOGNITION OF THE SOCIAL EFFECTS OF RULES

Finally, and perhaps most importantly, underpinning the land law system is, or should be, a recognition that these rules, ultimately, are serving a social purpose. This social purpose extends beyond the desire to create wealth. We must never forget that land is a limited and scarce resource; that it is proportionately very expensive to acquire; and that each piece of land is unique. As mentioned, for many, this aspect of land law is perceived as being subservient to the needs of the market. There is an extended critique in the literature on the basis that the land law system insufficiently services this principle, prioritising certainty and transactability at the expense of those whose homes are subject to the property rights of others. To a certain extent, the wider legal context is however helping to ensure that these concerns cannot be too far removed from the courts' and legislature's minds when creating land law rules.

---

[29] Law Commission report no. 307, 'Cohabitation: the financial consequences of relationship breakdown' (2007).
[30] Law Commission report no. 327, 'Making land work: easements, covenants and profits a prendre' (2011).
[31] Law Commission consultation no. 227, 'Updating the Land Registration Act 2002' (2016).

First, there is the influence of human rights within land law. Although not visible yet in certain areas, this has certainly provoked shifts in case law—for example in relation to the relationship between public authority landlords and their tenants[32]—and in the approach taken by those considering reform of land law (eg in relation to ownership of family homes).[33] The precise interaction between these two systems has been the subject of some controversy, for more on which see chapter 17 of this book. But no one thinks, quite rightly, that the wider context of civil and democratic society should not shape and influence private law interactions. Indeed, as Nield and Hopkins explain, whilst human rights rules might not have changed the practical consequences in some areas of land law, they do nevertheless challenge a 'property-focused' paradigm, which is centred around rights in land rather than the people who live on land. They reason that:

> 'In the stark logic of property law, legal issues relating to the home are often distilled into questions of the acquisition of property rights and the priorities of those rights between the parties. While the home is the subject of a canvas of regulation in which the rights-based approach of property law is sometimes displaced, it nevertheless remains the case that critical issues relating to the home fall to be determined through the property paradigm of rights and priorities… In this property rights-based approach, occupiers without such rights are frequently invisible'.[34]

However, the human rights legislation mandates that such occupiers are brought back into the picture.

Second, we can also see an increasingly sophisticated series of responses, particularly from the courts, in assessing how private law rules interact with the rapidly changing legal landscape in respect of environmental regulation,[35] planning law controls,[36] private agreements in respect of restrictive covenants,[37] and criminal law.[38] The courts have sought to provide stability in private law in the face of this evolving landscape, whilst respecting the goals of these other areas of legal regulation. To give two examples here, we can think first of the relationship between the rules relating to adverse possession (considered in chapter 6)—so fundamental to our understanding of the nature of title to land—and the criminal law prohibition on squatting in residential premises.[39] The courts have been required to assess which of these rules should be given priority, and have negotiated the political and social realities of squatting and adverse possession in so-doing.[40] Secondly, the courts, in relation to the tort of nuisance have long grappled with the question of how public law planning permissions should interact with a private law barrier to development.[41] Recent case law shows how the courts are able to adapt and direct their case law

---

[32] See the case law following *Manchester City Council v Pinnock* [2011] UKSC 6, [2011] 2 WLR 220 and *London Borough of Hounslow v Powell* [2011] UKSC 8, [2011] 2 AC 186.
[33] Law Commission report no. 307, 'Cohabitation: the financial consequences of relationship breakdown' (2007).
[34] Nield and Hopkins, 'Human rights and mortgage repossession: beyond property law using Article 8', (2013) 33 Legal Studies 431, 431.
[35] *Barr v Biffa Waste* [2012] EWCA Civ 312, [2013] QB 455.
[36] *Coventry (t/a RDC Promotions) v Lawrence* [2014] UKSC 13, [2014] AC 822.
[37] Law Commission report no. 349, 'Conservation covenants' (2014).
[38] *R (Best) v Chief Land Registrar* [2015] EWCA Civ 17, [2016] QB 23.
[39] Section 144 Legal Aid, Sentencing and Punishment of Offenders Act 2012.
[40] *R (Best) v Chief Land Registrar* [2015] EWCA Civ 17, [2016] QB 23.
[41] *Coventry (t/a RDC Promotions) v Lawrence* [2014] UKSC 13, [2014] AC 822.

in this area to continually strive to articulate the extent to which land law rules should constrain and shape public law, and vice versa.[42]

This last principle of land law, most fundamentally, however, is a question of fairness broadly defined. Part of fairness in this context of course is certainty, and there are many whose writings reflect a focus on certainty as being *the* defining feature of a fair and functioning land law system. Others focus on the effect of the rules on individuals, on flexibility in the face of unforeseen circumstances, and of the importance of housing. Indeed, as Gardner shows, we should be careful not to assume primacy for certainty and dynamic security without examining the social consequences of such a preference very carefully:

> The most obvious substantive reason, of any respectability, for favouring dynamic security is economic liberalism: the market, and all the boons that this is said to bring with it. Notwithstanding recent reminders that the market may not be a panacea, we might be broadly sympathetic to this, albeit with caveats. But until one begins, at a minimum, to actually talk in these terms, there is no hope of arriving at the plausible conclusion we are seeking as to the balance of advantage between the interests that are promoted by dynamic security, and those that it imperils.[43]

Neither protection of economic interests, nor support to those imperilled by the pursuit of such, can be achieved in its totality. They certainly cannot be pursued simultaneously with the expectation that they will always work hand in hand. Thus, the final principle is concerned with ensuring balance: balance between the need to be sensitive to context and to the fact that real people's lives are affected by land law rules, and the need to maintain a predictable and certain system as a whole. In this respect, the last principle can be seen as a *meta-principle*, one which encourages a thoughtful and open-minded application of the other principles. It should also be seen as a check on our analytical approach, in danger as it may be of failing to consider the human element. To that extent, the warning from Gardner, made in the context of land registration, but applicable beyond that issue, must be heeded:

> 'Finally, we must remember that 'land registration' [and land law as a whole] is, in less abstract terms, the set of rules controlling the operation of people's interests in the land that they have no alternative but to live on, and that comprises the locus of their society. And we must then insist that land registration's future is shaped by reflections sensitive to this recollection, and all it implies'.[44]

Summary: Principle 5—Recognition of the social effects of rules

The requirement that we take account of the social effect of rules is a reminder that land law affects, ultimately, people in their homes and workplaces. 'Tidy' and simple rules cannot be introduced if they sacrifice the social purposes for which we have these rules in the first place.

---

[42] See also E Scotford and R Walsh, 'The symbiosis of property and English environmental law—property rights in a public law context' (2013) 76 Modern Law Review 1010 and M Lee, 'The public interest in private nuisance: collectives and communities in tort' (2015) 75 CLJ 329.
[43] S Gardner, 'Alteration of the register: an alternative view', [2013] Conv 530, 536.
[44] S Gardner, 'The Land Registration Act 2002—the show on the road' (2013) 77 MLR 763, 779.

How are principles treated in this book?

This brief review of (some of) the principles underpinning land law is designed to give a sense of the nature of the debates which will be considered in the following chapters. It does not claim to be a comprehensive or uncontroversial description of what land law is designed to do. Far from it. It is instead an articulation of a series of perspectives on land law rules, all of which are defensible, and none of which is 'the be all and end all' of successful land law regulation. At the end of each of the chapters that follow, there is a box which contains some thoughts regarding how the law as explained in that chapter interacts with the principles. These thoughts are designed to provide a starting point for analysis to encourage engagement with these deeper questions about the functioning of the land law system.

1.4 THE LOGIC OF LAND LAW

The principles are explained here to act not only as a framework through which to approach analysis, but also as a 'way in' to the land law rules and the detail of their application as these principles underpin the logic of the system. It is to that logic that we now turn. It must be acknowledged from the outset, however, that not all of those who look at land law do so in the way explained here. There are a wide variety of different 'modes' of explanation of the ways in which the different pieces of the puzzle fit together. What follows here is simply one explanation of that jigsaw.

Land law cannot be explained in a linear fashion. There is no obvious starting point. For some, terminological problems in particular, suggest that the best place to start is the nature of rights in land, followed by an explanation of the particular rights that exist and their effect, before moving to analysis of their creation. For others, the starting point is a general framework as to how to create rights in land, before moving onto explanations of their nature and effect. Neither is perfect since the two issues are not really separate. The mode of creation of a right has a significant impact upon a right's effects and its relationship with other rights. To explain the rules relating to creation, one has to make reference to specific proprietary rights as these different rights have different formalities associated with their creation. Both issues presuppose the other. To understand land law then it is essential to (a) accept this total interdependency; and (b) to feel comfortable with terminology and the most basic of the rules as quickly as possible, so that one is able to learn a new rule which uses the terminology of concepts not yet encountered. Once that new rule is learnt it will build up a picture, so that it is possible then to return to the concept and understand it more fully.

1.4.1 LEGAL AND EQUITABLE RIGHTS

Let us start then with terminology. Two of the terms which cause the most significant problems are: 'legal' and 'equitable'. We have already seen earlier that land law draws a distinction between legal and equitable rights in terms of the mode of their creation, with legal rights generally requiring more formal steps. The terminology is a historical one. It reflects the fact that up until the 19th century there were two court systems in English law running parallel to one another. The first system, the Court of Common Pleas, was relatively rigid in its causes of action. It is not necessary to know the details of this, but the rigidity of some of the rules meant that the court simply could not answer certain kinds of legal disputes, and did not have certain kinds of remedies at its disposal. This created inconvenience and injustice. In response to that, amongst other issues, the Court of Chancery developed. This did not begin its life as a court per se, but rather as simply those individual arguments brought before the King which the legal system in the form of the courts were unable to solve, or to solve fairly. The burden of such decision-making being relatively high, the King delegated the authority to decide such cases to the Lord Chancellor—essentially one of the high ranking officials within the King's administration.

Unsurprisingly, increasing numbers of claims became too much also for the Lord Chancellor personally, so that a more formal system also emerged in this 'chancery' jurisdiction. The rules, at the origin of the court, were more flexible and perhaps more 'fair' than those applied at common law, but that flexible approach did not continue. Rather, as is inevitable in a system of judicial precedent, the Chancery Court began to develop clear and fixed rules, albeit ones with a different flavour to those created at common law in the Court of Common Pleas. Eventually, the inconvenience of having two different court systems became such that under the Supreme Court of Judicature Acts 1873 and 1875 the courts were merged. Where the rules conflicted, the rules developed in equity were to take precedence over those created 'at common law' (ie in the Court of Common Pleas).

However, the *language* of legal and equitable rights has been retained in land law because the distinction between the two categories of rights serves a useful purpose. That purpose has got *nothing* to do with the origins of the courts. Thus, it is a fundamental mistake to think that equitable rights are 'all about fairness', whereas legal rights are much more strict and rigid. In addition, the contrast between legal and equitable rights should not be taken to suggest that equitable rights are somehow not legal in the sense of being unenforceable before a court. This is simply false. Indeed, the retention of the labels of legal and equitable is singularly *unhelpful* in elucidating the difference between such rights. For all the assistance the labels bring, they may as well be called blue and yellow rights, or, perhaps slightly more helpfully, universal and dependent rights, or something similar. From the outset, to understand this terminology, and to understand the logic of land law, one must first eschew the connotations that the terminology conjures up.

Rather, the essence of the distinction is this. The legal system has decided that some rights are so critical to the functioning of the land law system as a whole that they should be applicable, universally, against all third parties regardless of whether those third parties are aware of such rights. However, other rights, whilst needing to be *capable* of having third party effects, do not necessarily need to have these effects *automatically*. Rather, we can have a system whereby conditions are put onto third party effects, such as a third party knowing about the right, being able to find out about the right, or perhaps where third parties do not make sufficient enquiries. Legal rights form this first category; equitable, the second. However, because of the automatic and universal nature of the effects of legal rights, it is also important that these rights receive a good deal of publicity, so that third parties are able to find out about the rights, even though they would be bound by them whether or not they knew about them. How best to achieve this publicity? In modern law, the answer to this question is to mandate that for universal effect to be achieved it is (for the most part) necessary to publicise the rights on the land register. The older rules relied upon mandatory documentation which could then easily be read by and provided to third parties, solemnly signed by the relevant parties to show their commitment to the contents of the document.

Equitable rights, however, being conditional on the existence of other factors before they would be binding on third parties, do not need to be created in the same way with such a high level of publicity, and indeed, in certain cases, do not require any formal documents at all. Equitable rights therefore can serve a variety of purposes, from distributing the wealth and interests in land amongst a multitude of persons, without that needing be revealed or reflected publicly, to assisting in the management of land as between family members, where the outside world did not need to be concerned with the ins and outs of that legal relationship. Both these purposes are achieved through the use of trusts, to which we return shortly. Other equitable rights include rights such as options to purchase land or restrictive covenants, rights which although potentially very significant for third parties *if bound*, are not so essential to the operation of the land law system as a whole that there is a need to make them automatically binding. In this way, the nature of the right in question, and its importance to the system as a whole, feeds into the mandatory means of its creation. The likely means of creation of an expectation of rights—deliberate, conscious or accidental—also feeds into the formalities required for their creation. Thus, the rules regarding formalities also have influence on the substance of the law. By limiting the numbers of situations where formalities can be avoided altogether, we shape the substance of rights which are likely to be created informally.

> **Summary: Legal and equitable rights**
>
> The language of legal and equitable rights is unhelpful. In essence, legal rights are rights which are universally binding, and as such require a high degree of publicity and formality. Equitable rights are conditional in their effects on third parties, and therefore can be created more privately, more informally, and more flexibly.

1.4.2 INTERESTS UNDER A TRUST

Of these equitable and legal rights, the terminology becomes the most difficult when we turn to the law of trusts. Trusts as a concept are not unique to land law. We consider the nature of the trust in detail in chapter 16. A trust exists when one person has 'legal title' to an estate in land—ie the title which for certainty and transactability reasons we made mandatorily public—and another has 'equitable title' to the land—ie a title that can be created without publicity, and which, due to its contingent third party effects, can operate more flexibly and unpredictably between others who may share equitable title in a property. The person with legal title is the trustee, and the relationship between them and the equitable title-holder(s) is managed by the imposition of trust duties. The fundamental underpinning of these is that the trustee, who is the legal title-holder, must act for the benefit of her beneficiaries, ie those with equitable title. Thus, any transactions with the legal title must be in the interest of the beneficiaries or the trustee will be liable for breach of trust. However, third parties, unless the conditions for being affected by the interest under the trust are met, do not need to be concerned with the identity of the beneficiaries, nor their dispute with the trustee. Rather, they need only be concerned with the identity of the trustee and the quality of her rights in land.

> **Summary: Trusts**
>
> A trust arises where one person holds 'legal title' to an estate and another person holds 'equitable title'. The trustee (legal title-holder) must act for the benefit of the beneficiary (equitable title-holder). Trusts are primarily used in land law to manage situations of multiple ownership.

The system has developed with this web of different kinds of rights so as to allow for easy transactability of land without it becoming overburdened, whilst also ensuring that those things which parties may seek to ensure in relation to land are possible. The rules relating to how such rights are created are shaped by this desire to distinguish between public, universal rights, and more private rights which are only binding upon others where certain conditions are met. The priority rules, ie the rules which explain the relationship between different property rights, also reflect this distinction as we shall see in chapter 15.

1.4.3 ESTATES IN LAND

A second aspect to the land law logic which must be internalised, and which again is difficult (partly due to terminology), is the idea of *estates* in land rather than *ownership* of land. To understand land law it is essential to get rid of the idea of ownership of land. There is no such thing as 'the owner' of a piece of land in English and Welsh land law. This does not mean that people are lying when they say they own their land, nor does it mean they are being inaccurate as such. This book will refer to landowners and owners of land. It is not that this term is wrong, it is that is has no *legal* definition. There is no legal concept of ownership, although of course there is a moral concept, and indeed the term is used as a shorthand for one or more concepts which do have a legal meaning—such as freeholder, leaseholder, owner of the freehold title, and registered proprietor. To a certain extent, all of these terms means 'owner', although not '*the* owner'.

This is a second aspect of this point about ownership. When someone says they 'own' property, they usually mean that they, or perhaps they and their spouse or partner, are *the* owner of the land. In this, they are legally inaccurate since English and Welsh law does not recognise this idea of absolute ownership of land. Rather, they are *an* owner of an *estate* in that land. They may be the only person with such an estate at the moment that they speak, but the law does not guarantee them that status. It does not promise that you are the *only* person with ownership-type rights in your land. In learning land law, if you can move away from the idea of ownership, and instead think of only of estates and titles to land, and interests in land, without being concerned with whether something constitutes *ownership* according to a pre-conceived idea of what owning land 'should' be like, then you will likely assimilate the rules more quickly.

> **Summary: Estates in land**
>
> The is no legal concept of absolute ownership in English and Welsh land law. Rather, one owns or holds title to an *estate* in land.

Finally, and this is very much a practical rather than a theoretical issue (and was mentioned earlier), it must be understood that most case law disputes, at least in the modern law, relate to the law 'at the edges', at the point where rights interact, or at the periphery of the core nature of a particular interest in land. To take the example of easements—the odd collection of a variety of historically and contemporarily important rights, which defy easy categorisation—one of the most important recent cases is concerned with whether it is possible to have an easement to use a tennis court.[45] The core cases of easements are rights of way, rights to run pipes under another's land, and the like. The question of tennis courts is a question of how far the courts are prepared to stretch this category of rights to fit new modes of living. To put this at its most basic: the cases you read and the questions you focus on are the 'hard bits' because it is here that there is analysis to be done, and law to be applied. In practice, in the day-to-day life of the law, most of the operation of these rules is really straightforward and, bearing mind the number of properties owned in England and Wales, and the enormous numbers of interests existing in the land, the relative paucity of land law case law and disputes, and the perceived specialist nature of this law, is testament to the fact that this area of law, mostly and with a few notable caveats works well, and works simply. Thus, when you look at the difficult areas of law, do not let this undermine your faith in the logic of the system. Rather, it is a question of seeing how the logic of the system responds to new challenges.

1.5 CONCLUSION

The purpose of this chapter has been threefold. First, it has introduced the three fundamental questions which arise in land law: 1) what is the nature and type of rights in land; 2) how are these rights created; and 3) how do they interact. It then sketched a very simplified answer to these questions, so that the overall picture of the 'jigsaw' in land law can be kept in mind whilst the detail of the rules within each question are studied and analysed. Second, it introduced five concerns of land law: 1) the importance of autonomy; 2) the protection of the vulnerable; 3) public resources; 4) the role of technology; and 5) potential for implicit or explicit prioritisation of certain economic interests, at the expense of others and other people who thereby become outsiders, exploited rather than protected by the system. These concerns have given rise to five principles of land law, principles to which this book will refer as we learn the rules in more detail. These principles are:

1) Certainty
2) Sensitivity to context
3) Transactability
4) Systemic and individual effects
5) Recognition of the social role of the land law system.

When these principles are taken together, they have formed a 'logic' within the system. This logic, far from being immune to criticism, is useful to get to grips with how land law, so far, has been

---

[45] *Regency Villas Title Ltd v Diamond Resorts (Europe) Ltd* [2017] EWCA Civ 238, [2017] Ch 516.

designed to as to attempt to achieve these principles, conflicting and incoherent at points as they may be, as far as possible. Understanding this logic begins with understanding the terminology, and this terminology is nowhere more unhelpful but essential than in the distinction between legal and equitable rights, and in the concept of ownership. Finally, this chapter closes with a reminder: law when studied academically, from the perspective of analysis, is a study of law which focuses on 'tricky' issues, on the edges of the normal operation of the rules, not on the central and normal operation of those rules.

1.5.1 HOW TO NAVIGATE THIS BOOK

From here, this book will now consider how these rules work in more detail. In the remainder of Part I we continue our introduction by, in chapter 2, explaining the nature of land as a legal concept, and the nature of rights in land. In chapter 3, we then explore the concept of registered land, and draw some parallels and contrasts with unregistered land. In Part II, we then look at how rights in land are created. Chapter 4 explores formalities for the creation of rights in land. Chapter 5 then examines the land register as part of the rights creation process, and looks at the certainty and guarantee which the register provides in creating rights. Chapter 6 then looks at the creation of rights through adverse possession. Chapter 7 explores the creation of trusts where no formalities are present. Chapter 8 concludes Part II with an examination of the rules relating to proprietary estoppel. Part III then explores the nature and effects of such land law rights once created. Chapter 9 looks at the right which is closest to 'ownership' in English and Welsh law, the freehold estate. Chapter 10 explores the ownership right which is limited in time, the leasehold estate. In chapter 11 we consider mortgages—the interest by which a person can created a secured debt in relation to land, and which forms the most important part of the operation of the financing of the housing market. Chapter 12 considers easements, the mixed bag of rights we mentioned earlier, which are so critical to the practical function of a system of land law. Chapter 13 then examines freehold covenants—rights which restrict what a person is able to do on their land. Chapter 14 looks at options to purchase and rights of pre-emption and a wider collection of rights known as estate contracts. In Part IV, we then consider the interaction between rights, considering first, questions of priority (chapter 15), and second, questions of co-ownership of rights in land (chapter 16). Part V then looks without land law per se, to highlight two important areas of interaction with the wider legal system. Chapter 17 considers the role of human rights in land law, and chapter 18 then explores the tort actions which exist to protect rights in land.

In navigating this book, it will be made clear in the introduction to some of the chapters that it may be necessary to read two or more chapters to fully grasp the nature of much of the discussion. Thus, chapter 2 is essential before chapter 3, and in turn chapter 3 essential before chapter 5. Similarly, reading chapter 10 without having read chapter 4 would be more difficult. In this sense, the work progresses according to the author's own choices as to the best 'order' in which to learn a series of related and interconnected issues, issues which cannot be properly understood in isolation. However, almost no land law course is taught with the instruction, 'start at the beginning of the textbook and keep reading to the end'. Rather, individual lecturers will alter the order in which they approach topics. The consequence is that the structure of this book may not fit exactly with your own course. For this reason, throughout there will be references to other chapters so that you are able to recognise areas within the book where some pre-existing knowledge from earlier chapters would be helpful or essential. Finally, the summaries, definitional tables, and charts, may help to accelerate learning in particular areas without having to assimilate all the detail of the operation of the rules. This will assist in a developing a quick overall picture of how the rules work.

TABLE OF DEFINITIONS

Freehold estate	Estate in land of unlimited duration. Considered the 'highest' form of ownership in English law, save for that of the Crown.
Leasehold estate	A property right arising where there is a consensual grant of exclusive possession for a limited duration.
Mortgage	An interest arising as a security for a debt.
Easement	A limited right to use another's property, or (more rarely) to prevent that person from using their property in a particular way.
Profit	A right consisting in the ability to take from another's land— eg fishing, timber, hunting, and grazing rights.
Freehold covenant (restrictive covenant)	A covenant which limits the use to which servient land can be put, and which does not require the covenantor to expend money.
Leasehold covenant	An obligation contained in a lease.
Option to purchase	An option to purchase is a right which entitles its holder to force the proprietor of an estate in land, be that freehold or leasehold, to transfer their estate in land. There is no requirement on the option-holder to purchase the land.
Right of pre-emption	A right which provides that if a vendor decides to sell their estate in the land, the purchaser must be able to buy that estate at a price previously or to be agreed.
Rentcharge	A right to receive income from the owner of a freehold estate in land.
Rights of re-entry	A right of a landlord to terminate a lease/to bring about forfeiture of that lease.
Right to set aside a transaction	A right to rescind a voidable transaction.
Right to rectify a document	A right to rectify a document relating to the relevant land, eg rectification of a deed of conveyance (and possibly the right to rectify the register).
Equity arising by estoppel	The property right which arises in response to estoppel, and which is extinguished upon the crystallisation of the estoppel and the grant of any remedy.
Interest under a trust of land	A right relating to the freehold or leasehold estate which consists in the ability to hold the legal owner of the estate to account for the manner in which he manages his right, and which is itself a proprietary interest.

FURTHER READING

There are many eminent land and property lawyers over the centuries who have put their mind to what property is, how it should work, and what principles and purposes it serves. It is impossible to provide a comprehensive list of such works here. However, it should be kept in mind that siting behind rules-based learning in relation to land law, there is a whole raft of what is referred to as property theory. Such theory is not concerned with the precise operation of individual rules, but with the legal and moral nature of ownership, of property rights, and of the nature of land as a scarce asset. This list can provide a starting point, and a range of perspectives, should you wish to take your own reading and understanding of property theory further but it should be kept in mind that these works are challenging, and what is listed does not even represent the tip of the iceberg!

ALEXANDER, G. S. and PEÑALVER, E. A., *An Introduction to Property Theory* (CUP, 2012).
DEMSETZ, H., 'Toward a Theory of Property Rights', (1967) 57 American Economics Review 347.
PENNER, J. E., *The Idea of Property in Law* (OUP, 1997).
UNDERKUFLER, L. S., *The Idea of Property* (OUP, 2003).

2

PERSONAL AND PROPERTY RIGHTS IN LAND

2.1	Introduction	25	2.5	Conclusion	53
2.2	Interests in Land	26		Principles	54
2.3	What is Land?	46		Table of Definitions	55
2.4	Relativity of Title	52		Further reading	56

CHAPTER GOALS

By the end of this chapter you should understand:

- The nature of property rights in terms of their effects on third parties;
- The concept of the *numerus clausus* and the list of rights in land which make up that list;
- The status of the four categories of licence;
- The blurred nature of the boundary line between property and personal rights;
- The horizontal and vertical boundaries of land;
- That land is made up of land itself and some features on the land (fixtures);
- A basic working concept of the idea of possession of land (considered in more detail in chapters 6 and 10), as opposed to occupation and use; and
- The basic principles of relativity of title in English land law.

2.1 INTRODUCTION

This chapter has two primary goals. Its first is to examine what is meant by 'property rights' in English law. A distinction is drawn between proprietary interests, or property rights, and personal rights. To this end, in 2.2, it considers the consequences of a right having proprietary status, and the sorts of rights which *do not* have such status. It will become clear that the line between the two is not always clear-cut. The second goal is to explain what *land* is, in the context of land law. This is examined in 2.3. It will be seen that whilst there is some debate about the scope of control given to a person with rights in land, and to those moveable items that can be treated as part of the land in question, rights in land are not really ownership of a physical space. Rather, they are a right to certain advantages in respect of that space. This chapter also examines the concept of relativity of title. For a full understanding of the way in which the concept of relativity forms the fundamental underpinning of English land law, this material should be read in conjunction with chapter 6 on adverse possession and chapter 9 which considers the freehold estate.

Before we delve into the detail of these issues, therefore, it is necessary to explain what this chapter is *not* about. Since the Greek philosophers, writers and thinkers have been exploring what it means to have property—to 'own' something. Some of the further readings in chapter one look at this question in respect of land. These questions form the basis of some of the most significant political ideologies of the past two hundred years. The discussions of the idea of ownership in current philosophical and legal discourse are many and varied. They ask: who owns land, and what are the obligations that come with such ownership? Given that English land law has no legal concept of ownership, these questions become questions for morality. Although they have and will continue to have an influence on the law, they are not determinative of it. This is not to say that law is irrelevant to the way in which the issue of *ownership* is discussed—far from it, it forms a central part—but, in many ways, philosophies around ownership are simply not part of what an understanding of land *law* entails. Whilst the laws as we see them have been shaped by the variations in these philosophical concepts over time (and for more on that, see the further reading in this chapter), the law is not a representation of any particular philosophical stance. In this sense, land law is far more prosaic than a discussion of what ownership means and entails. That question is answered by values, in politics and in society, and by the totality of obligations that rest on person with rights in relation to land—environmental, social, and economic.

2.2 INTERESTS IN LAND

Property rights in relation to land come in two forms: estates, and interests (with interests also being used as a generic description for both). Estates are rights which a person holds in their 'own land': interests are rights which a person holds in relation to another's land. Both of these are proprietary. Proprietary interests are those rights which are capable of having third party effects, and they do so, not because third parties have consented to their effects, or voluntarily acted in such a way as to 'bring the property right upon them', but rather, they have such third party effects because that is inherent in their nature. Thanks to this third party application, we seek to ensure that there is a closed list of such rights, as was explained in chapter 1 at 1.2.1. The fact that property rights can affect third parties also shapes their required nature, before they are accorded proprietary status.

2.2.1 NATURE OF PROPERTY RIGHTS

Therefore, the crucial distinction between personal and property rights is about the effect that these rights can have on third parties. Property rights bind third parties. Because of this, we seek to provide that our property rights have certain characteristics, so as to ensure that it is 'fair' that third parties are affected (and the legal and equitable distinction explored in the previous chapter at 1.4.1 feeds into this). In *National Provincial Bank v Ainsworth*,[1] Lord Wilberforce explained the test for the identification of property rights in English law. This relates both to legal property rights, and to those rights which are capable only of existing in equity. In so-doing, the House of Lords in this case effectively creates what is known as the *numerus clausus* ('closed list') of property rights. Whilst this list is not officially closed (statute could create new rights, and the Supreme Court could overturn its approach in *Ainsworth* so that in theory it is possible to create new property rights), for most practical purposes there is such a closed list. This makes the life of those learning and operating within the context of land law much easier.

> **Key case:** *National Provincial Bank v Ainsworth* [1965] AC 1175
>
> A lender sought to take over control of a property, and sell it, using the proceeds of sale to pay off the mortgage debt. Mrs Ainsworth, the wife of the borrower, and an occupant of the house, argued that she had a 'deserted wife's equity' in the property. This was a type of property right which the courts had never allowed before. Mrs Ainsworth argued that if she had such a right, being proprietary, it would be capable of binding the lender (see chapter 15 for explanation of why and when any particular facts would achieve this outcome as far as the lender is concerned if the 'deserted wife's equity' had been granted proprietary status). This right could not have been a legal property right. It does not appear in section 1 Law of Property Act 1925 which is a definitive list of legal property rights (see discussion to follow). Mrs Ainsworth sought an equitable property right, which as we explained at 1.2.1, would have been contingent in its third party effects. The court concluded, however, that the 'deserted wife's equity' did not form part of the numerus clausus (the closed list) and that it was not, therefore, capable of being a property right.
>
> In concluding that Mrs Ainsworth's claim to a property right arising through her status as the paper title-holder's (freehold owner's) wife could not be recognised, Lord Wilberforce explained the features which a right must have in order for it to be considered proprietary. He reasoned that property rights have to be:
>
> - Definable
> - Identifiable
> - Capable of binding third parties
> - Permanent and stable.[2]
>
> On close inspection of this test, it becomes clear that it is circular. For a right to be 'capable of binding third parties' it must, as explained earlier, be a property right. The circularity means that although we do not have a fixed number of property rights, we effectively have fixed classes or categories of property rights. It is also worth emphasising that many of the property rights we most certainly do have look somewhat dubious when compared against this list. Let us take only two brief examples. Easements, as explained in chapter 12 at 12.2, are a mixed-bag of rights which (mostly) allow a person to utilise another's land in a particular way, including rights of way, hanging out washing on a line, using an outside

---

[1] *National Provincial Bank v Ainsworth* [1965] AC 1175 (HL).
[2] *National Provincial Bank v Ainsworth* [1965] AC 1175 (HL), 1248.

> toilet, and using a swimming pool. Much of chapter 12, which explains the law relating to easements, is concerned with the challenges which exist in defining easements. Of this category, 'definable' is not the first adjective that springs to mind. Similarly, as we see in chapter 10, it is possible to have leases of a very short duration—weeks and even days—and even though such are rare, they are most certainly not 'permanent'. Lord Wilberforce's test then is not so much an explanation of what characteristics our current rights actually have, but a test of what any new property right would have to look like.

Given this closed list, it should be possible to explain what rights make up the list. This is not quite as straightforward as it first appears. There are a few categories of rights where we are not entirely certain whether or not they are property rights (the right to rectify the register being a clear example of this ambiguity, as is explained in chapter 5 at 5.3.4.2). However, we certainly know *most* of the rights which make up this list. Part of the list is to be found in statutory provisions, which although not responsible for the *creation* of these property rights, are nevertheless confirmation of both their existence, and in some cases, their nature as either legal or equitable.

Section 1(2) LPA 1925 gives a list of the legal (universally binding) property rights. A recurring theme of this book will be the critical importance of reading statutory provisions (rather than simply being familiar with them). It is not possible to understand the fundamental rules underpinning our land law system without engagement with the statutory provisions in this way. As a result, at various points through the book, statutory provisions are replicated either in full or almost in full, sometimes with annotations. Reading these provisions, and understanding their content is *without doubt* the most important step to successful performance in a land law exam, or to thorough and accurate analysis. Following the annotation of the following statute, the property rights mentioned here are explained.

> '1 Legal estates and equitable interests.
>
> (1) The only estates in land which are capable of subsisting or of being conveyed or created at law are—
>
> (a) An estate in fee simple absolute in possession;
>
> (b) A term of years absolute.'

The estate of fee simple absolute in possession is otherwise known as the 'freehold' estate. It is the closest which English law has to 'ownership' of land. The term of years absolute is the 'leasehold' estate—the 'term of years' here refers to the fact that leasehold interests, unlike the freehold, only last for a limitation duration (although this could be as long as 999 years).

> '(2) The only interests or charges in or over land which are capable of subsisting or of being conveyed or created at law are—
>
> (a) An easement, right, or privilege in or over land for an interest equivalent to an estate in fee simple absolute in possession or a term of years absolute;'

Easements, as mentioned earlier, are a mixed collection of rights, including rights of way, rights to light, and rights of support (where one 'piece of land' holds up another—eg in the case of a semi-detached house). They are economically very important, although somewhat difficult to summarise in a few sentences. Rights and privileges in the rest of this section refers mainly to profits à prendre. These are somewhat old-fashioned looking rights, such as the right to fish for salmon in another's river, or to cut wood from another's forest, but they can be enormously valuable.

> '(b) A rentcharge in possession issuing out of or charged on land being either perpetual or for a term of years absolute;'

A rentcharge is the right to receive payment from the proprietor of a freehold estate. These are largely of historical interest as no new rentcharges can be created.

> '(c) A charge by way of legal mortgage;'

The charge by way of legal mortgage is the modern form which mortgages take. The mortgage is the security interest which a person obtains to secure a debt against a property. Contrary to the colloquial way in which we speak about mortgages, it is the *lender* who receives the mortgage right.

> '(e) Rights of entry exercisable over or in respect of a legal term of years absolute, or annexed, for any purpose, to a legal rentcharge.'

Rights of entry are the ability of a freehold owner (or the owner of a legal rentcharge), to go into possession of land to bring the leasehold estate of another to an end.

> '(3) All other estates, interests, and charges in or over land take effect as equitable interests.'

This section makes clear that there are no other possible legal rights in land. We can take from this that the list encapsulated in this section is the list of the most important and economically significant rights in land law, since they are accorded universal application against third parties. Everything else exists only as an equitable property right.

Of the rights outlined in this section, four are practically the most significant, and are treated in their individual chapters in this book. These are: freehold (chapter 9), leasehold (chapter 10), mortgage (strictly, charge by way of mortgage) (chapter 11), and easement (chapter 12). The summary of these rights here is merely an introduction. Please refer to the relevant chapter for more detail.

2.2.1.1 Freehold

The freehold is the closest that English law gets to some concept of 'absolute' ownership of land. However, there can be multiple freehold titles in relation to a single piece of land. Whilst no one such title would make a person *the* owner of the land, they may have *the best title* to land. Freehold titles are, essentially, ranked according to the date of their creation, subject to a potential cut-off point (see chapter 6 for how this cut-off point works in modern law). To think of the freehold as ownership in the sense of there being only one single owner of the land is, therefore, wrong, but it can be a helpful 'shorthand', as long as the limitations of the shorthand are appreciated.

Since the freehold is the most extensive possible right in relation to land, it is important to know what is entails. There is a common understanding that being the common law equivalent of ownership, the freehold entitles the right-holder to use, abuse, destroy, and transfer, the property at will, absent the control of any other, and, depending on your political perspective, absent the control of the state (for more on this question, see the further reading section later). Furthermore, the scope of the freehold right is said to extend geographically from the centre to the Earth to the stars, so that the owner of surface rights also has control over sub-surface rights as well as controlling access to the airspace above their land. Both of these ways of understanding the operation of the freehold are wrong, at least in modern law, and it is doubtful whether they could ever be said to have been meaningfully true. The caveats to the description are explored in detail in chapter 9 at 9.2.2.

2.2.1.2 Leasehold

The lease is consensual exclusive possession of land for a limited duration. Without the limitation on the duration, there is a freehold. The test as to whether a lease has been created is entirely objective. It depends not on what the parties wished or intended to achieve by any agreement, but what the terms of a contract as performed and intended to be performed actually give rise to. This was developed in the famous decision of Lord Templeman in *Street v Mountford*,[3] of which much more in chapter 10, at 10.2. In that case, Lord Templeman reasoned that, 'the traditional distinction between a tenancy and a licence of land [lies] in the grant of land for a term at a rent with exclusive possession'.[4] In other words, whenever these features are present—exclusive possession, term, and rent—the parties have necessarily created a lease (subject to a few very narrow exceptions), whatever they chose to call what they have done. In chapter 10, there is discussion of when these features are *not* required in order to create a lease (see 10.2).

2.2.1.3 Mortgage

At its heart, a mortgage is simply a right given to a lender as security for a loan. Before 1925, a mortgage actually involved the handing over of title to the relevant land subject to the right to get it back should the money owed by paid back in full plus any interest. Statutory reforms mean that mortgages of the legal title at least do not operate in this way any more, but instead constitute the creation of an additional proprietary interest for the mortgagee (lender). The mortgage is at once a contract concerned with the loan of money, and a property right.

2.2.1.4 Easement

The 'central case' of an easement is a right which allows you to use another's land in a particular way. They arise between nearby landowners, and exist to benefit one piece of land, known as the 'dominant tenement', and burden another, the 'servient tenement'. The category of easements includes the ability to walk across another's land using a right of way; to run pipes under it; to string wires over it; to park your car or store belongings on their land; to use a tennis court or swimming pool; or to use the space provided by a garden or park. However, there are other types of easement which cannot be explained as a right to 'use' another's land, such as a right of support which exists to prevent one owner from knocking down their half of a semi-detached house, for example, or a right to light which will prevent the development of structures which will block the passage of the light. Further, some very rare easements may constitute the right to demand that your neighbour spend money on his own land for your benefit—again, the right of support may

---

[3] *Street v Mountford* [1985] 1 AC 809.
[4] *Street v Mountford* [1985] 1 AC 809, 816.

fall in this category if maintenance is needed to ensure the support is provided; and the so-called 'spurious' easement of fencing which will require the neighbour to maintain fencing on his own land for your benefit.

Numerous attempts have been made to provide a single clear test for what can be easements, but the most famous such attempt was articulated in the decision in *Re Ellenborough Park* where the court explained that there were four criteria for the creation of an easement. These are:

'(1) there must be a dominant and a servient tenement:
(2) an easement must 'accommodate' the dominant tenement:
(3) dominant and servient owners must be different persons, and
(4) a right over land cannot amount to an easement, unless it is capable of forming the subject-matter of a grant'.[5]

What is meant by these requirements is explained in chapter 12 at 12.2.1.

These four are the main legal property rights. There are also a large number of equitable property rights. The 'list' of such equitable property rights is not found in a single place, but many do appear in statutory provisions. Some are not the subject of statutory coverage, but instead find their source and description solely in the case law. This list of equitable property rights is not exhaustive, since the courts can add rights to this category (at least in theory, as explained earlier). However, the main equitable property rights are: restrictive covenants (chapter 13), options to purchase (chapter 14), rights of pre-emption (chapter 14), estate contracts (chapter 14), equities arising by estoppel (chapter 8), rights to rectify the register (chapter 5), rights to set aside documents, rights to rectify documents, and interests under trusts (chapters 7 and 16). Rights to set aside and rectify documents are not considered in separate chapters, but do form part of the discussion in chapters 5 and 11 in particular.

2.2.1.5 Restrictive (freehold) covenants

Freehold covenants are voluntary agreements entered into by one freehold owner with another person, according to which he promises to behave in a particular way in relation to his land. Strictly speaking, a 'covenant' is a promise made by deed (a special kind of document, explained in chapter 4 at 4.3.2). There are two types of freehold covenant: positive covenants and negative covenants. Only negative—restrictive—covenants are treated as proprietary rights.

2.2.1.6 Options to purchase

An option to purchase is a right which entitles its holder to force the proprietor of an estate in land, be that freehold or leasehold, to transfer their estate in land. There is no requirement for the option-holder to purchase the land. There are certain requirements which must be met before a contract can take the form of an option to purchase. First, if created before 6th April 2010, the option must be exercisable within a defined and limited period of time. For options created after this date, this rule no longer applies. Second, the option contract must specify a price either fixed, or determinable by reference to some neutral standard, and must identify property to be purchased.

---

[5] *Re Ellenborough Park* [1956] Ch 131 (CA), 140.

2.2.1.7 Rights of pre-emption

Rights of pre-emption are in some ways similar to options to purchase in that they are giving to one person a privileged position in respect of their ability to purchase the relevant title to land. However, they are also very different in that the vendor has significantly more control. There are two possible ways in which right of pre-emption can be structured. The first is as a right of first refusal, where the vendor has given the potential purchaser the ability to have a first chance to buy the land. However, the parties will still have to agree a price and this can of course be a stumbling block to agreeing the sale. The second type would have a pre-set price either determined or determinable by some objective measure in the contract for the right of pre-emption so that if the seller decides to sell their estate in the land, the purchaser must be able to buy that estate at the agreed price.

2.2.1.8 Estate contracts

Estate contracts are contracts in which a promise is made for the transfer or creation of an estate in land (ie the freehold or leasehold estate). Once the contract is formed, equity will treat the situation as though the estate has *already* been transferred, giving rise to an equitable version of that interest, albeit on the same terms as the legal interest would be once the deed and any other formality requirements were completed.

2.2.1.9 Equities arising by estoppel

Such rights are the 'unformed' property rights which arise when a person has the 'benefit of an estoppel'. Proprietary estoppel is a very flexible doctrine which allows the court to remedy injustice by giving a person a property right, a money award, and various other options. Equities by estoppel arise when a promisor has assured the promisee that they have or will have a particular right in land, the promisee has relied on that promise to their detriment, and the promisor has then attempted to go back on that promise. The estoppel will arise when it is 'unconscionable' (essentially, unfair) for the promisor to go back on their promise in this way. The equity arising by estoppel does *not* entitle the promisee to what they have been promised, but it *does* entitle them to something, which is later determined by the courts. The equity itself therefore acts as a sort of 'marker', protecting the promisee should the promisor sell their land, or otherwise transfer or transact with it, prior to the court's grant of a remedy.

2.2.1.10 Rights to rectify the register

As explained earlier, it is not entirely clear whether these are property rights or not. If they are, then they are the right of a person who has lost title to land, or an interest in land, through their name being taken off the register by mistake, to have their right returned to the register in the place that it ought to have been before.

2.2.1.11 Interests under a trust

The trust interest is, in many ways, the one with which newcomers to land law struggle the most. We discussed this terminology at 1.4.2 of chapter 1. It is essentially a *relationship* between the legal owner of the freehold or leasehold estate—the trustee—and the 'equitable owner'—the beneficiary. The nature of this relationship is that the trustee must act for the benefit of the equitable owner when dealing with the land. However, to add a layer of protection, the equitable owner has their own property right, so that third parties may be affected by that interest (if the conditions for the bindingness of equitable rights are met).

These brief descriptions of the property rights will, on first reading, be difficult to process. The terminology will be unfamiliar, as will any sense of the circumstances in which such rights arise, and what they mean for the people who hold such rights, or are burdened by such rights. However, it is useful to begin analysis of what rights in land are with an upfront explanation of these rights, which can be referred to for a potted summary of their nature where required. This information is summarised further in the table of definitions, at the end of the chapter. A fuller version of this table is available in the online resources, which also explains how such rights are created and the conditions for their impact on third parties.

> **Summary: Nature of property rights**
>
> Thanks to the decision in *Ainsworth*, there is an effectively closed list of property rights. In this list fall two types of rights: those which are capable of being legal property rights (of which the most important are freehold, leasehold, easement and mortgage) as defined by section 1 Law of Property Act 1925; and those which can only exist in equity. Both of these categories of rights are capable of binding third parties but legal rights are universally binding, whereas equitable rights depend on further conditions being satisfied before they will bind third parties.

2.2.2 LICENCES

If a right is not part of this list, then it is licence. Licences are the generic category of rights that relate to land but which are not property rights. None of these are binding on third parties (although third parties may, by their actions, bind themselves to honour such rights). Any attempt to render such rights into a species of property right has been confirmed as mistaken by the Court of Appeal in *Ashburn Anstalt v Arnold*[6]. Licences are hugely varied. They cover an enormous range of circumstances, and they come into and go out of existence without any requirements of formalities or solemnity. Their mode of creation is very different from most property rights (see chapter 4). However, it is useful to consider licences in more detail here, to set the scene for the distinction between personal and property rights discussion which follows. Many land law textbooks devote a chapter to licences, or include them in chapters on proprietary estoppel. They are included here, however, since understanding licences is very useful in appreciating where the boundary line between the personal and the proprietary lies.

There are different categories of licences which behave in particular ways. The existence of these categories, has, historically at least, led some courts to accord either full proprietary status, or a sort of modified proprietary status, to such rights. In this section of the chapter, we will be considering a series of cases which seem to suggest that some licences can bind third parties, that they are property rights. This is fundamentally wrong. To ask whether licences can be property

---

[6] *Ashburn Anstalt v Arnold* [1989] Ch. 1 (CA).

rights is a totally meaningless question. A licence is a personal right in land. It would be like asking whether a personal right was a property right. It just does not make sense. Nonetheless, there are some cases which do discuss this. Luckily, now, we have had a return to sense. It is worth tracing the history of these cases anyway to understand the development of the current rules as this gives a considerable deal of insight into the nature of rights in land, and to the logic of why they are treated as they are by the property rules which we discuss in the rest of this book.

There are four categories of licence that appear in the literature. Of these, the 'estoppel licence' is not, in this author's opinion, a separate category of licence and is instead a muddled label given to situations involving proprietary estoppel (see equities by estoppel earlier and chapter 8 generally). We therefore discuss this only very briefly. The other categories are:

1. Bare licences
2. Contractual licences
3. Licences coupled with an interest.

In relation to each of these, in this section we consider (a) the nature of the licence; (b) and when and how it can be revoked as against the original promisor (ie between the original parties to the licence).

2.2.2.1 Bare licence

A bare licence is simply a permission to be on land. For example, the permission you have to enter a shop, or for your friend to come round for tea, are bare licences. A bare licence is a right *in personam* (a personal right). It is revocable at will. Its effect is to provide a defence to an action in trespass. We consider trespass, the tort of entering onto land possessed by another, in chapter 18. A licence will be a bare licence where the transaction which creates that licence has no other legal effect—eg it is not a transaction which gives rise to a contract.

A bare licence could be given for a defined period of time—as may be the case in the example of the shop where although it is clear that the licence is implied and unspoken, it is nevertheless assumed to come to an end when the shop closes. If a licence is until a defined period, then it will expire at that time. However, it can be revoked any time before that 'expiry' as there is nothing in a bare licence which would justify holding the person giving permission to be on the land to their promise. If you cause disruption in the shop, the shopkeeper can make you leave earlier. If the duration of a licence is undefined—as may be the case with the friend coming round for tea—it is revocable at any time. However, the revocation will not necessarily have immediate effect in the sense that the friend would not necessarily be a trespasser immediately that you ask them to leave. Rather, you must leave enough time for the licensee to leave the premises, or, in some cases, to make arrangements for somewhere else to go.[7] The revocability of such licences, and their nature as merely defences to an action for trespass, is explored in the House of Lords decision in *Winter Garden Theatre v Millennium Productions*.[8]

---

[7] *Canadian Pacific Railway v The King* [1931] AC 414; *Governing Body of Henrietta Barnett School v Hampstead Garden Suburb Institute* (1995) 93 LGR 470.

[8] *Winter Garden Theatre v Millennium Productions* [1948] AC 173 (HL).

> **Key case:** *Winter Garden Theatre v Millennium Productions* [1948] AC 173
>
> In this case, Millennium Productions were given a licence to use the Winter Garden Theatre for producing plays for 6 months. The agreement (which was contractual) contained an option to continue for a further six months at an increased rent. The licence contained the provision that if the company wished not to take up the option of the extra six months, then they had to give one month's notice of the intention to bring the licence to an end. There was no express provision in the agreement for the licensor, ie Winter Garden Theatres, to bring the licence to an end. The theatre owners then served on Millennium Productions a notice trying to bring the licence to an end. They did not argue that there had been a breach of the licence agreement. Millennium Productions sought a declaration that the licence was not revocable except as a result of a breach of the contract, or that it was valid for a reasonable period after notice of the revocation. The court held that the licence was not perpetual and that it could be withdrawn, but that notice was required.
>
> Despite being a case concerned with contractual licences, this case has important consequences also for how we understand bare licences. First, it emphasises their fundamental nature as being merely a permission to be on land and nothing more. As Viscount Haldane explained, '[t]he effect of a licence to A to permit B to enter upon A's land or to use his premises for some purpose is in effect an authority which prevents B from being regarded as a trespasser'.[9] Second, the case gives indications that the 'grace period' which is given, even in the case of bare licences, allowing the licensee (the person with the licence) to leave, arises from a rule of law, not from some sort of implied agreement. The consequence of this is that the reasonable period will exist in all cases, whether or not there is any interaction between the parties.

In the aftermath of this case, and other cases such as *Canadian Pacific Railway Company*[10] (moving railway tracks) and *The Henrietta Barnett School* (moving a school),[11] it has become clear that in the case of bare licences, the law may insist on a lengthy period of time (calculated in years potentially) before the licensee would become a trespasser. This is because the law has recognised that in some bare licence cases, although there is no contractual promise, the licensee may nevertheless have relied on the existence of the licence in some respect. In the case of *The Henrietta Barnett School*,[12] the school had relied on the licence by not finding somewhere else to conduct the business of the school. Quite how the 'grace period' should operate in such cases has been the subject of some discussion. It seems, however, that the courts will take a common sense approach to this question, recognising detriment, without this somehow 'morphing' into a property right. However, one aspect of this, a potential requirement that not only the licensor give the licensee a reasonable 'packing up time', but also *notice* of the intention to revoke the licence, begins to fudge the distinction between personal and property rights in the eyes of some commentators. Thus, per Hill:

> 'it is far from clear that the licensor's obligation to give reasonable notice is required to ensure that a "two-sided" licensee [ie those cases where the licensee relies on the licence] does not suffer hardship… [However, all] the cases in which the basis of the court's decision has been either the doctrine of a licence acted upon or the licensor's obligation to give reasonable notice could have been decided

---

[9] *Winter Garden Theatre v Millennium Productions* [1948] AC 173 (HL), 188.
[10] *Canadian Pacific Railway v The King* [1931] AC 414.
[11] *Governing Body of Henrietta Barnett School v. Hampstead Garden Suburb Institute* (1995) 93 LGR 470.
[12] *Governing Body of Henrietta Barnett School v. Hampstead Garden Suburb Institute* (1995) 93 LGR 470.

equally (or more) satisfactorily by the proper application of the doctrine of proprietary estoppel or the packing-up period. Furthermore, there is no argument of principle in support of the proposition that a licensor should be under an obligation to give the licensee a period of notice before revocation of a bare licence is to take effect. It does not follow from the fact that a contractual licensee will normally be under an implied obligation to give the licensee a reasonable period of notice that a similar obligation arises in the context of bare licences. When bare licences are located in the broader picture of rights in relation to land, the notion that a bare licensee is entitled to a period of notice is illogical.'[13]

Even in this most simple of personal rights in land, we can see the dangers of not maintaining a strict and clear boundary between personal and property rights.

> **Summary: Bare licence**
>
> A bare licence is revocable at any time, and is merely a defence to an action in trespass. The licensor may have to give the licensee a reasonable amount of time to leave, and some cases suggest they may also have to give a reasonable notice period as well as a 'packing up' period.

2.2.2.2 Contractual Licences

This danger has, even more forcefully, manifested itself in the now, thankfully, resolved case law saga that resulted in contractual licences being treated as property rights for some purposes. Contractual licences are licences for which consideration has been given (for those not yet familiar with the rules of contract law, this basically means that payment or some other promise must be given in return for the licence) and which form part of a contractual agreement. The licence can be the main purpose of the contract, or a collateral issue. It can also be express or implied.[14] It can also be a right to enter the land and a duty to do so, as in cases involving a contractual licence to carry out building works.

The effect of contractual licences between the parties

The first thing to establish in relation to contractual licences is the effect that such will have in terms of the relationship between the landowner and the licensee. Can the original licensor revoke the licence other than in accordance with the terms of the contract? Is a licence irrevocable except as provided for by this contract? This is considered in *Hounslow v Twickenham Garden Developments*.[15]

> **Key case: *Hounslow v Twickenham Garden Developments* [1971] Ch 233**
>
> In this case, an architect was unhappy with progress on a building site and so wrote to the council (the landowner) to complain about the contractors. The council then wrote to the contractors attempting to bring the contract of employment to an end. The contractors refused to accept this and chose to carry on with the work on the site. The council sought to regain possession of the land and claimed an injunction to prevent trespass. The question for the court was whether the licence, which was generated

---

[13] J Hill, 'The termination of bare licences' (2001) 60 CLJ 89, 108.
[14] *Errington v Errington* [1952] 1 KB 290 (CA); *Chandler v Kerley* [1978] 1 WLR 693 (CA).
[15] *Hounslow v Twickenham Garden Developments* [1971] Ch 233 (Ch).

by the contract, could be revoked in this way. It was decided that the contract was one for the execution of specified works on the site with, therefore, at least an implied negative obligation on the council not to revoke any licence except in accordance with the contract (as revocation of the licence would prevent the contractors from carrying out their contractual duties). This shows the power of a contractual licence as between the contracting parties. It suggests that in this context, where the contractors were obligated to carry out works, and the whole relationship was governed by the contract of works, then the licence could only be revoked as part and parcel of either bringing the contract to an end as a whole, or otherwise in line with what the contract provides. In this sense, since the licence is part of the contract, it is governed by the contract.

Given the central importance of the contract to the relationship, what is the position where the contract, possibly implied, is silent as to when the licence can be revoked? This was considered in *Chandler v Kerley*.[16]

Key case: *Chandler v Kerley* **[1978] 1 WLR 693**

Mr and Mrs Kerley owned a house together. Mrs Kerley and Mr Chandler started seeing each other. It was agreed that Mrs Kerley would stay in the house but that Mr Chandler would then buy the house cheaply from Mr Kerley. Mr Chandler then wanted to sell the house at full value and for Mrs Kerley to leave. She tried to argue that Mr Chandler could not evict her on the basis that they had an agreement that she could stay and as a result Mr Chandler had been able to purchase the land more cheaply from Mr Kerley. The Court of Appeal decided that Mrs Kerley had a contractual licence to remain in the house. There was obviously no such thing in the sale—this involved quite a high degree of judicial intervention—but it nevertheless gave her a degree of protection. What did this mean in terms of revocation, however, since there was no explicit contractual agreement—written or otherwise—to which the court could refer? The court emphasised that a contractual licence can be terminated in accordance with the contract. If the contract is silent on the issue, it will normally be the case that the ability to terminate on reasonable notice will be implied. Quite apart from demonstrating the dangers of love life and land law colliding, this case demonstrates the creative ways in which courts can use licences to affect the rights and obligations of the parties to the contract to reflect the 'fairness' which is apparent in any situation. It is important to note, however, that this has no effect on third parties, since, by definition, they are not affected by the terms of the licence.

In short, a contractual licence is revocable only in accordance with the terms of the contract.

The effect of contractual licences against third parties

However, the effect of licences on third parties is significantly less potent. There is a complicated series of case law on this question but the answer is very firmly, and very clearly, that contractual licences are personal rights and cannot bind third parties *except* in cases where the third party acts in such a way as to *bind themselves* to the right. In other words, the bindingness of the licence depends upon the conduct of the third party, and does not in any way suggest that the

---

[16] *Chandler v Kerley* [1978] 1 WLR 693 (CA).

licence has some form of proprietary effect. It is necessary, however, to examine the history of this case law to understand some of the commentary, but also to explain the 'constructive trust' (in reality, nothing of the sort) which can arise in some circumstances.

1. The early case law

Early case law on the question of the status of the contractual licence vis-à-vis third parties was entirely orthodox. This was confirmed in the House of Lords decision in *King v David Allen Billposting*.[17]

> **Key case:** *King v David Allen Billposting* [1916] 2 AC 54
>
> The owner of a picture house gave David Allen Billposting permission to affix posters and advertisements to the flank walls of the picture house for a period of 4 years. They agreed that the owner would not, while the licence remained in force, permit any other person to affix any advertisement to the walls. The picture house company then transferred its lease, and the new lease contained no reference to the agreement for the adverts. The new company then refused permission for the adverts, and so David Allen brought an action. The court held that the agreement did not create an interest in land, but merely a personal obligation on the licensor to allow the licensees the use of the wall. As he had put it out of his power to fulfil his obligation under the agreement, he was liable in damages for breach of contract, but the third party was not affected by the agreement. In the words of Lord Buckmaster:
>
> > 'I have looked anxiously and carefully through this document to see whether it was possible to derive from its construction anything except the creation of a personal obligation between the appellant and the respondents with regard to the use of this wall, and I am unable to find it. this is nothing but a licence–a licence for a fixed term of years, but a licence which creates no estate or interest in the land'.[18]
>
> This decision is a completely straightforward explanation of how contractual licences work. The contracting parties were bound by the obligations through their acceptance of the contract, and would be liable for damages or another remedy in case of breach. The third party, however, was not automatically affected by the licence, and had not behaved in any way to voluntarily bind himself to the contract either.

2. The 'infusion of equity'

Here the matter should have rested, and since *King* is a House of Lords decision, there ought to have been no room for manoeuvre. However, in the Court of Appeal, there were developments which began to suggest that equity could intervene in some cases to make a licence binding upon a third party. This can be seen in *Errington v Errington*.[19]

> **Key case:** *Errington v Errington* [1952] 1 KB 290
>
> A father, wishing to provide a home for his son, purchased a house using a mortgage. He promised that if the son continued in occupation and paid the instalments, he would then transfer the property to him. When the father died, he left all his property to his widow. The son then, leaving his wife, went to live

---

[17] *King v David Allen & Sons Billposting Ltd* [1916] 2 AC 54 (HL).
[18] *King v David Allen & Sons Billposting Ltd* [1916] 2 AC 54 (HL), 59–60.
[19] *Errington v Errington* [1952] 1 KB 290 (CA).

with his widowed mother. The wife continued to live in the house and pay the instalments. The mother brought an action for possession against the wife. The court held the son and daughter-in-law were licensees entitled under a personal contract to occupy for as long as they paid the instalments. So far, so simple. However, Denning LJ tried rather hard to find a way for how this contract, made between the couple and the father, could affect the position of the widow. He argued that, in some way, equity would step in and prevent the contract being 'breached'. Thus, he explained:

> 'This infusion of equity means that contractual licences now have a force and validity of their own and cannot be revoked in breach of the contract.'[20]

In other words, Denning LJ is arguing here that the contractual licence can have a 'persistent' effect against third parties, and so will bind them equally as it would bind an original contracting party, except as the contract itself provides. This, in effect, gave the licence a proprietary status, and was entirely at odds both with the House of Lords decision in *King v David Allen*,[21] and with the logic of what licences are and how they work. It is widely accepted as having been a wrong turn.

3. Confirmation of the *numerus clausus*

The House of Lords was then given an opportunity to consider this issue in *National Provincial Bank v Ainsworth*,[22] discussed at 2.2.1. However, the court was reluctant to authoritatively pronounce on the status of contractual licences in domestic-style situations, and whilst highlighting that (obviously) rights which were non-proprietary could not have proprietary effects on third parties, they did not close the door entirely.

4. Licence and a constructive trust

This meant that the Court of Appeal, still spearheaded by Lord Denning, had an opportunity to build on *Errington*[23] in *Binions v Evans*.[24]

> **Key case:** *Binions v Evans* [1972] Ch 359
>
> Mrs Evans' husband was employed by a large estate and lived in a cottage owned by the estate paying no rent. He died, and Mrs Evans continued living in the cottage. In 1968, the trustees of the estate entered into an agreement to provide a temporary home for her and agreed to let her live there as a tenant at will free of rent for the rest of her life or as determined according to the terms of the agreement. In 1970, the trustees agreed to sell the cottage to Binions and gave Binions a copy of the agreement including a special clause in the contract of sale to protect Mrs Evans' occupation. As a result of this Binions paid a reduced price but then, in 1971, tried to evict Mrs Evans. It was held that the agreement between Mrs Evans and the estate created a contractual licence resulting in an equitable interest. When the cottage was sold to Binons subject to Evans' right under the agreement, Binions took the cottage on a constructive trust to permit Mrs Evans to reside there during her life or as long as she desired. Lord Denning

---

[20] *Errington v Errington* [1952] 1 KB 290 (CA), 299.
[21] *King v David Allen & Sons Billposting Ltd* [1916] 2 AC 54 (HL).
[22] *National Provincial Bank v Ainsworth* [1965] AC 1175 (HL).
[23] *Errington v Errington* [1952] 1 KB 290 (CA).
[24] *Binions v Evans* [1972] Ch 359 (CA).

stated that even if the contractual licence itself was personal, that a purchaser taking the land subject to the licence will be bound to honour it under a constructive trust. Thus,

> 'Whenever the owner sells the land to a purchaser, and at the same time stipulates that he shall take it subject to a contractual licence, I think it plain that a court of equity will impose on the purchaser a constructive trust in favour of the beneficiary'.[25]

This decision seems to show that in circumstances like those involving Mrs Evans, equity creates a new property right which she can use to defend herself against the third party purchaser. If this were to be true regardless of Binions' behaviour, then it would be a remarkable decision, inventing a new property right, and going very much against both the authority in *King* and the test in *Ainsworth*. However, the precise ratio of the case was, and remains, unclear, and so after this decision there was scope for the case law to move in a number of different directions.

5. Constructive trust exists at all times

Unfortunately, following from *Binions*,[26] in *DHN v Tower Hamlets*,[27] the court held that the constructive trust must have existed at all times alongside the licence, since there was no new event in these cases which 'triggered' the constructive trust (which, as highlighted earlier, is no such thing). This meant that the licensee has a property right at all times, the same 'shape and size' as the licence. The inevitable conclusion to this logic, as explained in *Midland Bank v Farmpride*,[28] was that contractual licences generate property rights.

6. Licences are personal rights

This was such nonsense, however, that a later Court of Appeal, in *Ashburn Anstalt*[29] rejected this approach holding that the earlier decisions were decided *per incuriam*. The court held that contractual licences are personal rights. In some cases, a third party may be affected by the 'constructive trust', but only where they promise to be so-bound, and pay less for the land as a result. It is their own behaviour, not the contract itself, which results in the obligation to uphold the licence falling on their shoulders.

> **Key case: *Ashburn Anstalt v Arnold* [1989] Ch 1**
>
> Arnold sold its leasehold interest in shop premises. The agreement provided that the vendor could remain in the property. The purchaser promised that it intended to redevelop the property and would grant the vendor the lease of a shop on the site once this was done. In 1985 Ashburn Anstalt purchased the freehold subject to this agreement. The court assessed whether there was anything which could be binding upon the purchaser. Fox LJ reasoned that if no tenancy (lease) was created, and that this was simply a contractual licence, although a licence is not binding even on a purchaser who has knowledge of the licence, appropriate facts might give rise to a constructive trust. This would only be done where it would be inequitable for the purchaser to deny the claimant an interest. In this case there was no such constructive trust as no inequity arose.

---

[25] *Binions v Evans* [1972] Ch 359 (CA), 368.
[26] *Binions v Evans* [1972] Ch 359 (CA).
[27] *DHN Food Distributors v Tower Hamlets LBC* [1976] 1 WLR 852 (CA).
[28] *Midland Bank Plc v Farmpride Hatcheries Ltd* (1980) 260 EG 493 (CA).
[29] *Ashburn Anstalt v Arnold* [1989] Ch 1 (CA).

> As Fox LJ highlighted, 'we do not think that there is any serious doubt as to the law. A mere contractual licence to occupy land is not binding on a purchaser of the land even though he has notice of the licence'.[30] The far-reaching statement of *Errington*[31] was, thus, contrary to authority. The finding on appropriate facts of a constructive trust may well however be regarded as a beneficial adaptation of old rules to new situations.

The critical issue in the modern law, therefore, is when this 'constructive trust' will arise. As *IDC v Clark*[32] and *Lloyd v Dugdale*[33] emphasise, it can only do so when there is a promise to honour the licence and a lower payment. This promise can be implied but the courts will very be reluctant to imply it. Furthermore, the courts have indicated that a subsequent purchaser who has not promised to be bound by the licence, will not be bound to it. In this sense, this constructive trust (merely an inconvenient label, and not indicative of proprietary status) does not mean that the licence has somehow become a property right.

> **Summary: Contractual licences**
>
> Contractual licences are binding as between the contracting parties under the terms of the contract. In some cases, a third party, may, by their own actions, bind themselves to such a contract. The mechanism by which this takes place is referred to in the case law as a constructive trust, even though nothing is held on trust.

2.2.2.3 Estoppel licences

The easiest thing with estoppel licences is to start off from the perspective that there is no such thing. You can have an estoppel, and you can a licence, but there is no hybrid concept. Nonetheless, because people do refer to them, it is worthwhile understanding what they might mean and what the relevance of this concept in your understanding of both licences, and estoppel (as explained in chapter 8).

One option is that this concept refers to a licence granted by a court following the successful invocation of the rules of equity relating to estoppel. This would mean that a claimant has shown that they have detrimentally relied on a sufficiently certain promise, and that an estoppel has arisen in their favour. The court then tries to work out how to remedy this estoppel. One option is that they may grant a licence as the remedy to the estoppel. If this is what is meant by estoppel licence then it might be more clear to refer to this as a licence arising in response to an estoppel, and the licence that emerges would certainly not have proprietary effects.

A second option is that the situation is one where a person has a licence, and then later relies on a promise to their detriment, so that an estoppel arises in their favour. At that time they would have a licence to be on the land and *separately* an equity arising by estoppel which is in itself a property right.

---

[30] *Ashburn Anstalt v Arnold* [1989] Ch. 1 (CA), 15.
[31] *Errington v Errington* [1952] 1 KB 290 (CA).
[32] *IDC v Clark* (1993) 65 P & CR 179 (CA).
[33] *Lloyd v Dugdale* [2001] EWCA Civ 1754, [2002] 2 P & CR 13.

The third option is that a person has a licence from an original landowner. The landowner then sells the land to a third party and the third party promises that they will give effect to the licence, paying a lower price as a result. In this case the 'licence' will bind the purchaser because of their promise. This is through the mechanism of a constructive trust, but because the constructive trust label is so inappropriate here, people may refer to it as an estoppel licence. Neither is a helpful term.

> **Summary: Estoppel licences**
>
> The term 'estoppel licence' is unhelpful and should be avoided.

2.2.2.4 Licences coupled with an interest

Licences coupled with an interest are, in some ways, property rights, but this is really because there is no independent licence in such a case. Instead there's just an interest, and the way that it is actually exercised, ie through entering onto another's land, requires that the person with the right not be a trespasser during the exercise of their right. For example, a profit to fell trees is a property right—profits are explained at 2.2.1 and in chapter 12—and the exercise of this right requires its holder to actually enter the servient land in order to fell the trees. Another example would be where A grants B a lease over A's barn, but to access the barn B has to cross A's land. This could be in the nature of a licence but it is integrally linked to the lease itself. The licence such as it is certainly has no existence independent of the property right.

> **Summary: Licences coupled with interest**
>
> Licences coupled with an interest are best understood as being simply expressions of the fact that some property rights entitle their holder to enter onto land belonging to another without being a trespasser. Any such 'licence' has no independent existence.

2.2.3 PROPERTY RIGHTS AND THIRD PARTY EFFECTS

Now that we know what the property rights are, it is essential to examine their defining characteristic in a bit more detail, to see how far the true boundary between licences and property rights is rigidly maintained. This key characteristic is, as explained earlier, the ability to bind third parties. However, is the distinction between property rights and personal rights as clear-cut as we think, and as it should be, in this respect? The boundary line between the two has, arguably, become somewhat blurred as a result of the decision in *Manchester Airport v Dutton*,[34] and the follow-up case law, including *Mayor of London v Hall*[35] and most recently *Manchester Ship Canal v Vauxhall*.[36] These cases show that even where a person does *not* have a property right, they may nevertheless be able to get *remedies* in relation to land which are, in effect, remedies against third parties.

---

[34] *Manchester Airport v Dutton* [2000] QB 133 (CA).
[35] *Mayor of London v Hall* [2010] EWCA Civ 817, [2011] 1 WLR 504.
[36] *Manchester Ship Canal v Vauxhall* [2018] EWCA Civ 1100.

Key case: *Manchester Airport v Dutton* [2000] QB 133

Manchester Airport had been granted a licence by the freeholder, the National Trust, to fell some trees in order to build a second runway. Before the Airport could begin works on the land some environmental protestors set up a camp in the trees. The natural outcome would have been for the National Trust to bring an action for possession against the trespassers, but the National Trust was reluctant to intervene. Manchester Airport could also have brought personal actions against the National Trust or against the trespassers (eg for tort of interference with contract) but these actions were not guaranteed of success, and did not give Manchester Airport a fast solution. Instead, Manchester Airport brought an action for possession against the trespassers. Traditional understandings of the situation would have said that since the Airport did not have a right to possession of the land, having only a licence, they ought not to have been able to obtain an order for possession. Indeed, Chadwick LJ in the dissent agreed that since Manchester Airport did not have a property right, they could not obtain a proprietary remedy in the form of an order for possession.

The majority however, Laws LJ and Kennedy LJ, granted the order for possession. Kennedy LJ, took a linguistic approach to the question relying on the rather imprecise wording of the particular order concerned. However, Laws LJ took a much more radical approach, complaining that the traditional rule—ie the rigid distinction between the person and the proprietary—is old-fashioned ('the rattle of medieval chains'[37]), and argued that in circumstances like this, a court should not be helpless to give effect to the right that Manchester Airport did have. Keeping this in mind, Laws LJ reasoned that:

> 'the true principle is that a licensee not in occupation may claim possession against a trespasser if that is a necessary remedy to vindicate and give effect to such rights of occupation as by contract with his licensor he enjoys. This is the same principle as allows a licensee who is in de facto possession to evict a trespasser. There is no respectable distinction, in law or logic, between the two situations. An estate owner may seek an order whether he is in possession or not. So, in my judgment, may a licensee, if other things are equal. In both cases, the plaintiff's remedy is strictly limited to what is required to make good his legal right. The principle applies although the licensee has no right to exclude the licensor himself. Elementarily he cannot exclude any occupier who, by contract or estate, has a claim to possession equal or superior to his own. Obviously, however, that will not avail a bare trespasser.
>
> In this whole debate, as regards the law of remedies in the end I see no significance as a matter of principle in any distinction drawn between a plaintiff whose right to occupy the land in question arises from title and one whose right arises only from contract. In every case the question must be, what is the reach of the right, and whether it is shown that the defendant's acts violate its enjoyment. If they do, and (as here) an order for possession is the only practical remedy, the remedy should be granted. Otherwise the law is powerless to correct a proved or admitted wrongdoing; and that would be unjust and disreputable.'[38]

The main consequence of this decision is that the court here gives Manchester Airport something that the National Trust did not give them—the right to control who is on the land. Furthermore, it blurs the boundary between personal and property rights—the personal licence is binding on the trespassers. As a result, this case has been the subject of sustained criticism.

Amongst such critics sits Swadling, who explains that this case is inappropriate in opening up the numerus clausus. However, he also sees it as evidence of a wider trend—a trend which we see occurring in other areas of this book, including in chapters 7 and 8, and indeed in *Chandler v Kerley*. The courts

---

[37] *Manchester Airport v Dutton* [2000] QB 133 (CA), 148.
[38] *Manchester Airport v Dutton* [2000] QB 133 (CA), 150.

44 Chapter 2 Personal and Property Rights in Land

occasionally look to the 'right' result and finding a way to achieve that outcome, rather than considering the content of the rules. This, Swadling explains, is inappropriate remedialism (focus on the remedy rather than the rule). Such a focus, in his view, results in an inappropriate change to the substance of rights.

> 'But it is not a question for the "law of remedies" to determine the nature of a claimant's right, and it is this concentration on remedies to the exclusion of rights which makes the case doubtful. If Laws L.J. had instead focused on the content of the right… then it would have been seen that the right was not one which by its nature was capable of binding a stranger to its creation… Once we decouple remedy from right, we begin more or less inadvertently to change the very nature of the right itself. And it was only by this means that a personal right was in this case elevated to the status of a property right. By the manipulation of remedies the closed number of proprietary rights has been inappropriately increased.'[39]

Given the negative reaction which emerged following *Dutton*, there was perhaps a feeling that the decision would be overturned should the Court of Appeal have the opportunity so to do. However, in *Mayor of London v Hall*[40] it became clear that far from wishing to distance itself from the *Dutton*-approach, the Court of Appeal gave that case support.

> **Key case:** *Mayor of London v Hall* [2010] EWCA Civ 817
>
> The Mayor of London brought an action for possession against protestors in Parliament Square Gardens (PSG). These protestors were trespassing on PSG and the Mayor claimed that he was not able to keep the square in good order, prevent vandalism etc. The Mayor did not have a property right in the land. The decision by Neuberger MR—that the Mayor of London was able to bring an action against the trespassers in this case—was ultimately decided on the basis of the provisions of the Greater London Authority Act 1999 but there is discussion of *Dutton*. Neuberger comments favourably on the earlier decision and this suggests that *Dutton* is now 'here to stay'. Furthermore arguably, the tone of the decision in *Hall* suggests that *Dutton* may be wider even than had been anticipated in the immediate aftermath of the case. This 'broadening' of the potential applicability of *Dutton* comes from an (implied) limitation suggested by the court in *Dutton*, that an individual could only bring an actin for possession on the basis of a contractual right if that right was rendered entirely useless by the existence of the trespasser. In *Hall*, however, the rights of the Mayor of London in respect of PSG were not rendered useless by the existence of the 'democracy villagers'. Rather, they were made more difficult in some respects, and continued relatively unhindered in others. By removing the direct relationship between interference with the totality of the personal right, and the possibility of acquiring a remedy in the form of a possession order, the court appears to go beyond the boundaries of *Dutton*.
>
> Furthermore, in so-doing, the court conflates and confuses a number of important legal concepts, which we discuss in more detail later. As I have argued elsewhere,
>
>> 'The logic of the distinctions being used here must then be examined. There are four different potential scenarios: (i) a person is in (non-exclusive) actual occupation of the land; (ii) a person has a personal right to be in actual (non-exclusive) occupation but is not in fact in actual occupation (as with a licensee who has not moved into a flat); (iii) a person has a right to possession and is in possession (as with the Mayor

---

[39] W Swadling, 'Opening the numerus clausus' (2000) 116 LQR 354, 360.
[40] *Mayor of London v Hall* [2010] EWCA Civ 817, [2011] 1 WLR 504.

> of London—this person can or can not be in occupation); and (iv) a person has a right to possession and is
> not in possession (as is the case where there is adverse possession). These scenarios each contain a mixture
> of "rights" and "facts". The fact of occupation can be distinguished from the right to occupation; similarly
> the fact of possession can, and here must, be distinguished from the right to possession. Crucially here
> also a right to occupation is something different from a right to possession. This is clearly true when we
> consider a licensee, and yet the line of cases from *Dutton* appears to conflate these issues.[41]

This conflation between what a licence can do—confer a right to occupy—and what the *fact* of being in possession (with or without consent) will achieve—ie the ability to defend that possession—is unfortunately all too apparent in the very recent decision in *Manchester Ship Canal v Vauxhall*.[42] This case is further evidence, if such is needed, of the conceptual muddle which can be caused by a failure to really keenly observe the concepts being employed, and their legal consequences.

> **Key case:** *Manchester Ship Canal v Vauxhall* [2018] EWCA Civ 1100
>
> Vauxhall operates a manufacturing plant at Ellesmere Port, on the edge of the Manchester Ship Canal. In 1962, Vauxhall and the canal owners reached an agreement which would allow Vauxhall to discharge material into the canal. This agreement was granted 'in perpetuity', ie forever, for an annual fee of £50. As one can imagine given the cost of environmentally friendly treatment of such material and the like, the real value of this ability to discharge is now estimated at around £400,000 a year. Manchester Ship Canal sought to bring this licence to an end, and Vauxhall applied for relief against forfeiture. Forfeiture is one of the means by which a lease is brought to an end: relief against forfeiture is the court's power to prevent the lease being terminated in this way. More detail on forfeiture is available in chapter 10 at 10.5.3. By applying for relief against forfeiture, Vauxhall, although clearly licensees, were asking the court to treat them as though they had a property in the form of a lease. The Court of Appeal held that relief from forfeiture was available. The reasoning was that although an earlier decision, *The Scaptrade*,[43] had concluded that relief from forfeiture was not available for 'mere contractual licences', that this case did not involve a 'mere' contractual licence. Rather, because the licence entitled Vauxhall to control, it granted a species of possession (albeit that it could not have been a lease because of the lack of limitation of time, and it could not have been a freehold because of the annual payment). This decision, as with *Dutton*, blurs a number of concepts. However, it is very difficult to define what rights Vauxhall really did have. The right was definitely not a lease. But by consensually conferring possession, it is difficult to deny that something 'more than' a licence was created by this agreement. One way of explaining the outcome—at least in terms of the proprietary status of the remedy given to Vauxhall—is that even if the agreement could not give a property right, because nothing within the confines of the numerus clausus was granted, the fact of Vauxhall being in possession gave them the right to defend it. This would mean that Manchester Ship Canal could not assert their own possessory rights against Vauxhall because their contractual agreement prevented them from so-doing. But this is not the reasoning used by the court, which instead focused on the 'possessory licence', with some proprietary and some personal consequences.

[41] E Lochery, 'Pushing the boundaries of *Dutton*?' [2011] Conv 74, 80.
[42] *Manchester Ship Canal v Vauxhall* [2018] EWCA Civ 1100. For discussion of the Supreme Court decision in this case, see the online resources.
[43] *Scandinavian Trading Tanker Co AB v Flota Petrolera Ecuatoriana* (The Scaptrade), [1983] 2 AC 694 (HL).

> **Summary: Property rights and third-party effects**
>
> In theory the line between licences—personal rights to use, occupy or visit land—and property rights, which bind third parties, is clear. In practice, however, cases such as *Dutton* and *Vauxhall* show that even the courts sometimes blur this line, and give a property remedy where only a personal right exists, or reach a proprietary conclusion on the basis of a personal contract. The consequence of this is a conceptual muddle, which damages the integrity of the *numerus clausus*.

2.3 WHAT IS LAND?

Having established what property rights are, the other important puzzle piece is the nature of land. Land, as defined in section 205 LPA 1925, includes both corporeal things—land, buildings etc—and incorporeal things—such as rights over land. Land law, in essence, is concerned with incorporeal rights relating to corporeal land and buildings. Both elements of land, therefore, require further definition.

2.3.1 LAND—CORPOREAL

There are two dimensions to the discussion, 'what is land?' First, you must assess the scope of land vertically and horizontally. Second, you must assess whether things present on the land are part of that land.

2.3.1.1 Horizontal and vertical scope

In relation to the horizontal scope of a part of land, this relates to questions of boundaries. For the most part such boundaries are clear. Where they are not clear, neighbours may agree to fix the horizontal boundaries, or adverse possession may be utilised to ensure that the legal boundary meets with the physical boundary. These issues are discussed in more detail in chapters 5 and 6. However, to summarise, in working out what the horizontal boundaries of a property are, there are three relevant sources of information: (1) the physical features present on the ground, such as fences, walls, and other boundary markers; (2) the documentation that details where land was divided when it was first split into multiple freehold plots—if such documentation can be found—and later documents were available, that show the relevant boundaries; and (3) the land registry record of where boundaries sit. *Prima facie* none of these is determinative, and indeed, it may be that it is almost impossible to tell in practice where the *true* boundary is. However, in such cases, the rules relating to adverse possession as explained in chapter 6 may well operate so as to change the legal boundary to fit with the physical features present on the land.

In relation to the vertical scope of land, the key cases are *Bernstein v Skyviews*[44] and *Star Energy v Bocardo*.[45] These cases are explained in detail in chapter 9 concerning the freehold estate as it is in relation to freeholds that these rules are most relevant. In the case of a leasehold

---

[44] *Lord Bernstein v Skyviews and General Ltd* [1978] QB 479 (QB).
[45] *Bocardo SA v Star Energy UK Onshore Ltd* [2010] UKSC 35, [2011] 1 AC 380.

estate, the geographical vertical scope of the estate in land is usually determined by reference to the contract which gives rise to the lease. To summarise here, *Bernstein* establishes that the property right in land extends as far into the sky as is necessary for the reasonable enjoyment and use of the land. This raises a question—can you extend the scope of your property rights by simply building a taller building? *Bocardo*[46] tells us that property in land extends as far into the centre of the earth as human endeavour allows. Beyond that point it is absurd to consider ownership since no human can utilise or control the matter concerned. As new technology is developed, so too will the scope of the property right expand. Since, however, there can be no dispute over land beyond the scope of human endeavour, this does not raise the same problems as the *Bernstein* test might.

> **Summary: Horizontal and vertical scope**
>
> The horizontal scope of the land may be revealed by examination of the physical features present on the ground, by documentation at the time the land was divided, and subsequently, and examination of the land register. The vertical scope of freehold land reaches as high as is reasonably necessary, and as low as human endeavour allows. More detail is given on this in chapter 9. The scope of leasehold land is primarily determined by the contract granting the lease.

2.3.1.2 Fixtures and fittings

As far as the things on land are concerned, we can divide such things into three categories: things that are part and parcel of the land (trees, grass, buildings etc); fixtures (items which thanks to the degree of annexation and purpose of annexation have become attached to the land); and chattels. This tri-partite division is important as it helps to demonstrate which items have become so much part of the land that when the land is sold, for example, the transferor of the land is unable to remove these items even if they are not specifically mentioned in the contract of sale. Spotting things which are part and parcel of the land tends to be easy—they have become so enmeshed with the land that they do not really have any independent identity. So, standard buildings, patios, established planting and the like, are as much part of the land than would be the soil and plants that would exist on the land were the land to be entirely unmarked by human hands.

Fixtures can pose more of a problem. These are essentially items which are not part of the land as such, but are attached to it in such a way that we treat them as though they were to be part of it. The boundary line between such fixtures and the land itself, on the one hand, and chattels which are not part of the land, on the other, can be very difficult to draw. Any assessment is generally impressionistic and based on common sense. We look to see whether removing the item would cause damage to it or the land, and whether the thing is simply resting on its own weight. This is sometimes explained as the test of 'degree of annexation'. But sometimes this degree of annexation test is not enough. Consider a dry stone wall. It is simply a pile of stones, arranged nicely. And yet, it becomes part of the land. The reason for this is that the degree of annexation is not the only factor to take into account. The purpose of annexation is also taken into account. The primary

---

[46] *Bocardo SA v Star Energy UK Onshore Ltd* [2010] UKSC 35, [2011] 1 AC 380.

authority for this approach is *Holland v Hodgson*[47]—the case which established the degree and purpose of annexation test—and very often a problem question will expect you to reason from first principles in this way.

The rules relating to the definition of land need not always be approached from first principles, however, as would be the case if one turned first to the degree and purpose of annexation tests. Sometimes it is easier and more accurate simply to reason by analogy with existing cases. Because of the impressionistic approach which the courts take to these questions, as highlighted earlier, it is sometimes better to look for cases sufficiently similar to the one in question. This section therefore covers some of the more common issues in respect of fixtures. It should be noted at this point also that the rules relating to fixtures in cases of a lease are somewhat different. These are explained in chapter 10, at 10.5.6.

House boats

The question as to whether house boats—moored in a fixed location, and very often physically attached to the land by means of a walkway, electricity and water services, or even in some cases by built living structures straddling the boundary between the boat and the riverbank—constitute fixtures or chattels has been the subject of perhaps a surprising amount of case law. Certain general principles seem to be emerging from the case law: for example, *Mew v Tristmire*[48] and *Chelsea Yacht and Boat v Pope*.[49] *Chelsea Yacht* explains that, 'a boat, albeit one used as a home, is not of the same genus as real property'.[50] In this respect, if the house boat is still more boat than it is land, then the courts are likely to conclude that it has not become attached to the land. *Mew* tells us that even if a boat becomes unable to operate as a boat (ie it would sink if moved), that does not mean that it has become part of the land. It is still a boat. Furthermore, these cases also emphasise that the relevant moment for assessing whether something is part of the land or not is its date of installation. In *Mew*, the boats had been still in the same place for a long time and had, in effect, been neglected as river craft in this time. The court was keen to emphasise that the fact that someone cannot be bothered to properly maintain their boat is not a reason to conclude that the boat has become part of the land to which it is moored. Similar arguments would apply to mobile homes and caravans as discussed later. Neglect does not, in this sense, alter the character of the chattel so as to turn it into land where otherwise it would not be.

Mobile homes, chalets, caravans, portacabins

The position in relation to mobile homes, cabins, and caravans is perhaps a little more complicated to navigate than the case law relating to house boats. This is because there is a fairly significant range involved in such structures: from a small mobile caravan which is generally taken away for weekends at a time, to portacabins being used on school sites for additional classroom space which may remain in the same place for decades. The courts have not, therefore, determined all these cases as sitting on one side of the line of another. However, some guidance was given in *Elitestone v Morris*.[51]

[47] *Holland v Hodgson* (1871–72) LR 7 CP 328 (Court of Exchequer).
[48] *Mew v Tristmire* [2011] EWCA Civ 912, [2012] 1 WLR 852.
[49] *Chelsea Yacht and Boat v Pope* [2000] 1 WLR 1941 (CA).
[50] *Chelsea Yacht and Boat v Pope* [2000] 1 WLR 1941 (CA), 1946.
[51] *Elitestone v Morris* [1997] 1 WLR 687 (HL).

Key case: *Elitestone v Morris* [1997] 1 WLR 687

Elitestone were freehold owners of a field divided into 27 lots. Morris was the owner of a chalet on one of these lots. Elitestone wanted possession of all the lots and brought possession proceedings. Morris argued that he had become a tenant. Whether or not this was the case boiled down to whether the chalet in which Morris lived was part of the land. The cabin rested on concrete pillars by its own weight. It was not attached to the land as such. However, the house was not like a portacabin or a mobile home. It could not be taken down and re-erected elsewhere—removal would involve its demolition.

In deciding that this cabin had become part of the land, the court gave some very useful guidance as to the distinction between chattels and fixtures.

First, Lord Lloyd emphasised that, '[i]f can structure can only be enjoyed in situ, and is such that it cannot be removed in whole or in sections to another site, there is at least a strong inference that the purpose of placing the structure on the original site was that it should form part of the realty of that site'.[52] In this sense, the likelihood of destruction of the object by its removal weighed strongly in favour of the conclusion that it had become part of the land. Lord Clyde agreed with this assessment, reasoning that, 'there are powerful indications that it and its constituent parts do not possess the character of a chattel'[53] of which one was the impossibility of removal without damage.

Second, the court was clear that the distinction between chattels and fixtures was not a matter for agreement between the parties, nor determined by their subjective intentions. It was a question of fact. However, the intention of the parties could be relevant to assessment of the purpose of annexation. In brief, express agreement cannot prevent a chattel from becoming part of the land. In the words of Lord Lloyd, 'the intention of the parties is only relevant to the extent that it can be derived from the degree and object of the annexation. The subjective intention of the parties cannot affect the question whether the chattel has, in law, become part of the freehold'.[54] Lord Clyde expressed this slightly differently, holding that: 'it is the purpose which the object is serving which has to be regarded, not the purpose of the person who put it there. The question is whether the object is designed for the use or enjoyment of the land or for the more complete or convenient use or enjoyment of the thing itself'.[55]

In this sense, the court emphasises that when thinking about the purpose of annexation, it is important not to confuse this with a consideration of whether the parties wanted the object to become part of the land. Rather, the question is one of the objective assessment of what purpose structures like the kind in question serve. Let us return to the school portacabin example. It is clear that from an objective assessment of purpose, the portacabin is being designed to operate in a way akin to a building. It may be that taking account of the very limited degree of annexation in such cases, the courts conclude that they are not attached. Their purpose nevertheless is one normally associated with fixtures on land, rather than chattels to be removed at will. This can be contrasted with the holiday caravan where the entire purpose of such is to be removed regularly.

Finally, all members of the court were keen to emphasise the fact and degree nature of the fixtures and fittings assessments. Lord Lloyd explained that the relationship between the two factors—degree and purpose of annexation—were themselves context dependent: 'the importance of the degree of

---

[52] *Elitestone v Morris* [1997] 1 WLR 687 (HL), 690.
[53] *Elitestone v Morris* [1997] 1 WLR 687 (HL), 697.
[54] *Elitestone v Morris* [1997] 1 WLR 687 (HL), 697.
[55] *Elitestone v Morris* [1997] 1 WLR 687 (HL), 698.

> annexation will vary from object to object'.[56] Lord Clyde also highlighted that the question is very fact and circumstance dependent:
>
>> 'the answer to that question is to be found by a consideration of the particular facts and circumstances... But each case in this matter has to turn on its own facts. Comparable cases are useful for guidance in respect of the considerations employed but can only rarely provide conclusive answer'.[57]
>
> And the answer to this simple question, as Lord Lloyd confirms, is highly impressionistic. Thus, he explained, 'in the case of the house the answer is as much a matter of common sense as precise analysis'.[58]

Statues, greenhouses, and other decorative and garden features

There are two different kinds of considerations at play in this sort of cases. The first consideration is similar to those explained earlier. Can the item be removed without destruction, and does it rest on its own weight or has it been physically attached to the land? In the case of greenhouses, it is clear, for example, that some are of a much more portable design than others. Whilst we can see from *Elitestone*[59] earlier that this is not determinative, where a greenhouse could not be removed without being destroyed, there would be a strong case for its having become part of the land. On the other hand, if the greenhouse could be easily moved, then the question becomes a more subtle analysis as to what function it plays in the property as a whole. Regarding the question in relation to statues and other forms of garden ornaments—ranging from large sculptures and fountains to garden gnomes—the courts have emphasised that where statues and garden features become an essential part of the design of the house and grounds, then they can become part of the land even if they have not been physically attached to the land but, in the case of a large statue for example, simply rest on their own weight.[60] Again, this will also be a very impressionistic assessment, turning on fine distinctions in individual cases.

Finally, in terms of fixtures and fittings, it is also important to remember that there will be some significance to the date at which an item is brought onto the land, and when the court's assessment as to its status is made. The houseboat cases suggest it is at the time when the item first arrives onto the land. Later decay or neglect does not mean that an item becomes part of the land. However, there must be a point when human endeavour can change an item for being a chattel to being a fixture—it just is not very clear when that is. The question will, perhaps unsurprisingly, be a question of fact and degree.

> **Summary: Fixtures and fittings**
>
> The general test for distinguishing between fixtures and fittings depends upon the degree and purpose of annexation. However, it is sometimes easier to reason by analogy to particular scenarios, such as those involving houseboats, mobile homes, greenhouses, and garden ornaments. The result is usually one based on common sense and impression.

---

[56] *Elitestone v Morris* [1997] 1 WLR 687 (HL), 692.
[57] *Elitestone v Morris* [1997] 1 WLR 687 (HL), 696.
[58] *Elitestone v Morris* [1997] 1 WLR 687 (HL), 692.
[59] *Elitestone v Morris* [1997] 1 WLR 687 (HL).
[60] *D'eyncourt v Gregory (No.1)* (1866–67) LR 3 Eq 382 (Ch).

2.3.2 LAND—INCORPOREAL, AND USE, OCCUPATION, AND POSSESSION

Turning now to the question as to what constitutes the 'incorporeal' side of 'land', this is essentially a reminder that when one purchases title to land, one is not buying a physical space. Instead, one purchases an estate in that land which is merely a legal construct entitling one to use (see later) and possess the land. Associated with this legal construct will be other associated rights which may have become 'attached' to the land. For example, when considering easements earlier, it was mentioned that one of the conditions for the existence of as easement is that there is a 'dominant' and a 'servient' tenement. This means, in basic terms, to use the example of a right of way, that there is one estate in land, the owner of which is entitled to use the right of way, and another, the servient owner, who as a result of owning a different estate in land is obligated to put up with that use. We can then say that when the dominant owner buys the relevant estate in land, they are acquiring not only the possession of the physical space—horizontally and vertically defined—but also the entitlements associated with that estate.

However, the mention here of entitlement to use and possess is a complicated issue. The question of entitlement to possess is considered in detail in the chapters concerning leasehold estates (the very definition of which is a grant of exclusive possession for a limited time), mortgages (since legal mortgages automatically give rise to a right to possession for a lender), and adverse possession (as possession as a factual state of affairs can generate a freehold title to land). This is a useful place to set the scene for that discussion with some consideration of the distinction that exists between use, occupation and possession, three of the most difficult concepts to 'pin down' when first considering land law.

Of these three, the most simple is occupation. Occupation as a legal concept is used in a variety of contexts. It defines the scope of protection for certain tenants, as explained in chapter 10, and it is a means by which equitable rights can be made enforceable against third party transferees of estates in land (assuming some other conditions are met—as explored in chapter 15). As you will see when you read these chapters, the courts have repeatedly insisted that the term occupation is not a term of art—it is simply an ordinary word of the English language and should be interpreted as such, taking account of the facts and circumstances of the case, and also the purpose to which the term is being put in the relevant legislation.

Use, by contrast, is much more nebulous in English land law. Indeed, some have argued[61] that English land law does not confer onto the holders of rights in land any entitlement to use. Such a 'bald' assessment of the right to use land is probably overstated in practice, but the uneasy place which use occupies in our understanding of how rights in land works is emphasised by the difficulty in pinning down what would constitute an unlawful interference with use and comfort as expressed in the tort of nuisance, and considered in chapter 18.

Finally, there is the factual concept of possession. The word 'possession' in English land law is a word which is used to mean subtly different things at different times. Sometimes is it used, as in the context of leases (see chapter 10), in opposition to 'occupation'. Here it describes a situation where a person is living in a residential property, for example, and their relationship with that property is not one akin to a lodger, or a hotel guest, but is more extensive than that, and has

---

[61] See discussion in chapter 18—S Douglas and B McFarlane, 'Defining Property Rights' in J Penner and H Smith, *Philosophical Foundations of Private Law* (OUP, Oxford, 2013).

become a lease. Sometimes it is used to describe a factual state of affairs. So when an individual has changed the locks of a property so that they are the only person able to obtain access to a property, they are factually in possession. Sometimes, finally, it is used to describe a *right* so that even though a person may not in fact have a physical presence on the land, because they are 'in possession' (in the sense that they have a right to possession) they are able, for example, to receive the rental income from the property. The multiplicity of ways in which this word is used can make study and understanding of 'possession' in the abstract problematic. At its heart, however, the word possession is always referring to the same idea: the ability whether in fact, in law, or both, to control access to property.

2.4 RELATIVITY OF TITLE

Finally, this chapter will now conclude with discussion of the concept of relativity of title in English land law. This is a foundational concept. It is the reason why we do not have 'an' owner of land. It is the explanation for the notion of adverse possession and for how freeholds (and indeed, albeit less commonly, leaseholds) work. The concept is covered in more detail in chapter 9. Nevertheless, in this introductory section of the book it is very important to get a sense of relativity as it will assist in quickly assimilating the logic of land law.

The idea behind relativity is that whenever there is a case before the court, the court will not be asking 'who owns this land'. Rather, which of the two parties before the court are *more* entitled to use the land. The courts are assessing *relative*, rather than absolute, merit. However, the consequences of this approach are to allow for the possibility of multiple titles to land to exist simultaneously, albeit that some are 'stronger' titles than others. Usually, the strongest title will be that which arises through paper-based transactions with the land, and in the case of registered title, as we explain in chapter 5, since registered title is in effect guaranteed, there is less scope for the application of the idea of relative title in registered land disputes. This is not to say that there is no relativity of title in registered land—it is still possible in a dispute between two persons with freehold *neither* of whom are registered title holders, that the question will be determined purely on the basis of their relative merits—but rather that the significance of this concept has lessened since the coming into force of the Land Registration Act 2002 on 1 October 2003.

The main result of the possibility of multiple, and relative, titles, is that English law is able to accept the possibility of titles being generated independently from the consent of a current titleholder. This is where adverse possession comes in. Adverse possession, as we see in chapter 6, is possession of land—in terms of factual control and an intention to exercise such control over access to the land—without permission of the 'paper title-holder' (ie the person who has received their title by entering into a consensual transaction with the previous owner, or who has inherited that title). In taking possession in this way, the adverse possessor will generate for themselves a freehold title to the land. This will rank relatively lower than the paper title, but would rank higher, for example, than another adverse possessor who came along later (subject to cut off dates as explained in chapter 6). Possession, therefore, takes on even more significance when considered from the perspective of relative title.

Why do we have such a system of relativity? The reasons behind this are explained more in chapter 9 in 9.3, but to summarise here:

1. Relativity of title helps to avoid problems of proof. Whilst this is less importance in modern law—since title is now recorded at the land registry—historically it was critical to examine the relevant paper-work. If title depends upon paper record, then without the records no transactions can take place in relation to the relevant land. Because of this, given how easy it is to lose pieces of paper over almost 1000 years of relevant English legal history, English land law has always given, in effect, a presumptive degree of control of land to the person in possession of land. There is therefore, partly for reasons of ease of proof, a presumption in favour of the *status quo* and this is embodied in the concept of relative title.

2. Another reason why this presumption exists is to prevent parties resorting to self-help to seize land from a person that they believe is not entitled to be in possession of that land. The fact that a person in possession has a title to that land, of some form or another, means that any person wishing to displace them will usually have to obtain an order for possession from a court.

3. Relativity of title reflects the fact that all land ownership in England is derivative on the title of the Crown to all land, at least in theory. This has very few practical consequences. (We consider some of these in chapter 9 at 9.6). Nevertheless, it is an important foundational principle in English land law and of course was of much more significance in the development of feudal land-holding, and therefore in the birth of land law in the medieval period. This should not be overemphasised.

4. Finally, the relativity of title principle is essentially a conclusion from, as well as a cause of, the fact that English law has no vindicatory action by which an individual is able to prove that they are the absolute owner of land. Their title can only be asserted in a practical dispute, rather than in the abstract in this sense. Without the action to support some concept of absolute ownership therefore, English law has developed a system which does not require one, reinforcing the fact that relativity of title is essential to the operation of English land law.

2.5 CONCLUSION

This chapter has explained the nature of property rights and emphasised their third-party effects. It has shown that there is effectively a closed list of such rights, allowing the creation of the table of property rights. It was then shown that despite some judicial controversy, licences—ie personal rights in land—are not property rights and cannot affect third parties in this way. This much is now clear. However, there are some cases where the distinction between the personal and the proprietary is not as sharp, as in the case of *Manchester Airport v Dutton*.[62]

When thinking about rights in land, however, it is crucial not only to think about the property rights themselves, but also the nature of land. The geographical scope of land—both vertical and horizontal—and which features on the land become 'part' of rights in that land, tell us a lot about the nature of property rights in English land law. The incorporeal rights also associated with land

---

[62] *Manchester Airport v Dutton* [2000] QB 133 (CA).

add to this picture of rights in land being a legal construct, not a physical connection with space per se. However, when we examined the crucial concepts of use, occupation, and possession, it is clear that English law does recognise that factual affairs can have legal consequences, and nowhere is this clearer than in relation to the acquisition of title by possession, and its relationship with the foundational concept of relativity of title.

PRINCIPLES

How does this discussion begin to shape our understanding of the principles explained in chapter 1? To recap, these principles were:

1. Certainty
2. Sensitivity to context
3. Transactability
4. Systemic and individual effects
5. Recognition of the social role of the land law system.

Even in the context of the very foundational concepts used in English law, we can begin to see how these principles are shaped by some of the decisions made. Most particularly this comes from the attitude of the courts to the *numerus clausus*, and to the nature of property rights as explained by Lord Wilberforce. The very idea of requiring rights to be definable and stable before they can acquire proprietary status is a reflection of the need for certainty. In this sense, much of what is achieved in relation to the list of property rights is done in pursuance of this principle. This can very much be to the detriment of the social function of property. Consider Mrs Ainsworth in this—through no fault of her own, she was deprived of her home thanks to the fact that the nature of her occupation was so precarious, being entirely parasitic upon the rights of her husband, that she was not deemed worthy of protection against a purchaser. This seems to be a harsh result, and indeed it almost certainly was in the instant case, but we ought not to lose sight of the fact that were the courts more flexible in this regard, and more willing to look at individual circumstances, the risks are significant, not only for individual purchasers, but for the system more generally.

Indeed, we can see how this flexibility pans out in the context of decisions like *Chandler v Kerley* and *Errington v Errington*. In both cases, the courts distort familiar legal concepts in pursuance of what is clearly a justified decision on the facts. Many writers, as we shall see throughout this book, bemoan the form of justifiable analysis of English law which prioritises certainty and clarity over all other concerns, and indeed, too narrow a focus on the purposes of land law does distort one's vision. But does this mean that the law should be manipulated in the way we see in these cases?

A different kind of distortion to achieve the 'right' result is present in *Manchester Airport v Dutton* where the court simply could not abide the trespassers succeeding and the 'rightful' licensee being left with no effective remedy. In this sense, much of this chapter has been about the ways in which English law, in its fundamental structures, balances certainty and flexibility and sensitivity to particular contexts.

In defining land too choices are being made. Let us consider the definition of fixtures from the perspective of transitory housing. What does the exclusion of caravans and mobile homes from the definition of land tell us about the law's attitude to housing, and housing for those of a lower income in particular, or of the travelling community? The social effect of these rules is to treat such persons as occupying a home in a different capacity from those able or willing to occupy in a more traditional way. This attitude has, over time, had powerful effects in terms of planning law, for example, as well, as we shall see in chapter 17, on the ways in which such communities' human rights are conceived.

Finally, in terms of transactibility, the whole notion of relativity of title has, in many ways, come about in pursuit of transactibility in land. In an era when proof of title would have been very difficult to come by, relativity of title allowed land to be bought and sold even when absolute ownership cannot be determined. This is interesting because, as we shall see in many other places in this book, transactibility and certainty very often work hand in hand. However, English law, in pursuit of a dynamic property market has in many ways eschewed the certainty which absolute title can bring.

Overall, whilst the details of the operation of these five principles will be given more detail and nuance in the specific rules explored in later chapters, even here in grappling with introductory ideas, we can see how these tensions have and continue to shape the relevant rules.

TABLE OF DEFINITIONS

Freehold estate	Estate in land of unlimited duration. Considered the 'highest' form of ownership in English law, save for that of the Crown.
Leasehold estate	A property right arising where there is a consensual grant of exclusive possession for a limited duration.
Mortgage	An interest arising as a security for a debt.
Easement	A limited right to use another's property, or (more rarely) to prevent that person from using their property in a particular way.
Profit	A right consisting in the ability to take from another's land—eg fishing, timber, hunting, and grazing rights.
Freehold covenant (restrictive covenant)	A covenant which limits the use to which servient land can be put, and which does not require the covenantor to expend money.
Leasehold covenant	An obligation contained in a lease.
Option to purchase	An option to purchase is a right which entitles its holder to force the proprietor of an estate in land, be that freehold or leasehold, to transfer their estate in land. There is no requirement on the option-holder to purchase the land.
Right of pre-emption	A right which provides that if a vendor decides to sell their estate in the land, the purchaser must be able to buy that estate at a price previously or to be agreed.
Rentcharge	A right to receive income from the owner of a freehold estate in land.
Rights of re-entry	A right of a landlord to terminate a lease/to bring about forfeiture of that lease.
Right to set aside a transaction	A right to rescind a voidable transaction.

(Continued)

Right to rectify a document	A right to rectify a document relating to the relevant land, eg rectification of a deed of conveyance (and possibly the right to rectify the register).
Equity arising by estoppel	The property right which arises in response to estoppel, and which is extinguished upon the crystallisation of the estoppel and the grant of any remedy.
Proprietary estoppel	An equitable doctrine which generates a property right in response to an assurance which has been detrimentally relied upon, where it would be unconscionable for the promisor to go back on their promise.
Interest under a trust of land	A right relating to the freehold or leasehold estate which consists in the ability to hold the legal owner of the estate to account for the manner in which he manages his right, and which is itself a proprietary interest.
Freehold estate	Estate in land of unlimited duration. Considered the 'highest' form of ownership in English law, save for that of the Crown.
Licence	A permission to be on land which operates as a defence to an action in trespass.
Bare licence	A mere permission to be on land.
Contractual licence	A permission to be on land for which consideration have been given and which forms part of a contractual relationship.
Licence coupled with an interest	A permission to be on land intrinsically part of a proprietary interest.
Land	The corporeal land and those objects on that land which have become part of the land, and the incorporeal rights in that land.
Possession	The right to, or the fact of, control of land characterised by the ability to exclude others
Occupation	A physical presence on relevant land that has features of continuity and stability.
Property right	A right which is enforceable against third parties.
Personal Right	A right which is not enforceable against third parties generally.
Legal right	Property rights which are universally binding on third parties.
Equitable right	Property rights which are conditional in their effects on third parties.

FURTHER READING

The further reading here is designed to give some insight into the idea of land as a subject of ownership-type interests, and of what obligations that entails, and of possession of land as a concept in English law.

GARNSEY P., *Thinking about Property From Antiquity to the Age of Revolution* (CUP, 2007).
HARRIS J., 'Ownership of Land in English Law' in MACCORMICK, N. and BIRKS, P. (eds) *The Legal Mind* (Clarendon Press, 1986).
HARRIS J., *Property and Justice* (OUP, 2002).
VAN DER WALT A., *Property on the Margins* (Hart, 2009).
WONNACOTT, M., *Possession of Land* (CUP, 2006).

3

REGISTERED AND UNREGISTERED LAND

3.1 Introduction 57
3.2 Land Law in the 20th and 21st Centuries 59
3.3 Registered Land 60
3.4 Unregistered Land 70
3.5 Conclusion 79
Principles 79
Table of Definitions 80
Further Reading 80

CHAPTER GOALS

By the end of this chapter, you should have:

- A basic understanding of the concept of registration of land, and of the difference between registration of title and title by registration;
- An appreciation of the goals of the Land Registration Act 2002, and the Law Commission reform proposals;
- Understanding of the three principles of land registration—the mirror, insurance, and curtain principles—and of how these principles have shaped the legislative provisions, as well as their limitations;
- An appreciation of the four guiding principles within unregistered land and how these are reflected in the rules; and
- Knowledge of points of comparison between registered and unregistered land.

3.1 INTRODUCTION

In this final introductory chapter, we explore not the fundamental principles which underpin our land law system, but rather examine one of its most important components—the registration of title to land. This is the system whereby rights in land are recorded on a publically available register. This chapter explains what the land register is, and how it fits into the system of rights in land. We consider also the policies which have motivated and shaped the relevant legislation. As part of this exploration, we will draw comparisons with unregistered land, and examine some of the history of English land law in the 20th and 21st centuries. Understanding the historical processes that have brought the law to where it is now can be helpful in analysing and applying the modern rules. As a result, in 3.2, a brief explanation of the process through the 1925 reforms, and to the modern law as encapsulated in the Land Registration Act 2002 (LRA 2002) is given. This is by no means comprehensive, but gives some insight into the changes in attitude to land law which have taken place over the past one hundred years. In 3.3, an explanation of the functioning of registered land is given, particularly focusing on the some fundamental principles of registered land and a glimpse of how this registration system works in the majority of cases is provided. Finally, in 3.4, a short account of the rules relating to unregistered land is given. This is not a detailed explanation, but instead focuses on the key components of unregistered land, to allow this discussion to act as a point of comparison with the registered land rules.

Over time, our system of land law has morphed. It began as a system which operated very well in the context of a small number of landowners with large estates; where occupation and ownership were largely independent concepts; and where finance, lending, and the real estate market formed a less significant part of the economic system, on the one hand, and of the process by which people acquire the ability to live in a permanent home on the other. However, land law now serves a multiplicity of social and economic roles. Furthermore, the structures within early 20th century society meant that, for women in particular, security in such a sense was provided through societal status and marriage, rather than through property. The modern law is much more reflective of the economic entanglement that exists between institutional lending and the ability of people to acquire title to a home, and of the consequences which the breakdown of relationships has in respect of rights in land.

In examining this history, and the registration system which has emerged from this social and legal development, this chapter is concerned with assessing two questions. First, what are the underpinning principles of land registration and to what extent, in general terms, do these principles actually feature in the practical operation of the rules? Second, how far does registration of title therefore represent an improvement on the system of unregistered land? The first element of this discussion therefore depends upon what the aims of the system actually were. According to the successive Law Commissions that shaped, established, and reformed the current land registration process, the key principles are the mirror, curtain and insurance principles. In considering how these fit within the LRA 2002, therefore, it is necessary not only to look at the Act itself, but also to make extensive consideration of the various Law Commission reports which explain the 'thinking' behind the provisions. This chapter therefore contains repeated references to both the Law Commission report establishing the LRA 2002, and to the recent report which suggests some potential changes within the new few years.

Before addressing these issues in detail, however, it is useful here to pause simply to get a sense of how the system works at its most basic. When parties decide they want deliberately to create a new right in land, or transfer an existing right, they have to undertake a number of steps. When trying to create a *legal* right in land (explained in the previous two chapters), given the universal applicability of such rights, one of the steps that must be taken is to give such rights an appropriate degree of publicity. For most legal rights, the degree of publicity required before they can be created so as to be universally applicable is entry on the land register. Once this is done, if any third party wants to find out what rights affect a certain piece of land, they can consult the register to see if any rights are recorded there. Unless such rights are registered, they will exist in an equitable form only and therefore may or may not be binding upon third parties. In this sense, the register is part of the process of *creating* rights. It also has a hugely significant effect in terms of managing conflicts *between* rights. This is because the register creates what are known as priority rules—that is, the rules which explain who wins in case of conflict between property rights. Although the detail of the operation of these rules is sometimes complex, in very basic terms, entry of a right on the register protects that right against someone who later acquires title to the land. Where a right is *not* present on the register, then the later purchaser is much less likely to be affected by that right. Let us explore this picture by considering an example.

In 2008 Mark became the registered freehold owner of Broadcasters' House. This means that when looking at the register, he would be listed there. In 2018, he decided that he wanted to move somewhere smaller, and so agreed to sell the property to Simon for £400,000. When Mark bought the house, he paid a neighbour for the ability to use a private road running across the neighbour's land and had agreed also that the neighbour could use his swimming pool. The right relating to the road also appeared on the register. Therefore, when Simon examined the register, he saw not only confirmation that Mark was the owner of the property, but also that it did indeed have the right (easement) across the neighbouring land. He saw nothing about the swimming pool.

Once negotiations were complete, the contracts exchanged, and the formal documents of transfer (deed) drawn up, Simon's name replaced Mark's on the register. This meant that Simon was now registered owner. The registration had ensured the *transfer* of the freehold title. When the neighbour attempted to use the swimming pool, and to prevent Simon using the private road, Simon pointed to the register, highlighting the proof of the agreement regarding the road to ensure he was able to use it. He also pointed to the register noting the absence of any right relating to the swimming pool. In these circumstances, whilst Simon would be able to use the road, he was not obliged to allow the neighbour to use the swimming pool. The role of the register in this was also to affect the position regarding the *conflict* between the rights.

In this whole transaction we can see how central the register is to the outcome. Its publically available nature means that Simon was able to find out in advance what his rights and obligations were. And it is here that we see the guiding philosophy behind land registration—it is designed to make information publicly available, at a low price, to make people's legal positions clearer and simpler to discover. This is supposed to make transacting with land cheap, easy, and effective. We will see in the following sections how the law has developed to reach this point.

3.2 LAND LAW IN THE 20TH AND 21ST CENTURIES

The land law system as it now exists has developed from the system of feudal land holding, where large estates were under the single ownership of a particular family. Many of the features of this system arose from historical accident, and there was an enormously complicated system with multiple forms of ownership-type rights in land, and a variety of different estates.

The unnecessary complexity of this was apparent following the industrial revolution, and recognised with full force in the run up to 1925. 1925 is a significant date in land law for it is here that 'modern' land law really begins with the Land Registration Act 1925 and the Law of Property Act 1925, the latter of which remains one of the most important statutes in land law. In the aftermath of the first world war, the old systems and societal structures began to break down, and it was recognised that the land law system needed to change to fit with the realities of 20th century Britain. The 1925 reforms therefore concentrated on two primary goals: first, to consolidate the rules so that the whole system was comprehensible and accessible in a single place; and second, to simplify the rules. The first goal was, in this sense, procedural. The second was however substantive, and some substantial changes emerged.

The first major development in 1925 was, as a result of section 1 Law of Property Act 1925, to reduce the possible estates in land to two: the freehold and the leasehold. The second was the clarification and limitation of the number of rights which could exist at law to those mentioned in that section. This, as was explained in the previous two chapters, reflects the facts that the universal bindingness of legal rules means that they are hugely significant not only for those who hold such rights, but also for third parties. It must, as a result, be possible for third parties to be able to find out about such rights, and to understand them, and be aware of what is required of them as a result of such rights. Limiting the number and type of rights which can exist in this form is a good way of limiting any injustice thereby caused to third parties, and of encouraging a degree of certainty and predictability in the operation of the rules.

The 1925 Act also contains a number of so-called 'word saving' provisions. Some of these existed in the older law, but their importance in the conveyancing system in 1925 is clear. They provided a means by which the actual creation of documents of transfer could be speeded up, and left less at the mercy of human error in copying old documents. It also recognised that the cost of a professional conveyancer drawing up documents like this was perhaps disproportionate to what was gained by repeating language in documentation over and over again.

Taken together, these rules made the buying and selling of land more straightforward, simpler, and cheaper. This had an important consequence: it made land a much more marketable asset. Furthermore, the 1925 reforms established the path to land registration, by introducing a limited and non-compulsory form of registration, albeit one that became more significant in the second half of the century. Of course, in part the 1925 reforms were driven by the real estate market, but they also facilitated it. The LRA 2002, which came into force in October 2003, can be seen as the ultimate expression of this. This Act heralded compulsory registration, and establishes the levels of publicity required today. The desire to protect purchasers of land is effectively a desire to make land a safe economic asset. We consider in 3.3 what the downsides of such a focus may be.

3.3 REGISTERED LAND

The 2002 Act was the result of extensive Law Commission activity, seeking to modernise the system and to make it easier for purchasers. It was also designed to allow the land law system to take advantage of new technology. Before we examine this modernisation process in more detail, it is useful to give now a slightly more detailed overview of how the land registration system works. This is merely a summary. The detail of these rules is provided in chapters 5 and 15 in particular.

The discussion here is designed to set the scene for what follows in the later chapters, and also to somewhat alleviate the problem of 'what to cover first'.

Land registration essentially contains three guiding rules. Certain rights must be registered to be *created* (at least in a certain form). Once registered, the effect of such rights is determined by their registered status. The relationship between the right-holder and third parties who later acquire rights in, or transact in relation to, the relevant land is, again, determined by registration. The register therefore has three functions: it controls creation of rights, the effects of such rights, and the interaction between rights. In this sense, registration fundamentally determines how land law works.

With regards to the first function, ie the land register as a mechanism controlling how rights in land are created, the land registration system requires that certain rights be registered before they can operate at law. These are, mainly, freeholds, leaseholds of a duration of more than seven years, mortgages, and easements. A failure to register does not mean that the right does not exist, merely that it operates only in equity. Equitable rights, as has been discussed, affect third parties in different ways from legal rights. The second function is then managed, primarily, through the effect of registration. In respect of *estates* in land, the consequence of registering title is that title is then guaranteed (although in practice this has not been as strong a guarantee as was perhaps envisaged as we explore in chapter 5 in 5.2 and 5.3). For *interests* in land, the process of registration does not guarantee their validity, but it does protect those rights against third parties if valid. Finally, the third function of land registration is a question of 'priorities'. In this sense, it is not about how various rights operate *in themselves*, but rather, how they interact with the rights of others in respect of the same land. In this regard, the LRA 2002 provides that, on transfers of title to registered land, only those rights which either appear on the register, or have been deemed worthy of special protection despite *not* appearing on the register, will bind the new owner of that title. This latter category of rights is known as overriding interests. This is a very important aspect of the operation of land law, particularly since one of these categories is rights belonging to a person occupying the relevant land. This is significant since it provides an additional layer of protection to persons occupying property as their home. These three functions together essentially describe the three main components of land law: the creation of rights; the operation of rights; and the interaction between rights. Land registration, in the modern law, sits at the centre of all of these.

3.3.1 AMBITION IN THE LAND REGISTRATION ACT 2002

The ambition of the LRA 2002 in shaping these functions is explained in the first paragraph of the Law Commission report:

> 'The purpose of the Bill is a bold and striking one. It is to create the necessary legal framework in which registered conveyancing can be conducted electronically. The move from a paper-based system of conveyancing to one that is entirely electronic is a very major one and it will transform fundamentally the manner in which the process is conducted. The Bill will bring about an unprecedented conveyancing revolution within a comparatively short time. It will also make other profound changes to the substantive law that governs registered land. These changes, taken together, are likely to be even more far-reaching than the great reforms of property law that were made by the 1925

property legislation. Not only will the Bill introduce a wholly different method of conveyancing, but... it will also alter the way in which title to land is perceived. The Land Registration Bill is the largest single law reform Bill and project that has been undertaken in the Law Commission since its foundation in 1965'.[1]

In the recent project considering reforms to the LRA 2002, this ambition is still evident. Nearly 15 years of experience with the LRA 2002, and the fundamental shift that this Act represented, has not dampened the collective enthusiasm for the potential within land registration. Thus, as the recent Law Commission consultation states:

> 'Title registration is far more than a collection of information... Even deeds registration.... was more than just information. It governed priority, and protected a purchaser from the effect of unregistered deeds. But because title registration is designed to eliminate the work of unregistered conveyancing it is far more than a record. The register is an active instrument which guarantees the validity of that which is registered'.[2]

Some elements of these reforms are still in progress—particularly electronic conveyancing, which has not yet been comprehensively introduced. This seriously undermines the overall project of the LRA 2002 which was fundamentally premised on the merits of e-conveyancing (on which more, later). Furthermore, the Law Commission argued in bringing the LRA 2002 forward, that the consequence of the legislation would be that there was a fundamental shift in understanding of what title to land in English law involves. This too is now problematic, as significant difficulties that have been experienced in using the system of guaranteed, public title to which the LRA 2002 was designed to give rise (see chapter 5).

However, in many respects the LRA 2002 has achieved many of its goals. It is important to remember that the majority of cases do not result in problems. Chapter 5 considers in detail cases at the 'edge' of the operation of the register, where there are challenges, errors, and fraud. In the vast majority of cases, however, the registration of title system, the guarantees which it provides, and the sharing of necessary information with third parties and the public at large has been a success story. The rules which the LRA 2002 puts in place are mostly simple and straightforward. There is a remarkably small amount of litigation concerning registered conveyancing considering how many transactions take place on a daily basis.

Further analysis: Advantages and disadvantages of e-conveyancing

E-conveyancing was an important element in persuading the legal community that reform would be beneficial in the late 1990s and early 2000s. E-conveyancing is the process by which any changes to the register are made simultaneously with the creation of a deed of transfer through the land registry databases. It results in the transfer happening simultaneously with its registration. This system is designed to speed up conveyancing, and to make the register accessible and understandable to all, even those without legal advice. It was, and to an extent still is, hoped that e-conveyancing would make the process cheaper and faster. It is also a reflection of the fact that law must move with the times. Society's

---

[1] Law Commission, 'Land Registration for the Twenty-First Century' (Report no. 271) (2001), [1.1].
[2] Law Commission, 'Land Registration for the Twenty-First Century' (Report no. 271) (2001), [2.27]–[2.28].

> expectations about how such important purchases and sales will take place increasingly do not involve an expectation of lengthy formal document creation which is then manually inputted into an electronic database. Such seems old-fashioned and unnecessarily cumbersome.
>
> However, the internet-based element of such a system is also the source of the challenges in implementing this system. The database, if accessible from external servers, is hackable from outside. Given the amount of wealth held in property in the UK, opening out the record to such hacks, and making the *record* of the register *proof* of title at the same time, is a risky business. Recognising this, the land registry and other interested parties have spent considerable time establishing a secure database and limiting access to the network under network access agreements (essentially limited to reputable solicitors' firms). The consequence of having to direct registration processes through such solicitors firms, however, means that the process for many people will become more, not less, expensive, undermining the entire point in the first place. This conundrum has meant that e-conveyancing has been intermittently progressed and stalled, and trialled, but never definitively introduced.

Shaping all these changes is a faith in what are known as the principles of land registration in a 'Torrens' system. Torrens here refers to Robert Torrens, a legislator in Australia who introduced the first system of 'title by registration' based on these three principles: the mirror principle, the insurance or indemnity principle, and the curtain principle. Many land law systems throughout the world now claim to have or aspire to have a fully 'Torrens' system based upon these principles, although it must be said that few, if any, entirely achieve it. The system of 'title by registration' can be contrasted with a system of 'registration of title' in which the register acts not as a *mode of creation* of rights, but merely *records* rights that are created 'off-register'. This is sometimes referred to as a system of deeds-based conveyancing. Whether or not English law has a system of 'title by registration' is a question dealt with in detail in chapter 5. Briefly here, the answer is that although formally it appears so to do, in practice, we have something of a hybrid between deeds-based and registration-based conveyancing. As a compromise, it has flaws, but again it must be reiterated that it does work well in most cases. The primary reasons for why title by registration has not been comprehensively introduced are both mechanical, and fundamental. The mechanical reason is that the full advent of title by registration will not be realised until e-conveyancing is introduced (at least under the system as it is currently designed). The second, much more fundamental reason, is that title by registration—ie a system which means that a person becomes owner of land as a result of registration, rather than as a result of anything which takes place 'in the real world'—runs up against the problem of human nature. Both mistakes and fraud are inevitable, and once this is accepted, the possibility of 'removing' title as a result of an 'off-register reality' becomes the only palatable option.

In this way, it is not particularly sensible or productive to spend a great deal of time assessing whether the LRA 2002, and the new Law Commission proposals, live up to the Torrens principles entirely. Such is impossible (not least because these principles are not even entirely mutually compatible), but a system which did achieve the principles to the fullest extent possible would not be one which fairly reflected the ways in which people very often behave where money and property is at stake. It is much more useful to consider whether the 'inroads' made into the relevant principles make sense, are balanced, and produce a coherent system overall.

> **Summary: Land registration principles**
>
> The Torrens principles of land registration are the mirror, insurance and curtain principles. Following these principles is designed to achieve a system of 'title by registration' whereby ownership of rights is conferred by their appearance on the register. This can be contrasted with registration of title systems where the register operates merely as a record of rights. English land law operates a system which is essentially a compromise between these two positions.

3.3.2 MIRROR PRINCIPLE

Let us begin with the mirror principle. The LRA 2002 was designed to produce a system whereby, 'the register should be a complete and accurate reflection of the state of the title of the land at any given time, so that it is possible to investigate title to land on line, with the absolute minimum of additional enquiries and inspections'.[3] Compliance with this principle would mean that the register would show who owned relevant rights on land, any limits on that ownership, and the interests of other people in relation to such land. The goal of this is to ensure that whenever someone looks at the register, they get a full picture of the rights and burdens associated with land.

However, on closer inspection, this principle is unachievable, and more complicated than this expression of it. It is more subtle than a blanket rule that the land register should simply be a perfect reflection of what rights in land exist. If we recall the table of property rights in the previous chapter, not all of these are deliberately created. The right to rectify the register only arises where a mistake is made on the register. Rights to set aside documents are a consequence of fraud or mistake arising between parties. There is no way to have a land registration system which could mirror these rights quite simply because the parties do not know about them until something has already gone wrong. Furthermore, the importance of rights in land as providing people with their home means that we do not want a rigid system which cannot flexibly respond to the wide variety of human relationships which can exist.

How does the land registration system account for this? Under the 1925 legislation, under the 2002 Act provisions, and under the new proposed Bill, there is a clear recognition that not all rights can reasonably be expected to appear on the register. The law responds to this by introducing the concept of so-called overriding interests. Recall that one purpose of registration is to manage the interaction *between* property rights in land. To achieve this, the register generally means that a purchaser of an estate in land—the freehold or leasehold—will be bound only by those rights which appear on the register. However, overriding interests are rights which are binding upon purchasers of estates in land *even though* they do *not* appear on the register. In this sense, overriding interests fundamentally undermine the idea of the mirror principle because they mean that a purchaser has to make 'off-register' investigations, and will be affected by some rights which do not appear there. Thus, whilst the mirror principle has at its heart the idea that everything which a purchaser might need to know about is continued on the register, that goal has not been pursued to its ultimate degree within the registration system.

---

[3] Law Commission, 'Land Registration for the Twenty-First Century' (Report no. 271) (2001), [1.5].

The significance of this inroad on the mirror principle, however, can only be revealed by an understanding of how broad or narrow this category of overriding interests is. The full details of the list—and the different rules which exist depending upon whether an estate in land is being entered on the register for the first time, or involves a transfer of an existing registered right—are explained in chapter 15 at 15.3. However, here we outline the most common overriding interests in the more usual situation, ie subsequent registration cases. The list of these appears in schedule 3 LRA 2002 and consists of: legal leases granted for a term of seven years or less (with some small exceptions); the interests of a person actually occupying the property; and legal easements created in a particular way. In practice, the most contentious of these is likely to be the interests of a person in occupation of the property, since this allows the informally created rights of such persons to bind the purchaser of the estate. This can include interests under trusts, and estoppel, both of which have the potential to be hugely problematic for the purchaser. As you might expect, the rules relating to when these interests will bind purchasers are carefully calibrated to produce a fair balance (again, see chapter 15), but it is important to recognise that they exist, and that they undermine the mirror principle in potentially very significant ways.

However, the mirror principle also demands that what *does* appear on the register is correct. This is, essentially, the notion of guaranteed title as explained in 3.3.1. As the Law Commission stated, the consequence of this is that the register must be trusted and trustworthy, so that, '[i]f, therefore, any person suffers loss as a result of some mistake or omission in the register of title, he or she is entitled to be indemnified for that loss'.[4] It is this aspect of the mirror principle that has proved most problematic in practice, as we see in chapter 5. In basic terms, it is very difficult for an administrative agency, such as the land registry, to ensure that each transaction which it registers is a genuine transaction, with valid consent from all parties, let alone to ensure that even in cases where all parties do genuinely consent, that no errors are made in the transaction process. It is therefore inevitable, as we have already noted, that, due to a combination of human error and human creativity, errors will appear on the register. This much is unavoidable. The question becomes how we should respond to this. The register is a publicly accessible database, and reliance on the register is central to the operation of almost all transactions in land. Do we say that even where there are errors on the register it should be trustworthy? Or do we say that errors on the register are effectively at the risk of the person reading it?

As we shall see in chapter 5, the LRA 2002 has not got a clear answer to this choice. On the one hand, it suggests in section 58 that even if a transfer was a forgery, and the original owner is totally unaware of the change of title, that title is guaranteed to belong to the person on the register. In a sense, this is confirmed by the provisions in schedule 8, which allow for indemnities to be paid by the land registry in cases where something has gone wrong on the register (considered in more detail in 3.3.3 later). On the other hand, schedule 4 makes provision for the register to be changed when errors do creep in. Furthermore, the case law on this question has taken a generous approach to such changes to the register, and has severely undermined the 'guarantee' in section 58, as explained in chapter 5. It is therefore somewhat difficult to pin down precisely where the balance has been struck between the rights of the person entitled to the land 'off register', and those entitled to the land through total reliance on the registration system. This lack of commitment is

---

[4] Law Commission, 'Land Registration for the Twenty-First Century' (Report no. 271) (2001), [1.7].

made more problematic by the fact that any indemnity must be paid by the land registry (subject to the possibility of recovery from a person who caused such an error through their own fraud or lack of proper care—a possibility that is somewhat remote given the likely circumstances of such cases). The land registry is both a public body, and a body with a limited budget. The answers to these fundamental questions as to how accurate the 'mirror' on the register is, therefore, has significant consequences in terms of cost to the public purse, as well as to the private parties involved.

> **Summary: The mirror principle**
>
> The mirror principle requires that the register be an accurate reflection of the rights benefitting and burdening any particular piece of land. The operation of overriding interests—interests which bind purchasers of land even though they do not appear on the register—and of the guarantee of title provisions, undermines the fulfilment of the mirror principle.

3.3.3 INSURANCE PRINCIPLE

The second relevant principle is the 'insurance principle'. This principle is intimately connected with the mirror principle, and essentially means that any person who suffers loss as a result of reliance on the register should be compensated. The Law Commission explains: '[p]eople dealing with land need to be able to rely on what the register says because they are unable to look behind the register to the deeds. The insurance principle means that if the register is shown to be incorrect, those who suffer loss as a result are compensated'.[5]

This principle is therefore about two separate issues: the value of reliance on the register (which is essentially the flip-side of the mirror principle, as discussed in 3.3.2); and the availability of compensation should it prove unreliable. The degree to which the LRA 2002 can be said to embody the first aspect of the insurance principle is considered in relation to the mirror principle, but it should be noted here that the insurance principle is essentially a paradox. How, at once, can a system both provide that the register be completely reliable, whilst at the same time accepting that it is not always reliable and therefore that compensation is available? In accepting the possibility of compensation for errors on the register, the system accepts that the register can be in error. It therefore accepts that title is not immediately indefeasible, that is, unchallengeable. This is not necessarily a criticism of the system—immediate and total indefeasibility is not a good response to the complex policy concerns which underpin land registration—but it does suggest that building policy on the basis of the insurance principle was always going to be problematic.

Indeed, in the recent Law Commission consultation, the authors of that report recognise this problem, and so unpick the goals behind making the register as reliable as possible, in order to allow for a nuanced response in the legal provisions themselves. Thus, it is said that indefeasibility serves four goals:

> '(1) Clarity: it should be possible to determine the answer in a given situation as easily and with as little litigation as possible.

[5] Law Commission, 'Updating the Land Registration Act 2002' (Consultation paper no 227) (2016), [2.19].

(2) Finality: there must come a point, at some stage in a chain of transactions, when there is no question of a registered proprietor losing his or her title because of a mistake that occurred.

(3) Fact-sensitivity: the rules used to determine who gets the land and who gets an indemnity need some in-built flexibility to ensure that the land should pass to or remain in the ownership of the person who most needs it or values it.

(4) Reliability of the register: to be able to rely on the register means knowing that if title is lost, either because the register transpires to have been wrong, or because something happens to remove a name from the register when it should not have been, then an adequate indemnity will be available. An adequate indemnity is one that fully compensates a person for his or her loss, in the cases where the party who takes an indemnity is not only innocent of fraud but also has taken all proper care'.[6]

It is in this last point that we see the true value of the insurance principle—ie the payment of money if something does go wrong. Absolute indefeasibility would be entirely contrary to the need for fact-sensitivity, and would give rise to the potential for absurd results. Thus, when considering the extent to which the LRA 2002 embodies the insurance principle, it is therefore important to consider the circumstances in which an indemnity is available, and how adequate that indemnity will be. These issues which are explained in chapter 5.

> **Summary: The insurance principle**
>
> The insurance principle requires that the register is accurate, and where inaccurate, that compensation must be paid. In English law, except in cases of fault or lack of proper care, this compensation is paid by the land registry.

3.3.4 CURTAIN PRINCIPLE

The final principle which is said to underpin the system of registration is the curtain principle. The Law Commission defined this principle as follows: '[t]his principle says that a curtain is drawn across the register against any trusts'.[7] As a definition of a principle, however, this is not particularly illuminating. Instead, it is best to understand the principle as a statement of a desire to keep a particular kind of interest *off* the register. The goal is to ensure that these rights do not affect purchasers of land so that there is no justification for their being registrable. This metaphorical principle alludes to the fact that the register is *not* supposed to be a record of the complex and relationship-dependent issues which can arise in relation to co-owned land, especially in a domestic situation. For this reason, the curtain principle refers to two notions. First, it holds that interests under trusts should not appear on the register. Second, it holds that such interests should not affect purchasers of the land without a further justification being present in any particular case.

---

[6] Law Commission, 'Updating the Land Registration Act 2002' (Consultation paper no 227) (2016), [13.15].
[7] Law Commission, 'Updating the Land Registration Act 2002' (Consultation paper no 227) (2016), [2.18].

This principle is essentially the principle which explains why we utilise trust interests as a very important aspect of English land law. Indeed, the 1925 reforms which we mentioned in 3.2 heightened rather than lessened this role. The separation between legal and equitable title means that the legal title becomes a question of transactability, security for a loan, and 'registry administration': equitable title is the explanation of who is entitled to reside in a property, and to the proceeds of sale should the property be sold. By separating these two functions—the administrative (who can buy, sell, borrow against, and transact with land) and the personal (who lives on the land, and is entitled to its value on sale)—the land law system makes transacting with land much simpler. It would entirely defeat this purpose were it either necessary or possible to register trust interests. Rather, what is essential is that, as far as is appropriate, any interests under trusts are of no consequence to purchasers.

How does the land registration system achieve this? First, and most importantly, the LRA 2002, in section 33, prevents the registration of any interest under a trust. It is therefore not possible for interests under trusts to bind purchasers of land, except in a relatively 'easy to spot' set of cases (ie when the person with the interest under the trust occupies the property). This means that it is usually straightforward for a purchaser to either know about the interest under the trust, and bargain accordingly, or for their solicitors or other conveyancing professional to at least be aware that questions needing to be asked. For more detail on the relevance of occupation, see chapter 15, section 15.3.3.

3.3.4.1 Overreaching

Second, the land registration system facilitates a process known as overreaching. Overreaching is a concept which proves difficult for many students throughout their time studying land law. Attempting to get to grips with it as early as possible is definitely the best plan! Overreaching is the mechanism by which certain equitable interests in land are 'transformed' upon the sale of that property into interests which relate to the *proceeds* of that sale, rather than the property. This means that whilst the equitable co-owners may be entirely unable to agree as to who has what percentage entitlement to these proceeds, this is not a dispute that is of any relevance to the purchaser. As long as the purchaser pays the *total* to the trustees, the on-going dispute will not affect them.

Furthermore, in cases where the trustee and the beneficiary are different people, the mechanism of overreaching means that purchasers do not need to be concerned with the potential for breach of trust to have occurred in such circumstances. Rather, the beneficiaries will only have an action against their trustees in respect of the proceeds of sale. For overreaching to take place, the transaction in question must involve the payment of money to at least two trustees. Such transactions, most commonly, therefore, are either sales of the title to the relevant estate, or the grant of a mortgage in such an estate. Certain other transactions are also overreaching transactions—eg the sale of legal title to mortgaged property (see chapter 11 at 11.4.4), and a sale resulting from a court order under section 14 Trusts of Land and Appointment of Trustees Act 1996 (see chapter 16 at 16.4.1).

Whilst this mechanism is mainly a product of the Law of Property Act 1925, particularly sections 2 and 27, the LRA 2002 assists through sections 23 and 24 which confer upon registered owners of land (ie owners of the freehold or leasehold estate) the so-called 'owners' powers.

Owners' powers are important in this respect. They take precedence over any limitation on the powers of the trustees that may appear in the document which establishes the trust but which a third party potential purchaser may be unable to access, and certainly about which they may reasonably be entirely unaware. This means that, most importantly, where land is transferred in breach of the duties of the trust, or even in breach of the *powers* conferred on the trustees by the trust itself, it will not matter to the quality of the title of the purchaser. This is also supported by the guarantee of title in section 58.

This fundamental idea is explained by the Law Commission:

'This general principle that a person's right to exercise owner's powers is unlimited unless there is some entry in the register... has effect for one specific purpose only. This is to prevent the title of the disponee being questioned. It follows that, if the person exercising owner's powers did not have unlimited powers, but there was no entry in the register to reflect this fact:

(1) the disponee's title could not be challenged; but
(2) the disposition would not be rendered lawful'.[8]

The consequence of this is that whilst the purchaser would be entirely unconcerned by any potential breach of trust or overstepping of trustees' powers, it would not prevent the beneficiaries suing for breach of trust. This is the very essence of the curtain principle.

A second mechanism by which the LRA 2002 facilitates overreaching is through the use of what are known as restrictions. Restrictions are, in essence, administrative instructions to the land registry not to register dispositions in relation to a particular piece of land *unless* certain conditions are met. To ensure that overreaching takes place, this could include a condition that the proceeds of a sale are paid to two trustees.[9]

However, it is also possible for restrictions to hinder the *wider* curtain principle (for this principle is more than ensuring the effective operation of overreaching). The restriction, in setting conditions before land can be transacted with, can act as a stifling of transfers of legal title without, for example, the consent of beneficiaries. This means that although a purchaser may not have to be concerned about the *precise* nature of any breach of trust in terms of the quality of their title should any sale actually occur, in the run up to such a sale, the need to consult with beneficiaries may slow proceedings, and may result in them ceasing all together. As a result, the curtain principle does not necessarily mean that in *practice* the purchasers will be unconcerned with the existence and nature of any interests under trusts relating to the estate in question. Rather, once a transaction occurs, where overreaching is possible, then the purchaser's new title will be unaffected by any such issues.

The recent Law Commission consultation on updates to the LRA 2002 contemplated taking this further, and considered whether interests under trusts *should* be capable of registration, suggesting that the appetite for the curtain principle is perhaps not as strong as it once had been. This is a reflection of the effect of the curtain principle, and overreaching in particular, which is to put vulnerable co-owners ay the mercy of perhaps unscrupulous trustees. However, the Law Commission felt that consideration of overreaching as part of the operation of the curtain principle in

---

[8] Law Commission, 'Land Registration for the Twenty-First Century' (Report no. 271) (2001), [4.9].
[9] Law Commission, 'Land Registration for the Twenty-First Century' (Report no. 271) (2001), [6.41].

registered land was beyond their remit. In reaching this conclusion, they emphasised the important policy tensions which exist in relation to this mechanism:

> 'The treatment of beneficial interests under the Act, however, reflects an ongoing debate about the correct balance to strike between the rights of purchasers and mortgagees on the one hand, and beneficiaries on the other, particularly in the context of beneficial interests that people may own in their home. That debate raises broad questions of social policy that ultimately touch on the appropriate balance the law strikes between property as a "home" and as a financial investment for homeowners to realise. The treatment of beneficial interests in the LRA 2002 sits within a much wider matrix of considerations of how the law balances the desire of home owners to secure their interest in the home, with the interests of purchasers and of those (such as mortgage lenders) with a financial interest in the property'.[10]

This approach has been maintained within the final report, and it is clear that there is little appetite for allowing registration of interests under trusts beyond that which the restriction mechanism can provide.[11]

Summary: The curtain principle

The curtain principle requires that interests under trusts do not appear on the register, and do not affect purchasers without more in any individual case. To reflect this, interests under trusts are not registrable. Where a transfer is made by two or more trustees, and money is paid to those trustees, interests under a trust will be overreached. If they are not overreached—because there is only one trustee, or no money is paid—they may acquire 'overriding' status through actual occupation. Interests under a trust can be protected by a restriction.

3.4 UNREGISTERED LAND

The final section of this chapter gives a brief overview of the principles of conveyancing in unregistered land. This is not supposed to be a definitive explanation of such rules—that would be a book in itself—but rather a guide to the general framework. This is intended to allow for comparison between the unregistered and registered land systems, as very few land law courses now anticipate understanding of unregistered land as a standalone topic. Nevertheless, it is useful to be aware of how unregistered land works, in order to understand some of the debate surrounding the conclusivity of the register, for example, as well as this giving insight into how English land law has developed over time.

There are essentially four fundamental elements of unregistered land conveyancing which must be appreciated. First, in unregistered conveyancing, legal interests are 'king'. They bind all parties. It matters not whether a third party purchases title to land with no knowledge of such rights, and no way of finding out about them (subject to the small category of legal rights which needed to be registered as Land Charges following the Land Charges Act 1972—a category which

---

[10] Law Commission, 'Updating the Land Registration Act 2002' (Consultation paper no 227) (2016), [1.21].
[11] Law Commission, 'Updating the Land Registration Act 2002' (Report no 380) (2018), [10.89].

represents an exception to, rather than an overturning of, this fundamental principle). They will nevertheless be bound. The second is that unregistered conveyancing is essentially private. There is no expectation that the transactions that take place will appear on any public register, *but*, this privacy has over the course of time been gradually eroded so that even in unregistered land, there is still mandatory registration of certain interests. This is a reflection of the third party effect of rights, and of the justice inherent in the ability of those bound by such rights to learn of their existence. Third, the unregistered land system treats 'equity's darling' differently from all other persons. Equity's darling is the purchaser of a legal title, who provides valuable consideration (money, or something calculable in money), is in good faith, and who has no knowledge or notice of any existing rights. Such a person would not be bound by any equitable rights of which they did not have notice. Fourth, given the general lack of a public record, the unregistered land system relies very heavily on the private record in the form of the deeds of transfer and other associated documents. This means that for unregistered land, the keeping of such records is absolutely critical. This can of course be problematic when many of these documents date back hundreds of years. Unregistered conveyancing, therefore, has something of a 'proof problem'. Many of the rules that apply to unregistered land are means by which such proof problems can be overcome.

3.4.1 LEGAL INTERESTS—UNIVERSAL APPLICATION

The first guiding principle for unregistered land is that all legal rights will bind all transferees of the land—even a purchaser without notice of such rights. The only exceptions to this principle relate to certain statutorily imposed charges (the most common of which are conditions on planning permissions), charges from the Inland Revenue (which are used to allow the recovery of tax arrears through property of the debtor), and the puisne mortgage (discussed in 3.4.2), which need to be registered under the Land Charges Act 1972. Otherwise, all legal rights will bind in all circumstances. The critical thing with such rights, therefore, becomes ensuring that (a) they can operate at law under section 1 Law of Property Act 1925 (see chapter 2 at 2.2.1); and (b) that they are created with the appropriate formalities to ensure that they do so operate (see 4.3), which in unregistered land means, in most cases, the use of a deed (explained in detail in chapter 4 at 4.3.2—essentially a formal document which is signed and witnessed in creating or transferring the relevant right).

> **Summary: Rights in unregistered land**
>
> In unregistered land, legal rights are universally binding (except statutory charges, Inland Revenue Charges, and puisne mortgages).

3.4.2 REGISTRATION IN UNREGISTERED LAND—THE LAND CHARGES ACT 1972

The mandatory registration to which we referred earlier is governed by the Land Charges Act 1972 (having been introduced in the Land Charges Act 1925). This Act provides that certain kinds of interests need to be registered even in unregistered land. Why is this the case? As we noted earlier, the bindingness of certain rights on third parties occurred—outwith the LCA system—under two conditions. First, all legal rights would bind all parties. Second, equitable rights would bind everyone *except* a good faith purchaser for value of the legal estate who had no notice of such rights. The critical thing for third parties, therefore, was the circumstances in which they could find out about such rights, and how far the 'doctrine of notice' would bind them to rights of which in fact they had no knowledge, but which they perhaps *ought* to have known about. But equitable rights can be enormously important. Right-holders are vulnerable where all they have is an equitable right as they are effectively at the mercy of a legal title–holder, despite the fact that they may have made a substantial investment to obtain the rights in the first place. If third parties cannot find out about such rights, it does not seem justified to bind them to these rights. How can these two problems be resolved? The answer is to make for a publicly searchable record of certain kinds of rights which, on the one hand, will bind any purchaser to those rights (thus protecting the equitable right-holder), and on the other hand, means that the purchaser has an easy and simple way of finding out about the right in the first place. Of course, this logic, if pushed to its ultimate conclusion, results in a complete system of land registration. However, the Land Charges Act 1972 is a sort of compromise in this respect in that it requires the registration of some kinds of rights, but *not* the registration of title to land.

In this compromise, a lot of problems emerged. The first is in the list of rights which must be registered in order to bind a purchaser. These are:

1. Some statutorily imposed charges;
2. A 'puisne mortgage' (we define this later);
3. Inland Revenue charge for inheritance tax;
4. A limited owner's charge;
5. An equitable charge (which affects the legal estate, but does not arise under a trust, and is not secured by deposit of the title deed);
6. Estate contract (as explained in chapter 14—this is a contract to convey or create a legal lease or to convey the freehold);
7. Restrictive freehold covenant;
8. Equitable easement.[12]

These interests were chosen because mostly they are difficult to 'spot' on an inspection of land. The lack of clear, consistent logic underpinning what is registrable and what is not, does not make it easier to operate within these rules. Importantly, the first three of these rights are legal rights, but which can only be binding if registered. Of these, the most significant in land law terms, is the puisne mortgage. This is a mortgage which is not protected by the deposit of title deeds. Deposit of title deeds is a method of mortgage which is no longer used, but essentially it used to be the case that the deeds to a property would be held by the lender until the loan was repaid. This was to allow the lender to sell title to the property to realise their security should the borrower fall into arrears, without having to get the title deeds from the borrower (who might, in such cases, be tempted to

---

[12] These are defined in section 2 Land Charges Act 1972.

'lose' the deeds to avoid a quick or easy sale on the lender's behalf—thus underlining the importance of documentation to unregistered land). However, since there would only be one original version of the title deeds, any subsequent mortgage—a second mortgage, for example, used to borrow on top of the first loan—would therefore not have the advantage for the lender of being able to retain the title deeds. Furthermore, it would be very difficult for a third party to know of this loan since they would not have the evidence of the lending in the form of the whereabouts of the title deed. This left such mortgages potentially unfair for purchasers (they are legal mortgages and therefore before the Land Charges Act 1972, automatically binding). As a result, these are one of the few legal rights that are not automatically binding on purchasers in unregistered land.

Once a right is registered on the land charges register, a number of consequences follow. First, regardless of whether the intending purchaser actually consults the register, they are deemed to have actual notice of the right. It will be binding upon even a purchaser for value. Second, the right will be registered against the *name* of the person entitled to the burdened estate.[13] This system is very problematic. First, names are not unique nor even necessarily stay the same through a person's ownership of land. Second, it is not always possible to discover the name of former owners and therefore not always possible to find the relevant rights. To compensate for some of these problems, and for the problems associated with variations of the same name, eg Jon or Jonathan, Tora and Victoria, etc, the purchaser will not be bound by any right which was not revealed to them on an official search if they did search under the correct name (and reasonable variations thereof). Finally, if a right is not registered when such was required, then it will be void as against a purchaser, even if the purchaser did not know about the right. Similarly, a purchaser acting in bad faith will also be protected, as the doctrine of notice in this sense does not apply in cases involving the LCA 1972.

> **Summary: Registration in unregistered land**
>
> Even in unregistered land, some rights are required to be registered on the land charges register if they are to affect purchasers of an estate in the land. The LCA system of registration under name rather than property is very problematic.

3.4.3 PURCHASER FOR VALUE WITHOUT NOTICE

The third guiding principle in unregistered land is that in cases where registration is not required under the LCA 1972, or prior to that Act, whilst all legal interests would bind a transferee, equitable rights would not bind in all circumstances. Rather, equitable rights would not bind a purchaser of the legal estate acting in good faith, and providing money or money's worth, who did not have notice of the right. This would be 'an absolute, unqualified, unanswerable defence'.[14] Most of these requirements are relatively straightforward. However, the 'without notice' qualification proved hugely difficult in practice, and this was one of the main drivers behind the switch to registered land.

---

[13] Land Charges Act 1972, section 3(1).
[14] *Pilcher v Rawlins* (1872) 7 Ch App 259, 269.

3.4.3.1 The doctrine of notice

The doctrine of notice is, in the case of rights which do not need to be registered under the Land Charges Act, therefore critical to the operation of priority disputes in unregistered land. This doctrine encompasses three different 'modes' by which we ascribe knowledge or a form of knowledge to an intending purchaser: actual notice, constructive notice, and imputed notice. Of these, constructive notice is by far the most controversial, as it involves a finding that despite the fact that the purchaser *did not* know about a right, we pretend that they did for the purposes of priority. If the justification behind the bindingness of such rights is knowledge, constructing knowledge in this respect is divorced from the justification. However, the whole doctrine of notice and its application has proved problematic. The central function which this a doctrine plays in unregistered conveyancing, when twinned with these problems, was therefore one of the main motivations behind a switch to registered land. As Howell explains:

> '[B]y the nineteenth century, the notice doctrine was acknowledged as causing considerable difficulties; it was identified in the earliest reports and proposals for reform in the nineteenth century as one of the major problems of real property. Difficulties arose mainly over the question of whether a person who was admittedly a purchaser for value of a legal estate in fact had "notice" of the prior equitable right. Actual notice, conscious knowledge of matters affecting the title, presented relatively few problems. The difficulties of "imputed" notice, that is, notice which came through an authorized agent and was imputed to the principal, were largely overcome by the Conveyancing Act 1882... It is constructive notice which has caused and continues to cause the most difficulty. The principle upon which it is based is eminently reasonable. If a purchaser is affected only by matters of which he actually knows, he will take care to ensure that he is without that knowledge. Since this could clearly lead to injustice, equity was prepared in certain circumstances to treat the purchaser as having knowledge which he did not in fact have. In order to satisfy the courts of equity, the purchaser was expected to inspect both the land itself and the documents of title to a standard of enquiry set by the courts, and that standard could be very high'.[15]

Thus, there is a tension in the idea of making the bindingness of rights dependent upon knowledge: if a purchaser does not want to be bound by any adverse rights, then the temptation will be for that person to seek deliberately to avoid acquiring any knowledge. In this sense, the doctrine of notice becomes, effectively, a form of incentive to make very careful inquiries. If the purchaser is going to be bound either way—through actual knowledge, or through constructive notice if they *do not* carry out careful inquiries—then it is in the purchaser's best interest to actually know about the rights. Then they can take appropriate steps to either renegotiate a price which reflects the bindingness of the prior right, or to negotiate with the right-holder to discharge the right, prior to purchase.

Actual notice

To explore how the doctrine of notice works, let us examine the three categories of notice in more detail. First, actual notice is distinguishable in theory from knowledge. Knowledge as both a legal test and a philosophical concept is difficult. For example, can we say that a person knows something if they have been told about it over and over again but fundamentally do not believe that

---

[15] J Howell, 'The doctrine of notice: an historical perspective' [2007] Conv 431, 431–2.

to be true? On the other hand, does a person know about something if they have been told it by a source which they do know to be entirely unreliable, so that usually everything that this person says is a lie? Thus, the law does not seek knowledge. Whilst the line between knowledge and notice is very fuzzy, strictly speaking, they are not the same thing. Thus, however a person heard about the right—whether from a reliable source or not—they can be said to have actual notice, except perhaps in cases where they only hear vague rumours of a right (although in such a case we may say that they did have constructive notice if they did not respond to the rumours by taking appropriate investigative steps). Furthermore, because what is sought is notice, not knowledge, if a purchaser is given a document which contains the transaction giving the right-holder the right, for example, then he will have actual *notice* of that right, even if he does not read the document so as to have subjective knowledge of it. That the having of a document must be enough is clear. Otherwise, it would be far too easy or a person to escape the doctrine of notice by simply saying that they had not read a document, a question which is effectively impossible to prove or disprove. Finally, as we discussed in 3.4.2 in relation to the Land Charges Act, where a right is registered on the land charges register, then whether or not they have read the register, they are treated as though they have actual notice of the right (which is entirely justifiable by the fact that it is usually very easy to search the register and therefore knowledge is straightforwardly acquired).

3.4.3.2 Constructive notice

Second, we must examine the doctrine of constructive notice. This is defined in *Hunt v Luck* as:

> 'the knowledge which the courts impute to a person upon a presumption so strong of the existence of the knowledge that it cannot be allowed to be rebutted, either from his knowing something which ought to have put him to further inquiry or from his wilfully abstaining from inquiry, to avoid notice'.[16]

Essentially constructive notice will arise where a person does not take sufficient care in investigating the presence of any rights in relation to land which they intend to purchase. It is a tool to ensure such care. The explanation of this is given by Sir James Wigram VC in *Jones v Smith*,[17] in a discussion which gets to the heart of constructive notice and the justifications behind it.

> **Key case: *Jones v Smith* (1841) 1 Hare 43**
>
> His lordship began by emphasising that it is not possible to determine in advance what will suffice for constructive notice. He then suggested, however, that such notice could be split into two classes.
>
>> 'First, cases in which the party charged has had actual notice that the property in dispute was, in fact, charged, incumbered or in some way affected, and the Court has thereupon bound him with constructive notice of facts and instruments, to a knowledge of which he would have been led by an inquiry after the charge, incumbrance or other circumstance affecting the property of which he had actual notice; and, secondly, cases in which the Court has been satisfied from the evidence before it that the party charged had designedly abstained from inquiry for the very purpose of avoiding notice'.[18]

---

[16] *Hunt v Luck* [1901] 1 Ch 45 (Chd), 52.
[17] *Jones v Smith* (1841) 1 Hare 43, 66 ER 943.
[18] *Jones v Smith* (1841) 1 Hare 43, 66 ER 943, [54].

> The first case is where a person is aware of a right binding the property but has not made full investigations of the nature of that right. In such cases, the court will conclude that he is aware of all the information he would have had if he had 'followed up' on the right about which he was aware. The second case is where an individual has not carried out inspections to avoid knowledge.
>
> His Lordship then went onto explain the justifications in these cases:
>
> 'The proposition of law, upon which the former class of cases proceeds, is not that the party charged had notice of a fact or instrument, which, in truth, related to the subject in dispute without his knowing that such was the case, but that he had actual notice that it did so relate. The proposition of law, upon which the second class of cases proceeds, is not that the party charged had incautiously neglected to make inquiries, but that he had designedly abstained from such inquiries, for the purpose of avoiding knowledge—a purpose which, if proved, would clearly shew that he had a suspicion of the truth, and a fraudulent determination not to learn it. If, in short, there is not actual notice that the property is in some way affected, and no fraudulent turning away from a knowledge of facts... if mere want of caution, as distinguished from fraudulent and wilful blindness, is all that can be imputed to the purchaser—there the doctrine of constructive notice will not apply'.[19]

However, in more recent explanations of the doctrine of notice, there has been more emphasis on carelessness being enough to give rise to constructive notice.

In order to avoid falling victim to the doctrine of constructive notice, a purchaser must do two things. First, they must inspect the land itself. Second, they must inspect the documentation which conferred title onto the vendor. It is in this sense both a real life and a paper-based exercise. The physical inspection of the land essentially allows the purchaser to see evidence of factors which are contrary to what the vendor says. For example, if the vendor indicates that they live alone in the property, but there is evidence of another person, that would be enough to require the purchaser to make further inquiries to be sure that the vendor's position was true. This can be a very difficult test for a purchaser to meet, however, since the vendor will be incentivised in some cases to disguise the right-holder's presence. This was discussed in the infamous case of *Kingsnorth Finance v Tizard*.[20]

> **Key case:** *Kingsnorth Finance v Tizard* [1986] 1 WLR 783
>
> This case involved a family home. It was in the name of the husband only, but the wife had contributed financially to its acquisition. When their relationship broke down, the wife moved out of the house, but came back daily to look after their two children. The husband entered into a mortgage transaction, telling the lender representative who came to look round that he had separated from his wife and that she lived elsewhere. The wife claimed that she had an equitable interest that took priority over the loan since the lender, she argued, had notice of her right.
>
> The court held that the fact that the property was occupied by the father and two children was enough to put the lender on notice so that they should have made further enquiries. As a result, they were taken

---

[19] *Jones v Smith* (1841) 1 Hare 43, 66 ER 943, [56] (from Hare report).
[20] *Kingsnorth Finance v Tizard* [1986] 1 WLR 783 (Chd).

to have notice of her right, so that they were bound by it. In reaching this conclusion, the court held that arranging an inspection with the vendor, in cases like this, was not enough:

> 'Such a pre-arranged inspection may achieve no more than an inquiry of the vendor or mortgagor and his answer to it. In the case of residential property an appointment for inspection will, in most cases, be essential... How then is a purchaser or mortgagee to carry out such inspection "as ought reasonably to have been made" for the purpose of determining whether the possession and occupation of the property accords with the title B offered? What is such an inspection "as ought reasonably to be made" must, I think, depend on all the circumstances. In the circumstances of the present case I am not satisfied that the pre-arranged inspection on a Sunday afternoon fell within the category of "such inspections which ought reasonably to have been made"'.[21]

This conclusion may seem somewhat harsh on the lender, since they did make inquiries about the wife's rights. The problem for them was the vendor's lie, not the failure to ask the question. Furthermore, the judge was critical of the lender's representative's failure to rifle through drawers, and open cupboards etc. As Thompson argues, this seems unfair:

> 'With respect, this seems to go too far. Suppose [he] had asked where the mother of the children was and had been told either that she was dead or that she had left years ago and her present whereabouts, or even whether she was still alive, was unknown. What then is he supposed to do? Clearly, an inspection of the property should take place. If the mortgagor says this can take place at the weekend, can it really be supposed that the mortgagee's agent must insist on calling at an alternative, unannounced time to check whether the mortgagor is lying? Similarly must he insist upon rifling through drawers and cupboards, inevitably causing offence? It is submitted that such behaviour goes far beyond what are reasonable inquiries.
>
> It is suggested that the onus on a purchaser of unregistered land is not this heavy. It is necessary that the vendor should be asked whether he shares the house with anyone else. Additionally he should be asked if he either is or was married. If the answers reveal the existence of anybody, then inquiries where possible should be made of that person. Further, an inspection of the property should be carried out ... For the purchaser to insist on doing more carries the inevitable implication that he suspects the vendor of deceit. Such demands should not be considered to be within the scope of reasonable inquiries'.[22]

The second aspect of constructive notice—proper examination of the title—since the Law of Property Act 1969, has been an obligation to ensure that the paper-based transactions prove good title to the land dating back at least 15 years. This is intended to exceed the period of adverse possess (see chapter 6), without leaving the purchaser with too burdensome a task in terms of completing an investigation where paperwork dating back furthermore may be missing or incomplete.

3.4.3.3 Imputed notice

The final type of notice is imputed notice. Imputed notice is notice acquired by an agent of the purchaser, which even if not communicated to the principal, is treated as though it had so been communicated. This is essentially a question of actual notice in relation to solicitors or buying agents. In cases where the agent does acquire actual notice of a right, and does not communicate this to the principal, then of course the principal may have an action against the agent, so that the principal themself, although bound by the right, is not without recourse.

---

[21] *Kingsnorth Finance v Tizard* [1986] 1 WLR 783 (Chd), 795.
[22] M P Thompson, 'The purchaser as private detective' [1986] Conv 283, 286.

In general then, the doctrine of notice ensures that rights will be binding far beyond cases where there is actual knowledge. Megarry & Wade (the leading practitioners' text) sums up the approach of the courts in this respect: '[t]he tendency of the Court of Chancery was constantly to extend and refine the doctrines of constructive and imputed notice'.[23] This broadening, so amply demonstrated by the facts of *Tizard*, eventually proved the downfall of the doctrine of notice, which plays almost no role in modern land law. Rather, the process of registration, both in unregistered and registered land, is seen as a vastly more satisfactory approach to managing the tension between third party rights and purchaser knowledge.

> **Summary: The doctrine of notice**
>
> A purchaser for value without notice of a right will not be bound by that right, in unregistered land, unless that right is a legal right, or appears on the land charges register. There are three species of notice: actual, constructive, and imputed. The operation of this doctrine was one of the main motivations for a move to registered land.

3.4.4 PROBLEMS OF PROOF IN UNREGISTERED LAND

Finally, many of the rules in unregistered land can be explained by the problems of proof associated with such a system. Two important features fall under this heading: the first is the 15-year root of title discussed earlier; and the second is the system of adverse possession.

3.4.4.1 15-year root of title

The first solution to the proof problem is to be found in the requirement that a purchaser only investigate title for at least 15 years. Of course, if within the fifteen year inspection window there is a clear problem with title, then the purchaser will be required to look further. However, if all appears well within 15 years, then further investigation is unnecessary. Given the relatively slow turnover of property (particularly in relation to the kinds of property which still remain unregistered), it is highly likely that proof dating for at least 15 years will be available. Furthermore, it must be remembered, that from now on any transaction in such land will mandate registration, so that the proof problem is a diminishing one.

3.4.4.2 Adverse possession

The other solution to the problem of proof in unregistered land is the operation of the rules relating to adverse possession. These are explained in detail in chapter 6, and indeed adverse possession is usually the only topic in relation to unregistered land still taught in many land law courses. The role of adverse possession in this context is effectively to 'wipe the slate clean' so that defects in any paper title do not persist potentially for many hundreds of years, only to resurface and cause problems for the current owner of an estate in land. This works because where a person is in possession of land for more than 12 years, whether or not they had paper title to that land, they will then have the strongest title to that land as all others would have been extinguished. Similarly, if there is a valid chain of conveyance which taken together adds up to 12 years, then the same reasoning applies.

---

[23] C Harpum et al, *Megarry and Wade: The Law of Real Property* (8th ed) (Sweet & Maxwell, London, 2012), [8.024].

3.5 CONCLUSION

To conclude this section, we can then take these features of unregistered land conveyancing and compare with registered land. First, registered land does not have a proof problem, and nor is knowledge relevant. This was one of the main motivations behind the wholesale switch to registered land in 2003, to avoid the problems and injustice caused by the doctrine of notice, whilst allowing for clear and certain knowledge of who had title. Whilst not 100 per cent successful, the degree to which the mirror and insurance principles are embodied, demonstrates that registered land is certainly an improvement on what went before. Second, for registered land, the first point of call for a purchaser will be the register. This makes conveyancing cheaper and more efficient, for whilst investigation of title and a physical inspection of the land remain important—to spot overriding interests—it is nevertheless a potentially less arduous task. Finally, there is a clear switch in policy from unregistered to registered land regarding the degree to which conveyancing land is seen as a public function. The registration system integrates public resources and administration into the conveyancing system, providing its guarantees, and changing its character from something private and hidden, to something public and open (at least to an extent). In this character change lies risks—fraud due to the ease of acquisition of information about title; identity theft; even privacy concerns, but the risks are seen as being vastly outweighed by the efficiency gains. Perhaps, however, it is now worth considering whether the reliance on technology which e-conveyancing represents, and the mass availability of data through the public register, holds more hidden risks than we might have thought in 2002.

PRINCIPLES

How does this discussion begin to shape our understanding of the principles explained in chapter 1? To recap, these principles were:

1. Certainty
2. Sensitivity to context
3. Transactability
4. Systemic and individual effects
5. Recognition of the social role of the land law system.

The system of land registration has a profound effect on these principles. Indeed, the modern law is so heavily influenced by the move from unregistered to registered land that the entire character of the system has shifted. The new system is much more commercially focused, with an emphasis on dynamic security and transactability which without any doubt poses risks for vulnerable users within the system, particularly those whose rights are held under a trust. Sensitivity to context is, in this sense, anathema to a land registration system since the flexibility and uncertainty that such sensitivity implies undermines the very philosophy behind registered land.

However, in the practical creation of a system of registered land, the drafters of the relevant legislation over the years have recognised that ignoring context is both unrealistic, and wrong. The shape of the mirror principle is evidence of this. Allowing overriding interests as it does, the principle bends to ensure that some comfort and protection is given to those occupying land. Furthermore, whilst the system of overreaching may seem to place many occupiers at serious risk, the ability to use restrictions again provides a degree of protection which a 'pure' Torrens system may not.

Most importantly for the principles here, however, the whole system of land registration tells us an awful lot about how land law is seen in the legal system as a whole. Whatever the merits or otherwise of thinking about land as a fungible asset, land registration is fundamentally about labeling land as *owned* and burdened by rights which other people own. It is not about shared use, about patterns of historical occupation, or about providing homes and safe spaces for people to spend their time. Thus the 'social purpose' of land law is revealed by the system of registered land to be, at least in part, the creation of wealth. This decision as to how we conceptualise land, as something which can be assigned a label of 'this is mine', in a publically accessible fashion, shapes much of the tone for the development of land law as a whole, and hugely influences critique of these rules.

TABLE OF DEFINITIONS

Overriding interest	An interest in land which binds a purchaser of registered land despite not appearing on the register.
Land registration	The process of creating a public record of titles to and rights in land.
Land registry	The public body responsible for managing the land register.
Mirror principle	Principle holding that the register should be an accurate reflection of the rights that exist in relation to a piece of land.
Insurance principle	Principle holding that the register should be accurate, and where inaccurate, that compensation should be payable to those who lose out as a result.
Curtain principle	Principle holding that interests under trusts should not appear on the register; and that such interests should not affect purchasers of the land without a further justification being present in any particular case.
Doctrine of notice	The doctrine ascribing knowledge of a right to a purchaser in unregistered land.
Land Charges Register	The register of certain rights relating to unregistered land.

FURTHER READING

The further reading section here is designed to give you some further information on the history of land registration in the UK and elsewhere:

BRIGHT, S. and DEWAR, J., (eds), *Land Law: Themes and Perspectives* (OUP, 1998).
COOKE, E., *The New Law of Land Registration* (Hart, 2003).
GRINLINTON, D., (ed), *Torrens in the twenty-first century* (Lexis Nexis, 2003).
SIMPSON, A. W. B., *A History of the Land Law* (OUP, 1986).

4

FORMALITIES AND THE CREATION OF RIGHTS IN LAND

4.1	Introduction	81	Principles	112
4.2	Purposes of Formality Rules	82	Table of Definitions	114
4.3	The Rules	86	Further Reading	114
4.4	Conclusion	112		

CHAPTER GOALS

By the end of this chapter you should be able to:

- Explain the possible purposes of formality rules, particularly in relation to transactions involving land;
- Understand the steps which must be taken to create an enforceable contract in relation to the creation or transfer of a right in land, and when this is required;
- Understand the steps which must be taken to create a valid deed in relation to rights in land, and when such is required;
- Have an appreciation of the formalities required to transfer or create an equitable interest in land; and
- Understand the consequences of a failure to comply with formality rules.

4.1 INTRODUCTION

Formality rules in relation to land serve a number of important purposes, but can also frustrate the wishes of parties who accidentally fail to meet their requirements. This 'frustrating effect' requires justification. This can be found in the fact that such rules help to ensure that the parties to a transaction have thoroughly and carefully considered the nature of the transaction. As a result, they play an important role in protecting vulnerable individuals; in ensuring caution; and in preserving the essence of an agreement should any future disputes arise. However, the existence of formality rules can, in some cases, be both intimidating and irksome, a barrier to speedy and efficient negotiations. There is, therefore, a constant tension in this area of land law between the certainty and predictability which formalities ensure and the need for flexibility to protect the expectations of those involved in a transaction. When thinking about formality rules, and how they operate in practice, this balance, and the importance of reaching a fair and predictable compromise, should always be kept in mind.

Furthermore, it is essential to understand how formality rules in relation to land operate in order accurately and swiftly to ascertain what rights or otherwise may have arisen in any particular situation, so that the on-going legal position of the parties can be accurately explained. These rules are sometimes technical and a little dry. Once learnt, they provide an essential foundation for considering issues such as registration of title. From a practical point of view, a thorough but clear knowledge of these rules makes problem questions, in particular, quicker and more straightforward.

This chapter outlines the general principles in relation to formalities and examines some specific instances of the operation of such rules. Section 4.2 considers the purpose of formality rules. Sections 4.3–4.5 then consider, in turn, the formalities required to create an enforceable contract in land; a deed; a and valid disposition of an equitable interest.

4.2 PURPOSES OF FORMALITY RULES

There have been a number of analyses regarding the purposes which formality rules serve. Of these, the most famous perhaps is that of Lon Fuller. He enunciated three primary functions for formality rules: the evidential function, the cautionary function, and the channelling function.[1] In analysing these different functions, Fuller explains the advantages not only of formalities in terms of a record of an agreement reached, but also in terms of the solemnity that such a process encourages for those entering into a contract in relation to land. For others, the distinctive nature of land makes formality rules all the more important in this context, thanks to its significance in economic and social terms, and the serious personal consequence that might emerge in cases where something goes wrong in a transaction involving land.

Citing Austin, Fuller explains the evidentiary function: '[t]he most obvious function of a legal formality is, to use Austin's words, that of providing "evidence of the existence and purport of the contract, in case of controversy"'.[2] Such an evidential function is clearly important to the parties to the transaction themselves. They will know with clarity what has been agreed. It is also helpful for the courts in their function as enforcers of the agreement. Without such written evidence, it would likely be both time-consuming and costly to examine witnesses, consider the relative merits of the parties' evidence, and to provide a clear and certain articulation of the respective rights and obligations of the parties to the dispute. It is therefore useful both in terms of the resources of the parties, but also in terms of the resources of the court, to by-pass the need for a review of evidence by limiting that evidence to a single, probative, document.

---

[1] L Fuller, 'Consideration and form' (1941) 41 Columbia Law Review 799.
[2] L Fuller, 'Consideration and form' (1941) 41 Columbia Law Review 799, 800.

The cautionary function is quite different. This function is not something with which the courts are concerned per se. Nevertheless, by requiring that parties take time and care in reaching their agreement, it is likely that they will express themselves more clearly than they otherwise might, thus assisting in terms of the usefulness of the document from an evidential perspective. Fuller describes this function as, 'a check against inconsiderate action'.[3] This is a useful and important function, especially in land law. Entering into a mortgage agreement, for example, is likely to constitute one of the most significant financial decisions an individual makes in her lifetime. However, on the other hand, the requirement of caution and care—and the advantages that this can bring in respect of a more vulnerable or less experienced party to a transaction—can be tempered with the frustrating effects of formality rules. The expectations of such inexperienced parties can be frustrated through a failure to comply with formality rules. It can therefore be argued that formality rules can and should only be required if and when they increase protection of such individuals, rather than in cases where they are used by the more experienced party as a weapon to avoid meeting their promises. For this reason, formality rules have an explicit or implicit fraud exception, whereby parties are unable to rely on the rule in order to perpetrate a fraud. When considering the way the rules are applied in case law, or in problem questions, it is therefore worth thinking whether the cautionary function of the rule is benefitting the less experienced party—ensuring care—or harming that person by giving the experienced party the upper hand.

The final function discussed by Fuller is the channelling function. In many ways, it is this function which is most specifically useful in cases of property law given the inability of parties to simply render proprietary any kind of agreement. Rather, as discussed in chapter 2, in order to have proprietary consequences, the rights and obligations which the parties agree must fit into one of the pre-defined categories of property right, such as a lease or a mortgage. As Fuller explains, 'in this aspect form offers a legal framework into which the party may fit his actions, or, to change the figure, it offers channels for the legally effective expression of intention'.[4] This is a complex way of saying that formality rules allow parties to 'sign up to' a pre-defined set of consequences from their agreement. To give an example, when parties agree that they want to create a lease, there are certain consequences of having a leasehold relationship which arise automatically. The parties do not have to spell them out. By requiring the agreement to be written down, parties have to articulate exactly what right it is they wish to create, and therefore which pre-determined set of consequences they wish to call into action. The combination of a *numerus clausus*, discussed in chapter 2, and formality requirements, therefore limits and channels the sorts of agreements which parties are able to create, producing a degree of predictability and clarity which may otherwise be absent.

However, it is possible to add to the list of functions for formality rules which was given by Fuller. We can also say that formality requirements are one method by which the more vulnerable members of the community are protected against deceitful actions of those around them. This goes further than the evidential or cautionary function, since such a vulnerable individual may very well be happily committed to the terms agreed between themselves and the other party. However, by requiring a written record of the transaction that has taken place, the courts are

---

[3] L Fuller, 'Consideration and form' (1941) 41 Columbia Law Review 799, 800.
[4] L Fuller, 'Consideration and form' (1941) 41 Columbia Law Review 799, 801.

more easily able to assess the balance of power created by the relationship. In a consumer context, for example, protection given to mortgagors by regulation of mortgage relationships, is assisted by the requirement that the mortgage transaction be written down.[5] Furthermore, the existence of formality rules has an important economic function in terms of the risk to which a transaction gives rise. For many conducting transactions in land—in particular, for banks and building societies when entering into mortgage transactions—whilst enforceability and caution are very important to them, above this there is a generalised need for them to calculate the risks associated with the grant of finance on the basis of a secured interest over land. This is not so much about minimising risk, although that is clearly important. Rather it is about providing a clear background against which the level of risk present can be measured. Part of this risk calculation relates to the likelihood of something going wrong with the agreement between themselves and the borrower such that the borrower is not required to pay. The existence of formality rules militates against this risk by fulfilling these functions described by Fuller but more importantly it limits and shapes the types of risks which can occur and the circumstances in which this might take place. Added together, therefore, the functions articulated by Fuller produce a sort of super function in the form of risk avoidance within the legal system.

Some have argued, however, that it is wrong to look at the formality rules through these traditional lenses. By focussing on certainty, predictability, risk avoidance etc, some scholars suggest that we 'take for granted' what we want our land law system to do.[6] In particular, these sorts of functions are focused on commerce, resource and investment, for the most part, rather than security, individual dignity, and the importance of land as a means of providing a home.[7] It is important, then, to recognise that whilst these may be the primary policy goals behind the existing formality rules, these are not the only principles against which formality rules can be judged. It is perfectly legitimate to come at the question of the success or otherwise of these rules from a perspective which has nothing to do with certainty.

Let us imagine an example. Anne is in negotiations with Mary to rent Mary's house. Neither party has much experience in property deals. Being of limited means, both are reluctant to incur expensive legal fees if they can help it. Using the internet, they think they have found out what they need to do to make the lease agreement legally binding. Unfortunately, they forget to put a vital detail into the document—how long the rental agreement is to last—although they had orally agreed it would be a 10-year lease. Anne moves into the house and uses her savings to pay for the removal men, and to buy furniture etc. Both women are very happy with the arrangement. However, sometime later, Anne wishes for her partner and his children to move into the house. Mary is anxious to prevent this as she is not keen for children to stay in the house as she believes they might do damage to the property. There is nothing in the written agreement about whether children are allowed but in investigating how she might stop the children moving in, Mary thinks that because there is no period of time listed in the agreement, she might be able to evict Anne. Anne and Mary have reached an impasse, and engage the assistance of lawyers.

---

[5] For example, under the Mortgage Credit Directive 2014, as implemented into UK law and as managed by the Financial Conduct Authority.

[6] D Cowan, L Fox O'Mahoney, and N Cobb, *Land Law* (London, Palgrave, 2016) 12.

[7] J Hohmann, *The Right to Housing: Law, Concepts, Possibilities* (Oxford, Hart Publishing, 2013).

There is a relatively simple solution to this problem. Since there is no term written down in the lease, the written contract is void as being uncertain. By failing to comply with an important aspect of the formality rules here, ie the inclusion of all the relevant terms within the written document, the parties are deprived of the certainty that the written contract would have provided for them. Instead, the law steps in to provide a default position. As a result, the court will look to see how often Anne pays rent—let us say monthly—and imply the creation of a periodic tenancy that rolls over from month to month. This means that with a month's notice, Mary is able to bring the periodic tenancy to an end (subject to any issues of security of tenure, discussed in chapter 10).

If Anne and Mary here had complied with the formality rules, by including all the relevant terms within the contract, this situation would not have arisen. There would have been clear evidence of the 10-year agreement which both they, and the court should things progress that far, could point to in settling the question as to how long the lease should last. This evidence would not have fallen foul of the statutory requirement that all the terms be recorded in this written form. Furthermore, in having to write this down, both may have been more conscious of the length of agreement to which they were signing up, and might have thought about what major issues might arise over the course of a ten-year period. Formalities, in short, would have helped here.

But this is not the only way to think about this scenario. The end result seems disproportionate, given the investment that Anne made in moving to the property and setting up her life there. The lack of formality is significantly more serious for her than it is for Mary in this situation. The 'fall back' position of the periodic tenancy is not what Anne wants. Mary is in the stronger position of the two as she can simply rent out her house again. Anne cannot recoup the money and effort she has spent in turning Mary's house into her home.

This example shows that just because the point of formality rules is to create certainty, caution etc, it is possible to consider whether they also contribute to or detract from other 'goods' in the property law system, such as a fair and equable distribution of housing, the ability for individuals to plan their lives because they have a stable 'home', and the security and privacy which a home can provide.

Summary: Functions of formality rules

1. Evidential function: proving what has been agreed. This provides certainty to the parties, and assists the courts.
2. The cautionary function: requiring reflection on the agreement before it is crystallised. The ensures that the parties know what they are agreeing, and are certain that they wish to go ahead.
3. The channelling function: directing the agreement the parties have reached into a particular legal form. This makes the operation of the property law system more simple.
4. Protecting vulnerable individuals by allowing courts to assess the balance of power in legal relationships, and to scrutinise particularly onerous terms.
5. Allowing accurate risk assessment through ensuring clarity in the terms of an agreement.

When we start to think about these different functions of formality rules, it becomes clear that the goals can be reached in a number of different 'formal' ways. The purposes of formality rules tell us that formality rules are required, but do not necessarily tell us what these should look like. For that, we must also take account of the distinctive nature of land, and in particular its permanence through time and the longevity of many of the agreements and rights created in relation to land. Indeed, a desire to ensure the functions are met even when the original parties are no longer connected to the land in question has a huge influence over the shape of the formality rules in land law.

It is important to understand also that land law does not just require one type of formal document. There is a range of documents, and they have different effects in different situations. The simplicity, certainty and clarity to which formality rules should give rise is undermined in land law by the fact that there are subtly, but importantly, different formality rules for the creation of different types of rights and different types of transactions. For example, creating a ten-year lease requires different documentation than does creating a two-year lease; transferring a mortgage requires different forms than does transferring an interest under a trust. It is therefore at least arguable that the policies behind formality rules, although perhaps met in relation to each individual rule discussed later, are not met *globally*. The whole land law system is not particularly clear and simple (except to those who already know it—and sometimes not even then). It is therefore important to analyse each rule individually, but also to think about the whole network of rules and how they interact.

4.3 THE RULES

There are many different areas in land law where formalities are required. Certain procedures must be followed when creating a trust in land; when creating a contract for an interest in land; or when attempting to transfer or create such an interest in cases where there is no contract, such as a will, or a gift. Furthermore, a failure to use these formalities does not give rise to homogenous consequences. Rather, for each of these categories there are subtly different effects arising from a failure to take all the formal steps required, a picture further complicated by the distinction between legal and equitable property rights. This can make study of these rules difficult, and it is important to keep two things in mind at all times: what are the relevant parties to the transaction trying to achieve, and which statutory provisions govern that process? From here, it ought to be simply a matter of engaging with the relevant statutory provisions in order to discern from them the outcome. Inevitably, however, the picture is rarely as straightforward as this. Case law interpretation, opaque statutory wording, and the fact that the distinctions between the relevant categories are not always clear cut, will make this somewhat more difficult in practice than it appears on paper. However, Table 4.1 will provide a starting point at least.

When considering this table, it is important to remember that this chapter in general refers to situations where the parties *deliberately* create the relevant property rights (even if they do not label them as such). There are many situations where property rights arise impliedly or automatically by statute and those situations are not within the scope of this chapter. This chapter will now consider each of these four categories in turn.

Table 4.1 Transactions and statutory provisions

Transaction	Statutory Provision
Creation of an enforceable contract concerning rights in land	Section 2 Law of Property Act 1989
Creation of a deed transferring or creating rights in land	Section 1 Law of Property Act 1989; Section 52 Law of Property Act 1925
Creation of a trust of land	Section 53 Law of Property Act 1925
Transfer of an interest under a trust of land	Section 53 Law of Property Act 1925

4.3.1 CONTRACTS

We begin with the creation of an enforceable contract for the sale, creation or other disposition of an interest in land. This can range from the very simple—A agrees that she will buy B's freehold title for a price of £100,000 on 1 January—to the highly complex—transactions involving multiple property development transactions, for example. However simple or complicated the transaction, there is a basic general rule: contracts disposing rights in land must be created in signed writing, in a single document, containing all the terms of the agreement. As is to be expected, there are exceptions to this general rule, and situations where it is not as clear as it seems on its face.

4.3.1.1 The general rule

First, we must examine what the general principles in relation to formalities and contracts relating to rights in land are. When entering into a transaction involving such property rights, the first step the parties will generally undertake is the reaching of an informal agreement. This informal agreement, often an oral agreement, constitutes the basis upon which a binding contract is later built. However, in certain circumstances this informal agreement itself may give rise to property rights. Such instances are however rare, and exceptions to the general rule that the creation of rights in land requires, at least, a written contract, are few and far between. We will discuss these circumstances in the next section. In this section we focus on the need to use a written contract as the first step in the rights-creation process.

Before examining the precise content of these rules, it is essential to note that there is a series of important categories of 'agreements' with which you might be asked to deal. Not all agreements are contracts. First, there is the explicit agreement which is detailed and tolerably clear with promises made on both sides. This sort of agreement is common in the negotiation of house sales, for example, where parties agree a price, the extent of the property to be sold, and dates, major terms, etc. Secondly, there is the implicit agreement where the parties simply perform in line with a shared but tacit understanding as to what is to happen, and actions are performed on both sides. For example, this could include a situation where a neighbour utilises a right of way by implicit consent, and, for example, contributes to the cost of maintaining the path, without there ever having been a firm and clear agreement that this practice will continue. In this sort of scenario, there is no contract. Finally, there is the promise relied on such that some sort of agreement can be inferred from conduct where the initial promise was explicit, but it was not an agreement as such.

These different kinds of 'bargains' are dealt with very differently by the legal system. Not all such *bargains* will give rise to *contracts* even in situations where no writing is required. Understanding this is essential to understanding the workings of the formality rules, but it can be somewhat difficult to negotiate the boundary lines between the various categories as they exist on a spectrum ranging from the extremely clear, to the entirely implied (see Figure 4.1).

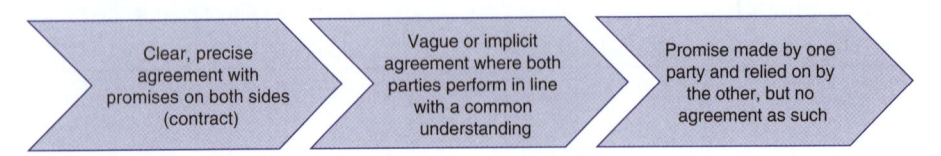

> Clear, precise agreement with promises on both sides (contract) → Vague or implicit agreement where both parties perform in line with a common understanding → Promise made by one party and relied on by the other, but no agreement as such

Figure 4.1 Categories of agreements

The differences between these situations can be seen in the following example:

Jane and Henry are neighbours. They moved in one year ago, and notice a newly constructed fence which is causing some problems. They are not sure where the boundary fence should go between their two houses but are happy to work together amicably to try to sort the situation out. There are (at least) three ways that they might deal with this situation.

1. Jane and Henry decide that the best thing to do is to agree that the fence that already exists is in the wrong place, and that it should be moved. They agree that because the moving of the fence will give Jane more land, it is only right that she should pay for the new fence, since neither of them is really sure how it got to be in the wrong place. This is what happens, and they are both happy with the new fence arrangement.

2. After a few vague discussions about the matter, both seem clear that the fence needs to move in such a way as to give Jane less land. They have not actually agreed that this will happen as such, but they both think that this is the right thing to do. So, Jane arranges for a new fencing contractor to come round and build a fence in the right place, and Henry then demolishes the fence on his side.

3. Henry comes to Jane and says something like, 'I promise that if you build a new fence, I will not object to it', and Jane goes ahead and builds the fence.

In only one of these scenarios is there a contract—scenario number one. It is an oral contract, so whether or not it is legally binding remains to be seen. The other two scenarios do not involve a contract—but that does not mean that they have no legal consequences. It simply means that the consequences which arise are not *contractual*. For how scenarios 2 and 3 might be solved, see chapter 8. The situation may also involve problems of adverse possession, explained in chapter 6, although we would need much more information on the relevant timescales of the fence, and evidence from the previous owners in order to determine this.

It is important to remember, therefore, the key elements of a contract in order to establish when you have an *oral contract* which may or may not give rise to binding proprietary interests and to determine whether the situation before you is one where the parties are attempting to create an enforceable contract. First, contracts require offer and acceptance: this is simply saying that the parties to the transaction must both have agreed on the same terms, at the same time. Second, there must be consideration, ie there must be rights and obligations on both sides. This can be an important stumbling block in property transactions (see later in relation to declarations of trust, for example), and means that whilst (almost) all contracts for the creation or disposition of rights in land require writing, contractual agreements are not the only method by which property rights are created. Sticking with contractual agreements for now, however, let us examine the rules regarding the creation of an enforceable contract relating to rights in land.

If the situation is one where a contract is being formed, the general rule is contained in section 2(1) Law of Property (Miscellaneous Provisions) Act 1989. It states that:

> 'A contract for the sale or other disposition of an interest in land can only be made in writing and only by incorporating all the terms which the parties have expressly agreed in one document or, where contracts are exchanged, in each'.

We can break this provision down into its constituent parts: 'sale or other disposition'; 'interest in land'; 'in writing'; 'all the terms expressly agreed'; and 'one document'. The following section discusses each of these elements of the provision.

Sale or Other Disposition

A disposition of an interest in land is the generic term given to all transfers, creations, disposals, etc. of such rights. It is defined in the Law of Property Act 1925, section 205(1)(ii):

> '"disposition" includes a conveyance and also a devise, bequest, or an appointment of property contained in a will'.

The next step, therefore, is to understand what a conveyance is. It too is defined in section 205(1)(ii):

> '"Conveyance" includes a mortgage, charge, lease, assent, vesting declaration, vesting instrument, disclaimer, release and every other assurance of property or of an interest therein by any instrument, except a will'.

Taken together, these statutory provisions mean that a contract for the disposition of an interest in land is a contract which, amongst other things, creates a mortgage, charge, or lease or relates to the transfer of the freehold interest. Indeed, it covers all 'assurances' of property or of an interest in property. Assurance is not defined in the Act, but it has been interpreted very widely. However, as Megarry and Wade (the leading practitioners' text) highlights, the most important thing is that the rule applies to 'a contract to *make* [emphasis in the original] a disposition, it does not apply to the disposition itself'.[8] This is a critical point. Understanding the distinction between a contract to dispose of an interest, and the actual carrying out of those promises, are two different stages in the conveyancing process. In layman's terms, this is the distinction between the 'exchange' stage and the 'completion' stage in a house sale process. The rule relating to contracts only applies to the *promise* to make the disposition as expressed through the contractual agreement. Different formality rules apply to the actual transferring process as will be seen later in the discussion relating to deeds. This point is emphasised in *Helden v Strathmore Ltd*.[9]

[8] C Harpum et al, *Megarry and Wade: The Law of Real Property* (8th edition) (London, Sweet and Maxwell, 2012).
[9] *Helden v Strathmore Ltd* [2011] EWCA Civ 452, [2011] HLR 41.

> **Key case:** *Helden v Strathmore Ltd* [2011] EWCA Civ 452
>
> This case highlights the important point that section 2 Law of Property (Miscellaneous Provisions) Act 1989 only applies to contracts and not to the actual disposition of interests in land. This case involved a series of mortgage agreements where the actual execution of the charge (ie the deed) did not contain all the relevant terms of the agreement which the parties had earlier reached. Lord Neuberger makes it clear in his judgment that this failure is completely outside the scope of section 2. He reasons that:
>
>> 'Section 2 is concerned with contracts for the creation or sale of legal estates or interests in land, not with documents which actually create or transfer such estates or interests. So a contract to transfer a freehold or a lease in the future, a contract to grant a lease in the future, or a contract for a mortgage in the future, are all within the reach of the section, provided of course the ultimate subject matter is land. However, an actual transfer, conveyance or assignment, an actual lease, or an actual mortgage are not within the scope of section 2 at all'.[10]
>
> In reaching this conclusion, Lord Neuberger relies not only on the wording of section 2, but also on its statutory history and the purpose for which the section was introduced. In short, section 2 is a rule about the creation of contracts, not a rule about the creation of property rights. This should be kept in mind at all times.

Interest in land

Interests in land are defined by the statute in section 205:

> '"interest in land" means any estate, interest or charge in or over land'.

Importantly, this means that contracts for licences, ie non-proprietary interests relating to land, are excluded from the scope of the Act. Such rights are not 'interests... in or over land'. Otherwise, the definition is clearly a broad one. Thanks to the fact that there is no statutory list of interests in land in English land law, there is theoretically an unlimited number and type of transactions which could fall within the statutory provision. However, as discussed in chapter 2 at 2.2.1, the effect of the decision in *National Provincial Bank v Ainsworth*[11] is that there is, in effect, a practical 'closing' of the potential categories of property rights, making it easier to determine in advance whether a transaction which parties intend to undertake is one which is covered by the scope of section 2(1).

There are however some categories of agreements which are difficult to classify in terms of whether they relate to the disposition of an interest in land or not. The most prominent of these historically has been the right of pre-emption. A right of pre-emption arises, essentially, from a promise by the proprietor of an estate in land to offer their right to a particular buyer, if they decide to sell. It is in effect a right of first refusal. The potential buyer is under no obligation to buy the right, and the proprietor under no obligation to sell. These rights are explained in more detail in chapter 14 at 14.4. Prior to the introduction of the Land Registration Act 2002 (LRA 2002), there was an on-going dispute as to whether such rights constituted immediate interests in land. Given the tenuousness of the situation, it was previously considered too 'conditional' to do so.

---

[10] *Helden v Strathmore Ltd* [2011] EWCA Civ 452, [2011] HLR 41.
[11] *National Provincial Bank v Ainsworth* [1965] AC 1175.

However, section 115 Land Registration Act 2002 states that rights of pre-emption as relating to registered land should be treated as giving rise to property rights immediately at the moment of the agreement and not, as some case law had suggested, at the moment at which the proprietor decides to sell their property. The position for unregistered land remains somewhat unclear. In registered land however it is now clear that a contract to create a right of pre-emption is a contract to create an interest in land, and therefore that it must be made in writing. The range of available property rights has already been covered in chapter 2 at 2.2.1. It may be useful here to refresh this information by consulting the table of definitions at the end of the chapter.

In writing

This requirement is straightforward, but it is useful to keep in mind that the rule does not require any special form of writing. The contract does not need to be typed, carried out by a lawyer, or be expressed in any particular way so long as the contract is sufficiently clear. Indeed, rough notes jotted on the back of an envelope will be enough, as long as the other requirements, such as the inclusion of all the terms, are met. This means that although there are some difficult technical issues surrounding section 2(1), compliance with it in most cases is very straightforward and is not costly to the parties. Arguments which suggest that formality requirements 'ask too much' of parties to a transaction are not particularly convincing in respect of section 2, since compliance with it is an easy matter. For example, the reasoning of Arden LJ in *Joyce v Rigolli*[12] (a case considered in more detail later) that because 'the area of land disposed of by both parties was of a very small amount [i]t would be unrealistic to require the parties to execute a transfer of the land',[13] appears to overstate the problems that arise in ensuring compliance with the provisions of section 2 where the parties are deliberately engaged in a transaction with proprietary consequences. The ease of compliance with section 2 is, therefore, something which ought to filter into the policy assessment of the merits or otherwise of requiring such writing.

All the terms

Again, in many cases, this requirement is straightforward. However, there are two difficulties which can arise in practice which require some analysis. First, parties may not expressly agree many of the elements of their transaction, but the law may imply additional terms from those expressly agreed. This happens regularly in relation to landlord and tenant contracts, for example. These terms do not need to be included in the contractual document. They are not expressly agreed. But this can mean that the document on its face can be misleading as to the respective rights and obligations of the parties. If one of the reasons for encouraging compliance with formality rules is that the parties to the transaction thereby achieve a degree of certainty as to what is expected from them as the contractual arrangements progress, it can be argued that not requiring the inclusion of *all* the terms undermines this. However, it is also totally impractical to require that parties include all of the implied terms which the law automatically inserts into their relationship. By definition, the parties may not be aware that these terms are being inserted into their agreement or have not agreed to that effect. A requirement that all the terms be included

---

[12] *Joyce v Rigolli* [2004] EWCA Civ 79, [2004] 1 P & CR DG22.
[13] *Joyce v Rigolli* [2004] EWCA Civ 79, [2004] 1 P & CR DG22, [32].

would be, in effect, a requirement of legal advice since a conveyancing specialist would be aware of the terms implied by law, and be able to insert them. This, naturally, would come at a cost, both in terms of cost to the parties, and in terms of diminishing the ease with which parties can comply with section 2.

Second, the requirement that all the terms be included in a single document raises the question as to what constitutes a 'single' contractual arrangement. What happens when parties to a transaction reach multiple agreements, all perhaps related to the same end goal, but theoretically separable. Which of these agreements must be included within the single document, if any? This issue is discussed in more detail later, when considering the extent to which separating out transactions in this way is possible as a 'workaround' or exception to section 2. One thing at least is clear: the contract *must* contain a statement of the identity of the parties, of the property, the interest or estate in that property to be disposed of, and of the price. These things must be certain and clear, or at least capable of being made certain without further agreement, in the contractual document.

One document

This final requirement, that the terms be contained in a single document (or, that the relevant contractual document refers to, thereby incorporating, another document which does contain all the terms—an approach which would often be used for a standard form contract), is one which has been examined by the case law, and is said to be simply a 'common sense' test. This test was articulated in *Firstpost Homes v Johnson*:[14]

> 'The point is a short one and largely one of first impression, though in considering whether the two sheets of paper are one document or two for the purposes of section 2 it is important to bear in mind that the section expressly contemplates that one document may incorporate the terms of a second document by reference'.[15]

A requirement that a particular transaction be recorded or created in writing is a relatively common one in the English legal system. A requirement that it be contained in a single document which contains all the terms of a particular transaction is, however, unusual. This requirement therefore can be thought of as requiring additional justifications on top of the general need for writing. It can be considered to serve two purposes. First, it reduces the potential complexities caused by a need to consult multiple documents. Secondly, and perhaps more importantly, it ensures that both parties to the transaction either have all the terms before them, or in cases of incorporation, know what document to refer to, when signing the contract (and thereby binding themselves to its terms). This easy accessibility of the terms of the contract should hopefully reduce the circumstances in which an individual signs up to an agreement without fully understanding what it will mean for them and what obligations they may fall under in so-doing. The function of formalities which can be seen as protective and cautionary is thereby well served.

---

[14] *Firstpost Homes v Johnson* [1995] 1 WLR 1567.
[15] *Firstpost Homes v Johnson* [1995] 1 WLR 1567, 1573.

> **Summary: A step-by-step guide to section 2(1):**
> 1. Is the contract for a disposition of an interest in land?
> 2. Is the contract made in writing?
> 3. Does the document contain all the relevant terms in a single document, or in a document which is incorporated into the contract?

Signed by both parties

Once this single document has been created, and the rest of the requirements of section 2(1) are met, section 2(3) then explains that the document must be signed by both parties, or by agents acting on their behalf:

> 'The document incorporating the terms or, where contracts are exchanged, one of the documents incorporating them (but not necessarily the same one) must be signed by or on behalf of each party to the contract'.

Perhaps surprisingly, 'signing' is not something which is defined in the statutory provisions. Rather, case law has developed in order to clarify what constitutes a valid signature. In *Firstpost Homes v Johnson*,[16] the case generally said to represent the leading authority on section 2, the court held that simply typing your name was not enough to be a signature. However, it is suggested that in the digital age, such an act could constitute a signature. If, for example, it was done in a specific box stating that it constituted a signature then it is likely to suffice. The difficulty with digital/typed signatures however is one of identity. It is clearly much more straightforward to forge a typed signature than it is to forge a handwritten one. The issue of e-signatures therefore brings to the forefront one of the purposes of the formality requirements in the first place: proof that the agreement has taken place.

> **Further analysis: E-signatures and typed signatures**
>
> The question as to how parties can sign their contract disposing of an interest in land seems, at first glance, to be one regarding which there could not be much controversy. And yet, the development of news forms of communication means that it is no longer clear whether a 'wet ink' signature, made by hand, onto paper, is required. *Firstpost Homes v Johnson* suggests that such is necessary in a transaction involving land. According to, Peter Gibson LJ: 'it is an artificial use of language to describe the printing or the typing of the name of an addressee in the letter as the signature by the addressee... Ordinary language does not, it seems to me, extend so far'.[17]
>
> However, case law is not all one way on this question, and there are strong policy reasons why we might want to regard typed signatures as sufficient. Although not a decision relating to land, there is some case law concerning charter party negotiations (a type of shipping contract) which holds that in certain cases a typed name can indeed suffice. In *Golden Ocean Group Ltd v Salgaocar Mining Industries*

---

[16] *Firstpost Homes v Johnson* [1995] 1 WLR 1567.
[17] *Firstpost Homes v Johnson* [1995] 1 WLR 1567.

Pvt Ltd,[18] the Court of Appeal considered whether the on-going exchange of email documents could constitute the formation of a contract in writing The court reasoned as follows:

> 'It was common ground both before the judge and before us that an electronic signature is sufficient and that a first name, initials, or perhaps a nickname will suffice. Mr Kendrick's point was that the affixing of Mr Hindley's name was not done in a manner which indicated that it was intended [emphasis added] to authenticate the document, that being the touchstone... In my judgment Mr Hindley put his name, Guy, on the e-mail so as to indicate that it came with his authority and that he took responsibility for the contents. It is an assent to its terms. I have no doubt that that is a sufficient authentication'.[19]

In other words, the court is highlighting that what matters is the *intention* of the party when she types her name. This provides a means by which the reasoning in *Firstpost Homes v Johnson*[20] can be distinguished. In that case it was fairly clear that the typed name was not intended to be a signature. As long as it is clear that a party *intended* to bind themselves to the relevant terms when typing her name, it seems such a typed name can be enough to constitute a section 2(3) compliant signature.

There is further authority which supports the approach in *Golden Ocean Group*.[21] For example in *Ramsey v Love*[22] the court considered whether an automatic signing machine would constitute a valid signature. Per Morgan J, '[i]t was accepted that for the purpose of signing a document... it was not necessary that the guarantor should sign the document with a pen held in his own hand'.[23] This, taken together with other recent cases such as *Mehta*[24] suggests that the quotation from *Firstpost Homes*[25] is wrong. However, the land registry requires a wet ink signature unless its official e-document procedure is followed. The prudent individual would use a wet ink signature for land transactions, just to be doubly sure.

> **Summary: A step-by-step guide to section 2(1) and section 2(3)**
>
> 1. Is there a contract—ie is there an offer and acceptance on the same terms, and consideration for the contract (promises on both sides)? Is that contract for the disposition of an interest in land? If yes, then the contract must be made in writing (subject to the exceptions later).
> 2. Does the written document contain all the terms of the agreement? As a minimum it must contain the parties, the property, and the price.
> 3. Has the written document been signed? This depends upon the intention of the party when putting their name to paper.

4.3.1.2 Exceptions

As mentioned earlier, there are, unsurprisingly, exceptions to the general rule expressed in section 2(1). Some of these are statutory exceptions. Others have arisen through case law. Before considering these 'exceptions' is it important to note that some of them, strictly speaking, are not *exceptions* to the general principle, but perhaps surprising applications of it or surprising interpretations of its key provisions. For example, one of the categories discussed later is 'disposing boundary

---

[18] *Golden Ocean Group Ltd v Salgaocar Mining Industries Pvt Ltd* [2012] EWCA Civ 265; [2012] 1 WLR 3674.
[19] *Golden Ocean Group Ltd v Salgaocar Mining Industries Pvt Ltd* [2012] EWCA Civ 265; [2012] 1 WLR 3674, [32].
[20] *Firstpost Homes v Johnson* [1995] 1 WLR 1567.
[21] *Golden Ocean Group Ltd v Salgaocar Mining Industries Pvt Ltd* [2012] EWCA Civ 265; [2012] 1 WLR 3674.
[22] *Ramsey v Love* [2015] EWHC 65 (Ch).
[23] *Ramsey v Love* [2015] EWHC 65 (Ch), [7].
[24] *J Pereira Fernandes SA v Mehta* [2006] EWHC 813 (Ch); [2006] 1 WLR 1543, [27].
[25] *Firstpost Homes v Johnson* [1995] 1 WLR 1567.

agreements'. These are agreements where the parties are trying to resolve some uncertainty as to the location of the boundary between their properties. In doing so, they may consciously transfer land, but they do not intend so to do. The courts have held that this is not a contract 'for' the disposition of an interest in land, and therefore, they reason, that on a strict reading of section 2(1) the requirement of writing does not apply. This reasoning is controversial, as will be discussed later, but it means that strictly the ability to create an enforceable contract to dispose of an interest in land orally in the context of boundary negotiations is not, according to the courts, an exception to section 2(1). In practice, however, it is. It is for that reason that it is included in this list. Similar comments can be made about the mixed contracts doctrine, if it still represents good law in domestic cases, and the question of collateral contracts and modifications to contracts. In strict terms these too do not represent exceptions to section 2(1). Rather, they fall outside that provision given its judicial interpretation. The practical effect however is the creation of enforceable contracts which, at least broadly, relate to interests in land and which do not need to be made in writing.

Some of the exceptions are genuine exceptions however, and it is with these that the analysis below starts. These are: short leases; contracts made in the course of a public auction; and certain contracts regulated by the Financial Services Act.

Short leases

First, we have the short lease. Under section 2(5) Law of Property (Miscellaneous Provisions) Act 1989, leases for a duration of three years or less (and meeting other additional requirements discussed immediately below), can be created or disposed of by contract without the need for a signed, written document which complies with the terms of section 2(1). The reason why no writing is required for transactions of this sort is that their short-term (and therefore relatively-speaking, trivial) nature means that both lessor and lessee will suffer little if there later emerges some doubt about the precise terms, at least in theory. Furthermore, the regularity with which such leases come into and out of existence means that a strict requirement that these contracts be written down in such a way as to comply with section 2(1) is thought to be an example of regulatory overkill. It is important to note, before examining this exception further, however, that section 2(5) does not mean that either such leases are not often written down. Usually, in fact, they are, if not in the precise way required by section 2(1). Nor does it dispense with the need for the other elements of a contractual agreement to be present. Thus, to create a lease by parol (ie orally) a contract is required. However, that contract does not need to take the form of a single document containing all the relevant terms, signed by both parties.

Furthermore, the exception in section 2(5) does not apply to all leases of a duration of three years or less. Section 2(5) holds that:

'This section does not apply in relation to—(a) a contract to grant such a lease as is mentioned in section 54(2) of the Law of Property Act 1925 (short leases)'.

It is essential therefore to consult section 54(2), which states that:

'Nothing in the foregoing provisions of this Part of this Act shall affect the creation by parol of leases taking effect in possession for a term not exceeding three years (whether or not the lessee is given power to extend the term) at the best rent which can be reasonably obtained without taking a fine'.

In addition to the length of term—three years or less—the lease must therefore also take effect immediately in possession, and be for the best rent reasonably obtainable. We can examine these rules in more detail.

The rule relating to the need for the lease to take effect immediately in possession, although expressed in a potentially obscure way, essentially rules out two situations. First, it rules out the situation whereby the lessor and lessee agree that the lessee will take a 2-year lease, for example, in ten years time. Second, it rules out situations involving concurrent leases. Concurrent leases are leases which co-exist, thanks to their different terms/different start and end dates. Instead of having a simple landlord and tenant relationship between a single freeholder and a leaseholder, there is a freehold landlord, an intermediary tenant, and the tenant in possession.

Let us consider an example. Evie, the freeholder, grants Luke a 2-year lease, to start immediately. However, as part of the transaction, he also grants Dylan, a 1-year lease, to start, equally, immediately. In such a situation, Evie, the freeholder, becomes landlord to Luke; Luke becomes landlord to Dylan. In this case, even though Luke's lease is only of a two-year duration, because it does not give him a right to possession of the land, thanks to Dylan's lease, it would need to be in writing. Given the relative complexity of such an arrangement, it is likely that the parties to such a transaction would be keen to reduce it to writing in any case, and will receive legal advice in so-doing. This 'exception to the exception' in section 2(5) is not, therefore, one which causes much difficulty in practice in relation to concurrent leases. As will be seen, however, it can cause quite some problems when parties attempt to create a short lease to start in the (very near) future.

The second requirement, that the lease be at the best rent reasonably obtainable without the taking of a fine, is somewhat difficult to apply in practice given the potentially vague nature of this requirement, as discussed later. However, case law has done much to clarify exactly what is required here. Before considering this, the term 'fine' requires some explanation. This is a lump sum, usually taken at the beginning of a lease, in return for a lower rent and is often called a premium.

> **Further analysis: Immediate possession and best rent—some practical problems**
>
> These two requirements, ie the need for the lease to go into possession immediately, and to be for a best rent without a premium, may seem 'technical' and somewhat peripheral to the operation of this exception to the need for a written contract (and, as will be seen, to the requirement for a deed). But thinking about these exceptions gives some insight into the operation and development of the formality rules in general. It can, therefore, be considered a useful 'window' through which these rules can be viewed.
>
> Brown and Pawlowski have examined the origin and practice of these requirements. They conclude that the provisions ought to be re-thought, such that there is a 'grace period' of three months in relation to the 'immediate possession' requirement and a complete abolition of the rent rule.[26] They argue,

---

[26] J Brown and M Pawlowski, 'Re-thinking s.54(2) of the Law of Property Act 1925' [2010] Conveyancer and Property Lawyer 146, 146.

beginning with the possession rule, that this rule only emerged as a historical accident, responding to an old common law rule with no on-going practical relevance. They also argue that it creates unnecessary complexity in the law, and has the potential, through rigid interpretation, to be an unwelcome complication.

> 'What is apparent is that the current requirement in s.54(2) that the lease "take effect in possession" does not reflect the realities of the short-term residential letting market and is at odds with the underlying rationale behind the short lease exception which is to allow the parties to short-term letting agreements to create indefeasible legal leases informally'.[27]

In part, they suggest, this is because the rule, when interpreted literally, prevents oral leases in cases where the lease is agreed perhaps a few days or weeks before the tenant is due to move in, from taking effect. In practice, this sort of very short delay is common simply due to practicalities such as the need for a clean of a rental property before the tenant moves in, or, even more prosaically, due to the availability of the parties. Brown and Pawlowski's analysis is more appropriately directed at the requirement for a deed for such leases perhaps, but it applies to a certain extent to the written contract requirement as well. Bright agrees with their approach. At the very least, the criticisms of the rule prompt some consideration as to why the rule exists in the first place, and what circumstances may fall foul of its operation.

The best rent requirement too comes under heavy criticism. Again, this rule appears, according to Brown and Pawlowski, to be a matter of historical accident. Its modern incarnation is however subject to potentially divergent case law interpretations. In *Fitzkriston v Panayi* the court treated best rest as being equivalent to market rent.[28] In *Looe Fuels Ltd v Looe Harbour Commissioners* however the court was happy to consider the subjective, agreed rent as being equivalent to the best rent available in the circumstances.[29] Brown argues that in these circumstances 'best rent' should indeed be a reference to the rent that the parties have in fact agreed. First, he argues, to respect the 'reasonably available' element of the test, one has to acknowledge the rent which is in fact agreed, as this was the rent which was available. Second, there is no clear indication from the statutory history nor policy as to what best rent is supposed to refer here. Third, too restrictive an approach has the potential to exclude many 'deserving' tenants from certain protections which arise once they have a lease (see chapter 10). In Brown's view, therefore, the attitude of the courts to the meaning of best rent in *Fitzkriston*, commonly considered to be the leading authority on the question, is wrong.

Summary: The short leases requirement

In order to create a valid contract of a lease of three years or less, there is no need to write that contract down in such a way as to comply with section 2(1). This applies as long as, first, the lease goes into possession immediately (ie on the day that the agreement is reached) and second, the lease is at the best rent, which probably means market rent. The reason for this exception to the need for a section 2-compliant contract is that such leases are of sufficiently short duration that prejudice is not often suffered as a

---

[27] J Brown and M Pawlowski, 'Re-thinking s.54(2) of the Law of Property Act 1925' [2010] Conveyancer and Property Lawyer 146, 153.
[28] *Fitzkriston LLP v Panayi* [2008] EWCA Civ 283, [2008] L & TR 26 (CA (Civ Div)).
[29] *Looe Fuels Ltd v Looe Harbour Commissioners* [2008] EWCA Civ 414, [2007] All ER (D) 263.

> result of informal creation. The hassle and cost of using formalities in such a situation may outweigh the certainty benefits thus achieved. However, the limitations on the section, and the 'immediate possession' rule in particular, have been the subject of sustained criticism for failing to reflect the reality of the residential letting market, where parties often reach agreement prior to the move-in date. A rigid interpretation of this rule is both potentially impractical, and can have serious consequences for tenants.

Before we move away from this requirement, however, two final issues require to be addressed. What happens if there is no valid written agreement in these cases? Very often, the tenant will nevertheless go into possession of the land, and will pay rent. This produces a tenancy of sort. In some cases, it will give rise to a tenancy at will; in others, a periodic tenancy with the period calculated on the basis of rent. This periodic tenancy may match the parties' expectations in terms of their oral agreement, or it may not, but it does not need to be made in writing as long as the period is itself three years or shorter. These two types of tenancy are considered in more detail in chapter 10 at 10.4. However, it is worth noting here when a tenant is a tenant at will, and when a periodic tenant, depends usually on the circumstances in which they go into possession. If, for example, the tenancy falls foul of section 2(5) because it does not involve best rent, but instead there is a single premium paid, it is highly unlikely that this would give rise to a periodic tenancy. There would be no 'period' on which to base such a tenancy. The tenant at will is in a much more vulnerable position that the periodic tenant, not least because they have no tenure so that at any point they can be evicted by the landlord. Second, it is important to note that these rules only apply to the *creation* of short leases, and not to their *transfer*. All attempted transfer contracts must be made in writing whatever the duration of the lease.[30]

> **Summary: A step-by-step guide to section 2(1) and section 2(5)—short leases**
>
> 1. Is there an agreement between the parties whereby there is an offer and acceptance on the same terms, with consideration provided on both sides? If so, there is an oral contract for the creation of the lease.
> 2. Is this lease for a duration of three years or less? If so, there is no need to write this contract down in order to render the contractual agreement enforceable unless either:
>   (a) The lease does not go into possession immediately (even by a few days); or
>   (b) The lease is not at the best rent available (market rent) without a fine (premium).
> 3. If the lease contract ought to have been put into writing but was not either (a) a tenancy at will or (b) a periodic tenancy calculated on the basis of the rental period, will come into existence.

Contracts regulated by the Financial Services and Markets Act 2000

Originally, this exception refered to the Financial Services Act 1986. However, this piece of legislation was superseded by the Financial Services and Markets Act 2000. Contracts regulated by the FMSA are essentially contracts relating to investment. As part of an investment process, it is

---

[30] *Crago v Julian* [1992] 1 WLR 372.

possible that interests pertaining to land or otherwise will be 'traded' without that being the deliberate or conscious intention of the parties to the transaction. It is for this reason that the bulk of the contracts made by a person carrying out a regulated activity under the Act are excluded from the scope of section 2(1). It is worth noting, however, that mortgage contracts are excluded from the exclusion, and continue to require a written contract whether or not the lender is regulated under the FSMA.

Sales a public auction

Sales at public auction do not need to be followed up with a written contract in order for the contract of sale to be binding. This is simply to reflect the fact that in the auction process the sale becomes binding on the fall of the hammer.

Boundary agreements

The short leases exception is, as a matter of practice, the most important exception to the requirement that a contract be made in writing if it is to be enforceable. However, there are a number of other, less common, situations, where the formality requirements can be avoided. One of the most controversial of these involves the situation where neighbours agree as to the whereabouts of the boundary between their two properties. In many cases, such an agreement can be said to be a 'demarcating' agreement. The parties simply do not know (within a 'zone of uncertainty') where the boundary line between their properties lies. In which case, they may, for some practical reason, simply agree that the boundary line is fixed along some physical feature, be that a fence or similar. This can be expressed visually in Figure 4.2. Here, the original boundary (unbroken) line between the spotty land and the checked land is entirely within the 'zone of uncertainty' (the 'bricked' area) but to the left of the tree. The parties might agree that it makes more sense for the tree to be within 'Party A's' land, but since the entire boundary remains within the 'zone of uncertainty' no one is sure whether any land has changed hand, and as such this is a demarcating agreement and does not require to be made in writing. This is relatively uncontroversial.

Alternatively, the parties could agree some placement for the boundary in such a way as the knew that the boundary between their properties was changing, but which, for some practical reason, makes more sense, or where the parties are simply happy to alter their respective entitlements. They might thereby agree, explicitly, to transfer some land for Party A to Party B in order that, for example, a fence can be built in such a way as to respect existing trees. Such an agreement

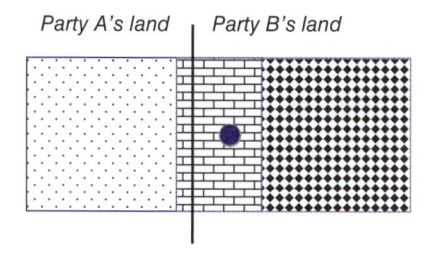

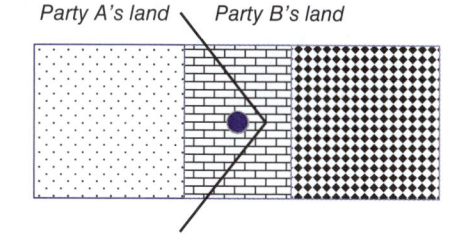

Figure 4.2 Example of a demarcating agreement

has of course to be written down and comply with section 2(1). This is referred to as a disposing agreement (shown in Figure 4.3), because of the explicit and deliberate transfer of land.

However, there is a third potential type of agreement. Here, the parties want, as in the first type of agreement, to settle the uncertainty as to the whereabouts of the boundary. However, in so-doing, they may both be aware that there is change in the entitlements to a certain extent to ensure that the new boundary line, in solving the uncertainty, makes sense in the context of the physical features present on the land (as shown in Figure 4.4). In these cases, existing case law tells us that the parties are not required to write this type of agreement down.

The division between the true demarcating and the hybrid demarcating/disposing case is a fine one. However, the issue was explored in *Joyce v Rigolli*[31] in the Court of Appeal and this, and the follow up case in *Yeates v Line*[32] now represent the leading authorities on the issue.

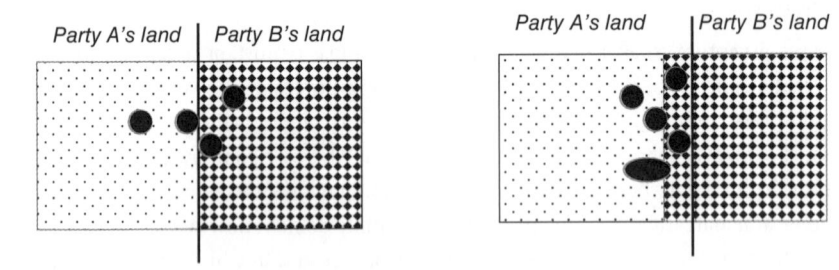

Figure 4.3 Example of a disposing agreement

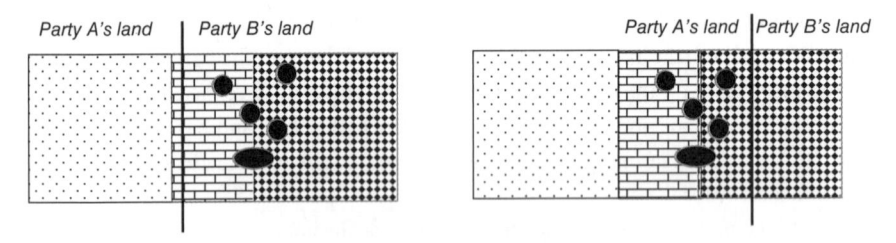

Figure 4.4 Example a hybrid demarcating/disposing agreement

Key cases: *Joyce v Rigolli* [2004] EWCA Civ 79 and *Yeates v Line* [2012] EWHC 3085

Joyce v Rigolli involved an oral boundary agreement between neighbours. In fixing the boundary between their properties it was likely that land was being transferred to one plot or the other, although since they did not know where the old boundary was, it was not possible to say how much land was being transferred. The parties' purpose was simply to fix the line of boundary. It is therefore a clear example of

---

[31] *Joyce v Rigolli* [2004] EWCA Civ 79; [2004] 1 P & CR DG22.
[32] *Yeates v Line* [2012] EWHC 3085 (Ch), [2013] Ch 363.

the 'hybrid' agreement referred to here. The parties were solving an issue of uncertainty. In this sense, the purpose of their agreement (at least, explicitly) was not to transfer land from one to another. However, in order to make sense of the physical features on the land, it was necessary for the parties to transfer land.

As the agreement was not made in writing, it did not comply with section 2 LP(MP)A 1989. Arguably, it was void. The Court of Appeal had to assess whether the boundary agreement could be enforced despite the lack of writing, and therefore, whether there were any exceptions to section 2(1) not expressed in the statute itself. The court reasoned as follows:

> 'As a matter of ordinary English usage, for a contract to be one "for" selling or disposing of land, it must have been part of the parties' purposes, or the purposes to be attributed to them, in entering into such a contract that the contract should achieve a sale or other disposition of land. The fact that the effect of their contract is that land or an interest in land is actually conveyed, when that effect was neither foreseen nor intended nor was it something which ought to have been foreseen or intended, is not the acid test....
>
> In this case, however, Mr Rigolli consciously thought that he was giving up a small triangle of land round the cherry tree... Even so, the area of land disposed of by both parties was of a very small amount. It would be unrealistic to require the parties to execute a transfer of the land... Further, to make the validity of a boundary agreement dependent on the preparation and execution of a written contract would be contrary to the important public policy in upholding boundary agreements... I do not consider that Parliament... could have intended section 2 to apply to transfers of land pursuant to boundary agreements... simply because a trivial transfer or transfers of land were consciously involved'.[33]

These comments highlight a number of key features about the formality rules, their purpose, and statutory interpretation. First, Arden LJ draws a link between the purpose of a transaction, and the need for it to comply with the formality rules. She does so on the basis that section 2(1) refers to a contract 'for' the creation or disposition of rights in land. The 'for' she reasons refers to purpose, not effect. This is far from certain as a matter of statutory history and interpretation! Second, she relies on the fact that the amount of land transferred was 'trivial'. She reasons that the public policy considerations which weigh in favour of formality requirements, in the instant case, were outweighed by the public policy requirements of upholding freely negotiated boundary agreements. What trivial means, and why this situation involved only a trivial transfer were not explained. Both the purpose element and the trivial element appear to be essential to her reasoning, as the final paragraph highlights.

Whatever the merits of the decision in *Joyce*, however, there is little doubt that some uncertainty remained in the aftermath of the decision as to the precise relationship between the two requirements referred to by Arden LJ. It was clear that for true demarcating agreements, a written agreement is not required. However, what was less clear was whether the Court of Appeal would suggest that all agreements whose purpose was simply to resolve uncertainty would escape the requirements of section 2(1).

This issue came before a subsequent court in *Yeates v Line*.[34] The neighbours here were disputing whether one of them had acquired land through adverse possession, but had come to an oral agreement to end this dispute. This agreement had the effect of transferring title of part of the land. The intention of

---

[33] *Joyce v Rigolli* [2004] EWCA Civ 79, [2004] 1 P & CR DG22, [31]-[32].
[34] *Yeates v Line* [2012] EWHC 3085 (Ch), [2013] Ch 363.

the parties had simply been to end their disagreement. The agreement had a 'disposing effect' and Kevin Prosser QC sitting as a Deputy Judge of the High Court had to decide whether this meant that the contract was void for not being made in writing and therefore not complying with s2. This is what he said:

> '*Joyce v Rigolli* is binding authority for the proposition that an oral demarcation agreement... is not void by virtue of section 2(1) of the 1989 Act even though the agreement has a disposing effect, because the words "a contract for..." in section 2(1) refer to an agreement which has a disposing purpose...
>
> ...my task is to interpret section 2(1), and to do so in the light of the reasoning of the Court of Appeal in *Joyce v Rigolli*, and I consider that I am therefore required to decide that a demarcation agreement is no more than an example of an agreement which does not fall foul of section 2(1), because it does not have a disposing purpose even if it has a disposing effect. The compromise agreement in the present case is another example'.[35]

Again, the judge here states that the agreement does not need to be in writing because of its purpose. He does not rely on the 'trivial' part of Arden LJ's judgment. He makes clear that the rule he articulates is not restricted to boundary agreements. This is highly controversial, and very difficult to apply. It relies on a subjective assessment of the purpose of a contract rather than an objective test as to the effect of that contract. The removal of the 'trivial' and boundary restrictions on the scope of this rule mean it has enormous potential to disrupt the system as it was previously understood. In particular, three issues emerge. First, what happens when the parties to the agreement have divergent purposes? Does this mean that section 2(1) does apply? Second, would this rule apply whatever the nature of the dispute in question? For example, would it apply if land was transferred as part of a settlement of an on-going dispute surrounding a bankruptcy? Third, and more positively, the removal of the 'trivial' limitation is welcome. As Dixon argues, '[i]f one is to ignore the words of s.2, better to do it on the basis of an all-encompassing subterfuge than a distinction based on the accident of the amount of land in dispute'.[36]

These two cases therefore, in relation to one small issue, show the trouble which can arise in relation to the formality rules in English land law. They raise the policy point highlighted at the end of the first section—if the operation of the rules is so complex as to be unpredictable, can the formality rules achieve their main functions even where the rule itself (ie write contracts down) is very clearly beneficial?

Summary: Section 2(1) and 'boundary agreements'

1. Is the agreement a demarcating agreement such that no land is consciously transferred? If yes, there is no need to put the agreement in writing.
2. Is the agreement a disposing agreement whereby land is deliberately transferred, and for the purpose simply of transferring it? If yes, then writing which complies with section 2(1) is required.
3. Is the agreement a hybrid agreement whereby land is consciously transferred but the *purpose* of that agreement is not to make such a transfer but, for example, to bring a dispute to an end? If so, then no writing is required.

---

[35] *Yeates v Line* [2012] EWHC 3085 (Ch), [2013] Ch 363, [29]-[35].
[36] M Dixon, 'To write or not to write?' [2013] Conv 1, 4.

Mixed contracts/performance

Another potential exception to the requirement of writing is the potential for contracts which are 'part performed' to be, in a certain way, excluded from the operation of section 2(1). Under the old statute, it was possible to, for example, create a mortgage without any writing through the action of depositing title deeds with the lender in return for the transfer of the relevant funds. This is no longer possible, as *United Bank of Kuwait v Sahib* confirms.[37] However, it has been argued that in cases where although there was no written contract at the outset, once all the 'land elements' of that contract have been performed, there is no need for a written document in order for the remaining elements of a contract to be enforceable. This is best explained with an example.

Lily, a freeholder, agreed with Felicity, that Felicity would purchase Lily's freehold title, but that in order to facilitate this, Lily would lend Felicity the purchase money. Felicity would then pay back the purchase money, with a very high rate of interest. No agreement was ever written down regarding the terms of the repayment of the loan. Lily then transferred her freehold interest to Felicity by means of a valid deed. Felicity became registered proprietor. Lily then accepted that she needed to pay the purchase money, but refused to pay the interest as had been agreed.

In such a case, Lily would argue that since there was no disposition of an interest in land left for the formality requirements to 'bite' on, there would be no reason to use the formality rules to stop the enforcement of the terms of the loan. On the other hand, Felicity would argue that the contractual agreement for the transfer of the property, along with the loan terms, was void for want of formality. Simply performing some elements of the contract could not 'bring it to life' such that although she would be bound to pay the purchase price (or return title), she would not be bound to pay the agreed interest.

This issue has appeared in a number of cases. It raises the question as to when different contractual terms can be separated out into 'collateral' and other contracts. The line of case law surrounding these rules is quite difficult. There appears to be a potential division emerging between the way in which the judiciary deal with this situation in a residential context, and its treatment in commercial cases. This can be seen if, for example, we consider the distinction between the reasoning in *Keay v Morris Homes*,[38] and *Mirza v Mirza*.[39]

The first thing to note, however, is that there is no doubt that if the two agreements are genuinely separate, and not part of the same transaction, then only the agreement containing terms relating to rights in land need to be made in writing. In other words, there is no *ex post facto* linking of two apparently unlinked agreements simply because they both, in practical terms, contribute to the overall transfer of the rights in land. Thus, if the agreement between Lily and Felicity in relation to the interest payments had been made some time after the deed of transfer of the title, for example, as a response to Felicity's inability to raise funds elsewhere, then of course that agreement would be enforceable.

The decision in *Tootal Clothing*[40] however had been interpreted to mean that wherever you have an agreement, if the 'land elements' of that agreement have already been performed, then

---

[37] *United Bank of Kuwait v Sahib* [1997] Ch. 107.
[38] *Keay v Morris Homes Ltd* [2012] EWCA Civ 900, [2012] 1 WLR 2855.
[39] *Mirza v Mirza* [2009] EWHC 3 (Ch), [2009] 2 FLR 115.
[40] *Tootal Clothing Ltd v Guinea Properties Management Ltd* (1992) 64 P & CR 452.

there is no justification for not allowing the parties to rely on the 'contract' to enforce any remaining obligations if they themselves do not relate to the disposition of an interest in land, whether or not the terms could be genuinely separated out. The decision in *Tootal*[41] had been subject to heavy criticism. For that reason perhaps, it was departed from in *Keay v Morris Homes*.[42] In between these two cases, however, the court in *Mirza v Mirza*[43] had held that it was possible to use performance as a work-around for the formality rules, at least in this sort of domestic situation. That decision was not itself considered in *Keay v Morris Homes*.[44] Since *Keay*[45] did not overrule *Tootal*,[46] on which *Mirza*[47] was based, it is possible that this decision survived and still represents good law.

Whatever the position in terms of authority, however, there is little doubt that logic demands that the approach in *Keay* be followed. The whole idea of the possibility of using performance as a way to solve a lack of formalities is illogical and wrong. How can performance 'unvoid' a contract that never existed? The agreement never gave rise to any obligations, so how can these later be 'enforced'? As I have argued elsewhere:

> 'In terms of the overall structure of how we deal with land "promises" where there is a lack of formalities such that any promise is not valid contractually, we can see that, as a result of the decision in *Keay*,[48] the division between "domestic" and "commercial" contexts may be widening'.[49]

However, it is suggested, that this does not make logical sense. Furthermore, the commercial/domestic distinction is not one which should be said to form a firm foundation upon which diverging rules are built. There is judicial appeal to this division, but on more than the most superficial examination it can be seen that there is indeed no such division. Rather, there is merely a spectrum which ranges from the intensely 'domestic' in cases of a romantically involved couple purchasing a family home, through situations where familial relations invest in property, to the wholly commercial involving the leasing of a large scale office building by a listed company. The logic of the formality rules, the reason for their existence, and thus their applicability, should not depend upon this distinction.

Modifications to contracts and collateral contracts

In addition to considering the position of mixed contracts, the decision in *Keay v Morris Homes*[50] is telling also for the question of modifications to or supplemental agreements relating to contracts involving the disposition or creation of an interest in land. In particular, they raise the question as to when parties can agree additional terms to their land contract given that section 2(1)

---

[41] *Tootal Clothing Ltd v Guinea Properties Management Ltd* (1992) 64 P & CR 452.
[42] *Keay v Morris Homes Ltd* [2012] EWCA Civ 900, [2012] 1 WLR 2855.
[43] *Mirza v Mirza* [2009] EWHC 3 (Ch), [2009] 2 FLR 115.
[44] *Keay v Morris Homes Ltd* [2012] EWCA Civ 900, [2012] 1 WLR 2855.
[45] *Keay v Morris Homes Ltd* [2012] EWCA Civ 900, [2012] 1 WLR 2855.
[46] *Tootal Clothing Ltd v Guinea Properties Management Ltd* (1992) 64 P & CR 452.
[47] *Mirza v Mirza* [2009] EWHC 3 (Ch), [2009] 2 FLR 115.
[48] *Keay v Morris Homes Ltd* [2012] EWCA Civ 900, [2012] 1 WLR 2855.
[49] E Lees, '*Keay v Morris Homes* and section 2 Law of Property (Miscellaneous Provisions) Act 1989' [2013] Conv 68, 73.
[50] *Keay v Morris Homes Ltd* [2012] EWCA Civ 900, [2012] 1 WLR 2855.

requires that the written, signed, contact contain all the terms of the agreement. Of course, if the parties agree to modify their contract and write that contract down containing all the terms, that new contract will, naturally, be binding. Otherwise, the new terms will not be valid in so far as they relate to land.

4.3.1.3 Consequences of a failure to comply

If the parties fail to create a written contract where it is required, then their contract per se will not be enforceable. That is not to say, however, that the *bargain*, cannot be enforced, at least to a certain extent (see earlier also in relation to the imposition of a periodic tenancy or tenancy at will, and chapter 10 at 10.4). The methods by which this enforcement may take place are either proprietary estoppel or, following recent case law, constructive trust. The specific rules relating to these are to be found in chapters 7 and 8. However, a basic outline will be given here so that it is possible to see how they relate specifically to 'failed' contracts.

Proprietary estoppel depends upon a promise, detrimentally relied on. Strictly speaking it is not a breach of the general principle in section 2. The enforcement of the equity which arises on the creation of an estoppel is not the enforcement of a contract as such. The result of this is that the remedy which is granted to the promisee may not map onto his expectation interest. In other words, the promisor may not have to do all that he promised. In some cases, he will simply have to ensure that the promisee is not left in a worse position than if the promise had never been made. In others, there may be no remedy at all. In this sense, proprietary estoppel is not a means by which failed contracts can be enforced through the back door. However, in practice, the result may look very close to such enforcement. There has been considerable case law and academic discussion of the relationship between proprietary estoppel and the legislative provisions. Again, for more on this, see chapter 8.

Before moving on from proprietary estoppel, however, it is important to note that the success of a claim in estoppel depends upon the presence of unconscionability such that it is unfair, broadly speaking, for the promisor to go back on his promise. The courts have been relatively clear that they are significantly less likely to find such unconscionability in cases either where the parties have deliberately chosen not to cement their relationship in a binding contract, as in *Cobbe v Yeoman's Row*,[51] or where the parties are experienced commercial parties who ought, all else being equal, to have known that unless or until they reduced their agreement to writing, it could not be enforced. The consequence of this is that successful estoppel cases are more common in the domestic/familial situation. The parties could not necessarily have been expected to be aware of the requirements of writing, and so the unconscionability 'factors' play out very differently from how they can be perceived in the commercial context.

The constructive trust 'route' for enforcement of the unwritten contract, is both rare, and controversial. It is a technique which has been employed in relation to informal agreements to create a trust, both express and implied, in relation, in particular, to rights in the family home. It is not however often used simply as a mechanism to solve the parties' failure to comply with section 2. This is true even though section 2 itself makes clear that nothing in it affects the operation of

---

[51] *Cobbe v Yeoman's Row* [2008] UKHL 55, [2008] 1 WLR 1752.

implied, resulting or constructive trusts. However, in recent case law—particularly *Matchmove v Dowding*[52]—the courts have held that constructive trusts can be used in this way. For detailed discussion of this, see chapter 8 at 8.6.

4.3.1.4 Consequences of compliance

We have considered therefore what occurs if the parties do *not* comply with the provisions in section 2. For the most part it will mean that their contract is unenforceable, unless they can bring their case within one of the exceptions earlier. If they cannot so do, then they may be able to rely on either proprietary estoppel or constructive trusts to give effect, to some extent, to their bargain. The outcome will not necessarily be the same as if they have used the proper formalities to give rise to the contract, however. Partly this is a result of the fact that there is discretion for the courts in remedying a proprietary estoppel, but mainly it is because the fact of having concluded a written contract in relation to an interest in land *itself* gives rise to property rights in the land. The position is relatively simple. Where there is a contract for a lease, an equitable lease will arise. Where there is a contract for a mortgage, an equitable mortgage will come into being; an easement, and equitable easement, etc. The contract 'stage' in the rights creation process is, in this sense, sufficient for the creation of an equitable right in land. For some types of rights, ie those which are only capable of existing in equity, there is no need to take any further steps in terms of creation. For example, options to purchase, not appearing in section 1(2) of the Law of Property Act 1925, cannot exist at law. It is therefore enough to use a written contract to create them. No further steps are required. It is possible to create them in other ways—including the use of a deed—but a written contract will suffice.

Where the goal of the parties is to create a legal interest, such as the creation of a legal lease, it may seem odd that the contract gives rise to a property right, but one which neither of the parties has in fact bargained for, ie an equitable version of that right. The reason why the contract is said to give rise to such an equitable right is the maxim, 'equity sees that which ought to be done as having been done' as explained in the case of *Walsh v Lonsdale*.[53] As between the parties, the distinction between the legal right and the equitable right arising by contract, is unimportant. Both give the parties remedies in case of failure to comply with the terms of the agreement. However, the distinction is potentially very significant when third parties become involved, as will be seen in chapter 15. To put it very crudely here and as we explained in chapter 1—an equitable right is more vulnerable in relation to third parties than is a legal right. For this reason, where a legal interest is sought, parties will generally proceed to the next 'stage' in the formalities process—the creation of a deed.

4.3.2 DEEDS

A written contract is one method by which rights in land are created. In cases where the parties are trying to create an equitable interest, the written contract will suffice to do so. However, when parties are trying to create a legal interest in land, then it may be necessary for the parties to use a deed. Before discussing the requirements for a valid deed, and the effect of a deed once created, it is useful

---

[52] *Matchmove v Dowding* [2016] EWCA Civ 1233.
[53] *Walsh v Lonsdale* (1882) 21 Ch D 9.

to think first about what a deed actually is. It is a written document. But unlike a written contract, it is not a *promise* to do something: it is actually *doing* it. The etymology of the word deed gives a clue here. A 'deed' is something which has been done. It is important to realise therefore that a deed is more than an 'extra formal' contract. In unregistered conveyancing, the creation and 'delivery' (see later) of a valid deed is enough to, for example, transfer freehold title to the house. In this sense, a deed should be thought of in active terms. It is the passing over of the property.

As highlighted, however, a deed is not always required. The consequences of having entered into a valid deed are hugely different depending upon whether the land is registered or not. These issues, and the requirements which must be met in order for a valid deed to be created, are discussed later.

4.3.2.1 The requirements of a valid deed

In order to be a valid deed, the document must meet the requirements in section 1(2) Law of Property (Miscellaneous Provisions) Act 1989. This section states:

'An instrument shall not be a deed unless—

(a) it makes it clear on its face that it is intended to be a deed by the person making it or, as the case may be, by the parties to it (whether by describing itself as a deed or expressing itself to be executed or signed as a deed or otherwise); and

(b) it is validly executed as a deed by that person or, as the case may be, one or more of those parties.'

Section 1(3) then explains what 'validly executed as a deed' entails:

'(3) An instrument is validly executed as a deed by an individual if, and only if—

(a) it is signed—

(i) by him in the presence of a witness who attests the signature; or

(ii) at his direction and in his presence and the presence of two witnesses who each attest the signature; and

(b) it is delivered as a deed'.

There are, therefore, four key elements: first, the document must be clearly intended to be a deed; second, it must be signed; third, it must be witnessed; and finally, it must be 'delivered' as a deed.

Intended to be a deed on its face

The most simple way, of course, to demonstrate on the face of the document that it is intended to be a deed is to label it 'deed'. This is the usual way that this requirement is met. As Dray highlights, 'this is not a very onerous obligation, especially in an era where standard, computer-generated documentation is the norm'.[54]

---

[54] M Dray, 'Deeds speak louder than words: attesting time for deeds?' [2013] Conv 298, 300.

Signed

The deed must also be signed. The question as to what constitutes a valid signature—be that a 'wet ink' signature done by hand, or a typed name, etc has been discussed earlier in relation to contracts. However, it is important to note in relation to deeds that since there is a requirement that the signature of the parties or party to the deed be *attested*, that the witness must actually have seen the signature take place. It is not possible therefore to simply type a name at the bottom of a document, later print that, and ask the witness to sign the piece of paper before them.

Witness

It is with the witnessing requirement that the rules regarding deeds become somewhat more complex. This is thanks to an ambiguity in the statutory language. The statute simply says that the witness or witnesses must 'attest' the signature. There is however no definition of 'attest' in the statutory provisions. There is therefore some debate, even if there is a widely accepted practice, as to whether this actually requires that the witness *sign* the deed also, or whether it is enough for that witness to simply have *witnessed*, ie seen, the signing by the parties to the deed. Furthermore, there is some uncertainty as to *who* can witness a deed. Can they be a party to the deed? On this first issue, the Law Commission stated that, '"Attestation" involves more than simply witnessing the execution of the deed; it also includes the subscription of the witness' signature following a statement (attestation clause) that the document was signed or executed in his presence'.[55] However, as Dray shows, there is some ambiguity and inconsistency present in the pre-1989 case law regarding the concept of attestation, and the earlier statutory provisions, such as the Statute of Frauds, had required both attestation and signature by the witness, suggesting that there is a distinction between the two concepts.[56]

Howsoever this may be, there is an accepted practice which is followed in the vast majority of cases, and is required by the land registry in terms of its own assessment as to the validity of a deed. Most deeds will contain an attestation clause, which is simply a statement that 'Witness A saw Party X sign the deed', will contain Witness A's own signature, and her name and address so that she can be contacted if a problem were to arise with the deed.

Delivery of a deed

Finally, the deed must also be 'delivered' before it is to be effective as a deed. This puzzling phrase does not, contrary to its 'natural sense', necessarily mean that the deed must be handed over to the other party to the transaction. Rather, as the case law highlights, '"[d]elivery does not mean "handed over" to the other side. It means delivered in the old legal sense, namely, an act done so as to evince an intention to be bound'.[57] Delivery, in this sense, is more akin to a public acknowledgement of the fact of the deed coming into effect. If we consider the fundamental point made in the introduction to the deeds section, the sense of this becomes somewhat clearer. The deed,

---

[55] Law Commission, Deeds and Escrows (HMSO, 1987), Law Com. No.163, HC Paper No.1, fn 18.
[56] M Dray, 'Deeds speak louder than words: attesting time for deeds?' [2013] Conv 298, 303.
[57] Per Lord Denning M.R. in *Vincent v Premo Enterprises* [1969] 2 QB 609.

as highlighted, is the method of the transfer of the property rights: it is the *doing* of the thing. In moveable property terms, it is the handing over of the object with a view to making it someone else's. Here, the physical handing over is replaced by a symbolic handing over in the sense of an expressed intention that ownership has changed hands. Of course, it is possible to 'hand over' the property right in the land by literally handing over deed which constitutes the transfer. However, it is possible to symbolically bring this about through a clear statement of the transfer having happened.

Once the logical leap is made from physical delivery, to symbolic delivery through expressed intention, however, the precise boundaries of the rule become less clear. The debate then becomes, what acts constitute a sufficiently clear signal of an intention to be bound that they suffice for the purposes of section 1(3)? Whilst in most cases the situation will be clear, there can be doubt in cases where a deed is prepared in advance of the intended day of transfer. Nevertheless, the deed comes into effect on the deed of its delivery, not the date of its preparation (and therefore may come into effect at some date *after* the witnessing of the signatures).

4.3.2.2 When is a deed required?

The previous section demonstrates what is required of a valid deed, but it is important to note also when such a deed is required. The position is very simple. Deeds are required in order to create or transfer any legal interest or estate in land, except for the creation of short leases (3 years or less) to go into possession immediately (see earlier). The provision requiring a deed for the creation or transfer of all other legal rights is section 52 Law of Property Act 1925. It states: '[a]ll conveyances of land or of any interest therein are void for the purpose of conveying or creating a legal estate unless made by deed'.

Although the 'list' of legal rights was given in chapter 2, it is therefore worth repeating the rights which will require a deed in order to operate at law. The list of such rights (Table 4.2) is taken from section 1(2) Law of Property Act 1925 combined with sections 52 and 54 LPA 1925. When considering whether or not a deed is required, simply refer back to this table.

4.3.2.3 Consequences of having used a deed

The use of a deed used to be sufficient to create or transfer the relevant legal interest in land. However, since the advent of compulsory registration, for registered land, this is no longer the case. Rather, the further step of registration is required. This is discussed in chapter 5. In this sense, for registered land at least, the deed in itself does not give rise to any additional rights on top of what arises on the formation of a valid, written contract. (We do consider the cumulative effect of a deed and the payment of money which may affect the legal position in relation to estate contracts in chapter 14 at 14.2.) However, there are cases where there either is no written contract and parties have progressed straight to a deed, or the situation is one in which a contractual agreement is unsuitable, eg the provision of a gift. In these cases, where there is no written contract, the deed will operate in equity, so as to create an 'equitable version' of whatever legal right the parties were seeking, or will be sufficient, to give rise to a right in equity. Thus, for example, a deed of gift of a freehold title would result in the current legal proprietor holding on trust for the transferee.

The only exception to this is the narrow class of cases where although a deed is required in order to create the relevant right, registration is not compulsory. This is the case for leases of over

Table 4.2 Rights which will require a deed in order to operate at law (Law of Property Act 1925, ss 1(2), 52 and 54)

The creation or transfer of a freehold estate (fee simple in possession)
The creation of a leasehold estate of a duration of more than 3 years
The creation of a leasehold estate to go into possession at some date in the future or which is not for best rent
The transfer of a leasehold estate of any duration
The creation or transfer of an easement or profit
The creation or transfer of a charge by way of mortgage
The creation or transfer of a rentcharge
The creation or transfer of a right of re-entry

3 years, but less than or equal to 7 years in duration where certain other conditions are met. For the creation of such leases at law, there must be a deed, but there is no need to register.

The statutory provision which governs this special class of leases is section 27(2) LRA 2002. It states:

'(2) In the case of a registered estate, the following are the dispositions which are required to be completed by registration—

...

(b) where the registered estate is an estate in land, the grant of a term of years absolute [ie a lease]—
   (i) for a term of more than seven years from the date of the grant,
   (ii) to take effect in possession after the end of the period of three months beginning with the date of the grant,
   (iii) under which the right to possession is discontinuous'.

Therefore, to meet the requirements of this section, a lease of over three years, but less than or equal to seven years need not be completed by registration as long as (a) it takes effect in possession within three months of the deed; and (b) the right to possession is continuous. If both of these apply, then the deed (ie the grant) will be sufficient to give rise to a legal lease. For all other legal rights where a deed is required, registration is also needed to give rise to the relevant right at law. More detail is given in relation to land registration in chapter 5.

> **Summary: Deeds**
> 1. Are the parties attempting to dispose of a legal interest in land? If no, no deed is required. If yes, then a deed is required except for leases of a duration of three years or less where the lease is to go into possession immediately and is at the best rent available.

> 2. If a deed is required, then the parties must:
>   (a) state on the face of the document that it is a deed;
>   (b) sign the document;
>   (c) witnesses must attest the signing of the document; and
>   (d) the deed must be 'delivered'.
> 3. In unregistered land, this will suffice for the creation of a legal right. In registered land, to complete the creation of the legal right, registration will be required, except in the case of leases of a duration of seven years or less where possession is continuous, and the lessee goes into possession within three months of the date of the deed.

4.3.3 INTERESTS UNDER A TRUST

The nature of trust interests is discussed in chapter 16. It is important to note that there are different formality rules relating to a declaration of trust, and to the *transfer* of interests arising under a trust (and indeed, other equitable interests, as discussed in the next section), than there are for other kinds of property transaction. The general principles are roughly the same: these transactions must take place in writing of some kind, but the rules are, to a certain extent, less prescriptive. The general rule is contained in section 53 Law of Property Act 1925 which states, '(b) a declaration of trust respecting any land or any interest therein must be manifested and proved by some writing signed by some person who is able to declare such trust or by his will'.

Much of the difficulty to which this section has given rise can be explained by the use of the 'manifested and proved' test (as opposed to 'created'). This means that the declaration of trust need not be contemporaneous with the creation of the relevant document, nor does the section mean that the trust is void for an absence of writing. It appears, from the wording of the provision at least, that the declaration of trust cannot be *proved* unless it is in an appropriate form. This is not quite the same thing as saying that the declaration of trust is void. This can lead to the rather strange situation where a person has orally agreed to take a legal property right but to hold that on trust for a third party (so, A transfers his freehold title to B on the basis of an oral declaration by B that he would hold on trust for C), the transfer of the freehold title is properly carried out so that B keeps the property, but C is unable to enforce the trust. However, because the trust *exists*, nor can A claim, for example, that there is a breach of the promise nor can A argue that the property should be held on trust for him.

The result of this is that an exception to this general principle, ie that the trust must be manifested and proved in signed writing or it is unenforceable, has arisen. The absence of writing cannot be invoked by the putative trustee as an instrument of fraud. This is a very uncertain principle, and its operation is the subject of much debate.

The other exception to the general requirement of writing for interests under a trust is the statutory exclusion of implied, resulting and constructive trusts. The operation of these types of trust is discussed in chapter 7. However, it is important to note here that these methods of creating trusts outwith the scope of section 53(1) are used very widely in land law.

4.3.4 DISPOSITIONS OF EQUITABLE INTERESTS

We have now considered how equitable property rights are created through the use of a contract; how they are created if a deed is used; and how, specifically, interests under a trust can be created. However, there is a final category of potential transaction, and that is the disposition of a *subsisting* equitable interest. That is, what formalities must parties use in order to deliberately transfer an existing equitable interest (which may have been created either through contract, through a deed, by will, or by a trust instrument complying with the requirements of section 53(1)(b)). Section 53(1)(c) states that, 'a disposition of an equitable interest or trust subsisting at the time of the disposition, must be in writing signed by the person disposing of the same'. Thus, signed writing is clearly required. However, this is demonstrably different from section 53(1)(b) which only requires that the declaration of trust be *manifested and proved* in signed writing. Section 53(1)(c) actually requires signed writing to carry out the disposition, not only to prove it. Furthermore, unlike section 2 LP(MP)A 1989, in reference to contracts, there is no explicit stipulation that the written document explain the terms of the disposition. However, if there are terms for the disposition, then, in all likelihood, the transaction will be a contractual one, and compliance with section 2 would suffice. Section 53(1)(c) is therefore only relevant where there is no contract for the disposition. Rather, the written document here serves roughly the same purpose as a deed does for the completion of a disposition of a legal interest.

4.4 CONCLUSION

The rules relating to formalities are essential to the operation of the land law system in practice. Getting these rules wrong causes an enormous amount of difficulty for parties. For the most part, it is very straightforward to comply with the rules, and anyone with competent legal advice is unlikely to encounter any problems in this respect. However, in a more general sense, the formality rules give us a window into the various purposes to which rules in land law are put. They also emphasise that even the most seemingly straightforward statutory provisions can encounter issues surrounding definition, interpretation, and application to unusual facts.

PRINCIPLES

How does this discussion shape our understanding of the principles explained in chapter 1? To recap, these principles were:

1. Certainty
2. Sensitivity to context
3. Transactability
4. Systemic and individual effects
5. Recognition of the social role of the land law system.

In one sense, the formality rules in general are clearly targeted at achieving all of these principles. Indeed, in most cases, formality rules will both make a situation more clear and certain, whilst also creating a degree of protection for those who are transacting in relation to their homes, for example. It is in the precise detail of the operation of the rules however that we begin to see where the law is more consciously responding to these different principles in different places.

Let us take the exceptions to the need for a written contract rule. For the most part these exceptions—auctions, FSMA regulated transactions, boundary agreements and mixed contracts—are relatively narrow in the sense that they do not relate to those kinds of transaction with which land law is centrally concerned. Short leases, however, are one of the most common transactions and furthermore, the consequences for at least one party is likely to be that any error in this process will result in them losing their home in circumstances which they did not expect. Thus, in making this transaction one for which no formality is required, the law has made an explicit choice not to pursue certainty, caution and protection in this particular area. This is surprising, for it is entirely reasonable to argue that it is in relation to this kind of low value, consumer-style transaction that inequalities of bargaining power and the force of the market on individuals are most likely to be felt. Against this background, the reason for excluding short leases from such rules, ie that it would be too much trouble to make people write these down, does not appear particularly convincing.

However, there is a more rational explanation which is in the flexibility that short leases created, not necessarily in a 'fixed term' contract (where the duration of the lease is determined in advance where the expectation is that the lease would not be renewed), but in cases of periodic tenancies. These are explained in chapter 10 at 10.4.1, but their essence is that their short period (usually a month or a quarter) gives all parties flexibility. In this flexibility lies protection for both. The idea that people should write down a new tenancy every month, however, does seem excessive given that the inherent flexibility of such tenancies is something which both parties might legitimately seek. Furthermore, as explained in chapter 10, there are special rules giving statutory protection of tenure to residents in some cases, so that they cannot be evicted even once the contractual term had ended. Might it not be better to leave the protection to these rules, so that formality rules become, in the context of leases, one of certainty alone? This argument shows the importance of putting all the jigsaw pieces into place before reaching a definitive conclusion on the balance struck by the law!

There are however some areas where the law is manifestly failing to meet any of these principles. The boundary agreements case law is a classic example of this, where the court has clearly decided the outcome on the basis of what seems 'fair' in the instant case with very little consideration given to what this means for the system as a whole. The rules produced massively sacrifice clarity for an individual outcome. Furthermore, as we mentioned at the outset, whilst formality in general can provide certainty, having such a range of formality rules for subtly different transactions, does not provide certainty, at least not the kind of moral certainty we explained in chapter 1.

Finally, we can see in this chapter some of the struggles that the law has in keeping up to pace with modern business and social practices. Email communication is now itself almost old-fashioned in some contexts, and yet legal practice has not yet fully determined whether typing an email name is enough to constitute a signature for land law. This might be quite right—perhaps we want to ensure parties sit down in front of a piece of paper with a pen and a solicitor, to achieve the cautionary and protection functions discussed earlier, thereby advancing the social purposes of land law—but to punish parties for a failure to do so when the popular expectation might be that a typed signature would be enough perhaps takes this all too far.

TABLE OF DEFINITIONS

Contract	An agreement between two or more parties with promises (consideration) arising on both sides.
Written contract	A contract which complies with section 2 Law of Property (Miscellaneous Provisions) Act 1989 by being in writing, containing all the relevant terms, in a single document, signed by both parties.
Deed	A document which complies with section 1 Law of Property (Miscellaneous Provisions) Act 1989 by stating on its face that it is a deed, being signed by the parties and witnessed, and having been effectively delivered as a deed.
Consideration	An obligation or performance undertaken in return for the imposition of a contractual obligation.

FURTHER READING

Much of the recommended further reading for this chapter is footnoted above. Particularly useful are:

FULLER, L., 'Consideration and Form' (1941), 41 Columbia Law Review 799.
LAW COMMISSION, Deeds and Escrows (HMSO, 1987), Law Com. No.163.

It might also be useful to consider the further reading in chapter three, as a historical overview of the development of English land law shows how the formality rules have morphed over time.

5

LAND REGISTRATION

5.1	Introduction	115	5.5	Conclusion	159
5.2	Registration and Rights-Creation	116		Principles	160
5.3	Errors on the Register	127		Table of Definitions	161
5.4	Reform of the Rectification and Indemnity Provisions	157		Further Reading	161

> ### CHAPTER GOALS
>
> By the end of this chapter, you should understand:
>
> - The function of the land register as regulating methods of rights creation, as an extension of the formality rules discussed in chapter 4;
> - Which rights must be registered in order to be validly created at law, both on first registrations and on subsequent registrations;
> - What the effect of registration will be;
> - How errors might emerge on the register and how they are fixed;
> - Indemnities consequent on errors in registered land;
> - The effect of errors on the register for our understanding of the system as a whole; and
> - Reform proposals.

5.1 INTRODUCTION

In chapter 3, we explored the aims and principles which underpin registered land, comparing such an approach with that of unregistered conveyancing. This chapter, rather than looking at the principles of registration, explores how the English land law land registration system works in practice. To this end, it is important to begin this discussion with a basic structural point. The land registration system achieves three goals. The first is as a method of controlling the way in which rights are *created*. The second is in terms of managing the *effect* of such rights, once they have been created. The third is as a means to regulate the *interactions* between different proprietary rights which exist in relation to the same piece of land. This last function of the registration system is a question of priorities, and is considered in chapter 15. The first two functions—mode of rights creation, and effect of rights creation—are considered here in 5.2 of this chapter. Section 5.3 then explores what happens when these functions go wrong within the system—how do the principles of registered land interact with the inevitable reality of both human error and human creativity? In answering this issue, the chapter considers how the register is rectified and altered. Section 5.4 then examines potential reforms, including those proposed by the Law Commission, and the possibility of the advent of e-conveyancing, before 5.5 concludes.

It will be seen that whilst, in many respects, the governing statute—the Land Registration Act 2002 (LRA 2002)—has been remarkably successful, in the over fifteen years since it came into force, problems have begun to emerge at the fringes of its operation. For this reason, the Law Commission has now begun the process of bringing about reform of the LRA 2002, to allow for the smoother operation of the registration system in cases of error. In addition, a fairly unwieldy body of case law has emerged which attempts to navigate these statutory provisions and to reach a solution in a particular dispute which seems both to be fair, and in line with the policies behind the enactment of the LRA 2002 in the first place.

It is important to note at this point that this chapter, in terms of the overall effect of land registration on the land law system, should be read in conjunction with the priorities chapter, chapter 15. A full understanding of the priorities chapter is however only sensibly possible once the nature of rights in land is at least known in outline. This chapter is concerned with the effect of registration as a method of *rights creation*, not of *rights protection*. These two functions are separable. However, it may be useful to refresh an understanding of the overall land registration system explored in chapter 3 in introductory form before reading this chapter, in order successfully to maintain a separation between these two functions. It is also important to emphasise, ahead of tackling this chapter, that not all land law courses will expect knowledge of registration error to the same detailed level that is present here. Much depends upon the way that individual courses have prioritised consideration of different land law issues. If this applies to your personal course, then the summary boxes will provide a good flavour of the debate, so that registration error is understood in outline.

5.2 REGISTRATION AND RIGHTS-CREATION

One of the major impacts of the LRA 2002 was to mandate that certain rights be registered before they can be created at law. As we saw in chapter 4, the process to create legal rights already involved more formalities than did the process of creating equitable rights, even before the coming into force of the LRA 2002. Indeed, this reflects the logic of the distinction between such rights which we considered in chapter 1 at 1.4.1. It highlights the universal bindingness of legal rights, when compared with the dependent bindingness of equitable rights. The LRA 2002 has continued this distinction. It is now necessary to register (almost) all rights in order for them to operate at law. This registration may take place in two forms: an estate in land can be registered under its own title number; or an interest in land can be registered as a notice against an existing registered title. The effects of these two processes are very different in terms of what the registration system guarantees about the quality of these rights. The first question to which the land registration rules give rise, therefore, is the question of which interests must be registered in order to operate at law.

5.2.1 INTERESTS WHICH MUCH BE REGISTERED

One of the fundamental goals of land registration, as explained in chapter 3 at 3.3.1, is that as many rights as is possible and reasonable appear on the register. This is to ensure that the register is an accurate representation of the proprietary interests which exist in relation to a particular piece of land (with the notable exception of interests arising under trusts which are consciously kept off the register). In order to ensure this, the LRA 2002 instituted a regime of mandatory registration for the creation of certain such important legal rights.

The requirements of mandatory registration are stated in sections 4 and 27 LRA 2002. It is here that we see the ambition of the LRA 2002 as controlling the means by which rights in land are created. In applying these rules, it is important to distinguish between rights which must be registered when, at the moment at which the rights are granted by deed, the *title* to the relevant estate is *not* registered (ie what are the triggers for first registration?); and the rights which must be registered in cases where the title to the land is already on the register, prior to the creation of the right. It is important to remember that these rules are only applicable where one seeks for the transaction in question to operate *at law*.

5.2.1.1 First registration

This section explores what is required in cases of first registration.

The requirement to register

The governing section in relation to the triggers for first registration is section 4, which explains when title to land must be registered for the first time. It is the trigger for compulsory registration. To understand these provisions it is essential to read them, not merely to read a summary of how they work. Section 4 states:

> 'When title must be registered
>
> (1) The requirement of registration applies on the occurrence of any of the following events—
>
>   (a) the transfer of a qualifying estate—
>
>   ...
>
>   (c) the grant out of a qualifying estate of an estate in land—
>
>   (i) for a term of years absolute of more than seven years from the date of the grant
>
>   (d) the grant out of a qualifying estate of an estate in land for a term of years absolute to take effect in possession after the end of the period of three months beginning with the date of the grant;
>
>   ...
>
>   (g) the creation of a protected first legal mortgage of a qualifying estate.
>
> (2) For the purposes of subsection (1), a qualifying estate is an unregistered legal estate which is—
>
>   (a) a freehold estate in land, or
>
>   (b) a leasehold estate in land for a term which, at the time of the transfer, grant or creation, has more than seven years to run.'

The purpose of section 4 is to set the conditions for first registration. Essentially, it provides that title must be registered where either the estate itself is transferred—with the relevant estates being freehold estates and leasehold estates of a duration of more than 7 years remaining—or where certain kinds of interest are created out of that estate. In this latter category we can include the creation of a leasehold estate of more than 7 years in duration, or where a lease of any length goes into possession more than three months after the grant, and the grant of a first legal mortgage (meaning a mortgage which ranks in priority ahead of any other mortgages).

The requirement that the estate be registered on the transfer or creation of that estate is a means of ensuring that as much 'land' as possible finds its way onto the register, even though freehold title to such land may not have been conveyed for many hundreds of years (thanks, for example, to family trusts). The consequence of this, however, as we have explained in chapter 3, is that when we talk of registered *land*, this is something of a misnomer in so far as we are really concerned with registered *estates* in land. The geographical scope of the land is relevant to the process of registration, obviously, but as we see later, boundaries on the register are not conclusive. Registration is less concerned with the creation of a perfect map in the form of a cadastral system, as it is with reflecting the different layers of ownership which are present in relation to a single geographical space. The triggers for first registration reflect this.

The effect of first registration

The effect of registration of title is explained by sections 11 and 12 LRA 2002. In respect of freehold title, the effect of registration is to ensure that the legal estate is vested in the legal proprietor, along with all rights which benefit that estate. It will also ensure that the registered proprietor has the owner's powers as explained in sections 23 and 24 LRA 2002, as discussed later. The proprietor will be affected by any rights already listed on the register. For example, where a long leasehold estate has been registered but the freehold title has not yet been registered, upon registration of the freehold title, the freehold would remain subject to the lease. They will also be bound by any right listed in schedule 1 LRA 2002 (see chapter 15 at 15.3). In the case of first registrations, the proprietor will also be bound by any titles acquired through adverse possession of which they have notice. In respect of leasehold title, the proprietor will similarly be bound by any rights which appear on the register, and by any rights protected as overriding interests under schedule 1, but they will also be bound by any covenants which exist in respect of the leasehold estate itself (we consider leasehold covenants in chapter 10 at 10.5.1), the bindingness of which is not a matter for land registration, but for the law relating to leases.

There are different categories of title with which a person may become registered. For freehold title, there are three such categories. These are absolute, qualified, and possessory title. For leasehold estates, there are four titles: absolute, good, qualified and possessory title. The distinction between absolute and good titles reflects the fact that a leasehold title is by its nature not absolute in the sense that it is subject to the right of reversion which the freeholder has, and therefore is dependent, to an extent, upon the quality of the freehold title. Thus, an absolute leasehold title is granted where the registrar is convinced that the *freehold* title is itself an absolute title. A good title is given where the leasehold estate meets all the relevant requirements, but there is a lower degree of certainty in relation to the freehold estate.

Registration with absolute title is essentially confirmation from the registrar that they are of the opinion that a subsequent purchaser of that title could be assured that it was a valid title.

Qualified title, by contrast, would be granted if the registrar felt that there were reservations regarding the title which ought not to be ignored. A person will be registered with possessory title if they are in possession of the land, but are not otherwise able to be registered with absolute or qualified title. It is important to note that qualified titles in particular are rare. The registrar is unlikely to register with qualified title. However, it may occur where, for example, the chain of conveyance presented to the register appears on its face to be good, but it does not go back at least 15 years. Here the registrar is perhaps unconvinced in respect of the possibility of a superior title existing either through adverse possession, or because the person with superior title has not been out of possession for the required time.

Possessory title is more common and is likely to be the case where a person claims under adverse possession to be entitled to be the first registered proprietor of that estate. The consequence of a possessory title is that it may be challenged if any estate or interests existed at the time of first registration. The example given by Megarry and Wade, the leading practitioners' text relating to land law, is the case where a person is registered as freehold proprietor on the basis of adverse possession, when it later transpires that in fact they were in adverse possession as against a leasehold estate, such that they should have been registered as leasehold proprietor and were subject to the non-barred freehold title.[1] In such a case, the 'registered freehold proprietor' would remain subject to the unregistered but superior freehold title. As we note later, however, even if someone were to be registered with absolute title in such cases, the mistake made in registering with freehold title would mean that the register would almost certainly be subsequently rectified.

The effect of being registered with these different kinds of title is that whereas a person with good or absolute title is subject only to those binding rights explained in chapter 15 and earlier (ie rights appearing on the register and those protected in schedule 1), the title will not be subject to any other limitations. For qualified title, the title-holder will be in the same position as one with absolute title except that rights which are exempted from the effect of registration will be enforceable as against a person with qualified title.

Cautions against first registration

In order to prevent a first registration, and the effect that such may have on the beneficiaries of a trust, for example, it is possible to enter what is known as a 'caution' against first registration.[2] There is a separate register for such cautions. Any person with an interest in the relevant estate is able to lodge such a caution. The effect of such a caution can be to ensure that the interest of this person is entered onto the register, so that they are protected on any disposition, or, in the case of an interest under a trust which cannot be registered, so that a restriction may be entered to protect that beneficiary going forward (for more in relation to restrictions, see later and chapter 16 at 16.2.4). The level of protection given by cautions is relatively weak. This is because the primary consequence of a caution is that the registrar must give notice to the person with the benefit of the caution that an application to register has been made so that they can object to the application. It does not operate as a substantive means of protection in itself.

---

[1] C Harpum et al, *Megarry & Wade: The Law of Real Property* (8th ed) (Sweet & Maxwell, London, 2012), [7–035].
[2] Land Registration Act 2002, section 19.

> **Summary: First registration**
>
> First registrations are required upon the grant or transfer of a qualifying estate. These are: a freehold; a leasehold estate of more than 7 years; a leasehold estate due to go into possession more than 3 months after the grant; and a first legal mortgage.
>
> A person will be registered with—for freeholds—absolute, qualified, or possessory title. In the case of a leasehold estate, they will be registered with absolute, good, qualified or possessory title. Charges will appear on the charges register.
>
> The effect of such registration is to vest title in the registered proprietor, subject only to any right appearing already on the register, or which overrides under schedule 1.

5.2.1.2 Registrable dispositions

This section explores what is required in cases involving dispositions relating to registered titles.

Requirement of registration

Where title to land is *already* registered, certain dispositions in relation to that land also need to be completed by registration in order for the disposition to have effect at law. This is a result of section 27, which states that:

> 'Dispositions required to be registered
>
> (1) If a disposition of a registered estate or registered charge is required to be completed by registration, it does not operate at law until the relevant registration requirements are met.
>
> (2) In the case of a registered estate, the following are the dispositions which are required to be completed by registration—
>
>   (a) a transfer,
>
>   (b) where the registered estate is an estate in land, the grant of a term of years absolute—
>
>   (i) for a term of more than seven years from the date of the grant
>
>   (ii) to take effect in possession after the end of the period of three months beginning with the date of the grant,
>
>   (iii) under which the right to possession is discontinuous,
>
>   ...
>
>   (d) the express grant or reservation of an interest of a kind falling within section 1(2)(a) of the Law of Property Act 1925 (c. 20), other than one which is capable of being registered under Part 1 of the Commons Act 2006,
>
>   (e) the express grant or reservation of an interest of a kind falling within section 1(2)(b) or (e) of the Law of Property Act 1925, and
>
>   (f) the grant of a legal charge.
>
> (3) In the case of a registered charge, the following are the dispositions which are required to be completed by registration—
>
>   (a) a transfer, and
>
>   (b) the grant of a sub-charge.'

To summarise, this provision requires the registration of certain rights before they can operate at law. To that extent, this provision has no effect on the creation of rights in equity. If all the other proper formalities are completed for the creation of a registrable disposition, then that right will operate in equity notwithstanding the failure to register.

The registrable dispositions are, most importantly, the transfer of a registered estate; the grant of the leasehold estate which is more than seven years in duration, or where it is to go into possession more than three months after the grant, or where possession under the lease is discontinuous; the transfer of any registered lease; the creation of a right which falls under section 1(2)(a) LPA 1925, ie the grant of an easement, right or privilege (such as a profit); the creation of a right under section 1(2)(b) LPA 1925, ie the grant of a rentcharge in possession; the creation of a right under section 1(2)(e) LPA 1925, ie the grant of a right of re-entry; and the grant of a legal charge. Most land law courses focus on four key aspects of this: transfer of freehold estate; creation or transfer of a relevant leasehold estate; the express grant, transfer, or sub-charge of a legal charge; and the express grant of an easement. It matters not to the requirement of registration whether or not the interest in question was transferred or created for valuable consideration.

Effect of registration—estates and charges

The effect of registering such rights is that they can take effect at law. In the case of an estate in land—ie the freehold and leasehold estates—the consequence will also be that the proprietor is registered with one of the classes of title explained earlier. They will be guaranteed as proprietor of the estate under section 58 LRA 2002 (considered in detail later), and as having owner's powers as provided for by sections 23 and 24. The effect of registration of a charge on the charges register mirrors the effect in respect of estates.

Effect of registration—interests protected by a notice

Whilst estates in land are entered under their own title number when registered, and thus engage the guarantees provided by the register in respect of guarantee of title, it is possible to enter an interest as the subject of a notice on the register, so that it is lodged against the estate in question. This will protect the priority of that right as against subsequent registered purchasers of the estate (as explained in chapter 15), but it does not ensure the validity of those rights, as provided for in section 32 LRA 2002.

Interests which cannot be entered as the subject of a notice

It is possible (although not necessary) to enter a notice onto the register in respect of almost all kinds of property rights which can affect land, whether legal or equitable in nature. If a notice is entered in relation to a right which cannot operate at law (because it does not appear in the list of legal property rights in section 1 Law of Property Act 1925), then its quality as an equitable right will not be altered by entry on the register. Rather, its priority will be protected. However, certain interests *cannot* be entered as the subject of a notice (Law of Property Act 1925, s 33):

> 'Excluded interests
>
> No notice may be entered in the register in respect of any of the following—
>
> (a) an interest under—
>
> (i) a trust of land, or
>
> (ii) a settlement under the Settled Land Act 1925 (c. 18),

> (b) a leasehold estate in land which—
>> (i) is granted for a term of years of three years or less from the date of the grant, and
>> (ii) is not required to be registered,
>
> (ba) an interest under a relevant social housing tenancy,
>> (c) a restrictive covenant made between a lessor and lessee, so far as relating to the demised premises,
>
> …'

This is an extremely important provision, despite its apparently innocuous nature. It is critical to the functioning of the register in terms of administrative ease, and to one of the principles underpinning the whole land registration system—the curtain principle—as discussed in chapter 3. By preventing notices relating to interests arising under trusts of land, the register, to a large extent, operates as a 'curtain'. Purchasers do not need to be concerned with such interests (except to the extent to which they may be protected as a result of the beneficiary's discoverable actual occupation, see chapter 15 at 15.3.3 and chapter 3 at 3.3.4.1 for a summary of the rules). It is also very important to keep this provision in mind when considering problem questions and questions of priority. In chapter 15, we explain the 'process' by which priority questions are resolved in registered land. One aspect of this is the question as to whether or not a right has been registered. When dealing with a trust of land, however, it is important *not* to ask whether the right has been registered, since section 33 provides that such is impossible.

The second crucial feature of this section is the inability to register the creation of a lease of a duration of three years or less, unless the lease must otherwise be registered. This would be because it is to go into possession more than three months after the date of the grant, or because possession under that lease is discontinuous. The sheer number of such leases created would make the task of the land registry administratively impossible were such rights routinely registered. There is no need to register them from the perspective of the leaseholder. Legal leases of this duration are automatically overriding, ie binding on a subsequent purchaser notwithstanding the fact that such rights do not appear on the register, under schedule 1 paragraph 1 and schedule 3 paragraph 1, or will likely override due to the actual occupation of the leaseholder (for more, see chapter 15 at 15.3.1 and 15.3.3). Were a practice to emerge whereby such rights were registered, then the land registry would be utterly overwhelmed.

Categories of notice

As with freehold and leasehold titles, there are different forms of notice which reflect the different circumstances in which a person might apply for a notice to be entered onto the register. This can be seen in section 34:

> 'Entry on application
>> (1) A person who claims to be entitled to the benefit of an interest affecting a registered estate or charge may, if the interest is not excluded by section 33, apply to the registrar for the entry in the register of a notice in respect of the interest.
>> (2) Subject to rules, an application under this section may be for—
>>> (a) an agreed notice, or
>>> (b) a unilateral notice.'

The effect of an agreed notice—ie one where both the registered proprietor and the right-holder agree to the entry or the registrar is otherwise convinced as to the validity of the right—is to protect that right against subsequent attempts to have it removed by the registered proprietor. In the case of a unilateral notice, the registered proprietor can apply for the cancellation of the notice (subject to notification of the right-holder by the registrar). A right-holder may object to this attempt to cancel the notice, and the matter will then be resolved by reference to the relevant documentation to consider the validity of the right.

> **Summary: Registrable dispositions**
>
> Certain dispositions of registered estates must be registered in order to operate at law. These are (mainly): the transfer of a freehold estate; the grant of a leasehold estate of more than 7 years in duration, or which is to go into possession more than three months after the grant or is discontinuous; the transfer of any existing registered easement; the grant or transfer or a legal charge; and the grant of an easement.
>
> The freehold and leasehold estates will be registered as estates in land. The charge will appear on the charges register. Any other legal interests will be entered as the subject of a notice. Notices can be either agreed or unilateral.
>
> The effect of registration of estates and charges is to guarantee title to those estates, and to confer priority over any right which is not either registered, or appears in schedule 3 LRA 2002. The effect of registration of interests is to confer priority to the registered interest-holder should the estate in question be transferred to another for valuable consideration. Registration of an interest as a notice will also allow it to operate at law if it is in its nature capable of being a legal right (section 1 LPA 1925).
>
> Whilst it is possible (although not necessary) to enter a notice to protect most legal and equitable rights in this way, it is not possible to enter a notice in relation to leaseholds of a duration of three years or less; of interests under a trust of land; and of interests arising under the Settled Land Act (outwith the scope of this book).

5.2.1.3 Restrictions

Restrictions are also considered in chapter 16 at 16.2.4. These are an essential element in the functioning of the system in respect of disputes between beneficiaries of trust of land, their trustees, and third parties, but restrictions are not limited to this context. A restriction is simply the entry of a limitation onto the register which, in effect, prevents the registrar from entering transactions onto the register unless certain conditions are met. It is in this sense a procedural protection. It does not prevent the substantive dealing with land, but rather prevents the registrar from giving full effect to such dealing through engagement with registered title, unless the conditions of the restriction are met.

Common conditions expressed in a restriction are that transfer of freehold title should not be registered without consultation with the beneficiaries of a trust in relation to that land, or may reflect a prohibition on dealings with the title at all during a specified period of time (prior to the grant of probate, for example, in cases involving contested wills). Such 'freezes' on the land can operate to provide a great deal of protection in practice in cases where a person either does not *yet* have a right in land (but expects so to do under the provisions of a will, for example). They are also effective where a person does have a right in land which is vulnerable to third parties, but they are unable to protect it through some other means, such as the entry of a notice (because, most commonly, the right in question cannot be entered as a subject of a notice on the register because it is an interest under a trust). Persons can apply for restrictions. The registrar is also able to enter restrictions onto the register of their own volition. In some cases the registrar is *mandated* to enter a restriction.

Restrictions can be entered to prevent invalid or unlawful dispositions. This may be, to utilise the example provided by Megarry and Wade, where a public authority has limited powers to dispose of their land, so that any transfer would be *ultra vires*.[3] In such a case, a restriction may be entered to highlight the nature of that limitation. An alternative example would be the case where the registrar was concerned, perhaps due to previous attempts to register transfers, that a particular title was particularly susceptible to fraudulent dealings. In such cases, the registrar may enter a restriction to prevent dealings with that title unless the true registered proprietor was first individually consulted.

5.2.2 OWNER'S POWERS AND GUARANTEE OF TITLE

The registration system provides that once a person becomes registered, they *are* proprietor of the relevant title for all purposes, even if they should not be registered. This is the guarantee of title provided by section 58 LRA 2002.

> 'Conclusiveness
>
> (1) If, on the entry of a person in the register as the proprietor of a legal estate, the legal estate would not otherwise be vested in him, it shall be deemed to be vested in him as a result of the registration.'

This section appears to hold that any person registered is guaranteed to have title. On the one hand this could be read as the ultimate expression of indefeasibility. Title, once registered, becomes sacrosanct (this concept is explained further in chapter 3 at 3.3). But that was not the intentions of the drafters of the Act, and nor is it consistent with the other provisions of the Act, especially schedule 4. However, quite how far the guarantee extends, and what it means in practice, remains far from clear as we see later.

The consequence of this provision in simple cases is that even if there was a flaw in the underlying transaction (a flaw which may never come to light, and which may have been merely technical, with all parties validly consenting to the transaction in question), then registration will have the effect of conferring legal title. Without such registration, no title can be conferred. This guarantee of title only applies to registration of estates. It does not confer validity onto interests which become registered.

One extremely important consequence of becoming a registered proprietor is that the proprietor becomes entitled to use the owner's powers. These powers form an important element of the conclusivity of the register debate too. However, since in most cases there will *not* be an error on the register, it is useful to explain what these powers achieve here. In effect, the owner's powers are the flip side of the guarantee of title. Sections 23 and 24 provide that when a person either is

---

[3] C Harpum et al, *Megarry & Wade: The Law of Real Property* (8th ed) (Sweet & Maxwell, London, 2012), [7-078].

registered with title, or is entitled to be so registered, then they are then able to complete certain transactions in relation to the land. If they are not so-registered, or entitled to be registered, since they do not have an interest in the land which enables them to create the rights in question, then they would not have such powers. In this sense, it could be argued that the inclusion of a specific list of owner's powers in the land registration legislation was strictly unnecessary. However, what these provisions do is to explain the scope of possible transactions in relation to registered land (precluding, for example, the possibility of the creation of a mortgage by the grant of a long lease).

'23 Owner's powers

(1) Owner's powers in relation to a registered estate consist of—

(a) power to make a disposition of any kind permitted by the general law in relation to an interest of that description, other than a mortgage by demise or sub-demise, and

(b) power to charge the estate at law with the payment of money.

(2) Owner's powers in relation to a registered charge consist of—

(a) power to make a disposition of any kind permitted by the general law in relation to an interest of that description, other than a legal sub-mortgage, and

(b) power to charge at law with the payment of money indebtedness secured by the registered charge.'

This provision is important to the registered land debate because it suggests that the ability to transact in relation to an estate in land comes from the registration system itself, not because the power to transact has been passed through proprietors by virtue of the principles of off-register conveyancing. However, in practice, this section has not had the effect of making any valid transaction by a registered proprietor indefeasible. The unregistered land conveyancing rules have altered how we understand this section. Instead, now, it may be better to understand this section as clarifying the scope of owner's powers, without necessarily guaranteeing that any exercise of those powers will lead to good title.

'24 Right to exercise owner's powers

A person is entitled to exercise owner's powers in relation to a registered estate or charge if he is—

(a) the registered proprietor, or

(b) entitled to be registered as the proprietor.'

This section, taken together with sections 58 and 23 earlier, appears to 'close the circle'. It seems to explain the power of a person with registered title, whether or not they 'should' have been registered, being able to conduct onwards transfers of that title without the transferee having to worry about any off-register problems, and without constraints on that power other than those appearing on the register itself. This is not how the provisions have been interpreted, as we shall see later.

In theory, the effect of owner's powers is to ensure that where a person is registered as proprietor, even if the document which led to their registration (such as the establishment of a trust with them as trustee), attempts to limit their powers, the fact of their being registered means that a purchaser is entitled to rely on the transaction without investigating any such limitations, unless, of course, they appear on the register.

> **Further analysis: Title by registration or registration of title**
>
> Sections 23, 24, and especially section 58 are designed to produce a shift in philosophy in the land law system. Rather than resulting in a process where what occurs off register—dispositions effected by deeds—are prioritised, the system is designed to shift the locus of conveyancing onto the register itself. Later we explore the heated debate as to how this shift in philosophy affects our approach to when and why changes should be made to the register through the process of alteration.
>
> The debate that exists between the different approaches to rectification of the register is really a debate between those who see the register as the *source* of title, and those who see it as a record of title. Of those who fall into the former camp, some see the register as fulfilling this role because that is what the Law Commission itself was recommending when compulsory registration was established: others because they believe this is the best way to ensure justice in the system. Few argue that the Law Commission wished to maintain an approach which saw the register merely as a record. Some do advocate this position on the grounds that they think registration of title too blunt a tool when compared to centuries of judge-made rules capturing the multiplicity of concerns with which any land law system must contend. There are also those who take an 'if it ain't broke don't fix it approach' to the unregistered land system, arguing that the unregistered land principles were mostly satisfactory, and that in shifting to the registered land approach we have lost much that is valuable.
>
> The fault lines of this debate are captured by Dixon:
>
>> 'A lingering and unresolved tension in the system of registered title in England and Wales is to the extent to which the title register should be conclusive of all matters concerning ownership of a registered title. Should registration as proprietor be conclusive irrespective of the circumstances in which the registration came about, subject only to the possibility of alteration of the register in conformity with the statutory scheme? Or should the register be regarded as a record of title, such that the record should be corrected if there is a fault in the underlying validity of the proprietor's title when judged by reference to pre-registration principles of property law and conveyancing?'.[4]
>
> In analysing these issues yourself, and in engaging with the academic literature mentioned in here, it is essential that you decide for yourself which of these positions you adopt. It is also critical to note at this point however that mostly things do not go wrong in the registration process. Where there are no human errors and no fraud, the system produced is smooth and harmonious. Sections 23, 24 and 58 are the linchpins of this harmony.

5.2.3 BOUNDARIES

Whilst the register may guarantee title, it is important to note that it does not guarantee boundaries. Section 60 LRA 2002 states that boundaries as represented on the registration map are not conclusive. The geographical scope of registered land is not guaranteed. The consequence of this is that to determine the precise scope of any estate, it is necessary to look both at the physical layout on the ground. This takes account of the possibility that adverse possession has altered the boundaries over time in a way which is not reflected in the conveyancing documentation. It is also important to consider deeds of transfer and documents explaining the scope of land if and when title to a particular estates was divided. It is possible for parties with registered title to

---

[4] M Dixon, 'A not so conclusive title register?' (2013) 129 LQR 320, 320.

formally agree boundaries through the registration system, in which case at that point the boundaries would become conclusive. This general approach to boundaries is reflected in the special exception for adverse possession in boundaries cases as provided for by schedule 6, paragraph 5 LRA 2002, and as discussed in chapter 6 at 6.3.

> **Summary: Consequences of registration**
>
> In most cases, there will be no error or flaw on the register. In such cases, the consequences of registration will be:
>
> 1. That any right capable of operating at law, and required to be registered in order to so operate, does so operate;
> 2. In the case of estates in land, the register will guarantee title to the relevant estate, and will confer owner's powers onto the registered proprietor;
> 3. The priority rules in the LRA 2002 will 'kick in' so that disputes between a registered estate-holder, and a third party, will be regulated by the registration system. This effect is explained in chapter 15.

5.3 ERRORS ON THE REGISTER

However, the register is not always error-free. The rules relating to errors on the register, broadly defined, have proved to be the most problematic and controversial of the 2002 Act regime. In many ways this is testament to the high quality of the legislation as it only encounters problems in its operation, effectively, where there is a problem off-register. Fraud, forgery, the need to rectify documents, or land registry operational errors all make the register, in some sense, inaccurate. However, the way in which the LRA 2002 deals with these errors is not entirely satisfactory. There is a proposed bill from the Law Commission which aims to alter some aspects of the LRA to make the process of dealing with such errors more in line with the overall aims of land registration.

5.3.1 THE SYSTEM OF ALTERATION AND RECTIFICATION IN OUTLINE

The first step in working one's way through these debates is to understand, in very simple terms, what the scheme introduced by the LRA 2002 is, and how it was *supposed* to operate. We have already outlined what will happen when there are no errors on the register. According to the Act, any person with title is guaranteed to have that title and to be able to deal with that title for as long as they remain registered. This is the fundamental principle of title by registration. However, the Act accepts that errors may arise in relation to the register. As such, there is provision for the register to be changed, and guaranteed titles to be removed, against the consent of their proprietor. This can happen in two ways: alteration, and rectification.[5] Alterations will happen where the

[5] LRA 2002, schedule 4, paras 1 and 2.

register needs to change because it has become out of date (amongst other reasons).[6] The classic example of this would be where title is held as joint tenants and one of the joint tenants dies. In such a situation the register is wrong because of events off-register. If there is an alteration of the register, then no indemnity will be available to anyone who loses out as a result of the alteration. This is based upon the understanding that there are few circumstances in which alterations are made where there would be any loss since events off-register mean that the change to title merely reflects what has already happened.

Rectifications, on the other hand, are possible when two conditions are met. First, there must be a mistake on the register.[7] Second, the rectification of that mistake must be capable of having an adverse affect on a registered proprietor.[8] If these are conditions are met, then the additional rules relation to the rectification of the register come into play. Where rectification is possible, the court is able to order a rectification of the register but its discretion in so-doing is a directed discretion. As the rectification may prejudicially affect a proprietor in possession of land, then the register cannot be rectified unless that proprietor caused or contributed to the mistake by their own fraud or lack of proper care, or where it would be unjust otherwise not to rectify the register.[9] If the proprietor is not in possession, then the court (or registrar) will rectify as long as there are no exceptional circumstances.[10] Whether or not the register is in fact rectified, the *ability* to rectify triggers the ability for an indemnity to be granted to someone who loses out as a result of the decision to (or not to) rectify.[11] If an indemnity is available, then the claimant will be entitled to the value of what they have lost, as long as they did not contribute to their loss through their own fraud or lack of proper care.[12] If they did so contribute, then the amount of indemnity available would be reduced accordingly. The indemnity is paid by the land registry, as part of what is effectively a state-sponsored insurance system for the quality of titles to land. However, the registry is able to attempt to recover the cost of the indemnity from third parties if it is as a result of the behaviour of the third party that the mistake came about in the first place.[13]

> **Summary: Changes to the register**
>
> The land register can be changed in two ways, alterations and rectifications.
>
> 1. Alterations can be made where the register is out of date, to correct a mistake, or to give effect to a right exempted from the effect of registration.
> 2. Rectifications can be made where there is a mistake on the register, and correction of that mistake would prejudicially affect the title of a registered proprietor.

---

[6] LRA 2002, schedule 4, paras 2.
[7] LRA 2002, schedule 4, para 1(a).
[8] LRA 2002, schedule 4, para 1(b).
[9] LRA 2002, schedule 4, para 3(2).
[10] LRA 2002, schedule 4, para 3(3).
[11] LRA 2002, schedule 8, para 1.
[12] LRA 2002, schedule 8, para 5.
[13] LRA 2002, schedule 8, para 10.

On paper this system works well. However, the difficulties which have emerged have done so because there is no commitment in the registration system as to whether what is being established is indefeasible or defeasible title, and if the former, whether this is immediate or deferred indefeasibility. Indefeasible title is title which cannot be challenged once registered. Very few systems, if any, have a system of total indefeasibility. However, some systems provide for title which can be questioned only in cases where there is fraud, for example. Other systems introduced deferred indefeasibility, which makes the original transferee's title questionable in cases where there is a flaw in a transfer, but makes any subsequent transferees safe, even sometimes in cases of fraud. There is no expression in the LRA 2002 as to when, if ever, title becomes indefeasible in this way. For that reason it appears that the section 58 guarantee of title does not in fact give rise to total protection or indeed to guarantee of title in any meaningful sense. If that title is ultimately undermined by fraud or some other vitiating factor, since the guarantee is always affected by the off-register position, then the title is not guaranteed. This fundamental lack of commitment within the legislation has led to what is essentially a mess in the case law. This mess has been extensively scrutinised within the literature. To understand the current case law however, and the multitude of academic responses to the problems, it is necessary to begin with discussion of how errors can arise in relation to the register.

5.3.2 TYPES OF REGISTRATION ERROR

We begin with an attempt to categorise errors which can emerge in relation to the land register.

First, it is possible for such errors to arise *entirely* due to the fault of a land registry official, eg a misreading of a document, a typographical error, or the input of faulty information. We can call this error type 1(a). This kind of mistake appears to be rare, and is fairly easy to deal with as long as no subsequent transactions have taken place. The position is made more complicated where a variation on this kind of error emerges and the wrongly registered person then transacts with the land, so as to sell it onto a third person, to grant a mortgage in relation to it, and the like. This is error type 1(b). In both of these cases, the 'responsible party' is the land registry:

- Error type 1(a): land registry error, no onwards transfer
- Error type 1(b): land registry error, onwards transfer

Second, it is possible for such an error to arise where a transfer of property is void. Such cases might emerge because a transfer is a forgery, or because the transaction was void for mistake. In this case, error type 2(a) is defined by a situation where the person now registered ought not to be registered because the transfer *to them* was void. It may be that this is their fault, or they may be an innocent 'victim' of the void transaction and is referred to in the literature very often as the classic 'A-B' situation. Error type 2(b) emerges where the person registered by mistake then transacts with the land, be that innocently or with knowledge of the error, so that a third party, C, now appears on the register, either as proprietor of the estate in question, or with a mortgage, lease, etc. This situation is sometimes referred to as the A-B-C scenario:

- Error type 2(a): void transaction, no onwards transfer
- Error type 2(b): void transaction, onwards transfer

Third, it is possible for an error to arise where a transfer of property is *voidable* and has now been rescinded. To refer to this type of error as a 'mistake' is problematic—both in theory and in terms of the case law as discussed later—but it is part of the package of 'registrations in error' and it is useful to consider it here. Again, this can be split into error type 3(a) where the person entitled to rescind the transfer is the current registered proprietor, or where the current proprietor transacted with another who is able to rescind the contract, and type 3(b) where the registered proprietor has created a further transaction in relation to the title, which has been subsequently registered. In both of these situations, the 'victim' who is entitled to rescind the transaction may opt rather to continue with the contract. In such cases, the register will be entirely accurate:

- Error type 3(a): voidable transaction, no onwards transfer, attempt to rescind the transaction
- Error type 3(b): voidable transaction, onwards transfer, attempt to rescind the transaction

Fourth, it is possible for errors to arise where there is no transaction at all. Rather, the land registry has wrongly responded to some other form of documentation which does not demonstrate what it claims to demonstrate. This could arise, for example, where the land registry is sent a certificate from a bailiff's company confirming that a lease has been forfeited by a landlord (see chapter 10 at 10.5.3), or where a person claims that they are entitled to be registered as a result of adverse possession, but where the claims made in the application form are false, either deliberately or otherwise. Into this category as well we can perhaps put cases where there is a valid transaction, but it is not between the registered proprietor and another person, but between two strangers to the property. This could be the result of a transaction created by an agent, which is not binding upon the principal, where it is the principal that is the registered proprietor. The transaction in such cases is not void, it is just not a transaction involving the proprietor of the land. Such a situation can involve no onwards transfer (4(a)), or a subsequent transfer (4(b)):

- Error type 4(a): documentation error, no onwards transfer
- Error type 4(b): documentation error, onwards transfer

Finally, errors can arise on the register where the land registry has correctly responded to the paperwork as sent to them, but that paperwork itself contains an error and is susceptible to being rectified. This is not a situation involving a void or voidable transaction. Rather, it is a situation where the documentary evidence of what was agreed contained errors. There is, in such cases, a valid and enforceable agreement. An example could include a deed granting a lease where the term of that lease is wrongly recorded. Another example would be a case where a mortgage deed failed to specify the correct sum due on the mortgage. In such a case, when the document itself is rectified to reflect what the parties genuinely intended at the time of the transaction, the register may become inaccurate through its reflection of the original documentation. Again, this could be of the type (a) variety, where no further transaction has taken place, or of the type (b) variety where, for example, the lease in question has been assigned and the assignee believes that they are entitled to the 100-year lease which appeared in the original documents, rather than the 10-year lease which was intended:

- Error type 5(a): documentation susceptible to rectification, no onwards transfer, documentation is rectified
- Error type 5(b): documentation is susceptible to rectification, onwards transfer, documentation is rectified

In errors type 2-5, the error did not *originate* with the land registry, but rather from the 'real world' transactions. We may question, therefore, what the availability of an indemnity from the registry means in such situations in terms of the overall principles driving the land registration system. Errors of the type (a) variety tend to be theoretically easy to solve. This is the case even though there are difficult questions to answer in terms of how we should compensate anyone who loses out as a result of such a transaction, and how we decide whether A or B should be entitled to be the registered proprietor. However, errors of the type (b) variety are hugely problematic. There are usually at least two innocent parties, one of whom will certainly lose out, as well as there being the additional 'complication' of a guaranteed registration. In such situations, although the land registry as an administrative body may not be at fault, there is a reliance on what the register provides. That reliance is entirely justified in the context of what the register promises, ie guaranteed title with the registered proprietor entitled to exercise their owner's powers.

Fundamentally, the LRA 2002 does not handle happily the type (b) errors. In working out a resolution to type (b) errors, the case law has also had fundamental impacts on the ways in which type (a) errors are resolved. A complex web of case law has emerged, which although not openly inconsistent, is at least challenging to resolve and is premised upon conflicting policy goals.

We now work through the different solutions, without suggesting that any one solution is preferable to any other. As will be seen in the further analysis boxes, however, bringing a 'neutral' perspective to these questions is difficult. We can see this even if we consider the cartographical exercise earlier. Some authors would draw these categories differently and would consider that some of these were not instances of registration error at all. This means that reading about this issue in the academic literature can be very difficult. Often authors who disagree are disagreeing not about result, but about the 'route' by which a result can be achieved, or suggest that one case can stand for three or four different and potentially conflicting points of law. This is not a criticism of those writing and thinking about this issue—I am as much part of this—but rather it is to say that if you read something which appears to be at odds with what is written here it does not necessarily mean that either you have not understood what the textbook is saying, nor does it mean that the other author is wrong, nor that the textbook is wrong! Rather, this is an area in which there are many different possible interpretations, and no clear-cut answers.

5.3.3 THE STATUTORY FRAMEWORK

The starting point for working through these issues is the statutory framework. Section 58 LRA 2002 guarantees the validity of registered titles, and sections 23 and 24 confer power to deal with that title onto such registered proprietors. Schedule 4 then explains the circumstances in which the register can be changed, and schedule 8 explains the indemnities from the land registry which may be given on the occasion of such change.

> Schedule 4:
>
> 'Introductory
>
> 1 In this Schedule, references to rectification, in relation to alteration of the register, are to alteration which—
>
> (a) involves the correction of a mistake, and
>
> (b) prejudicially affects the title of a registered proprietor.'

The definition of rectification given in this paragraph is essential. Rectification is an alteration where there is both a mistake, and a prejudicial effect on the title of a registered proprietor.

> 'Alteration pursuant to a court order
>
> 2(1) The court may make an order for alteration of the register for the purpose of—
>
> (a) correcting a mistake,
>
> (b) bringing the register up to date, or
>
> ...'

This paragraph, which defines alteration, first emphasises that the correction of a mistake is an alteration in itself, which, in accordance with paragraph 1, becomes a rectification where that alteration has a prejudicial effect on a registered proprietor. The most common form of alteration is under subparagraph b, however, as this allows for changes to the register when circumstances in real life render the register inaccurate, such as the death of a co-owner or, as we shall see, the rescission of a voidable transaction.

> '3(2) If alteration affects the title of the proprietor of a registered estate in land, no order may be made under paragraph 2 without the proprietor's consent in relation to land in his possession unless—
>
> he has by fraud or lack of proper care caused or substantially contributed to the mistake, or
>
> it would for any other reason be unjust for the alteration not to be made.'

This paragraph effectively institutes a presumption in favour of a proprietor in possession. Where there is a rectifiable mistake, if that proprietor is in possession, then correction should not be made without the proprietor's consent unless either they contributed to the mistake, or it would be unjust not to rectify. This presumption in favour of the proprietor in possession is, in practice, a weak one, as we shall see.

> '(3) If in any proceedings the court has power to make an order under paragraph 2, it must do so, unless there are exceptional circumstances which justify its not doing so.'

This is essentially a counter-presumption, meaning that in cases where there is a registered proprietor not in possession, or where it would be unjust not to rectify, then unless exceptional circumstances are present, the register should be rectified.

> 'Rectification and derivative interests
>
> 8 The powers under this Schedule to alter the register, so far as relating to rectification, extend to changing for the future the priority of any interest affecting the registered estate or charge concerned.'

This paragraph effectively provides that where the register is rectified, the court is empowered to make adjustments to the priorities between competing rights when ordering that rectification. Quite what 'adjustments' means here was unclear prior to the decision in *Gold Harp*.[14] We now know that in cases involving mistaken de-registration, for example, it means that the courts are able to ensure that the right

---

[14] *Gold Harp Properties Ltd v MacLeod* [2014] EWCA Civ 1084, [2015] 1 WLR 1249.

in question has the priority which it ought to have had had no mistake been made, taking account of the date at which the various rights were created.[15]

'Schedule 8 - Indemnities

'Entitlement

1(1) A person is entitled to be indemnified by the registrar if he suffers loss by reason of—

    (a) rectification of the register,

    (b) a mistake whose correction would involve rectification of the register,

…'

This paragraph explains the circumstances in which a person is entitled to an indemnity from the land registry. The power to grant an indemnity is not limited to cases involving mistakes on the register. It can include mistakes made in the process of a register search, and the like. However, the most contentious aspect of this provision has been the link made between the recovery of loss and either the rectification of the register, or the existence of a mistake which would involve rectification where the court or registrar has exercised their discretion not to rectify notwithstanding the existing of the mistake.

'(2) For the purposes of sub-paragraph (1)(a)—

    (a) any person who suffers loss by reason of the change of title under section 62 is to be regarded as having suffered loss by reason of rectification of the register, and

    (b) the proprietor of a registered estate or charge claiming in good faith under a forged disposition is, where the register is rectified, to be regarded as having suffered loss by reason of such rectification as if the disposition had not been forged.

(3) No indemnity under sub-paragraph (1)(b) is payable until a decision has been made about whether to alter the register for the purpose of correcting the mistake; and the loss suffered by reason of the mistake is to be determined in the light of that decision.'

This paragraph highlights that the question as to whether the register is going to be rectified is logically prior to the question of the availability of an indemnity. This much is obvious, not least because usually it will be different people who lose out when the register is rectified and when it is not.

'…

Claimant's fraud or lack of care

5(1) No indemnity is payable under this Schedule on account of any loss suffered by a claimant—

    (a) wholly or partly as a result of his own fraud, or

    (b) wholly as a result of his own lack of proper care.

(2) Where any loss is suffered by a claimant partly as a result of his own lack of proper care, any indemnity payable to him is to be reduced to such extent as is fair having regard to his share in the responsibility for the loss.

…'

---

[15] *Gold Harp Properties Ltd* v MacLeod [2014] EWCA Civ 1084, [2015] 1 WLR 1249, [96].

This paragraph emphasises that in cases where an indemnity is available to a claimant, it will nevertheless be reduced in cases where the claimant is somehow at fault in the existence of the mistake on the register, or in the scale of their loss.

> 'Valuation of estates etc.
>
> 6 Where an indemnity is payable in respect of the loss of an estate, interest or charge, the value of the estate, interest or charge for the purposes of the indemnity is to be regarded as not exceeding—
>
>   (a) in the case of an indemnity under paragraph 1(1)(a), its value immediately before rectification of the register (but as if there were to be no rectification), and
>
>   (b) in the case of an indemnity under paragraph 1(1)(b), its value at the time when the mistake which caused the loss was made.'

This paragraph gives guidance in terms of determining the size of an indemnity. It is clear that the indemnity cannot exceed the value of the estate. This is potentially problematic, as can be seen in cases like *Barclays Bank v Guy*[16] later where the mistake on the register consists in the registration of a charge where the sums lent may vastly outstrip the value of the land. In such a case, even if the claimant did not contribute to their own loss in any way, they may not receive full compensation. The paragraph also gives guidance as to the value date and timing, as well as 'fictions' employed in order to value the estate in question.

> '...
>
> Recovery of indemnity by registrar
>
> 10(1) Where an indemnity under this Schedule is paid to a claimant in respect of any loss, the registrar is entitled (without prejudice to any other rights he may have)—
>
>   (a) to recover the amount paid from any person who caused or substantially contributed to the loss by his fraud, or
>
> ...'

This paragraph provides that the registry is able to recover the costs of an indemnity from third parties, where appropriate.

5.3.4 THE FRAMEWORK IN PRACTICE

These statutory provisions, although lengthy, do not set up a complicated scheme. The premise is simple. Where the register contains a mistake, if removal of that mistake does not prejudicially affect anyone, then the register should be changed, and no indemnity given. If the change to the register *will* affect someone, then the register should only be changed against that person, if they are in possession, if they either caused or contributed to the mistake themselves, or there is a reason based in justice why it should be changed. In such a case, however, given the prejudice caused, the title-holder will receive an indemnity from the land registry. If there are no reasons based in justice why the register should be changed, then another person may be entitled to an

---

[16] *Barclays Bank v Guy* [2008] EWCA Civ 452, [2008] 2 EGLR 74.

indemnity. This is a carefully thought through scheme, *but*, it does not cover all eventualities, Most importantly of all, there is no statutory definition of mistake. It is with this omission that the difficulties started. We explore this by, first, looking at the history of the case law to determine how the current position has come to be. Second, we examine the current solutions to the error types identified earlier, and third, we explore how these solutions affect our overall understanding of what sort of land registration system the LRA 2002 establishes by returning to the academic commentary.

5.3.4.1 Understanding the history

The starting point for the difficulties emerging was the decision in *Barclays Bank v Guy*,[17] and the 'revelation' in that case that the word 'mistake' defined not only the availability of rectification of the register, but also of indemnity. This linking together means that the scope of the power to rectify the register also defines when compensation is available from the land registry. The problems that this link causes can be seen all too clearly from the facts of *Guy*.

> **Key case:** *Barclays Bank v Guy (no 1)* [2008] EWCA Civ 452
>
> This case involved 48 acres of development land in Manchester. The land was originally acquired by Trevor Guy. In 2004, there was an agreement between Mr Guy and Ten Acres Ltd for the sale of the land, for £15,000,000. Consequent upon this, Ten Acres Ltd became registered proprietors of the land. However, this company was under the control of a fraudster. In fact, Ten Acres later went into liquidation without having paid the purchase price. In 2005, Ten Acres executed a charge in favour of Barclays and this charge was duly registered. Sums due under the charge exceeded £100,000,000. Mr Guy claimed that the transfer was the result of a fraud, and that it should be overturned and title to the land returned to him. He also alleged that he had priority over the bank's charge. The bank, by contrast, seeking to realise its security, wanted to sell the land.
>
> The Court of Appeal proceeded on the basis that Mr Guy had at least an arguable case that the transfer was indeed void. As such, it was clear that the transfer to Ten Acres was invalid. Had matters rested there, Mr Guy would have regained title, and all would have been well. However, as the Court of Appeal acknowledged, the subsequent dealings with Barclays meant that the guarantee of title in section 58 was engaged. Thus, 'the register is conclusive, subject only to its rectification pursuant to the provisions of the Act itself'.[18]
>
> When these provisions are examined, the Court of Appeal reasoned, it becomes clear that any change to the register in respect of Barclays' charge would be a rectification because it would adversely affect their title. As a result, in order to allow rectification, it would be necessary to show that there was a mistake on the register. The dilemma that the court faced in this respect is neatly encapsulated in the words of Lloyd LJ:
>
>> 'What Mr Guy would have to show is that the order for the removal of the charge from the Register could be made for the purposes of correction a mistake. He therefore has to show that the registration of the

---

[17] *Barclays Bank v Guy* [2008] EWCA Civ 452, [2008] 2 EGLR 74.
[18] *Barclays Bank v Guy* [2008] EWCA Civ 452, [2008] 2 EGLR 74, [9].

charge was a mistake. I can see that he could well arguably show that the registration of the original transfer was a mistake. There is no question of that kind as regards the charge. It was properly executed by Ten Acre Limited. It is in proper form and there is nothing intrinsically wrong with it. What is wrong with it, according to Mr Guy, is that Ten Acre Limited did not have good title to the land itself. It's title was subject to rectification on the part of Mr Guy'.[19]

However, the effect of section 58 is to say clearly that there was nothing wrong with Ten Acre's title at the time of the registration of the charge. Thus, in respect of the charge itself, per Lloyd LJ again,

'I cannot see that it is arguable that the registration of the charge can be said to have been a mistake, or the result of a mistake... I simply cannot see how it could be argued that if the purchaser or charge knows nothing of the problem underlying the intermediate owner's title, that the registration of the charge or sale to the ultimate purchaser or charge can be said to be a mistake.'[20]

The tone of the comments of Lloyd LJ have shaped the land registration debate since this case. The distinction alluded to in the case between void and voidable transfers, and the analysis of the consequence of the conclusivity of the register, have proved difficult to undermine despite the unsatisfactory (in many ways) outcome of this case.

However, the judgment itself, despite being in the Court of Appeal, was not of binding force, as it was a permission to appeal case. This allowed other courts to take a different approach to these questions. However, the Court of Appeal got another opportunity to comment on the statutory provisions in *Barclays Bank v Guy (no 2)*,[21] in a case concerned with the analysis of reopening permissions to appeal. This second case (*Guy no 2*), being a practice direction, is not binding on subsequent courts either in respect of the law in relation to land registration. The comments made by the court are nevertheless a useful element in understanding what followed.

> **Key case:** *Barclays Bank v Guy (no 2)* [2010] EWCA Civ 1396
>
> Here, Lord Neuberger MR explored what was meant by mistake in this context, and why that was proving problematic in case law terms:
>
> 'There is no doubt that, under the provisions of the Land Registration Act 2002, registration is normally conclusive... However, paragraph 2(1)(a) of Schedule 4 of the Act enables the court to [rectify in cases of mistake]... The central issue is, therefore, whether Mr Guy could get the registration of the bank's charge... removed under the provisions of this paragraph. This issue can fairly be said to turn on whether the concept of "correcting a mistake" is given a wide or a narrow meaning'.[22]

---

[19] *Barclays Bank v Guy* [2008] EWCA Civ 452, [2008] 2 EGLR 74, [19].
[20] *Barclays Bank v Guy* [2008] EWCA Civ 452, [2008] 2 EGLR 74, [23].
[21] *Barclays Bank v Guy (no 2)*, [2010] EWCA Civ 1396, [2011] 1 WLR 681.
[22] *Barclays Bank v Guy (no 2)*, [2010] EWCA Civ 1396, [2011] 1 WLR 681, [16]-[17].

> This comment makes it clear that the definition of mistake is critical, emphasising the problems caused by the absence of such a definition within the statute itself.
>
> Lord Neuberger then went onto analyse what the alternative conceptualisations of this dispute may be. He highlighted that:
>
>> 'there are other ways of putting Mr Guy's case, namely (a) that the removal of his name from the proprietorship register was a mistake and, in order to correct that mistake, the charge would have to be removed from the charges register, or (b) that the registration of the charge flowed from the mistake of registering the transfer, and therefore should be treated as part and parcel of that mistake'.[23]
>
> These two options (that the removal of the charge was necessary to correct a mistake, or that the charge itself was part of the original mistake), have both appeared in different forms in the case law which follows. In effect, in this case though, Neuberger MR is departing from the approach of Lloyd LJ. He thinks that the position within the statutory provisions is perhaps less clear-cut than appeared in the earlier judgment. However, in terms of result, nothing changed here for Mr Guy.

The consequence of the decision in *Guy* was that Trevor Guy, who had lost his land perhaps as a result of being somewhat naïve, but certainly not through fraudulent activity of his own, was left with the option of either regaining title to the land, but without the availability of any indemnity, or not regaining the land. This was problematic. If he regained the land, that land would still be subject to the charge and so in the very likely event that Guy was unable to pay Barclays the sums due, he would lose the land to Barclays. Without an indemnity, the land was effectively worthless. In deciding that he was not entitled to an indemnity, the Court of Appeal highlighted the consequences of linking together the ability to rectify and the ability to obtain compensation for loss should something go wrong with the registration process.

It is useful to highlight at this point, however, that as unpalatable a result as this is for Guy, the land registry was not in fact complicit in *his* loss. Guy lost money as a result of entering into a transaction with a fraudster. The land register intervention comes into the picture only by guaranteeing Ten Acres' title for the purposes of the grant of the charge to Barclays. In this way, whilst Barclays had relied upon the guarantee of title expressed in the register, Guy had not. This consideration may not change what we consider the right result in this case, but it is an important factor in how the law in this area develops.

Following the decision in *Guy*, there were a number of decisions made by what was the Adjudicator to the Land Registry, and what is now the First Tier Tribunal (Property Chamber) which developed the jurisprudence in a variety of different ways.[24] Much of that case law has now been superseded by developments in the High Court and Court of Appeal. Nevertheless, it is important to appreciate that the general tenor of this case law was a muddled one. No consensus emerged in respect of how mistake should be defined.

---

[23] *Barclays Bank v Guy (no 2)*, [2010] EWCA Civ 1396, [2011] 1 WLR 681, [35].
[24] See *Paton v Todd* [2012] EWHC 1248 (Ch); *Ajibade v Bank of Scotland & Endeavor Personal Finance* HM Land Adjudicator, REF/2006/0163/0174; *Odogwu v Vastguide* [2009] EWHC 3565 (Ch); and *Stewart v Lancashire Mortgage Corp* HM Land Adjudicator, REF/2009/0086 and 1556.

The most important decision to come from the adjudicator, however, is that in *Knights Construction v Roberto Mac*.[25] This decision is significant because although not binding itself, it has been given strong support in the leading Court of Appeal case in *Gold Harp v McLeod*.[26] It is, for the moment at least, generally considered to represent that law on the question of rectification of the register in cases involving type (b) errors.

> **Key case:** *Knights Construction v Roberto Mac* REF/2009/1459, [2011] 2 EGLR 123
>
> This case concerned a rectangle of land behind an old Salvation Army (SA) chapel in March. The deeds relating to ownership of this land had been destroyed during bombing in WWII. In 2007, the SA considered selling the chapel and so applied for voluntary first registration. The plan submitted to the registry in this application included the disputed land. The SA were then entered as proprietors of the land on the register albeit that this should not have happened. The SA had not been in possession of this land and never had title to it. In 2009 the SA sold the land to Roberto Mac, which then became registered title-holder.
>
> In resolving whether title should be registered in favour of Knights Construction (the true owner) or remain with Roberto Mac, HM Adjudicator began by highlighting that whether or not the Salvation Army should have had title, they certainly did have title as soon as they were registered as a result of section 58.[27] This reference to the conclusivity of section 58 is important.
>
> The next step in Deputy Adjudicator Michael Mark's approach was to highlight that if the mistake had come to light prior to the transfer to Roberto Mac, there would have been no problem. This would have been because Knights Construction would have had a, 'cast iron case for alteration of the register. There was a plain mistake, there were no exceptional circumstances, and the rectification provisions in paragraph 6 of Schedule 4 to the 2002 Act would not have applied as... [the SA] were not in possession of that land'.[28]
>
> However, the further transaction had taken place, and this made the situation much more difficult in registration terms. Furthermore, an additional consideration in the adjudicator's approach was the consequences of a finding their neither rectification nor indemnity were available. Per Michael Mark:
>
>> 'There was a potential problem as to the relationship between the provisions as to rectification and those as to indemnity, in that in one construction of the provisions, a party might end up without the land or an indemnity as a result solely of the provisions of the 2002 Act, although wholly without fault. I was concerned as to a possible conflict in this respect both between the losing party in the future and the Land Registry, and, if the result of the 2002 Act was that an innocent party lost its property without qualifying to obtain an indemnity under Schedule 8, between the legislation as so interpreted and Article 1 of Protocol 1 of the Human Rights Convention'.[29]
>
> This emphasis on the fact that the linking of mistake and rectification could have the effect of depriving a person of property without their being entitled to compensation is critical to the generous interpretation of mistake which has been adopted by the courts here.

---

[25] *Knights Construction v Roberto Mac* REF/2009/1459, [2011] 2 EGLR 123.
[26] *Gold Harp Properties Ltd v MacLeod* [2014] EWCA Civ 1084, [2015] 1 WLR 1249.
[27] *Knights Construction v Roberto Mac* REF/2009/1459, [2011] 2 EGLR 123, [39].
[28] *Knights Construction v Roberto Mac* REF/2009/1459, [2011] 2 EGLR 123, [40].
[29] *Knights Construction v Roberto Mac* REF/2009/1459, [2011] 2 EGLR 123, [61].

> Michael Mark then made an extensive survey of the policies as expressed in the Law Commission report, and in land registry guidance. He was seeking to ascertain what the intention of the drafters of the legislation was in cases such as this, where there was a flaw in a chain of conveyances, but where the conclusivity of title provisions in the 2002 Act had, to a certain extent, intervened. He reasoned that the Law Commission and land registry reports all demonstrated that the intention had not been to remove the ability of a party in the position of Knights Construction to recover their land. Furthermore, there was no clear indication in the case law leading up to this case what the right answer should be. Rather, there were a number of decisions, from the Adjudicator, the High Court, and the Court of Appeal in the all of which pointed in different directions. The analysis of these conflicting approaches is careful and thorough. Having reviewed this material, Michael Mark concluded:
>
> 'There are various ways of approaching the construction of paragraph 2(1)(a) of Schedule 4 to the 2002 Act... I am satisfied that I can and should construe the provision in a manner which gives effect to the intention of the Law Commission in its Bill and which ensures that where a person is deprived by legislation of property to which they would otherwise have title, then they should be compensated appropriately at least if they are not at fault. That is so whether the person deprived is the original owner or the subsequent purchaser of registered land who finds that his title has been removed by rectification, and where her or not there is an error as to the amount of land included in the title... Schedule 4 and Schedule 8 need to be read together for this purpose.
>
> I am therefore satisfied that the remedy of rectification is available in the present case to Knights Construction. It would be so available whether, adapting the two possible interpretations suggested by Lord Neuberger, (a) the original registration of the Salvation Army was a mistake, and, in order to correct that mistake, which here persists, the register should be corrected by removing this part of the land, which should never have been registered at all, from the title, or (b) that the registration of Roberto Mac as proprietor of the land flowed from the mistake of including the land in the original title, and therefore should be treated as part and parcel of that mistake'.[30]

In this case, therefore, the adjudicator was clear that in type (b) cases, whether or not C's registration is a mistake in itself, or a consequence of a mistake, C's interest should be removed from the register. In order to correct the mistake of registering title with B, C's interest would have to be removed. In effect, this interpretation results in a 'flaw' in the chain of conveyancing rendering subsequent registrations susceptible to being rectified off the register without limit. This is hugely significant. It would not have been the case in unregistered land that there was no limit to the scope of registration thanks to the adverse possession provisions as considered in chapter 6.

The decision in *Knights Construction*,[31] therefore, whether right or wrong as an interpretation of the LRA 2002, almost certainly leads to the Law Commission reforms which we discuss later in this chapter. It also acts as a framework within which the courts have developed solutions to the other types of land registration error which were mapped out above.

---

[30] *Knights Construction v Roberto Mac* REF/2009/1459, [2011] 2 EGLR 123, [131]-[132].
[31] *Knights Construction v Roberto Mac* REF/2009/1459, [2011] 2 EGLR 123.

5.3.4.2 The law as it now stands

As explained above, understanding the history of the debate surrounding the LRA 2002, a debate which is only around 8 years old, is necessary to allow a full appreciation of the shape of the academic literature, whist also explaining the nature of the current reforms. It does not necessarily assist in explaining what the law *is* now. This section will consider what the law currently does in response to the error types explained earlier.

Error type 1—pure land registry error (a) and (b)

In a pure land registry error case, in (a) situations, the answer is simple. Title will be rectified unless circumstances are such that the court relies upon the presumption in favour of the proprietor in possession to decide *not* to rectify the register notwithstanding the fact that as a matter of conveyancing history, the register is now 'wrong'. In such cases, the original registered proprietor, or, in cases of first registration, the paper title-holder will be entitled to an indemnity if the register is not rectified in their favour. In cases where the register is rectified, then the mistaken registered proprietor, now removed, will be entitled to an indemnity. In such cases, the statute is effectively applied as written.

In type 1(b) cases, ie where the land registry error has not been spotted before land was subsequently transferred to a third party, then as we have seen above, the position appears to be dictated by the decision in *Knights Construction v Roberto Mac*.[32] The register will indeed be rectified, along with any subsequently registered rights (although we do not know how 'far back' such a rectification chain may go), unless there is some reason why it would be unjust to rectify the register in such a case if the mistaken registered proprietor happens to be in possession. This is not a straightforward meaning of the statute and requires either an extended reading of 'mistake', so that the subsequent onwards transfer is characterised *itself* as a mistake, or an extended reading of 'correcting' a mistake. The case law has not committed itself to one or other of these positions.

A difficult position can now emerge, however, not where there is a subsequent onwards transfer per se, but in terms of trying to decide what a registered proprietor, not in fact entitled to be registered on the basis of the conveyancing situation, 'has' during the currency of their registration. This issue came to the fore in *Parshall v Hackney*,[33] (see later), a case which raises the issue of so-called 'double' registrations. This case also highlights that once we have made a determination that in error type 1(a) cases, the practical presumption is in favour of the original proprietor, and in type 1(b) situations, that the removal of later parties down the chain is likely, we have also, deliberately or otherwise, made a decision about where the principles of unregistered conveyancing sit within our land registration system, and as to the quality of the titles that thereby emerge.

---

[32] *Knights Construction v Roberto Mac* REF/2009/1459, [2011] 2 EGLR 123.
[33] *Parshall v Hackney* [2013] EWCA Civ 240, [2013] Ch 568.

Key case: *Parshall v Hackney* [2013] EWCA Civ 240

In this case, the land registry had, in error, registered two different proprietors as owning the same plot of land. The person entitled to be registered on the basis of the conveyancing history was not in possession of that land. Rather, the mistakenly registered person was in possession. The question for the court was whether these facts involved adverse possession or something else, and if something else, how the position between the two parties was to be resolved.

The court began by assessing the nature of the problems involved in rectification of the register.[34] From here, the focus of the court was first to establish whether this situation could properly be understood as a case of adverse possession. The difficulty with this is, of course, that it is not possible to be in adverse possession of land to which you have paper title. Furthermore, whilst the concept of relativity of possession is critical and central to our understanding of the doctrine of estates in land, in practice it plays second fiddle to the statutory schemes, at the heart of which sits the LRA 2002. In answering this question, Mummery LJ also gave an indication as to his view as to the effect of registration. In an infamous passage, his lordship reasoned:

> 'This is a case of equality of registered titles, rather than the normal case of relativity of titles. The two registered titles co-exist on the register unless and until corrected by rectification. The determination of the question of rectification is logically prior to the determination of the question of possessory title. It has to be decided who was entitled to be registered as proprietor of the disputed land before it can be decided whether the right of the proprietor to recover the disputed land is statute barred. If, for example, the rectification issue regarding registration is resolved in favour of the respondent, the question of the respondent's claim to a possessory title would never arise for determination'.[35]

The key point is the court's assessment as to the possibility of equally valid co-existing freehold titles in relation to the same piece of land, with the rectification provisions being determinative in assessing how the position should be resolved. In cases where the rectification position puts a strong presumption in favour of the proprietor in possession, then the fact that there could be no adverse possession may not have significant consequences in practice. However, as we have seen above, this presumption is very weak, if it exists at all in reality. So, in effect, in cases like this, the determining factor is the off-register position, not the registration of title. The reliance upon registration to prevent adverse possession sits at odds with the overall outcome of this case law taken as a whole. Furthermore, as Kester Lees has argued, it is difficult to see why this case was not treated as being a consequence of the non-conclusive nature of boundaries represented on the register. 'The general boundaries rule provided a quick, simple and easy solution to the dilemma facing the Court of Appeal that would have avoided the unnecessary complication of the dual registration of title in the instant case'.[36]

---

[34] *Parshall v Hackney* [2013] EWCA Civ 240, [2013] Ch 568, [9].
[35] *Parshall v Hackney* [2013] EWCA Civ 240, [2013] Ch 568, [89].
[36] K Lees, '*Parshall v Hackney*: a tale of two titles' [2013] Conv 222, 227.

> **Summary: Error type 1**
>
> Error type 1(a): title will usually be transferred to A, with an indemnity for B.
> Error type 1(b): title will usually be returned to A, with an indemnity for C on the basis either that C's registration was a mistake, or rectification and indemnity would be required to correct the mistaken transfer to B.

Error type 2 cases—void transaction

Where there is an error type 2 case, then the answer appears to be that in almost all cases the register will be rectified so that A regains title to the land, and B receives an indemnity from the land registry for their losses, as long as they did not contribute to the loss themselves. It makes no difference to this that the error originated without rather than within the land registry. This means that in cases of a void transfer, the presumption in favour of the proprietor in possession appears to be a fairly weak presumption. The 'spoken' presumption in the statute is effectively overtaken by an unspoken presumption that relies on the fact that where there is a void transaction the law is reluctant to uphold the consequences of that transaction since it would result in a person losing title without their consent.

1. Error type 2(a)—no trust

We also know after some problematic case law, that there is no trust in such a circumstance (this has significant consequences for the type (b) error discussion later). This issue was considered in *Malory v Cheshire Homes*,[37] and *Fitzwilliam v Richall Holdings*.[38]

> **Key case:** *Malory v Cheshire Homes* [2002] EWCA Civ 151
>
> Malory is one of the most maligned decisions in land law. The case involved Malory Enterprises obtaining, from the land registry, a certificate of title to development land in Manchester. Malory Enterprises was a fraudulent company, set up, in effect, as an imitation of Malory BVI. Malory Enterprises then sold title to the land to Cheshire Homes. However, Malory BVI was in occupation of the relevant land at all material times. The question became the resolution of the dispute between Malory BVI and Cheshire Homes. There was no doubt that the registration of Malory Enterprises was a mistake. The question was how this mistake affected the title of Cheshire Homes.
>
> This decision is made under the 1925 Act. One of the arguments presented by Malory BVI was that it was the beneficiary of a trust, so that upon the wrongful registration of Malory Enterprises, they immediately became trustees of the land for Malory BVI. Then, upon registration of Cheshire Homes' title, Malory BVI's interest under the trust would take priority over Cheshire Homes by virtue of their actual occupation. The Court of Appeal accepted this formulation, reaching two significant conclusions. First, the circumstances of the void application to register would mean that the newly registered proprietor

---

[37] *Malory Enterprises v Cheshire Homes* [2002] EWCA Civ 151, [2002] Ch 216.
[38] *Fitzwilliam v Richall Holdings* [2013] EWHC 86 (Ch), [2013] 1 P & CR 19.

would hold on trust for the benefit of the original proprietor.[39] Second, this trust interest could be binding upon the new registered proprietor. If the first conclusion is correct, then there is little doubt that the second is also correct. However more significantly for the current case law, as we shall see later, the court also held that even if they were wrong with regards to the interest under the trust, that it might be possible for Malory BVI to have an interest which could be protected as overriding as a result of their actual occupation in the form of a right to rectify the register.[40]

This argument is hugely controversial, not least because it is very difficult to explain why a trust would arise in such circumstances.[41] This part of the case has now been overruled by *Swift 1st* which we explain later.

On the second point, which survived *Swift 1st*, Arden LJ explained, when considering the argument that a right to rectify cannot be proprietary because it is discretionary in nature:

> 'a distinction is to be drawn between a right to seek rectification and the fulfilment of that right. The exercise by the court of its discretion is necessary for the fulfilment of the right (and if exercised in a manner which is adverse to the holder will result in extinction of the right) but the exercise by the court of its discretion is not necessary to bring the right into existence… In my judgment, the right to seek rectification to reflect a proprietary interest in land fulfils the criteria approved in *Williams & Glyn's Bank Ltd v Boland* [1981] AC 487, namely that it is a right in reference to land which is capable of transmission through different ownerships of land'.[42]

Although strictly obiter, the conclusion that Arden LJ reaches here does have a certain appeal. As we discuss later, it allows for a relatively subtle approach to type (b) scenarios, where there is an onwards transfer following mistake. The discretion point is however a sound one, and there are certainly some difficulties in justifying a conclusion that the right to rectify can be a property right.

Given that *Malory* was decided under the 1925 Act, and the controversy surrounding the decision, it was perhaps expected that should a decision on the same question be addressed by the courts, that the courts would depart from the approach in *Malory*. However, Newey J in the High Court, although acknowledging the difficulties with *Malory*, felt that the Court of Appeal authority binding upon him could not be distinguished in this case.

Key case: *Fitzwilliam v Richall Holdings* [2013] EWHC 86

Fitzwilliam had been the registered proprietor of a property in London. He had let the property to tenants whose occupation continued until the time of the litigation. In 2008, Fitzwilliam was arrested. Whilst in prison, Mr Fitzwilliam authorised Mr George to manage some of his interests. George (unauthorised) sold the title to Richall Holdings, forging the transfer documents. Richall Holdings became registered proprietor.

---

[39] *Malory Enterprises v Cheshire Homes* [2002] EWCA Civ 151, [2002] Ch 216, [65].
[40] *Malory Enterprises v Cheshire Homes* [2002] EWCA Civ 151, [2002] Ch 216, [67]-[68].
[41] See E Lees, 'Richall Holdings v Fitwilliam: Malory v Cheshire Homes and the LRA 2002' (2013) 76 MLR 924.
[42] *Malory Enterprises v Cheshire Homes* [2002] EWCA Civ 151, [2002] Ch 216, [67]-[68].

The question for the court was whether or not Richall held on trust for Fitzwilliam. This was significant, albeit that unlike in *Malory* above, even if there was no trust in place, there seems little doubt that the registration of Richall was a mistake on the grounds that there was no valid transfer (Mr George not himself becoming registered at any point). Newey J, as mentioned above, reached the conclusion that there was a trust in this case on the basis of the authority in *Malory*. He was of the view that the 2002 Act and the 1925 Act could not sensibly be distinguished. Indeed, that Newey J did not feel particularly enthusiastic about the decision in *Malory* is clear from his extensive citation of the arguments against the result in the case.[43] However, Newey J concluded, '[f]or what it is worth, I can see considerable force in some of the arguments advanced by *Malory's* critics. Whatever merit the criticisms of *Malory* may have, however, I am bound by the decision'.[44]

To say that this decision resulted in academic consternation is something of an understatement.[45] Most commentary focused on three key issues: the bindingness of *Malory*, which most felt could have been distinguished if absolutely necessary, but did feel sympathy with the High Court; the legal justifications for the outcome in *Malory* itself; and finally, the need for this approach to resolve the dispute in *Fitzwilliam* at all, given that it was a type (a) not a type (b) case.

It is not just theoretical issues which caused disquiet to those commenting on the decision, however. The practical outcomes too were hugely problematic. As Dixon explains,

> 'Clearly, whatever decision the court might reach on this, one innocent party is going to suffer, Fitzwilliam if there is no alteration, Richall if there is. But there are, it is submitted, three advantages to this way of looking at the case. First, it upholds the strength of the guarantee of registered title on which the LRA 2002 is based and does not require a purchaser to seek to go behind the register to investigate the validity of the vendor's title. Secondly, it applies the 2002 Act in a simple and straightforward way and avoids an unnecessary and complex diversion into the nature of legal and equitable title and a forensic examination of the meaning of a 'disposition'. Thirdly, and perhaps most importantly, the losing innocent party can claim a full indemnity from the Land Registry, because the counterpart to a strong title register is compensation for those suffering loss thereby. This is a matter apparently ignored in *Fitzwilliam* as the case appears to proceed on the basis that the 'loser' loses everything'.[46]

This is because obtaining an indemnity from the land registry depends upon loss. In cases where a person loses their registered title because the right of another person took priority, then since that right always had priority over them, the change to the register in line with such priority rules would not have resulted in any substantive loss, hence Dixon's comments regarding the loser also losing their indemnity. Indemnities are explained later at 5.3.6.

However, that jurisprudence has now been overtaken to an extent by the decision in *Swift 1st v Chief Land Registrar*.[47] It is critical to note here that in terms of the type (a) cases, the consequence

---

[43] *Fitzwilliam v Richall Holdings* [2013] EWHC 86 (Ch), [2013] 1 P & CR 19, [75].
[44] *Fitzwilliam v Richall Holdings* [2013] EWHC 86 (Ch), [2013] 1 P & CR 19, [76].
[45] See, E Lees, 'Richall Holdings v Fitwilliam: Malory v Cheshire Homes and the LRA 2002' (2013) 76 MLR 924; M Dixon, 'A not so conclusive title register?' (2013) 129 LQR 320; S Gardner, 'Alteration of the register: an alternative view' [2013] Conv 530; E Cooke, 'The register's guarantee of title' [2013] Conv 344. Of these, only Gardner is supportive of the trust analysis.
[46] M Dixon, 'A not so conclusive title register?' (2013) 129 LQR 320, 324–5.
[47] *Swift 1st v Chief Land Registrar* [2015] EWCA Civ 330, [2015] Ch 602.

of *Swift 1st* is to overrule *Fitzwilliam*. In cases of a void transfer from A to B which is subsequently registered, whilst B will be title-holder during the time for which they remain on the register, they will not hold on trust for A. Their title will be subject to the strong likelihood of rectification. For type (b) cases, however, the case raises the possibility of the right to rectify the register itself becoming a proprietary interest which can then be binding upon subsequent transferees. In this sense, whilst *Swift* overturns *Malory* in respect of the generation of the trust, in fact it gives support to the other conclusion in *Malory* regarding rights to rectify.

> **Key case:** *Swift 1st v Chief Land Registrar* [2015] EWCA Civ 330
>
> Registered title in this case remained at all times with Mrs Rani. She occupied this property throughout. However, a fraudster had registered a charge against the property. The charge was clearly a mistake, and there is little doubt that it would have been rectified off the register. However, the difficulty emerged in respect of the valuation of the indemnity. The question was essentially whether this charge, vulnerable as it was to rectification, was ever worth anything. To put this another way, the court was required to assess whether the loss of a void but registered charge was a substantive loss entitling the registered proprietor to compensation from the land registry.
>
> The Court of Appeal concluded that although the charge was valueless, the provisions of the 2002 Act allowed for a 'fictional' value to be created so that an indemnity was available. It was also given the opportunity to assess the 'trust' approach in *Malory* and *Fitzwilliam*. In so doing, it concluded that *Malory* was decided *per incuriam*, and should be overruled. This aspect of the decision has been warmly welcomed.
>
> However, the court in *Swift 1st* also took a wrong turning. Just like *Fitzwilliam*, this is a type 2(a) case. In type 2(a) cases there is the mistaken registration of an interest, and no onwards transfer. Here, the mistaken registration was of Swift 1st's charge, and this charge was not subsequently transferred. However, the court treated the case as though there had been an onwards transfer. They focused on Mrs Rani's actual occupation (for detailed discussed of the effect of actual occupation, see chapter 15 at 15.3.3) as protecting her entitlement to remove the charge from the register. However, this approach makes no sense on the facts, since the right to rectify could only ever have arisen after the registration of the charge.
>
> Furthermore, the court's conclusion that whilst the fact of Mrs Rani's actual occupation rendered the charge worthless, the lender was nevertheless able to obtain an indemnity, creates a strange fictional value approach which is particularly odd given that at no point did the lender rely on register. The court establishes this fictional value through reliance on paragraph 1(2)(b) of Schedule 8. As we shall see, this provides that where an interest is created through a forgery, for the purposes of establishing an indemnity, it is treated as though it were of value. The consequence of the judicial reliance on this section is that cases of forgery are now treated differently when registered than other void transactions (eg transactions void for mistake).

Whatever one's views as to the rightness of the implicit presumption that the most just result is to rectify title and return title to A, whilst giving B compensation from the land registry, the law in type 2(a) cases has the merits of being clear and relatively straightforward to apply. The tone of these cases is that whilst no trust arises, it is almost always justified to 'return' title to the original registered proprietor.

> **Summary: Error type 2(a)**
>
> Error type 2(a): no trust arises, and title is usually returned to A with an indemnity for B.

2. **Error type 2(b)—rights to rectify and presumptions in favour of the original proprietor**

Presumptions in favour of original proprietor—correcting a mistake Despite the relatively settled nature of these rules now, there are still issues to be ironed out. Although we know from *Knights Construction v Roberto Mac*[48] that in order to correct the mistake of registering B, it is necessary to rectify C off the register, and to provide an indemnity 'up the chain' to those who lose out, as a result of *Swift*, we do not always know the *value* of what is lost up the chain. Therefore we do not know whether a substantive indemnity will be forthcoming. Furthermore, the *Knights Construction* line of case law also does not define which step in the chain is the mistake. This matters because, under schedule 8, a person will not be entitled to an indemnity if they contributed to the *mistake* themselves. If the registration of C is not itself a mistake, but merely a consequence of it, does the limitation on personal fault indemnity recovery apply only to B? Finally, it is problematic to simply rely on a very strong presumption that title will be returned to the original proprietor in the type (b) cases. The relative merits between the parties is very finely balanced. C has no control of or knowledge in relation to the transaction between A and B. Indeed, in this sense, in A-B cases, B relies on the *bona fides* of A, and of the soundness of the transaction. In A-B-C cases, C relies on the *register* in terms of needing to deal only with B. In this sense, the position is very different. In such cases C has not only relied upon the seemingly valid transaction between themselves and B. They have done their research into B's *bona fides*, but have also relied on what section 58 has promised, ie that B has title to the land whether or not they ought to have been registered in the first place. In theory, B may have been in a position to discover the void nature of the transaction, but C cannot be in a position to discover that the transfer between A and B was in fact void. The policy concerns in A-B-C situations are much more finely balanced.

Rights to rectify as overriding interests This difficulty in reaching a blanket or even presumed solution (ie A or C) is one of the key reasons as to why there is no clear solution in the law here. The LRA 2002 has not committed to always finding in favour of C. The case law and the academic literature has responded by attempting to create a series of more nuanced solutions or guides to show when the answer should be A and when C. One possibility is to rely on the idea that the resolution between A and C should be one of priorities rather than a question for schedules 4 and 8 LRA 2002. This approach relies on the possibility that A has a proprietary interest in the form

---

[48] There is detailed discussion of these arguments in S Cooper and E Lees, 'Interests, powers and mere equities in modern land law' (2017) 37 OJLS 435.

of a right to rectify the register, which would then form the basis of the priority dispute between A and C.[49]

Deciding on a case-by-case basis An alternative more nuanced approach is simply to allow the courts to examine each situation to determine where the justice in the case lies. This approach has the advantage of being 'honest'—rather than relying on technical property rules to assess when A will win, when C, the courts are explicitly mandated to reach the 'right' result on the facts. Such a 'genuine look' approach has been advocated by Cooper. Instead of using a blanket A or C rule as a proxy for what is likely to be the fairest outcome in any particular case, the law would be better served by attempting to discover what the actual fairest outcome might be. He acknowledges that this would lead to more and lengthier litigation. But, he reasons, given that there are relatively few cases of this type to be considered, the additional burden on the courts is outweighed by the merits of the decisions which will thereby be reached.[50]

The A-B-C situation is therefore not susceptible to a ready answer, either as a matter of case law, or as a matter of policy. Equally, it is difficult to determine a principled and predictable approach which allows for the creation of a sensible middle ground.

> **Further analysis: Is there a middle ground?**
>
> Cooper has considered what is 'really' going in in rectification cases in the sense. He explains the 'poverty' of strict approach in favour of C in terms of its in ability to capture the real nature of land and what property rights mean to those who acquire them. He highlights that a more sensitive and flexible approach to rectification can better encompass such a range of roles, arguing that:
>
> > 'The truncated rectification model [ie prioritising C's claim] would preclude the original owner from recovering the land by rectification proceedings once a mistakenly-entered registered proprietor had made a disposal. It would create a rule that the new acquirer takes all, leaving the former owner to indemnity, without regard to their relative positions. The criticism might be defended by pointing out the availability of indemnity, but that is not accepted here. The idea that land is to be equated with its market value, or indeed any level of monetary substitute, has never entirely dominated property thinking and modern legal developments suggest we are receding from its high water mark. It is, for example, an axiom of human rights that full compensation does not prevent a governmental expropriation from being arbitrary, but must also be strictly justified by public interest. The resurgent critical legal scholarship on "place" has also argued for attentiveness to the physical setting of land as the material basis for human activity and as a concept invested with social meaning, rather than as an abstract, bureaucratic representation of the land as mere spatial volume. Both of these forces suggest that law recognises the importance of land rights as constitutive of unique and important social values. To respect those values, the adjudication of rectification claims should involve an individualized assessment of the relative positions of owner and acquirer'.[51]
>
> To accept such a view, however, requires accepting also that it is in fact possible to find a 'middle ground' which would allow the development of such a fact sensitive framework. Cooper advocates a genuine

---

[49] S Cooper, 'Resolving title conflicts in registered land' (2015) 131 LQR 108.
[50] S Cooper, 'Resolving title conflicts in registered land' (2015) 131 LQR 108, 131.
[51] S Cooper, 'Resolving title conflicts in registered land' (2015) 131 LQR 108, 113–14.

judicial discussion as to where the relative merits of these claims should lie. He acknowledges too however that such would increase litigation cost and time, and is not therefore without its downsides as an approach.

Goymour has also advocated a 'middle road'. She states that:

> 'The third - and preferable - option is to devise a system that integrates the best parts, and avoids the pitfalls, of both the "title by registration" and general property law schemes. This might be achieved by (i) abandoning the artificial, formalist notion that title stems from the Register, and instead rooting title openly in the rules of general property law, whilst also (ii) recognising that the rules of general property law might themselves be modified for registered land cases, to respond to the unique policy concerns raised by the registration system.
>
> Following this route, the rules of general property law would, by default, give title to A in the A-B-C scenario, but be tweaked for registered land cases, to give C the title in certain exceptional circumstances. Neither A nor C would then be favoured in any blanket, abstract fashion; rather the legislature would have the opportunity to define precisely when C should win based on carefully worked-through and openly-discussed policy reasons'.[52]

Again, the appeal of such an approach is clear, but Goymour does not go on to elaborate what the policy reasons might be, and how they would mutually interact.

Thus, arguments for a middle ground run against two problems. The first is a logistical one. The difficulty in adjudicating on these cases will make for lengthy and expensive case law, and the pressures on court time are already such that the legal system is struggling to cope. The second, more significant one in many ways, is that the goal of a middle road is essentially a goal that begs the question: why do we want to have a land registration system in the first place? If the reason for a land registration system is to ensure certainty, transactiblity of land, and security of title for purchasers, then it goes without saying that those are the values that should be prioritised in the resolution of disputes within that system. If however the nature of the disputes is such that we do not want certainty or security, but rather sensitivity to the human cost of such disputes—a perfectly valid response to the difficulty of disputed claims by innocent parties to the same piece of land—then we might ask, however, whether the problem is really that we do not want a system of title by registration in the first place. To put this another way, a sensitive, nuanced and highly flexible approach to resolving disputes between innocent parties in registered land is not just the opposite of having a blanket rule in favour of A or C, it is the opposite of having title by registration.

Summary: Error 2(b)

There are two solutions present in the case law:

i. Either the courts will rectify in line simply with the statute, with a weak presumption in favour of a proprietor in possession almost always 'trumped' by the policy arguments in favour of A. C will be able to obtain an indemnity; or

ii. A is treated as having a proprietary interests in the form of a right to rectify. The register can then be rectified if A was in actual occupation at the time of C's registration. However, *Swift 1st* suggests that in such cases, C will only obtain a substantial indemnity if the registration of B was based on a forgery.

---

[52] A Goymour, 'Mistaken registrations of land: exploding the myth of "title by registration"' (2013) 72 CLJ 617, 650.

Error type 3: voidable transactions

Voidable transactions are, in many ways, even more controversial than the type 2 errors considered above. These are difficult because of how voidable transaction are conceptualised. A voidable transaction is valid until it is made void. That means that it is capable of producing legal effects. A void transaction, by contrast, is said to have no effect. Furthermore, where a transaction is susceptible to being rescinded, it is equally open to the person entitled to rescind to elect to maintain the transaction. As a result, the bringing to the end of the contractual relationship is voluntary.

The poses a problem for the registration system because it is clear that until a transaction is indeed rescinded, registration on the basis of that transaction is not a mistake. It only becomes erroneous once the person elects to rescind the transaction. Furthermore, many people would argue that at the time when the registration takes place, it is not mistaken, and it does not become so because the transaction is later rescinded. Rather, the rescission of the transaction means that the contract *no longer* exists, and as a result, the register is now out of date in that it fails to reflect the *new* state of affairs, ie that there is no longer a valid transaction underpinning the registration.

The ways in which voidable transactions should be handled is considered in *NRAM v Evans*.[53]

> **Key case: *NRAM v Evans* [2017] EWCA Civ 1013**
>
> Mr and Mrs Evans granted a first legal charge in 2004. In 2005 a new loan agreement was reached, acting as a consolidation of debts. However, the charge as it appeared on the register was not altered. A bank employee then applied to the land registry to discharge the charge. That employee was unaware of the 2005 loan and did not appreciate that the charge was intended to secure that loan in place of the first. As a result, the charge was removed, rather than amended.
>
> The court considered how these facts should be accommodated within the alteration and rectification schemes, and concluded that it is important to distinguish between void and voidable transactions. Critically, this is because whilst, in respect of a void transaction, the registrar would not have made an entry had all the facts been known, this will not be the case with voidable transactions. The registration of a voidable transaction is 'correct at the time it is made'.[54]
>
> The result of this was that the court held that there is no mistake, for the purposes of schedule 4, in registering a voidable but not rescinded transaction. In the words of the court:
>
>> 'Such a voidable disposition is valid until it is rescinded and the entry in the register of such a disposition before it is rescinded cannot properly be characterised as a mistake. It may be the case that the disposition was made by mistake but that does not render its entry on the register a mistake, and it is entries on the register with which Schedule is concerned. Nor, so it seems to me, can such an entry become a mistake if the disposition is at some later date avoided. Were it otherwise, the policy of the LRA 2002 that the register should be a complete and accurate statement of the position at any given time would be undermined'.[55]

---

[53] *NRAM v Evans* [2017] EWCA Civ 1013, [2018] 1 WLR 639.
[54] *NRAM v Evans* [2017] EWCA Civ 1013, [2018] 1 WLR 639, [53].
[55] *NRAM v Evans* [2017] EWCA Civ 1013, [2018] 1 WLR 639, [59].

Kester Lees has commented on this decision, arguing that the position with voidable transactions is certainly different from those involving void transactions. He demonstrates in particular that this approach 'feels' appropriate in *NRAM v Evans* itself because the bank, who loses out, was entirely at fault in the error. Why should they be compensated? This will not always be the case however, as transactions will be voidable (rather than void) in cases involving undue influence. As a result, given that rescission in this sense is a prospective rather than a retrospective remedy, the victim of undue influence would be left without recourse. Ultimately, however, Lees concludes, in asking whether the registrar would really to register such 'tainted' transactions if they knew all the facts (and therefore whether or not there was a mistake), that:

> 'Of course, the answer is, and ought to be, a resounding yes. Whilst this may seem harsh in hard cases, it is nonetheless logically coherent and necessary in order to preserve the strength of the title guarantee of the Register. The separate doctrines of duress, undue influence etc. have developed to provide a remedy in the form of rescission; ie setting aside. Until the remedy is claimed and awarded the transaction is valid and so the Registrar must register it. Indeed, the remedy is a discretionary one (albeit to be exercised judicially) and, therefore, it is not for the Registrar to second-guess either a potential claimant (who may prefer to rely upon the document rather than have it set aside) or the court's discretion'.[56]

These comments highlight that in cases involving voidable transactions, as with void transactions considered above, the human cost of a clear and certain answer must be weighed against the merits of such an answer. Again, there is no easy solution here.

Summary: Error type 3

The alteration of the register to reflect the rescission of a voidable transaction is treated as an alteration, not a rectification. No indemnity will be available. It is not clear what the position is in error type 3(b) cases.

Error type 4: misleading documentation

As explained above, however, registration can happen in error even where there has been no transaction of any kind, without this being a pure registry mistake. Examples of this in the case law include the situation where a person has sent in forged documents purporting to show a valid forfeiture of a lease;[57] an application for adverse possession which alleged the relevant degree of factual possession whereas in fact that had been absent;[58] and a situation where a transfer supposedly executed on behalf of a principal by an agent was in fact not binding upon the principal.[59] In such cases, the courts seem happy to simply apply the presumption in the LRA 2002 as explained in that provision. This can be seen most clearly in *Walker v Burton*.[60]

---

[56] K Lees, '*NRAM v Evans*: there are mistakes and mistakes...' [2018] Conv 91, 95–6.
[57] *Gold Harp Properties Ltd v MacLeod* [2014] EWCA Civ 1084, [2015] 1 WLR 1249.
[58] *Baxter v Mannion* [2011] EWCA Civ 120, [2011] 1 WLR 1594.
[59] *Knightsbridge Property Development Corp (UK) Ltd v South Chelsea Properties Ltd* [2017] EWHC 2730 (Ch).
[60] *Walker v Burton* [2013] EWCA Civ 1228, [2014] 1 P & CR 9.

> **Key case:** *Walker v Burton* [2013] EWCA Civ 1228
>
> In this case, the proprietors of a small manor in a village in Yorkshire believed that registration as proprietors of the manor brought with it title to the Ireby Fell, an area of fell-land. They applied to the registry on this basis and were subsequently registered with title to the Fell. The local villagers objected to this registration. On further investigations, it seemed that the Earldom upon which the Burtons had based their claim to the land had in fact fallen into abeyance some centuries earlier, so that they were wrong about their entitlement to the Fell land. Rather, the person truly entitled to be registered appeared to be either the Duchy of Lancaster or the Crown. The Duchy/Crown were not particularly interested in pursuing the claim to the land however, and so the dispute was really between the Burtons and the villagers in respect of this land.
>
> The court concluded that although they were not entitled to be registered, they should be left on the register on the grounds that all the circumstances meant that the presumption in favour of the proprietor in possession in this case should be upheld, and as a result it would not be unjust not to rectify the register. In considering the justice in the case, Mummery LJ highlighted (amongst other reasons), the importance of the fact that the 'true' owner did not particularly wish to recover the land, stating:
>
>> 'First, there was no prospect of anyone else except the Burtons being registered as proprietors of the Fell. On the one hand, while the appellants had standing to make the application to correct the mistake in the Register, they did not have, or even claim to have, title to the Fell. On the other hand, the Crown, which in the submission of the appellants and in the view of the Deputy Judge has a valid title to the Fell, showed (and still shows) no sign of asserting title against the Burtons, or wishing to engage in this dispute. In those circumstances it was a relevant consideration that the Fell should be owned by someone rather than left in limbo with continuing uncertainty about title to it'.[61]

In this case, the apathy of the 'true' owner seemed to weigh quite heavily in the court's considerations, but it will not always be the case that there will be apathy, as we see later in *Gold Harp* for example.[62] However, the approach of the court in *Walker v Burton* creates a problem. It is clear that whilst the court did not exercise its discretion to rectify in this case, that did not mean either that they decided that the Burtons in fact had a conclusive title to the land. Rather, it is possible that if the Crown/Duchy brought an action that the court would re-consider how they used their discretion. The point would probably not be *res judicata* on the grounds that the way that the court's discretion plays out alters according to the identity of the claimant.

How these considerations play out in type (b) scenario becomes apparent from the decision in *Gold Harp*[63] which is now one of the leading Court of Appeal decisions in this area.

---

[61] *Walker v Burton* [2013] EWCA Civ 1228, [2014] 1 P & CR 9, [102].
[62] *Gold Harp Properties Ltd v MacLeod* [2014] EWCA Civ 1084, [2015] 1 WLR 1249.
[63] *Gold Harp Properties Ltd v MacLeod* [2014] EWCA Civ 1084, [2015] 1 WLR 1249.

> **Key case: *Gold Harp v MacLeod* [2014] EWCA Civ 1084**
>
> In this case, the claimants, schoolteachers, had taken respectively a lease each in relation to the top floor of a property. This property was owned freehold by Mr Ralph senior. Seeing the redevelopment potential of the property, Mr Ralph senior wished to evict the claimants, but did not have grounds to do so. As a result, he alleged that they had not paid their rent on time, and proceeded to forfeit, obtaining a certificate from the bailiffs regarding successful regaining of possession. Mr Ralph then applied to the land registry to have the leases removed from the register. Mr Ralph senior then granted a lease to his son, Mr Ralph junior, which was due to last the same length of time exactly as the claimants' leases. Subsequently the wrongful removal of the claimants' leases came to light.
>
> The fact that the removal of the leases was a mistake was straightforward. The land registry removed the leases on the basis of the forfeiture, but since such had not in fact validly taken place, there ought to have been no removal. This part was not difficult. Much more difficult was the question as to relative priorities as between the claimants, and Mr Ralph junior's lease. It was necessary to know which lease had priority in order to determine who was entitled to possession of the land.
>
> This question is made difficult because of two considerations. First, in accepting the lease, Mr Ralph junior, in theory, relied upon the register to demonstrate that there was no legal lease with superior priority, and could have made an inspection of the land to determine whether, for example, there was a person in actual occupation who may have had an equitable lease protected through that occupation. The fact that in the case itself Mr Ralph junior appears to have been somewhat complicit does not alter this theoretical reliance on the register. Second, the statutory provisions are themselves confusing in relation to this question. Schedule 4, paragraph 8 states that priorities of rectified interests can be 'adjusted' 'for the future only'. The problem therefore is the interaction between 'adjusted' and 'for the future' since it is difficult to see how priorities could be adjusted in such a way as to only have effects for the future.
>
> In response to this, Underhill LJ reasoned that the key word was 'adjust'. Were the claimants' leases to rank after Mr Ralph junior's lease, then would, the Court of Appeal highlighted, be no 'adjustment'—it would simply be a natural consequence of the fact that the claimants' leases would be put back onto the register after Gold Harp's lease had been registered. Thus, to 'adjust' priorities, the claimants would have to rank before Gold Harp. However, what did 'for the future' add to this explanation? According to the court, for the future here would mean that the consequences of priority would only operate once the court's order had been made. In the case of the conflicting leases, this would mean that Gold Harp would be treated as though it was not trespassing when in possession prior to the court order.

The consequence of the decision in *Gold Harp* was to prioritise A in what is effectively an A-B-C type scenario, albeit configured differently from those seen in *Knights Construction v Roberto Mac*[64] and *Barclays Bank v Guy*.[65] A different approach emerges in *Antoine v Barclays Bank* (see later),[66] as in this case, the court treated the wrongful documentation, which had been provided to a court, who then made a vesting order, as being akin to a voidable transaction, and therefore subject to *NRAM v Evans*.[67]

---

[64] *Knights Construction v Roberto Mac* REF/2009/1459, [2011] 2 EGLR 123.
[65] *Barclays Bank v Guy* [2008] EWCA Civ 452, [2008] 2 EGLR 74.
[66] *Antoine v Barclays Bank* [2018] EWHC 395 (Ch).
[67] *NRAM v Evans* [2017] EWCA Civ 1013, [2018] 1 WLR 639.

Key case: *Antoine v Barclays Bank* [2018] EWHC 395

In this case, the forged documentation was provided not to the land registry itself, but to the court. On the basis of this, the court made a vesting order, which was then put into effect by the land registry.

In considering whether this could constitute a mistake (since by definition the registrar had no option whatever to refuse the registration consequent upon the vesting order), the court analysed the meaning of mistake within the LRA, and gave support to the recent case law, such as *NRAM v Evans*[68] discussed above, and the general approach emerging in relation to this term. The conclusion that such a registration is not a mistake, despite the forgery, may appear surprising. However, on closer inspection, it is clear that, like the registration of a voidable transaction, where the mistake is made by the court, until the court decision is overturned ('rescinded, in that sense'), then the registrar is doing what they have to, and there is no mistake.[69] In this regard, the judge gave a number of reasons why the vesting order was akin to a voidable transaction, and thus any change to the register would be an alteration, not a mistake.[70] In short, because the register had to register the vesting order, it could not possibly be a mistake.

Finally, the judge concluded:

> 'whether or not it is right as a matter of terminology to refer to a court order as being "voidable", the July 2007 Order was certainly akin to a voidable transaction for the purposes of the analysis of whether it amounts to a mistake under LRA Schedule 4, para 2(1)(a). I accept that the *NRAM* principles as to the distinction between void and voidable transactions thus apply either directly, or by analogy, in this new factual context'.[71]

This confirmed the void/voidable distinction in *Evans*.

Summary: Error type 4

Error type 4(a) cases: where wrongful documentation is relied upon, it will be treated as a void transaction (akin to error type 2(a)), where the result of the documentation is a *direct* amendment to the register. Where the faulty documentation is provided to a court, which then makes a vesting order, the situation will be treated akin to a voidable transaction (error type 3(a)).

Error type 4(b) cases: A will be prioritised in these disputes, even to the extent of altering priorities to put A into the position that they would have been in had the register not be mistakenly changed.

Error type 5: documentation susceptible to rectification

Finally, there is the possibility of mistakes arising on the register where the registration is an accurate reflection of the documentation sent by the parties—and those transactions were perfectly valid—but where the documentation thus provided did not represent an accurate picture of what the parties' genuine intentions had been at the time of contracting so that the documentation

---

[68] *NRAM v Evans* [2017] EWCA Civ 1013, [2018] 1 WLR 639.
[69] *Antoine v Barclays Bank* [2018] EWHC 395 (Ch), [92].
[70] *Antoine v Barclays Bank* [2018] EWHC 395 (Ch), [116.3].
[71] *Antoine v Barclays Bank* [2018] EWHC 395 (Ch), [116.5].

would be susceptible to rectification. This error type raises questions not only of potential changes to be made to the register where errors are apparent, but also the issue of how documents and rights appearing on the register should be interpreted and understood. Thus, whilst the register may be mistaken when containing evidence taken from a document susceptible to rectification, it is also conceivable that whilst the information strictly speaking is accurate, it may be misleading due to unusual or unclear phraseology.

These issues were considered in *Cherry Tree v Landmain* where Longmore LJ reasoned that: '[t]he omission of the details of the sums to be paid may in one sense be a "mistake" but it is not a very important mistake. It was not suggested that the charge was legally ineffective because the sums, for which the property was to be charged, were omitted'.[72] However, in commenting on these kinds of 'information' mistakes, I have argued elsewhere that:

> 'There is no clear division, at least in terms of impacts on the parties themselves, and on third parties, between information being missed off in its entirety, and information containing a serious flaw, and information simply being misleading in terms of ancillary rights. Although we may want to allocate risk differently depending upon where on the spectrum the problem with the registration lies, the lack of clear delineation suggests that we may want to utilize a single framework of principles to allocate this risk. Not only will this render the system more simple and clear, but it will also be more predictable for the parties. The key to developing such a system is to recognise that questions of mistake, and of priority, are part and parcel of the same question'.[73]

This demonstrates the problem of information mistakes. That is, the register is not wrong in terms of the titles it records, but it is problematic in terms of the information that it provides to those viewing it.

Summary: Error type 5

The register, if changed, will be changed on the basis of alteration not rectification. However, it may be that third party-focused interpretation of the documents does not take account of the particular intention of the parties.

5.3.5 CONCLUSIONS ON LAND REGISTRATION—TITLE BY REGISTRATION OR REGISTRATION OF TITLE

The pattern of the case law here is without doubt difficult. There is no easy route through it precisely because there is no clear answer. The structural approach to the question of rectification of the register can be approached from many different angles: prioritisation of off-register conveyancing; the centrality of the guarantee of title; priority disputes; and responsiveness to individual circumstances. Which of these or other approaches one takes fundamentally alters which rules

---

[72] *Cherry Tree Investments v Landmain* [2012] EWCA Civ 736, [2013] Ch. 305, [142].
[73] E Lees, 'The public face of the register: confidence in the Land Registration Act 2002' in A Wudarski (ed) *Das Grundbuch im Europa des 21. Jahrhunderts*, (Duncker & Humblot, 2016) 371.

one sees as being relevant to the resolution of the dispute at hand. What is important, therefore, is to undertake two separate tasks. The first task is a categorisation task: by ascertaining the 'essential' facts of existing case law, we can categorise different land registration disputes according to their core components. Then, when a problem question or new case emerges, if it shares the core components with an earlier case, we can ascertain how the courts will solve that case even if there is no clearly discernible underlying principle which links, unifies, and renders coherent the relationship between the different 'models' apparent in the cases. The second task is an analytical one—what are the merits of the range of approaches available to us, and what does that mean the result *should* be in different models. This approach attempts to unify outcomes to these cases under a single principled approach, but it is very unlikely that it would be consistent with all the case law which currently exists. Accepting this does not mean accepting that the law should be unprincipled in this way, but rather accepting that the case law cannot necessarily be made consistent in principle, even if in terms of result there is no direct conflict.

5.3.6 AVAILABILITY OF INDEMNITIES

There are three aspects to consideration of the possibility of an indemnity. First, it is important to ascertain when what has been or might be lost as a result of rectification or a decision not to rectify even in cases of mistake is something of value. Second, it is important to consider the circumstances in which the behaviour of the claimant may mean that they are awarded compensation to a value less than the value of the right they have lost. Third, the process of valuation itself must be examined. When considering all these questions we must also keep something fundamental in mind, and that is that the Land Registry is a public body whose income comes only from its own fees. Thus, whilst it guarantees £trillions of property, it does not have the resources to effectively insure all landowners against every kind of problem which might emerge. It is tempting to think of indemnity cases as involving an individual, deprived of their home, looking for comparatively meagre compensation from a well-resourced public body, leading most to 'root for' the individual to succeed in their compensation claim. Whilst many are indeed deserving, it is also possible to argue that the land registry is being required to prop up individuals where they have naively entered into a bad bargain which although not careless, is merely a consequence of their lack of commercial sense or of deliberately risky decision-making. We can ask therefore whether it is right for the land registry to be helping people in this situation.

First, then, in what circumstances will the right lost be a right with value? This is really the flipside of the question we considered above regarding the possibility of rights to rectify the register being property rights, and the conflicts between A and C in circumstances like this being questions of priority. The question as to the value of rights 'inherently limited' by their vulnerability to rectification was considered in *Swift 1st*.[74] We addressed these issues earlier, however it is useful here to consider the aspects of the decision concerned with valuation of indemnity. This arises because of the slightly strange reasoning which the court engages in here. The court holds that Mrs Rani (the freehold proprietor of the property) obtained, on the mistaken registration of

---

[74] *Swift 1st v Chief Land Registrar* [2015] EWCA Civ 330, [2015] Ch 602.

Swift 1st's charge, a right to set aside the charge and this right, according to the court, would have priority over the bank because of Mrs Rani's actual occupation. This reasoning is really difficult to follow, not least because the right to set aside the charge could only, by definition, arise *after* the charge was registered, and therefore could not be said to have priority over the change. Nevertheless, the court's reasoning could equally apply in other circumstances where there was a genuine priority dispute thanks to an onward transfer or subsequent right-creation. Given this, the court's next conclusion, that the fact of the right with priority meant that the bank's charge was worthless, is hugely significant. If correct, it would mean that in any case where the courts characterised the conflict between A and C as being about priority, and not about mistake per se, then C, were they to lose title, would lose a title already inherently limited in terms of its value as a result of A's having priority over them, and as such, although ostensibly entitled to an indemnity, would receive no money from the registry since the right lost would be valueless.

The court avoids this conclusion in *Swift 1st* itself, by relying on schedule 8, which states that in cases where a right is created by forgery, it should be treated as though it was a valid right for the purposes of calculating the indemnity due. As a result, since the mortgage in *Swift 1st* was a forgery, the court could use this fiction to give it value where otherwise it would have been valueless always being limited by the possibility of rectification. The problem is of course that if this argument is correct, in any cases where A has priority over C in respect of the ability to rectify the register (if these disputes are conceptualised as priority disputes), then unless the transfer to C was forged (which would not make sense since by definition in A-B-C disputes, the transaction between B and C is itself valid), there could be no indemnity in such cases. This would be ironic since the courts have worked hard to ensure that indemnity is available by manipulating the meaning of the word 'mistake' to make it cover the registration of C! It is suggested, however, that the courts would not follow this approach, despite the support apparently given to it in *Swift 1st*.[75]

The second question is when will the claimant's own behaviour reduce the amount of indemnity to which they are entitled. This is a question for the statutory provisions. It is clear that where claimant's loss is caused entirely or in part by their own fraud or lack of proper care, then the indemnity will not be available or will be reduced. In making this assessment, the courts will apply the usual principles of careless and fraudulent behaviour. Again, however, depending upon how one conceptualises when rectification is available, it is possible to argue that B or C's loss is *always* caused, to a certain extent, by a lack of proper care on their part. This is not true with A of course. If a fraudster forges A's signature on a document and does nothing to prevent this document being registered, we can hardly say that A has not been careful! A is not in a position to even know that there is any risk about which he must be vigilant. By contrast, where B transacts with A, if A is a fraudster, then it may be that more steps were required from B in terms of confirming A's identity, and the like. In A-B-C cases, depending upon whether one sees this as a question of priority, or of an extended meaning of 'mistake' then again we could say C always had the opportunity to protect themselves. If the question is one of priorities, then in order to insulate themselves against such losses, C merely has to ensure that there is no person in discoverable actual occupation of the land by making a reasonable inspection of the land and making inquiries. If however one sees

---

[75] *Swift 1st v Chief Land Registrar* [2015] EWCA Civ 330, [2015] Ch 602.

this as mistake, and there is no priority dispute (in contrast to what is said in *Swift 1st*), then C has acted entirely properly, because they have relied upon the only thing on which they were entitled and mandated to rely, ie the register, which simply raises the question again as to whether their registration in such circumstances can and should be considered a mistake at all.

The final question in respect of indemnity is how rights are valued for the purposes of calculating the indemnities due. This may be no simple matter in situations where, for example, there is a mistaken registration of an easement. How does one calculate the value of land without an easement present as compared to one where there is an easement present? The courts in such cases will be mandated to rely on evidence from valuation experts.

5.4 REFORM OF THE RECTIFICATION AND INDEMNITY PROVISIONS

5.4.1 LAW COMMISSION PROPOSALS

The Law Commission has recently concluded that reform of the LRA 2002 is needed.[76] The primary proposals in the consultation in respect of the rectification and indemnity process are as follows, although we await the full response from Government and so it may be that no reform is in fact forthcoming. Note, the discussion here is designed merely to provide an insight into the reform proposals. Complete coverage of this content would not be possible within this work.

First, the Law Commission clearly rejects the 'right to rectify' as an overriding interest solution. Second, they propose that a presumption be put in place that where a person has been *removed* from the register by mistake (or never registered in the first place), then that person should become the registered proprietor, as long as they are in possession of the land and there are no exceptional circumstances. Similarly, if a person is successor in title to someone who was wrongly removed from the register, then they too should become registered proprietor, as long as they are in possession and there are no exceptional circumstances. In cases where it has been more than ten years since the mistake in removing a person, the register will not them be rectified except where the registered proprietor (ie the person not in possession) either consents to the rectification or they caused or contributed to the mistake by their own fraud or lack of proper care. Third, where the *registered* proprietor is in possession of the land, they should remain so (unless they consent to the change) except in cases where they caused or contributed to the mistake through fraud or lack of proper care or, and this is a significant change to the current rules, where it is less than ten years since the original mistake, and it is unjust not to rectify. Effectively, this means that a presumption is created in favour of registered proprietors in possession, and unless they caused the mistake themselves, that presumption basically becomes irrebuttable after ten years. The consequence of this is that there is effectively a ten-year conclusivity cut off. Fourth, in cases like *Parshall v Hackney*,[77] where two or more titles are registered in relation to the same piece of land, then the proposal is that these cases will be treated in the same way as all other registration

---

[76] Law Commission, report 380, 'Updating the Land Registration Act 2002' (2018).
[77] *Parshall v Hackney* [2013] EWCA Civ 240, [2013] Ch 568.

mistake, ie the question of possession is central, except where a person in possession caused the mistake through their own fraud or lack of proper care. The consequence of this is that there will be no adverse possession in such cases. The ten-year period will also be determinative in these cases. Fifth, the Commission recommends that these rectification provisions should take precedence over the priority scheme in section 29. In effect this is a decision that the priority scheme does not operate in cases where there is a mistake on the register. Finally, on the question of competing interests, such as was the case in *Gold Harp*,[78] the Law Commission proposes that the rectification should operate retrospectively so as to give the interest the priority it ought to have had, had no mistake been made. In respect of the indemnity provisions, the Commission suggests a limited statutory tort to take reasonable care in making land registry applications resting on professional conveyancers to allow easier recourse by the registry to third party sources of finance.

These proposals have not been universally welcomed with some seeing them as unnecessary, and others as not ambitious enough. In many respects, they represent a practical compromise between the various competing principles and approaches to the conclusivity of the register, but they still do not represent a principled commitment to any one form of land registration. This can be seen most particularly in the ten-year long-stop rule. Whilst this would provide welcome clarity and certainty in many cases, it is not a principled solution. The ten-year rule is based upon convenience, and ease, not on the basis that a title ten years old is somehow superior in quality to one nine years and eleven months. This is not to say that pragmatism is not welcome here—a solution is better than no solution, and this solution certainly has its advantages, but it should not be seen as more than a pragmatic pursuit of a limited form of indemnity. Furthermore, there is still a potential problem which is that there is still no statutory definition of mistake. The Law Commission recognises this, and it was a deliberate choice based upon the fact that any attempt to define mistake in advance inevitably runs into the complex realities of real life. However, it is problematic, even with the ten-year long-stop in place, because the ten-year period runs from 'the original mistake'. Without knowing what a mistake is, we cannot know what the original mistake is. The meaning in the majority of cases is tolerably clear, but as we have seen with our experience of the LRA 2002, comprehensibility in the majority of circumstances can cause problems in the few.

5.4.2 THE ADVENT OF E-CONVEYANCING?

Recent communications coming from the land registry, along with the grant of significant powers from the ministry to the registrar, suggest that the advent of e-conveyancing may be closer to hand than some had assumed.[79] E-conveyancing was one of the central planks of the intended 2002 Act scheme, and provision is made within section 93 for a move to e-conveyancing. Under this system, a single conveyancing process would merge the stages of contract, deed and registration, so that property rights could only be created if simultaneously registered (except, of course, from those rights not required to be registered). This process was intended to move us on from a conveyancing process which is slow and cumbersome, to one which could be concluded more

---

[78] *Gold Harp Properties Ltd v MacLeod* [2014] EWCA Civ 1084, [2015] 1 WLR 1249.
[79] https://www.gov.uk/government/news/hm-land-registry-moves-forward-with-digital-conveyancing, published 23 Jan 2018, accessed 25 April 2018.

swiftly. Furthermore, the e-conveyancing process would mean direct contact with the land registry throughout the transaction, hopefully minimising delays on the register, and ensuring that the register provides an up-to-date record of all transactions in relation to land.

However in the immediate aftermath of the coming into force of the 2002 Act, it become apparent that the software required to safely and efficiently operate such a system required considerable investment in time and design, and the economic and political will for such a system seemed to peter out. One particular problem was that of access to land registry servers from external computers—as would be necessary were e-conveyancing to be even remotely practical—and the possibilities to which this would give rise in terms of fraud, identity theft, and large-scale hacks. The enormity of the value of property which would be entirely at the mercy of the land registry's internal computer security (valued in the trillions of pounds), was too high to risk on an uncertain technology. E-conveyancing was then put on hold.

The land registry has now announced that it is moving forward with the simplification of its electronic processes. Whilst this is not a move to e-conveyances in its full form, it appears from the tone of what has been put into the press, that the intention is not to abandon e-conveyancing altogether.

5.5 CONCLUSION

Some of the issues raised in this chapter are very difficult—and the solutions provided in the case law hard to unravel. The relatively straightforward rules concerning when estates and interests must be registered in order to exist at law, the effect of such registration in terms of the classes of titles, and the theoretical effect of such registration in terms of guarantee of title and owner's powers, has, through case law, morphed into a very difficult substantive question of what it actually means to have guaranteed title when something has gone wrong. Partly this question is hard to answer because of the lack of commitment within the statutory provisions as to how such guarantees should be treated, but it is also difficult because the underlying policy arguments are themselves nuanced and certainly do not all go in one direction. Whilst it is possible to make a convincing argument that the intention behind the 2002 Act was to create a system of title by registration, the reality of what that means for those who lose their land through no fault of their own, has proved unpalatable, and for good reason.

Furthermore, the interaction between the principle of guaranteed title in section 58, of owner's powers in sections 23 and 24, and the rectification scheme in schedule 4, has been supplemented with the indemnity provisions in schedule 8, and the priority scheme established in sections 28 and 29. Taking into account the wider statutory context, and in particular the potential for rights to rectify to constitute overriding interests, and the link made between the definition of mistake in schedule 4, and in schedule 8, the drafting of the statute has meant that the courts have the opportunity to be, and in many ways, the obligation to be, creative in finding solutions to land registration problems. Although some may see this judicial creativity as problematic, leaving behind as it does the intention of Parliament, at least as expressed through the Law Commission, it is a creativity borne, to an extent, of necessity. The law in this area is hard to apply and it is necessary to trace the different threads through the case law. The courts are essentially juggling plates. But if we compare the way that outcomes have morphed over the years since *Barclays Bank v Guy*,[80] the results of these cases in terms of what happens to the individuals involved seems to have reached a good balance. The challenge now is whether we can replicate this balance in terms of outcome, with a more clear and predictable statutory scheme, and with the removal of the enormous variety of options that exist when attempting to manage a system of land registration.

PRINCIPLES

How do these rules shape the balance of the principles operating in relation to land law? To recap, these principles were:

1. Certainty
2. Sensitivity to context
3. Transactability
4. Systemic and individual effects
5. Recognition of the social role of the land law system.

There are two aspects to land registration and its influence on the principles of land law. The first is the general system created by land registration—and the shape this gives to land law as a whole when there are no errors or problems in the system. In these cases, there has been an attempt to balance certainty and transactability on the one hand, and recognition of the social elements of people's homes on the other. The first goal is achieved through the mandatory registration of estates in land before any disposition can operate at law. This ensures that as many rights as is reasonably useful appear on the register, making the whole process of transacting with land cheaper and more streamlined, thus reducing transactions costs whilst at the same time not affecting certainty or conclusivity in a search for such a speedy process. The second goal is achieved through the recognition that not every right can or should reasonably be registered, and that instead a number of rights which arise in relation to land do so without the conscious volition of the parties. Such rights are not thereby given 'lower' status within the land law system, and as explained in chapter 3 briefly and considered again in chapter 15, they are protected against third parties in very many cases through the actual occupation of the right-holder. However, it ought to be recognised that in explicitly prohibiting the registration of interests under a trust through the use of the notice, and the prioritization given to the curtain principle in this respect, the system implicitly suggests that the integrity of such rights *may* be appropriately sacrificed to the alternative goal of certainty and transactability.

When there are problems or errors in the system, however, the degree to which any of these principles are reached suffers enormously. Indeed, the debate surrounding the conclusivity of the register is in many ways a debate between these competing principles, but the current law, in failing to have a single predictable or even structured outcome in respect of how errors are handled

---

[80] *Barclays Bank v Guy* [2008] EWCA Civ 452, [2008] 2 EGLR 74.

means that none of the principles are being actively pursued. Instead, the law is uncertain and unpredictable, but not in such a way that ensures sensitivity to context. In this respect, the law reform proposals from the Law Commission are very significant in that their very pragmatism, as mentioned above, means that they are not identifiably driven by any of the principles so central to the proper functioning of our system. This is not to suggest that the reforms are not welcome—they are in so far as they improve upon the current position—but the failure to commit to a particular form of land registration hinders the ability of the law in this area to achieve not only certainty, but the other goals mentioned here too.

TABLE OF DEFINITIONS

Registered estate	An estate, title to which appears on the register.
Registrable estate	An estate which must be registered if a transfer or creation of that estate is to operate at law.
Registrable interest	An interest which must be registered if a transfer or creation of that interest is to operate at law.
First registration	The first time that title to an estate appears on the register.
Rectification	The process by which the register is altered following the presence of a mistake on the register whose correction would involve prejudice to the estate's proprietor.
Mistake	An error on the register (not clearly defined in case law or statute).
Alteration	The process by which the register is changed, to correct a mistake, or to keep the register up to date.
Indemnity	A payment from the land registry in cases of rectification or where rectification is possible but does not in fact take place.

FURTHER READING

There is a lot of potential further reading in relation to this topic, however for recent analysis of the case law and issues, this list provides a good place to start:

COOPER, S., 'Resolving title conflicts in registered land' (2015) 131 LQR 108.
COOPER, S. and LEES, E., 'Interests, powers and mere equities in modern land law' (2017) 37 OJLS 435.
GOYMOUR, A. et al, *New Perspectives on Land Registration* (Hart, 2018).
LAW COMMISSION, 'Updating the Land Registration Act 2002' (report no. 380, 2018).

6

ADVERSE POSSESSION

6.1 Introduction	162	6.5 Adverse Possession and Criminal Law 184
6.2 Adverse Possession and Unregistered Land	163	6.6 Explanations for Adverse Possession 185
		6.7 Conclusion 188
6.3 Adverse Possession and Registered Land	174	Principles 189
		Table of Definitions 190
6.4 Adverse Possession and Leases	181	Further Reading 190

CHAPTER GOALS

By the end of this chapter, you should be able to understand:

- How the principle of relativity gives rise to the possibility of adverse possession;
- The nature of adverse possession, and the meaning of factual possession and intention to possess;
- How these rules operate in relation to unregistered land;
- How these rules operate in relation to registered land;
- The relationship between the rules relating to adverse possession and leases, and between adverse possession and the criminal law; and
- The potential justifications for adverse possession as they have evolved over time.

6.1 INTRODUCTION

Adverse possession is obtention of title to land by means of possession without permission. Upon first encountering adverse possession many students' reaction is one of surprise: 'is that not simply legitimised "theft" of land'? Indeed, that is one way of considering or understanding adverse possession. However, it is also the natural and logical consequence of the combination of the principle of relativity of title, and of limitation (time limits) on actions. To explain further, as discussed in chapters 2 and 9, the heart of the principle of relativity of title is the idea that more than one person can have title to the same estate in land at the same time. There is no one 'owner', and indeed the common law does not have a concept of 'ownership' in this sense. Person A's title may be better than person B's, but they are both valid titles. The second aspect to adverse possession is the concept of limitation on actions. A time limit on actions exists to prevent a right-holder coming along 30 years after an event which caused them loss and demanding a remedy. It ensures certainty and prevents the property market becoming stagnant. The time limit for actions involving land is 12 years. As a result, before the advent of registered land (as is discussed in more detail later), if, in our example earlier, person A failed to sue B for possession if B had 'taken over' the possession of that land without A's permission for 12 years, A is no longer able to assert their title as against B. Following the logic of relativity through, this means that A no longer has a title superior to that of B. This is the fundamental operation of adverse possession.

Adverse possession as an area of land law raises both interesting questions of law (very often assessed through problem questions) and critical policy questions. Furthermore, recent developments mean that there is a now a certain degree of conflict between adverse possession as a rule in land law, and 'squatting' (the act of taking up residence in another's land without their permission) and the criminal law. This is an intensely political issue, touching on ideas such as: homelessness; the importance and merits of protecting what some refer to as the 'property-owning class'; human rights, and, as will be seen, local authority resources and austerity politics. It is not possible to fully analyse adverse possession divorced from this wider context. It is also important to note that although there is relatively little case law on the topic in the modern law, in practice adverse possession is very significant and common, albeit largely confined to 'boundary' cases as we explore in detail later.

This chapter will begin by analysing and explaining the rules relating to adverse possession, considering both unregistered land, in 6.2, and registered land in 6.3. Adverse possession is one of the few areas where the unregistered land rules are still regularly taught. Section 6.4 will then consider the special situation which emerges when the rules on adverse possession interact with leases. Section 6.5 then examines the relationship between the adverse possession rules and criminal law. Section 6.6 concludes by looking at the justifications or explanations behind adverse possession, including the relationship between these rules and human rights.

Note: for discussion concerning the relationship between adverse possession and human rights in more detail, see chapter 17 at 17.3.1.

6.2 ADVERSE POSSESSION AND UNREGISTERED LAND

Partly because of the continued teaching of the rules of unregistered land in relation to adverse possession, and partly because understanding the unregistered land rules is essential to a proper understanding of the *registered* land rules, this chapter will begin by explaining what adverse possession is and how it operates in the context of unregistered land. The definition of adverse possession can be broken down into two constituent parts (and the clue is in the name!): adverse, and possession. It makes more sense to discuss the meaning of possession first.

6.2.1 POSSESSION

The word 'possession' in English land law is a word which is used to mean subtly different things at different times as we have already explained in chapter 2 at 2.2. Sometimes is it used, as in the context of leases (see chapter 10), in opposition to 'occupation'. Here it describes a situation where a person is living in a residential property, for example, and their relationship with that property is not one akin to a lodger, or a hotel guest, but is more extensive than that, and has become a lease. Sometimes it is used to describe a factual state of affairs, as when an individual has changed the locks of a property so that they are the only person able to obtain access to a property. Sometimes, finally, it is used to describe a *right* so that even though a person may not in fact have a physical presence on the land, because they are 'in possession' (in the sense that they have a right to possession) they are able, for example, to receive the rental income from the property. The multiplicity of ways in which this word is used can make study and understanding of 'possession' in the abstract problematic. At its heart, however, the word possession is always referring to the same idea: the ability whether in fact, in law, or both, to control access to property. Importantly, we must always be keen to distinguish between possession on the one hand, and occupation and use on the other.

To begin to understand possession as both a right and a factual state of affairs, it is sometimes useful to think not of land, but of a chattel instead. For example, let us consider a mobile phone. If someone on the bus were to take my mobile phone out of my bag and slip it securely into their own bag, possession of that phone has transferred from me to them as a matter of fact. I have not lost my *right* to possess it: it is, after all, my phone, but physical possession (ie control) has moved to them. Now let us imagine that they get on a second bus, and a third person steals the phone from their bag. Does the second person have the right to take the phone back from the third? Some may argue that they do not—the second person should never have had the phone, and so they should not be able to get it back. Others might say that neither the second nor the third person ought to have the phone. But we are not asking an absolute question here, 'who is the owner', but an easier question, who is 'better' out of person two and person three? The answer which English law gives to this question is that out of these options, person two is better simply by virtue of the fact that they had the phone before person three did and there was no voluntary transfer between the two. This is the idea of relativity of title. However, this situation also gives us a clue to the different ways in which we can understand the meaning of the word possession. I never lost my 'right to possession' in this situation, but I lost my physical control of the phone as soon as it was taken out of my bag. Person two never had a right to possession, but upon seizing control of the phone they obtained not only factual possession, but in a strange way, a right to protect that physical or factual possession as against all third parties (apart from me).

Transferring this understanding to situations involving land, adverse possession is about the latter understanding of possession: physical possession, ie practical control of a piece of land. It is not asking who has the *right* to possess, but rather, who is in fact in possession. Once that is understood, explaining the meaning of possession in this context becomes so much the easier.

Despite being somewhat nebulous in theoretical terms, the case law has developed a definition of possession in the adverse possession context which is relatively straightforward to apply. The question which must be asked is first, whether the claimant is in factual possession of the land, and second, whether they have the intention to possess. The clearest enunciation of these rules is to be found in the decision of Slade J in *Powell v MacFarlane*.[1]

---

[1] *Powell v McFarlane* (1979) 38 P & CR 452.

Key case: *Powell v MacFarlane* (1979) 38 P & CR 452

In this case, a young man (the first relevant facts in the case occurred from when Powell was 14-years old) did a variety of acts on the land including: grazing the family cow on the land; mowing it for hay; repairing the fencing surrounding the land to make it stock proof; shooting pigeons and rabbits on the land; cutting down trees; and using farm vehicles on the land to clear certain areas. The land did not belong to him on paper, but he claimed to have acquired it using adverse possession.

Slade J outlines the following general principles in explaining when a person will be in possession of land. First, he emphasises that all else being equal, a person with paper title is assumed to be in possession of land. So, if you can demonstrate paper title, then without more you will be deemed to be in possession. Second, in order to displace this assumption regarding the possession of the paper title-holder, a person must show both factual possession and intention to possess. The judge then discusses what it means to be in factual possession, and to have this intention.

> 'Factual possession signifies an appropriate degree of physical control. It must be a single and conclusive possession, though there can be a single possession exercised by or on behalf of several persons jointly. Thus an owner of land and a person intruding on that land without his consent cannot both be in possession of the land at the same time. The question what acts constitute a sufficient degree of exclusive physical control must depend on the circumstances, in particular the nature of the land and the manner in which land of that nature is commonly used or enjoyed.... Everything must depend on the particular circumstances, but broadly, I think what must be shown as constituting factual possession is that the alleged possessor has been dealing with the land in question as an occupying owner might have been expected to deal with it and that no-one else has done so.
>
> ... [T]he animus possidendi involves the intention, in one's own name and on one's own behalf, to exclude the world at large, including the owner with the paper title if he be not himself the possessor, so far as is reasonably practicable and so far as the processes of the law will allow'.[2]

In concluding that the young man did not have an intention to possess in this case, the court clearly relied, in part, on his age at the time of the relevant acts on the land. The suggestion is that a child of 14 cannot have the intention to possess, but this is clearly false. Most 14 year-olds will be acutely aware of the difference between 'mine' and 'yours' and the notion of taking control of an object. Even though we may doubt the actual result in this case, the guidance given as to what intention to possess means in general has not been doubted, and forms the foundation of the modern law on the question.

The following section will explain these concepts in more detail.

6.2.1.1 Factual possession

Factual possession is, as Slade J highlights earlier, simply being in control of land. In particular, it means the ability to exclude all others as far as is reasonable. However, as Slade J also highlights, what constitutes sufficient control in this respect will vary according to the nature of the land and the uses to which it can be put. There is a difference, for example, in terms of the physical steps which would constitute taking factual possession of a residential flat when compared with an empty field. The courts have repeatedly confirmed that in each case the question as to whether a

---

[2] *Powell v McFarlane* (1979) 38 P & CR 452, 470–2.

claimant is in possession of land will be a question which depends upon all the facts of that individual case and will be dealt with on a case-by-case basis. There are no 'hard and fast rules' and no definitive tests to be applied, beyond that already described. However, we can look at a number of cases and begin to consider the sorts of things which are usually considered to be sufficient to constitute factual possession.

Open farm land, fields, forests, etc

In many ways, the issue as to whether an individual possesses open, undeveloped land is one of the most difficult in defining possession. The issue of 'who is in control' will very often be easier to establish where the question involves a residential property, for example, where the property is likely to be secured in some way. The difficulty with open or otherwise empty land, is that acts of control can be very subtle and invisible. This can be seen from *Powell*[3] itself. Each individual act here is in some respects quite minor—at least in the context of trying to establish who is in exclusive control of a piece of land—but taken together they indicate a pattern of behaviour which does indicate a degree of factual control. In *Powell*,[4] Slade J concluded that these acts were not sufficient to demonstrate the *intention* to possess, as will be discussed later, but they probably were enough to constitute factual possession of the land if they had been accompanied by an appropriate intention. Indeed, in some cases simply taking hay from land has been held to be enough (*Umma v Appu*[5]) albeit that the result in this case was in part dictated by the particular understandings and patterns of use of land present in that particular area of Sri Lanka. A similar result was reached in *Adams v Batt*.[6] Even shooting on land can be enough where that is the only reasonable use to which the land can be put.[7]

Recent case law confirms that in relation to this sort of property, the acts which are said to constitute evidence of factual possession can be relatively minor. In *King v Suffolk County Council*[8] (as case to which we will return later), the disputed land concerned some unused deciduous forest land. The claimant had cultivated this land, planted flowers, put up a fence, laid down some wood chippings to act as a path, and installed a swing and other similar garden features. A similar approach was taken in *Gott v Lawrence*[9] even though in that case the court's assessment of the facts resulted in a different conclusion. As with *Powell*,[10] these acts are innocuous in themselves perhaps—even fencing can be done for purposes other than controlling access to property (like keeping animals in)—but as a package, the court concluded that this was enough to constitute factual possession of this land. That such an 'in the round' assessment ought to be taken is confirmed in *Heaney v Kirkby*[11] where Kaye QC states that, '[i]n my judgment what matters is an objective assessment of the circumstances and all the circumstances taken as a whole. It is not just a question of taking isolated items'.[12]

[3] *Powell v McFarlane* (1979) 38 P & CR 452.
[4] *Powell v McFarlane* (1979) 38 P & CR 452.
[5] *Umma v Appu* [1939] AC 136.
[6] *Batt v Adams* (2001) 82 P & CR 32.
[7] *Red House Farms (Thorndon) Ltd v Catchpole* (1976) 121 Sol Jo 136, [1977] 2 EGLR 125.
[8] *King v Suffolk County Council* FTT Ref No 2015/0867, 13 October 2016.
[9] *Gott v Lawrence*, [2016] EWHC 68 (Ch).
[10] *Powell v McFarlane* (1979) 38 P & CR 452.
[11] *Heaney v Kirkby* [2015] UKUT 0178 (TCC).
[12] *Heaney v Kirkby* [2015] UKUT 0178 (TCC), [38].

However, in relation to agricultural land at least, the courts have held that certain acts will be very strong evidence of adverse possession. In the famous words of Cockburn CJ in *Seddon v Smith*,[13] 'enclosure is the strongest possible evidence of adverse possession'.[14] It should be noted though that this comment is *obiter* and was in fact made in the context of the court's conclusion that it is possible to demonstrate factual possession even if enclosure does not take place. So, whilst it is useful for demonstrating factual possession and is very strong evidence thereof, enclosure is not conclusive, nor is it essential.

Riverbed

The somewhat unusual question as to whether land making up the riverbed can be adversely possessed through the mooring of boats has arisen in a number of cases. One of the difficulties relates to what acts are required to demonstrate factual possession in such situations. How, in short, can one 'act as an owner' in relation to the riverbed? That such is even possible appears to have been accepted in both *Port of London Authority v Ashmore*[15] and *Moore v British Waterways Board*.[16] However, in *Tower Bridge Yacht and Boat Company v Port of London Authority*,[17] Mann J concluded that in many of these situations the mere act of mooring a boat, or using concrete pillars to, for example, support the boat at times of low tide (on a tidal river such as the Thames), would not be enough. Rather, there would need to be a clear 'taking of control' of the land. Although, as is clear from Mann J's judgment, this is not impossible in such a claim, it will certainly be difficult to demonstrate.

Furthermore, in this sort of situation, very often the precise shape, location, and extent of moorings, blocks etc. may change over time (a wooden post would rot, for example). This means that there was no defined space over which the supposed factual possession takes place. Whilst, again, this is not an insurmountable barrier—it may be that very precise evidence can demonstrate an area which has been continuously possessed for the relevant period—it is a challenge which presents itself in this sort of case. Finally, the case emphasises an important wider point as, Mann J highlights: '[such acts were] more in the nature of user, which is not sufficient to amount to possession; or it is conceivably occupation. The distinction between those concepts and possession in any given case may be a fine one, and differences hard to articulate, but it exists'.[18] We can, therefore, add another guide to the assessment as to what constitutes factual possession—would the facts be more comfortably described as use or occupation rather than possession? Whilst use of land may be evidence of possession, it is not constitutive of possession in itself. Therefore, as Lord Neuberger highlighted in *Tower Hamlets London Borough Council v Barrett*: '[f]actual possession involves some sort of physical presence or at least being in physical control in some real way'.[19]

---

[13] *Seddon v Smith* (1877) 36 LT 168 (CA).
[14] *Seddon v Smith* (1877) 36 LT 168 (CA), 169.
[15] *Port of London Authority v Ashmore* [2010] EWCA Civ 30; [2010] 1 All ER 1139.
[16] *Moore v British Waterways Board* [2013] EWCA Civ 73; [2013] Ch 488.
[17] *Tower Bridge Yacht and Boat Company v London Port Authority* [2013] EWHC 3084 (Ch).
[18] *Tower Bridge Yacht and Boat Company v London Port Authority* [2013] EWHC 3084 (Ch), [282].
[19] *Tower Hamlets London Borough Council v Barrett* 2006 1 P&CR 9 at 54.

6.2.1.2 Intention to possess or 'animus possedendi'

Like all intention-based questions in law, the test for whether a potential adverse possessor has an intention to possess can be difficult and complex to establish because the judge's task is to ascertain, from external evidence, what a person was thinking during the period of their use of the relevant land. This means that the intention to possess, despite being about the claimant's state of mind, is usually determined according to external evidence, and in many cases the evidence considered will be the *same* as that considered in relation to factual possession. As Lord Hope explains in *Pye*: 'acts of the mind can be, and sometimes can only be, demonstrated by acts of the body'.[20] For example, changing all the locks on a house is not only likely to be enough to ensure that there was factual possession of the house (as no one else is able to enter), but is also the strongest evidence possible of an intention to possess (see further later). The intention to possess therefore has both a subjective and an objective side. Objectively, it must be clear from the squatter's actions what their intention was, but subjectively, it must also be clear that they genuinely did have the relevant intention.

In respect of a general test for what constitutes sufficient intention, again *Powell* itself is instructive. This is because although the acts carried out by the boy when he was 14 and then later could, from the tone of the judgment, have been said to have constituted factual possession of the land, Slade J reached the conclusion that they were not enough to demonstrate an intention to possess as we explained earlier. Part of the reason why Slade J reached this conclusion was the age of the claimant at this time and so we can say that the judge took a subjective approach, considering not 'what might a person do if they intended to exercise control over the land' but rather, 'did the things that this particular person did show that they so intended'. If, as in Powell's case, that person's age, mental state, or other relevant factor meant that these acts were perhaps more ambiguous than if they had been carried out by an older person, then that may be enough to prevent a court from concluding that there was a relevant intention to possess. Furthermore, Slade J in that case highlighted the importance of the subjective intention being evidenced by outward signs, so that it can be said that the claimant 'made such intention clear to the world'.[21]

However, there are some specific questions that have arisen in the case law which allow us to go beyond this general test. We can explain the meaning of intention to possess by considering five issues.

First, the claimant must intend to control access to the property on their own behalf. Essentially, the claimant must show that they intended to control access to the property *in their own name*. If, for example, they are acting as agent, or in some sense in their own mind on behalf of the true owner (even if the true owner is unaware of their actions), they cannot be said to have the relevant intention.

Second, the claimant must intend to have the ability to exclude all others (subject to what is said here about the paper title-holder). In this respect, the intention must encompass a desire to exclude all others as far as is reasonably practical. This intention may be manifested

---

[20] *J A Pye (Oxford) v Graham* [2002] UKHL 30, [2003] 1 AC 419, [70].
[21] *Powell v McFarlane* (1979) 38 P & CR 452, 472.

by enclosure (see further later), changing the locks on a property, or simply using the land in such a way as to make it clear to the outside world that the squatter's permission would be required before a third party could access the land. However, this aspect of the *animus possidendi* does not require the squatter to intend to keep out the paper title-holder. This was made very clear in the House of Lords decision in *Pye v Graham* where the court held: 'it is not necessary to show that there was a deliberate intention to exclude the paper owner or the registered proprietor'.[22]

Third, if the claimant believes that they are the true owner of the land, this will not prevent the relevant intention being present (in fact, usually this would be enough to prove the existence of the relevant intention). This is because if the claimant believes the land to be theirs, then they quite obviously would intend to control access to it. In such cases however it is important to keep in mind that this subjective belief is not enough. This is not simply because it may be hard to prove if there were to be no outward actions demonstrating this belief, but because the intention to possess is only part of the story, and factual control must also be present.

Fourth, on the other hand, there is no need for the claimant to intend to *own* the land—only to possess it. This issue was also raised in *Pye*, as in that case the claimants very clearly did not intend to own land: indeed, they had offered to pay rent. The House of Lords in *Pye* was unanimous however that the relevant intention is one of possession, not 'ownership'. This gives support to the comments of Hoffman J in *Buckinghamshire County Council v Moran* that, 'what is required for this purpose is not an intention to own or even an intention to acquire ownership but an intention to possess'.[23]

Finally, it does not matter if the claimant thinks that they have permission to be present on the land, eg under a tenancy, as long as they have an intention to exclude. This is demonstrated by the decision in *Tower Hamlets London Borough Council v Barrett*.[24] As with a belief in ownership, belief that the land was being occupied and possessed as a tenant is a belief that the squatter has a right to exclusive possession of the land, as this is the very hallmark of the lease (see chapter 10). Per Neuberger LJ (as he then was) in that case, '[t]hey believed their tenancy included the area. Hence they thought they were enjoying exclusive possession of it'.[25]

> **Further analysis: Enclosure**
>
> One of the issues which comes up regularly in adverse possession cases, with regards both to the factual and mental elements of possession, is the relevance of enclosure. Enclosure is essentially the process by which a squatter can turn land from being, in practical terms, freely accessible by all, to one which only persons with permission may be able to enter, through the addition of fencing, gates or locks. Indeed, this example demonstrates an important point: not all squatting involves adverse possession.

---

[22] *JA Pye (Oxford) Ltd v Graham* [2002] UKHL 30, [2003] 1 AC 419, [71].
[23] Cited with approval in the Court of Appeal decision in the case by Slade LJ at 463.
[24] *Tower Hamlets London Borough Council v Barrett* 2006 1 P&CR 9.
[25] *Tower Hamlets London Borough Council v Barrett* 2006 1 P&CR 9, 42.

In many cases there are statements to the effect that enclosure is the strongest possible evidence of possession. This can be seen, for example, in *Seddon v Smith*,[26] *London Borough of Hounslow v Minchinton*,[27] and in *Buckinghamshire County Council v Moran*.[28] In this last case, Slade LJ explains that, 'enclosure by itself *prima facie* indicates the requisite *animus possidendi*'.[29] In almost all cases, therefore, an act of enclosure would be extremely good evidence of adverse possession.

Even in cases where there is an act falling slightly short of enclosure per se, acts which have a similar goal in mind will also be strong evidence of possession. Thus, in *Powell* the squatter repaired fencing so as to ensure that it was stock proof, and in *Pye v Graham*,[30] although the Grahams did not plant the enclosing hedging, they did ensure that it was in good condition. In both of these cases these acts were taken to be good evidence that the squatter was in possession of the land (albeit that in *Powell*,[31] as seen earlier, the court held that for other reasons the relevant *animus possidendi* was missing).

However, in *Inglewood v Baker*,[32] the court held that in some cases enclosure will be insufficient where, for example, it is done for the purpose of keeping livestock *in* rather than keeping third parties *out*. This suggests that enclosure will not always be unambiguous evidence in favour of possessory intent. This case is controversial. In many ways, the idea of keeping livestock in has a similar 'controlling' element, as does the idea keeping third parties out. For this reason, some commentators have argued that this case does not represent the best way of understanding the role of enclosure in establishing possession. Jourdan and Radley-Gardner comment that, 'the fact that the intention to make exclusive use of the land is formed because of a desire to keep animals in does not affect the nature or quality of that intention'.[33]

6.2.1.3 Continuity of possession

The final issue to consider before moving on from the definition of possession, is the question of continuity. In order to be the foundation for a successful adverse possession claim, the squatter's possession of the land must be continuous (subject to what is said about chains of possession later). This is because the possession of the paper title-holder is presumed. If, therefore, the squatter abandons their possession at a certain point, the law will presume that the paper title-holder is back in possession and the clock of limitation will restart at this point. This much is clear. However, it is important to note that, as Jourdan and Radley-Gardner highlight, 'a squatter can be in continuous possession even if he does not use the land continuously'.[34] Just as use and possession are different things in terms of the definition of possession, so too they can be separated when assessing the continuity of possession.

6.2.2 ADVERSE

The requirement that possession be 'adverse' is relatively straightforward. It means simply that the claimant cannot be possessing the land with permission from the paper title-holder (otherwise of course the paper-title holder would not have an action for possession against the adverse possessor

---

[26] *Seddon v Smith* (1877) 36 LT 168 (CA).
[27] *London Borough of Hounslow v Minchinton* (1997) 74 P & CR 221 (CA).
[28] *Buckinghamshire County Council v Moran* [1990] Ch 623 (CA).
[29] *Buckinghamshire County Council v Moran* [1990] Ch 623 (CA), 641.
[30] *JA Pye (Oxford) Ltd v Graham* [2002] UKHL 30, [2003] 1 AC 419.
[31] *Powell v McFarlane* (1979) 38 P & CR 452, 472.
[32] *Inglewood v Baker* [2002] EWCA Civ 1733, [2003] 2 P & CR 23.
[33] S Jourdan and O Radley-Gardner, *Adverse Possession (2nd edition)* 205.
[34] S Jourdan and O Radley-Gardner, *Adverse Possession (2nd edition)*.

which would later become barred through limitation). The meaning of adverse is explained by Lord Millet in *Ramnarace v Lutchman*: 'adverse possession is possession which is inconsistent with and in denial of the title of the true owner'.[35] Does it make any difference to this if the adverse possessor, knowing full well that the land is not 'theirs' contacts the paper title-holder and offers to pay rent? Is the possession still adverse in these circumstances? This was the issue considered by the leading case of *Pye v Graham*,[36] a case which was particularly significant for Pye since the land in question was development land on the outskirts of Oxford. In that case, Lord Browne-Wilkinson explains the 'adverse' issue in an even more straight-forward way: 'ordinary possession of the land ... without the consent of the owner'.[37] It makes no difference to this assessment whether the paper title-holder is 'inconvenienced' in any way or whether the use of the land is inconsistent or consistent with his own plans. All that matters is whether the possession is without consent and as such, is adverse.

In most circumstances this will be very straight-forward, but there are a few circumstances in which the question as to whether possession is adverse or not may be slightly more complicated. These are: first, in cases where although the owner has not given explicit permission for the possessor to be on their land, they are aware of their presence and have chosen to do nothing about it (acquiescence). In such cases as these, it can be difficult to establish whether the adverse possessor has permission to be on the land and the line between acquiescence and permission can be very fine. However, the principle is clear. Acquiescence is not enough to prevent the squatter's possession from being adverse, active permission is required. Second, in cases where the claimant entered the land with permission and their permission has run out (holding over), it is possible to infer from this that they have a sort of implied permission to be on land by the fact that the paper title-holder has not acted to evict them? That the answer to this is 'no' was made very clear from *Pye v Graham*. In that case, the Grahams had originally had a lease over the relevant property, allowing them to use the land as part of their farm business. At the end of the original lease, the Grahams contacted the paper title-holder to ask what they should do in order to renew the lease and how much rent they should pay. They did not receive a reply to this and so continued to use the property as they had before. This offer to pay rent, which was not acknowledged by Pye, was held insufficient to suggest that the possession was with the consent of the owner (nor did it indicate that the Grahams were lacking sufficient intention to possess the land, as discussed earlier).

Summary: Adverse possession

The definition of adverse possession essentially encompasses three elements: factual possession of land; an intention to possess; and a lack of permission for that possession from the paper title-holder. Factual possession is characterised by physical control over access to the relevant land, but exactly what acts are required to show that will depend on the characteristics of the land itself. Intention to possess is an intention to exclude all others as far as is reasonably possible, but it does not require an intention to own, or indeed to exclude the paper title-holder if challenged. Finally, mere acquiescence by the paper title-holder is not enough to prevent possession from being adverse. As long as the possession is without consent, it will be adverse.

---

[35] *Ramnarace v Lutchman* [2001] UKPC 25, [2001] 1 WLR 1651, [10].
[36] *Pye v Graham* [2002] UKHL 30, [2003] 1 AC 419.
[37] *Pye v Graham* [2002] UKHL 30, [2003] 1 AC 419, [36].

6.2.3 CONSEQUENCES OF ADVERSE POSSESSION

Once it has been shown that the claimant has been in adverse possession, the next stage is to establish whether this possession has been enough to deprive the paper title-holder of their rights. Whether or not this has happened depends, primarily, at least in the case of unregistered land, on time. According to the Limitation Act 1980, sections 15 and 17, in almost all cases the paper title-holder's title will be extinguished if their land has been adversely possessed for 12 years. Special rules apply to the Crown however, for whom the time period is 30 years for most land, and 60 years in relation to the foreshore. In most cases, possession for the requisite period of time will mean that the adverse possessor now has the 'best' title to the land and is safe from challenge from all others. In cases where a single squatter has been in possession for twelve years, the matter is simple. That squatter can now be considered to be the 'owner' of that land.

It is therefore important, from the perspective of a paper title-holder, to know how to 'stop time running' so as to prevent extinction of title. There are a number of different ways in which this can happen. First, if the squatter acknowledges the title of the true owner in writing, this will stop time running. So too will payment to the paper title-holder as this will usually mean that there is an implied license in place. In fact, it is not even necessary for the paper title-holder to require payment: if they simply give the possessor permission to be on the land, then the possession will no longer be adverse, and the clock will stop. The clock also stops running (or more accurately, fails to start running) in certain specific situations where the paper title-holder is prevented by their age or a disability from having capacity to act. This incapacity must exist from the outset however. Finally, the clock will stop running if the squatter deliberately conceals their possession of the land from the true owner.

If the paper title-holder fails to stop the clock running such that their title is extinguished, the final issue is what rights this means that the adverse possessor now has. According to *Titchborne v Weir*,[38] the possessor does not obtain the paper title-holder's title, but instead obtains a new title by virtue of their possession. Furthermore, as can be seen in *Asher v Whitlock*,[39] the title obtained by the possessor is presumptively, a freehold title (for situations when an equivalent to leasehold title arises, see later).

6.2.3.1 Multiple Squatters

It is important to note, however, that this possession can be carried out by one, or more than one either connected or independent possessors, so long as each has a period of exclusive possession and there is no gap between them. This is an important consequence of the fact that adverse possession in unregistered land is about *extinction* of title (not acquisition). Instead of asking how long has the squatter been in possession, it is better to think of this in terms of how long has the paper title-holder *not* been in possession. If the paper title-holder has been 'absent' for twelve years or more, then their title is extinguished and they can no longer sue for possession. What this means is that, in cases where there are multiple squatters, any one of these can only be 'safe' as against the others when that one person has been in adverse possession for twelve years (or has been transferred, gifted, or has inherited so many years). There are essentially two situations to

---

[38] *Tichborne v Weir* (1891) 94 All Er Rep 449 (CA).
[39] *Asher v Whitlock* (1865–66) LR 1 QB 1 (QBD).

be discussed here. The first is cases where there is a chain of conveyance or wills between the first squatter and the current squatter, so that they are connected and there is a single possessory title transferred between them. The second is in cases where one adverse possessor loses their possession to another adverse possessor as a result of the later possessor seizing possession from them.

Consensual subsequent adverse possessor

In cases where there as a transfer of the first squatter's possessory title, such consecutive, continuous periods of possession are treated as though they were a single act of possession, so that the periods of time are added up to work out whether the current possessor has the 'best' relative title. This makes no difference to the paper title-holder. If they have been out of possession for twelve years then their title is extinguished regardless of the interactions between the possessors, but for the squatters, it means that the earlier squatters are unable to sue on the basis of their own possessory title for they have voluntarily transferred this to another. This is logical, but it can make for difficult problem questions.

To give an example. Imagine that Aruna is the paper title-holder to a field surrounded by dilapidated fences. Sylvia decides to start growing crops on the field. To keep it all looking neat and to keep dog walkers out, she repairs the fences and installs a lock on the gate. This continues for five years until Sylvia's death. In her will, Sylvia left all of her property to her son, Rohan. Rohan, wishing to continue his mother's legacy on the field continues to cultivate it for another five years. At this point, Rohan, who has no idea that his mother did not have paper title to the land, decides to sell the field to a charity which helps young people learn how to grow their own food. The charity then continues to cultivate the field for another five years.

None of the individuals involved here is in adverse possession of the land for twelve years. However, Aruna, the paper title-holder, has not asserted her right to possession of the land for fifteen years. As a result of this, under the Limitation Act 1980, her title is extinguished. Since the transfers between Sylvia and Rohan (by will) and Rohan and the charity (*inter vivos*) all followed the correct procedures, the single possessory title which Sylvia acquired has been passed on now to the charity. This means that the charity is now the best title-holder and there is no one who is able to sue the charity for possession.

Non-consensual subsequent adverse possession

On the other hand, where subsequent squatters are not connected to one another, and there is no transfer of rights between them, each acquires their own possessory title which rank, as usual, according to which was created first. This means that it is necessary to examine each squatter in order to ask, has their title been extinguished? It is only once one individual squatter (or a chain of consensual possessors) has been in possession for a total of twelve years that they can be considered to have a title which cannot be defeated by one of the earlier possessory titles. It is important to remember however that the periods of adverse possession must be continuous: if there is a break in the chain of possession, time will begin to run again. Let us consider an example.

Gianpaolo is the paper title-holder to a cottage in a small village in Devon. He is never there however as he lives in Italy. He had bought the cottage in order to use it as a holiday home, but decided, on reflection, that he preferred Italy. He does not rent out the property, and having lain empty for a number of years, it is now falling into disrepair. Seeing this dilapidated cottage, Ivana decides that she will move in there for a few months as she cannot find a house to rent. She enters the property easily as all the locks on the doors have rotted away, and secures the property, adding new locks, fixing the windows etc. In total, she spends a year in the property. Ken, another resident of the village, sees Ivana entering the property one day, and knowing it is not hers, when she is out, changes the locks on the doors having broken in. He is now the only key-holder and he keeps an eye on the property making sure it is safe. This continues for ten years until Ken dies, leaving all his property to his son, Keith. Keith does not visit the cottage as he does not know about it. Shortly after Ken's death, Remy breaks into the cottage and secures it for his own use. He has been living there for the past two years.

In this situation it is necessary to build a small timeline. Gianpaolo has not been in possession of the property for 13 years. His title is therefore extinguished. Ivana obtained a possessory title. She has been absent from the property for 12 years. Her title too is extinguished. Ken (and therefore Keith) obtained a possessory title. This title has not been asserted for only two years. It has not therefore been extinguished. Finally, Remy has a possessory title. This means that the 'best' title here belongs to Keith. Keith's title will not be extinguished for another ten years, but Remy can defend his possession against all apart from Keith.

These problems demonstrate the critical importance of the underlying explanation for adverse possession in unregistered land, ie extinction of title. It is now time to turn to registered land, where underlying logic is somewhat different.

> **Summary: Adverse possession in unregistered land**
>
> Adverse possession in unregistered land results in the paper title-holder's title being extinguished after 12 years of continuous dispossession. If factual possession, an intention to possess by a third party, and a lack of permission continue, then the paper owner can no longer assert their title to the land. Whether the adverse possessor is able to assert title against all others depends upon them demonstrating that no other, unconnected, person has been in possession during the past 12 years.

6.3 ADVERSE POSSESSION AND REGISTERED LAND

Once the rules relating to adverse possession and unregistered land are fully understood, it becomes much easier to follow the process in relation to registered land. The Land Registration Act 2002 made a number of fairly fundamental changes in relation to the rules on adverse possession. At the heart of this is a switch in philosophy from the idea of extinction of title, to the idea of acquisition by possession. This is a very important change, because it means that where title is registered, unless the procedures in the LRA 2002 itself are followed, the registered proprietor cannot lose their title by adverse possession. There were some arguments at the time at which these changes were made whereby some argued that this represented an end to the idea of relativity of title in English land law since there would be an 'owner' in the form of the registered proprietor. However, this change does not remove the idea of relativity of title altogether. For example, a squatter still obtains a possessory title once they go into adverse possession and is still able to defend that possession against a third party. What has changed, fundamentally, is the consequence of being in adverse possession as far as the registered proprietor is concerned (ie the 'paper title-holder' in unregistered land terms).

There are two potential situations which can arise in relation to registered land. If the period of adverse possession, ie 12 years, was completed before the 1 Oct 2003, then the registered proprietor will hold on trust for the squatter and the squatter becomes entitled to apply to the registry to become registered proprietor. If the period of possession was *not* completed by this date, then the new rules in the LRA 2002 will apply to the squatter's claim, and, fundamentally, they cannot obtain title to the land simply by virtue of their possession.

This is because sections 95 and 96 of the LRA 2002 disapply the Limitation Act 1980 as far as registered land is concerned (that is, land where the freehold or leasehold title to that land is registered). The new rules on how adverse possession works are found in Schedule 6 of the 2002 Act:

Right to apply for registration

1(1) …a person may apply to the registrar to be registered as the proprietor of a registered estate in land if he has been in adverse possession of the estate for the period of ten years ending on the date of the application.

(2) …a person may also apply to the registrar to be registered as the proprietor of a registered estate in land if—

(a) he has in the period of six months ending on the date of the application ceased to be in adverse possession of the estate because of eviction by the registered proprietor, or a person claiming under the registered proprietor,

(b) on the day before his eviction he was entitled to make an application under sub-paragraph (1), and

(c) the eviction was not pursuant to a judgment for possession.

(3) However, a person may not make an application under this paragraph if—

(a) he is a defendant in proceedings which involve asserting a right to possession of the land, or

(b) judgment for possession of the land has been given against him in the last two years.

(4) For the purposes of sub-paragraph (1), the estate need not have been registered throughout the period of adverse possession.

Notification of application

2(1) The registrar must give notice of an application under paragraph 1 to—

(a) the proprietor of the estate to which the application relates,

(b) the proprietor of any registered charge on the estate,

(c) where the estate is leasehold, the proprietor of any superior registered estate,

(d) any person who is registered in accordance with rules as a person to be notified under this paragraph, and

(e) such other persons as rules may provide.

(2) Notice under this paragraph shall include notice of the effect of paragraph 4.

Treatment of application

- 3(1) A person given notice under paragraph 2 may require that the application to which the notice relates be dealt with under paragraph 5.
- (2) The right under this paragraph is exercisable by notice to the registrar given before the end of such period as rules may provide.
- 4 If an application under paragraph 1 is not required to be dealt with under paragraph 5, the applicant is entitled to be entered in the register as the new proprietor of the estate.'

Importantly, the definition of adverse possession itself has not changed. Thus the case law concerning the meaning of intention to possess and factual possession remains just as relevant as it was to the unregistered land rules. If such adverse possession is shown to have carried on for 10 years, then the squatter is able to apply to the land registry in order to become registered proprietor (paragraph 1). Having the right to apply to become registered proprietor does not however guarantee that this application will succeed.

Rather, on receiving this application, the land registry is then required to notify both the registered proprietor and, for example, a registered charge-holder, of the application.[40] Such persons are sent a notice. This notice requires action from them (within 65 working days) if they are to prevent the applicant becoming the new registered proprietor.[41] If the registered proprietor does not respond to the notice, then the applicant is automatically registered.[42] If the proprietor does respond, they have three options. First, the current proprietor can consent to the application. This may be the case, for example, where the application relates to a boundary situation where all parties are happy to regularise the legal position so that it matches up with practice 'on the ground'. Second, the current proprietor may make an objection. This objection, in effect, alleges that the adverse possessor has not in fact been in adverse possession for the required ten years such that the grounds for the application are not made out. Finally, the registered proprietor may serve a counter-notice.[43] If they take this last option, the adverse possessor cannot become registered proprietor unless one of three exceptions explained later applies. The operation of this notice procedure is neatly demonstrated by the facts of *Baxter v Mannion*.[44]

> **Key case:** *Baxter v Mannion* [2011] EWCA Civ 120
>
> In this case, Baxter applied to the Registry under the schedule 6 procedure. Whilst the notice was sent to Mannion, he did not respond within the required 65 days so that Baxter was automatically registered. However, Mannion then later argued that the Register should be altered because (a) he had legitimate reasons for not having responded, including family tragedies and (b) because Mannion had not in fact been in adverse possession for the required ten years. Both of these arguments were potentially significant for the operation of the 2002 Act. The first argument impliedly asked the court to exercise discretion

---

[40] Schedule 6, paragraph 2.
[41] Land Registration Rules 2003, rule 189.
[42] Schedule 6, paragraph 4.
[43] Schedule 6, paragraph 3 and Land Registration Rules 2003, rule 190.
[44] *Baxter v Mannion* [2011] EWCA Civ 120, [2011] 1 WLR 1594.

based on fairness to 'soften' the automatic procedures which schedule 6 establishes. The second asks a broader question about whether there was a 'mistake' on the register even if the procedures in schedule 6 had been followed correctly (the issue of the role of mistake in land registration is discussed in more detail in chapter 5).

On the first issue, the court had to consider whether to take account of the fact that Mannion did not respond, in part, because of his brother's death and the death of his three week-old grandson. In other words—is there discretion to extend the time limit in relation to the notice procedure in schedule 6? The court confirmed that there is not.

However, on the second issue, the court held that in cases where there is a substantive mistake, but the procedures have correctly been followed, the court nevertheless has the ability to require that the register be altered. Otherwise, on the reasoning of the court, despite Baxter never having had the ability to apply to be registered, would succeed in this, and that cannot have been in the intention of the drafters of the 2002 Act.

This conclusion is undoubtedly correct. It would be absurd if 'mistake' referred only to procedural errors. However, as we explored in chapter 5, concluding that substantive errors of this sort can lead to rectification of the register has led to a great deal of difficulty in deciding where exactly the line should be drawn. What this case emphasises is that the fact of being in adverse possession for the required time is absolutely essential, whatever the response of the land registry is to a false claim in that respect.

If the true owner has served a counter-notice, and fails to bring possession proceedings against the adverse possessor within the next two years, then the adverse possessor is able to apply to become registered proprietor once again and in this case registration would be automatic.[45] If the squatter is registered—either because the current registered proprietor fails to respond, consents to the application, or because the squatter has applied again following the two-year period—then the squatter will take the registered title subject to all pre-existing rights, apart from registered charges.[46] Unlike in unregistered land, the squatter here does not get a 'new' title to land. Rather, there is a deemed statutory assignment of the current registered title.

What this system establishes, in effect, is a mandatory warning system. It gives a registered proprietor a notification that there is someone on their land who has a possessory title to that land and who is claiming rights in it. If the registered proprietor still fails to take proper care of their land, they will lose title to it. The fastest this can be done given the ten-year rule for applications, and the two-year grace period for registered proprietors, is twelve years, and the parallel with unregistered land in this respect is deliberate. However, unlike with unregistered land, if the squatter of the registered land *never* applies to be registered, no matter how long his adverse possession continues, the registered proprietor's title will never be extinguished.

As is clear from the preceding discussion, the operation of the 'exceptions' in relation to the notification and counter-notice process is obviously essential in determining how likely a registered proprietor is to lose their land to an adverse possessor. On close inspection, these exceptions seem to be just that—a narrow range of circumstances in which the normal rules will not apply. Indeed, only one of these seems to be capable of constituting a genuine exception to the rules. The three exceptions are: first, where there is a proprietary estoppel such that it would be unjust not to register

---

[45] Schedule 6, paragraph 6.
[46] Schedule 6, paragraph 9.

the applicant as proprietor; second, where the applicant is entitled to be registered for some other reason; and third, in respect of boundaries. Let us now consider these exceptions in more detail.

The first exception, is in schedule 6, paragraph 5(2). It states that:

'The first condition is that—

(a) it would be unconscionable because of an equity by estoppel for the registered proprietor to seek to dispossess the applicant, and

(b) the circumstances are such that the applicant ought to be registered as the proprietor'.

At first glance, this exception seems odd. If the applicant has the benefit of an estoppel (for the rules regarding proprietary estoppel, see chapter 8), then why would they need additionally to rely on adverse possession in order to attempt to obtain a right in the relevant land? Certainly, the examples given by the Law Commission in their report explaining the provisions of the 2002 Act seem to fall foul of this argument.[47] However, on closer inspection there is a cogent argument that this exception means something more specific than merely the existence of a proprietary estoppel. Rather than covering proprietary estoppel in general, it may cover situations where the estoppel relates specifically to the application to become registered.

For example, let us imagine that Clare, a registered proprietor, discovers that Lindsay, a squatter, is likely shortly to make an application to be registered. Wishing to resolve matters in a way which makes everyone happy, Clare approaches Lindsay and suggests that, whilst Lindsay has been in possession of the whole of the relevant land, if Lindsay only applies to be registered as proprietor of half, gives up her claim to the other half, and pays Clare £10,000 to cover some damage done to the half which Clare will keep, then Clare will not object. They do not write this agreement down, but Lindsay goes ahead and submits an application to be registered as proprietor and pays Clare £10,000. Clare, having changed her mind, serves a counter-notice. It is suggested that, in this scenario, it may be concluded that Clare's actions resulted in an equity by estoppel arising in Lindsay's favour (as Lindsay gave up her right to apply in relation to the rest of the land and paid Clare £10,000 on the basis of a promise made by Clare). It would also seem in such a case to be a proportionate response to the injustice caused to Lindsay, and the loss suffered by Clare (it is important to keep in mind that Clare has been sufficiently disinterested in her land for at least ten years to allow Lindsay to build up the right to apply), to allow Lindsay to succeed in her application.

It appears then, that if this estoppel exception is limited to specific assurances relating to the application itself, then this exception may have a very limited, but nevertheless, useful, function to play.

The same cannot really be said of the second exception contained in schedule 6, paragraph 5(4)(b). This states that:

'The second condition is that the applicant is for some other reason entitled to be registered as the proprietor of the estate'.

---

[47] Law Commission, Land Registration for the Twenty-First Century: A Conveyancing Revolution, Law Commission Report No. 271 (London, 2001), [14.40].

It is difficult to ascertain what was intended by this exception. If the applicant is entitled to be registered as proprietor for some reason other than adverse possession, then it would seem very strange for them to be relying on adverse possession at all. Rather, they will just rely on the transfer by deed or by will which constituted the reason why they were entitled to be registered in any case. This suggests that the reason for the existence of this exception may well be to explicitly allow such persons to be registered even if they do not succeed in their adverse possession claim.

Finally, and by far the most important in practice, there is the boundary exception contained in schedule 6, paragraph 4(5)(c). This states that:

'The third condition is that—

(a) the land to which the application relates is adjacent to land belonging to the applicant,

(b) the exact line of the boundary between the two has not been determined under rules under section 60,

(c) for at least ten years of the period of adverse possession ending on the date of the application, the applicant (or any predecessor in title) reasonably believed that the land to which the application relates belonged to him, and

(d) the estate to which the application relates was registered more than one year prior to the date of the application'.

In its most basic terms, this exception refers to cases where some physical feature on the land, or previous documentation, made it look as though the boundary line between two pieces of land was in a particular place but where this was an error. For a number of years (at least ten), all concerned will likely have continued on in ignorance of the error, perfectly happy with the status quo. Then, likely due to a transfer of neighbouring land, or an investigation into the possibility of development or planning permission, it comes to light that the fence is in the wrong place. What this exception allows for is the adverse possessor to succeed in their claim to become registered proprietor of the disputed land. The reason for this is that, first, it helps to protect good neighbourly relations (remember again, to succeed, the registered proprietor will likely have been relatively happy with the current situation for a long period of time). Second, it allows the legal rights position to catch up with practical reality. This is a function which the law of adverse possession has been playing for many years. In English law, practical solutions are usually selected over precise and perfect theoretical frameworks. This boundary exception rule is a pragmatic response to a fear that the very useful role of adverse possession in regularising boundaries would be lost in the search to achieve perfect security of title.

In order to strike the right balance, however, the paragraph imposes a number of conditions before the applicant can become registered proprietor. First, the disputed land must be adjacent to land 'belonging to' the application (we will return to the meaning of belonging to shortly). Second, there has been no determination of the exact boundary under section 60 of the LRA 2002 (the official procedure by which boundaries are fixed as the register itself is not conclusive as to boundaries). Third, for at least ten years ending on the date of the application (or, in reality, shortly before the date of the application), the applicant must have reasonably believed that the disputed land belonged to them (again, we will return to the key aspects of this conditions shortly). Finally, the disputed land must have been registered for at least a year before this condition can apply.

The second and fourth conditions of this paragraph are relatively straightforward and are certainly easy to establish in any particular case. Much more problematic are conditions one and three. The first is difficult because of the imprecision in the language, 'belonging to'. This language could mean simply, 'is registered proprietor of'. This is a simple and easy to apply test. However, one assumes that the drafters of the LRA 2002 avoided this formulation on the basis that they did not want to exclude the operation of paragraph 5(4) in cases where the applicant's adjacent land was unregistered, for example. However, by failing to define this precisely, the situation arises where an applicant may be able to argue that the adjacent land 'belongs to them' by virtue of a *possessory* title, so that where an application is adversely possessing *two* adjacent plots of land they may be able rely on paragraph 5(4) in relation to both. It is unlikely that a court would adopt this interpretation—it is probably not what was intended by the drafters of the statute—but it is a consequence of the ambiguity of 'belonging to' here.

The third condition has a number of potentially complex elements in it also. The first is the requirement that the ten years of reasonable belief end 'on the date of the application'. In practical terms, this is not possible. Rather, it has been interpreted to mean within a short time frame after the truth comes to light. The second issue relates to the reasonable belief requirement. The test for such reasonable belief has been discussed in the case law, and we will discuss is shortly. Before that though it is interesting to note that again the reasonable belief is that the land 'belonged to' them. This, as before, raises the issue as to what belonging to means in this context, why that language was chosen rather than a more precise label, and what exactly, therefore, it is that the applicant needs to have believed.

Notwithstanding this, it is the meaning of the reasonableness requirement which has raised the most difficulties in terms of the application of these provisions. We can see this in *IAM Group v Chowdery*.[48]

> **Key case:** *IAM Group v Chowdery* [2012] EWCA Civ 505
>
> In this case, the error as to boundaries would have been apparent had the squatter carefully consulted the documentation regarding their purchase. Their solicitor would have been aware of the real location of the boundary between the two relevant properties if they were reasonably competent (no evidence was given in the case as to what the solicitor actually knew).
>
> Etherton LJ on behalf of the court held that what mattered was the reasonableness of the claimant's belief, not questions of constructive knowledge. The squatter here had 18 years of unchallenged occupation of the land, and that in itself was said to form part of the 'reasonableness' assessment. The decision also confirms the approach in *Zarb v Parry*,[49] where the court held that merely being challenged as to your ownership will not necessarily be enough to render your belief in your ownership unreasonable.

---

[48] *IAM Group v Chowdery* [2012] EWCA Civ 505, [2012] 2 P & CR 13.
[49] *Zarb v Parry* [2011] EWCA Civ 1306, [2012] 1 WLR 1240.

> In that case it was also confirmed that the presence of physical features on the land (in that case, a hedge) will feed into the question of reasonableness of belief.
>
> Whilst this case clearly comes down on the side of the applicant to the land registry given their own subjective knowledge, it is perhaps a little surprising that a lack of knowledge consequent upon a failure either to examine or to obtain detailed legal advice on the conveyancing documentation was considered reasonable. In most areas of land law, we operate under the '*caveat emptor*' approach which is that it is your fault if you do not know a relevant fact about what you are buying. In this case though, it could perhaps be said that the fact of asking and employing a relatively competent solicitor ought to be enough for you to acquire the relevant knowledge.

Finally on the exceptions in paragraph 5(4), we must think more broadly about the question as to what constitutes a 'boundary' for the purposes of this exception and whether this will apply to disputes involving adjacent land no matter how large and extensive the land relating to the application is. Certainly, this would feed into the question of reasonableness and so in practice there may be very few cases where a substantial amount of land was acquired through adverse possession through reliance on this sub-paragraph. However, it does raise the issue as to precisely what the purpose of this exception is, whether it is really about boundaries and the fact that land registry plans are not conclusive as to boundaries, or is it really about ensuring that in 'neighbours' cases, the legal rights are altered to fit practice.

The final issue to deal with in relation to registered land is the question of multiple squatters. Unlike in unregistered land where the underlying logic is one of extinction of title, because here we are considering *acquisition* of registered title through possession, the rules operate differently. The wording of schedule 6 makes it clear that it is the applicant themselves who must have been in possession for the required ten-year period. The general rule therefore is that the squatter cannot add periods of possession to their own to reach ten years. This general rule is modified by two exceptions which allow the squatter to 'add up' time in certain specific cases. The first is what was referred to earlier as a consensual transfer.[50] That is, the when the current squatter is successor in title to an earlier squatter or multiple earlier squatters. The second case, which is much less significant, is that a squatter can add up periods of possession in cases where she is in possession, another squatter then comes into possession, and then she returns to possession as long as the whole chain is a continuous one.[51]

6.4 ADVERSE POSSESSION AND LEASES

So far, we have considered the situation where adverse possession takes place 'against' a freeholder. However, it is of course possible to have a situation where someone goes into adverse possession in relation to land in which there is a lease. Furthermore, there are situations in which a tenant himself may go into adverse possession either against his own landlord—ie he goes into

---

[50] Schedule 6, paragraph 11(2)(a).
[51] Schedule 6, paragraph 11(2)(b).

possession of land which was not granted to him as part of the lease—or against a third party, for example in a situation involving a mistaken boundary. What happens in these cases? The rules regarding the interaction between adverse possession and leases are somewhat complex and in many cases do not entirely follow the 'logic' of extinction of title and possessory titles to land being acquired through adverse possession. Therefore, it is useful to simply think of these rules as being their own separate category of rules. Let us break these down into three categories.

6.4.1 ADVERSE POSSESSION AGAINST A TENANT

First, there is the situation where an adverse possessor goes into possession of land in which there is a lease. Here, since the freeholder has voluntarily transferred his right to exclusive possession to the tenant (see chapter 10), the freeholder cannot lose his title through the Limitation Act since there is no failure to exercise his rights in such cases. Rather, the tenant has the right to exclusive possession and it is his right which is to be extinguished. What this means is that when an adverse possessor goes into possession against a tenant, the estate in which he obtains a possessory title is the leasehold estate, and the most he can acquire, as a result, is title for the remaining term of the lease. This is entirely logical, with the twist that strictly speaking the case law holds that he obtains a *freehold* title which will come to an end at the date at which the lease would have come to an end. This linguistic complication does not particularly add to our understanding of what the adverse possessor has, however, so that we can conclude that *in effect*, he acquires the leasehold estate.

However, this brings with it its own complications. What happens, for example, in cases where the landlord has a right to bring the lease to an end early (called a right of re-entry or forfeiture, explained in chapter 10 at 10.5.3) in certain situations, such as the non-payment of rent, or has the benefit of a break clause. Can the landlord exercise these rights thereby bringing the adverse possessor's title 'to an end' early? The answer from the case law appears to be yes. Again, this is entirely logical, but it can sometimes be difficult to apply these rules in practice.

In registered land, although there appear to be no decided cases on the point, we can assume that the adverse possessor acquires the right to apply to become registered proprietor of the registered leasehold estate.

6.4.2 ADVERSE POSSESSION BY A TENANT AGAINST HIS LANDLORD

The second way in which leases and adverse possession can interact is in cases where the tenant adversely possesses against his landlord. We have already considered the case where the tenant 'holds over' after the end of his tenancy and continues in possession, as in *Pye v Graham*.[52] This is a perfectly normal adverse possession situation. What is being referred to here is the case where a tenant goes into possession of land, title to which belongs to his landlord, but which was not included in the grant of the original lease. In such cases as these, rather than giving the tenant a freehold title to the land possessed, the law effectively extends the scope of his lease so that the leasehold estate becomes physically larger. This somewhat anomalous result is difficult to explain.

---

[52] *Pye v Graham* [2002] UKHL 30; [2003] 1 AC 419.

The possessory title which the tenant obtains on going into possession should be a freehold title, since he is possessing as against a freeholder. However, the explanation seems to lie in something akin to estoppel, so that the tenant is estopped from denying the landlord and tenant relationship between himself and the landlord given that it is the existence of the lease which has afforded him access to the land in the first place.

Whilst this rule is relatively well established in relation to unregistered land, it is very uncertain how the rules operate in registered land. The Law Commission report does not hugely assist in terms of analysing how the new approach of application will work in such cases. Does the tenant apply to be registered of a leasehold estate if the 'lease' they have acquired is over seven years' duration? What happens if their remaining leasehold term is shorter than this? How does this interact with the fact that the case law has concluded that strictly speaking there is a freehold in situations like this, albeit a time limited one? The answer, with some uncertainty, appears to be that the tenant in these circumstances is unable to apply to be registered under the rules on adverse possession. He may however be able to apply on the basis of an estoppel or something akin to an estoppel.[53]

6.4.3 ADVERSE POSSESSION BY A TENANT AGAINST A THIRD PARTY

This final situation is the strangest of all. In such cases, the tenant, through being on land over which he has a lease, is able to access land belonging to a third party, and extending his use of the leasehold land, goes into possession of the third-party land. In such cases, as with the previous scenario, we might expect the law to conclude that the tenant has a possessory freehold title in the third party land which then becomes a superior title when the freeholder's title is extinguished after 12 years (the position in relation to registered land is considered later). However, that is not what the rules establish in these cases. Rather, the tenant is said to obtain a leasehold estate in the land and his *landlord* obtains the freehold estate. In effect, the adverse possession of the tenant is said to be 'on behalf' of his landlord. Again, this could be explained by something akin to estoppel—the tenant is estopped from denying the landlord and tenant relationship and since there is an intimacy of connection between his squatting and the existence of the lease, that explains why he is only treated has having a leasehold estate. This does not really explain why the landlord is able to obtain the freehold title however, as the landlord does not have a possessory title of any kind.

Again, how these rules operate in relation to registered land is uncertain. Although it appears to be the landlord who is entitled to the freehold estate in such land, on a strict reading of schedule 6, they do not have the ability to apply. However, the estoppel which exists between the landlord and tenant so as to prevent the tenant from denying his status means that the tenant seems unable to apply either. The Law Commission, however, has indicated that it does not regard legislative reform as necessary to allow the landlord to apply. Instead, there is a suggestion in the recent report that the preferred option is simply for the land registry to amend its policies in this regard.[54]

---

[53] For more detail, see E Lees, 'Encroachments and schedule 6 LRA 2002: unknotting the tangle' (2015) 79 Conveyancer and Property Lawyer 110.

[54] Law Commission, 'Updating the Land Registration Act 2002' Law Commission Report no. 380 (July, 2018), 400–401.

6.5 ADVERSE POSSESSION AND CRIMINAL LAW

The next issue which this chapter will consider is the interaction between adverse possession and the criminal law. In many situations, an adverse possessor is likely to have committed a criminal offence in the course of their possession. This could be as a result of having damaged property belonging to the paper title-holder, of having broken into the property, or, in the case of residential properties, sometimes by virtue of being in possession of that land in itself. This chapter will outline some of the key criminal offences which apply in this area, before considering the general question of how this impacts upon the land law rules. Does the fact that an adverse possessor has committed a criminal offence prevent them from acquiring title to land under the adverse possession rules or applying to the land registry in order to become registered proprietor?

The most significant criminal law provision in this context is section 144 Legal Aid, Sentencing and Punishment of Offenders Act 2012. We will return to that shortly. It is important to remember that it is not the only provision which may criminalise some of the activities of a squatter. Prominent amongst these alternative provisions is the offence contained in section 7 Criminal Law Act 1977. This applies where an individual enters land as a trespasser (thereby excluding, for example, tenants holding-over after the end of their lease) and fails to leave the property when asked to do so by a displaced residential occupier. Whilst it is clear that in many adverse possession situations there would be no such request (in such cases one would imagine that the displaced occupier would bring an action for possession against the squatter), it is possible to imagine situations where that would be the case, not least where the occupier is not a freeholder or leaseholder, but a licensee who, on being displaced, may not have a big incentive to pursue an action for possession themselves. It can also be a criminal offence to damage property (eg breaking down a door) in order enter onto premises (Criminal Damage Act 1971), and if a person objects to an entry and violence is threatened to secure it, it will be an offence under section 6 Criminal Law Act 1977. All of these offences may be committed in the process of going into adverse possession, depending upon the circumstances.

The most important offence in the context of adverse possession is, however, the offence in section 144 of LAPSOA 2012. Before this offence, as we have seen, whilst in many cases a criminal offence would be committed in the act of going into adverse possession, LAPSOA makes the act of squatting itself the criminal offence. The only exceptions are those found in the statute itself, ie in cases where the squatting consists of a tenant holding on after the end of their lease, and in cases where the squatter did not enter the land as a trespasser, but as an invited visitor, for example, who subsequently refuses to leave.

The advent of this particular offence however brought to the fore the difficult issue of the interaction between adverse possession and the criminal law. Whilst there was already a significant degree of cross-over, as indicated, never before have the two things been so explicitly linked. As a result of this the land registry was left with a problem. In cases involving a claim for adverse possession, should they accept an application from an adverse possessor to become registered since they would (almost) definitely have committed a criminal offence in the process of acquiring their possessory title and as such, allowing them to be registered would allow them to profit from their own wrongdoing? This would run contrary to an importance principle of English law, that a criminal should not profit from his crime. Allowing a squatter to become registered in these circumstances, would, on this argument, be tantamount to saying: what you are doing is a crime, but if you keep it up for a really long time, then we will reward you with a big windfall in the form of title to the land. On the other hand, section 144 is arguably tackling a somewhat different issue than is present in adverse possession cases which continue for ten years. Section 144 was introduced, in part, as a response to the 'Occupy' protests and was designed to allow residential occupiers to enlist the help of the police in evicting trespassers from their property. Without this offence, the trespass itself would not have been a crime so that rather than involving the police, the residential occupier would have had to obtain an order for possession through the courts, a much slower and more costly process. The interaction between the two sets of rules was considered by the Court of Appeal in *Best v Chief Land Register*.[55]

> **Key case: *Best v Chief Land Registrar* [2015] EWCA Civ 17**
>
> In the decision in *Best v Chief Land Registrar*, the Court of Appeal was required to assess the validity of this argument. The court concluded that in situations such as these, the land law rules should prevail so that the adverse possessor is entitled to become registered proprietor (or at least apply to be so registered). This is in many ways a surprising conclusion, and the reasons of the Court of Appeal are not entirely convincing, even though in reality, the problem being tackled by section 144 is miles removed from the situation where an individual manages to possess residential land for ten or twelve years. The Court of Appeal justified its conclusion, essentially on the basis, that the public interest in continuing to allow adverse possession claims to succeed outweighed the principle of *ex turpi causa*.
>
> *Best* has been largely welcomed. The failure of the drafters of the 2012 Act provisions to examine the interaction between these rules and the rules on adverse possession was roundly criticised. There are however some remaining questions from *Best*, as Goymour explains:
>
>> 'Most problematic is the fact that, even though Mr. Best's criminal conduct did not bar his civil law claim, he remains vulnerable to criminal prosecution and, should his Schedule 6 application for title succeed, might have to give up the profits of his crime under the Proceeds of Crime Act 2002'.[56]
>
> Whilst Mr Best could successfully apply to be registered through the land registration provisions, therefore, this does not mean that he is immune from subsequently having to give up that title later, and as such, the interaction between these different areas of law is not yet entirely settled.

6.6 EXPLANATIONS FOR ADVERSE POSSESSION

The adverse possession rules are, in places, technical, but at their heart is the idea that an individual can lose title to their land, be that registered or unregistered, through simple inaction. This idea requires some explanation as it is both surprising and some would say, a sort of state-sanctioned theft of land. How can we justify or explain this? First, it is important to recognise that although there

---

[55] *Best v Chief Land Registrar* [2015] EWCA Civ 17; [2016] QB 23.
[56] A Goymour, 'Squatters and the criminal law: can two wrongs make a right?' (2014) 73 Cambridge Law Journal 484, 486.

is one single idea behind all these rules, adverse possession may be performing different functions in the different contexts in which it arises. Specifically, adverse possession in a boundary situation, for example, operates simply to ensure that the legal rights reflect reality on the ground, a situation which the relevant parties may often be perfectly happy with, being unaware of any problem. At the other extreme, the rules allow for a situation where a relatively 'minor' act of 'taking control' (such as changing locks and supervising access to an empty house) results in an individual acquiring title to what may be very valuable property without the paper title-holder even being aware of the risks. We may say, and with some justification, that the same arguments cannot apply in these two hugely divergent practical situations. However, it is important to think about the role which adverse possession plays in general, and how this affects the way in which we should analyse the relevant rules.

The first potential justification, or explanation, for the adverse possession rules lies in the problems of proof of title associated with unregistered land. For unregistered land, it can be very difficult to 'prove' title in the sense that where a chain of conveyance relies on the passing on of physical deeds in the form of a bundle of papers, over time, it can be very easy for some of the papers to be lost. Furthermore, there is always the risk with unregistered land (and, as was seen in chapter 5, with registered land), that transactions have taken place where the 'true' paper title-holder did not consent to a sale or other transfer of the land and there was, for example, a forged deed. This transaction may have taken place so far in the distant past, however, that no one still living can be sure whether the transaction was valid or not. There are a number of different ways of solving these problems—one such is to impose a 'cut-off' date in terms of chains of conveyance so that the court would be satisfied if a chain of conveyance can be proved going back, eg 15-years or so. Another way of solving this problem is adverse possession. As long as the 'current owner' is able to show a continuous and consensual chain of possession tracing back twelve years, thanks to the possibility of extinction of title, there is no one who can defeat her. This 'proof-based' justification has been the subject of a number of academic articles. As Ballantine states, '[i]t is one thing to have the rightful ownership and just title to land; it is another thing to have the proof of that right which can be laid before a purchaser or before a jury'.[57] Harpum agrees with this: '[t]he policy which justifies this is the facilitation of conveyancing by narrowing the range and timespan of enquiries which have to be made when investigating a title'.[58] This explanation for the development of the adverse possession rules is historically convincing. It is not however enormously helpful in the era of registered land where proof of title is a much less significant problem. This can help to explain therefore why the LRA 2002 makes such a radical change to the rules regarding adverse possession: the extinction of title process is (arguably) no longer required.

The second potential justification given for adverse possession is that, given the scarcity of land, if someone does not make use of their land for a twelve year (or ten year) period, and does not even pay sufficient attention to that land so that they are completely unaware that another person has been in possession of that land for the relevant period, then we would be 'better off' to ensure that the land was in the hands of someone who makes good economic use of it. This can in turn be explained in two ways. First, there is the idea of 'just deserts': because the squatter has put their time and effort into the land, and made economic use of it, they deserve title after a sufficiently long period of time. Second, on an efficiency analysis, ownership of the land by the squatter who uses the land is more

---

[57] H W Ballantine, 'Title by adverse possession' (1918) 32 Harvard Law Review 135, 136.
[58] C Harpum, 'Adverse possession and future intentions' (1990) 49 Cambridge Law Journal 23, 23.

efficient. These are two different justifications—one is based on a sense of fairness, the other on an economic analysis (or assumption) as to the best possible use of the land—but they are both focussing on the same sort of justification, which is that there is a moral or economic reason (as opposed to a legal reason) as to why adverse possession is possible. We could also think of this in terms of scarcity and housing need, since adverse possession of residential properties is most likely to occur in cases involving squatters. The further reading section in this chapter gives some additional reading on the role of squatting in English law, but it is useful to note here that whilst some squatting does indeed involve adverse possession, much does not since the population of squats is often transient, and no one person or group of persons together seizes control of access. Given this, whilst there may good reasons for arguing that a person who ignores their property should, in some way, face a sanction given the lack of quality housing for all, tying that specifically to adverse possession requires some sensitivity as to the precise conditions in which the adverse possession is taking place.

A third way of thinking about the role of adverse possession is to distinguish between the negative operation of the Limitation Act itself which is all about preventing a previous title-holder (be that a paper title or a possessory title) from asserting that, and the positive effect of possessory title existing at all, which means that if all other titles fall away through limitation, only the possessor retains a title at all. There are, in effect, two separate things occurring, which combine to produce the consequence what we refer to as 'adverse possession'. But they are two functions which are not necessarily dependent upon each other, and as such, we can justify them separately. Limitation of actions is justified on the grounds that there would be paralysing uncertainty in relation to the use, transfer, and disposition of land if there was a fear that at any moment a successor in title from a long distant proprietor of the land could turn up and demand its return to them. Possessory title is justified as a response to the dangers of self-help. By allowing a person in possession to defend that possession, we prevent others attempting to forcibly remove them from the land. Furthermore, possessory title in some situations may be all there is since no paper record is available. In such cases, it is important for there to be *someone* who is able to evict trespassers on the land and be responsible for safety and other issues on the land. Adverse possession as a means by which someone with a possessory title becomes the 'best' relative title-holder is merely a consequence of limitation and possessory title, on this approach.

Whichever of these justifications is chosen, however, there is a final concern with these rules, which is the extent to which they are compliant with human rights. More detail is given on how human rights operate in this context in chapter 17 at 17.3.1. To summarise, however, article 1 protocol 1 of the European Convention on Human Rights introduces a 'right to property'. In other words, this allows the holder of rights (be they in land or in chattels or indeed in intellectual property), to retain those rights except in cases where depriving them of their rights is a proportionate response to a legitimate need in a democratic society. That this protection is part of English law was ensured by the Human Rights Act 1998. This requires, in section 3, that all legislation be interpreted in such a way as to ensure compliance with human rights. Section 6 provides that all public authorities (including the courts) comply with human rights. Which of the justifications is the best explanation of adverse possession therefore shapes the enquiry as to whether adverse possession can be seen as a proportionate response to a legitimate need in a democratic society (there is no doubt that a person is being deprived of their property). This issue was addressed in the case of *Pye v UK*,[59] ie the follow up to *Pye v Graham*.[60]

---

[59] *Pye v UK* (2006) 43 EHRR 3, [2005] ECHR 921.
[60] *J A Pye (Oxford) v Graham* [2002] UKHL 30, [2003] 1 AC 419.

> **Key case:** *Pye v UK* (2006) 43 EHRR 3
>
> The decision of the Grand Chamber of the European Court of Human Rights represents the end of a long line of judicial decisions considering the question as to whether the adverse possession rules in unregistered land represent a breach of human rights. By a narrow margin, the court concluded that they did not. Taking into account that margin of appreciation given to signatory states, the court held that the determination made here that practical possession was more important after a certain point that formal title was a legitimate one for a state to make. In reaching this conclusion, the court highlighted the general importance of limitation of actions and the ease with which a paper title-holder could protect themselves.
>
> In respect of this former point, the court cites its own judgment in *Stubbings*[61] where it stated:
>
>> 'They [limitations on actions] serve several important purposes, namely to ensure legal certainty and finality, protect potential defendants from stale claims which might be difficult to counter and prevent the injustice which might arise if courts were required to decide upon events which took place in the distant past on the basis of evidence which might have become unreliable and incomplete because of the passage of time'.[62]
>
> In essence, the court was of the view that limitations on actions, and the consequential interaction with possessory title, was in itself sufficient justification for the adverse possession rules, giving some support to the third explanation. This explanation does not work for registered land, however, since there is no limitation in this context. The explanation for the on-going possibility of adverse possession in registered land, albeit with the warning system in place, does therefore demand a different explanation. The court was however clear that the new system definitely complied with the relevant human rights controls.

6.7 CONCLUSION

Overall, adverse possession is surprising, and to many, counter-intuitive. Once the logic behind it and the reason behind the development of the rules are understood, it becomes not only relatively easy to justify *in certain situations*, but also the precise shape of the rules becomes more understandable. Adverse possession is a classic situation where English land law has chosen to prioritise flexibility, responsiveness to facts on the ground, and a certain degree of pragmatism, over the absolutes which a registered land system may be said to provide. Indeed, by allowing some, albeit limited role, for adverse possession in the LRA 2002, the legislature has demonstrated a clear recognition that adverse possession as a doctrine has some very important and useful functions to play in English land law, especially in relation to the regularisation of boundaries.

Beyond this however, adverse possession is also an almost inevitable outcome of the twin ideas of limitations of actions and relativity of title, and as such can be seen to be a classic expression of the effects of the underlying doctrines. This is not to say, however, that the law is unsympathetic to those who lose their land through mere inaction. It is very straightforward for the paper title-holder to land to maintain their title by, in unregistered land, simply giving the possessor

---

[61] *Stubbings v UK* (1996) 23 EHRR 213, [1996] ECHR 44.
[62] *Stubbings v UK* (1996) 23 EHRR 213, [1996] ECHR 44, [51].

permission, for example, and in registered land, by replying to the notice provided by the land registry. Understanding adverse possession is not only important in itself, it is important as an insight into the fundamental workings, and logic, of English land law.

PRINCIPLES

How does this discussion shape our understanding of the principles explained in chapter 1? To recap, these principles were:

1. Certainty
2. Sensitivity to context
3. Transactability
4. Systemic and individual effects
5. Recognition of the social role of the land law system.

As noted earlier, and referred to in the further reading section later, the first thing that we must establish in exploring the relationship between the principles of land law, and the rules explained in this chapter, is that squatting—unlawful occupation of property, a consequence most often of the lack of availability of housing, of economic inequality, and of wider social problems such as drug addiction and abuse—and adverse possession are not the same thing. Indeed, a discussion as to how the principles of land law are reflected in our legal approach to squatting would be very different from that which follows here. However, adverse possession—being as it is both a wider and narrower phenomenon—engages these principles in a different way.

The rules of adverse possession are fundamentally about certainty. In unregistered land they provided a way of ensuring that the loss of paper documents relating to title to land is not fatal either to establishing the relative merits of claims, or to the proper functioning of the market in land. Even in registered land, the rules do still have this in their sights in respect of boundaries. The operation of the exceptions in paragraph 5 of schedule 6 is so unclear, except in relation to boundaries however, that we can perhaps say that the *only* time when acquisition of registered title through adverse possession in registered land is now effectively automatic, as long as the possessor applies to the registry, is in the case of boundaries. The certainty that this system provides—both in formal and moral terms—cannot be overstated and it is an enormously important function. With this certainty, comes transactibility. Furthermore, in the case of registered land, the fact that title acquisition is not automatic, means that purchasers of land will not accidentally acquire land from one not entitled to the paper title, on the grounds that such a person appears to be able to prove title through possession. The narrowing of the rules in relation to registered land therefore actually supports transactibility, and the different rules in the different types of land can be supported on that basis.

However, not all areas of the rules relating to adverse possession are clear and certain. The rules relating to the interaction between registered land, leases, and adverse possession are frankly, a mess. The fact that we have not had the benefit of significant amounts of case law on this question suggests that there are few problems in practice, but that does not justify a failure to clearly explain the new system in this context. In a different way, the very definition of adverse possession itself could be said to be uncertain, relying as it does on very precise facts. It is however very sensitive to the precise context, as we saw in relation to the discussion of adverse possession of the river bed.

In the more unusual cases involving adverse possession of larger strips of land or whole plots, as in *Pye*, however, the arguments from our principles are less clear, and depend very much on how one views what adverse possession rules are designed to achieve. From an economic perspective, we could say that the rules act as long term incentive to take care of, pay attention to, and possibly even use, one's land. Whilst the rules do not precisely require this, by making a consequence of inaction and ignorance of the state of one's land the possibility of loss of title to that land, the rules may ensure that landowners pay more attention to their land than they might otherwise do so. The counter argument to this of course is that the adverse possession rules require only that: attention, and they do not require use, and so the arguments of 'best economic use' are not entirely convincing in that respect. However, if one does take this 'use-focused' economic justification seriously, then this would demonstrate land law responding positively to the social function of land, by attempting to ensure that this scarce resource is utilised, to some extent, efficiently. On the other hand, in those cases where we are dealing with a situation involving squatting, the position from a social purpose angle is more mixed, as squatting is only really possible in properties which are otherwise unoccupied or derelict. By focusing on *control* rather than *use*, the adverse possession rules in this way do not assist those in desperate housing need.

TABLE OF DEFINITIONS

Possession	The right to, or the fact of, control of land characterised by the ability to exclude others.
Factual possession	The physical ability to exclude others from land.
Intention to possess	The intention to exclude others from land as far as reasonably possible.
Adverse	Without the consent of the paper title-holder.
Extinction of title	The process by which a paper title is extinguished through limitation. To be contrasted with a process of acquisition of title.

FURTHER READING

Whilst much of the discussion in this chapter has been concerned with adverse possession, behind the scenes adverse possession is very closely linked to squatting. The two are not necessarily present together. The economic reality of land, however, is that squatting can lead to adverse possession, and it is in this particularly contentious area that many of the discussions surrounding the justifications for adverse possession are to be found. This further reading list suggests some starting points for examining the issue of squatting, its relationship to land law, and of the arguments surrounding responsible and socially-aware use of lands.

ALEXANDER, G., 'The Social-Obligation Norm in American Property Law' (2009) 94 Cornell L Rev 745.
FOX O'MAHONEY, L. and COBB, N., 'Taxonomies of squatting: unlawful occupation in a new legal order' (2008) 71 MLR 878.
FOX O'MAHONEY, L., O'MAHONEY, D. and HICKEY, R., *Moral Rhetoric and the Criminalisation of Squatting* (Routledge, 2016).

7

IMPLIED TRUSTS

7.1 Introduction	191	7.6 Reform	228
7.2 Express Trusts	192	7.7 Conclusion	230
7.3 Statutory Trusts	194	Principles	231
7.4 Constructive Trusts	195	Table of Definitions	232
7.5 Resulting Trusts	220	Further Reading	232

> **CHAPTER GOALS**
>
> By the end of this chapter you should understand:
>
> - How express trusts are created;
> - The statutory trust which arises under the Law of Property Act 1925;
> - The circumstances which will give rise to a constructive trust;
> - The circumstances which will give rise to a resulting trust; and
> - The plans regarding reform of the law in this area.

7.1 INTRODUCTION

As we have seen in chapter 4, rights in land are, for the most part, created by following a number of formal steps. These formal steps help to ensure certainty, clarity for the parties, and a degree of caution and deliberateness in the relevant process, all of which are enormously welcome in the day-to-day operation of the land law rules. However, too rigid an insistence on formality rules can facilitate one party taking advantage of another; can frustrate parties' expectations; and can produce unwelcome consequences when a relationship breaks down, for example, which may result in one person being left with no home, and no resources to acquire another. As we have and will see across this book, the socio-economic consequences of land law rules can be enormously significant—the law relating to mortgages shows this all too clearly (see chapter 11)—but there is perhaps no more acute a clash between the 'emotional reality' of people's 'lived experience' and the systemic focus of the principles of land law, than in respect of division of property on relationship breakdown. Thus, whatever the merits of formality rules in general, the law has recognised

192   Chapter 7   Implied Trusts

that there are certain circumstances where the informal interactions between parties justifies the creation or adjustment of property rights outwith the normal process. The law relating to implied trusts is one such example. Another, proprietary estoppel, is explored in the next chapter.

In this chapter we will recap, first, on the creation of express trusts (see also chapter 4 at 4.3.3). Second, we discuss the statutory trust of land arising through the Law of Property Act 1925. The chapter will then explore the law relating to constructive trusts in 7.4. In 7.5, we will consider the rules surrounding resulting trusts, before turning to questions of reform in 7.6. The chapter should be read in conjunction with chapter 16 which is concerned with the nature of the trust. It must be noted from the outset that this chapter is case law-heavy. The law relating to implied trusts is almost entirely a judicial invention, and perhaps even more importantly, the relative vagueness of many of the rules means that a knowledge of how they work in practice from existing case law is essential. Appreciating the rich tapestry of this case law is crucial to a robust analysis of the doctrines.

7.2 EXPRESS TRUSTS

Before we look in detail at constructive and resulting trusts, it is useful briefly to recap on how trusts are expressly created (also explained in chapter 4 at 4.3.3) and to consider why parties may end up in the situation where they have not made an express trust regarding the nature of their relationship with the 'co-owned' property. In order to create an express trust there must be a declaration of trust manifested and proved in signed writing in accordance with section 53(1)(b) Law of Property Act 1925. This does not mean that the trust must actually have been created in writing, but rather that the court will not enforce a trust where there is no proof of its creation in the form of signed writing.[1] The statute does not explain what is actually required from an express declaration of trust. However, it is clear that there is no precise form of words needed for the relevant document to produce an express trust.[2] Neither does it matter when a trust is created—it can be at the time of purchase of the property, or it can be subsequent to this—as long as the legal title-holders to the property follow the required steps at the relevant time. In relation to registered land, the easiest and quickest way to achieve this declaration of trust is simply to indicate how the property is to be held on the land registry form.[3] There is a tick-box for whether parties want a joint tenancy or a tenancy in common, and if the latter, in what shares. Joint tenancies and tenancies in common are discussed in chapter 16 at 16.3. However, it is useful to summarise here. Joint tenancies (possible at law and in equity) are a conceptualisation of co-owners which involve the co-owner both holding a single indivisible whole. Tenancies in common, by contrast, which can only exist in equity, are conceptualised with each party holding their own share. The primary consequence of this distinction is that where a joint tenancy exists, should one joint tenant die, the other will automatically hold the single whole. As such it is not possible

---

[1] *Gissing v Gissing* [1971] AC 886 (HL), 905.
[2] *Bannister v Bannister* [1948] 2 All ER 133.
[3] For more on the operation of the TR1 form, see A Moran, 'Anything to declare? Express declaration of trust on Land Registry form TR1: the doubts raised in Stack v Dowden' [2007] Conv 364, and also the comments of Lady Hale in *Stack v Dowden* [2007] UKHL 17, [2007] 2 AC 432, [53].

for the deceased joint tenant to leave their interest to a third party in their will. This is known as the right of survivorship.

If there is an express trust, the courts have made it clear that such a trust will be conclusive.[4] This is a general proposition relating to the fact that in both resulting and constructive trust situations, the apparent basis for the law's intervention to imply a trust is based on the parties' intentions[5]—express, implied, or presumed. If there is an express trust, there is no evidential gap in respect of the parties' intentions into which the law relating to implied trusts can step. Like all documents, of course, there are many reasons why such would be overturned by the court: forgery, mistake, undue influence, fraudulent misrepresentation and the like. These possibilities are all wholly uncontroversial and entirely in line with the law's treatment of all transactions. However, there is one development which has caused disquiet,[6] and this relates to the possibility of overturning or amending the consequences of an express trust on the basis of a proprietary estoppel. This possibility was raised in *Clarke v Meadus*.[7] We consider this in more detail later at 7.4.4.7, when exploring the overlaps between proprietary estoppel and constructive trusts, an issue explored from the perspective of proprietary estoppel in chapter 8 at 8.6.

Section 53 does contain an exception to the general formality requirements, however, stating, at section 53(2): '[t]his section does not affect the creation or operation of resulting, implied or constructive trusts'. The taxonomical indication of this section is that there are three types of trust which fall without the formality rules of section 53—implied, resulting, or constructive. However, it is commonly accepted that this is not an accurate reflection of how the different categories of trusts sit together.[8] Rather, implied trusts is an umbrella term for both resulting and constructive trusts. There is also the possibility that certain statutory trusts (ie those created by operation of law rather than through the deliberate act of the parties) would fall under the heading of 'implied trusts'. This structure is set out visually in Figure 7.1. We discuss one important situation relating to statutory trusts at 7.3.

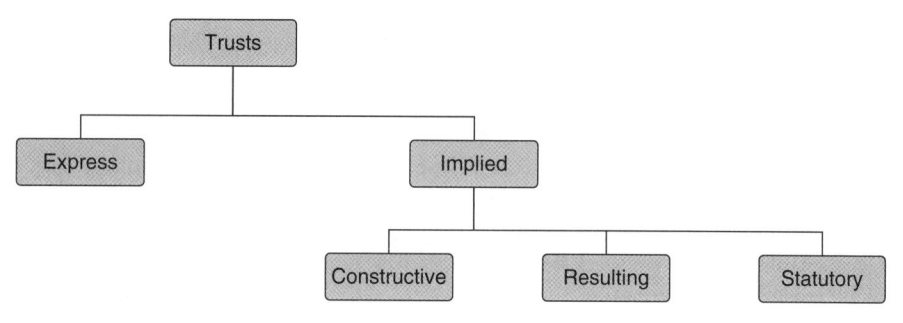

Figure 7.1 Types of trust

---

[4] *Goodman v Gallant* [1986] Fam 106; *Roy v Roy* [1996] 1 FLR 541.
[5] The role of intention in respect of the creation of resulting trusts is considered in J Mee, 'Presumed resulting trusts, intention and declaration' (2014) 73 CLJ 86; R Chambers, *Resulting Trusts* (Oxford, OUP, 1997); and W Swadling, 'Explaining resulting trusts' (2008) 124 LQR 72.
[6] M Pawlowski, 'Informal variation of express trusts' [2011] Conv 245.
[7] *Clarke v Meadus* [2010] EWHC 3117 (Ch), [2011] 1 P & CR DG18.
[8] See eg K Gray and S F Gray, *Land Law* (7th ed) (Oxford, OUP, 2011), 326, [7–008].

Given how easy it is to create an express trust, it is worth exploring why parties may find themselves in a situation where there is a question of co-ownership and no express trust in place. First, the parties may simply not know that such formal steps would be useful. In newly acquired land, this means that the parties have not filled out the very simple box on the land registry form discussed earlier. It is very unlikely that a conveyancing solicitor would submit a form to the land registry without this being completed. This suggests that in such circumstances, for the parties to end up without an express trust, either they have had very poor legal advice, or they have had no legal advice. Furthermore, in cases where the property is being acquired with the help of a mortgage, it is usual for mortgage companies to insist on professional conveyancing. It is therefore a very narrow class of cases where land is acquired as a couple, but no express trust is in place. Second, one party may have acquired title to the property in advance of the relationship commencing. In this case, many couples may simply 'never get round' to formalising their respective entitlements to the property. This circumstance is likely to be more common than the first. Third, and perhaps most seriously, the relationship between the parties may be such that there is a significant imbalance of power between them, either as a result of the individual personal circumstances applicable to the couple, or because of the cultural or social landscape surrounding the relationship, which means that one or the other feels unable to insist on the security which an express trust would bring, even if they were aware of the need for a formal document of this type. Thus, some couples will be without the benefit of an express trust due to a lack of knowledge; others due to a romantic reluctance to specify property ownership on the development of the relationship; and others still due to one party, either deliberately or not, to an extent taking advantage of the other. This background ought to lead some context to the question of how and when implied trusts arise.

7.3 STATUTORY TRUSTS

Statute can impose trusts outside the will or intention the parties. This will happen whenever there is co-ownership of legal title to land.

This is a result of section 34(2) Law of Property Act 1925 which states that:

> 'Where, after the commencement of this Act, land is expressed to be conveyed to any persons in undivided shares and those persons are of full age, the conveyance shall (notwithstanding anything to the contrary in this Act) operate as if the land had been expressed to be conveyed to the grantees, or, if there are more than four grantees, to the four first named in the conveyance, as joint tenants in trust for the persons interested in the land'.

The consequence of this for the law relating to implied trusts is that whilst statute provides that there must be a trust in case of joint ownership of legal title, it does not tell us what that trust looks like. It is partly for this reason that the court in *Stack v Dowden*[9] (see 7.4.2) was very anxious to establish what the correct starting point is in cases like this. Whilst statutory provisions tell us that any co-ownership of legal title will result, unavoidably, in a trust, it does not tell us who is

---

[9] *Stack v Dowden* [2007] UKHL 17, [2007] 2 AC 432.

entitled to benefit under that trust, nor what shares any respective parties would have. However it is important to note that the mandatory statutory trust provides, in effect, a default position should the courts be unable to identify the evidence to give rise to an implied trust.

7.4 CONSTRUCTIVE TRUSTS

The law relating to constructive trusts is uncertain; relies on judicial discretion; and has been criticised in the strongest possible terms by a number of academics.[10] This does not mean, however, that we cannot start to impose some more or less predictable rules onto how this *process* is managed by courts, even if the actual decision they will reach is very unpredictable. The law in this area has been fundamentally affected by the House of Lords decision in *Stack v Dowden*[11] and the Supreme Court decision in *Jones v Kernott* (see further at 7.4.2).[12] These decisions render much of the historical case law somewhat otiose, particularly that of the Court of Appeal. However, it is useful to understand some of the history behind these rules in order to appreciate not only how they work, but also why they have proved so controversial.

Before we delve into this history, however, it is very useful to get a sense of how constructive trusts work. As a very basic proposition, they will arise when, in the absence of an express trust, the parties have a common intention (express or implied) as to how the property is held—an intention not reflected in the legal title—which has been detrimentally relied upon. There are therefore a number of 'layers' to the creation of the constructive trust, and each layer has a different impact upon the eventual outcome.

> **Summary: Constructive trust**
>
> A constructive trust arises where legal title does not reflect a common intention shared between the parties as to their respective entitlements in equity, where that intention has been detrimentally relied upon.

7.4.1 THE HISTORY OF THE CONSTRUCTIVE TRUST

This 'common intention constructive trust' is of relatively recent inception. Prior to the Second World War, the sorts of concerns which now motivate the courts to examine the possibility of a constructive trust—contributions to household and property expenses without the security of a defined

---

[10] See, amongst much else, W Swadling, 'The common intention constructive trust in the House of Lords: an opportunity missed' (2007) 123 LQR 511; M Dixon, 'The never-ending story - co-ownership after *Stack v Dowden*' [2007] Conv 456; A Briggs, 'Co-ownership and an equitable non sequitur' (2012) 128 LQR 183; J Mee, 'Ambulation, severance, and the common intention constructive trust' (2012) 128 LQR 500; M Dixon, 'Editor's notebook (March/April)' [2011] Conv 87; S Bridge, '*Jones v Kernott*: fairness in the shared home - the forbidden territory or the promised land?' [2010] Conv 324. Not all commentary is critical of the case. Even whilst acknowledging the uncertainty to which it gives rise, Gardner for example argues that the case can be explained on a more principled basis than that present in the judgments, S Gardner, 'Family property today' (2008) 124 LQR 422; and S Gardner and K Davidson, 'The future of *Stack v Dowden*' (2011) 127 LQR 13. See also, M Harding, 'Defending *Stack v Dowden*' [2009] Conv 309.

[11] *Stack v Dowden* [2007] UKHL 17, [2007] 2 AC 432.

[12] *Jones v Kernott* [2011] UKSC 53, [2012] 1 AC 776.

property right; increasing recognition of the economic importance of childcare; the possibility of the breakdown of a relationship where the couple lived together but were not married—were not often relevant. In a society where (well-off) women did not work, it was not seen as important to consider how their (well-off) husbands held the family property. The couple would be unlikely to divorce, and so it simply did not matter whether the woman had an interest in the family home or not, since her security in this respect was provided by marriage. Of course, many women did work, but these women tended either to be unmarried and therefore very unlikely to be co-habiting with a partner, or to be in a relationship with another who was themselves unlikely to acquire property rights. Thus, questions of ownership of land only arose for the wealthy, and such wealthy women tended to be financially secure either through their parents or through their husband.

However, following the War, the patterns of women's work changed and more women stayed in the formal forms of employment which they had taken up during the war. Furthermore, society's attitude to cohabitation, marriage, and divorce, began to change, a process accelerated during the 1960s with increasing emancipation of women. The result of this was that whilst society's attitudes to the role of women had shifted, the law's treatment of property had not. As a consequence, on the breakdown of a relationship, many women who either had worked consistently providing part of the family income, or who had given up work in order to raise children, were left with no interests in the property to which they had contributed, and insufficient personal wealth to secure a home for themselves and potentially any children. The emancipation of women in this sense also removed a degree of security. For this reason, starting in the Court of Appeal in the 1950s, but firmly established in the House of Lords in the late 1960s and early 1970s, the courts began to see the importance of examining the way in which parties intended to hold their property, and to respond accordingly outwith the strictures of the formal requirements of an express trust.

We can see this impetus present in the comments of Denning LJ in *Eves v Eves*: '[e]quity is not past the age of child bearing. One of her latest progeny is a constructive trust of a new model'.[13] However, at this point in the development of the rules, they were unstable. It fell to the House of Lords to impose structure onto this discretion in the twin cases of *Pettitt v Pettitt*[14] and *Gissing v Gissing* (see the key cases boxes that follow).[15]

It is usual in much that is written about constructive trusts to commence with an analysis of these cases. Further, in accordance with the idea that the House of Lords binds itself, the tendency is to interpret subsequent case law, including the highest court decisions in *Lloyds Bank v Rosset*[16] (see the following key case boxes) and *Stack*[17] and *Kernott*,[18] in the light of what was held in *Pettitt*[19] and *Gissing*.[20] The problem with taking this approach to the interpretation of subsequent case law—formally correct as it is in terms of precedent—is that it tends to present an unrealistic picture of how the law actually operates post-*Stack*.[21] This chapter, therefore, will take the view

---

[13] *Eves v Eves* [1975] 1 WLR 1338, 1341.
[14] *Pettitt v Pettitt* [1970] AC 777 (HL).
[15] *Gissing v Gissing* [1971] AC 886 (HL).
[16] *Lloyds Bank v Rosset* [1991] 1 AC 107 (HL).
[17] *Stack v Dowden* [2007] UKHL 17, [2007] 2 AC 432.
[18] *Jones v Kernott* [2011] UKSC 53, [2012] 1 AC 776.
[19] *Pettitt v Pettitt* [1970] AC 777 (HL).
[20] *Gissing v Gissing* [1971] AC 886 (HL).
[21] *Stack v Dowden* [2007] UKHL 17, [2007] 2 AC 432.

that although understanding this history is important from an analytical perspective, any attempt to 'fit' the various cases together will likely produce an inaccurate picture of the rules as they play out in modern case law. In this sense, whether for good or for bad, we accept that 'the law has moved on'[22] since *Rosset*[23] (and, by definition, from *Pettitt*[24] and *Gissing*[25]).

To understand this case law, it is important to grasp the distinction between an implied intention and an imputed intention. Implied or inferred intentions are intentions which the court concludes the parties genuinely had, but which they did not say out loud. Imputed intentions are invented for the parties by the court, on the basis of what a 'reasonable person' would have thought in the circumstances. In order to establish an imputed intention, it is necessary for a court first to have established that they could not discern any intention from the way the parties actually behaved.

Summary: Intentions

Express intention—an intention where parties have open discussions in which they consider their respective shares in the property.

Implied intention—an intention which is discerned from the ways in which the parties have behaved, but which does not depend on an express discussion.

Imputed intention—an imputed intention is an intention which was *not* held by the parties, but which the courts conclude they *would* have held had they, as reasonable persons, turned their minds to the question.

The starting point for considering these rules is *Pettitt v Pettitt*[26]:

Key case: *Pettitt v Pettitt* [1970] AC 777

In this case, the property in question had been purchased using the proceeds of sale from a previous property owned by Mrs Pettitt only. The new property was conveyed into her name only. Mr Pettitt claimed an interest in the property by virtue of the fact that he had carried out improvement and renovation works.

On these facts the court held that there was no common intention that the parties would share the beneficial interest in the property. However, they did give guidance on when and how such a common intention could be found, and the consequences of such a finding.

The ambiguity present in the approach of the House of Lords is clear from the approach of Lord Reid. He reasoned that:

> 'even where there was in fact no agreement, we can ask what the spouses, or <u>reasonable people in their shoes, would have agreed</u> if they had directed their minds to the question of what rights should accrue to the spouse'.[27] (emphasis added)

---

[22] *Stack v Dowden* [2007] UKHL 17, [2007] 2 AC 432, [26] and [60].
[23] *Lloyds Bank v Rosset* [1991] 1 AC 107 (HL).
[24] *Pettitt v Pettitt* [1970] AC 777 (HL).
[25] *Gissing v Gissing* [1971] AC 886 (HL).
[26] *Pettitt v Pettitt* [1970] AC 777 (HL).
[27] *Pettitt v Pettitt* [1970] AC 777 (HL), 795.

This is a significant statement, as it suggests that the foundation of the constructive trust is not in the actual intention of the parties, but rather in some other consideration based in objective reasonableness. We can draw a distinction between this, and the approach of Lord Morris, who was much more hesitant to look for a 'fair' solution in light of what reasonable people would have thought in the situation in which the parties found themselves.

He reasoned, first, that it was perfectly possible for a court to conclude that parties had indeed reached an agreement, even if this was not said in express words. However, he emphasised that it would be necessary for there to be evidence upon which a finding of such an agreement could be based. Otherwise, on his approach, there would be no justification in allowing a person to make a claim to property which, on its face, belonged to another. Thus:

> 'The mere fact that parties have made arrangements or conducted their affairs without giving thought to questions as to where ownership of property lay does not mean that ownership was in suspense or did not lie anywhere. There will have been ownership somewhere and a court may have to decide where it lay. In reaching a decision the court does not find and, indeed, cannot find that there was some thought in the mind of a person which never was there at all. The court must find out exactly what was done or what said and must then reach conclusion as to what was the legal result. The court does not devise or invent a legal result'.[28]

Similarly, Lord Upjohn highlighted that it was a question of finding the parties' true agreement, not imposing a fair solution upon them in the teeth of the evidence.

However, the most problematic statements in the case came from Lord Diplock, who stated that:

> 'The common situation in which a court has to decide whether or not a term is to be implied in a contract is when some event has happened for which the parties have made no provision... Nevertheless the court imputes to the parties a common intention which in fact they never formed and it does so by forming its own opinion as to what would have been the common intention of reasonable men as to the effect of that event upon their contractual rights and obligations'.[29]

It was this statement that led to much of the difficulties that followed *Pettitt* and, if correct, would be a clear indication that the court was not really basing a constructive trust on intention properly so-called at all.

This case was followed by *Gissing v Gissing*.[30]

Key case: *Gissing v Gissing* [1971] AC 886

The parties, a married couple, lived in a home owned by the husband at law. The wife had worked throughout the relationship. When the relationship broke down, the wife claimed that she had an interest in the property.

The case allowed an extended House of Lords the opportunity to comment on *Pettitt*. In particular, Lord Diplock clarified the place of imputation of intention in this are of the law. He explained that:

> 'I did, however, differ from the majority of the members of your Lordships' House who were parties to the decision in *Pettitt v. Pettitt* in that I saw no reason in law why the fact that the spouses had not applied their

---

[28] *Pettitt v Pettitt* [1970] AC 777 (HL), 804.
[29] *Pettitt v Pettitt* [1970] AC 777 (HL), 823.
[30] *Gissing v Gissing* [1971] AC 886 (HL).

> minds at all to the question of how the beneficial interest in a family asset should be held at the time when it was acquired should prevent the court from giving effect to a common intention on this matter which it was satisfied that they would have formed as reasonable persons if they had actually thought about it at that time. I must now accept the majority decision that, put in this form at any rate, this is not the law'.[31]
>
> Despite the clarity of this statement, however, some of the other members of the court used the language of imputation (Lords Reid and Pearson) and it is clear that there was no consensus as to what imputation actually meant. As we shall see, this lack of clarity produced some challenges for the later interpretation of these rules.

In the aftermath of these cases, the Court of Appeal seized on a number of ambiguities in the judgments to expand the jurisdiction to which they gave rise. This can be seen, for example, in *Eves v Eves*,[32] *Grant v Edwards*[33] and *Springette v Defoe*.[34] This process, creating uncertainty and overstepping the 'spirit', if not the precise *ratio*, of these cases, led to the House of Lords addressing the issue once more in *Lloyds Bank v Rosset*.[35] In this case, Lord Bridge attempted once again to impose a degree of clarity and predictability onto the operation of the common intention constructive trust.

> **Key case:** *Lloyds Bank v Rosset* **[1991] 1 AC 107**
>
> A husband and wife purchased property as a home for themselves and their children using money from the husband's family trust in Switzerland. The Swiss trustee insisted that the purchase be made solely in H's name. The wife carried out work almost daily on the property but made no contribution to the purchase price nor to the cost of renovation. The husband left the house because of marital difficulties and the lender claimed for repossession. The question was whether the facts allowed the wife to claim an interest in the property.
>
> Lord Bridge concluded that she did not have such an interest. First, he relied upon the circumstances of the requirements of the Swiss trust fund and its insistence on sole ownership by the husband. In light of this, it would take very strong evidence to establish that it was their common intention to defeat the conditions imposed by the trustee and treat the property as being beneficially owned. Even if there had been such an agreement however, this would have been ineffective as there was no written document complying with s53(1) LPA 1925. Thus, to establish a constructive trust, it would also be necessary to show that the wife had acted to her detriment in reliance on the agreement.
>
> The judge concluded however that there was no express agreement. The next question was then whether the conduct of the parties was enough to establish a common intention. Lord Bridge doubted whether W's contribution to the work was sufficient to claim under a constructive trust. His lordship

---

[31] *Gissing v Gissing* [1971] AC 886 (HL), 904.
[32] *Eves v Eves* [1975] 1 WLR 1338.
[33] *Grant v Edwards* [1986] Ch. 638 (CA).
[34] *Springette v Defoe* [1992] 2 FLR 388.
[35] *Lloyds Bank v Rosset* [1991] 1 AC 107 (HL).

explained, considering what evidence can suffice to show the common intention necessary to give rise to the trust:

> 'In this situation direct contributions to the purchase price by the partner who is not the legal owner, whether initially or by payment of mortgage instalments, will readily justify the inference necessary to the creation of a constructive trust. But, as I read the authorities, it is at least extremely doubtful whether anything less will do'.[36]

Post-*Rosset*, once again, the Court of Appeal began to expand the jurisdiction, relying on the 'doubtful' (as opposed to explicit prohibition) element of Lord Bridge's comments. This reached its apogee in *Oxley v Hiscock*,[37] where Chadwick LJ concluded: 'each is entitled to that share which the court considers fair having regard to the whole course of dealing between them in relation to the property'.[38] This is a fairly radical departure from that which was said by Lord Bridge in *Rosset*. The state of the case law at this point was such that it was felt appropriate for the House of Lords to have another look at the issue. Furthermore, changes in society, in particular in relation to the cohabitation of unmarried couples, meant that the need for further consideration came not only from case law, but also from changing demographics. The result of this was the seminal decision in *Stack v Dowden*[39] which was followed, in 2011, by a further decision of the Supreme Court in *Jones v Kernott*.[40]

7.4.2 STACK V DOWDEN AND JONES V KERNOTT

The importance of these cases—*Stack v Dowden* and *Jones v Kernott* cannot be overstated, and it is very important to know them in detail.

> **Key case:** *Stack v Dowden* [2007] UKHL 17
>
> In 1983 a house was bought and conveyed into Ms Dowden's sole name. The parties had 4 children. This house was sold in 1993 and another property was bought as a family home in joint names. The registration contained no express declaration of trust. The parties kept separate bank accounts and made separate investments and savings.
>
> The end result in the case was to divide the proceeds of sale 65 per cent (Ms D): 35 per cent (Mr S), a figure which actually matched their contributions to the purchase price. However, the route by which the court reached this decision took into account much more than this simple financial measure.
>
> Furthermore, there was considerable variation between the different judgments in the case. For this reason, we consider the approaches of the individual judges.

---

[36] *Lloyds Bank v Rosset* [1991] 1 AC 107 (HL), 132–3.
[37] *Oxley v Hiscock* [2004] EWCA Civ 546, [2005] Fam 211.
[38] *Oxley v Hiscock* [2004] EWCA Civ 546, [2005] Fam 211, [69].
[39] *Stack v Dowden* [2007] UKHL 17, [2007] 2 AC 432.
[40] *Jones v Kernott* [2011] UKSC 53, [2012] 1 AC 776.

7.4 Constructive Trusts

Baroness Hale

The main judgment was given by Baroness Hale with whom Lords Hoffman, Hope and Walker agreed. She reasoned as follows.

First, if there is an express declaration of a trust this will be conclusive unless there has been a subsequent variation as a result of proprietary estoppel. It should also be assumed that where people do not make an express trust, that is because in most circumstances they will wish their beneficial interests to mirror their legal titles. This, according to her Ladyship, was not a controversial proposition. Thus, the starting point for sole legal ownership would be sole ownership. The starting point for joint legal ownership, is joint equitable ownership.

The second step would then be to establish whether the contrary had been proven: 'to ascertain the parties' shared intentions, actual, inferred or imputed, with respect to the property in the light of their whole course of conduct in relation to it'.[41] The goal, her Ladyship explained, would be to prove that a common intention existed as between the parties that would justify concluding that the equitable interests were other than the legal title suggests at face value.

Thus, in cases such as *Oxley v Hiscock*,[42] where the transfer was into a sole name, her Ladyship continued, the first stage is to prove that the claimant has any equitable interest at all, before it can be decided what this interest is. This hurdle can easily be surmounted by showing that the claimant had made some financial contribution. However, the courts ought not to be trying to discover what is 'fair' as had been said in *Oxley*. Rather, the purpose was to look for a genuine intention shared between the parties, taking into account their behaviour and its context. It is better, according to Baroness Hale, to see this process as a holistic one, looking at the whole course of dealing to see what was intended.

In joint names cases, on this approach, the position is the same in terms of the process which must be followed. There are however differences in joint and sole name cases in trying to divine the common intentions or understandings between the parties. It will almost always have been a conscious decision to put the property into joint names. Further, unlike in sole names cases where a clear financial contribution will usually be very good evidence that a particular person was intended to have some right in the relevant land, in joint names cases, since such an interest is already presumed, the challenge will be finding evidence which shows that it should be more than the 50 per cent which the legal title indicates is appropriate. According to Baroness Hale, '[i]n joint names cases it [a full examination] is... unlikely to lead to a different result unless the facts are very unusual'.[43]

Her ladyship emphasised that in asking this question, many more factors than financial contributions will be relevant. These include:

– advice or discussions at the time of transfer

– purpose for which the home was acquired

– the nature of the relationship

– whether they had children

– how the purchase was financed

– how the parties arranged their finances

– how they discharged the outgoings on the property and household expenses

---

[41] *Stack v Dowden* [2007] UKHL 17, [2007] 2 AC 432, [60].
[42] *Oxley v Hiscock* [2004] EWCA Civ 546, [2005] Fam 211.
[43] *Stack v Dowden* [2007] UKHL 17, [2007] 2 AC 432, [68].

- where the couple are joint owners it may be easier to conclude that each was intended to share the benefit and burden equally
- the parties' individual personalities.

Her Ladyship then made clear that this was not an exhaustive list, and concluded: '[a]t the end of the day, having taken all this into account, cases in which the joint legal owners are to be taken to have intended that their beneficial interests should be different from their legal interests will be very unusual'.[44] In the instant case, she found that the facts, particularly the fact that the parties had kept their finances entirely separate, were indeed unusual enough in this case to justify a departure from the 'default' position (or in the words of the court, the 'presumption'), that equitable title and legal title are the same.

Lord Hoffman

Lord Hoffman agreed with Baroness Hale. In the course of his judgment, he also mentioned that the constructive trust is ambulatory. This is not taken up by the other members of the court in *Stack*, but is relevant once we look at *Kernott* as we shall see later. Ambulatory in this sense means that, as the parties' intentions could change over time, so would the size of their respective shares.

Lord Hope

Lord Hope also agreed with Baroness Hale and made some additional comments. He reasoned, rightly, that the key to success in this area is finding the correct starting point. Where the parties have dealt with each other at arm's length, the correct approach is the resulting trust approach (an approach which we explain later at 7.5). In a domestic, romantic context, according to his Lordship, there is a very different sort of relationship in place, and as such, a very different serious of assumptions: thus, '[w]ho pays for what in regard to the home has to be seen in the wider context of their overall relationship'.[45]

Keeping in mind that the starting point here is very different from that in resulting trust/arm's length cases, the next question which Lord Hope examined was whether the situation involved a property in joint or in sole legal ownership. Where there is joint legal ownership, there will a presumption that the house is held in equal shares. Where there is sole legal ownership, the presumption will be that the other party has no beneficial interest. The legal title determines the right starting point.

Lord Hope then applied this reasoning to the particular case. He reasoned that in this case it would be perhaps appropriate to stick to this presumption, but it that it could not be ignored that the parties' contributions to the purchase price of the property were not equal. It was also important, on Lord Hope's account, that they maintained their financial independence. He reasoned that indirect contributions should be taken into account here, as should any complete pooling of money. He then agreed with Chadwick LJ in *Oxley v Hiscock* that 'regard should be had to the whole course of dealing between them in relation to the property'.[46] In this case there was never a stage when the parties intended that their beneficial interest in the property should be shared equally.

Lord Walker

Lord Walker also agreed with Baroness Hale, and he too made separate comments of his own. These are particularly worthy of note, as in *Jones v Kernott* discussed later, Lady Hale and Lord Walker give a joint judgment which represents the views of the majority.

---

[44] *Stack v Dowden* [2007] UKHL 17, [2007] 2 AC 432, [69].
[45] *Stack v Dowden* [2007] UKHL 17, [2007] 2 AC 432, [3].
[46] *Oxley v Hiscock* [2004] EWCA Civ 546, [2005] Fam 211, [39].

Lord Walker first approached this issue by examining, again, what the starting point should be. He reasoned that there will be a considerable burden, in joint names cases, on the person arguing that the beneficial interests do not mirror the legal interests where the courts are asked to deal with a cohabiting couple where there has been no express declaration of trust. He then went on to examine the theoretical underpinning to this area of law, considering the judgments in *Gissing*[47] and *Pettitt*.[48] In his view these cases did not provide a single coherent picture as to how the common intention constructive trust operates.

He then considered *Lloyds Bank v Rosset*.[49] In this case, Lord Walker commented, Lord Bridge highlighted that if there is to be a finding of actual agreement, arrangement or understanding, such as to form evidence of a common intention, it must be based on evidence of express discussions between the parties. If there is no evidence to support the finding of such an agreement, according to Lord Bridge, the court must rely on the conduct of the parties to infer a common intention to share the property beneficially. Direct contributions would justify the inference necessary but, as Lord Walker emphasised, Lord Bridge was doubtful whether anything less would do. Lord Walker expressed his doubts as to the correctness of this view of the law in *Gissing*,[50] but, perhaps more importantly reasoned: '[w]hether or not Lord Bridge's observation was justified in 1990, in my opinion the law has moved on'.[51]

Thus, per Lord Walker, the correct approach in this area is to take a broad view as to what contributions are to be taken into account. His Lordship then commented with approval on *Grant v Edwards*,[52] *Midland Bank v Cooke*[53] and, significantly, *Oxley v Hiscock*.[54] These cases advocated a 'whole course of dealing approach' to ascertaining the parties' true intentions, in cases where these have not been expressed. Applying this to the facts of the case before him, a claimant must show that there was an intention that the property should be held otherwise than as beneficial joint tenants. This can be judged from the very different financial contributions and the way they kept their finances separate. Once this was established, the quantum could be calculated on the basis of more than just the respective financial contributions.

Further analysis: Post-*Stack* questions

In the immediate aftermath of the decision in *Stack*[55] there was considerable academic consternation.[56] In particular, the prevailing view was that the judgments and their mutual interaction left a great deal that was uncertain and much apparent contradiction. These issues can be summarised into four key questions:

1. Did the new approach in *Stack* apply both to cases where the property was in a sole name, as well as joint names cases?

2. Was it possible to impute an intention to the parties that they share in some way other than the legal title would suggest?

---

[47] *Gissing v Gissing* [1971] AC 886 (HL).
[48] *Pettitt v Pettitt* [1970] AC 777 (HL).
[49] *Lloyds Bank v Rosset* [1991] 1 AC 107 (HL).
[50] *Gissing v Gissing* [1971] AC 886 (HL).
[51] *Stack v Dowden* [2007] UKHL 17, [2007] 2 AC 432, [26].
[52] *Grant v Edwards* [1986] Ch. 638 (CA).
[53] *Midland Bank v Cooke* [1995] 4 All ER 562 (CA).
[54] *Oxley v Hiscock* [2004] EWCA Civ 546, [2005] Fam 211.
[55] *Stack v Dowden* [2007] UKHL 17, [2007] 2 AC 432.
[56] See fn 10.

3. When would circumstances be unusual enough to 'rebut the presumption that equity follows the law'?
4. At what point in the course of the relationship of the parties, and their course of dealing with the property, would the calculation as to the interaction between the various factors be made?

The levels of dissatisfaction with this case is no more clearly demonstrated than by Swadling:

'What we have… is more unfocused tinkering with Lord Denning's (not Lord Diplock's) mutant child, and the creation of even finer and more unintelligible distinctions. Until a fundamental analysis of this subject is undertaken, we will never properly understand the common intention constructive trust… Moreover, we still need to know to what category of event this trust responds. Is it unjust enrichment, wrongdoing, or something in the miscellany? But most of all, we need to know whether it should exist at all… until such an enquiry is undertaken, we are doomed to continue lurching from one seemingly arbitrary precedent to another'.[57]

Key case: *Jones v Kernott* [2011] UKSC 53

As a result of this post-*Stack* furore, the Supreme Court considered the issue again in *Jones v Kernott*. The case essentially serves two purposes: first, it cements the decision in *Stack* which some had seen as vulnerable to narrow or restricted interpretation on the basis that the court did not explicitly overrule *Pettitt*,[58] *Gissing*,[59] or *Rosset*.[60] Second, it provided a means by which the remaining uncertainties from *Stack*[61] could be explored. The leading judgment was given jointly by Lord Walker and Lady Hale.

Comments on Stack v Dowden

First, Lady Hale and Lord Walker commenced with discussion of *Stack* itself. They reasoned that Lady Hale's comments in that case were directed at a joint legal names case and that her comment regarding imputation in particular should be seen in that light. Thus, in such joint names cases, in order to rebut the presumption that equity follows the law a genuine common intention must be shown. Unequal contributions to the purchase price will not normally be sufficient to show this. The task must also not be undertaken lightly. There is unlikely to be a different result other than 50/50 in joint names cases unless the facts are very unusual. To ascertain whether such an intention is present, the court must look at the parties' whole course of conduct to ascertain what the parties' common intentions were.

Stack, on the analysis of Lady Hale and Lord Walker, also established that the approach to be taken in both sole and joint name cases is that the legal and equitable titles are mirrored. This is based, first, on the fact that the parties in a loving relationship have bought a property together. This sort of arrangement without more can be assumed to be an arrangement which will lead them to share 50/50. Second, making an account of the payments each party makes is an almost impossible task and there will be

---

[57] W Swadling, 'The common intention constructive trust in the House of Lords: an opportunity missed' (2007) 123 LQR 511, 518.
[58] *Pettitt v Pettitt* [1970] AC 777 (HL).
[59] *Gissing v Gissing* [1971] AC 886 (HL).
[60] *Lloyds Bank v Rosset* [1991] 1 AC 107 (HL).
[61] *Stack v Dowden* [2007] UKHL 17, [2007] 2 AC 432.

variations over time with each party doing what they can. We should respect the 'ups and downs' of such a relationship and assume that the parties intended to share 50/50 in cases of joint legal title.

Lord Walker and Lady Hale also reasoned that *Stack* suggests that resulting trusts should no longer be used in the domestic homes context. This is because 'it is not possible at one and the same time to have a presumption or starting point of joint beneficial interests and a presumption (let alone a rule) that the parties' beneficial interests are in proportion to their respective financial contributions'. We will see when considering *Collie v Marr*[62] that future cases do not read *Stack* as having introduced such a rigid distinction.

Possibility of imputation?
On the question of imputation, Lady Hale and Lord Walker explained that the law imputes intentions all the time. For example, the presumption in relation to resulting trusts is simply an imputed intention as it is based not on the parties' actual intentions but on a broad statement about human motivation. We consider whether this is a true statement in respect of resulting trusts later. However, the court in *Kernott* highlighted that the first step will always be to find the parties' actual shared intentions, whether express or inferred from their conduct:

> 'The primary search must always be for what the parties actually intended, to be deduced objectively from their words and their actions. If that can be discovered... it is not open to a court to impose a solution upon them in contradiction to those intentions merely because the court considers it fair to do so'.[63]

The court will not impose a solution which is contrary to what the evidence shows was actually intended. If we examine this in the context of the first stage, which is to go beyond the *prima facie* starting point that legal and equitable titles will be mirrored, then, as a matter of logic, the evidence must show one of two things. Either, it will show that the parties had a common intention that the property be shared differently from what it appears on the legal title; or, it will show that they had no such intention. When reasoning on the balance of probabilities, one of these must be the outcome of the evidence. If a common intention is found, then it will give rise to a constructive trust if it has been detrimentally relied upon. If no common intention is found, then the court cannot go beyond the *prima facie* situation from legal title because it has been proved that the parties did not intend to go beyond it. In this sense, there is no room to impute intention, because the parties' intention is known, one way or the other.

However, as *Kernott* makes clear, there is a moment in this process where imputation may not only be appropriate, but in fact necessary, and that will be where the evidence proves on the balance of probabilities that the parties shared other than legal title, but there was no shared intention as to what their actual shares would be. As Lady Hale and Lord Walker explain:

> 'But if [the court] cannot deduce exactly what shares were intended, it may have no alternative but to ask what their intentions as reasonable and just people would have been had they thought about it at the time. This is a fallback position which some courts may not welcome, but the court has a duty to come to a conclusion on the dispute put before it'.[64]

We explore this sort of imputation, and how common it is likely to be, later.

---

[62] *Collie v Marr* [2017] UKPC 17, [2017] 3 WLR 1507.
[63] *Jones v Kernott* [2011] UKSC 53, [2012] 1 AC 776, [46].
[64] *Jones v Kernott* [2011] UKSC 53, [2012] 1 AC 776, [47].

Finally, Lord Walker and Lady Hale provide a summary of their views:

'The starting point is that equity follows the law and they are joint tenants both in law and in equity.

That presumption can be displaced by showing (a) that the parties had a different common intention when they acquired the home, or (b) that they later formed the common intention that their respective shares would change.

Their common intention is to be deduced objectively form their conduct…

In those cases where it is clear either (a) that the parties did not intend joint tenancy at the outset, or (b) had changed their original intention, but it is not possible to ascertain by direct evidence or by inference what their actual intention was as to the shares in which they would own the property [the court should decide what is fair considering the whole course of dealing]…

Each case will turn on its own facts. Financial contributions are relevant but there are many other factors…'.[65]

Lord Wilson

Lord Wilson broadly agreed with Lady Hale and Lord Walker, but took a different view in respect of imputation. He reasoned that the first question will be whether it can be shown that there was a common intention that the shares in the property should be in proportions other than joint and equal. The second is to calculate these proportions. Imputation is relevant to the second question. This case, his Lordship reasoned, did not require him to answer the question as to whether imputation was possible at the first stage. However, he took a different view as to what imputation involves, explaining that: '[w]here equity is driven to impute the common intention, how can it do so other than by search for the result which the court itself considers fair?'[66] In this way, Lord Wilson more explicitly drew a connection between imputation and notions of fairness than did Lady Hale and Lord Walker.

Lord Collins

Lord Collins agreed with Lord Walker and Lady Hale, but commented that he did not believe that the difference between imputation and implication will be hugely significant in practice.

Lord Kerr

Lord Kerr highlighted that in his view, unlike in Lord Collins', the differences between Lord Wilson and Lord Walker and Lady Hale are both terminological and conceptual differences which will have important practical consequences. He also explored the question of imputation in more detail, asking, how far should the court go in attempting to infer actual intentions rather than simply accepting that imputation is the only possible outcome on the facts? There is a natural inclination to prefer inference to imputation, according to Lord Kerr, but he cautioned that the court should not say that it is inferring an intention where it is really imputing one: '[i]t would be unfortunate if the concept of inferring were to be strained so as to avoid the less immediately attractive option of imputation'.[67] If the court is going to impute, per Lord Kerr, it should make sure that there is a clear line between imputing and inferring. An imputed intention is one 'which was attributed to the parties, even though no such actual intention could be deduced from their actions and statements, and even though they had no such intention'.[68] Imputing, on Lord Kerr's analysis, has nothing to do with finding the parties' views.

---

[65] *Jones v Kernott* [2011] UKSC 53, [2012] 1 AC 776, [51].
[66] *Jones v Kernott* [2011] UKSC 53, [2012] 1 AC 776, [87].
[67] *Jones v Kernott* [2011] UKSC 53, [2012] 1 AC 776, [72].
[68] *Jones v Kernott* [2011] UKSC 53, [2012] 1 AC 776, [73].

Further analysis: *Kernott*, and the uncertainties of *Stack*

We noted the following four big questions which remained after *Stack*. Were they now answered after *Kernott*? In short—mostly, yes—but for many the answers to these questions were not what they were hoping for, and new uncertainties have—perhaps inevitably—emerged.

1. Did the new approach in *Stack* apply both to cases where the property was in a sole name, as well as joint names cases? Both the court in *Stack*, and again in *Kernott*, emphasised that the 'starting point' in these two types of cases is the same. Equitable title will be assumed to be the same as legal title. However, both courts also recognise that this produces a very different context for a decision as to shares in the two situations. In a sole names case, if the claimant fails to establish that there was a common intention to share, then they will be left with nothing. In a joint names case, worst case scenario, if there is no common intention to go beyond legal title, the claimant will have a 50 per cent share in the property. This is a very different prospect. Furthermore, in sole names cases, even a small financial contribution to the purchase of property will look very odd if it is not accompanied by either a clear intention to give, or be on the basis of a common understanding that the parties will share. In joint names cases, unequal contributions to purchase price would not look strange, and can be explained as simply an incidence of what is clearly a 'sharing' relationship in general.

   In this sense, the general approach of *Stack* applies to both cases, but the way in which the rules operate may be different given the different starting points. We shall see that subsequent case law agrees with this assessment.

2. Was it possible to impute an intention to the parties that they share in some way other than the legal title would suggest? The short answer to this question is, 'no'. It is not possible to impute a common intention to act as the foundation for a common intention constructive trust. However, in cases where a common intention to share other than legal title indicates has been established, but the courts for some reason simply cannot discern an intention as to quantification, either expressly or impliedly, then it will be possible to impute an intention as to the size of the share.

3. When would circumstances be unusual enough to 'rebut the presumption that equity follow the law'? The 'unusual' nature of the circumstances is emphasised in both cases, without a clear explanation as to what makes them unusual. Nevertheless, we can reason from *Stack* that the unusual feature was the separateness of the parties' finances. In *Kernott*, the unusual feature appears to be the length of period between relationship breakdown and the attempt to divide the proceeds of sale. Neither of these features, one would imagine, would be all that unusual in the context of a cohabiting couple and relationship breakdown, but perhaps this simply means that we take the word 'unusual' with something of a pinch of salt.

4. At what point in the course of the relationship of the parties, and their course of dealing with the property, would the calculation as to the interaction between the various factors be made? This is the point which becomes the most contentious following *Kernott*. As highlighted earlier, Lord Hoffman in *Stack* mentioned the possibility that the constructive trust in these cases is ambulatory. This idea was adopted by the court in *Kernott*. The whole idea of the ambulatory constructive trust is hugely problematic. *Kernott* makes it clear that there should be a constant re-assessment of the parties' intentions as their relationship with each other and the property develops.

7.4.3 POST-*STACK* CASE LAW—THE RULES IN PRACTICE

There have been a significant number of post-*Stack* cases in the High Court and the Court of Appeal and Privy Council. We concentrate here on the patterns emerging in the higher courts. The decisions can be split into three categories: sole names constructive trust cases; joint names constructive trust cases; and cases where the courts concluded that resulting trusts provided a better solution.

7.4.3.1 Sole names cases

We consider three cases here: *Geary v Rankine*,[69] *Thompson v Hurst*,[70] and *Agarwala v Agarwala* (see the key cases that follow).[71] There are many others, but these cases demonstrate the operation of the *Stack* rules in useful ways. *Geary*[72] highlights the importance of the common intention; *Thompson*[73] emphasises the starting point in sole names cases, as well as demonstrating how imputation of intention may operate at the quantification stage of the process; and finally, *Agarwala*[74] shows how constructive trusts operate in a commercial or quasi-commercial context, in cases where there is an express agreement as to how property is held.

> **Key case: *Geary v Rankine* [2012] EWCA Civ 555—commonality of intention**
>
> Mrs Geary (G) and Mr Rankine (R) began a relationship but did not marry. R had invested some of his own money into a business in Hastings (a guest house). G helped in the business from time to time, but she was not paid a wage. She argued that as a result of this, she had acquired an interest in the property on the basis of a common intention constructive trust.
>
> The Court of Appeal held that at the time of purchase there was certainly no intention that G would acquire an interest in the property which was simply being bought as an investment by R and under his sole responsibility. G must therefore have been arguing that an intention had arisen subsequent to purchase. In concluding that there was no such common intention in the case, the Court of Appeal highlighted the important of the 'common' nature of such an intention. Furthermore, the court was clear that the relevant intention must have been an intention to share in 'ownership' of the property, not simply an intention that they work together to rescue the business. Lewison LJ expressed this in the following terms:
>
>> 'It is an impermissible leap to go from a common intention that the parties would run a business together to a conclusion that it was their common intention that the property in which the business was run, and which was bought entirely with money provided by one of them, would belong to both of them'.[75]
>
> Whilst, therefore, the Court of Appeal reasoned, G may have felt she was entitled to such an interest at many points, there was no intention on R's part that she should so share in the property and his

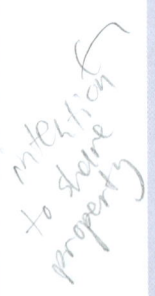

---

[69] *Thompson v Hurst* [2012] EWCA Civ 1752, [2014] 1 FLR 238.
[70] *Agarwala v Agarwala* [2013] EWCA Civ 1763, [2014] 2 FLR 1069.
[71] *Geary v Rankine* [2012] EWCA Civ 555, [2012] 2 FLR 1409.
[72] *Thompson v Hurst* [2012] EWCA Civ 1752, [2014] 1 FLR 238.
[73] *Agarwala v Agarwala* [2013] EWCA Civ 1763, [2014] 2 FLR 1069.
[74] *Geary v Rankine* [2012] EWCA Civ 555, [2012] 2 FLR 1409.
[75] *Geary v Rankine* [2012] EWCA Civ 555, [2012] 2 FLR 1409, [22].

continued failure to provide assurances to G in this respect meant that she ought to have been under no illusion as to the nature of R's intentions. This highlights that in sole names cases where there is no contribution to purchase price, proving the commonality of any intention may be a significant hurdle for claimants.

Key case: *Thompson v Hurst* [2012] EWCA Civ 1752—imputation at the quantification stage in sole names cases

In this case, a couple had intended to purchase in joint names but had not done so on the advice of a mortgage broker. H had entered the property as a local authority tenant and T had later moved into the property, and they had two children. The mortgage had been obtained in H's sole name. Their relationship later broke down. T argued that as the parties had intended to purchase in their joint names, even though they had not in fact done so, the correct starting point would have been the same as if they had been joint tenants, ie a joint tenancy in equity.

The Court of Appeal did not accept that the correct starting point in this case was that the parties were joint tenants in equity. The fact that the transfer had not been in joint names meant that the 'presumptions' in place were of sole beneficial ownership, not joint tenancy in equity. However, the court did go onto conclude that the parties had indeed intended that T have some interest in the property. Having established this, however, the court highlighted that the parties had not turned their mind to the size of T's interest. As a result, the court accepted the approach of the first instance judge which had been to impute an intention as to quantity, giving T a 10 per cent interest, rather than the 50 per cent to which he suggested the intentions at the time of purchase had entitled him.

Some very useful guidance in this respect is given by Etherton LJ, who demonstrates when and how any question of imputation will arise:

> 'In the case of joint legal ownership, the property is necessarily held on trust and the only question is as to the size of the respective beneficial interests of the parties. In the case of a single legal owner, such as the present, where there is no express declaration of a trust, the claimant has first to establish some sort of implied trust... The claimant must show that it was intended that he or she was to have a beneficial interest at all. That can only be achieved by evidence of the parties' actual intentions, express or inferred, objectively ascertained. If such evidence does show a common intention to share beneficial ownership, but does not show what shares were intended, then each of them is to have that share which the court considers fair, having regard to the whole of dealing in relation to the property'.[76]

Key case: *Agarwala v Agarwala* [2013] EWCA Civ 1763—common intention constructive trust in a business context

A bed and breakfast in Cambridge was bought in the name of Jaci Agarwala (Jaci). This purchase was part of an arrangement with her brother-in-law, Sunil Agarwala (Sunil). The purchase had been his idea, but unable to finance it himself, he had approached his sister-in-law to join in. The mortgage and title to the house were in Jaci's name. Jaci argued that the express agreement was that the business and property

---

[76] *Thompson v Hurst* [2012] EWCA Civ 1752, [2014] 1 FLR 238, [22].

were to be hers entirely. She argued that Sunil was involved in the transaction only to provide him with free spillover for his own bed and breakfast business. In return, Sunil would run the business for free. Sunil argued that the property was purchased for his own purposes. The property was put into Jaci's name and the mortgage was in her name because Sunil could not obtain the lending required. In return for this Sunil would pay Jaci a monthly salary for doing the accounts of the property. The mortgage was paid out of the proceeds of the business.

The judge at first instance had been convinced by Sunil's account. Thus, the court determined that there was an agreement between them that the property was held on trust 100 per cent for Sunil by Jaci.

The presumption in this case, as in all such cases, will be that the legal owner owned 'outright', and that her title was not subject to a trust. In order to rebut this presumption, Sunil had to show on the balance of probabilities that there was an agreement that he have equitable title to the property. It then had to be shown that the appropriate legal mechanism here was a constructive, not a resulting trust. Finally, Sunil had to show that he had relied to his detriment on this agreement.

Sullivan LJ reasoned that:

'The weight to be given to the presumption will depend upon the facts of the particular case. In a conduct case, where no prior agreement is alleged, and where the parties' conduct is ambivalent, the presumption is likely to be decisive. But in a case such as the present, where it is common ground that there was an agreement as to how this business asset was to be bought, held and used, the presumption is only the starting point'.[77]

On the basis that Sunil proved the existence of the common intention, the presumption was thereby rebutted. In many ways, therefore, this is an entirely orthodox application of the 'rules' established by *Stack*.[78] This is however an unusual case in which to find reliance on the common intention constructive trust. The commercial context may have indicated that it was more likely to be a resulting trust. Sullivan LJ reasoned that what is critical here is not the nature of the agreement, commercial or otherwise, but the fact of the agreement.[79] He held that:

'in a case in which it was common ground that a property was being purchased as a commercial venture and where there was no dispute that the parties had entered into an agreement as to the terms on which it was to be bought, held and used, the judge correctly focused on ascertaining what, on the balance of probabilities, were the terms of that agreement'.[80]

This approach is of note because of the clear indication that the common intention constructive trust is not confined to the domestic context, but will be appropriate wherever there is an express agreement as to equitable ownership which is not formalised in the form of an express trust where that agreement is relied upon. Sullivan LJ also highlighted the critical importance of detriment to this doctrine. Detriment is as much a part of the establishment of the constructive trust as is the common intention. This is a useful confirmation given that in many cases where the question of detriment arises, the detriment is evinced by the behaviour that constitutes evidence of the common intention. In many cases, including in *Stack* itself, the role of detriment in the trust is not clear. Here, the court makes it very clear that detriment is essential to the establishment of a trust even where there is an express agreement.

---

[77] *Agarwala v Agarwala* [2013] EWCA Civ 1763, [2014] 2 FLR 1069, [13].
[78] *Stack v Dowden* [2007] UKHL 17, [2007] 2 AC 432.
[79] *Agarwala v Agarwala* [2013] EWCA Civ 1763, [2014] 2 FLR 1069, [16].
[80] *Agarwala v Agarwala* [2013] EWCA Civ 1763, [2014] 2 FLR 1069, [24].

7.4.3.2 Joint names cases

In respect of joint names case, we consider *Barnes v Phillips*[81] and *Fowler v Barron*,[82] both of which demonstrate the emerging orthodoxy from *Kernott*.

> **Key case:** *Barnes v Phillips* [2015] EWCA Civ 1056—imputation at the first and second stages
>
> Here, an unmarried couple purchased a family home for themselves and their children in joint names. The house was purchased with a deposit to which they both contributed and with the aid of a mortgage for which they were jointly responsible. After the relationship broke down, Ms B sought a declaration as to the respective shares in the property. The judge at first instance concluded that the initial starting point that the parties held as joint tenants in equity had been rebutted by the existence of a common intention, and, through imputation as to the size of the relevant share, he concluded that Mr Barnes was entitled to 15 per cent and Ms Philips 85 per cent, taking account of the dealings with the property and the difficulties in relation to child maintenance payments.
>
> The first issue for the Court of Appeal was the question of the role of imputation at the first stage of the process, ie the 'rebuttal of the presumption' stage. The Court of Appeal confirmed that, '[t]he majority in *Jones v Kernott* held that imputation of intention was permissible only at the stage of ascertaining the shares in which property was held following the demonstration of an actual intention to vary shares in the property'.[83]
>
> This much was entirely consistent with the rules as clarified in *Kernott*. However, a very interesting feature of the case was whether Mr B's non-payment of his children maintenance obligations could be taken into account at the second, ie quantification, stage. The Court of Appeal held that this was a legitimate consideration, highlighting that *Stack v Dowden* gives courts a wide discretion in taking into account a potentially unlimited range of factors. As Lloyd Jones LJ reasoned:
>
>> 'I consider that, in principle, it should be open to a court to take account of financial contributions to the maintenance of children (or lack of them) as part of the financial history of the parties save in circumstances where it is clear that to do so would result in double liability'.[84]

> **Key case:** *Fowler v Barron* [2008] EWCA Civ 377
>
> Here the parties had been in a relationship for 23 years, commencing when Ms F was 17, Mr B, 43. They cohabited for 17 years in a property, title to which was in joint names. There was no express trust. On the breakdown of the relationship Mr B contended that the property was held on trust for him alone, since he had effectively provided the entirety of the purchase money and had paid the relevant expenses.
>
> In the case, Arden LJ emphasises that after *Stack*, whilst the evidence which can be reviewed has expanded from *Rosset*, the goal is still the same, ie to uncover what the parties really intended. Her Ladyship also emphasised that in cases such as this it is important to keep in mind that we are looking for a joint

---

[81] *Barnes v Philips* [2015] EWCA Civ 1056, [2016] 2 FLR 1292.
[82] *Fowler v Barron* [2008] EWCA Civ 377, [2008] 2 FLR 831.
[83] *Barnes v Philips* [2015] EWCA Civ 1056, [2016] 2 FLR 1292, [26].
[84] *Barnes v Philips* [2015] EWCA Civ 1056, [2016] 2 FLR 1292, [41].

intention. Therefore, 'any secret intention of Mr Barron, that Miss Fowler should only benefit in the event of his death and on the basis that they were then still living together, does not provide the evidential basis for rebutting the presumption, since it is not evidence of the parties' shared intention'.[85] Keeping this in mind, and examining the other facts of the case, including Ms Fowler's contributions to mortgage payments at various points, the Court of Appeal concluded that the presumption of joint tenancy at equity could not be rebutted, and that a narrow focus on financial contributions only was an error.

7.4.3.3 Resulting trust cases

The final group of cases to consider in respect of the post-*Kernott* developments is those cases where the court concludes that even though the relationship between the parties is a close or familial one, the resulting trust is nevertheless the more appropriate response to the facts. We consider *Laskar v Laskar*,[86] and the very significant *Collie v Marr*.[87]

> **Key case:** *Laskar v Laskar* [2008] EWCA Civ 347
>
> The mother, who had been a secure tenant of a council house for about 20 years, sought to buy the house. Her income alone was insufficient to fund the purchase, so she agreed to buy the property jointly with her daughter. It was not intended by the parties that they would use the property as their home.
>
> The court held that although where members of the same family purchased in joint names a property which they intended to be and in fact was occupied by them as a home there was a presumption of equality, where the property was primarily intended as an investment that presumption did not apply but it was presumed that their respective beneficial shares reflected the size of their contributions to the purchase price. In other words, because this property was bought as an investment to rent out, and not as a family home, the resulting trust was appropriate.
>
> According to Lord Neuberger:
>
> > 'In this case, the primary purpose of the purchase of the property was as an investment, not as a home. In other words this was a purchase which, at least primarily, was not in "the domestic consumer context" but in a commercial context. To my mind it would not be right to apply the reasoning in *Stack v Dowden* to such a case as this, where the parties primarily purchased the property as an investment for rental income and capital appreciation, even where their relationship is a familial one'.[88]
>
> The consequence of this case is that there seemed to be a less rigid distinction between commercial and domestic cases than the dicta in *Kernott* had indicated. Nevertheless, Lord Neuberger's approach still focused on the investment motive behind acquisition of the property, suggesting that the resulting trust may not have been appropriate if there had been mixed motivations behind purpose, including that the property provide a home for the parties. The approach that there should be no rigid line between commercial and domestic contexts is taken further in *Collie*.[89]

---

[85] *Fowler v Barron* [2008] EWCA Civ 377, [2008] 2 FLR 831, [37].
[86] *Laskar v Laskar* [2008] EWCA Civ 347, [2008] 1 WLR 2695.
[87] *Collie v Marr* [2017] UKPC 17, [2017] 3 WLR 1507.
[88] *Laskar v Laskar* [2008] EWCA Civ 347, [2008] 1 WLR 2695, [17].
[89] *Collie v Marr* [2017] UKPC 17, [2017] 3 WLR 1507.

Key case: *Collie v Marr* [2017] UKPC 17

Marr, a banker, had purchased a number of properties in the Bahamas. He was in a personal relationship at this time with Collie, a building contractor. The relationship subsequently broke down, and the question emerged as to the respective ownership of these properties and of a number of other items such as paintings and a boat.

The properties were acquired in joint names, and so the question for the Privy Council was, first, whether the presumptions explained in *Stack* applied in this case, and if so, whether the correct route for 'moving beyond' those presumptions lay in the rules relating to resulting or to constructive trusts. In this sense, the case is really concerned with whether there is a rigid distinction between commercial and domestic properties in respect of implied trusts, and if so, where this case fall on that line.

The Privy Council held that there is no such rigid distinction, and that, in line with both *Laskar v Laskar*[90] and indeed the comments in *Stack* itself, whilst the starting point in joint names cases will be a joint tenancy in equity, this is no more than a starting point and that the task for the court, whatever the context, will be to find the true intentions of the parties and to respond accordingly. It is notable in this respect, that the Privy Council quite explicitly refers to the starting points/presumptions as '*prima facie*' positions, and this does indeed seem to be the most accurate way of explaining what is meant by 'presumption' in *Stack*. The key comments in this respect are:

> 'The Board considers that, save perhaps where there is no evidence from which the parties' intentions can be identified, the answer is not to be provided by the triumph of one presumption over another. In this, as in so many areas of law, context counts for, if not everything, a lot. Context here is set by the parties' common intention - or by the lack of it. If it is the unambiguous mutual wish of the parties, contributing in unequal shares to the purchase of property, that the joint beneficial ownership should reflect their joint legal ownership, then effect should be given to that wish. If, on the other hand, that is not their wish, or if they have not formed any intention as to beneficial ownership but had, for instance, accepted advice that the property be acquired in joint names, without considering or being aware of the possible consequences of that, the resulting trust solution may provide the answer'.[91]

Although the precedent value of a Privy Council decision means that the matter is not now beyond doubt, it seems likely that subsequent courts will indeed focus on questions of intention, rather than drawing rigid lines based on context.

Further analysis: Commentary on *Collie v Marr* [2017] UKPC 17

The decision in *Collie v Marr* has caused some to regret what they see as a 'backwards' step towards the focus on financial contributions being *the* determining factor in implied trusts cases. However, in this author's opinion, this is a misrepresentation of what the court in *Collie* actually says and others have been somewhat more positive. As Roche explains,

> '[f]irst, the Boards reconciliation of Lady Hale's and Lord Neuberger's reasoning reminds us that the presumption arising from joint names and the presumption of resulting trust are merely different starting

---

[90] *Laskar v Laskar* [2008] EWCA Civ 347, [2008] 1 WLR 2695.
[91] *Collie v Marr* [2017] UKPC 17, [2017] 3 WLR 1507, [54].

points for the same process - namely working towards an evidence-based conclusion as to the intentions of these particular parties regarding this particular property.'[92]

This search for intention, by using context as a guide to how behaviour should be interpreted, is really what these cases are about. This is why imputation was and remains controversial. It is no less artificial to mandate the use of constructive trust in a domestic context, and a resulting in a commercial, than to simply impute intentions on the basis of what is fair. To put this another way, if the doctrines are based on intention, then the courts must be open to the possibility that a domestic couple intend their shares to be determined solely by their contributions.

However, George and Sloan explain that one result of *Collie* is, despite the Board's comments to the contrary, to create a clash of presumptions. They explain that:

> 'While it is true that some basic reference to the parties' intentions in relation to the property is necessary in order to decide whether the case is domestic or commercial, their purpose in buying it can be distinguished from their intended ownership, and the factual inquiry for the former is likely to be more straightforward, broader brush and less realistically the subject of a dispute. For the latter, the essential problem is that while both the resulting trust and the *Stack* presumption could be rebutted by evidence of some contrary common intention about their ownership, their very purpose is to provide a starting point where such evidence might be insufficiently clear. If both presumptions depend on an analysis of the parties' common intention before they arise in the first place, even after a case has been categorised, that function is lost. That leads to a logical flaw in the interaction between the two types of trust, as the presumption of a resulting trust can be displaced by the existence of an agreement which gives rise to a constructive trust'.[93]

This reveals one of the major difficulties in this area, and that relates again to the problem of presumptions, and as to what is being presumed, and how the presumption can be rebutted. The language of presumptions is only helpful where its parameters are clear, and in implied trusts, the term covers a range of different legal conclusions. The first, the presumption that equity follows the law, is not a presumption at all, but rather a statement of starting point for a court's inquiry. No facts are presumed. The second, the presumption of resulting trust, is, as we shall see, itself contentious and the subject of a sustained academic debate. Similarly, the presumption of advancement which again we discuss later, providing as it does an 'assumption' that money provided within the context of certain relationships should be seen as a gift, is criticised as being anachronistic.

7.4.4 THE 'RULES'

We can now use the information derived from this case law to build a simple breakdown of the rules. Each rule will then be explained in turn.

> Rule 1(a). If there is an express declaration of trust, the court will not interfere with that and utilise the implied trust to 'get round' the express trust—*Goodman v Gallant*[94] *Roy v Roy*[95] (and confirmed in *Stack*). There are some exceptions to this, eg where the declaration

---

[92] J Roche, 'Returning to clarity and principle: the Privy Council on Stack v Dowden' (2017) 76 CLJ 493, 494.
[93] M George and B Sloan, Presuming too little about resulting and constructive trusts? [2017] Conv 303, 309.
[94] *Goodman v Gallant* [1986] Fam 106.
[95] *Roy v Roy* [1996] 1 FLR 541.

of trust is the result of fraud, undue influence, mistake, forgery, and the like, or, possibly, where there is a proprietary estoppel, *Clarke v Meadus*.[96]

Rule 1(b). At this point, it is necessary to determine whether the best route to take to the question is a resulting trust or a constructive trust approach. If the conclusion is a constructive trust, then proceed to rule 2.

Rule 2. If there is no express declaration of trust, there is a 'presumption' that equity follows the law. This means that in joint names cases there is a presumption that there is a joint tenancy in equity; and in sole names cases there is a presumption that the person with no legal ownership similarly has no equitable interest. On sale, this would result in 50:50 of the proceeds of sale, or 100:0 respectively.

Rule 3. The next stage is for the claimant to rebut this presumption. This will only happen in 'exceptional circumstances' and is based on a finding of an express or implied common intention that the property be held in some way other than the 100:0 or 50:50 earlier.

How can we find this common intention? Direct contributions to purchase price, mortgage payments, expenditure on the house, separate finances etc all appear to be relevant, but we do not know exactly.

In *Stack* it appears that it was the separate finances that were the key to the decision. In *Kernott*[97] it appears to have been the fact that she had responsibility for the mortgage for 14 years.

Rule 4. If the presumption has been rebutted you want to quantify the shares. The shares will be quantified in the basis of a 'holistic approach' based on an express, implied, or imputed intention that takes into account the whole course of dealings of the parties in relation to the property.

Rule 5. From *Kernott* we know that this common intention constructive trust can be ambulatory. In other words, the respective shares, once the presumption is rebutted and the common intention constructive trust has been established, can change over time. In *Kernott* the man's share got smaller and smaller the longer he did not contribute to the cost of the house.

7.4.4.1 Rule 1(a)—express trusts are conclusive

This rule is explained earlier at 7.2.

7.4.4.2 Rule 1(b)—is the case a resulting or a constructive trust case?

Following *Collie v Marr*,[98] we can say that whilst *Kernott* and *Stack*, taken together with *Laskar v Laskar*[99] suggest that a resulting trust will normally be appropriate in commercial cases, whereas a constructive trust will be appropriate in domestic cases, it is not possible to draw a fixed rigid line between the two. Rather the search in every case will be to find the best reflection of what the parties truly intended. This does not mean, however, that we should ignore context in attempting

---

[96] *Clarke v Meadus* [2010] EWHC 3117 (Ch), [2011] 1 P & CR DG18.
[97] *Collie v Marr* [2017] UKPC 17, [2017] 3 WLR 1507.
[98] *Collie v Marr* [2017] UKPC 17, [2017] 3 WLR 1507.
[99] *Laskar v Laskar* [2008] EWCA Civ 347, [2008] 1 WLR 2695.

to ascertain what those intentions would be, and in cases of arm's length dealing, the logic behind the resulting trust does seem more appropriate than it does in cases where parties are in a closer relationship.

7.4.4.3 Rule 2—the presumption that equity follows the law

There is considerable academic disquiet about this phrase. As Swadling has analysed, albeit in a different context, presumptions in law are presumptions about a particular fact being true, where there is an evidential gap.[100] The only justified application of presumptions is to solve evidential problems of this type. The 'presumption' applied in co-ownership cases is not a presumption as to a particular fact. Furthermore, in *Collie* the court refers instead to the '*prima facie* position', suggesting that the court there is uneasy with the language of presumption. For that reason, if may be easier (and indeed, more informative) to use a more neutral terminology here. The best way to think of rule 2 is simply to see the legal title as the starting point, and that is completely uncontroversial. In the absence of any other information, the best way to see who has equitable interests in a particular piece of land is to start by considering who has legal title.

Legal title in sole name: 'sole names cases'

At first glance sole names cases suggest that the legal owner is the sole owner. When a person simply has legal title, we do not think of them as 'holding on trust for themselves'. Rather, there is no trust and it is assumed that no one else has a property right in the land unless and until evidence comes to light to suggest that is incorrect.

Legal title in joint names: 'joint names cases'

At first glance, joint names cases suggest that the property is held on trust for the legal co-owners. The starting point is that the two parties will hold on trust for each other as joint tenants. If no more is established, then the joint tenancy would result in a 50:50 division of proceeds of sale, and a 50 per cent share should the joint tenancy be severed. It is essential in cases like this for there to be a trust of some sort. As we explained earlier, as soon as there is more than one legal owner, statute demands that the property is held on trust. The reason for this, to allow for relatively easy resolution of any disputes which arise, and to facilitate the process of overreaching, as considered in more detail in chapters 15 and 16. Given that there must be a trust, however, it makes sense for this to be 50:50 unless anything else is proved.

The approach of the courts is, in this sense, merely a reflection of common sense and of what most people would assume presented only with information about the legal title. Dressing this up in the language of 'presumptions' does not make this more clear.

7.4.4.4 Rule 3—rebutting the presumption (or moving away from the starting point/default position)

When we talk about rebutting the presumption, what we are considering here is whether there is any evidence which justifies finding that the parties do not hold the property in the way in which legal title would suggest that they do. The justification for 'rebutting this presumption' is

---

[100] W Swadling, 'Explaining resulting trusts' (2008) 124 LQR 72.

an evidential finding that the parties shared a common intention that the equitable title would be held differently from legal title. Thus, in sole names cases, the relevant common intention is that the parties intend that the claimant have some interest in the property, however small. In joint names cases, the relevant intention is that the parties intend that they do not share the property equally. It is not necessary at this point to demonstrate that the parties had an active, shared, intention as to how much each had. Rather, it is enough simply to show that they did not intend either 100:0 or 50:50.

The evidence which can be used to prove the existence of this common intention can be found in payments to purchase (which would be especially persuasive in a sole name case), in express discussions about how the property is held, or, since *Stack*, by reference to the 'whole course of dealing in relation to the property'. This might therefore take account of mortgage payments, of contributions to renovation works and the like, as well as non-financial dealings with the property, including how decisions are made about what to do with the property. However, it is important to note that this is not necessarily the same information that is taken into account later when 'quantifying' the share. Rather, the evidence at this point in the process should, it seems, relate to the parties' relationship with the property.

7.4.4.5 Rule 4—quantifying the shares

Once it has been established that the starting point of legal title is not an accurate reflection of the parties' intentions, then it will become necessary to quantify the shares. In order to do this, a huge number of factors are relevant, and the courts are not restricted to analysis of financial contributions, even though evidence based on such contributions will usually be fairly weighty as seen in *Stack*. The main goal of the court will be to ascertain what the parties intended, either expressly, or more usually, impliedly in terms of their respective proportions. However, if the evidence shows that the parties had reached no such intention, or that they had different intentions, then it may be necessary to impute an intention based on what reasonable people would have concluded was an appropriate share on the facts. It is easiest to see how this works with an example.

Imagine that Emilio and Maja decided to purchase a rural estate in Wales to use as a holiday home for themselves, and as a business. It is conveyed into their joint names. Emilio contributes 70 per cent of the purchase price; Maja 30 per cent, but post acquisition, Maja spends the equivalent of 10 per cent on renovations to the properties. At the time of purchase, Emilio went to see his solicitor and had a conversation about how they would hold title to the property, a conversation which was fortuitously recorded. He stated that he was contributing more of the purchase price, and that therefore they both intended that he should have a larger share of the equity. He stated that he expected to have a 70 per cent share. Maja also went to see her own solicitor, and this conversation too was recoded. She stated that they both intended that Emilio would have a larger share of the equity, thanks to his greater contribution to the purchase price, but that it would be 60:40 thanks to her expected expenditure on renovations (expenditure which did indeed take place). In this case, there is very clear evidence that the intention of the parties was not equality as would be suggested by legal title. The courts would therefore go beyond the *prima facie* starting point. However, a problem would then emerge that whilst there was a common intention that the title was not held 50:50 in equity, there was *no* common intention as to respective shares. As a result, the court would need to impute an intention, at least with regards to one or the other of them.

218 Chapter 7 Implied Trusts

This example shows the narrowness of the situation where imputation will be the only way to resolve the question of the parties' respective shares. Imputation is only possible in the face of evidence on the balance of probabilities that whilst the parties had a shared intention that the property would not be held 50:50, they had simply not turned their collective minds to the question of what the shares would be, or had formed different views as to what the shares should be. It is unlikely that the evidence would be able to show this clearly, and instead it is more likely that the courts will look at the factors that allowed them to go beyond the *prima facie* starting point, and conclude that those same factors also point to the size of the shares. This would be a case of implying rather than imputing an intention as to quantity.

7.4.4.6 Rule 5—ambulatory constructive trust

Finally, we know from the operation of the rules in *Kernott* that the trust here was ambulatory—that is, the shares of the parties changed over time as their intentions as to how the property was shared also altered. This makes it necessary to look not only at the parties' intentions at the time of purchase, but also to consider evidence about those intentions over time.

> **Further analysis: Quantification and acquisition—language and process**
>
> Some discussing these cases will refer to the distinction between 'quantification' and 'acquisition' cases. The idea behind this language is that in sole names cases, the claimant has to first prove that they are entitled to any interest in the property, and must then proceed to demonstrate the size of that interest. In quantification cases, the person already has an interest, and the question merely relates to the size of that interest. Drawing a dichotomy between cases of this type is misleading. Rather, it is much better to think of all cases of this type as involving two *stages*: stage one involves going beyond legal title; and stage two involves working out the shares. It makes no difference whether the property is held in sole or joint names cases: both cases will involve these two steps assuming a constructive trust is established.
>
> Thinking of the distinction between quantification and acquisition as being a question of 'stages' rather than types of cases, will produce a much clearer explanation of the way in which *Stack* operates, and also allows for a more concrete understanding of when imputation is permitted, and when the various presumptions in play might be relevant.

7.4.4.7 Analysis of these rules

These rules have received sustained criticism, as highlighted earlier. This criticism tends to fall into four categories: first, because they produce uncertainty; second, because of the possibility of imputation of intention; third, due to the uncomfortable relationship between these rules and resulting trusts and proprietary estoppel; and fourth, due to the apparently 'ambulatory' nature of this trust. We consider these in turn.

Uncertainty

There are two levels of uncertainty in play here. The first level of uncertainty concerns the sort of uncertainty that springs from novelty. This can be resolved by further judicial consideration of the cases, and we can see this happening already in the follow-up decisions. The second form of uncertainty concerns unpredictability of result. The levels of discretion mean that it is very difficult to predict what the result in the cases will be. It also makes it difficult for third parties, eg banks who have lent to a co-owner. We can see the nature of this uncertainty in the comments of Behrens J in *Aspden v Elvy*[101] who concludes an assessment as to quantity with the following statement: '[t]he figure is somewhat arbitrary but it is the best I can do with the available material'.[102] Anything which a judge describes as arbitrary cannot be considered a good basis for the law going forward!

Imputation

The second reason given by many for criticising these cases is the fact that imputation of intentions is seen as an illegitimate overstepping of the role of the court. Therefore, we must ask whether it is acceptable for a court to impute intentions. This question can be answered in two ways. The first is to consider how the possibility of imputation interacts with the previous case law, especially *Gissing v Gissing*,[103] *Pettitt v Pettitt*,[104] and *Lloyds Bank v Rosset*,[105] those cases being the foundation stone of this jurisdiction. How much of a change does *Stack* actually introduce in this respect? The answer to this really depends upon how 'seriously' you take the limiting phrases in these cases, and how narrowly you interpret the *ratio* of the case law. There is no *one* correct answer to this question. The second is to consider whether, regardless of previous case law, it would *ever* be acceptable for a court to impute intentions in this way. For some, the idea of imputing intentions is wholly illogical. The theory behind constructive trusts is that they are giving effect to the parties' intentions subsequently relied on. That is the justification for going beyond the mandated formality rules. Without the presence of intentions, the courts are in effect saying that they can simply ignore the formality rules where it looks unfair to insist upon them but where that fairness is simply a judicial 'intuition' in an instant case, and this is hardly a sound basis for jettisoning statutory rules. Where an intention is imputed, that is necessary because the evidence has *shown* that *no* intention existed. In this way, the courts justify the imposition of a trust on the basis of intention in the teeth of the evidence that there was no intention. This is illogical at best, and subterfuge at worst.

Resulting trusts and proprietary estoppel

How do the rules relating to constructive trusts interact with resulting trusts and with estoppel? This is certainly a point of continuing confusion. We consider the relationship from the perspective of estoppel in chapter 8 at 8.6. It may be helpful to read, in summary form at least, around the topic of proprietary estoppel in order to fully understand the analysis here. From the perspective of trusts, the reason why the decision in *Clarke v Meadus* has proved so controversial is the similarity of fact patterns which can give rise to a proprietary estoppel and a constructive trust. The constructive trust depends, as we have seen, on a common intention which has been detrimentally relied upon. Estoppel, by contrast, will arise where there has been a promise or assurance detrimentally relied upon. The distinction between 'express agreement' constructive trusts, and express assurance proprietary estoppel cases, will be fine at best and non-existent at

---

[101] *Aspden v Elvy* [2012] EWHC 1387 (Ch), [2012] 2 FLR 807.
[102] *Aspden v Elvy* [2012] EWHC 1387 (Ch), [2012] 2 FLR 807, [128].
[103] *Gissing v Gissing* [1971] AC 886 (HL).
[104] *Pettitt v Pettitt* [1970] AC 777 (HL).
[105] *Lloyds Bank v Rosset* [1991] 1 AC 107 (HL).

worst. This matters because of the different remedies which emerge in the two types of cases, and, more fundamentally because whilst a constructive trust cannot be used to subsequently alter an express trust, estoppel can so undermine the express trust. This means that in many situations the very same facts which would have given rise to a constructive trust had there been no express trust, would instead give rise to a proprietary estoppel.

In respect of the distinction between resulting and constructive trusts, much guidance has now been given in *Collie v Marr* as explained earlier, and the analysis of that case present in the literature shows that a recognition that the distinction between commercial and domestic contexts in this respect cannot be rigid, is a welcome one. However, being more flexible in this respect raises another set of questions, not least what presumptions will be in play in any particular case.

Ambulatory constructive trust

The ambulatory nature of the trust is now likely to be at the forefront disputes in relation to the size of the parties' respective shares. This will be particularly important where, in cases following relationship breakdown, one party leaves the family home, ceasing payments towards the mortgage and household expenses, instead providing their own accommodation at cost. If this continues for a long period of time, as *Kernott* shows, that party is at risk of their share in the property diminishing on the grounds that the parties' intentions have changed. However, this is a doubtful interpretation of the *common* intention of the parties, and even on a purely 'fairness' assessment, seems to be a wrong step for the law to take. In cases where parties are joint legal title-holders and (as a starting point) joint tenants in equity, both has a right to occupy the property by virtue of their rights in it. When the relationship breaks down, such that it is not practical for them both to occupy simultaneously, and one leaves, spending their own money on alternative accommodation, were they to continue to contribute to the cost of the original property, eg by paying towards the mortgage, they would be paying *twice* for an occupation right: once in relation to their new home, and again in relation to the original home. The occupier of the original home, however, would only be paying once, in the form of their own contribution to the expenses associated with that home.

To conclude that ceasing to pay expenses in respect of the original property is evidence of an intention to relinquish rights in their former shared home is, therefore, to misrepresent what the consequence of relationship breakdown is in these cases. Where the couple can no longer live together, their collective resources must now provide two separate accommodations. Since both have equal rights to occupy the original family home, moving out and spending money on alternative accommodation cannot be seen as evidence of an intention of giving up one's rights to that home. This suggests that the approach taken in *Kernott* is not, in fact, based on the parties' *common* intentions at all, but rather is, contrary to the court's outward statements, an assessment as to the fairest outcome taking account not only of the parties' intentions, but also of the quality of their behaviour.

7.5 RESULTING TRUSTS

The rules relating to resulting trusts, unlike those considered immediately previously, tend to produce certain and easily applied rules albeit that, as we discussed, a difficult initial decision will be whether a resulting or constructive trust solution is more appropriate in an instant case.

The only real issues in respect of resulting trusts themselves are, first, establishing when the presumptions underpinning the resulting trust apply; and, second, explaining what those presumptions actually are and why. When dealing with land law and co-ownership of land, the usual situation in which resulting trusts arise is when parties contribute to the purchase price of a property without that contribution being reflected in the way in which the legal title is conveyed. In the absence of an express trust, the courts will presume that the parties intended to hold the equitable title in proportion to their contributions to purchase. The outcome—that a person will be entitled to a share of the property proportionate to their contribution to its acquisition—is therefore generally simple to establish. Resulting trusts will also arise when a person transfers legal title in land to another, without there being a gift intended; or where a party attempts to set up a trust by conveying title to intended trustees, but the trust itself fails. The bulk of this part of the chapter focuses on the first species of resulting trust—the purchase money resulting trust.

7.5.1 EXPLANATION FOR RESULTING TRUSTS

Resulting trusts are, on one theory at least, all about the undoing of apparent gifts. Thus, when A gives either money to B, or transfers title to him, without any explanation in the form of an executed transfer expressed with an intention to give, or a relationship between the parties which would make a gift the most likely explanation from the circumstances, 'equity' assumes that no gift was intended, and tries to 'undo' the transfer of legal title by imposing a resulting trust. 'Resulting' in this sense means not 'as a result of', but rather implies a springing back action. So, when a person gives away title to property without so intending, or without properly executing the transfer in certain circumstances, a resulting trust will spring back in their favour. This sort of 'gift-based' rationale is a very accurate explanation of how parties usually tend to deal with one another in commercial situations. Especially where parties are dealing at arms length, it is very unusual for one to simply pass property to another without their being a clear explanation for that in the form of a bargain struck between them. Let us consider how this rationale works in the land law context.

Imagine that Chocolate Ltd enters into an agreement with Sweets Ltd that they will work together to buy title to a large warehouse in Birmingham, so that they can both use the property to store goods to be transported. Chocolate contributes 70 per cent of the purchase price; Sweets, 30 per cent. There is no mortgage. The property is then registered in joint names but the parties fail to make an express declaration of trust in the proper form. If no trust is implied by the courts, then when the property is sold, the proceeds of sale would be split 50:50—a trust is mandatory thanks to section 34 LPA 1925 as we explained earlier, and all else being equal, the presumption would be joint tenants in equity severing to equal shares on division. This would mean, in effect, that Chocolate had 'given' 20 per cent of the value of the property to Sweets. Without there being a clear explanation for this in the dealings between the two, 'equity' will presume that this was not what was intended, and will therefore impose the resulting trust. The resulting trust will then give Chocolate a 70 per cent share of the equitable title; and the trust will operate as tenants in common in unequal shares.

However, the rationale employed here, ie the assumption that no 'gift' was intended, runs into difficulties where the situation is more ambiguous than that involving Chocolate and Sweets.

Indeed, as we shall see later, Swadling argues that the vast majority of resulting trust cases actually involve ambiguous transfers, rather than *not a gift* transfers, meaning that the justification for the trust becomes unclear.[106] Very often, parties will neither intend that there is a gift, nor that the contribution is explicitly *not* a gift, but will instead see payments as being a sort of joint enterprise where ownership and precise contribution are related but not necessarily determinative. We saw how the law treats these ambiguous situations earlier, with the focus being on a search for the parties' true intentions, rather than by reliance on a series of presumptions. We consider in this section, however, how resulting trusts work in cases where the courts have concluded that this is the most accurate characterisation of the parties' intentions.

> **Further analysis: Lack of intention to give versus presumed intention that a resulting trust arise**
>
> There is a considerable amount of literature on the question as to whether resulting trusts arise as a result of an *absence* of an intention to give, or whether they respond to a presumption that the parties intended to hold on trust in proportion to their shares. It may seem at first glance that this is a narrow distinction, and in many cases it may well be, but the distinction between the two matters when we consider what evidence is required in order for a party to argue that the resulting trust is inappropriate. If the first explanation is true, only a clear demonstration of an intention to give would prevent a resulting trust arising should the other elements be present. If the second is correct, then evidence of any intention inconsistent with a resulting trust would suffice. The courts in *Collie* and *Stack* appear to be of the latter view, recognising that 'gift or no gift' is not necessarily an appropriate dichotomy to draw in the complex situations which arise in both commercial but primarily in domestic situations.
>
> There is, as explained by Swadling, a third option, and that is that there is no single explanation as to why resulting trusts arise. He argues, in effect, that we are led astray in this area by an unwarranted focus on 'presumptions' and their effects, without a proper understanding of what presumptions are and how they work. This disquiet about the role of presumptions in this area is perhaps reflected in the comments in *Collie v Marr* that the operation of the rules relating to implied trusts cannot and should not be seen merely as a clash of a variety of presumptions. Swadling goes further than this, however, and disputes the very core of the 'equity undoes apparent gifts' explanation of the resulting trust. Thus, he explains:
>
> > 'Five separate propositions seem to be involved here: that gratuitous transfers are "apparent gifts"; that equity is suspicious of gifts; that equity consequently presumes that "apparent gifts" are "not gifts"; that the presumption of "not-gift" is a presumption of "non-beneficial transfer"; and that a "presumption" of "non-beneficial" transfer triggers a trust in favour of the transferor'.[107]
>
> He then concludes that none of these propositions is true on a close analysis of the case law. According to this approach, the analysis of why resulting trusts arise explained at the outset of this chapter is wrong on essentially all counts. Swadling's conclusion therefore is that the law in this area is essentially based on a 17th and 18th century presumption that the party has declared trust in his own favour but that the evidence of that trust in the appropriate form is absent. But, as he acknowledges, this is far from a realistic presumption on the facts of these cases and nor does he suggest that this *should* be how we conceptualise such trusts. Rather, he explains, it is the only explanation which makes sense on the existing case law.

---

[106] W Swadling, 'Explaining resulting trusts' (2008) 124 LQR 72, 86.
[107] W Swadling, 'Explaining resulting trusts' (2008) 124 LQR 72, 85–6.

7.5.2 WHEN WILL A RESULTING TRUST ARISE?

Resulting trusts will arise in a land law context in three circumstances, and most land law courses focus on the first two. First, a resulting trust will be the 'right solution' where there is a contribution to purchase price, where that was not actively intended as a gift, and where on the evidence, taking account of context, the parties' intention was most likely that they share in accordance with their contributions. This contribution could come in two forms. First it could be a direct monetary payment. Similarly, where property is purchased from the proceeds of sale of a previous property in which the relevant person had an interest, they will be treated as a having contributed to the purchase of the new property in proportion to the size of their share in the old property. Second, such a trust will arise where there is transfer of title to property for no money where the title was not given as a gift. In this circumstance, a trust will arise in favour of the transferee (we examine the operation of this rule in the context of registered land later). Third, a resulting trust will arise where a person attempts to set up a trust, and transfers title of the purported trust property to a trustee, but the trust itself fails for some reason (want of formalities, for example). The first type of trust is the 'purchase money resulting trust'. The second type is the 'voluntary conveyance resulting trust'. The third is the 'failed trust resulting trust'.[108]

7.5.2.1 Purchase money resulting trust

As noted, purchase money resulting trusts arise where there are direct contributions to the purchase price at the time of purchase. It is this temporal question which has been seen as preventing the flexible application of resulting trust principles to the domestic homes context, since most properties of this type are purchased with the help of a mortgage.[109] If the person contributes part of the cost of the purchase, he will obtain a resulting trust proportionate to that contribution.[110] This does not apply if either there is clear evidence of a contrary intention[111] or if the purchaser is the wife or child of A and there is no evidence that it was not a gift.[112]

What happens where the parties contribute equally to the purchase price and you find a resulting trust? In these cases, there is (another!) weak presumption that the resulting trust gives rise to a joint tenancy.[113] The rules relating to the distinction between a joint tenancy and a tenancy in common are explained in chapter 16 at 16.3. This presumption can be rebutted by evidence from the surrounding circumstances as was seen in *Edwards v Fashion*.[114] Let us examine the different options with some examples.

First, Michal becomes sole legal title-holder to a warehouse. 100 per cent of the purchase price was given by Eda. There is no evidence that this was intended as a gift. In this case, Michal will hold the property on trust absolutely for Eda. Eda will, for example, receive 100 per cent of the

---

[108] W Swadling, 'Explaining resulting trusts' (2008) 124 LQR 72, 73.
[109] *Laskar v Laskar* [2008] EWCA Civ 347, [2008] 1 WLR 2695; *Springette v Defoe Springette v Defoe* [1992] 2 FLR 388; *Dyer v Dyer*.
[110] *Malayan Credit v Jack Chia* [1986] AC 549.
[111] *Fowkes v Pascoe* (1874–75) LR 10 Ch App 343.
[112] *Ashe v Mumford* (2001) 33 HLR 67.
[113] *Aveling v Knipe* 34 ER 580, (1815) 19 Ves Jr 441.
[114] *Edwards v Fashion* 24 ER 156, (1712) Prec Ch 332.

proceeds of sale should the property be sold, and, in line with the rule in *Saunders v Vautier*,[115] would be able to require that Michal transfer legal title to her.

Second, Michal becomes sole legal title-holder to the warehouse. He has contributed 20 per cent of the purchase price, and Eda, 80 per cent. There is no evidence that Eda intended for the money contributed to be a gift. Michal would hold on trust in the shares 20 per cent for himself, and 80 per cent for Eda. This would give rise to an equitable tenancy in common. Both Eda and Michal can deal separately with their own shares.

Third, Michal becomes sole legal title-holder to the warehouse. Eda had contributed 80 per cent of the purchase price, and Donovan, 20 per cent. There is no evidence that either Eda or Donovan intended their contributions to be a gift to Michal. Michal would hold on trust 80 per cent for Eda and 20 per cent for Donovan. This would be in the form of an equitable tenancy in common. Both Eda and Donovan can deal separately with their own shares.

Finally, Michal becomes sole legal title-holder to the warehouse. He had contributed 50 per cent of the purchase price, and Eda, 50 per cent also. There is no evidence that Eda's contribution was intended as a gift. Michal would hold on trust for himself and Eda. There is a weak presumption that this gives rise to an equitable joint tenancy given the equality of the contribution. This can be rebutted. If it is rebutted, there will be a tenancy in common at 50:50.

As we can see from these examples, these rules are predictable and easy to apply, even if, as discussed earlier, their theoretical underpinning is somewhat murky. However, there are some remaining uncertainties in the law. The primary amongst these has already been discussed earlier, ie when will a resulting trust be the appropriate outcome: when a constructive trust? There are also some other issues which require resolution. First, how do mortgage or other staged payments fit into a resulting trust analysis? Second, what evidence is required in order to rebut the various presumptions which a resulting trust approach puts in place?

On the first question, there are two possible approaches to this. On the one hand, it is possible to argue that mortgage payments should count towards the proportions of the resulting trust because, in modern law at least, that is the reality in terms of how people purchase their property. Indeed, were property to be held solely in one person's name (in terms of legal title), but another paid all of the mortgage instalments over a very long period of time, it seems just as, if not indeed *more* clear, that this is unlikely to have been intended as a gift unless there was specific evidence of that effect. The precise role of mortgages within the resulting trust doctrine was considered by Lord Neuberger in *Stack*, and there he did suggest that mortgage payments should be considered in the application of the doctrines. However, given that the rest of the House of Lords explicitly moved away from the resulting trust, it is unlikely that we will be given a clear resolution to this question in the context of domestic homes at least.

On the other hand, it could be argued that the real relevance of payments towards mortgages is not actually about where the relevant money comes from, but rather, who is obliged to provide that money. Thus, whatever money someone actually provides in relation to a mortgage, they are in a very different position from the person who is *obliged* so-to-do. Let us explore this with an example.

Imagine that Rayhana purchases legal title to a property, providing 20 per cent of the purchase price as a deposit from her savings, and paying the rest with the help of a mortgage. She signs this mortgage herself, and is the sole person responsible for its repayment. However, her sister,

---

[115] *Saunders v Vautier* 49 ER 282, (1841) 4 Beav 115.

Amna, moves into the property and in return for Rayhana's patience, Amna pays the mortgage for two full years. This represents 5 per cent of the purchase price. Amna then later moves out, and Rayhana, struggling to repay the mortgage, falls into arrears. The bank exercises its remedies as a secured creditor and sells the property. There is a £75,000 surplus following discharge of the mortgage debt. Would we say that it would be right for Amna to receive 5 per cent of this surplus? Certainly, she paid towards the mortgage, and that payment was not intended as a gift per se. However, we can also say that if Amna did have 5 per cent of the property, she was not under obligations as far as the mortgage was concerned. The lender could not sue her personally. Thus, in this situation, Amna gets the benefits of rights in this property, by virtue of mortgage payments, but does not suffer the downside of having to make such payments. This does not seem to be an intuitively 'fair' approach to how mortgage payments should sit within the resulting trust rules. We could put this another way—Amna 'got what she paid for' when she contributed to the mortgage, ie permission to occupy. Should she also obtain rights in the property? If not, how do we articulate the division between the 'deserving' and the 'undeserving' case?

The second issue, ie what evidence must be brought if the various presumptions are to be rebutted, is equally difficult to resolve. The relevant presumptions may be, first, that payments towards purchase price, or transfer of title, are presumed not to represent gifts unless the contrary is proven; second, that in the absence of a gift intention, the parties intended for rights under a trust to result to the person providing such funds; and third, that in cases of equal contributions to purchase price, it is presumed that the intention is for a joint tenancy to exist. Of these, the first two presumptions are much more important in the practical operation of these rules. It may also be the case that both presumptions are not actually relevant—this depends upon which understanding one adopts as to why resulting trusts arise in purchase money cases, as discussed earlier. However, either way, the question can be boiled down to one of the strength of these presumptions, and what sorts of evidence can be brought to demonstrate that the presumption should be overcome.

The first answer to this comes in the form of a countervailing presumption, that is, the presumption of advancement, and in the rules relating to loans. The presumption of advancement is, essentially, an out-dated rule, which assumes that certain kinds of relationship will mean that ambiguous transfers should be conceptualised as a gift. The presumption applied from parents to children, and from husband to wife, but not the other way around (hence its out-dated nature). The presumption was intended to be abolished by section 199 Equality Act 2010. However, as Blackham highlights, that section has never been brought into force and so strictly-speaking the presumption still applies. However, it should be acknowledged that the presumption is very easily rebutted, perhaps a result of this out-dated and discriminatory nature. In the recent decision of *Wood v Watkin*, the court explained, however, that this reasoning does not necessarily apply in cases where the transfer is between parent and child.[116] Nevertheless, in any cases where you are asked to consider a situation where a husband provides part of the purchase price for property, or transfers title to property to his wife, or a parent to their child, the presumption is that this was intended as a gift and therefore that the resulting trust should not arise.

The second answer to the rebuttal of the resulting trust presumption is one of context. Thus, in a situation where two commercial parties are dealing at arm's length, we may we expect extremely clear evidence that the intention was a gift were the presumed resulting trust to be rebutted. This

---

[116] *Wood v Watkin* [2019] EWHC 1311 (Ch).

is because the apparent inappropriateness of any gift would be particularly strong in such a case. By contrast, in a situation where two close friends purchase a property together with a view to starting a business, and see themselves as 'joint' in that initiative, we may say that inferences from inequality of contribution to purchase price may be relatively easily rebutted. For example, they might bring evidence that they saw themselves in the form of a partnership or as having equal stakes in the enterprise, especially, if, for example, they had already determined that business profits would be split equally.

Finally, it could be that the correct answer here is not to consider how the presumption is rebutted per se, but rather to consider whether we are dealing with presumptions at all. Instead, following cases such as *Collie* it may be that the language of presumptions is not an accurate presentation of how the law works. Rather, the courts will look at the facts of the case, and try to ascertain from the context within which it occurs, and the behaviour of the parties of the time, what the parties genuinely intended. In such a case, it may not be necessarily to rely on presumptions at all, but simply to examine the facts.

Whichever of these options is selected, we can however give a relatively clear sense of the route that the courts will take in establishing whether a resulting trust has arisen in a purchase price contribution context. A remaining difficulty is what happens where the supposed contributions to purchase were made subsequently to the acquisition of title. This might be either by contributions to a mortgage, or by contributions to renovations or improvements which substantially increase the value of the property. On sale, the 'price achieved' is a reflection of the money put in at the time of purchase, and of the money put in subsequently to the value of the property. Historically there was little doubt that the only relevant contribution would be a contribution made at the time of the purchase. It would only be at this point that the transferee of legal title would obtain something without the recognition in place that they did not pay for it in its entirety. Indeed, the rigidity of the law in this respect goes a long way to explaining why the common intention constructive trust rules were needed to go beyond that which resulting trusts could achieve. However, some later case law suggests that resulting trusts ought not to be as tightly constrained as this. Lord Neuberger in *Stack* certainly took the view that resulting trusts could arise through contributions to mortgage payments, recognising the critical role which mortgages play in the modern property market. The support given to Lord Neuberger's judgment in this case in *Collie* may give some hope that the law on resulting trusts may develop in this way.

Summary: When will a purchase money resulting trust arise?

1. Where X contributes to the cost of acquiring title to property at the time of purchase and,
    a. there is no evidence that this was intended as a gift;
        i. in cases where the money was provided by husband to wife, or father to child, there is a weak presumption that this will indeed have been intended as a gift
    b. there is no evidence that this was intended as a loan.
2. Then, a resulting trust will arise in favour of that person, according to the percentage of purchase money which they contributed.

7.5.2.2 Voluntary conveyance resulting trust

The second category of resulting trust, less common in the land law case law, emerges where a person transfers title to another where that transfer was not made for consideration, nor was there an intention that the title be transferred as a gift. This may occur, for example, where the intention of the transferor was that the transferee would simply 'keep property safe' for them. Perhaps more commonly in land law, it might be where there was some factor in the transfer which vitiated the consent of the transferor and no money was provided to the transferor. It is said in the commentary and the case law that this sort of trust too rests of a presumption that unless it was made clear that a gift was intended in such circumstances, or where payment was made, that a resulting trust should emerge.

How does this interact with the recent case law on the question of the conclusivity of title in respect of land registration? The issue as to whether a forged transfer, which resulted nevertheless in registration of the transferee's title, would automatically give rise to a resulting trust under this doctrine? Under pre-registration law, the question would be moot since the void transfer would not result in conveyance of title. However, because section 58 LRA 2002 guarantees title to the land, the conveyance would nevertheless be effective. This argument was considered in *Swift 1st v Chief Land Registrar*,[117] following its apparent acceptance (although not necessarily in those terms) in *Fitzwilliam v Richall Holdings*[118] (itself based on the 1925 Act decision in *Malory v Cheshire Homes*[119]). In *Malory*[120] and *Fitzwilliam*,[121] the courts concluded that a trust would arise in these cases (although they do not use the label 'voluntary conveyance resulting trust' because of course in these cases, there was no such conveyance). However, the Court of Appeal in *Swift* confirmed that no trust arises in these cases because, first, there is no intention to trigger the trust.[122] Rather, the void nature of the conveyance means that apart from the register, nothing has happened. Wrongful registration does not, in itself, result in the creation of a trust.[123]

Thus, the voluntary conveyance resulting trust will only arise where there is indeed a validly created conveyance, but where either directly on the evidence, or through the imposition of presumptions regarding gifts and advancement, it is clear that the transferor did not intend to part with the value of the title conveyed.

> **Summary: When will a voluntary conveyance resulting trust arise?**
>
> 1. Where X transfers legal title to property to another in return for no consideration, and,
>   a. there is no evidence that this was intended as a gift;
>   i. in cases where the money was provided by husband to wife, or father to child, there is a weak presumption that this will indeed have been intended as a gift
>   b. there is no evidence that this was intended as a loan.
> 2. Then, a resulting trust will arise in favour of the transferor.

---

[117] *Swift 1st v Chief Land Registrar* [2015] EWCA Civ 330, [2015] Ch 602.
[118] *Fitzwilliam v Richall Holdings* [2013] EWHC 86 (Ch), [2013] 1 P & CR 19.
[119] *Malory v Cheshire Homes* [2002] EWCA Civ 151, [2002] Ch 216.
[120] *Malory v Cheshire Homes* [2002] EWCA Civ 151, [2002] Ch 216.
[121] *Fitzwilliam v Richall Holdings* [2013] EWHC 86 (Ch), [2013] 1 P & CR 19.
[122] *Swift 1st v Chief Land Registrar* [2015] EWCA Civ 330, [2015] Ch 602.
[123] *Swift 1st v Chief Land Registrar* [2015] EWCA Civ 330, [2015] Ch 602.

7.5.2.3 Failed trust resulting trust

The failed trust resulting trust tends to arise less often in relation to land, thanks to the requirements of formalities in particular and so we consider it here essentially for completeness. This kind of resulting trust arises where a person transfers property to another with the intention that the transferee should hold on trust for a third party but the formalities required to create the trust for the third party are not properly fulfilled. The trust arises because whilst on the evidence it is very clear that the transferee was not entitled to the benefit of the property, nor could a trust arise in favour of the third party due to the lack of proper declaration of trust. As a result, equity will create a resulting trust as the 'best solution' to the problem.

7.6 REFORM

The decision in *Stack*, and judicial comment in those cases that true reform of these rules was something long overlooked by Parliament, prompted the Law Commission to consider the issue of how property should be handled on the breakdown of a co-habiting relationship. It seems highly unlikely that the changes proposed by the Law Commission in this respect will be adopted in the near future, being potentially controversial given the view of some that they would make co-ownership very or too close to the rules relating to matrimonial property. It is nevertheless useful to be aware of the changes outlined by the Commission, as they provide insight into both the policy concerns with the existing law, and into the strengths and weaknesses of various alternative approaches. It should be noted, that whilst this chapter has dealt with implied trusts generally in land law, the Law Commission was particularly concerned with the breakdown of cohabiting relationships. Their proposals should therefore be read in that light.

The basic approach they suggested was that there should be an opt-out scheme for cohabiting couples which would 'kick in' after a minimum term of cohabitation (suggested by the Commission to be somewhere between 2 and 5 years), or where the child had a couple together. This would then allow either party to apply for financial relief on the breakdown of the relationship, unless they had followed the specified opt-out procedure. If financial relief were so available, then the courts would be entitled to use a structured discretion to handle the division of assets.

> **Further analysis: Law Commission's proposals for reform**
>
> The precise text of the Law Commission's recommended changes are cited here.
>
> 'An eligible cohabitant applying for relief following separation ('the applicant') must prove that:
>
> (1) the respondent has a retained benefit; or (2) the applicant has an economic disadvantage as a result of qualifying contributions the applicant has made
>
> A qualifying contribution is any contribution arising from the cohabiting relationship which is made to the parties' shared lives or to the welfare of members of their families. Contributions are not limited to financial contributions and include future contributions, in particular to the care of the parties' children following separation.

> A retained benefit may take the form of capital, income or earning capacity that has been acquired, retained or enhanced.
>
> An economic disadvantage is a present or future loss. It may include a diminution in current savings as a result of expenditure or of earnings lost during the relationship, lost future earnings, or the future cost of paid child-care.
>
> The court may make an order to adjust the retained benefit, if any, by reversing I in so far as that is reasonable and practicable having regard to the discretionary factors listed later. If, after the reversal of any retained benefit, the applicant would still bear an economic disadvantage, the court may make an order sharing that loss equally between the parties, in so far as it is reasonable and practicable to do so, having regard to the discretionary factors.
>
> The discretionary factors are:
>
> (1) the welfare while a minor of any child of both parties who has not attained the age of eighteen;
> (2) the financial needs and obligations of both parties;
> (3) the extent and nature of the financial resources which each party has or is likely to have in the foreseeable future;
> (4) the welfare of any children who live with, or might reasonably be expected to live with, either party; and
> (5) the conduct of each party, defined restrictively but so as to include cases where a qualifying contribution can be shown to have been made despite the express disagreement of the other party.
>
> Of these discretionary factors, item (1) earlier shall be the court's first consideration.
>
> In making an order to share economic disadvantage, the court shall not place the applicant, for the foreseeable future, in a stronger economic position than the respondent'.[124]
>
> As mentioned previously, although it is unlikely that these proposals will be taken forward, it is nevertheless indicative that the focus of the Law Commission is first, on the importance of children's welfare on the division of property of co-habiting couples, something notably lacking in the current approach to the constructive trust; and secondly, the focus on an attempt to achieve some form of parity in treatment between the two parties, regardless of their respective personal wealth. That is not the same thing as saying that assets will be divided equally of course, but rather that the courts should approach the matter with the interests of both in mind.

Absent these reforms, it seems likely that we will be left with the land law rules developed through implied trusts as the only way to manage the breakdown of relationships in these circumstances. Is this an acceptable outcome? Many have argued that it is not, both from the perspective of the parties concerned, required to litigate and engage in contentious discussions to ensure their mutual financial security, and from the perspective of any children of that relationship. The almost inevitable outcome of litigation is a further deterioration of the relevant relationship. This can hardly be considered a desirable outcome. Some of the literature on this topic is passionate in its condemnation not only of the precise rules, but of underlying assumptions, and even attitude of the legal system in this area. As Cowan et al argue:

---

[124] Law Commission, 'Cohabitation: The Financial Consequences of Relationship Breakdown' Report no. 307 (2007), 74–6.

> 'The starting point of the approach taken by law to human motivation seems so banal, monochrome, one-dimensional, irrelevant to lived experience and requires subjective opinion which merely exposes the prejudice/s of the speaker. It ignores the complicated narratives of the parties, fixes on certain matters which may have been an afterthought (if they gave any thought to it or its implication) and, despite the (sometimes) best intentions of the judges to do 'the right thing', the law just is plain stupid'.[125]

There is some force in this criticism. There is no doubt that the law in this area is premised on a series of rationalist assumptions, but the operation of romantic relationships can hardly be considered the place where human rationality is at its strongest. Furthermore, there has been considerable criticism of the rules on the grounds that, from the outset perhaps consciously, and since then, implicitly, they are biased against women. This is because the continuing attention paid to financial contributions, even if their significance has decreased following *Stack*, on average would disadvantage women. The response that women in such situations can protect themselves by insisting on the creation of an express trust, may be true but frequently will not represent the reality of the relationship within which such women find themselves. Inequality in the relationship; cultural assumptions about the place of women within certain groups; and a persistent emotional link between a romantic partner and financial security, will all combine to produce reluctance to insist upon formalising proprietary relationships in this way. Furthermore, even in cases where there is a relatively even balance of power between the parties, where one person has acquired title solely before the commencement of the relationship, and the other moves in later, it takes a good deal of courage to commence a 'when does this property become mine' conversation. In situations where the non-owner also on average earns less, or has given up work for the purposes of childcare, the consequences of failing to ensure their financial security by commencing on an uncomfortable conversation of this type, are consequently more severe. This is one of the big advantages of the Law Commission's solution in that the 'opt out' nature of the scheme produces default protection rather than requiring that a person in need of the law's help persuade their partner to allow them.

7.7 CONCLUSION

The law relating to implied trusts, along with that which we consider in the next chapter, proprietary estoppel, demonstrates that even when the focus of so many of these rules is on land as a marketable commodity, the importance of people to this equation is not forgotten. That does not mean, however, that the rules operate perfectly, nor that the balance is necessarily struck in the right place. The rules are highly unpredictable and often apparently arbitrary. The reform proposals which exist do not represent a clear improvement either, however, and so in this area it is perhaps best to see the law as it exists as a series of compromises borne out of a combination of political unwillingness to tackle the issues of cohabitation and imbalance in relationships head on, and of the common law's reluctance in respect of, and the constitutional impropriety of, judicially created 'revolutionary' rules.

---

[125] D Cowan et al, *Great Debates in Land Law* (London, Palgrave Macmillan, 2016), 225.

PRINCIPLES

How does this discussion shape our understanding of the principles explained in chapter 1? To recap, these principles were:

1. Certainty
2. Sensitivity to context
3. Transactability
4. Systemic and individual effects
5. Recognition of the social role of the land law system.

Implied trusts do not achieve certainty and they do not achieve transactibility. The degree to which they act as a brake on such is determined on the one hand by the priority rules, and especially those relating to overreaching (explained in chapters 15 and 16) and by the flexibility and lack of precision inherent in the rules relating to such trusts themselves. To ask that such rules be entirely certain would be to defeat their object—but that does not mean that the current position is acceptable. As we can see in relation to the question of when the starting point that equity follows the law will be departed from; to the problem of quantifying parties' shares; and to the initial choice between a resulting and a constructive trust analysis, predictability is far from achieved. Whilst this is welcome to a degree, it also causes significant problems for those vulnerable or ill-informed persons which the rules are designed to help.

In such cases as these, the first step taken by a person claiming an interest in a house to which they do not have title, or in relation to which they believe that are entitled to more than the legal title appears to give them, will be to consult a solicitor. Already the process now involves some degree of cost. But solicitors can operate cheaply and swiftly where the rules are clear and easy to apply: advice becomes straightforward and persons claiming an interest are able to know whether or not it is in their interest to persue their case further. In relation to constructive trusts, this is simply not possible. A consultation with a solicitor is likely to lead to more not less uncertainty, and to a likely unproductive and time-consuming trawl through a relationship history. This will be costly. Even if the claimant does win at any trial so that the other side will pay their costs, the totality of their outlay will very likely not be covered. Certainly, there will be no compensation for the time and effort involved in such protracted litigation.

Perhaps more seriously, the question as to the existence or otherwise of an implied trust arises almost solely in the cases of either bankruptcy/severe financial difficulties in relation to a lender on the one hand, or relationship breakdown on the other. Both situations are enormously stressful in any case. Adding into this litigation concerning proprietary interests in land is likely to make the situation almost, if not entirely, unmanageable for those caught into this web. In the worst case scenario of a relationship breakdown where there are children of the relationship caught between their parents, a fight regarding property rights which cannot sensibly be settled or negotiated (since no one knows what is likely to happen in court) can very quickly make the future dealings between the parties so antagonistic that a civilised and amicable co-parenting situation can become impossible. The social consequences of uncertainty here stretch very far beyond mere economic costs. If we compare this to the popular wisdom surrounding how to achieve a 'friendly and fair' divorce, the rules in relation to cohabiting couples are certainly less well-calibrated to achieving such an end to a relationship.

Having said that, however, the courts are very clearly responding to social need in creating these rules. The changes in living patterns and relationship forms experienced over the last thirty years cannot simply be ignored by the law. To treat such relationships as though they were purely commercial enterprises would be unrealistic and a dereliction of duty by the courts, and yet the strictures of precedent and the lack of action by Parliament means that the solution they have reached is not a good one. Furthermore, in individual cases whilst we may welcome condemnation of poor behaviour, or taking of advantage, and of bullying by depriving such a person of property rights and wealth 'through the back door', is this really what land law should be about? We may well see that Mr or Ms X should not 'hold onto' wealth obtained through deceit or abuse of power, but the system that this produces is not satisfactory for the 'victim' of such abuses either. These rules may well be a work in progress, but there is certainly work still to be done.

TABLE OF DEFINITIONS

Interest under a trust	Relationship between trustee (legal owner) and beneficiary (equitable owner) whereby the legal owner has to act for the benefit of the equitable owner, and the equitable owner has a right in the property which can be enforced against third parties.
Express trust	A trust which arises through the express volition of the parties. It must be expressed in a written form to be enforceable under section 53 Law of Property Act 1925.
Implied trust	A trust which arises not from the express wishes of the parties in an appropriate form.
Constructive trust	A trust which arises in response to evidence of a common intention which is detrimentally relied upon.
Resulting trust	A trust which arises to un-do an apparent gift in circumstances where a gift would be an inappropriate outcome and there is no evidence that one was intended.

FURTHER READING

Much of the discussion surrounding implied trusts is concerned with the relationship between the new rules as expressed in *Stack* and *Kernott* with the previous authorities. As analytically insightful as much of this is, it is perhaps now slightly out of date given the way the Court of Appeal authorities have responded to the House of Lords/Supreme Court decisions. This further reading is therefore concerned with the broader question of how implied trusts is responding to societal pressures and the consequences of this for the shape of the law in general.

BARLOW, A. et al, *Cohabitation, Marriage and the Law* (Hart, 2005).
FOX O'MAHONY, L. 'The politics of Lloyds Bank v Rosset', in Douglas, S., Hickey, R. and Waring, E. (eds), *Landmark Cases in Property Law* (Hart, 2015).
GARDNER, S., 'Family property today' (2008) 124 LQR 422.
LIEW, Y. K., *Rationalising Constructive Trusts* (Hart, 2017), chapter 4.

8

PROPRIETARY ESTOPPEL

8.1 Introduction	233	8.6 Relationship between Estoppel
8.2 Requirements of Estoppel	234	and Constructive Trusts 266
8.3 Consequences of Estoppel	257	8.7 Conclusion 270
8.4 Effect of the Estoppel on Third Parties	262	Principles 271
8.5 Relationship between Estoppel and Formalities	265	Table of Definitions 272
		Further Reading 272

CHAPTER GOALS

By the end of this chapter, you should be able to understand:

- The three forms of proprietary estoppel;
- The primary elements of estoppel by assurance (assurance, detriment, reliance and unconscionability);
- The consequences of estoppel arising in terms of remedies and effects on third parties; and
- The relationship between estoppel and formalities, and estoppel and constructive trusts.

8.1 INTRODUCTION

Proprietary estoppel is one of the land law doctrines which allows for the creation of rights in land without a written contract or other formal document. It arises when a person (the promisor) makes a promise to another (the promisee) in relation to their land, and then attempts to go back on that promise in circumstances where it was unfair to do so. Given the general policy of formality, with its associated benefits of certainty and clarity, we must consider the rules relating to proprietary estoppel from the perspective not only of *when* proprietary estoppel generates rights in land, but also *why* it does so. This is particularly important in relation to estoppel since it represents a general and potentially broad exception to the formality rules discussed in chapter 4.

In broad brush terms, as explained earlier, proprietary estoppel operates to generate proprietary interests where an informal representation has been detrimentally relied on by the person to whom that promise was made. However, as McFarlane has highlighted, the label 'proprietary estoppel' may be better understood as the name given to three separate forms of rights generation[1]—estoppel by representation, estoppel by acquiescence, and estoppel by assurance or promise. Of these, the most wide-reaching in terms of its effect is estoppel by assurance, and this will be the focus of this chapter. The other doctrines, to the extent which they are subtly different, will be discussed at various points. Estoppel by assurance arises where an assurance (promise) has been detrimentally relied upon by the promisee in circumstances where it would be unconscionable for the promisor to go back on their promise. The right which arises as a result is an 'equity arising by estoppel'. The courts then have discretion to determine what remedy, if any, should be given to the promisee in such cases to satisfy this equity and 'crystallise' the estoppel.

In terms of when estoppel will arise, the rules are relatively straightforward to understand, even if the precise result in each case can be hard to predict. Similarly, the principles at play in terms of remedies are clear even if, again, the actual outcome can vary on a case-to-case basis. However, the underlying justification for estoppel; its interaction with formality rules; and the nature of rights which estoppel generates, can be controversial. Furthermore, the relationship between the different branches of estoppel has, at least historically, generated some difficulty in terms of tracing the historical development of this doctrine. Some cases which have been treated as estoppel cases previously might now be considered constructive trust cases, for example. This chapter will therefore explain these rules from a modern perspective, rather than being concerned with the historical development of these rules per se.

To explore these issues, this chapter will begin, in 8.2, by considering when an estoppel arises, looking first briefly at estoppel by representation and acquiescence, before turning to estoppel by assurance and at the questions of assurance, detriment, reliance and unconscionability in this context. Section 8.3 explores the consequences of an estoppel having arisen. Section 8.4 considers the effect of proprietary estoppel on third parties. Section 8.5 considers the relationship between proprietary estoppel and the formality rules—section 2 Law of Property (Miscellaneous Provisions) Act 1989 in particular. Finally, section 8.6 will then analyse the relationship between proprietary estoppel and constructive trusts in terms of when such rights will arise, as this is a difficult and controversial area.

8.2 REQUIREMENTS OF ESTOPPEL

This section considers the different 'requirements' for establishing estoppel whilst recognising three key issues. First, estoppel is not established in a formulaic, 'tick-box' way. Rather, the courts apply it in a flexible and discretionary fashion. Speaking of 'requirements' is therefore a somewhat misleading term to give to the reality of the judicial approach. Second, it is a matter of some controversy as to whether, in relation to modern proprietary estoppel, there are in reality three separate forms of estoppel. This issue is discussed fully at 8.2.1 and 8.2.2. Finally, the section discusses unconscionability in relation to 'estoppel by assurance'. However, unconscionability permeates the whole doctrine and so, in theory, is required in order to establish the other two forms

---

[1] B McFarlane, *Proprietary Estoppel* (OUP, Oxford, 2014). The extent to which the tripartite classification is useful is discussed later.

of estoppel as well. However, since the criteria for estoppel in the other two cases are relatively narrow, the courts do not normally have recourse to unconscionability as a separate 'requirement' for the establishing of the estoppel. Rather, in those cases, unconscionability is treated as though it were a conclusion arising from the fact that the other relevant criteria are met. For this reason, it makes sense to consider what unconscionability means, and how it is applied by the court, primarily in relation to estoppel by assurance.

8.2.1 ESTOPPEL BY ACQUIESCENCE

First, estoppel by acquiescence arises when a landowner, for example, stands by and watches whilst another builds on or otherwise improves that land, without intervening. McFarlane defines this strand as follows: '[i]t applies where B adopts a particular course of conduct in reliance on a mistaken belief as to B's current rights and A, knowing both of B's belief and of the existence of A's own, inconsistent right, fails to assert that right against B'.[2] In circumstances like this, A is unable to assert his right against B, at least, not fully. An alternative mode of expressing the test for estoppel by acquiescence is found in *Willmott v Barber*[3] where the court lists five necessary features: i. B must have made a mistake as to his rights; ii. B must spent money or done acts on the faith of this belief; iii. the possessor of the right must know of his own inconsistent right; iv. A must know of B's mistaken belief; and v. A must have encouraged B in his expenditure of money or effort. However, care must be taken in expressing the test this way. As will be seen, all types of proprietary estoppel are imbued with an inherent flexibility. To treat the establishment of an estoppel as a 'tick box' exercise is to underestimate the discretion which the courts have, and have regularly displayed, in shaping the rules in any particular case. That does not mean that it is 'easy' to demonstrate that estoppel has arisen. Simply, it means that the words used by Fry J in *Willmott v Barber*[4] should not be treated as though they were a statutory provision, capable of precise and formulaic application.

Let us explore this type of estoppel with an example. Ole and Magdalena are joint legal titleholders to a plot of land. Their next-door neighbour, Simon, mistakenly believes that a patch of land at the end of his garden forms part of his own freehold title. Ole and Magdalena know that this is not the case. They stand by and watch whilst Simon spends many hours cultivating this patch, turning it into a beautiful rose garden. They even nod and smile when Simon tells them that he is very proud of the Lady of Shallot and Summer Song roses he has planted 'in his garden'. They then decide that they will try to evict Simon from the land once his work is complete so that they can enjoy the garden which he has built.

In this situation, Simon will have little difficultly in establishing that he has made a mistake as to his own rights. Ole and Magdalena did not take the reasonable opportunity presented to them to correct this, knowing as they did that the land in question did not form part of Simon's title. However, it is important to note here, and this is a theme to which we will return later, that the *remedy* which Simon will get in this case is not necessarily the title to the relevant land.

---

[2] B McFarlane, *Proprietary Estoppel* (OUP, Oxford, 2014), [1.06].
[3] *Willmott v Barber* (1880) 15 ChD 96 (ChD).
[4] *Willmott v Barber* (1880) 15 ChD 96 (ChD).

Apart from remedy, another issue which this scenario raises is the level of the distinction between this form of estoppel and the promise or assurance-based form of proprietary estoppel. In this case, there is clearly no express promise made by Ole and Magdalena to Simon. However, recent developments in relation to the assurance requirement of assurance-based estoppel (particularly in *Thorner v Major*, see later at 8.2.3.1), mean that the assurance can be implied, making the two types of estoppel very close in practice. Later we consider whether it therefore makes sense to continue to think of there being three types of estoppel.

8.2.2 ESTOPPEL BY REPRESENTATION

Estoppel by representation is, in many ways, very similar to promise-based estoppel which we discuss next. However, the *consequence* of an estoppel by representation is somewhat different, and so it is worth briefly considering this. Estoppel by representation is said to arise where A makes a statement to B about a state of fact or law, or both, on which B then relies. Estoppel by representation results in a bar arising which means that A cannot deny the truth of that fact, or the correctness of his statement as to the law. It does not guarantee B rights in the land as a remedy, but will prevent A from making a statement inconsistent with his earlier one.

This is an old form of estoppel and is very closely related to the foundation of estoppel. The clue is in the word itself. E*stop*pel arises in order to *stop* a person from raising an argument in court. This form of estoppel is only established in relatively narrow circumstances. Indeed, because the effect of it is rather limited, in most circumstances a person who believes that an estoppel has arisen in their favour in a case like this will more likely rely on the rules relating to promise-based estoppel. Primarily the limitation in cases like this is the requirement, established in a number of cases, that the statement made be unequivocal. This means that not only must it be very certain, it must relate to a statement of fact or fact and law and cannot relate to a statement of opinion or intention.

> **Further analysis: Are there three forms of estoppel or one?**
>
> There have been a number of calls to unify estoppel into a single concept—with some even going as far as to suggest proprietary and promissory estoppel be amalgamated. One of the most prominent calls for such a change to the law is to be found in the extra-judicial comments of Lord Neuberger. Thus, he puts forward the case for approaching all kinds of estoppel 'in the round', arguing:
>
> > 'may not estoppel now be seen to be a generic term for a claim by a claimant who has changed his position in the reasonable and foreseeable belief that a defendant's act, statement, silence or inaction has a particular consequence, so that it would now be unconscionable for the defendant to repudiate that consequence (wholly or to an extent), at least without giving the claimant some compensation'.[5]
>
> However, there are some who treat proprietary estoppel as a single concept. The authors of the 8th edition of Megarry & Wade (the leading practitioners' guide) take this approach, for example.[6]

---

[5] Lord Neuberger of Abbotsbury, 'The stuffing of Minerva's owl? taxonomy and Taxidermy in equity' (2009) 68 CLJ 537, 547–8.

[6] C Harpum et al, *Megarry & Wade—The Law of Real Property* (Sweet & Maxwell, London, 2012), 711.

However, such unification faces a number of problems, even if the unification is limited to proprietary estoppel. For this reason, McFarlane has argued forcefully that conceptual clarity can only be achieved by separating the different strands of estoppel.[7] There are three reasons for this distinction. First, the different strands of estoppel have different effects (particularly estoppel by representation). Second, the *belief* which the claimant holds is different in acquiescence cases, since in such cases the claimant must make a mistake about his current rights (not future promised rights). Finally, there is an important distinction between estoppel by representation and assurance on the one hand, and by acquiescence on the other in terms of the passive or active nature of the representation. As Samet has argued, estoppel by acquiescence involves, in effect, liability for an *omission*, ie a failure to speak up. The other two forms of estoppel relate to active promises, even if such promises are implied.

If, as McFarlane and others show, it is right to conclude that there are indeed three different forms of estoppel, with related, but subtly different effects, then we must perhaps examine the justifications for the different forms of estoppel. In particular, estoppel by acquiescence seems hard to explain given that, in a way unusual for private law, it involves liability for an omission. This issue has been considered in detail by Samet, who concludes that it is difficult (although not impossible) to justify this form of estoppel. It is certainly very problematic to justify the remedial preference in relation to estoppel by acquiescence to confer onto the promisee either title to or a long term right to use the relevant land (in contrast, for example, to providing a remedy which reflects the detriment suffered—for more on the different remedial approaches possible in relation to estoppel, see 8.3.2). Thus, she argues:

> 'The acquiescence category of PE is... justified on a principle that is essentially different from the principle that stands at the basis of liability for active encouragement of reliance. It is a principle which is relatively weak, at least in the sense that it cannot fully suppress the weighty general considerations against legal liability for omission. This relative weakness, in comparison with the heavy-duty principle that supports liability for active encouragement to rely, ought to be reflected in the remedy that is on offer for the successful claimant. A nuanced result can be reached by limiting the measure of the remedy for acquiescence to the reliance value, and by downscaling it from proprietary to personal'.[8]

8.2.3 PROMISE OR ASSURANCE-BASED ESTOPPEL

By far the most common, and most commonly discussed, form of estoppel is promise-based estoppel. The terms 'promise' and 'assurance' are used interchangeably here. Indeed, in many cases the line between the three different forms of estoppel is not clear-cut. Some acquiescence and representation cases could be recast as assurance-based estoppel cases. Consider the problem involving Simon and Ole and Magdalena described previously. Rather than seeing their nodding and smiling as being representative of a 'standing by', it would also be possible to interpret that behaviour as an implied assurance that the land in question 'belonged to' Simon. This implied assurance could then form the basis of an assurance-based estoppel claim. Certainly, the line is not clear-cut.

Furthermore, it is in relation to assurance-based estoppel that the courts most readily flex their discretionary muscles, and context and a general attitude to 'fairness' in equity pervades the application of this doctrine. This means that it is both dangerous and inaccurate to try to build a precise 'test' as to when an estoppel will arise. However, we can break down the various factors which are

---

[7] B McFarlane, *Proprietary Estoppel* (OUP, Oxford, 2014), [1.24]–[1.27].
[8] I Samet, 'Proprietary estoppel and responsibility for omissions' (2015) 78 MLR 85, 111.

said to make up an estoppel, even if these are not applied in a strict, rigid fashion, but rather as forming part of an overall, holistic assessment as to whether there is unconscionability present in a particular case. Thus as Walker LJ (who we may consider to be the 'father' of the modern estoppel doctrine) states in *Gillett v Holt* (see later): 'it is important to note at the outset that the doctrine of proprietary estoppel cannot be treated as subdivided into three or four watertight compartments'.[9]

Estoppels arise when there has been an assurance which has been detrimentally relied upon so that it would be *unconscionable* for the promisor to go back on her promise. In early case law, the courts seemed to take the view that unconscionability in these circumstances was, in effect, a conclusion from 'adding up' the assurance and the detrimental reliance. Any time that these elements were present, it would *always* be unconscionable for the promisor to go back on their promise. However, over time, the definitions of assurance and detrimental reliance have expanded (as it natural in a system based on precedent and reasoning by analogy). This has left the potential scope of proprietary estoppel very wide. As a result, the courts have begun to recognise that it is necessary to treat unconscionability not as a *conclusion*, but as an additional overarching factor which must be proved before an estoppel will arise. This, whilst useful in terms of limiting the scope of estoppel to the cases where it genuinely seems appropriate, has given rise to its own challenges, not least because there is no clear definition of unconscionability present in the case law (nor, arguably, could there ever be).

8.2.3.1 Assurance

An assurance is a statement or conduct which the promisee has reasonably taken to mean that the promisor was promising some right in property to the promisee. This promise can relate either to land which the promisor already owns, or to land which he intends or expects to acquire. All that matters is whether the promisee reasonably believes from that assurance that either they currently do have a proprietary interest in the relevant land, or that they will acquire such in the future.[10] The test for an assurance in the context of proprietary estoppel is, somewhat unhelpfully, that the promise be 'sufficiently certain'. This is unhelpful in the sense that, as a definition, it presupposes the question. Nevertheless, it does give a clue as to how estoppel operates. The courts have a great deal of discretion and flexibility, and the test for the assurance and how clear it must be, and what form it must take, will vary depending upon the circumstances in which it was given. To demonstrate this further, it is useful to begin with an examination of the two leading cases in proprietary estoppel: *Cobbe v Yeoman's Row*[11] and *Thorner v Major*.[12]

> **Key case: *Cobbe v Yeoman's Row* [2008] UKHL 55**
>
> This case involved property owned by Yeoman's Row Management in Knightsbridge, London. Mrs Lisle-Mainwaring, a shareholder and director of Yeoman's Row Management, conducted negotiations with Mr Cobbe, an experienced property developer. The intention was that Mr Cobbe would commission architects' drawings, obtain planning permission etc. for the development of the property into flats.

---

[9] *Gillett v Holt* [2001] Ch 210 (CA), 225.
[10] *Re Basham* [1986] 1 WLR 1498 (Ch).
[11] *Cobbe v Yeoman's Row Management Ltd* [2008] UKHL 55; [2008] 1 WLR 1752.
[12] *Thorner v Major* [2009] UKHL 18; [2009] 1 WLR 776.

If this was done, then Yeoman's Row would sell the property (which was made up of six terraced houses) to Mr Cobbe for £12mn upfront, and then a share of the profits once the development had taken place and the flats sold. This agreement was referred to by the parties as a 'gentleman's agreement' and was never written down.

Mr Cobbe did obtain the relevant permissions and plans, but at this point Mrs Lisle-Mainwaring decided that she would demand an up-front price of £20mn to reflect the fact that the properties now had the benefit of planning permission for development and were thus worth more than previously, albeit that she also offered to take a lower percentage of the eventual profits of the development. Mr Cobbe, concerned that paying such a large sum up front would affect his ability to make a profit from the transaction, did not agree to the new terms. Instead, he brought a claim based on proprietary estoppel, arguing that an estoppel arose in his favour on the basis of the assurance in the original agreement which, in obtaining planning permission and the architects' plans (and spending hundreds of thousands of pounds in the process), he had relied upon to his detriment. The case eventually reached the House of Lords where, amongst a number of other issues, the court was required to assess whether this sort of 'gentleman's agreement' contained a sufficiently certain assurance in order to give rise to an estoppel. The court concluded that it did not. In this case, the parties were experienced property developers. They all knew, or ought to have known, that this sort of transaction must be recorded in a signed, written contract before it can be enforceable in accordance with section 2 of the Law of Property (Miscellaneous Provisions) Act 1989. Whilst this feeds into the assessment of unconscionability in the case, as we will see later, it also affects the way in which the 'sufficiently certain' test plays out. An assurance would need to be very different in a commercial context than in a domestic context to be sufficient to found the basis of a proprietary estoppel.

Furthermore, the court also considered whether the assurance needs to be about specific property/a specific property right. If that is necessary for a proprietary estoppel, then it would be difficult in this case for Cobbe to argue that such a promise was made to him. What right was promised? It seems to have been something akin to an option to purchase, but at the very least it was a conditional option on his having obtained the relevant planning permissions. Discussing these issues, Lord Scott reasoned:

> 'Proprietary estoppel requires, in my opinion, clarity as to what it is that the object of the estoppel is to be estopped from denying, or asserting, and clarity as to the interest in the property in question that that denial, or assertion, would otherwise defeat. If these requirements are not recognised, proprietary estoppel will lose contact with its roots and risk becoming unprincipled and therefore unpredictable'.[13]

On this approach, it is clear that Lord Scott saw the need for the promise to relate to a specific proprietary interest as being paramount. This was because Lord Scott focused in his judgment on, as he refers to it, the 'root' of estoppel, ie the role of estoppel as preventing someone from relying on a fact, statement, or legal rule, when they had promised that they would not so rely. In *Cobbe*, Lord Scott highlighted, it was difficult to point to exactly what Mrs Lisle-Mainwaring would be prevented from arguing. She would not be prevented from arguing that the agreement they reached was not binding in contract. Neither party thought this to be the case, and section 2 of the Law of Property Act 1989 would in any case make this argument impossible. Nor could she be prevented from arguing that she had flexibility as to whether or not to sell at all—that was clear, and Mr Cobbe did not dispute that. In short, the argument between the parties here was about price, not about a proprietary interest, and so, in Lord Scott's view, proprietary estoppel could not arise here. This reasoning as to what will suffice to ground an estoppel

---

[13] *Cobbe v Yeoman's Row Management Ltd* [2008] UKHL 55; [2008] 1 WLR 1752, [28].

is not an approach which has been taken forward wholesale. Many see Lord Scott's approach as being far too rigid and, importantly, wrong as a matter of historical precedent. Lord Scott's analysis relies very much on seeing proprietary estoppel as a specific subspecies of promissory estoppel.[14] However, many doubt whether this is an accurate reflection as to how the law of proprietary estoppel has developed in distinction to the narrower promissory estoppel. Furthermore, if Lord Scott's analysis was a correct interpretation of previous case law, then there would be very few successful estoppel claims, whereas cases like *Gillett v Holt*[15] show that estoppel can arise in cases even where all parties know perfectly well that the promises in question are not binding in law (because, for example, they relate to a will) and where the precise proprietary rights being granted were uncertain. The difficulties with the judgment of Lord Scott in this respect are explained in detail by McFarlane and Robertson.[16]

The result of this was that the court held that Mr Cobbe was not entitled to the benefit of a proprietary estoppel. He did however receive some compensation to reflect the time and money spend in obtaining the planning permission on the basis of a quantum meruit (ie the cost of the services provided).

As will be seen next, the impact of *Cobbe* on the role and scope of proprietary estoppel was significantly curtailed by the decision in *Thorner*,[17] which undermines the reasoning in *Cobbe* and returns our understanding of estoppel to the pre-*Cobbe* position. However, some lessons can still be taken from *Cobbe*, and it is important to realise that whilst much of the reasoning from this case has been questioned, the result has not. This is because, in a commercial context like this, when parties are of equal bargaining power, and dealing at arm's length, the justification for granting rights in the face of an absence of formalities become harder to meet, and the degree to which there is unconscionability in going back on a 'promise' which both parties knew was not binding, and indeed which both parties intended not to be binding, is, at the very least, doubtful.

Key case: *Thorner v Major* [2009] UKHL 18

The decision in *Cobbe* can be very clearly contrasted, both in tone and result, with the decision in *Thorner v Major*. This case involved a large farm in Somerset. The original owner of the farm was Mr Peter Thorner (Peter). When Peter died, his cousin, David, expected that he would inherit the farm because of the relationship between himself and Peter; David's working on the farm for many years without pay; and various oblique promises which had been made to him. However, Peter died without a will, so that the property would go to his next of kin. Major was one of the personal representatives managing P's estate. The question was whether there was enough here to form the basis of a proprietary estoppel. Considering the assurance question (we will also return to this case often throughout this chapter), the court held that the assurance in this case was partly one arising through conduct and partly arising through vague and oblique statements. For example, Peter at one point handed a piece of paper to David with the words, 'that is for my death duties'. The paper was an insurance certificate. This was held by the court to be an indication to David that the insurance policy would cover inheritance tax when David

---

[14] *Cobbe v Yeoman's Row Management Ltd* [2008] UKHL 55, [2008] 1 WLR 1752, [14].
[15] *Gillett v Holt* [2001] Ch 210 (CA).
[16] B McFarlane and A Robertson, 'The Death of Proprietary Estoppel' [2008] LMCLQ 449 and B McFarlane and A Robertson, 'Apocalypse averted: proprietary estoppel in the House of Lords' (2009) 125 LQR 535.
[17] *Thorner v Major* [2009] UKHL 18, [2009] 1 WLR 776.

inherited. When this is compared with the promise made in *Cobbe v Yeoman's Row*[18] it is clear that, in some respects, the promise in *Cobbe* was much stronger. However, it must be noted that what matters is not what the promisor said as such, but what the claimant reasonably understood by such a statement. In *Thorner*, David reasonably understood from this statement that Peter intended him to inherit the farm. In *Cobbe*, Mr Cobbe cannot have reasonably understood that their oral agreement would guarantee him a right to purchase the land at the agreed price, because he was perfectly well aware that there was no binding legal agreement between the parties. However, the two major problems for Mr Cobbe—that he ought not to have thought that the promise was legally binding (and that therefore there could be no grounds for estoppel) and that the right promised to him was imprecise in its scope and nature—applied with equal force to the arrangement in *Thorner*. Thus, whilst the context was hugely different, the central questions were very similar.

On the first issue, ie the extent to which it matters that the parties do not consider their agreement to be legally binding, the court demonstrates the flexibility of the doctrine and how a wrong turn can be taken by being too rigid in the application of the various 'tests' discussed in the case law. The court highlighted that whilst David did not believe that the promise was irrevocable, in the sense that a will can be changed right up until the moment of death, he did nevertheless take the promise to be a firm commitment as to what was to happen. Focussing on whether the parties believed the promise to be revocable is, in this sense, a red-herring. It does not matter whether they believed the promise to be legally binding. Rather, what matters is whether the circumstances were such, taking account both of what was believed and the circumstances which gave rise to that belief and reliance on that belief, it would be unfair or unconscionable to allow the promise to be reneged upon. As a result, Lord Walker reached the conclusion that, 'I would prefer to say (while conscious that it is a thoroughly question-begging formulation) that to establish a proprietary estoppel the relevant assurance must be clear enough. What amounts to sufficient clarity, in a case of this sort, is hugely dependent on context'.[19]

On the question as to whether the promise has to relate to a specific property right, that was made difficult in this case because, as is common with many farms, the precise scope of the farm business changed over time, expanding and contracting in line with the commercial needs of the farm business. This, combined with the fact that the promises made to David were implied over a long period of time, made it difficult to say with precision exactly what rights had been promised and in relation to what land. However, the court did not see this as a barrier to the creation of an estoppel. As Lord Walker explains, it is necessary for the promise to relate to identifiable property: 'In my opinion it is a necessary element of proprietary estoppel that the assurances given to the claimant (expressly or impliedly, or, in standing by cases, tacitly) should relate to identified property owned (or, perhaps, about to be owned) by the defendant'.[20] However, this is not the same thing as saying that the promise must relate to a specific proprietary interest. Thus, if the land can be labelled and identified, eg 'the farm', that will suffice. Lord Scott explains this:

'Peter's representation that David would inherit Steart Farm speaks, at least where Peter remained the owner of an agricultural entity known as Steart Farm, as from his death and if, at that time, evidence were available to identify Steart Farm with certainty, David's claim to be entitled in equity to Steart Farm cannot, in my opinion, be rejected for want of certainty of subject matter'.[21]

---

[18] *Cobbe v Yeoman's Row Management Ltd* [2008] UKHL 55, [2008] 1 WLR 1752.
[19] *Thorner v Major* [2009] UKHL 18, [2009] 1 WLR 776, [56].
[20] *Thorner v Major* [2009] UKHL 18, [2009] 1 WLR 776, [61].
[21] *Thorner v Major* [2009] UKHL 18, [2009] 1 WLR 776, [18].

> **Summary: Assurance after *Thorner v Major* [2009] UKHL 18**
>
> Combining these two key cases tells us three important features of the 'assurance' in estoppel cases.
>
> 1. The assurance need only be 'certain enough' to found the estoppel. Whether this test is met will depend upon all the circumstances. However, in commercial contexts, generally the promise will have to be very firm before it will be enough to ground an estoppel.
> 2. It is not necessary for the parties to believe that the promise is irrevocable in law. What matters is whether the circumstances are such that if the promise is reneged upon that would be unconscionable.
> 3. The promise must relate to identified or identifiable land, but it does not need to relate to a specific proprietary interest.

Context and Assurance

The comparison between these two cases shows very clearly the importance of context in assessing the quality of an assurance. One way of thinking about the relevance of context here is to consider not only whether the promisee was reasonable in relying on the promise given its content, but whether B 'was entitled to rely'.[22] This expression emphasises the normative weight of the content and mode of expression of the promise. It is only in cases where unconscionability and the content of the promise 'meet' that the promise will be certain enough to form the basis of an estoppel.

This means, as has been emphasised, that it is somewhat difficult to predict in advance, and devoid of context, when a particular course of conduct will fall on one side of the line or the other. What is clear is that although it can be implied, there must be an assurance of some kind. This is an essential element of a successful assurance-based estoppel claim. This means that there can be no estoppel (except in the relatively few cases which amount of estoppel by acquiescence) where the promisor has not actually made any *promise* in relation to the land. This will make it very difficult to claim an estoppel in relation to very heavily qualified promises. This was a clear issue in *Cobbe v Yeoman's Row*[23] (see earlier), where the qualification was obvious, or could be problematic in cases where the promisee intended (and it was clear that they intended) that their promise be morally binding perhaps, but certainly not legally binding. In terms of labelling however, the commercial/domestic distinction is said to form a central role in relation to context.

> **Further analysis: Domestic and commercial distinction**
>
> The commercial/domestic distinction is one which plays a significant role in relation to proprietary estoppel, just as it does in relation to implied trusts (see chapter 7). It plays both a practical and an explanatory/normative role. The courts rely on the distinction as a justification for the outcome reached. This is because, as highlighted earlier, some approach the concept of unconscionability, the foundation

---

[22] B McFarlane, *Proprietary Estoppel* (OUP, Oxford, 2014), [2.95].
[23] *Cobbe v Yeoman's Row Management Ltd* [2008] UKHL 55, [2008] 1 WLR 1752.

stone for proprietary estoppel, from the perspective that the concept can only be defined by reference to the context within which any particular dispute has arisen. This means that there is a very intimate connection between context and unconscionability. Following the decisions in *Cobbe v Yeoman's Row*[24] and *Thorner v Major*,[25] there this is thus an intimate connection between the meaning of unconscionability and the commercial/domestic distinction. This is particularly so in relation to the nature of the assurance and whether or not it meets the sufficiently certain test once unconscionability is used as a crosscheck. This distinction is therefore one which is said to have an enormous amount of explanatory power.

Lord Neuberger, for example, sees the merit in this distinction, arguing:

> 'The notion that a claimant takes his chance, where he knows that he has no legally enforceable right, is easier to accept in the context of a commercial and arm's length relationship than in a domestic or familial context. In a commercial situation, the absence of a contractual relationship normally arises from the parties, with easy access to legal advice, considering themselves better off, or at least choosing to take a risk, rather than being bound'.[26]

Furthermore, he highlights the normative importance of this distinction, as well as its practical effects:

> 'It may very well be that proprietary estoppel will not often assist a claimant in a commercial context, but that is probably all to the good: in the business world; certainty and clarity are particularly important, and judges should be slow to encourage the introduction of uncertainties based on their views of the ethical acceptability of the behaviour of one of the parties'.[27]

However, on closer inspection, this distinction runs into some difficulties, both as a justificatory tool, and as a means of explaining current case law. First, it is problematic because it is not a clear-cut distinction. There are many situations which can be described as both domestic and commercial. Some of the most significant estoppel cases in fact fall into this category—*Gillett v Holt*[28] and *Thorner v Major*[29] involve significant personal relationships but they are also relationships which take place in the context of *commercial* activity, that is, farm businesses. Consider also an example—let us imagine four friends purchase property together in order to do it up to make a profit. Is that a commercial or a domestic situation? Similarly, what about a situation where two business partners work together in a business for a number of decades? Their relationship, by this point, is likely to be more friend than colleague, and so reliance on the commercial/domestic distinction is not as convincing as it may be in purely theoretical terms.

Furthermore, it is not a particularly useful distinction in terms of explaining why the current case law is as it is. Certainly, it is harder to prove an estoppel in a commercial situation. As Dixon has argued, however, this does not appear to be because of the commercial context per se, but because reasonable reliance on an assurance such that it would be unconscionable not to follow through with that promise is more unlikely in the commercial context. Consider *Cobbe*, (see earlier). In that case it was not unconscionable for Mrs Lisle-Mainwaring to go back on her promise precisely because she had never suggested that her promise was irrevocable, and nor did Mr Cobbe believe it was irrevocable. The experience of the parties

---

[24] *Cobbe v Yeoman's Row Management Ltd* [2008] UKHL 55, [2008] 1 WLR 1752.
[25] *Thorner v Major* [2009] UKHL 18; [2009] 1 WLR 776.
[26] Lord Neuberger of Abbotsbury, 'The stuffing of Minerva's owl? Taxonomy and taxidermy in equity' (2009) 68 CLJ 537, 542.
[27] Lord Neuberger of Abbotsbury, 'The stuffing of Minerva's owl? Taxonomy and taxidermy in equity' (2009) 68 CLJ 537, 543.
[28] *Gillett v Holt* [2001] Ch 210 (CA).
[29] *Thorner v Major* [2009] UKHL 18, [2009] 1 WLR 776.

meant that they were all aware of the reality of the agreement that they had reached. Furthermore, they had *intentionally* reached an informal agreement. Both parties did not desire it to be binding at the stage at which they agreed it. Similar arguments can be made about the agreement reached in the recent Court of Appeal decision in *Generator Developments v Lidl*,[30] where the court emphasised the relevance of the arms' length dealings and the deliberate choice to make an agreement binding 'in honour' only.

This kind of approach is perhaps more likely in the commercial context, but does not really have anything to do with that context. Families may reach exactly the same kind of conclusion. They want a flexible, adaptive legal framework within which things can change as circumstances develop so they do not make their agreement binding. It is not only in a commercial context that flexibility may be desired. Furthermore, the idea that in a domestic context parties do not have knowledge of what is required is not borne out in the case law either. In *Gillett v Holt*,[31] (see 8.2.3.3). Mr Gillett was fully aware that there needed to be a formal will if he was to inherit the farm property. Indeed, much of the parties' collective effort (prior to the falling out) was spent in trying to construct the inheritance in such a way as to limit the tax liability of Mr Gillett on Mr Holt's death. To suggest that the unconscionability in going back on the promise arises here because of the domestic context, and thus the 'inexperience' of the parties flies in the face of the facts. In other words, the domestic/commercial distinction may express whether an estoppel is or is not more likely, but it does not necessary tell us *why* it is more likely in terms of explaining current case law.

8.2.3.2 Reliance

In addition to the assurance, in order to give rise to an estoppel there must also be detrimental reliance. We will consider the 'detrimental' aspect of this later, but first this section considers the meaning of reliance. By reliance is meant a causal link between the promise made and some act or other detriment carried out or suffered by the promisee. As with other areas of law, there are many different tests which can be used in order to determine whether a causal link can be established. The usual test for causation, used both in contract and tort law, as well as in relation to estoppel, is the 'but for' test for causation. This can be expressed as meaning that, 'but for' the promise, the promisee would not have behaved in the way that they did, such that there is a link between the promise and their action. In the majority of situations the causal link between the two is clear. For this reason, generally speaking, reliance will be presumed and it is usually up to the promisor, in cases where the promise and the detriment are manifest, to *disprove* the causal connection between the two. However, in some situations there will be doubt about the causal link. This generally occurs in two types of situations. The first is in cases where there is the possibility of 'mixed motives' in terms of the promisee's actions. The second is in cases where the outward assurance takes place *after* some of the acts said to constitute the reliance. Furthermore, there are some cases where the 'but for' test fails entirely. This last situation will be discussed towards the end of this section.

Let us consider the first case by thinking about an example. George and Mary are in a romantic relationship and live together. After many years of happiness, George falls ill and needs caring for. Mary looks after him. During this time, George promises Mary that she will inherit all of his property when he dies (he has a substantial personal fortune). At this point, Mary decides that to look

---

[30] *Generator Developments Ltd v Lidl UK GmbH*, [2018] EWCA Civ 396, [2018] 2 P & CR 7.
[31] *Gillett v Holt* [2001] Ch 210 (CA).

after him properly she will need to give up her job. George recovers and then later informs Mary that he is going to leave all his property to a charity in his will. It is clear here that Mary is looking after George out of love and affection, but is she also looking after him in part in reliance on his promise? Certainly, this appears to be the explanation for her giving up her job and caring for him full time.

Because of the difficulties in this sort of 'mixed motive' case, the courts have explored a slightly different test from usual. Rather than thinking about whether the claimant would have acted as they did had there been no promise (which, very often, it is clear they would have), instead the courts sometimes ask, would the claimant have acted differently if the promise had been withdrawn explicitly? This test was developed in *Wayling v Jones*,[32] but a number of commentators have doubted whether this is a sound test to use in this context. That means that some other tests have been proposed for mixed motives cases, including whether the promise 'contributed to' the promisee's course of conduct, and whether the promise played a 'significant' part in their decision-making.

Tests for causation

Articulating and utilising an appropriate test for causation is a problem which exists in many different areas of the law. This is especially so where there are multiple stages in a causal chain between the actions of a defendant in a particular case, and the loss which the claimant alleges that they have suffered. So, for example, in cases of pollution, there will be the problem where the owner of a storage tank fails to properly secure the tank, but a third party vandal turns on the tap which results in the river becoming polluted. In this case, did the owner of the tank cause the pollution? On the one hand, 'but for' their failure to secure the tank, the pollution could not have happened. However, on the other hand, they neither invited nor permitted the third party vandal to behave the way that they did, and the intervention of a deliberate act of this type could be said to break the causal chain. To take another example, consider air pollution: does Mrs Smith's driving her car cause Ms Jones' asthma, where the asthma has arisen as a result of years of exposure to car fumes, of which Mrs Smith's emissions constitute only a very tiny part? We have no clear and consistent legal test by which we ought to assess the causal links in these cases, and the same is true of estoppel.

According to McFarlane, one way in which the courts have attempted to deal with this problem of finding the 'best' test for causation is simply to avoid asking what the appropriate test is. The presumption of causation in an estoppel case once the promise and detriment have been demonstrated can, to an extent, be seen as a reflection of the court's uneasiness in being drawn into a clear articulation as to which test for causation they are applying in any particular case. However, as McFarlane explains, there are five possible tests which, at various times, the courts appear to be utilising.

1. **'Would the promisee have changed their behaviour had the promise been withdrawn?'**

This is the test developed in *Wayling v Jones*[33] and utilised in *Ottey v Grundy*[34] as discussed later.

The academic reaction to this approach is mixed to say the least. As Cooke has argued, it is a test which essentially downplays the importance of the promise.[35] The reason for this is that

---

[32] *Wayling v Jones* (1995) 69 P & CR 170 (CA).
[33] *Wayling v Jones* (1995) 69 P & CR 170 (CA).
[34] *Ottey v Grundy* [2003] EWCA Civ 1176; [2003] WTLR 1253.
[35] E Cooke.

withdrawing the promise is not just a statement in relation to the property promised. It will also likely affect the whole basis of the parties' relationship so that it would almost unthinkable that the promisee not change their behaviour if the promise was withdrawn, whether or not the promise was motivating them in the first place. Either they would change their behaviour because the promise was withdrawn, or they would change it because they no longer liked or trusted the promisor. It would be impossible to tell which, and so the test does not really provide any insight into the causes of the earlier behaviour of the promisee.

2. The 'sole motivating factor' test

The second possible test for causation could be that the claimant is required to show that the sole motivating factor for their actions was the promise. This is a very impractical test. It will be almost impossible for someone to prove this, especially in the kind of domestic/family situation where estoppel is more likely to succeed. This argument was made forcefully in *Campbell v Griffin* where Walker LJ said that, 'it would do no credit to the law if an honest witness who admitted that he had mixed motives were to fail in a claim which might have succeeded if supported by less candid evidence'.[36]

3. The contributory cause test

This is a test which establishes that the promise was one cause of the claimant's actions. McFarlane rejects this test because in accepting that the claimant's behaviour would have been the same even if the promise was not made, there is an acknowledgement that in fact there is no causal relationship between the promise and the actions taken by the claimant. In other words, a contributory cause test (which does not require 'but for' causation) removes the need for reliance.

4. The substantial factor test

This is a modification of test three, as it requires a more robust link between the act and the promise. However, on McFarlane's view, even this does not ensure that there is a sufficiently robust link between the promise and the claimant's actions. This is not least because,

> 'It is very difficult to test reliably for the presence of the adjectives' in this test, i.e. substantial or significant. Instead, it is likely to mirror the contributory cause test with the courts having discretion as to whether to attribute normative significant to the link. It still does not require the demonstration of a change of behaviour by the claimant in reliance on the promise'.[37]

5. The 'but for' test

The 'but for' test is the standard test of causation present in most areas of the law where causal links require to be proved. It faces some difficulties in cases where multiple parties have contributed to the same outcome but in general it is a very useful test for causation. Indeed, in advocating this test in an estoppel context, McFarlane is essentially arguing that there is nothing peculiar to an estoppel context which requires a departure from the standard test for causation. In other areas of law, this test is not used because of difficulties of scientific evidence or because the causal mechanisms involved in a particular outcome are so complex that a search for a precise causal

---

[36] *Campbell v Griffin* [2001] EWCA Civ 990, (2001) 82 P & CR DG23, [29].
[37] B McFarlane, *Proprietary Estoppel* (OUP, Oxford, 2014).

link is doomed to fail. That is not the case with estoppel and so there is no justification for departing from the normal test.

This does not mean that the 'but for' test is free from controversy or academic criticism. Some accuse it of being too technical and legalistic. However, one way of getting round this problem is to consider the burden of proof, as opposed to the test being applied. Alternatively, the courts can simply be realistic and apply common sense to their application of the test. Since it is very difficult (or indeed impossible) to prove what is going on inside someone's head at any particular time, it seems legitimate in this context for the courts to utilise the presumption of reliance in *Wayling v Jones*[38] and *Greasley v Cooke*.[39]

Whichever of these tests is used, however, the answer is almost always that there is a causal relationship of some sort between the promise and the behaviour. This means that at least part of their motivation, to a greater or lesser extent, was the promise which had been made to them. The application of some of these tests can be seen in the cases discussed here. First, in *Wayling v Jones*[40] and *Ottey v Grundy*,[41] the hypothetical, 'would the claimant have behaved differently had the promise been withdrawn?' test discussed earlier is applied. In *Campbell v Griffin*[42] a more standard 'but for' test is used in a mixed motivation context.

> **Key case:** *Wayling v Jones* (1995) 69 P & CR 170
>
> *Wayling v Jones* involved a proprietary estoppel claim in relation to a hotel. Paul Wayling claimed that an estoppel had arisen in his favour in relation to the estate of Daniel Jones. Wayling and Jones had been in a relationship for some 15 years prior to Jones' death. In addition to the close personal relationship, Wayling also worked for Jones as his chauffeur and was generally his 'companion' through a series of businesses, including a café, shop, and eventually the hotel in question, the Royal Hotel, Barmouth. Wayling did not receive a substantial wage for this work, but did receive a small allowance and most of his expenses were covered by Jones. Wayling managed this hotel for Jones, who was now in poor health. When Wayling said to Jones that he deserved more money for doing this extra work, Jones told him not to worry as it would all be his one day. When Jones died, his will did leave property to Jones but it referred to the Glen-Y-Mor hotel, a business which they had previously run together, but which Jones had sold in order to fund the purchase of the Royal Hotel. Jones had not changed his will to reflect this, and so Wayling received nothing of value under the will, and due to outstanding liabilities, was declared bankrupt. The question for the court was whether a proprietary estoppel had arisen in these circumstances in relation to the Royal Hotel.
>
> The difficulty for the claimant arose in relation to reliance, because he admitted that he would have lived and stayed with Jones even if no promise had been made. The court got round this problem by treating the causal test as being whether Wayling would have left Jones if the promise had been withdrawn meaning that they could make a finding that there was reliance in this case.
>
> This approach is clear too in the decision in *Ottey v Grundy*.[43]

---

[38] *Wayling v Jones* (1995) 69 P & CR 170 (CA).
[39] *Greasley v Cooke* [1980] 1 WLR 1306 (CA).
[40] *Wayling v Jones* (1995) 69 P & CR 170 (CA).
[41] *Ottey v Grundy* [2003] EWCA Civ 1176; [2003] WTLR 1253.
[42] *Campbell v Griffin* [2001] EWCA Civ 990, (2001) 82 P & CR DG23.
[43] *Ottey v Grundy* [2003] EWCA Civ 1176; [2003] WTLR 1253.

> **Key case:** *Ottey v Grundy* [2003] EWCA Civ 1176
>
> In this case, Ms Ottey cared for her lover Mr Andreae, who suffered health problems arising from alcoholism. She did this partly out of love and affection, and partly because Mr Andreae supported her financially and had promised that she would inherit some of his property, including a flat in Jamaica, on his death.
>
> In considering this, Arden LJ stated that:
>
> > 'In order to show that the person to whom the assurance was made was induced to act to his detriment, it is not necessary to show that he would have left the maker of the assurance if the promise had not been made, but only that he would have left the maker of the assurance if the promise had been withdrawn'.[44]
>
> This approach meant that there was an estoppel in this case.

> **Key case:** *Campbell v Griffin* (2001) 82 P & CR DG23
>
> A similar 'mixed motives' approach arose in *Campbell v Griffin* but the court's analytical approach is somewhat different.[45] In this case, Mr Campbell was the lodger of a Mr and Mrs Ascough. As they became older and more frail, Mr Campbell increasingly took on the burden of caring for them. They had assured him that he would inherit their property if he did so.
>
> It was clear from the evidence in the case that Mr Campbell was acting from mixed motives—he cared about the couple and would not have left them to suffer even if he had no expectation of inheritance. However, as the court highlighted, this this not enough to prevent an estoppel arising in his favour. If estoppel was not possible in situations of mixed motives, then only those motivated only by money or the promise of property would succeed, and this seems to be a perverse kind of reward in cases involving a carer/caree relationship. Thus, the court simply highlighted that where there is a mixed motivation, that will not prevent the formation of an estoppel. In many ways, therefore, they by-pass the issues which arise by using such a 'multiple cause' approach, ie that at no point is it actually established that reliance is present. This may ensure that a common sense attitude is taken so that the law does not reward callous behaviour more than generous behaviour in this sense, but it is problematic nevertheless.

The presence of multiple causes for the claimant's behaviour is not the only causal difficulty which can emerge in relation to estoppel. What about the situation where some of the acts which are said to constitute the reliance take place *before* the relevant promise is made? Surely in this situation the courts could not conclude that there was a causal link between the two. This was certainly an issue for Ms Ottey in *Ottey v Grundy*[46] and likely added to the motivation for the court to depart from the but for test for causation in that case. The issue was considered in some detail in *Chun v Ho*.[47]

---

[44] *Ottey v Grundy* [2003] EWCA Civ 1176, [2003] WTLR 1253, [56].
[45] *Campbell v Griffin* (2001) 82 P & CR DG23.
[46] *Ottey v Grundy* [2003] EWCA Civ 1176, [2003] WTLR 1253.
[47] *Chun v Ho* [2002] EWCA Civ 1075, [2003] 1 P & CR DG2.

> **Key case:** *Chun v Ho* [2002] EWCA Civ 1075
>
> In this case, Ms Chun claimed that she was entitled to an equitable interest in a property called Hill House either arising through proprietary estoppel or as a constructive trust (for more on the relationship between these two, see later 8.6). Ms Chun had originally been Mr Ho's assistant, but when he was imprisoned for bribery and corruption, she continued his business for him from outside prison, communicating with him by letter. By this time, the two had become lovers. Once Mr Ho was released from prison, a property was acquired in the name of a company owned by Mr Ho. Ms Chun was not registered as joint legal owner, nor was an express trust made conferring on her an equitable interest in the property. She claimed that Mr Ho had promised her a share in his property if she helped with his business whilst he was in prison and that they had agreed that she would have a 51 per cent share in Hill House. The difficulty for Ms Chun was that her acts of helping with his business took place before the acquisition of Hill House and before the agreement that she would have a 51 per cent share.
>
> The Court of Appeal admitted that this was a challenge for Ms Chun, but concluded that on considering the entirety of the relationship between the parties, there was reliance here. This is because the court construed the detriment not as the carrying out of the work whilst Mr Ho was in prison, but in allowing him to become sole registered proprietor of Hill House against the background of the work that she had done. This case therefore shows that in some circumstances, the court will consider subsequent acts as being indicative of reliance against the background of prior very substantial acts.

8.2.3.3 Detriment

If the assurance is the foundation of the estoppel, then detriment constitutes the justification for the courts enforcing the promise notwithstanding the lack of formalities present. In this sense, the presence of detriment is the core of proprietary estoppel. However, over time, the courts' assessments as to what constitutes sufficient detriment to found an estoppel has become more and more generous to claimants. The current state of the law is such that 'detriment' is perhaps not the best label here. Rather, it is better to think of this as being a change of position which occurs in reliance on the promise. We can see this if we delve a bit deeper into what is required to demonstrate that detriment is present. First, does detriment need to be financial? Second, in cases where the claimant has suffered both losses and advantages as a result of their relationship with the promisor, does the loss have to outweigh the advantages so that, overall, they are 'worse off' in order for the courts to conclude that detriment exists? Finally, what happens in cases where the detriment suffered is out of all proportion to the promise made?

Forms of detriment

On the first question, the courts have been very clear that the detriment suffered need not be a financial one. Rather, the 'losses' suffered by the claimant can be simply lost opportunities, for example. This has been demonstrated in a number of cases, including one of the most seminal estoppel cases—*Gillett v Holt*.[48]

---

[48] *Gillett v Holt* [2001] Ch 210 (CA).

Key case: *Gillett v Holt* [2001] Ch 210

In *Gillett v Holt*, the claimant was a farm hand, labourer and subsequently manager, who had worked on Mr Holt's farm for approaching 40 years. Mr Gillett had left school at 15 in order to work on Mr Holt's farm. At family occasions over many years, Mr Holt told Mr Gillett that he would inherit the farm. This promise was made in front of many people on numerous occasions. There was no doubt whatsoever that there was an assurance in this case. What was slightly more difficult was the question of detriment. Mr Gillett had certainly taken lower wages for his work than he otherwise might, but he had also received accommodation at a lower price. In financial terms, overall, the judge at first instance had concluded that he was not substantially worse off than he would have otherwise been. However, other aspects of his course of conduct were said to constitute the detriment in this case, such as not seeking employment elsewhere, carrying out expenditure on Mr Gillett's home situated on Mr Holt's land, and making limited provision for a pension.

The Court of Appeal considered whether this was enough to constitute detriment for the purposes of establishing an estoppel. In doing so, Walker LJ gave some general guidance:

> 'The overwhelming weight of authority shows that detriment is required. But the authorities also show that it is not a narrow or technical concept. The detriment need not consist of the expenditure of money or other quantifiable financial detriment, so long as it is something substantial. The requirement must be approached as part of a broad inquiry as to whether repudiation of an assurance is or is not unconscionable in all the circumstances'.[49]

In taking this broader approach, Walker LJ concluded that Mr Gillett's detriment had been, 'unusually compelling'[50] and that he had an 'exceptionally strong claim'.[51] In this case, therefore, not only did the court conclude that there was detriment, but that this was a very strong case of estoppel.

It may be worth examining what features of this case make it a particularly clear example of a 'deserving' estoppel case. First, it is suggested, the most significant element of this case was the fact that Mr Gillett, and later Mr and Mrs Gillett had effectively arranged their whole lives around their relationship with Mr Holt, his business, and the promises of future inheritance. This was not, like in *Cobbe v Yeoman's Row*,[52] for example, merely a commercial transaction. It involved the parties' family, social and business lives. Second, the promises in this case were repeated and given on occasions where Mr Gillett was thinking about arranging things differently, or seeking written assurances as to his future position. The promises, rather than being background motivation for the overall choices Mr Gillett made, were, on many occasions, the specific reason why a particular decision was made. There was a close intimacy between the promise and the detriment, closer than in many estoppel cases. Finally, this was a situation where, at the commencement of the relationship at least, there was a huge imbalance of power. Mr Gillett left school and did not seek further formalised training (except a limited number of additional night classes) in order to work with Mr Holt. Mr Holt, as the court explains, in the manner of a patron, supported him. At that moment, the future course of Mr Gillett's life was essentially dictated by Mr Holt's plans for and with him. In such a situation, as the court highlights, when you take a 'step back' and look at all the matters in this case in the round, it is clear that there was enormously detrimental reliance on Mr Gillett's promises, and therefore, a very good case of estoppel.

---

[49] *Gillett v Holt* [2001] Ch 210 (CA), 232.
[50] *Gillett v Holt* [2001] Ch 210 (CA), 234.
[51] *Gillett v Holt* [2001] Ch 210 (CA), 234.
[52] *Cobbe v Yeoman's Row Management Ltd* [2008] UKHL 55, [2008] 1 WLR 1752.

It is clear, therefore, from *Gillett v Holt*,[53] and numerous other cases, that the detriment in estoppel cases does not need to be financial. Similarly, the claimant does not need to be overall 'worse off' as a result of the estoppel, albeit that this may be taken into account at the remedy stage. This can be seen in *Henry v Henry* (see 8.3.2.1), for example. However, it is also important to note that the concept of detriment is not unlimited. In *Coombes v Smith*,[54] Ms Coombes argued that she had suffered detrimental reliance on a promise by leaving her husband having become pregnant with her lover's child. She had also moved into the house which it had been promised she would later share with her lover (and the legal title-holder of the property, who, in fact, never moved into the property). The court was wholly unconvinced by these arguments, especially the fact of becoming pregnant. It made it clear that this could not constitute detriment for the purposes of proprietary estoppel.[55] Similarly, in *Hunt v Soady*,[56] payment of mortgage payments when the promisee was already obligated to make such payment was held not to constitute a detriment.

Finally, we must assess what happens where although there is a promise, the reliance on that promise is out of all proportion to the promise made. In such cases, the courts have been clear that the remedial discretion which the courts have in this area allows the court to take account of such a disproportionate detriment. This means that acting out of proportion in this way will not prevent the formation of an estoppel, but it may mean that even once the equity has been satisfied, the claimant cannot be said to have had the totality of her detriment remedied.

Examples of Detriment

The theories in relation to what the court is assessing in terms of detriment have been discussed in the previous section. However, it is often useful to be able to reason by analogy in cases like this, and so in this section we explain some different kinds of detriment and the cases where they arise.

1. Expenditure

The most obvious, and easily calculable, kind of detriment is where there has been expenditure in reliance on the promise. This can, and often does, relate to the land in relation to which the promise was made. For example, in *Bradbury v Taylor*,[57] the claimants spent £100,000 improving the relevant land. However, it is not necessary that the expenditure relates to that land. It can include expenditure on other things which would not otherwise have been bought had the promise not been made (always bearing in mind that the courts will take a second look at detriment which is out of all proportion to the promise made). It is also useful to consider that in cases where the expenditure which was alleged to have taken place in reliance on the promise is wholly unconnected with the land ('I bought this Ferrari because I thought I was getting a house for free'), the courts will be very vigilant in ensuring that there is a causal relationship between the expenditure and the promise. In addition, it must be shown that the claimant has actually suffered detriment in spending the money. In cases where the claimant uses money to purchase another, albeit different, asset, it may be that they have suffered no detriment at all, even if they could be said to have made a poor decision.

---

[53] *Gillett v Holt* [2001] Ch 210 (CA).
[54] *Coombes v Smith* [1986] 1 WLR 808 (Ch).
[55] *Coombes v Smith* [1986] 1 WLR 808 (Ch), 820.
[56] *Hunt v Soady* [2007] EWCA Civ 366.
[57] *Bradbury v Taylor* [2012] EWCA Civ 1208, [2013] WTLR 29.

2. Effort

It is not just money which may be spent in reliance on an estoppel, however. Another potential form of detriment lies in effort and the provision of time and services. This can be seen in both *Jennings v Rice* and *Campbell v Griffith* where the claimant spent time and effort in caring for the promisor(s) for no pay. Similarly, in *Thorner v Major* and *Gillett v Holt*, the primary detriments related to the work done on the farms for little or no pay.

3. Missed Opportunities

The most difficult kind of detriment to assess, however, will very often be detriment suffered as a result of missed opportunity. This can relate to the opportunity passed over to get a job elsewhere—as in *Henry v Henry*, *Gillett v Holt* and also arguably *Thorner v Major*. This sort of loss can be very speculative. It is for this reason that the guidance earlier regarding thinking of 'detriment' as not just a calculable balance sheet of whether the claimant is overall better or worse, but rather seeing whether the estoppel has in some sense determined the overall course of their life in the alternative emerges. Certainly, if there was substantial expenditure, there would be no need to rely on this alternative approach to the question of detriment, but in cases where what is alleged is a lost opportunity to seek a better life elsewhere, it may be more appropriate to think of detriment in this way. The courts will, as with expenditure not relating to the land, be especially suspicious of speculative detriments, and the usual standards of proof will apply so that the claimant has to demonstrate that the lost opportunities of which they speak are real in some sense.

> **Summary: Detriment**
>
> Detriment will be demonstrated where the claimant has changed the course of their life in reliance on a promise, even if overall they may be better off as a result of that choice. This will be relatively easy to establish where the losses are financial or in terms of opportunity, but they can also exist in re-centring a life around a promised situation.

8.2.4 UNCONSCIONABILITY

Unconscionability lies at the very heart of estoppel—it is the explanation for why estoppel can be used to generate rights in property. In one of the founding cases for modern proprietary estoppel, *Taylor Fashions v Liverpool Victoria Trustees*, Oliver J stated:

> 'whether you call it proprietary estoppel, estoppel by acquiescence or estoppel by encouragement is really immaterial—[estoppel] requires a very much broader approach which is directed rather at ascertaining whether, in particular individual circumstances, it would be unconscionable for a party to be permitted to deny that which, knowingly, or unknowingly, he has allowed or encouraged another to assume to his detriment than to inquiring whether the circumstances can be fitted within the confines of some preconceived formula serving as a universal yardstick for every form of unconscionable behaviour'.[58]

---

[58] *Taylor Fashions v Liverpool Victoria Trustees* [1982] QB 133 (Ch), 151–2.

However, it is also an elusive concept. It can be very difficult to pin down, and is hard to define/indefinable. There is also a question about what role unconscionability plays in estoppel. Is it, as earlier cases seem to treat it, effectively a conclusion to be drawn from analysis of the three factors of assurance, detriment and reliance? Or is it a fourth and separate requirement in estoppel cases which must be assessed *in addition to* assurance, detriment and reliance? As discussed earlier, at this precise moment, it seems to be more the case that unconscionability is treated as a fourth and separate essential element which must be demonstrated before the court will allow an estoppel to arise. This raises its own challenges, however, in terms of definition. We can see this in, *Suggitt v Suggitt*.[59]

> **Key case:** *Suggitt v Suggitt* [2012] EWCA Civ 1140
>
> This case demonstrates the problem of ambiguous assurances and of 'satisfying the equity' and considers how unconscionability feeds into this process. Importantly, the decision also raises questions as to how estoppel should operate in cases of potentially incompatible assurances to different people.
>
> The case involved a dispute between the estate of Frank Suggitt (Frank), and Frank's son, John Suggitt (John). John claimed that despite not inheriting the farmhouses and business under his father's will, that he was entitled to them as a result of proprietary estoppel. Certainly, Frank had intended that his son would indeed become proprietor of the farm at some time in the future, but had deliberately omitted him from the will. The will, under which John's sister Caroline inherited the estate, stipulated Caroline ought to transfer the farm estate to John when he appeared ready to take over the business, but expressly no trust to this effect was established, as a result of John's deficiencies as a farmer.
>
> Throughout John's life however, despite John's shortcomings, Frank had made it clear to John that he would have the farm one day. Not only did his father make statements to this effect (although not perhaps in the years leading up to Frank's death), he encouraged John to attend agricultural college, and also to set up a business managing 50 acres of the farm estate, the land provided rent-free.
>
> The court had to determine whether the assurances given to John, which, had become less certain over the years, nonetheless gave rise to an estoppel. Secondly, there was the matter of the terms of the will. Thirdly, Frank had also assured Caroline that she was to be a 'rich woman' following his death suggesting that she was likely to inherit the farm estate, as indeed happened.
>
> At first instance, the judge concluded that there was a valid estoppel claim, dividing the estate between John and Caroline in order to satisfy this equity. In doing so, he explained that the overarching question was whether 'in the circumstances that have happened, it would be unconscionable for the promise not to be kept'.[60]
>
> The discussion primarily focussed on the assurance. The judge, taking his guide from *Thorner v Major*,[61] highlighted that in this area, context is everything. He concluded that 'it is more likely than not that Frank did make some kind of repeated promise or assurance to John that led him reasonably to expect that someday at least the farmland ... would definitely be his following his, Frank's, death'.[62] In order to bolster his conclusion on this point, the judge cross-checked through the use of unconscionability as something which

---

[59] *Suggitt v Suggitt* [2012] EWCA Civ 1140, [2012] WTLR 1607.
[60] *Suggitt v Suggitt* (first instance) [2011] EWHC 903 (Ch), [2011] 2 FLR 875, [43].
[61] *Thorner v Major* [2009] UKHL 18, [2009] 1 WLR 776.
[62] *Suggitt v Suggitt* (first instance) [2011] EWHC 903 (Ch), [2011] 2 FLR 875, [53].

could be independently assessed. He did not assume that detriment, plus assurance, plus reliance, means that withdrawal of that assurance would amount to unconscionable conduct.

The Court of Appeal agreed with this 'cross-check' approach. Arden LJ stated: '[w]here doubt is raised as to whether assurances have been given then the court may wish to look for confirmation to the strength of the evidence about reliance and detriment'.[63]

The decision does not fully address one of the real difficulties in the circumstances, the existence of the two inconsistent assurances. The flexibility provided by the discretion to satisfy the estoppel gave rise to an attempt to compensate for a weak estoppel claim with a weaker remedy. It is suggested that the additional role given to detriment in particular, (proving the existence of the estoppel, but also guiding the judge in how to remedy it) required a more detailed discussion of the detriment suffered. The judge appears to have attempted to strike a balance between the interests of Caroline and John bearing in mind the quality of the detriment suffered by John where both had relied on assurances. We ought to consider whether cases of inconsistent assurances can and should be balanced at the 'satisfying the equity stage', and if so, how the competing assurances are to be juggled. For more on the relationship between competing equities in estoppel, see the article by Pawlowski and Brown in the further reading section later.

It is therefore clear that in addition to performing the cross-check function outlined earlier, unconscionability is also a criterion *in itself*, constraining the availability of proprietary estoppel. However, in this latter role, the definition of this term is all the more important. There are a number of potential 'definitions' for unconscionability that exist. Some of these are more convincing, and more explicatory, than others. Some, merely restatements of the term, suggest that unconscionability is a case where allowing the promisor to go back on their promise would 'shock the conscience of the court' or where it would be 'inequitable' to allow them to do so. Others, like Dixon[64] attempt to give unconscionability a very precise definition but this may run into conflict or at least not sit happily with some of the existing decisions. This of course does not mean that such is not a good definition in terms of the *future* direction of estoppel, but rather that it is not an entirely convincing explanation of the *current* case law. Finally, other approaches suggest that unconscionability is no 'one' thing, but is instead a flexible concept which responds to, and is dictated by, the context within which it arises. So, for example, the definition of what constitutes unconscionable conduct could be different in a commercial or domestic environment. The merits of this distinction as both a theoretical and a practical explanatory tool were discussed at 8.2.3.1.

> **Further analysis: 'The double assurance'**
>
> As this section has shown, it can be very difficult to define unconscionability. Indeed, it may fairly be said that there is no *one* case law definition. Rather, it is a shortcut explanation for a range of different factors. However, some academic analysis does attempt to provide a concrete definition of this term, so as to prevent proprietary estoppel becoming 'penicillin', that is, a cure-all remedy which is given whenever a court thinks a situation involving land looks 'unfair'. One example of such an approach is that of Dixon.[65]

---

[63] *Suggitt v Suggitt* [2012] EWCA Civ 1140, [2012] WTLR 1607, [30].
[64] M Dixon, 'Confining and defining proprietary estoppel: the role of unconscionability' (2010) 30 Legal Studies 408.
[65] M Dixon, 'Confining and defining proprietary estoppel: the role of unconscionability' (2010) 30 Legal Studies 408.

He argues that in order to fully understand proprietary estoppel, and, as a result, the notion of unconscionability, we need to take a step back and consider what role estoppel plays in our land law system as a whole. He notes that proprietary estoppel is the primary means by which proprietary rights in land can arise where the formality rules are not complied with. Thus, we must justify and explain proprietary estoppel by reference to its role as a means to get around a failure to comply with formality rules. By making this argument, he then concludes that there must be some relationship between the notion of unconscionability, and the formality rules themselves.

As Dixon says:

'If statute requires the claimant's alleged property right to have been created with a certain type of formality, why, in the absence of such formality, can the claimant run to the back door, break in using estoppel as a jemmy, and run off with some or all of the landowner's proprietary valuables?'.[66]

He then examines the formality rules to consider why it might be unconscionable for someone to rely on a failure of formalities to deny the grant of a proprietary right. He concludes that this will be the case not only when someone has only promised another a proprietary interest, but rather where they have also promised that the promisee need not worry about the absence of formalities. In other words, Dixon argues that in successful estoppel cases there should be a 'double assurance'. First, there must be a rights assurance—'I promise you will inherit my land'—and then there must be a formalities assurance, 'Don't worry, we don't need to write this down now. I will take care of it all in my will, it is all in hand'.[67] However, recognising that is unlikely, although not impossible, that such an explicit formalities assurance will be made (there was such an explicit assurance in *Gillett v Holt*,[68] see earlier), Dixon then acknowledges that such an assurance may be implied.[69]

How convincing is this account of the meaning of unconscionability? On the one hand, it may be that this is an excellent way of reconciling the tensions at the heart of proprietary estoppel. It is a means by which people can get around statutory requirements that they write their land transactions down, and, critically, that they can do so in cases where the promises made, and the losses suffered are sometimes very vague and imprecise. Yet, the more 'commercial' or precise an agreement, in some cases, the harder it can be to prove an estoppel precisely because in these situations we have a greater expectation that the parties write their arrangements down. By focusing on the relationship between formalities and estoppel, we can begin to understand the ways in which estoppel relates to contracts, for example, an issue which his discussed further later. Dixon argues that:

'It is not readily apparent why the law should be happy to give some validity to entirely non-contractual promises by reason of proprietary estoppel—without any explanation of the basis of the doctrine—but at the same time refuse to act in relation to more formal (but failing) agreements because they might amount to a contract regulated by s2'.[70]

However, one issue with Dixon's definition, as he admits, is that parties very rarely explicitly make formalities assurances.[71] It may be, therefore, that allowing such a promise to be implied simply defers the 'fairness' assessment so that instead of saying, 'is it unfair to allow the promisee to go back on their promise

---

[66] M Dixon, 'Confining and defining proprietary estoppel: the role of unconscionability' (2010) 30 Legal Studies 408, 409.
[67] M Dixon, 'Confining and defining proprietary estoppel: the role of unconscionability' (2010) 30 Legal Studies 408.
[68] *Gillett v Holt* [2001] Ch 210 (CA).
[69] M Dixon, 'Confining and defining proprietary estoppel: the role of unconscionability' (2010) 30 Legal Studies 408.
[70] M Dixon, 'Confining and defining proprietary estoppel: the role of unconscionability' (2010) 30 Legal Studies 408, 415.
[71] M Dixon, 'Confining and defining proprietary estoppel: the role of unconscionability' (2010) 30 Legal Studies 408.

here', the question becomes, 'is it fair to imply a formalities assurance in this case'. This is a particular problem in cases like *Thorner v Major*[72] where the entire relationship between the parties takes place at a very uncommunicative level so that not only is the formalities assurance implied, so too is the rights assurance. The precision of Dixon's definition may not, therefore, lead to the predicted certainties in practice.

If Dixon's approach is not the right one, however, what other approaches are there, except to take unconscionability on a case-by-case basis so that individual circumstances are merely addressed afresh each time to see whether some abstract concept of unconscionability is present? First, as unconscionability does have this flexible meaning, it may encompass within it a variety of different considerations. These might include the imbalance of power between the parties—as seen, for example, in *Gillett v Holt*. It may also include the nature of that relationship, be it commercial or domestic, dependent in some sense (a caring relationship might fall into this category). Finally, the repeated or public nature of the relevant assurances may also go to unconscionability. In this sense, unconscionability may be treated as a catch-all term describing various different considerations some, but probably not all, of which will be relevant in any particular case.

Finally, as discussed earlier, unconscionability may be all about context in the sense that it is primarily determined by the commercial/domestic distinction and what that implies about the respective parties' likelihood of obtaining legal advice; experience and knowledge of the rules regulating property transactions; the degree to which they are dealing at arm's length; and the expectations and motivations of the parties in terms of what they expect to gain from a transaction. In particular, the references in the carer relationships to the complexity of motive in such situations may weigh in favour of the granting of an estoppel when compared to a situation like *Cobbe* where the motive is purely financial.

Even if unconscionability does exist in a particular case, however, it is important to remember that unconscionability *in itself* does not give rise to an estoppel. Rather, the estoppel jurisdiction requires the assurance which is relied on to the promisee's detriment: not unconscionability in the abstract. This was made clear in the very early estoppel case of *Ramsden v Dyson*.[73] Lord Neuberger, writing extra-judicially, has confirmed that unconscionability is not a grounds for a remedy without more:

> 'Equity is not a sort of moral US fifth cavalry riding to the rescue every time a claimant is left worse off than he anticipated as a result of the defendants behaving badly, and the common law affords him no remedy... unconscionable behaviour is not always enough to give rise to an estoppel. I suggest that, before he can establish a proprietary estoppel claim, a claimant must show that he acted in the belief that he has something which can be characterised as a legal right'.[74]

> ### Summary: Approaches to unconscionability
>
> 1. Unconscionability is 'shorthand' for a wide range of disparate considerations, taking into account issues such as equality of bargaining power, the degree to which parties have knowledge and experience of the relevant transaction processes, the degree to which parties are dealing at arm's

---

[72] *Thorner v Major* [2009] UKHL 18, [2009] 1 WLR 776.
[73] *Ramsden v Dyson* (1866) LR 1 HL 129 (HL).
[74] Lord Neuberger of Abbotsbury, 'The stuffing of Minerva's owl? Taxonomy and taxidermy in equity' (2009) 68 CLJ 537, 540–2.

length, etc. There is, therefore, no single test for unconscionability, but rather each individual decision will involve a weighing of factors.
2. 'Double assurance'—unconscionability relates to formalities in the sense that estoppel is only possible in situations where a 'formalities' assurance was made so that the promisee reasonably believes that they need not be concerned with the formality requirements.
3. Unconscionability is a function of various factors, of which the most important is *context*, in the sense that there is a distinction between commercial and domestic contexts.

8.3 CONSEQUENCES OF ESTOPPEL

Once the courts have established that a proprietary estoppel has arisen, that does not guarantee that the promisee will get what they have been promised. Far from it. Instead, there are two stages to the consequences of an estoppel. First, immediately once the 'unconscionability' arises, the promisee will have the benefit of an equity arising by estoppel. This is a proprietary interest which is itself capable of binding third parties. When it does so is discussed later in this chapter and in chapter 15 on priorities. This equity by estoppel gives the claimant a right to come to court to seek relief to 'satisfy the equity'. Once the claimant does this, then their estoppel will be crystallised. This is step two. At this point, the courts will satisfy the equity by giving to the claimant some remedy. This could be a proprietary right in the relevant land, such as the freehold, or a leasehold interest, or it could be a personal right, such as a monetary award. As will be seen later, it may also result in no award. These stages will be examined here in turn.

8.3.1 THE EQUITY ARISING BY ESTOPPEL

Prior to the introduction of the Land Registration Act 2002 (LRA 2002), there was some doubt as to whether the equity arising by estoppel was itself a property right. In some cases, the estoppel was given 'proprietary force' by adding a constructive trust (*Yaxley v Gotts*[75]). However, since 1st October 2003, it is now certain that the equity arising through estoppel is a proprietary interest in the sense that it is capable of binding third parties (at least for registered land). This is because section 116 LRA 2002 states that: 'It is hereby declared for the avoidance of doubt that, in relation to registered land, each of the following—(a) an equity by estoppel, and, (b) a mere equity, has effect from the time the equity arises as an interest capable of binding successors in title'. What this means for third parties is discussed later. However, it is also important to establish what exactly this means that the claimant has. Clearly they do not have an equitable share in the property in the sense of an interest under a trust, but nor do they have some other kind of defined proprietary interest which entitles them to use, deal with, or occupy the land in some way. In this respect, it is a strange kind of right. Indeed, it might be better explained as a power in the sense that it gives the claimant the ability to go to court to ask the court to grant them a remedy. It does not guarantee what that remedy is, nor, importantly, does it guarantee that they in fact get any remedy at all,

---

[75] *Yaxley v Gotts* [2000] Ch 162 (CA).

258   Chapter 8   Proprietary Estoppel

as *Sledmore v Dalby*[76] shows. However, what it does do is ensure that, in effect, the claimant has a transferrable and identifiable claim in relation to the land which persists with the land rather than being unique to themselves and the relevant promisor. This suggests, that it is possible, for example, to inherit the benefit of a proprietary estoppel.

Let us demonstrate how this might work in practice with an example. Sahila, the owner of land, promises her close friend Thies that he will inherit her land when she dies if he cares for her and helps to look after her animals. Thies duly cares for Sahila and the animals and receives no pay. He has to give up his work as a fashion designer to do this. Unfortunately, Sahila dies without leaving a will. Before the issue as to the inheritance of the property is resolved, Thies also dies, leaving his property in his will to his goddaughter, Anjali. Anjali then comes to court seeking a remedy from Sahila's estate.

In this case, at the time of Sahila's death, Thies already has an equity which has arisen as a result of the proprietary estoppel. The assurance which Sahila made to him, and his subsequent substantial detrimental reliance on that would render it unconscionable for Sahila to revoke the promise made to him. Similarly, the trustees of her estate are bound by this estoppel since they merely step into Sahila's shoes. When Thies therefore leaves all his property to Anjali, part of what her leaves her is the benefit of the estoppel. This should allow Anjali to seek a remedy from the Sahila's estate.

This first stage of the estoppel process is therefore the emergence of the equity arising by estoppel.

8.3.2 REMEDY

The second stage is the crystallisation of the equity by the court in the process of awarding a remedy to the claimant.

8.3.2.1 The remedial approach

What will happen once the promisee goes to court and seeks a remedy to satisfy the equity which has arisen in their favour? The courts clearly have a great deal of flexibility in deciding what the remedy will be. They may for example grant a proprietary interest in the relevant land, they may give the claimant money or a personal occupation right, and they may also give the claimant nothing if they think that events subsequent to the estoppel having arisen mean that the equity has already been satisfied. Furthermore, the courts may in fact give the claimant an interest under a trust. In these cases, proprietary estoppel and constructive trusts are almost indistinguishable (see 8.6).

What test or tests do the courts employ when deciding what remedy to give? The usual test is expressed to be that the court will do the minimum necessary to satisfy the equity. However, in some judgments, the courts have referred to the need for the remedy granted to be 'proportionate' to the detrimental reliance and the assurance made. Whether this is a different test, or a different way of expressing the same test, is somewhat unclear. The different modes of expression can however be analysed by considering *Henry v Henry (St Lucia)*.[77]

---

[76] *Sledmore v Dalby* (1996) 72 P & CR 196 (CA).
[77] *Henry v Henry* [2010] UKPC 3, [2010] 1 All ER 98.

Key case: *Henry v Henry (St Lucia)* [2010] UKPC 3

This case, heard before the Privy Council and relating to land in St Lucia, involved Calixtus Henry, the claimant, arguing that he had the benefit of a proprietary estoppel arising because of his conduct subsequent to an assurance made to him by Geraldine 'Mama' Pierre, a relative and friend of his grandmother'. Calixtus' grandmother had built a house on land part-owned by Geraldine Pierre. Calixtus was born and grew up in that house and in turn had his own children whilst living there. Calixtus claimed that he had been told repeatedly by Mama that if he cared for her, farmed and looked after the land, then he would inherit from her. He worked on this land, grew food there (giving some of the food to Mama) and generally made a small living operating essentially as a subsistence farmer. In making this choice, he gave up the opportunity to produce for himself a 'better life' on a different island.

Taking all this into account the Privy Council had to assess what the appropriate remedy was in the case, bearing in mind that the land had potential development value as well as the conflicting claims of the other potential owners of the land. In reaching the conclusion that Henry would be entitled, in effect, to a one-quarter share in the property, the court highlighted that, '[p]roportionality lies at the heart of the doctrine of proprietary estoppel and permeates its every application'.[78] This approach echoes the sentiment in *Jennings v Rice* that: 'uncertain, or extravagant or out of all proportion to the detriment which he has suffered, the court can and should recognise that the claimant's equity should be satisfied in another (and generally more limited) way'.[79]

In addition to the question as to the proportionality of the remedy, however, some courts have engaged with the controversial question as to whether the primary aim of estoppel is to provide a remedy which confers what was expected onto the promisee, or one which 'undoes' any detriment which they have suffered. This issue was considered by the Court of Appeal in *Davies v Davies*.[80]

Key case: *Davies v Davies* [2016] EWCA Civ 463

In this case, Ms Davies worked on the family farm for no or less money than she might receive working elsewhere, and for longer hours than other jobs would require. However she also received free accommodation, amongst other benefits. She had also left the farm, following disputes with her parents, without intending to return, on a few occasions. Ms Davies expected that she would inherit the farm land and the business. However, the Court of Appeal held that this expectation was not 'equivalent'[81] to the detriment she had suffered. Ms Davies claim was valued at approximately £4.4mn for the farm land and the business. Her parents argued she was entitled to £350,000. The first instance judge decided that the appropriate remedy lay somewhere between Ms Davies' expectation and a rough calculation of her detriment, and valued it at £1.3 mn.

The Court of Appeal, in deciding whether this was an appropriate remedy, gave some general guidance in terms of what the remedial preference should be in relation to proprietary estoppel, ie whether we should be seeking to grant the expectation interest or the reliance interest. Lewison LJ was of the

---

[78] *Henry v Henry* [2010] UKPC 3, [2010] 1 All ER 98, [65].
[79] *Jennings v Rice* [2002] EWCA Civ 159, [2003] 1 P & CR 8, [50].
[80] *Davies v Davies* [2016] EWCA Civ 463, [2016] 2 P & CR 10.
[81] *Davies v Davies* [2016] EWCA Civ 463, [2016] 2 P & CR 10, [33].

> opinion that there would be cases where the expectation interest would represent the best remedial option. He reasoned that, 'the clearer the expectation, the greater the detriment and the longer the passage of time during which the expectation was reasonably held, the greater would be the weight that should be given to the expectation'.[82] However, in this particular case, given the uncertainty of Ms Davies' expectation in light of the 'to and fro' nature of the relationship with her parents, twinned with a small overall detriment, the expectation measure seemed all out of proportion. As a result, the court concluded that even the £1.3mn figure was too high, and awarded Ms Davies £500,000.
>
> This decision suggests that the court, in cases where the expectation is out of all proportion to the detriment, will be more likely to award the reliance measure.

This issue is one which has been discussed in more than the case law, however. It is a topic of much academic debate and appears to be an issue which cannot be resolved without a clear pronouncement from the highest court. Some argue that the expectation measure is the appropriate remedial approach (or at least the preferred judicial approach), so that where possible the claimant will be given what they were promised.[83] However, recent case law shows that the picture is more nuanced than this, and it can cogently be argued that it is more common for the detriment to be remedied except in cases where the claimant's detriment cannot easily be calculated, in which case their expectation may be the simplest way to ensure that they no longer are suffering a detriment. Arguably, *Thorner v Major*[84] is a case of this type. Robertson neatly articulates that argument:

> 'the fundamental goal in giving effect to an equity arising by way of proprietary estoppel is to prevent harm resulting from reliance on inconsistent conduct. In most proprietary estoppel cases, the claimant stands to suffer substantial non-financial detriment if the representor is allowed to behave inconsistently. In those circumstances the claimant's reliance interest is better protected by fulfilling the claimant's expectations than by attempting to quantify the detriment'.[85]

In reality, English law has not committed to any one approach in this regard, and it may be better not to attempt to impose a single approach, but rather to recognise, as Lloyd LJ does, that the degree to which we wish to reward the claimant with their expectation interest will depend on the certainty of the promise, the scale of the detriment, and the clarity of the link between the two. In *Habberfield v Habberfield*, however, the Court of Appeal gave some useful guidance, emphasising that the closer the detriment came to the performance of a 'bargain', the closer to the expectation interest the remedy should be. As Lewison LJ explains:

> 'Looking back from the moment when assurances are repudiated, the nearer the overall outcome comes to the expected reciprocal performance of requested acts in return for the assurance, the stronger will be the case for an award based on or approximating to the expectation interest created by the assurance. That does no more than to recognise party autonomy to decide for themselves what a proportionate reward would be for the contemplated detriment.'[86]

---

[82] *Davies v Davies* [2016] EWCA Civ 463, [2016] 2 P & CR 10, [41].
[83] E Cooke, *The Modern Law of Estoppel* (Oxford, OUP, 2000), 151; S Gardner, 'The remedial discretion in proprietary estoppel' (1999) 115 LQR 438.
[84] *Thorner v Major* [2009] UKHL 18, [2009] 1 WLR 776.
[85] A Robertson, 'The reliance basis of proprietary estoppel remedies' [2008] Conv 295, 318.
[86] *Habberfield v Habberfield* [2019] EWCA Civ 890, [68].

8.3.2.2 Types of remedy

The types of remedy available to a claimant in relation to estoppel essentially range from full title to the land—*Thorner v Major*[87] and *Pascoe v Turner*[88] are both examples of this remedy—to no award at all, as in *Sledmore v Dalby*.[89] Here the court held that the many years of essentially free accommodation that the claimant had received meant that the equity had already been satisfied. Furthermore, in the recent Court of Appeal decision in *Moore v Moore*, the fact that a promise involved a promise of a *future* benefit was also relevant to the type of remedy which will suffice.[90] There is however a range of remedies available, all of which assist the court in achieving a flexible, proportionate outcome.

Proprietary interests

In addition to those cases where a full title to the land is conferred on the claimant, there are also situations where different potential proprietary interests are granted. For example, in *Crabb v Arun DC*[91] and *Chaudhary v Yavuz*,[92] easements were granted to remedy the estoppel. In *Suggitt v Suggitt*[93] the claimant was awarded a part share in the land. This was a similar outcome to that in *Gillett v Holt*[94] where the claimant was not awarded their full expectation interest but was awarded a full interest in the farmhouse and a monetary award to compensate for his loss of involvement in the business. In *Ottey v Grundy*[95] too Ms Ottey was awarded part of the proprietary rights which she was seeking, obtaining title to a flat in Jamaica but not to other property.

Personal rights to occupy land

The fact that courts are sometimes willing to grant personal rights to occupy the relevant land for life is a source of some difficulty. These rights are sometimes referred to as estoppel licences and seem, in this sense, to sit somewhere between personal and property rights. The concept of the estoppel licence is discussed in more detail in chapter 2 at 2.2.2.3. However, it suffices here to say that the analysis of these rights as being personal rights to occupy, somehow 'bolstered' by estoppel, is wrong. Rather, they ought to be seen as leases for life which are non-assignable, so that the claimant is granted a proprietary interest, albeit one which cannot be assigned.

Monetary awards

In some cases, the courts will grant a right unconnected with the land itself. In *Jennings v Rice*[96] the court awarded the claimant £200,000 (rather than a proprietary right in relation to property worth in excess of £1mn). This award was calculated by making reference to the number of years for which the claimant had cared for the promisor, and working out a rough wage on that basis.

---

[87] *Thorner v Major* [2009] UKHL 18, [2009] 1 WLR 776.
[88] *Pascoe v Turner* [1979] 1 WLR 431 (CA).
[89] *Sledmore v Dalby* (1996) 72 P & CR 196 (CA).
[90] *Moore v Moore* [2018] EWCA Civ 2669, [2019] 1 FLR 1277.
[91] *Crabb v Arun DC* [1976] Ch 179 (CA).
[92] *Chaudhary v Yavuz* [2011] EWCA Civ 1314, [2013] Ch 249.
[93] *Suggitt v Suggitt* [2012] EWCA Civ 1140, [2012] WTLR 1607.
[94] *Gillett v Holt* [2001] Ch 210 (CA).
[95] *Ottey v Grundy* [2003] EWCA Civ 1176, [2003] WTLR 1253.
[96] *Jennings v Rice* [2002] EWCA Civ 159, [2003] 1 P & CR 8.

In *Campbell v Griffin*[97] a similar approach was taken, albeit this time with the assistance of an equitable charge over the property to ensure that the monetary award came from the proceeds of sale of the land.

8.4 EFFECT OF THE ESTOPPEL ON THIRD PARTIES

There are two situations in which an estoppel may have an effect on a third party at stage one. Whether or not the estoppel affects third parties at stage two depends upon the remedy which the court grants. First, the estoppel may be binding on a third party in some way, be that a new purchaser of land or a lender or subsequent beneficiary of a trust, for example. Second, a third party may claim that they have acquired the benefit of an estoppel. This could happen where they inherit the promisee's estate, or where they acquire land belonging to the claimant and allege that the estoppel 'stayed with' the land on that purchase as it was concerned, for example, with the location of boundaries or similar.

8.4.1 BURDEN OF AN ESTOPPEL

On the first issue, again, the question can be broken down into two further scenarios. The first involves the situation where the third party, although not the promisor, is somehow involved in or is aware of the promise and the claimant's reliance so that there is a sufficient link between the third party and the promise that we might conclude that they are *directly* liable to respect the estoppel. The second scenario involves the case where there is no involvement between the third party and the facts which are said to constitute the estoppel so that they cannot be considered to be directly and personally liable to respect the estoppel. Instead they will be liable so to do because of the proprietary, ie persistent, characteristic of the equity arising by estoppel.

Section 116 and the preceding section in this book make clear that the equity arising by estoppel is *capable* of binding third parties. That does not mean that it will in fact always do so. Instead, whether it will do so depends upon the usual priority rules. This section will discuss these rules in the context of registered land only, and this is meant only as a summary. A full explanation of the priority rules is to be found in chapter 15. A summary was also given in chapter 3. There are three questions which need addressing here. First, is it possible to enter a proprietary estoppel itself as a notice on the register (so that the right is 'registered' and therefore protected, as explained briefly in chapter 3 at 3.1)? Second, under what circumstances will a proprietary estoppel bind a third party as an overriding interest (an interest which binds even though it is not registered, see 15.3)? Finally, how will the courts adapt the remedy given, if at all, to reflect the fact that the land in question is now owned by a third party?

Before considering all these issues, it must be noted first that the questions mainly arise in the context of third party purchasers of estates in land—be that a new freeholder, leaseholder, or a registered charge-holder. In cases where a person obtains title to land under a will, or by

---

[97] *Campbell v Griffin* [2001] EWCA Civ 990, (2001) 82 P & CR DG23, [29].

gift, they will automatically be bound by any interests binding the estate immediately prior to the disposition (section 28 Land Registration Act 2002). This means that in these cases the estoppel will be automatically biding. However it does raise a somewhat difficult question, and that is the timing of the estoppel. When precisely does an estoppel arise? This is a question to which it appears there is no clear answer, and it is one with potentially significant consequences in priority cases.

Let us move onto the three questions outlined earlier. First, is it possible to enter proprietary estoppel as a notice on the register? It appears that the answer to this is yes. Certainly, there is nothing in the legislation to prohibit such an entry, and indeed, section 116 seems to encourage such an approach. However, it is of course unlikely that someone with the benefit of an estoppel would register their interest as they would not know of a potential dispute about the land until it was too late to take such formal steps.

Second, when might an interest under an estoppel be binding on a future purchaser of an estate in land as an overriding interest? As with all priority disputes in registered land, this is regulated by the priority rules in section 29 and 30 (depending on whether the purchaser acquires the freehold or leasehold estate, or a charge). These sections explain that a right will be binding and have priority over a purchaser if that interest is either entered on the register or if it is overriding. Schedules 1 and 3 list the overriding interests (depending on whether the situation is a case of first or subsequent registration). Schedule 3 (the more common situation in practice now) will be focussed on here. Schedule 3 explains that leases granted by deed for a duration of seven years or less; the interests of a person in actual occupation; and implied legal easements, will be binding upon the new registered proprietor. The only one of these which could apply in the case of an estoppel is clearly the second category, ie the interests of a person in discoverable actual occupation, regulated by schedule 3, paragraph 2 Land Registration Act 2002. There are a number of additional requirements before actual occupation will be enough to render the estoppel binding on a third party, and these (including the question of discoverability) are discussed in chapter 15 at 15.3.3.

Finally, will the courts take account of the fact that the land is now owned by a third party when assessing how to crystallise the estoppel? This is not a question which would usually arise because in most cases of proprietary rights, the right itself dictates what the claimant has, whether this entitles them to use the land, to receive proceeds of sale, to mortgage or lease the land, etc. However, because in relation to estoppel the remedy is discretionary, the courts do have some flexibility to adapt the remedy that they give. Will the identity and circumstances of the new owner of the land encourage them to make such an adjustment? This was discussed in *Henry v Henry*[98] where the Privy Council stated that, 'The Board does not rule out the possibility that cases may arise in which the particular circumstances surrounding a third party purchase may, notwithstanding the claimant's overriding interest, require the court to reassess the extent of the claimant's equity in the property'.[99] However, the court gives no guidance in what these circumstances might be and so the question seems to be an open one.

---

[98] *Henry v Henry* [2010] UKPC 3, [2010] 1 All ER 98.
[99] *Henry v Henry* [2010] UKPC 3, [2010] 1 All ER 98, [56].

8.4.1.1 Overreaching and estoppel

The issue as to whether an equity arising by estoppel can be overreached is one which was discussed in *Birmingham Midshires v Sabherwal*.[100] Overreaching in general is considered in in chapters 15 and 16 at 15.6.4 and 16.4.3.1. The possibility of overreaching equities arising by estoppel was in doubt because although an interest arising by proprietary estoppel is not an interest under a trust, if there are two or more owners of the relevant title to land, the land *will* be held on trust, and that triggers the possibility of overreaching in section 2 Law of Property Act 1925. In *Sabherwal*,[101] the court considered whether equities arising by estoppel were, as result, overreachable in principle. The court held that they were, but only where the particular estoppel in the case was an interest in some senses, akin to a trust,[102] in the sense that it related to a family home-type case. Thus, per Walker LJ: '[t]he essential distinction is, as the authors of Megarry and Wade note, between commercial and family interests. An equitable easement or an equitable right of entry cannot sensibly shift from the land affected by it to the proceeds of sale'.[103]

Assuming that this distinction is correct, and it is given muted support in the subsequent decision in *Mortgage Express v Lambert*,[104] this means that *certain* equities arising by estoppel can be overreached and others cannot.

8.4.2 BENEFIT OF THE ESTOPPEL

The second issue that we mentioned earlier was the question as to when a third party may be able to acquire the benefit of the estoppel. If the estoppel has already been crystallised by the court, then whether or not this has proprietary consequences for a disponee of the promisee's estate depends upon what the nature of the remedy was, and whether it makes sense to conceive of this as being a right which persists in relation to some land of the promisee, rather than being personal to the promisee. To give an example, in *Chaudhary v Yavuz*[105] and *Crabb v Arun DC*,[106] the rights in question were easements which were granted as a remedy to an estoppel. Since easements cannot exist in gross (ie a person without an estate in land cannot acquire the benefit of an easement—see chapter 12 at 12.2.1.1), it would be impossible for the promisee themselves to somehow retain the benefit of the easement were they to subsequently transfer the estate in land to which the benefit of the easement attached. In this sort of situation, it is clear that the transferee would obtain the benefit of the easement under the transfer, even if this were not explicitly mentioned in the transfer deed, as a result of section 62 Law of Property Act 1925 (see chapter 12, 12.3.2.3). If, however, the award given to the promisee was a monetary award, as in *Jennings v Rice*[107] or *Ottey v Grundy*,[108] it would again, fairly obviously, be somewhat absurd to suppose that a transferee of the land belonging to the promisee would be entitled to that money if it had

---

[100] *Birmingham Midshires v Sabherwal* (2000) 80 P & CR 256.
[101] *Birmingham Midshires v Sabherwal* (2000) 80 P & CR 256.
[102] *Mortgage Express v Lambert* [2016] EWCA Civ 555, [2017] Ch 93.
[103] *Birmingham Midshires v Sabherwal* (2000) 80 P & CR 256, [28].
[104] *Mortgage Express v Lambert* [2016] EWCA Civ 555, [2017] Ch 93.
[105] *Chaudhary v Yavuz* [2011] EWCA Civ 1314; [2013] Ch 249.
[106] *Crabb v Arun DC* [1976] Ch 179 (CA).
[107] *Jennings v Rice* [2002] EWCA Civ 159, [2003] 1 P & CR 8.
[108] *Ottey v Grundy* [2003] EWCA Civ 1176, [2003] WTLR 1253.

already been paid to the promisee. Slightly more complicated is the situation where the money has not yet been paid and the promisee themselves has died, for example. Can the person who inherits their estate enforce the judgment for money made in crystallising the estoppel? It is suggested that they would be able so to do. The promisee has the benefit of a judgment against the promisor in such a case, and as such the judgment would benefit their estate.

What about the situation where the estoppel has not yet been crystallised and the promisee merely has the benefit of the equity arising by estoppel. In these cases, does the uncrystillised estoppel pass with the promisee's land, if any, and even if the promisee does not have any land, are they able to assign the benefit of their estoppel either expressly or impliedly by will, for example? Again, this may depend on the type of estoppel which is being claimed. Since estoppels are, in many cases, personal remedies in the sense that the facts as they have arisen involve a very personal kind of unfairness which it would make no sense to assign, then it may cogently be argued that there is no blanket rule as to whether the benefit of an estoppel can be assigned or not. Certainly, we know that *some* equities arising by estoppel are assignable. This was made clear in *Lester v Woodgate*.[109] What we do not know is whether *all* such rights are assignable.

8.5 RELATIONSHIP BETWEEN ESTOPPEL AND FORMALITIES

One of the great controversies relating to proprietary estoppel is the relationship between estoppel and formalities. The central role which this tension has played in the development of some of the key concepts relating to estoppel is discussed earlier in relation to Dixon's definition of unconscionability (see 8.2.4). However, this issue is one which cannot be avoided by simply defining and moulding the estoppel rules to such a point where we are most comfortable with the role that estoppel plays when contrasted with the policies behind formality rules. Instead, the issue must be faced head-on. No matter how estoppel is defined, the consequence of finding an estoppel is that a property right is generated without the need for writing in any form and this goes against the principles of formality rules. What it does not do, however, is breach the statutory rules expressing those formality principles in *specific* contexts. This is where the statement that estoppel 'gets around' or 'breaches' formalities rules is shown to be a red herring. True enough, estoppel is not mentioned in section 2(5) LP(MP)A 1989 as an exception to the rule that all contracts involving the dispositions of an interest in land, except those explicitly exempted by statute, must be written down in a form which contains or refers to the totality of the contractual terms and is signed by both parties. However, estoppel is *not* a contract. Therefore, estoppel is not a way of getting round section 2. It has nothing to do with section 2. When looked at in this way the relationship between estoppel and the formality rules in section 2 is simple: they simply do not engage one another. Theoretically then, the answer is a straightforward one.

In practice though, as we might expect, the answer cannot be quite as simple as that. Neuberger has been very disparaging about this complexity, arguing, 'by needlessly meddling, Parliament, with misconceived drafting, and the courts, through inconsistent decisions, have had their

---

[109] *Lester v Woodgate* [2010] EWCA Civ 199, [2010] 2 P & CR 21.

wicked ways with section 2, we are worse off than we ever were with section 40'.[110] The reason for this is that in some estoppel cases, the assurance takes the form of a promise which if written down would be a contractual promise, with the detrimental reliance taking the form of the consideration which it was intended would provide the countervailing obligations within that contract. In such cases, the *only* flaw in the transaction (from the perspective of enforceable contracts) is that the parties failed to write their agreement down in the required manner. If, in such a case, the court not only decides to award the claimant the benefit of a proprietary estoppel, but also decides to award the claimant their expectation based upon that bargain, then what is the court doing but, in effect, enforcing the contractual arrangement? It is this situation which causes the problem for the relationship between proprietary estoppel and formality rules.

Similarly, the strict theoretical distinction between estoppel as a means of generating rights in land, and the formality rules governing other means of generating such rights, is stretched in cases involving wills, such as *Thorner v Major*[111] and *Gillett v Holt*.[112] In *Thorner v Major*[113] in particular, all that the uncle, Peter, had failed to do in that case was write a valid will. His intentions and desires for his cousin David to inherit the farm on his death were clear. This was not a situation like *Gillett* where there was a deliberate and conscious attempt to go back on an earlier promise regarding inheritance. Rather, in *Thorner*,[114] all that went wrong was that there was no valid will achieving the outcome which all parties desired. In such a case, allowing, as the court did, for David to become title-holder to the farm and business, effectively enforcing his expectation interest, has the practical effect of producing the effect which otherwise would need to take effect by will.

What we have then here is a practical challenge, not a theoretical one. The theory here—that the estoppel does not enforce the contract—is entirely correct and therefore there is no clash between estoppel and the rules relating to formalities. The situations involving wills do not involve the promisee inheriting the land in the absence of a will and in contravention of the rules relating to intestate inheritance, but they have the same practical effect. This means that whilst we do not need to explain, in terms of the statute, *how* estoppel can 'get around' proprietary estoppel, but rather *why* we allow them to have this practical effect, and this means we must return to the question of unconscionability discussed earlier. Unconscionability is the explanation as to why the practical effect of estoppel can be to get around formalities rules.

8.6 RELATIONSHIP BETWEEN ESTOPPEL AND CONSTRUCTIVE TRUSTS

Another difficulty which the decision in *Cobbe v Yeoman's Row*[115] considered is the relationship between estoppel and constructive trusts. Again, in theory, the distinction is an easy one. Estoppels arise when there is an assurance or representation which has been detrimentally relied upon.

---

[110] Lord Neuberger of Abbotsbury, 'The stuffing of Minerva's owl? Taxonomy and taxidermy in equity' (2009) 68 CLJ 537, 545.
[111] *Thorner v Major* [2009] UKHL 18, [2009] 1 WLR 776.
[112] *Gillett v Holt* [2001] Ch 210 (CA).
[113] *Thorner v Major* [2009] UKHL 18, [2009] 1 WLR 776.
[114] *Thorner v Major* [2009] UKHL 18, [2009] 1 WLR 776.
[115] *Cobbe v Yeoman's Row Management Ltd* [2008] UKHL 55, [2008] 1 WLR 1752.

8.6 Relationship between Estoppel and Constructive Trusts

Constructive trusts (in this case, the common intention constructive trust, see chapter 7) arise where there is a common intention and this is detrimentally relied upon. Whilst in both there is a need to demonstrate detrimental reliance—this is to be expected given the context, ie the creation of property rights in the absence of a formal document—in one a unilateral promise as to current or future rights in land is required, and in the other, what is needed is the proof of a *common* intention as to the *current* equitable title. Furthermore, the outcome of each is different. Where a constructive trust is established the claimant obtains an interest under a trust. There is no other option. Where an estoppel is established, the claimant obtains an equity by estoppel, but this estoppel is crystallised, as has been discussed earlier, into a variety of forms. This could be an interest in the relevant land, or it could be a money award, or nothing, depending on what the courts consider to be the minimum necessary to satisfy the equity. Finally, where a constructive trust is formed, the legal title-holder(s) will become trustees (albeit under a bare trust) so that the duties of a trustee apply and they can be sued for breach of trust where appropriate. This does not happen with a proprietary estoppel.

The differences in terms of formation and consequences therefore mean that it is important to distinguish between these two concepts carefully. The difficulty in so-doing arises from two factors. First, the historical development of both assurance-based estoppel and the common intention constructive trust mean that at various times the concepts have been conflated and used simultaneously. Some of the case law can be very difficult to explain on the basis of the distinguishing features discussed earlier.[116] Second, the fact situations which give rise to the two concepts, although separable in theory, will often be very close in practice. Indeed, in many constructive trust cases, there will almost always be a valid argument that there could also be a proprietary estoppel. This means that the two are often pleaded in the alternative, and on a few occasions the court has declined to decide precisely whether it is basing its decision on the rules of common intention constructive trust or on estoppel. The consequence of this is that it is not really possible to divide *definitively* all cases into being either constructive trust or estoppel cases. Nor is it possible to explain completely the language used by the judiciary in these cases. Some, it is suggested, must simply be seen as wrongly decided, or at least wrongly explained when viewed through the lens of the modern case law on both estoppel and trusts. Whilst this may be a problem in terms of precedent, it should not result in us muddling up the distinctions between the two concepts are far as far as we can avoid so-doing.

However, a major problem for comes from cases where the courts seem to conclude that proprietary estoppel generates its proprietary status by 'sitting behind' a constructive trust. This does

---

[116] An example of this is the decision in *Pascoe v Turner* [1979] 1 WLR 431 (CA) which would probably now be seen as a constructive trust case under the approach represented by *Stack v Dowden* [2007] UKHL 17, [2007] 2 AC 432 not withstanding the discussion in *Pascoe* about the role of constructive trusts in perfecting imperfect gifts (436) For more on that discussion, see *Dillwyn v Llewleyn* 45 ER 1285, (1862) 4 De GF & J 517 which highlighted the importance of detrimental reliance in relation to estoppel (at 521) to avoid breaching the principle that equity does not perfect such gifts. *Dillwyn* is also seen by many as the founding case of modern proprietary estoppel. Another example can be found in *Inwards v Baker* [1965] 2 QB 29 (CA), where the reasoning appears to be that Mr Baker acquired licence, protected, through the elements of estoppel, by the 'infusion' of an equity, drawing on the (now largely discredited) approach in *Errington v Errington* [1952] 1 KB 290 (CA). As Megarry and Wade argues, 'proprietary estoppel came to be employed to protect the rights of occupation of licensees' (C Harpum et al, *Megarry & Wade: The Law of Real Property*, Sweet & Maxwell, London, 2012) [16.006], and this is no longer the focus of the doctrine.

not make sense. But it is important to understand where this idea comes from in order to navigate some of the case law, including some of the most recent decisions in this area (eg *Matchmove v Dowding*[117]—see later). The reason why the courts have been tempted to conflate the two ideas, beginning arguably with Lord Denning, is the fact that constructive trusts are explicitly exempted from the formality requirements in section 2 LP(MP)A 1989 and section 53 Law of Property Act 1925. As a result, courts appear to have felt the need to 'force' proprietary estoppel into the statutory exceptions by concluding that they are 'supported by' or exist behind a constructive trust. This is however a dangerous mode of analysis for it means that trust duties may be present in situations where there is no justification in terms of the policies behind the imposition of trusts to impose such duties. Let us explore this line of case law by considering *Matchmove v Dowding*,[118] and its predecessor authorities in *Herbert v Doyle*[119] and *Yaxley v Gotts*.[120]

> **Key case:** *Matchmove v Dowding* [2016] EWCA Civ 1233
>
> In this case, Matchmove was a company wholly owned and controlled by Mr Francis. Mr Francis was close friends with the claimants, Mr Dowding and Ms Church. Ms Church and Mr Dowding were looking for a property in Bristol with some land to allow them to keep Ms Church's horses at home. They found a suitable property, but they were unable to buy the entirety of the land themselves. Mr Francis therefore offered to buy the whole site, and then transfer part of it to Ms Church and Mr Dowding in due course. Mr Francis duly purchased the relevant title, and Mr Dowding and Church contributed £66,000 to this initial purchase. They then sold their house, and constructued a new home for themselves on the site. The land on which this house sat was transferred to them. However, the agreement that they had reached with Mr Francis included his transferring a further plot of land where the horses would be kept. The transfer of this had been held up by a rights of way dispute with a neighbour. By the time that this dispute had been resolved, Mr Francis and Mr Dowding had fallen out, and Mr Francis refused to transfer the extra land. However, Mr Dowding and Ms Church had by this time paid Mr Francis £200,000, the total agreed amount for both their building plot and the extra land. None of this had been written down. Mr Dowding and Ms Church claimed that they had the benefit of either a proprietary estoppel or a constructive trust. The first instance judge had proceeded on the basis that both applied.
>
> The Court of Appeal, wishing to 'avoid' the issue as to whether section 2 prevented the formation of a proprietary estoppel in cases such as this, reached its decision solely on the basis of a constructive trust. However, it must be acknowledged that the facts in this case appear to be a completely orthodox situation of proprietary estoppel where a very clear promise was made and detrimental reliance occurred. The approach and outcome in this case therefore raises the issue which was thought resolved after *Thorner v Major*[121] and the Supreme Court's attitude to its earlier judgment in *Cobbe v Yeoman's Row*,[122] ie whether it is not possible to rely on proprietary estoppel in cases where there is a failed contract.
>
> In terms of the specific conclusion in the case that a constructive trust arose, this too is difficult. This is because on the facts of the case it was difficult to establish exactly when the trust arose, and what in fact was held on trust.

---

[117] *Matchmove v Dowding* [2016] EWCA Civ 1233, [2017] 1 WLR 749.
[118] *Matchmove v Dowding* [2016] EWCA Civ 1233, [2017] 1 WLR 749.
[119] *Herbert v Doyle* [2010] EWCA Civ 1095, [2011] 1 EGLR 119.
[120] *Yaxley v Gotts*, [2000] Ch 162 (CA), 175.
[121] *Thorner v Major* [2009] UKHL 18, [2009] 1 WLR 776.
[122] *Cobbe v Yeoman's Row Management Ltd* [2008] UKHL 55, [2008] 1 WLR 1752.

> It appears that the chosen analysis, given the agreement detrimentally relied upon, was a constructive trust, and not an estoppel, but it difficult to see why this would not be an ordinary proprietary estoppel case. One issue in such cases, as is clear from cases such as *Kinane v Mackie-Conteh*,[123] is the extent to which estoppel is 'permitted' to perfect what would otherwise be merely a contractual agreement and contractual performance into a binding agreement notwithstanding the fact that there is no written document. Furthermore, enforcing this promise harks back, in effect, to the doctrine of part performance which has clearly been rendered impermissible by section 2. This was the argument put forcefully by the court in *Yaxley v Gotts*,[124] in the judgment of Walker LJ:
>
>> 'Parliament's requirement that any contract for the disposition of an interest in land must be made in a particular documentary form, and will otherwise be void, does not have such an obviously social aim as statutory provisions relating to contracts by or with moneylenders, infants, or protected tenants. Nevertheless it can be seen as embodying Parliament's conclusion, in the general public interest, that the need for certainty as to the formation of contracts of this type must in general outweigh the disappointment of those who make informal bargains in ignorance of the statutory requirement. If an estoppel would have the effect of enforcing a void contract and subverting Parliament's purpose it may have to yield to the statutory law which confronts it, except so far as the statute's saving for a constructive trust provides a means of reconciliation of the apparent conflict'.[125]
>
> However, in this particular case, the reliance went beyond merely contractual performance. Part of the reliance, ie the payment of the total £200,000 was clearly merely that envisaged by the contract. If that was all that had happened, then arguably the court could not use proprietary estoppel (or a constructive trust) for that matter, because all that would have occurred would be perfection of the contract. However, on the facts Mr Dowding and Ms Church went beyond that: they sold their other property and they constructed their house on the understanding that the house would also have access to the extra land. This means that it would have been possible for the courts to generate an explanation for the finding of a proprietary estoppel which did not come into direct or indirect conflict with section 2.

Whatever one concludes about the rights or wrongs of finding a constructive trust in these cases, the fact that the court relies on this doctrine and not proprietary estoppel, in short, raises two questions. First, when can proprietary estoppel be relied upon in cases where parties have failed to write down what would otherwise amount to a contractual agreement as discussed earlier? Second, when, in such cases, will a constructive trust have arisen? If the answer to these is first—never, at least in commercial cases—and second, whenever the agreement was regarded to be certain and immediately binding, and was then detrimentally relied upon, a constructive trust will still arise in many cases (although it would not arise in a case like *Cobbe*[126] where the parties quite demonstrably did not consider the agreement to be immediately binding).

There is also a practical problem in distinguishing constructive trusts and estoppel, and this arises most pertinently in relation to problem questions, where it can be difficult to know whether the primary mode of analysis you should use is one based on estoppel or one based on constructive trusts. We can see this by looking at two examples.

---

[123] *Kinane v Mackie-Conteh* [2005] EWCA Civ 45, [2005] 2 P & CR DG3.
[124] *Yaxley v Gotts*, [2000] Ch 162 (CA), 175.
[125] *Yaxley v Gotts*, [2000] Ch 162 (CA), 175.
[126] *Cobbe v Yeoman's Row Management Ltd* [2008] UKHL 55, [2008] 1 WLR 1752.

First, imagine that Saddiq is the sole freehold proprietor of a large cottage in the countryside from which he runs a B & B business. His boyfriend Conrad moves into the property and begins to work for the business in return for no pay. He does this for 20 years. At no point do the parties discuss ownership of the house as such but they have repeated conversations during which Saddiq reassures Conrad that his financial position is secure. As Conrad's help in the business has meant that an additional three rooms can be used as guest accommodation, his contribution has made it significantly easier for Saddiq to pay the mortgage.

Second, imagine that the scenario is the same as earlier, except that rather than working for the B & B business for no pay allowing the business profits to pay off the mortgage, Conrad looks after the couple's adopted children, freeing up Saddiq to concentrate on the business so that the profits increase and the mortgage payments can be met.

The couple then splits up, and Conrad claims that he has a 30 per cent ownership share in the property or that he should be paid money equivalent to that value. Should this be treated as proprietary estoppel, a constructive trust, or neither? This is not an easy question. On the one hand, the lack of an express assurance as to ownership of the property would seem to preclude proprietary estoppel. However, the decision in *Thorner v Major*[127] shows that the assurance can be implied, and it may be possible to imply from Saddiq's reassuring Conrad as to his financial position a promise that Conrad has a share in the property. Certainly this is a more explicit assurance than that found in *Thorner*.[128] Furthermore, in that case the court had relied heavily on the continued implied nature of the promise in the way in which the parties worked together over such a long period of time. The same may be said here. On the other hand, this is a domestic homes situation, and the implication is that Conrad has an *immediate* interest in the property, rather than a future interest or similar, such that an implication of a constructive trust may be more appropriate.

There is no case law resolution to this problem, at least not a definitive one. Instead, the tactic can only be to reason by analogy and highlight the difficulties that exist in this area, without getting too bogged down in them.

8.7 CONCLUSION

The estoppel rules are designed to best capture when we feel 'going back on promises' is unfair, even if those promises are not cemented in the usual formalities which English law requires. The most common type of estoppel—estoppel by assurance—requires that the promisor make a sufficiently certain promise upon which the promisee acts to her detriment, so that it is unconscionable for the promisor to go back on her promise. The boundaries of these terms are not entirely clear, but very often the courts are taking a common sense approach to establishing when an estoppel would be appropriate. The consequence of such arising, however, is the generation of a persistent proprietary interests which is capable of binding third parties in certain circumstances. When crystallised, the courts may grant the claimant a very wide range of remedies. This maintains estoppel's focus on flexibility and responsiveness to fact and to context.

---

[127] *Thorner v Major* [2009] UKHL 18; [2009] 1 WLR 776.
[128] *Thorner v Major* [2009] UKHL 18; [2009] 1 WLR 776.

PRINCIPLES

How does this discussion shape our understanding of the principles explained in chapter 1? To recap, these principles were:

1. Certainty
2. Sensitivity to context
3. Transactability
4. Systemic and individual effects
5. Recognition of the social role of the land law system.

Estoppel is characterised by its lack of precision. This is precisely the point. It is impossible to definitively explain the requirements of the doctrine, or to give a precise definition to unconscionability. Were it possible so to do, then estoppel would be unable to fulfill its purpose as the expression of flexibility in land law. In this respect, we may argue that not only are the rules of estoppel representative most clearly of sensitivity to context, they *are* the overall system's response to this principle. This is how land law ensures that it does not lose perspective on the fact that the enforcement of rights, and arguments about the precise parameters of section 2 Law of Property (Miscellaneous Provisions) Act 1989 have effects on real people's lives and livelihoods. If this is right, then since life is messy, so too must the law be and certainty and transactibility must take a back seat here.

This does not mean, though, that we cannot have some defined or at least thought-through idea as to when and why people at the risk of losing their home, or suffering huge detriment because promises are not kept, should be helped by the law, and when not. In this respect, although we ought not to seek certainty in this area, we can seek certainty about *why* the estoppel rules exist, and that we certainly do not have. This lack of clarity of vision is also clearly apparent when we consider the boundaries of estoppel and its relationship with other key concepts making up our land law system: constructive trusts and the formality rules. We do not know precisely how these rules interact because, in effect, no one has decided what the point of those rules is in the first place. It is right to say, of course, that in a system of common law which develops organically over time in response to circumstances as they arise, too rigid a search for consistency of explanation is dangerous as it may stifle innovation in the law just when it is needed most. The culmination of this uncertainty is to be found in the notion of unconscionability. Some explanation consistently applied as to what this means would certainly enhance the normative clarity of the rules.

We can also see the power of individual cases having radical effects within the system as a whole in the estoppel case law. In the aftermath of *Cobbe*, the academic community was predicting that estoppel would no longer serve an important purpose in our legal system since it could no longer 'get around' section 2 formality rules. The decision itself, in terms of results, is clearly correct, but the reasoning sent shockwaves. In a context where there is no certainty, the importance of keeping an eye on the systemic effects of any decision becomes all the more important.

Finally, when we think of estoppel's place within land law we cannot help but feel that this is land law's social conscience. It is these rules which help to prevent the powerful taking advantage of the vulnerable by destroying their reasonable expectations. It may not achieve this in all contexts, but that is very much one of its aims.

TABLE OF DEFINITIONS

Estoppel by assurance	Estoppel which arises in response to a promise detrimentally relied upon where it would be unconscionable to revoke the promise.
Assurance	The sufficiently clear promise made by the promisor to found an estoppel.
Detriment	The setback to interests or change of course suffered by the promisee.
Reliance	The causal link between the promise and the detriment suffered by the promisee.
Unconscionability	The 'unfairness' that exists in going back upon a promise detrimentally relied upon where circumstances are such that the court cannot allow the promise to be revoked (not susceptible of of a clear definition!).
Equity by estoppel	The property right which arises in response to estoppel, and which is extinguished upon the crystallisation of the estoppel and the grant of any remedy.
Promissory estoppel	A form of estoppel which does not generate property rights, but which prevents a person from going back upon a promise they have made where that promise has been detrimentally relied upon. This can act as a defence, but not a cause of action.

FURTHER READING

The further reading in this section is devoted to exploring the flexible aspects of estoppel, and how these have shaped the doctrine.

BIEHLER, H., 'Remedies in cases of proprietary estoppel: towards a more principled approach?' (2015) 54 Irish Jurist 79.

DIXON, M., 'Confining and defining proprietary estoppel: the role of unconscionability' (2010) 30 Legal Studies 408.

HOPKINS, N., 'The relevance of context in property law: a case for judicial restraint?' (2011) 31 Legal Studies 175.

PAWLOWSKI, M. and BROWN, J., 'Proprietary estoppel and competing equities' [2018] Conv 145.

9

FREEHOLD ESTATE

9.1	Introduction	273	9.6	Commonhold	284
9.2	The Content of the Freehold Estate	274	9.7	Termination of the Freehold Estate	285
9.3	Multiple Freeholds and Relativity of Title	279	9.8	Conclusion	287
				Principles	288
9.4	The Transfer and Registration of Freehold Interests in Land	282		Table of Definitions	289
				Further Reading	289
9.5	Flying Freehold	283			

CHAPTER GOALS

By the end of this chapter you should have an understanding of:

- The nature of the freehold as land law's 'highest' right in land;
- The scope of the freehold estate geographically and theoretically;
- How multiple freeholds are managed;
- How freeholds are transferred;
- The concepts of the commonhold and flying freehold; and
- The process of termination of the freehold estate.

9.1 INTRODUCTION

The purpose of this chapter is to explore English land law's understanding of the concept of 'ownership' of land as developed through the freehold estate. We have already explored the nature of rights in land in chapter 2, and considered the terminology of estates and ownership there. This chapter is very much an extension of that discussion. It is odd that despite being land law's 'highest' right in land, it is very difficult to explain what the freehold is and how it works. The information provided in the introductory chapters is essential to a good understanding of the freehold. This chapter is designed to represent a deeper analysis of how the freehold works in practice. It is important from the outset therefore to see that this chapter is really concerned with two separate issues. First, it is about how English law understands title to land, considering the issue of relativity of title. Second, it considers the rules relating to the freehold estate, English law's 'most extensive' right in land, and therefore what most people refer to as and consider to be 'ownership' in this sense. The sections considering relativity of title should be read alongside the discussion in chapter 2 and 6.

There are two estates in land in English law—freehold and leasehold. This chapter is concerned with the freehold estate, which is also referred to as the 'fee simple absolute in possession'. For discussion of the leasehold estate and the legal mechanisms managing the various rights to which it gives rise, see chapter 10. As noted earlier, the freehold estate is the 'highest' estate in land available in English law. It is what most people would commonly refer to as ownership of land. However, to think of it like this is, in many ways, misleading. Having a freehold estate does not entitle that freehold proprietor to ownership. English law does not see ownership as being a single, absolute state. In part, this is because English land law has never recognised a legal action allowing an individual to obtain a confirmation from a court that they are *the* owner of the thing concerned. English courts will not decide who is the absolute owner of a piece of land. Rather, they will make an assessment as to who of the parties before the court has a better title to the land such that they are entitled to the remedy sought or to resist the application of their opposing party. This is a very important feature of English land law. It is what defines the features of the freehold right and explains why much of land law operates as it does.

In this chapter, we consider what it means to have a freehold estate, and some of the rules relating to transfers, ownership and the operation of this estate. Section 9.2 asks what does having a freehold right, all else being equal (no trusts over the land, no leasehold estate in place, for example) entitle the owner of that right to do? Section 9.3 considers whether is it possible for more than one person to have a freehold right in the land and, if so, how are the mutual conflicts between these two 'equal' rights managed? Section 9.5 considers the flying freehold, section 9.6 the commonhold, and section 9.7 the termination of the freehold estate.

9.2 THE CONTENT OF THE FREEHOLD ESTATE

Before the legislative reforms in 1925 it used to be possible to have a number of different forms of freehold estate. Since the coming into force of the Law of Property Act 1925, however, there is now only one form of freehold ownership—the fee simple absolute in possession.

The freehold is the closest that English law gets to some concept of 'absolute' ownership of land. However, since there can be multiple freehold titles, to think of the freehold as ownership in the sense of there being only one single owner of the land is wrong. Nevertheless, as the freehold is the most extensive possible right in relation to land, it is important to know what is entails. There is a common understanding in relation to the freehold interest, that being the common law equivalent of ownership, it entitles the owner of that right to use, abuse, destroy, and transfer, the property at will, absent the control of any other, and, depending on your political perspective, absent the control of the state. Furthermore, the scope of the freehold right is said to extend geographically from the centre to the Earth to the stars, so that the owner of surface rights also has control over sub-surface rights as well as controlling access to the airspace above their land. Both of these ways of understanding the operation of the freehold are wrong, at least in modern law. It is doubtful whether they could ever be said to have been meaningfully true. Let us commence with the modern understanding of what freehold owners are entitled to do in relation to their land, before considering the space encompassed within the freehold title. We conclude this part by considering rights of re-entry and reversion which form the residual entitlement of a freehold once possession has been granted to another.

9.2.1 LIMITATIONS ON USE

First, considering the ability to use land, it is obvious that a freehold proprietor, despite having the most extensive right in relation to the relevant land cannot simply do anything he likes on that land. He cannot, for example, build in a way which breaches planning law; carry out industrial processes on his land without an appropriate pollution permit; and, most obviously, he cannot cause personal injury to another on his land regardless of the fact that he has a property right in it. Perhaps more significantly in land law terms, he cannot use his land in a way which impinges on the reasonable user of his neighbour. This relationship between neighbours is governed by the laws concerning nuisance discussed in chapter 18.

It is therefore important to keep in mind that whilst the freehold does entitle the freehold proprietor to use the land, it does not entitle him to absolute liberty from control on that land. This much however is not particularly controversial. It is a necessary feature of society which operates on the basis of rule of law guaranteeing, at a minimum, protection for its citizens against the violence of others, wherever that violence takes place. In this sense, restrictions on use which exist to prevent harm to others are generally accepted. Much more controversial are rules which limit the owners' use rights where the goal is either to protect the owner themselves, or to protect some more nebulous (though not necessarily less important) interests such as the environment, cultural and architectural heritage, and the like. This sort of control is the subject of intense debate in the United States, for example, where the Constitutional provisions protecting property are the subject of intense scrutiny in relation to issues such as zoning laws, compulsory purchase, and use restrictions.[1] This debate has been less intense in the United Kingdom. Partly this is a result of the historical background to ownership of land discussed in the introductory chapters; partly it is a result of the lack of a written constitution and a differing political climate. Nevertheless, there are discussions about what can be fairly termed the difference between seeing ownership of land as entailing rights and obligations as part of a social contract, sometimes referred to as a 'progressive property' perspective, and those who believe that the role of the state should be minimising, allowing the free market and negotiated entitlements to strike an appropriate balance.[2] There is reference to this wider debate in the further reading section later.

---

[1] There is an extensive debate in the literature about the interaction between the US constitution and public regulation of land use. For a starting point, see Alexander, *The Global Debate over Constitutional Property: Lessons for American Takings Jurisprudence* (University of Chicago Press, Chicago, 2006).
[2] The progressive property concept emerges from a paper issued by Alexander et al in the Cornell Law Review which lists the obligations which exist as a result of owning property. Alexander at al, 'A statement of progressive property' (2009) 94 Cornell Law Review 743.

> **Further analysis: Conceptualising ownership**
>
> At the heart of this debate about how we should understand what ownership of land means in English land law, lies a tension. The tension is this: rights in land are at once technical and neutral, but they are also a means by which scarce resources are allocated and decisions are made about who is entitled to which benefits in our society. Cowan et al discuss this problem, emphasising that if we reconceived the question so that instead of asking, 'who owns this land', instead we asked, 'whose house is this', we may abandon the (so-called) technical and narrow questions with which our land law is concerned and instead focus on the implications in terms of fairness, equality, and opportunity which these rules engender. They ask, 'what would land law look like if, rather than labeling it like that, we labeled it "the law of the home" or "the law of place"?'.[3]
>
> Whether or not one agrees that this focus of English land law is indeed hiding these big questions behind technical ones, whenever considering what the freehold estate is, and how it can be transferred in terms of formalities, and the like, the potential for the rules to have significant effects in practice, however dry and dusty they appear, should be kept in mind.

9.2.2 GEOGRAPHICAL SCOPE

The second issue is the geographical scope of that control. This issue can arise in relation to leasehold estates, but generally the geographical scope of a lease is determined as a matter of construction of the grant as explained in chapter 10. In relation to the freehold, there is no such document to which we can refer. The traditional maxim is *cujus est solum, ejus est usque ad coelom et ad infeors* ('the owner of the soil is presumed to own everything up to the sky and down to the centre of the earth'[4]). In relation to what is included 'with' land, see the discussion at 2.3.1 in chapter 2. This is said to be the delineation as to what constitutes the scope of the freehold right, case law has shown this to be an overstatement both 'upwards' and 'downwards'. In relation to control of the airspace above land in which a particular person has a freehold estate, let us consider an example.

Suppose that Esther has a freehold estate in land and wishes, as a result of that, to build for themselves an enormous tower. However, in order to do this, they will need to swing a crane over Thomas' land. Thomas objects to this and wishes to obtain an order from the court that Esther is not entitled to swing this crane over their land. This crane is far taller than the height of the existing buildings on Thomas' land. Since Thomas is 'only' a house-owner Thomas never makes use of the airspace in which the crane is seeking to encroach. The works are anticipated to take about 6 months. Can Thomas complain?

The answer to this question lies in case law. The general principle, however, is that Thomas can prevent this. The swinging crane would be committing a trespass by encroaching on Thomas' ability to control rights of access to his land, and this includes the right to control access to the airspace within their sphere of control.

---

[3] Cowan et al, *Great Debates in Land Law* (2nd ed) (Palgrave Macmillan, London, 2016), 23.
[4] Harpum et al, *Megarry and Wade: The Law of Real Property* (8th ed) (Sweet and Maxwell, London, 2012), [3.037].

However, there have been two developments which alter this general position. First, government has enacted statute to clarify that the navigation of commercial flights is not dependent on individual landowners granting permission for the flights to cross over their land. That this is an essential element of modern air transport is obvious. The second development is the more significant one that the owner of the freehold right in land is only entitled to control access to a 'reasonable' height. This emerged in the case of *Bernstein*.[5]

> **Key case: *Bernstein of Leigh v Skyviews* [1978] QB 479**
>
> In this case, Skyviews were a company which flew over the countryside taking photographs of houses, and then attempted to sell those photos as a memento to their owners, so that they could appreciate their property from the air. The owner of the land, Lord Bernstein, objected to this claiming that it was a trespass on his land, being an invasion not only of his property rights, but also of his privacy.
>
> In assessing whether this was a trespass, the court held that Bernstein was only entitled to control access to the height necessary for his reasonable use and enjoyment. Skyviews' aircraft was flying above this height.
>
> It is somewhat difficult to see what the limitations on the reasonable use and enjoyment of land are in this sense, particularly if we consider the crane example earlier. Furthermore, this case raises the question as to whether different 'types' of freehold owner (commercial, residential, owner of a tower block) should be treated differently in terms of the vertical scope of their ownership since they have different needs in terms of the reasonable uses and enjoyment of the land. Does this height increase as development on the land takes place, or when land is transferred to another person wishing to carry out a tall development on the property? In all likelihood, these problems would be resolved, looking not to the principled underpinning in any particular case, but rather reaching a pragmatic conclusion based upon a fair balance between the needs of all parties. The flexibility of the rules as to what a freehold estate entitles you is revealed in considering these questions.

Similar pragmatism from the judiciary, along with statutory intervention (in relation to fracking, for example, in the Infrastructure Act 2015), has emerged in relation to the question of 'downwards' ownership as well. Unsurprisingly, this question tends to be of much more commercial and financial significance than does the question of height. This is because of the value of many substrate minerals and mining interests. In terms of statutory intervention in this question, as with height, the question of ownership to depth has not been definitively determined by the legislature (rather, specific kinds of substances are excluded from freehold ownership). Instead the general principle is one which has been determined by case law. The case of *Bocardo*[6] however substantially modifies the general principle expressed in the 'to the centre of the Earth' maxim, relating to sub-strata ownership of land.

---

[5] *Bernstein of Leigh v Skyviews* [1978] QB 479 (QBD).
[6] *Bocardo SA v Star Energy UK* [2010] UKSC 35, [2011] 1 AC 380.

> **Key case: *Bocardo v Star Energy* [2010] UKSC 35**
>
> In this case, the energy company wished to drill a pipe underneath the relevant land. The question therefore depended upon how deep the freehold ownership of the land reached.
>
> The court held that in general the ownership extends as far down as the owner could make use of that land.
>
> This, in contrast to the *Skyviews*[7] approach is not a question of reasonableness. It is, instead, a question of technology. The reasoning behind this is that given the current state of technology, the idea of owning to the centre of the Earth is essentially meaningless since nothing can be done more than a few kilometres beneath the surface of the Earth. It is not inconceivable that the position in this respect will be different in the future. In fact it is very likely. Given this, it can be argued that the freehold owner may as well own as far down as the centre of the Earth, for as soon as someone else could reach deeper than previous technology allowed, so too would the scope of their ownership. However, the articulation of the rule has changed since *Bocardo*.[8]

> **Summary: Geographical scope of the freehold**
>
> 1. The freehold extends vertically upwards as far as the owner can reasonably make use of the airspace above.
> 2. The freehold extends vertically downwards as far as human endeavour means it is possible for the freehold owner to make use of the land.
>
> Both of these principles are limited in relation to specific substance and specific kinds of uses by statutory intervention.

9.2.3 THE RIGHT OF REVERSION AND RIGHTS OF RE-ENTRY

What happens when a freehold owner is bound by other rights, particularly the leasehold? The nature of the freehold title in such cases is contained in the rights of reversion and re-entry. The freehold reversion is the right of the landlord to regain possession of property on the termination of a lease. The reversion is freely assignable by the landlord, as long as the appropriate formalities are followed. If the reversion is assigned, then, in accordance with the rules relating to leasehold covenants (agreements made between the original landlord and tenant) which are discussed in chapter 10 at 10.5.1, the new freeholder may be able to sue on such covenants. If the property is a dwelling, then it is important for the landlord to give the tenant notice of the transfer of title.

The right of re-entry is the landlord reversioner's ability to go back into possession of land upon the early termination of a lease following successful forfeiture. This is discussed in chapter 10 at 10.5.3. Nevertheless, it is an important incident of the freehold and is described by Gray and

---

[7] *Bernstein of Leigh v Skyviews* [1978] QB 479 (QBD).
[8] *Bocardo SA v Star Energy UK* [2010] UKSC 35, [2011] 1 AC 380.

Gray as: 'his ultimate security against the non-payment of rent and his ultimate insurance in respect of the commercial investment represented by the lease'.[9] This right is itself a property right and appears in the list of legal property rights in section 1(2) LPA 1925.

It is also possible to have a right of re-entry affecting a freehold title, as strange as this may seem. This is a hangover from the old law, and is a consequence of parties attempting to finance acquisition of title by granting the seller a right of re-entry should the purchase price not be paid in accordance with pre-determined instalments. The 1925 reforms did not abolish this possibility although they did emphasise that the freehold subject to a right of re-entry would nevertheless still be considered a fee simple absolute. Similarly, in respect of adverse possession of leasehold land, the adverse possessor will, in accordance with the normal adverse possession rules, obtain a possessory freehold title on going into possession. This will be subject to a right of re-entry exercisable by the paper title-holder at the coming to the end of the lease.[10] Thus, rights of re-entry are property rights which a freeholder acquires on the grant of a lease, but also rights to which they might be subject in certain rare circumstances.

Summary: Right of reversion and rights of re-entry

The right of reversion is the characterisation of the landlord's interest during the currency of a lease, and essentially is his right to return into possession once the lease comes to an end. A right of re-entry is a right entitling a landlord to bring a lease to an end on the occurrence of certain events, eg non-payment or rent resulting in forfeiture.

9.3 MULTIPLE FREEHOLDS AND RELATIVITY OF TITLE

In relation to all rights in land, whether of the same or different types, there will also be questions of priority. Multiple mortgages created in relation to the same piece of land will, all else being equal, rank according to the date at which they were created. All the mortgages if created in accordance with the proper formalities will however be perfectly valid. The same applies to leasehold estates. As can be seen in chapter 10, there is nothing to stop the simultaneous running of multiple leases. Can the same be said to be true of the freehold estate? Instinct tells us that there cannot be two 'equally good' owners. However, as noted earlier, the holder of the freehold estate is not considered to be an absolute owner in this sense. For this reason, two simultaneous freeholds is perfectly possible, although, by some method or another, it will (almost—see *Parshall v Bryans*,[11] key case box later, also discussed in chapter 5 in 5.4.3.2) always be possible to determine which of the freehold interests in the land is the 'better' right. This is because of the concept of relativity of title. The following discussion should be read in conjunction with chapter 6 concerning adverse possession which reveals one of the most important consequences of the possibility of multiple

---

[9] Gray and Gray, *Land Law* (4th ed) (Oxford, Oxford University Press, 2011), [4–110].
[10] The consequences of this principle are considered in *Fairweather v St Marylebone* [1963] AC 510 (HL).
[11] *Parshall v Bryans* [2013] EWCA Civ 240, [2013] Ch 568.

freeholds, and chapter 2 which discusses the nature of rights in land and relativity at 2.4. Indeed, since relativity of title is the logical underpinning of land law, understanding how it operates is essential to understanding land law in general. However, its most important consequences arise in relation to the freehold estate hence the short re-cap here.

Relativity of title is the principle whereby the question as to who is the *best* owner of land is never asked. Rather, the question becomes, of the two people in front of a court, which has a better title to land? Immediately a person goes into possession of land in a situation where they have not been given permission to do so by a person with a possessory title in that land (such as a freeholder or a leaseholder) they obtain at that moment their own possessory interest in land. Thus, a freehold title can be acquired through a formal transfer (as we see later) or by what is sometimes referred to as original acquisition in that a new title arises by virtue of possession.

There are a number of reasons why English law adopts this approach. The first is a problem of proof, of less significance now than historically. Where title is obtained *only* by demonstrating the relevant paper work, it becomes very important that the paper work is not lost. If title depends upon paper record, then without the records no transactions can take place in relation to the relevant land. Because of this, given how easy it is to lose pieces of paper over almost 1000 years of relevant English legal history, English land law has always given, in effect, a presumptive degree of control of land to the person in possession of land. If another person is able, by showing the relevant pieces of paper, to demonstrate that they have a *better* title that the person currently in possession, then that person will be evicted. This is explained neatly by Fox:

> 'In the common law, possession of property could be treated as evidence of a good title arising from some underlying proprietary interest, notwithstanding that there was almost certainly some other claimant who could assert an equivalent proprietary interest in the asset. To a large extent, presumptions of evidence determined a claimant's right of recovery rather than any conceptual theory of substantive proprietary interests'.[12]

There is therefore, partly for reasons of ease of proof, a presumption in favour of the *status quo*.

Another reason why this presumption exists is to prevent parties resorting to self-help to seize land from a person that they believe is not entitled to be in possession of that land. The fact that a person in possession has a title to that land, of some form or another, means that any person wishing to displace them will usually have to obtain an order for possession from a court. Finally, relativity of title reflects the fact that all land ownership in England is derivative on the title of the Crown to all land. This has very few practical consequences, and we consider these later, but it is an important foundational principle in English land law and of course was of much more significance in the development of feudal land-holding, and therefore in the birth of land law in the medieval period.

Finally, the relativity of title principle is essentially a conclusion from, as well as a cause of, the fact that English law has no vindicatory action by which an individual is able to prove that they are the absolute owner of land. Their title can only be asserted in a practical dispute, rather than in the abstract in this sense. Without the action to support some concept of absolute ownership

---

[12] Fox, 'Relativity of title at law and in equity' (2006) 65 Cambridge Law Journal 330, 335.

therefore, English law has developed a system which does not require one, reinforcing the fact that relativity of title is essential to the operation of English land law.

As mentioned earlier, however, the concept of relativity of freehold titles in relation to registered land is challenged by the guarantee of title which the register represents (see chapter 5). The consequence of this for freehold ownership is demonstrated by the decision of the Court of Appeal in *Parshall v Bryans*.[13]

> **Key case: *Parshall v Bryans* [2013] EWCA Civ 240**
>
> In this case, the land registry (see also chapter 5, 5.4.3.2) had, in error, registered two different proprietors as owning the same plot of land. The person entitled to be registered on the basis of the conveyancing history was not in possession of that land. Rather, the mistakenly registered person was in possession. The question for the court was whether these facts involved adverse possession (see chapter 6) or something else, and if something else, how was the position between the two parties to be resolved. In essence, it was a question as to how relativity of title should operate in relation to registered titles.
>
> This case is very important to this chapter, as it explains how registration has affected how we conceive of the nature of the freehold estate, and how the guarantee of title in section 58 interacts with what we have said here about relativity being the bedrock of the freehold.
>
> In deciding that there was no adverse possession in this case, Mummery LJ reasoned that: '[t]his is a case of equality of registered titles, rather than the normal case of relativity of titles'.[14] This suggests that in registered land, at least, there can be two equally valid freehold titles, at least until the register is rectified. As a result, the court held, there was no adverse possession and therefore the 'true' owner was able to recover their land despite the long held possession of the other.
>
> Commentators on this case have noticed both practical and theoretical problems arising from the outcome. Xu notes some consequences of this decision:
>
> > 'First, having no title is actually better than having a valid and legitimate title. If the owners of No.31 never had title and were only squatters, they would have acquired the disputed land before the commencement of the Land Registration Act 2002. The same would apply if they ignored requirements of compulsory registration and never bothered to register their title, because then the legal title would not pass to them and their possession would be, happily, "unlawful"... Their failing lies in remaining lawful all this time and abiding by the law of land registration'.[15]
>
> Kester Lees has also analysed this case and argues that there are six reasons why the court's approach in this case was wrong. First, the court asked the wrong question since they examined not whether the possession was adverse as against the paper title-holder, but merely whether it should be considered 'adverse' in general. For more on this, see chapter 6. Second, he highlights that registration as a freehold proprietor does not necessarily bring with it an immediate right to possession. Third, and most important for this chapter, he highlights that:

---

[13] *Parshall v Bryans* [2013] EWCA Civ 240, [2013] Ch 568.
[14] *Parshall v Bryans* [2013] EWCA Civ 240, [2013] Ch 568, [89].
[15] Xu, 'What do we protect in land registration?' (2013) 129 LQR 477, 479–80.

'whilst the two titles may enjoy an "equality" nonetheless they also have a relativity. The appellant's title was prior and clear from any defects. By contrast, the respondent's title was created later, in error, and subject to an inherent defect that it was always susceptible to rectification. The statutory magic cannot in reality make these titles equal. There may well be two separate and distinct titles, but they do not exist in isolation of each other. All the statutory magic can do is to result in both parties enjoying absolute freehold titles to the same parcel of land. There is no reason in principle or authority for this affecting the court's (necessary) ability to examine, as between themselves, who has the better right to immediate possession'.[16]

Fifth, Lees points to the consequences for guarantee of title, which we consider more in chapter 5. Finally, he highlights that the policy choices in the case are not all in one direction.[17]

Summary: Relativity of title

In unregistered land, relativity of title is used to determine the relationship between multiple freeholds. In registered land, whilst the principle of relativity of title is still crucially important when dealing with multiple 'off-register' possessors, as in the case of two squatters (see chapter 6), where title is registered, the Court of Appeal has suggested that such titles rank equally until the register is changed (see chapter 5).

9.4 THE TRANSFER AND REGISTRATION OF FREEHOLD INTERESTS IN LAND

This discussion in this part is intended to be recap only. It should be read in conjunction with chapter 4 concerning formalities, which examines the steps required in order to create a contract to transfer a freehold right in land, and then the steps by which a deed, the actual process of transferring, is created. Chapter 5 explains the registration requirements in relation to freehold interests, and the consequences of this. However, the important steps in relation to the transfer or creation (following division of an existing freehold) of a freehold interest in land are: first, a written contract which complies with section 2 Law of Property (Miscellaneous Provisions) Act 1989 is required. Next, a deed which complies with section 1 of the same Act will be needed. Finally, the transferee needs to be registered as freehold proprietor before the transfer will take effect at law (section 4 and 27 LRA 2002).

Unlike in relation to the creation of an easement or a lease, failure to carry out these steps as required does not give rise to an 'equitable freehold'. Indeed, there is no such thing as an equitable freehold. Rather, following the creation of a contract to transfer the right in land, which is then acted upon by the transferee on payment of the contract debt, a so-called vendor-purchaser trust is created so that the vendor will hold on trust for the buyer until the formalities are complete.

---

[16] Lees, 'Parshall v Hackney: a tale of two titles' [2013] Conv 222, 230.
[17] Lees, 'Parshall v Hackney: a tale of two titles' [2013] Conv 222, 228–31.

Prior to the payment of the contract debt, strictly speaking no trust arises, rather the contract itself will be an 'estate contract' which is itself a form of equitable property right arising under the doctrine of *Walsh v Lonsdale*.[18] This is explored in detail in chapter 14 at 14.2.1.

The registration requirements in relation to the freehold estate also have consequences for the type of title which the proprietor is treated as having. As discussed in chapter 5, there are three classes of title: absolute, qualified, and possessory. A registered proprietor will be registered as having one of these titles, although it is important to highlight that these are all valid freehold titles. For more information on the operation of these different classes of title, see 5.2.1.

9.5 FLYING FREEHOLD

The flying freehold is a rare occurrence. Essentially it involves the situation where one person is freehold proprietor of land which sits above land which is subject to the title of another person. For example, this could occur where a person's property reaches over the top of an alleyway with the alleyway belonging to another, or where a person's bedroom extends above the property below belonging to another. Generally speaking, flying freeholds are not now created deliberately because they caused problems in situations involving attempted maintenance of common parts. However, they may have arisen historically on the division of buildings, or, as is the case in *Lambeth LBC v Blackburn*,[19] in situations involving adverse possession. The leading case in modern law is *Abbahall Ltd v Smee*,[20] which attempts to provide a practical solution to some of the problems caused by these rights.

> **Key case:** *Abbahall Ltd v Smee* [2002] EWCA Civ 1831
>
> This is a case involving a flying freehold arising due to adverse possession. The flying freehold comprised the first and second floors of a building and the roof. The freeholder of these areas had not maintained the roof, and as a result, water was leaking into the ground floor flat, and the roof posed a danger to users of the ground floor. The question for the court was whether the freehold owner of the ground floor could obtain payment from the freeholder of the roof to compensate them for the works carried out.
>
> The court held that in cases such as these, in an attempt to act fairly and reasonably, the costs should be shared between the parties.
>
> Mumby J reasoned as follows:
>
> 'In a case such as this, where the roof serves equally to protect both the claimant's premises and the defendant's premises, common sense, common justice and reasonableness as between neighbours surely all suggest that those who are to take the benefit of the works ought also to shoulder the burden of paying for them. In principle, in a case such as this, it is, in my judgment, fair, just and reasonable to require that those who will share the benefit of the works should also share the burden of paying for them. To throw the entire burden either onto the claimant or onto the defendant would be unjust, unfair and unreasonable. It would also be unneighbourly.

---

[18] *Walsh v Lonsdale* (1882) 21 ChD 9.
[19] *Lambeth LBC v Blackburn* [2001] EWCA Civ 912, (2001) 33 HLR 74.
[20] *Abbahall Ltd v Smee* [2002] EWCA Civ 1831, [2003] 1 WLR 1472.

> In principle, therefore, the burden of meeting the cost of the necessary works in a case such as this... ought to be shared between those who will benefit from the works...
>
> On what basis ought the costs to be shared? It seems to me that, other things being equal, the costs should be shared equally'.[21]
>
> Given the relative paucity of case law on the topic of flying freeholds, the extensive quotation here is useful in giving guidance as to how the relationship between the various parties is managed at law.

9.6 COMMONHOLD

Since 2004, it has been possible to create what is referred to as freehold ownership of commonhold land. This is a result of the Commonhold and Leasehold Reform Act 2002. This type of ownership was designed to provide a new means of managing ownership of flats in blocks and the like. It was designed to reproduce some features of condominium ownership used in the United States for example. However, the rules have not really been utilised and very few commonhold interests have been created. The way that the commonhold works is for the owner of each individual unit to have what is effectively a freehold in that unit and also to become a member of a private company which then owns and manages the common parts.

Commonhold interests can only be created deliberately, and require there to be a commonhold association and a community statement which defines the units within the commonhold, and the rights and duties of the association members. If these are present, then a person can apply to be registered proprietor of a freehold interest of the individual unit and the community association will be registered as freehold proprietor of the common areas. The management of the relevant land will then run in accordance with the community statement.

> **Further analysis: Why has commonhold been unpopular?**
>
> As highlighted earlier, the operation of these rules is not covered in detail here precisely because so few people have decided to use the commonhold mechanism. According to Megarry and Wade, by 2011 there were only 17 registered commonholds.[22] This is somewhat strange because using the commonhold system is so much simpler than the normal freehold/leasehold approach to managing blocks of flats, for example, which entails a lot of administrative difficulty. Driscoll has examined why the commonhold has been unpopular, and explains that partly this is a result of 'bad press' and misconceptions about its operation. He explores these—which are largely to do with the level of control that a developer or potential freeholder of the common parts would have in a commonhold scenario—and concludes: '[t]he message is a simple one: what's to be lost by trying a modern new system which has been

---

[21] *Abbahall Ltd v Smee* [2002] EWCA Civ 1831, [2003] 1 WLR 1472, [38]-[41].
[22] Harpum et al, *Megarry and Wade: The Law of Real Property* (8th ed) (Sweet and Maxwell, London, 2012), [33.001].

specifically designed for the ownership and management of interdependent buildings such as blocks of flats'.[23] It is also important to recognise, as has been apparent in the press recently, that landlords seek on occasion to take advantage of the freehold/leasehold management structure of apartments to charge very high ground rents depriving the leasehold of much of its value. This 'abuse' (if one conceives of it in that way) of the freehold rights are part of the motivation for the on-going Law Commission investigation into reforms of commonhold to make them more popular and suitable for managing these issues going forward.

9.7 TERMINATION OF THE FREEHOLD ESTATE

We mentioned earlier that the freehold estate ought not to be considered ownership in any absolute sense. Primarily this is because of relativity of title, but it is also a consequence of the fact that all estates in land in English land law are conceptualised as being grants from the Crown. The practical consequence of this emerges in cases where land falls *bona vacantia* because either the freehold owner has died without leaving any heirs or has gone bankrupt, or because a company which owned the land has been dissolved, or gone insolvent and entered liquidation, and the land has been disclaimed by the liquidator. In these circumstances, the law ensures that land will never be without an owner. There will never be a vacuum. In cases where a company goes insolvent, or a person goes bankrupt, the trustee in such cases is able to 'disclaim', ie give up, property which is onerous (eg is subject to a mortgage). Any disclaimed freehold estate will also pass to the Crown. We consider these principles in more detail in this part.

The 'return' of title to the crown, so that no estates exist in the land, is called 'escheat'. Escheat to the Crown occurs when land is *bona vacantia* either due to a lack of heirs or due to disclaimer. Upon the dissolution of a company any leasehold and freehold interests of the company will vest in the Crown in the person of the Treasury Solicitor. It has never been determined authoritatively whether upon the property vesting in the Treasury Solicitor he becomes liable for it and under any covenants binding on the property, such as any landlord's repairing covenants or, where the onerous property is a lease, for the payment of rent. In *Toff v McDowell*[24] without the benefit of argument, it was assumed that the Crown was subject to the burden of the landlord's covenants in the lease. However, the general view taken (and adopted by the Treasury Solicitor) is that until some positive act of management is taken no liabilities arise. Given the uncertainty in this situation, the Crown may itself decide to disclaim the property.

Thus, there are three ways in which land can be disclaimed so as to render it *bona vacantia*. This could be:

(1) disclaimer by a Liquidator;

(2) disclaimer by a Trustee in Bankruptcy; or

(3) disclaimer by the Crown after the dissolution of a company as mentioned earlier.

---

[23] Driscoll, 'Whatever happened to commonhold?' (2008) 7333 NLJ 1137, 1139.
[24] *Toff v McDowell* (1993) 25 HLR 650.

The effect of a valid disclaimer by the Treasury Solicitor is that the onerous property is deemed never to have vested in the Crown under Companies Act 2006, s 1012. However, for freehold property, the disclaimer will trigger a 'boomerang effect' in that whilst the property has been disclaimed by the Crown in the person of the Treasury Solicitor, the property reverts back to the Crown in the person of the Crown Estate Commissioners. This is explained in *SCMLLA Properties Ltd v Gesso Properties (BVI) Ltd*.[25]

> **Key case:** *SCMLLA Properties Ltd v Gesso Properties (BVI) Ltd* [1995] BCC 793
>
> In *SCMLLA Properties Ltd v Gesso Properties (BVI) Ltd*, the Deputy Judge, considering a case of the disclaimer of freehold titles by a liquidator pursuant under section 178 Insolvency Act 1986, provided the following comprehensive exposition on the effect of a disclaimer of freehold property: 'Since disclaimer of a freehold ipso facto determines the company's interest in the land, this general proposition requires title on disclaimer to be immediately and automatically in the Crown...'.[26]
>
> The effect of disclaimer on a freehold interest therefore is:
>
> (1) to terminate as from the date of disclaimer the rights, interest and liabilities of the company in respect of the freehold;
>
> (2) the entire freehold interest determines as at the date of disclaimer;
>
> (3) upon termination there is a 'boomerang effect' as the freehold interest escheats to the Crown, now in the person of the Crown Estate Commissioners, as opposed to the Treasury Solicitors;
>
> (4) the escheat is automatic, pursuant to the underlying principle that there must never be a vacuum of ownership of land; and
>
> (5) finally, the freehold interest is deemed never to have vested in the Treasury Solicitor at all.

Upon the disclaimer the Crown will have no liability for the freehold property. The Treasury Solicitor is protected to the effect that the property is deemed never to have vested in him. The Crown Estate is protected in that, until such time as the Crown Estate takes possession or carries out acts of control over the property, it incurs no liability for it.

Further, it is important to appreciate that the Crown does not have the same freehold interest in the disclaimed property. The old freehold interest, formerly belonging to the now dissolved company, is determined. All the 'authorities indicate that the freehold determines on an escheat; indeed, it is the determination of the freehold which brings about the escheat'.[27] In *UBS Asset Management Ltd v Crown Estate Commissioners*[28] Roth J summarised the position:

> 'Escheat, in essence, is a form of reversion in that when there is no longer any tenant holding the land the fee simple estate returns to the lord by whom the tenure was originally created. And as all land is originally derived from the Crown and it is assumed that there is no intermediate lord between

---

[25] *Scmlla Properties Ltd v Gesso Properties (BVI) Ltd* [1995] BCC 793.
[26] *Scmlla Properties Ltd v Gesso Properties (BVI) Ltd* [1995] BCC 793, 804.
[27] *Scmlla Properties Ltd v Gesso Properties (BVI) Ltd* [1995] BCC 793, 800.
[28] *UBS Asset Management Ltd v Crown Estate Commissioners* [2011] EWHC 3368 (Ch).

the Crown and the freehold owner, the estate returns to the Crown upon the termination of the freehold. However, the Crown takes the land subject to subordinate interests, such as, for example, a subsisting lease'.[29]

It is also worth noting that a mortgage of the former freehold will survive and (at least until the relevant limitation period has expired) the mortgagee will have the power to sell the freehold pursuant to the mortgage; if such a sale takes place it is (perhaps curiously) the original freehold which is transferred.[30]

The Crown also acquires the power to grant a new freehold of the same property it may do so on any terms. The common practice of the Crown Estate is to grant such new freehold interests to those who can show an interest in the property; usually lessees or mortgagees.

Where land has escheated to the Crown, however, this raises the spectre of how the register should be altered. Unless the registered title is closed it will look to any people who examine the register like the freehold property continues in the original company's ownership, whereas the whole title will have determined and the property will vest in the Crown. In practice, however, the title is not closed. Instead, where a freehold estate has determined, the registrar may enter a note on the register, together with a note of any inferior affected title. If the registrar is uncertain as to the validity of any disclaimer, it is mandatory that the registrar also records this concern. Given such an entry subsists on the register, the registrar will not close the title until an application is made to him to do so and even then the registrar usually will only close the title after the Crown has granted a new freehold and this has been registered itself. Given the Crown Estate could become liable upon taking an act of possession or control, the Crown Estate Commissioner will rarely make any applications to the land registry until such time as a sale is negotiated, as discussed earlier. The first and last act of control will be the grant of a new freehold estate.

Once a sale has been negotiated, the Crown Estate Commissioners will make a grant of the new freehold estate, which will fall within section 4 LRA 2002 and, therefore, require compulsory registration. However, strictly speaking such a grant is not a 'transfer' as it is the creation of a new estate. The newly granted estate will be registered under a new title number and the title of the determined estate will be closed. The new registered title will be registered subject to any burdens which affected the former freehold estate.

9.8 CONCLUSION

In many respects it is very difficult to explain what a freehold is and what a freeholder can do. It is really a 'negative space' in that it is residual entitlement to use land as desired within the confines of the other property rights described in this book, those tort and other private law limitations on such action, and public land use regulations. However, there are certain peculiar features of the freehold, such as the possibility of flying freeholds and commonholds, which require examination and it is important also to understand the ways in which the freehold represents an 'ownership' interest in the colloquial sense or not. Much of what is said in this chapter about the

---

[29] *UBS Asset Management Ltd v Crown Estate Commissioners* [2011] EWHC 3368 (Ch), [8].
[30] *Scmlla Properties Ltd v Gesso Properties (BVI) Ltd* [1995] BCC 793.

freehold should be read alongside the other chapters in the first half of this book, for the management of the freehold estate is a question of formalities and registration, of adverse possession, and of examining the competing interests explained in this book. What is a freehold is a question without an easy answer.

PRINCIPLES

How does this discussion shape our understanding of the principles explained in chapter 1? To recap, these principles were:

1. Certainty
2. Sensitivity to context
3. Transactability
4. Systemic and individual effects
5. Recognition of the social role of the land law system.

As difficult as it is to get a hold on the nature of the freehold estate, this is as good a place as any to consider what this slippery nature means for the principles explored throughout the book. Oddly, whilst it is very difficult if not impossible to define the freehold estate, this is partly because remarkably few disputes arise on that subject. This is primarily because the statutory and common law hemming in of land use *in general* means that the question of what private law rights in land entitle one to do essentially becomes redundant in the face of questions arising from planning law, environmental law, and tort law. Furthermore, most of the questions about how far a freehold extends in terms of the powers given to the freehold owner arise because of a dispute not with another freehold owner, but with the holder of another right in land. In such cases, the dispute will usually centre of the content of the *competing* right, not of the freehold itself. In this lack of disputes there is an indication that for practical purposes the content of the freehold is certain enough, at least in land law terms.

On the other hand, the tacit assumption in much of this, ie that the freehold entitles one to do whatever one likes with one's land, unless that is prohibited, is one that can be questioned. This attitude to property rights in land is one with a long history. It was first explored in the seminal case of *Entick v Carrington* (see 17.2.2), a case more likely to be encountered in constitutional law than in a land law course, but which emphasises that unless the law *prohibits* something, you are free to do it. It also places great weight on the zone of control given to an individual by the fact of their having property rights in land. However, the assumption of liberty is not all one way. It also brings with it an assumption of liberty at the expense of others unless that is specifically prohibited. For those researching the law relating to housing, to the environment, and to access to space, for example, this assumption of dominium is far from welcome. For such writers, the argument is that property should and does entail social responsibility and as such the assumption, embodied in the 'negative space' characteristics of the freehold, is a dangerous one for society as a whole. The inability to define the freehold, therefore, may, perhaps contrary to one's expectations, not cause a lack of certainty, but perhaps does limit the degree to which land law is able to properly balance a range of competing policy objectives.

TABLE OF DEFINITIONS

Freehold estate	Estate in land of unlimited duration. Considered the 'highest' form of ownership in English law, save for that of the Crown.
Commonhold	The ownership structure which confers a freehold right over a unit in a larger structure, with membership of the management group of that structure.
Flying freehold	A freehold interest extending above the freehold interest of another.

FURTHER READING

The further reading here is concerned with analysis of statutory limitations of the freehold right in terms of the scope of that right, to give a sense of where Parliament has intervened to limit such rights and of what this means for how we think of what land is. Of course, this list could cover the entirety of planning law, much of environmental law, and tort law as explained in chapter 18, and should therefore be seen only as a sample, focused on the private law issues which emerge in relation to this wider question. It focuses particularly on the relationship between law and geography, that is, law as a constructor of space.

BLOMLEY N., *Law, Space and the Geographies of Power* (The Guilford Press, 1994).

HOLDER, J. and HARRISON, C., *Law and Geography* (OUP, 2003).

LAYARD, A., 2016, 'Public Space: Property, Lines, Interruptions'. Journal of Law, Property and Society, vol 2., pp. 1–47s.

10

LEASES

10.1	Introduction	290	10.6 Sub-Leases, Concurrent Leases, and	
10.2	The Nature of the Lease	291	Reversionary Interests	327
10.3	Creation of Leases	303	10.7 Conclusion	328
10.4	Forms of Leases	305	Principles	328
10.5	Relationship Between Landlord and		Table of Definitions	329
	Tenant and Bringing a Lease to an End	311	Further Reading	330

CHAPTER GOALS

By the end of this chapter, you should understand:

- The essential elements of a lease and how these interact and have been interpreted by the courts;
- How leases are created;
- The different types of leases and how they may arise;
- How the relationship between landlord and tenant is managed both during and after the contractual term of the lease; and
- How the law manages multiple leases.

10.1 INTRODUCTION

The leasehold estate is one of the two possible estates in land. The other, the freehold estate, was discussed in chapter 9. It is important to appreciate from the outset what a versatile concept the leasehold estate is. The purposes to which leases are put range from very short-term occupation agreements, to leases lasting hundreds of years. Some are a flexible way of conferring all the practical qualities of 'ownership' whilst, for example, allowing for a single freehold over an entire block of flats, simplifying the maintenance of common areas etc. Others range from from storage agreements to commercial occupation of landmark buildings in the City of London.

The lease, as a single legal concept, is required to achieve a lot of different purposes. Understanding this range is an important part in understanding how leases operate both in theory and in practice. And yet, despite the multiplicity of pressures and uses to which this single concept is put, it is remarkably successful. Indeed, the fundamental structure of how leases operate is largely without controversy.

There is however a much higher degree of controversy regarding what is known as security of tenure—the ability of a tenant to stay in occupation of property after the term which was contractually agreed has expired. Whilst this topic could be (and indeed, is) the subject of an entire textbook in itself, and as such it is not possible to cover all the issues in detail here, it is important nevertheless to have an awareness of these rules as they are essential to how leases work in practice. They provide the modulation to the fundamental concept of the lease which makes it easy to tailor to the specific context within which it is being used. Furthermore, there are also controversies which have arisen, both historically and today, in the mechanisms which owners of land sometimes use to *prevent* an occupant of that land from having a lease, so that they have only a licence, ie a personal right to use land.

This chapter will discuss these issues by first, in 10.2, considering the nature and essential requirements of the lease. Section 10.3 then looks at the formality requirements which must be met in order to create a lease (these are discussed in much greater detail in chapter 4, but it is useful to mention them again here for the purpose of reminder). Section 10.4 considers some different types of leases. Section 10.5 looks at the relationship between the leasehold and freehold, including consideration of the methods by which a lease is brought to an end and security of tenure. It also explores covenants in leases. Finally, 10.6 considers the issue of concurrent and sub-leases and the reversionary interest.

10.2 THE NATURE OF THE LEASE

The lease is, essentially, consensual exclusive possession of land for a limited duration. Without consent, the situation is one of adverse possession. Without the limitation on the duration, there is a freehold. It is important however to realise that not only can a range of occupation and use situations constitute the relevant exclusive possession here, but also that the limitation duration can range from the very short, to hundreds of years.

One issue which has been a problem over the years, although less so now for reasons which will be discussed later, is the tendency for parties to sometimes mislabel what rights they are creating when they create a right which looks a lot like a lease. Very often, for reasons of avoiding security of tenure—that is, the ability of the tenant to remain in possession of the relevant land beyond the contractually agreed date—the parties label their agreement as a licence (ie a personal right in land). The courts were, and to a slightly lesser extent, still are, very wary of this tactic. For that reason, the test as to whether a lease has been created is entirely objective. It depends not on what the parties wished or intended to achieve by their agreement, but what the terms of the contract as performed and intended to be performed actually gives rise to. This approach is essentially the approach which results in the *numerus clausus* discussed in chapter 2. It has also resulted in a clear 'test' for the presence of a lease. This was developed in the famous decision of

Lord Templeman in *Street v Mountford*.[1] In that case, his Lordship reasoned that, 'the traditional distinction between a tenancy and a licence of land [lies] in the grant of land for a term at a rent with exclusive possession'.[2] In other words, whenever these features are present—exclusive possession, term, and rent—the parties have necessarily created a lease (subject to a few very narrow exceptions), whatever they chose to call what they have done.

> **Key case:** *Street v Mountford* [1985] 1 AC 809
>
> In this leading case in relation to the law of leases, Mr Street granted Mrs Mountford the right to occupy two rooms. There were other conditions in the agreement which was labelled the licence agreement. It also contained a clause that stipulated that Mrs Mountford accepted that she was not protected by the Rent Act. However, it is not possible to contract out of the Rent Act, and so the question became whether this was a lease or a licence. If it was a licence, the Rent Act would not apply. If it was a lease, Mrs Mountford would have the benefit of both security of tenure and rent control. The issue turned on whether the parties' labelling the agreement as a licence agreement was determinative of whether or not they had created a licence. Lord Templeman, giving judgment of the Court, concluded that it did not mean this. Rather, the Court would judge objectively what the parties had created by looking at the reality of their agreement and the rights and obligations which it created. The many consequences of this judgment are discussed and analysed throughout this chapter.

What Lord Templeman does not say, however, is that all of these features are necessary for a lease, and indeed, over time, it has become clear that there is certainly no rent requirement. Rent can serve a useful function in establishing a lease, however, and so we return to this later. Let us examine each of these elements of the lease in turn.

10.2.1 EXCLUSIVE POSSESSION

By far the most important, and the most difficult, requirement in relation to leases is the requirement of exclusive possession. Without a grant of exclusive possession in the relevant land, there is no lease. It is very important to highlight here that what we are talking about is the *right to* exclusive possession (as opposed to the factual state of being in exclusive possession). The difference between these two ways of thinking about possession is discussed in detail in chapter 2 at 2.2.3. For now, it is important to be clear exactly what must be present in order for the possession to form the basis of the lease.

First, the possession must be with consent of another with a right to such possession. Usually this would be the freehold owner who automatically has a right to possession unless he has voluntarily limited that right or has lost his title entirely to adverse possession. However, in some circumstances it could also be a leaseholder, where a sub-lease is granted (see later at 10.6) or a mortgage lender where that lender has used their right to possession under a mortgage (see chapter 11, 11.4.3) and has in turn granted a lease to a tenant. If the 'tenant' obtains their

---

[1] *Street v Mountford* [1985] 1 AC 809.
[2] *Street v Mountford* [1985] 1 AC 809, 816.

right to occupy property from someone who does not themselves have an existing right to possession, they will not have a proprietary estate in land in the form of a lease. They may however have a strange legal construct referred to as a *Bruton*[3] tenancy. This is discussed in more detail later. Second, the consequence of the test for the presence of a lease being the existence of a *right to* exclusive possession vis-à-vis the grantor, rather than the fact of having gone into exclusive possession, means that a lease can arise even in cases where the 'tenant' never in fact goes into physical possession of the property but, for example, immediately sublets. Finally, in looking to see whether the grant in question confers a right to exclusive possession onto the purported tenant, the courts look primarily to what is agreed in the contract. They do this, however, in a common sense and open-minded way. If, as will be seen, the contract is full of terms which are never intended to be realistic, then the courts will side-line those terms in their search for what the 'truth' of the matter is.

With those points in mind, let us consider what exclusive possession actually means in this context. To a certain extent, we can draw some parallels with the possession requirement of adverse possession which we explored in chapter 6 at 6.2.1. There, the focus is on the ability to exclude the world as large as far as is reasonable, and the concomitant intention so to do. In relation to leases, the underlying concept is the same, but the way it looks on the ground, as a result of the consensual nature of the possession, may be somewhat different. However, at all times the courts are looking for a physical presence on the land, or a controlling influence in relation to that land, which means that it is the tenant, and not the landlord, who has to the right to control and does in fact control access to the land. In relation to residential occupiers, the distinction is sometimes said to lie between the tenant, who does have exclusive possession, and the lodger, who does not. This expression of the distinction is perhaps less helpful now where fewer people will be familiar with the practice of taking in a lodger. It is also not particularly helpful in a commercial context. Beyond this general guidance, we must look to the case law in order to demonstrate what constitutes exclusive possession in the leasehold context, with always the caveat in mind that the nature of the land will in part determine what constitutes exclusive possession of that land.

First, it is helpful when thinking about exclusive possession to remember that exclusive possession (or simply, possession) is not the same as exclusive occupation. Just as a person in exclusive occupation of land may not be in possession of that land, so too a person who shares his occupation may be in exclusive possession. Whilst the two concepts share certain 'on the ground' features, especially in relation to residential properties, and it can therefore be easy to confuse the two or use the term occupation where what is meant is possession, it is critical to distinguish clearly between the two. They have very different consequences in legal terms. We can demonstrate this with an example.

Kareem and Sophie occupy a flat together. Kareem signed an agreement with their 'landlord', William. Sophie only began to occupy the flat much later and never herself reached an agreement with the landlord. William had not entered the property since Kareem moved in two years ago, and the contract only allows the landlord the right to access the property without permission in an emergency. In this situation, where there is nothing to suggest that the terms of the contract

---

[3] *Bruton v London & Quadrant Housing Trust* [2001] 1 AC 406 (HL).

are not to be taken seriously, it is very clear that the landlord is no longer in possession of the land. He has voluntarily given that right away.

What, however, is the situation as between Kareem and Sophie? At first glance, since both parties live in the flat, it is perhaps tempting to consider that they both have exclusive possession of the land. This would be a misinterpretation of the facts. Rather, Kareem has exclusive possession and Sophie is merely a licencee with a right to occupy thanks to Kareem's consent that she do so. The fact that Kareem lets Sophie stay means that he no longer has exclusive occupation of the flat. However, it does not mean that he is no longer in exclusive possession. In fact, his letting Sophie occupy is actually an exercise of his right to possession. The reason why this is the correct legal conclusion is discussed in detail in the 'shared accommodation' section later, but it is useful as an example to show the critical importance of distinguishing between occupation and possession when attempting to determine the nature of a 'residential' relationship.

It can also be useful, rather than referring always to the fundamental question as to whether the 'tenant' has exclusive possession in the sense of a right of control of access, to reason by analogy to existing case law. If taking this approach, there are a number of different factors which appear to be important to the question of exclusive possession.

10.2.1.1 Provision of services

In some cases, the 'landlord' will agree to provide services to the 'tenant', such as cleaning or the provision of food in the case of a boarding house. In situations like this the courts are very unlikely to conclude that the tenant has exclusive possession. Usually no lease will arise. This applies both in residential and commercial situations. A good example of a commercial situation where there will be no exclusive possession is the position regarding 'stalls' in the common hallway areas of shopping centres. In a residential situation, the classic situation where the 'tenant' will not be in exclusive possession is a hotel room. Quite obviously the owner of the hotel will have the ability not only to enter the room at will, but also to remove the occupant of the room should they wish, as well as asking them to swap rooms for example. It is really in this kind of situation that the language of Lord Templeman in *Street v Mountford*[4] regarding 'lodgers' is at its most helpful.

The difficulty comes, of course, when the situation is on the borderline. There are a few prominent cases where the landlord does provide some services to the tenant, and yet it is concluded there is still a lease because of the nature of these services. A good example of this is the situation where a tenant takes a lease of commercial premises but the landlord operates a reception service (perhaps for other tenants as well). In this sort of situation, whilst services are provided, and the tenant would not be considered to have exclusive possession of the reception area, there would nevertheless be no barrier to the tenant having exclusive possession of the premises which they alone occupy.

10.2.1.2 The keeping of keys

The fact that a landlord may keep a set of keys is not, in itself, particularly significant. Even in very long leases it is usually just good common sense for a landlord to keep a copy of keys in case of emergency or if the tenant were to lose their own keys. More significant is the situation where the

---

[4] *Street v Mountford* [1985] 1 AC 809.

landlord keeps a set of keys in order to allow them to have access to the property without the consent of the tenant. In this situation, it cannot be truly said that the tenant has control over access to the property, since they are unable to keep their landlord out. We can explore the significance of keys by looking at the decision in *Aslan v Murphy*.[5]

> **Key case: *Aslan v Murphy* [1990] 1 WLR 766**
>
> In this case, the agreement between the landlord and tenant provided not only that the landlord would keep the keys to the room, but also that the tenant was required to vacate the room for 90 minutes each day. In discussing whether the court would take these factors into account, the court engaged with the distinction between shams and pretences (discussed later), but also considered the nature of the arrangement as a whole to assess whether it was realistic. Specifically, Lord Donaldson, discussing the relevance of the landlord's keeping the keys, first emphasised that keeping keys is not determinative in itself. There is no 'magic' in it. He then stated that:
>
> > 'What matters is what underlies the provisions as to keys... A landlord may well need a key in order that he may be able to enter quickly in the event of emergency: fire, burst pipes or whatever. He may need a key to enable him or those authorised by him to read meters or to do repairs which are his responsibility. None of these underlying reasons would of themselves indicate that the true bargain between the parties was such that the occupier was in law a lodger. On the other hand, if the true bargain is that the owner will provide genuine services which can only be provided by having keys, such as frequent cleaning, daily bed-making, the provision of clean linen at regular intervals and the like, there are materials from which it is possible to infer that the occupier is a lodger rather than a tenant.'[6]

10.2.1.3 Shared Accommodation

The most difficult situations regarding whether or not a tenant has exclusive possession arise when talking about multiple occupation situations. These are difficult because not only is it necessary to work out what the respective entitlements are as between landlord and tenant, but also between the various tenants, to ascertain whether one, all, or none of the occupiers has exclusive possession of the property. These issues are explored in the box through consideration of case *AG Securities v Vaughan and Antoniades v Villiers*.[7]

> **Key case: *AG Securities v Vaughan and Antoniades v Villiers* [1990] 1 WLR 766**
>
> These two cases were addressed simultaneously by the House of Lords. They both involved situations involving multiple occupiers, albeit that the fact patterns are very different into the two cases. In the first, *AG Securities*, the landlord had granted four different people the right to occupy a particular property. Each of them had signed the leases on different dates. The amounts owed in rent were different although each occupant was entitled to occupy for a six-month term. In the second case the landlord had given a man and his girlfriend a right to occupy a one-bedroomed flat. They had signed separate but identical

---

[5] *Aslan v Murphy* [1990] 1 WLR 766 (CA).
[6] *Aslan v Murphy* [1990] 1 WLR 766, 773.
[7] *AG Securities v Vaughan and Antoniades v Villiers* [1990] 1 AC 417 (HL).

agreements on the same day. The agreements referred to the arrangement as licences, and the landlord purported to reserve to himself the right to introduce another licensee at any time at his discretion. The House of Lords gave general guidance as to how to resolve such situations. First, they highlighted that in order for there to be a single lease over the entirety of a property, the tenants must be able to hold such a lease as joint tenants. This requires the four unities to be present since it is not possible to hold legal title to an estate in land as tenants in common. The details of these rules are discussed in chapter 16 at 16.3, but to summarise, the four unities are: possession, interest, title and time. For both of these cases, this requirement posed a problem. In particular, title and time were in issue. This is because unity of title requires the interest to have been derived from the same document. Time requires that the interests be granted simultaneously. However, in these cases there were separate documents.

The court concluded, however, that in the second case, separating the documents had in itself been a pretence to allow the landlord to evade the protections granted to the tenant by the Rent Act (essentially, security of tenure and protection against rent increases). In the first case, the separation of the agreements was genuine however. This prevented a joint lease of the whole.

Thus, when attempting to establish whether there is a lease of a whole, the first step is to establish whether, in cases of separate documents, the separation of the documents was a pretence or a genuine reflection of the type of occupation being offered in each case. Second, the court highlighted that in relation to joint occupation, where the property is unsuitable for additional occupiers, as was the case in *Antoniades v Villiers*,[8] any term which purported to allow the landlord to bring in an additional occupier would be ignored. As Lord Oliver stated:

'These clauses cannot be considered as seriously intended to have any practical operation or to serve any purpose apart from the purely technical one of seeking to avoid the ordinary legal consequences attendant upon letting the appellants into possession at a monthly rent. The unreality is enhanced by the reservation of the right of eviction without court order, which cannot seriously have been thought to be effective, and by the accompanying agreement not to get married, which can only have been designed to prevent a situation arising in which it would be quite impossible to argue that the "licensees" were enjoying separate rights of occupation. The conclusion seems to me irresistible that these two so-called licences, executed contemporaneously and entered into in the circumstances already outlined, have to be read together as constituting in reality one single transaction under which the appellants became joint occupiers.'[9]

As one might imagine, the issue of shared accommodation comes most prominently to the fore in two situations. The first, that of a cohabiting couple, is generally straightforward to resolve. If the couple enter into the lease agreement together, and there is nothing else to suggest that they have a licence, then they will most likely be joint tenants of the lease. The second, that of multiple individuals in a flat-share scenario is less clear. There are four options in such cases. One of these individuals may be the tenant of the whole, and the other occupants licensees. This outcome will be the most likely if there is effectively a 'chief' occupier who is the only person to have negotiated and dealt directly with the landlord. A second option is that each person is a tenant of their individual room. This would be the case in some student accommodation where there might be a shared kitchen within a 'staircase' or 'corridor' but where each student has control of access over

---

[8] *AG Securities v Vaughan and Antoniades v Villiers* [1990] 1 AC 417.
[9] *AG Securities v Vaughan and Antoniades v Villiers* [1990] 1 AC 417, 468.

their own room, including as against the landlord within reason. The third is that the occupants together all have a tenancy of the whole thing. This would probably be the case if a group entered into negotiations together with a landlord, were all responsible directly for paying the rent, but where none could realistically expect to 'keep the others out' of their room (except as the conventions of privacy and politeness dictate). A student house with a small number of rooms is likely to fall into this category. Finally, it may be the case that none of them have a tenancy, and that all are simply licensees. This is usually the case in University-provided student halls, where a number of services such as cleaning, maintenance, etc, are provided by the University to the students. Whether this is the case will be determined, again, by considering questions of exclusivity of possession in relation to those spaces.

10.2.1.4 Pretences

Finally, when considering whether an individual or group have exclusive possession, it is essential to be aware of the possibility that the terms of a contract are a pretence. This is where a term is put into a contract to make it appear that the agreement reached between the parties is something other than what is really going to take place, or which gives a different 'flavour' to the agreement. Such terms are never really intended to be relied upon and are, in this sense, not genuine. An example of this is to be found in *Aslan v Murphy*[10] discussed immediately earlier. There has been some difficulty in the past created by the inconsistent use of the word 'sham' in this context. A sham, strictly speaking, is a situation where a document is created or an act is done merely with the aim of tricking a third party (potentially including a court) into believing that an agreement or term exists when it does not. The key to the definition of shams is that both parties understand and intend for the clause to be included merely to achieve this outcome.[11] However, very often the sorts of clauses introduced into tenancy agreements do not generally have this purpose, or at least, the tenant does not also intend that they have this purpose. They are not trying to trick third parties as such, rather they often represent a disingenuous attempt to disguise the nature of the agreement on behalf of the landlord, with the tenant unable to utilise their bargaining power to exclude the term (or being ambivalent as to its inclusion thinking it is not a genuine representation of what will happen in practice). That the language of and rules relating to shams are perhaps not the most appropriate way of explaining the outcomes in many lease/licence distinction cases is confirmed in *AG Securities v Vaughan and Antoniades v Villiers*.[12] However, some situations are still considered under the general banner of 'shams', particularly cases where a residential premises is let to a company formed by the occupying tenant in order that the tenant not have security of tenure (since a company cannot have the benefit of security of tenure for residential premises). The operation of these rules is considered in detail in *Hilton v Plustitle*[13] and *Kaye v Massbetter*.[14]

---

[10] *Aslan v Murphy* [1990] 1 WLR 766.
[11] A very clear explanation of the test for 'shams' is found in *Mikeover v Brady* [1989] 3 All ER 618 (CA).
[12] *AG Securities v Vaughan and Antoniades v Villiers* [1990] 1 AC 417.
[13] *Hilton v Plustitle* [1989] 1 WLR 149 (CA).
[14] *Kaye v Massbetter* (1992) 24 HLR 28 (CA).

Further analysis: The role of intention

One question which emerges from this review of the case law, and which is important in general in getting to grips with the subtle interactions between objective and certain standards in land law, and the need and desire of the legal system to give effect to the expressed intentions of parties to a transaction, is the role of intention. As Hill has considered, in many areas of law, the parties' intention in terms of what they have created is the primary driver in terms of how their agreement will be interpreted and given effect. In some areas, as in relation to implied trusts, intention is, essentially, the very foundation of the rights-creation process, even where the appropriate formalities are not followed. Why then in relation to leases have the courts decided that an intention-focused, subjective approach is inappropriate?

Some insight can be gained from the context within which the leading decision, *Street*,[15] was made. This decision was made at a date when the rent and tenure controls in relation to leases were very generous to residential occupiers thanks to the Rent Act 1977. This legislation gave landlords, usually both more sophisticated in terms of their access to legal advice and experience, and with a greater power in terms of the negotiation process, especially in relation to low value housing, a very big incentive to grant occupiers licences rather than leases. This is because licences were not protected. The courts have however been traditionally unwilling to explicitly recognise that the decision to focus on objective tests rather than subjective intention in this context is based on a policy-based conclusion about inequality.

Thus, as Hill argues:

> 'the most honest approach to the lease/licence distinction would be for the courts to recognise more explicitly the basis of their intervention. Unless external factors suggest that the parties' expressed wishes should be overridden, there is no reason why an agreement which confers exclusive possession for a term at a rent should not take effect as a licence if that is what the parties intend to create. Where a transaction is freely entered into on the basis of commercial considerations there is no justification for the law's disregard of the parties' intentions. However, where there is inequality between the parties—as is the case in the private sector of the housing market—the law is entitled to look behind the form of the agreement'.[16]

Bright too sees the policy behind the decision in *Street*[17] and the follow-up case of *Antoniades v Villiers*[18] as being primarily based on the inequality of bargaining power which exists in such cases:

> 'Freedom of contract has not, however, always been paramount and is a particularly inappropriate model when dealing with the consumer as a contracting party. The whole focus of the housing legislation is to provide protection based on status as a residential occupier and not to allow market-place forces to dominate'.[19]

This perhaps explains why there remains the slightly uncomfortable interaction between the wholly objective test used to establish the occupation rights of a individual, the somewhat less rigidly objective approach used by the courts when they asses the same questions in a commercial context, and the underlying additional requirement that the parties must have intended to create a legal relationship at

---

[15] *Street v Mountford* [1985] 1 AC 809.
[16] J Hill, 'Intention and the creation of proprietary rights: are leases different?' (1996) 16 Legal Studies 200, 217.
[17] *Street v Mountford* [1985] 1 AC 809.
[18] *AG Securities v Vaughan and Antoniades v Villiers* [1990] 1 AC 417.
[19] S Bright, 'Beyond sham and into pretence' (1991) 11 Oxford Journal of Legal Studies 136, 141.

all. Thus, the objective approach, which *Street v Mountford*,[20] represents is really about ensuring that landlords do not evade security of tenure provisions by falsely portraying their relationship as not involving a lease.

One may wonder, however, whether, especially in the commercial context, there is some value in allowing parties to define the nature of their relationship by intentionally explaining that the relationship is not a lease. Indeed, as Bright and Hill both highlight,[21] it is perfectly possible for parties to prevent an agreement giving rise to proprietary consequences in relation to easements, for example, as is exemplified by *IDC v Clark*.[22] Furthermore, the importance of preventing parties from escaping from their obligations through falsely construing their arrangement as a licence is much diminished since 1996 and the rules in the Housing Act 1996 relating to Assured Shorthold Tenancies.

Summary: Exclusive possession

Exclusivity of possession is characterised by the right to control access to the property. In considering whether a purported tenant has exclusive possession or not it is useful to consider: the provision of services; the reasons for any retention of keys; the relationship between and with other occupiers of the property; and the objective reality of an agreement as it genuinely operates as between the parties.

10.2.2 TERM

The requirement for a limited duration for a lease is very often expressed as meaning that there must be certainty of term. Whilst in many ways that is true, the label 'term certain' can be somewhat misleading. What is required is that both parties must be able to know, either because the contract provides as such, or there is some rule of law in place which determines, the maximum possible duration of the arrangement should one of them wish to get out of it. To put this another way, each party to the lease must be able to tell what the maximum amount of time that they are 'tied into' the agreement (at least as a matter of contract). This can be demonstrated by the decision in *Lace v Chantler*,[23] where a lease for the duration of the Second World War was held to be void for uncertainty of term. However, the leading case law expression of this rule is to be found in *Prudential Assurance v London Residuary Body*.[24]

Key case: *Prudential Assurance v London Residuary Body* [1992] 2 AC 386

In this case, the House of Lords declined to modify or adjust the certainty of term rule to reflect the potential commercial inconvenience this rule cased. In this case, the contract stated that the lease would last until the public authority required the land in question for the purposes of widening a road.

---

[20] *Street v Mountford* [1985] 1 AC 809.
[21] J Hill, 'Intention and the creation of proprietary rights: are leases different?' (1996) 16 Legal Studies 200 and S Bright, 'Beyond sham and into pretence' (1991) 11 Oxford Journal of Legal Studies 136.
[22] *IDC Group Ltd v Clark* (1993) 65 P & CR 179 (CA).
[23] *Lace v Chantler* [1944] KB 368 (CA).
[24] *Prudential Assurance v London Residuary Body* [1992] 2 AC 386 (HL).

> It was not clear that this land would ever be required for this purpose. There were therefore two difficulties with the lease as contracted for. First, there was no maximum duration on the term of the lease. Second, it was not certain that there would ever be a termination point for this lease so the lease was also potentially indefinite. These are two separate problems, and this case therefore gave the court the opportunity to decide whether both of these problems are fatal to a contractual lease, or whether only the second would be. This is particularly important since there is no doubt whatever that a lease cannot be indefinite: an indefinite lease is a freehold, but that does not mean that the term has to be certain, at least in logical terms.
>
> On this point, the court decided that the requirement of knowledge of the maximum duration on the lease was necessary for a valid contractual lease. Lord Templeman stated: 'an uncertain term which takes the form of a yearly tenancy which cannot be determined by the landlord does not create a lease'.[25] In reaching this decision, the Court relies on a combination of the principle in *Lace v Chantler*[26] (and the cases which preceded it) and the wording of the Law of Property Act 1925. In doing so, however, the Court did not explicitly or consistently distinguish between the two different problems present in this case. Notwithstanding this, however, the case now stands as authority for both the principle that the maximum duration of a lease must be known, and for the principle that the lease must be of determinate duration.

Saying that there must be a maximum duration, however, is not the same thing as saying that the parties must know how long their arrangements will last. This means that the parties do not need to be aware of the *minimum* duration of their agreement. Let us demonstrate this with some examples.

Vinh owns a number of freehold properties in Lincoln. He decides that he wants to 'rent them out' to make some money. He agrees with Sabrina that she can occupy the property until he requires it for a development which he has planned, or for three years, whichever is sooner. He agrees with Johanna that she can occupy on a rolling contract for one month at a time. Finally, he agrees with Wupya that she can occupy until she gets married.

In none of these situations does Vinh know how long each of these occupiers will stay in his property. However, as a result either of statutory rules or of the way the contract is expressed, he knows the *maximum* amount of time that he will have to allow each of these occupiers to stay if he decides to evict them, subject to any tenure protection that may have from statute. In the first case, the longest that Sabrina can stay is three years. In the second, if Vinh wishes to evict Johanna, the longest she can stay is one month after he reaches this decision. Similarly, if Johanna decides she wants to leave, the maximum amount of time she has to continue paying rent is one month. Finally, there is a statutory rule (section 149(6) Law of Property Act 1925) which tells us that any lease which expresses itself to be a lease until marriage is turned into a lease for 90 years or marriage, whichever is sooner. Again, the maximum duration of the lease is therefore 90 years.

These scenarios show that the term certain requirement does not mean certain knowledge about the length of the lease therefore. Furthermore, recent judicial developments mean that the operation of this rule is substantially modified in respect of leases granted to individuals. Most significant in this is the Supreme Court decision in *Berrisford v Mexfield*.[27]

---

[25] *Prudential Assurance v London Residuary Body* [1992] 2 AC 386 (HL), 395.
[26] *Lace v Chantler* [1944] KB 368 (CA).
[27] *Berrisford v Mexfield Housing Co-operative Ltd* [2011] UKSC 52, [2012] 1 AC 955.

> **Key case: *Berrisford v Mexfield* [2011] UKSC 52**
>
> The tenant in this case occupied property as part of a mutual housing scheme. As part of the scheme, the tenant, Ms Berrisford, was required to be a member of the mutual housing association. If she ceased to be a member, then the housing association, Mexfield, could bring her occupation to an end. They could also do so if Ms Berrisford was in arrears of rent for a certain period of time. Alternatively, Ms Berrisford herself could bring her occupation to an end by serving one month's notice. There were no other provisions as to the length of the term. The first problem which the court was required to address was whether there could be a periodic tenancy in this case, as this is the usual solution to leases where there is no term. The court held that this was not possible because of the fetters on Mexfield's ability to bring the lease to an end. Since both parties were not able freely to serve notice on the monthly periodic tenancy, it was not possible to imply such a tenancy in this case. Secondly, then, the court assessed whether there was any alternative solution in the case so as to allow the lease to comply with the requirements outlined in *Prudential Assurance v London Residuary Body*[28] whilst also remaining in-keeping with the terms of the agreed lease. The court held that such a solution could be found, first, in the common law rule that an uncertain lease granted to an individual would be treated as a lease for life, and section 149(6) LPA 1925 which converted leases for life into leases of 90 year duration determinable.

The '*Berrisford* workaround' will not however solve all problems of uncertainty of term. First, it will not solve the problem for companies. Because the process by which the lease is rendered certain involves the common law rule of a lease for life, the rule cannot apply to companies since companies are, obviously, not alive. Secondly, it is arguable whether the *Berrisford* workaround can apply where the contractual term is not only uncertain in terms of length, but is also uncertain more generally. Let us examine this with an example.

Peter and Jasmine enter into a contract whereby Peter will take a lease of Jasmine's farm. They agree that Peter will be lessee until 'growing conditions improve'. In this situation, it is highly unlikely that a court would conclude that the rule in *Berrisford* can render this uncertain lease certain. This is because even when turned into a 90-year lease determinable on 'growing conditions improving', it is still totally uncertain as to when growing conditions improve. Whilst the lease would still be determinable upon Peter's death, the uncertainty as to whether growing conditions had 'improved' or not, would be so uncertain as to be unworkable.

The need for provision of this sort is not unique to leases, nor indeed to land law. A term in a contract which is hopelessly vague will either be void in itself, or where the term is essential to the contract, will render the contract void.

The rule regarding the need for a certain term has the potential to be commercially inconvenient. The fact that it is a long-standing rule helps to solve this to a certain degree—those who receive legal advice on the drafting of their lease agreement will simply work around the issue by the use of break clauses, or simply use a long stop maximum date to provide the required certainty. However, in some cases those drafting a lease will either be unaware of the rule, or will fail to properly comply with it. What happens then? Certainly we know that the lease as contracted for is void, but that does not necessarily mean that there is no lease. This is because, likely unaware of

---

[28] *Prudential Assurance v London Residuary Body* [1992] 2 AC 386 (HL).

the flaw in their contractual arrangements, the purported tenant will go into exclusive possession of the property and will pay rent. In these circumstances, the court may imply a periodic tenancy. These are considered later at 10.4.1.

> **Summary: Leases**
>
> For leases granted to companies, the maximum duration of the contractual lease must be known from the outset. For leases granted to individuals, if the maximum contractual term is not known from the outset, the law will transform the lease into a 90-year lease, determinable upon death or upon the conditions as specified in the contract.

10.2.3 RENT

As stated earlier, rent is not strictly required for there to be a valid lease. This is made clear in section 205(1)(xxvii) Law of Property Act 1925, and was confirmed in the decision in *Ashburn Anstalt v Arnold*.[29] Apart from anything else, it is very common for leases to be granted in return for what is known as a premium or a fine, which is essentially a lump sum at the commencement of the lease. This kind of lease is perfectly valid and there is no need for a rental payment in such cases. What about leases where no money is paid at all? It is clear that this in itself will not necessarily be a barrier to the creation of a valid lease. However, the absence of rent (or payment in some other form) may cause the court to pause and consider what the parties' intentions were in any particular case.

This is because, like all contractual arrangements, in order to create a valid lease, there is a requirement that there must be an intention to create a legal relationship. Where there is no such intention, there can be no lease. We discuss this requirement next. Rent is also useful in cases where the parties allege that their relationship is a periodic tenancy. As explained earlier, in the absence of an express contractual term as to the length of a period, where the courts imply a periodic tenancy they will do so on the basis of the frequency with which rent is due.

> **Summary: Rent**
>
> Rent is not necessary for the creation of a valid lease, but it can be useful in demonstrating intention to create a legal relationship and in calculating the duration of a periodic tenancy.

10.2.4 INTENTION TO CREATE A LEGAL RELATIONSHIP

In the box in the previous section, we discussed the role of intention in the creation of the leasehold relationship. It was clear there that unlike in many areas of property law, intention is almost irrelevant in terms of the creation of leases. In particular, there is no requirement that the parties

---

[29] *Ashburn Anstalt v Arnold* [1989] Ch. 1 (CA).

intend to create a lease in order to create a lease. However, the parties need to intend to create *something* in terms of their legal relationship. To show how important rent is to the establishment of this requirement, we can consider an example.

Diana allows her sister Vera to come and stay in her spare room. When Vera moves in, Diana tells her not to worry about privacy and that she has the only key to the spare room and she can do what she likes with it. Diana assures Vera that she, Diana, will only go into the spare room in an emergency. She tells Vera that she can stay for six months and then they will revisit the situation. Vera pays no rent to Diana.

In this case, we do seem to have an agreement which is conferring upon Vera some form of exclusivity of possession. However, it does not seem realistic to think that either party sees this arrangement as legally binding. Diana does not expect to be able to sue Vera for breach of contract should Vera leave early, nor vice versa should Diana go into Vera's room to clean and tidy. The nature of the relationship between the parties mean that there is no intention to create legal relations. Our attitude to this arrangement may well be different, however, if Vera made Diana a lump sum up front, or a monthly payment, to reflect her accommodation. In such a case, we might well think that both parties intended to be bound by their agreement given that money has changed hands. The seriousness of the arrangement is increased by the presence of rent or a premium. Thus, whilst rent is not necessary, it is a useful way to demonstrate an intention to create a legal relationship where otherwise we might think that intention is lacking, in arrangements between close family members, for example.

10.3 CREATION OF LEASES

This section should be read in conjunction with chapter 4 on formality requirements and chapter 5 on land registration. The details of when certain formalities are needed, and the rules as to precisely what is required, in order to create a valid lease, are contained in those sections. The following should therefore be considered as merely an outline of the very most basic requirements. As a reminder: leases of 3 years' or less duration, to go into possession immediately, for best rent, do not require any written formalities for their creation; leases of more than 3 years but 7 years or less in duration require a written contract (section 2 Law of Property (Miscellaneous Provisions) Act 1989) and a deed (section 52 Law of Property Act 1925); leases of more than 7 years' duration require a written contract and a deed, but also that they be registered to operate at law. For leases of more than 3 years' duration, if there is a written contract which complies with section 2, there will be an equitable lease if no other formalities are created. There are some further exceptions and modifications to these general principles which, again, are discussed in detail in chapter 4.

Thus, in order to create a valid lease, the formalities which are required will depend upon the length of the lease which the parties are attempting to create and the type of lease to which they wish to give rise, as well as the nature of the rights which they currently have. There are three possible ways in which a lease may be created or transferred. First, a transaction may give rise to or result in the transfer of a legal lease. Second, a transaction may give rise to or result in the transfer of an equitable lease. Third, a transaction may result in the creation of or transfer of an interest under a trust of a lease. Whilst both the second and third options will result in what we may term, broadly, equitable leases, they are two different things and it is important to keep this in mind, not least because in the third situation the presence of the trust will mean that there is a legal leaseholder who falls under trust duties, whereas that will not be the case in option two. In many ways it is simplest to express this visually (see Figure 10.1).

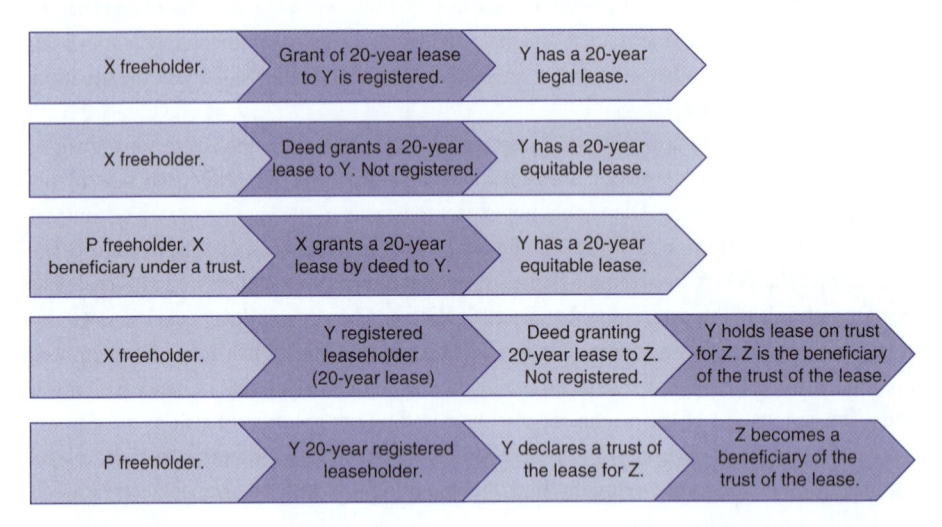

X freeholder.	Grant of 20-year lease to Y is registered.	Y has a 20-year legal lease.
X freeholder.	Deed grants a 20-year lease to Y. Not registered.	Y has a 20-year equitable lease.
P freeholder. X beneficiary under a trust.	X grants a 20-year lease by deed to Y.	Y has a 20-year equitable lease.
X freeholder.	Y registered leaseholder (20-year lease)	Deed granting 20-year lease to Z. Not registered.	Y holds lease on trust for Z. Z is the beneficiary of the trust of the lease.
P freeholder.	Y 20-year registered leaseholder.	Y declares a trust of the lease for Z.	Z becomes a beneficiary of the trust of the lease.

Figure 10.1 Equitable leases and trusts of leases

In terms of the relationship between landlord and tenant, it matters little whether the lease which is created is a legal or an equitable lease (except for the transmission of covenants in some cases as we explain at 10.5.1), although if the lease is held on trust, this will have significant impacts for the relationship between beneficiary and trustee (which will not be landlord and tenant). Let us consider these two issues in turn, for it is only in relation to the leasehold estate that such a wide variety of options is possible, thanks to its being itself an estate in land, and being derivative on the freehold estate.

First, then, what are the consequences for the tenant of having an equitable rather than a legal lease? The main consequence is that, as we shall see in the priorities chapter, chapter 15, if the freeholder sells their freehold estate, an equitable leaseholder will be vulnerable to the purchaser of that estate since their lease will not be registered. Depending upon why the lease is equitable, it may be possible to protect the equitable lease in terms of priority by entering a notice on the register. In cases where this is not possible (for example, where there is a trust of a lease), the tenant may protect their priority if they are in discoverable actual occupation at the time of the transfer (see chapter 15, 15.3.3—these rules were also explained in summary form in chapter 3 at 3.3.2). However, there is also a further consequence arising from the fact that certain equitable interests can be overreached. Overreaching as a mechanism is discussed in detail in in chapter 15 at 15.6.4 and chapter 16 at 16.4.3.1, and its primary application is in relation to interests under a trust. However, following the decision in *Mortgage Express v Lambert*,[30] we know that more than trust

---

[30] *Mortgage Express v Lambert* [2016] EWCA Civ 555, [2017] Ch 93.

interests or interests akin to trust interests (*Birmingham Midshires v Sabherwal*[31]) can be overreached. This can include certain forms of equitable lease (as long as the other requirements of overreaching are met—ie that money is paid to at least two legal owners). This means that the rules regarding overreaching of leasehold interest are highly complex, and a clear understanding of the mechanism by which the lease is created is required to establish whether the lease can be overreached. These are shown in figure 10.2.

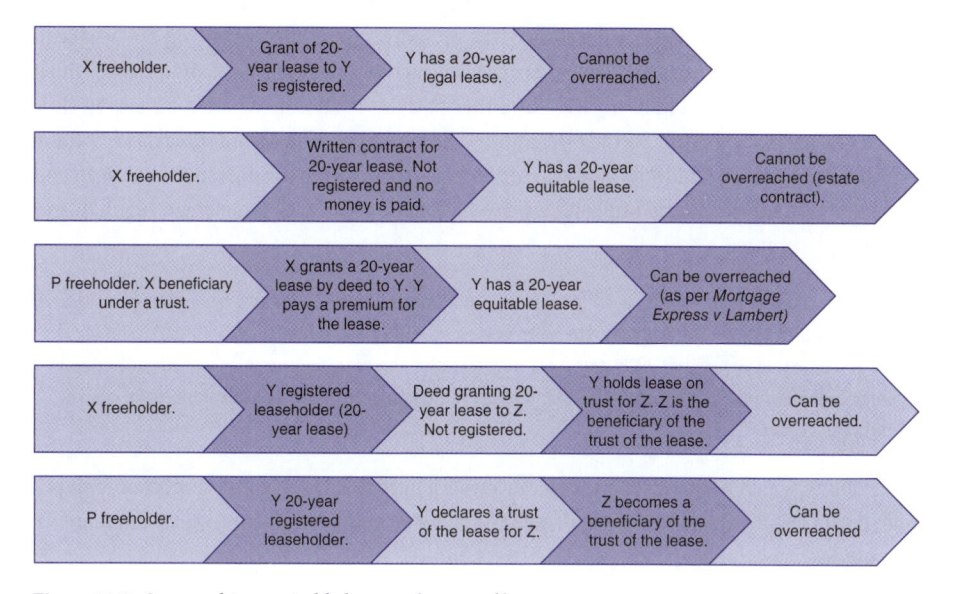

X freeholder.	Grant of 20-year lease to Y is registered.	Y has a 20-year legal lease.	Cannot be overreached.		
X freeholder.	Written contract for 20-year lease. Not registered and no money is paid.	Y has a 20-year equitable lease.	Cannot be overreached (estate contract).		
P freeholder. X beneficiary under a trust.	X grants a 20-year lease by deed to Y. Y pays a premium for the lease.	Y has a 20-year equitable lease.	Can be overreached (as per *Mortgage Express v Lambert*)		
X freeholder.	Y registered leaseholder (20-year lease)	Deed granting 20-year lease to Z. Not registered.	Y holds lease on trust for Z. Z is the beneficiary of the trust of the lease.	Can be overreached.	
P freeholder.	Y 20-year registered leaseholder.	Y declares a trust of the lease for Z.	Z becomes a beneficiary of the trust of the lease.	Can be overreached	

Figure 10.2 Overreaching equitable lease and trusts of leases

10.4 FORMS OF LEASES

10.4.1 PERIODIC TENANCIES

Periodic tenancies are a very useful and very common type of lease. They are essentially a rolling contract for a certain period of time. For example, a monthly periodic tenancy might arise where a tenant goes into exclusive possession and pays rent on a monthly basis where there is no contractual term, the contractual lease is void for some other reason, or where the parties expressly agree a monthly periodic tenancy. In this case, either party is free to walk away from the lease arrangement at the end of each period, provided that they give sufficient notice (subject to the rules relating to security of tenure which we consider at 10.5.5).

Where a periodic tenancy is expressly contracted for, the contract itself will stipulate the period of the rolling term. However, where a periodic tenancy is implied, either due to no contractual term at all, or a contractual term void for uncertainty, then the period is usually calculated

---

[31] *Birmingham Midshires Mortgage Services Ltd v Sabherwal* (2000) 80 P & CR 256 (CA).

on the basis of the frequency with which rent is due. So, if rent is due monthly then there will be a monthly periodic tenancy; where quarterly, a quarterly tenancy and so on. This arrangement can then continue indefinitely. This provides a highly flexible way of managing a lease arrangement, but of course does not provide the certainty or security that some landlords and tenants may seek.

There are some circumstances however where a periodic tenancy cannot be implied so as to prevent this being used as a solution to an 'uncertainty of term' problem. First, a periodic tenancy cannot be implied where no rent is payable, for example, since in that situation there will be no evidence upon which to imply the duration of the period. Secondly, the courts will not be able to use the periodic tenancy arrangement where the contractual agreement contains a clause which prevents the free termination of the lease by either party in relation to a particular period. This was the reason for which no periodic tenancy could be implied *Berrisford v Mexfield*.[32] There were limitations on the landlord's ability to serve notice to bring the lease arrangement to an end and this prevented the courts implying a periodic tenancy. As Lord Templeman highlights in *Prudential Assurance*:

> 'A tenancy from year to year is saved from being uncertain because each party has power by notice to determine at the end of any year. The term continues until determined as if both parties made a new agreement at the end of each year for a new term for the ensuing year. A power for nobody to determine or for one party only to be able to determine is inconsistent with the concept of a term from year to year.'[33]

The flexibility which periodic tenancies allow raises a particular problem in respect of *joint* periodic tenancies, as explained here in relation to *Hammersmith & Fulham v Monk*[34] and *Sims v Dacorum BC*.[35]

> **Key cases: *Hammersmith & Fulham v Monk* and *Sims v Dacorum* BC [2014] UKSC 63**
>
> The detail of the interaction between property law and human rights law as modulated through the Human Rights Act 1998 is discussed in chapter 17. However, there is one aspect of the relationship between leases and human rights which should be noted here, since it is an important aspect of the regulation of periodic tenancies and gives insight into how such rights work. In *Hammersmith & Fulham v Monk*,[36] Mr Monk and Mrs Powell were joint periodic tenants of a lease granted by the Council. As periodic tenants they were of course able to terminate the tenancy by serving one period's notice. In this case, Mrs Powell wanted to leave the property and be re-housed elsewhere. As a result, the Council encouraged her to serve notice to quit, terminating the tenancy for both herself and for Mr Monk. The consequence of this for Monk was that he was deprived without his consent of his own rights to occupy the property. However, this outcome was, in effect, a necessary feature of the fact that he occupied under a periodic tenancy. The very point of a periodic tenancy is that the parties can chose to terminate at any time because, in theory, a new lease arises with each period. Given this, Mrs Powell could not be forced

---

[32] *Berrisford v Mexfield Housing Co-operative Ltd* [2011] UKSC 52, [2012] 1 AC 955.
[33] *Prudential Assurance v London Residuary Body* [1992] 2 AC 386 (HL), 394.
[34] *Hammersmith & Fulham lbc v Monk* [1992] 1 AC 478 (HL).
[35] *Sims v Dacorum bc* [2014] UKSC 63, [2015] AC 1336.
[36] *Hammersmith & Fulham lbc v Monk* [1992] 1 AC 478 (HL).

to consent to a new lease. This meant that no joint periodic tenancy would arise without her consent. Of course, Mr Monk could negotiate a new sole-owned tenancy with the Council, but it would not be the same tenancy as before. On the other hand, the outcome allowed the Council to evict Mr Monk, avoiding the controls usually imposed onto the ability of a Council to evict a residential tenant under the security of tenure provisions (discussed later in the chapter at 10.5.5). Some therefore see this rule as merely a mechanism by which councils limit the scope of tenant's security of tenure. This dilemma is summed-up by Lord Bridge:

> 'the effect of the determination will be to deprive the other joint tenant of statutory protection. This may appear an untoward result... But the statutory consequences are in truth of no relevance to the question which your Lordships have to decide. That question is whether, at common law, a contractual periodic tenancy granted to two or more joint tenants is incapable of termination by a tenant's notice to quit unless it is served with the concurrence of all the joint tenants'.[37]

Whatever the merits of this approach, however, their Lordships were persuaded that: 'logic seems to me to dictate the conclusion that the will of all the joint parties is necessary to the continuance of the interest'.[38] This appeal to the logic of the periodic tenancy settled the matter. The rule came before the Supreme Court however in *Sims v Dacorum BC*, where Mr Sims argued that this rule breached his human rights. The facts were very similar to *Monk*. Mr and Mrs Sims were joint periodic tenants of a Council property. They separated and Mrs Sims wished to leave the property. This was particularly pressing for her since Mr Sims had, she alleged, committed acts of domestic violence. Mrs Sims moved into a refuge, and sought different Council accommodation from Wycombe Council. Wycombe informed her that she could not be granted new accommodation unless she served a notice to quit in relation to the Dacorum property.

Against this background the Supreme Court was required to assess whether this deprivation of Mr Sims' accommodation rights breached his article 8 (right to a private life) and article 1 protocol 1 (right to possessions) rights. The detail of how these articles operate to constrain and shape property law, if at all, is discussed further in chapter 17, but it suffices here to explain that the Supreme Court gave such arguments very little credence. As Lord Neuberger, giving judgment for the Court, explains: '[g]iven that Mr Sims was deprived of his property in circumstances, and in a way, which was specifically provided for in the agreement which created it, his A1P1 claim is plainly very hard to sustain'.[39] Similarly, in relation to the article 8 claim, the Court placed much importance on the fact that the tenancy was brought to an end precisely in line with the contractual agreement giving rise to that tenancy.

From these two cases then it is clear that the rule that one of two or more joint periodic tenants can terminate the tenancy with regards to the other co-owners by serving notice to quit does not breach human rights and indeed is a necessary consequence of the logic of the periodic tenancy.

10.4.2 TENANCIES AT WILL

The tenancy at will is a strange legal concept. It is very often referred to as an estate in land without tenure. The tenant in such a situation has no right to remain in possession of the land from the moment that the landlord indicates that they wish for the tenant to leave. Given the lack of

---

[37] *Hammersmith & Fulham LBC v Monk* [1992] 1 AC 478 (HL), 482–3).
[38] *Hammersmith & Fulham LBC v Monk* [1992] 1 AC 478 (HL), 484).
[39] *Sims v Dacorum BC* [2014] UKSC 63, [2015] AC 1336, [15].

conceptual clarity as to precisely what a tenancy at will is, it is perhaps fortunate that they arise only in a relatively narrow range of circumstances. The primary situation in which tenancies at will arise is when a potential tenant goes into possession of land whilst the parties are negotiating the terms of a formal lease. This can be exemplified by the case of *Javad v Aqil*.[40]

> **Key case:** *Javad v Aqil* [1991] 1 WLR 1007
>
> In *Javad v Aqil*, the landlord had agreed that the prospective tenant could go into occupation of the land pending on-going negotiations for a long-term lease of the property. The tenant went into possession, paying money which was expressed to constitute three-months' rent. On two further occasions, a quarter's rent was paid. However, the parties failed ever to reach agreement as to the contractual lease. The question in the case was whether the tenant was occupying under a periodic tenancy, or whether instead a tenancy at will arose. The court concluded that there was no way in the situation to imply a periodic tenancy, despite the regular payment of rent, since the periodic tenancy is based on the presumed intentions of the parties in all the circumstances of the case. In this situation, the implication of a periodic tenancy would have been inconsistent with what the parties wanted. In the particular case the distinction was very important as the periodic tenant has the benefit of the protection of the Landlord and Tenant Act 1954 so that they have security of tenure if they are occupying for the purposes of a business (as discussed later in this chapter at 10.5.5). The tenant at will, by contrast, does not have the benefit of security of tenure.
>
> As Nicholls LJ explained:
>
> 'Where parties are negotiating the terms of a proposed lease, and the prospective tenant is let into possession... the fact that the parties have not yet agreed terms will be a factor to be taken into account in ascertaining their intention... depending on all the circumstances, parties are not to be supposed thereby to have agreed that the prospective tenant shall be a quarterly tenant. They cannot sensibly be taken to have agreed that he shall have a periodic tenancy, with all the consequences flowing from that.'[41]
>
> The risks of taking any other approach were discussed by the court. Again, per Nicholls LJ:
>
> 'Otherwise the court would be in danger of inferring or imputing from conduct, such as payment of rent and the carrying out of repairs, whose explanation lies in the parties' expectation that they will be able to reach agreement on the larger terms, an intention to grant a lesser interest, such as a periodic tenancy, which the parties never had in contemplation at all.'[42]

10.4.3 THE '*BRUTON* LEASE'

It is somewhat difficult to know where in a land law textbook to situate discussion of the *Bruton* 'lease' arising from the decision in *Bruton v London & Quadrant Housing Trust*.[43] For many discussion of this concept should be found alongside discussion of licences in land, since the *Bruton* tenancy is, in reality, not a tenancy at all, but rather a non-proprietary right. However, in this

---

[40] *Javad v Aqil* [1991] 1 WLR 1007 (CA).
[41] *Javad v Aqil* [1991] 1 WLR 1007, 1012–13.
[42] *Javad v Aqil* [1991] 1 WLR 1007, 1013.
[43] *Bruton v London & Quadrant Housing Trust* [2001] 1 AC 406.

infamous decision of the House of Lords, Lord Hoffman referred to the *Bruton* tenancy as a 'non-proprietary lease', and it is for that reason that this concept is considered here. What is a *Bruton* tenancy?

> **Key case:** *Bruton v London & Quadrant Housing Trust* [2001] 1 AC 406
>
> Mr Bruton had taken what he believed to be a lease from the Housing Association. The contractual agreement between them, although labelled a licence agreement, conferred upon Mr Bruton (at least as far as the wording was concerned), a right to exclusive possession of the property. London & Quadrant, however, were incapable of actually granting Mr Bruton a tenancy since they themselves had only a personal right in the land. This was because the freeholder, Lambeth Borough Council, was, as a result of statute, incapable of granting property rights in this land to the housing trust. Thus, London & Quadrant did not have a lease. By virtue of the principle that you cannot give that which you do not have, London & Quadrant could not have conferred upon Mr Bruton a right to exclusive possession of the land, which at all material times rested with Lambeth Borough Council. However, as a matter of fact, Mr Bruton did go into possession of the land, and this was done consensually in the sense that it was accorded by the contract between Bruton and London & Quadrant. When London & Quadrant sought to evict Bruton, he alleged that they could not as he had the protection of the Housing Act 1988 (see 10.5.5.2) which conferred on him security of tenure. The question in the case, therefore, was whether Bruton had a lease such that he could claim security of tenure and this came down to whether it was possible for a contract between a licensee and a purported 'tenant' of theirs to give rise to a lease. The court held that it could but that it would be a special kind of lease which did not have proprietary effects. Later, we return to the question of what this means in terms of the ongoing debate as to whether the lease is primarily a construct of contract, or property. For now, we can focus on what right this meant that Mr Bruton actually had, and what the logic behind this idea is, and whether it can be supported in legal and in policy terms.
>
> In respect of what Mr Bruton actually had, some significant guidance was given in the follow up case of *Kay v Lambeth Borough Council*[44] which involved an identical situation, albeit with a different tenant. In that case, the court confirmed the personal status of the *Bruton* tenancy. That is, it reasoned that this tenancy could have no binding effects beyond the parties to the contract, so that Lambeth Borough Council could obtain an order for possession against the 'tenant' without having to comply with security of tenure provisions or similar.

> **Further analysis:** Lease—contract or property? Explaining *Bruton*
>
> A number of different explanations have been put forward justifying the decision in *Bruton*. The first explanation is essentially the one given in the case, ie that Mr Bruton had a non-proprietary lease. By this, Lord Hoffman meant that whilst the contractual arrangement between the parties was one of landlord and tenant, this did not necessarily mean that the tenant had a proprietary interest in the land. This was based on the very old common law rules which emerged in the medieval period as a result of which a lease was treated as being a personal right relating to land, not giving the tenant the right to possession of that land. For this reason, Dixon describes the effect of the decision in *Bruton* as 'their Lordships

---

[44] *Kay v Lambeth LBC* [2006] UKHL 10, [2006] 2 AC 465.

[identifying] the continuing existence of a beast long thought extinct: the lease as pure personality, not even a "chattel real".[45] The legal basis for such an approach does therefore exist. However, the 'lease as contract' approach is far from universally accepted.

To reflect this there are, essentially, two alternative explanations for the outcome in the case, if not the reasoning. First, it has been argued that *Bruton* can be justified on the grounds that the housing association was estopped from denying its own status as a landlord for the purposes of the applicability of security of tenure. This argument was explored by the judges in the Court of Appeal, and in the House of Lords, Lord Hoffman highlights the problem that the housing association explicitly held itself out *not* to be a landlord.[46] However, Bright has argued that the language of the agreement is not necessarily fatal to an estoppel-based argument on the grounds that the estoppel can be found not in the language used by the housing association, but by the fact that it did in fact confer on Mr Bruton the rights associated with exclusivity of possession, and therefore, a lease.[47]

Second, it has been argued that the decision can be explained on the basis of relativity of title. The idea of relativity of title is considered in chapter 2 at 2.4. The applicability of this concept to the *Bruton* situation is considered by Roberts amongst others.[48] He argues that the housing association, although granted only a licence by the local authority, nevertheless went into possession of the land. As a result, they obtained a possessory title to that land, and Bruton's lease was then derivative upon that possessory freehold title. This would mean that Mr Bruton had a perfectly valid lease—and a proprietary lease at that—but it would not be a lease which could be binding upon one with a relatively superior right to possession, as the local authority did. That the 'non-proprietary' lease could not bind the freeholder was confirmed in *Kay v Lambeth LBC*,[49] albeit that the relativity of title reasoning was not supported.

None of these explanations is perfect—the explanation from the case itself is neither clearly articulated by the court, nor is it one really supported in authority according to the way the law has developed since the Tudor times. The estoppel argument struggles to be convincing because London & Quadrant had quite clearly *not* held themselves out to be a landlord—they had described the agreement as being a licence agreement. This of course does not mean that there could be no lease, but it makes it difficult for the explanation of the case to lie in London & Quadrant's conduct in this sense. Finally, the relativity of title point, whilst potentially working in theory, does not fit neatly with what the court actually says it is doing. Furthermore, it depends upon London & Quadrant obtaining a possessory title even though their occupation was demonstrably derived from a licence agreement since the local authority could not grant a lease themselves to the housing association thanks to statute.

Furthermore, whichever of these explanations is chosen, it does not help with the fundamental question raised by *Bruton*, which is whether the contractual or proprietary elements of the lease take precedence in terms of how we understand the operation of the lease. This issue is an on-going tension, as can be seen also in relation to issues such as security of tenure, the objectivity of the test for the existence

---

[45] M Dixon, 'The non-proprietary lease: the rise of the feudal phoenix' (2000) 59 Cambridge Law Journal 25, 27.
[46] *Bruton v London & Quadrant Housing Trust* [2001] 1 AC 406, 414–15.
[47] S Bright, "Exclusive possession, true agreement and tenancy by estoppel" (1998) 114 LQR 345, 349–50.
[48] N Roberts, 'The Bruton tenancy: a matter of relativity' [2012] Conv 87. For objections to this approach, see A Baker, 'Bruton, licensees in possession and a fiction of title' [2014] Conv 495. A slightly different, but related approach, is taken by J P Hinojosa, 'On property, leases, licences, horses and carts: revisiting *Bruton v London & Quadrant Housing Trust*" [2005] 69 Conv 114. All explanations are covered in detail by A Goymour, '*Bruton v London & Quadrant Housing Trust* [2000]: relativity of title, and the regulation of the 'proprietary underworld' in S Douglas et al, *Landmark Cases in Property Law* (Hart Publishing, Oxford, 2015).
[49] *Kay v Lambeth LBC* [2006] UKHL 10, [2006] 2 AC 465.

> of a lease, and restrictions on uncertainty of term. Parties may wish to contract for a very wide range of rights, and the principle of freedom of contract which underpins contract law suggests that they should be able to do so. However, the proprietary character of the lease means that we try to ensure that the lease is of a recognised form, lying comfortably within the implied *numerus clausus* (discussed in chapter 2 at 2.2.1). The tension between freedom of contract therefore, and the third party effects and burdensome nature of potential proprietary interests is an on-going one in relation to leases.

10.5 RELATIONSHIP BETWEEN LANDLORD AND TENANT AND BRINGING A LEASE TO AN END

Covenants contained in a lease agreement are promises made binding through the deed creating the relevant lease, or implied into a lease agreement through operation of law. They regulate the position between landlord and tenant during the currency of the lease. The rules relating to when these obligations will benefit and bind subsequent landlords and tenants are difficult. They are also very detailed if considered fully. For that reason, this book summarises these rules, giving a sense of the policy concerns at play, and of the ways in which reforms have altered these rules over time, rather than giving full detail. We mention also the remedies which are available for breach of such obligations. Similarly, the law relating to the bringing to an end of a lease is complex, and there are many different elements to this issue, not all of which can be covered here. For a fuller explanation not only of the rules relating to termination of a lease but also of security of tenure, you should consult a landlord and tenant textbook which will go through these issues in much more detail. Nevertheless, it is important to have a sense as to how such issues work, at least in outline, as this will give a much more realistic picture as to how leases work in practice than simply focussing on the issues as to what a lease is and how it is created.

10.5.1 COVENANTS BETWEEN LANDLORD AND TENANT

The law relating to covenants between landlord and tenant is not easy, nor is it particularly sensible in many cases. Nevertheless, the importance of these rules cannot be overstated. They govern when a landlord and tenant—whether the original parties, or transferees of the freehold or leasehold estate—are able to sue and be sued in respect of obligations laid out in the lease agreement. The rules are radically different depending upon whether the lease was entered into before or after 1 January 1996. If before, the common law rules apply (with a few minor statutory amendments). If after, then the statutory rules in the Landlord and Tenants Covenants Act 1995 determine the outcome. The following sections explain these rules. A complete flow chart explaining these rules is available in the online resources.

10.5.1.1 Original landlord and tenant

Where the original landlord and tenant both retain possession of the property, all covenants contained in the lease are enforceable between each other, regardless of when the lease was entered into, and regardless of the kind of term in question. This is a consequence of the binding nature of the contract into which the parties voluntarily entered.

10.5.1.2 Subsequent landlord and/or tenant—pre-1996 leases

The rules relating to the 'running' (ie continuing bindingness of covenants post-transfer of the lease or of the reversion) prior to 1996, are governed by the common law, by section 141 Law of Property Act 1925, and by the law relating to restrictive covenants (most commonly encountered in relation to freehold property) explained in chapter 13.

In essence, where the tenant has assigned the lease, that *original* tenant will *remain* liable in respect of *all* the covenants contained in the lease. This is because under the old rules, assignment of the *property* of the lease, does not release the *contractual* obligations contained therein. The new tenant will also be liable to perform some obligations in the lease. Which obligations bind the tenant depend, first, on whether the tenant takes the assignment of the lease at law or in equity. If they take the assignment of the lease in law, then the new tenant will be *bound* by any obligation which 'touches and concerns' the land as a result of section 141 Law of Property Act 1925. The new tenant may also have the *benefit* of certain obligations (ie they are able to sue an original or subsequent landlord for breach). This will be the case where the obligations 'touch and concern' the land (as long as the relevant landlord remains or has become bound as we consider later). If the tenant takes the assignment in equity, he will only be bound by covenants which pass under the rule in *Tulk v Moxhay*, explained in chapter 13 at 13.4.4. Since this situation is relatively uncommon in relation to leases it is not necessary to give the details here, but essentially it allows for the burden of *negative* or *restrictive* covenants to pass, where those covenants relate to the land.

Where the landlord has assigned the lease, in theory she will remain liable, as a result of the contractual relationship, in respect of all the obligations contained in the lease. However, this liability often limited by (a) indemnity from any subsequent landlord, and (b) from the nature of the lease and the sorts of obligations resting on landlords (which are usually related to ensuring peaceful possession of the land, and to repairs to the property, in respect of both of which it is likely to be more productive for a tenant to sue a subsequent landlord). Where the landlord has assigned the lease, the new landlord will be bound and benefitted, as with tenants, by any obligations which touch and concern the land. You can visit the online resources to see a flowchart of these rules.

10.5.1.3 Subsequent landlord and tenant—post-1996 leases

Under the new law, the rules relating to the running of covenants are to be found in the Landlord and Tenants Covenants Act 1995. These rules are reproduced and annotated here, and explained in more detail later.

> '2 Covenants to which the Act applies.
>
> > (1) This Act applies to a landlord covenant or a tenant covenant of a tenancy—
> >
> > > (a) whether or not the covenant has reference to the subject matter of the tenancy, and
> > >
> > > (b) whether the covenant is express, implied or imposed by law...'
>
> This section explains the scope of the Act, emphasising that it applies to all the obligations in a leasehold contract.

'3   Transmission of benefit and burden of covenants.

(1) The benefit and burden of all landlord and tenant covenants of a tenancy—

    (a) shall be annexed and incident to the whole, and to each and every part, of the premises demised by the tenancy and of the reversion in them, and

    (b) shall in accordance with this section pass on an assignment of the whole or any part of those premises or of the reversion in them.'

This sub-section makes clear that not only will both the benefit and burden of relevant covenants be 'attached' to every part of the land, but that they will pass regardless of the nature of the assignment. As a result, we know that there is no distinction between how these rules operate in respect of an assignment at law or in equity.

'(2) Where the assignment is by the tenant under the tenancy, then as from the assignment the assignee—

    (a) becomes bound by the tenant covenants of the tenancy except to the extent that—

        (i) immediately before the assignment they did not bind the assignor, or

        (ii) they fall to be complied with in relation to any demised premises not comprised in the assignment; and

    (b) becomes entitled to the benefit of the landlord covenants of the tenancy except to the extent that they fall to be complied with in relation to any such premises.'

This sub-section results in a new tenant being bound and benefitted by any obligations binding/benefitting the original tenant.

'(3) Where the assignment is by the landlord under the tenancy, then as from the assignment the assignee—

    (a) becomes bound by the landlord covenants of the tenancy except to the extent that—

        (i) immediately before the assignment they did not bind the assignor, or

        (ii) they fall to be complied with in relation to any demised premises not comprised in the assignment; and

    (b) becomes entitled to the benefit of the tenant covenants of the tenancy except to the extent that they fall to be complied with in relation to any such premises.'

This sub-section results in a new landlord being bound and benefitted by any obligations binding/benefitting the original tenant.

'…

(6) Nothing in this section shall operate—

    (a) in the case of a covenant which (in whatever terms) is expressed to be personal to any person, to make the covenant enforceable by or (as the case may be) against any other person; or

…'

This is a very important sub-section, as it means that any obligation which is expressed to be personal cannot pass under the provisions of the Act. We explain what this means later, and analyse what this seemingly small caveat means for the degree to which the new law represents and improvement on the old rules.

> '5 Tenant released from covenants on assignment of tenancy.
>
> (1) This section applies where a tenant assigns premises demised to him under a tenancy.
> (2) If the tenant assigns the whole of the premises demised to him, he—
>   (a) is released from the tenant covenants of the tenancy, and
>   (b) ceases to be entitled to the benefit of the landlord covenants of the tenancy, as from the assignment.
>
> . . .'
>
> This section results in a tenant being released from their obligations when they assign the tenancy. This is a very important development from the old law, under which a tenant would be bound by all obligations under the original contract, whether or not the retained the property rights associated with the lease.
>
> '6 Landlord may be released from covenants on assignment of reversion.
>
> (1) This section applies where a landlord assigns the reversion in premises of which he is the landlord under a tenancy.
> (2) If the landlord assigns the reversion in the whole of the premises of which he is the landlord—
>   (a) he may apply to be released from the landlord covenants of the tenancy in accordance with section 8; and
>   (b) if he is so released from all of those covenants, he ceases to be entitled to the benefit of the tenant covenants of the tenancy as from the assignment.
>
> . . .'
>
> Similarly, landlords can be released from all obligations under the lease on assignment of the reversion if they follow the appropriate procedure and request release under section 8. However, it is important to emphasise that whilst the statutory procedure is one way in which the courts have held landlords can be released from their obligations, case law has also resulted in the creation of alternative methods. The consequence of these alternative methods is that landlords are almost always automatically released on assignment of the reversion, as we shall see later.

The consequence of the new rules is that whilst original landlord and tenant will be benefitted and bound by obligations if both retain their rights in respect of the property, on assignment the new landlord and tenant will be benefitted and bound by any obligations not expressed to be personal. The old tenant will be automatically released from their obligations, although, as we explain later, they can be required to enter into an authorised guarantee agreement which can make them liable for performance of obligations by a future tenant. The old landlord, to be released under the Act, has to go through the procedure explained in section 8 of the Act. You can visit the online resources to see a flowchart of these rules.

However, in practice, it is now more normal for landlords to introduce what is called an 'Avonridge clause' into their lease agreements, which is a contractual method by which they will ensure their release from such obligations on assignment of the reversion. This is a result of the controversial decision in *Avonridge*.[50]

> **Key case: *London Dioscesan Fund v Avonridge* [2005] UKHL 70**
>
> This case involved an attempted contractual release from obligations of the original landlord under a lease. The House of Lords held that it was possible for landlords to release themselves from liability even though they had not followed the statutory procedure in section 8 LCTA 1995. The reason for this is that the court concluded that even though the purpose of the statute was to provide a route by which the landlord could ensure that they were released from such obligations, it did not aim to provide the only route. Its overall policy was to allow landlords to be released from liability, so the use of a contractual rather than statutory mechanism was therefore deemed a legitimate means to achieve this goal. This decision is extremely controversial. This is because it allows the landlord to simply by-pass the statutory procedure by using superior bargaining power to insert an Avonridge clause into the lease. In the House of Lords, the reason given for allowing such a by-pass was the view that the 1995 Act was never intended to be the only route by which liability could be excluded, merely 'a' route. Thus, Lord Nicholls explained:
>
>> 'the mischief at which the statute was aimed was the absence in practice of any such exit route. Consistently with this the legislation was not intended to close any other exit route already open to the parties: in particular, that by agreement their liability could be curtailed from the outset or later released or waived. The possibility that by agreement the parties may limit their liability in this way was not, it seems, perceived as having unfair consequences in practice, even though landlords normally have greater bargaining power than tenants'.[51]
>
> The majority of the Court agreed with this assessment, although Lord Walker dissented.[52] The 'merits' of this decision are marginal, since both avenues make sense depending upon one's perspective. If one wishes for the statute to cover all scenarios, then of course Avonridge is wrong, but if one focuses on the question of freedom of contract, then its appeal is clear. As Dixon explains,
>
>> 'Avonridge is a case which is not reducible to the simple question of whether the answer is "right"... It is what it is: an interpretation of a statute that does no violence to the statutory language and no violence to the statutory purpose. What may be said, however, is that a chance was missed, possibly deliberately, to establish the 1995 Act as a self-contained scheme free from the dictates of privity of estate and privity of contract'.[53]
>
> However, as Dixon emphasises, the consequence of this case is certainly that the contractual element of the lease are brought to the fore. He argues that:
>
>> 'The case is another example of how the judiciary currently are content to analyse the landlord and tenant relationship more as a matter of contract than of real property. Leases are now more readily seen as contractual bargains than the establishment of a proprietary relationship with its own fundamental incidents. That is not to say that the proprietary nature of leases is denied, but rather that where proprietary principles and contractual principles conflict, the latter take precedence'.[54]

---

[50] *London Diocesan Fund v Avonridge Property Co Ltd* [2005] UKHL 70, [2005] 1 WLR 3956.
[51] *London Diocesan Fund v Avonridge Property Co Ltd* [2005] UKHL 70, [2005] 1 WLR 3956, [16]–[17].
[52] *London Diocesan Fund v Avonridge Property Co Ltd* [2005] UKHL 70, [2005] 1 WLR 3956, [35].
[53] M Dixon, 'A failure of statutory purpose or a failure of professional advice?' [2006] Conv 79, 84–5.
[54] M Dixon, 'A failure of statutory purpose or a failure of professional advice?' [2006] Conv 79, 84.

Expressed to be personal

In addition to the *Avonridge* controversy, problems have also emerged in relation to the innocuous 'expressed to be personal' qualification in section 3(6). The policy behind the inclusion of this caveat is simple. Where a clause is something negotiated between the individual original landlord and tenant, and it is entirely dependent upon their identities and wishes, it would make no sense for it to transmit to future landlords and tenants. For example, it would not make sense for an obligation that the tenant walk the landlord's dog be assigned along with the reversion or lease. However, the way this term has been interpreted means that it gets very close to mirroring the 'touches and concerns' test considered earlier, thus limited the clarity which was sought by the drafters of the Act. This can be seen in *Chesterfield Properties v BHP*.[55]

> **Key case: *Chesterfield Properties v BHP Petroleum* [2001] EWCA Civ 1797**
>
> Under a lease agreement, responsibility for the repair of the building constructed by the landlord rested on the landlord's shoulders. Specifically, the repairing clause in question referred to any problems occurring within a six-year period which were the result of defective design, materials, or workmanship. The question for the court was whether this obligation was 'expressed to be personal' so that it would be excluded from the operation of the 1995 Act, meaning that the original landlord would remain bound by the covenant, and it would not bind successors in title to the landlord. The Court of Appeal concluded that this term was expressed to be personal, and that automatic release did not therefore occur on the assignment of the reversion. Per Jonathan Parker LJ,
>
> > 'A covenant which relates to the land may nevertheless be expressed to be personal to one or other or both of the parties to it. That is a matter for the contracting parties.
> >
> > Nor can we see anything in the 1995 Act to fetter the freedom of contracting parties to place a contractual limit on the transmissibility of the benefit or burden of obligations under a tenancy.'[56]
>
> In other words, the parties can, even under the 1995 Act provisions, either expressly or impliedly limit the power of the Act by indicating in their contract that a particular term is 'personal'.
>
> The consequences of this case are two-fold. First, the distinction between a test which considers implied 'labels' that an obligation is personal, and the touches and concerns test, is a fine one. Many of the same considerations will be brought to bear in assessing whether a term is caught by the 1995 Act or not. In this way, the interpretation that the Courts have given to the statutory terms may have the impact of reducing the law to the same state of fine lines and subjectivity which prompted the drafting of the 1995 Act in the first place. Second, and on the other hand, the Courts here, as with *Avonridge* earlier, are clearly prioritising freedom of contract and there is clear merit in this.

Authorised Guarantee Agreements

As highlighted earlier, whilst a tenant will be automatically released from obligations upon assigning a lease, they can be obligated by their landlord as part of a process by which permission for an

---

[55] *BHP Petroleum Great Britain Ltd v Chesterfield Properties Ltd* [2001] EWCA Civ 1797, [2002] Ch 194.
[56] *BHP Petroleum Great Britain Ltd v Chesterfield Properties Ltd* [2001] EWCA Civ 1797, [2002] Ch 194, [61]–[62].

assignment is obtained, to enter into an authorised guarantee agreement (AGA), under which they act as guarantor for the obligations of a new tenant. This is explained in section 16 LTCA 1995.

> '16   Tenant guaranteeing performance of covenant by assignee.
>
> (1) Where on an assignment a tenant is to any extent released from a tenant covenant of a tenancy by virtue of this Act ("the relevant covenant"), nothing in this Act (and in particular section 25) shall preclude him from entering into an authorised guarantee agreement with respect to the performance of that covenant by the assignee.'
>
> An AGA is an agreement under which an original tenant (T1) agrees to guarantee performance of the obligations by the next assignee (T2), as held in *Good Harvest*.[57] An important qualification is that T1 cannot be forced to guarantee performance of any later assignees, T3, T4 etc. T2 is able to guarantee performance of T3, and so on.
>
> '...
>
> (3) Those circumstances are as follows—
>
> (a) by virtue of a covenant against assignment (whether absolute or qualified) the assignment cannot be effected without the consent of the landlord under the tenancy or some other person;
>
> (b) any such consent is given subject to a condition (lawfully imposed) that the tenant is to enter into an agreement guaranteeing the performance of the covenant by the assignee; and
>
> (c) the agreement is entered into by the tenant in pursuance of that condition.'

This section emphasises that an AGA can be required as part of the process of ensuring that a landlord gives permission for an assignment of the lease. This allows a landlord to demand that an AGA be entered into before assignment can take place.

The key feature of AGAs is that they give landlords a degree of comfort should their tenant seek to assign, as it reassures them that the new tenant is likely to be trustworthy, or the original tenant would not be willing to undertake to guarantee their performance of the obligations of the lease. However, this will only last until T2 assigns the lease, for at that point T1 will be released from their AGA.

> **Further analysis: Do the rules in the Landlord and Tenant Covenants Act 1995 represent an improvement on the old law?**
>
> The short answer to this is, not really. The main reason why the Act itself does not achieve its primary goals—to simplify the law, to prevent original tenants (in particular) from remaining liable under the lease post-assignment, and to adjust the balance of power between landlord and tenant—is that its drafting process was one dominated by compromise. However, the other problem has been the approach to the courts in relation to this Act. In effect, they have not seen it as a single statutory scheme designed to represent the *totality* of the relevant rules, but rather as only part of a wider set of rules governing the

---

[57] *Good Harvest Partnership LLP v Centaur Services Ltd* [2010] EWHC 330 (Ch), [2010] Ch 426.

landlord and tenant relationship. This can be seen particularly in relation to the 'expressed to be personal' test and the rules relating to *Avonridge* clauses. In both of these cases, the courts have emphasised that approaches to interpretation of contractual terms within a lease are not dependent solely on the policy concerns expressed in the lease itself.

Slessenger expresses the results of the compromises which the Act represents following the decision in *Avonridge*:

> 'For landlords it is obviously good news that they can avoid the uncertainties of the statutory release scheme... In particular, the decision deals with a problem which meant that landlords of multi-let buildings often did not apply for release at all. A landlord using the statutory mechanism might be released by some but not all of the tenants... But the decision is bad news for tenants, particularly those with little bargaining power or who are unrepresented... they will lose the protection against being stranded with a worthless landlord which Parliament seems to have intended. For the future, the statutory release scheme may be an irrelevance'.[58]

10.5.1.4 Remedies for breach of covenant

Finally, when dealing with covenants between landlord and tenant, it is important to be aware of the range of remedies available. Of these, the most important for the landlord is the possibility of forfeiture. We consider this in detail in 10.5.3, since it is a means by which a lease is brought to an end. Otherwise, the primary remedies for a landlord will be actions for arrears of rent, damages for breach of covenant, commercial rent arrears recovery (CRAR) and injunctions or specific performance. With the exception of forfeiture and CRAR, these remedies operate effectively in the same way as all remedies in cases of breach of contract. CRAR is essentially a scheme under which a landlord is able to recover chattels in respect of commercial property to reflect the amount of rent owing.

10.5.2 TERMINATING LEASES—EFFLUXION OF TIME

The most straightforward way in which a lease can be brought to an end is by the process of effluxion of time. This is simply the process whereby the lease ends in accordance with the contractual provisions as to its length. However, in a very great number of cases, there will be security of tenure in place which means that a lease does not end on the date of its contractual expiry (see 10.5.5). Furthermore, even in cases where the contractual lease does come to an end on the date specified, the parties may chose to remain in place and continue their occupation in a more informal way. Thus, for example, in a business context where the parties have contracted out of the protection of the Landlord and Tenant Act 1954 (see later), even when the contractual term comes to an end, the tenant may remain in possession and a periodic tenancy will likely arise on the basis of the regularity with which rent is due.

---

[58] E Slessenger, '*London Diocesan Fund and others v Avonridge Property Company Ltd*' (2006) 10 Landlord and Tenant Law Review 46, 48–9.

Effluxion of time therefore becomes particularly important for establishing when the contractual regulation of the lease ceases on its terms and when statutory regulation of the lease takes over. Once this contractual lease comes to an end and either an informal or a statutory regulation of the lease comes into place instead, the grounds on which and procedures by which the parties can bring the lease to an end will then be regulated by different provisions.

10.5.3 TERMINATING LEASES—FORFEITURE AND NOTICES

Another way in which a leasehold relationship can be brought to an end is by the landlord exercising his right of re-entry and forfeiting the lease. Forfeiture of a lease is possible in cases where the contract has been breached in such a way as to trigger the landlord's contractual right of re-entry. This depends usually on the nature of the breach, and not all breaches will trigger this ability. Indeed, special language has been developed in the process of drafting leases to signal to the parties which of the terms of the agreement are considered sufficiently important by the parties to trigger the possibility of forfeiture if breached. These terms are labelled, 'conditions'. Another option is to have a general forfeiture clause in the lease signalling that any breach of covenant can be enough to trigger the landlord's right of re-entry. If such a clause is triggered of course the landlord has an option whether or not to bring the lease to an end. In order to actually complete the process of forfeiture, however, the landlord has to actually go into possession of the relevant land. This means that they must either enter peacefully (that is, without committing a criminal offence—possible only in relation to unoccupied commercial premises), or they must go to court to obtain an order for possession.

10.5.3.1 Forfeiture process

Depending upon whether the forfeiture action is being brought consequent upon a breach of an obligation to pay rent, or a breach of some other term, the precise process which must be followed in order to successfully forfeit the lease will be different. If rent is due, and unless the lease dispenses with this requirement, the landlord must first make a formal demand for the rent unpaid if the arrears are less than six months. In the case of a long lease of residential property there are additional hurdles to overcome in the Commonhold and Leasehold Reform Act 2002. Where the breach relates other than to payment of rent, the process in section 146 Law of Property Act 1925 must be followed. The most important elements of this provision are provided and annotated here.

'Section 146 Restrictions on and relief against forfeiture of leases and underleases.

(1) A right of re-entry or forfeiture under any proviso or stipulation in a lease for a breach of any covenant or condition in the lease shall not be enforceable, by action or otherwise, unless and until the lessor serves on the lessee a notice—

    (a) specifying the particular breach complained of; and
    (b) if the breach is capable of remedy, requiring the lessee to remedy the breach; and
    (c) in any case, requiring the lessee to make compensation in money for the breach; and the lessee fails, within a reasonable time thereafter, to remedy the breach, if it is capable of remedy, and to make reasonable compensation in money, to the satisfaction of the lessor, for the breach.'

Therefore, the landlord can only bring an action for forfeiture in cases to which section 146 applies if she has served a notice which specifies the breach complained of; gives the opportunity for the tenant to remedy the breach if such if possible; and specifies that the tenant should provide compensation to reflect any breach, as well as carrying out any remedial works, giving the tenant reasonable time so to-do. This means that where a breach is 'capable of remedy', the landlord will have to allow the tenant the chance to remedy the breach, making the process of forfeiture either impossible or at the least more time-consuming. The distinction between remediable and non-remediable breaches is considered later.

> '(2) Where a lessor is proceeding, by action or otherwise, to enforce such a right of re-entry or forfeiture, the lessee may, in the lessor's action, if any, or in any action brought by himself, apply to the court for relief; and the court may grant or refuse relief, as the court, having regard to the proceedings and conduct of the parties under the foregoing provisions of this section, and to all the other circumstances, thinks fit; and in case of relief may grant it on such terms, if any, as to costs, expenses, damages, compensation, penalty, or otherwise, including the granting of an injunction to restrain any like breach in the future, as the court, in the circumstances of each case, thinks fit.'
>
> This section confers a statutory power onto the courts to grant relief from forfeiture in appropriate cases. The circumstances taken into account when assessing whether relief is possible are considered later.
>
> '...
>
> (11) This section does not, save as otherwise mentioned, affect the law relating to re-entry or forfeiture or relief in case of non-payment of rent.'
>
> This sub-section confirms that section 146 notices are not required in cases of non-payment of rent.
>
> '(12) This section has effect notwithstanding any stipulation to the contrary.'
>
> This sub-section emphasises that parties cannot, by the lease agreement, follow a procedure different from that in section 146.

One of the key questions arising from section 146 actions, therefore, is when a breach will be remediable or not. Where a term of the contract requires the tenant *to do* something, these will generally be remediable—since the tenant can simply do whatever they ought to have done in the first place. Where the breach consists of something which the tenant has done which they ought *not* to have done, it is generally more likely that the courts will consider that the breach is not remediable. This would be the case, for example, where the tenant had sublet or where some action of the tenant has left a 'taint' on the property. This is easiest seen by an example. Consider case *Patel v K&J Restaurants Ltd*.[59]

> **Key case:** *Patel v K&J Restaurants Ltd* [2010] EWCA Civ 1211
>
> This case involved the alleged use of a property for the purposes of prostitution. The landlords brought an action for forfeiture and argued that the breach was irremediable because of the 'taint' that was left on the property from this use, and that therefore the landlord did not need to give the tenant time to

---

[59] *Patel v K&J Restaurants Ltd* [2010] EWCA Civ 1211, [2011] L & TR 6 (CA (Civ Div)).

remedy the breach. The Court of Appeal in this case concluded that the breach was indeed capable of remedy. In part, this was because the use as a brothel had been through a sub-tenant, and generally the courts will be reluctant to hold that a breach cannot be remedied for reasons of 'taint' where a sub-tenant carries out the relevant breaches. In part also, the Court of Appeal, unwilling to interfere with the findings of fact of the court at first instance, was taking account of the comments by that judge that the location of this flat (Tottenham Court Road), meant that it was much less likely to suffer from 'stigma' than would be the case in some other locations. This case shows the subjective nature of the 'remediable' test. Whilst in most cases it is straightforward, where the breach results in some sort of diminution in the perceived character or value of the property, much will depend upon the location of the property, the type of property, and indeed the judge's own assessment of those factors and on the nature of the breach. The consequences of this for a landlord may be inconvenient, as they will be required to allow the tenant time to remedy the breach. However, it ought to be remembered that this will all be bounded by the court's ability to give relief from forfeiture in any case.

10.5.3.2 Relief from forfeiture

The courts have a well-established jurisdiction to provide a tenant with relief from forfeiture. Again, the rules are different depending on whether the landlord seeks forfeiture on the grounds of non-payment of rent, or for breach of some other term of the lease. In relation to the former, the statutory powers are constructed on top of a general equitable power vesting in the courts to refuse possession. Where a tenant pays the rent owed prior to the court action, then relief is almost certain to be granted, and in some cases, it is mandatory. In relation to the latter, the courts' power to grant relief from forfeiture is derived wholly from statute as have seen earlier in section 146. The operation of these rules is complex and potentially uncertain in its scope, although a good general rule of thumb is that the court leans against forfeiture. The courts have also refused to provide strict guidelines as to when they will exercise their discretion to provide relief against forfeiture, although it is clear that the court will take into account factors such as the seriousness and nature of the breach and the general conduct of the tenant. You can visit the online resources to see a flowchart explaining this further.

10.5.3.3 Notice

However, another way in which the parties can voluntarily bring their lease to an end is by serving notice in compliance with the terms of the lease. This could include a break notice where available under the terms of the lease, or, in cases of periodic tenancies, giving one period's notice. It is important to realise, however, that the ability to serve notices in this way is significantly constrained by security of tenure provisions, which are discussed later. In cases where there is no security of tenure, however, the ability to serve notice would be determined by the nature of the lease and its specific terms.

10.5.4 TERMINATING LEASES—SURRENDER

A tenant may also surrender their lease if they no longer wish to remain in possession of the land. If the landlord accepts this surrender, then the lease will be at an end. To surrender a lease, the surrender must be carried out by deed, even if the lease itself was created orally. It is also very important to remember that this is a consensual process—the surrender is only effective if the landlord is happy to accept it. It is however possible for *implied* surrender to take place. The most common situation in which this occurs is where the landlord and tenant agree to change the duration of the lease. Since it is not possible to simply amend an existing lease in this way, the agreement will take effect as a surrender and re-grant, so that a new lease is created for the new duration. The same would occur if the parties attempted to change the physical scope of the lease to include more or less of the landlord's land.

10.5.5 SECURITY OF TENURE

As mentioned in the introduction, security of tenure is the concept by which a tenant is able to remain as tenant of a property even once the contractual term has come to an end. Provided the relevant statutory tests are met, there can be security of tenure in many different contexts: business, agriculture, and residential, both private and public. However, the precise mechanisms which make up this security vary according to the context and each sector has its own specific rules, carefully tailored to the needs of both landlords and tenants in these areas.

It may be thought that the ability of a tenant to require the landlord to allow them to stay in possession of land after the contractual term of a lease comes to an end is hugely inconvenient for a landlord. What if they wish to re-let the property on the basis that the market has improved? What about in cases where the property in question is a residential property and the landlord himself wishes to move in? In part, these difficulties are accounted for in the shape of the statutory schemes. Intended occupation by the landlord herself, is, for example, one of the 'grounds for possession' which exists across these sectors. In part, the difficulties can be contracted out of. In relation to business tenancies, for example, it is possible to contract out of the protection of security of tenure entirely. In this case you might argue that the security of tenure provisions are doing nothing more than altering the bargaining position between the parties, they are not guaranteeing security in any real sense.

This is a potentially valid criticism, but it raises the issue as to what the purpose of security of tenure actually is. Like the rules, this varies according to context. In particular, there is a division between security of tenure which is directed at commercial enterprises, be that business tenancies or agricultural tenancies, and residential tenancies. Let us start with commercial tenancies. There are really three reasons why we might seek to ensure that a tenant can remain in occupation even on the expiry of the contractual term of the lease. First, many businesses depend on their location for the success of their business.

Think for example of a high street bakery. If such a bakery is successful, it is likely because it has built up a consistent local clientele who visit the bakery on a regular basis. Partly this will be possible because the bakery is sited in a particularly convenient location so that people can drop in without having to travel specifically to get there. Partly also it will be successful because it has become a 'feature' of the local area. Now imagine that the bakery is required to move due the expiry of their lease. The only suitable premises which they can find are in a neighbouring town. The bakery business is likely, in these circumstances, if not to fail, then at least to struggle for a while before they find their feet in a new area. This prevents the business from investing, expanding, or hiring more employees. It also deprives the residents of the first town of a valued business. This dependence on locality is sometimes referred to as the 'goodwill' of a business.

Second, security of tenure gives a business the sense of security required to allow them to invest in their premises, be that a farm or a business. For example, a tenant farmer is unlikely to upgrade his milking machinery if he knows that he cannot depend upon being a farmer of that particular plot of land. A business tenant is unlikely to install new equipment or improve the décor of his workplace if he knows he could be evicted at any moment. Without such investment not only do businesses suffer, but the local area will suffer too as there is a risk that commercial property is being left to fall slowly into disrepair rather than being renewed and refreshed. Finally, security of tenure is an important bargaining chip in the landlord and tenant relationship. In a commercial context, the landlord is very often an institutional investor, such as a pension fund or real estate firm, and this means that they have a huge bargaining power. The tenant, by contrast, is very likely to have considerably less clout to wield in any negotiations. The security of tenure provisions, whether contracted out of or not, try to balance the playing field somewhat. This should, in theory, produce a better outcome in terms of efficiency etc, since the tenant is not made to accept whatever conditions the landlord wishes to provide, limiting the tenant's own ability to improve his business etc.

Similar, although not identical, arguments can be given in the residential context. Here, the primary reason why security of tenure is provided is, essentially, to allow residential tenants to plan their lives and to settle in a particular area safe in the knowledge that they can remain there for the foreseeable future as long as they comply with the terms of their contract. This is most important for families, where access to schooling often depends upon residency but also for those in employment, for example, who need to know that they can get to their place of work in a timely and affordable fashion. It is also important for developing a sense of 'pride' in a living space, and this can be very useful if the landlord wishes to rely on the tenant maintaining the property to a high standard (as is often the case for public sector rental where the landlord is unlikely to have sufficient resources to maintain all properties within their portfolio given that rental values are not high in this sector).

10.5.5.1 Business Tenancies

Security of tenure in the business context operates as a sort of background presumptive security, but since 2003, it has been possible to contract out the protection of the Landlord and Tenant Act 1954 without the consent of the court. This meets very often with the goals of the parties, both of whom seek flexibility if required. However, the fact that the protections under the Act operate as the default unless the parties agree can give the tenant a powerful bargaining chip in negotiations the terms of their lease. Furthermore, in practice, there are still a great number of tenants who have the protection of the 1954 Act, and so it is important to understand, at least in general terms, when the protection of the Act can apply, and what the confers upon the tenant in terms of their ability to resist attempts by the landlord to bring the lease to the end.

When does the Act apply?

The Act applies, broadly, when there is a lease of premises occupied by the tenant for the purposes of a business. This applies to both fixed-term and periodic tenancies, but does not apply to tenancies at will. The meaning of occupation in this context has proved somewhat difficult, and it is not necessary to go into detail here, but it is important to realise, as with elsewhere in land law, the meaning of occupation is not treated as a term of art. Rather, the courts will look at all the circumstances of the case to assess whether the requirement of occupation is met.

One area which has caused some difficulty is in respect of the degree to which multiple persons can be in actual occupation of property simultaneously. The sort of situation where this arises is, for example, the situation where a single shopping centre is rented out wholesale to a single tenant, and then individual shop units are sub-let to individual tenants. Ought we to conclude in such cases that the tenant of the whole, or tenants of the shop, or both, are in occupation of the land at the relevant time? Again, the courts will look at this on a case-by-case basis, but in general we can note that only one person can be occupation of premises for the purposes of the Act at any one time. Furthermore, because occupation must be for the purposes or partly for the purposes of a business, where a tenant remains in occupation only of the common parts (like corridors and stairs), because the purpose of their business is effectively renting out space to third parties, the courts will conclude that their occupation of the common parts will be insufficient to protect their business, and therefore that the Act does not apply. This was decided in the leading case of *Graysim Holdings*.[60]

The other issue which can prove somewhat difficult for courts to resolve is the question as to what activities can count as a business. Fortunately, there is an easy answer in the case of corporate or incorporate bodies. For such tenants, any activity which they carry out, be it for profit or not, will constitute a business. For individuals, an activity will count as a business where it is a trade, profession or employment.

If all these requirements are met, then unless the activity is otherwise excluded from the protection of the Act (eg because the tenant is using the premises as a business in breach of an express, comprehensive condition that he not use the premises for the purposes of a business), or the parties have voluntarily contracted out of the protection of the Act, then the tenant will be able to remain in possession of the land once the contractual tenancy comes to an end.

The effect of security of tenure

If the tenant has security of tenure, the effect of that will be that the landlord cannot evict the tenant unless the landlord can rely on certain 'grounds' for possession. These are: tenant's failure to repair; persistent arrears; other substantial reasons (such as illegal use) or breaches; if the landlord is able to provide suitable alternative accommodation; where the current tenancy is created by sub-letting part of the holding; where the landlord intends to carry out demolition, reconstruction, or substantial construction works; and where the landlord intends to occupy the property for himself. The detail of these rules is beyond the scope of this work, but this list demonstrates that the grounds upon which the landlord can rely are fairly narrow, and do not take account, for example, of significant shifts in the value of the rental property due to market changes. For this reason, many landlords even if they do not contract out of the protection of the Act, will insist on rent review clauses within their lease to ensure that even if the tenant is allowed to remain in possession of the property, they will do so paying a market rent.

---

[60] *Graysim Holdings Ltd v P&O Property Holdings Ltd* [1996] AC 329 (HL).

10.5.5.2 Residential tenancies

There are two categories of residential tenants: private sector tenants, and public sector tenants. However, after reforms carried out in 2016, although not yet in force, the protections given across the two sectors are being increasingly brought together in that, whilst at the time of writing public sector tenants have a fairly substantial degree of security, especially when compared with private sector tenants who assuredly do not, if the reforms in the Housing and Planning Act 2016 come into force, public sector tenants too will have very limited security of tenure.

Private sector tenants

Whilst some private sector tenants still have the protection of the Rent Act (which we have mentioned in passing in earlier sections of this chapter), the number for whom this very high degree of protection continues to apply is now small. Instead, most private sector tenants will either have an assured tenancy, or an assured shorthold tenancy (AST). The assured tenancy is the default option, but it is comparatively rare. The vast majority of private sector tenants occupy under an AST.

Section 1, Housing Act 1988 defines assured tenancies.

> 'A tenancy under which a dwelling-house is let as a separate dwelling is for the purposes of this Act an assured tenancy if and so long as:
>
> (a) the tenant or, as the case may be, each of the joint tenants is an individual; and
>
> (b) the tenant or, as the case may be, at least one of the joint tenants occupies the dwelling-house as his only or principal home.'

as long as the tenancy is not otherwise excluded.

The same tenancies will automatically be ASTs if appropriate notices are not served at the time of the creation of the lease. The key issues in terms of the application of the Act are, as is apparent from the statutory provisions, what constitutes a dwelling, what constitutes a separate dwelling, and when a tenant will be considered to occupy as his only or principal home. On the first issue, the courts have gradually relaxed the definition of what constitutes a dwelling, recognising that the most vulnerable tenants are the most likely to occupy 'a-typical' property. This is exemplified by the leading case of *Uratemp*[61] where the House of Lords held that since the whole point of security of tenure provisions is to assist the most vulnerable, 'a-typical properties' could be considered dwelling houses so long as they provided a 'home' for the tenant. In that case itself this meant that the tenant, who occupied a hotel room with no bathroom and only minimal cooking facilities (kettle, toastie maker, etc.), could nevertheless be considered as occupying a dwelling.

The effect of the Act applying is that the tenant will have an AST unless the appropriate notices were served to create an assured tenancy. If an assured tenancy is created, then the landlord can only obtain possession against the tenant if the grounds for possession listed in the Act are made out. There are many of these, but they include non-payment of rent, disrepair, landlord's own occupation, and an intention to carry out construction works. A full list of these grounds can be found in schedule 2 Housing Act 1988.

---

[61] *Uratemp Ventures Ltd v Collins* [2001] UKHL 43, [2002] 1 AC 301.

If an AST has come into existence, then the landlord can terminate the tenancy after six months by serving a section 21 notice and waiting two months. The only restrictions on this are the requirements that the landlord must protect the tenant's deposit in accordance with the tenancy deposit scheme and must also provide the tenant with information during the currency of their lease as to how renting residential properties works. In addition, if the tenant has registered a complaint with the local authority as to the state of repair of the property so that the Council has concluded that the property represents a health hazard, the landlord will be unable to evict the tenant until the condition of the property has improved (Deregulation Act 2015).

Public sector tenants

A tenant who rents from a public sector landlord, such as a district council, will have security of tenure if, 'the tenant is an individual and occupies the dwelling-house as his only or principal home; or, where the tenancy is a joint tenancy, that each of the joint tenants is an individual and at least one of them occupies the dwelling-house as his only or principal home' (section 81 Housing Act 1985). This is known as the 'tenant condition' and the terms in the section are interpreted in a very similar way to those in relation to private sector tenants. In addition, the landlord condition in section 80 Housing Act 1985 must also be met. This depends on the identity of the landlord and is mainly concerned with local and county councils and other similar bodies. As with private sector tenancies, even if these terms are met there are some exclusions from the protection of the Act.

If the Act does apply, as earlier, the landlord will only be able to seek possession against the tenant if certain grounds, contained in schedule 2 Housing Act 1985 are met. Again, there are many of these, including those listed earlier, plus others relating more specifically to the local authority context. Importantly, however, local authorities also have a degree of flexibility both at the time of the creation of the lease, and subsequently, in cases where the tenant does not appear suitable to have security of tenure. Thus, the local authority is able to use introductory tenancies in particular problem estates, and flexible tenancies as introduced in the Localism Act 2011 which allow the landlord to obtain possession against the tenant in a much wider range of circumstances. Furthermore, if the tenant commits an offence or behaves in such a way as to result in their being subject to a criminal behaviour order, the tenant may be put onto a demoted tenancy so that they lose their security of tenure for a limited period of time.

This will all become much more flexible for local authorities, at least in theory, when (and indeed if) the reforms in the Housing and Planning Act 2016 come into force since these provisions will, in effect, put to an end security of tenure in the public sector. If these provisions do come into force, all new tenancies will have to be fixed term tenancies of (usually) between two and ten years (with a norm of five years). At the end of the fixed term the local authority will have an unconstrained discretion (subject to the overarching public law standards of legality, reasonableness, and the principles of natural justice) to decide whether to renew the lease, grant the tenant a new lease of different property, or evict the tenant. There will no longer be a need to rely on any particular grounds. This is obviously an enormously significant development in terms of security of tenure.

It will mean, importantly, that there is very limited security of tenure in all three contexts. In the business tenancies sector, it is possibly simply to contract out of the Act. In the private rental sector, ASTs provide very limited security of tenure and are the norm. In the public rental sector there will be merely a fixed-term contractual tenancy and a mandatory review process, not providing any genuine security of tenure.

10.5.6 TENANTS' FIXTURES AT THE END OF A LEASE

At the end of the lease, tenants may wish to argue that they can remove certain items brought to the land by them during the lease. Whether or not they can do so depends upon whether the goods remain chattels or have become part of the land. We considered the distinction between moveables and land in chapter 2, but there are special rules in respect of leases which are summarised here. Whilst fixtures in general are items which have become part of the land, and therefore would not be removeable, where a fixture is a 'tenant's fixture' it can be removed. This will be the case where the item was brought onto the land as part of a trade or business, for ornamental or decorative purposes, or for agricultural purposes, and can be removed without causing substantial damage to the land.

10.6 SUB-LEASES, CONCURRENT LEASES, AND REVERSIONARY INTERESTS

The final issue to consider is one of the most flexible and useful aspect of leases, the ability to sublet, to create concurrent leases, and the nature of the reversionary interest (ie the interest of the freeholder) during the currency of the lease.

A sub-lease exists where a tenant (T1) grants to another tenant (T2) a term *shorter* than T1's term. For example, T1 has a ten-year lease and sub-lets to T2, granting them a three-year lease. This can be contrasted with an assignment of the lease, which would be where T1 grants the remaining time left on their lease to another person. Very often, sub-letting is prohibited in a lease contract, at least without the consent of the landlord. Furthermore, the security of tenure provisions contain limitations on the ability to sub-let (except to spouses, for example, where this is generally possible). This is because the purposes of the residential protections for tenants is to allow that person to remain in their home unless the grounds for possession apply. It is not to allow them to take *financial* advantage of the rental value of that property. In relation to Council properties in particular, allowing free sub-letting may result in a protected tenant, T1, paying below market rent for their property, and then sub-letting at market rent, thus making a profit at the expense of the Council and the public purse.

Concurrent leases are slightly different. A concurrent lease arises where an initial lease is granted to T1 for, say, 10 years. The freeholder then grants another lease to T2 for 15 years. Depending upon the relevant priority rules (see chapter 15), if T1 has priority over T2, in this situation T2 will be treated as having a concurrent lease which goes into possession at the end of T1's term. Until that point, T2 is unable to go into possession of the land. This is a different position from a sub-let because the second lease is granted by the landlord.

Finally, we can consider the position of the freeholder during the currency of the lease. Her interest at this time is described as a reversionary interest because the right to possession of the land reverts to her once the lease(s) come to an end. This interest is itself assignable, so that the freeholder can transfer her freehold interest to a third party, and subject to the priority rules, the new freeholder will be bound by those lease(s). A superior tenant (T1) in a sub-leasing situation also has a reversionary interest during the currency of the sub-lease. This too can be assignable depending upon the terms of the head lease (T1's lease).

10.7 CONCLUSION

This chapter has covered a lot of ground. Unlike the freehold estate, where the rules are essentially a 'negative space' in that the freehold owner is able to do with the land anything not otherwise specifically limited, either by public policy or by the rights of others, the leasehold estate is constrained in a number of ways. As noted in the introduction, the concept has to operate in a very wide range of circumstances, meaning that a range of rules have developed to cater for these different contexts. The overall picture is one which is hard to master, and yet the fundamentals of leases are relatively straightforward: consensual possession of land for a limited duration. This relationship is at once a proprietary one, and one hemmed in by contract. From the former we derive protections for tenants in the form of security of tenure, and we understand the rules relating to forfeiture: from the latter have developed the rules relating to enforcement of leasehold covenants, and the essentials of term and scope. How leases are created, operate, and eventually come to an end is also fundamentally simple, even if once the details are examined a great deal of complexity emerges. Leases are created by a consensual agreement—depending upon the length and type of the lease, a greater or lesser degree of formality is needed. Leases operate according to the terms of the contract—where leases and reversions are assigned, in essence, the new landlord and tenant will be affected only by those aspects of the leasehold contract that were related to the property, whilst those who have assigned will be released from on-going obligations unless they chose to retain duties. Finally, the lease will come to an end through time, through breach of obligations, or through a process shaped by statutory rules but which, in effect, try to reach a fair compromise between the landlord and their tenant.

PRINCIPLES

How does this discussion shape our understanding of the principles explained in chapter 1? To recap, these principles were:

1. Certainty
2. Sensitivity to context
3. Transactability
4. Systemic and individual effects
5. Recognition of the social role of the land law system.

Given the breadth of the rules considered here, to sum up how the operation of the leasehold estate operates within the principles of land law is a challenging task. In places, clearly, the social role of the law is paramount: residential security of tenure, particularly in a public residential context, is a reflection of the fact that such leases represent the provision of housing to the most vulnerable. On the other hand, the ways in which the Landlord and Tenant Covenants Act 1995 has been interpreted—particularly in *Avonridge* is an expression of the importance of the commercial certainty and risk, to the detriment of those which the relevant rules were, from the outset, designed to protect.

However, if we look to the fundamentals of the leasehold relationship, its essence is one of ensuring certainty. By dismissing the subjective intentions of the parties in favour of an objective assessment of the nature of the agreement reached, the courts give primacy to the *numerus clausus*, and to the idea that in order to be capable of conferring a proprietary interest onto an individual, an agreement must fall into certain 'forms'. Furthermore, by focusing on the need for a certain maximum duration, whether a result of the agreement or of statutory workarounds, again the law is highlighting that leases cannot be created in a manner which undermines the certainty of the content of that right for all concerned.

In considering the means by, and circumstances in which, leases can be brought to an end, however, this pursuit of certainty is replaced by a focus on individual circumstances, albeit filtered through structured rules. Thus, the rules relating to relief from forfeiture are not susceptible to certain guidance: rather the courts will look at individual circumstances. Similarly, when we consider security of tenure, whilst the 'grounds' upon which a landlord can rely in attempting to bring a lease to an end are clear, the interpretation of these in practice can be somewhat more of a lottery.

In respect of transactiblity, the primary area where this becomes relevant to leases is in the rules relating to covenants and even in the 'summary' given here there is an enormous amount of complexity. The law here is really unsatisfactory, not least because it is so hard to provide a concise and comprehensible explanation! This is not just a problem for those learning the rules, but also for companies and individuals attempting to plan on the basis of these rules. The 1995 Act does however make a leasehold interest more transactable by giving the original landlord and tenant the ability to release themselves from the obligations under the lease. Without this, both parties would be very nervous about assigning their interest, in case they should be sued under obligations owed under the original contract but without any longer be able to benefit from the land itself.

Having said all of this, whilst there are problems without a doubt, in the operation of leases, the lease is also one of the triumphs of English land law in its sheer usefulness and versatility. It is perhaps for this reason that we 'muddle along' with some of the more problematic aspects.

TABLE OF DEFINITIONS

Lease	A property right arising where there is a consensual grant of exclusive possession for a limited duration.
Possession	The right to, or the fact of, control of land characterised by the ability to exclude others.
Term	The duration of a lease.

Rent	Sums regularly due under a lease.
Premium/fine	A sum paid at the commencement of a lease.
Forfeiture	The process by which a landlord goes into possession of tenanted land, so as to bring the lease to an end.
Covenant	A promise made by deed.
Touches and concerns	The requirement that a covenant must benefit land, not persons only, and must do so from its inception.
Fixed term tenancy	A lease where the contractual term of the lease is for a single, fixed duration.
Periodic tenancy	A lease where the leasehold agreement 'rolls over' from period to period. This is usually calculated on the basis of the regularity with which rent is due.
Tenancy at will	An estate in land where the tenant has a right to possession but no tenure so that the lease may be brought to an end at any time.

FURTHER READING

The further reading in this section is designed to provide a starting point in relation to some of the areas of this chapter where only the first basic steps are explained: landlord and tenant covenants, remedies and forfeiture, and security of tenure. These are specialist landlord and tenant law issues, and few land law courses cover them in detail. However, in practice they are very important rules and are essential to the value of leases.

HALEY, M., 'Business Tenancies: Parting with Occupation' [1997] Conv. 139.
REYNOLDS, K. and CLARK, W., *Renewal of business Tenancies* (5th ed) (Sweet & Maxwell, 2016).
GARNER, S. and FRITH, A., *A Practical Approach to Landlord and Tenant* (8th ed) (OUP, 2017).
BLANDY, S., BRIGHT, S., and NIELD, S., 'The dynamics of enduring property relationships in land' (2018) 81 MLR 85.

11

MORTGAGES

11.1 Introduction	331	11.6 Position of the Mortgagor	358
11.2 Nature of Mortgages	332	11.7 Mortgages and Third Parties	368
11.3 Formalities for the Creation of a Mortgage	333	11.8 Conclusion	373
11.4 Remedies of the Legal Mortgagee	336	Principles	373
11.5 Remedies—Equitable Mortgages and Charges	356	Table of Definitions	375
		Further Reading	375

CHAPTER GOALS

By the end of this chapter, you should understand:

- The idea of the mortgage as a secured debt in relation to land;
- The steps required in order to create a valid mortgage, in law and in equity;
- The remedies of a lender, considering actions on the contract debt, foreclosure, sale, possession, and the appointment of receivers, and how these alter in cases involving equitable mortgages;
- The position of the mortgagor; and
- The interaction between rights arising under a mortgage and third parties.

11.1 INTRODUCTION

Mortgages are fundamental to the functioning of modern land law. They are the means by which most people finance the acquisition of their property. They therefore underpin the enormous amount of wealth wrapped up in our land law system. But mortgages are more than simply a commercial transaction between a lender and a homeowner. They are also a property right in themselves and this brings with it a wide variety of options for the lender in terms of recovering their security. They also pose huge risks for the borrower. The focus in UK culture on home ownership in this sense does bring with it problems for those who struggle to afford their repayments. We will consider these different aspects of mortgages throughout this chapter. In 11.2 we examine the nature of the mortgage right and in particular consider what terms can and cannot form part of a mortgage agreement. In 11.3 we consider the formal requirements of mortgages in terms of their creation. Section 11.4 considers problems in the creation of a mortgage and the effects of these, looking in particular at the issues caused by undue influence. Section 11.5 considers the rights and obligations of the borrower in a mortgage (mortgagor), and section 11.6 considers the rights and obligations of the lender (mortgagee). Section 11.7 then considers third party effects of a mortgage, priorities, and land registration. The last of these issues is one of the most difficult areas of land law, and, as a result, one of the areas most tested in problem questions. However, it is considered in much more detail in the priorities chapter (chapter 15). The discussion in this chapter should be seen only as a starting point.

11.2 NATURE OF MORTGAGES

Like all property rights, thanks to the *numerus clausus*, mortgage agreements must contain certain elements and must not contain certain other elements in order to constitute a valid mortgage. At its heart a mortgage is simply a right given to a lender as security for a loan. Before 1925, a mortgage actually involved the handing over of title to the relevant land subject to the right to get it back (the right of redemption) should the money owed be paid back in full plus any interest. Statutory reforms mean that mortgages of the legal title at least do not operate in this way, but instead constitute the creation of an additional proprietary interest for the mortgagee. However, appreciating that as a matter of history the mortgage involved the handing over of title helps to navigate some of the issues surrounding the remedies of the lender in particular.

There are certain rules surrounding the mortgage that limit what can be agreed as part of a mortgage transaction. Not least amongst these is the fundamental principle that, 'once a mortgage, always a mortgage'. This rule means that a mortgage must have, at its core, the right for the borrower to discharge the mortgage interest, having a 'clean' title, once all the monies are repaid. Anything which prevents this is not in the nature of a mortgage. It would therefore be either fatal to the creation of the relevant agreement as a property right, or will be rendered a void term by the courts if the lender attempts to enforce it. It is also critical to understand that the mortgage is at once a contract and a property right.

Throughout this chapter we will refer, generically, to mortgages. However, the term is used inaccurately, but commonly, to describe a number of subtly different security interests. The most important terminological distinction is that between mortgages and charges. This distinction is of largely historical importance, and many now use these terms interchangeably. Understanding it is nevertheless useful especially in relation to equitable rights. A mortgage used to involve the conveyance of title to the land to the lender, subject to the right of redemption of the borrower. Thus, the mortgagee would be title-holder to the land, be that freehold or leasehold, and the borrower would have an equitable proprietary right in the land allowing him to regain title should the mortgage money be repaid. A charge, by contrast, was a right which attached to the land of another entitling the charge-holder to certain remedies.

In modern land law, it is now only possible, since 1 October 2003, to create legal mortgages in the form of a charge by deed expressed to be by way of legal mortgage. The consequence of creating a mortgage in this way is that the mortgagee is treated *as though* they had a 3000-year lease in relation to freehold land, and a term of years in relation to leasehold land. The consequence of this is to give the mortgagee the same rights as a long leaseholder, albeit that statutory provisions supplement and constrain these rights in various ways. The most fundamental of these rights is, as the chapter concerning leaseholds explains, the right to exclusive possession of the land. This rather convoluted way of conceptualising the nature of a mortgage may seem to be an unnecessary series of fictions. However, given that the practical consequences of the mortgage are almost all a matter for statutory regulation and contractual agreement, it is simply useful to understand this 'leasehold fiction' to explain why the mortgagee has an immediate right to possession of the land, and to understand the statutory language.

Equitable 'mortgages', by contrast, arise in a wide variety of ways. It is important to realise that equitable mortgages generally fall into four categories: (1) mortgages of equitable rights, ie a mortgage created by a beneficiary of a trust over their trust interest; (2) an equitable mortgage created by a legal owner where a deed was used (but the mortgage was not registered); (3) an equitable mortgage created by a legal owner where only a section 2 LP(MP)A 1989-compliant contract was used; and (4) an equitable charge. As we shall see later, both the formal requirements for the creation of these rights, and the rights and remedies associated with them differ according to which of these has arisen. Before we go on to examine these in more detail, it may be useful to consult the table of definitions at the end of the chapter, because the language is particularly 'counter-intuitive' in this area of the law.

11.3 FORMALITIES FOR THE CREATION OF A MORTGAGE

The creation of mortgages, as with other property rights, is a question of following the appropriate formalities. It used to be possible to create a mortgage by other means. For example, this could be done through the deposit of title deeds with the lender as security for the debt, but this is no longer possible following the introduction of section 2 Law of Property (Miscellaneous Provisions) Act 1989. If a contract is created which complies with this section, then an equitable mortgage will be created, be that an equitable mortgage of a legal estate, or an equitable mortgage of an equitable interest (such as an interest under a trust).

In order to create a 'legal mortgage' (strictly, a registered charge by way of legal mortgage) then the further steps of the creation of a deed (as per section 87 LPA 1925) which is duly registered will be required. The terminology here is important. As noted previously there are subtle differences between charges and mortgages (particularly in equity). However, since the LRA 2002, it has been clear that just as there is only one conceptualisation of the legal mortgage, ie the charge by deed expressed to be by way of legal mortgage duly registered, so too there is only one methodology for creating such rights. This involves the creation of a deed which complies with section 1 Law of Property (Miscellaneous Provisions) Act 1989, and the registration of that deed in line with section 4(1)(g) (first registration upon the grant of a first legal mortgage) and section 27(2)(f) (registrable dispositions) LRA 2002 (for more on first and subsequent registrations in terms of the process of rights creation see chapter 5 at 5.2).

For unregistered land (keeping in mind that a new first mortgage now would trigger compulsory registration), and for any mortgage entered into before the coming into force of the LRA 2002, there remains another method of mortgage creation: a demise of term of years, ie the demise of a leasehold estate in the lender subject to the right to redeem. This method too required the use of a deed although as was noted earlier, as a result of section 23 LRA 2002, it is no longer possible to use this method of creating a mortgage. Under both of these methods the mortgagor keeps his legal title. This was the fundamental change brought about by the 1925 legislation. It is a reflection of the ways in which the mortgage has changed in terms of its commercial role since its inception in the 12th and 13th centuries. One very significant consequence of retaining title of course is the ability to grant subsequent mortgages over the same property, giving rise to the possibility of multiple lenders having mortgage-based remedies in relation to the same piece of land. As we shall see, this possibility is the source of much grief in the operation of the law. It is usually in cases of multiple mortgages that the borrower is risk of losing their property and the greater number of lenders vastly increases the possibility that the property is in negative equity.

As highlighted earlier, in cases where the formal requirements needed to create a legal mortgage are not met, the consequence will, as a result of the doctrine in *Walsh v Lonsdale*,[1] be an equitable mortgage as long as there is a contract which complies with section 2 LP(MP)A 1989. There are however other methods by which an equitable mortgage can be created. The first of these is express creation of such a mortgage. This would be rare as most lenders would not be willing to lend on the basis of an equitable mortgage only, given the consequences that this has for the potential priority of their right as we discuss in chapter 15 and briefly at 11.5 in this chapter. However, it does happen in cases of co-ownership for example. In order for a valid legal mortgage to be granted in respect of co-owned land, all legal title-holders would be required to execute the mortgage deed. This means that the creation of the mortgage depends upon the consent of all legal owners. Where this consent cannot be obtained, it is still possible for one co-owner to create a mortgage over his own equitable 'share' in the property. This is an equitable mortgage over an equitable interest in the land. In cases where the parties hold as joint tenants at equity, the entering into the mortgage will itself have the effect of severing the joint tenancy (see chapter 16 at 16.3.3.2). In cases where the parties hold as tenants in common, the co-owners are of course at liberty to deal with their own equitable interest in the property as they wish without the consent of the other. Thus, in cases where one co-owner wishes to borrow, as long as the lender is satisfied about the commercial risks of such a lending, it is possible to create an express equitable mortgage. To achieve this it will only be necessary to use section 2-compliant contract. However, as we shall see later, it is possible in relation to some equitable mortgages for the lender to have the same remedies as a legal mortgagee as long as the mortgage is made by deed. This is the consequence of the decision in *Swift 1st v Colin*[2] (see the key case box). This means that there is a certain incentive to utilise a deed even in cases of a deliberate equitable mortgage.

---

[1] *Walsh v Lonsdale* (1882) 21 Ch D 9.
[2] *Swift 1st v Colin* [2011] EWHC 2410 (Ch), [2012] Ch 206.

It is also the case that an equitable mortgage will arise when all that the borrower has is an equitable interest—either an interest under a trust of the freehold or leasehold estate, or an equitable lease—and here the same rules apply in relation to the use of contracts and deeds. However, it should be noted that because the 1925 legislation did not change the fundamental nature of equitable mortgages, equitable mortgages of equitable estates are still conceptualised as a transfer of the equitable estate subject to a *new* right arising in the borrower, that is, the right to redeem their title on repayment of loan and interest. As a result of this, there are two methods by which such a mortgage can be created. First, in cases where the parties seek a contractual agreement outlining their rights and responsibilities in respect of the lending, they should use a section 2-compliant contract. Such a contract would likely also suffice for the formalities required for the transfer of an equitable estate in land as required by section 53(1)(c) LPA 1925. In a commercial transaction it would be usual to have both documents for the peace of mind of the lender. Second, however, the parties could simply use a form which met only with the requirements of section 53(1)(c), ie was made in writing. This would mean that they did not have an enforceable contract, but it would not prevent there being a valid disposition of the equitable interest. Nor would it prevent the equitable right of redemption vesting in the borrower. It would produce some problems however, not least as cases like *Mirza v Mirza*[3] show in respect of attempts to enforce terms regarding payment of interest, for example.

Finally, it is possible to create an equitable charge. Equitable charges can be created simply by contract and there is no conveyance of any title either legal or equitable consequent upon this. As long as the contract complies with section 2, there are no further requirements to create such an interest.

Summary: Formalities for the creation of mortgages

1. Legal mortgage. To create a legal mortgage, a contract which complies with section 2 LP(MP)A 1989; a deed which complies with section 1 LP(MP)A 1989; and registration of the mortgage is required per section 4 and 27 LRA 2002.

2. Equitable mortgage.
   (a) To create an equitable mortgage of a legal interest, a contract which complies with section 2 LP(MP)A 1989 or a deed which complies with section 1 LP(MP)A 1989 is required. If a deed is present, then the mortgagee will be able to take advantage of the remedies implied by section 101 LPA 1925 (see later).
   (b) To create an equitable mortgage of an equitable interest, a document which complies with section 53(1) LPA 1925 is required. A section 2-compliant contract would suffice.

3. Equitable charge. A contract which complies with section 2 LP(MP)A 1989 is required to create an equitable charge.

---

[3] *Mirza v Mirza* [2009] EWHC 3 (Ch), [2009] 2 FLR 115.

11.4 REMEDIES OF THE LEGAL MORTGAGEE

For practical purposes, the most important element of the mortgage relationship will be how strong are the remedies available to the lender. This is because the stronger the remedies are, the less risky the lender will perceive the transaction to be. As a result, interest rates will be theoretically lower, giving access to such borrowing to a wider range of persons. In English land law, the remedies for the lender are very strong. We will consider them in turn in this section, before examining how they interact. They are: the ability to sue on the contract debt; foreclosure; the right to possession; the power to sell; and the power to appoint a receiver.

11.4.1 ACTION ON THE CONTRACT DEBT

As mentioned earlier, the mortgage is both contract and property. The right to sue on the contract debt is the ultimate expression of the contractual nature of the promises entered into. The borrower agrees, as per the contract, to repay the sums lent. The contract will usually state the date at which this money is due, whether by instalments or as a lump sum, and what interest is due. Even if the mortgage does not expressly provide terms relating to repayment, the obligation to repay will be implied. If the mortgagor fails to pay according to these terms, the lender can bring a personal action against them demanding such payment. Although very simple, this is usually not a very effective remedy in itself. The borrower will rarely have the funds available to repay the loan on demand like this. If they did, the lender would probably not need to bring an action against them! However, that does not mean that this remedy is not useful. It may not, in most cases, produce payment of the sums due, but it does have a number of other consequences. Of these, probably the most significant is the potential to hasten bankruptcy or insolvency in the case of a corporate borrower, which can itself be a desired outcome for the lender. This is shown by the case *Alliance & Leicester v Slayford*.[4]

> **Key case:** *Alliance & Leicester v Slayford* [2001] 1 All ER (Comm) 1
>
> Mr Slayford had mortgaged the property, legal title to which was in his sole name. Mrs Slayford had an equitable interest in the property. She had signed a priority waiver at the time of the mortgage, but claimed that as she did not understand this waiver it had been ineffective. The court agreed that the waiver was ineffective as Mrs Slayford had been misled by her husband. As a result, the mortgagee could not obtain a possession order against Mrs Slayford. To get around this problem, the mortgagee decided to sue Mr Slayford on the personal covenant for the debt, a move which they knew would render him bankrupt. The consequence of this would be that even though the mortgagee did not have priority over Mrs Slayford, by relying on section 335A Insolvency Act 1986, the mortgagee would be able to obtain possession and sale of the property much more easily than if they had to rely on the factors in section 15 Trusts of Land and Appointment of Trustees Act 1996 (TOLATA 1996) (discussed in detail in chapter 16). The question for the court in this case, therefore, was whether this deliberate tactic to avoid any protection given to Mrs Slayford by tactically rendering her husband bankrupt was an abuse of process.

---

[4] *Alliance & Leicester v Slayford* [2001] 1 All ER (Comm) 1 (CA).

The Court of Appeal was very clear that this was not an abuse of process, and highlighted that lender's remedies are cumulative and can be applied until the sums due are repaid.[5] Furthermore, the judge was clear that the personal circumstances of the borrowers did not affect the legitimacy of the mortgagee's actions:

> 'By that he [counsel for Mrs Slayford] means their age (Mr. Slayford is 65, Mrs. Slayford 52), Mrs. Slayford's epilepsy, the effect on Mrs. Slayford if litigation is prolonged and their financial circumstances. I am afraid that these matters, taking singly or cumulatively, do not seem to me to begin to justify denying a secured creditor who has not hitherto proceeded on the personal covenant against the mortgagor the opportunity to obtain a judgment against the mortgagor for what is due. It is simply not an abuse of process to sue a mortgagor of Mr. Slayford's age and lack of resources when he has on any footing defaulted so massively on his obligations'.[6]

It is notable that at first instance the judge in this case had been extremely critical of the bank. He stated that:

> 'I have to say that I find the approach of the [Bank] disgusting beyond belief and I shall say so. Right, and I do not care who knows it and I do not care whether you are right as a matter of law or not it is disgusting to try and obtain possession by the back door against an elderly couple of this kind. It is revolting beyond belief'.[7]

This sort of language is very rare. The Court of Appeal certainly attempts to distance itself from such criticisms of the lender's actions. Importantly, the court emphasises that notwithstanding Mr Slayford's age, he has voluntarily entered into the mortgage transaction and as a result the bank must be legitimate in expecting those sums to be repaid.

Another useful element of the remedy in contract for the lender is the ability to continue to pursue a borrower even once the property has been sold, for any shortfall. This is important in cases of negative equity in ensuring that the mortgagee is able to recover the entirety of the sums due, regardless of the sale price of the house. Again, the mortgagor may not have sufficient funds available, but the possibility is itself useful to the mortgagee. Furthermore, because the proprietary rights arising through the mortgage relate to the specific land subject to the mortgage, the lender cannot use their proprietary remedies to force a sale of property or other assets belonging to the mortgagor. However, suing on the contract debt, either by forcing a bankruptcy, or by giving the courts the possibility of making a charging order in respect of other property, would allow the mortgagee to tap into these otherwise inaccessible sources of wealth.

11.4.2 FORECLOSURE

Just as the ability to sue on the contract debt is the ultimate expression of the nature of the mortgage as a contractual agreement, so too is the remedy of foreclosure the ultimate expression of the mortgage as a proprietary interest. It is the essence of a secured debt: 'if you do not pay me, I get

---

[5] *Alliance & Leicester v Slayford* [2001] 1 All ER (Comm) 1 (CA), [28].
[6] *Alliance & Leicester v Slayford* [2001] 1 All ER (Comm) 1 (CA), [30].
[7] *Alliance & Leicester v Slayford* [2001] 1 All ER (Comm) 1 (CA), [5], cited in M Thompson, 'The cumulative range of a mortgagee's remedies' [2002] Conv 53, 56.

to keep your thing', and of course has its roots in the original form of the mortgage involving conveyance of legal title. In such cases, foreclosure would extinguish the right to redeem. However, in modern law, foreclosure is actually very rare. A lender has to apply to the court to be granted the right to foreclose. The courts usually refuse this and instead order a sale under section 91 Law of Property Act 1925. This is because foreclosure involves the mortgagee being transferred title to the property, and with it, the entire value of the property regardless of how much was owing to them. We can see the problem with this with an example.

Imagine that Phil, purchasing a property outright in 2010 for £500,000, decided in 2015 to borrow £100,000 on the security of a mortgage against the property to carry out development works on the property. The value of the property increased to £1,000,000 as a result of these works, but unfortunately Phil is unable to keep up with the mortgage payments due to a change in his circumstances. In this situation, if the bank were to be able to foreclose on the mortgage, they would become outright owner of a £1,000,000 asset whereas the sums owed would be somewhere in the region of 10 per cent of that.

As a result of this potentially unfair outcome—remember, the modern law is very strict to ensure that a mortgage transaction is really there as a means for the lender to ensure recovery of the money lent, it is not there to secure some other advantages for the lender—the courts have a power to order sale in lieu of foreclosure. Because, as we shall see, mortgagees will generally have a power of sale themselves which does not require a court action for its exercise, it is now therefore rare not only for a court to allow foreclosure, but in fact for a lender to even apply for it.

11.4.3 RIGHT TO POSSESSION

Like the remedy of foreclosure, the right of the mortgagee to go into possession of the mortgaged property is an inherent consequence of the mortgage as a proprietary interest. We discussed earlier the fact that the conceptualisation of the mortgage in modern law is *as if* the lender has the benefit of a 3000-year lease (in respect of freehold property). This brings with it a right to possession as soon as the mortgage is created. This means that the mortgagee is able to go into possession of the mortgaged property at any time during the currency of the mortgage unless they have contractually or otherwise voluntarily limited the availability of that right. It is a common misconception that the mortgagee cannot go into possession unless the borrower is in default.

However, it should be noted that, first, there is usually very little incentive for a lender to go into possession unless the mortgagor is in default or otherwise threatening to be unable to pay the sums due, at least in a residential context. This is because, once in possession, the lender falls under a duty to achieve maximum income from the property in order that the property 'pays its way' in terms of paying down the mortgage debt. It is therefore usually more trouble that it's worth to go into possession of mortgaged property unless it is with a view to sale in due course (see later). In respect of commercial property, there may be more sense in the mortgagee going into possession to ensure, for example, that the property is being effectively rented out to maximise the income from the property.

Furthermore, the consequence of a lender going into possession of mortgaged land, can be, and indeed usually is, 'traumatic' (in the words of Gray and Gray) for the mortgagor and any other residents of the property.[8] For this reason, and generally in line with modern law's recognition of the weak bargaining power of consumers in many contexts, the law has limited the ways in which the lender can exercise their right to possession. It must be noted from the outset, however, that these limitations—which stem from both the criminal law and property law—only apply where either the lender has had to 'force' their way into possession in some way, or where the lender has applied to the court for an order for possession. The fundamental ability of the lender simply to go into mortgaged property and remain there, is still present in modern law. We can see this if we consider *Ropaigealach v Barclays Bank*.[9]

> **Key case:** *Ropaigealach v Barclays Bank* [2000] QB 263
>
> Mr and Mrs Ropaigealach had granted to the bank a registered charge in respect of a property in Cardiff. They had failed to pay sums due under the mortgage and were almost £64,000 in arrears. At the relevant time they were not living in the property, as it was being refurbished. The bank decided to sell the property by auction and although they sent letters to this effect to the mortgagors, the mortgagors claimed to be unaware of what was happening until after the sale was complete. The question for the court was (a) whether the bank was able to sell the property without first going into possession and (b) whether the bank was able to go into possession of the property without first seeking a court order. Chadwick LJ made a very thorough examination of the background to and purpose of section 36 AJA 1970 (a section we discuss in more detail later, and which constrains the ability of a lender to go into possession of residential property in cases where a court order is sought). He reasoned, first, that Parliament did not intend here to make it necessary for a lender to go to court to exercise a right to possession. Rather, he argued, it is clear that Parliament had not considered whether a borrower needed protection against a lender who took possession without a court order, not least because the majority of residential occupiers would have had the protection of the Criminal Law Act 1977. As a result, the court concluded that a literal interpretation of the statutory provisions was the most appropriate.[10]
>
> The other judges agreed with this conclusion, although Clarke LJ was extremely reluctant to do so, and highlighted the consequences of interpreting the statute in this way:
>
>> 'It seems to me that if a mortgagor needs that relief he needs it whether the mortgagee chooses to exercise his right of possession by entering into possession with or without an order of the court. Indeed he also needs it if instead of doing either the mortgagee sells the property to a purchaser leaving the purchaser to take possession.'[11]
>
> Both Dunn[12] and Dixon[13] in their comments on this case recognise that although perhaps regrettable, there was really no other interpretive option open to the Court of Appeal in this case. It is also important to realise that the facts of this case inevitably make it unusual. As we discuss later, it will be very rare that a lender is able lawfully to go into possession without a court order, and therefore without the possibility of borrower reliance on section 36 being triggered.

---

[8] Gray and Gray, *Land Law* (7th ed) (Oxford University Press, Oxford, 2011), 304.
[9] *Ropaigealach v Barclays Bank* [2000] QB 263 (CA).
[10] *Ropaigealach v Barclays Bank* [2000] QB 263 (CA), 282–3.
[11] *Ropaigealach v Barclays Bank* [2000] QB 263 (CA), 286.
[12] Dunn, 'No tempering of the wind for the shorn lamb' [1999] Conv 263.
[13] Dixon, 'Sorry, we've sold your home: mortgagees and their possessory rights' (1999) 58 CLJ 281.

The limitations on the right of possession are fivefold. First, section 6 Criminal Law Act 1977 limits the circumstances in which a lender can go into possession of residential land. Second, if the lender applies to the court for an order for possession (and so avoiding conflict with the first rule), then the borrower may be able to rely on the Administration of Justice Act 1970, section 36, to obtain a delay in the lender going into possession. Third, there is the court's inherent jurisdiction to delay possession for a very short period to allow time for the mortgagor to raise finance. Fourth, there are certain 'soft law' controls on the ways in which lenders behave, such as Council of Mortgage Lenders code of practice, the pre-action protocol, and the requirement of a published policy in line with the Financial Services and Markets Act 2000. Finally, and controversially, there is an argument that human rights controls may limit the ability of the lender to go into possession. We will consider these in turn.

11.4.3.1 Criminal Law Act 1977

Section 6(1) controls the ability of a lender to simply go into possession without a court order. It states that:

'(1) ...any person who, without lawful authority, uses or threatens violence for the purpose of securing entry into any premises for himself or for any other person is guilty of an offence, provided that—(a) there is someone present on those premises at the time who is opposed to the entry which the violence is intended to secure'.

'Violence' here is not necessarily referring to physical violence or threats of such violence, but can include also violence to the property (section 6(4)(a)). Therefore it would cover things like breaking a down door, damaging a lock, etc. It is very difficult to see how a lender could in fact secure possession of premises where there is an unwilling occupant without resorting to violence or threats of violence in some way. In any case, whether or not the mortgagee would in fact breach this provision, the *possibility* of such a breach means that in almost all cases involving a residential occupier, they will simply obtain a court order. Such a proceedings is usually not too lengthy or expensive, and it saves a lot of problems should the lender 'get it wrong' and breach section 6(1).

11.4.3.2 Administration of Justice Act 1970, Section 36

As soon as the mortgagee seeks a court order for possession, however, in respect of residential property, this brings the possibility of the mortgagor resisting an order for possession on the grounds of section 36. This section states that:

'(1) Where the mortgagee under a mortgage of land which consists of or includes a dwelling-house brings an action in which he claims possession of the mortgaged property, not being an action for foreclosure in which a claim for possession of the mortgaged property is also made, the court may exercise any of the powers conferred on it by subsection (2) below if it appears to the court that in the event of its exercising the power the mortgagor is likely to be able within a reasonable period to pay any sums due under the mortgage or to remedy a default consisting of a breach of any other obligation arising under or by virtue of the mortgage.

(2) The court—

    (a) may adjourn the proceedings, or

    (b) on giving judgment, or making an order, for delivery of possession of the mortgaged property, or at any time before the execution of such judgment or order, may—

        (i) stay or suspend execution of the judgment or order, or

        (ii) postpone the date for delivery of possession, for such period or periods as the court thinks reasonable'.

This provision allows a residential occupier to argue that because they will be able to pay back any sums due within a reasonable time, the mortgagee's order for possession should be delayed to allow that to happen. It is critical therefore, to understand what the central terms mean here: dwelling-house; reasonable period; and sums due.

Dwelling-house

The meaning of the term dwelling-house has been litigated about for many years, albeit not always in the context of section 36. This term is critical in determining the scope of residential security of tenure for tenants and is discussed in chapter 10 at 10.5.5.2. The courts used to determine the meaning of dwelling-house by ascertaining, in a rather formulaic way, whether the property provided all the facilities required by the residential occupier, including kitchen and bathroom facilities. However, this approach was changed in the seminal House of Lords decision in *Uratemp*[14]. In that case, the court concluded that the test for a dwelling-house was not functional, but rather, one of perception. They shifted the focus to the question as to whether the occupant perceived the property to be their 'home'. This decision assisted those living in precarious environments (such as long-term occupants of hotel rooms). However, in the context of section 36, that issue is less likely to arise simply because it is very unlikely that a lender would lend on the security of such a property.

Rather, in this context the debate tends to be more around work-live spaces, where the property is a mixture of residential and commercial. The section is clear that just because the property also contains commercial space is not enough to take the facts outside of the scope of section 36.

Reasonable period

How the courts interpret the terms 'reasonable period' is essential to the operation of this section. Not only does it determine when the protection for the borrower applies, but it also determines how likely it is that they will be able to pay the sums back. Thus, if the reasonable period of time is relatively short—in a mortgage context, one or two years—then it is highly unlikely that the borrower can show that they can pay back. On the other hand, if the reasonable period

---

[14] *Uratemp Ventures Ltd v Collins* [2001] UKHL 43, [2002] 1 AC 301.

is 20 years say, then the borrower will likely be in a stronger position. The court's answer to this question has changed over the years, but the decision in *Cheltenham & Gloucester v Norgan*[15] now represents settled law.

> **Key case:** *Cheltenham & Gloucester v Norgan* [1996] 1 WLR 343
>
> The facts of this case are unremarkable. They involved a straightforward mortgage granted by a couple to the lender, sums on which were owing. The lender sought a possession order against the couple. Although this was granted, it was suspended twice on the basis that the borrowers argued that they could pay back sums due. The suspensions were for a relatively short period of time.
>
> This pattern reflected the prevailing approach to section 36 at the time, which was to give one or two year suspensions to possession orders in the hope of payment by the borrower. However, courts, recognising the enormous effect that a possession order would have on a borrower were generous in granting repeated suspensions, as here. This was inconvenient for all parties. The lender spent time and money in bringing more than one action and the borrower had a sword of Damocles above their head knowing that they were unlikely to be able to pay back all the money within a short period of time, even if they made progress. As a result, the court changed its approach here, and instead reasoned that the starting point for calculating the reasonable time should be the remaining term of the mortgage. However, the court also emphasised that in shifting the presumption, they would need to be more rigorous than in the past in ensuring that borrowers' finances were such that the repayment over this longer period of time were reasonably assured. Again, per Waite LJ:
>
>> 'I would acknowledge, also, that this approach will be liable to demand a more detailed analysis of present figures and future projections than it may have been customary for the courts to undertake until now. There is likely to be a greater need to require of mortgagors that they should furnish the court with a detailed "budget" of the kind that has been supplied by the mortgagor in her affidavit in the present case'.[16]
>
> As Morgan highlights, therefore, 'Norgan will be of assistance only to those borrowers who are able to present to the judge a sensible, workable budget'.[17] She also emphasises, as did the court, that the new approach is very much a 'one-strike' approach. If the borrower fails to meet their new payment 'schedule', then they will not be given a second chance. Thompson agrees with this assessment, cautioning that:
>
>> 'It would seem that, for the future, a mortgagor will only have one bite of the cherry which, although preventing the steady escalation of costs which, ultimately will be borne by the mortgagor, may cause hardship in certain cases and it is to be hoped that an inflexible practice with regard to this matter does not develop'.[18]
>
> Fisher & Lightwood, the leading practitioners' text on mortgages, explains the considerations now relevant to the determination of a 'reasonable period' as follows, showing that whilst the whole length of the term is the right starting point, the courts can take a range of factors into 'modifying' that starting point:
>
>> '(a) How much can the borrower reasonably afford to pay, both now and in the future?;
>>
>> (b) If the borrower has a temporary difficulty in meeting his obligations, how long is the difficulty liable to last?

---

[15] *Cheltenham & Gloucester v Norgan* [1996] 1 WLR 343 (CA).
[16] *Cheltenham & Gloucester v Norgan* [1996] 1 WLR 343 (CA), 353.
[17] Morgan, 'Mortgage arrears and the family home' (1996) 112 LQR 553, 557.
[18] Thompson, 'Back to square two' [1996] Conv 118, 123.

(c) What was the reason for the arrears which have accumulated?

(d) How much remains of the original term?

(e) What are the relevant contractual terms...?

(f) Is it a case where the court should exercise its power to disregard accelerated payment provisions (s. 8 of the Act of 1973)?

(g) Is it reasonable to expect the lender, in the circumstances of the particular case, to recoup the arrears of interest: (i) over the whole of the original term, or (ii) within a shorter period, or even (iii) within a longer period, ie by extending the repayment period?

(h) Is it reasonable to expect the lender to capitalise the interest or not?

(i) Are there any reasons affecting the security which should influence the length of the period for repayment?'.[19]

Sums due

Finally it is important to consider exactly how much is meant by 'sums due' on the mortgage. This is not necessarily the entirety of the mortgage sum. Rather, in an instalment mortgage, thanks to the Administration of Justice Act 1973, this may mean simply the payments missed. All will depend upon the contract itself and the ways in which the parties have agreed that the mortgage money will be repaid. Similarly, in an interest only mortgage, it would relate only to the interest payments missed.

It is worth noting at this juncture that the rule does not only apply to missed monetary payments. Although this is the most likely species of breach of the mortgage agreement, triggering the mortgagee's desire to go into possession, the jurisdiction extends to other breaches. Examples could include failures to insure the property, or to let the property fall into disrepair. In these cases, the court is looking for whether the mortgagor is able to remedy the breaches within a reasonable time.

This section is therefore potentially a powerful way of preventing a mortgagee from going into possession. But it has its limitations. First, from *Ropaigealach*,[20] we know that if the lender does not in fact go to court to obtain an order for possession, then the jurisdiction of section 36 does not apply. The section is dependant upon the lender seeking an order for possession. Secondly, since *Norgan*,[21] the courts have been relatively strict in terms of the proof sought to justify the mortgagor's assertion that they are able to pay back what they owe, usually with a forensic accounting exercise. This means that in cases where the mortgagor has simply 'borrowed too much', the courts are very unlikely to step in to prevent or delay the possession action. Rather, the section only really provides assistance to those who are in temporary financial difficulties but who have now come out of those difficulties. Examples of this may include a self-employed person who was

---

[19] Clark et al, *Fisher & Lightwood's Law of Mortgages* (14th ed) (Lexis Nexis, London 2014), [29.44], 642–3.
[20] *Ropaigealach v Barclays Bank* [2000] QB 263 (CA).
[21] *Cheltenham & Gloucester v Norgan* [1996] 1 WLR 343 (CA).

ill and unable to work, or unexpected one-off expenses which caused a cash-flow problem. To put this another way, the section is not as generous to borrowers as it might appear at first glance. In cases of serious default it does not usually provide any comfort to the mortgagor.

One question which has posed significant difficulties, however, is the extent to which a mortgagor is able to argue that they will sell the mortgaged property and that this will represent the means by which they can 'prove' that they are able to pay back the sums due in the reasonable time. This argument is a difficult one for borrowers to make. It is very contingent upon not only finding a willing buyer, but also on the lender giving them permission to proceed with the sale, or the court ordering a sale at the petition of the mortgagor. None of these are guaranteed. This poses particular difficulties where the property either is in negative equity (where the debt is greater than the value of the property), or risks being so if the right buyer cannot be found. As a general rule, we can say that the courts will usually allow a mortgagor to proceed to sale if the property is in positive equity. If the property is in negative equity then it is very unlikely that the court will allow the buyer to use a potential sale as an argument for delaying mortgagee possession. There is also a 'timing' element to the mortgagor's raising the possibility of sale, which is demonstrated by the case of *Krausz*.[22] In exceptional circumstances, however, the court may grant a delay in possession to allow a sale even in cases of negative equity, as we see from *Palk*.[23]

> **Key case:** *Cheltenham & Gloucester v Krausz* [1997] 1 WLR 1558
>
> In this case, after multiple suspensions of the lender's possession order, the borrowers argued as a last resort that they should receive the benefit of another suspension on the basis that they would sell the property and that would allow them to repay the sums due. The debt was much larger than the projected sale price. The court was required to assess whether it would (a) make an order for sale; and (b) suspend the order for possession, in these circumstances. Philips LJ in the Court of Appeal highlighted that the court would be very reluctant to make such an order for sale when the property was in negative equity. Indeed, as we shall see later when considering *Palk*, a case discussed in *Krausz*, the circumstances must be exceptional indeed to justify the court ordering such a sale. The judge considers the potential effects of allowing sales in such cases:
>
>> 'In any case in which there is negative equity it will be open to the mortgagor to resist an order for possession on the ground that he wishes to obtain a better price by remaining in possession and selling the property himself. In not every case will the primary motive for such an application be the wish to obtain a better price than that which the mortgagee is likely to obtain on a forced sale. Often the mortgagor will be anxious to postpone for as long as possible the evil day when he has to leave his home... There will be a danger, if the mortgagee does not obtain possession, that the mortgagor will delay the realisation of the property by seeking too high a price, or deliberately procrastinating on completion.'[24]
>
> Although some commentators, eg Kenny,[25] have expressed dismay at this decision, there is a clear justification behind the court's approach. Philips LJ is right to highlight the practical quagmire to which allowing a mortgagor to sell in these circumstances might give rise. This will cause hardship without doubt, especially

---

[22] *Cheltenham & Gloucester v Krausz* [1997] 1 WLR 1558 (CA).
[23] *Palk v Mortgage Services Funding* [1993] Ch 330 (CA).
[24] *Cheltenham & Gloucester v Krausz* [1997] 1 WLR 1558 (CA), 1564.
[25] A Kenny, 'No postponement of evil day' [1998] Conv 223.

given that a mortgagee sale is likely to raise a much lower price that one conducted by the mortgagor themselves. But putting the responsibility of supervising such sales onto the shoulders of the courts would be a heavy administrative burden. Even in *Krausz* however, the court recognises that there are cases where even in negative equity, a sale should be ordered. One example of this is *Palk*, and although the court in *Krausz* casts doubts on the generality of the application of the rule in that case, they do not overrule it. In the most egregious of cases, section 91 may still provide an 'escape route' for the mortgagee.

We can now explore this in case *Palk v Mortgage Services*.[26]

Key case: *Palk v Mortgage Services* [1993] Ch 330

In this case, the court allowed the mortgagor to obtain a delay in possession proceedings on the basis that they would use a court-ordered sale to finance repayment of the mortgage money due despite the fact that the property was in negative equity. The reasoning behind the court's approach here was due to the fact that the lender, in proposing to go into possession, was planning not to sell the property, but to rent it out. The reason why this was problematic was because the projected rent was not going to be enough to cover the interest on the mortgage. This meant that the money due under the mortgage would increase exponentially for however long the renting lasted. But the mortgagor would have no control over when the mortgagee decided to stop renting out the property and sell it. The justification given by the lender for this plan was that they wanted to wait on a potential market rise so that the property would rise in value and cover the entirety of the mortgage debt. If this happened then it would be a positive outcome for both lender and borrower. However, as the court highlighted, the 'gamble' of this happening was a gamble entirely at the borrower's expense, and the court was very reluctant to allow this entirely one-way risk. As a result, they accepted that the lender should not be allowed to go into possession and instead relied on the possibility of the sale to recover the mortgage debt.

There was also an important timing element to this process which fell in the Palks' favour. First, they had already negotiated a sale. The agreed price was lower than the mortgage debt but there was a strong prospect that the sale would actually take place. This was not an entirely speculative plan, in other words, which provides a contrast with *Krausz*.[27] Second, the bank had already obtained an order for possession, and the Palks had applied for the possibility of a court ordered sale under section 91 LPA 1925 (see later). This was not the situation in *Krausz*[28] as we noted, as in that case, the mortgagor there had not yet applied for a court ordered sale, and so the fact of them bringing that action was also speculative. The general tone of the court's approach here is interesting, and arguably is not one which is mirrored in all disputes between lender and borrower (see *Alliance & Leicester v Slayford*[29] previously as an example). Per Sir Donald Nicholls VC:

'a mortgagee can sit back and do nothing. He is not obliged to take steps to realise his security. But if he does take steps to exercise his rights over his security, common law and equity alike have set bounds to the extent to which he can look after himself and ignore the mortgagor's interests. In the exercise of his rights

---

[26] *Palk v Mortgage Services Funding* [1993] Ch 330 (CA).
[27] *Cheltenham & Gloucester v Krausz* [1997] 1 WLR 1558 (CA).
[28] *Cheltenham & Gloucester v Krausz* [1997] 1 WLR 1558 (CA).
[29] *Alliance & Leicester v Slayford* [2001] 1 All ER (Comm) 1 (CA).

over his security the mortgagee must act fairly towards the mortgagor. His interest in the property has priority over the interest of the mortgagor, and he is entitled to proceed on that footing. He can protect his own interest, but he is not entitled to conduct himself in a way which unfairly prejudices the mortgagor.'[30]

As a result of this general approach, and of the specific reluctance that the court felt in subjecting Mrs Palk to this risk, the court utilised its very wide discretion under section 91 LPA 1925 regarding orders for sale. This is itself interesting. We consider this jurisdiction in more detail later. However, it is also important to consider how the court's very wide discretion in respect of section 91 interacts with the relatively narrow discretion conferred upon it by the strict terms of section 36, bearing in mind that the *Palk* process was now at the second, 'sale' stage, whereas *Krausz*[31] was at the first, 'delay in possession order' stage. It is clear that the consequence of the court ordering a sale under section 91 was going to be that the mortgagee's possession order would remain suspended. There is no mention in the case of section 36 however. The court seems to base its decision solely on its discretion under section 91. This suggests, hence the doubt cast on *Palk* in *Krausz*,[32] that the courts have an additional, inherent discretion, not only to delay for a short period of time to allow the mortgagor to move in a fair and sensible fashion, but more substantially to delay orders for possession when faced the possibility of a mortgagor sale. This is a discretion which certainly does not appear in the terms of section 36, unless is it demonstrated that this sale will guarantee repayment of the sums due under the mortgage in the reasonable time envisaged by that section.

Further analysis: Court's jurisdiction to suspend possession proceedings

This possibility is examined by Dixon. He explains that, '[u]nderstandably, perhaps, the use of the power to direct sale in destruction of the mortgagee's right to possession generated much concern among commercial lenders, not least because termination of the security by sale in 'negative equity' cases forces reliance on the mortgagor's personal covenant to repay.'[33] He then assesses whether, as *Krausz*[34] suggests, the only mechanism by which a court can delay an order for possession is section 36, or whether such a broader, general discretion exists as *Palk*[35] seems to suggest. He concludes that there are three different jurisdictions at play here. First, the jurisdiction under section 36; second, the 'inherent jurisdiction' to suspect possession orders (interpreted more or less broadly); and third, the possible discretion which section 91(2) confers when it states that a court ordered sale may be made on 'any terms' as the court sees fit.

This last argument is contrary to the *dicta* in *Krausz*,[36] but Dixon looks at the purpose of section 91(2), which is to protect borrowers, and argues that,

'[s]een in this context, it is perfectly sensible that the power to order sale under s 91(2) should carry with it an ancillary power to suspend the mortgagee's possession (or interfere with 'any other action' of the mortgagee)

---

[30] *Alliance & Leicester v Slayford* [2001] 1 All ER (Comm) 1 (CA), 337.
[31] *Cheltenham & Gloucester v Krausz* [1997] 1 WLR 1558 (CA).
[32] *Cheltenham & Gloucester v Krausz* [1997] 1 WLR 1558 (CA).
[33] Dixon, 'Combating the mortgagees's right to possession: new hope for the mortgagor in chains?' (1998) 18 Legal Studies 279, 281.
[34] *Cheltenham & Gloucester v Krausz* [1997] 1 WLR 1558 (CA).
[35] *Palk v Mortgage Services Funding* [1993] Ch 330 (CA).
[36] *Cheltenham & Gloucester v Krausz* [1997] 1 WLR 1558 (CA).

independent of any other jurisdiction, particularly as the powers of s 91 are exercisable expressly when 'any other person dissents... In short, s 91(2) and its suspensory power is needed precisely because the security is deficient. It is submitted, therefore, that the essence of the court's unfettered discretion under s 91(2) is a discretion to determine whose rights shall prevail, even if the security will not thereby be discharged in its entirety. In a suitable case, possession can be suspended in order that the mortgagor's right to sell might prevail.'[37]

It should not be assumed, however, that the policy arguments in favour of a discretion like this in section 91 all go in one direction. Yes, certainly, it provides a means by which the courts can respond to particular unfairness in specific cases. This is almost certainly a good thing in the instant case. However, when looked at systemically, this may be disadvantageous for both borrowers and lenders. For borrowers, it raises the possibility that pursuing potentially costly and time-consuming litigation is a worthwhile prospect. If the mortgagor loses, they will have to cover the costs of the bank (probably added onto the mortgage debt). For mortgagors already in dire financial straits, this is an outcome to be avoided. For lenders, it imposes a delay on obtaining possession, usually with a view to a sale. This will limit their ability to recover the sums due. This has two potential consequences. First, lenders may lend to fewer individuals seeking to avoid risky situations where they cannot recover the loan. Second, they may raise interest rates in such circumstances to reflect the risk. Neither of these outcomes is good for borrowers. Thus, whenever we consider how to ensure that individuals like Mrs Palk are not subject to the risks the mortgagee sought to subject her to, we must note that this sort of decision does not happen in a vacuum. By opening out the possibility of section 91(2) containing a wide-ranging discretion to suspend orders for possession in cases where the mortgagor seeks sale, we raise the possibility of uncertainty and risk. For this reason the balance struck when *Palk*[38] and *Krausz*[39] are considered together is a good one. Only in exceptional circumstances can section 91(2) be used to 'defeat' section 36 in cases where a property is in negative equity, with these exceptional circumstances kept within tight bounds.

As Cowan et al note, however, there are alternative perspectives on the effects of providing the lender with strong remedies in this way. They argue that

> 'a rather circuitous form of reasoning [has] developed, maintaining that if creditors were not protected by the law in the event of debtor default, this would adversely affect the availability of credit, which would ultimately harm the consumer. From a social perspective, the expansion of low-income ownership also exploded the myth that the status of owner could be viewed as providing a reliable indication of socio-economic wellbeing.'[40]

11.4.3.3 Inherent jurisdiction of the courts

We tangentially considered the inherent jurisdiction of the courts above, in exploring whether this was the explanation for the delay in possession proceedings in *Palk*.[41] However, in most cases, the sorts of delays which the courts grant by using this discretion is a matter of weeks. It is usually to allow the mortgagor a reasonable opportunity to take every last chance to raise available finance before they lose their home. It is a reflection of the seriousness of the consequences for the

---

[37] Dixon, 'Combating the mortgagees's right to possession: new hope for the mortgagor in chains?' (1998) 18 Legal Studies 279, 291.
[38] *Palk v Mortgage Services Funding* [1993] Ch 330 (CA).
[39] *Cheltenham & Gloucester v Krausz* [1997] 1 WLR 1558 (CA).
[40] Cowan et al, *Great Debates in Land Law* (2nd ed) (Palgrave Macmillan, London, 2016), 206.
[41] *Palk v Mortgage Services Funding* [1993] Ch 330 (CA).

borrower, and an attempt to allow them every chance to keep their home, not a serious limitation on the lender's ability to regain the money lent. The leading case on the exercise of this jurisdiction is *Birmingham Citizens' Permanent Bulding Society v Caunt*[42] which highlights that the courts can really only use this discretion to delay for a matter of weeks.

11.4.3.4 Soft law options

Whilst soft law options, such as voluntary pre-action protocols and guidance issued by bodies such as the Council of Mortgage Lnders are not binding per se, many of these have their grounding in statutory legal rules. The consequences for a lender of not complying with them (at least, systematic non-compliance) will be serious in terms of reputational damage and competitiveness within the market.

11.4.3.5 Human rights

The arguments surrounding the role which human rights law may and does play in relation to mortgage lending are very difficult. The detail of this discussion is to be found in chapter 17 at 17.3.5. They are made difficult by the existence of a multiplicity of fundamentally inconsistent case law, which fails properly to systematise its discussion of human rights. Many cases talk 'at cross purposes'. There is little recognition of two fundamental points in relation to mortgages. First, although most cases are brought by a private individual against another private individual (so that we are considering questions of horizontal effect), in many of these cases there is a statutory provision or a common law rule underpinning the argument of the lender. Since statutory provisions are subject to the interpretation obligation in section 3 HRA 1998, and common law is potentially subject to the section 6 duty to comply with human rights which rests on all public authorities including courts, the position is not as simple as merely saying that article 8 does not have horizontal effect in a property context. Second, there is a tension in mortgages which is that the mortgage agreement is, in theory, freely negotiated, or at least freely signed. The mortgagor has voluntarily given to the lender the right to go into possession of their land from the outset. This 'freely negotiated' contractual element of the relationship is one aspect in particular which the courts recognise affects the way in which human rights arguments play out in this area.[43] We discuss these in much more detail in chapter 17. However, it is useful here to note some of the case law on the question, and to highlight, in very simple terms, that to date, human rights arguments have held no sway in respect of the courts adjusting their approach or re-interpreting statute. We can see this if we consider *Horsham Properties v Clark*.[44]

> **Key case: *Horsham Properties v Clark* [2008] EWHC 2327**
>
> In this case, the mortgage company sold title to the property to a third party, Horsham Properties, by auction. At no point did they obtain an order for possession against the mortgagors. Horsham then sought possession against the mortgagors. The question was whether sale without an order for possession breached the mortgagors' human rights, or whether the 'by-pass' to section 36 which resulted meant

---

[42] *Birmingham Citizens Permanent Building Society v Caunt* [1962] Ch 883 (ChD).
[43] See *Sims v Dacorum BC* [2014] UKSC 63, [2015] AC 1336.
[44] *Horsham Properties Group Ltd v Clark* [2008] EWHC 2327 (Ch), [2009] 1 WLR 1255.

that section 101 should be interpreted as requiring a court order. The court held that the mortgagee did not have to seek court approval to exercise its power of sale, and that section 36 could not be used to restrain a sale in these circumstances. The purchaser of the title from the mortgagee was therefore entitled to possession and section 36 was irrelevant to that since there was no longer any money owing on the mortgage. As Briggs J explained:

> 'any deprivation of possession constituted by the exercise by a mortgagee of its powers under section 101 of the LPA after a relevant default by the mortgagor is justfied in the public interest, and requires no case-by-case exercise of a proportionality... First, it reflects the bargain habitually drawn between mortgagors and mortgagees for nearly 200 years, in which the ability of a mortgagee to sell the property offered as a security without having to go to court has been identified as a central and essential aspect of the security necessarily to be provided if substantial property based secured lending is to be available at affordable rates of interest. That it is in the public interest that property buyers and owners should be able to obtain lending for that purpose can hardly be open to doubt, even if the loan-to-value ratios at which it has recently become possible have now become a matter of controversy'.[45]

The nuances in this conclusion are nicely captured by Greer who, in commenting on this case, concludes that:

> 'The difficulty is, of course, that the lending institutions are commercial operations... They are not philanthropic institutions with a mission to provide homes for all. Their primary concern is to make a profit... [I]t will fight hard to protect its existing legal rights. Even more significant, given that the current crisis has deepened by the increasing unwillingness of lenders to lend, the lending industry retains the upper hand: if Parliament acts in a way which lenders feel undermines their security, they will become much more careful about whether to lend at all. Although many might say that this would be a positive measure-given that irresponsible lending contributed to the mess that we are in a confident lending market may well be one of the essential keys to economic recovery'.[46]

Thus, from this case we can conclude that not only can a lender sell without a court order, or indeed without obtaining an order for possession, so too can they provide to that purchaser the ability to evict the mortgagor, and none of this breaches their rights to a home under the Human Rights Act 1998.

Summary: Right to possession

1. This right is a necessary consequence of our conceptualisation of mortgages and arises 'as soon as the ink is dry' on the mortgage deed, (*Four Maids v Dudley Marshall*).[47]

2. The lender can exercise this right without a court order at any time they wish, whether or not the borrower is in default.

---

[45] *Horsham Properties Group Ltd v Clark* [2008] EWHC 2327 (Ch), [2009] 1 WLR 1255 [44].
[46] Greer, '*Horsham Properties Group Ltd v Clark*: possession - mortgagee's right or discretionary remedy?' [2009] Conv 516, 523–4.
[47] *Four Maids v Dudley Marshall* [1957] Ch 317.

> 3. However, if they do so, the lender risks breaching the Criminal Law Act 1977, section 6. As a result, most lenders seek a court order before going into possession. This raises the possibility of the borrower raising three arguments:
>   a. That they can pay back the sums due in a reasonable time, justifying a delay or suspension etc of the order for possession under section 36 Administration of Justice Act 1970 as amended;
>   b. That the court would be justified in delaying possession because they (the borrower) intends to proceed immediately to sell and has made an application under section 91 LPA 1925 to this effect. The court will likely allow this if either i. the property is in positive equity; or ii. there are very exceptional circumstances; and
>   c. That the court should use its inherent power to delay possession for a very short period to give the borrower one last chance to raise the necessary finance.
> 4. The borrower may also seek to rely on their human rights. This argument will almost certainly fail.

If the mortgagee does succeed in their action for possession, then once in possession, they will fall under a general duty to maximise the profits from their possession, so as to allow those profits to pay down the mortgage money, as per *White v City of London Brewery Company*.[48]

11.4.4 POWER OF SALE

Mortgagees generally seek to go into possession of land as a precursor to the exercise of a power of sale. Given the practical impossibility of achieving foreclosure, the power of sale is really the mortgagee's best chance of realising the security so as to get the money which they are owed. The advantage of the sale procedure over foreclosure of course is that the mortgagor will get any surplus which arises after the sale. Because the value which the sale realises is critically important therefore, for both parties, not only has the law imposed limits on *when* a mortgagee can exercise its power of sale, but also *how* it exercises it. We will consider these issues here in turn.

11.4.4.1 When can a mortgagee exercise its power of sale?

A mortgagee generally has a power of sale either because it is expressly provided for in the mortgage contract and deed, or, as a result of section 101 LPA 1925, because it is implied into the mortgage deed by statute.

This section states that:

> '(1) A mortgagee, where the mortgage is made by deed, shall, by virtue of this Act, have the following powers, to the like extent as if they had been in terms conferred by the mortgage deed, but not further (namely):
>
>   (i) A power, when the mortgage money has become due, to sell, or to concur with any other person in selling, the mortgaged property'.

---

[48] *White v City of London Brewery Company* (1889) 42 Ch D 237.

The implied power of sale therefore only arises where the mortgage is made by deed (as we discuss later). This means that some equitable mortgages will also involve this implied power of sale. The consequence of this section is that even if the parties do not expressly mention a power of sale, then the lender will nevertheless be able to sell the property. However, it is worth noting that section 101(4) highlights that this implied power of sale only operates so far as is consistent with the mortgage deed.

It is also important to note from section 101 that the power of sale will only arise once the 'mortgage money has become due'. This refers to what is known as the legal date of redemption. Normal practice would be that the legal date for redemption is about 6 months after the mortgage was entered into. As soon as the power of sale has arisen, the mortgagee is able to sell the title subject to the mortgage. This does not mean that they will not face liability for selling in an improper fashion. In certain extreme circumstances, also, the sale may be set aside. The consequence of the power of sale *arising* however, is that if the purchaser is in good faith, then their title cannot be questioned.

In order to be completely secure the lender will usually want to ensure that not only has the power of sale *arisen*, but that it has also become *exercisable* in accordance with section 103 LPA 1925. This will (subject to the duties arising from case law), prevent them from facing any claim from the mortgagor for improper sale. Section 103 states:

'Section 103 Regulation of exercise of power of sale.

A mortgagee shall not exercise the power of sale conferred by this Act unless and until—

(i) Notice requiring payment of the mortgage money has been served on the mortgagor or one of two or more mortgagors, and default has been made in payment of the mortgage money, or of part thereof, for three months after such service; or

(ii) Some interest under the mortgage is in arrear and unpaid for two months after becoming due; or

(iii) There has been a breach of some provision contained in the mortgage deed or in this Act, or in an enactment replaced by this Act, and on the part of the mortgagor, or of some person concurring in making the mortgage, to be observed or performed, other than and besides a covenant for payment of the mortgage money or interest thereon.'

The section therefore lists three conditions, the fulfilment of any one of which will result in the power of sale being exercisable: first, that a notice has been served on the borrower stating that the entirely of the mortgage money is due, and the money has not been paid within three months; second, that the interest under the mortgage is two months in arrears; and third, that some other term of the mortgage deed has been breached. This last condition would usually be something like a breach of a requirement to insure the property; renting out of the property without permission of the lender; or letting the property fall into serious disrepair.

11.4.4.2 How should the power of sale be exercised?

Once the power of sale becomes exercisable, it is then important that the mortgagee comply with the common law duties that fall on them when it comes to exercising their power of sale. These can broadly be termed as a requirement to act in good faith. The case law has developed a series of more specific requirements to give guidance to a lender to indicate when these good faith requirements have been met. First, the lender is required to engage in an honest sale not to a connected person.[49] Second, the lender has to take steps to ensure that the best price reasonably available is achieved on the sale. Third, the lender must ensure that the motivation behind exercising the power of sale is partly based on a desire to realise their security. Let us consider these in more detail.

Honest sale to an unconnected person

The requirement that the sale be an honest one is always difficult to prove. Essentially it boils down to the lender taking appropriate steps to ensure that they treat the borrower fairly. The most important element of this honesty relates to the identity of the buyer. In cases where the mortgagee and the purchaser are connected in some way, the courts will look at the transaction very closely. In some cases of course, the fact that there is a link between the mortgagee and the purchaser will not mean that there has been any impropriety. It is not suggested, for example, that a relative of an employee of a very large bank should be unable to buy property for sale on the open market simply because it happens to be for sale through that bank. Nevertheless, the courts will be particularly cautious to ensure fair play in cases such as this.

If the courts conclude that the transaction is dishonest in this way, then the next question is what the remedy will be for the borrower. In most cases the borrower would likely seek to set aside the sale. Whether this is possible depends not on the conduct of the mortgagee, but on the conduct of the purchaser. We can see this from *Corbett v Halifax*.[50]

> **Key case:** *Corbett v Halifax* **[2002] EWCA Civ 1849**
>
> In this case, following default by the mortgagor, the mortgagee bank sought to sell the property. An employee of the lender wanted to purchase the property, but since this was a breach of his terms of employment, he instructed his uncle to buy it for him. The estate agent, knowing that the employee was prohibited from purchasing the property, asked whether he had obtained consent to the purchase and the employee (falsely) stated that he had. The uncle then bought the title and immediately sold it to the employee. Unknown to the employee, the sale had been made at an undervalue, and the question was whether the sale could be set aside in these circumstances.
>
> The court held that despite the fact that the sale was to a connected person, and at an undervalue, the sale could not be set aside. They reached this conclusion on the basis that there was in fact no link between the employee's breach of his terms of employment, and the undervalue in the sale. To put this another way, the employee was in bad faith, but he was in bad faith vis-à-vis the lender. As far as the borrower was concerned, he thought he was purchasing the property in a fair transaction and so was not in bad faith vis-à-vis the borrower. The remedy for the mortgagor was therefore in damages.
>
> Pumfrey J reached this conclusion by first giving a general guide as to when a sale can be set aside, stating:
>
>> 'It would seem to follow from this that a completed sale by a mortgagee is not liable be set aside merely because it takes place at an undervalue. Impropriety is a pre-requisite, and section 104(2) makes it clear that the purchaser is not protected if he has actual knowledge of the impropriety... Thus, the completed sale by a mortgagee pursuant to his statutory power is vulnerable only if the purchaser has knowledge of, or participates in, an impropriety in the exercise of the power.'[51]

---

[49] *Williams v Wellingborough BC* 73 LGR 33 (ChD).
[50] *Corbett v Halifax* [2002] EWCA Civ 1849, [2003] 1 WLR 964.
[51] *Corbett v Halifax* [2002] EWCA Civ 1849, [2003] 1 WLR 964, [26].

> Applying this to the instant case, the court reasoned that whilst the purchaser had knowledge of an impropriety, he had no notice of the relevant impropriety, ie the undervalue. Thus, the purchaser could take advantage of the protection afforded to him by section 104. Scott Baker LJ expressed this very neatly: 'In short, the Halifax's in-house rules and whether they were properly applied had nothing to do with the Corbetts'.[52]

Best price reasonably available

The selling mortgagee is also under a duty to ensure that the transaction realises the best price reasonably available. This does not mean that they have to do up the property, wait for a market rise, apply for planning permissions to increase the value of the land, and the like.[53] Rather, it means that the mortgagee has to take reasonable steps to open the property out to the market. The market can set a price on that property at the time which fairly reflects the state of the property and the state of the wider market. In reality, this tends to boil down to a requirement that the mortgagee either use an estate agent, or sell the property through a public auction properly advertised. The nature of this duty is very well explained by the decision in *Bishop v Blake*.[54]

> **Key case: *Bishop v Blake* [2006] EWHC 831**
>
> This case represents an almost perfect example of how not to handle a sale as a selling mortgagee. It is also an unusual example of a case involving an individual lender as mortgagee. Here, the property was originally owned by Mrs Blake. Mrs Blake sold title to Mrs Bishop, but lent her the purchase money, being granted a mortgage. So, Bishop was the mortgagor and Blake the mortgagee. Bishop declined to pay some of the sums due, and so Blake decided to sell the property. She sold the property to Gillie's Inns, which was a company connected to the tenants of the property (a pub), the Brinds. Blake, Gillie's Inns and the Brinds effectively worked together on the sale, and the property was sold at a price which discharged the mortgage money and nothing more. Thus, Bishop argued that the sale was to a connected person and at a serious undervalue.
>
> In terms of the actual process of sale, at some point after the sale had effectively been agreed, a very small advert was put into a trade paper stating that a property was for sale but without giving any details, including location, price etc. There was significant disagreement however as to whether there was actually an undervalue as two competing valuations had been given. The court reasoned that looking at competing valuations was not the best way to assess undervalue. Rather, the court should look to the process leading to sale. In this case, there was no doubt that the process was flawed.

---

[52] *Corbett v Halifax* [2002] EWCA Civ 1849, [2003] 1 WLR 964, [48].
[53] *Silven Properties Ltd v Royal Bank of Scotland Plc* [2003] EWCA Civ 1409, [2004] 1 WLR 997; and *Cuckmere Brick Co v Mutual Finance* [1971] Ch 949 (CA).
[54] *Bishop v Blake* [2006] EWHC 831 (Ch), [2006] 17 EG 113 (CS).

> Dixon summarises the flaws in this case:
>
> 'Applying the proper method in *Bishop* itself, an examination of the process of sale made it clear that there was virtually no likelihood that the best price had been obtained. The collusion between mortgagee and purchaser prior to the sale, the absence of any serious advertising, the virtual transfer of the conduct of the sale to the purchaser's solicitors, and the mortgagee's solicitor's obsession with realising an amount necessary to redeem the charge with the minimum of effort clearly indicated that the conduct of the sale had fallen far below that which was required'.[55]

Motivation

Finally, the selling mortgagee must act in good faith in the sense that their motivation for selling the property must be to realise their security. This is, in a way, the flipside of the requirement that a mortgage transaction is 'only' a mortgage in respect of clogs and fetters on the equity of redemption (see later). The duty here is not a 'pure' one, however, as Gray and Gray highlight when commenting on *Meretz*:[56] 'The demands of good faith also necessitate that a desire to recover the debt secured must be at least some part of the motivation of the selling mortgagee, but 'purity of purpose' on his part is not essential'.[57]

11.4.4.3 Remedies for the mortgagor

Assuming that the duties of the selling mortgagee are breached, we must now consider what the remedies of the mortgagor are in such a situation. We have already highlighted that unless the purchaser of the title is themselves in bad faith, then the only available remedy is in damages. This much is made clear by section 104 LPA 1925.

This section states that:

'(2) Where a conveyance is made in exercise of the power of sale conferred by this Act, or any enactment replaced by this Act, the title of the purchaser shall not be impeachable on the ground—

(a) that no case had arisen to authorise the sale; or

(b) that due notice was not given; or

(c) where the mortgage is made after the commencement of this Act, that leave of the court, when so required, was not obtained; or

(d) whether the mortgage was made before or after such commencement, that the power was otherwise improperly or irregularly exercised;

and a purchaser is not, either before or on conveyance, concerned to see or inquire whether a case has arisen to authorise the sale, or due notice has been given, or the power is otherwise properly and regularly exercised; but any person damnified by an unauthorised, or improper, or irregular exercise of the power shall have his remedy in damages against the person exercising the power'.

---

[55] Dixon, 'Mortgage duties and commercial property transactions' [2006] Conv 278, 284.
[56] *Meretz Investments NV v ACP Ltd (No 3)* (2006) at [314] per Lewison J.
[57] Gray and Gray, *Land Law* (7th ed) (Oxford University Press, Oxford, 2011), 312.

It is important also to consider the scope of such remedies for, as in most areas of English law, damages are calculated not on the basis of an attempt to punish the mortgagee, but rather to calculate the loss to the mortgagor. The loss to the mortgagor in these cases is likely to be the difference in value between the property on the open market, and the property as sold. However, this is unlikely to be a true reflection of what has gone wrong for the mortgagor here. Rather, the mortgagor wants to be compensated for the fact that, in her eyes, she has been wrongly deprived of her house in such circumstances. Nevertheless, as mentioned, this will not be possible unless the purchaser is in good faith.

Once the property is sold, the sale money will be used first, to pay off any secured creditors in the order of priority, and the costs for such lenders, and then any surplus will be given back to the borrower as per section 105 LPA 1925.

11.4.5 POWER TO APPOINT A RECEIVER

The final remedy on which a mortgagee can rely is the power to appoint a receiver. The power to appoint such receivers is contained in section 101(1)(iii) LPA 1925. This power arises under the same circumstances as when the power of sale arises. This is relatively uncommon in residential transactions, because the receiver must be remunerated for the service which they provide. This is usually done through receiving pay from the proceeds of sale of any property, or in appropriate cases, from the income generated by renting out the property. It is seen as an expense of the mortgage rather than a cost which the lender must bear. The purpose of a receiver is to shift the risk of breach of mortgagee's duties away from the mortgagee themselves. This works because the receiver is treated for most purposes as though they are an agent of the mortgagor, and as such fall under different duties in respect of how they conduct the management of the property than does the lender. By divesting themselves of the practical control over this management however, the mortgagee removes itself from a position where it could breach these duties. Furthermore, as long as the mortgagee acts in good faith, he will not fall under a duty of care in respect of the appointment of receivers.[58]

For this reason, it is more common for receivers to be appointed in respect of commercial property, particularly where the property appears on its face to be capable of generating sufficient income to service the mortgage debt but where it will require careful and intensive management to do so. It is also a good option for the lender where the borrower appears to be in a position where bankruptcy (in the case of an individual) or insolvency (in the case of a company) look likely. This is because there are tight rules as to what can be done with property in these cases so as to not unfairly disadvantage other creditors. The lender may wish to the leave the navigation of these rules to the experts in the form of their appointed receivers.

The nature of this receivership is explained by section 109 LPA 1925:

'109 Appointment, powers, remuneration and duties of receiver.

(1) A mortgagee entitled to appoint a receiver under the power in that behalf conferred by this Act shall not appoint a receiver until he has become entitled to exercise the power of sale conferred by this Act, but may then, by writing under his hand, appoint such person as he thinks fit to be receiver.

---

[58] *Re Potters Oils (No 2)* [1986] All ER 890.

(2) A receiver appointed under the powers conferred by this Act, or any enactment replaced by this Act, shall be deemed to be the agent of the mortgagor; and the mortgagor shall be solely responsible for the receiver's acts or defaults unless the mortgage deed otherwise provides.'

The decision in *Medforth v Blake*[59] provides guidance as to how the receiver should operate when acting in this way as agent.

> **Summary: Remedies of a mortgagee—legal mortgages**
> 1. Sue on the contract debt. This is useful for recovering any remaining debt after sale; to accelerate bankruptcy; and as means to obtain a charging order in respect of other property belonging to the mortgagor.
> 2. Foreclosure. This brings the mortgage to an end by transferring legal title to the mortgagee. The courts usually order sale in lieu of foreclosure under section 91 LPA 1925.
> 3. Right to possession. This arises as soon as the ink is dry on the mortgage, but there are a number of restrictions on the mortgagee's right in practice, particularly for residential land. If the mortgagee goes to court for an order for possession, the court has a discretion to delay the possession order in certain circumstances. Possession is usually sought as a precursor to sale.
> 4. Power to sell. This arises if the mortgage is made by deed and the contractual date for redemption has passed. It becomes exercisable if one of the three conditions in section 103 LPA 1925 is met. The mortgagee falls under a number of duties on sale, largely to ensure that they obtain the best price reasonably available and act in good faith.
> 5. Power to appoint a receiver. This arises at the same time as the power of sale. The receiver becomes agent of the borrower, and as such this allows the lender to divest itself of risk involved in managing mortgaged property.

11.5 REMEDIES—EQUITABLE MORTGAGES AND CHARGES

The remedies available to the lender in cases of an equitable mortgage are importantly different. However, following the advent of the LRA 2002, some equitable mortgagees will have remedies by virtue of the fact that despite not having a legal mortgage, because the mortgage was made by deed, section 101 operates. We discuss this later. In cases where the mortgage was not created by deed, but rather only by a contract which complies with section 2 LP(MP)A 1989 or by a document which meets the requirements of section 53 LPA 1925, then the remedies of the mortgagee will be constrained by the need, in most cases, to obtain a court order.

To obtain a sale of the property in such cases, the lender may apply to the court under section 91 LPA 1925. As we see in chapter 16, however, it is also very common for the lender to approach this situation though TOLATA 1996. The reason for this is that in many cases where an equitable mortgage has arisen, it is as a result of a co-ownership situation. As we discuss later, often such

---

[59] *Medforth v Blake* [2000] Ch 86 (CA).

situations involve undue influence or the forgery of a mortgage deed by one co-owner. An equitable mortgagee does not have a right to possession of the land. This is logical since equitable interests do not generally entitle the holder to possession of the relevant land. As a result, they must apply to the court for an order for possession if they wish to go into possession of the land. The court will usually order this as a precursor to sale, but it is not guaranteed. The position in this respect is complicated however by the fact that the logic behind the rule in *Walsh v Lonsdale*,[60] ie that equity treats that which ought to be done as having been done. This would suggest that equity should treat the mortgagee as though they have a right to possession of the land if that was part of the contractual agreement. Much will depend as we have said on the precise manner in which the mortgage has in fact come to be equitable. Certainly, in cases where the mortgage was created by a document which complied with section 53 but not with section 2, then the *Walsh v Lonsdale*[61] argument would not apply.

However, the equitable mortgagee can generally rely on the remedy of foreclosure. This is because in such circumstances they will not become *legal* owner of the property, but rather will become absolutely entitled to the equitable interest, putting an end to the right of redemption of the mortgagor. This will generally result in the mortgagor holding on trust for the equitable mortgagee, with the trust duties associated with such a position.

In cases where the mortgage was made by deed, but is not legal either because it was not subsequently registered, or because it was granted in respect only of equitable property, then section 101 will still operate however. This was made clear in the controversial case of *Swift 1st v Colin*,[62] which tends to blur the line between the equitable and the legal mortgage in terms of their effects.

> **Key case: *Swift 1st v Colin* [2011] EWHC 2410**
>
> The case raises two difficult issues. First, does section 101 imply a power of sale into an equitable mortgage where that mortgage is created by a deed? And second, if it does imply a power of sale into the deed, what is it that the mortgagee is able to sell—legal or equitable title?
>
> The court concluded that not only does section 101 give the equitable mortgagee a power of sale in cases where that mortgage was created by deed, it also gives them the ability to sell legal title. Whilst the first part may be uncontroversial in so far as it is always subject to contrary intention in the deed, it is certainly not self-evident that this power would be a power to sell the legal title. The authority that they can do so is obiter comments in *Re White Rose Cottage*[63] but the matter now appears to be beyond dispute. As Evans notes:
>
> > 'Not only does the Land Registry now regard the case [*Colin*] as resolving the issue of an equitable mortgagee having an inherent right to possession without any court order, but also that...an equitable mortgagee can sell that which he or she does not have, namely the legal estate'.[64]

---

[60] *Walsh v Lonsdale* (1882) 21 Ch D 9.
[61] *Walsh v Lonsdale* (1882) 21 Ch D 9.
[62] *Swift 1st v Colin* [2011] EWHC 2410 (Ch), [2012] Ch 206.
[63] *Re White Rose Cottage* [1965] Ch. 940.
[64] Evans, 'A scrutiny of powers of sale arising under an equitable mortgage: a case for reining these in' [2015] Conv 123, 132.

> **Further analysis: How should we treat equitable mortgagees?**
>
> Evans is highly critical of the result in *Swift 1st v Colin* case. He argues that, first, since mortgage fraud is on the increase, the ability for an equitable mortgagee to sell title to a mortgaged property without engaging with the judicial process is likely to increase the risks here. Second, he highlights that protections for residential borrowers will be absent if a court order for sale is not required. This, he argues, is especially concerning in cases involving equitable mortgages because of how they are likely to have arisen.
>
>> 'An equitable mortgage may have been created in more questionable, informal and unsupervised circumstances than a legal mortgage. The case for scrutiny by a court (save for instances where a mortgagor gives informed consent to a repossession) is particularly compelling if the mortgage is only an equitable one. Swift 1st Ltd ought not to be given any especial significance, and the undesirable prospect of sales which may have been kept hidden from other legal or equitable owners of the property concerned should be reined in.'[65]
>
> These arguments are a reflection of the fact that there are a multitude of ways in which equitable mortgages arise. Many of these are informal, are potentially based on an imbalance of power in situations involving two co-owners, and the like.
>
> However, as a matter of statutory interpretation, it is important to highlight that the statutory provision quite explicitly does not mention legal mortgages, but rather mortgages made by deed. Although most mortgages made by deed pre the coming-into-force of the LRA 2002 would have been legal mortgages, not all would have been. Thus, the argument that the drafters of the 1925 legislation cannot have intended this power to extend to equitable mortgages is not entirely convincing, even if there are strong arguments that they *ought* to have restricted the power in this way. Whatever the merits of extending the power of sale to the equitable mortgagee however, it is certainly what the statute says.
>
> The real controversy is therefore the question of what can be sold and it is clear that this is Evans' primary objection[66] to the decision in *Colin*.[67]

Finally, an equitable charge can apply to the court for sale of the relevant property, but he is not entitled to possession of the land.

11.6 POSITION OF THE MORTGAGOR

Many works will refer to this as being a question of the 'rights' of the mortgagor. Indeed some of the legal concepts referred to in this part are indeed rights which vest in the mortgagor, of which the rights of redemption in their various forms are the most prominent. However, it is important to note that the mortgagor is protected in ways beyond these rights. Rather rules surrounding the fundamental nature of mortgages help to keep any 'abuse' of the mortgage construct in check. We commence the part with this issue, which is often referred to as the doctrine of 'clogs and fetters'.

---

[65] Evans, 'A scrutiny of powers of sale arising under an equitable mortgage: a case for reining these in' [2015] Conv 123, 132.

[66] Evans, 'A scrutiny of powers of sale arising under an equitable mortgage: a case for reining these in' [2015] Conv 123, 132.

[67] *Swift 1st v Colin* [2011] EWHC 2410 (Ch), [2012] Ch 206.

11.6.1 CLOGS, FETTERS, AND OTHER LIMITATIONS ON RIGHTS TO REDEEM

As we noted in 11.2, the nature of the mortgage is such as that it can *only* be a mortgage. Any term of the mortgage which goes beyond the idea of a secured debt will not be enforced by the courts. This is generally known as the doctrine of clogs and fetters, although a range of issue falls under this umbrella. In very simple terms, clogs and fetters are terms of the mortgage which limit the ability of the mortgagor to redeem, either openly, or in effect, in such a way as to skew the nature of the transaction. Let us show this with a simple example.

Hugh has decided to fulfil a lifelong dream and open a public house. He finds the perfect pub, and the brewer which controls this pub, Tasty Beer Ltd, offers to lend him the money to purchase the leasehold interest in the pub. As part of this mortgage agreement, Hugh is also bound to purchase all his beer directly through the brewer, at a price to be determined. Is this right for the brewer to demand that Hugh purchase beer through them a clog on Hugh's rights to redeem?

This issue has been a difficult one for the courts, recognising that there is a fine line between a commercial motivation for lending, and a distortion of the mortgage structure to achieve a different end. The question of *solus* ties, which arise in respect of pubs, petrol stations, and the like, has been particularly problematic. However, there are also more obvious strategies used by lenders such as that in *Swan Brewery v Fairclough*.[68]

The courts do however take a 'common sense' approach to this rule. They recognise that in some commercial transactions, both parties may well have freely and deliberately agreed to the limitation on redemption within the contract. Where there is a certain equality of bargaining power, it would seem that the courts are somewhat reluctant to interfere with freedom of contract in this respect even in cases where the date of redemption is delayed by decades (*Knightsbridge Estates v Byrne*[69]). This approach to the relevance of bargaining power is mirrored in the comments of Lord Halsbury LC in *Samuel v Jarrah Timber*[70] when he noted that it he was very reluctant to reach a decision which would mean that '[a] perfectly fair bargain made between two parties to it, each of whom was quite sensible of what they were doing, is not to be performed because at the same time a mortgage arrangement was made between them'.[71]

What about the collateral advantages discussed earlier? This issue has most recently been discussed in *Jones v Morgan*.[72]

> **Key case:** *Jones v Morgan* [2001] EWCA Civ 995
>
> In *Jones*, the court was required to assess whether an agreement to transfer half of the mortgaged property to the lender constituted a clog on the equity of redemption, notwithstanding the fact that strictly speaking the transfer and the mortgage constituted two separate agreements. In concluding that this was

---

[68] *Fairclough v Swan Brewery Co Ltd* [1912] AC 565 (PC).
[69] *Knightsbridge Estates v Byrne* [1940] AC 613 (HL).
[70] *Samuel v Jarrah Timber & Wood Paving Corp Ltd* [1904] AC 323 (HL).
[71] *Samuel v Jarrah Timber & Wood Paving Corp Ltd* [1904] AC 323, at 325.
[72] *Jones v Morgan* [2001] EWCA Civ 995, [2002] 1 EGLR 125.

a clog on the equity of redemption, and inconsistent with the fundamental nature of the mortgage, the court highlighted that this doctrine, rarely relied upon in modern law, was still alive and well.

Chadwick LJ gave extensive consideration to the earlier decision in *Kreglinger v New Patagonia Meat Company*,[73] and concluded that:

> '(i) there is a rule that a mortgagee cannot as a term of the mortgage enter into a contract to purchase, or stipulate for an option to purchase, any part of or interest in the mortgaged property; (ii) the foundation of the rule is that a contract to purchase, or an option to purchase, any part of or interest in the mortgaged property, is repugnant to or inconsistent with the transaction of mortgage of which it forms part... (iii) the reason why the contract or option to purchase is repugnant to or inconsistent with the mortgage transaction is that it cannot stand with the contractual proviso for redemption or with the equitable right to redeem... and (iv) it is essential, in any case to which the rule is said to apply, to consider whether or not the transaction is, in substance, a transaction of mortgage.'[74]

In applying these principles to the instant case, the court concluded (Pill LJ dissenting as to result), that the agreement to transfer part was inconsistent with the mortgage transaction.

This decision caused a degree of surprise, with many thinking that the doctrine had been effectively sidelined in the modern law of mortgages.

Further analysis: Should we move on from the clogs and fetters rule?

The issue of clogs and fetters has long been the subject of criticism. Lord Mersey in *G&C Kreglinger v New Patagonia Meat & Cold Storage Co Ltd*[75] famously stated that, '[i]t is like an unruly dog, which, if not securely chained to its kennel is prone to wander into places where it ought not to be.'[76] Thompson clearly sets us this debate, explaining that:

> 'Mortgage terms which were vulnerable to being categorised as clogs on the equity of redemption fall into one of three broad categories. These are attempts to restrict or deny the mortgagor the right to redeem the mortgage at all, the securing of collateral advantages for the mortgagee in the mortgage, and the reservation of a right by the mortgagee, at some time in the future, to acquire the mortgaged property free from the rights of the mortgagor. The whole doctrine, however, developed against a background where the mortgage was seen as instrument of oppression and the intervention of equity was necessary to prevent the exploitation of the mortgagor by the mortgagee, whose bargaining position was much stronger. As such, however, it represented a considerable interference with the notion of freedom of contract, whereby parties are free to contract on whatever terms they choose, and the clash between the two approaches, the paternalistic attitude of equity and the more robust view of the common law of affording sanctity to what the parties had agreed, is very evident in the development of this branch of the law.'[77]

---

[73] *Kreglinger v New Patagonia Meat & Cold Storage Co Ltd* [1914] AC 25.
[74] *Jones v Morgan* [2001] EWCA Civ 995, [2002] 1 EGLR 125, [55].
[75] *G&C Kreglinger v New Patagonia Meat & Cold Storage Co Ltd* [1914] AC 25 (HL).
[76] *G&C Kreglinger v New Patagonia Meat & Cold Storage Co Ltd* [1914] AC 25 (HL), 46.
[77] Thompson, 'Do we really need clogs?' [2001] Conv 502, 502–3.

Thompson's own view on this is very clear. He states that, when concluding on the merits of *Jones v Morgan*:[78]

> 'Unfortunately, the present case is another modern example of the ancient doctrine of clogs upsetting an otherwise unobjectionable commercial contract... It seems clear, however, that the courts do not feel able with regard to clauses... to perform the necessary judicial surgery. We are, therefore, left with a position whereby a rule which has been criticised for over a century, which was devised to deal with completely different socio-economic circumstances, continues to exercise its baleful function of upsetting commercial contracts. Sadly, it seems that the courts, at least below the House of Lords, are constrained by authority to apply rules which have outlived their usefulness.'[79]

One particularly interesting development, however, has been the possibility of using the clogs and fetters doctrine to tackle what are seen as oppressively high interest rates. The starting point is *Cityland and Property (Holdings) Ltd v Dabrah*.[80]

Key case: *Cityland and Property (Holdings) Ltd v Dabrah* [1968] Ch 166

This case concerned not interest rates, but a premium. The level of the premium imposed on the borrower was, in the words of the court, out of all proportion to prevailing interest rates. The court assess whether this constituted such a limitation on the equity of redemption that it could not be permitted. Per Goff J: 'it must be borne in mind that this premium was so large that it forthwith destroyed the whole equity and made it a completely deficient security.'[81]

This was further considered in *Multiservice Bookbinding v Marden*.[82] Some see this as representing a potential route to ensuring consumer protection in mortgages in respect of extortionate rates of interests. This is a problem which is particularly acute for those taking out second mortgages or with a poor credit history. However, the court in *Marden* in fact declined to intervene in the instant case.

Key case: *Multiservice Bookbinding v Marden* [1979] Ch 84

In this case, the court examined the decision in *Dabrah*, and particularly the reliance on the 'unreasonable' nature of the premium in that case. In *Marden*, the court was of the view that an unreasonable

---

[78] *Jones v Morgan* [2001] EWCA Civ 995, [2002] 1 EGLR 125.
[79] Thompson, 'Do we really need clogs?' [2001] Conv 502, 514–15.
[80] *Cityland and Property (Holdings) Ltd v Dabrah* [1968] Ch 166 (ChD).
[81] *Cityland and Property (Holdings) Ltd v Dabrah* [1968] Ch 166 (ChD), 181.
[82] *Multiservice Bookbinding Ltd v Marden* [1979] Ch 84 (ChD).

interest rate was not enough to attract the intervention of the court. Rather, the bargain had to be unconscionable. Per Browne-Wilkinson J:

> 'I therefore approach the second point on the basis that, in order to be freed from the necessity to comply with all the terms of the mortgage, the plaintiffs must show that the bargain, or some of its terms, was unfair and unconscionable: it is not enough to show that, in the eyes of the court, it was unreasonable. In my judgment a bargain cannot be unfair and unconscionable unless one of the parties to it has imposed the objectionable terms in a morally reprehensible manner, that is to say, in a way which affects his conscience.'
>
> The classic example of an unconscionable bargain is where advantage has been taken of a young, inexperienced or ignorant person to introduce a term which no sensible well-advised person or party would have accepted. But I do not think the categories of unconscionable bargains are limited: the court can and should intervene where a bargain has been procured by unfair means.'[83]

In assessing this, the court emphasised that it would take into account not only the size of the interest rate itself, but also the nature of the parties, their commercial experience, and the context within which the loan was granted.

Thus, in respect of clogs and fetters we can summarise as follows:

1. The doctrine is a way of ensuring that the mortgage transaction is a simple secured debt, so that there are no limits on the right of the borrower to bring the mortgage to an end if the debt is repaid.
2. There are four ways in which this right to redeem can be 'fettered'
   a. Explicit limits on the date at which the mortgage can be brought to an end. The courts will allow these if either they are reasonable in terms of the length of the limit, or even in cases where the delay is very lengthy, if the parties dealt at arms' length in a commercial transaction.
   b. An attempt by the lender to secure a 'collateral advantage'. This will generally be permitted so long as the term does not act as a restraint of trade or make it practically impossible for the borrower to repay the sums due.
   c. An attempt by the lender to introduce a rate of interest or some other term so impossible to meet in practice that it has the effect of preventing redemption. Such terms will only be struck down if the interest rate is unconscionable or oppressive, rather than simply unreasonable.
   d. An attempt for the lender to reserve for themselves the right to purchase the mortgaged property. Such terms will not be enforced.
3. There is sustained criticism of this doctrine, from both the courts and academic commentators. In commercial contexts this criticism appears to have a great deal of weight, but they may still perform a useful function in a consumer context, even if the rules are not really well-designed to reach that end.

---

[83] *Multiservice Bookbinding Ltd v Marden* [1979] Ch 84 (ChD), 10.

11.6.2 INTEREST RATES

The rule on clogs and fetters may not be the only 'route' by which a borrower can attempt to obtain some relief from an extremely high interest rate however. In some cases, the courts have indicated that they have an inherent jurisdiction to strike down such terms merely because they are oppressive, rather than having to demonstrate that in some way they are repulsive to the nature of the mortgage.

It is also relatively clear that it will not be possible for a lender to have an *arbitrary* right to vary interest rates. Let us show this with an example.

Mary Brown undertook to pay a rate of interest that was variable at the sole discretion of the Bank. Last year the Bank trebled its interest rate for all customers whose surname began with 'B'. The question arises as to whether this is a legitimate step for the bank to take, or whether the courts will intervene to prevent it.

That this would not be legitimate is demonstrated by the decision in *Nash v Paragon Finance*.[84]

> **Key case:** *Nash v Paragon Finance* [2001] EWCA Civ 1466
>
> The mortgage agreement in this case contained a term allowing unfettered interest rate adjustments on the part of the mortgagee.
>
> Here it was held that 'the discretion to vary interest rates should not be exercised dishonestly, for an improper purpose, capriciously or arbitrarily'.[85] By way of example, Dyson LJ suggests that, '[a]n example of a capricious reason would be where the lender decided to raise the rate of interest because its manager did not like the colour of the borrower's hair'.[86]
>
> This suggests that the courts will utilise their inherent jurisdiction to strike down arbitrary terms. The basis upon which they will do so, however, is perhaps somewhat unclear. One explanation is that there is an implied term in the mortgage that any powers in the mortgage will not be used capriciously. This is considered in *Paragon Finance v Pender*.[87]

> **Key case:** *Paragon Finance v Pender* [2005] EWCA Civ 760
>
> Mr and Mrs Pender were registered proprietors of the property. They granted a charge to Paragon. Paragon was entitled, according to the contract, to vary the interest rates howsoever and whensoever they wished. It was accepted by counsel for Paragon that this power was limited by an implied obligation that it would not, 'be exercised improperly, capriciously or arbitrarily, or in a way which no reasonable mortgagee, acting reasonably, would do'.[88] In this case, the lender had a policy of raising interest rates in cases where the borrower was in repeated arrears, as a means of encouraging repayment. The court concluded that this was a legitimate use of the power to raise interest rates and was in no sense improper or arbitrary.

---

[84] *Nash v Paragon Finance* [2001] EWCA Civ 1466, [2002] 1 WLR 685.
[85] *Nash v Paragon Finance* [2001] EWCA Civ 1466, [2002] 1 WLR 685, [32].
[86] *Nash v Paragon Finance* [2001] EWCA Civ 1466; [2002] 1 WLR 685, [31].
[87] *Paragon Finance v Pender* [2005] EWCA Civ 760, [2005] 1 WLR 3412.
[88] *Paragon Finance v Pender* [2005] EWCA Civ 760, [2005] 1 WLR 3412, [118].

> This case shows us that whilst it may be possible to use the implied obligation to limit interest rate rises which are based on no rational commercial reason, it is not a mechanism to prevent the imposition of high interest rates where there is a good reason for the lender to wish to raise such interest rates.
>
> It is worth noting in this case that the court also held that this was not an extortionate credit bargain under the Consumer Credit Act 1974 (now an unfair credit relationship following the Consumer Credit Act 2006). We return to this legislation next.

11.6.3 CONSUMER PROTECTION LEGISLATION

There is also now a good deal of consumer protection legislation which constrains the terms which lenders can rely on in a consumer context. Some of this relates specifically to the mortgage market, but much arises from wider consumer protection measures, such as the Consumer Rights Act 2015 which governs 'unfair terms' more generally.

The Financial Services and Mortgages Act 2000 provides that first mortgages granted to institutional lenders will be regulated by the Financial Conduct Authority. This applies to mortgages created after 31 October 2004. However, as a result of the Mortgage Credit Directive 2014, most second mortgages are now also regulated by the FCA where entered into after 21 March 2016. If a mortgage which falls within the scope of the regulatory power of the FCA is created without the consent/rules of the FCA, then the lender risks committing a criminal offence. However, the FCA handbook protections are not comprehensive. They are largely focused on ensuring that individuals are given sufficient information to make proper decisions, rather than on actually affecting the balance of power between the lender and the borrower in a more comprehensive way. It is important to emphasise here also that in giving the regulatory power to the FCA, the FSMA 2000 and associated legislation removes the jurisdiction of the courts in this area. As a result, the majority of 'normal' mortgages will not be subject to court scrutiny as to the fairness or otherwise of the mortgagee's conduct, except in so far as the equitable doctrines discussed in the preceding sections apply.

Until the Consumer Rights Act 2015 came into force, it was also clear that interest rates could not be reviewed by the courts generally under provisions relating to unfair contract terms. However, from 1st October 2015, the new legislation makes it clear that whilst *generally* such terms will be excluded from consideration by the courts, it appears from section 64 Consumer Rights Act 2015 that where interest terms are not presented in a transparent and prominent position, then they will be susceptible to review by the courts under these provisions.

Whatever the potential benefits of these consumer-focused rules, however, we should note that they have not had a significant impact in practice beyond the controls which the common law and equity already provided. Rather, we may say that the advantage of these rules has been the mandatory provision of information to the consumer so that they are more aware of the risks that they take on when granting a mortgage.

11.6.4 UNDUE INFLUENCE

It is of course possible that a mortgage transaction would be flawed for some reason. This could include cases of fraud, forgery, mistake, and the like. This is particularly problematic in situations involving undue influence. It is relatively common in cases of mortgages involving co-ownership for one co-owner to have been pressured into entering into the mortgage transaction without either genuinely consenting to that transaction, or without really understanding what the nature of the transaction was. There are two sides to this issue. First, under what circumstances can we say that there was undue influence? Second, since the undue influence is between two mortgagors, rather than mortgagee and mortgagor, under what circumstances will the undue influence affect the mortgagee?

11.6.4.1 When does undue influence exist?

The courts have developed a two-strand test for the presence of undue influence in a transaction. Undue influence can be presumed, or actual. Presumed undue influence exists where there is a transaction which is not explicable on its face, puts one party at a manifest disadvantage and where the parties are in a close relationship (one of trust and confidence). In such cases, the burden of proof will fall onto the primary borrower to demonstrate that there was no undue influence. Actual undue influence depends upon proof that undue influence has in fact taken place and the burden of proof in these situations lies upon the person alleging that there has been undue influence. The latter is relatively rare. It is hard to prove undue influence because it can be very difficult to prove what was said or done between two parties in private. Presumed undue influence is more common in this context.

Megarry and Wade explain the nature of presumed undue influence:

'According to *O'Brien*, undue influence will be presumed in two types of case...

(i) as a matter of law from certain relationships... This "presumption" is really a reflection of "a sternly protective attitude towards certain types of relationship in which one party acquires influence over another person who is vulnerable and dependant"; and

(ii) as a matter of fact where one person reposed trust and confidence in another and the impugned transaction called for an explanation. This is effectively a rebuttable evidentiary presumption which shifts the burden of proof to the person trying to uphold the impugned transaction.'[89]

The requirements of actual undue are as follows:

1. The party who brought about the transaction had the capacity to influence the supposed victim of the undue influence;
2. That such influence was in fact exercised;
3. That this influence was undue; and
4. The exercise of the undue influence had a casual effect in relation to the transaction.

Undue influence can arise in cases not only where the 'victim' enters into a mortgage directly, but also where they stand as surety or guarantor for the mortgage of another. This was the case in *Barclays Bank v O'Brien*,[90] for example, a leading modern case on the existence of undue

---

[89] Harpum et al, *Megarry and Wade: The Law of Real Property* (8th ed) (Sweet and Maxwell, London, 2012), [23–123].
[90] *Barclays Bank v O'Brien* [1994] 1 AC 180 (HL).

influence. Undue influence can also be relevant in cases where an individual waives their priority to a mortgage. The waiver can itself be vitiated by undue influence, and if that affects the lender as discussed later, then the waiver will be ineffective. We can see the principles at work in *O'Brien*.[91]

> **Key case:** *Barclays Bank v O'Brien* [1994] 1 AC 180
>
> In this case Mr and Mrs O'Brien agreed to enter into a second mortgage in order to secure money which was owed by Mr O'Brien's company. Mrs O'Brien did not really understand the nature of the transaction, and was induced to enter into it by false representations made by her husband as to its scope and intended duration. The House of Lords held that in cases such as these, where there was evidence of undue influence in a surety transaction, equity would allow the victim to set aside the transaction as against the primary debtor. Furthermore, in such situations where the transaction involved only risk for the victim, the lender would be put in inquiry and had to take reasonable steps to ensure that victim's consent to the transaction was legitimately obtained.
>
> Lord Browne-Wilkinson, with whom the rest of the court agreed, explains the policy considerations at play in this area and it is clear that social context is critical to the operation of the rules relating to undue influence. He reasoned that changes in social attitudes to property meant that increasing numbers of cases involving undue influence were appearing before the courts. This is because wealth was more evenly spread, and a high proportion of this was in the form of the family home. Given the direction of travel towards gender equality, these homes were then also in the name of both parties. As a result, for one party to raise finance for a business, or similar, it was usual for both parties to need to consent to borrowing against the security of the home. However, this attitude to gender equality is only successful if there is also parity between the parties in their dealings with one another in the instant relationship, and that is not always the case. As the court reasons:
>
> > 'The number of recent cases in this field shows that in practice many wives are still subjected to, and yield to, undue influence by their husbands. Such wives can reasonably look to the law for some protection when their husbands have abused the trust and confidence reposed in them.'[92]
>
> However, his Lordship then emphasised that it is important to ensure that this tension does not result in the stagnation of the property market, with 'the wealth currently tied up in the matrimonial home does not become economically sterile.'[93]
>
> His Lordship then went onto explain the two categories of undue influence: Class 1, actual undue influence; and class 2, presumed undue influence. Class 2 can then be further divided into class 2A where certain relationships, such as that of solicitor and client and doctor and patient automatically raise the presumption that undue influence exists; and class 2B where there is a relationship of trust and confidence between the parties so that the presumption of undue influence is justified. Whilst husband/wife relationships do not raise the class 2A presumption, they would typically be a relationship of class 2B type, which itself would highlight the likelihood of undue influence.

---

[91] *Barclays Bank v O'Brien* [1994] 1 AC 180 (HL).
[92] *Barclays Bank v O'Brien* [1994] 1 AC 180 (HL), 188.
[93] *Barclays Bank v O'Brien* [1994] 1 AC 180 (HL), 188.

Finally, Lord Browne-Wilkinson summarised the applicable rules:

> 'Where one cohabitee has entered into an obligation to stand as surety for the debts of the other cohabitee and the creditor is aware that they are cohabitees: (1) the surety obligation will be valid and enforceable by the creditor unless the suretyship was procured by the undue influence... (2) if there has been undue influence... unless the creditor has taken reasonable steps to satisfy himself that the surety entered into the obligation freely and in knowledge of the true facts, the creditor will be unable to enforce the surety obligation because he will be fixed with constructive notice of the surety's right to set aside the transaction; (3) unless there are special exceptional circumstances, a creditor will have taken such reasonable steps to avoid being fixed with constructive notice if the creditor warns the surety (at a meeting not attended by the principal debtor) of the amount of her potential liability and of the risks involved and advises the surety to take independent legal advice'.[94]

11.6.4.2 When will the undue influence affect the lender?

However, just because undue influence is proven between two mortgagors, this does not mean that the mortgagee is affected by the undue influence. Rather, the courts have established what is known as the *Etridge* protocol to determine when a mortgage will be set aside because it was procured through undue influence on the part of someone other than the lender themselves. These rules were developed in the leading case of *Royal Bank of Scotland Plc v Etridge (No.2)*.[95]

> **Key case: *Royal Bank of Scotland Plc v Etridge (No.2)* [2001] UKHL 44**
>
> *Etridge* determined that even where there is undue influence present in a particular case, that does not mean that the lender will be affected. The case establishes a series of steps which a lender can follow to provide themselves, in effect, with immunity against the impact of undue influence on the part of either one of two borrowers, or a third party. Underpinning these steps is a requirement that the lender attempt to discover the presence of any undue influence, and take reasonable measures to satisfy themselves that none is present. The steps are as follows:
>
> 1. Whenever a wife agrees to stand surety for her husband's debt (or to become a party to a mortgage which does not benefit her), then the bank should take steps to be sure that undue influence is not a factor. This applies equally to homosexual and heterosexual couples, and to unmarried couples where the lender is aware of the relationship.
>
> 2. If the bank is put on inquiry, then:
>
>   'a bank can reasonably be expected to take steps to bring home to the wife the risk she is running by standing as surety and to advise her to take independent advice... a bank satisfies these requirements if it insists that the wife attend a private meeting with a representative of the bank at which she is told of the extent of her liability as surety, warned of the risk she is running and urged to take independent legal advice. In exceptional cases the bank, to be safe, has to insist that the wife is separately advised'.[96]

---

[94] *Barclays Bank v O'Brien* [1994] 1 AC 180 (HL), 198–9.
[95] *Royal Bank of Scotland Plc v Etridge (No.2)* [2001] UKHL 44, [2002] 2 AC 773.
[96] *Royal Bank of Scotland Plc v Etridge (No.2)* [2001] UKHL 44, [2002] 2 AC 773, [50].

3. The bank may also be advised to seek confirmation from the 'victim's' solicitor regarding the genuine nature of that person's consent to the transaction. This can put a heavy burden onto the shoulders of solicitors in this context and raises the difficult question as to whether both parties should be represented by separate solicitors.

If undue influence is shown to exist, and the undue influence affects the lender, then the mortgage will be unenforceable as against the victim. However, this does not necessarily mean that the victim has priority over the mortgage. This will depend on the usual priority rules. In cases where the mortgage in question involved two legal owners, one of whom was induced to enter the transaction by undue influence, then the legal mortgage will be set aside (and the register rectified), However, an equitable mortgage will arise in respect of the genuinely consenting owner's share. The operation of this rule is neatly demonstrated in the recent case of *Santander v Fletcher*.[97] This will result in the lender becoming an equitable co-owner, and able, as a result, to rely on the court's jurisdiction under section 14 TOLATA 1996 (chapter 16). This means that even if the lender does not have priority over the victim, they may still be able to obtain sale of the property.

11.7 MORTGAGES AND THIRD PARTIES

This part is concerned with priorities, and as such we only give a summary here since the matter is dealt with in detail in chapter 15. There are really three key situations in which a mortgage right will come into conflict with the property right of another: mortgages versus leasehold estates; mortgages versus an interest under a trust; and mortgages versus purchasers of land. We consider these in turn. Remember, as we discussed in chapter 1 at 1.2.3, a priority dispute is not concerned so much with the individual right, but the modalities of interaction between one kind of property right and another. In modern registered land, the priority rules are contained in sections 28–30 LRA 2002, but where mortgages are concerned, there are some additional layers to priority disputes which arise as a result of the fact that (a) the mortgagee obtains an immediate right to possession in the mortgaged land which takes priority over the mortgagor's right to possession, but that does not tell us about third party possessory interests and (b) many mortgages in which priority disputes arise are situations involving co-ownership. We discuss the priority rules that are specific to mortgages here, but this section should be read in conjunction with chapters 15 and 16.

11.7.1 MULTIPLE MORTGAGES

First, though, we consider the situation where there are multiple mortgages granted over a single property. The starting point is that they will rank, first, according to the order in which they were created. If all the mortgages are registered as charges, then section 48 LRA 2002

---

[97] *Santander UK Plc v Fletcher* [2018] EWHC 2778 (Ch), [2019] 2 P & CR 4.

provides that they will rank according to which they were registered, rather than the order in which they were created. If not all of the charges are registered, then the charges which are registered will be able to take advantage of the priority rule in section 30 (see chapter 15).

For mortgages which operate in equity only because they have not been registered, then they will again take priority according to the order in which they were created (section 48 does not affect this), but unless the mortgage is somehow entered as a notice on the register (although not substantively registered as a charge) then this equitable mortgagee will likely lose priority to any later registered legal mortgage.

11.7.2 SUBROGATION

The ability to subrogate is a very powerful weapon in a mortgagee's armoury. It affects their priority regardless of the nature of the third party's rights. In its most basic terms, subrogation is the ability to 'step into the shoes' of a former lender and take advantage of their 'higher' priority position. It is easiest to demonstrate this with an example.

Ralph is the registered proprietor of King's Cottage. He purchased the cottage in 2012 with the help of a mortgage granted to Drosselmeyer Bank. This was registered as a legal charge. In 2013 Ralph granted Clara a 30-year lease over the property, without the consent of Drosselmeyer Bank. In 2015, Ralph declared a trust of the property in favour of Fritz. In 2017, short of funds, Ralph decided to re-mortgage the property. Fritz and Clara both live in the property now. Ralph has moved out. Sugar Plum Bank lent him enough to pay off the remaining loan amount with Drosselmeyer plus an additional £50,000. Sugar Plum has now found out about the lease and the declaration of trust and are concerned that they do not have priority over the rights of Clara and Fritz.

Subrogation will be very helpful to Sugar Plum bank here. It allows them to 'step into the shoes' of Drosselmeyer Bank for the purposes of priority because their funds were used in order to pay off the original loan. It is important to note, however, that this ability to subrogate to the priority of the original lender only applies to the money used to pay off the loan. This means, in a order of priority, it would go:

- Sugar Plum Bank (original loan)
- Clara's Leasehold interest
- Fritz's trust interest
- Sugar Plum Bank (additional £50,000)

In order for subrogation to have this effect however, it is very important that there is a causal connection between the subsequent loan and the original loan being repaid. This justifies the treatment of the subsequent lender as though the original mortgage was assigned to him, rather than there being a new loan. The operation of these rules is considered in detail in *Cheltenham & Gloucester v Appleyard*.[98]

---

[98] *Cheltenham & Gloucester v Appleyard* [2004] EWCA Civ 291, [2004] 13 EG 127 (CS).

> **Key case:** *Cheltenham & Gloucester v Appleyard* [2004] EWCA Civ 291
>
> Neuberger LJ in this case gives a lengthy analysis of the fundamental principles of subrogation. These are:
>
> 1. Subrogation can emerge from the contract, or it can emerge from equity. The term potentially covers a number of different situations. However, courts are usually concerned with the equitable principle.
> 2. This has arisen to undo unjust enrichment.
> 3. Subrogation is flexible, but we should attempt to apply it in a principled way.
> 4. A lender may seek to rely on subrogation for a variety of reasons, including their own ineptitude or their having been misled.
> 5. Subrogation is not limited to property rights.
> 6. Just because a lender has a secured right, it does not mean that he is unable to claim a superior security on the basis of subrogation.
> 7. However, if the lender has all that he bargained for, he cannot seek to rely on subrogation to improve his position.
> 8. The fact that the lender may have been negligent does not prevent his relying on subrogation.
> 9. It is not necessary for there to be a common intention between the parties that the lender should have some security in order for him to rely on subrogation.
> 10. Subrogation cannot put the lender in a better position than that which he bargained for.
> 11. Lenders will struggle to rely on subrogation if it will not leave them better off than their original security.
> 12. The sum to which a lender is subrogated cannot be greater than the amount of the debt discharged.
> 13. As this is an equitable remedy, the normal equitable principles apply and the principles of priority are determined according to normal equitable rules.[99]

11.7.3 MORTGAGES AND TRUST INTERESTS

The interaction between mortgages and interests under trusts operate in exactly the same way as all other priority disputes. However, since it is such a common issue to arise both in real life and in problem questions, we include the most important considerations here. For a full picture however it is essential to read chapters 15 and 16.

First, in any case where a mortgage is granted in relation to land in which there is a trust, it is critical to ascertain whether overreaching has taken place. This will occur if the loan money was given to two or more legal owners. If this has happened, then the mortgage will rank above any trust interest, whether that be a co-ownership situation where the two legal owners hold on trust for themselves, or whether the beneficiary of a trust be one or more third parties. The mechanics of overreaching are discussed in chapters 2, 15, and 16.

---

[99] *Cheltenham & Gloucester v Appleyard* [2004] EWCA Civ 291, [2004] 13 EG 127 (CS), [32]–[44].

Second, even in cases where the interest under the trust is not overreached, that does *not* mean that the interest will be binding on the mortgagee. This will depend, first and foremost, on whether the mortgage is subsequently registered. If it is, then the priority rule in section 30 LRA 2002 means that the chargee will be bound only by those interests the priority of which is protected at the time of the disposition. When thinking about interests under a trust, since they cannot be the subject of a notice on the register (section 33 LRA 2002), this means that the beneficiary will only be protected if they are in actual occupation in such a way as to comply with the requirements of schedule 3, paragraph 2 LRA 2002 at the relevant date. If they are, then the beneficiary will be protected. If not, the priority of their equitable interest will be postponed to the charge. This means that the lender will be able to exercise the 'normal' remedies of the legal mortgagee against both the mortgagor and any beneficiary(ies).

Third, where money is advanced in order to facilitate the *purchase* of a property, then as a result of the rule in *Abbey National v Cann*,[100] confirmed *obiter* in relation to post-2002 Act situations by *Scott v Southern Pacific*,[101] all equitable interests will rank behind the mortgagee, even if strictly-speaking the charge was created fractionally after any declaration of trust. The effect of this is to close what is known as the *scintilla temporis*, ie the 'slither' of time which exists between multiple documents created on purchase of land which may include a declaration of trust. The logic behind this rule relation to 'acquisition mortgages' is that where an individual becomes the beneficiary of a trust in relation to property acquired by mortgage, there would be no property in question were it not for the mortgage. As a result, the mortgagee should take priority.

> **Further analysis: Acquisition mortgages**
>
> The policies behind the rules relating to acquisition mortgages have a certain appealing logic. It does make sense for a lender whose loan has made the purchase of a property possible to have priority over a beneficiary under a trust in the majority of cases. However, in some situations, the 'justice' of the situation is less clear. For example, in *Scott v Southern Pacific*,[102] the situation did not involve the 'new' purchase of a property. Rather, in that case, title to the properties were transferred to fraudsters as part of an equity release scheme. The original owners were promised that they would be granted leasehold interests for life in the property. The properties were acquired using a mortgage, and when the fraudsters then defaulted on the loans, the mortgagee sought possession of the land against the original owner. It is not as clear here to say that, 'but for' the loan the original owners would not have had any interest at all in the property, as it is in simple acquisition cases.
>
> Smith, in commenting on *Abbey National v Cann*,[103] considers what the alternatives might be to a 'one size' approach.
>
> > 'We may start by saying that where finance is required to complete a purchase, then the mortgagee should to that extent have priority... If there are overlapping sources of finance then three solutions offer themselves... First, we could simply favour the mortgagee. As has been argued, it is difficult to support this conclusion in terms of legal logic or economic reality. A second solution is to favour the source of finance

---

[100] *Abbey National v Cann* [1991] 1 AC 56 (HL).
[101] *Re North East Property Buyers Litigation* [2014] UKSC 52, [2015] AC 385.
[102] *Re North East Property Buyers Litigation* [2014] UKSC 52, [2015] AC 385.
[103] *Abbey National v Cann* [1991] 1 AC 56 (HL).

> that is first in time. The difficulty here is partly that establishing a time order may be difficult and partly that it is difficult to reconcile with [*Cann*]... The final solution is to accord the sources of finance equal priority (proportionate to their quantum)... It is worth noting that if a mortgagee fails to obtain possession then he is likely to bankrupt the mortgagor. Almost inevitably, the house will be sold and an equal priority analysis can be applied to the proceeds of sale. The third solution seems most likely to do justice, although it would require considerable elucidation. It has to be recognised, however, that it is at odds with other real property priority rules, which invariably strive to prefer one proprietary claim to another. On the other hand, once the scintilla temporis doctrine (designed to provide us with a preference) is dismissed, the law appears to be at a loss as to what to put in its place'.[104]
>
> This shows the dilemma of the *scintilla temporis*/acquisition mortgage rule. It produces a generally fair rule of thumb, but it does not necessarily reflect the realities of an existing case.

Fourth, in cases where notwithstanding the operation of these three rules it appears that a beneficiary may still have priority over a chargee, the courts will inquire as to whether the beneficiary has waived their priority over the bank. Very often there would be an express waiver to this effect. As long as that waiver was not itself obtained by undue influence, for example, (see earlier), and was itself valid, then it will have the effect of giving the lender priority. Implied waiver is also possible.[105]

11.7.4 MORTGAGES AND TENANTS

As with other priority disputes discussed in this section, the general rules relating to priority disputes between mortgagees and tenants are the same. A leasehold interest registered or otherwise protected at the time of the charge would take priority over a registered charge. One created after the charge would not have priority. In cases of an equitable mortgage, priorities will be determined by the order of creation (or waiver and *scintilla temporis* rules discussed immediately previously). However, statute has determined that certain *consequences* of priority will be slightly modified in relation to this interaction. Furthermore, in cases of a subsequent lease, if the mortgagee consents to that lease, then they will be unable to exercise the right of possession against the tenant, for example. The Mortgage Repossessions (Protection of Tenants) Act 2010 provides that in cases of an unauthorised subsequent lease, the courts have discretion to delay a possession order for up to two months to provide the tenant with sufficient time to plan their move. This does not mean that the tenant has priority over the mortgagee of course, but it does limit the potential severe consequences of their lack of such priority.

In cases of equitable mortgages, if the equitable mortgage is created before a registered lease, then the tenant will take priority over the equitable mortgage as long as the priority of the mortgage was not protected at the time of the disposition by a notice on the registered or by actual occupation of the mortgagee.

---

[104] Smith, 'Mortgagees and trust beneficiaries' (1990) 106 LQR 545, 549.
[105] *Paddington Building Society v Mendelsohn* (1985) 50 P & CR 244 (CA).

11.7.5 MORTGAGES AND PURCHASERS

A mortgage will have priority against a subsequent purchaser of the estate subject to the mortgage if that mortgage is either registered or if the mortgagee was in actual occupation at the time of the disposition in accordance with schedule 3 paragraph 2 LRA 2002 (very unlikely). Of course, this is only relevant if the mortgage was not discharged on the sale of the property as it usually would be.

11.8 CONCLUSION

Throughout this chapter we have discussed the consequences of the mortgage being both a contractual agreement and an element of property law. At times, the freedom of contract of the parties and the proprietary entitlements to which that contract gives rise work together. However, in some situations we can see that there is a conflict. This arises not least in respect of the rules in relation to clogs and fetters, where, as we discussed, the parties are not free to agree what they like as part of a mortgage transaction, even in cases of commercial 'arms' length' dealing. Consumer protection legislation and soft law mechanisms have, to a certain extent, modified the freedom of contract of parties, although this is generally welcomed given that in the consumer context there is a huge inequality of bargaining power. These rules reflect the reality of the real estate market today and the fact that almost all home-buyers have no choice but to use a mortgage as a means to facilitate that acquisition. However, there are also areas where parties can contractually agree to modify what would otherwise be the 'default' position in relation to mortgages. Should it be desired by the parties they can modify both the lender's right to possession and the operation of the power of sale, fundamentally shifting the nature of the remedies which a lender has. It would be rare for a lender to agree to voluntarily curtail their rights in this way, but it is not impossible as a matter of law. In this respect, the fundamental proprietary rights can be modified by contract. In this sense, in terms of understanding the rules regulating mortgages, the most important message from this chapter is precisely this: mortgages are a creation of contract. Just as with leases in the previous chapter, the contract and the property cannot be separated, and it is the combination of the 'system-wide' property rules, and the individualistic contract rules which has created the mortgage as it exists today.

PRINCIPLES

How does this discussion shape our understanding of the principles explained in chapter 1? To recap, these principles were:

1. Certainty
2. Sensitivity to context
3. Transactability
4. Systemic and individual effects
5. Recognition of the social role of the land law system.

In relation to the law of mortgages we see a strong clash between these principles. This is because in mortgages rests the most important commercial aspect of property from an institutional perspective, and the most important aspect of property in respect of people's relationship with their own home. Since almost all residential property is acquired with the aid of a mortgage, we see here how sensitive the balance must be between the requirements of certainty and transactability on the one hand, and of sensitivity to context and recognition of social effects on the other. For a lender to be sure of their ground, the rights associated with a mortgage need to be very clear so that there is very minimal risk—or at least so that any risks there are, such as the risk of market falls, or of 'untrustworthy' borrowers—are risks which are left to the lender themselves to assess and manage. The law, in this sense, should provide them with a clear and predictable position which allows for the accurate calculation of risk, a calculation which will then be reflected in the interest rates charged by lenders to ensure the profitability of their enterprise. We can of course validly criticize the role that institutional lending plays in relation to residential property. We could argue that the system would be fairer to individuals and 'socially' more effective, were such lending to operate on a not-for-profit basis, for example. But under the current economic structures in relation to property ownership, certainty is absolutely critical from a lender perspective.

Furthermore, when we think about transactability, a mortgage could heavily impinge on the buying and selling of land if either the mortgage itself was too flexible a concept, so that each transaction involved lengthy and complex negotiations, thus raising the transaction costs associated with dealings in land. Such transaction costs can be off-putting to those engaged in property transactions, and by having a relatively settled system of inflexible rules (including, for example, the prohibition on clogs and fetters on the right to redeem), such transaction costs are reduced, albeit to the detriment of contractual flexibility. In this way, if we regard property as an asset, to be bought, sold and lent on in order for profits to be made, then certainty and security in terms of mortgages are absolutely critical.

On the other hand, this certainty must be examined closely against the associated costs. For individuals who find themselves in very difficult personal circumstances, often through no fault of their own, the effect that losing their home in addition to any other problems can be devastating. It is easy to imagine the circumstances in which such might arise: relationship breakdown and illness are circumstances which spring to mind. In both of these situations, a person's ability to afford their mortgage may be severely hindered by events beyond their own control in their personal life. This means that in addition to having the problem itself, the borrower will also have the risk of losing their home weighing on their shoulders. The law makes no allowance for these circumstances. Some argue that it could not do so: the vicissitudes of life are such that it would be impossible to tailor provision to all deserving cases, and the consequences for the system as a whole were such an attempt to be made would be so disruptive as to make lending on land extremely problematic, if not impossible. Others however would say that this structural argument overstates the position. They would suggest that the law of mortgages does not currently have the balance right. In completely ignoring the personal circumstances of borrowers, the law may cause enormous injustice and unfairness at a moment in people's lives when they most need support. In reality, probably both arguments are true in different places and at different times. The problem is in allowing for nuance in addressing these issues, and the fast turnover of commercial lending transactions is not the place for nuance.

Another very important theme which permeates the law of mortgages is the distinction which the law implicitly or explicitly draws between the domestic and commercial contexts.

Thus, section 36 AJA 1970 only applies to dwelling houses, as does section 6 Criminal Law Act 1977. The doctrine of clogs and fetters and limitations on the right to redeem are dealt with more strictly in the context of a domestic/consumer setting. Occupiers of property are treated differently than all others as a result of the priority rules expressed in the LRA, something which can have particular significance for property in which there is sole legal ownership but co-ownership in equity (as explained in chapters 15 and 16). By contrast, in commercial cases, not only is it significantly easier for a lender to go into possession without a court order, the borrower will have no avenues to limit the lender's right to possession. This suggests that whilst the law has not produced a position where individual nuance is possible, there are signs that a sort of contextual responsiveness has developed over time to reflect the needs present within the different 'industries' depending upon the land law rules.

TABLE OF DEFINITIONS

Mortgagor	The person creating a mortgage, ie the borrower. This feels somewhat counterintuitive according to a lay understanding of how mortgages work, so useful rule of thumb is to think of bOrrOwer = mortgagOr.
Mortgagee	The person in whom the security interest vests, ie the lender. Again, think lEndEr = mortgagEE.
Legal right to redeem	The is also known as the contractual date of redemption, and is a date specified in the contract after which as a matter of contract the mortgagor is able (and obliged) to pay back the sums due. The practical importance of this date relates more to the remedies of the lender than it does the rights of the borrower.
Equity of redemption	The proprietary interest that consists of the 'residual' entitlement to property mortgaged. Developed against the background of mortgages involving the transfer of legal title, this term is now used to describe the totality of the mortgagor's interest in the land and the courts are wary of attempts to limit the scope of the equity of redemption.
Equitable right to redeem	This is a specific right which arises once the contractual date of redemption has passed, and forms part of the equity of redemption.

FURTHER READING

The further reading in this section is designed to give a range of perspectives on the wider social impacts of lending in relation to land, as well as more detail on the law of mortgages if required:

BRIGHT, S., 'The dynamics of enduring property relationships in land' (2018) 81 Modern Law Review 85.
CLARK, W., *Fisher & Lightwood: Law of Mortgage* (14th ed) (Lexis Nexis Butterworths, 2014).
NIELD, S., 'Responsible Lending and Borrowing: Whereto Low-Cost Home Ownership?' (2010) 30(4) Legal Studies 610.
WHITEHOUSE, L., 'The Mortgage Arrears Pre-Action Protocol: An Opportunity Lost' (2009) 72(6) Modern Law Review 793.

12

EASEMENTS AND PROFITS

12.1	Introduction	376	12.7 Reform of the Law	
12.2	The Nature of Easements and Profits	377	of Easements	414
12.3	The Creation of Easements	394	12.8 Conclusion	415
12.4	The Use of Easements	405	Principles	415
12.5	Extinction of Easements	410	Table of Definitions	416
12.6	Transfers, Priorities, and Third Parties	410	Further Reading	416

CHAPTER GOALS

By the end of this chapter you should understand:

- What easements and profits are, and have an appreciation of their fundamental characteristics;
- How such rights are created expressly, impliedly, and by prescription;
- How such rights are used;
- The circumstances which will lead to the extinction of easements;
- How such rights are transferred, and how they affect third parties; and
- The current reform proposals.

12.1 INTRODUCTION

Easements and profits à prendre constitute a miscellaneous category of rights which can be legal in nature and which are exercised in relation to land, title to which belongs to someone else. This is most easily explained by the example of the right of way, which is an easement. The title-holder to one parcel of land may have the benefit of a right of way over his neighbour's land. This right is a property right and it will therefore remain the case that the owner of parcel A has a right of way over parcel B regardless of their individual identities. The fact that it is not possible to give a definition as to what an easement *is*, beyond that it is a right relating to land belonging to another, is a big clue to some of the problems encountered in relation to this category of rights. As will be seen, although there are certain shared characteristic features, the category is not a particularly coherent one, being, rather, the product of historical necessity and need. To put this another way—easements and profits constitute a 'rag bag' of rights, but the value of this bag ought not to be underestimated. Indeed, some of the most valuable rights it is possible to have are in the nature of an easement, including rights of way, rights to light (which can perhaps be better understood as, in effect, a right to prevent certain kinds of development on neighbouring land), and rights of support. Without such rights, it would be impossible to operate a system of land law with the majority of land in private ownership, as land would become landlocked, inaccessible, and development difficult.

Profits, by contrast, are of much more historical relevance than modern. Nevertheless, they are also capable of being legal rights. Profits are, again, a somewhat disparate group but essentially consist of the right to use, hunt, or take away something from another's land. The rights to cut crops, fish salmon, or fell trees on land belonging to another all constitute profits. These rights reflect a use of land which whilst still prevalent in the UK of course, is not necessarily typical of most people's day-to-day experience of urban living. This is not to say that they are not valuable. Timber and hunting rights in particular still constitute enormously valuable rights. They are not however part of the 'core' of land law in the way that easements are. It is unlikely that on a daily basis you would not benefit from one or more easement either on your own land or another's, be it in the form of a right of way, the running of water pipes through another's soil, or telephone wires above. The same cannot be said of profits.

This chapter is divided into two fundamental parts. The first part is concerned with the nature of these rights. It explores what sorts of rights can be easements and profits and considers the modern development relating to easements in particular. The second part is concerned with the creation of such rights and their interaction with the rights of others.

12.2 THE NATURE OF EASEMENTS AND PROFITS

The nature of these rights is not something which is susceptible of a simple comprehensive definition. Rather, it is best to understand what easements are by considering those rights which are already easements, and reason by analogy to new or unknown situations.

12.2.1 WHAT RIGHTS CAN BE EASEMENTS?

The 'central case' of an easement is a right which allows you to use another's land in a particular way. This includes the ability to walk across it using a right of way; to run pipes under it; to string wires over it; to park your car or store belongings on their land; to use a tennis court or swimming pool; or to use the space provided by a garden or park. However, there are other types of easement which cannot be explained as a right to 'use' another's land. Rather, they may by more naturally characterised (even if it is strictly possible to explain them according to the 'use' paradigm) as the ability to prevent another using their own land or dealing with features on their land in a particular way. This would include a right of support which exists to prevent one owner from knocking down their half of a semi-detached house or a right to light which will prevent the development of structures which will block the passage of the light. Further, some very rare easements may constitute the right to demand that your neighbour spend money on his own land for your benefit. Again, the right of support may fall in this category if maintenance is needed to ensure the support is provided. The so-called 'spurious' easement of fencing, which will require the neighbour to maintain fencing on his own land for your benefit, is also an easement of this type.

Numerous attempts have been made to provide a single clear test for what can be easements, but the most famous such attempt was articulated in the decision in *Re Ellenborough Park*[1] which has now been extensively reviewed in the recent Supreme Court decision in *Regency Villas*.[2]

> **Key case: *Re Ellenborough Park* [1956] Ch 131**
>
> The case of *Ellenborough Park* involved the use of a recreational area situated in the centre of a town square in Weston-Super-Mare. The houses surrounding the park claimed that they had an easement to use the park area. In concluding that the surrounding owners did have such a property right, Evershed MR listed the criteria (taken from Cheshire's textbook) which he applied in order to ascertain whether or not the right claimed was susceptible of being characterised as an easement. However, it is important to realise that this guidance was not, and is not, a statutory test to be applied rigidly. Rather, it is indicative of what easements will look like, and it does highlight some of their necessary features, albeit subject to interpretation in an instant case.
>
> The four criteria are:
>
> '(1) there must be a dominant and a servient tenement:
>
> (2) an easement must "accommodate" the dominant tenement:
>
> (3) dominant and servient owners must be different persons, and
>
> (4) a right over land cannot amount to an easement, unless it is capable of forming the subject-matter of a grant'.[3]
>
> In the case itself, the main issue was whether the right to use the park as suggested by the claimants was in the nature of a mere *ius spatiendi*. This 'right to wander' is traditionally a right which cannot constitute an easement, being at once too vague, too extensive, and to antithetical to the nature of an easement as a right which benefits land, rather than the people who own that land from time to time. In general terms, this falls under the second requirement, but can also been seen as forming a concern relevant to the fourth requirement which (in part) requires that an easement be definable. As we shall see later, however, the concerns regarding recreational space expressed in *Ellenborough Park*,[4] whatever one's view as to the way they fit into the decision in the case itself, have been superseded by the recent decision in *Regency Villas*.[5] That decision of the Supreme Court has redefined the way which the courts consider recreational or 'leisure-based' rights.
>
> Nevertheless, in respect of both the outcome of the case, and the four critera expressed in the generic formula earlier, the case is the starting point for understanding what kinds of rights can be easements.

---

[1] *Re Ellenborough Park* [1956] Ch 131 (CA).
[2] *Regency Villas Title Ltd v Diamond Resorts (Europe) Ltd* [2018] UKSC 57.
[3] *Re Ellenborough Park* [1956] Ch 131 (CA), 140.
[4] *Re Ellenborough Park* [1956] Ch 131 (CA).
[5] *Regency Villas Title Ltd v Diamond Resorts (Europe) Ltd* [2018] UKSC 57.

12.2.1.1 There must be a servient and dominant tenement

To understand what this requirement means it is necessary first to get to grips with the terminology (see also the table of definitions at the end of the chapter). The servient tenement is the land which is *burdened* by the relevant easement. The servient tenement can be either of a freehold or leasehold estate. It is the land which suffers the burden of the use. Thus, in the case of a right of way, or the use of a garden as in *Ellenborough Park*,[6] it would be the land over which the right of way runs, or where the garden itself was situated. However, in those atypical cases where the easement is not in the nature of a use of the other person's land, it may very well be that the dominant owner is not actually permitted to enter onto the servient tenement, as in the case of a right to light or a right of support. In such cases, the servient tenement is the land where use by the title-holder is limited by the existence of the easement. In essence, the servient tenement is the land where the title-holder is limited in some way in their ability to use their land, either by the right of someone else to use it or merely in order to maintain the status quo.

The dominant tenement by contrast, is the title benefitted by the easement. Again, the dominant estate can be a freehold or a leasehold estate. However, there *must* be a dominant tenement for an easement to exist. Easements cannot exist *in gross*, ie without a dominant tenement. This is a key difference between profits and easements since profits can exist *in gross*. The reason for this, however inconvenient it can sometimes be, is to ensure that land is not overburdened. The flipside of the requirement that there must be a servient and dominant tenement therefore is that easements can be brought to an end by merger of two previously separate estates. This is discussed in more detail later in the chapter at 12.5.

It may also be useful, especially in problem questions, to keep in mind the need for two separate estates in land. This does not necessarily mean that there will be two wholly separate pieces of *land* and in some cases the freeholder of both sites may be the same person. Thus it would be possible for tenant A to have a right of way over tenant B's land even though freeholder X was proprietor of the whole. Similarly, where freeholder X granted a tenancy over part of his land to tenant A, freeholder X may obtain the benefit of an easement over the part rented out even though he is freehold owner of that land.

12.2.1.2 The dominant and servient tenement must be in separate ownership

Although this is the third criterion on Evershed MR's list, it makes since to discuss this next. It is for the most part a simple requirement and merely requires assessing whether the two relevant estates are separately owned. However, it can sometimes be a stumbling block in complex chains of conveyance, especially when a single plot is being divided into multiple plots and can prevent the creation of a series of easements on an estate development, for example, prior to the first conveyance to the first purchaser. In problem questions, it can be treated as a 'sanity check' and merely requires ensuring that at no time is any person seemingly enjoying the benefit of an easement over their own estate. The case of *London & Blenheim Estates Ltd v Ladbroke Retail Parks Ltd*[7] demonstrates how this rule can trip people up.

---

[6] *Re Ellenborough Park* [1956] Ch 131 (CA).
[7] *London & Blenheim Estates Ltd v Ladbroke Retail Parks Ltd* [1994] 1 WLR 3.

> **Key case: *London & Blenheim Estates Ltd v Ladbroke Retail Parks Ltd* [1994] 1 WLR 3**
>
> This case is notable for a number of discrete reasons, and will be discussed again in the section concerned with the implied creation of easements by section 62 Law of Property Act 1925. However, it is an important case in demonstrating the need for the dominant and servient tenement to be in separate ownership and remain so.
>
> The case involved a claim that a right of parking had been created in relation to land in Leicester. The purported grant of the easement contained a number of conditions which were required in order for the rights to be created. However, by the time these conditions were met, the land had changed hands and so the agreement between the original parties could not have effects on the third party title-holders.
>
> The question was therefore whether the agreement gave rise to an easement prior to the meeting of the conditions. The court concluded that it could not do so whatever the interpretation of the relevant clause since at that time there was only one tenement and so the dominant and servient land were not in separate ownership.
>
> Thus, if attempting to create a future easement, it is critical that the land be separated and in separate ownership before such easements are drafted. Otherwise, they cannot exist and will not exist when the land is separate unless specific provision is made in the deed which results in the division of the land itself.

12.2.1.3 The easement must 'accommodate' the dominant tenement

This requirement is more colloquially expressed as meaning that the easement must benefit the dominant land. By this is meant that not only is the benefit accorded one which is of benefit regardless of who owns the dominant tenement, but also that the right must be of some value beyond being merely 'more pleasant' for the dominant owner. It is for this reason, for example, that doubts about the ability of a right to wander to exist as an easement emerged. We can therefore divide this requirement into two separate but related parts: first, a right cannot be an easement if it is insufficiently beneficial; and second, the benefit must in some sense be related to an existing, established or clearly potential use of the relevant land, a use which is not dependent upon the grant of the easement itself. This second more complex requirement is considered next.

First, however, we can consider what it means for the easement to be beneficial to land, rather than to persons. This requirement means, in part, that the easement cannot be something which is dependent upon the particular characteristics or identity of the current owner of the dominant tenement. To give an example, the right to allow springer spaniels to run on the neighbouring land is one which is only beneficial to a specific owner with a springer spaniel. It is, in this sense, too personal to constitute a valid easement. The boundary line on this one is of course fine. A vehicular right of way, for example, is quite demonstrably a valid easement but its usefulness does depend on the dominant owner having a vehicle. This is what is meant by the *Re Ellenborough Park*[8] requirements not being statutory rules susceptible to strict interpretation, but rather, very often, are a matter of common sense and 'gut instinct'.

Similarly, this aspect of the criteria is often called upon to explain why a right of way can only exist if the relevant tenements are geographically proximate, although not necessarily adjacent.

---

[8] *Re Ellenborough Park* [1956] Ch 131 (CA).

Whilst it is clearly beneficial to land to have a right of way passing over neighbouring land, it is clearly not for the benefit of the owner of the dominant land if the two parcels of land are 400 miles apart. This rule was discussed in the case of *Bailey v Stephens*.[9]

Finally, the rule that the easement must benefit the land itself, rather than the persons occupying the land, is also said to encapsulate the idea that the easement cannot be 'purely recreational'. The exclusion of 'recreational' easements has always been somewhat dubious. The right in *Re Ellenborough Park*[10] itself can reasonably be considered to be a recreational easement, allowing, as it did, use of a garden for pleasure. Later cases confirm that the position is not as simple as saying that recreational easements cannot exist. In *Mulvaney v Gough*,[11] for example, the court held again that it was possible to have an easement to allow for use and enjoyment of a garden (although not carrying out gardening, see later). Indeed, one can rationalise the use of gardens for example as being, in reality, about enlarging the space that can be used by a property and as such as being of intrinsic value regardless of the actual use to which that space is put (be it picnicking, BBQ, playing ball games etc). What matters, according to this line of reasoning, is the value of space and freedom to choose the activities carried on within that space, rather than the activities themselves. However, the 'prohibition' on recreational easements cannot not be considered to represent the law following the Supreme Court decision in *Regency Villas v Diamond Estates*.[12]

Key case: *Regency Villas v Diamond Estates* **[2018] UKSC 57**

Here, the Supreme Court was required to decide whether the use of a swimming pool, tennis courts, Italianate gardens, and other recreational areas such as squash courts and a gym could constitute a valid easement.

In answering this question, the court began by highlighting that easements are always a product of their historical context. Furthermore, Lord Briggs emphasised that whilst it was true that there was suspicion of recreational easements in the case law, this was because it is was difficult to show that such easements benefitted the dominant tenement. He reasoned that:

> 'it [*Re Ellenborough Park*] is not fatal to the recognition of a right as an easement that it is granted for recreational (including sporting) use, to be enjoyed for its own sake on the servient tenement. The question in every such case is whether the particular recreational or sporting rights granted accommodate the dominant tenement'.[13]

Keeping this in mind, access to and use of leisure and exercise facilities, in modern conditions, is not considered to be 'recreational' in the sense of being purely for fun. Rather, the ability to exercise and enjoy outdoor space is seen as being intimately connected to what it means to live a good and fulfilling life. This had led the Court of Appeal to conclude that it is perfectly possible to have an easement which allows for the use of recreational facilities as long as this does not require the servient owner to spend

---

[9] *Bailey v Stephens* 142 ER 1077, (1862) 12 CB NS 91 (Court of Common Pleas).
[10] *Re Ellenborough Park* [1956] Ch 131 (CA).
[11] *Mulvaney v Gough* [2002] EWCA Civ 1078, [2003] 1 WLR 360.
[12] *Regency Villas Title Ltd v Diamond Resorts (Europe) Ltd* [2018] UKSC 57.
[13] *Regency Villas Title Ltd v Diamond Resorts (Europe) Ltd* [2018] UKSC 57, [48].

money on the maintenance of such facilities (see later), and the Supreme Court agreed with this (Lord Carnwath dissenting). Per Lord Briggs:

> 'Whatever may have been the attitude in the past... recreational and sporting activity of the type exemplified by the facilities at Broome Park is so clearly a beneficial part of modern life that the common law should support structures which promote and encourage it, rather than treat it as devoid of practical utility or benefit'.[14]

This decision is perhaps unsurprising in the sense that the 'purely recreational' rule has always appeared somewhat arbitrary, especially when attempts are made to distinguish between a garden, for example, and a tennis court space. However, the reasoning of the court, focussing as it does on modern conditions is notable. It is reflective of an aspect of the law relating to easements highlighted earlier, ie that easements have always been the category most responsive to changes in technology and needs through history. To take a very simple example, it is possible to have an easement of use of an outdoor toilet[15] and a washing line.[16] These easements today look odd—it would be strange indeed for a total stranger to be able to use their neighbour's toilet as of right—but at the time when such technology was new and the ability to use a flushing toilet novel, it would be a valuable right.

In respect of the 'land related' aspects of this requirement, we can look to the contrast between two cases to explain the nature of this rule—*Hill v Tupper*[17] and *Moody v Steggles*.[18] Again, it is not one which is capable of 'bright line' explanation, but is, instead, one which we can only approach in a pragmatic and common sense way.

> **Key case:** *Hill v Tupper* 159 ER 51
>
> This case concerned the use of pleasure boats on a canal. The claimant alleged that he had the right to sole use of the canal on the basis of an easement. The servient land was the canal itself, and the dominant land was a small area of the bank where the claimant kept the hut from which he sold tickets and arranged the use of the pleasure craft. The question for the court was whether the right to the sole use of the canal constituted a right capable of benefitting the dominant land, ie the hut. The court held it could not do so. The reasoning was that sole use of the canal was purely for the benefit of the business, and not for the dominant land. Pollock CB stated that, 'it is not competent to create rights unconnected with the use and enjoyment of land, and annex them to it so as to constitute a property in the grantee'.[19] In itself, this case is not particularly troubling. It is perfectly reasonable to draw a theoretical line between rights which benefit land, and which benefit a business carried out on that land, even if it can be difficult to articulate the line in practice. However, it interacts in an uncomfortable way with the later decision in *Moody v Steggles*.[20]

---

[14] *Regency Villas Title Ltd v Diamond Resorts (Europe) Ltd* [2018] UKSC 57, [81].
[15] *Miller v Emcer Products Ltd* [1956] Ch 304 (CA).
[16] *Drewell v Towler* 110 ER 268, (1832) 3 B & Ad 735 (King's Bench).
[17] *Hill v Tupper* 159 ER 51, (1863) 2 Hurl & C 121.
[18] *Moody v Steggles* (1879) 12 ChD 261 (ChD).
[19] *Hill v Tupper* 159 ER 51, (1863) 2 Hurl & C 121, 127.
[20] *Moody v Steggles* (1879) 12 ChD 261 (ChD).

> **Key case:** *Moody v Steggles* (1879) 12 ChD 261
>
> In this case, the question for the court was whether the agreement to allow the 'dominant owner' to erect a pub sign on the servient land could be in the nature of an easement. Following *Hill v Tupper*,[21] it appeared this would not be allowed since it is a right which benefits not the land, but a business carried out on the land. However, the court concluded that in this case, because the use of the land as a pub was well-established and had been carried out for many years, that the right could be an easement. As Fry J explains:
>
>> 'the house can only be used by an occupant, and that the occupant only uses the house for the business which he pursues, and therefore in some manner (direct or indirect) an easement is more or less connected with the mode in which the occupant of the house uses it'.[22]
>
> What is the difference between these two cases? It seems as though it depends not on whether the easement benefits the business per se, but rather, whether, if it does, that the business has become part and parcel of the land. In this case, if one were advertising the land with the pub on it as being for sale, for example, one would say that this was 'a pub for sale'. By contrast, if one were selling the part of the riverbank with the office hut on it, one would say, 'piece of riverbank for sale', not 'canal pleasure boat business for sale' because the two things are separable. The pub and the land are one thing: the hut and the canal boat business are not the same thing.
>
> However, it is not always going to be easy to apply in practice. Consider, for example, the decision in *P&S Platt Ltd v Crouch*[23] (a case to which we return in detail later). This case involved the question as to whether it was possible for a hotel to have the benefit of a right to moor boats on a river for use by the hotel guests. Certainly, the business of a hotel is, one would assume, to provide lodging, food and perhaps activities to their guests. The provision of the use of leisure craft is part of the hotel business in this case. It is not however inseparable from it—the hotel could have a policy of occasionally renting out such boats to non-residents for example, charging for use. Doing this would not fundamentally change the day-to-day nature of the business being carried out on the land but it would take some of the cases where the boats were used onto the *Hill v Tupper*[24] side of the line. Neither *Moody v Steggles*[25] nor *Hill v Tupper*[26] were considered in the case, but certainly the outcome in *Platt*,[27] that the use of the moorings could constitute an easement, is one which demonstrates how fine the line is in practice.

12.2.1.4 The right must be capable of being the subject matter of a grant

This obscure sounding requirement is actually critical to the nature of easements. In essence, what this requirement states is that the right must be sufficiently 'easement-like' in order to qualify as an easement. In order to be the 'subject matter of a grant', a right must be proprietary, and to be proprietary, the right must be easement-like. Expressed in this way, this test appears entirely circular. In fact, it is susceptible to breaking down to constituent parts, each of which is perfectly intelligible if not straightforward to apply in practice. First, the easement must be sufficiently

---

[21] *Hill v Tupper* 159 ER 51, (1863) 2 Hurl & C 121.
[22] *Moody v Steggles* (1879) 12 ChD 261 (ChD), 266.
[23] *P&S Platt Ltd v Crouch* [2003] EWCA Civ 1110, [2004] 1 P & CR 18.
[24] *Hill v Tupper* 159 ER 51, (1863) 2 Hurl & C 121.
[25] *Moody v Steggles* (1879) 12 ChD 261 (ChD).
[26] *Hill v Tupper* 159 ER 51, (1863) 2 Hurl & C 121.
[27] *P&S Platt Ltd v Crouch* [2003] EWCA Civ 1110, [2004] 1 P & CR 18.

well-defined that it is capable of clear expression in a written document. Second, the easement must not stray too far from the existing categories of easements. Third, the right must not be so extensive as to be too burdensome to constitute an easement. We will consider these in turn.

Clear, defined, and capable of certain expression

On the first point, the easement must be clear, defined, and capable of certain expression. It is for this reason that easements such as, 'children playing' are excluded. What does that actually mean the children can do on the relevant land? What portion of the land are they able to access? This can be contrasted with the right of children to use a defined playground, for example, which following *Regency Villas*[28] does appear to be capable of being an easement and is, clearly, capable of being sufficiently defined in a document to be the subject matter of a grant.

Similar to existing forms of easement

The second requirement, that the claimed right must not stray too far from the existing categories of easements is more difficult. It is difficult because, as highlighted, since there is no clear 'definition' of easements as such, it is hard to assess when the right has gone 'too far' in this respect. However, case law has developed some 'rules of thumb' which can be applied. First, the courts have held that it will be highly unusual, if not impossible, for a new easement to arise which requires the servient owner to expend money for the benefit of the dominant owner. Whilst it is true that the easement of support and the easement of fencing may require such expenditure, these, according to settled case law, are to be seen as anomalous rights. This rule of thumb was confirmed in *Regency Villas*[29] as the Supreme Court made it clear that responsibility for the costs of maintaining the facilities in that case would rest solely on the shoulders of the dominant owner. Second, the courts are wary of creating new so-called 'negative' easements. These are easements which prevent the servient owner from doing something on their own land, rather than allowing the dominant owner to use the servient land. A good example of a negative easement is the right to light and many negative easements exists. However, in *Phipps v Pears*[30] the court held that it would not be possible to extend the right of support (which is also a negative easement) to create a new easement which would be a right to protection from the weather. Similarly, it has been held that it is not possible to have an easement to protect a view, for the same reason.

This, 'sufficiently easement-like' requirement is, therefore, like much else in the law relating to easements as much a matter of instinct as it is capable of precise articulation. This can make it a difficult rule to apply with certainty to problem questions. However, it can also be a very useful rule since it can provide a 'short cut' to deciding whether a right before you is in fact capable of being an easement. We can demonstrate this with an example.

Imagine Filip agrees with Aditya that Aditya—the owner of a parcel of land including a large salmon farm—can use his land for the purposes of smoking fish on a line over a fire. They formalise this agreement in a deed, believing that it can constitute an easement. Subsequently, Filip transfers title to has land to Mayra. Mayra does not like the smell of smoked fish and therefore wishes to bring Aditya's use to an end. Can she do so?

---

[28] *Regency Villas Title Ltd v Diamond Resorts (Europe) Ltd* [2018] UKSC 57.
[29] *Regency Villas Title Ltd v Diamond Resorts (Europe) Ltd* [2018] UKSC 57.
[30] *Phipps v Pears* [1965] 1 QB 76 (CA).

In this case, it is unclear whether the ability to smoke fish is capable of constituting an easement. It seems to be highly personal, and does not seem, at first glance, to benefit Aditya's land. This in itself would potentially be a good reason to discount the possibility of this being an easement. Indeed, that is probably the correct answer. However, in an exam setting, it can be a useful 'cross-check' to compare the features of this claimed right with those rights which you know either can or cannot be an easement. For example, it is clearly possible to have a right to use a washing line. In a sense, hanging fish on a line to dry them by smoking is not miles away from hanging clothes on a land to dry them. If it is possible to have an easement for the latter, why not the former? Similarly, it is possible to draw a parallel here with *Moody v Steggles*.[31] Aditya's land comprises a lake in which the salmon farm is situated. Like a pub, the business and the land are one and the same thing. Without the smokery, Aditya still has a salmon farm (and thus the *Hill v Tupper*[32] exclusion does not seem to apply). The right to use the line for smoking is clearly related to a well-established business on the site. However, we could say it is rather an idiosyncratic right and does seem to depend on the salmon farmer wanting not only to conduct a salmon farm, but also to smoke his fish, thus indicating that the right may be too personal. By reasoning by analogy here, however, rather than starting from the 'first principles' of *Re Ellenborough Park*,[33] the discussion about whether or not this right is capable of being an easement is more nuanced and shows more knowledge.

It may be useful here to give a list of the sorts of rights which, according to existing case law, can or cannot be easements (Tables 12.1 and 12.2). This list is not exhaustive, but will provide a starting point for 'reasoning by analogy' with existing cases. For a fuller list, see Megarry and Wade[34] or Gale on Easements.[35]

Table 12.1 Rights which can be easements

Rights which can be easements	Case law examples
Rights of way (general)	*Nickerson v Barraclough*,[36] *Manjang v Drammeh*[37]
Rights of way (foot only)	*MRA Engineering v Trimster*,[38] *Cousens v Rose*[39]
Rights to light	*Colls v Home and Colonial Stores Ltd*[40] (the law relating to rights to light is highly complex and not the subject of detailed treatment in this book—for more extensive comment see Karas, *The Law of Rights to Light*[41]).

(Continued)

---

[31] *Moody v Steggles* (1879) 12 ChD 261 (ChD).
[32] *Hill v Tupper* 159 ER 51, (1863) 2 Hurl & C 121.
[33] *Re Ellenborough Park* [1956] Ch 131 (CA).
[34] Harpum et al, *Megarry & Wade: The Law of Real Property* (8th ed) (Sweet & Maxwell, London, 2012).
[35] Gaunt and Morgan, *Gale on Easements* (20th ed) (Sweet & Maxwell, London, 2016).
[36] *Nickerson v Barraclough* [1981] Ch 426 (CA).
[37] *Manjang v Drammeh* (1991) 61 P & CR 194 (PC).
[38] *MRA Engineering v Trimster* (1988) 56 P & CR 1 (CA).
[39] *Cousens v Rose* (1871) LR 12 Eq 366 (Chancery).
[40] *Colls v Home and Colonial Stores Ltd* [1904] AC 179 (HL).
[41] Karas, *The Law of the Rights to Light* (Wildy, Simmonds and Hill, London, 2016).

386   Chapter 12 Easements and Profits

Right to water through a pipe	*Goodhart v Hyett*[42]
Right to discharge water onto the land of another	*Mason v Shrewsbury & Hereford Railway Company*[43]
Right of support	*Dalton v Angus & Co*,[44] *Lemaitre v Davis*[45]
Rights of fencing	*Crow v Wood*[46]
Right to hang washing on a neighbour's line	*Drewell v Towler*[47]
Right to hang a sign	*Moody v Steggles*[48]
Right to store coal in a coal shed	*Wright v Macadam*[49]
Right to park	*London & Blenheim Estates Ltd v Ladbroke Retail Parks Ltd*,[50] *Moncrieff v Jamieson*,[51] *Batchelor v Marlow*,[52] *Virdi v Chana*[53]
Right to use a kitchen	*Heywood v Mallalieu*[54]
Right to use a toilet	*Miller v Emcer Products Ltd*[55]
Right to use ventilation	*Hervey v Smith*,[56] *Wong v Beaumont Property Trust*[57]
Right to enter neighbour's land to complete repairs	*Ward v Kirkland*[58]
Right to use a garden	*Re Ellenborough Park*,[59] *Mulvaney v Gough*[60]
Right to use a swimming pool, tennis court etc	*Regency Villas v Diamond Resorts*[61]

---

[42] *Goodhart v Hyett* (1883) 25 ChD 182 (ChD).
[43] *Mason v Shrewsbury & Hereford Railway Company* (1870–71) LR 6 QB 578.
[44] *Dalton v Henry Angus & Co* (1881) 6 App Cas 740.
[45] *Lemaitre v Davis* (1881) 19 Ch D 281.
[46] *Crow v Wood* [1971] 1 QB 77 (CA).
[47] *Drewell v Towler* 110 ER 268, (1832) 3 B & Ad 735 (King's Bench).
[48] *Moody v Steggles* (1879) 12 ChD 261 (ChD).
[49] *Wright v Macadam* [1949] 2 KB 744 (CA).
[50] *London & Blenheim Estates Ltd v Ladbroke Retail Parks Ltd* [1994] 1 WLR 3.
[51] *Moncrieff v Jamieson* [2007] UKHL 42, [2007] 1 WLR 2620 (HL).
[52] *Batchelor v Marlow* [2001] EWCA Civ 1051, [2003] 1 WLR 764.
[53] *Virdi v Chana* [2008] EWHC 2901 (Ch), [2008] NPC 130.
[54] *Heywood v Mallalieu* (1883) 25 ChD 357 (ChD).
[55] *Miller v Emcer Products Ltd* [1956] Ch 304 (CA).
[56] *Hervey v Smith* 69 ER 510, (1855) 1 Kay & J 389 (ChD).
[57] *Wong v Beaumont Property Trust* [1965] 1 QB 173 (CA).
[58] *Ward v Kirkland* [1967] Ch 194 (ChD).
[59] *Re Ellenborough Park* [1956] Ch 131 (CA).
[60] *Mulvaney v Gough* [2002] EWCA Civ 1078, [2003] 1 WLR 360.
[61] *Regency Villas Title Ltd v Diamond Resorts (Europe) Ltd* [2018] UKSC 57.

Table 12.2 Rights which cannot be easements

You cannot have an easement to receive radio or telephone signals across a neighbour's land. We can assume that the same applies to wireless internet connectivity.	*Hunter v Canary Wharf* [62]
Whilst it is possible to have an easement to use a garden space, it is not possible to have an easement of gardening. This is because such an easement would give the dominant owner control over (at least) the aesthetics of the garden, and would therefore go beyond the accepted categories of easement.	*Mulvaney v Gough* [63]
A mere *jus spatiandi*—a right to wander—cannot be an easement	*International Tea Stores v Hobbs* [64]
You cannot have an easement to protection from the weather	*Phipps v Pears* [65]

> **Further analysis: Easements to create a nuisance—*Coventry v Lawrence* [2014] UKSC 13**
>
> Chapter 18 of this book considers the relationship between tort law and land law, and looks at some of the torts which exist to both constrain and protect uses of land. One such of these is the tort of nuisance. In very rough terms, nuisance allows a claimant to obtain an injunction or an award of damages to prevent unreasonable use of neighbouring land which is interfering with his own reasonable enjoyment of his land. In this sense, nuisance polices the boundary between neighbouring landowners to ensure that each other's use respects the property rights of the other, always taking account of the need for give and take.
>
> One interesting development in this respect is the decision in *Coventry v Lawrence*.[66] Here, the Supreme Court postulated that it might be possible to have an easement to make a noise, thus, in effect, providing a defence to what otherwise might be a nuisance. Whilst there has long been the theoretical possibility of an easement to pollute, for example, this is really saying that there is a possible easement to discharge water or other substances onto a neighbour's land, and that is clearly within the well accepted nature of easements. This easement of noise development is interesting because, as with the outcome in *Regency Villas*,[67] it shows the ways in which our law adapts to new understandings in society. The most easily recognisable easement is, of course, the right of way, and that involves the passage of persons over land. Other prominent easements, such as rights of drainage, and the passing of pipes and wires, also involve 'travel' across such land. In *Coventry v Lawrence*,[68] the Supreme Court highlights that noise too involves such travel depending as it does on the passage of sound waves. If noise nuisances are understood in this way, then it is entirely natural that there could also exist an easement to make noise. On the other hand, noise, unlike water or electricity through wires, or light through a window, or a person on a roadway, does not travel along a defined path.

---

[62] *Hunter v Canary Wharf* [1997] AC 655 (HL).
[63] *Mulvaney v Gough* [2002] EWCA Civ 1078, [2003] 1 WLR 360.
[64] *International Tea Stores v Hobbs* [1903] 2 Ch 165.
[65] *Phipps v Pears* [1965] 1 QB 76 (CA).
[66] *Coventry (t/a RDC Promotions) v Lawrence* [2014] UKSC 13, [2014] AC 822.
[67] *Regency Villas Title Ltd v Diamond Resorts (Europe) Ltd* [2018] UKSC 57.
[68] *Coventry (t/a RDC Promotions) v Lawrence* [2014] UKSC 13, [2014] AC 822.

> The comments of Lord Neuberger in *Coventry*[69] are *obiter*, and cannot therefore be said to represent the law. Even the possibility of an easement being a defence to a nuisance (as opposed to a trespass) is interesting, and shows the symbiotic relationship between land law and tort law, with each supporting and shaping the other.

Easement must not be 'too extensive'

Finally, and most importantly in practice, the easement must not be too extensive a right in order to be considered an easement. This requirement is critical in distinguishing between estates in land and easements, and as such is concerned with the degree of physical control over a property which the claimed right confers onto a purported dominant owner. Too much, and the handing over of possession which results means that the right would be better conceived as a lease or a transfer of the freehold title. The goal of this requirement is therefore relatively simple. However, the courts have had some difficulty in explaining where the line lies, and have expressed the test in a variety of ways. This issue has come up most regularly in respect of potential easements of storage in general, and of easements of car parking in particular. Of course, such rights are enormously valuable in the modern age, and also very common. The precise test which the courts settle on will therefore have significant implications in practice.

The starting point is the decision in *Copeland v Greenhalf*.[70] In this case, the court held that a purported easement for a wheelwright to park wagons on a strip in an orchard failed as it conferred onto the dominant owner too great a power over the servient land. The court expressed it thus:

> 'I think that the right claimed goes wholly outside any normal idea of an easement... This claim... really amounts to a claim to a joint user of the land by the defendant. Practically, the defendant is claiming the <u>whole beneficial user</u> of the strip of land on the south-east side of the track there; he can leave as many or as few lorries there as he likes for as long as he likes; he may enter on it by himself, his servants and agents to do repair work thereon. In my judgment, that is not a claim which can be established as an easement. <u>It is virtually a claim to possession of the servient tenement, if necessary to the exclusion of the owner; or, at any rate, to a joint user</u>, and no authority has been cited to me which would justify the conclusion that a right of this wide and undefined nature can be the proper subject-matter of an easement'.[71] (Emphasis added.)

The intention of this passage is clear. Upjohn J is highlighting that a right which is too extensive, and confers possession onto the dominant owner cannot be in the nature of an easement. On close inspection of this passage though there are three different ways of expressing the test. First, that the dominant owner is claiming 'the whole beneficial user'; second, that it is 'virtually a claim to possession'; and third, 'a joint user'. Two of these expressions are referring to use: one to possession. The tenor of this passage however seems to be that the extensive nature of the 'use' is

---

[69] *Coventry (t/a RDC Promotions) v Lawrence* [2014] UKSC 13, [2014] AC 822.
[70] *Copeland v Greenhalf* [1952] Ch 488 (ChD).
[71] *Copeland v Greenhalf* [1952] Ch 488 (ChD), 498.

the real problem. Subsequent courts, therefore, adopted a use-based test (eg *London & Blenheim Estates v Ladbroke*).[72] The leading case on this test now is *Batchelor v Marlow*,[73] albeit that the comments of the Supreme Court in *Regency Villas*[74] have added to the complexity in this area.

> **Key case: *Batchelor v Marlow* [2001] EWCA Civ 1051**
>
> This case involved a potential easement of parking. The agreement allowed the potential dominant owner to park their car from 9.30am – 6pm on weekdays. The court held that this was too intrusive a right to constitute an easement. Tucker LJ expressed his views as follows:
>
>> 'If one asks the simple question: "Would the plaintiff have any reasonable use of the land for parking?" the answer, I think, must be "No". He has no use at all during the whole of the time that parking space is likely to be needed. But if one asks the question whether the plaintiff has any reasonable use of the land for any other purpose, the answer is even clearer. His right to use his land is curtailed altogether for intermittent periods throughout the week. Such a restriction would, I think, make his ownership of the land illusory'.[75]
>
> Hill-Smith, commenting on this case, suggests that *Batchelor* should not be followed.
>
>> 'It is submitted that contrary to the *Batchelor* case, the courts should not be reluctant to find an easement of parking and that the drawing of fine distinctions in this area is inimical to the sensible development of the law. Indeed it would be better if the courts found that the ouster principle did not apply at all in the context of an easement of parking. In any event, the court should not be too ready to find on the facts that the owner's use of the land has been rendered illusory'.[76]

This Court of Appeal decision was, for a long time, the leading English authority on the point. In the mid-2000s, however, the House of Lords sitting as the final court of appeal for Scotland was given the opportunity to consider the test in relation to servitudes in Scotland. As the court itself highlights, the law in England and Scotland is, in this respect, identical. The reasoning in *Moncrieff v Jamieson*[77] is therefore very significant for English law, even if it is not strictly binding.

> **Key case: *Moncrieff v Jamieson* [2007] UKHL 42**
>
> In *Moncrieff v Jamieson*, the court was required to answer the question as to whether there could be an easement of parking when the parking of the car would take up the entirety of the relevant space. The space in question was necessary for the driver of the car, the purported dominant owner, because their own house was perched on the edge of a cliff. There was nowhere else to put the car. According to the

---

[72] *London & Blenheim Estates Ltd v Ladbroke Retail Parks Ltd* [1994] 1 WLR 3.
[73] *Batchelor v Marlow* [2001] EWCA Civ 1051, [2003] 1 WLR 764.
[74] *Regency Villas Title Ltd v Diamond Resorts (Europe) Ltd* [2018] UKSC 57, [61].
[75] *Batchelor v Marlow* [2001] EWCA Civ 1051, [2003] 1 WLR 764, [18].
[76] Hill-Smith, 'Rights of parking and the ouster principle after *Batchelor v Marlow*' [2007] Conv 223, 234.
[77] *Moncrieff v Jamieson* [2007] UKHL 42, [2007] 1 WLR 2620 (HL).

reasoning in *Copeland v Greenhalf*,[78] this right would be too extensive to constitute an easement. The use would deprive the servient own of all 'beneficial user' of his land, since whenever the car was parked in the space it would be impossible to use that space for anything else. In this sense, it amounted to 'joint user'. However, as the House of Lords articulated, the 'use' test was never really getting to the heart of what was at stake here. The question was not one of use, but rather of possession and control of the relevant land. In the following quotation, the court is highlighting that the 'ouster' principle only makes sense if it is understood as meaning removal of possession and control from the servient owner.

> 'I must later examine the so-called "ouster" principle, the principle which, it is said, prevents the creation of a servitude if the servitude contended for would prevent any reasonable use being made of the servient land, and some of the authorities relating to that principle. To the extent, however, that the "ouster" principle is asserting that a servitude must not be inconsistent with the continued beneficial ownership of the servient land by the servient owner, I would unreservedly accept it. If, for example, the nature of the purported servitude were to place the dominant owner in such occupation of the servient land as to bar the servient owner from possession or control of the land I would find it very difficult to accept that the right could constitute a servitude'.[79]

The difference in terms of consequence between the two expressions is captured neatly in Lord Scott's analysis of the decision in *Wright v Macadam*,[80] where it was concluded that it is possible to have an easement of storage not withstanding the obvious difficulty that an item stored takes up the entirety of the space in which it is stored.

> 'it is difficult to see any difference in principle between a case in which the dominant owner has sole use of a patch of ground for storage purposes, e g a coal shed, and a case in which the dominant owner is the only user of a strip of road for access purposes or of a viaduct for the passage of water. Sole user, as a concept, is quite different from, and fundamentally inferior to, exclusive possession. Sole use of a coal shed for the storage of coal does not prevent the servient owner from using the shed for any purposes of his own that do not interfere with the dominant owner's reasonable use for the storage of coal'.[81]

Lord Scott therefore concluded that sole use would not be inconsistent with the servient owner still being in possession of land, and would not, as a result, prevent the right allowing such use from being an easement.[82] As a result of taking this line of reasoning, Lord Scott eventually advocated an abandonment of the 'reasonable user' test as articulated in *Batchelor v Marlow*.[83] He did so not because the test of reasonable user because it is uncertain—which it undoubtedly is—but rather because he did not see that there was any good reason to prevent a landowner from granting an extensive right, as long as it did not amount to the grant of an alternative proprietary interest by conferring possession onto the dominant owner.[84]

The merits of this approach are explained in the further analysis box.

---

[78] *Copeland v Greenhalf* [1952] Ch 488 (ChD).
[79] *Moncrieff v Jamieson* [2007] UKHL 42, [2007] 1 WLR 2620 (HL), [47].
[80] *Wright v Macadam* [1949] 2 KB 744 (CA).
[81] *Moncrieff v Jamieson* [2007] UKHL 42, [2007] 1 WLR 2620 (HL), [55].
[82] *Moncrieff v Jamieson* [2007] UKHL 42, [2007] 1 WLR 2620 (HL).
[83] *Batchelor v Marlow* [2001] EWCA Civ 1051, [2003] 1 WLR 764.
[84] *Moncrieff v Jamieson* [2007] UKHL 42, [2007] 1 WLR 2620 (HL).

However preferable the test in *Moncrieff*[85] may be, being a decision of the House of Lords in a Scottish case, it would not be open to an English court to simply ignore the Court of Appeal authority of *Batchelor*.[86] This was the dilemma which faced the court in *Virdi v Chana*.[87]

> **Key case:** *Virdi v Chana* [2008] EWHC 2901
>
> In this case, the space over which the easement was claimed was in fact smaller than the width of the car being parked on it. If *Copeland v Greenhalf*[88] and *Batchelor v Marlow*[89] were followed, at least in terms of the outcome in those two cases, then there could not possibly be an easement. However, inspired by *Moncrieff*,[90] the court, whilst recognising that it was bound by the 'reasonable user' test took a much broader interpretation as to what constituted reasonable use than had appeared in previous decisions. Thus, Judge Purle QC explains that, in exploring what 'reasonable use' the servient owner would retain in this case. It is worth reading this list carefully, for the 'narrowness' of some of these uses shows how far the jurisprudence on this question has shifted since *Copeland*.
>
>> 'there is a tree on the servient land, in the corner of the gravelled area, which appears from the photographs to have been planted relatively recently. The planting of that tree (or any replacement), and going on to the servient land to tend to it during its life, is not an illusory right. The same could be said of other shrubs or trees that might be planted on other parts of the servient land, so long as this did not (which it need not) obstruct the right to park. Some limitation on the servient owner's user is a common feature of easements generally, and applies (for example) to all rights of way.
>>
>> The Appellant could also come on to the servient land for the purpose of maintaining or repairing the fence which abuts it, or replacing the fence with a wall. She could also go onto the gravelled area (so far as within her ownership) to erect signs, or place decorative flower pots on the land, subject again to not obstructing the ability to park on the gravelled area, which none of this need do.'[91]
>
> The same would certainly be true of the land in *Copeland v Greenhalf*[92] of course. The significance of the *Virdi*[93] decision therefore is that it shows the extent to which the courts can in effect apply a possession-based test whilst paying lip-service to the 'reasonable user' test.
>
> Arguably, however, again following *Regency Villas*,[94] there is no longer even a need to pay lip-service to the reasonable user test. The Supreme Court in that case, although not explicitly overruling *Batchelor v Marlow*,[95] and thus creating an arguably inconsistent line of precedent, applies a possession and control/management and control test.

---

[85] *Moncrieff v Jamieson* [2007] UKHL 42, [2007] 1 WLR 2620 (HL).
[86] *Batchelor v Marlow* [2001] EWCA Civ 1051, [2003] 1 WLR 764.
[87] *Virdi v Chana* [2008] EWHC 2901 (Ch), [2008] NPC 130.
[88] *Copeland v Greenhalf* [1952] Ch 488 (ChD).
[99] *Batchelor v Marlow* [2001] EWCA Civ 1051, [2003] 1 WLR 764.
[90] *Moncrieff v Jamieson* [2007] UKHL 42, [2007] 1 WLR 2620 (HL).
[91] *Virdi v Chana* [2008] EWHC 2901 (Ch), [2008] NPC 130, [20]–[21].
[92] *Copeland v Greenhalf* [1952] Ch 488 (ChD).
[93] *Virdi v Chana* [2008] EWHC 2901 (Ch), [2008] NPC 130.
[94] *Regency Villas Title Ltd v Diamond Resorts (Europe) Ltd* [2018] UKSC 57, [61].
[95] *Batchelor v Marlow* [2001] EWCA Civ 1051, [2003] 1 WLR 764.

The overall result of this jurisprudence can therefore be said to be that in all likelihood, an English court will now apply *either* an explicit 'possession and control' test or will in effect use such a test taking the broad approach in *Virdi v Chana*.[96]

> **Further analysis: 'Reasonable user' or 'possession and control'**
>
> Whatever the case law position between these two tests, it is important to consider the impacts of the adoption of such tests. The primary reason for adopting a possession and control test is essentially that this is the only test which precisely calibrates the distinction between the grant of an estate in land, ie a freehold or a leasehold estate, and the grant of an easement. To understand why this matters, it is necessary to return to the idea of the *numerus clausus*. To recap, the *numerus clausus* is the 'closed list' of property rights which exists in English law. For legal rights the list is a statutory one, contained in section 1 Law of Property Act 1925. For rights which exist in equity, there is no closed list per se, but the effect of the decision in *National Provincial Bank v Ainsworth*[97] is to limit the creation of new property rights. In the context of easements, the requirement that the right 'be capable of being the subject matter of a grant', reinforces the numerus clausus.
>
> The consequence of having a closed list of property rights, however, is that there is always a danger that a valuable or practically significant right will 'fall through the gap'. In sense, it is useful to recall the metaphor of the *numerus clausus* as creating a series of 'lily pads' in a pond. The lily pads represent property rights, the water surrounding them the array of personal rights which can exist in land and which are collectively referred to as licences. If a right therefore falls without the definition of a specific property right, it will 'fall into the water' and be a licence, and will not, without more, be enforceable against third parties as explained in chapter 2. In the context of storage and car parking easements, the test in *Batchelor v Marlow*[98] was resulting in lots of valuable parking rights falling between the different rights, thus being 'only' a licence and therefore not binding on third parties. The 'possession and control' test closes this gap.
>
> The Supreme Court in *Regency Villas* has added to this debate. Lord Briggs in that case explains that:
>
>> 'Leaving aside cases where the grant confers exclusive possession, which cannot by definition be an easement, the ouster principle rejects as an easement the grant of rights which, on one view, deprive the servient owner of reasonable beneficial use of the servient tenement or, on the other view, deprive the servient owner of lawful possession and control of it.'[99]
>
> The argument that the easements in that case deprived the servient owner of control was rejected in the case on the facts, but the court seems to express itself using 'management and control' as a third alternative to possession and control or reasonable use.

12.2.2 WHAT RIGHTS CAN BE PROFITS?

The category of rights referred to as profits à prendre, is much less dynamic than is that relating to easements. Profits, whilst potentially very valuable, are not of enormous amount of *legal* interest and as such, most land law courses deal with them only briefly. It is nevertheless very useful

---

[96] *Virdi v Chana* [2008] EWHC 2901 (Ch), [2008] NPC 130.
[97] *National Provincial Bank v Ainsworth* [1965] AC 1175.
[98] *Batchelor v Marlow* [2001] EWCA Civ 1051, [2003] 1 WLR 764.
[99] *Regency Villas Title Ltd v Diamond Resorts (Europe) Ltd* [2018] UKSC 57, [61].

to know what rights can constitute profits, not least because it may help distinguish them from easements, as with the easement to garden mentioned earlier. As the name indicates, the most usual types of profits involve the right to take (prendre) something from another's land. Hunting, fishing, and grazing rights (the animals take the grass) can all be seen in this light. Profits can either be granted in such a way as to preclude the servient owner from also fishing in the river, for example, or can be 'in common' so that both the dominant and servient owners are able to fish. It is also important to note that profits, unlike easements, can exist 'in gross'. That is, for a valid profit there is no need for a dominant owner to hold title to nearby land. In this sense, there is an important conceptual difference between the easement and the profit. Easements are granted, in theory, for the benefit of the *land* over which the dominant owner has title: profits, by contrast, are for the benefit of a *person*, and can be transferred without the need for title to the dominant land to be transferred.

Whilst there is little controversy in relation to most profits, some difficulty has been encountered concerning profits relating to the use of water. It is possible to have a profit to take water from another's land, usually from a watercourse of some description. The reason why water in particular can cause difficulties is that the boundary line between easements and profits is very narrow here, as shown by the case *Mitchell v Potter*.[100]

> **Key case:** *Mitchell v Potter* [2005] EWCA Civ 88
>
> In this case, the claimant was a farmer who had a right to draw water from a small spring on his neighbour's land. The water was drawn from the spring to the farmer's land through a pipe, travelling by gravity. The neighbour then decided to allow another neighbour also to use the water from the spring. The question arose as to whether this right was the right to the passage of water through the pipe, ie an easement, so that it would only be relevant if there was water to pass along the pipe; or whether it was a right to the water itself, ie a profit. The Court of Appeal concluded that this was a profit, and therefore a right to water, not a right to the passage of water through the chanel, but this was simply a matter of interpretation of the words of the deed of grant, and it is clear that in vaguely worded agreements some confusion might arise.

> **Further analysis: Do easements and profits have to be exercised reasonably?**
>
> Although this question applies equally to profits and easements, the relevant case law has arisen primarily with regard to profits. The reason for this is the rule in *Harris v Flower*[101] discussed later in relation to easements which limits the ability of a dominant owner to increase their use of an easement beyond that envisaged at the time of its grant. Usually this means that the question simply does not arise for easements. In relation to profits, however, the question as to 'how many fish can I take'?; or 'how many animals may I graze on the field?' obviously arises as soon as the profit is granted.

---

[100] *Mitchell v Potter* [2005] EWCA Civ 88.
[101] *Harris v Flower* (1904) 91 LT 816.

> The matter is the subject of somewhat inconsistent case law. In *Gardner v Davis*[102] for example, it was held that there was an obligation to use a profit of sewerage (the right to use another's septic tank in this case) reasonably. The question arose because the defendants' use of the tank had led to a number of 'overflows' in the servient owner's garden. The court concluded that the scope of the profit did not extend so far, and that the action of the dominant owner could therefore be considered a nuisance. By contrast in, *Pole v Peake*,[103] the Court of Appeal held that in relation to a profit to 'rear game', as long as *reasonable care* was exercised, that is the dominant owner was not negligent, then they could rear as many game birds as they so desired and could not be held liable for any damage caused by the fact of so-doing. This suggests that there was no limitation on the *scale* of the operation based upon the profit, only on the manner of carrying out that operation. Even then the manner was only constrained by the usual standards of negligence. To put this another way, whilst the profit in this case could not be a defence to liability for damage caused by negligence, it could be a defence to any amount of damage caused as long as reasonable care was taken.

12.3 THE CREATION OF EASEMENTS

The creation of easements is a seemingly complex topic, and a favourite of examiners, especially for problem questions. On closer inspection though, it is not particularly difficult. The rules, whilst at times odd and apparently somewhat arbitrary, are relatively straightforward to understand. In essence, the key to success in relation to this topic is just to *learn* the rules and practice applying them to get used to the process by which you ascertain whether an easement has been validly created.

12.3.1 EXPRESS EASEMENTS

Of course, many easements will be expressly created. These will be expressed in a deed and deliberately put into place either between existing landowners, or on the division of land where one parcel of a single piece of land is divided off and sold. In both of these cases, the respective parties have recognised that it is to their mutual benefit to ensure that questions regarding access, drainage, sewerage, electricity provision etc are resolved clearly within the document. The relatively small amount of inconvenience that the existence of such rights usually poses encourages parties to negotiate reasonably on these points.

The formalities required for express easements depends, first, on whether the grant is to take place in law, or in equity only. In order to create an express legal easement, first, a written and signed contract may be required (although, as explained in chapter 4, this contract may be contained in the same document as a deed) if the parties are intending the grant to be one made for valuable consideration, ie payment. If the grant of the easement is gratuitous, then obviously a contract is not possible (since there is no consideration), and the terms of the grant of the

---

[102] *Gardner v Davis* [1999] EHLR 13 (CA).
[103] *Pole v Peake* [1998] EG 125 (CS) (CA).

easement will simply be contained in the relevant deed. To confirm, if a contract is being used, to be a valid contract relating to the disposition of an interest in land, the contract must comply with section 2 Law of Property (Miscellaneous Provisions) Act 1989. For more on the operation and requirements of this section, see chapter 4.

The second stage in contractual transactions, and the first in gratuitous grants, is the creation of the deed. As a result of section 1 and 52 Law of Property Act 1925, a deed is required to create a legal interest. The deed must appear on its face to be a deed, be signed by the parties, witnessed, and delivered as a deed (see chapter 4). Following the Land Registration Act 2002 (LRA 2002) however, it is not enough simply to create the relevant deed in order to ensure that the easement operates at law. Rather, the easement must also be registered in order to take effect as a result of section 27 LRA 2002. The easement is entered as a notice on the title of both the benefitted and burdened land, and this will ensure first that it is a legal easement, and second, will protect the priority of the easement should a priority dispute arise.

If the easement is to take effect in equity only, then a section 2-compliant contract will suffice if the transfer was for valuable consideration. If the easement is gratuitous, then a deed will be required. It is also possible for an easement to arise in equity by virtue of proprietary estoppel. It is perhaps unwise to refer to these as 'equitable easements' however, since it will depend upon the terms of the court order 'satisfying the equity' as to whether the easement will, in the fullness of time, take effect in equity or at law. It is conceptually more sound to keep the two-stage process of estoppel in mind in line with the discussion in chapter 8 at 8.3. First, the equity by estoppel arises. This inchoate right, is, as confirmed by section 116 LRA 2002, a property right it itself and it is certainly equitable in nature. Second, following crystallisation of the equity by a court, a new property right *may* arise. This could be in the nature of an easement, as in *Crabb v Arun DC*,[104] and its 'final form' (ie legal or equitable) will depend on the terms of the court order. For example, the court may order that the easement be registered and therefore it may be a legal easement.

12.3.2 IMPLIED EASEMENTS

Implied easements are easements which have arisen completely outwith the express or implied *discussions* of the party. The implication is, in this sense, an implication of law, not an implication of what the parties actually decided as is the case in relation to the creation of implied trusts or estoppel for example. That is not to say that the implication here is unrelated to intention. Express contrary intention will prevent the operation of the rules relating to implied easements as we shall see. Rather the implication as to intention here does not depend on any evidence that the parties actually had the relevant intention. Instead, the existence of the intention is *presumed* unless contrary intention appears expressed in words within a binding document. To put this another way, the rules here operate automatically unless the rules are expressly excluded in the relevant deed of transfer or the relevant contract.

Before we examine the methods by which easements are impliedly created, it is critical to understand the precise factual context within which this question arises. Easements cannot be

---

[104] *Crabb v Arun DC* [1976] Ch 179 (CA).

implied between neighbouring landowners simply because it looks sensible for such an easement to exist. Rather, easements are implied *into* a deed or a contract. Which of these exists determines the character of any easement which emerges, ie legal or equitable. This deed or contract must be between a putative servient owner and a putative dominant owner but can only happen when land is being divided because the deed or contract must be one which transfers either a legal or an equitable estate in land. It is absolutely critical that this understood, or the rules relating to implied easements will forever pose significant problems.

> **Summary: Implied easements**
>
> Implied easements are created by the implication of *words* into a document—be that a contract or a deed—the effect of which is to divide land. The methods of implication are routes by which the words which would give express effect to an easement are assumed to exist in this document. The easement will therefore take on the character of the document into which it is implied. Easements implied into a contract will be equitable in nature: easements implied into a deed will be legal.

There are four 'methods' of implication.

1. Easements of necessity
2. Easements of common intention
3. Section 62 Law of Property Act 1925
4. The rule in *Wheeldon v Burrows*.[105]

The methods are explained in detail later. Whether or not it is possible to rely on any of these four methods, depends, first, on whether you are dealing with an implied *grant* or an implied *reservation*. Implied grants occur where the seller of the land becomes the *servient* owner. That is to say, when they divide their land and give or sell title to part of their land to another, they *also* give or sell—or *grant*—them the benefit of an implied easement. Implied reservations occur where the seller of the land becomes the *dominant* owner. That is, when they divide their land and give or sell title to part of their land to another, they *keep*—or *reserve to themselves*—a right over the land which they have given away or sold. Figure 12.1 demonstrates this distinction. The black line represents a right of way, and the arrow head shows the direction of travel.

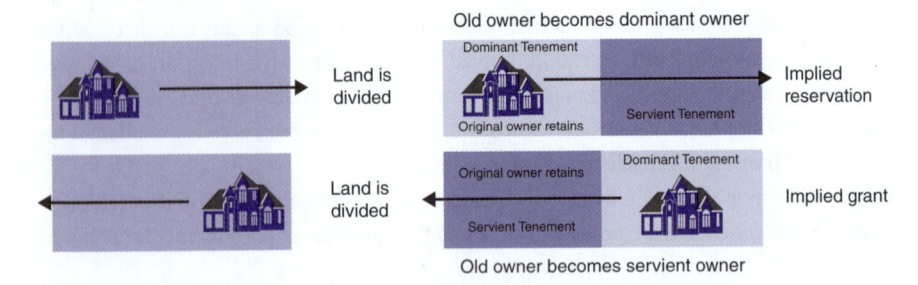

Figure 12.1 Grants and reservations

---

[105] *Wheeldon v Burrows* (1879) 12 ChD 31.

Just as it is absolutely essential to get to grips with the idea that implied easements are implied *into* a document, so too is it critical to understand the difference between implied grants and reservations, and to be able to determine in a problem question which you are dealing with. This is because whilst it is possible to use all four methods of implication in relation to implied *grants*, it is only possible to use the first two for implied *reservations*.

> **Summary: Methods of implication in grants and reservations**
>
> **Grants:**
> 1. Easements of necessity
> 2. Easements of common intention
> 3. Section 62 Law of Property Act 1925
> 4. The rule in *Wheeldon v Burrows*
>
> **Reservations:**
> 1. Easements of necessity
> 2. Easements of common intention

> **Further analysis: Reservations versus grants**
>
> It may be helpful, in learning this distinction, to consider the logic as to *why* the law is so much more disposed to favour the creation of implied grants than reservations. As will be seen, it is not only that fewer methods are available in relation to implied reservations, but also that the methods which are available for reservations are very narrow and hard to establish. By contrast, section 62 Law of Property Act 1925 in particular is very broad in its scope.
>
> The 'legal' justification given for the difference is that there is a general principle of law that you should not 'derogate from a grant' without expressly saying so. This principle essentially means that if you give something away or sell something, you give 'all' of it without keeping part for yourself unless you expressly say you are keeping that part. Referring to this legal maxim does not take us very far however: *why* does this principle exist?
>
> In relation to land, at least, there are two relatively convincing explanations. First, there will always be an imbalance of knowledge between a seller and a buyer in land transactions. The seller is much better placed to know what rights they will need once the land is divided because they are more familiar with the topography of the site, its geographical connections with access routes, the whereabouts of pipes etc which run underground; and whether there is any need for special provision to be made to ensure that the amenity value of the land they retain will be diminished. By contrast, a prospective buyer, particularly one without legal assistance, will probably have visited a site at most three times, be at the mercy of the seller in terms of available documentation, and is unlikely to be equally knowledgeable of the difference in terms of amenity to which failing to specify rights may give rise.
>
> Second, and perhaps more importantly given the theoretical basis of these rules in intention (to a limited extent), the buyer, when visiting a site, is 'presented' with a package. So, for example, when touring a house, the package presented is one which includes drainage and sewage pipes; running water; and, perhaps, access to a convenient road. When the buyer makes an offer on that property, he is, he believes, buying that package as seen. Most likely he does not think that there is a risk that once the property is divided he may buy a property which is landlocked, or which has no drainage, unless he is told that there is

> a risk of such. The seller, on the other hand, will know perfectly well that if he cuts off access to the main road following division, that the buyer may well find their land landlocked. If land law is attempting to protect, within reasonable bounds, the expectations of parties to a transaction, then the non-derogation from grant principle helps to ensure this.

12.3.2.1 Easements of necessity

The first method of implication is that relating to easements of necessity. This method, to repeat, is available for both implied grants and implied reservations. Necessity here really does mean necessity. The method can be used where land would be completely unusable without the implication of the easement. As such, it only really relates to two types of easement: rights of support, and rights of way. To give an example, if a seller sells half of his house so as to create two semi-detached properties, even if it is not specified in the grant that there is a right of support between the two, this will be implied on the basis of necessity so that neither party is able simply to knock their half down. Similarly, if land is being sold so that either the retained part or the sold part would become landlocked, that is, completely inaccessible from a public highway or private land over which a right of way already exists, then a right of way would be implied.

The courts have been very strict in considering what constitutes landlocked for these purposes. It must be that the land is *completely* inaccessible. This can been seen by examining two cases: *Manjang v Drammeh*[106] and *MRA Engingeering v Trimster*.[107] In the former, access by river prevented the court implying a land-based easement of necessity, and in the latter the possibility of access on foot prevented the courts implying a vehicular right of way under this doctrine.

The justification for this rule is to keep land usable, as much as it is about respecting parties' presumed intentions upon the division of the land. The question has arisen in case law, however, whether intention is wholly irrelevant such that this is really a question of public policy. The court in *Nickerson v Barraclough*[108] concluded that this is not a rule of public policy and an expression of contrary intention in a conveyance will preclude the operation of the rule. This case also makes clear that the right cannot be implied into a conveyance *retrospectively*. That is, in *Nickerson*,[109] the land only became landlocked sometime after transfer due to changes in respect of access rights relating to other, unrelated land. The claimant argued that due to the land *now* being landlocked it would be appropriate to go back to the conveyance dividing the land and assume that a right of way was intended. The court refused to do so.

12.3.2.2 Easements of common intention

Whilst the rules relating to easements of necessity are easily applied to any instant case given the strictness of these rules, the rule relating to common intention requires a more subjective assessment. Again, this method can be used for both reservations and grants. For those who have

---

[106] *Manjang v Drammeh* (1991) 61 P & CR 194 (PC).
[107] *MRA Engineering v Trimster* (1988) 56 P & CR 1 (CA).
[108] *Nickerson v Barraclough* [1981] Ch 426 (CA).
[109] *Nickerson v Barraclough* [1981] Ch 426 (CA).

already studied implied trusts, however, and are familiar with the common intention constructive trust (see chapter 7), it is useful to keep in mind that the 'common intention' requirement with easements is *much* more rigorous, especially in implied reservation cases. The 'fairness' based approach which seems to drive much that happens in relation to family homes is absent here. Rather, it is perhaps better to think of these cases as being closer to a joint venture situation.

The way that this rule works is that if the parties are dividing the land on the basis of a common plan that either the sold or the retained part will be used for a particular purpose, and the easement is strictly necessary for that purpose to be realised then an easement will be implied. There are therefore two aspects: when is a common intention present? And when is an easement *necessary* to give effect to that purpose? These requirements are discussed in *Wong v Beaumont Properties*.[110]

> **Key case: *Wong v Beaumont Properties* [1965] 1 QB 173**
>
> Notwithstanding the fact that in the judgment in this case the easement here is sometimes referred to as an easement of necessity, this is clearly a case of an easement arising by common intention. The property concerned was a basement, a lease of which was granted to the claimants in order that they could carry on a Chinese restaurant on the premises. To operate such a restaurant, health and safety rules required that there was adequate ventilation from the kitchens through a ventilation shaft. This shaft went into the high floors of the building. The claimants alleged that they had an easement to use the ventilation shaft. This could not be an easement of necessity as explained earlier since the property was usable without the ventilation: it just would not be useable as a restaurant. However, the restaurant business would not be operable without the ventilation. Furthermore, the purpose for which the original lease was granted was in order of the basement to be specifically used as a Chinese restaurant. This was enough, the court concluded, to allow an easement to be implied into the conveyance of the lease.

12.3.2.3 Section 62, Law of Property Act 1925

The third method of implication is the section 62 of the Law of Property Act 1925. This can only be used for implied grants. This section began life as a 'word-saving' provision. In the days when deeds were drafted by hand and written out, changes to deeds would be very expensive. The more information contained in the deed, the longer it would take a clerk to transcribe. As a result, property legislation contained provisions designed to cut down on the length of transfer deeds by allowing reference to previous deeds. Section 62 is one of these. Its original intention was basically to confirm that even if a particular right was not mentioned in a later conveyance, if it was mentioned in an earlier conveyance and nothing had happened to suggest that the right had disappeared or been abandoned, then it would be presumed that the property right would be transferred in the conveyance. Indeed, section 62 still performs this role as we shall see later in relation to the benefits of easements for purchasers of the dominant land.

---

[110] *Wong v Beaumont Property Trust* [1965] 1 QB 173 (CA).

However, case law, commencing with *International Tea Store v Hobbs*[111] and *Wright v Macadam*[112] expanded the role of section 62 to mean that it is now capable of turning previous *use* into a crystallised *right* on the transfer of land. This is a controversial development. It has been described as a 'trap for the unwary'. It does not, however, necessarily pose undue problems in practice for the reason that anyone receiving legal advice will almost certainly exclude the operation of this section in a deed of conveyance, and make express provision for any easements which they envisage being created on the division of land. Nevertheless, the 'upgrading' power of this section—from mere usage to rights—can be criticised and for this reason the Law Commission has suggested that the law of easements be reformed so as to abolish this effect as we explore later at 12.7.

When will section 62 perform this role? In the early case law concerned with this section, two conditions were set on its operation. First, there must have been prior diversity of occupation of the relevant land. Second, the use of the easement must have been continuous and apparent. We explore these requirements in more detail later, for even in the modern case law, which has modified the test somewhat, these factors will still have a critical role to play. The difference is now that they need not both be present. However, the most important condition which *must* be met in order for section 62 to operate is that a deed has been used. If no deed is used, section 62 *cannot* apply.

The consequence of this requirement is that any time a deed is used, and section 62 applies, the easement which is implied as a result will be a legal easement if a legal estate is being transferred. In the case of registration, this means that the transfer of the estate must be registered. Essentially, we return to how implication of easements works in order to understand this. If implication works by pretending that certain words existed in a document when in reality they did not, then the effect of those words will depend on the nature and fate of the document. If the words are implied into contract, then the effect of that cannot be to create a legal easement since a contract alone cannot create legal easements. By contrast, if the words are implied into a deed, that will be enough to create a legal easement but, one assumes, following the requirements of section 27 LRA 2002, it is essential to register the transfer created by that deed in order for the deed to take effect at law, including any easements implied into it.

> **Summary: Section 62, Law of Property Act 1925**
>
> A deed is essential for the operation of section 62. Whether this produces a legal or an equitable easement depends upon the estate being transferred and the formality requirements relating to that deed.

Prior diversity of occupation

Prior diversity of occupation means that someone other than the person dividing their estate in land must have been occupying the part being divested and that person must have been using the land in the same way as the purported easement. This use without the grant of the formal easement is sometimes referred to as a quasi-easement. This occupation can take two forms. First, it

---

[111] *International Tea Stores v Hobbs* [1903] 2 Ch 165.
[112] *Wright v Macadam* [1949] 2 KB 744 (CA).

could be occupation under a lease, where the freeholder of the entire site then later transfers the freehold to the part of his land subject to the lease or where the leaseholder of the entire site has sub-let and transfers leasehold title of the part subject to the sub-lease. Second, the occupation could be on the basis of a licence, that is, a mere permissive personal right which confers no estate on land. Either will be sufficient to give rise to the 'prior diversity of occupation'. It is very important to note that prior diversity of occupation is *not* the same thing as prior diversity of *ownership*.

As for the meaning of occupation, this is a word which is not readily susceptible of a legal definition. In this context and others, including land registration and the test for 'actual occupation' in schedule 1 paragraph 2 LRA 2002 and schedule 3 paragraph 2 LRA 2002 (see chapter 15 at 15.3.3), the courts have continually stated that occupation is a 'common word of English' and should be interpreted as such, without rigid definition. It is important to note however that it is not essential for someone to *live* in a property in order for them to occupy it. This much is obvious if we think of commercial premises. It is very unlikely that any of the employees will live in their office, but we certainly would say that the business is occupying such an office. Rather, you should think of occupation as connoting a stable and relatively continuous physical presence on the land, either of people or property.

Continuous and apparent

The 'continuous and apparent' requirement is considerably more nebulous. There is also a lack of clarity in the case law as to whether it is necessary that *both* be present for section 62 to operate, or whether it suffices if one only exists in any given scenario. Let us explain with an example.

Jerome is the proprietor of a large farm with a house in the North-Western corner and a large barn in the South-East. Access to the main road is in the South-Eastern corner near the barn. Jerome decides that he no longer wishes to live on site. He agrees to sell freehold title to a small plot, including the house, to Floella. Floella, having moved in, is disappointed to learn that Jerome will not allow her to use the track across the field, which he himself had previously used, to get from the house to the main road. Instead, she must take a substantial diversion using a small and poorly-surfaced road which adds 15 minutes to her journey time. She argues that an easement arose by implication on the transfer of title to the North-Western plot. Putting aside the 'prior diversity of occupation' requirement for the moment—as we shall see, recent case law has made it clear that it is not necessary for *both* prior diversity and continuous and apparent usage—can we say that the use of the track has been 'continuous and apparent'?

On the one hand, we may argue that it is not continuous. Imagining that Jerome uses the track at most three or four times a day, his use is in no sense continuous. Contrast this, for example, with a right to light where the passage of light through a window is continuous. The track is apparent however, in that it has left physical traces on the land. On the other hand, it could be said that the use is continuous in that it is continuously available. It is not as though Jerome has limited his own use by expressly only using the track between certain hours, for example. Which of these is the correct interpretation of the test?

Case law tells us that 'continuous' in this sense, means continuously available.[113] Otherwise, the test would limit the types of easement which can pass under section 62, and that would defeat the

---

[113] *Wood v Waddington* [2015] EWCA Civ 538, [2015] 2 P & CR 11.

object of the provision (as interpreted by the courts at least). Thus, we may say that continuous and apparent use, means continuously available and leaving physical traces on the land so that someone visiting the land would be able, without too much difficulty, to say that the previous occupier of the land used in a particular way. They might, based on this, build up an expectation that they would be entitled to do the same, hence the justification for the rules relating to implication to intervene.

The operation of these rules was, however, substantially and rather radically modified by the decision of the Court of Appeal in *Platt v Crouch*.[114]

> **Key case:** *Platt v Crouch* [2003] EWCA Civ 1110
>
> As mentioned earlier at 12.2.1.3, this case involved the question as to whether a hotel was entitled, by virtue of an easement, to use of a mooring. In this case, Peter Gibson LJ held that:
>
> > 'To my mind the evidence is clear that the rights in question did appertain to and were reputed to appertain to and were enjoyed with the hotel, being part of the hotel business and advertised as such and enjoyed by the hotel guests. The rights were continuous and apparent, and so it matters not that prior to the sale of the hotel there was no prior diversity of occupation of the dominant and servient tenancies.'[115]
>
> However, the authority for the proposition that it does not matter that there was no prior diversity is unclear. Certainly, in *International Tea Stores v Hobbs*[116] (the first case to use section 62 in this way), the court relied on the diversity of occupation (or indeed in that case, possession) as being of great significance to the possibility of section 62 converting the permissive use into an easement on conveyance. It was also inconsistent with dicta of the House of Lords in *Sovmots Investments*[117] and some cases which followed, including *Kent v Kavanagh*.[118]

Controversial as this decision was, and uncertain its authority, it was nevertheless followed by another Court of Appeal in *Wood v Waddington*.[119] We can now conclude that this case represents good law.

One thing that remains somewhat unclear following the decision in these cases, however, is whether it is necessary in cases where there *is* prior diversity, for the right to be continuous and apparent, or, whether in such cases, there is no need for the continuous and apparent tests to be met. In other words, are the tests alternative tests, or is prior diversity of occupation in effect irrelevant, because all that matters is whether the use was continuous and apparent?

Whatever the resolution to the remaining uncertainties in relation to the operation of section 62, there is no doubt that its operation is wide in its scope. The original purpose of section 62, as we have explained, was to ensure that rights which already existed would pass on conveyances of the land even where they were not expressly mentioned in a deed of transfer. This was to save

---

[114] *P&S Platt Ltd v Crouch* [2003] EWCA Civ 1110, [2004] 1 P & CR 18.
[115] *P&S Platt Ltd v Crouch* [2003] EWCA Civ 1110, [2004] 1 P & CR 18, [42].
[116] *International Tea Stores v Hobbs* [1903] 2 Ch 165.
[117] *Sovmots Investments Ltd v Secretary of State for the Environment* [1979] AC 144 (HL).
[118] *Kent v Kavanagh* [2006] EWCA Civ 162, [2007] Ch. 1.
[119] *Wood v Waddington* [2015] EWCA Civ 538, [2015] 2 P & CR 11.

on the need for lengthy documents in the era of hand writing. The purpose of the section is now to upgrade precarious and merely permissive use into a right which cannot be discharged regardless of how inconvenient it is for the servient owner without the express agreement of the dominant owner. For this reason, with the increasingly broad scope of section 62, in addition for calls to reform the operation of that section itself, there have also been calls for the power of the courts to discharge obsolete restrictive covenants (see chapter 13 at 13.6), to be extended to cover easements. We discuss possible avenues for reform of easements in more detail later in this chapter.

12.3.2.4 The rule in *Wheeldon v Burrows*

The final method by which easements are implied is by the rule in *Wheeldon v Burrows*.[120] This rule will apply where the quasi-easement, ie the use of the land prior to the transfer, is both continuous and apparent and necessary for the reasonable enjoyment of the land. The first requirement is interpreted in the same way as in relation to section 62 as considered earlier. The second requirement is, again, an impressionistic assessment rather than a strict test. It has however been taken to mean that the easement must do more than make the land 'more convenient'. It is certainty not a strict test of necessity in the same way as in relation to easements of necessity however.

The situations when this rule will apply are very narrow following the decisions in *Platt v Crouch*[121] and *Wood v Waddington*.[122] This is because since continuous and apparent quasi-easements will crystallise into implied easements under section 62, there are no circumstances where a deed is used that *Wheeldon v Burrows*[123] will allow for the creation of an implied easement but section 62 would not. The same is not true the other way around: because of the 'necessary for reasonable enjoyment' test, *Wheeldon*[124] is narrower than section 62. However, since section 62 requires a deed, any time there is a written contract only, *Wheeldon v Burrows*[125] will apply. The consequence of this is that any easement implied under the rule in *Wheeldon*[126] will necessarily be equitable in nature.

> **Summary: Methods of implication**
>
> 1. Easements of necessity (grants and reservations). An easement will be implied where land is unusable without the easement. This only really applies to easements of right of way and of support.
> 2. Easements of common intention (grants and reservations). An easement will be implied where that easement is necessary to give effect to a clear joint plan in relation to the future use of the divided land.

---

[120] *Wheeldon v Burrows* (1879) 12 ChD 31.
[121] *P&S Platt Ltd v Crouch* [2003] EWCA Civ 1110, [2004] 1 P & CR 18.
[122] *Wood v Waddington* [2015] EWCA Civ 538, [2015] 2 P & CR 11.
[123] *Wheeldon v Burrows* (1879) 12 ChD 31.
[124] *Wheeldon v Burrows* (1879) 12 ChD 31.
[125] *Wheeldon v Burrows* (1879) 12 ChD 31.
[126] *Wheeldon v Burrows* (1879) 12 ChD 31.

3. Section 62 Law of Property Act 1925 (grants only). An easement will be implied into a deed of transfer where the use of the quasi-easement prior to the division of the land was continuous and apparent.
4. The rule in *Wheeldon v Burrows*[127] (grants only). An easement will be implied into a transfer where the use of the quasi-easement was continuous and apparent, and the easement would be necessary for the reasonable enjoyment of the land.

12.3.3 BY PRESCRIPTION

Prescriptive easements are extremely important in practice because they allow for the creation of easements by long use (subject to the conditions explained later) in situations where land has long been divided. This means that it performs a substantially different role to the methods of implication discussed earlier. It can also be reasonably described as unnecessarily complex. The general principle behind the various different rules relating to prescription is that if an easement has been used for a sufficiently long time, openly and without deceit, to the mutual satisfaction of all the relevant parties, then it ought to be treated as though a right to do so has arisen, effectively by either implicit consent, or by acquiescence at the least, on the part of the servient owner.

The period for prescription of easements is 20 years, and the easement must have been used regularly, if not incessantly, during that time. Furthermore, for any route to prescription, the right must have been used '*nec vi, nec clam, nec precario*', or, more helpfully, without force, secrecy, or permission. Lord Hoffman explains the rationale behind these requirements:

> 'The unifying element in these three vitiating circumstances was that each constituted a reason why it would not be reasonable to expect the owner to resist the exercise of the right—in the first case, because rights should not be acquired by the use of force, in the second, because the owner would not have known of the user and in the third, because he had consented to the user, but for a limited period.'[128]

If these features are shown to exist, then there are three 'methods' of prescription which might apply. First, there is common law prescription. In order to succeed under this approach, the claimant must show 20 years' usage of the right. However, if the defendant can show that the right was not used at sometime after 1189 (as they very likely can), then the claim will fail. This date is significant as being the date of 'time immemorial'. In other words, if something can be shown to have existed as far as 1189, then the law treats it as though it has always existed. The second method is the doctrine of 'lost modern grant'. This is based on the legal fiction that there was an express deed of easement at some time in the modern past but that it has been lost. As long as the 20 years' use in the appropriate manner exists, this method will succeed as long as it would not have been legally impossible for the easement to have been granted prior to that time. This 20-year period can be any time 20 years in the past, and the use does not have to continue up to the date of the claim. The third method is a claim under the Prescription Act 1832. To succeed under the Act, the claimant must show that their use continued up until the date of the application. The only advantage of using the Act, therefore, relates to the fact that it is possible to claim a prescriptive

---
[127] *Wheeldon v Burrows* (1879) 12 ChD 31.
[128] *R v Oxfordshire CC Ex p Sunningwell PC* [2000] 1 A.C. 335 at 350.

easement if the use has continued for forty years, even in cases where there was oral permission to use the right, ie the 'nec precario' requirement is absent. Thus, most successful claims will be made under the doctrine of lost modern grant, but in cases where there is an oral permission, the claimant will need to rely on the Prescription Act 1832.

> **Further analysis: The Prescription Act 1832**
>
> This Act is famously appallingly drafted and there have been a number of calls for its abolition. However, as it remains on the statute books, it is essential to understand its operation and purpose. It was intended to improve upon the rather odd situation which had developed in common law in relation to the doctrine of lost modern grant. In such cases, even where it could be proved that no grant was made, the doctrine would apply unless it was impossible that such a grant could have been made. This absurdity—a rule based on a grant which in many if not most cases quite patently did not exist—was pure fiction and courts knew it. Thus, the legislature introduced legislation to put prescription on a more 'honest' footing. In doing so, however, it enormously complicated the law of prescription and has certainly not got rid of the lost modern grant doctrine.
>
> For one thing, the Act introduces two periods of prescription, as mentioned earlier. After 20 years, the Act merely says that a defendant cannot resist a claim to prescription by proving that user began after 1189. After 40 years, the Act provides that the prescriptive right will be 'absolute and indefeasible'. Thus, after 20 years, the Act prevents a defendant from relying on one specific argument. After 40 years, the Act provides that the claimant must succeed as long as forty years of prescriptive use can be proved. It therefore does not prevent reliance on the existing common law rules, and instead adds an in some ways inconsistent alternative route to proving an easement by prescription.

> **Summary: Easements by prescription**
>
> Easements by prescription arise when an easement has been used without force, secrecy or permission for twenty years. There are three methods by which this use becomes determinative of an easement:
>
> 1. Common law. This can be excluded by proof that the easement did not exist at some time since 1189.
> 2. Lost modern grant. This can be excluded if the grant of the easement would have been impossible prior to the 20 years' usage.
> 3. Prescription Act 1832. Where a claimant relies on this Act, they can claim an easement after 20 years' use if the only barrier under the common law was that there was proof that the easement did not exist at some time since 1189. After 40 years' use, the claimant can establish an easement under this Act even if the use was based on oral permission.

12.4 THE USE OF EASEMENTS

Once it has been established in any particular case that an easement has arisen, it is still important to ascertain precisely what that entitles both the dominant and servient owner to do. For example, is it possible in situations involving rights of way, for the servient owner to change the route of that right of way in order to carry out development on their land? And if so, how extensive can a diversion be? In cases of car parking, can the dominant owner decide to increase their usage from parking one car to two, or more? Finally, in situations where a dominant owner for example acquires a further plot of land, can they use an existing right of way as a 'cut through' to land not originally intended to be benefitted by that easement? These questions are all significant in practice, especially when we consider that the existence of old easements can be very restrictive to development of previously occupied sites, given the importance of development on brownfield for the purposes of provided city housing etc.

Of course, the first place to turn in order to answer these questions will be the deed of conveyance itself. If the deed does not answer this problem, however, then the starting point is the rough rule of thumb that a dominant owner is entitled to full use of the easement as it was when it arose, either expressly, impliedly or by prescription, and no more. This means that the servient owner cannot diminish their use, but equally nor can the dominant owner increase it. The easement is also for the benefit of the original dominant tenement, and cannot be used for the benefit of other land even where the owner of the land is the same.

This rule of thumb is, however, as one would expect, subject to certain modifications in particular circumstances. Let us begin with consideration of the question of diversion of easements involving passage over the servient land—be that water through a defined channel, electricity wires, sewage pipes, light, or a right of way. This situation was discussed by the High Court in *R (Gloucester CC) v Secretary of State for the Environment, Transport and the Regions*.[129] In this case, the court held that in cases where the need for a diversion of the right of way is caused by natural forces, the dominant owner will be unable to demand a new route on a different path. Thus, if the right of way becomes unusable due to natural causes, the dominant owner will lose their right. In other cases, the servient owner is unable to change the course of the right of way.

Secondly, is it possible for the dominant owner to increase their usage of the property? Let us imagine an example where this might arise.

Graham runs a bed and breakfast from his house in the Lake District. He has an express easement of parking for the cars of his guests in a neighbouring farmer's field. His house has always been able to house four or five guests at any time, and typically this would mean three cars parked in the farmer's field. The field is very large, and this never caused the slightest inconvenience to the farmer. However, given the success of the business, and Graham's ambitions to open a gastropub in an adjacent property, Graham has now built an extension on his house to house a further twenty-five guests. He envisages advertising this particularly to coach trips, bringing business to his restaurant and ensuring his hotel is full. Can he park the coach and any additional cars on the farmer's land?

There are three potential issues in this problem. The first is the change of vehicle; the second, the increase in the number of cars, and the third is the possibility of parking for restaurant guests who are not hotel guests. We deal the last of these issues later, but what about the intensification of the use? The guiding principle, as explained in Gale on Easements, the leading practitioners' guide, is that, 'no alteration can be made in the mode of enjoyment by the owner of the dominant

---

[129] *R (Gloucester CC) v Secretary of State for the Environment, Transport and the Regions* (2001) 82 P & CR 15 (QBD).

tenement, the effect of which will be to increase such restriction [on the servient owner's use of his land] beyond its legitimate limit'.[130] The key word here, of course, is 'legitimate', and to ascertain how far modifications can be made to the use of the easements we need to explore the case law. One 'test' used to explore the issue of illegitimate changes to use is the notion of 'excessive' use. This is demonstrated by the decision in *McAdams Homes Ltd v Robinson*.[131]

> **Key case:** *McAdams Homes Ltd v Robinson* [2004] EWCA Civ 214
>
> In this case Lord Neuberger gives extensive guidance as to the principles which govern changes to the use of an easement. These principles have been paraphrased in Gale by Gaunt QC and Morgan J, and we cite the most important elements of these principles here:
>
> > '(1) where the dominant land is used for a particular purpose at the time an easement is created, an increase, even if substantial, in the intensity of that use... cannot of itself be objected to by the servient owner;
> >
> > (2) excessive use of an easement by the dominant land will render the dominant owner liable in nuisance...
> >
> > (3) where there is a change in the use of, or the erection of new buildings on, the dominant land, without having any effect on the nature or extent of the use of the easement, the change, however radical, will not affect the right of the dominant owner to use the easement;
> >
> > ...
> >
> > (5) the issue as to the extent of an easement acquired by implied grant or by prescription should be determined by answering two questions;
> >
> > (6) the first question was: whether the development of the dominant land represented a "radical change in the character" or a "change in the identity" of the dominant land as opposed to a mere change or intensification in the use of the dominant land;
> >
> > (7) the second question was: whether the use of the dominant land as redeveloped would result in a substantial increase or alteration in the burden on the servient land;
> >
> > (8) it is only if the redevelopment of the dominant land resulted in a radical change in its character and would lead to a substantial increase in the burden that the dominant owner's right to enjoy the easement would be suspended or lost'.[132]
>
> This lengthy citation is warranted by the clarity of the expression here, and it is a very good guide as to how to handle possible increases in use in a problem question.

Let us apply this guidance to our discussion of Graham's hotel. The first principle—that in itself increased use followed by a mere intensification of use of the dominant land, where that use has not changed—seems to be determinative. However, we could say that a small bed and breakfast arrangement is not the same usage as a hotel, nor is the use of a coach an 'intensification' of

---

[130] Gaunt and Morgan, *Gale on Easements* (20th ed) (Sweet & Maxwell, London, 2016).
[131] *McAdams Homes Ltd v Robinson* [2004] EWCA Civ 214, [2005] 1 P & CR 30.
[132] Gaunt and Morgan, *Gale on Easements* (20th ed) (Sweet & Maxwell, London, 2016).

parking cars—it is a substantial change in the identity of the vehicle which may have implications, for example, for damage done to the land by the weight of the coach. To explore this, we can consider Lord Neuberger's sixth principle, which highlights that we must examine whether there is a 'radical change of character' in the identity of the dominant land. If this change in identity results in a substantial increase in burden (we can probably say that it does here), then the use for coach parking may not be permitted. However, this is a very impressionistic, general and uncertain assessment. Thus whilst it seems possible, if not probable, that Graham would not be allowed to increase his use in this way, it is by no means certain.

Does it make a difference to our approach to Graham's use of his land that the increase in parking is for the benefit of other land as well? This question is in part answered by the rule in *Harris v Flower*,[133] albeit that this rule is primarily concerned with rights of way and as such our assessment of car parking rights involves reasoning by analogy. In *Harris*, Romer LJ states that, '[i]f a right of way be granted for the enjoyment of close A, the grantee, because he owns or acquires close B, cannot use the way in substance for passing over close A to close B'.[134] To put this another way, just because the owner of Whiteacre happens also to own Blackacre, and Blackacre has the benefit of an easement, it does not mean that Whiteacre has the benefit of an easement 'by proxy'. Thus, in the case of Graham, restaurant guests cannot park their car on the farmer's field. The operation of this rule is however murky and deeply contested and the case law contains many contradictions and apparent exceptions.

In *Macepark (Whittlebury) Ltd v Sargeant*[135] the judge summarised the law as follows:

'(a) An easement must be used for the benefit of the dominant land.

(b) It must not "in substance" be used for the benefit of non-dominant land.

(c) Under the "ancillary" doctrine, use is not "in substance" use for the benefit of the non-dominant land if (1) there is no benefit to the non-dominant land or if (2) the extent of the use for the benefit of the non-dominant land is insubstantial, ie it can still be said that in substance the access is used for the benefit of the dominant land and not for the benefit of both the dominant and the non-dominant land.

(d) "Benefit" in this context includes use of an access in such a way that a profit may be made out of the use of the non-dominant land, e.g. as a result of an arrangement with the owner of the dominant land.

(e) The application of these principles can involve potentially difficult questions of fact and degree'.[136]

This is a useful guide to the operation of the *Harris v Flower*[137] rules, but it must be acknowledged that subsequent case law has not followed these to the letter. For example, in *Giles v Tarry*[138] the Court of Appeal applied the rule in *Harris v Flower*[139] quite rigidly.

---

[133] *Harris v Flower* (1904) 91 LT 816.
[134] *Harris v Flower* (1904) 91 LT 816.
[135] *Macepark (Whittlebury) Ltd v Sargeant* [2003] EWHC 427 (Ch), [2003] 1 WLR 2284.
[136] *Macepark (Whittlebury) Ltd v Sargeant* [2003] EWHC 427 (Ch), [2003] 1 WLR 2284, [50]-[51].
[137] *Harris v Flower* (1904) 91 LT 816.
[138] *Giles v Tarry* [2012] EWCA Civ 837, [2012] 2 P & CR 15.
[139] *Harris v Flower* (1904) 91 LT 816.

Key case: *Giles v Tarry* [2012] EWCA Civ 837

The facts of this case show the potentially absurd nature of the *Harris v Flower*[140] rule, albeit that the result does seem to attempt to take a common sense attitude to how these rules work. In the case, a farmer had a right of way over a field (for clarity let us call it the Pink field). This right of way took him to a public highway. He subsequently acquired another field (the Blue field) and wished to use the right of way to go directly from his other field (the Yellow field), to the second (the Blue field). The owner of the Pink field claimed this constituted an impermissible extension of the dominant tenement as it would mean that the Blue field also had the benefit of the right of way. The farmer argued that even if it was not possible for him to go directly from the Yellow to the Blue fields, there was nothing that prevented him from going from the Yellow field onto the public highway, and then simply returning onto the public highway and not making it all the way along the track and 'nipping' into the Blue field. Since he had control of access to the Blue field, it simply meant that he would not use the 'whole' of his right of way back to the Yellow field. The idea that the decision in this case could rest on so fine an argument demonstrates quite how difficult this rule can be in practice. However, the Court of Appeal attempts to handle this in a sensible way. Norris LJ began by reasoning:

> 'the law contemplates that the rights they have over each other's lands will be reasonably exercised and reasonably allowed. It is not for this court to create a detailed regulatory regime by reference to what either of them might or might not do.'[141]

The guiding approach therefore is one of reasonableness. Furthermore, it is possible, said the Court of Appeal, to take into account the intention of the dominant owner. Thus, per Neuberger LJ: 'although the language in which the critical question is posed varies from case to case, the underlying thrust of the question is the same: what in substance and intention is the dominant owner's use?'[142]

Once intention is taken into account, therefore, the intention of the farmer here would be a single operation, an operation which was not permitted by the rule in *Harris v Flower*,[143] ie to use the right of way for the benefit of another, even if the precise mechanics by which this were done could artificially appear to get round the rule.

It is clear, however, that the Court of Appeal does not appear to be particularly enthusiastic about the operation of the rule, and it cites both academic and Law Commission arguments against the rule. Nevertheless, as they acknowledge, they have to apply the rule as it exists.

Summary: Use of easements

In general, easements can only be used according to the route and extent envisaged in the original grant, and for the benefit only of the original dominant tenement. However, these principles are applied in a common sense manner, and courts will take account of any change in character of the land, and use, as well as an on the ground assessment of practicalities, in cases of dispute.

---

[140] *Harris v Flower* (1904) 91 LT 816.
[141] *Giles v Tarry* [2012] EWCA Civ 837, [2012] 2 P & CR 15.
[142] *Giles v Tarry* [2012] EWCA Civ 837, [2012] 2 P & CR 15, [56].
[143] *Harris v Flower* (1904) 91 LT 816.

12.5 EXTINCTION OF EASEMENTS

Just as it is very important to know when an easement arises, be that expressly or impliedly, it is critical to know when they will come to an end. First, of course, such easements may be brought to an end expressly. This will require a deed if the easement was a legal easement, but it may be that a contract suffices to in effect bring the easement to an end if, for example, the courts conclude that the dominant owner thereby becomes estopped from reliance on the easement. Whether this kind of estoppel would have binding effects on future owners of both the dominant and servient land would depend, in part, on questions of priority.

Secondly, easements can be extinguished by abandonment. This is very hard to prove and the circumstances when a court will conclude that an easement has been truly abandoned are very narrow. Case law highlights that such abandonment can only be proved by evidence of both acts or omissions by the dominant owner which are indicative of abandonment, and evidence of a subjective intention to abandon. One example of this might be where the dominant owner changes the use or layout of his own land so as to render use of the easement impossible. The operation of this rule was discussed in the recent case of *Annetts v Adeleye*.[144]

An easement will also be extinguished where the dominant and servient lands come into the ownership and possession of the same person. This is a necessary consequence of the rule that it is not possible for an easement to exist unless there is a dominant and servient tenement in separate ownership. Since this method of extinction of easements is automatic, however, it might reasonably be supposed that it may catch people out, especially in complex transactions where land moves to and fro between different parties.

12.6 TRANSFERS, PRIORITIES, AND THIRD PARTIES

Finally, easements may 'come to an end' in a manner of speaking, if they lose priority following a disposition of the servient land. It is important therefore to understand the consequences of transfers of land both benefitted and burdened by easements.

12.6.1 EXPRESS LEGAL EASEMENTS

The most simple situation in this regard is in cases where an easement, expressly created, is registered. If it is created by a person capable of creating a legal right in the relevant land, and the proper formalities are complied with, then any easement which is registered will be legal in nature. Without such registration, an express easement cannot be legal. The necessity therefore that an express legal easement will *always* be registered means that they will *always* take priority on dispositions of the land.

---

[144] *Annetts v Adeleye* [2018] EWCA Civ 555, [2018] 2 P & CR DG9.

12.6.2 IMPLIED LEGAL EASEMENTS

The situation here is somewhat more complex because, by virtue of the fact that such easements are implied, they will not appear on the register. Nevertheless, as explained in this chapter, they may be legal easements by virtue of the formalities associated with the document into which they are implied.

Let us set the scene with an example. In 2012, Agatha was the registered proprietor of a large property containing a manor house and a gamekeeper's cottage. Finding this too much to maintain by herself, she decided to sell the gamekeeper's cottage to Paige by registered disposition. No express easements were created in the deed. On moving in, Paige discovered that there was no access to the cottage except along the road running across the retained land. Agatha did not object to Paige driving along this road however, just as she herself had done. In 2016, Agatha decided to move to Italy and sold the manor house and retained land to Kirsten, who duly became registered proprietor. Finally in 2017, Paige sold the gamekeeper's cottage to Darya. Darya's title was also registered and she now wishes to use the road.

In establishing whether Darya is entitled to use the road over what is now Kirsten's land, we must first establish whether a right of way was created by implication on the division of the land by Agatha. It seems tolerably clear that it was. First, we know that a right of way is capable of being an easement, and there is nothing to suggest here that the right was in reality benefitting Paige herself rather than the gamekeeper's cottage. Second, we know that any easement which is created by implication, since there are no express easements, would be implied into the deed of transfer, which itself was registered, meaning that any easements thus created would be legal. Finally, whilst it is highly likely that an easement of necessity has arisen in this case, given that the land would otherwise be landlocked, the use of the land by Agatha prior to the transfer, and the fact that the roadway would be obvious and continuous in the relevant sense, an easement would be created by section 62 in any case. Thus, we have an implied easement, legal in character, but which is not expressed on the register.

Implied legal easements form their own category of overriding interests (see chapter 15 at 15.3.4), precisely because their very important but hidden social functions (think here, for example, of drainage and sewage rights) mean that there is an important policy goal to ensure that land remains benefitted and burdened by such rights even if they do not expressly appear in the conveyancing documentation.

First, on the question of benefit, whilst it is not necessary to register the benefit of an easement, whenever an express easement is registered, the title to the benefitted land will be amended to that effect. Where this is not present on the register, it does not matter that the rights do not appear in the transfer of the benefitted land however (in this case, the transfer from Paige to Darya) as a result of section 62. This is, in effect, an example of the original purpose of section 62 at work. It ensures that rights which are attached to the relevant land are not lost simply because they are not mentioned in a deed of transfer. Thus, given that Paige appears to have had the benefit of an implied legal easement, so too does Darya.

What about the burden? This is more complex. What priority rules govern this situation? In schedule 1, paragraph 3 and schedule 3, paragraph 3 LRA 2002, special provision is given specifically for implied legal easements. These paragraphs provide that in cases of implied legal easements, the purchaser of a burdened estate will be bound by these easements if any of the following three conditions are met:

1. The easement would have been obvious on a reasonably careful inspection nof the land (as, in all likelihood, would be the case with the road here)
2. The purchaser knew about the easement; or
3. The easement has been used any time within the last year.

This last condition in particular may seem very broad. Indeed, it is perhaps surprising given the general policy of the Law Commission when implementing the LRA was to limit the number of overriding interests (see chapter 15). However, the hidden nature of many implied easements makes this last condition a very useful catch-all for rights which may not be visible on a physical inspection of the land but which are critical to its use. If any of these three conditions are met, then the purchaser of the relevant land—Kirsten, in this case—is bound to allow the purchaser of the dominant land to continue to use their easement.

What happens if the conditions are not met? The question as to the 'fate' of an otherwise valid proprietary interest which loses its priority on the disposition of a registered estate is a complex issue, and is addressed fully in chapter 15 at 15.3. The issue, as highlighted there, is whether, following a transfer, the right is merely 'postponed' to the estate in question, or whether it is destroyed. The difference between these two determines whether the right can subsequently be revived and take priority once again on a subsequent transfer. For example, if an easement does not meet any of the conditions detailed earlier, but following transfer, begins to be used again, can it take priority on a subsequent transfer? We can return to the example earlier to explain this further.

Imagine now that at the time of the transfer to Kirsten, Paige has been away for over a year and has not used the roadway. In this time, being merely an un-surfaced road, the grass has grown over the road and no physical signs of it remain. Furthermore, Kirsten is wholly unaware of the road. When Paige transfers title to Darya, and Darya realises that the roadway is the only point of access to the cottage, after making inquiries, Darya informs Kristen. Kristen is perfectly happy for Darya to use the road although it is clear that she is not legally bound to let her do so as the easement has lost its priority. Darya then uses the road daily. Subsequently, Kristen transfers registered title to Alex. Is Alex bound by the right of way over the road?

The answer to this depends upon the meaning of 'postpones' in section 29 LRA 2002. The issue is discussed fully at 15.7.

12.6.3 EXPRESS EQUITABLE EASEMENTS

Moving away from legal easements, we must now consider the circumstances in which an express equitable easement will have priority over a transfer of registered title to the servient land. First, it is important to note that it is not impossible to register such rights. It will of course be highly unusual for an equitable easement to be registered (in most cases, the act of registration will be a precursor to the easement taking effect at law), but it is not impossible.

If, as is much more likely, the easement is not registered due to a failure to complete the relevant formalities (most likely the requirement of registration itself), then the only way in which the interest can bind a purchaser of registered title to the land is by virtue of actual occupation that complies with the requirements of schedule 1 paragraph 2 in cases of first registration, or schedule 3 paragraph 2 for subsequent registrations. The requirements of these paragraphs are explained fully in chapter 15.

The essential question is this: in what circumstances can the dominant owner be considered to be in actual occupation of the *servient* land, and how does this relate to the nature of the easement which they have. To put this another way—does the dominant owner occupy the servient land when he uses his right of way? Does he occupy when he parks his car on the land in compliance with an easement of parking? The key case on this is *Chaudhary v Yavuz*.[145]

> **Key case: *Chaudhary v Yavuz* [2011] EWCA Civ 1314**
>
> In this case, an equitable easement existed and the claimant alleged that this right was binding on the new proprietor of the dominant tenement on the basis that he had occupied the relevant land at the time of the disposition. The nature of this occupation, it was alleged, was the staircase that the claimant had built to allow him to use his right of way. In other words, he argued that he occupied the site with the physical structure that constituted his right of way. The court held that this did not amount to actual occupation.
>
> Lloyd LJ gives some useful guidance:
>
> 'There was no indication that it was used otherwise than for passing and repassing between the street and the relevant flat or flats. In my judgment such use does not amount to actual occupation. I dare say that no-one else was in occupation of the metal structure either, but not every piece of land is occupied by someone, let alone in someone's actual occupation (as distinct from possession).'[146]
>
> In making this argument, Lloyd LJ specifically refuses to comment on correctness of the earlier case of *Saeed v Plustrade*[147] in which it was held that it was possible to occupy servient land by using the land for parking in cases of an easement of parking. Of the two, the stronger authority is that of *Chaudhary v Yavuz*,[148] but it is not too difficult to reconcile the two judgments, given the differing use which occurs in a right of way situation (passing and re-passing) and parking which does involving stationary use of land for an extended period of time.

What is certainly possible is that a dominant owner can protect their easement if they happen to be in actual occupation of the servient land *for some other reason*. This would be unusual, but it is not inconceivable. For example, in cases involving farming, very often neighbouring farmers will occupy fields belonging to another when the field needs resting from its usual purpose. It may be put to grazing for example to allow the soil to recover for subsequent arable use. In such a case, it may be that the dominant owner, farmer A, has a right of way over Pink field, created by deed but not registered. He then occupies Pink field under a grazing licence for a two-year period. Farmer B, the proprietor of Pink field, then transfers title by registered disposition for value to Farmer C. Farmer C would then be bound by the express equitable easement by virtue of Farmer A's occupation of Pink field.

---

[145] *Chaudhary v Yavuz* [2011] EWCA Civ 1314, [2013] Ch 249.
[146] *Chaudhary v Yavuz* [2011] EWCA Civ 1314, [2013] Ch 249, [31].
[147] *Saeed v Plustrade* [2001] EWCA Civ 2011, [2002] 2 P & CR 19.
[148] *Chaudhary v Yavuz* [2011] EWCA Civ 1314, [2013] Ch 249.

12.6.4 IMPLIED EQUITABLE EASEMENTS

Finally, we consider implied equitable easements. Remember, these will arise when land is divided *but* there is no deed of conveyance, only a contract, or where there is a deed but that deed is not subsequently registered. In such cases, it is crucial to realise, the *legal title* to the divested land will not change since there is no registration. It appears that whilst a person can have the benefit of an easement against land of which he is only trustee, it may not be true the other way around, ie where the purported dominant owner *only* has an interest under a trust in the purported dominant land, as would be the case in a vendor-purchaser trust for example.

12.7 REFORM OF THE LAW OF EASEMENTS

We conclude this chapter with a brief consideration of the proposals made by the Law Commission to reform the law of easements—brief because they are increasingly unlikely to be taken up by Parliament. The Commission was of the view in its report that four key changes were required in relation to the law of easements: (1) that section 62 would no longer transform use into rights; (2) that a new method of implied easements be created and the other methods overturned; (3) that the courts be given jurisdiction to discharge obsolete easements in line with the power in section 84 LPA 1925 relating to restrictive covenants; and (4) reform of the creation of easements by prescription. Of these proposals, the second is the most interesting. The Law Commission concluded that:

> 'We recommend that an easement shall be implied as a term of a disposition where it is necessary for the reasonable use of the land at that date, bearing in mind:
>
> (1) the use of the land at the time of the grant;
>
> (2) the presence on the servient land of any relevant physical features;
>
> (3) any intention for the future use of the land, known to both parties at the time of the grant;
>
> (4) so far as relevant, the available routes for the easement sought; and
>
> (5) the potential interference with the servient land or inconvenience to the servient owner.'[149]

It is notable that these to a certain extent mirror features of the existing law, but do not replicate it exactly.

On prescription, the Law Commission recommended that the current law be abolished and replaced with a single statutory method for prescription:

> 'We recommend that:
>
> (1) an easement will arise by prescription on completion of 20 years continuous qualifying use;
>
> (2) qualifying use shall be use without force, without stealth an without permission; and
>
> (3) qualifying use shall not be use which is contrary to the criminal law, unless such use can be rendered lawful by the dispensation of the servient owner.'[150]

---

[149] Law Commission, *Making Land Work: Easements, Covenants and Profits à Prendre* report no. 327 (London, 2011), [3.45].

[150] Law Commission, *Making Land Work: Easements, Covenants and Profits à Prendre* report no. 327 (London, 2011), [3.123].

Given the simplicity of this approach, it could hardly fail to be an improvement on the current rules, but as highlighted earlier, is unlikely to happen.

12.8 CONCLUSION

The information in this chapter has a slightly different character to some of the other chapters. If we consider the leasehold estate, for example, the rules in relation to easements are at once less contentious, and more settled, as well as having considerably fewer social impacts. In this respect, we can say that any discussion of the law of easements is less 'analytical' than some other chapters. In exams, very often, examiners use the detail of the technical aspects of the law to test students' ability to reason with and apply the rules, rather than considering the rules from a policy perspective. In part, this is because the rules relating to easement are mostly well-settled so there is no need to analyse recent changes—the decision in *Regency Villas* represents an obvious exception to this. However, more generally, it is because of the social function which easements play. They are not determinative of a person's home, nor mostly of the economic value of land except in so far as land without access, for example, would significantly lose its value. Rather, the law relating to easements is an example of a structural choice by the land law system about *how* to achieve certain clearly necessary functions in relation to land. The fact of needing easements or rights like easements is completely uncontentious. The only issue then becomes the precise structures given to such rights, and given how long we have had to develop these rules, over time, responding to changing social conditions, it is little wonder that, for the most part, their operation is satisfactory.

PRINCIPLES

How does this discussion shape our understanding of the principles explained in chapter 1? To recap, these principles were:

1. Certainty
2. Sensitivity to context
3. Transactability
4. Systemic and individual effects
5. Recognition of the social role of the land law system.

As noted, the law relating to easement has a less obvious, more subtle effect on how the principles of land law play out than does the law relating to implied trusts, to leases, or to proprietary estoppel, for example. That is not to say, however, that they are not shaping these principles. Indeed, the rules relating to easements, being relatively clear and settled (albeit only really to those with the benefit of legal advice), allow for a predictable risk assessment, giving parties sufficient confidence in the system. This encourages transactions in land, and drives down the cost of doing such transactions in the form of legal time and insurance. However, this does not mean that there are not areas of contention. Primarily problems arise in relation to easements arising by prescription, as here it is not as easy as in the other cases for parties to make appropriate investigations to discover whether or not their land is affected by certain rights. Furthermore, the on-going uncertainty as to the precise potential scope of very valuable rights, such as car parking, is commercially inconvenient even if it is possible in most cases for the parties to design a system which avoids a clash with these rules. Nevertheless, easements are an instructive case where we can see a good balance being drawn between the need of sensitivity to context—consider the rules relating to what can be an easement, and also to the use of easements—but where that contextual analysis is bounded by predictable principles which shape any consideration of the particular context. It is perhaps unsurprising, therefore, that the common-sense changes to the rules suggested by the Law Commission have not been taken up: yes those rules would represent a marginal improvement, but the current law causes comparatively few difficulties and so the appetite for change simply is not there.

TABLE OF DEFINITIONS

Dominant tenement	The land for the benefit of which an easement exists.
Servient tenement	The land burdened by the existence of an easement.
Express easement	An easement created as a result of express dealings between parties and formalised using the appropriate documentation.
Implied easement	An easement which arises outside the expressed will of the parties, and which is implied into a document the result of which is to divide title to land. The methods for implication are: necessity; common intention; section 62; and the rule in *Wheeldon v Burrows*.
Prescription	A method allowing for the creation of easements through long use.
Profit	A right consisting in the ability to take from another's land—eg fishing, timber, hunting, and grazing rights.

FURTHER READING

In line with the comments in the concluding section to this chapter, the further reading here is designed to assist in the analysis of the precise details of the rules discussed, rather than giving a more socially-focused analysis of the effects of these rules.

DOUGLAS, S., 'Reforming implied easements' (2015) 131 LQR 251.
GAUNT, J. and MORGAN, P., *Gale on Easements* (20th ed), (Sweet & Maxwell, 2016).
PULLEYN, S., 'Equitable easements revisited' [2012] Conv 387.
SPARK, G., 'Easements of parking and storage: are easements non-possessory interests in land?' [2012] Conv 6.

13

FREEHOLD COVENANTS

13.1	Introduction	417	13.6 Modification and Discharge of	
13.2	The Nature of Freehold Covenants	418	Covenants—Section 84 LPA 1925	441
13.3	Creation and Interpretation		13.7 Reform of Freehold Covenants	442
	of Freehold Covenants	421	13.8 Conclusion	444
13.4	Transmissibility of Freehold		Principles	444
	Covenants	422	Table of Definitions	445
13.5	Positive Covenants	438	Further Reading	445

CHAPTER GOALS

By the end of this chapter you should understand:

- The nature of freehold covenants and the distinction between positive and negative covenants;
- How such covenants are created and interpreted;
- The different routes by which the benefit and burden of these rights attaches to land, and how this affects successors in title;
- The rules relating to positive covenants and the limited ability of such rights to bind successors in title;
- The power of the court to modify or discharge restrictive covenants; and
- The proposals for reform.

13.1 INTRODUCTION

The law relating to freehold covenants is complicated largely by its history. Such covenants provide a 'private' mechanism for controlling use of land, which sit alongside planning and environmental controls and they therefore have a very important practical role. As Gray and Gray explain: 'covenants... provide a means of binding adjacent landowners to a common plan for the user of their respective lands and often operate effectively as a form of private legislation affecting successive generations of owners'.[1] It is important, therefore, to understand this history in

---

[1] Gray and Gray, *Land Law* (7th ed) (Oxford University Press, Oxford, 2011), 126 [3–043].

order nimbly to navigate the case law and statutory provisions, and to analyse the somewhat odd distinctions which exist in relation to these rules. Furthermore, freehold covenants, like leases, are both property rights and contractual agreements, and the tensions between the principles which underpin these different areas of law is itself a source of much of the difficulty in relation to restrictive covenants. The fundamental point, however, is this: restrictive covenants, ie covenants which limit what a freehold owner is able to do in relation to their land, are, in effect, proprietary interests which can bind future holders of that land, and benefit successors in title to the original covenantee. In order to do so, a number of requirements must be met, and in modern law, the most important of these will usually be the need for the priority of such a covenant to be protected by the entry of a notice on the register. Positive covenants, ie the obligation for a freeholder owner to do something on his land, will very rarely bind future owners.

Keeping this general position in mind, there are a number of different questions which arise in relation to all freehold covenant situations. First, is the right in the nature of a freehold covenant, and, where appropriate, is it a negative or restrictive covenant? Second, has the right been created with all the appropriate and necessary formalities? Third, has the benefit of the covenant run with the land? Fourth, has the burden of the covenant run with the land? Finally, how do the priority rules affect the instant case? We will discuss these issues in turn, before considering how these rules are different in relation to positive covenants and when and how such covenants are discharged and modified. We consider issues surrounding potential reforms in the final part.

13.2 THE NATURE OF FREEHOLD COVENANTS

Freehold covenants are, at their heart, voluntary agreements entered into by one freehold owner with another person, according to which she promises to behave in a particular way in relation to her land. Strictly speaking, a 'covenant' is a promise made by deed. We discuss this formality requirement in 13.3.

There are two types of freehold covenant: positive covenants and negative covenants. The law treats these two types of promise very differently. Only negative—restrictive—covenants are treated as proprietary rights which persist with the burdened land. However, it is perfectly possible to agree a positive covenant in relation to land, and for that covenant to be enforceable by the original promisee (covenantee) as against the original promisor (covenantor). Just because the burden cannot be transmitted, that does not mean that these rights are ineffective or lacking value, and it is important to remember that the *benefit* of a positive covenant is something which can be assigned or attached to benefitted land. A negative covenant is one by which the covenantor agrees *not* to use his land in a particular way. Some very common examples relate to agreements to limit development on a site to no more than x houses; not to use a property for a particular business, such as a pub; and not to use land in such a way as to disturb the peaceful enjoyment of neighbouring properties. Positive covenants, by contrast, require (according to the rough 'shorthand' employed as a guide by the courts) that the promisor 'put his hand in his pocket' and pay money to achieve a certain end. Examples might include a promise to maintain a common access route; an agreement to maintain fencing for the benefit of a neighbour; or an agreement to keep one's land in a good condition for the benefit of the rest of an area or estate. The distinction between these two, central as it is to the operation of the rules, is one of substance not form, so that it is not possible to 'word' a covenant as being negative—not to let a fence fall into disrepair—to conceal its positive nature.

Thus, it is possible validly to create a very wide variety of covenants in relation to land which will be enforceable as between the promisor and promisee as would be the case with any promise made by deed in this way. Some, but not all of these, will be proprietary interests. However, in order to be a valid proprietary interest (or, perhaps more accurately, in order to ensure that the benefit and burden of the covenant attach to the relevant land), it is usually necessary for some further requirements to be met.

First, the covenant must be negative, that is, restrictive, in nature (except in a very narrow range of circumstances which are discussed later) in order for the burden of that right to attach to the relevant land. Secondly, it must relate to an identifiable 'dominant tenement' (to utilise the language of easements). There must also be a servient tenement equally identifiable. This requirement means that although covenants in general can be created 'in gross' (no dominant land), that is not possible if the parties wish the benefit and burden of the covenant to pass with the land. Third, it must benefit that dominant tenement. As with easements (see chapter 12), this generally means that the areas land cannot be too far apart geographically, for if they are, it is very difficult to see how the *land* (as opposed to the parties) would be benefitted by the existence of the relevant obligation. The particular wording of this test has varied over the years—originally phrased as being a question as to whether the obligation 'touched and concerned' the dominant land, it is now more usually expressed as depending upon whether the covenant was created for the benefit of that land. In practice, as long as there is an identifiable dominant tenement which would be benefited by the covenant, the fact of that benefit is effectively presumed and is usually very straightforward to demonstrate. This is logical: the nature of the real estate market means that the very fact of retaining some degree of control, however limited, of the activities of a neighbour necessarily enhances the value of the dominant land. However, as Gray and Gray highlight, the very limited function of this requirement has the benefit of filtering out ideological or prejudiced restrictions.[2] Finally, the covenant must have been made with the intention of creating a right which would bind and be enforceable by the successors in title to the original parties. As a result of the Law of Property Act 1925, this has effectively been presumed unless it is clearly expressed in the deed that the parties did not intend for the right to pass with the land. We consider these requirements in more detail throughout the chapter.

If a right meets these fundamental requirements, then it is likely, although not guaranteed, that the benefit and burden of that right will pass with the land albeit that the precise mechanics by which this occurs do present a significant degree of complexity. In certain very restricted circumstances, the benefit or burden of rights which do not meet these requirements will also pass with the land as we shall see. As mentioned earlier, the rules in general in respect of these rights has been significantly complicated by their history. In particular, there is a deep-rooted division

---

[2] Gray and Gray, *Land Law* (7th ed) (Oxford University Press, Oxford, 2011), 138.

between the rules which have developed 'at law' and those which emerged 'in equity'. This history is neatly described by Francis:

> 'First, because of the limits on enforceability [in contract]… which the Common Law imposed on such covenants… [t]he Common Law allowed the benefit of any covenant (whether positive or restrictive) to run, but not the burden. The Courts of Equity devised the rules in the first half of the nineteenth century to overcome the limitation as to the running of the burden. Since 1875, when Common Law and Equity were fused… we should not really need to worry about the historic difference nearly 140 years later. But there are some circumstances when we need to remember the distinction between the rules at Common Law and in Equity'.[3]

It is fair to say that the equitable rules are, on the whole, more 'generous' in respect of the burden of the relevant covenant, whereas the rules at law are more simple in respect of the benefit. This mismatch between the two systems can cause some confusion. This division emerged as a consequence of the fact that in the early years of the creation of these rights, they were seen more in the nature of contractual promises than in the nature of property rights. As a result, the common law in particular struggled to overcome the fundamental principle of privity of contract (ie the principle that a person not party to a contract cannot be affected by its terms). Indeed, this problem was only overcome, by equity in relation to the burden of such covenants, in the middle of the nineteenth century.[4] When compared to the much older proprietary interests such as the leasehold estate and the easement, it could be argued that up until even the 1980s there was still a fairly significant degree of uncertainty as to precisely how and when equity and the common law, as supplemented by statute, would ensure that the a restrictive covenant 'attached' to the land.[5] This means that there is still a tendency to consider these rules by reference to the historical division between law and equity, and this makes navigating the rules unnecessarily difficult. In terms of practical consequences, however, the division itself is not significant. In the majority of cases as there is no need, for instance, to match the 'route' by which the rights are being enforced. Thus, it is possible for a claimant to rely on the rules developed at law with regards to the *benefit* of the covenant to justify his bringing an action against a successor in title to the covenantor who is only *bound* by the covenant through the rules in equity. In cases where a transfer takes place in equity only, however, the distinction will become important.

Summary: Fundamental requirements in order for covenants to attach to the land

1. Covenant must be restrictive/negative in nature.
2. There must be an identifiable dominant and servient tenement.
3. The covenant must benefit the dominant tenement.
4. The covenant must have been made with the intention of creating a right which would bind and be enforceable by successors in title.

Covenants will be very unlikely to affect successors in title if these requirements are not met. However, depending on how the land is transferred amongst other factors, more may be needed in order to ensure that such successors are bound.

---

[3] Francis, *Restrictive Covenants and Freehold Land* (4th ed) (Jordans, London, 2013), 6.
[4] *Tulk v Moxhay* 41 ER 1143, (1848) 2 Ph 774 (ChD).
[5] See *Federated Homes Ltd v Mill Lodge Properties Ltd* [1980] 1 WLR 594 (CA).

13.3 CREATION AND INTERPRETATION OF FREEHOLD COVENANTS

Like almost all proprietary interests, the creation of a freehold covenant is subject to rules relating to formalities. Unlike easements, leaseholds, freeholds and mortgages however, the freehold covenant cannot exist at law. Rather, since it is excluded from section 1(2) LPA 1925, it can only exist in equity. This does not have profound effects for the operation of such rights as between the parties, but it does impact upon the formalities which are required to validly create these interests, and, of course, for how the principles of land registration operate in relation to such rights.

Because these rights are (sometimes) treated as encumbrances on land, if one seeks to create a contract for the creation of a restrictive covenant, it is necessary to create a contract which complies with section 2 Law of Property (Miscellaneous Provisions) Act 1989. As long as consideration is provided for this contract, and the contract is otherwise enforceable, this will have the effect of creating a valid restrictive covenant under the doctrine of *Walsh v Lonsdale*.[6] However, the more usual step is simply to incorporate the terms of such a covenant into a deed of covenant, thus meaning that strictly speaking no consideration is necessary in relation to the covenant itself. It will then be critical to comply with section 1 Law of Property (Miscellaneous Provisions) Act 1989 so as to create a valid deed (see chapter 4 at 4.3.2). The fact that the promise is covenanted for in a deed means, amongst other things, that there is no need for consideration to pass from the promise to the promisor, and so some restrictive covenants are 'gratuitous' in the sense that the promisee does not provide anything in return for the promisor's voluntary assumption of such obligations. Usually, such covenants are insisted upon as part of the negotiations surrounding sale of land.

It is also important to consider how such covenants are construed. This is critical, since many are drafted in rather vague wording, and it may be that the 'easiest' solution to any particular problem is simply to conclude that whether or not the relevant covenant attaches to the land, the particular plan of the successor in title to the covenantor is not actually covered by the wording of the covenant in any case. This is simply a matter of contractual interpretation, but the courts appear to be cognisant in this area in particular that a 'sensible' and practical approach is usually better than a highly technical one. Furthermore, this interpretation will take place in light of the factual matrix surrounding the agreement in order to give the words the meaning the parties intended (objectively ascertained). These principles were explained by Lord Hoffman in the famous *Investor Compensation Scheme v West Bromwich Building Society*[7] decision.

It is particularly important to think about contractual interpretation in property law in the context of freehold covenants because the scope of those rights is not determined by property law rules. We can contrast this with mortgages, leases and easements, where property law rules exist to determine the 'kinds of' terms which can form part of the agreement to create these rights. So, mortgages cannot involve terms which constitute a fetter on the equity of redemption (see chapter 11); and leases must by definition involve the grant of exclusive possession to the tenant, and must be for a defined or definable duration (see chapter 10). It is true that in order for the covenant to be one which is susceptible of transmission—both in relation to the benefit and the

---

[6] *Walsh v Lonsdale* (1882) 21 ChD 9.
[7] *Investor Compensation Scheme v West Bromwich Building Society* [1998] 1 WLR 896, 912–13.

burden—the covenant needs to be related to the land, but to be valid as an enforceable agreement this relationship to the land is not necessary. Thus, the parties are entirely in control of the content of their agreement, making the terms of that agreement critical, and the process of interpretation especially important.

13.4 TRANSMISSIBILITY OF FREEHOLD COVENANTS

Before we move on to consider the precise rules which allow for the passing of burden and benefit in relation to covenants, it is useful here to pause to consider the range of circumstances which can emerge in relation to the transmission of such rights. This is shown in diagrammatic form in the online resources. It is possible that there will be disputes between original covenantor and covenantee; between successors in title to each of those, or to just one of these; or between those deriving title from such persons, or multiple combinations of these. Thus, when you are required to assess whether parties A and B are benefitted or burdened by the relevant covenant, it is necessary as a first step to ensure you know what relationship each party is in vis-à-vis the original parties.

13.4.1 LIABILITY AND REMEDIES OF ORIGINAL COVENANTOR AND ORIGINAL COVENANTEE

The original covenantee can always enforce any express covenant against the original covenantor, provided that there has been no assignment of the benefit of rights under the contract. This is a consequence of the privity of contract rule which means that as long as the *contractual* rights are still 'in place' (have not been assigned as a matter of contract law) then the parties can still sue on the contract. This does not however tell us what remedy the covenantee will receive in circumstances where either they, or the original covenantor, have transferred their rights in the land to a third party. In cases where the covenantee has transferred the dominant land, then whilst he is able to sue for breach of covenant, he will only receive nominal damages as he has not suffered any loss. In cases where it is the original covenantor who has divested himself of the land, then he will be liable to anyone who is able to sue on the original covenant (ie who is now in privity of contract with him). In such a case however the remedy will lie only in damages so that it may be of little value to a person seeking to enforce the covenant.

The common law has always allowed parties to sue on the covenant in this way. We are concerned in this section with *personal liability* (as distinct from proprietary liability) and therefore need to know how the concept of privity of contract operates in this context. It is clear from the case law that certain modifications to the general principle that only those persons who sign the original covenant are those able to be sued and sue on it. The following sections explain when others may be considered original parties. We consider the effects of section 56 LPA 1925 and the Contracts (Rights of Third Parties) Act 1999.

Given then that the original covenantor, except in cases of (usually, authorised) assignment of the burden, will be bound always to the terms of the covenant, and the original covenantor, unless again she has assigned her rights, will also always be able to sue on the covenant, it is essential to know exactly who the original covenantor and covenantee actually are. Ninety-nine per cent of the time this is really obvious, but some difficulty has arisen when one of these parties purports, in the deed, to be executing the deed on behalf of themselves and some other subset of persons, eg the current leasehold proprietors of a subset of the freehold estate.

Let us show this with an example. In 2008 Paula became registered proprietor of a site bordering the River Welland. She was concerned about the state of the river, and entered into a covenant with her neighbours that they would ensure that their land was not put to any use which could pollute the river. In the covenant, it was stated that the covenant was made for the benefit of Paula and Paula's land (the Mill House) but also that the covenant was made with all properties backing onto the river within a particular postcode.

Is it possible to extend the 'definition' of the original covenantor/convenantee in this way? Would it make a difference if the covenant simply said that the covenant was made 'for the benefit of' the other owners, rather than 'with' them? The answer to this, effectively, is that it is possible to so-extend the class of covenantee, although not covenantor. This distinction is a result of the fact that it is generally much harder to impose an obligation onto someone without their explicit consent than it is to confer a benefit upon them.

> **Summary: Original parties**
>
> The original covenantor and covenantee can sue on the covenant, as long as the rights under the covenant have not been assigned.

13.4.1.1 Section 56, Law of Property Act 1925

The effect of section 56 Law of Property Act 1925 has been the subject of some controversy and difficulty, thanks, in part, to the inconclusive line of authority around *Smith and Snipes v River Douglas Catchment Board*.[8] Certainly, this section allows for persons other than the actual signatories to the original deed to be treated as though they were original covenantee for the purposes of privity.

The section reads as follows:

> 'A person may take an immediate or other interest in land or other property, or the benefit of any condition, right of entry, covenant or agreement over or respecting land or other property, although he may not be named as a party to the conveyance or other instrument'.

The wording of this section appears rather broad, not least because it does not specifically identify *when* this extension of the original class of covenantees can come about. However, case law tells us that it is possible when a person or group of persons is specifically identified as a party, exists, and is identifiable at the time at which the covenant was entered into. This means it is not possible to use section 56 to make a *future* owner an 'original convenantee' in this sense. Quite when someone is mentioned in a covenant with the intention that they be treated 'as a party' and when they are simply mentioned as someone who may 'benefit from' the covenant

---

[8] *Smith v River Douglas Catchment Board* [1949] 2 KB 500 (CA).

can be unclear however, despite the critical importance for this distinction for the operation of section 56. The distinction, as Megarry and Wade (the leading practitioners' guide) label it, is that between a covenant made *for* someone, and a covenant made *with* them.[9] In the previous example, this would mean that the current neighbouring owners could enforce the covenant as original parties since the covenant was expressed to be made *with* them. The case law on this distinction is however somewhat inconclusive. We consider these rules as developed through three cases: *Smith v River Douglas Catchment Board*;[10] *Beswick v Beswick*;[11] and *Beswick v Beswick*[12] in the House of Lords.

> **Key case: *Smith v River Douglas Catchment Board* [1949] 2 KB 500 and the Court of Appeal decision in *Beswick v Beswick* [1966] Ch 538**
>
> In *Smith*, the Catchment Board covenanted with the owners of lands susceptible to flooding that, in consideration for the landowners contributing to the cost of certain repairs, that they would maintain the brook. One of the covenantees transferred her land to Mr Smith. It was held that the Board was in breach of the contract and that this breach had caused damage, but the critical question was whether this allowed Mr Smith to take action against the Board. The majority of the court considered whether the benefit of the covenant had become annexed to the land (the problem being that there was no servient tenement in this case), and concluded that it had done so. Denning LJ, however, chose instead to consider whether the class of original covenantees would include Mr Smith as a successor in title. He reasoned that:
>
>> 'Section 56 means, therefore, that a person may enforce an agreement respecting property made for his benefit, although he was not a party to it. So construed it is a clear statutory recognition of the principle to which I have referred and it is applicable to this case... it should, I think have been held there that the daughters had a right at common law to sue for their pension, a right which was reinforced by s. 56. I cannot believe that the covenantors there could break their contract with impunity.'[13]
>
> He thereby suggested that successors in title could be included in the class of original covenantees where a covenant was made 'only' for someone's benefit and not *with* them, per se. This was considered by the Court of Appeal in *Beswick v Beswick*.[14] In this case Peter Beswick agreed with his nephew John Beswick that he would transfer to him the goodwill and trade of his coal business in consideration for John's employing him for the rest of his life and agreeing to pay an annuity to Peter's wife. The nephew took over the business but then refused to pay the annuity after his uncle had died. The question was whether the wife, not having signed the relevant covenant, could nevertheless enforce it.
>
> This is not a restrictive covenant case, but it did give the Court of Appeal the opportunity to revisit the argument based on section 56. Lord Denning MR therefore said of section 56: '[i]f there was, therefore,

---

[9] Harpum et al, *Megarry and Wade: The Law of Real Property* (8th ed) (Sweet and Maxwell, London, 2012), [32–007].
[10] *Smith v River Douglas Catchment Board* [1949] 2 KB 500 (CA).
[11] *Beswick v Beswick* [1966] Ch 538 (CA).
[12] *Beswick v Beswick* [1968] AC 58 (HL).
[13] *Smith v River Douglas Catchment Board* [1949] 2 KB 500 (CA), 517.
[14] *Beswick v Beswick* [1966] Ch 538 (CA).

any doubt as to her ability to sue at common law or equity, that doubt is removed by this section.'[15] Danckwerts LJ was even more forthright in reaching this conclusion:

> 'Why should the section not be taken to mean what it says? There really is no ambiguity. The section says that "A person may take ... the benefit of ... any agreement over or respecting land or other property, although he may not be named as a party to the conveyance or other instrument." The section seems to have come as a shock to conventional lawyers who could not believe their eyes, but the section does say that a person not a party can take the benefit of a contract. Faced with the unexpected and unfamiliar, there has been a tendency to take a timorous view of the provisions of this section.'[16] These two cases taken together would have given a radical role to section 56. However, as we shall see, the House of Lords did not adopt this approach.

Key case: *Beswick v Beswick* [1968] AC 58 in the House of Lords

These cases then came before the House of Lords in *Beswick*.[17] The court held that section 56 did not allow a third party to sue on the contract unless they were identified as a party. The court reasoned that section 56 had been intended merely to consolidate existing legislation, and so without clear words, ought not to be seen as having resulting in the change to the law. Thus, whilst it was clear that Parliament did accidentally alter the law, the extent of the change should be kept to the minimum which the wording of the statute permitted. Lord Reid explains this position:

> 'The context in which this section occurs is a consolidation Act. If the definition is not applied the section is a proper one to appear in such an Act because it can properly be regarded as not substantially altering the pre-existing law. But if the definition is applied the result is to make section 56 go far beyond the pre-existing law. Holding that the section has such an effect would involve holding that the invariable practice of Parliament has been departed from *per incuriam* so that something has got into this consolidation Act which neither the draftsman nor Parliament can have intended to be there.'[18]

For a third party covenantee to sue on the covenant therefore, the court held that three requirements needed to be met:

1. The beneficiary does not need to be a party to the deed. The covenant must purport to be made *with* the third party however. The person with whom the covenant is made must exist and be identifiable.

2. The section only applies to conveyances of land (rather than covenants in general) and the covenant must have been made in the form of a deed.

3. The section only applies to a deed between more than one party.

Thus, the court held that Lord Denning's approach to section 56 in *Smith*[19] was wrong.

---

[15] *Beswick v Beswick* [1966] Ch 538 (CA), 557.
[16] *Beswick v Beswick* [1966] Ch 538 (CA), 562.
[17] *Beswick v Beswick* [1968] AC 58 (HL).
[18] *Beswick v Beswick* [1968] AC 58 (HL), 77.
[19] *Smith v River Douglas Catchment Board* [1949] 2 KB 500 (CA).

As a result of these decisions, a consensus seems to have emerged, as shown by *Amsprop Trading Ltd v Harris Distribution Ltd*,[20] that the scope of persons allowed to sue as a result of the 'expanding' power of section 56 is rather limited. This makes sense: it should not be the case that a covenantor leaves themselves liable to be sued by an group of persons to which he did not intend to give such a power. However, the limitation is not one which appears naturally on a straight reading of section 56 which is rather expansive in its wording.

> **Summary: The effect of section 56, LPA 1925**
>
> This section will extent the class of original covenantees as long as they are:
>
> 1. In existence and identifiable at the time of the deed;
> 2. The covenant is one which can be considered related to property; and
> 3. The covenant is made *with* (rather than *for*) the potential claimant.
>
> Furthermore:
>
> 4. The covenant must be made in a conveyance of land; and
> 5. The covenant must be between more than one party.

13.4.1.2 Contracts (Rights of Third Parties) Act 1999

In relation to contracts entered into after 11th May 2000 it may be possible to utilise the extension of the privity rules in the Contracts (Rights of Third Parties) Act 1999, as long as a the covenant entered into in the deed constitutes a contract for the purposes of section 7(3) of that Act. There is no case law applying this statute in this way. Under these provisions, provided that the contractual agreement states that a party is able to enforce the obligations under that contract, they will so be able. Furthermore, if there is a term which purports to confer a benefit on any person, then they will also be able to sue unless there is a contrary intention expressed in the contract. This will be the case even if the person is not specifically named, but rather fits a general description, such as 'successor in title'. This has a certain potential advantage over the extension in section 56 because it does not demand that the person be in existence at the time of the contract.

Clearly the scope of this is potentially very wide, but it is important to note that again, the principle of extension of the original parties only extends to the *covenantee*. Furthermore, whilst opening out the original contractual benefit to a wide class of persons may seem to impose undue disadvantage on the original covenantor, he has of course voluntarily agreed to this in the contract. This is very different from liability which arises as a result of the proprietary nature of covenants in land, since there the original covenantor has not been able to voluntarily shape the class of persons who are able to hold him to his contractual promise.

---

[20] *Amsprop Trading Ltd v Harris Distribution Ltd* [1997] 1 WLR 1025 (ChD).

> **Summary: The liability of original covenantor and covenantee**
>
> Under the rules of privity of contract it is always possible for the original covenantor and covenatee to sue on the obligations contained in the covenant. When both parties retain possession of the relevant land, this is very simple. However, there are qualifications to this simple principle.
>
> 1. As well as the original covenantee, it is also possible for certain other persons to sue on the contract as though they were original covenantees as a result of section 56 LPA 1925. This applies to persons who are named as a party to the covenant, so that the covenant was not made *for* them, but rather was made *with* them, even if they did not sign it. The person must exist at the time of the convenant and be identifiable in order for this rule to apply.
> 2. As well as the original covenantee, it is also possible for certain other persons to sue on the contract if either they are named as a beneficiary, or a term of the contract purports to confer a benefit on them, then they will also be able to sue on the contact unless a contrary intention appears in the contract itself. This may even be the case for future persons.

13.4.2 RUNNING OF THE BENEFIT—SUCCESSOR IN TITLE TO ORIGINAL COVENANTEE SUES ORIGINAL COVENANTOR

What happens when the original covenantee has transferred their land? Is the successor in title able to sue on the covenant? In this section we consider the position where the successor in title is a legal freehold proprietor. In almost all cases the benefit of the covenant will have passed to the new owner of the freehold title. We consider three 'routes': assignment, annexation, and building schemes.

13.4.2.1 Assignment of the benefit of the covenant

First, it is possible for the benefit of the covenant to be assigned as a chose in action. This is an express transfer of the right to sue on the covenant, and it will have the consequence of bringing to an end the contractual ability of the original covenantee to sue on the contract. Assignment will normally be achieved by way of statutory assignment under section 136 LPA 1925 and so must be made in writing with written notice to the covenantor. This is an assignment of the benefit at law, and as long as the covenant was not expressly personal to the covenantee, then it will be possible to assign. The effect of this is to completely and permanently remove the ability of the covenantee to sue. This may not be the desired outcome of a covenantee dividing his land, for example, and so may not be the best solution in an instant case. We can show this with an example.

Let's imagine John owns a large estate. He divides this estate into multiple plots and wishes to bind all the new owners of the plots to a series of obligations. He sells one plot to Bruno. If he were to assign the benefit of the covenant to Bruno, he would not be able to retain the benefit himself, and therefore could not further assign the benefit onto the purchasers of another plot of land. It is therefore inconvenient to use assignment in some cases since it leaves the original covenantee without any rights, and they cannot therefore further assign.

> **Summary: Assignment**
>
> The ability to sue on a covenant can be contractually assigned.

13.4.2.2 Annexation of the benefit to the freehold estate

We are now concerned with the passing of the benefit of the ability to sue on a restrictive covenant, not in cases where that ability arises as a matter of *contract*, but where it arises as a matter of property as a result of the purported beneficiary of the covenant having become freehold owner of the dominant land. Thus, we assume here that there has been no express assignment of the rights under the covenant. We will deal with this question first *at law* on the premise here that the person attempting to enforce the covenant has become freehold legal owner. Such a person will be able to sue on the covenant if the following conditions are met:

1. The covenant touches and concerns the land of the covenantee;
2. The covenantee has a legal estate in the land benefited; and
3. There must be an intention that the covenant run with the land.

Let us consider these in turn.

The covenant must 'touch and concern' the land of the covenantee

The 'touch and concern' test, howsoever worded, is intended to express the fact that the covenant must benefit *land*, not persons only, and must do so from its inception. To put this another way, the covenant must be designed to benefit both the original covenantee and his successor in title. This will be readily assumed to be the case if the covenant increases the value of the land, for example. Where it is clear that the covenant does benefit the land, then following the decision in *Federated Homes v Mill Lodge Properties*,[21] a presumption arises that the covenant is intended to benefit each and every part of the land. This means that if land is later divided, all parts of the land will continue to have the benefit of the covenant. We consider case law on the 'touch and concern' test later (see the key case box at 13.4.4.2 on *P & A Swift Investments*).

The covenantee must have a legal estate in the land benefited

In order for the benefit of the covenant, annexed to the land, to pass to the successor in title, that person must have a legal estate in the land benefited. We consider later the circumstances where the purported claimant is not a successor in title to the original covenantee (ie legal title) but rather derives title from them. This would be the case in circumstances where the claimant takes an equitable title in the land in the absence of a valid registration of the transfer of the freehold title, for example. Whether or not this requirement is met is a function of the nature of the conveyance which has taken place, and the formalities used.

---

[21] *Federated Homes Ltd v Mill Lodge Properties Ltd* [1980] 1 WLR 594 (CA).

13.4 Transmissibility of Freehold Covenants

It must be intended that the covenant run with the land

In order for the benefit of the covenant to be annexed to the land so that it is possible for a subsequent freehold owner to be able to sue on the covenant, it is also essential that there is an intention that the covenant should run. The law on this question was significantly changed by the decision in *Federated Homes*[22] which held that the effect of section 78 Law of Property Act 1925 is to introduce a presumption that such covenants are indeed annexed to the land.

This section states:

'A covenant relating to any land of the covenantee shall be deemed to be made with the covenantee and his successors in title and the persons deriving title under him or them, and shall have effect as if such successors and other person were expressed. For the purposes of this subsection in connexion with covenants restrictive of the user of the land 'successors in title' shall be deemed to include the owners and occupiers for the time being of the land of the covenantee intended to be benefitted'.

This overturned the burden of proof explained in *Smith v River Douglas Catchment Board*[23] where Tucker LJ stated that, 'it must be shown that it was the intention of the parties that the benefit thereof should run with the land'.[24]

> **Key case:** *Federated Homes v Mill Lodge Properties* [1980] 1 WLR 594
>
> In *Federated Homes* the owner of a site which included the red, green and blue land obtained planning permission to develop the site and erect a number of dwellings. The blue land was conveyed to D. The conveyance contained a restrictive covenant. By a series of transfers, P became owners to the red and green lands. In respect of the red land the chain of assignments of the benefit of the covenant had been broken. Was the owner of the red land able to sue of the covenants? Did the benefit run with the land? The consequence of this decision has been to vastly simplify the rules relating to the passing of the benefit of a covenant. It was held that there was a restrictive covenant which related to or touched the covenantee's land and so section 78 had the effect of annexing the benefit to the covenantee's land. It was annexed to every part of the land also. This is a much wider effect than section 79 has, in relation to the burden, as we shall see. There the effect of the section is merely to introduce a presumption that the covenant was not intended to be purely personal unless it is expressed to be so. Section 78 has a substantive, rather than a probative effect, according to *Federated Homes*, which will mean that in almost all cases the benefit of a covenant will become annexed to the land.
>
> As Brightman LJ reasons: 'if the condition precedent of s78 is satisfied, that is to say, there exists a covenant which touches and concerns the land of the covenantee, that covenant runs with the land for the benefit of his successors in title, persons deriving title under him or them and other owners and occupiers'.[25]

---

[22] *Federated Homes Ltd v Mill Lodge Properties Ltd* [1980] 1 WLR 594 (CA).
[23] *Smith v River Douglas Catchment Board* [1949] 2 KB 500 (CA).
[24] *Smith v River Douglas Catchment Board* [1949] 2 KB 500 (CA), 505.
[25] *Federated Homes Ltd v Mill Lodge Properties Ltd* [1980] 1 WLR 594 (CA), 605.

Following *Federated Homes*,²⁶ there was some concern expressed that it would not be possible to contract out of the effect of section 78 since the court there had indicated that it was not subject to 'contrary intention' expressed in the covenant itself. However, it has now been held, in *Roake v Chadha*,²⁷ that in cases where a covenant is stated not to benefit the land, it would not be annexed to the land, providing a route to achieving 'contracting out'.

> **Key case: *Roake v Chadha* [1984] 1 WLR 40**
>
> In this case, the question arose as to whether it is possible, in effect, to contract out of the automatically annexing effect of section 78. The question arose because the covenant in question was expressed not to be for the benefit of subsequent purchasers. In this case, Judge Paul Baker QC said that although section 78 was not subject to a contrary intention per se, on a proper construction a covenant may not automatically be annexed where it is stated not to benefit the land as it would not meet the requirement expressed in *Federated Homes* that the covenant had to benefit the land. It would therefore be possible to contract out in fact.

This was taken further in the subsequent decision in *Crest Nicholson Residential (South) Ltd v McAllister*,²⁸ where Chadwick LJ reasoned that there was no reason to make section 78 mandatory, so that he would permit the effect of the section to be simply excluded by express words.

> **Key case: *Crest Nicholson Residential (South) Ltd v McAllister* [2004] EWCA Civ 410**
>
> In this case two brothers bought an estate and formed a company to sell off the land in plots. Three individual purchasers each acquired a plot and then by three more conveyances each acquired a further plot. All the conveyances contained restrictive covenants. Three of the conveyances contained express words of annexation. The court held that section 78 only operated to annex the benefit to such land as the conveyance identified as intended to be benefitted and only in so far as the conveyance did not express a different intention. Furthermore, section 78 does not get rid of the requirement that the benefitted land be ascertainable. Kenny explains the result of this decision:
>
> > 'The judgment of Chadwick L.J. in *Crest Nicholson* is a model of clarity. It explains what is meant by saying that s.78 of the Law and Property Act 1925 causes 'automatic statutory annexation'. He makes it clear that annexation takes place under s.78 only in respect of the land of the covenantee which is intended to be benefited. It is still necessary to construe the conveyance or transfer as a whole to identify what the land is which is intended to be benefited'.²⁹

These rules have been very recently considered by the Chancery Division in *Doberman v Watson*.³⁰

---

[26] *Federated Homes Ltd v Mill Lodge Properties Ltd* [1980] 1 WLR 594 (CA).
[27] *Roake v Chadha* [1984] 1 WLR 40 (ChD).
[28] *Crest Nicholson Residential (South) Ltd v McAllister* [2004] EWCA Civ 410, [2004] 1 WLR 2409.
[29] Kenny, 'Conveyancer's notebook (January/February)' [2006] Conv. 2006 1, 6.
[30] *Doberman v Watson* Ref. HC-2017–000370.

13.4 Transmissibility of Freehold Covenants

> **Key case:** *Doberman v Watson* Ref. HC-2017–000370
>
> This case highlights the importance of ensuring that land is identifiable at the time of the covenant in order for it to be annexed to the land. Halpern QC sitting as a deputy judge of the High Court emphasised the importance of the land being identifiable from the conveyance. Commenting on *Crest Nicholson*, he reasoned:
>
> > 'the land to be benefited must be defined so that it is readily ascertainable. In this case, as I have already said, the land to be benefited is identified in some conveyances at the vendor's building estate but it is not clearly defined in any of them and in some of them there is no mention of it at all'.[31]
>
> Taking *Crest Nicholson* and *Doberman* together, we can say that section 78 will only have the effect of automatically annexing the benefit of a covenant to benefitted land if (a) there is no contrary intention expressed in the conveyance showing either that the covenant should not be annexed, or that the covenant is purely personal; and (b) the benefitted land can actually be identified from the conveyance. A covenant saying that the covenant is for the benefit of 'nearby land' for example, would not result in annexation as it would be completely unclear what land was intended to be benefitted.

If these requirements are met, then the consequence is that the benefit of the covenant will automatically pass at law and will attach to the freehold title to this property. It is immaterial to the operation to this rule whether the covenant is positive or negative. It is also irrelevant, in fact, whether the covenantor has any land.

> **Summary: Benefit of a covenant**
>
> The benefit of a covenant will be annexed to the land, so that it passes to the successor in title without contractual assignment, if there is no contrary intention expressed in the covenant, and as long as the benefitted land can be identified from and is benefitted by the covenant.

13.4.2.3 Building schemes

Although in cases where there is a legal transfer of title to land, section 78 will usually assist the claimant, it may sometimes be necessary to utilise the rules relating to building schemes in case where, for example, the order in which various plots were sold make it problematic to conclude that the claimant is entitled to the benefit of the covenant (it was entered into after the potentially benefitted land was carved off from the common whole). It should be noted here that it is not easy to meet the requirements of building schemes.

We can explore this with an example. Imagine Kit purchases a large development site outside Stratford-upon-Avon. He decides that he wants the site to retain a Shakespearian character and so drafts a series of restrictive covenants limiting what purchasers of property on the site can do with the outsides of their homes and gardens. He sells the first plot to Portia who covenants for the benefit of Kit's land and his successors in title. Kit then sells the second plot to Mercutio.

---

[31] *Doberman v Watson* Ref. HC-2017–000370, [16].

Mercutio signs the same covenant. This would mean that Portia was unable to sue Mercutio for breach of the covenant, although Kit's intention was that the covenants would be enforceable not only by him but by all other residents of the estate so as to ensure enforcement of the covenants both now and into the future.

The key case in relation to building schemes is *Elliston v Reacher*.[32]

Key case: *Elliston v Reacher* [1908] 2 Ch 665

This case establishes four requirements before the courts will find that a building scheme has been created.

1. Both plaintiff and defendant derive title from a common vendor.
2. Prior to the sale of the estates to the respective parties, the common vendor laid out his estate or part thereof for sale in lots 'subject to restrictions intended to be imposed on all the lots, and which … are consistent and consistent only with some general scheme of development'.
3. The general restrictions were intended to be for the benefit of all the lots.
4. Both parties or their predecessors in title purchased the lots upon the understanding that the restrictions were for the benefit of other lots included in the general scheme and that there was a degree of reciprocity in this.

Summary: Passing of the benefit at law

There are three routes by which the benefit of a covenant can be passed on to a successor in title to the freehold estate at law. First, the benefit may pass by express assignment made with the appropriate formalities. Second, it may pass by annexation of the benefit to the freehold title. In order for annexation to occur, three requirements must be met:

1. The covenant must touch and concern or benefit the land of the covenantee. This land must be reasonably identifiable.
2. The original covenantee and the successor in title must have a legal estate in the land.
3. It must be intended that the covenant pass with the land. This intention is presumed as a result of section 78 Law of Property Act 1925.

Third, the successor in title may rely on the rules relating to building schemes.

13.4.3 RUNNING OF THE BENEFIT—PERSON DERIVING TITLE FROM THE ORIGINAL COVENANTEE SUES ORIGINAL COVENANTOR

In the previous section we were considering the situation where the purported claimant is a *successor* in title to the original covenantee. This has two consequences. First, in cases of transfer of freehold estate, this means we are talking about a legal transfer, and therefore the

---

[32] *Elliston v Reacher* [1908] 2 Ch 665 (CA).

rules earlier were concerned with the situation in which the benefit of a covenant can pass at law. Second, it was assumed that the original covenantee and the claimant had the same estate in land, both physically in terms of its scope, and legally (freehold not leasehold). What happens when one, or both, of these features are missing? We consider here the passing of the benefit where the covenantor has a different estate in geographical scope, and the passing of the benefit in equity.

13.4.3.1 Geographical scope

We are concerned here with whether the fact that the claimant has a different estate in terms of size from the original covenantor affects the annexation of the benefit at law. This is relevant when an original covenantee, or a successor in title to them, divides their land. We can see an example of this in Kit's Shakespearian estate earlier. It has been held that the effect of section 78 LPA 1925 in this context is that there is no need for the claimant and the original covenantee to have the same estate. This is the consequence of the decision in *Federated Homes*[33] that the covenant is presumed to be annexed to each and every part of the covenantee's land.

13.4.3.2 Different legal estate—tenancies

It is also immaterial to the passing of the benefit at law that the purported claimant has a tenancy rather than succeeding to the freehold title. All that matters is that the lease is a legal one, and this depends on the manner of the creation of the lease, and the property rights of the grantor.

13.4.3.3 Claimant only has an equitable interest in the land

What about cases where the 'difference' between the original convenantor's estate and the claimants is not one of geographical scope per se, but where the conveyance to the claimant was one made at equity so that they must demonstrate that the benefit passed in equity. How might this situation arise?

Imagine that Gavin, registered freehold proprietor of a large and luxurious country estate, covenants with Douglas that Douglas will not build more than five houses on his neighbouring property. Gavin, tiring of the country life, decides to sell his property to Lynne. The parties execute a deed of transfer, but absent-mindedly forget to register the transfer. At this point, Gavin will hold the property on trust for Lynne. Is Lynne able to sue on the covenant?

There are three ways in which the benefit can be passed in equity.

Annexation

Once annexed to the land the benefit will always be annexed. This means that as soon as the benefit of the covenant attaches to the land, any person deriving equitable title 'from then on' will have the benefit of the relevant rights. This annexation can be express or implied. Annexation in equity can be more problematic than at law. First, it is essential that there is an intention in the covenant to benefit the covenantee by benefitting his land. Without this, annexation in equity is not possible as explained in *Re Union of London and Smith's Bank Ltd's Conveyance*[34] and *Newton*

---

[33] *Federated Homes Ltd v Mill Lodge Properties Ltd* [1980] 1 WLR 594 (CA).
[34] *Re Union of London and Smith's Bank Ltd's Conveyance* [1933] Ch 611 (CA).

Abbott Cooperative Society Ltd v Williamson & Treadgold Ltd[35] Secondly, the scope of the benefitted land must be reasonably ascertainable from the terms of the covenant. Bearing in mind that we are dealing in this section with cases where the benefitted land is potentially not the same as the original land of the original covenantee, this may be somewhat difficult to prove. The difficulties which can arise in this respect are demonstrated by *Newton Abbott Cooperative Society Ltd v Williamson & Treadgold Ltd.*[36]

> **Key case:** *Newton Abbott Cooperative Society Ltd v Williamson & Treadgold Ltd* [1952] Ch 286
>
> In this case an ironmonger conveyed property opposite these premises to a purchaser. The conveyance contained a covenant by the purchaser not to carry on the business of an ironmonger. The relevant land was then passed under will to the ironmonger's son, but there was never any assent in writing in respect of the restrictive covenant. The owners of the premises opposite started to sell ironmongery items. The question which arose was whether there was an annexation of the benefit of the covenant in this case. It was held that there was nothing in the conveyance which identified the land for the benefit of which the covenant was alleged to be taken. Where a person is suing on the basis of annexation of the benefit of a covenant there must be something in the deed containing the covenant to define the land for the benefit of which the covenant was entered into. The court will however be reasonable and will look to the surrounding circumstances to determine this to see if the land can be identified with reasonable certainty. That was the case here and so the claimant could enforce the covenant. Thus, in cases of annexation, this case highlights that the benefitted land must be clear, but this can be determined from both the circumstances of the case and the wording of the conveyance itself.

Assignment

It is also possible to assign the benefit of a covenant in equity. This would not have the effect of attaching the right to the land per se, but it would give the transferee the ability to sue whilst also depriving the original covenantee of their ability so to do.

Building schemes

Finally, it is possible for the benefit of a covenant to pass in equity if the rules relating to building schemes discussed earlier are met.

> **Summary: Passing of the benefit in equity**
>
> There are three methods by which the benefit of a covenant can pass in equity.
>
> 1. Annexation
> 2. Assignment
> 3. Building schemes

[35] *Newton Abbott Cooperative Society Ltd v Williamson & Treadgold Ltd* [1952] Ch 286 (ChD).
[36] *Newton Abbott Cooperative Society Ltd v Williamson & Treadgold Ltd* [1952] Ch 286 (ChD).

13.4.4 RUNNING OF THE BURDEN—RESTRICTIVE COVENANTS

Very simply, at law, the burden of a covenant will not run as held in *Austerberry v Oldham Corp*.[37] Equity has intervened to mean that the burden of restrictive covenants can run in equity as a result of the decision in *Tulk v Moxhay*.[38] The consequence of this is that the burden of positive covenants will never run but under some circumstances, the burden of negative covenants will do so. It is important however to remember that even if the burden of a covenant does run with the land, it will only be binding upon a future purchasers of registered land if the priority rules in the Land Registration Act 2002 (LRA 2002) protect the covenant upon transfer, as explained in detail in chapter 15.

At the time of the decision in *Tulk v Moxhay*,[39] the explanation for the case was unclear, and the court in *Tulk* itself seemed to base the decision in whole or in part on the conscience of the purchaser. However, over time, the courts have accepted that the restrictive covenant should now be treated as a species of proprietary entitlement. In order for this proprietary right to emerge, the requirements established in *Tulk v Moxhay*[40] are: (1) that the covenant is restrictive; (2) that there are two plots of land, one servient, one dominant; (3) the dominant land is benefitted by the covenant; (4) that it was intended that the covenant run with the land/the covenant is not purely personal; and (5) the priority of the covenant is protected under section 28-30 LRA 2002 (registered land).

13.4.4.1 There is a servient and a dominant tenement

We have already considered the meaning of requirement (1). Some guidance is given on the second requirement by *London CC v Allen*.[41]

> **Key case: *London CC v Allen* [1914] 3 KB 642**
>
> In this case the owner of certain land applied for permission to lay a new street on the land. The council agreed to give their sanction on the condition that the owner entered into a covenant not to build on a plot of land that lay across the end of the proposed street. The owner then entered into a covenant to this effect. The Council did not possess any neighbouring land for the benefit of which the covenant was imposed. The owner then sold this plot with notice of the covenant. The purchaser then built the houses on the land without the council's consent. The court decided that where the owner of land who derives title under a person who has entered into a restrictive covenant, which does not run with the land at law, is not bound in equity even if he took notice of its existence, if the covenantee is not in possession of or interested in land for the benefit of which the covenant was entered into. Per Buckley LJ: 'where the covenantee has no land, the derivative owner claiming under the covenantor is bound neither in contract nor by the equitable doctrine which attaches in the case where there is land capable of enjoying the restrictive covenant'.[42]

---

[37] *Austerberry v Oldham Corp* (1885) 29 Ch D 750 (CA).
[38] *Tulk v Moxhay* 41 ER 1143, (1848) 2 Ph 774 (ChD).
[39] *Tulk v Moxhay* 41 ER 1143, (1848) 2 Ph 774 (ChD).
[40] *Tulk v Moxhay* 41 ER 1143, (1848) 2 Ph 774 (ChD).
[41] *London CC v Allen* [1914] 3 KB 642 (CA).
[42] *London CC v Allen* [1914] 3 KB 642 (CA), 653.

13.4.4.2 The dominant land is benefitted by the covenant

From the case law, there is effectively a presumption that a covenant relating to specified land will also benefit that land. Where, however, the land benefitted is unclear from the covenant itself, the position will be more complex for the claimant. Exactly what 'benefit' means in this context, however, has historically been somewhat difficult thanks to the archaic language of the 'touch and concern' test. Some guidance is provided in the modern context by *P & A Swift Investments v Combined English Stores Group*.[43]

Key case: *P & A Swift Investments v Combined English Stores Group* [1989] AC 632

This case is actually concerned with landlord and tenant covenants rather than freehold covenants but it nevertheless gives very useful assistance in determining when a covenant will 'touch and concern' land and therefore benefit it. Lord Oliver proposes a 'test' (or at least, a guide) to help determine whether a covenant does so touch and concern.

> 'Formulations of definitive tests are always dangerous, but it seems to me that, without claiming to expound an exhaustive guide, the following provides a satisfactory working test for whether, in any given case, a covenant touches and concerns the land: (1) the covenant benefits only the reversioner for time being, and if separated from the reversion ceases to be of benefit to the covenantee; (2) the covenant affects the nature, quality, mode of user or value of the land of the reversioner; (3) the covenant is not expressed to be personal (that is to say neither being given only to a specific reversioner nor in respect of the obligations only of a specific tenant); (4) the fact that a covenant is to pay a sum of money will not prevent it from touching and concerning the land so long as the three foregoing conditions are satisfied and the covenant is connected with something to be done on to or in relationto the land'.[44]

Francis gives some guidance as to the sorts of categories of benefit which the courts have recognised:[45]

1. Protection from competing trade;[46]
2. Protection from certain forms of development;[47]
3. Use of conditions (eg relating to approval of plans);[48] and
4. Protection of the neighbourhood generally.[49]

---

[43] *P & A Swift Investments v Combined English Stores Group* [1989] AC 632.
[44] *P & A Swift Investments v Combined English Stores Group* [1989] AC 632, 642.
[45] Francis, *Restrictive Covenants and Freehold Land* (4th ed) (Jordans, London, 2013), [7.55].
[46] *Newton Abbott Cooperative Society Ltd v Williamson & Treadgold Ltd* [1952] Ch 286 (ChD).
[47] *Wrotham Park Estates Co v Parkside Homes* [1974] 1 WLR 798.
[48] *Marten v Flights Refuelling Ltd* [1962] Ch 115.
[49] *Wrotham Park Estates Co v Parkside Homes* [1974] 1 WLR 798.

13.4.4.3 It was intended that the covenant run with the land/the covenant is not purely personal

In relation to the running of the burden, the intention requirement is affected not by section 78 Law of Property Act 1925, but by section 79. The consequence of this section is, as we have noted, that the intention that the covenant pass with the land is presumed. The effect of section 79 can be rebutted by express or implied words in the conveyance, as demonstrated by *Morrells of Oxford v Oxford United FC*.[50] As Francis expresses this: 'this section does not have the effect of making a personal covenant one which binds successors to the original covenantee'.[51] Rather, the effect of section 79 is to presume an intention that the covenant is not personal.

> **Key case:** *Morrells of Oxford Ltd v Oxford United Football Club Ltd* [2001] Ch 459
>
> Morrells owned a pub in Blackbird Leys, Oxford. In 1962 the land was transferred from Oxford City Council to Morrells' predecessor. Oxford United FC had covenanted with the Council that no land within ½ mile of the land that owned by the football club would be used for selling liquor. Oxford United bought land within ½ mile of the pub from the Council. The Court of Appeal was required to assess whether the Council could be liable for the operation of the pub by Morrells. The court considered whether section 79 could be impliedly excluded. Robert Walker LJ held that it could be, recognising that a fair reading of the contract here would prevent section 79 operating to extend the liability. He also gave some guidance on the effect of section 79, stating:
>
>> 'My tentative view, therefore, coinciding, I think, with the judge's, is that section 79, where it applies, and subject always to any contrary intention, extends the number of persons whose acts or omissions are within the reach of the covenant in the sense of making equitable remedies available, provided that the other conditions for equity's intervention are satisfied'.[52]
>
> Walker LJ also examined the House of Lord's judgment in *Earl of Sefton v Tophams*,[53] examining the divergences between the judges there. In minimising the significance of these differences, he concluded:
>
>> 'Section 79 is concerned with simplifying conveyancing by creating a rebuttable presumption that covenants relating to land of the covenantor are intended to be made on behalf of successors in title, rather than be intended as purely personal. That is a necessary condition, but not a sufficient condition, for making the burden of the covenants run with the land'.[54]
>
> In this respect, and in respect of the effect of section 79 regarding original covenantors, however, we can certainly take from this case that it can be impliedly excluded.

---

[50] *Morrells of Oxford Ltd v Oxford United Football Club Ltd* [2001] Ch 459 (CA).
[51] Francis, *Restrictive Covenants and Freehold Land* (4th ed) (Jordans, London, 2013), [7.61].
[52] *Morrells of Oxford Ltd v Oxford United Football Club Ltd* [2001] Ch 459 (CA), [35].
[53] *Earl of Sefton v Tophams Ltd (No.2)* [1967] 1 AC 50 (HL).
[54] *Morrells of Oxford Ltd v Oxford United Football Club Ltd* [2001] Ch 459 (CA), [40].

13.4.4.4 Notice and registration

A restrictive covenant which is otherwise enforceable will always retain priority against a donee or devisee because they are not purchasers. In registered land, this is the principle enshrined in section 28 LRA 2002 which emphasises that the normal priority rule (ie cases not covered by section 29 or 30—see chapter 15) will be a 'first in time rule'. By definition, the covenant was created prior to the relevant transfer or there would be no need to consider the transmission of the burden. If, however, the transferee provides valuable consideration for the acquisition of the estate or interest there must be registration of the covenant in order for the covenant to bind. Where title to the land is unregistered, any restrictive covenants will be registerable as land charges under the Land Charges Act 1972. Where title is registered, a restrictive covenant requires protection by means of a notice against the burdened title, LRA 2002 s32(1). Of course, it is possible that the beneficiary of the covenant could be in actual occupation of the burdened land at the time of the disposition so that the requirements of schedule 3 paragraph 2 are met, but this is extremely unlikely.

> **Summary: Burden of a covenant**
>
> The burden of a covenant cannot pass at law. It is possible for the burden of restrictive covenants to pass in equity. This will occur if:
>
> 1. The covenant is restrictive
> 2. There are two plots of land, one servient, one dominant
> 3. The dominant land is benefitted by the covenant
> 4. It was intended that the covenant run with the land/the covenant is not purely personal; and
> 5. The priority of the covenant is protected.

13.5 POSITIVE COVENANTS

As noted, the general rule is that it is not possible for the burden of positive covenants to run at all. It is possible however to circumvent this rule—indeed, this is one of the main justifications cited by those advocating reform (see 13.7). For example, it is possible to use a chain of covenants, or to make acceptance of the burden of a covenant a condition for the enjoyment of the benefit, as demonstrated by *Halsall v Brizell*.[55] Chain of covenants pose an inherent risk but are in practice extremely common. Once the chain is broken it is not possible to revive it but a failure on the part of a conveyancing solicitor to monitor the chain in this way would almost certainly constitute negligence on their part, offering an alternative route of redress.

The jurisprudence surrounding the benefit and burden principle is somewhat difficult to navigate. There is a dispute in the literature as to what qualifications and requirements the leading

---

[55] *Halsall v Brizell* [1957] Ch 169 (ChD).

cases in this area—*Halsall v Brizell*[56] and *Rhone v Stephens*[57]—mandate in order for the principle to operate. The principle is relatively intuitive at first glance. As Gravells explains it:

> '[p]ursuant to the so-called "pure principle", a benefit conferred by a transaction and a prima facie independent burden imposed by the same transaction may become linked, so that successors in title to the original parties who wish to enjoy the benefit are bound also to assume the linked burden, even where that burden involves a positive obligation'.[58]

According to Gravells, the independence of the benefit and the burden is important, or otherwise it could simply be argued that the benefit/burden principle is nothing more than a way of explaining conditional rights. This may be entirely correct, but it makes it difficult to determine whether *Halsall v Brizell*,[59] which shows the inter-connectness of the rights, is a case involving the principle at all, even though it is said to be the foundational case for that principle!

Key case: *Halsall v Brizell* [1957] Ch 169

This case involved an estate known as Cressington Park in Liverpool. The purpose of the covenant was to ensure that the purchasers of plots on the estate would contribute to the cost of upkeep of a promenade and the estate roads. The court held that if the residents wished to use these roads and other facilities, then they would need to accept the reciprocal obligation to pay for their upkeep. Per Upjohn J:

> 'If the defendants did not desire to take the benefit of this deed… they could not be under any liability to pay the obligations thereunder. But, of course, they do desire to take the benefit of this deed… Therefore, it seems to me that the defendants here cannot, if they desire to use this house, as they do, take advantage of the trusts concerning the user of the roads contained in the deed and the other benefits created by it without undertaking the obligations thereunder. Upon that principle it seems to me that they are bound by this deed, if they desire to take its benefits'.[60]

This element is relied upon by later courts, particularly in *Rhone v Stephens*.[61]

Key case: *Rhone v Stephens* [1994] 2 AC 310

This case gives us further guidance on the operation of the benefit and burden principle and on the debate surrounding what *Halsall v Brizell*[62] actually decided. The case involved a covenant requiring the holder of land to pay for the upkeep of roof overhanging her land belonging to a neighbour. The court refused to enforce the obligation, upholding the general principle in *Austerberry v Oldham Corp*[63]

---

[56] *Halsall v Brizell* [1957] Ch 169 (ChD).
[57] *Rhone v Stephens* [1994] 2 AC 310 (HL).
[58] Gravells, 'Enforcement of positive covenants affecting freehold land' (1994) 110 LQR 346, 348.
[59] *Halsall v Brizell* [1957] Ch 169 (ChD).
[60] *Halsall v Brizell* [1957] Ch 169 (ChD), 182–3.
[61] *Rhone v Stephens* [1994] 2 AC 310 (HL).
[62] *Halsall v Brizell* [1957] Ch 169 (ChD).
[63] *Austerberry v Oldham Corp* (1885) 29 Ch D 750 (CA).

that the burden of a positive covenant could never run with the land, and refusing to apply the benefit and burden principle to the case on the grounds that there was no intimate link between the supposed benefit and burden. This called into question how we should understand what *Halsall v Brizell*[64] actually decided.

On that case, in *Rhone*,[65] Lord Templeman stated that:

> 'I am not prepared to recognise the "pure principle" that any party deriving any benefit from a conveyance must accept any burden in the same conveyance.... Conditions can be attached to the exercise of a power in express terms or by implication. *Halsall v Brizell* was just such a case and I have no difficulty in wholeheartedly agreeing with the decision. It does not follow that any condition can be rendered enforceable by attaching it to a right nor does it follow that every burden imposed by a conveyance may be enforced by depriving the covenantor's successor in title of every benefit which he enjoyed thereunder. The condition must be relevant to the exercise of the right'.[66]

In other words, Lord Templeman seems to be of the view that *Halsall*[67] is not an example of the principle of benefit and burden at play, but rather is an example of a conditional right. Snape, in analysing this case, sees Lord Templeman's comments as an outright rejection of the possibility of the pure benefit and burden principle,[68] although Gravells does not think the case goes as far as that.[69] Either way, considering *Rhone v Stephens*,[70] it is clear that the court sees the benefit burden principle as being limited in its scope, albeit that its precise parameters remain somewhat unclear.

This was considered further in *Thamesmead Town v Allotey*.[71]

Key case: *Thamesmead Town v Allotey* (1998) 30 HLR 1052

The case concerned the possibility of enforcing two payments: one for the upkeep of roads and sewers within the estate, and the other for the upkeep of general and common areas. This case gives further guidance on how we should interpret *Rhone v Stephens*'[72] approach to the benefit and burden principle. Peter Gibson LJ here reasons that there are two requirements for the enforceability of a positive covenant. The first is that the discharge of the burden must be relevant to the exercise of the rights which enables the benefit to be obtained. In Dixon's words, the one must be the 'flipside' of the other.[73] The second is that the successors in title must have the opportunity to chose whether to take the benefit or to renounce it so as to escape the burden. He thus highlights both the reciprocity and the optional nature of the obligation, bringing the interpretation closer to the 'conditional benefit' approach rather than the 'pure' benefit and burden principle interpretation of what this rule achieves.

---

[64] *Halsall v Brizell* [1957] Ch 169 (ChD).
[65] *Rhone v Stephens* [1994] 2 AC 310 (HL).
[66] *Rhone v Stephens* [1994] 2 AC 310 (HL), 322.
[67] *Halsall v Brizell* [1957] Ch 169 (ChD).
[68] Snape, 'The burden of positive covenants' [1994] Conv 477.
[69] Gravells, 'Enforcement of positive covenants affecting freehold land' (1994) 110 LQR 346.
[70] *Rhone v Stephens* [1994] 2 AC 310 (HL).
[71] *Thamesmead Town v Allotey* (1998) 30 HLR 1052 (CA).
[72] *Rhone v Stephens* [1994] 2 AC 310 (HL).
[73] *Thamesmead Town v Allotey* (1998) 30 HLR 1052 (CA), 337.

It is also possible for the burden of a positive covenant to pass in relation to leasehold estates as we explained in chapter 10. For this reason, a very common technique in new housing estates is for the developer to sell long leaseholds rather than freeholds. This allows the developer to retain a degree of control over the aesthetics of an estate, assisting them should they still be selling housing on the estate.

> **Further analysis: Should the burden of positive covenants run?**
>
> The justification behind this rule is summarised by Lord Templeman in *Rhone v Stephens*:[74]
>
>> 'For over 100 years it has been clear and accepted law that equity will enforce negative covenants against freehold land but has no power to enforce positive covenants against successors in title of the land. To enforce a positive covenant would be to enforce a personal obligation against a person who has not covenanted. To enforce negative covenants is only to treat the land as subject to a restriction.'[75]
>
> This justification is not, however, universally accepted and it is certainly inconvenient in many commercial situations for positive covenants to be so difficult to enforce directly. The reliance on leasehold estates to allow for the enforcement of such covenants in particular is seen as an unnecessarily cumbersome device. Thus, as Gravells argues:
>
>> 'Few would dissent from the view that in appropriate circumstances positive covenants should be capable of enforcement against successors in title to the original covenantor; that enforcement should be through direct means rather than through indirect means, which are artificial and frequently unreliable; and that the continued absence of such direct means is inconvenient and potentially unjust. Since the House of Lords has now clearly ruled out a judicial solution, it is for Parliament to provide a legislative solution.'[76]
>
> Indeed, it seems that it is only a failure of Parliament to intervene that has prevented the creation of such a rule. As we shall see later, in its most recent report the Law Commission has advocated the changing of the law in this respect, but whether or not this will actually happen remains to be seen.

> **Summary: Positive covenants**
>
> The burden of a positive covenant will run either through a chain of express assignments, or, very rarely, under the benefit and burden principle.

13.6 MODIFICATION AND DISCHARGE OF COVENANTS—SECTION 84 LPA 1925

Many of the millions of historic restrictive covenants which burden land in the UK are, for all practical purposes, obsolete and very unlikely to affect the land at all, or are significantly burdensome in respect of reasonable uses of land. For this reason, many people seek to have such

---

[74] *Rhone v Stephens* [1994] 2 AC 310 (HL).
[75] *Rhone v Stephens* [1994] 2 AC 310 (HL), 321.
[76] Gravells, 'Enforcement of positive covenants affecting freehold land' (1994) 110 LQR 346, 350.

covenants discharged so that they can be removed from the title, largely as a matter of conveyancing simplicity, or to have them modified to permit a particular use or development. Often this can be done merely by agreement between the parties. However, there are also more contentious claims for a covenant to be modified or discharged. These matters are dealt with under the jurisdiction of section 84 LPA 1925 which allows the Upper Tribunal (Lands Chambers) to make such an order. This provision has not been a total success. It is relatively difficult and expensive to have a covenant discharged or modified in this way. Nevertheless, the Law Commission at least recommended retaining the jurisdiction and indeed hopes to extend it to a wider class of rights. The four grounds upon which the covenant can be discharged appear in the statute.

They are (appearing in section 84(1)):

'(a) that by reason of changes in the character of the property or the neighbourhood or other circumstances of the case which the Upper Tribunal may deem material, the restriction ought to be deemed obsolete, or

(aa) that in a case falling within subsection (1A) below the continued existence thereof would impede some reasonable user of the land for public or private purposes... or, as the case may be, would unless modified so impede such user; or

(b) that the persons of full age and capacity for the time being or from time to time entitled to the benefit of the restriction, whether in respect of estates in fee simple or any lesser estates or interests in the property to which the benefit of the restriction is annexed, have agreed, either expressly or by implication, by their acts or omissions, to the same being discharged or modified; or

(c) that the proposed discharge or modification will not injure the persons entitled to the benefit of the restriction'.

It is very rare for a claimant to succeed under paragraph (a) here, and if a claimant does succeed this tends to be under ground (aa) and to result in a modification of the covenant rather than a full discharge and with a compensation payment.

13.7 REFORM OF FREEHOLD COVENANTS

In 2011 the Law Commission produced a report recommending reform of the law relating to covenants.[77] There has been no legislation in response to this report. It is still nevertheless useful to consider the Law Commission's findings as starting point for unlocking your own analysis of these rules. First, and inevitably, the Law Commission criticised the law relating to freehold covenants as being unduly and inappropriately complex and messy. This it undoubtedly is, and, (arguably) unlike the law relating to easements causes significant problems in practice, particularly with the law relating to the running of the benefit and the identification of a claimant to enforce such covenants. Secondly, they are critical of the rule against the running of the burden of positive covenants.

---

[77] Law Commission, *Making Land Work: Easements, Covenants and Profits à Prendre* report no. 327 (London, 2011).

'(1) It is difficult to identify who has the benefit of a restrictive covenant for two reasons:

   (a) there is no requirement that the instrument creating the covenant should describe the benefited land with sufficient clarity to enable its identification without extrinsic evidence; and

   (b) the benefit of a restrictive covenant, being an equitable interest, cannot be registered as an appurtenant interest on the register of title to the dominant land.

(2) There are differing and complicated rules for the running of the benefit and burden of restrictive covenants.

(3) The contractual liability between the original parties to a covenant persists despite changes in the ownership of the land; when the land is sold, the original covenantor remains liable.

(4) Whereas the benefit of a positive covenant can run at law, the burden of a positive covenant does not run so as to bind successors in title.'[78]

As a result of these arguments, they conclude that a new right in land should be created, the 'land obligation'.

Given that it is now somewhat unlikely that any action will emerge in respect of this new right (unless certain reforms relating to the commonhold estate- explained in chapter 9- later come to fruition), it is perhaps unnecessary to consider the structures that the Law Commission wanted to introduce. It is however still important to think, in particular, about their arguments in favour of allowing positive covenants to run with land. It is very difficult to think of any reason why it would not be better for the law relating to restrictive covenants to be more straightforward! The main argument presented by the Law Commission in favour of making positive covenants run is in fact the complex nature of the workarounds which parties employed to avoid this rule. As the Law Commission themselves state, the question is not really whether they *should* run, since parties already employ a wide range of structures to attempt to achieve this and will continue to do so, but rather whether there should be a clear and easy mechanism to bring about this outcome:

> 'The "workarounds" described above are products of the determination of practitioners in the face of a prohibition imposed by *Keppell v Bailey*[79] that impedes the arrangements that their clients want to make. So the task for this project is not to justify positive obligations, starting from a clean slate, but to recommend reforms that would provide a simpler and more practicable method to achieve what can already be done, in a way that minimises the economic burden upon properties and their owners.'[80]

However, the Law Commission did recognise that there are a number of challenges with making such obligations into property rights, not least the potential for an increased amount of litigation and potential difficulties of enforcing such covenants. To avoid these issues, the Commission considered whether it would be appropriate to limit the types of obligations which could be enforced

---

[78] Law Commission, *Making Land Work: Easements, Covenants and Profits à Prendre* report no. 327 (London, 2011), [5.4].
[79] *Keppell v Bailey* 39 ER 1042, (1834) 2 My & K 517.
[80] Law Commission, *Making Land Work: Easements, Covenants and Profits à Prendre* report no. 327 (London, 2011), 5.38.

as positive covenants. By and large the Commission rejected this approach, stating only that the covenants would be controlled by the 'touch and concern' test, a solution which takes advantage of the existing expertise of the courts.

Whether or not the Law Commission proposals do ever come to fruition, we can say that the law relating to freehold covenants is not straightforward to explain. There are a number of frankly needless complications which linger in modern law thanks to the historical, and relatively recent, development of the rules. However, in practice, the vast majority of restrictive covenants not expressed to be personal will run with the land—both benefit and burden—and be enforceable by and against original covenantor and covenantee and their successors in title. Given the social and economic benefits of such rights, simplicity in achieving this outcome would indeed be welcome.

13.8 CONCLUSION

In a way similar to the previous chapter, the law regarding restrictive covenants is analytically interesting from the perspective of the complexity and 'piecemeal' nature of the rules. The policies behind the rules are fairly straightforward, and the practical effects do not cause any major discomforts within the wider land law system. In short, whilst it cannot be denied that the rules are a mess, and they cause problems in practice because of that, they do not significantly undermine or shape the way the law operates as a whole. From an examiners' perspective this makes them ideal for problem questions.

PRINCIPLES

How does this mean that restrictive covenants shape the balance of the principles operating in relation to land law? To recap, these principles were:

1. Certainty
2. Sensitivity to context
3. Transactability
4. Systemic and individual effects
5. Recognition of the social role of the land law system.

The answer is that restrictive covenants do not have an enormous impact on these principles. The principles which are compromised by restrictive covenants are without a doubt those of certainty and transactability. Indeed, the cost associated with untangling a mess of restrictive covenants can be high. However, in practice many people will either simply negotiate on a 'without prejudice' basis with their neighbours, to get permission to carry out development even if it does breach a covenant which no one ever decides is actually binding, or they will pay money to a neighbour to discharge any covenant where it is inconvenient. If this does not work, many parties will simply take out insurance. This means that the costs of the transaction might be high, but the risks relatively low. This allows parties to make a valid assessment of the merits of carrying out any particular development in the 'shadow' of a covenant, without ever having to determine its real legal effects. Furthermore, in lots of cases, parties will simply not know that a covenant existed at some point, and thanks to the effects of registration on priority disputes, the covenant will become postponed to the freehold estate and therefore practically irrelevant.

We might say that this is not enough and that the law should be reformed in line with Law Commission proposals so that parties do not need to operate in the 'shadows' like this, but rather will know their legal position and respond accordingly. Part of the problem with this is that many restrictive covenants are historical—the Law Commission proposal will not remove the problem of determining whether the covenant has become annexed to the land at some time in the past, nor will it undo decades of drafting in light of these rules. Thus, it may be simpler to leave things as they are, even though some practical problems are caused.

TABLE OF DEFINITIONS

Covenant	A promise made by deed.
Covenantor	The person making a promise by deed.
Covenantee	The person to whom a promise is made in a deed.
Assignment	The process by which the benefit and burden of rights is contractually assigned.
Annexation	The process by which the benefit and burden of rights becomes attached to the land and therefore passes regardless of the contractual position.
Restrictive/ negative covenant	A covenant which limits the use to which servient land can be put, and which does not require the covenantor to expend money.
Positive covenant	A covenant which requires the coventantor to expend money.
Touches and concerns	The requirement that a covenant must benefit land, not persons only, and must do so from its inception.

FURTHER READING

Similar to easements, the further reading here focuses on giving more detail in the operation of the rules, rather than in respect of analysis considering the social effects of these rules.

CASH, A., 'Freehold covenants and the potential flaws in the Law Commission's 2011 reform proposals' [2017] Conv 212.

FRANCIS, A., *Restrictive Covenants and Freehold Land* (5th ed) (Jordan Publishing, 2019).

O'CONNOR, P., 'Careful what you wish for: positive freehold covenants' [2011] Conv 191.

14

ESTATE CONTRACTS, OPTIONS TO PURCHASE, AND RIGHTS OF PRE-EMPTION

14.1 Introduction	446	14.5 Conclusion	460
14.2 Estate Contracts	447	Principles	460
14.3 Options to Purchase	455	Table of definitions	461
14.4 Rights of Pre-Emption	458	Further Reading	461

CHAPTER GOALS

By the end of this chapter, you should understand:

- The different kinds of estate contract;
- The rights which arise from estate contracts and their potential effects on third parties; and
- How options to purchase and rights of pre-emption work in practice.

14.1 INTRODUCTION

This short chapter is concerned with estate contracts, options to purchase and rights of pre-emption. For many land law courses, these rights only need to be understood in outline detail. However, having some understanding as to how such rights operate is actually very important for two reasons. First, it gives an insight into the commercial reality of many transactions in relation to land, and the mechanisms which exist in respect of land as an asset (rather than the rules relating to implied trusts (chapter 7) and estoppel (chapter 8), for example, which are more directly focused on land as home). Second, recent case law has meant that issues have arisen surrounding the question of overreaching in relation to such interests. A deeper understanding of the structural implications and features of these rights will allow a more thorough analysis of that case law. The debates surrounding the issues of the proprietary status of such rights, their nature, and the way they interact with the general principles of land law, give a good deal of insight into the nature of property rights in general.

'Estate contracts' is a generic term given to contracts relating to the intended transfer of estates in land, ie the freehold and leasehold estate. The consequence of an estate contract varies depending upon the kind of interest which it is intended will be created and the precise nature of the agreement reached between the parties. This can lead to some conceptual difficulties.

Options to purchase and rights of pre-emption are two kinds of estate contract. Both involve an agreement between a freehold or leasehold proprietor, and a potential purchaser in relation to that estate. An option to purchase entitles its holder to demand that the proprietor sell that estate to them, usually within a defined time period, for a pre-determined or determinable price. The right of pre-emption is, in effect, a right of first refusal. It does not allow its holder to force the proprietor of the estate in land to sell, but means that if that person does decide to sell, it must first be offered to the holder of the pre-emption right. More detail on the precise requirements of these rights will be given in 14.3 and 14.4. Section 14.2 is concerned with the generic category of estate contracts and the complexities which arise in relation to these.

14.2 ESTATE CONTRACTS

Estate contracts are, as the name implies, contracts in which a promise is made for the disposition of an estate in land. On the grounds that 'equity sees that which ought to be done as having been done' (see chapter 4, 4.3.1.3), once the contract is formed, assuming that it is a contract which could be specifically enforced (as is the case with almost all contracts involving land given the uniqueness of land as an asset), equity would treat the situation as though the estate had *already* been transferred. This would give rise to an equitable version of that interest, albeit on the same terms as the legal interest would be once the deed and any other formality requirements were completed. This so-called 'accelerating effect' is also referred to as the rule in *Walsh v Lonsdale*.[1] At first glance, it would seem to make sense that this doctrine applied only to contracts relating to estates in land, that is to say, contracts to transfer or create a freehold or a leasehold interest.

14.2.1 INTERESTS OTHER THAN FREEHOLD AND LEASEHOLD ESTATE

However, the position appears more general than this, and an equitable easement, for example, will arise in cases where there is a failure to complete all the required formalities but there is a binding written contract to that effect. This is not without controversy however, and it is not entirely clear, as Pulleyn explains, whether:

> 'in equity, easements are assimilated to leases so as to fall wholly within the scope of the rule in *Walsh v Lonsdale* or whether they are (in the alternative or additionally) assimilated to some other species of equitable right. Either outcome will have consequences for the formalities needed. If an equitable easement is like an equitable lease, the former will only arise where there is a specifically enforceable contract to create one'.[2]

---

[1] *Walsh v Lonsdale*, (1882) 21 ChD 9.
[2] S Pulleyn, 'Equitable Easements Revisited' [2012] Conv 387, 387.

Certainly, on analysis of the case law it is clear that an equitable easement will arise if a section 2 Law of Property (Miscellaneous Provisions) Act 1989-compliant contract is present. Whether less will suffice, such as a document which complies with section 53(1)(a), is unclear. Gardner and Mackenzie suggest that this would be enough.[3] Pulleyn argues, however, that the grant of an equitable easement in this way requires a contract.[4] Thus, although strictly speaking it may not be legitimate to refer to such agreements as 'estate contracts', it is nevertheless important to recognise what the effect of such agreements will be.

14.2.2 NATURE OF THE RIGHT WHICH ARISES

Turning now to contracts relating to the freehold and leasehold estate, the operation of the rule relating to estate contracts about the coming into being of an equitable interest in the relevant land as soon as the contract is agreed (in a valid form), looks very simple. In basic terms it means that a contractual agreement gives rise to an equitable version of whatever legal right the parties have contracted to grant. This has already been discussed in chapter 4 at 4.3.1.3. However, on closer inspection, the operation of this rule is not nearly as simple as it looks. This is because, on the execution of the contract, if the remedy of specific performance is indeed available and the purchase price has been paid, in cases where what is involved is the *transfer* of an existing legal interest (rather than the creation of a new one), a so-called 'vendor-purchaser constructive trust' arises.[5] But it may be, that the rights from estate contracts are *different* from the rights arising under this trust. This section considers the nature of such rights.

14.2.2.1 Separate rights–estate contract and trust

Important for this chapter is the analysis present in cases such as *Sookraj v Samaroo*[6] that the equitable interest arising from the specifically enforceable contract is something *different* from the trust which arises when the pre-completion payment of (some) purchase money is made. As Lord Scott explains,

> '[a] purchaser who enters into a specifically enforceable contract for the sale of land acquires an equitable interest in the land and retains that interest for as long as the contract remains enforceable. On making pre-completion payments on account of the price the purchaser acquires also an equitable lien on the land to secure their repayment'.[7]

Gray and Gray have agreed with this analysis it appears, to a certain extent seeing the equitable interest arising as part of the specifically enforceable contract as being something different from the 'trust' which emerges (and which develops through the different stages of the

---

[3] S Gardner and E MacKenzie, *Introduction to Land Law* 4th Ed.
[4] S Pulleyn, 'Equitable Easements Revisited' [2012] Conv 387, 404.
[5] The foundational case for this is *Lysaght v Edwards*, (1876) 2 ChD 499.
[6] *Sookraj v Samaroo* [2004] UKPC 50, [2005] 1 P&CR DG11.
[7] *Sookraj v Samaroo* [2004] UKPC 50, [2005] 1 P&CR DG11, [15]. See also C Harpum et al, *Megarry & Wade: The Law of Real Property* 8th ed (Sweet & Maxwell, London, 2012), [15.054].

conveyancing process from something akin to a purchaser's lien to a bare trust).[8] Similarly, Thompson reasons:

> '[t]he beneficial interest that the purchaser acquires is dependent on payment of the purchase price and not simply upon the entry into the contract of sale. It is the equivalent of a lien. The beneficial interest that the purchaser acquires seems to be independent of the notional ownership acquired simply by entry into the contract of sale'.[9]

If this is right, then the estate contract has an existence which is separate from the vendor-purchaser constructive trust. It may bind a purchaser in its own right. If the contractual right and the trust have, in a sense, an independent existence, arising from different 'triggering events', then the situation for both third parties and the proposed vendor becomes problematic. This makes it important also to establish when an estate contract comes to an end, ie to determine when the contract is complete. In registered land, the case law suggests that this is probably when payment is made and the deed is executed, rather than when the title is actually registered (*Abbey National v Cann*[10] and *Scott v Southern Pacific*[11]). We can discern from this three separate stages in the development of these rights (assuming that the estate contract and the trust do have some sort of existence independent from one another—or at least, have different effects). The conceptual confusion about the precise nature of these rights can give rise to practical problems on closer inspection, as we can see in *Baker v Craggs*.[12]

Key case: *Baker v Craggs* [2016] EWHC 3250 (Ch), [2018] EWCA Civ 1126 in the High Court and Court of Appeal

Briefly, this case involved a contract to transfer title to the freehold estate of a farm. Once the deed had been created, but before the legal title was registered, the vendors purported to grant the benefit of an easement over the land to be transferred. The question for the court was first, whether the grant of an easement in this way could be an overreaching transaction (the High Court said yes, and critically the Court of Appeal said no). If this was an overreaching transaction, then the question emerged as to whether the rights under a estate contract could be overreached (it is clear that the rights under a vendor-purchaser constructive trust can be). Overreaching was summarised in chapter 3, and is explained in more detail in chapter 15 at 15.6.4 and chapter 16 at 16.4.3.1. The High Court held that grant of the easement constituted a grant of a legal estate for the purposes of overreaching, and so considered whether the interest of the potential purchaser, ie either their estate contract or their vendor-purchaser trust, could be overreached.

Newey J reasoned as follows. He first analysed the existing case law to determine what kind of interest the purchaser had at the time of the grant of the easement. Considering *Scott v Southern Pacific*[13] and

---

[8] K Gray and S Gray, *Elements of Land Law* 5th ed (OUP, Oxford, 2009), [8.1.62]–[8.1.66].
[9] M P Thompson, 'The widow's right' [1996] Conv 295, 300.
[10] *Abbey National v Cann* [1991] 1 AC 56 (HL), 85.
[11] *Re North East Property Buyers Litigation (Scott v Southern Pacific Mortgages Ltd)* [2014] UKSC 52, [2015] AC 385.
[12] *Baker v Craggs* [2016] EWHC 3250 (Ch), [2017] 2 WLR 1483; [2018] EWCA Civ 1126.
[13] *Re North East Property Buyers Litigation (Scott v Southern Pacific Mortgages Ltd)* [2014] UKSC 52, [2015] AC 385.

Abbey National v Cann,[14] he held that at the completion of the deed and the payment of the purchase money, the contractual agreement no longer had any 'force' so that the only interest that the purchaser had would be an interest under a trust which could be overreached.[15] The decision of the High Court was widely criticised, and the decision of the Court of Appeal, which is completely orthodox on the question of overreaching, has been welcomed. The Court of Appeal is also clear that the relevant interest was the trust arising *on completion* of the sale (ie the conveyance in the deed, and the payment of purchase money). The decision of the Court of Appeal is primarily significant for questions around the scope of overreaching. However, from the question of the estate contract, it emphasises analysis elsewhere that there are three stages to a transaction: the creation of a contract (from which is derived a property right in the form of an estate contract); the completion of the sale through the deed and payment of the purchase money (from which is derived a property right in the form of a vendor-purchaser constructive trust); and registration, the result of which is to transfer legal title and collapse the trust. Whilst the Court highlights that the trust can be overreached, the question as to whether the estate contract could be is not addressed. This is in doubt because of the statutory provisions which we shall now explore.

To examine this further, a good starting point is to begin with a more detailed examination of each of the stages in a conveyance.

Step one: exchange of contracts. At this point, as long as a binding contract which complies with section 2 Law of Property (Miscellaneous Provisions) Act 1989 and is otherwise specifically enforceable has been created, the purchaser will have the benefit of an equitable interest arising under an estate contract. At this point in the conveyancing process, assuming *Baker v Craggs*[16] is correctly decided (or, under an alternative analysis in line with *Lloyds Bank v Carrick*[17] where the Court of Appeal reasoned that the purchaser in this position has nothing more than a contractual right), then the purchaser's interest cannot be overreached on a transfer of title to the property by two trustees. This is because it seems beyond doubt that estate contracts as a generic category cannot be overreached. For more on the types of interest which cannot be overreached, see chapters 15 and 16. Thus, the prospective purchaser would actually be in a better position, since his interest could not have been overreached.

Step two: completion of the conveyance and the creation of the trust. The vendor will now become subject to a form of trust (or, as Gray and Gray imply, this may be better considered to be a lien,[18] agreeing with *Sookraj v Samaroo*[19] cited earlier). Furthermore, that this relationship is something different from the estate contract itself is supported by the Law Commission in Law Com No 191,[20] and by the decision in *Cumberland Consolidated Holdings Ltd v Ireland*[21] which

---

[14] *Abbey National v Cann* [1991] 1 AC 56 (HL).
[15] *Baker v Craggs* [2016] EWHC 3250 (Ch), [2017] 2 WLR 1483.
[16] *Baker v Craggs* [2016] EWHC 3250 (Ch), [2017] 2 WLR 1483.
[17] *Lloyds Bank v Carrick* [1996] 4 All ER 630 (CA).
[18] K Gray and S Gray, *Elements of Land Law* 5th ed (OUP, Oxford, 2009), [6.1.46] and [8.1.62] (the purchaser's lien does not require a specifically enforceable contract, although it may better capture the nature of the purchaser's rights on exchange of contracts).
[19] *Sookraj v Samaroo* [2004] UKPC 50, [2005] 1 P&CR DG11.
[20] Law Commission, 'Transfer of Land: Risk of Damage after Contract for Sale', Law Commission Report no. 191 (1990), [2.7].
[21] *Cumberland Consolidated Holdings Ltd v Ireland* [1946] KB 264 (CA).

seems to result in the imposition of (some) fiduciary duties onto the vendor. These duties which would not arise purely by virtue of the contract, suggesting that the obligations arising by the trust go beyond those arising in the contract itself.

At this point, there is little doubt that the vendor becomes a bare trustee, holding on trust for the purchaser under a constructive trust.[22] There is nothing to suggest that the trust itself cannot be overreached. Therefore, the most critical question becomes whether the estate contract essentially disappears on the creation of the deed and the payment of the purchase money. Certainly, this is the apparent view of the Supreme Court in *Scott v Southern Pacific*,[23] where Baroness Hale highlights that at the point where all that is left is the 'conveyancing machinery' of registration, such that the interest is one vulnerable to be overreached:

> '[a]ssuming that all relevant registration requirements are met, the purchaser has now acquired an absolute right to the legal estate (and the mortgagee an absolute right to the charge). Her interest is of a different order from that of a purchaser before completion, who has the contractual right to have the property conveyed to her but may never in fact get it.'[24]

In becoming an interest 'of a different order', as explained in *Baker v Craggs*,[25] the interest becomes one which is vulnerable to overreaching. This is also the approach taken in *Abbey National v Cann*,[26] where it is submitted that the estate contract 'folds' on the completion of the deed.

However, that this is what happens in registered land is not a matter beyond doubt. There is a cogent argument that there are still contractual obligations regulating the parties' relationship up until the point where title is registered, not least an implied term that the vendor not attempt to prevent registration of the title by, for example, contacting the land registry. Thus, even if the interests are two separate interests, there is an argument that the estate contract survives the completion of the deed and payment of the purchase money, so that whilst the interest under the trust could, in theory, be overreached, the interest arising by virtue of the estate contract could not.

Step three: registration. For completeness, at this point, it is certain that the contract and the transfer merge, so that there is only the estate in land granted where the grant was completed by registration.

Finally, it is important to realise that the precise operation of the estate contract as an independent interest is one which has not been subjected much to the scrutiny of the courts in cases where a trust has arisen. In many situations, whether it is the contract or the trust which does it, the proprietary reach of both would be sufficient to protect the prospective purchaser against a third party. Only in cases where there are two trustees of the relevant land does the question arises as to whether the interest of the purchaser, whatever it is, may be overreached. In many circumstances, therefore, the complexity of the nature of the right arising by the estate contract is not one which causes problems, and in many estate contract cases, ie in cases

---

[22] *Bridges v Mees* (1957) Ch; *Lloyds Bank v Carrick* [1996] 4 All ER 630 (CA).
[23] *Re North East Property Buyers Litigation (Scott v Southern Pacific Mortgages Ltd)* [2014] UKSC 52, [2015] AC 385.
[24] *Re North East Property Buyers Litigation (Scott v Southern Pacific Mortgages Ltd)* [2014] UKSC 52, [2015] AC 385, [113].
[25] *Baker v Craggs* [2016] EWHC 3250 (Ch), [2017] 2 WLR 1483.
[26] *Abbey National v Cann* [1991] 1 AC 56 (HL), 85.

involving a contract to do something other than transfer an existing legal estate, the question simply does not arise since there is no doubt that the interest arising by the estate contract cannot be overreached.

14.2.2.2 There is only one interest

However, there is a very cogent argument that there are not two interests in play here, and that the division between steps one and two is illusory. This argument posits that the interest arising under the estate contract, which is designed to transfer an estate in land, *is* a trust. This means that estate contracts relating to the attempted transfer of an estate in land do not result in the 'normal' equitable property right arising through the contract, but instead simply give rise to a trust. In such a case, the interest under the trust would be capable of being overreached, regardless of the fact that it as a trust interest arising as a result of a contract. This is certainly the most simple outcome, but it is not one which sits comfortably with some of the case law. Ferguson explains the appeal of this argument: '[t]o argue that the trust continues to bind the land in the hands of a purchaser when the contract has ceased to do so is to neglect this dependence upon contract, treating the trust instead as a wholly free-standing legal relationship'.[27] Note, however, in making this argument, Ferguson appears to accept that it is possible that the estate contract can be overreached.[28]

14.2.2.3 A practical approach

Whichever of these options is correct, it is useful to be able to navigate the various options in play. We will now examine this by considering a conveyance involving a transfer of a lease. The options are 'labelled' according to the case which best supports the outcome, without suggesting that this case is binding authority for this option.

The following diagrams explain this:

In figure 14.1, there is no problem, since although there is a contractual agreement which results in the grant of the lease by deed, since the formality requirements of registration are complete, we can say Ys no longer have an interest emerging under the contract itself, since the

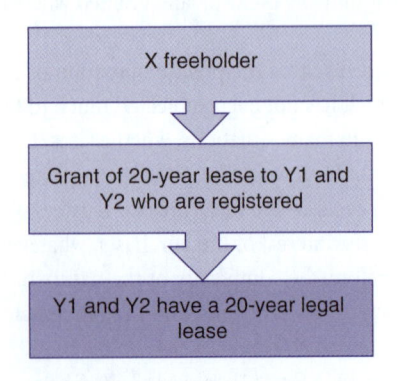

```
X freeholder
    ↓
Grant of 20-year lease to Y1 and
Y2 who are registered
    ↓
Y1 and Y2 have a 20-year legal
lease
```

Figure 14.1 Completed transfer

---

[27] P Ferguson, 'Estate contracts, constructive trusts and the Land Charges Act' (1996) 112 LQR 549, 550.
[28] P Ferguson, 'Estate contracts, constructive trusts and the Land Charges Act' (1996) 112 LQR 549, 551.

contract is completed in that sense. Since legal interests cannot be overreached (except in a very limited set of circumstances, primarily involving a mortgage, see chapter 11), the lease cannot here be overreached. This much is entirely uncontroversial.

In figure 14.2, the position is more difficult. If *Baker v Craggs*[29] (and this is supported by the approach in the Court of Appeal, albeit not decided there) is right, then the estate contract would have ended through completion of the deed. If that analysis is correct, then Z's interest, being only an interest under the trust and having no other equitable interest in the land, would be overreached on the further conveyance by Y1 and Y2 to O. This is the most simple explanation, but it is controversial, not least because it means that Z is actually in a *worse* position once the purchase money is paid and all the formalities, apart from registration itself, are complete.

A similar outcome is reached (shown in Figure 14.3) if we consider that the interest under the trust and the estate contract are really one and the same thing so that there is only one interest, the trust interest, albeit that this interest shifts in terms of the obligations arising as a result of the trust relationship through the various stages of the conveyance. Again, if this is correct, then the trustees of the trust of land are able to overreach the interest under the trust. This might be best

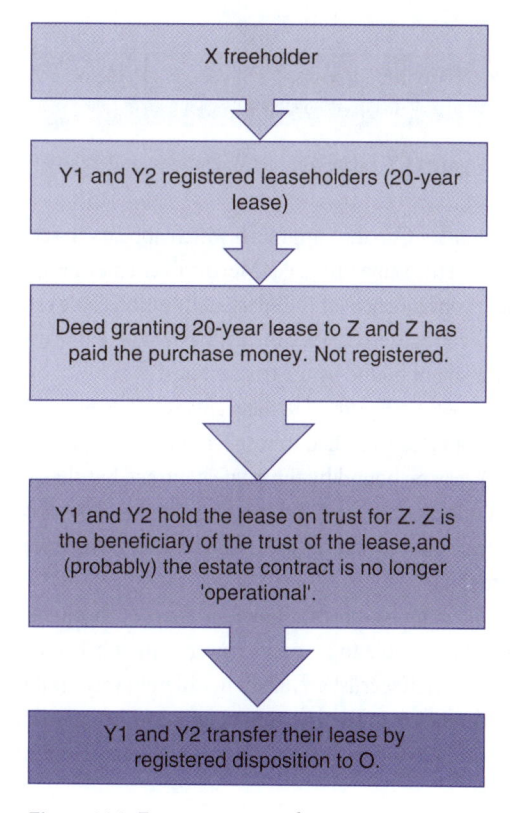

```
X freeholder
    ↓
Y1 and Y2 registered leaseholders (20-year lease)
    ↓
Deed granting 20-year lease to Z and Z has paid the purchase money. Not registered.
    ↓
Y1 and Y2 hold the lease on trust for Z. Z is the beneficiary of the trust of the lease, and (probably) the estate contract is no longer 'operational'.
    ↓
Y1 and Y2 transfer their lease by registered disposition to O.
```

Figure 14.2 Estate contract and trust are separate

---

[29] *Baker v Craggs* [2016] EWHC 3250 (Ch), [2017] 2 WLR 1483.

```
┌─────────────────────────┐
│      X freeholder       │
└─────────────────────────┘
            │
            ▼
┌─────────────────────────────┐
│ Y1 and Y2 registered        │
│ leaseholders (20-year lease)│
└─────────────────────────────┘
            │
            ▼
┌─────────────────────────────────┐
│ Estate contract and trust are   │
│ one interest granting 20-year   │
│ lease to Z and Z has paid the   │
│ purchase money. Not registered. │
└─────────────────────────────────┘
            │
            ▼
┌─────────────────────────────────┐
│ Y1 and Y2 hold the lease on     │
│ trust for Z. Z is the           │
│ beneficiary of the trust of the │
│ lease arising through contract. │
└─────────────────────────────────┘
            │
            ▼
┌─────────────────────────────────┐
│ Y1 and Y2 transfer their lease  │
│ by registered disposition to O. │
└─────────────────────────────────┘
```

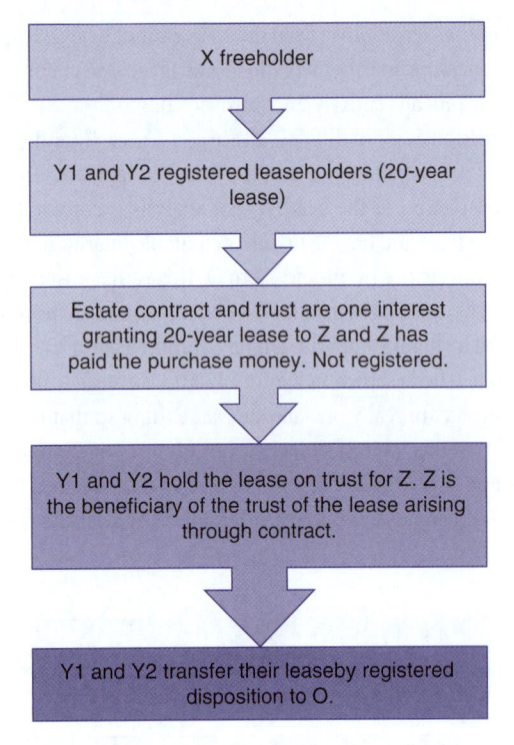

Figure 14.3 Estate contract and interest under the trust merge

described as the *Lloyds Bank v Carrick*[30] approach which appears to see the estate contract and the trust interest as one and the same thing. Per Merritt LJ cited by Ferguson,[31] 'the trust interest was merely an "equitable consequence" of the specifically enforceable estate contract, which was registrable but had not been registered. Since the bank could take free of that contract (by virtue of L.C.A., s.4(6)), it was also not bound by the trust interest'.[32]

Under the approach shown in Figure 14.4, the rights which Z has, although overreachable in respect of the trust, cannot be overreached in respect of the estate contract. This could result in the odd situation that O may be bound by the estate contract, but that Y1 and Y2 hold the proceeds of the subsequent sale on trust for Z. This precise outcome does not appear to be present in the case law, but is a logical consequence of cases like *Samaroo*[33] which see the estate contract and the trust as two separate rights.

Whichever of the explanations is correct, however, there is absolutely no doubt that the position is one which is not amenable to an easy answer. This is because the estate contract and the vendor-purchaser constructive trust are, albeit in different ways, both outcomes which cause conceptual difficulties. In relation to the first, we do not know its nature, if it is something different from the trust. In relation to the second, this trust is an unusual one, not giving rise to the full range of fiduciary duties.

---

[30] *Lloyds Bank v Carrick* [1996] 4 All ER 630 (CA).
[31] P Ferguson, 'Estate contracts, constructive trusts and the Land Charges Act' (1996) 112 LQR 549.
[32] P Ferguson, 'Estate contracts, constructive trusts and the Land Charges Act' (1996) 112 LQR 549.
[33] *Sookraj v Samaroo*, [2004] UKPC 50, [2005] 1 P&CR DG11.

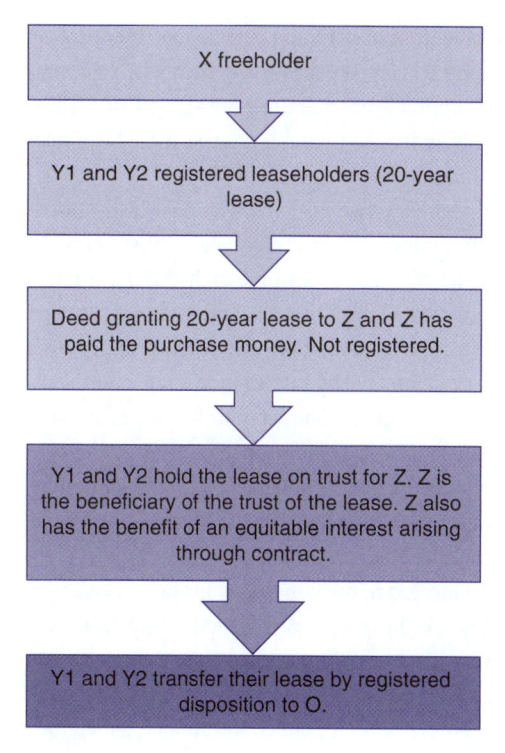

```
┌─────────────────────────┐
│      X freeholder       │
└─────────────────────────┘
            │
            ▼
┌─────────────────────────────────────┐
│ Y1 and Y2 registered leaseholders   │
│          (20-year lease)            │
└─────────────────────────────────────┘
            │
            ▼
┌─────────────────────────────────────┐
│ Deed granting 20-year lease to Z    │
│ and Z has paid the purchase money.  │
│           Not registered.           │
└─────────────────────────────────────┘
            │
            ▼
┌─────────────────────────────────────┐
│ Y1 and Y2 hold the lease on trust   │
│ for Z. Z is the beneficiary of the  │
│ trust of the lease. Z also has the  │
│ benefit of an equitable interest    │
│         arising through contract.   │
└─────────────────────────────────────┘
            │
            ▼
┌─────────────────────────────────────┐
│ Y1 and Y2 transfer their lease by   │
│     registered disposition to O.    │
└─────────────────────────────────────┘
```

Figure 14.4 Persistent estate contract

Summary: Estate contracts, vendor-purchaser trusts, and overreaching

There are three stages in the conveyancing process: the creation of a contract which gives rise to an estate contract; the completion of the deed and the payment of the purchase money which gives rise to a trust; and registration which dissolves the trust and fulfils the contract by transferring legal title. The main problem which emerges from this is that estate contracts cannot be overreached, whereas trust interests can be overreached. As a result, there is uncertainty at stage two, whether the potential purchaser has *two* interests—the estate contract, and an interest under a trust—or just one, the interest under the trust. This question is not fully resolved in the case law.

If the former option is correct, then the strange position emerges whereby although the trust interest is overreached, the estate contract would not be, leaving purchasers potentially bound. If the latter is correct, then a similarly strange result emerges, which is that the purchaser is *worse off* for having paid the purchase money.

14.3 OPTIONS TO PURCHASE

As stated earlier, an option to purchase is a right which entitles its holder to force the proprietor of an estate in land, be that freehold or leasehold, to transfer their estate in land. There is no requirement on the option-holder to purchase the land. In this sense, the option can be distinguished from conditional contracts, where the obligations to buy and sell may only come into being upon certain events, eg the obtention of planning permission. There are certain requirements which must be met before a contract can take the form of an option to purchase (and thereby obtain its *in rem* status). Since the option is not mentioned in section 1(2) Law of Property Act 1925, once created, the right can only exist as an equitable interest. It can be protected by the entry of a notice on the register and it cannot be overreached.

In order to be valid, there are two essential features which must be present. First, if created before 6th April 2010, the option must be exercisable within a defined and limited period of time. It cannot be available to be exercised at any time in the future, or it would offend the rule against perpetuities. For options created after this date, the rule against perpetuities no longer applies thanks to the Perpetuities and Accumulations Act 2009. Second, the option contract must specify a price either fixed, or determinable by reference to some neutral standard, the property to be purchased, etc. In essence, the option contract must be precise as to its terms. An option which is not precise on such matters may be void for uncertainty. In order to create a valid option, some formalities must be complied with. It is possible to grant an option by deed, but it is more usual to use a contract, in which case the requirements of section 2 Law of Property (Miscellaneous Provisions) Act 1989 must be met.

One problem which emerged in relation to options to purchase immediately after the coming into force of section 2 Law of Property (Miscellaneous Provisions) Act 1989, was the issue as to whether a decision to exercise the option needed to be in signed writing, specifically, whether it needed to be signed by *both* parties, despite being an essentially unilateral act. This may sound like a somewhat trivial problem, but it pointed to and highlighted the difficulty that exists in determining what an option to purchase actually is: is it a contract for sale, albeit a conditional one (so that the exercise of the option would not constitute a contract in itself), or is it a offer to sell which cannot be revoked, so that the exercise of the option would be the acceptance of the offer, requiring the signature of both parties and all the terms of the sale to be contained in a single document before it could be considered a valid contract? The slippery nature of the option to purchase is famously captured in the words of Jordan CJ, that an option is 'nearly always a ticklish thing'.[34] This issue was considered in *Spiro v Glencrown*.[35] Here Hoffman J concluded that, 'an option is not strictly speaking either an offer or a conditional contract'.[36]

> **Key case:** *Spiro v Glencrown* [1991] Ch 537
>
> In this case, the owner of a freehold estate in a property in Finchley in North London granted an option to purchase, which was exercisable by 5pm on that same day. The purchaser attempted to exercise the option by giving written notice of his intention by 5pm. However, the purchaser subsequently changed his mind and no longer wished to exercise the option. The purchaser argued that his exercise of the option was not binding as it did not meet the requirements of section 2 Law of Property (Miscellaneous Provisions) Act 1989. The vendor argued that it did not need to so-comply, and that he was therefore entitled to damages from the purchaser.

---

[34] *Mackay v Wilson* (1947) 47 SR (NSW) 315, 318.
[35] *Spiro v Glencrown* [1991] Ch 537 (ChD).
[36] *Spiro v Glencrown* [1991] Ch 537 (ChD), 544.

In answering this question, Hoffman J, as he then was, first explained that, absent authority to the contrary, his assessment was that section 2 was intended to apply to the contract for the option, and not the exercise of that option. He reasoned as follows:

> 'Section 2, which replaced section 40 of the Law of Property Act 1925, was intended to prevent disputes over whether the parties had entered into a binding agreement or over what terms they had agreed. It prescribes the formalities for recording their mutual consent. But only the grant of the option depends upon consent. The exercise of the option is a unilateral act. It would destroy the very purpose of the option if the purchaser had to obtain the vendor's countersignature to the notice by which it was exercised. The only way in which the concept of an option to buy land could survive section 2 would be if the purchaser ensured that the vendor not only signed the agreement by which the option was granted but also at the same time provided him with a countersigned form to use if he decided to exercise it. There seems no conceivable reason why the legislature should have required this additional formality.'[37]

Hoffman J then reviewed the authorities to assess whether the he was obligated to conceptualise an option as an irrevocable offer, rather than a form of conditional contract, in the sense explained earlier. The key case was *Helby v Matthews*,[38] where the option was so described. However, Hoffman J explained: '[t]hey [the judges in that case] were not using "offer" in its primary sense but, as often happens in legal reasoning, by way of metaphor or analogy. Such metaphors can be vivid and illuminating but prove a trap for the unwary if pressed beyond their original context.'[39]

Not all commentators are convinced by this explanation of the previous authority, however, and the matter remains somewhat controversial.

Stark, for example, analysing this case, concludes:

> 'We may, however, be some way to discovering the true nature of an option to purchase. It is indeed a relationship *sui generis*. It is not a contract for the sale of the land itself but a contract granting a right to call for the sale of the land. On the one hand, the courts have regarded the purchase of an option as being the purchase of an interest in the land, whereby the purchaser acquires rights over the land. On the other, the courts have recognised that an option does not confer the same rights in the land as are conferred by an ordinary contract for the sale of land. That is why for example the courts have refused to hold that options grant the purchaser a beneficial interest in the property as would be the position between contract and conveyance in an ordinary contract for the sale of land. The option is a legal hybrid. Perhaps it would have been preferable, rather than to characterise it as a conditional contract, to recognise that although it is indeed only an offer for sale, it is a unique offer in that it is enforced by a contract.'[40]

Once an option has been entered into, it fetters the proprietor's ability to sell and it has the potential to bind third parties so that any subsequent purchaser of the estate in breach of the option, may well be subject to the option, depending on the priority rules. Per Jessel MR in *London and Southwestern Railway Company v Gomm*: 'the right to call for a conveyance of the land is an equitable interest… In the ordinary case of a contract for purchase, there is no doubt about this.'[41]

In terms of the priority rules, if the land is registered then the question as to whether the option to purchase is capable of binding the purchaser of the title to the land depends on whether, first,

---

[37] *Spiro v Glencrown* [1991] Ch 537 (ChD), 541.
[38] *Helby v Matthews* [1895] AC 471 (HL).
[39] *Spiro v Glencrown* [1991] Ch 537 (ChD), 543.
[40] J Stark, 'The Option to purchase—a legal chameleon' [1992] Journal of Business Law 296, 301.
[41] *London and South Western Railway Company v Gomm* (1882) 20 ChD 562, 581.

the option is the subject of a notice, or, second, if not, whether the option-holder is in discoverable actual occupation at the time of the disposition in such a way which meets the requirements of schedule 3, paragraph 2, LRA 2002. More detail on these rules is to be found in chapter 15.

14.4 RIGHTS OF PRE-EMPTION

Rights of pre-emption are in some ways similar to options to purchase in that they are giving to one person a privileged position in respect of their ability to purchase the relevant title to land. However, they are also very different in that the vendor has significantly more control. There are two possible ways in which rights of pre-emption can be structured. The first is as a right of first refusal, where the vendor has given the potential purchaser the ability to have a first chance to buy the land. However, the parties will still have to agree a price and this can of course be a stumbling block to agreeing the sale. The second type would have a pre-set price either determined or determinable by some objective measure in the contract for the right of pre-emption so that if the seller decides to sell their estate in the land, the purchaser must be able to buy that estate at the agreed price. Rights of pre-emption, at least in respect of registered land (see later), being interests in land, must, it seems, be created in an appropriate form, be that by deed or by a section 2-compliant contract, although the matter is certainly not beyond doubt.

There is a long running debate as to whether such rights should be properly considered to be proprietary interests. Whilst options to purchase have long been considered to have this status, given the degree of control that passes to the purchaser when an option is created, the same cannot be said of the pre-emptive right. Whilst the vendor has constrained their choice of purchaser to a greater or lesser extent, they have not constrained their choice about whether to sell or not, and are therefore perfectly entitled never to sell the land.

Before the coming into force of the Land Registration Act 2002 (LRA 2002), the position was unsettled and the subject of much academic and judicial discussion. However, as a result of section 115 LRA 2002, rights of pre-emption created in relation to registered land at least, must be considered to have proprietary status and be capable of binding future disponees or legatees in relation to the relevant estate in land. The section states: '[a] right of pre-emption in relation to registered land has effect from the time of creation as an interest capable of binding successors in title'. The matter is therefore beyond debate in a registered land context. It is still useful to consider why the debate about rights of pre-emption existed nevertheless. Partly this is because it is still of relevance to unregistered land and rights created prior to the coming into force of the LRA 2002, but mainly because it gives insight into the question considered earlier about the proprietary status of estate contracts in general.

> **Further analysis: The proprietary status of rights of pre-emption outside the LRA**
>
> The strongest indication that such rights should be considered as proprietary is to be found in the Law of Property Act 1925 which states that rights of pre-emption should 'remain in force as equitable interests only'. This implies, at the very least, that rights of pre-emption are equitable interests in land. However, it does not demand that this is so, and may instead be read as excluding legal status from such rights if they

are indeed of proprietary status. However, the case law is relatively well-settled in the other direction, so that at common law a right of pre-emption is treated as merely a contractual right unless something occurs or is present in the contractual dealings to indicate otherwise.

Most importantly, they can take on such a status once the triggering act of a decision to sell has taken place. This was decided, albeit obiter, in *Pritchard v Briggs*,[42] where the Court of Appeal highlighted that once the triggering event has taken place, the vendor no longer has the same degree of freedom which they enjoyed prior to the triggering decision to sell, such that the interest could at that moment be considered proprietary. This decision has been the subject of much criticism, both academic and by implication by the judiciary, eg by Mummery LJ in *Dear v Reeves*.[43] Nevertheless, cases such as *Kling v Keston Properties*[44] have followed the approach in *Pritchard*.[45] The academic response to these various cases has been luke-warm, with Kenny noting that such analysis, 'reminds us of the unsystematic, pragmatic or perhaps chaotic way in which English property law develops without ever finding any clear conceptual foundation'.[46]

Any right of pre-emption with proprietary status (be that by virtue of LRA 2002, or because a triggering event has occurred), is capable in theory of binding a transferee of the relevant land, depending upon the priority rules discussed in chapter 15. As with options to purchase, therefore, in respect of registered land the right will bind a purchaser if either it is the subject of a notice on the register, or if the right-holder is in discoverable actual occupation which meets the requirements of schedule 3 paragraph 2 at the time of the disposition. The operation of these rules can be seen in the case of *Law v Haider*.[47]

Key case: *Law v Haider* [2017] UKUT 212

This case has a complicated history, involving a boundary dispute between the parties and a subsequent mediation at which a settlement was reached. As part of this settlement, there was a right of pre-emption in favour of Mr and Mrs Law in relation to some meadow land. Mr and Mrs Law attempted to protect this right by means of a unilateral notice on the register, as well as a restriction. The question before the Upper Tribunal was whether this, ie entry of a restriction, was possible since the purpose of a restriction is not to protect priorities should a sale occur, but rather to prevent a sale from taking place in breach of the right of pre-emption. In holding that a restriction should be possible in such a case, Morgan J, after making a very extensive review of the relevant authorities, gives a full explanation of rights of pre-emption and their nature. The significance of the case lies in the confirmation that it is possible to enter a restriction. It is also important to note from the case that Morgan J takes a very narrow definition as to what constitutes 'sale' in breach of a pre-emptive right. He highlighted that a gift of the freehold or a lease would not constitute 'sales' for this purpose.[48] The consequence of this decision is that whilst it is possible to enter rights of pre-emption as notices, there are other ways in which such rights can be protected—preventing a sale, rather than protecting priority should such a sale take place.

---

[42] *Pritchard v Briggs* [1980] Ch 338 (CA).
[43] *Dear v Reeves* [2001] EWCA Civ 277, [2002] Ch 1.
[44] *Kling v Keston Properties* (1985) 49 P & CR 212 (Ch).
[45] *Pritchard v Briggs* [1980] Ch 338 (CA).
[46] P H Kenny, 'What is a right of pre-emption' [2001] Conv 295, 296.
[47] *Law v Haider* [2017] UKUT 212 (TCC).
[48] *Law v Haider* [2017] UKUT 212 (TCC), [84].

14.5 CONCLUSION

This brief chapter is designed to give a more detailed flavour of estate contracts than is present in the majority of land law courses. The purpose of so-doing is to allow a fuller understanding of these rights, as well as highlighting certain areas of controversy in relation to such rights. The primary area of controversy historically was the proprietary status of such rights, but this issue has now been resolved. The remaining uncertainty that exists, however, relates to precisely how and when such rights come into and go out of existence, and this is an issue which has not been fully resolved. Indeed, in relation to the generic 'estate contract', emerging from contractual dealings in relation to transfers or creation of estates in land, the precise timings of this are very unclear, notwithstanding a number of decisions on the matter. In almost all cases the practical significance of this lack of clarity is minimal, but in cases where problems emerge at some point during the conveyancing process, the question of precisely what rights a transferee has, their status, and the operation of the priority rules in relation to such rights becomes critical.

PRINCIPLES

How does this mean that options to purchase shape the balance of the principles operating in relation to land law? To recap, these principles were:

1. Certainty
2. Sensitivity to context
3. Transactability
4. Systemic and individual effects
5. Recognition of the social role of the land law system.

As with the previous chapter concerned with restrictive covenants, the law relating to estate contracts, and the timings and nature of the various rights is not generally hugely influential on the overall balance within the system between the competing principles. This is not to say that estate contracts are not important: commercially, options to purchase in particular are hugely important in the structuring of many transactions and their practical uses should not be overlooked. However, because they are used primarily in commercial contexts, they tend to arise in circumstances where parties have the benefit of high quality legal advice and so, generally speaking, not too many problems arise. Furthermore, because options do arise in this context and do not tend to arise in relation to private residential properties, the question of the social impact of such rights on the relation between individuals, each other, and their home, rarely arises.

Where these questions have arisen, however, rare though that occurrence is, the lack of conceptual clarity in the law has been problematic. This is evidenced by the decision in *Scott v Southern Pacific* where the Supreme Court was required to assess whether an estate contract could give rise to a right in one's own land. The answer (no) is far from controversial, but the fact that the question was addressed to Supreme Court level is an indication that the underlying uncertainties, when they do cause problems, result in expensive, lengthy and drawn out litigation. In this respect, the uncertainties which do exist in the law result in disproportionate problems resting on the shoulders least able to bear the consequences of such uncertainty, ie those without access to high quality legal advice before entering into potentially prejudicial transactions.

TABLE OF DEFINITIONS

Estate contract	Contracts for intended transfers of estates in land.
Option to purchase	An option to purchase is a right which entitles its holder to force the proprietor of an estate in land, be that freehold or leasehold, to transfer their estate in land. There is no requirement on the option-holder to purchase the land.
Right of pre-emption	A right which provides that if a vendor decides to sell their estate in the land, the purchaser must be able to buy that estate at a previously agreed price.
Right of first refusal	A right which provides that the potential purchaser will have a first chance to buy the land, at a price to be agreed.

FURTHER READING

There is little written specifically about estate contracts. Nevertheless, the following will provide useful in exploring the issues raised in this chapter in more detail:

DRAY, M. et al, *Barnsley's Land Options* (6th ed) (Sweet & Maxwell, 2016).
STARK, J., 'The option to purchase - a legal chameleon?' [1992] Journal of Business Law 296.

15
PRIORITIES

15.1	Introduction	462	15.6	Exceptional Cases of Priority	480
15.2	First in Time—The Basic Priority Rule	464	15.7	Consequences of a Loss of Priority	488
15.3	Purchaser of a Legal Estate who Later Becomes Registered—The Special Priority Rule	465	15.8	Conclusion	491
				Principles	493
				Table of Definitions	494
15.4	Priorities on First Registration	479		Further Reading	495
15.5	Rules Applicable to Registered Charges	480			

CHAPTER GOALS

By the end of this chapter you should understand:

- Why the three guiding questions of priority disputes are so critical;
- How the basic priority rule operates, and how this is modified in relation to registered purchasers of registered estates in land;
- How overriding interests operate;
- How waivers or consent affect priority; and
- The consequences of a loss of priority.

15.1 INTRODUCTION

So far in this book we have essentially been concerned with the rules regarding the creation and operation of 'single' property rights. That is to say, we have examined the nature of a mortgage, of an easement, of leases, etc and have considered what this entitles the holder of these rights to do in relation to the relevant land. This chapter explores the issue of how such rights *interact*, and how conflicts between rights-holders are resolved. This is not a question of competing validity, but rather, of competing priorities. Understanding how priority rules operate is one of the most significant elements of land law. It is critical to problem questions in particular. The rules are also occasionally difficult to apply, especially when priority rules are combined with the rules relating to co-ownership and mortgages as will be discussed in the chapter which follows this. As a result, a flow chart assisting in the application of these rules appears in the online resources. The choice to site this discussion of priority so far away from chapter 5 on registered land may seem an unusual choice but it has been done for two reasons, as explained there also. First, in order to appreciate the importance of any priority dispute, there is merit in understanding the individual rights which conflict as a starting point. Without understanding these rights, it is difficult if not impossible to appreciate the consequences of the priority question. Second, it is important to keep the two functions of registered land—that of rights creation, and that of rights protection—separate. They are both questions surrounding the rules in registered land, but that does not mean it makes sense to treat them as a single whole for they are tackling and addressing two entirely different problems.

The structure of this chapter is as follows. First, we explain the general priority rules for registered land (unregistered land is considered in summary form only in chapter 3 at 3.4 where you can find a summary of the rules relating to registered land also). We then look at the special priority rules in place first, in cases involving dispositions of registered land; second, for cases involving registered charges; and third in cases involving first registrations (many works begin with discussion of first registration, but such cases are now becoming relatively less common). We then explain some exceptional cases where these normal priority rules are supplanted by rules bespoke to particular scenarios. Here, this chapter discusses priority searches; waiver and consent; the special rules relating to acquisition mortgages; the registration gap; overreaching; and subrogation (considered in more detail in chapter 11 at 11.7.2). Finally, the chapter explains the consequences of a loss of priority. Once these general rules are understood, the chapter which follows examines, amongst other issues, how these rules play out in the specific context of co-owned land.

A fundamental point to keep in mind about priorities as you read this chapter is that the interaction between rights, the way the priority schemes operate, and the effect of rights which do bind, is determined, most significantly, by the mode of that right's creation, and the nature of the right itself. Furthermore, the rules contained in the Land Registration Act 2002 (LRA 2002) regarding the *creation* of rights are critical in explaining how the logically dependent priority rules work. It is therefore essential to keep the information in chapters 4 and 5 in mind when reading this chapter to understand the *nature* of the rights in question.

One of the purposes of the LRA 2002 was to improve upon the operation of the priority rules under the previous land registration regimes. It was designed to produce simple and easy to apply rules to allow for straightforward determination of priority conflicts with a reduction in the list of 'overriding interests'. This is a concept which we introduced in chapter 3, and to which reference has been made throughout the book.[1] To a very large extent, this has succeeded. Priorities in registered land are, at least in the vast majority of cases, simple. To understand these rules, however,

---

[1] Strictly speaking, these are unregistered interests which override, but they are commonly referred to as overriding interests in line with the approach taken under the 1925 legislation.

it is critical to keep in mind three central points at all times: first, the most important determinant of priorities between any property rights is the date of their creation; second, those who purchase and become registered proprietors of registered estates in land are put into a special position as they may be able to assert priority over a right which was created prior to their purchase of the estate; and third, priority rules are relevant only in so far as the parties have not validly consented or contracted to lose priority to a newer right or some other 'exceptional' priority rule applies. If these three points are kept in mind, then we can see that three questions emerge which should be asked in every situation where you are required to assess relative priority.

1. When were the rights created?
2. Is there a purchaser of a registered estate?
3. Is there a valid waiver of priority or consent to the creation of a new right or some other exceptional priority rule applicable to the situation?

15.2 FIRST IN TIME—THE BASIC PRIORITY RULE

As section 28 LRA 2002 explains, the basic priority rule which determines the interaction between property rights in registered land is the 'first in time' rule. This means that a right will take priority over rights created after it, and will rank after those created before it. This first in time rule is the fundamental starting point and is entirely sensible. It applies to all rights in registered land, whether those rights are themselves registered or not. It was explained by the Law Commission as follows:

> 'It follows therefore, that in cases that fall within this general rule, the priority of any interest in registered land is determined by the date of its creation... this rule is an absolute one, subject only to the exceptions provided for by the Bill. No question arises as to whether "the equities are equal".'[2]

The consequence of this rule, therefore, is that there is no scope within the LRA 2002 for weighing up the relative merits of one or another claimant in respect of the 'quality' of their claim, their behaviour etc. This is a priority rule based not on who 'deserves' to succeed, but rather on clear and easily applied rules. In answering any problem question, as a result, the first and essential step is to make a timeline of the rights which have arisen and been transferred on the facts. Unless either the 'special' priority rule for purchasers of registered estates, or one of the exceptional priority rules applies, then this timeline will determine priorities.

> **Summary: Basic priority rule**
>
> The normal priority rule is that rights take priority over those created later, and are subject to those created before. This is known as the 'first in time' rule.

---

[2] Law Commission report no. 271, 'Land Registration for the Twenty-First Century' (2001) at 78, [5.5].

15.3 PURCHASER OF A LEGAL ESTATE WHO LATER BECOMES REGISTERED—THE SPECIAL PRIORITY RULE

This basic priority rule is however modified in the vast majority of purchases of land in cases involving subsequent registrations. We consider the priority rules in relation to the (less common) situation of first registration later in this chapter. When a purchaser of a legal estate, where that estate is required to be registered, then becomes registered proprietor, the completion of that purchase by registration brings into play a the special priority rule in section 29 LRA 2002. This section states (emphasis added):

'Effect of registered dispositions: estates

(1) If a *registrable disposition* of a *registered estate* is made for *valuable consideration, completion of the disposition by registration* has the effect of postponing to the interest under the disposition any interest affecting the estate immediately before the disposition whose priority is not protected at the time of registration.

(2) For the purposes of subsection (1), the priority of an interest is protected—

  (a) in any case, if the interest—

   (i) is a registered charge or the subject of a notice in the register,

   (ii) falls within any of the paragraphs of Schedule 3, or

   (iii) appears from the register to be excepted from the effect of registration, and

  (b) in the case of a disposition of a leasehold estate, if the burden of the interest is incident to the estate.

(3) Subsection (2)(a)(ii) does not apply to an interest which has been the subject of a notice in the register at any time since the coming into force of this section.

(4) Where the grant of a leasehold estate in land out of a registered estate does not involve a registrable disposition, this section has effect as if—

  (a) the grant involved such a disposition, and

  (b) the disposition were registered at the time of the grant.'

This section establishes two sets of rules. The first relates to the conditions for the application of section 29. These are (highlighted earlier in italics):

1. That there is a disposition of an existing registered estate;
2. That this disposition is itself required to be registered;
3. That the disposition is made for valuable consideration; and
4. The disposition is completed by registration.

The second set of rules, in sub-section (2), explains the consequences of the section 29 priority rule applying. In such cases, in summary, the new proprietor will only be bound by those rights which were themselves registered, or which were overriding. In order for a right to be registered, it might be registered as an estate in its own right, as would be the case with a leasehold estate of a duration of more than 7 years, for example, or it may be entered as the subject of a notice on the register. We considered the process of registering in chapter 5 at 5.2, where we also explore what is meant by registrable dispositions.

Spotting registered interests is, of course, easy, since they appear on the register. Much more difficult is the question relating to overriding interests. As has been explained elsewhere, overriding interests are those interests which are binding upon a purchaser of a legal estate even though they do not appear on the register. In other words, they are given special status within the system as a whole, as they appear as an exception to two fundamental priority rules—the first in time rule, and the rule that a purchaser would only be bound by those interests which appear on the register. The main categories of overriding interest are: short legal leasehold estates of a duration of 7 years or less; the interests of a person in actual occupation; and implied legal easements and profits. There are other categories as we mention later, but this book will not consider these in detail.

15.3.1 SHORT LEGAL LEASES OF A DURATION OF 7 YEARS OR LESS

'Leasehold estates in land

1 A leasehold estate in land granted for a term not exceeding seven years from the date of the grant, except for—

(a) a lease the grant of which falls within section 4(1)(d), (e) or (f);

(b) a lease the grant of which constitutes a registrable disposition.'

Schedule 3, paragraph 1, LRA 2002 protects the priority of any legal leasehold estate of a duration of seven years or less as long as that lease does not fall within section 4(1)(d)–(f) or was not otherwise registrable. The relevant statutory provisions in section 4 state:

'(d) the grant out of a qualifying estate of an estate in land for a term of years absolute to take effect in possession after the end of the period of three months beginning with the date of the grant;

(e) the grant of a lease in pursuance of Part 5 of the Housing Act 1985 (the right to buy) out of an unregistered legal estate in land;

(f) the grant of a lease out of an unregistered legal estate in land in such circumstances as are mentioned in paragraph (b)'.

The most significant of these in practice is likely to be (d), since this relates to circumstances where the lease as granted, even if only 6 months in duration, will not be protected in terms of its priority where the tenant did not go into possession within a 3 month period of the grant. This, as we considered in relation to the slightly different rules in section 54 Law of Property Act 1925 in respect of the requirement of deeds in leases, in chapter 4 (see 4.3.1.2), is actually likely to be fairly common if the relevant paperwork is completed sometime before a person goes into possession of a lease. The fact that the lease does not meet this condition, however, so as to prevent it falling under the scope of schedule 3 paragraph 1, does not mean that it cannot be an overriding interest under schedules 3, paragraph 2 as we shall see. If the lease in question is a residential lease, those provisions make it likely that it would still be protected.

The requirement that the relevant lease be 'legal' is not immediately apparent from the text of the provision itself. However, this is how the provision is widely interpreted thanks to its use of the word 'grant', as in *City Permanent Building Society v Miller*.[3] Under ordinary circumstances, if a lease which is not required to be registered is created by deed, which is implied by the word 'grant', then that lease would be legal. However, there are a small number of circumstances where parties may choose to use a deed, but where nevertheless an equitable lease is created. For example, the parties may stipulate expressly that they wish the lease to be equitable, or the lessor may not have a legal estate in the relevant land so that they are not able to create a legal lease. In such circumstances, it may be that the 'grant' requirement is interpreted in such a ways as to protect these leases against the purchaser. However, this does not seem to have been the intention of the drafters of the Act, and it does not fit well with the justification behind the protection of these short leases.

These leases are protected for two reasons. First, positively, these leases tend to be residential, and are of enormous practical and legal significance since short leases makes up the bulk of the residential rental market. Given this, we might expect that a high degree of protection would be given to those renting on a short leases as against a purchaser. This takes account of the relevant balance of power within the relationship between landlord and tenant in these circumstances, particularly when it comes to protections against assignment of the reversion. Second, the sheer number of these means that it is perhaps unrealistic to expect the land registry to efficiently manage registration requests in relation to all such leases. This means that it is probably a more efficient use of the land registry's resources to render all such short lease automatically overriding so that there is no need to register them. This is combined with the fact that from the purchaser's perspective, it is very unlikely to be significantly onerous to either carry out relevant inquiries to find out about the lease, or, if not, to simply put up with the tenant until the short lease runs its course. It may be enormously disappointing to a purchaser to discover that there is a tenant with 5 years left on their lease with priority over the new freeholder, but in terms of the long-term value of the asset, the landlord will be able usually simply to wait until the lease comes to an end. The Law Commission sums up these policy concerns: '[t]he policy behind this class of overriding interest has been to keep the register free of such leases because of their short duration and the risk that they would clutter the register'.[4]

15.3.2 RELEVANT SOCIAL HOUSING LEASES

One of the very few amendments to the 2002 Act since its coming into force has been to add a provision relating to the overriding nature of social housing leases. Public private partnership leases also receive special protection through section 90 Land Registration Act 2002. Schedules 3 paragraph 1A states that the following will be protected against a purchaser:

> 'Relevant social housing tenancies
>
> Paragraph 1A Leasehold estate in land under a relevant social housing tenancy.'

The paragraph was introduced by the Localism Act 2011, and the relevant social housing tenancy relates to those tenancies defined in section 134 Localism Act, which states:

---

[3] *City Permanent Building Society v Miller* [1952] Ch 840 (CA).
[4] Law Commission report no. 271, 'Land Registration for the Twenty-First Century' (2001), 142, [8.9].

"'relevant social housing tenancy" means—

(a) a flexible tenancy, or

(b) an assured tenancy of a dwelling-house in England granted by a private registered provider of social housing, other than a long tenancy or a shared ownership lease.'

We considered the flexible tenancy and the assured tenancy in chapter 10 earlier in this book (see 10.5.5.2). The purpose of including these leases within the category of overriding leases is merely to reflect the risk of the landlord changing identity in these types of situation and as a corollary to the fact that they cannot be registered as explained in chapter 5 thanks to section 33 LRA 2002.

15.3.3 THE INTERESTS OF A PERSON IN ACTUAL OCCUPATION

In order for the interests of a person in actual occupation to be protected in priority terms, it is necessary for a number of conditions to be met. First, and critically, the person in actual occupation must have a *property right*. Actual occupation *by itself* is not a right which can be protected. It is a factual state of affairs which is a means to protection. Second, the person must be in actual occupation. We discuss the definition of actual occupation later. It is worth highlighting here that this is a factual question and is determined according to the ordinary meaning of 'occupation'. Third, that person must have been in actual occupation at the *relevant date*. When precisely is the relevant date has been the subject of some case law difficulties. Fourth, the purchaser will then be bound by the property right of a such a person if *either* the purchaser knows about the right, or the actual occupation of the right-holder would have been obvious on a reasonably careful inspection of the land. If either of these conditions is met, then the purchaser will be bound *unless* they made inquiries of the right-holder during the purchase process, and the right-holder did not inform them of their right, and the right-holder did not have a good reason to withhold this information. If all these requirements are met, then the right will have priority over the purchaser's estate. If however they are not met, and there is no other basis for the right in question to override the disposition then it will lose its priority. According to the language of section 29, this means that the right will be 'postponed' to the right under the disposition. We consider later what postpone means in this context, at 15.7.

15.3.3.1 Property rights

The first criterion does not need further explanation, except to say that this means it is necessary to familiarise yourself with Table 15.1 as a starting point at least (see also chapter 2). This is not an exhaustive list.

Table 15.1 Property rights

Property Right	What is it?	Requirements
Freehold estate	Estate in land of unlimited duration. Considered the 'highest' form of ownership in English law, save for that of the Crown.	A valid title or grant from the Crown. A new title created by mere possession is a freehold title.
Leasehold estate	Estate in land of limited duration.	Exclusive possession for a defined or definable term.

15.3 Purchaser of a Legal Estate who Later Becomes Registered—The Special Priority Rule

Mortgage interest	Security for a debt.	
Easements	An easement is an interest in the land of another. For example, a right of way, right to light, right to pass water through a defined channel etc.	For an interest to be capable of being an easement: (a) you need a dominant and servient tenement; (b) the dominant and servient tenements must be in separate ownership; (c) the easement must benefit the dominant tenement; and (d) it must be capable of being the subject matter of a grant.
Option to purchase	Gives the right holder an ability to force a sale.	The right must be exercisable within a specified time period and the price specified or calculable.
Right of pre-emption. These are only automatically interests in land capable of binding a purchaser if created after Oct 13 2003.	Covers two rights—rights of pre-emption (grantee has a right to purchase at a fixed price before the grantor can sell to anyone else) and right of first refusal where the grantor is able to set the price himself at the time at which he decides to sell the land.	
Right to set aside a transaction.	Allows the right-holder to 'go back in time' and set aside a transaction—gift, sale, mortgage etc, and is itself a property right such that it may be binding on third parties.	The main reasons for this would be undue influence, fraud, *non est factum*, and mistake.
Right to rectify the register	Will allow the register to be altered prospectively—see chapter 5 for discussion of the proprietary status of such rights.	The conditions for the ability to rectify the register are laid out in sch 4, LRA 2002. The main one is rectification on the basis of a mistake.
Interest under a trust of land	Equitable title where a legal estate is held on trust.	A valid written declaration of trust, or a trust created through implication.
Proprietary estoppel	A flexible jurisdiction which allows the court to act to give effect to promises which would not otherwise be binding.	It depends upon promise + detriment + reliance + unconscionability.

15.3.3.2 Actual occupation—a factual test

The second criterion is that the person must be in actual occupation. The courts have repeatedly highlighted that actual occupation is not a term of art. Rather, it is an ordinary word of the English language and should be understood as such. Whilst this may be an accurate reflection of how the courts envisage their approach to this term, it is not necessarily particularly helpful in demonstrating how the word should be applied. Some rules do in fact appear to be developing in determining the parameters of actual occupation. Furthermore, whilst there is a now a growing body of case law under the 2002 Act for the meaning of occupation, it is also useful to consider that case law which exists in relation to other contexts. This includes the pre-2002 Act rules (where actual occupation was also relevant), and the rules relating to security of tenure in relation to leases (discussion in chapter 10, where the scope of protection under those provisions depends upon the existence and scope of occupation). Whilst the 'rules' from other contexts may not be directly applicable when considering priorities under the LRA 2002, therefore, the fact that in this wide variety of legislative contexts the courts see themselves as applying a 'common English word' means that there is no reason why such case law *cannot* provide a valid point of comparison or evidence for a particular approach.

It is critical to note, however, three important things about actual occupation. First, it is possible for more than one person to occupy land at one time, and in different capacities. Thus, a licensee and a freeholder may both occupy land, sharing the use of relevant spaces. Occupation, unlike possession, is not a concept that encompasses the idea of 'keeping others out'. Second, it is possible for one person to be in occupation of more than one space at the same time. We might see, for example, that a single person occupies the office that they rent, as well as their home, simultaneously. Occupation in this sense does not mean 'main home', for example. Finally, whilst we would typically associate occupation with residential accommodation, it is perfectly possible to 'occupy' other spaces, including commercial and agricultural land. However, the *mode* of occupation will of course be very different. The factors that a court may look at to determine occupation in such contexts will differ. This is what is meant by the case law reminders that all will depend upon the nature of the land in question, and the nature of the 'person' who holds the relevant right (a company, not being a physical person, cannot *itself* occupy, but it does occupy through the occupation of its employees, for example).

Furthermore, the courts have indicated that certain features may be helpful in assessing whether or not a person is in actual occupation, even if these do not coalesce into a 'test' to be applied rigidly. First, the courts will consider the nature of the land and its use. Second, they will examine the presence of belongings or the person themselves on the site. Third, the courts will look at the intention behind the physical presence on the land, to ascertain whether the right-holder has an 'intention to occupy'. This is not a determinative test by any means. Indeed it is usually used to show that occupation is present when on its face it may not appear to be. Fourth, the courts will look at the permanence of the links between the right-holder and the land in terms of their occupation. This may be particularly relevant in relation to land where the existing physical presence is somewhat minimal, but there has been extensive physical presence formerly. In such cases, the courts will also examine the reason behind any absence. Finally, the courts will consider whether or not there is any agent on the land who may be said to be occupying 'on behalf of' the right-holder, where the right-holder is not themselves present at the relevant time. This is far from an exhaustive list, and some or all of these factors may be entirely unhelpful in an instant case. Nevertheless, it is useful to keep them in mind as a starting point. It is only really by getting to grips with the relevant case law, however, that the nebulous nature of the occupation test becomes clear. This is shown most clearly by *Link Lending v Bustard*.[5]

---

[5] *Link Lending Ltd v Hussein* [2010] EWCA Civ 424, [2010] 2 EGLR 55.

15.3 Purchaser of a Legal Estate who Later Becomes Registered—The Special Priority Rule

Key case: *Link Lending v Bustard* [2010] EWCA Civ 424

In this case, Ms Bustard had unfortunately been hospitalised against her will and taken into psychiatric care due to complications arising from her alcoholism. She was unable to look after herself or to function outside of the hospital environment. The evidence presented to the court by her doctors was that she was unlikely to return to living outside the hospital. Whilst she was suffering through this illness, her 'friend' had contracted with the lender to take a mortgage out on the property, and had encouraged Ms Bustard to transfer title to her.

The question for the court was whether Ms Bustard had been in actual occupation at the time of the disposition to the mortgage company (there was no doubt that the transfer of title to the friend could be overturned). The reason why this case was problematic for the court was that, in reality, Ms Bustard no longer lived at the property in question. Since she was unlikely ever to return, it was difficult to see this as her 'occupied home'. However, the court demonstrated that it is willing to be flexible in the application of the actual occupation test.

Thus, the court relied on the fact that Ms Bustard's belongings were still present in the property. She did also return there approximately once a week (intermittently, and supervised) in order to collect her post and the like. Furthermore, there was nowhere else that Ms Bustard would call 'home' and in this sense her intention added to the presence of her belongings to 'create' occupation. The court was also persuaded that the reason why Ms Bustard was absent was relevant here, as was the fact that she desired to return to the property should she be well enough to do so. In the words of Mummery LJ:

> 'The trend of the cases shows that the courts are reluctant to lay down, or even suggest, a single legal test for determining whether a person is in actual occupation. The decisions on statutory construction identify the factors that have to be weighed by the judge on this issue. The degree of permanence and continuity of presence of the person concerned, the intentions and wishes of that person, the length of absence from the property and the reason for it and the nature of the property and personal circumstances of the person are among the relevant factors... The judge was, in my view, justified in ruling... that Ms Bustard was a person in actual occupation of the Property. His conclusion was supported by evidence of a sufficient degree of continuity and permanence of occupation, of involuntary residence elsewhere, which was satisfactorily explained by objective reasons, and of a persistent intention to return home when possible, as manifested by her regular visits to the property'.[6]

The operation of these rules in a somewhat different can be seen in *Thompson v Foy*,[7] which also gives very useful general guidance.

Key case: *Thompson v Foy* [2009] EWHC 1076

Mrs Foy was registered proprietor of a house in Derbyshire. Her mother, Mrs Thompson, claimed that she had a right to set aside the transaction by which her daughter became registered proprietor. She also argued that, on the grant of a registered charge by Mrs Foy, as a result of Mrs Thompson's actual occupation, that right would take priority over the charge. The details regarding the dispute surrounding the validity over the transaction are not important here. Rather, the discussion of the court as to whether or not Mrs Thompson was in actual occupation at the relevant date is where the importance of the case lies.

---

[6] *Link Lending Ltd v Hussein* [2010] EWCA Civ 424, [2010] 2 EGLR 55, [27–30].
[7] *Thompson v Foy* [2009] EWHC 1076 (Ch), [2010] 1 P & CR 16.

This was because, first, it was questionable whether Mrs Thompson's actual occupation had come to an end, and because the date at which she went out of actual occupation appeared to be before the date of registration. We consider the case further later, but here it is useful to explain the general guidance given by the court regarding the meaning of actual occupation. This is also a helpful paragraph as a reference source for the relevant authorities. Lewison J explained:

'i) The words "actual occupation" are ordinary words of plain English and should be interpreted as such. The word "actual" emphasises that physical presence is required...

ii) It does not necessarily involve the personal presence of the person claiming to occupy. A caretaker or the representative of a company can occupy on behalf of his employer...

iii) However, actual occupation by a licensee (who is not a representative occupier) does not count as actual occupation by the licensor...

iv) The mere presence of some of the claimant's furniture will not usually count as actual occupation...

v) If the person said to be in actual occupation at any particular time is not physically present on the land at that time, it will usually be necessary to show that his occupation was manifested and accompanied by a continuing intention to occupy'.[8]

Lewison J also explained that where a person leaves a property, and does so with the firm mindset that they will never seek to return, the fact that some belongings may remain is not enough to overcome this intention.[9]

Further analysis: Discretion in the priority scheme

As we have seen earlier, there is very little room for discretion in the application of the priorities scheme, a theme to which we return when considering the rules relating to acquisition mortgages in *Abbey National v Cann*[10] and *North East Property Buyers*[11] later. Indeed, one of the only places where the courts have interpretive flexibility is in relation to the meaning of actual occupation. Whether a lease is 7 years or less in duration is not something about which there can be interpretive disagreement; but the courts are able to take a more fact-sensitive approach in relation to actual occupation. This sensitivity is seen, without a doubt, in *Bustard*.[12] Ms Bustard in this case was in a very vulnerable position. Her mental and physical health meant that it was very easy for others to take advantage of her. The courts were aware of this. The interpretation of actual occupation that this resulted in is extremely broad. Indeed, it is difficult to think of a circumstance where a person could have a more minimal physical connection with residential property where it could be concluded that they were still in actual occupation. Ms Bustard did not live in the property and was in all likelihood never going to live there again. Nevertheless, the courts supported her arguments.

This has led some to consider the court's use of their discretion in cases such as this. Bevan for example has argued that the piecemeal approach of the courts has resulted in 'a vastly more subjective

---

[8] *Thompson v Foy* [2009] EWHC 1076 (Ch), [2010] 1 P & CR 16, [127].
[9] *Thompson v Foy* [2009] EWHC 1076 (Ch), [2010] 1 P & CR 16, [131].
[10] *Abbey National v Cann* [1991] 1 AC 56 (HL).
[11] *North East Property Buyers* [2014] UKSC 52, [2015] AC 385.
[12] *Link Lending Ltd v Hussein* [2010] EWCA Civ 424, [2010] 2 EGLR 55.

15.3 Purchaser of a Legal Estate who Later Becomes Registered—The Special Priority Rule

assessment of the intentions, wishes and feelings of the parties in order to determine question of actual occupation'.[13] He argues that this interpretation is wrong, and that we should return to 'a more tightly defined, less elastic, less subjective determination of actual occupation'.[14] The current approach, Bevan highlights, appears to be inconsistent with the aims of land registration as a whole, and with the increasingly narrow approach taken to overriding interests in reforms of the law.[15] Most importantly, he suggests that the courts are moving from an objective assessment of the fact of actual occupation, to a subjective approach which focuses on intentions to occupy. The danger of such an approach is that the entire reason why actual occupation is a basis for the protection of rights is that, in theory, it should be discoverable by a purchaser. Yes, actual occupation is also a proxy means to protect those with the greatest emotional and personal stake in the land, but is not supposed to be a one-way street in this respect.

Bevan explains his objections to the subjective approach based on four grounds:

'First, for its inconsistency vis-à-vis the clear direction of travel within modern land law towards a narrowing, reduced role for overriding interests... secondly, for its apparent results-orientated focus and its failure to articulate precisely how such subjective notions are to be discerned and employed as part of an actual occupation analysis. Thirdly, the current, more subjective approach is challenged as resting on shaky foundations stemming from landlord and tenant law rather than rooted in principles of land registration; and, finally, for permitting policy arguments to trump principle in determinations of actual occupation'.[16]

Bevan's third criticism is particularly interesting, as the more subjective approach to occupation is certainly one which is evinced in a landlord and tenant context, as part of a broader understanding of the role of such rules, as we have seen in chapter 10, in *Uratemp*.[17] In that case, the courts were focussed on the fact that the protections given to tenants by the security of tenure provisions would be denied those most in need of them were too restrictive an approach to be taken to the interpretation of the key terms of the relevant provisions: dwelling and occupation. Bevan argues, agreeing with Hayton,[18] that the analogy apparently drawn by Mummery LJ in *Bustard*[19] between the landlord and tenant context and the land registration context, is inappropriate, and that the principles and policies in play in the two places are very different. However, that is an argument which is difficult to substantiate.[20] Both areas of law are focused on how to balance the needs of potentially vulnerable occupiers, subjected to market forces beyond their control and the acts of third parties, against the importance of certainty, transactability, and the smooth functioning of the real estate market.

Bogusz has taken a different approach, supporting the court's seemingly generous attitude in cases of vulnerable parties stating that, 'frustrating as it may seem for lawyers, the lack of a "single legal test" provides for a degree of much needed flexibility and latitude for the judicial interpretation' of the actual occupation test'.[21] The consequences of such an approach are, as she highlights, 'First, the judicial use of a reflexive factual and contextual analysis serves as a potential antidote to alleviate the harshness of the

---

[13] C Bevan, 'Overriding and over-extended? Actual occupation: a call to orthodoxy' [2016] Conv 104.
[14] C Bevan, 'Overriding and over-extended? Actual occupation: a call to orthodoxy' [2016] Conv 104.
[15] C Bevan, 'Overriding and over-extended? Actual occupation: a call to orthodoxy' [2016] Conv 104–5.
[16] C Bevan, 'Overriding and over-extended? Actual occupation: a call to orthodoxy' [2016] Conv 112.
[17] *Uratemp Ventures Ltd v Collins* [2001] UKHL 43, [2002] 1 AC 301.
[18] D Hayton, *Registered Land* (3rd ed) (Sweet & Maxwell, London, 1981), 87–91.
[19] *Link Lending Ltd v Hussein* [2010] EWCA Civ 424, [2010] 2 EGLR 55.
[20] C Bevan, 'Overriding and over-extended? Actual occupation: a call to orthodoxy' [2016] Conv 114–15.
[21] B Bogusz, 'Defining the scope of actual occupation under the LRA 2002: some recent judicial clarification' [2011] Conv 268, 274.

rule where the actual occupier's undiscoverable rights are not protection. Secondly, this flexibility acts as a means of redressing the policy bias towards the protection of disponee [sic] from undiscoverable rights.'[22] Thus, Bogusz argues that it is in departing from the Law Commission's stated goals in enacting the LRA 2002 that the case law in fact achieves a welcome outcome in the state of the law. In making this analysis, Bogusz draws an analogy with the case law in *Stack*[23] (see chapter 7 at 7.4.2) where the courts are deliberately limiting the effects of strict and seemingly rigid statutory provisions to ensure some flexibility in the law in the context of residential and familial situations.[24]

Finally, in terms of what can constitute sufficient factual occupation, the temptation is to focus on residential occupation where the relevant property rights tend to be an interest under a trust, a lease, or a proprietary estoppel. However, it is possible to encounter situations where a person seeks to protect a different kind of right through actual occupation. We can see this in *Chaudhary v Yavuz*,[25] a case also discussed in chapter 12 at 12.6.3.

Key case: *Chaudhary v Yavuz* [2011] EWCA Civ 1314

This case involved a dispute in connection with an equitable easement. The easement in question was a right of way over a staircase (this staircase itself having been erected by the dominant owner). The question before the court was whether the use of the staircase, and even its erection in the first place, could constitute actual occupation for the purposes of schedule 3 paragraph 2.

The court was unconvinced. Per Lloyd LJ:

'There was no indication that it was used otherwise than for passing and repassing between the street and the relevant flat or flats. In my judgment such use does not amount to actual occupation. I dare say that no-one else was in occupation of the metal structure either, but not every piece of land is occupied by someone, let alone in someone's actual occupation (as distinct from possession).'[26]

Further, his Lordship went onto reason:

'The metal structure became part of the land on any basis, regardless of whether any part of it, as a chattel... to the owner of number 37, as opposed to his neighbour on whose land it was placed. It thus became part of what could be used or occupied. It makes no sense to say that its presence on the land of the Defendant was itself occupation of that land by the person who paid for it to be put up in the first place. Occupation must be, or be referable to, personal physical activity by some one or more individuals... The only such activity in the present case was that of the Claimant's tenants and their visitors (and of course those of the Defendant) coming to and fro on the staircase... That is use, not occupation.'[27]

This reasoning sits somewhat at odds (although is not entirely conflicting with) the approach taken by the court in *Saeed v Plustrade*[28] where it was accepted (but not decided) that parking a car in line with an easement of parking could constitute actual occupation of the relevant land.

---

[22] B Bogusz, 'Defining the scope of actual occupation under the LRA 2002: some recent judicial clarification' [2011] Conv 268, 274–5.
[23] *Stack v Dowden* [2007] UKHL 17, [2007] AC 432.
[24] B Bogusz, 'Defining the scope of actual occupation under the LRA 2002: some recent judicial clarification' [2011] Conv 268, 284.
[25] *Chaudhary v Yavuz* [2011] EWCA Civ 1314, [2013] Ch 249.
[26] *Chaudhary v Yavuz* [2011] EWCA Civ 1314, [2013] Ch 249, [31].
[27] *Chaudhary v Yavuz* [2011] EWCA Civ 1314, [2013] Ch 249, [32].
[28] *Saeed v Plustrade* [2001] EWCA Civ 2011, [2002] 2 P & CR 19.

15.3.3.3 The relevant date

It is necessary that the right-holder not only be in actual occupation of the land, but that it can be shown that they were in actual occupation at the relevant date. Precisely when this is has been the subject of some controversy, as a result of the somewhat ambiguous wording of the provisions of the 2002 Act in this respect. The question, as the courts highlight, is whether the assessment date for actual occupation is the date of the contract between the parties, of the date of the deed of transfer, of registration, or of some combination of two or possibly even all three of these. If we examine the wording of the LRA 2002 the difficulty is that in schedule 3 paragraph 2 the rules state that the interest must belong to the right-holder 'at the time of the disposition' and is protected in relation to land in which she is in actual occupation. The implication we can take from this is that the relevant date for that occupation is the date of the disposition, which ordinarily we would interpret to meet the date of the deed (the contract being the promise to dispose of the interest). However, the wording of section 29 casts some doubt on this interpretation. It states that the priority of a right should be protected 'at the time of registration'. Furthermore, it speaks of 'completion' of a disposition 'by registration' suggesting that the disposition itself takes place over the period of time commencing with the deed (or possibly even with the contract given that the contract will generate equitable rights) and concluding with registration.

These issues have been discussed at length in the decision of Lewison J (as he then was) in *Thompson v Foy*[29]). We considered this case earlier when looking at the interpretation of the test for actual occupation employed there. It is worth re-visiting this case here, however, for an examination of the discussion relating to the timing of actual occupation.

Key case: *Thompson v Foy* [2009] EWHC 1076

The facts of this case are explained earlier, so there is no need to repeat them here. This box is concerned with those aspects of Lewison J's approach which focused on the question of the timing of the actual occupation. Lewison's starting point was, examining section 27, that the provision indicates that the disposition is the *grant*, ie the deed itself, and not its completion by registration. Thus, the disposition and the completion are treated, in section 27(2)(f), as being two separate stages. Furthermore, it is clear from section 29(1) that the timing of these two events is seen as being potentially different. Finally, schedule 3 paragraph 2(c) refers to inspection at the time of the disposition. Thus, Lewison concluded, 'if actual occupation must exist at one date only, then in my judgment the date of the disposition...is the relevant date.'[30]

However, he then went onto examine whether there was a need, in fact, for the occupation to exist not only at the date of the disposition but also at the date of registration. This was based on recognition of the fact that section 29 seems to contain *two* requirements: first, that the interest binds the estate immediately prior to the disposition; and second, that its priority must be protected at the time of registration. Furthermore, the order of the wording in schedule 3 seems to suggest that the fact that the interest belongs to the person at the time of the disposition is not itself enough. Lewison J compared that actual wording of schedule 3, '[a]n interest belonging at the time of the disposition to a person in actual occupation' with what may appear to be a more natural wording should actual occupation at the time of

---

[29] *Thompson v Foy* [2009] EWHC 1076 (Ch), [2010] 1 P & CR 16.
[30] *Thompson v Foy* [2009] EWHC 1076 (Ch), [2010] 1 P & CR 16, [121].

the deed be the only relevant date, ie '[a]n interest belonging to a person in actual occupation at the time of the disposition'.[31] He explains, therefore, that the way schedule 3 is worded seems to leave the date of the actual occupation open, so that the relevant date is therefore determined by section 29, 'so that actual occupation at the date of the disposition would be required in order for the right to affect the estate immediately before the disposition; and actual occupation at the date of registration would be required in order for that interest to be protected at the time of the registration'.[32]

This reasoning is not particularly convincing, especially since if the statutory provisions in schedule 3 do indeed leave open the date of the actual occupation, then there is no reason for the occupation at the date of the disposition in order for the interest to affect the estate at that time. Obviously actual occupation is only necessary for the purposes of protecting priority: it does not affect the bindingness of a right *prior to* any disposition. Furthermore, this does seem to be a somewhat artificial reading of the statute. If the statute is read strictly, then the relevant date appears that of registration, but this is both impractical in practice (since once the deed has been created the parties cannot back out of the purchase and so the registration gap would become a very serious issues) and inconsistent with the approach taken under the 1925 legislation. Given that there appears to have been no intention to change the law on this issue, it would therefore be preferable to interpret the statute in line with the earlier law if possible.

This case does not appear, however, to have put the matter beyond doubt, and that is because there is conflicting case law, or at least, case law which may put Lewison's comments into question. This comes from two sources. First, *Abbey National v Cann*[33] suggests that Lewison J is correct to conclude that the relevant date is the date of the deed, but certainly provides no support for Lewison's 'preferred' option of actual occupation existing across the time period to encompass also the date of registration. Second, the decision in *Link Lending v Bustard*[34] earlier seems to focus on the relevant date as being the date of registration.

Further analysis: The timing of actual occupation

As Lewison J highlights himself in his judgment on this issue, the leading practitioners' books in this area do not support his 'both dates' approach. Thus Megarry and Wade state that,

'it is the date of the *disposition* that is relevant, not the date of the registration of that disposition. This is because of the so-called registration gap... Although it has been suggested... that from the wording of para.2 actual occupation may also be required at the date of registration of the relevant disposition... it is clear that this was not Parliament's intention'.[35]

In making this comment, it is worth noting that the lead author on the 8th edition of Megarry & Wade, Charles Harpum, was the Law Commissioner responsible for the Bill which became the 2002 Act.

Bogusz, however, seems supportive of Lewison J's view, and is convinced by his interpretation of the statutory provisions, arguing that, 'this interpretive interaction between the two statutory provisions is

---

[31] *Thompson v Foy* [2009] EWHC 1076 (Ch), [2010] 1 P & CR 16, [124].
[32] *Thompson v Foy* [2009] EWHC 1076 (Ch), [2010] 1 P & CR 16, [125].
[33] *Abbey National v Cann* [1991] 1 AC 56 (HL).
[34] *Link Lending Ltd v Hussein* [2010] EWCA Civ 424, [2010] 2 EGLR 55, [3].
[35] C Harpum et al, *Megarry & Wade: The Law of Real Property* (8th ed) (Sweet & Maxwell, London, 2012).

credible because it takes in to account the fundamental important efforts of both ss.27(1) and 29(1) of the LRA 2002 as defining the specific dates at which the priority of interests are determined'.[36]

Furthermore, as Dixon has highlighted, the question of the timing of actual occupation is relevant not only for overriding interests protected under schedule 3 paragraph 2, but potentially also for those rights which may be protected under the other paragraphs in schedule 3, such as short leases.[37] What impact does the case law following *Thompson v Foy*[38] on the question of timing have on such issues? Dixon highlights that if *Thompson* were to apply to all overriding interests, that would conflict with the decision in *Barclays Bank v Zaroovabli*[39] where priority of a lease was given even though the lease postdated the disposition.[40] It is unclear whether that approach survives *Thompson*.[41]

15.3.3.4 Relevance of knowledge, inquiries, and discoverability of actual occupation

The statutory provisions explaining the operation of actual occupation as a means to protecting rights, whilst very well-drafted, are somewhat difficult to read. The reason for this is that they are expressed using double negatives at certain points, which can be misleading if the section is not read in its entirety. This is a salutary lesson in the right way to read statutes, but it also means that the rules appear somewhat less intuitive and sensible than in reality they are. In fact, the caveats put into place in terms of the protection given by the fact of actual occupation are very logical.

First, the purchaser of the property will be bound by the right of the person in actual occupation if they have actual knowledge of that right. Critically, this is not a test of notice, or indeed of knowledge on its own. It is actual occupation plus knowledge which is necessary here.

Second, the purchaser of the property will be bound by the right of the person in actual occupation if that actual occupation would have been obvious on a reasonably careful inspection of the land. This is a hypothetical test. It is not determinative either way whether or not the purchaser has in fact carried out a reasonably careful inspection (although if they have carried out such an inspection and they did not discover the actual occupation of the right-holder than that may be evidence that it was not in fact obvious). It is also important to note that whilst the relevant knowledge of the purchaser earlier is knowledge of the *right*, in relation to this aspect of the rules, what needs to be obvious is the occupation. Whilst there is little case law concerning the interpretation of this test, we can perhaps reason by analogy with the case law on occupation earlier to state that the courts are likely to interpret this test flexibly. The approach is likely to be one which treats 'obvious' and 'careful' as being ordinary words of the English language. It is also probably fair to say that the courts will focus on the nature of the land in question in order to assess what sorts of steps would be needed to constitute a reasonably careful inspection.

We can imagine, for example, the situation where a person has an interest under a trust in relation to a warehouse. They store items for distribution in the warehouse as and when stock

---

[36] B Bogusz, 'Defining the scope of actual occupation under the LRA 2002: some recent judicial clarification' [2011] Conv 268, 272.
[37] M Dixon, 'Editor's notebook (July/August)' [2009] Conv 283, 290.
[38] *Thompson v Foy* [2009] EWHC 1076 (Ch), [2010] 1 P & CR 16.
[39] *Barclays Bank Plc v Zaroovabli* [1997] Ch. 321, ChD.
[40] M Dixon, 'Editor's notebook (July/August)' [2009] Conv 283, 290.
[41] *Thompson v Foy* [2009] EWHC 1076 (Ch), [2010] 1 P & CR 16.

arrives. This means that from time to time the warehouse may be empty. When the warehouse is empty, a security guard is employed at night time to protect the warehouse from squatters. No one is present during the day. Would a reasonably careful inspection of this property discover the security guard?

Third, even in cases where the actual occupation of the right-holder would have been obvious on a reasonably careful inspection of the land, it may be possible that the purchaser will still not be bound by that right. This is because the purchaser will not be bound if, upon making inquiries of the right-holder, the right-holder does not reveal the right when they 'should' have done. How we interpret 'should' here is obviously important. It determines the scope of the protections given to the purchaser. It could simply be seen as a question of knowledge. Where the right-holder is aware that they have a proprietary interest in the property, they should reveal it when asked. This would mean that a person with a proprietary estoppel, for example, may be unaware that this is a proprietary interest and so may be justified in not explaining their position. However, it could also be interpreted more sensitively to the different pressures which may rest on the shoulders of the rights-holder in such a situation. This may take account of the fact that a person may be pressured by the vendor not to reveal any rights to the purchaser.[42]

15.3.4 IMPLIED LEGAL EASEMENTS AND PROFITS

The provisions of schedule 3 paragraph 3 are discussed in chapter 12 concerning easements (at 12.6.2). To summarise here, where an easement or a profit is implied into a deed of transfer, and that deed is then registered, the easement or profit thus created will be a legal easement or profit, but will of course not be registered (since it was not created deliberately by the parties). Such easements will be binding upon subsequent purchasers of estates in the land if one of three conditions is met. First, the purchaser knows about the easement at the time of purchase; second, the easement would have been obvious on a reasonably careful inspection of the land; or third, the easement has been used at any time in the year prior to the disposition of the servient the land. These requirements are straightforward in terms of interpretation, with the possible exception of the second, which would be interpreted in line with the considerations outlined in the previous section regarding the hypothetical nature of the reasonable inspection test, and the sorts of factors that the court would take into account in determining what a reasonable inspection of the relevant land would be.

15.3.5 OTHER UNREGISTERED INTERESTS WHICH MAY OVERRIDE

The following are also protected in schedule 3. These rarely pose problems, and it is not necessary to consider them in detail here.

> '4 A customary right.
>
> 5 A public right.

---

[42] *Begum v Issa*, unreported, recorded on westlaw as 2014 WL 5833780.

Local land charges

    6 A local land charge.

Mines and minerals

    7 An interest in any coal or coal mine, the rights attached to any such interest and the rights of any person under section 38, 49 or 51 of the Coal Industry Act 1994 (c. 21).

    8 In the case of land to which title was registered before 1898, rights to mines and minerals (and incidental rights) created before 1898.

    9 In the case of land to which title was registered between 1898 and 1925 inclusive, rights to mines and minerals (and incidental rights) created before the date of registration of the title.'

15.4 PRIORITIES ON FIRST REGISTRATION

For cases involving first registrations, the priority rules are slightly more generous to existing rights-holders. This is because the categories are overriding interests are wider. All other rules remain the same. For first registrations, the list of rights which will override is contained in schedule 1. This provides that the following rights will be protected.

'Leasehold estates in land

    1 A leasehold estate in land granted for a term not exceeding seven years from the date of the grant, except for a lease the grant of which falls within section 4(1) (d), (e) or (f).

Relevant social housing tenancies

    1A A leasehold estate in land under a relevant social housing tenancy.

Interests of persons in actual occupation

    2 An interest belonging to a person in actual occupation, so far as relating to land of which he is in actual occupation, except for an interest under a settlement under the Settled Land Act 1925 (c. 18).

Easements and profits a prendre

    3 A legal easement or profit a prendre.

Customary and public rights

    4 A customary right.

    5 A public right.

Local land charges

    6 A local land charge.

Mines and minerals

    7 An interest in any coal or coal mine, the rights attached to any such interest and the rights of any person under section 38, 49 or 51 of the Coal Industry Act 1994 (c. 21).

    8 In the case of land to which title was registered before 1898, rights to mines and minerals (and incidental rights) created before 1898.

    9 In the case of land to which title was registered between 1898 and 1925 inclusive, rights to mines and minerals (and incidental rights) created before the date of registration of the title.'

The categories are therefore the same as for subsequent dispositions, but critically there are fewer conditions to be met. This can be seen clearly in paragraphs 2 and 3 when compared with the rules in schedule 3 as discussed earlier. Thus, for actual occupation both discoverability and inquiries are irrelevant. Similarly, for easements, there is no need for discoverability, knowledge, or use.

15.5 RULES APPLICABLE TO REGISTERED CHARGES

For registered charges, the priority rule is explained in section 30. This applies to dispositions of registered charges. The rules are exactly the same as for subsequent registrations under section 29.

15.6 EXCEPTIONAL CASES OF PRIORITY

15.6.1 OFFICIAL SEARCHES

Official searches do not produce an exception to the priority rules in theory. They are simply a means by which a person can obtain what is in effect a land registry-certified confirmation of the content of the register at a particular date. However, the consequence of such a search is to give a person priority over any subsequently registered interests for a certain period of time (30 days from the day on which the application was lodged). It also prevents a person being bound by a right which was in fact registered, if the land registry fails to inform them of its registration. The land registry practice guide explains the effect:

> 'An official search certificate with priority grants priority to the protected registrable disposition over other registrable dispositions, rights, interests or matters that have not been entered on the day list before the official search with priority and are not themselves protected by an earlier official search with priority (if capable of being protected by an official search)'.[43]

The official search does not therefore protect a purchaser in respect of overriding interests.

15.6.2 WAIVER AND CONSENT

As we noted earlier, in addition to the two central rules of the importance of the timing of the creation of rights on the one hand, and the special protections given to purchasers of registered legal estates on the other, the third critical feature of the priority regime is that where a person waives their priority or consents to the creation of a right, they will not be able to assert priority regardless of the rules as expressed in section 28 and 29 LRA 2002. This makes the forms required of waivers, and the policy considerations which have shaped our attitudes to, for example, undue influence in respect of waivers, critical to the operation of the priority rules in practice. Furthermore, in certain kinds of cases, there can be an implied waiver, as considered in *Paddington Building Society v Mendelsohn*.[44]

---

[43] Land Registry, Practice guide 12, official searches https://www.gov.uk/government/publications/official-searches-and-outline-applications/practice-guide-12-official-searches-and-outline-applications#priority-and-priority-periods.

[44] *Paddington Building Society v Mendelsohn* (1985) 50 P & CR 244 (CA).

Key case: *Paddington Building Society v Mendelsohn* (1985) 50 P & CR 244

In this case, a mother and son agreed that they would purchase a leasehold interest in a flat. The mother provided a deposit of approximately half the purchase price, and the remainder was provided by a mortgage. The transfer was made and executed and the son agreed to pay the mortgage instalments. The building society was unaware of the mother's involvement which had been kept secret due to the mother's age and her inability to take out a mortgage in her own name. The son, his girlfriend, and the mother then all moved into the flat. The mother carried out considerable improvements on the flat. The son and girlfriend then later moved out, and the mother agreed to his taking out a second mortgage. A deed was then executed setting out the beneficial entitlement of the mother. The mortgage payments then fell into arrears and the building society sought possession. The Court of Appeal was required to assess the nature of the mother's interest, and the question of any priority between the mother and the lender. The court reasoned as follows on that point:

> 'There being no express declaration of trust or agreement as to the beneficial interests of the mother and the son at the time of the acquisition of the flat, the nature of the mother's equitable interest must depend on the intention to be imputed to the son and the mother at the time of the acquisition. Since the mother knew and intended that them mortgage was to be granted to the society and that without the mortgage on the flat in which she claims a beneficial interest could not have been acquired, the only possible intention to impute to the parties is an intention that the mother's rights were to be subject to the rights of the society'.[45]

The fact that this case involved registered and not unregistered land did not, in the view of the court, alter this conclusion at all. The wording that Browne-Wilkinson LJ uses in this case is perhaps unfortunate in modern terms, particularly the use of 'impute' in relation to the parties' intentions, since we know now from *Jones v Kernott*[46] that imputation in the way indicated here in inappropriate. However, when the actual reasoning is examined, it is clear that this is not a case of imputation at all, but rather an implied intention based on what the court assesses the parties must actually have been thinking. Indeed, it is clear that the mother had an express intention that the mortgage be created. Furthermore, in the academic commentary which arose in the aftermath of the Court of Appeal's decision, it is clear that many saw this case as a misleading expression of the earlier case law (particularly *Gissing v Gissing*[47]), and a retreat from the protection given to third parties in *Boland*.[48] Indeed, post-*Mendelsohn*,[49] Thompson reasoned that *Boland*[50] had 'become something of a damp squib',[51] a gloomy prediction which proved to be untrue. The point from this case which appears to have survived into the modern law however is this idea that certain facts can give rise to, in effect, an implied waiver of priority in respect of rights arising on the creation of a mortgage. That is certainly how Snell's equity interprets the case, citing it as authority for the point that, 'where a beneficial co-owner of a property agrees to a sum being raised on the property by way of mortgage in priority to the beneficial interest the mortgagee has priority'.[52]

---

[45] *Paddington Building Society v Mendelsohn* (1985) 50 P & CR 244 (CA) (citation taken from official transcript).
[46] *Jones v Kernott* [2011] UKSC 53, [2012] 1 AC 776.
[47] *Gissing v Gissing* [1971] AC 886 (HL).
[48] *Williams & Glyn's Bank Ltd v Boland* [1981] AC 487 (HL).
[49] *Paddington Building Society v Mendelsohn* (1985) 50 P & CR 244 (CA).
[50] *Williams & Glyn's Bank Ltd v Boland* [1981] AC 487 (HL).
[51] M P Thompson, 'The retreat from *Boland*' [1986] Conv 57, 61.
[52] J McGhee, *Snell's Equity* (Sweet & Maxwell, London, 2017), [4.051].

15.6.3 IMPLIED CONSENT—THE ACQUISITION MORTGAGE

There are some cases, however, where the law takes the rules relating to waiver and consent one step further, and relies on the idea of implied consent to justify the alteration of the usual priority rules even where the third party was unaware of or did not explicitly consent to the creation of the mortgage. One example of this is the acquisition mortgage. Acquisition mortgages are mortgages granted at the time of the acquisition of title to property. The theory behind the rules, as explained in *Abbey National v Cann*[53] and *North Eastern Property Buyers*,[54] is that where a person purchases property with the aid of a mortgage, any person deriving an interest as a result of that purchase only does so because the title-holder is able to rely on the mortgage to assist in the purchase. As a result, whatever the precise timings with regards to the creation of such interests, the mortgage will take priority over the derivative interest.

> **Key case:** *Abbey National v Cann* [1991] 1 AC 56
>
> In one of the most significant land law cases, the House of Lords was required, essentially, to consider the operation of priorities in the context of mortgages. The case involved a mortgage of a property on the outskirts of London. The grantor of the charge was registered as proprietor of the property on the same day as he granted the charge. He defaulted on the mortgage and the lender sought possession. However, his mother, who in fact lived in the property, and her now-husband argued that they had an equitable interest in the property which took priority over the lender as they had lived in the property from the date of purchase.
>
> Mrs Cann (the mother) was aware of and acquiesced in the mortgage but George Cann (the son) had not informed the lender of her presence, and had stated that the purchase of the property was for his own sole occupation. Mrs Cann argued that her priority over the lender could be established because, first, according to her, she had been in actual occupation prior to completion of the purchase. The court found that this was impossible that the completion had taken place at around 12.20 p.m. on the relevant day and she had not moved in by that point (she was in The Netherlands on holiday). However, George Cann and Mrs Cann's husband, Abraham Cann (the brother of Mrs Cann's first husband), did arrive at the property at 10 a.m. on the relevant day with a van including Mrs Cann's belongings and they started moving these into the house at around 11.45. However, she was certainly in actual occupation at the date at which the purchase and the charge were registered. In assessing whether these facts allowed Mrs Cann to claim priority over the lender, Lord Oliver began by considering what the appropriate date would be when considering the question of actual occupation. As we noted earlier, Lord Oliver stated that the relevant date would be the date of the disposition, not of registration. He reasoned that this 'produces a result which is just, convenient and certain, as opposed to one which is capable of leading to manifest injustice and absurdity'.[55] The absurdity in question is that a mortgagee should, 'after completion and after having made all possible inquiries and parted with his money, by bound by the interest asserted by a newly-arrived occupation coming in between completion and the registration of the charge'.[56] However, Lord Oliver did acknowledge that the statutory wording produced some difficulties in supporting such

---

[53] *Abbey National v Cann* [1991] 1 AC 56 (HL).
[54] *North East Property Buyers* [2014] UKSC 52, [2015] AC 385.
[55] *Abbey National v Cann* [1991] 1 AC 56 (HL), 83.
[56] *Abbey National v Cann* [1991] 1 AC 56 (HL), 83.

an interpretation of the provisions and that the date for assessing the overriding quality of a right must be the date of registration. However, that did not mean, as the court highlighted, that the date for assessing actual occupation must also be the date of registration. Rather, Lord Oliver reasoned:

> 'It is not the actual occupation which gives rise to the right or determines its existence. Actual occupation merely operates as the trigger, as it were, for the treatment of the right, whatever it may be, as an overriding interest. Nor does the additional quality of the right as an overriding interest alter the nature or equality of the right itself'.[57]

As a result of this, the existence of the right can be assessed at any point in the conveyancing chain. Given the absurdity of expecting physical inspection post-completion, there is no reason why the question of actual occupation cannot be answered at the time of the conveyance, rather than at the time of its registration.

The second issue which Lord Oliver then examined, was the order in which these relevant rights arose. After considering a number of earlier cases including *Church of England Building Society v Piskor*[58] and *In re Connolly Brothers (no 2)*[59] and *Security Trust Co v Royal Bank of Canada*,[60] Lord Oliver concluded that, 'a person cannot charge a legal estate that he does not have'[61] but:

> 'In the vast majority of cases, the acquisition of the legal estate and the charge are not only precisely simultaneous but indissolubly bound together. The acquisition of the legal estate is entirely dependent upon the provision of funds which will have been provided before the conveyance can take effect and which are provided only against an agreement that the estate will be charged'.[62]

Indeed, in some cases, the charge will actually have been executed before the transfer of title, subject to that transfer. This means that:

> 'The reality is that the purchaser of land who relies upon a building society or bank loan for completion of his purchase never in fact acquires anything but an equity of redemption, for the land is, from the very inception, charged... The 'scintilla temporis' is no more than a legal artifice'.[63]

As a result, according to the court, Mrs Cann's interest did not arise prior to the charge, but rather simultaneously with it, and therefore could not have had priority.

Key case: *Re North East Property Buyers* [2014] UKSC 52 (also known as *Scott v Southern Pacific*)

This case involved an agreement between a home-owner vendor, and a purchaser in an equity release scheme. The purchaser promised that the home-owners would be entitled to live in their properties indefinitely, through the granting of a lease for life post-completion of the sale. However, the vendor charged the relevant properties to assist with purchase, the charge being granted prior to the grant of the tenancy (which was in fact a 2 year assured shorthold tenancy). The purchaser then fell behind on

---

[57] *Abbey National v Cann* [1991] 1 AC 56 (HL), 87.
[58] *Church of England Building Society v Piskor* [1954] Ch 553 (CA).
[59] *In re Connolly Brothers (no 2)* [1912] 2 Ch 25 (CA).
[60] *Security Trust Co v Royal Bank of Canada* [1976] AC 503 (PC).
[61] *Abbey National v Cann* [1991] 1 AC 56 (HL), 92.
[62] *Abbey National v Cann* [1991] 1 AC 56 (HL), 92.
[63] *Abbey National v Cann* [1991] 1 AC 56 (HL), 92.

the mortgage, and the mortgage company sought possession of the property against the vendor. The question was whether the vendor had any proprietary interests which took priority over the lender's charge. On the facts of the case, there was no proprietary interest in existence prior to the grant of the mortgage, and so there could be no priority dispute in the case. However, the court gives some guidance on the role of the acquisition mortgage rule in post-2002 Act cases. The court gives support to *Cann*, and concludes that the scintilla temporis approach is still applicable in the modern law. However, it is clear that Baroness Hale in particular felt that the approach as expressed in *Cann* was not entirely satisfactory. She reasoned:

> 'I confess to some uneasiness about even that conclusion, for two reasons. First, *Cann* was not a case in which the vendor had been deceived in any way or been made promises which the purchaser could not keep. Should there not come a point when a vendor who has been tricked out of her property can assert her rights even against a subsequent purchaser or mortgagee? Second, *Cann* was not a case in which the lenders could be accused of acting irresponsibly in any way. Should there not come a point when the claims of lenders who have failed to heed the obvious warning signs that would have told them that this borrower was not a good risk are postponed to those of vendors who have been made promises that the borrowers cannot keep? Innocence is a comparative concept. There ought to be some middle way between the "all of nothing" approach of the present law'.[64]

These comments by Baroness Hale highlight the consequences of treating the interactions between lender and third parties of being 'mere' priority disputes in the sense that no account is taken in the rules as to the relative power of such parties in disputes, and their relative abilities to ensure that their own interests are protected. Furthermore, as Televantos and Maniscalco reason, the approach of Baroness Hale in this case was to suggest that the operation of the rule in *Cann* is a question of interpretation of the facts, not of the application of a concrete rule.[65] Essentially, under Baroness Hale's approach, it would be a factual question as to whether any concrete, deed and mortgage would be treated as indivisible, with no scintilla temporis, or not. Under Lord Collins' approach (which on this question appears to have been the minority view), the indivisibility of these steps would be a rule of law, not a question of fact.

Further analysis: The acquisition mortgage

Although the difference in opinion between Lord Collins and Lady Hale in *North Eastern Property Buyers*[66] is strictly obiter, their discussion is important for how the case law surrounding *Cann* is to be interpreted under the 2002 Act provisions. As noted earlier, Televantos and Maniscalco discuss the differing approaches and argue that Lord Collins' view, more certain and predictable as it is in its operation, is the preferred option.[67] Hopkins disagrees. He argues that Baroness Hale's view is more persuasive, stating:

> 'For the parties, contract, completion and mortgage are stages in a composite transaction, and the vendor-purchaser constructive trust, which was the focus of the Supreme Court's attention in its answer to the first question [ie whether the vendor had a proprietary interest prior to the completion of the sale] continues to define the relationship between the two parties until legal title passes by registration. To this extent, there is perhaps an even greater sense of proximity between contract and completion than exists between the "indivisible" stages of completion and mortgage. Notwithstanding, the different legal effects of the contract,

---

[64] *North East Property Buyers* [2014] UKSC 52, [2015] AC 385, [122].
[65] A Televantos and L Maniscalco, 'Proprietary estoppel and vendor purchaser constructive trusts' (2015) 74 CLJ 27, 29.
[66] *North East Property Buyers* [2014] UKSC 52, [2015] AC 385.
[67] A Televantos and L Maniscalco, 'Proprietary estoppel and vendor purchaser constructive trusts' (2015) 74 CLJ 27, 30.

> acknowledged by Lord Collins, lean towards keeping the contract separate and distinct. That is reflected by the fact that the nature of the relationship between vendor and purchaser under the trust changes significantly at the point of completion... If the matter retained practical significance, treating the contract as divisive from completion and mortgage could, no doubt, create difficulties.'[68]
>
> Acknowledging these difficulties, however, Hopkins then concludes, 'in answering priority questions, where a "dead heat" is not permitted, the courts cannot shy away from the fact that the outcome of cases may be dependent upon fine distinctions'.[69]
>
> Sparkes, however, agrees with Hale in so far as he argues that the current approach, which treats both 'innocent' parties in these questions as being 'equally innocent', is misplaced.[70] He highlights that since the coming into force of the 2002 Act, and the sidelining of the concept of notice (see chapter 3, 3.4.3.1 for the position in unregistered land – once again, the doctrine of notice is irrelevant in registered land), that 'the irrelevance of notice has morphed into the idea that registered land priorities begin and end with the provisions of ss. 28 and 29. A literal reading of this legislation is impossible... Clearly s.28 and 29 priorities can be modified by waiver or estoppel; and an implied subordination may be inferred from the circumstance that a contributor knows that a mortgage is needed to buy the property to which his or her equity will attach'.[71]
>
> Thus, if we can include some aspects beyond the legislative scheme in determining the relative priorities of parties, as there is no doubt that we do, why not others? In short, Sparkes reasons, 'the simple priority scheme in ss.28 and 29 of the LRA 2002 is much too simplistic'.[72] He highlights that the real core of this issue, had the court not felt so bound by the strictures of priority rules as expressed in the statute, would have been whether the priority rules could be varied by estoppel.[73] Whether or not one agrees with this analysis of the facts in the case, there is a valid argument to be made that the priority scheme in section 28 and 29 is 'too simplistic'. However, this simplicity also brings its own benefits, and that lies in the ease of conveyancing which a simplistic scheme like this produces. Certainly such certainty and simplicity has the risk of disadvantaging vulnerable home-owners like those in the *North East Property Buyers* litigation, but it also allows for cheaper conveyancing for all. Like the arguments which persist in relation to mortgages and the easy functioning of the mortgage market, there is no 'cost free' solution to priority disputes. The question must be rather where the system's priorities lie when trying to resolve them.

Whatever one's views of the rule relating to acquisition mortgages as a policy, it is worth examining whether the decision in *Cann* itself stands up to scrutiny. In the immediate aftermath of the decision, many whilst supportive of the outcome, were sceptical regarding the basis for the decision, and the search for an alternative explanation for *Cann* continues.

Goldberg, for example, has sought to explain the result in *Cann* on the basis of the effect of contracts in relation to interests in land in equity. Thus, he argues that:

> '[the] legal estate, in the *scintilla temporis* between its being obtained by the purchaser and its being subjected to the legal charge of the lender, by clothing the lender's existing equitable interest [arising

---

[68] N Hopkins, 'Priorities and sale and lease back: a wrong question, much ado about nothing and a story of tails and dogs' [2015] Conv 245, 251.

[69] N Hopkins, 'Priorities and sale and lease back: a wrong question, much ado about nothing and a story of tails and dogs' [2015] Conv 245, 251–2.

[70] P Sparkes, 'Reserving a slice of cake' [2015] Conv 301.

[71] P Sparkes, 'Reserving a slice of cake' [2015] Conv 301, 312.

[72] P Sparkes, 'Reserving a slice of cake' [2015] Conv 301, 315.

[73] P Sparkes, 'Reserving a slice of cake' [2015] Conv 301, 315.

through contract], enabled the latter (because of the priority of its creation) to prevail over the equitable interest of the actual occupier of the land, which had admittedly been created only "on or immediately prior to completion" of the purchase'.[74]

The steps, therefore, according to Goldberg would be as follows:

1. Creation of a contract for the sale of legal title to the purchaser. At this point the vendor would hold on trust for the purchaser.
2. Creation of a contract for the mortgage, which under the authority of *Tailby*[75] becomes enforceable as soon as the property is acquired, and therefore creates an equitable charge as soon as the equitable title is acquired through the contract: 'the charge is precisely simultaneous, and indissolubly bound together, not with the acquisition of the legal estate, but with the acquisition of the equitable... immediately on making the contract of sale'. At this point, the lender would therefore have an equitable mortgage.
3. The disposition vesting legal title in the purchaser.
4. The creation of an equitable interest in the land binding the purchaser's title in favour of the beneficiary of the trust.

On such an approach, the timing means that the lender has priority by virtue of the fact that their interest was created first.

However this approach does encounter some difficulties, not least the fact that if this is a correct analysis of the timings, then whilst an equitable mortgage might have had priority over the interest under the trust, that equitable mortgage would have disappeared on the creation of the legal mortgage. That legal mortgage would, one assumes, be subject to the usual priority rules. Another potential issue with this approach is the idea that the purchaser becomes subject to an equitable mortgage as soon as they acquired equitable title to the property. This would be surprising since by necessity the funds which would justify the existence of a mortgage would not have been released at this point, an understanding supported by that in *North East Property Buyers*.

Smith has also analysed the decision, and considers whether the real justification for the case is actually a simple policy argument: 'the mortgagee wins because he is a mortgagee'.[76] This reasoning was particularly apt on the facts of *Cann* itself because in fact the source of finance for the property was two-fold—part of the money was provided through the mortgage, but the other part was provided by Mrs Cann from the sale of her former home. Per Smith, 'George Cann had two overlapping sources of finance: the proceeds from the previous home and the mortgage. What logic or sense is there in saying that the mortgagee must have priority'.[77] As such, in questioning the basis for the House of Lords seeming rejection of the scintilla temporis analysis, Smith highlights that the explanation for the decision in case is not as simple as may appear from Lord Oliver and Lord Jauncey's judgments.

---

[74] G D Golberg, 'Vivit ac vivat scintilla temporis' (1992) 108 LQR 380, 382.
[75] *Tailby v Official Receiver* (1888) 13 AppCas 523.
[76] R J Smith, 'Mortgagees and trust beneficiaries' (1990) 106 LQR 545, 548.
[77] R J Smith, 'Mortgagees and trust beneficiaries' (1990) 106 LQR 545, 548.

15.6.4 OVERREACHING

We considered the rules relating to overreaching of interests under trusts in chapter 3 at 3.3.4.1 and consider them in relation to co-ownership in the chapter which follows. However, it is not just interests under trusts which are susceptible to being overreached, as *Mortgage Express v Lambert*[78] highlights. For the purposes of clarity, overreaching is the mechanism by which interests under a trust are transferred into the proceeds of sale when property is sold, or otherwise lose priority on a disposition of an estate in the relevant land. The mechanism is provided for in the Law of Property Act 1925, section 2, which states that:

'(1) A conveyance to a purchaser of a legal estate in land shall overreach any equitable interest or power affecting that estate, whether or not he has notice thereof, if—

…

(ii) the conveyance is made by trustees of land and the equitable interest or power is at the date of the conveyance capable of being overreached by such trustees under the provisions of subsection (2) of this section or independently of that subsection, and the requirements of section 27 of this Act respecting the payment of capital money arising on such a conveyance are complied with'.

Thus, for overreaching to occur, the interest in question must be capable of being overreached, and there has to be a disposition of an estate in land. The nature of rights that can be overreached is considered in *Mortgage Express v Lambert*.

> **Key case: *Mortgage Express v Lambert* [2016] EWCA Civ 555**
>
> Ms Lambert had a lease in a flat in Maidstone. The flat was worth approximately £120,000, but she agreed to sell the flat for £30,000 due to financial problems. The purchasers promised that upon completion, she would be able to remain living in the flat. Title was transferred to Sinclair and Clement. They then granted a mortgage to Mortgage Express for £104,550. Title was then transferred into Sinclair's sole name. Sinclair fell into arrears and the lender sought possession. Amongst other questions, the court had to determine whether Ms Lambert's equitable right was binding upon the lender. In order to answer this question, the court was required to determine whether (a) this interest was capable of affecting the estate in land; (b) whether it had been overreached; and (c) whether, if not overreached, it was overriding on the grant of the mortgage. In making this assessment, the court interpreted equitable interest broadly, and did not confine the operation of overreaching to interests under a trust. Per Lewison LJ:
>
> 'It is clear from the opening words of that section that it applies to "any equitable interest" affecting the estate; and equitable interests are themselves widely defined by section 1 (8) of that Act. Moreover the express list of exclusions from overreaching in section 2 (3) (which includes such matters as easements, equitable charges protected by deposit of deeds, and estate contracts) demonstrates that the ambit of overreaching is wide, otherwise those exclusions would not have been necessary'.[79]
>
> The result of this decision is that the scope of overreaching is potentially somewhat wider than may have been thought. Furthermore, there is now an uneasy interaction between the mere equity right which

---

[78] *Mortgage Express v Lambert* [2016] EWCA Civ 555, [2017] Ch 93.
[79] *Mortgage Express v Lambert* [2016] EWCA Civ 555, [2017] Ch 93, [37].

Ms Lambert was said to have, and other kinds of equitable rights, such as those arising under estate contracts, which are not susceptible to overreaching as discussed in chapter 14 at 14.2. As I have argued elsewhere, this is particularly problematic in the case of leases:

> 'Furthermore, problems are also likely to arise in relation to the leasehold estate in particular. There are essentially five ways in which an equitable lease could arise: first, an attempt to create a legal lease can fail for want of formalities giving rise to an equitable lease on the same terms; secondly, an equitable lease could be deliberately created by stipulation in the contract that the lease would only take effect in equity; thirdly, the beneficiary of a trust of a freehold or a leasehold estate could grant a lease such that there was an equitable lease of the trust property; fourthly, the holder of a legal lease could declare a trust of that lease (or a trust of the lease could arise by implication or by statute); and finally, an equitable lease could be granted as a remedy following the crystallisation of an equity arising by estoppel. Following *Lambert* and *Sabherwal*,[80] what is the outcome in each of these scenarios?
>
> In the first, there would be an estate contract, and the lease would not be overreached. There would be no trust duties present in this case. In the second scenario, there would be no trust duties, but the lease could be overreached as there is no contract to 'create or convey the legal estate' (LPA 1925 s.2(3)). In the third case, the position would be the same: no trust duties, but overreaching would occur. In the fourth case, there would be overreaching, because the lease would be an interest under a trust, but the trustees would, without question, be susceptible to fiduciary duties. Finally, in the estoppel case, the equity arising by estoppel could be overreached unless the court concluded that the equitable lease granted as a remedy was 'commercial' in the sense explained in *Sabherwal*. Although not impossible as a matter of logic, the range of options here as to what will happen to 'an equitable lease' in terms of overreaching, can hardly be described as a model of clarity or simplicity'.[81]

15.6.5 SUBROGATION

Another special priority rule which exists in relation to mortgages, and for that reason we consider it in chapter 11 at 11.7.2, is the rules relating to subrogation. These allow for a by-passing of the normal priority rules in cases where, in effect, a lender is able to 'buy' the priority of an earlier lender.

15.7 CONSEQUENCES OF A LOSS OF PRIORITY

If, for some reason, a right is neither registered, nor overriding, then that right will lose priority to the purchaser of a relevant estate if that purchase is subsequently registered. This balance has been carefully struck, and the rights which can bind the purchaser are generally those which are either discoverable through physical inspection without too much difficulty, or where they appear on the register themselves. However, the precise nature of the loss of priority, and what happens to the 'losing' right is not entirely clear from the statutory provisions. Section 29 states that such a right will be 'postponed to the estate under the disposition', which is a slightly odd

---

[80] *Birmingham Midshires Mortgage Services Ltd v Sabherwal* (2000) 80 P & CR 256.
[81] E Lees, 'Overreaching mere equities: *Mortgage Express v Lambert* [2016] EWCA Civ 555' [2017] Conv 72, 81.

way of phrasing a loss of priority. The question is essentially as to whether the right is effectively destroyed, in so far as it can never have priority again, or whether it is merely postponed in respect of the current owner of the relevant estate. For example, can the right-holder later make an entry of a notice on the register where appropriate and ensure that their right was protected as against subsequent purchasers? This approach would see 'postponing' as meaning that the right is effectively put into 'freeze' and can be revived but not in respect of the current estate-holder. Another approach would be to say that once a right loses its priority to an estate, such as 'the freehold' it can never take priority over that freehold again. Finally, as mentioned, it could be interpreted so as to mean 'destroy'.

> **Further analysis: The meaning of postpone**
>
> Dixon has explained the various possibilities as to what section 29 and the word postpone might mean in this context. Thus,
>
> > 'Possibility 1... it could be that s.29 effectively destroys *as property rights* all prior unprotected proprietary interests on the occasion of a registered disposition for valuable consideration. In other words, s. 29 postulates a voidness rule.[82]
>
> This possibility, Dixon highlights, is 'unambiguous and simple to apply'.[83] The problem is that this is not what the statute seems to say. Therefore, there is possibility 2.
>
> > 'Another view is that s.29 does not cause an unprotected right to be void as an interest against the land, but merely—as the section says—postpones it. The interest continues to exist as a property right, but cannot be enforced against any "interest under the disposition"... Thus, where the first disposition is the grant of a lease of the whole... an unprotected priori interest that binds the freehold will not bind the leasehold... but when the lease determines, the interest will resume its effect against the freehold'.[84]
>
> This possibility could be preferred because it best meets the language of the statutory provision. However, it is certainly more complicated in practice, and could lead to rights being revived many years later.
>
> We can also add a possibility three, which is that the right is postponed to the estate under the disposition *for now*, but can be revived as against that estate on a subsequent disposition should its priority then be protected. So, for example, we can imagine a scenario in which a person has an interest under a trust in relation to the relevant freehold land. The freehold title is transferred to a third party, at a time when the beneficiary of the trust was not in actual occupation. It is possible that the beneficiary of the trust could then subsequently go into actual occupation (although admittedly unlikely unless the third party was somehow connected to the vendor of the land or the beneficiary themselves). What then if the third party should sell the freehold title again onto another 'fourth' party? Would the interest under the trust somehow revive and bind the 'fourth' party thanks to the actual occupation of the beneficiary? This would be a very problematic outcome for the simplicity of the law, and would mean that rights could exist in abeyance for a number of years before being 'revived'. However, if Dixon is right that the section 29 effect is merely one of priority, and not validity, then surely such an option is not a logical impossibility.

---

[82] M Dixon, 'Priorities under the Land Registration Act 2002' (2009) 125 LQR 401, 404.
[83] M Dixon, 'Priorities under the Land Registration Act 2002' (2009) 125 LQR 401, 404.
[84] M Dixon, 'Priorities under the Land Registration Act 2002' (2009) 125 LQR 401, 405.

These different options were considered by the Court of Appeal in *Halifax v Popeck*.[85] However, the interpretation given by the court in that case has been case into doubt by what was HM Adjudicator in *Rosefair v Butler*.[86]

> **Key case:** *Halifax v Popeck* [2008] EWHC 1692
>
> This case concerned a fraud perpetuated by John and Tracy Whale with the help of solicitors who were either themselves fraudulent or totally incompetent. The fraud was conducted as follows. Mr and Mrs Whale were registered proprietors of a property in Hornchurch. The property was a house with a large garden, at the bottom of which were three garages. Against the house they had secured two mortgages from Cheltenham & Gloucester. John was then declared bankrupt. Subsequently, Mrs Whale applied to Halifax for a mortgage which purported to be a mortgage over the bungalow. However, the mortgage was created in favour of Halifax but was registered not against the title of the bungalow but against another title which was in fact a strip of land at the end of the garden and one of the garages and Tracy became sole registered proprietor of this strip.
>
> This having worked well, Tracy and John decided to perpetrate the same fraud for a second time, this time registering the title of the bungalow in the name of a company of which John was the sole director and Tracy the sold shareholder and then making the purchase, this time of the bungalow, to 'John Sinclair' which was in fact John Whale under an assumed name. John Sinclair then granted a mortgage over another strip at the bottom of the garden to the Bank of Scotland. The question in the case, the Bank of Scotland having obtained charges over the bungalow itself and Halifax having the benefit of a proprietary estoppel in relation to the bungalow, was how the relative priorities between the respective banks operated given the transfer of title to the bungalow from Tracy and John, to the company, and then to John Sinclair. This mattered notwithstanding the merger between Halifax and Bank of Scotland because the fraudulent/incompetent solicitor had moved firms during these fraudulent transactions and so it was relevant to determine which firm of solicitors should bear the cost of his incompetence.
>
> In determining this, the court's starting point was the general priority rule as explained in section 28, ie that the priorities is determined first by the order in which equitable interests are created. However, section 29 creates an exception to this general rule, and whilst that was not determinative of the position between Halifax and Bank of Scotland since neither was a purchaser of a registered estate duly registered in relation to the bungalow itself, it was important because Tracy and John transferred the freehold in the bungalow to John after the creation of Halifax's proprietary estoppel but before the creation of the equitable charge in favour of Bank of Scotland. The question was whether this meant that the Halifax claim was postponed to the freehold estate and, if so, what was the consequence of this postponement for the relationship between BoS and Halifax. This depended upon two things. First, was the transaction in this case one to which section 29 applied? Second, what was the effect of 'postponement' on a right?
>
> On the first question, the court concluded that the purported consideration provided in this case was part of the fraudulent transaction, and as such, there was no true consideration. As the court highlighted:
>
>> 'none of the conveyancing documents can be trusted and there is an equally, if not more, compelling analysis, namely that this is simply the execution of a fraudulent enterprise in the context of which the concept

---

[85] *Halifax Plc v Curry Popeck (A Firm)* [2008] EWHC 1692 (Ch), [2009] 1 P & CR DG3.
[86] *Rosefair v Butler* REF/2013/0046, 49, 50, 51, 52, 53.

of "consideration" is meaningless. I would according decide this case on the footing that the general rule set out in section 28 applies because Bank of Scotland cannot bring itself within the provisions of section 29'.[87]

Thus, in this case, the test for valuable consideration in section 29 was said to be one of substance, not form. As such section 29 could not be used in cases of fraud like this.

However, the court nevertheless went on to address the second question, considering, obiter, the meaning of postpone within the relevant legislative provisions. The court reasoned as follows:

> 'On the assumption of a transfer for valuable consideration, equitable interests binding the disponor do not bind the disponee as interests in land, even if the disponee was a party to the creation of those interests. This will mean that if the disponee then creates a subsequent equitable obligation binding the estate, there will be no question of competing equities. The obligation which the disponee created will continue to bind him as a personal obligation'.[88]

In other words, when an interest is 'postponed' to an estate on transfer, and the purchaser takes the estate in land free from that interest even if he was party to the interest's creation, that equitable interest cannot subsequently be said to bind the estate and in that sense as a proprietary interest it cannot bind the land again. This interpretation is certainly possible on the way that the legislation is worded. It is, as explained by Dixon earlier, is the simplest approach to the relevant provision. It relies on a conceptualisation of equitable interests and other derivative rights being 'formed out of' an estate in land, which are then postponed to that estate when section 29 intervenes. This does not affect their validity as a matter of contract law, for example, but it does mean that they lose their proprietary status. As noted earlier, however, this is a somewhat difficult interpretation and is not one which has been accepted in all subsequent case law. For example, in *Rosefair v Butler*,[89] Martin Dray siting as a Deputy Adjudicator reasoned:

> 'I consider that there is a fundamental difference between postponement on the one hand and the termination of a contract/property interest on the other. Despite the want of protection by notice, the head contract remains a valid, subsisting contract. It remains enforceable as against SJC. Indeed, in an appropriate case (albeit not this case), depending on the relationship between the original vendor and the current owner of the freehold estate, a postponed contract could be ordered to be specifically performed at the suit of the purchaser (with the original vendor being required to procure the new owner to transfer the property in completion of the contract)'.[90]

15.8 CONCLUSION

The priority rules can be applied in a relatively formulaic way. As long as the questions are approached in the right sequence: order of creation; applicability of the special priority rule for registered purchasers; and then exceptional priority rules, there is little scope for diversion from the right course. It is in this lack of flexibility, however, that many of the criticisms of the priority schemes may lie. We have seen how the academic community is split on whether these rules should prioritise the simplicity of their application, or the sensitivity of their results. In applying these rules, therefore, understanding of such analysis is critical to a thoughtful consideration of the outcomes.

---

[87] *Halifax Plc v Curry Popeck (A Firm)* [2008] EWHC 1692 (Ch), [2009] 1 P & CR DG3, [46].
[88] *Halifax Plc v Curry Popeck (A Firm)* [2008] EWHC 1692 (Ch), [2009] 1 P & CR DG3, [51].
[89] *Rosefair v Butler* REF/2013/0046, 49, 50, 51, 52, 53.
[90] *Rosefair v Butler* REF/2013/0046, 49, 50, 51, 52, 53, [96].

Summary: LRA 2002 priority rules

Remember to check also whether any of the exceptional priority rules apply.

(1) Do you have a disposition of a registered estate in land?

Disposition is defined in the LPA 1925. For any disposition of a registered estate in land the registration provisions will be relevant. See section 27(1) LRA 2002 for which estates require to be registered.

(2) What interests bind the registered estate immediately prior to the disposition in question?

This preliminary question is one you must answer in every problem question. For the interest to 'bind the estate' it must be a property right. If you are thorough with this question you will avoid using the LRA 2002 to suggest that disponee is bound by interests which are either personal in nature or which arise after the transfer. In the latter case, although P might be bound by these interests, he will not be bound thanks to the LRA 2002.

(3) Was the transfer made for valuable considered? (Money, or money's worth).

If no, then the question of priority of interests will be dealt with under section 28 whereby the priority of the interests will not be affected by the disposition. In other words, the disponee will be bound by those interests that bound the estate prior to the disposition. Section 28 applies to those taking under a gift, those taking under a will, and those who although in form have provided valuable consideration, have not in fact done so as a matter of substance (*Halifax v Popeck*[91]).

If yes, then you must turn to section 29 (or, if you are dealing with a registered charge, section 30).

(4) What rights are binding upon P?

Section 29 provides that P will only be bound by those interests that are (a) registered charges; (b) the subject of a notice on the register; or (c) are interests that override under schedule 1 and schedule 3. The first two will be easy to spot, but remember, some interests cannot be the subject of a notice—see section 33 (interest under a trust of land, interest under the Settled Land Act 1925, legal leases of 3 years or less).

If you are not dealing with a registered charge, or the interest is not the subject of a notice, then you must turn to the relevant schedule. We focus here on schedule 3.

(5) Are there any overriding interests?

Sch 3 protects as overriding interests (primarily) (a) short legal leases (7 years or less); (b) the interests of those in actual occupation; and (c) implied legal easements.

For (b), remember, first, that the meaning of actual occupation depends on the type of property concerned, and second, that circumstances are everything here—there are no hard and fast rules.

(6) Is R in actual occupation?

There are certain factors that are taken into account by the courts—for example: the presence or absence of belongings; intention to occupy or to return to occupation; permanence and continuity of occupation; reason for any absence; and the type of land. It is also possible to occupy through agents or employees. If an agent or employee is in occupation it is important to

---

[91] *Halifax Plc v Curry Popeck (A Firm)* [2008] EWHC 1692 (Ch), [2009] 1 P & CR DG3.

ascertain whether they are occupying for their own or their employer's benefit. When someone leaves actual occupation, that will be characterised by the intention never to come back.

(7) Is R in actual occupation at the relevant time?

There is some dispute as to what constitutes the relevant date—the date of the disposition (deed), or registration, or both. *Abbey National v Cann*[92] (and good sense), suggest that it should be the date of the deed. However, Lewison J in *Thompson v Foy*[93] suggests it is both the date of the deed and of registration. This is based on the wording of section 29. It is not however binding, and has not been generally accepted.

(8) If R does have an identifiable right, and is in actual occupation, then you must look at Sch3(2) to determine whether his actual occupation is sufficient to protect his interest.

   a) Has P made inquiry of the right-holder (R)? This is not a hypothetical question. If P has made no inquiry then it does not matter what R would have said had he been asked. If P does make inquiry, and R does not reveal their interest in the land when they ought to have done (ought to is probably concerned with R's knowledge of their rights and the circumstances surrounding P's inquiry), then P will not be bound by R's interest.

   b) Did P know about R's right? If the answer to this is yes then P will be bound by R's interest, whether or not R's actual occupation would have been obvious on a reasonably careful inspection.

   c) Was R's actual occupation obvious on a reasonably careful inspection of the land? This may prove to be a difficult question and is largely a matter of looking at all the circumstances to make a hypothetical judgment.

(9) What are the consequences?

If the right is not binding on the disponee, it will be postponed to the estate under the disposition. It is not clear what postponed means from the case law. *Halifax v Popeck*[94] suggests (obiter) that it means the right is extinguished; *Rosefair v Butler*[95] takes a different approaching, focusing on the estate under the disposition.

PRINCIPLES

How do these rules shape the balance of the principles operating in relation to land law? To recap, these principles were:

1. Certainty
2. Sensitivity to context
3. Transactability
4. Systemic and individual effects
5. Recognition of the social role of the land law system.

---

[92] *Abbey National v Cann* [1991] 1 AC 56 (HL).
[93] *Thompson v Foy* [2009] EWHC 1076 (Ch), [2010] 1 P & CR 16.
[94] *Halifax Plc v Curry Popeck (A Firm)* [2008] EWHC 1692 (Ch), [2009] 1 P & CR DG3.
[95] *Rosefair v Butler* REF/2013/0046, 49, 50, 51, 52, 53.

Priority disputes are at the very core of the land law system. Yes, the system is made up of a series of blocks, but we only know the content of each of those blocks by reference to what happens when different rights in land come into conflict. Thus, we only know the content of the right of lender in a mortgage situation by analyzing what that means they are able to do in respect of the freeholder or leaseholder borrower. Similarly, the rights arising under a restrictive covenant do not exist in isolation, but are instead a right limiting the right of a freeholder. Priority disputes, therefore, are about much more than who wins in any particular scenario. Instead, they are the forum by which the content of rights are shaped. This makes the ways in which priority disputes are resolved particularly critical to the functioning of the system as a whole, rather than as constituent parts.

In creating such a system the primary goals have been to achieve a degree of certainty so that needless litigation is avoided. The costs of parties attempting to navigate their various rights are kept low. This is primarily achieved through the two critical rules: that rights rank above rights created after them in priority terms, all else being equal; and that purchasers of land are treated differently from other persons, are both geared at creating that predictability within the system. However, the attempt to achieve such certainty has not been pursued blindly without recognition of what that might do to individuals with particularly vulnerable kinds of rights, such as proprietary estoppel, where the fact of even having that right may be unknown to its holder. In such cases, the rules relating to actual occupation aim to protect those persons against purchasers. Actual occupation of land is a very useful tool to achieve this aim, precisely because it is likely to be indicative of a close personal relationship between that person and the land in question, rather than a relationship formed only of investment value, for example. Furthermore, by treating the definition of actual occupation flexibly and responsively, the courts are able to use this test to ensure that the law is achieving true sensitivity to the context of land and the variety of ways in which people can use land.

This is not to say that the law in this area is without its flaws—there are specific issues which remain somewhat murky, not least the effect of a loss of priority, and in some areas we may say that protection of purchasers goes to far, for example in cases where overreaching occurs despite fraud—but in general the priority rules are sensibly but sensitively constructed to produce a system which balances the different principles. In this ways, the priority rules are remarkably successful.

TABLE OF DEFINITIONS

Priority dispute	A dispute which involves a clash of property rights and which is usually resolved according to the order of creation, should an alternative priority rule not apply.
Overriding interest	An interest in land which binds a purchaser of registered land despite not appearing on the register.
Actual occupation	The factual state of affairs characterised by the occupation of land, which, when appropriate conditions are met, will be sufficient to protect the priority of an interest following a disposition of registered land.

(Continued)

Overreaching	The process by which an interest loses priority on a disposition of an estate held on trust, and in cases of sale, is transferred into the proceeds of that sale.
Postpone	The 'ranking behind' an estate in land of an interest which has lost priority to a registered on a disposition of that estate.
Waiver	The consent given by a holder of a right to a loss of priority to a subsequently created right. These can be express or implied.
Acquisition mortgage	A mortgage which is used to acquire title to land, and which will take priority over any interest created as part of that purchase, regardless of precise timings.

FURTHER READING

The further reading in this section explores a number of the issues raised in this chapter, and should provide a starting point for analysing priority issues in more detail:

BEVAN, C., 'Overriding and over-extended? Actual occupation: a call to orthodoxy' [2016] Conv 104.
BOGUSZ, B., 'Defining the scope of actual occupation under the LRA 2002: some recent judicial clarification' [2011] Conv 268.
DIXON, M., 'Priorities under the Land Registration Act 2002' (2009) 125 LQR 401.
GOYMOUR, A. et al, *New Perspectives on Land Registration* (Hart, 2018).

16
CO-OWNERSHIP

16.1	Introduction	496	16.5 Conclusion	541
16.2	Interests Under a Trust of Land	497	Principles	541
16.3	Forms of Co-Ownership	503	Table of Definitions	544
16.4	Disputes Relating to Co-Owned Land	517	Further Reading	544

CHAPTER GOALS

By the end of this chapter, you should understand:

- The nature of trust interests, and the function that they play in relation to the management of co-owned land;
- How trusts are created and their priority protected against third parties;
- The powers of trustees;
- The different forms of co-ownership in terms of legal and equitable title;
- The process by which a joint tenancy in equity can be transformed into a tenancy in common; and
- How disputes are resolved in relation to co-owned land.

16.1 INTRODUCTION

In this book, in chapters 2, 4, and 7, we have already considered questions as to the nature of equitable interests in land, and issues as to how these arise, both expressly and impliedly. The purpose of this chapter is to consider the operation of one particular form of equitable interests, ie the trust of land, and how this legal structure is used to manage co-ownership of land. The chapter is divided into three main parts. Section 16.2 explains the nature of interests under a trust of land, and the rights and obligations for trustees and beneficiaries which arise as a result of the creation of such a trust. Section 16.3 then considers the different forms of concurrent co-ownership which can exist in relation to land, looking at joint tenancies and tenancy in common and the process of severance. Since co-ownership cannot exist without a trust, it is useful to have understood trusts generally before examining their use as a tool to manage co-ownership situations. Section 16.4

therefore explores the regulation of disputes between trustees, beneficiaries, and third parties. Partly these disputes relate to questions of priority, and so it is useful to read this chapter in conjunction with chapter 15 concerning the general priority rules, but there are also specific kinds of dispute which arise when land is held on trust which are considered here. It would also be useful to consult with chapter 3, where the concept of overreaching is introduced and explained in general terms. It is considered again here, and so a refresher will be helpful.

The complication involved in the application of many of the rules in this chapter is probably the main part of the law which those studying land law find really difficult, even once the revision period cements understanding of the majority of the rules considered in the other chapters in this book. The reason for this is that the operation of priorities, formalities, the law relating to mortgages, and to implied trusts and equity, all combine in co-ownership situations to produce a web of legal relations. It can be difficult to untangle this web. For this reason, in the online resources you will find a 'flow chart' which assists in the navigation of these rules. Available there also is a table which summarises the factors and their relevance to a series of decisions made under sections 14 and 15 of TOLATA.

16.2 INTERESTS UNDER A TRUST OF LAND

16.2.1 THE NATURE OF A TRUST OF LAND

One of the first questions which many people ask in the early stages of a land law course is 'what is a trust'. We have already begun to answer this question in chapter 2 when considering the respective roles of law and equity in land law. Of course it also arose when we considered the question of the creation of implied trusts in chapter 7. But we have not yet confronted it head on. This question, unfortunately, is also one of the most difficult to answer, and it is the subject of long standing debates in the academic literature and is, in a sense, irresolvable.[1] Part of the problem with attempting to answer this question is that a trust is many different things, depending upon the perspective one brings and what one is using the trust for. It is, to a certain extent, a malleable concept which allows it to function in a variety of contexts and for a variety of purposes. This very usefulness of the trust, however, is what makes it somewhat difficult to define. It is therefore helpful to try to boil down the trust to its essentials without claiming that this is necessarily a 'definition' of a trust. This will help understand trusts, but more importantly for this chapter, it will help understand how trusts work to manage co-ownership of land. It is also useful, and we discuss this later, to remember that when dealing with trusts in relation to estates in land, the Trusts of Land and Appointment of Trustees Act 1996 (TOLATA) goes a long way to defining the mutual rights and obligations of beneficiaries and trustees. So, to that extent, the rules considered in relation to trusts in land can be seen as much a consequence of statutory provisions (including the Land Registration Act 2002 (LRA 2002) and the Law of Property Act 1925 (LPA 1925)) as they are a consequence of the inherent nature of the trust.

---

[1] For recent discussion of this problem, see B McFarlane, *The Structure of Property Law* (Hart, Oxford, 2008). For a wider range of perspectives, so also F Maitland, *Equity* (2nd ed) (CUP, Cambridge, 1936), A W Scott, 'The nature of the rights of the "cestui que trust"' (1917) 17 Columbia Law Review 269; and H G Hanbury, 'The field of modern equity' (1929) 45 LQR 199, and R Nolan, 'Equitable Property' (2006) 122 LQR 232.

Nevertheless, in essence, a trust, in whatever legal context, arises where one person, a trustee, holds property, but is mandated to use that property for the benefit of another or multiple others (or possibly for both themselves and another person). The legal owner therefore falls under *trust duties* in relation to the property.[2] At the same time, the beneficiary of the trust, ie the person on whose behalf the legal owner operates, also obtains a species of property interest in the property. As is confirmed in Snell's Equity (the leading practitioners' guide in relation to trusts):

> 'The interest of a beneficiary under a trust is the paradigm of an equitable interest in property. Modern legislation often treats the beneficiary's right as an interest in the property bound by it. The beneficiary's interest is generally transmissible to and enforceable against third parties, which gives it some of the defining features of a proprietary interest'.[3]

It is this latter aspect of the trust which has proved particularly difficult to pin down. Some authors emphasise the aspect of the trust which relies upon the *duties* of the trustee and the ability of the beneficiary to assert rights as against the trustee. Others emphasise the proprietary aspects of the trust.[4] Whilst the two aspects may in many cases be simply two sides of the same coin, the degree to which a beneficiary really is an *owner* of the property, is significant in terms of their power to act in relation to that property, and in respect of the remedies which are available for breach of trust. Perhaps, however, the best starting point is to recognise that it is not possible to give a black and white response to questions as to the nature of the trust. Per Snell's Equity again:

> 'Any attempt to explain the beneficiary's interest solely as a personal right against the trustee or solely as a proprietary interest enforceable against third parties fails to do justice to all the features of the interest. It does not lend itself to simplistic reduction into just one kind of right'.[5]

The primary remedy which will arise when trust property is 'mis-managed', is, unsurprisingly, an action against the trustees for breach of trust. In many, if not all (and the caveat regarding the potential existence of a trust without fiduciary duties arising is controversial), instances involving a trust, the trustee will be under what are known as fiduciary duties. These duties are equitable obligations which constrain the 'trustee's conscience' and mandate that he act both with proper motivation, and also objectively for the benefit of the beneficiary. It is sometimes said that some forms of trust—eg a remedial constructive trust responsive to fraud—do not necessarily involve fiduciary duties.[6] This is controversial however, and it may be better said that the content of fiduciary duties is not the same in all contexts. Either way, in cases where the trustees are fraudsters, or act in a deliberately malicious way towards their beneficiaries, they are likely also to have taken sufficient steps to prevent the beneficiaries being able to obtain genuine and meaningful compensation from the trustees in respect of a breach of trust. In practice, therefore, in such deliberate malfeasance cases, the beneficiary may be left with no remedy from the trustees. In cases where the breach of trust was not calculated, or the trustees have assets, then an action for breach of trust can be very valuable however. It will require the trustee to 'compensate' the trust out of their own

---

[2] See generally, J McGhee, *Snell's Equity* (33rd ed) (Sweet & Maxwell, London, 2017) at chapter 7.
[3] J McGhee, *Snell's Equity* (33rd ed) (Sweet & Maxwell, London, 2017), [2–002].
[4] For further discussion, see B McFarlane and R Stevens, 'The nature of equitable property' (2010) 4 Journal of Equity 1; and T Cutts, 'The nature of equitable property: a functional analysis' (2012) 6 Journal of Equity 44.
[5] J McGhee, *Snell's Equity* (33rd ed) (Sweet & Maxwell, London, 2017), [2–002].
[6] See P Millett, 'Equity's place in the law of commerce' (1998) 114 LQR 214.

pocket for the consequences of their mismanagement. In cases where the breach of trust consists of a negligent management decision this is useful for beneficiaries as they would effectively be insulated from loss resulting from trustee action, whilst at the same time obviously being able to benefit from that action should the trust property increase in value.

However, the existence of the proprietary element of a trust gives rise to an alternative approach to ensure that a beneficiary does not lose out as a result of a breach of trust, deliberate or otherwise. This is the mechanism of tracing. Tracing is the process by which 'trust property' can be followed to ensure that the beneficiary always has a proprietary entitlement to an asset.[7] Thus, if a house is bought and held on trust, and then later sold, the beneficiary's interest will now lie in the proceeds of the sale. If the proceeds are then used to buy another property, that second property will be held on trust and the trustee would then be held liable for breach of trust were they to use the second property for a reason other than for the benefit of the trust, and so on. This can be very useful for beneficiaries, especially when dealing with money, since it allows the 'trail' of the trust assets to be followed. However, it can also be problematic, especially when the trust property becomes somehow mixed with assets belonging solely to the trustee, or to a third party. This book is not the place to discuss the complexity of these rules, but it is useful to be aware of the remedies available for breach of trust, since it helps to give some concrete meaning to the question of the nature of the trust.

In describing the nature of the trust here, the reader may feel that the context being described is one where a trustee has been consciously and deliberately appointed to manage a specific asset. It is therefore in that sense a description which accurately captures the operation of trusts in a commercial or 'trust fund' context. In land law many trusts do not in practice operate in this way. Rather, the trustees and the beneficiaries are often the same people, and they do not necessarily have any skill in terms of management of the asset concerned. The way that the trust mechanisms operate in this context, whilst formally the same, adjust according to context and rather than being about management of assets on behalf of others, the role of the trust changes. It becomes a dispute resolution mechanism in relation to co-ownership of land, first and foremost, with a secondary purpose of insulating third parties from the effects of the existence of the proprietary interests arising under the trust. The dispute resolution aspect of trusts is land is governed by TOLATA. The insulating effect of the trust is a consequence of the possibility of overreaching, both of which we discuss in more detail later in this chapter. This 'repurposing' of the trust in land law has proved very useful in attempting to strike a balance between the needs of co-owning parties, especially those in a romantic or familial relationship, where the complexities of personal relationships and family life meet the commercial assert-based aspects of land law head on.

> **Further analysis: Why do we use trusts in relation to land?**
>
> Before we examine the rights and duties which arise under this bespoke form of the trust especially designed to operate within this field, it is useful to think about *why* trusts are used in more detail. In 1925, when fundamental reforms were made to the ways in which rights in land were held, there was an opportunity, if so-desired, radically to re-think the role of trusts in land law. Rather than limiting the role

---

[7] *Foskett v McKeown* [2001] 1 AC 102 (HL).

of trusts, however, the law reforms put trusts front and centre in the operation of land law. This was done, primarily, because at the time co-ownership and trusts of land operated in a very different context to how they do now. Perhaps most significantly, there was little by way of 'clash' between the principles governing co-ownership, and those concerned with mortgages in relation to land. The authors of Megarry and Wade explain this context, stating that:

> 'At the time of the 1925 property legislation, co-ownership of land did not normally arise because of a desire for joint-ownership of the family home in the modern sense, but rather as a device for the management of a major asset for the benefit of a number of persons, often but not exclusively the extended family. Possession was not as important as income generation and capital preservation. The original scheme of the 1925 legislation reflects this'.[8]

In modern land law, where almost all residential property is acquired with the help of a mortgage, and couples are increasingly purchasing property together without the (legal) security provided by marriage and the legislation which regulates the division of property on the breakdown of a relationship, the pressures on the rules relating to trusts of land have morphed and multiplied. Do they stand up to these pressures?

Many would argue that they do not. The underlying principle of the trust is, at its heart, one which sees a division between trustees and beneficiaries, both in terms of identity and in terms of needs and interests. The idea that trustees should be neutral arbiters as to the 'best' decision for the trust itself is premised upon that person having no personal interest in the land. But when we are dealing with co-ownership of residential land, very often the trustees are not neutral in this way. Rather, they are also beneficiaries. This blurring of rules means that the fundamental structure of the trust is put under pressure. As Cobb et al argue, 'nowhere in land law is the tension between the theme of rationality and the emotional dimensions of property more exposed'.[9] Many of these criticisms relate to the means by which rights in land are acquired (implied trusts, and the like), but it can also be said that the way in which the trust sometimes operates is, as we shall see, to impliedly or expressly prioritise the commercial value of land ahead of the needs and wishes of those who occupy property as a home.

16.2.2 CREATION OF TRUSTS OF LAND

Before we move onto a more detailed consideration about the nature of co-ownership interests in land, and the ways in which these are managed through the trust, it is useful here to recap on how trusts are created and the circumstances which may give rise to trusts without the conscious efforts of the parties. First, it is crucial to remember, as we discussed in chapter 7 at 7.3, that whenever more than one person holds legal title to land there *must* be a trust.[10] This is a statutory trust, and it is mandatory (precisely because this allows for the creation of the dispute resolution function). However, knowing that a trust exists tells us nothing more than that there must be beneficiaries. It does not tell us who those beneficiaries are, nor the nature of the rights that they have in the property. Second, whether or not there is a sole legal owner or joint legal owners, it is possible expressly to create a trust in writing, as long as that declaration of trust complies

---

[8] Harpum et al, *Meggary and Wade: The Law of Real Property* (8th ed) (Sweet and Maxwell, London, 2012), [12–001].
[9] Cobb et al, *Great Debates in Land Law* (2nd ed) (Palgrave, London, 2016), 222.
[10] Law of Property Act 1925, section 36.

with section 53(1)(b) Law of Property Act 1925. It is not necessary for there to be more than one trustee for a trust to exist. Rather, if there is more than one trustee that it is necessary for there to be a trust. Third, in cases where there is a sole legal owner and *no* declaration of trust, the starting point will be that the legal owner does not hold the land on trust.[11] However, in some cases the facts may be such that the starting point is overturned, and a trust is implied. This may be a resulting trust, where the trust interest is calculated according to the percentage contribution made to the purchase price; or a constructive trust, where the courts will establish a trust on the basis of a common intention shared between the parties that the non-legal owner have a share in the property, where that intention has been detrimentally relied upon by the person claiming the right. Fourth, in cases where there is joint legal ownership but *no* declaration of trust, the starting point will be that the parties hold the equitable interest in a way which matches the legal title, ie the legal owners will hold for themselves as joint tenants in equity.[12] However, this starting point too may be overturned by the implication of either a resulting or constructive trust as explained earlier. The nature of the trust, therefore, is established either by reference to a written declaration of trust, or by an implied trust. However, the fact that there is a trust does not tell us how that operates, nor what the nature of the interests in relation to that trust are. Furthermore, it is important to consider also the relationship between joint owner trustees in such a situation, as well as considering the relationship between the trustees and the beneficiaries, and these and third parties as is explained later in this chapter.

16.2.3 RIGHTS AND POWERS OF TRUSTEES

As legal owners, trustees are effectively empowered to do anything which a legal owner would be able to do did a trust not exist. According to TOLATA, this means that they are entrusted with the powers of an absolute owner. In the case of registered land, these powers are conferred by virtue of the trustee's status as a person registered with title. This is the consequence of sections 23 and 24 Land Registration Act 2002. However, TOLATA also makes clear, in section 6, that the powers of the trustees can be expressly limited by the provisions establishing the trust in cases where the trust was set up by a settlor. How do these two statutory provisions interact? Essentially, from a third party perspective, these powers will not be limited unless there is express reflection of that fact on the register.[13] The mechanism for achieving such a limitation is the restriction.[14] We return to the role of the register in relation to the management of co-owned land towards the end of this section. From a third party perspective, therefore, unless there is a restriction apparent from the register, or a limitation imposed by the land registration rules themselves, it will not matter to the quality of the transferee's title or interest that any disposition may have been made in breach of trust. That of course does not answer the question about *priorities* conferred or altered by any such disposition, as we discuss later, it merely answers to the question as to *validity*.

---

[11] *Stack v Dowden* [2007] UKHL 17, [2007] 2 AC 432 (HL) and *Jones v Kernott* [2011] UKSC 53, [2012] 1 AC 776, as applied in *Geary v Rankine* [2012] EWCA Civ 555, [2012] 2 FLR 1409, amongst others. For more details see chapter 7.
[12] Ibid.
[13] Land Registration Act 2002, section 24.
[14] Land Registration Act 2002, section 40.

The rules relating to the powers of trustees also do not explain when and how a trustee will be in breach of trust when exercising those powers. Again, a third party would not be affected by any such breach of trust, but the beneficiaries would of course have an action against the trustees as we have explained. In order to ensure that there is no such breach, trustees generally have to:

(1) Do as beneficiaries say if they are all of full capacity and are all unanimous;
(2) Do as the settlor outlined in cases where the trust was created by a third party as a result of section 8 TLATA 1996; and
(3) Failing that:
   a. Act for the beneficiaries' interests,[15]
   b. Be even handed between the beneficiaries,[16]
   c. Act with degree of care and skill under the Trustee Act 2000, s1(1);
   d. Consult the adult beneficiaries and comply with the majority by share unless it breaches the terms of the settlement and it must also be consistent with the general interest of the trust, s11(1).

Let us examine these requirements in more detail. First, there is a general principle that the trustees should do as beneficiaries require as long as they are of full capacity, unanimous and absolutely entitled to the property. This is effectively linked to the fact that such beneficiaries would, if so absolutely entitled, be able to force the trustee to transfer the legal title to them. If they have the power to collapse the trust in this way, then it makes sense for them also to be able to dictate the way in which the property is managed. However, when we are dealing with rights in land, it is important to remember that because both of the mandatory statutory trust whenever there is more than one legal owner of land, and the operation of the rules relating to implied trusts, very often, the trustees and the beneficiaries will be the same people. As a result, it becomes somewhat meaningless in that context to say that the trustees should act in accordance with the wishes of the beneficiaries. By definition, if there is a dispute, in such cases, the beneficiaries are not unanimous and this situation is considered in 16.4. Nevertheless, there are of course multiple circumstances in relation to rights in land where this principle will be important.

Second, the trustees must act in accordance with the duties of the trust as expressed in any settlement document. This is, as mentioned in the opening section of the chapter, unlikely to exist in concurrent co-ownership of a residential family home, but it is important to be aware that trusts of land arise in other circumstances (including in relation to successive co-ownership, a topic not covered in this book), where a settlement document would be enormously important. Crucially, the effect of section 8 of TOLATA is to exclude or restrict any of the powers of the trustees in accordance with the document establishing the trust. Although in theory this could not be used to restrict the owners' powers conferred by the land registration provisions per se, it could mandate the entry of a restriction on the register itself, which would have that effect in practice.

---

[15] *Cowan v Scargill* [1985] Ch. 270 (ChD).
[16] *Raby v Ridehalgh* 44 ER 41, (1855) 7 De GM & G 104 (QBD).

Third, the trustees must act for the benefit of the beneficiaries and have regard to their rights when exercising these functions. This is essentially a consequence of the nature of fiduciary duties, but it is specifically provided for in section 6(5) of TOLATA. To achieve these duties they must also be even-handed between the beneficiaries. This does not mean treating them equally in terms of outcome. Rather, it means not prioritising the interests of one over the other without that overall being in the best interests of the trust. In exercising this even-handed approach, the trustees may be obligated to consult with the beneficiaries (except where the trustee intends to transfer land to beneficiaries who are absolutely entitled to that land). The consultation duty in section 11 TOLATA states that the trustees must consult beneficiaries of full age entitled to an interest in possession in the land (ie are entitled to an interest now, rather than in the future), and must then, as long as it complies with the general interest of the trust, give effect to the wishes of those beneficiaries or where there is disagreement, the wishes of the majority according to the percentage of their combined interests. As noted earlier, this consultation requirement could be excluded expressly in a settlement.

16.2.4 REGISTERED LAND AND THE USE OF RESTRICTIONS

Restrictions are used for many different purposes in relation to registered land, but one of the most important is as a means to limit the scope of trustees' powers which would otherwise be those of an absolute owner under sections 23 and 24 Land Registration Act 2002. Whilst the restriction, if 'breached' does not affect the quality of the disposition as such, it will prevent the registration of a disposition unless the terms of the restriction are met in the process of the creation of that disposition. The restriction does not, therefore, have a priority function. Rather, it has a *power* function, in that it prevents the registrar from registering a transfer in breach of a restriction under section 40 LRA 2002. Restrictions can be entered on the register either by trustees—voluntarily, or as mandated in a settlement—or by the beneficiaries themselves if that restriction is justified under the terms of the trust. Restrictions are very commonly used to enhance the operation of the overreaching rules which we discuss later.

16.3 FORMS OF CO-OWNERSHIP

16.3.1 LEGAL TITLE

Land can be co-owned in law; in equity; and in both. Where there is a 'sharing' of legal title, this must take the form of a joint tenancy.[17] Equitable interests, by contrast, can be held as joint tenants or as tenants in common. We explore these two concepts in the following section, but in essence, a joint tenancy is conceptualised as all parties owning a single undivided whole. The tenancy in common, by contrast, involves each person owning a defined share. This restriction on the types of co-ownership at law is critical. The fact that there can only be a joint tenancy at

---

[17] Law of Property Act 1925, section 34.

law has a number of fundamental consequences. We discuss these in this section, both in terms of how land co-owned at law must be dealt with, and in terms of how co-ownership at law may be created in the first place.

Before we consider the nature of the joint tenancy, however, it is useful to begin with the rules relating to the *number* and nature of legal owners of land. Under section 34 LPA 1925, it is not possible to have more than four persons be legal owners. This is essentially a question of maintaining simplicity, and of facilitating the transactability of land (since the consent of all legal owners will be required before the estate can be transferred, or a right created out of that legal estate). Indeed, it is a reflection of the very logic behind using a trust to manage co-ownership situations, as was discussed earlier. If there is an attempt to transfer the legal title of land into the names of more than four persons, then the law simply states that the first four named transferees on the deed will become proprietors and trustees.[18] If such a transfer did not specify a trust, then it is assumed that the land would then be held on trust for all the persons named in the transfer.[19] Depending upon the context this would either be as joint tenants or as tenants in common in equity, as we discuss later.

In order for a joint tenancy to be possible, the four unities must be present.[20] These unities are: unity of interest, title, possession, and time. Without these four being present, no joint tenancy can exist. Since this is the only way of co-owning legal title, without the four unities there cannot be a sharing of the legal title either. First, unity of interest means that all parties are entitled to hold the same interest in the relevant land. Thus, both must have contracted for freehold title, for example, rather than one having freehold and another leasehold title. In such a case there would, fairly obviously, be no sharing of the legal title to either the freehold or the leasehold estates. Unity of title means that the parties derived their current interest under the same title. This means that the title must have been conveyed to them using the same instrument of transfer. It is for this reason, for example, that we do not think of adverse possession giving rise to co-ownership, despite the fact that the adverse possession will generate multiple freehold titles vesting in both the paper title-holder and the adverse possessor(s). Whilst both parties in this example would have the same interest—ie a freehold—they would not have unity of title since the interests would not have been generated by the same conveyance from the same original title. Unity of possession means that neither party is able to keep the other out of possession. When dealing with co-ownership of leases this is a particularly helpful test, as it assists in distinguishing between cases involving a single co-owned lease over premises, and individual leases over rooms or spaces within a single building, as discussed in chapter 10 at 10.2.1.3. Finally, unity of time means that the parties must have obtained the interest at the same time, and it must last the same amount of time. In the case of the freehold, the 'duration' of the interest is clearly straightforward, since the very essence of the freehold is that it is not limited in terms of time. For leasehold estates, the leases must have commenced and finish on the same day. Since a joint tenancy is the only possible means of holding as co-owners at law, the consequence of the four unities is that there can be no 'adding' a person onto legal title, nor

---

[18] Law of Property Act 1925, section 34(2).
[19] Law of Property Act 1925, section 34(2).
[20] *AG Securities v Vaughan* [1990] 1 AC 417 (HL).

a taking away (except by death in the case of survivorship as we consider later, or as a result of a court appointment or replacement of trustees[21]). Thus, in any case where a party wants to obtain a 'share' of the legal ownership of a property, it is necessary for a re-conveyance into the joint names to take place.

> ### Summary: The four unities for a joint tenancy
> 1. Unity of interest—all parties must share the same interest;
> 2. Unity of title—all parties must have obtained their interest from the same transaction;
> 3. Unity of possession—no party is able to keep another out of possession; and
> 4. Unity of time—all parties' interests must be of the same duration.

How do we conceptualise the joint tenancy? A joint tenancy is built upon the idea that neither party has a 'share' in the relevant property. Rather *both* are owners of *the whole*. In this way, they are treated as though they are a single unit, and of course, the consent of both would be required in order for any transaction to take place in relation to the estate. A tenancy in common, by contrast, is based upon the idea that each person holds a distinct *share* in the property, which is capable of being dealt with independently and with only the consent of the respective owner of that share. It is for this reason that the unity of possession is the only unity required in order for a valid tenancy in common to exist. Crucially, such a form of ownership cannot operate at law.

Second, in terms of the most significant practical consequence of the distinction, the right of survivorship is a key feature of the joint tenancy. The right of survivorship, perhaps better termed the 'rule' of survivorship, is essentially a consequence of the way in which we conceive of a joint tenancy, as explained earlier. The rule means that whenever one of two or more joint tenants dies, the remaining joint tenants simply remain joint tenants of the whole. The deceased is unable to transfer his interest in the estate to another person through his will, since that would be an attempt to add a person to a title without a re-conveyance, and that is not possible in cases involving a joint tenancy. This can be best demonstrated with an example.

Jonathan and Madi held joint title to Windy Mill in Suffolk. On purchasing the property, they completed a declaration of trust, stating that they would hold as joint tenants in equity as well. After five years, the relationship between the couple broke down, and Madi moved out. She wrote a will, leaving all of her property to her sister, Carla. Sadly, a few months later, Madi was killed in a car accident. The result of this situation, thanks to the right of survivorship, would be that Jonathan would be the sole legal owner of the property, and there would be no trust in relation to it. Carla would be entitled to no interest in Windy Mill.

> ### Summary: Legal title
> Co-ownership of the legal title must take the form of a joint tenancy. This means that the four unities must be present, and the right of survivorship will operate on the death of one of the joint tenants.

---

[21] This is made possible under TOLATA, section 19.

16.3.2 EQUITABLE TITLE

Equitable title, by contrast, can exist both as a joint tenancy and as a tenancy in common. It is possible for either to be deliberately put in place from the outset through a written declaration of trust, or for either to arise through the creation of an implied trust as explained in chapters 4 and 7. Furthermore, in certain contexts, the courts may assume that a tenancy in common exists even where there is no need to rely on the implied trusts rules per se, in order to reflect what is generally thought of as the equitable 'preference' for a tenancy in common,[22] particularly in commercial cases where the right of survivorship seems more inappropriate.[23] In any case where the parties 'start off' with a joint tenancy in equity, it is also possible for severance to take place, which has the consequence of turning a joint tenancy into a tenancy in common. To re-emphasise, this is only possible in relation to the equitable estate. However, the possibility of severance is an important one, since it radically alters not only how we conceive of the respective entitlements of the parties, but also has significant practical consequences upon the death of one of the parties.

To demonstrate this, let us change the facts slightly for the Jonathan and Madi example. Imagine that just before Madi moved out, the parties had expressly agreed that they would sever their joint tenancy in equity and had signed a deed to that effect (the methods of severance are discussed later—but this would certainly achieve it). In this case, on Madi's death, whilst Jonathan would still become sole legal owner as explained earlier, he would hold the property on trust for himself and Carla in equal shares. This would entitle Carla to 50 per cent of the proceeds of sale, for example, should the property be sold, and would give her an equal right to occupy the property. The courts would then resolve any dispute between Carla and Jonathan as to how the property should be managed, in accordance with the rules we discuss in 16.4.

From the outset, it may be the case that the parties take equitable title as tenants in common rather than joint tenants however, so that severance is not necessary. This occurs where either the express words in a conveyance, or the implication from that conveyance, is such that a joint tenancy would be inappropriate. The authors of Megarry and Wade (the leading practitioners' text in relation to land law) highlight some of the words which parties could use in their conveyance to ensure a tenancy in common at the outset, in addition to specific stipulation to that effect. Thus, words such as 'in equal shares', 'equally', and 'to be divided between' would all give rise to tenancies in common.[24] Furthermore, in cases where there is a resulting trust, as we discussed in chapter 7 at 7.5, it may be that in cases involving equal contributions the courts conclude that a joint tenancy would be inappropriate given the intentions of the parties. In general, this would arise because equity has a preference for the tenancy in common. Equitable title can exist as a joint tenancy or a tenancy in common. If the latter, then the right of survivorship will not operate.

---

[22] See comments in *Burgess v Rawnsley* [1975] Ch. 429 (CA), and *Gould v Kemp* 39 ER 959, (1834) 2 My & K 304 (Ch).

[23] *R v Williams* (1735) Bunb 342, 343.

[24] Harpum et al, *Megarry and Wade: The Law of Real Property* (8th ed) (Sweet and Maxwell, London, 2012), [13–017].

16.3.3 SEVERANCE

As noted earlier, legal title in a co-ownership situation can only be held as joint tenants. This requires that the four unities be present before it is possible to have any kind of co-ownership of land. However, in relation to equitable title, this can be co-owned in two ways: joint tenants, or tenants in common. The question to be addressed in this section, therefore, is how parties can move from joint tenancy to tenancy in common in equity, a process known as severance.

There are four primary methods of severance arising through statute and from the decision in *Williams v Hensman*:[25] written notice; acting on your own share; mutual agreement; and mutual conduct. Of these, the first two involve unilateral action by one of the co-owners in equity which results in the joint tenancy between the parties being brought to an end. The latter two, as their name suggests, are premised upon an implied or express agreement between the parties that the joint tenancy would be severed. The importance of severance, as we have noted, lies in the fact that where a tenancy in common in equity exists, the right of survivorship will not operate in relation to the equitable interest, allowing the equitable co-owner to dispose of their interest under a will. We will now consider the methods of severance in turn.

16.3.3.1 Written notice

Under section 36 Law of Property Act 1925, it is possible to effect severance of the equitable title by following a written notice procedure. This provision states, at section 36(2):

> 'Provided that, where a legal estate (not being settled land) is vested in joint tenants beneficially, and any tenant desires to sever the joint tenancy in equity, he shall give to the other joint tenants a notice in writing of such desire or do such other acts or things as would, in the case of personal estate, have been effectual to sever the tenancy in equity'.

The essential elements of this statutory process therefore are: (i) the requirement of writing; (ii) expression of an immediate desire to sever; and (iii) communication of this to the other joint tenants.

In respect of the requirement of writing, there is no specific further requirement other than that of writing. However, the other two requirements have caused some issues in the case law. First, the expression of an immediate desire to sever will not be present if the notice served appears to suggest that the severance will take place at some future date.[26] In this case, no severance would be effected, either immediately, or indeed, on the coming to pass of the date itself or of some act which was said in the notice to be the condition for severance. Let us consider this with an example.

Franziska, Alex and John are equitable joint tenants of an inherited property. As none live there, nor have a strong connection with the property itself, they have decided to sell the property and use their respective shares of the proceeds of sale to purchase separate properties. In line with this plan, Franziska writes to Alex and John saying: 'in light of our intention to sell the property and

---

[25] *Williams v Hensman* 70 ER 862, (1861) 1 John & H 546 (QBD).
[26] *Harris v Goddard* [1983] 1 WLR 1203 (CA).

use the proceeds individually, I hereby confirm in writing that on the event of the sale, our mutual interests in the property will be severed and I will utilise my share of the proceeds separately'.

This letter would be insufficient to effect severance under section 36(2) as the intention regarding severance clearly relates to severance occurring in the event of sale and not before. Whether or not it would constitute evidence of mutual agreement to sever should the parties agree to a sale with a purchaser is however another matter.

The third requirement is that the notice actually be delivered to the other joint tenants. This can be split into two rules. First, it must be delivered to *all* the joint tenants. This may be very problematic in situations involving a large number of beneficiaries. It is also, at first glance, of dubious merits as a rule. It is entirely understandable for a person to seek to sever the joint tenant vis-à-vis a single individual, whilst leaving the rest of the joint tenancy intact. However, if we explore this desire further, it becomes clear that it is not possible to achieve this outcome, regardless of the rule relating to written agreement to sever. Let us return to Franziska and John.

Imagine now that Franziska wishes to work together with Alex in respect of their interest in the property, but for John to deal separately. She sends the letter of severance to John, but no such letter to Alex. Let us assume, for the moment, that this letter would have some effect. What would be the outcome? In the case of Franziska's death, her entitlement in the property would transfer without the need for a will automatically to Alex (or, more accurately, would simply be subsumed into Alex's existing entitlement). It would not do so to John. However, because John and Alex are still joint tenants under this model, in fact, Fransizka's share would *also* transfer automatically to John because he and Alex had undivided shares. So the result would be that John and Alex held the entirety of the interest under the trust as joint tenants *regardless* of Franziska's 'severance' note. For this reason, the law makes it clear that it is *not* possible to sever as against one co-owner only. It is of course possible for one co-owner to sever their own interest by communicating with all other co-owners, who many chose to remain as joint tenants in respect of their collective interest.

The second aspect of this rule is that the notice must be *effectively* delivered to the parties. This requirement is the subject of some case law, but even more exam problem questions, because it raises a number of potentially knotty problems. The first, considered in the case of *Kinch v Bullard*,[27] is what happens where a letter of severance is put into the post, and either never reaches the relevant address, or does arrive, but is not in fact read.

Key case: *Kinch v Bullard* [1999] 1 WLR 423

This case is memorable, not least for the dishonourable conduct in this case. Here, a couple's relationship had broken down. Upon hearing that she was suffering from a terminal illness, Mrs Johnson sent a letter to Mr Johnson severing their joint tenancy in their former home in order to ensure that he did not become absolutely entitled to the property on her death. However, after she had posted the letter, but before Mr Johnson had read it, Mr Johnson suffered a serious (and ultimately fatal) heart attack. On hearing of Mr Johnson's demise, Mrs Johnson rushed around to the property to retrieve the severance note,

---

[27] *Kinch v Bullard* [1999] 1 WLR 423 (ChD).

claiming that this meant that she was entitled to the whole of the property under the right of survivorship, notwithstanding the indisputable proof of her intention to sever the joint tenancy. The court was unpersuaded by her argument. Instead, they reasoned that in cases where a written notice of severance is posted, the notice is deemed to have been delivered as soon as it is entrusted to the postal service. This sits in line with the postal acceptance rule in contract law, although is clearly inconsistent with the idea that the severance must be communicated in order to be effective. Furthermore, the Law of Property Act itself contains rules relating to the use of postal communication in section 196. The consequence of this case is, essentially, that the posting of a severance notice will suffice, as long as the process of posting is itself reasonable, and the letter is sent to the right address.

This requirement of effective delivery is tempered by the rules relating to the means of delivery as well. *Kinch v Bullard*[28] demonstrates that using the post will suffice, but there have been cases where the person attempting to sever has used the post, but some error has arisen. This can be seen in the case of *Quigley v Masterson*.[29]

Key case: *Quigley v Masterson* [2011] EWHC 2529

Mr Pilkington (now deceased) and Mrs Masterson had started a relationship and lived together for many years. They were both divorced and had children from their previous relationships. They purchased a property together, in joint names in law and as joint tenants in equity. Their relationship later broke down, and the question then emerged, following Mr Pilkington's death, whether the joint tenancy had been severed. This was in doubt because although there was an attempt by Mr Pilkington to sever using a section 36 notice, the name on the communication was wrong. Mrs Masterson was, at the time, employed as cleaner at the University of Warwick. The letter was sent to Mrs *Masterton* at the University accommodation services address. It was held by the court that this was insufficient to meet the requirements of section 196(3) (since, the court emphasised, delivery to a place of employment under the wrong name could not really be considered effective delivery to the co-owner's 'last known place of business'). The joint tenancy had not therefore been severed by the service of the notice (although the court did conclude that the tenancy had been severed by other means). This case emphasises, however, the importance of using the correct name and address when attempting to rely on communication through the post.

From this case law taken together, we can build a number of requirements for the effective operation of written notice of severance in terms of the means of its communication: (1) it is sufficient that the notice be delivered to the co-owner—it is not necessary for the co-owner actually to have read the notice; (2) effective delivery can be effected by sending the letter to the last known address of the co-owner; (3) if using the postal delivery method, it is necessary to use the registered post as proof of the delivery by this means; and (4) if the postal delivery method is not used, then it may still be possible to demonstrate effective communication, but in such cases it is likely that the letter will have to actually be read.

---

[28] *Kinch v Bullard* [1999] 1 WLR 423 (ChD).
[29] *Quigley v Masterson* [2011] EWHC 2529 (Ch), [2012] 1 All ER 1224.

> **Further analysis: The use of the post**
>
> The relationship between the law and the postal service is an interesting one. In the nineteenth and early twentieth century, the law began to grapple with the fact that many legal documents were posted, but would not immediately arrive at the recipient's address, and in some cases, would not arrive at all. Thus, a decision was made in relation to contract law, to treat the act of posting as an act of communications for some purposes, whether or not the letter actually arrived and was read.[30]
>
> This became known as the postal acceptance rule. It operates effectively to presume that acceptances to contractual offers are properly communicated where the post is used. This fiction, however, is problematic. It is problematic for two reasons. First, since it only applies to contractual acceptances and not, crucially, to withdrawal of offers, situations may arise where an individual offers to contract with another, that other decides to accept the contract and posts acceptance.[31] However, whilst the offeree was deciding whether to enter into the contract or not, the offeror may have attempted to withdraw the offer and might have posted a communication to this effect. In such a situation, there would be two documents making their way through the postal service. One of these is deemed to already have had legal effects despite not being delivered and read. The other does not have such legal effects, and as a result, the contract would be treated as concluded and binding. The disparity of treatment between types of documents, whilst explicable taking account of the history of the case law, is not necessarily satisfactory. Second, this rule is problematic precisely because it is fictional. It binds parties to contracts without their knowledge, and potentially without their on-going consent.
>
> How do these arguments affect the operation of the 'postal rule' in relation to severance? First, we could say that the 'policy arguments' here are not significant. Severance, whilst having some legal consequences, does not in itself change what the parties own. It merely changes the *way* that they own it. Second, since, as we have seen, the consequence of severance is that the right of survivorship no longer applies, the parties are still able to ensure that their intentions are preserved through the writing of a will. This is very different from being bound to contractual performance! The fact of severance means that survivorship is not automatic, but it does not mean that the parties are unable to leave their respective interests to each other in their wills. Third, if we accept that severance can happen unilaterally—as we do both through the written notice method, and the acting on your own share method (which does not even require communication to the other co-owner)—then the fact that a notice of severance has not in fact been read does not alter the fact that the unilateral method has been followed. In the creation of contracts, where mutuality of acceptance of obligations is essential, the same reasoning does not apply. We can say, therefore, that whilst rules relating to the use of the post are problematic in contract law, in relation to severance, the rule is more readily justified. Finally, whilst the postal acceptance rule in contract is a development of the case law, the postal rule in severance is a direct consequence of section 196 Law of Property Act 1925. The statutory authorisation of the use of the registered post as a method of communication means that this rule is not only acceptable in policy terms, but also a rule which is comparatively easy to find out about, at least in theory.

16.3.3.2 Acting on your own share

The written notice of severance method is the most 'certain' way to ensure that a joint tenancy is brought to an end. However, it is also possible unilaterally to sever a joint tenancy by acting in relation to a 'share' by concluding a binding legal transaction in respect of that interest. This

---

[30] *Adams v Lindsell* 106 ER 250, (1818) 1 B & Ald 681 (KBD).
[31] *Henthorn v Fraser* [1892] 2 Ch. 27 (CA).

method can also be done without an active intention to sever per se. Rather, it is a consequence of the legally binding nature of the transaction. This is best explained by an example.

Antonin and Johann acquired title to a property on the Swan Lake Estate. This property was purchased expressly as joint tenants at law and in equity. Some years later, Johann wanted money for a personal project, and so entered into an agreement with Danube Bank Ltd to borrow against the property. As Antonin did not consent to this mortgage, this could only be a mortgage operating in equity. The entering into of the contract for the loan however had the effect of severing the joint tenancy in equity, even if Johann was not thinking about severance at the time of the transaction.

To explore the rules relating to acting on your own share a little further, it is useful to consider what acts will and will not be sufficient to sever the joint tenancy. The two most straightforward acts which will result in severance in this way will be an agreement to sell an equitable interest in the property,[32] or an agreement to mortgage that interest as considered earlier.[33] However, it is possible that such severance would occur, eg through the grant of a lease of the equitable interest.[34] Furthermore, it is also possible that any binding legal act which attempts to limit or circumvent the fact that the property is co-owned will also sever the joint tenancy. Secondly, any forgery or attempt to contract in relation to legal title without the consent of the other will also constitute an act on your own share.[35] It will also produce effects in equity in relation to the transaction which was forged, eg an equitable mortgage of the co-owner's share,[36] rather than a legal mortgage of the whole. Finally, the act of falling bankrupt will also be enough to sever a joint tenancy.[37] This is because the consequence of going bankrupt is that all the bankrupt's assets are transferred into their trustee in bankruptcy and therefore are effectively no longer in the hands of the original co-owner.

The precise moment at which such unilateral act of severance takes place can be critical. When we consider acts relating to your own share, the relevant moment is the moment at which the binding legal transaction is concluded.

16.3.3.3 Mutual agreement

That covered the unilateral methods of severance. However, it is also possible for both parties to act together in a way which will bring the joint tenancy to an end under the methods of mutual agreement and mutual conduct. Due to the mutuality involved here, unlike in relation to the unilateral methods of severance, the courts are more open to interpreting conduct, rather than looking for a binding single moment of severance. The line between these two methods of severance is a fine one, with no clear distinction existing as for when the moment a discussion tips from mutual conduct to mutual agreement. However, since the consequences of both are the same, it is usually not necessarily to pin down this precise dividing line. Having said this, mutual agreement

---

[32] *Re Wilks* [1891] 3 Ch. 59, 61 (ChD).
[33] *York v Stone* 91 ER 146, (1709) 1 Salk 158 (KBD).
[34] *Gould v Kemp* 39 ER 959, (1834) 2 My & K 304 (Ch).
[35] *Bankers Trust Co v Namdar* [1995] NPC 139 (ChD).
[36] As in *Bank of Ireland v Bell* [2001] 2 All ER (Comm) 920 (CA).
[37] *Re Gorman* [1990] 1 WLR 616 (DC).

is usually less 'ambiguous' than conduct can be. This can mean that a situation may fall somewhere between the two without a clear agreement but also without sufficient acts to show the mutual intention between the parties. It is also very important to keep in mind with mutual agreement cases, that the mutuality element requires all the relevant joint tenants to be involved in the discussions. It is not enough for one of a subset of joint tenants to have reached an agreement.

The agreement must be enough to demonstrate a mutual desire to sever. It does not, however, need to be made in writing in accordance with section 2 LP(MP)A 1989. The reason for this is that the severance of a joint tenancy is *not* a disposition of an interest in land. Rather, it is merely a change in the way in which existing rights are held. It does not engage the formality rules at all. This can of course give rise to problematic questions of proof, but that is something which the courts are fairly well-equipped, and certainly well-used, to handling.

What must the actual agreement be, in order to result in severance? Certainly, it is possible for there to be an explicit agreement between the parties that they will transform the way that they hold their rights, from joint tenants to tenants in common. However, any other agreement that indicates that the parties no longer wish a joint tenancy will also suffice, particularly where the primary consequence of a joint tenancy, ie the right of survivorship, would be inconsistent with the way that parties have explicitly agreed to manage their affairs. Thus, for example, where the parties agree that they will each leave their respective shares to a specified third party, that obviously cannot happen in the absence of severance, and the courts will treat this as sufficient mutual agreement.

One situation which has caused some difficulties in terms of mutual agreement is the situation where negotiations are on-going for one party to 'buy the other out'. The fact that the parties are even having this conversation may be evidence that they are both treating their joint tenancy as severed. However, during the negotiations period, they have clearly not reached total agreement. The courts have tended to treat such situations as potential applications of the rule relating to severance by mutual conduct, which we consider later. However, in *Burgess v Rawnsley*,[38] it is clear that the courts will occasionally stretch the mutual agreement tests in order to meet cases of this type.

Key case: *Burgess v Rawnsley* [1975] Ch 429

In this case, Mrs Rawnsley and Mr Honick, both in their sixties, and a widow/widower met at a scripture rally in Trafalgar Square. The parties began a friendly relationship, although it seems from the court report that, at least on her behalf the beginning, the motivation for the relationship was largely pity. They decided together to purchase the property which had been Mr Honick's home. They agreed both to contribute. The intention was that Mrs Rawnsley would live in the upper flat; Mr Honick in the lower. The property was then transferred into joint names. As Mr Honick had explained to his solicitor, the conveyance into joint names made sense to him because he fully believed that himself and Mrs Rawnsley would be married. This does not appear to have been her intention. Rather, she wanted to

---

[38] *Burgess v Rawnsley* [1975] Ch 429 (CA).

contribute to the purchase of the property so that she would be able to live in the upper flat. Both parties were disappointed. Eventually, Mr Honick approached Mrs Rawnsley with the view to his buying her interest in the property. They appeared to reach agreement on this point, but there was dispute as to the price for the interest. Mrs Rawnsley wanted £1000 and Mr Honick only wanted to pay £750. The parties remained on friendly terms, however, and nothing more was done. Some three years later, Mr Honick died. The question now was whether the joint tenancy had been severed, so that Mr Honick's daughter would inherit his interest in the property (and be entitled to 50 per cent of the proceeds of sale), or whether the joint tenancy remained, such that Mrs Rawnsley would now be entitled to the whole. The court, in analysing the situation, was divided with Lord Denning taking a different approach from the other judges. He began by highlighting that, 'equity leans against joint tenants and favours tenancies in common'. Taking this starting point into account, and considering the case law on mutual conduct and mutual agreement, he reasoned that:

> 'I think there was evidence that Mr. Honick and Mrs. Rawnsley did come to an agreement that he would buy her share for £750. That agreement was not in writing and it was not specifically enforceable. Yet it was sufficient to effect a severance. Even if there was not any firm agreement but only a course of dealing, it clearly evinced an intention by both parties that the F property should henceforth be held in common and not jointly'.[39]

In other words, he concluded that even if any agreement reached here was not firm enough and lacked the relevant formalities to be enforced in itself, it could nevertheless be enough to sever the joint tenancy. If not, however, he felt certain that the behaviour of the parties was enough to evince a common intention that they had indeed severed.

One particularly controversial aspect of Lord Denning's judgment, however, is his reasoning in respect of the mutuality of conduct needed to meet the conduct requirement:

> 'That shows that a "course of dealing" need not amount to an agreement, expressed or implied, for severance. It is sufficient if there is a course of dealing in which one party makes clear to the other that he desires that their shares should no longer be held jointly but be held in common.'[40]

We consider the mutual conduct requirement next, but it is worth highlighting here that the statement by Lord Denning that mutual conduct may not require both to actually intend to sever—rather in cases where one party actively wants to change the position, and the other is aware of that and does not act contrary to that intention and desire, then that may suffice to give rise to a tenancy in common. The importance of mutuality in explaining the parameters of the severance rules would suggest that this reasoning was wrong.

In any case, the other members of the court took a different approach, and relied much more heavily on the mutual agreement rules. As Browne LJ explained:

> 'An agreement to sever can be inferred from a course of dealing...and there would in such a case ex hypothesi be no express agreement but only an inferred, tacit agreement...the agreement establishes that the parties no longer intend the tenancy to operate as a joint tenancy and that automatically effects a severance'.[41]

Pennycuik VC was doubtful regarding the finding of an agreement on the facts, but did highlight that the finding of an agreement could be based on implication.[42]

---

[39] *Burgess v Rawnsley* [1975] Ch. 429 (CA).
[40] *Burgess v Rawnsley* [1975] Ch. 429 (CA).
[41] *Burgess v Rawnsley* [1975] Ch. 429 (CA).
[42] *Burgess v Rawnsley* [1975] Ch. 429 (CA).

16.3.3.4 Mutual conduct

Finally, it is possible for parties to sever by mutual conduct. This is constituted by a pattern of behaviour demonstrating an unambiguous, mutual, intention to sever. This is very often the most difficult severance to 'spot' because it can be hard to interpret the behaviour of parties. Whilst the courts refer to the need for unambiguous conduct in this respect, the strictness of the test is tempered by the fact that the courts, generally speaking, will favour a tenancy in common rather than a joint tenancy. This is because, as we have highlighted, the consequence of a joint tenancy in the form of the right of survivorship may frustrate the intentions and wishes of the parties upon their death, whereas a tenancy in common allows the parties the freedom to leave their property to whomever they wish, including the co-owner of the property. Thus, freedom is limited in the case of a joint tenancy, but not in the case of a tenancy in common. Nevertheless, the courts have held that inconclusive negotiations, or negotiations revealing a future plan, may not be enough to constitute severance by mutual conduct. The rules relating to mutual conduct and mutual agreement were considered by the Court of appeal in *Smith v Davis*.[43]

> **Key case: *Smith v Davis* [2011] EWCA Civ 1603**
>
> In this case, Mr and Mrs Smith had been joint tenants of a property in Suffolk. The question was whether this joint tenancy had been severed before her death so that her property could pass under her will, or whether the right of survivorship would operate. Before Mrs Smith's death, the marriage had started to fall apart, and Mr Smith had moved out. Both parties had contacted solicitors who had advised severance. No notice was served in this respect, however. There was correspondence between the parties, however, as a result of Mr Smith's financial hardship, about the sale of the property in order to allow the proceeds of sale to be divided. All parties seemed to agree that sale of the property was inevitable. However, agreement was not reached as to the precise mechanics of how the proceeds would be divided, notwithstanding the fact that a payment was made to Mr Smith and the property was put on the market. Nothing significant happened after this point before Mrs Smith's death. The court assessed the case law in light, particularly, of the approach in *Burgess v Rawnsley*,[44] in attempting to ascertain whether there was enough in this case to give rise to severance. First, the court was clear that the simple fact of proceeding to sale is not enough to constitute severance by mutual conduct or agreement: 'a sale could be said to have been entirely consistent, on the face of it at least, with the joint tenancy continuing and applying to the proceeds of sale'.[45] However, in this case, more took place than simply the parties putting the property on the market. Taking these actions together, there was, according to the court: 'a common and expressed intention and expectation that the house would be sold and the proceeds of the sale would be divided equally between them'.

One pattern of behaviour that does seem to be accepted by the courts as constituting severance by mutual conduct is the writing of mutual wills. We have highlighted that it is not possible to sever by will per se. This is because a will only has legal effects upon the death of the executor of

---

[43] *Smith v Davies* [2011] EWCA Civ 1603, [2012] 1 FLR 1177 (CA).
[44] *Burgess v Rawnsley* [1975] Ch 429 (CA).
[45] *Smith v Davies* [2011] EWCA Civ 1603, [2012] 1 FLR 1177 (CA), [14].

that will. Once a joint tenant dies, then the right of survivorship is automatic, and there will be no co-ownership to sever in the will.[46] However, the writing of mutual wills, whilst not productive in itself of a binding legal document in respect of the will, does demonstrate that both parties believe that they have something to leave in their wills, thus constituting clear evidence of an intention that they hold as tenants in common.

16.3.3.5 Other 'methods' of severance

We have considered in detail four methods of severance here—written notice; acting on your own share; mutual agreement; and mutual conduct. However, the case law shows that there are other means by which severance can be affected. The first, most importantly, appears to be the creation of an implied trust. The precise relationship between the implied trusts rules, and the severance rules, is however, vexed.

Further analysis: Severance and implied trusts

The problem being considered here is this: if, in line with what we considered in chapter 7, the 'presumption' in joint names cases is that, at least in a domestic context, the parties hold as joint tenants in equity, and, further, that at some point the courts conclude that a tenancy in common arises so that the parties hold in unequal terms, then, by implication, at some point also the tenancy must have been severed. But, as Briggs highlights, we do not know when this is. As he states,

'the initial presumption was that the co-owners were joint tenants in equity... It is therefore surprising to observe that although the Justices [in *Jones v Kernott*[47]] insisted that the starting point in equity was a joint tenancy, and the end point a tenancy in common in shares of 9 to 1, the term "severance" is not found anywhere in their judgments. The result seems to be that an equitable tenancy in common results from beneficial joint tenants just drifting apart. Neither the Law of Property Act 1925 s.36(2), nor *Williams v Hensman*... really prepared us for that'.[48]

The problem with this lack of precision on behalf of the Supreme Court, a lack of precision not subsequently rectified by later decisions, is that the consequences of the shift from joint tenancy to tenancy in common are not restricted to the size of the parties' respective shares in the property for the purposes of division upon sale. Rather, the existence of a tenancy in common has, as we have seen, a fundamentally different outcome upon the death of one of the parties. If we cannot pinpoint the precise moment of *severance*, in the gradual accumulation of behaviour leading to evidence of an implied but common intention to share other than as joint tenants, then it is not too difficult to construct a hypothetical situation where the question of severance becomes more critical than the question of the size of the respective parties' shares.

Furthermore, the problem of the 'presumption' of a joint tenancy in cases involving conveyance into joint names with no express trust—ie the presumption that equity follows the law—does not sit comfortably with the considerations we discussed earlier regarding equity's natural disinclination

---

[46] *Gould v Kemp* 39 ER 959, (1834) 2 My & K 304 (Ch).
[47] *Jones v Kernott* [2011] UKSC 53, [2012] 1 AC 776.
[48] A Briggs, 'Co-ownership and an equitable non sequitur' (2012) 128 LQR 183, 183.

to impose a joint tenancy in equity unless that seems appropriate in the context. Again, as Briggs reasons:

> 'Survivorship within a beneficial estate, equity's uncharacteristic concession to games of chance, has no role in their rational world. Indeed, survivorship often seems so odd an incident of equitable ownership that unless a conveyance invokes it in express words, a better starting point—a presumption, if that is helpful--would be that co-ownership in equity will be in common'.[49]

Thus, we can see, that in cases involving disputes as to the existence of *severance*, the methods outlined in section 36 and *Williams v Hensman*,[50] may not be the only relevant information to be taken into account.

Can this problem be resolved by simply bringing the behaviour giving rise to an implied intention to share other than as joint tenants as being evidence enough to satisfy the mutual conduct requirement of severance? The problem here is that behaviour which demonstrates that parties intended not to share 50:50 does not tell us very much about their intention regarding *survivorship*. Of course, one party believes that they are entitled to a much larger share in the property than the other party, you may think that this lack of a 'sharing attitude' would also be inconsistent with the desire that the party with the smaller share be deprived of that share upon death of the co-owner. However, the mere fact that one party does not want the other to acquire their interest in the property upon death has never been enough to constitute effective severance. Even where that intention is expressed in its clearest and most obvious form, ie in a will, that will not result in severance. Why then would a common intention that one party have a larger share in the property—often implied, and very often unclear—be enough when a *much* clearer expression of intention will not be?

A further act which will result in severance is the unlawful killing of one co-owner by the other.[51] This results in severance not precisely because of the effect it has on the respective proprietary entitlements of the parties, but rather because the law will not allow a murderer to take advantage of their killing by benefitting from their right to survivorship.

Summary: Severance

There are four primary methods of severance:

1. Written notice;
2. Acting on your own share;
3. Mutual conduct; and
4. Mutual agreement.

Severance also (seems) to occur on the implication of a trust in cases where title is co-owned at law, and definitely occurs where one party unlawfully kills the other.

---

[49] A Briggs, 'Co-ownership and an equitable non sequitur' (2012) 128 LQR 183, 184.
[50] *Williams v Hensman* 70 ER 862, (1861) 1 John & H 546 (QBD).
[51] For discussion, see Harpum et al, *Meggary and Wade: The Law of Real Property* (8th ed) (Sweet and Maxwell, London, 2012), [13–049].

16.4 DISPUTES RELATING TO CO-OWNED LAND

The position between trustees and beneficiaries is a delicate one. The trust is an appropriate name for this legal construct because, to a large extent, it depends upon the benevolence of the trustee in managing the property concerned. In relation to land, this becomes all the more important because of the statutory powers conferred through registered title. Where title to land is transferred, and subsequently registered, the fact of that registration will give rise to a different set of problems than would a transfer of land held on trust under the unregistered land rules. However, there are general principles which apply to the ways in which trustees should manage trust property, and how they should use the owners' powers conveyed on them by section 23 LRA 2002 in respect of registered land. How are disputes between trustees, beneficiaries, and potentially third parties resolved, and who decides what should happen to land where there is a 'deadlock'?

16.4.1 APPLICATIONS UNDER SECTION 14 TOLATA 1996

In some cases, the dispute between the trustees and the beneficiaries will be such that the courts need to intervene to find a resolution. The power to be able to bring such an action is conferred onto all interested parties by section 14 TOLATA 1996. Section 14 allows the court to take decisions regarding the management of the trust in lieu of the trustees and the court, in exercising such a power, is able to do anything which the trustees themselves could do. Thus, as section 14 itself states:

'(1) Any person who is a trustee of land or has an interest in property subject to a trust of land may make an application to the court for an order under this section.

(2) On an application for an order under this section the court may make any such order—

　(a) relating to the exercise by the trustees of any of their functions (including an order relieving them of any obligation to obtain the consent of, or to consult, any person in connection with the exercise of any of their functions), or

　(b) declaring the nature or extent of a person's interest in property subject to the trust, as the court thinks fit.'

16.4.1.1 General approach under section 14—shift from section 30 Law of Property Act 1925 to section 14 TOLATA 1996

The court has a great deal of discretion in exercising its powers under this section. Next, we discuss the principles which both statute and case law have suggested should direct and constrain this judicial discretion. This discretion sits in contrast to the position prior to the coming into force of the 1996 Act. Under section 30 of the Law of Property Act 1925, there was a general discretion for courts to prevent sale of land in exceptional circumstances where the original purpose of the trust was no longer operative, but otherwise, sale would be presumed. The effect of this was that the courts were very strict in ordering anything other than sale. This can be seen in *Re Citro*.[52]

---

[52] *Re Citro* [1991] Ch 142 (CA).

> **Key case: *Re Citro* [1991] Ch 142**
>
> (Note: this decision pre-dates section 335A Insolvency Act 1986—for explanation, see 16.4.1.5.)
>
> In this case, two brothers became bankrupt, with their only assets being their respective shares in their family homes. One brother, D, was separated from his wife and she remained in their house along with their three children (youngest of 12). The other brother, C, lived in the family home with his wife and their three children (youngest of 10). The debts were larger than their shares in the property. The trustee in bankruptcy applied for sale.
>
> The court was required to assess whether the property should be sold, and what the relevant considerations in these circumstances were. Nourse LJ began his analysis by highlighting that the relevant statutory provision was section 30 Law of Property Act 1925. The rule provided that the property could not be sold if the original purpose for the trust still existed but that otherwise there would be a sale unless there were exceptional circumstances. According to the court, the original purpose could not exist if there were other parties now beneficially entitled in respect of the property, as in this case due to the bankruptcy. Furthermore, the case law was consistently clear that the interests of a creditor would usually prevail over the interests of the wife and any children and this would be true whether or not the bankrupt person still resides within the family home. Thus, on a review of the relevant authorities, Nourse LJ summarised the relevant law as follows:
>
>> 'Where a spouse who has a beneficial interest in the matrimonial home has become bankrupt under debt which cannot be paid without the realisation of that interest, the voice of the creditors will usually prevail over the voice of the other spouse and a sale of the property ordered within a short period. The voice of the other spouse will only prevail in exceptional circumstances. No distinction is to be made between a case where the property is still being enjoyed as the matrimonial home and one where it is not'.[53]
>
> In considering what could constitute exceptional circumstances, the court highlighted that children needing to move school, finding a new home etc, whilst 'melancholy',[54] would not be 'exceptional' in the sense required. Whilst the strictness of this exceptional circumstances test now finds itself mirrored in the Insolvency Act, the general approach of the court, ie to look for a reason *not* to sell the property, has now been overtaken by the coming into force of TOLATA.

The 1996 Act, in abolishing trusts for sale and instead instituting the new regime of trusts of land, has created, at least in theory, a much greater degree of flexibility for the courts. It is useful here however to explore the range of orders which the court is able to make under its powers in section 14. First, the court is able to make an order for sale. Any order which the court does make in this way will be an overreaching transaction, so that the purchaser is able to take free of the interests of the beneficiaries regardless of the actual occupation or otherwise of the beneficiaries at the time of the sale. This will be the case even if there is only a single trustee, who would otherwise be unable to sell the land in such a way as to allow for overreaching (see later). Second, the court is able to make an order for sale but put conditions onto that sale, so that it is, for example, delayed for a defined period of time, or by reference to some objectively ascertainable criteria. Third, the

---

[53] *Re Citro* [1991] Ch 142 (CA), 157.
[54] *Re Citro* [1991] Ch 142 (CA), 157.

court can make an order regarding occupation of the property, so that they can suggest that one beneficiary is able to occupy; the other required to find alternative accommodation. This sort of order would also be likely to be accompanied by another order the court is able to make regarding occupation rent. Fourth, the court is explicitly permitted by section 14 to make a declaration regarding the equitable shares held by the respective parties in relation to the property. This is an unusual kind of declaration for English law, since, as we have seen in chapter 1, there is no action by which one can claim ownership of a thing. Finally, the court is able to combine these powers, and make a 'package' deal which resolves the totality of the parties' disputes. In putting together such a package, the court may well encourage the parties to negotiate for themselves with the court order acting as a 'default' solution should an alternative arrangement not be made. This sort of approach was taken by the court in *Mortgage Corporation v Shaire*.[55]

> **Key case:** *Mortgage Corporation v Shaire* [2001] Ch 743
>
> In this case, Mr and Mrs Shaire had purchased the property to live in together as their family home. After some time, their relationship broke down and Mrs Shaire started a new relationship with Mr Fox. Mr Fox moved into this property, and with the agreement of Mr Shaire, became co-owner of the family home. To facilitate this, Mrs Shaire and Mr Fox took out a mortgage and these payments were met by Mr Fox. Sometime later, Mr Fox died from a heart attack, and in sorting out the estate, it became apparent that Mr Fox had entered into a number of transactions without Mrs Shaire's knowledge or consent, and it seemed that he had forged her signature on these. One of these was a mortgage with the Mortgage Corporation.
>
> In concluding that Mrs Shaire had priority over the TMC mortgage for at least part of the sums lent, Neuberger J had to assess whether section 15 TOLATA had changed the law from the previous position in section 30 LPA 1925, which we discussed earlier, and then, second, if so, what the most appropriate order was in the case.
>
> On the first issue, Neuberger J reasoned that section 15 was certainly intended to result in a change to the law. He reasoned that: 'section 15 has changed the law. As a result of section 15, the court has greater flexibility than heretofore, as to how it exercises its jurisdiction on an application for an order for sale'.[56] The section has introduced certain considerations which a court must take into account, but there may be other relevant considerations which can be given weight in individual cases.
>
> Furthermore, the consequence of this is that the case law under the previous rules was not seen by the court as being helpful in giving guidance as to how the court's discretion under section 14 should be exercised. Again, per Neuberger J:
>
>> 'A difficult question, having arrived at this conclusion, is the extent to which the old authorities are of assistance... On the one hand, to throw over all the wealth of learning and thought given by so many eminent judges to the problem which is raised on an application for sale of a house where competing interests exist seems somewhat arrogant and possibly rash. On the other hand, where one has concluded that the law has changed in a significant respect so that the court's discretion is significantly less fettered than it was, there are obvious dangers in relying on authorities which proceeded on the basis that the court's discretion was more fettered than it now is. I think it would be wrong to throw over all the earlier cases without paying

---

[55] *Mortgage Corporation v Shaire* [2001] Ch 743.
[56] *Mortgage Corporation v Shaire* [2001] Ch 743, 760.

them any regard. However, they have to be treated with caution... and in many cases they are unlikely to be of great, let alone decisive, assistance'.[57]

Thus, it was not inevitable in the circumstances before the court that the property would have to be sold. Furthermore, according to the judge, the powers under section 14 are very wide, and the court is in a position to do more than simply decide between sale and no sale. Rather, it can be more creative in establishing a position which can best resolve the dispute between the relevant parties. This creativity was used to full advantage by the court.

> 'This idea is that the house is valued at a specific figure (rather than the range I have mentioned) and that TMC is effectively taken out by having its equity converted into loan, and Mrs. Shaire then has to pay interest on that loan. In my judgment, unless Mrs. Shaire is in a position to agree that course and to meet the payments which that course would involve, I would not be prepared to refuse the order for sale'.[58]

The court here effectively altered the bargaining position between the parties to allow that Mrs Shaire could stay in the property only if she agreed to bargain with TMC to ensure that their security was realised. If such an agreement could not be reached, then Mrs Shaire would be required to sell her home of more than 25 years, an outcome which Neuberger wished to avoid, but not at the entirety of the expense of the lender.

16.4.1.2 Who can make an application under section 14?

If the trustees themselves cannot agree what should be done with the land, then they can ask the court to adjudicate. Similarly, a beneficiary or the beneficiaries as a group, can apply to court to overrule the trustees' decision and the courts will exercise their powers as outlined here. Lenders can fall into this category as well, depending upon the nature of the mortgage rights that they have. The need for the trustees to be able to have a dispute resolution mechanism is clear—if there are two trustees and they cannot agree what to do, then someone must decide or the situation will become paralysed. However, we can ask whether it is justified for beneficiaries to have access to the courts' jurisdiction in this way. On the one hand, it seems important for beneficiaries, just as trustees, to be able to request the courts' assistance in the management of land where deadlock seems likely. On the other hand, the very essence of the trust is that management questions are taken out of the hands of the beneficiaries, and so it seems odd that the beneficiaries can attempt to overrule the trustees' decisions, even in cases where there is no *breach* of the trust, merely a decision with which the beneficiaries do not agree.

There is also a further problem with co-owned land, which is that very often the trustees and the beneficiaries will be the same people. This is the result of the mandatory trust arising as soon as there is more than one legal owner. It puts the parties into a difficult position regarding the management of the land. The fact that the courts are able to resolve these disputes for the parties prevents deadlock, and it is irrelevant whether the application strictly speaking is being made by the person in their capacity as trustee, or in their capacity as beneficiary. Furthermore, in

---

[57] *Mortgage Corporation v Shaire* [2001] Ch 743.
[58] *Mortgage Corporation v Shaire* [2001] Ch 743.

applications being made under section 14 by trustees and beneficiaries, however, it is also possible for applications to be made by lenders (although this is perhaps because in the case of an equitable mortgage, the lender does in fact *become* a beneficiary and co-owner) and this conflict of interests of course complicates the exercise of the court's discretion further.

16.4.1.3 Factors to be considered under section 14

Section 14 does not require that the court act as the trustees should. The court's discretion is different to the trustees'. Section 15 tells the court what to take into account, but it should be kept in mind that this is a non-exhaustive list. The courts are able to consider any factor which appears to them to be relevant in the circumstances. The factors listed in section 15 are:

> '(1) The matters to which the court is to have regard in determining an application for an order under section 14 include—
>
> (a) the intentions of the person or persons (if any) who created the trust,
>
> (b) the purposes for which the property subject to the trust is held,
>
> (c) the welfare of any minor who occupies or might reasonably be expected to occupy any land subject to the trust as his home, and
>
> (d) the interests of any secured creditor of any beneficiary.'

Furthermore, under section 15(3):

> '(3) In the case of any other application, other than one relating to the exercise of the power mentioned in section 6(2), the matters to which the court is to have regard also include the circumstances and wishes of any beneficiaries of full age and entitled to an interest in possession in property subject to the trust or (in case of dispute) of the majority (according to the value of their combined interests)'.

The reference to the power in section 6(2) is to the ability of the trustees to transfer title to the land to the beneficiaries. In applications for any other kind of order, the court will also take account of the wishes of the beneficiaries, or to the majority of those.

None of the factors listed in section 15(1) nor in section 15(3) are definitive, however. Rather, they form the matrix of considerations which the court will take into account when deciding how the dispute in question should be resolved under the discretionary approach discussed earlier. Indeed, the courts have shown in the case law that they will take a highly pragmatic approach. Each case is resolved on a case-by-case basis, rather than by reliance on strict rules. However, the courts have given some guidance on how the factors listed in section 15 should be understood, which in turn can give some assistance in predicting how the court's discretion may be exercised in any particular case (or problem question).

The intentions of the person who created the trust at the time of creation—s 15(1)(a)

The case law has emphasised that the intentions of the persons who set up the trust should be examined not at the time at which the dispute arises, but rather that the relevant intention was that expressed at the time of the establishment of the trust.[59] There are essentially two situations

---

[59] *White v White* [2003] EWCA Civ 924, [2004] 2 FLR 231.

here. The first is where you are dealing with a trust established by a *settlor*. This is someone who transfers property to trustees, or who acquires property to be vested in trustees, and their intentions will usually be expressed in the deed establishing the trust, or in some other kind of written document. In cases where no such expressed intention exists, the courts will often be able to ascertain those intentions from the circumstances surrounding the creation of the trust. The second situation is where multiple parties acquire title to land so that a trust arises automatically. In such cases, the reason for the co-ownership will also be the reason for the establishment of the trust, but very often, this reason will be silent in terms of the documentation. So, for example, where a couple purchase the property together, their intention at the time when they set up the trust, will usually be for them to share the property as their home together, but is highly unlikely that this purpose will be specified in any document. Rather, it is established by reference to the surrounding context. Because this factor, like all the factors in section 15, is not determinative as to outcome, the courts can be very flexible in establishing what the intention is. In cases where the intention is not clear at the time of purchase, this factor will simply not weigh strongly in the court's eventual assessment as to the best way to resolve the co-ownership dispute.

The purpose for which the trust is held at the time of litigation—section 15(1)(b)

The second factor in section 15 is the purpose for which the property is held *now*. In cases of dispute, very often land will be serving a variety of purposes, which is why a dispute has arisen. But there may be a clear 'principal' purpose, which the courts will use to help guide them in the exercise of their discretion. It is important to note that usage is not necessarily sufficient to show what the purpose of a property is. Even in cases where property is used solely as a family home, it will also be serving the function as an asset, or, where a mortgage has been granted in relation to the property, as security for a debt. Thus, this factor is very rarely the main consideration for the courts. However, it may well be used *negatively*, especially when the intention of the persons setting up the trust is compared to the current purpose of the land. Let us demonstrate this with an example.

Emma and Ali purchase a property together to live in it as their home. They spend many happy years there, and have a small mortgage taken out subsequent to the purchase which facilitated some building works. They have now fallen out, and each is seeking to live in the property to the exclusion of the other, although both are happy for the property not to be sold, as they recognise that the value of the property is rapidly increasing and they both wish to retain the asset. In this case, the courts will say that the original purpose of the property—ie as a family home—is no longer possible since neither wishes to live together. As such, that purpose provides very little assistance in resolving the dispute. In this sense, the intention and the purpose factors have 'ruled each other out'.

However, we can also say that there is a common purpose still remaining, albeit one which is not the same as that when the property was originally acquired—ie the asset which is appreciating in value. This value-accruing function was only a secondary consideration at the time of purchase, but is now the parties' *joint* purpose. Thus, whilst in cases where a relationship breaks down like this the usual response from the court would be to sell the property (as this is usually the most efficient and cleanest way to solve the problem), in this case, the continuing purpose of the property as an asset would weigh in the court's thinking and may well prompt them to reach an alternative resolution rather than sale to the dispute before them.

Welfare of any children who occupy or who might occupy—s 15(1)(c)

Section 15(1)(c) requires the court to take account of the welfare of any children who either occupy or who might be expected to occupy the property. This is very explicitly a question about *welfare*, not existence, and the courts are vigilant in explaining that in most cases the requirement to sell a property will not affect the welfare of children occupying that property. The majority of children will move house at some point in their life without it adversely affecting them. Thus, the courts will look for something additional to the fact of a move when assessing how and whether the welfare of children has been affected. The case law shows that a number of different issues may be considered to affect welfare in this way. First, in cases where children are at school, a requirement that they move during a sensitive time in their education (mid-exam year, for example), or where there is a particular reason why the child will be substantially affected by having to move from a particular school (eg in cases of special mental or physical needs), then the courts will usually ensure that there is a delay before the property can be sold. This will allow either for the child to finish their education entirely in particularly acute cases, or will allow them to reach a point where any move can be more easily managed. Second, the courts will take account of the fact that in cases where section 14 orders are being used to result in the sale of a property, this will usually be either because the relationship between a couple has broken down, or because a lender is seeking sale in circumstances where they cannot use their usual remedies (see later). In such cases, the children are likely to be depending upon the finances of just one adult in terms of acquiring a new residence. Either the couple will be splitting up so the children's main home is likely to be with one parent only, or (at least) one of the couple is in dire financial circumstances. In such cases, the possibility of children having to move districts; the possibility of one parent being realistically able to fund the purchase of suitable new accommodation, and the like, will all be taken into account in assessing any affect on the children's welfare.

It is important to note at this point that there is a temptation when discussing welfare of children to fall into the trap of immediately considering whether the impact on the children constitutes something 'exceptional' justifying a refusal to sell the property. This temptation arises because in relation to a different statutory provision (section 335A Insolvency Act 1986—as discussed later), much of the case law is concerned with circumstances in which sale of the relevant property will detrimentally affect children in an 'exceptional' way. There is a tendency to conflate the judicial approach under these two provisions. This temptation must be avoided, as it is an entirely inaccurate representation of how the courts handle simple claims under sections 14 and 15. In cases where there is no bankruptcy, the courts will be generous in cases involving children. There is no need to show that circumstances are exceptional in order to justify a delay to sale. Rather, the courts will simply look at the whole picture in the round to assess what is the best thing to be done.

The application of the children's welfare test can be demonstrated by two important cases: *First National Bank v Achampong*[60] and *Edwards v Lloyds TSB*.[61]

---

[60] *First National Bank v Achampong* [2003] EWCA Civ 487, [2004] 1 FCR 18.
[61] *Edwards v Lloyds TSB* [2004] EWHC 1745 (Ch), [2005] 1 FCR 139 (ChD).

Key case: *First National Bank v Achampong* [2003] EWCA Civ 487

The Achampong family had purchased a property and granted a charge to the bank. Mr and Mrs Achampong were joint legal owners of this property and they lived there with their children. The mortgage was taken out, however, in order to help fund some business interests of a third party, Mr Owusu-Ansah. Mrs Owusu-Ansah's signature appeared on some of the relevant documentation, but it appears that these had been forged. Everyone had proceeded on the basis that Mr Owusu-Ansah would pay the instalments, and he did do so for a time, but eventually he fell into arrears and the bank tried to realise its security. By this point, Mr Achampong and Mr Owusu-Ansah both lived in Ghana. The bank eventually brought possession proceedings against Mrs Achampong. She alleged that she had entered into the relevant transaction as a result of undue influence. The court accepted this, and held that as the bank had failed to take appropriate steps to ensure that her consent was genuine, they were affected by the undue influence. As a result, the bank applied for sale under section 14.

The question for the court was whether the fact that Mrs Achampong occupied the property with her infant grandchildren was enough to justify a delay in the sale of the property. On the facts, the court concluded that the sale should take place, keeping in mind the guidance given in *Bank of Ireland v Bell*[62] (see later) that a bank should not be kept out of its money indefinitely. On the question of the relevance of the occupation of the grandchildren, the court reasoned:

> 'While it is relevant to consider the interests of the infant grandchildren in occupation of the property, it is difficult to attach much if any weight to their position in the absence of any evidence as to how their welfare may be adversely affected if an order for sale is now made'.[63]

The fact that one of Mrs Achampong's adult children was mentally disabled did not affect the court's reasoning either.

From this case, we can see two features of the court's assessment under section 15(1)(c): first, it is for the person resisting sale to bring evidence as to how the welfare of any children will be affected—the courts will not assume that there is such an effect merely because there are children who occupy; and second, the courts are very explicitly concerned with welfare and not merely the existence of children. This seems to make this approach rather strict, not least because on the facts Mrs Achampong was unduly influenced to enter into a transaction in relation to her family home by her husband and a third party where neither is now being held to account for the loan repayment. However, this is the consequence of a system of strong lender remedies, important to the functioning of the mortgage market (although see chapter 11 for discussion as to the ways in which this argument may be rebutted).

Key case: *Edwards v Lloyds TSB* [2004] EWHC 1745

Mr and Mrs Edwards had purchased a small terrace house in Ilford in Essex. After their relationship broke down, Mrs Edwards lived there with her two children. There was a mortgage over the property to Alliance & Leicester, which appeared to have been a valid mortgage. However, shortly after the husband left the house, he entered into transactions with the lender and forged his wife's signature on the relevant documentation. Given the invalidity of these, when the lender sought possession of the property, the court was required to consider the factors in section 15 of TOLATA.

---

[62] *Bank of Ireland v Bell* [2001] 2 All ER (Comm) 920 (CA).
[63] *First National Bank v Achampong* [2003] EWCA Civ 487, [2004] 1 FCR 18, [65].

16.4 Disputes Relating to Co-Owned Land 525

> In making this assessment, the court began with consideration of the sums due, and the amount of money which would be left for Mrs Edwards after the sale of the property. Mr Edwards provided no financial support to his former wife and children, and there was no contact between them. Having taken this and Mrs Edwards' monthly income from her part time job into account, the court then considered the factors in section 15 and explained its discretion under these provisions. The court reasoned as follows:
>
>> 'First, if the house was sold now it is hard to see how Mrs Edwards could find the money to buy another smaller one ... the house is a two-bedroom house in which Mrs Edwards already has to share a bedroom with her daughter.... I very much doubt that she would be able to find another house which she could afford to buy and which would be adequate to accommodate her and her children'.[64]
>
> This, according to the court, was enough to show that the welfare of the minors would be affected, and more generally that the sale would be 'unacceptably severe' in terms of its consequences for Mrs Edwards and her family.[65] As a result of this, the court used its discretion to postpone sale for 5 years to allow the youngest child to reach majority. However, the court emphasised that at the end of that 5-year period, it would not mean that the interests of the children became irrelevant.[66] Rather, they would be different because at that time, their own needs will have changed. Nevertheless, the court explicitly allowed Mrs Edwards to make an application to vary the order for sale should circumstances change, making the sale in 5 years problematic (if, for example, either child was still in full-time education).
>
> This is a very different approach that than seen in *Achampong*, albeit that clearly the circumstances of the parties were very different.

Interests of the beneficiaries' secured creditors—s 15(1)(d)

Section 15(1)(d) requires the court to take account of the interest of any secured creditors. We consider the situation where there is a dispute between mortgagee and beneficiaries/trustees later, where this factor carries a significantly higher degree of weight. Where, however, the parties have been paying any secured debt, and will continue to do so as far as is ascertainable, then the interests of a secured creditor will not weigh very heavily in the minds of the court. Such cases would likely involve the breakdown of a romantic relationship and the courts will be more keen to ensure that a settlement is reached which allows the parties to handle this breakdown as cleanly and amicably as possible. However, if the breakdown makes it likely that the mortgage will not be paid, then this may be a factor that the courts will consider in deciding whether or not to sell the property.

In almost all cases, the interests of a secured creditor will weigh in favour of sale—regardless of whether the mortgage is currently being paid or not, the realisation of a security will often be the 'safest' option for a lender where there has been a relationship breakdown. However, in cases where the property is in question is in negative equity, but property prices are rising, it may be in the interests of the creditor for a delay to be imposed, preventing sale until property prices have risen. This is also likely to be better for the borrower. Thus, even in relation to secured creditors, this factor does not always weigh in favour of sale.

This likelihood of sale is clear from the tone of the case law in cases where sections 14 and 15 of TOLATA are invoked by a lender seeking sale of co-owner property where they do not

---

[64] *Edwards v Lloyds TSB* [2004] EWHC 1745 (Ch), [2005] 1 FCR 139 (ChD), [31].
[65] *Edwards v Lloyds TSB* [2004] EWHC 1745 (Ch), [2005] 1 FCR 139 (ChD), [33].
[66] *Edwards v Lloyds TSB* [2004] EWHC 1745 (Ch), [2005] 1 FCR 139 (ChD), [33].

have priority over one of the co-owners. The courts have emphasised that the introduction of TOLATA 1996 means that there is no presumption that in cases of dispute the land should be sold. This is a divergence from the previous position under the Law of Property Act where section 30 provided for sale unless agreement between the trustees could be reached or there were other circumstances justifying a delay. Under sections 14 and 15 there is no such presumption in favour of sale, as we saw with the approach of Neuberger J in *Mortgage Corp v Shaire*[67] earlier. However, there is the inevitable reality that unless the property is indeed sold, a lender in circumstances such as this is highly unlikely to be able to realise their security and recover the sums due (in cases where the borrower is not meeting the instalments) unless the property is sold. As such, a delay in sale is effectively a delay in the realisation of the security. The courts have highlighted that a lender should not be kept out of its money indefinitely in situations like this. This became clear in the leading decision in *Bank of Ireland v Bell*.[68]

Key case: *Bank of Ireland v Bell* [2001] 2 All ER (Comm) 920

Mr and Mrs Bell purchased a long lease of a property to live in together as their home. The finance for this purchase was made by a mortgage. Mrs Bell did not consent to the mortgage, and her signature on the relevant documents had apparently been forged by Mr Bell. Mr Bell then abandoned the property and Mrs Bell, and the bank sought an order for sale. The question was how the court ought to exercise its discretion under section 14, taking account of the factors in section 15, in cases such as this.

The court, in reviewing the various factors, reasoned (per Peter Gibson LJ):

'Prior to the 1996 Act the courts under section 30 of the Law of Property Act 1925 would order the sale of a matrimonial home at the request of the trustee in bankruptcy of a spouse or at the request of the creditor chargee of a spouse, considering that the creditors' interest should prevail over that of the other spouse and the spouse's family save in exceptional circumstances. The 1996 Act, by requiring the court to have regard to the particular matters specified in section 15, appears to me to have given scope for some change in the court's practice. Nevertheless, a powerful consideration is and ought to be whether the creditor is receiving proper recompense for being kept out of his money, repayment of which is overdue... In the present case it is plain that by refusing sale the judge has condemned the bank to go on waiting for its money with no prospect of recovery from Mr and Mr Mrs Bell and with the debt increasing all the time, that debt already exceeding what could be realised on a sale. That seems to me to be very unfair to the bank'.[69]

Further analysis: Priority given to secured creditors

The decision in *Bank of Ireland v Bell* effectively results in the interests of creditors being prioritised, or at least, in the words of Probert, creditors become 'first among equals', in the balancing act carried out by the courts.[70] Probert highlights what the effect of this preference may be, ie to effectively make each

---

[67] *Mortgage Corporation v Shaire* [2001] Ch 743.
[68] *Bank of Ireland v Bell* [2001] 2 All ER (Comm) 920 (CA).
[69] *Bank of Ireland v Bell* [2001] 2 All ER (Comm) 920 (CA), [31].
[70] R Probert, 'Creditors and section 15 of the Trusts of Land and Appointment of Trustees Act 1996: first among equals?' [2002] Conv 61.

case a balancing act between the welfare of any children, if there are any, and the interests of creditors. She argues:

> 'The danger in the reasoning lies in the way that it downgrades the purpose of providing a family home as against the interests of the creditors. If the purpose of providing a family home comes to an end upon the departure of one of the parties and only the original purposes are to be taken into account, then when one party has left and there are no children, the only relevant factor remaining is the interests of the creditors. Even where there are children the dispute is reduced to a straightforward contest between the welfare of any minors who might wish to occupy the property and the interests of the creditors. If these two factors are given equal weight then it is possible that either may prevail in the short term. In the long term, the minors will grow up and their interests will cease to be a relevant concern'.[71]

The effect of this case law, therefore, is to make the welfare of those occupying the house a secondary concern, and this is potentially worrying given that in most cases where a lender brings an action under section 14 for sale of property, it is because the situation involves a co-owner with priority over that lender. If that is the case, then it is difficult to see why the creditors' interests should nevertheless prevail. It is true that the fact of having priority will mean that the co-owner is entitled to their share of the proceeds of sale before the mortgage has been discharged, but that, as was seen in *Edwards v Lloyds TSB*[72] for example does not necessarily mean that they will be in a position to afford alternative accommodation.

Dixon agrees with this assessment. He argues that:

> 'There appears to be no recognition of the fact that the equitable owner has proprietary priority over the mortgage and that forcing him or her to take the priority in money [rather than in possession of the home] effectively ignored the abolition of the trust for sale... More importantly perhaps, there is no consideration of why the lender has filed to achieve the priority it surely intended to obtain'.[73]

It should be remembered, however, that the lender is not in a 'win-win' situation here either. Because in such circumstances the co-owner will usually remain entitled to a substantial proportion of the proceeds of sale, the lender is unlikely to realize the totality of their security. The question then becomes one of who should lose out and in what ways, following the often dubious dealings of a co-owner of property: their partner, or their lender?

Circumstances and wishes of the majority of adult beneficiaries

Finally, under section 15(3), unless the application involves a transfer of title to the beneficiaries, the court must also take account of the wishes and circumstances of the beneficiaries, with an additional factor being the view of the majority of those (calculated according to the percentage share which they own). In the majority of cases not involving a third party, the dispute would be one between beneficiaries (who would probably also be trustees) such that there is no clear answer to be determined according to this factor.

As we noted earlier, this list is not exhaustive and the court has considerable discretion over the relative weight which it affords to the various factors.

---

[71] R Probert, 'Creditors and section 15 of the Trusts of Land and Appointment of Trustees Act 1996: first among equals?' [2002] Conv 61, 66.

[72] *Edwards v Lloyds TSB* [2004] EWHC 1745 (Ch), [2005] 1 FCR 139 (ChD).

[73] M Dixon, 'To sell or not to sell: that is the question. The irony of the Trusts of Land and Appointment of Trustees Act 1996' (2011) 70 CLJ 579, 605.

16.4.1.4 Bankruptcy—section 335A Insolvency Act

In circumstances involving bankruptcy of one of the co-owners, the situation will be very different. In such cases, where an application for sale under section 14 is made by the bankrupt's trustee in bankruptcy, the court is directed to consider not the factors in section 15, but those in section 335A Insolvency Act 1986. This section provides that:

'(1) Any application by a trustee of a bankrupt's estate under section 14 of the Trusts of Land and Appointment of Trustees Act 1996 (powers of court in relation to trusts of land) for an order under that section for the sale of land shall be made to the court having jurisdiction in relation to the bankruptcy.

(2) On such an application the court shall make such order as it thinks just and reasonable having regard to—

   (a) the interests of the bankrupt's creditors;

   (b) where the application is made in respect of land which includes a dwelling house which is or has been the home of the bankrupt or the bankrupt's spouse or civil partner or former spouse or former civil partner—

      (i) the conduct of the spouse, civil partner, former spouse or former civil partner, so far as contributing to the bankruptcy,

      (ii) the needs and financial resources of the spouse, civil partner, former spouse or former civil partner, and

      (iii) the needs of any children; and

   (c) all the circumstances of the case other than the needs of the bankrupt.'

In many respect these factors are very similar to those contained in section 15, with the notable difference that the court is *not* permitted to consider the needs of the bankrupt person as demonstrated by *Everitt v Budhram*.[74] As the case law has demonstrated, this includes their physical needs in case of serious ill health, and the like, and can therefore be very detrimental to the welfare of the bankrupt person, as *Everitt* demonstrates. The court is required to consider the need of other inhabitants of the property, including the need of any children, amongst other factors. However, the court's ability to 'balance' these various needs is limited to the first year following the bankruptcy. After that point, the court is mandated by section 335A to act in accordance with the needs of the creditor (ie effectively ordering sale of the property) unless the circumstances are exceptional.

The ability of other residents to stay in the property longer term following bankruptcy is therefore almost entirely dependent upon the scope of this exceptional circumstances test. The more generous the courts are with this provision, the greater the provision for remaining in the home. However, case law to date has shown that the courts will interpret this provision very narrowly indeed. Cases such as *Barca v Mears*[75] show that the courts consider exceptional to mean *both* very severe *and* very unusual. It is usually this latter consideration which limits the ability of a

---

[74] *Everitt v Budhram* [2009] EWHC 1219 (Ch), [2010] Ch 170.
[75] *Barca v Mears* [2004] EWHC 2170 (Ch), [2004] All ER (D) 153.

particular inhabitant of the property to rely on the court's discretion here. Indeed, the courts have held that, in effect, only cases of terminal or very serious illness will be enough to allow a resident of such property to remain once the one year period has expired, as shown for example by *Claughton v Charalambous*.[76] As is perhaps to be expected, the very restrictive attitude that the courts have taken to this provision has resulted in claims being made that this provision breaches the protections given to individuals by the Human Rights Act 1998, so that the courts should exercise their discretion more generously to ensure that, in particular, the article 8 right to a private life (part of which is a right to the home), is not breached. We consider this line of case law more in chapter 17, but it useful to note here simply that the courts have shown very little movement in response to this issue. They have acknowledged that the section has the potential to breach human rights, but that as long as the courts genuinely consider the possibility of exceptional circumstances (rather than assuming that they do not exist), then the balance between the needs of mortgage lenders to ensure security in the most extreme of cases, and the needs of co-habitees with bankrupts person, has, according to the courts, been struck in the right place.

16.4.2 RIGHTS OF OCCUPATION AND OCCUPATION RENT

TOLATA also makes provision in relation to co-owned land to ensure that disputes regarding *occupation*, rather than management of the land as an asset, can also be effectively resolved. The resolution is provided through section 14 as earlier, but the background 'rights' in respect of occupation are established by sections 12 and 13 of the 1996 Act. Section 12 states that:

'(1) A beneficiary who is beneficially entitled to an interest in possession in land subject to a trust of land is entitled by reason of his interest to occupy the land at any time if at that time—

   (a) the purposes of the trust include making the land available for his occupation (or for the occupation of beneficiaries of a class of which he is a member or of beneficiaries in general), or

   (b) the land is held by the trustees so as to be so available.'

This ensures that even if a beneficiary is not currently occupying, due to decisions made by herself, or the trustees, then she has the *right* so to do. This sets the context for section 13, which states:

'(1) Where two or more beneficiaries are (or apart from this subsection would be) entitled under section 12 to occupy land, the trustees of land may exclude or restrict the entitlement of any one or more (but not all) of them.

(2) Trustees may not under subsection (1)—

   (a) unreasonably exclude any beneficiary's entitlement to occupy land, or

   (b) restrict any such entitlement to an unreasonable extent.

(3) The trustees of land may from time to time impose reasonable conditions on any beneficiary in relation to his occupation of land by reason of his entitlement under section 12.

---

[76] *Claughton v Charalambous* [1999] 1 FLR 740 (ChD).

(4) The matters to which trustees are to have regard in exercising the powers conferred by this section include—

(a) the intentions of the person or persons (if any) who created the trust,

(b) the purposes for which the land is held, and

(c) the circumstances and wishes of each of the beneficiaries who is (or apart from any previous exercise by the trustees of those powers would be) entitled to occupy the land under section 12.

(5) The conditions which may be imposed on a beneficiary under subsection (3) include, in particular, conditions requiring him—

(a) to pay any outgoings or expenses in respect of the land, or

(b) to assume any other obligation in relation to the land or to any activity which is or is proposed to be conducted there.

(6) Where the entitlement of any beneficiary to occupy land under section 12 has been excluded or restricted, the conditions which may be imposed on any other beneficiary under subsection (3) include, in particular, conditions requiring him to—

(a) make payments by way of compensation to the beneficiary whose entitlement has been excluded or restricted, or

(b) forgo any payment or other benefit to which he would otherwise be entitled under the trust so as to benefit that beneficiary.'

It is worth replicating this section in full to demonstrate the careful balance which has been struck in this Act between the needs and wishes of a wide variety of parties.

Taken together, these two provisions provide that any beneficiary can occupy where that is one of the purposes of the trust, as long as the property is available and suitable for occupation given the type of property it is, and any existing residents. The trustees are authorised to give one or more persons the ability to reside, provided of course that it is possible for more than one person to reside in the property. Where not all beneficiaries can occupy, the trustees must choose who occupies and can require others to be compensated. Where a beneficiary is in occupation he cannot be removed except by a court order and any claim in respect of this is brought under section 14, and the court will, as is normal, have regard to the factors in section 15 in determining the outcome of the case.

> **Further analysis: Valuation of occupation rent under TOLATA**
>
> Bright has analysed the case law in which orders relating to occupation rents have been made and has analysed the trends that seem to be emerging in this respect. She argues that:
>
> > 'Both under TLATA and the equitable principles there are few signs that the courts are willing to depart from the idea that the compensatory payment should be based on the rental value of the property. There has not (yet) really been a break from this past, notwithstanding both the clear direction in TLATA to have regard to the circumstances and wishes of the co-owners and the welfare of children, and judicial

> remarks that the equitable accounting jurisdiction aims to do what is fair between the parties. It is sensitivity to these kinds of financial and welfare considerations that undoubtedly shape the agreements reached informally between the co-owners. If courts are to move towards making these wider enquiries, then they will need to be supplied with evidence that enables them to have detailed information about the parties' circumstances, and the impact that a requirement to pay an occupation rent will have on the ability to provide for children'.[77]
>
> The possibility of an occupation rent under this section is an interesting one. It is designed to ensure that where there is a class of beneficiaries, and only one or a subset can occupy, the others do not lose out. It is based on the logic that as section 12 confers on all beneficiaries the right to occupy, those who are not occupying have their own rights limited for the benefit of others, despite a theoretically equal starting point. However, in asking a beneficiary in occupation to pay, we are in effect requiring that they pay for a right which they already had, and indeed, may have already paid for in the shape of contributions to the acquisition of the title. How can that discrepancy be explained?
>
> This answer to this is to be found in the distinction which we can draw between the benefit of rights in the land, and the benefit of being able to occupy that land. The contribution to purchase price explains the share in the equitable title that a person may have. That entitles them to occupy where suitable, but it does not *pay for* that occupation. This is why, when we deal with multiple beneficiaries entitled to occupy, but unable to share, the law recognises that the one who does *not* occupy the trust property, must pay to reside elsewhere. Thus, it is only fair that the one who does reside in the trust property should pay that other some compensation. However, it could not be market rate—the statute does not provide any guidance on this—because otherwise the one residing elsewhere would effectively be left with a net loss of zero (payment for alternative accommodation being offset by the occupation rent they receive), but the one occupying the trust property would be left with a loss. Thus, the rate of rent charged must be lower than market rent, but we do not know precisely how it ought to be calculated.

16.4.3 PRIORITY DISPUTES BETWEEN CO-OWNERS AND THIRD PARTIES

The regulation of disputes between co-owners and third parties is determined by two sets of rules: those relating to priorities; and those relating to co-ownership. For this reason, these rules can be particularly difficult to navigate as it will often be a case of switching between these two sets of rules to find the right answer. The general priority rules are considered in detail in the previous chapter. It is useful here to examine how the priority rules play out in a co-ownership context, and more importantly, how this means they affect the rules regulating co-ownership. We consider this here by examining the relationship between beneficiaries under a trust and third parties, both lenders, and disponees of title to the land. We commence our discussion with consideration of overreaching. This topic is explained elsewhere in this book, see eg chapters 3 and 15, but it is of such importance in practice, and so significant to the issues covered in this chapter, that it is useful to recap on this mechanism again here and to consider its particular application in relation to trusts of land.

---

[77] S Bright, 'Occupation rents and the Trusts of Land and Appointment of Trustees Act 1996: from property to welfare?' [2009] Conv 378, 395.

16.4.3.1 Overreaching

Requirements of overreaching

Overreaching is the mechanism by which interests under a trust are transferred into the proceeds of sale when property is sold, or otherwise lose priority on a disposition of an estate in the relevant land. The mechanism is provided for in the Law of Property Act 1925, section 2, which states that:

> '(1) A conveyance to a purchaser of a legal estate in land shall overreach any equitable interest or power affecting that estate, whether or not he has notice thereof, if—
>
> ...
>
> (ii) the conveyance is made by trustees of land and the equitable interest or power is at the date of the conveyance capable of being overreached by such trustees under the provisions of subsection (2) of this section or independently of that subsection, and the requirements of section 27 of this Act respecting the payment of capital money arising on such a conveyance are complied with'.

Thus, for overreaching to occur, the interest in question must be capable of being overreached. For the purposes of this chapter, which is concerned with disputes arising in relation to co-owned land, the relevant interests are interests under a trust and they are certainly capable of being overreached. Section 2 then provides that in order for such overreaching to occur in cases involving a trust of land, it is necessary for the requirements of section 27 to be met.

This section states:

> '(1) A purchaser of a legal estate from trustees of land shall not be concerned with the trusts affecting the land, the net income of the land or the proceeds of sale of the land whether or not those trusts are declared by the same instrument as that by which the trust of land is created.
>
> (2) Notwithstanding anything to the contrary in the instrument (if any) creating a trust of land... the proceeds of sale or other capital money shall not be paid to or applied by the direction of fewer than two persons as trustees, except where the trustee is a trust corporation...'

Section 27(1) explains what overreaching means in the context of the purchaser of a legal estate in the land subject to the trust (including of course one who purchases a leasehold estate or mortgage which is treated as an estate in land for these purposes), ie that person will not be 'concerned' with any interests which exist under a trust. Section 27(2) explains that for this effect to occur, the money in the transaction must be paid to at least two trustees. Thus, for overreaching to occur in relation to land in which there is a trust, two requirements must be met: first, the purchaser must provide valuable consideration to acquire a legal estate in the relevant land; and second, that money must be paid to at least two trustees.

When we consider these requirements in the context of co-owned land, we can see that wherever there are two trustees, those trustees hold considerable power in relation to the 'fate' of the beneficiaries' interest in the land. Where those trustees and beneficiaries are the same people, overreaching has a very limited role to play in so far as the consent of the trustees will be necessary for a legal estate to be granted. It is only therefore where the trustees and the beneficiaries are different people, that overreaching will have significant effects in relation to co-owned land.

Furthermore, it is important to always keep in mind that overreaching can only operate where there are at least two trustees. This distinction is shown by reference to the famous and very important cases—*Boland*[78], and *Flegg*[79]. We discuss these here, followed by a recent case which seems to cast some doubt on the current state of the law (*Wishart*[80]).

> **Key case: *Williams & Glyn's Bank Ltd v Boland* [1981] AC 487**
>
> This case involved a series of situations concerning wives with a co-ownership interest in a property, and a dispute over priority between such co-owners and lenders, where the mortgage was a legal mortgage validly granted by the sole legal owner.
>
> In the case, the House of Lords emphasised that since there was only one trustee in each case granting the legal mortgage in question, the mechanism of overreaching could not be used and as such the question of whether or not the lender was bound depended upon the actual occupation of the co-owner. Before *Boland*, the position of an equitable co-owner in circumstances like this was unclear, and it is therefore a significant case in effectively protecting the interests of one co-owner against the machinations of the other.
>
> It is interesting to note the role that policy concerns reached in the court's decision here, with Lord Scarman reasoning:
>
> > 'But the importance of the House's decision is not to be judged solely by its impact on conveyancing, or banking, practice. The Court of Appeal recognised the relevance, and stressed the importance, of the social implications of the case. While the technical task faced by the courts, and now facing the House, is the construction to be put upon a sub-clause in a subsection of a conveyancing statute, it is our duty, when tackling it, to give the provision, if we properly can, a meaning which will work for, rather than against, rights conferred by Parliament, or recognised by judicial decision, as being necessary for the achievement of social justice. The courts may not, therefore, put aside, as irrelevant, the undoubted fact that, if the two wives succeed, the protection of the beneficial interest which English law now recognises that a married woman has in the matrimonial home will be strengthened whereas, if they lose, this interest can be weakened, and even destroyed, by an unscrupulous husband. Nor must the courts flinch when assailed by arguments to the effect that the protection of her interest will create difficulties in banking or conveyancing practice. The difficulties are, I believe, exaggerated: but bankers, and solicitors, exist to provide the service which the public needs. They can - as they have successfully done in the past - adjust their practice, if it be socially required. Nevertheless, the judicial responsibility remains - to interpret the statute truly according to its tenor. The social background is, therefore, to be kept in mind but can be decisive only if the particular statutory provision under review is reasonably capable of the meaning conducive to the special purpose to which I have referred. If it is not, the remedy is to be found not by judicial distortion of the language used by Parliament but in amending legislation'.[81]
>
> Keeping these considerations in mind, and looking at the wording of the relevant provisions, the court concluded that in cases such as those in *Boland*, the interests under the trusts could not be overreached. The key to the outcome in the case, it must be emphasised, was the combination of **no overreaching**, the possibility of the interest under a trust being an **overriding interest**, and the protection of that interest being achieved by the wives' **actual occupation**. These latter two conditions were explained in chapter 15.

---

[78] *Williams & Glyn's Bank Ltd v Boland* [1981] AC 487 (HL).
[79] *City of London Building Society v Flegg* [1988] AC 54 (HL).
[80] *Wishart v Credit and Mercantile Plc* [2015] EWCA Civ 655, [2015] 2 P & CR 15.
[81] *Williams & Glyn's Bank Ltd v Boland* [1981] AC 487 (HL).

> **Key case:** *City of London Building Society v Flegg* [1988] AC 54
>
> *Flegg* demonstrates what happens when one seemingly small change in the facts pattern has a radical alteration in the outcome. In *Flegg*, a couple purchased a property to house themselves, and the wife's parents. The parents had contributed a significant amount to the purchase price, and occupied the property throughout. However, the couple executed charges secured against the property without the knowledge or consent of the parents. The question was whether the lender could exercise their security in relation to the property, and this depended upon whether the parents had priority over the lenders.
>
> The court, in concluding that the parents did not have priority over the lenders, focussed on the fact that unlike in *Boland*,[82] there were two legal owners and as such, the parents' interest had been overreached. As Lord Templeman explained:
>
> > 'The respondents claim to be entitled to overriding interests because they were in actual occupation of Bleak House on the date of the legal charge. But the interests of the respondents cannot at one and the same time be overreached and overridden and at the same time be overriding interests. The appellants cannot at one and the same time take free from all the interests of the respondents yet at the same time be subject to some of those interests. The right of the respondents to be and remain in actual occupation of Bleak House ceased when the respondents' interests were overreached by the legal charge save in so far as their rights were transferred to the equity of redemption'.[83]
>
> In effect, the court here concluded that 'overreaching trumps overriding'—to put this another way, if an interest is overreached, the question as to whether it can override on a transfer or grant of a legal estate in land is irrelevant. This meant that the parents being in actual occupation was completely inconsequential to the outcome of the case. The question simply could not arise, since their interests had already been overreached, and this was because, unlike in *Boland*,[84] there were two trustees.

Many see the outcome in *Flegg*[85] as being harsh on co-owners. There is little doubt that it is a consequence of a straight reading of the statutory provisions, but it also meant that the statutory provisions could assist, in effect, in facilitating a breach of trust. Furthermore, the policy concerns expressed by Lord Scarman in *Boland*[86] are just as a relevant on the facts of *Flegg*[87] as they had been in that earlier case. The concerns that their Lordships in *Boland*[88] felt for the ability of one co-owner to ride roughshod over the rights of another are not particularly alleviated by the fact that there is a requirement that two trustees agree to this harsh treatment. Nevertheless, *Boland*[89] and *Flegg*[90] have represented the settled law for a number of years. However, recent case law has begun to cast a small amount of doubt in respect of the precise operation of these rules, particularly the decision in *Wishart v Credit and Mercantile Plc*.[91]

---

[82] *Williams & Glyn's Bank Ltd v Boland* [1981] AC 487 (HL).
[83] *City of London Building Society v Flegg* [1988] AC 54 (HL).
[84] *Williams & Glyn's Bank Ltd v Boland* [1981] AC 487 (HL).
[85] *City of London Building Society v Flegg* [1988] AC 54 (HL).
[86] *Williams & Glyn's Bank Ltd v Boland* [1981] AC 487 (HL).
[87] *City of London Building Society v Flegg* [1988] AC 54 (HL).
[88] *Williams & Glyn's Bank Ltd v Boland* [1981] AC 487 (HL).
[89] *Williams & Glyn's Bank Ltd v Boland* [1981] AC 487 (HL).
[90] *City of London Building Society v Flegg* [1988] AC 54 (HL).
[91] *Wishart v Credit and Mercantile Plc* [2015] EWCA Civ 655, [2015] 2 P & CR 15.

Key case: *Wishart v Credit and Mercantile Plc* [2015] EWCA Civ 655

The property in question in this case was called Dalhanna. The registered proprietor of Dalhanna was Kaymuu, a company controlled by Sami Muduroglu (Sami). Sami was a close friend of Mr Wishart. Mr Wishart believed Sami was acting on his behalf, whereas in fact, Sami was a fraudster. Sami borrowed £500,000 from Credit and Mercantile, secured against Dalhanna. Mr Wishart was in occupation of Dalhanna at this time. Following Sami's disappearance and loss of all the money, C&M exercised their security and sold Dalhanna. Mr Wishart claimed he was entitled to the proceeds of this sale, alleging that his actual occupation gave him priority over the lender. The court therefore had to establish two things: first, did Mr Wishart have part or all of the equitable interest in Dalhanna; and second, did his actual occupation protect that against C&M. The judge at first instance had concluded that whilst Mr Wishart did have the beneficial entitlement to the property, this could not bind C&M even though Wishart was in actual occupation, because of a rule akin to estoppel known as the *Brocklesby* principle.

The starting point for the Court of Appeal was this:

'Despite the importance of actual occupation evident upon reasonably careful inspection as the principal mechanism under the 2002 Act to test whether an innocent third party acquiring legal title should be protected, the words in italics indicate that, in order to establish that an overriding interest exists, the occupier has to show that he has relevant rights capable of binding the purchaser of the legal title in equity, subject only to the question of actual occupation. Therefore, there is scope for the operation of any rule of law which prevents the occupier from having a relevant right as against the purchaser before one comes to apply the actual occupation test, which may have the effect of preventing a finding that there is an overriding interest under the statute'.[92]

In other words, whilst *Boland* indicates that actual occupation will protect the priority of a right not otherwise overreached, *Wishart* suggests that there are many other rules which can prevent that protection. Indeed, the primary rule cited by the court to support this is the possibility of an implied waiver, and that a waiver would prevent the co-owner from asserting priority must be correct. However, the breadth of the exception in *Wishart* is what has caused some disquiet. The principle applied by the court is summarised as follows:

'The *Brocklesby* principle is not based on actual authority given to the agent, but rather on a combination of factors: actual authority given by the owner of an asset to a person authorised to deal with it in some way on his behalf; where the owner has furnished the agent with the means of holding himself out to a purchaser or lender as the owner of the asset or as having the full authority of the owner to deal with it; together with an omission by the owner to bring to the attention of a person dealing with the agent any limitation that exists as to the extent of the actual authority of the agent'.[93]

The key features of the court's decision, therefore, are first, that Wishart gave authority to Sami for Sami to deal with the property; that Sami became registered proprietor on this basis thus giving himself the means of showing that power to third parties; and Wishart had not brought the fact that Sami was supposed to be acting on behalf of Wishart to the lender's attention. The problem which the commentators on this case highlight is that it is difficult to conceive of many situations where a trust would fall outside the parameters of this principle since this is precisely what a trust is designed to do, ie to give one person the actual and apparent authority to act on behalf of another. If this is a correct reading of what is said in *Wishart*, then the principle as expressed in *Boland*,[94] and the protection, limited though it is, which co-owners may receive from *Boland*,[95] would be significantly eroded.

---

[92] *Wishart v Credit and Mercantile Plc* [2015] EWCA Civ 655, [2015] 2 P & CR 15.
[93] *Wishart v Credit and Mercantile Plc* [2015] EWCA Civ 655, [2015] 2 P & CR 15.
[94] *Williams & Glyn's Bank Ltd v Boland* [1981] AC 487 (HL).
[95] *Williams & Glyn's Bank Ltd v Boland* [1981] AC 487 (HL).

> **Further analysis: The rights and wrongs of *Wishart***
>
> A number of commentators have doubted both the reasoning and the outcome in *Wishart*.[96] The reasons for rejecting its approach vary however. First, Televantos argues that the principles expressed in *Wishart*,[97] and in *Brocklesby*[98] by extension, are best seen as being principles relating to agency, and as rules expressing the position between agents and third parties, should be considered correct. However, Televantos continues, the error of the court in *Wishart*[99] was to hold that all situations involving a trust also involved agency such that the principles would apply *en bloc* to all trust cases.[100] He argues that, 'applying ostensible authority to all trusts arising from B holding assets for A's benefit would fundamentally alter the nature of such trusts', and that this is inconsistent with the Land Registration rules; with common law; and with the policy concerns so critical to the outcome in *Boland*.[101]
>
> Furthermore, Televantos highlights that the very structure of the LRA is premised on specific treatment of trusts interests in land. He argues:
>
> > 'The current English law regime for trusts of registered land take as a starting point that trustees can freely dispose of the trust assets, binding the beneficiaries. Beneficiaries will typically only be able to claim they keep their beneficial interest and priority where: (i) there has not been a disposition by two trustees or trust corporation; and (ii) the beneficiaries are in actual occupation of the land. The regime is designed to promote the marketability of land, and so favours third party purchasers over beneficiaries except in cases of owner-possessors. It goes without saying that the policies behind the rules governing priorities disputes in the context of trusts of land are specific, and very different to those underlying the doctrine of ostensible authority. The provisions of the LRA 2002 on point are clearly driven by a recognition that there is need to protect beneficiaries who live in the property in which they have an interest under a trust'.[102]
>
> Dixon's response to this case has been even stronger. He commented that the decision all but overrules *Boland*,[103] so that '[n]o amount of wailing and gnashing of teeth could bring it back from the grave—for that is where it might now be'.[104] This, he argues, represents a seriously wrong step for the law, not least because it ignores the careful balance struck between co-owning occupiers and third parties as expressed in the Land Registration Act.

In cases where overreaching has occurred, there will be two consequences for the beneficiaries. First, they will lose priority to whatever legal estate was conveyed as part of the overreaching transaction regardless of the registration priority rules. This will make the presence or absence of a restriction on the register particularly important, since the restriction, whilst unable to protect priority, can prevent an overreaching transaction taking place in the first instance. Second, in cases where it is the estate which was held on trust itself which has been conveyed, then any dispute between the beneficiaries will now relate either to the money paid, or to any property subsequently acquired by trustees with that money. In this sense, the interests under the trust 'follow'

---

[96] *Wishart v Credit and Mercantile Plc* [2015] EWCA Civ 655, [2015] 2 P & CR 15.
[97] *Wishart v Credit and Mercantile Plc* [2015] EWCA Civ 655, [2015] 2 P & CR 15.
[98] *Brocklesby v Temperance Permanent Building Society* [1895] AC 173 (HL).
[99] *Wishart v Credit and Mercantile Plc* [2015] EWCA Civ 655, [2015] 2 P & CR 15.
[100] A Televantos, 'Trusteeship, ostensible authority, and land registration: the category error in Wishart' [2016] Conv 181, 182.
[101] *Williams & Glyn's Bank Ltd v Boland* [1981] AC 487 (HL).
[102] A Televantos, 'Trusteeship, ostensible authority, and land registration: the category error in Wishart' [2016] Conv 181, 186.
[103] *Williams & Glyn's Bank Ltd v Boland* [1981] AC 487 (HL).
[104] M Dixon, 'The Boland requiem' [2015] Conv 285, 285.

the money, rather than the original trust property. In cases where the conveyance occurred in breach of trust, the effect of the overreaching transaction will be to protect a good faith purchaser, regardless even of bad faith or fraud on behalf of the trustees. Avoiding fraud is the reason for the two trustee requirement—the theory being that a sole trustee is much more likely to be tempted by the allure of a bad faith transaction than are two together—but fraud itself will not undermine the transaction as long as the *purchaser* is in good faith. The very fine line which can emerge in relation to the role of purchaser bad faith in respect of overreaching is, however, demonstrated by the decision in *HSBC v Dyche*.[105]

Key case: *HSBC v Dyche* [2009] EWHC 2954

In this case, D was the freehold proprietor of a house. HSBC had two mortgages over the house. C, who was D's father, claimed that he was the sole beneficial owner of the house under a constructive trust, and that he had priority over the mortgages so that the lender could not realise its security. The circumstances came about because, in 1994 as a result of C's bankruptcy, the property was transferred into the joint names of D and her husband. The common understanding between the parties at this time, the court concluded, was that at some point the property would be transferred back to C. The court was satisfied that this did indeed give rise to a constructive trust in favour of C. However, the more critical question was whether the transactions entered into with HSBC took priority over this interest under the trust.

In 2002, the property was transferred from Mrs D and her husband, just to Mrs D, as part of a divorce settlement between the two. Mrs D paid £5000 to her husband on the occasion of the transfer. On the same date, Mrs D granted a first legal mortgage to HSBC, claiming that Mr C was a tenant on the basis of a forged tenancy agreement. It was concluded by HHJ Purle QC, that this transfer from Mr and Mrs D to just Mrs D was a breach of trust given that it coincided with the grant of the mortgage. Similarly, Mr D must also have known that he was acting in breach of trust at the time.

The question to which these transactions gave rise, however, is whether C's interest under the trust was overreached as a consequence of the transfer from Mr and Mrs D to Mrs D for £5000 even though there was without doubt a breach of trust here.

This, in turn, depended upon whether the requirements of section 2(1)(ii) of the Law of Property Act 1925 were met. This provision requires transfer to a purchaser, ie a person providing valuable consideration in good faith, as defined in section 205 LPA 1925. In this case, given that Mrs D was acting in breach of trust, she could not have been described as being 'in good faith'. The judge explains the consequences if any other conclusion was reached here:

> 'I should, perhaps, mention that the definitions in section 205 apply "unless the context otherwise requires". Here, the context positively requires the definition to apply, as otherwise a trustee could overreach the beneficiary's interest in favour of himself'.[106]

According to the court, therefore, the significant feature of this case is that Mrs D was in bad faith *qua* purchaser. It makes no difference to the operation of overreaching that the trustee is in bad faith: rather, what matters is the good faith or otherwise of the purchaser. As a result of this, since Mr C's interest was not overreached, and given his occupation at the time of the disposition, his interest took priority over the mortgagee's charge.

---

[105] *HSBC v Dyche* [2009] EWHC 2954 (Ch), [2010] 2 P & CR 4.
[106] *HSBC v Dyche* [2009] EWHC 2954 (Ch), [2010] 2 P & CR 4, [40].

> **Further analysis: Overreaching and good faith after *Dyche***
>
> This decision has not proved to be universally welcome, as it muddies the water between the seemingly automatic operation of overreaching rules, to add aspects of good faith and knowledge where such are not immediately apparent from the statutory provisions in section 2 (albeit that the court in *Dyche* is right that the definition in section 205 would indeed preclude the operation of overreaching here). The dispute therefore is whether the court was right to say that the context did not require a different interpretation of purchaser. Of this decision, Dixon has said that: 'while the result may well be correct, the reasoning has the potential to undermine the security of mortgages and present as a direct challenge to a fundamental precept of the Land Registration Act 2002—the power of a registered proprietor to deal with their land'.[107] He elaborates further, arguing that the context did require a different interpretation of purchaser:
>
>> 'Otherwise, every purchaser who knows, or ought to have known, about the existence of an equitable owner who did not agree with the proposed transaction by the trustees could find that the overreaching machinery did not protect them. "Good faith" may have been the mainstay of unregistered conveyancing, but it has no significant role in respect of land of registered title'.[108]
>
> What other options are there, then, for explaining why overreaching did not take place in this case? One option, following *Halifax v Curry Popeck*,[109] would be to conclude that there was no true valuable consideration here given the bad faith. Second, it could be possible simply to say that there was no overreaching here because otherwise the statute would be used as an instrument of fraud—but that approach is not really so very different from saying that overreaching could not occur because of the bad faith of the purchaser. In fact, allowing a generalised 'fraud' exception to the operation of overreaching may indeed by *wider* than the reasoning in *Dyche*.[110] Finally, according to Dixon, it would be possible to argue that Mrs Dyche was not a 'third party' for the purposes of the overreaching machinery so that overreaching could not work.[111]
>
> Whilst these arguments may well represent alternative modes of reasoning from that present in *Dyche*,[112] it is not altogether clear that this solves the problem that Dixon identifies in terms of limiting the 'inroads' which this case makes into the certainty of the powers of the trustees, and the security of lending.

Consequences of no overreaching

In cases where no overreaching has occurred, then the regulation of the dispute between the beneficiaries under the trust and the third party will depend, first, upon any interactions between those parties during the transaction. If, in the course of discussions, for example, the beneficiary can be said to have either impliedly or expressly waived their priority, then regardless of the priority rules within the Land Registration Act 2002, the co-owner will rank behind the purchaser of the estate. This section will be much easier to follow if read in conjunction with chapter 15 but it is considered here to act as a useful reference guide to the specific questions which arise in relation

---

[107] M Dixon, 'Editor's notebook' [2010] Conv 1.
[108] M Dixon, 'Editor's notebook' [2010] Conv 1, 5.
[109] *Halifax v Curry Popeck* [2008] EWHC 1692 (Ch), [2009] 1 P & CR DG3.
[110] *HSBC v Dyche* [2009] EWHC 2954 (Ch), [2010] 2 P & CR 4.
[111] M Dixon, 'Editor's notebook' [2010] Conv 1, 6–7.
[112] *HSBC v Dyche* [2009] EWHC 2954 (Ch), [2010] 2 P & CR 4.

to co-owned land when considering priority rules. It will also be useful when reading this section, to make reference to the diagram contained in the online resources which charts the rules relating to priority, co-ownership, and lending.

If no waiver can be found, or the waiver was produced as a result of undue influence in such a way as to affect the third party (see chapter 11), then the relationship between the third party and the beneficiary will depend upon the normal rules of priority in registered and unregistered land. Given the focus of this book, we consider here only briefly those relating to registered land. For a fuller explanation, see chapter 15.

The first question to ask whenever there is a priority dispute not resolved by reference to the rules relating to overreaching, nor by the existence of a valid waiver, the next step is to ascertain whether the third party provided valuable consideration as part of a disposition of a registered estate, and subsequently themselves became the registered proprietor of that estate. If those conditions are met, then the dispute will be regulated by the rules in section 29 LRA 2002. If those conditions are not met, most likely because the disponee did not provide valuable consideration as part of the transaction, then the question will be resolved by reference to section 28. Under section 28, the disponee will be bound by any rights which were binding upon the relevant estate immediately prior to the disposition, which would naturally include any interests under a trust in respect of that estate. Section 28 cases are, in this way, pretty straightforward.

Where the conditions of section 29 are met, the position is slightly more difficult. In most cases, the 'route through' section 29 involves consideration of any interests either registered or which override the relevant disposition. However, when dealing specifically with interests under a trust, these *cannot* be registered as a notice. This is a result of section 33 LRA 2002 which states (amongst other things) that: 'No notice may be entered in the register in respect of any of the following—(a) an interest under—(i) a trust of land'. The consequence of this is that interests under a trust can only ever be protected as overriding interests. Since the only potentially relevant category of overriding interests is that contained in schedule 1 paragraph 2 and schedule 3 paragraph 2, ie the interests of a person in actual occupation, if a beneficiary of a trust wishes to assert priority against a third party, it is essential and unavoidable that they be in actual occupation at the time of the disposition so that the requirements of schedule 1 or schedule 3 paragraph 2 are met. The detail on this requirement is explained in chapter 15.

If the beneficiary is not in actual occupation at the time of the disposition, then they will lose priority to the estate under the disposition. In cases involving transfers of the freehold, that will mean that the beneficiary is no longer able to assert any rights against the freehold owner. In cases involving a mortgage, the position is slightly more complicated in that the beneficiary is still able to assert rights against the trustee as freeholder of the land, but they would be subject to the rights of the mortgagee. In particular this would mean that the mortgagee would be able to exercise its normal remedies under the mortgage, most importantly, sale and possession. On the other hand, if the beneficiary does have priority over either a new purchaser of the freehold estate, or a mortgagee, then that person will be severely restricted in what they are able to do with their rights. This is particularly significant for mortgagees because whilst they are entitled to their normal remedies by virtue of the legal status of the mortgage, they will be unable to *exercise* them against a beneficiary with priority. In such cases, what remedies will the lender have? This is one of the most significant questions when dealing with priority disputes in land law.

The first option for a lender in this situation will be to apply to the court for an order for sale under section 91(1), LPA 1925. The court will make a decision whether or not to order sale in these circumstances through the usual exercise of its discretion, but of course, in cases where there is a co-owner with priority over a valid legal mortgage, it will be that the lender is entitled to only part of the proceeds of sale, and thus the sale of the land may not cover the debt. An alternative approach is to rely on section 14 and 15 of TOLATA and bring an action requesting that the court order sale. Again, the lender may not recover the entirety of the debt in such a case. We have discussed earlier, however, that the lender is very likely to obtain a sale in such circumstances, following the decision in *Bank of Ireland v Bell*.[113]

We have assumed thus far that the mortgage in question is a valid legal mortgage on the grounds that the trustees, having all the powers of an absolute owner as per section 6 TOLATA, and, in cases of registered land, having all the owners' powers under section 23 LRA 2002, have validly granted such a mortgage to the lender. However, there are a number of circumstances in which the fact of co-ownership of the property will mean that there is no valid legal mortgage, such that the priority questions becomes one for the interests in equity only (thus rendering the principal rule that in section 28 LRA 2002, ie first in time). This could happen, first, where the legal title is held by more than one person. In such a case, all holders of the legal title must consent to the creation of the mortgage, and must validly execute the deed. If they do not do so, and their signature is forged for example, then the legal mortgage will be void *ab initio*. In this case, the mortgage, if registered, will first be rectified off the register. Once this has happened, the position between the lender and the borrower will depend upon the nature of the true borrower's interest. If they are a co-owner of the legal title, but have no equitable interest, then the mortgage will simply be worthless in terms of its proprietary status. The lender would of course have an action in contract against the borrower. Where that co-owner is also a beneficiary of the trust, however, then by virtue of the borrower's expressed agreement and contractual promise in relation to the mortgage, an equitable mortgage will arise in respect of the co-owner's share. As we noted in 16.3, entering into a mortgage in this way will sever a joint tenancy in equity if there was one, but it will also entitle the mortgagee to certain remedies.

To understand how these remedies work, it is useful to consider chapter 11 on mortgages, and in particular, to consider how equitable mortgages work. Equitable mortgages operate by the mortgagee *becoming* an equitable co-owner *subject to* the borrower's equitable right to redeem their interest should the sums owed by repaid. Thus, when there is an equitable mortgage in this co-ownership situation, the trustees will now only hold on trust for the lender, and any other co-owners. Since the lender will then themselves become a beneficiary of that trust, the natural 'route' to achieving sale of the relevant estate in land, is to apply to the court for a sale under section 14 and 15, since the nature of the equitable mortgage in this type of situation means that, in effect, the dispute in such cases has become a co-ownership dispute. This is different from the legal mortgage situation discussed earlier precisely because whilst in terms of priorities the lender and non-bound co-owner are in the same position, in terms of the nature of the lender's rights, there is a fundamental difference.

---

[113] *Bank of Ireland v Bell* [2001] 2 All ER (Comm) 920 (CA).

There are other ways in which a mortgage of this type could arise. The first is where one co-owner simply deliberately creates an equitable mortgage of their share only. It is highly unlikely that an institutional lender would be willing to lend on the basis of such a precarious security, but it is not legally impossible. Second, an equitable mortgage of this type might arise where the transaction is a voidable one, eg a misrepresentation, so that it is a valid legal mortgage until it is set aside, upon which point as long as there was genuine consent from one of the co-owners, the mortgage would operate in equity to affect that co-owner only. Third, this kind of equitable mortgage may arise in circumstances involving undue influence, where the lender is affected by that undue influence. We discussed the rules as to when such undue influence will arise in chapter 11. In all of these circumstances, what is in reality a dispute between a lender and a non-bound third party, morphs into, in effect, a co-ownership dispute between the non-bound co-owner, and the lender as equitable owner by virtue of their equitable mortgage.

The variety of ways in which lender rights and co-owner rights can interact means that this is one of the most difficult, and common, scenarios which is to be addressed in problem questions. For that reason, it is useful to build a 'route through' such rules, so that you can systematically consider all the options. A diagram representing one such route is available, as mentioned earlier, in the online resources.

16.5 CONCLUSION

This chapter, considering as it does co-ownership of land, has both introduced new concepts—such as the process of severance, and the nature of joint tenancies and tenancies in common—as well as integrating concepts already considered in this book, such as implied trusts, and mortgages. This makes co-owned land the most difficult to understand, since it requires understanding of almost all of the other issues in land law. For students encountering this material for the first time (and indeed for academics encountering them for the umpteenth time!) unravelling which rules must be applied and in what order can be a real challenge. The diagram should assist with this. The complicated nature of these rules makes them ideal targets for problem questions, and so the majority of this chapter has focussed on explaining how the rules work, rather than focusing on the consequences of these rules more broadly. The principles box which follows brings the context of these rules to the fore.

PRINCIPLES

How do these rules shape the balance of the principles operating in relation to land law? To recap, these principles were:

1. Certainty
2. Sensitivity to context
3. Transactability
4. Systemic and individual effects
5. Recognition of the social role of the land law system.

Assessing this balance requires a recognition that the rules in this chapter can be broken down into different concerns: the use of trusts to manage co-ownership, the different forms of co-ownership in terms of joint tenancy and tenancy in common, and the ways in which disputes in respect of co-owned land are solved. The first two concerns do not present much difficulty in terms of the principles: the fact of using trusts to manage co-ownership does not tell us very much without reference to the method of dispute resolution. The different forms of co-ownership operate relatively simply and without too many difficulties. Severance is usually straightforward and easy to achieve should parties desire it. Rather, the challenges for the principles considered in this book emerge when we look in detail at the means by which disputes in relation to co-owned land emerge and are managed.

Again, this question can be broken down, first, into disputes *between* co-owners, be they trustees, beneficiaries, or both, and disputes between a co-owner and a third party, usually a lender. In respect of both of these aspects, the law presents challenges. When dealing with the former, the law is clearly and deliberately neutral—the interests of the two parties are presented as ranking equally, and the considerations to be taken into account are premised upon, first, attempting to establish what the *common* interest is. This is, in many circumstances, entirely appropriate. However, it ought to be recognised that in very many circumstances involving co-ownership the position between the parties is not equal: either one is likely to suffer much more than the other from any decision being made in relation to the land, due to an inequality of income, or of alternative assets; or there may be an imbalance of power in the relationship, a factor which the current law does not explicitly take into account. Of course, many will argue, and with some justification, that land law is not the place to resolve these inequalities, but that does not necessarily mean that we should proceed on the basis that they do not exist, and that they are not the preserve of property rights to handle. We see in chapter 17 which explores the relationship between human rights and property law that land law is often most unable to help those who need its help the most. When we deprive the rules and operation of co-ownership of the context of the relationship in question, we may inadvertently exacerbate this problem.

This is even more apparent in disputes between third parties and a co-owner, which almost always arise because the act of another co-owner has left the first in a vulnerable position in terms of their rights. In cases, for example, where a non-bound co-owner wishes to remain in occupation of land to which they are entitled, and in relation to which they have not borrowed or contracted with another, it may seem unfair for that person to nevertheless be deprived of the ability to live in that house as a result of the dealings of their co-owner when as a matter of land law priority, those dealings 'rank behind' the co-owner. Indeed, there is a lot of force in this argument. However, in many areas of land law we are always trying to strike a balance between different interests within the system. The occupational rights of beneficiaries, and the emotional and social links that a person will build with a particular house, are weighed against the financial interests of the lender, and the needs of the wider mortgage market to allow lenders to realise their security, at least to a certain extent, regardless of the existence of co-ownership of the property.

The mechanism of overreaching can be criticised in similar terms, for the result of this is that a co-owner who does not consent to a transaction, can nevertheless lose priority on that transaction merely as a result of the fact that they were 'unlucky enough' to be in a situation where there were two trustees of the land, rather than one. The co-owner is left with recourse only against the trustees and the proceeds of sale, and if the trustees are acting in bad faith, that money and the trustees themselves, may well 'disappear' leaving the beneficiary without any recourse. The cause of this is the fact that we have chosen to use the trust, a mechanism first created with quite a different purpose in mind, as our dispute resolution mechanism for co-ownership situations. Whilst TOLATA introduces special rules for such disputes in relation to trusts of land, it does not remove the underpinning of the ownership structure, which means that 'power' and 'benefit' are inevitably separated, regardless of whether they usual reasons why we might *want* to separate those two aspects of ownership of land are present. To put this another way: we utilise trusts to separate different functions in relation to ownership of property. In the case of trusts of land, we also use trusts to facilitate a dispute resolution function in relation to co-ownership. The two needs within the land law system are separable, but there are consequences of our choice to use the trust as the solution to both problems.

Let us explore this in slightly more detail. The first consequence of using trusts as both a means of allowing co-ownership with management and benefit functions vesting in different people, and using this separation to manage disputes, is that in cases where the beneficiaries and the trustees are the same people, there is an inevitable blurring of management and benefit. This much is unavoidable. However, the dispute resolution side of trusts management is premised on the idea that the trustees, and the courts as proxy for the trustees, are able objectively to assess what is in the best interests of the trust as a whole. When the issues are finely balanced—as would often be the case in a situation involving two co-owners and decision-making deadlock—such an objective standard is illusory. Rather, the courts have to decide which of the co-owner's interests and desires should succeed over the other. Whilst this is perfectly normal in a dispute between two parties, especially where the needs of those parties is dictated as much by the strains and pressures on their personal relationship as it is by their proprietary investment goals, it does not sit comfortably with the notion that the very purpose of the trust is to prioritise no *one* beneficiary, but rather the trust as a whole.

The second consequence is that in situations involving lenders, where one trustee, who is also a beneficiary, acts outwith the powers of the trust, they will nevertheless affect the substance of the trust property in their capacity as beneficiary of that trust, since the beneficiary is of course able to transact with their own equitable interest in the property. When a debt is secured against a property, it matters not to the other beneficiary whether that mortgage affects them because their co-owner is a trustee, or because their co-owner is a beneficiary: the outcome is the same. Their home is likely to be sold as a result of a transaction to which they did not consent and which constituted a breach of the trust.

Even if this consideration did not weigh heavily on the court's mind, the statutory provisions themselves emphasise that the needs of any secured creditors should be taken into account when decisions are made as to whether property should be sold or not in section 15(1)(d). Furthermore, as we saw earlier, in cases involving bankruptcy, the needs of the secured creditor effectively take priority in all but the most exceptional of circumstances notwithstanding the fact that disputes of this type only arise where the secured creditor does *not* have priority over a co-owner as we discussed earlier.

As a result of these considerations, we can see that despite the complexity of the rules, the outcome in these areas is usually fairly certain. One way or another the property in question will likely be sold and the proceeds of sale will be divided between a non-bound co-owner who as a result loses their home, and a lender. Lenders are able, on the basis of this relative certainty, to calculate risk and act accordingly. Furthermore, transactions in co-owned land are made easy and straightforward in the majority of cases thanks to overreaching. However, when it comes to the individual circumstances of the occupiers of the land, even with the flexible jurisdiction of section 15, we can see from the case law that the focus is still on ensuring that lenders are left with powerful remedies. Sensitivity to context, in this sense, only goes so far.

TABLE OF DEFINITIONS

Joint tenancy	A means by which both legal and equitable title can be jointly owned, characterised by each party holding an undivided whole, which requires the presence of the four unities, and to which the right of survivorship applies.
Tenancy in common	A means by which equitable title can be jointly owned, characterised by each party holding an individual share, and to which the right of survivorship does not apply.
Interest under a trust	Relationship between trustee (legal owner) and beneficiary (equitable owner) whereby the legal owner has to act for the benefit of the equitable owner, and the equitable owner has a right in the property which can be enforced against third parties.
Severance	The process by which a joint tenancy in equity is converted into a tenancy in common.
Overreaching	The process by which an interest loses priority on a disposition of an estate held on trust, and in cases of sale, is transferred into the proceeds of that sale.
Overriding interest	An interest in land which binds a purchaser of registered land despite not appearing on the register.

FURTHER READING

Given the piecemeal nature of some of the rules discussed here, and the fact that much of the discussion requires engagement with rules from other areas of land law, the further reading recommended here is designed to give a range of voices considering these topics and therefore to present a starting point for taking analysis further:

DIXON, M., 'To sell or not to sell: that is the question. The irony of the Trusts of Land and Appointment of Trustees Act 1996' (2011) 70 CLJ 579.
HARPUM, C., 'Overreaching, trustees' powers and the reform of the 1925 legislation' (1990) 49 CLJ 277.
OWEN, G., 'A new paradigm for overreaching—some inspiration from Down Under' [2013] Conv 377.

17

PROPERTY LAW AND HUMAN RIGHTS

17.1 Introduction	545	17.4 Conclusion	579
17.2 Modes of Influence—Property and Human Rights	547	Principles	579
		Table of Definitions	581
17.3 Areas of Influence	559	Further Reading	581

CHAPTER GOALS

By the end of this chapter you should understand:

- The different modes of interaction between property law and human rights law, considering the range of potential sources, and the distinction between human rights as a 'support' for property rights, and human rights as a source of conflict with property rights;
- The mechanics of interaction, including the distinction between the different forms of horizontal and vertical effect; and
- How human rights arguments have played out in the key areas of: adverse possession, leases and licences, mortgages, and actions for possession against trespassers.

17.1 INTRODUCTION

The question as to the interaction between human rights and property law is a controversial one. Many doubt whether arguments about human rights have any role to play in private law disputes about rights in land. But this premise is false. It is false for two reasons. First, the idea that property law is only about private law is quite demonstrably wrong. Property law is as much a matter of state administration of rights in land as it is about freely negotiated rights between two private parties. For proof of this we need look no further than the role of the land registry, on the one hand, and the extensive regulatory scheme which bounds residential leases on the other. There is no residential lease granted which is not in some way or another shaped by statutory rules concerning the ability of the landlord to take possession against his or her tenant. To see this as being purely a question of private law is, therefore, to underestimate how 'political' regulation of rights in land has been, and continues to be.

Secondly, it is by no means self-evident that human rights are irrelevant in dealings between private parties, even if a clear bright line could be drawn between the public and the private in this context. Private law rules are always, at their foundation, state-backed, in the sense that the wheels of the legal system will be put in motion to uphold them. This by itself makes any call to the fact that such rights are *only* a matter for private negotiation, doubtful. In reality, even the most private of transactions is enforced publically and by state actors. Furthermore, to think that private actors cannot breach human rights as defined by law may well be correct in any particular state. A state could integrate human rights into its legal system in such a way as to make it impossible to argue that private individuals could ever breach human rights. Some will say that the English legal system has done this, and we return to this argument later. However, even if that is a valid legal argument (and we doubt whether it is in an English context), it does not make it a sound political or moral argument. If we take modern human rights to be the creation of an international politic which emerged after the Second World War, then there is no doubt that this was intended to cover private parties just as much as public. The debate about human rights is about recognising the ability which the powerful have to commit untold atrocities against the weak. Power does not necessarily equate to state power in this debate. If modern human rights documents are seen not as a political response to past events, but as part of an accepted common moral imperative, then again there is no reason why that moral imperative is one restricted to the state alone.

Whatever one's views as to how the English legal system should treat concerns regarding human rights, especially in those areas of law which are traditionally labelled as 'private law', it is important to realise therefore that there *is* a debate to be had as to the extent and shape of the interaction between the two sets of rules. To argue that there should be no interaction at all and that human rights should 'keep out' of property law, is both unrealistic and, in many ways, pointless, for that interaction already exists. This chapter will explore the frontiers of this interaction, and explain the many ways in which property law has been and continues to be shaped by the law relating to human rights.

Section 17.2 will consider the different mechanisms by which the law may be shaped by human rights and the general structural implications of this for English land law. Section 17.3 then considers how human rights arguments have had influence in particular areas of land law, focussing on adverse possession, leases, actions for possession against trespassers, and mortgages. This chapter takes this structural approach because, as we shall see, there is a huge divergence in how extensive the 'intrusion' into private law principles has been in relation to these different areas of law. With the exception of the context of leasehold arrangements where the landlord is a public or a quasi-public authority, we will see that to date the influence has been rather limited. Furthermore, the different areas of law demonstrate a different 'mode' of interaction, with some focusing on the substantive content of the rules without consideration of the precise identities of the parties, and in other areas the structure of the interaction becomes determinative of outcome. To attempt to deal simultaneously with these areas of law would produce confusion precisely because even though the way human rights interacts with each of these areas is becoming increasingly settled, a cross-topic explanation is impossible as there is no homogeneity. Rather, we must first think about how human rights *might* influence property law—addressing the initial structural question as to the modes of such influence—before then examining how this structure plays out in respect of the different areas of land law.

17.2 MODES OF INFLUENCE—PROPERTY AND HUMAN RIGHTS

Our starting point, therefore, is that property law and human rights can interact in a number of different ways. The major division distinguishes those cases where human rights arguments are made to 'bolster' an existing property law-based argument, and those where the human rights argument is made to attempt to limit the scope of a property right. Thus we can see the rules of property law and human rights working together, or they can be in conflict. In this part, we first consider the sources of human rights in English law, and then we consider which rights are particularly important in relation to property law. Following that discussion, we consider the mechanics by which key human rights interact with property law, and examine the question of horizontal effect in that context.

17.2.1 SOURCES

To talk about 'human rights' as if there is a single, definitive list of these is to underestimate the variety of different sources from which such rights may arise. To a certain extent, such rights are embedded in English common law, even if only in vague and possibly unenforceable ways. As such, they may shape and bound the way in which the courts exercise their discretion and approach the question of interpretation of statutory provisions, in a way which is essentially hidden. The seminal decision in *Entick v Carrington*[1] may well be seen in this light, even if at the time at which the decision was made, the judges would not have expressed themselves as having been concerned with human rights. Secondly, and most importantly, such rights arise, through the Human Rights Act 1998, from the European Convention on Human Rights. This document was drafted by the Council of Europe in the aftermath of the Second World War—a drafting processing in which the UK was one of the leading voices—and has been amended by its protocols a number of times since. Thirdly, and for as long as the UK remains a member of or subject to EU law in some form or another, rights arise from the European Charter of Fundamental Rights, albeit that these rules have not, to date, had a significant influence on property law. This is because the relevant (enforceable) rights largely mirror those within the ECHR. Finally, the UK is also a signatory state to a number of other human rights instruments which may be enforceable as a matter of international law, but which are not directly implemented into English law through statutory means. We can therefore put these aside for the purposes of our discussion.

---

[1] *Entick v Carrington* (1765) 2 Wilson, KB 275, 95 ER 807.

> **Summary: Sources of human rights law in England and Wales**
>
> 1. Common law
> 2. European Convention on Human Rights
> 3. European Charter of Fundamental Rights
> 4. Other international human rights agreements to which the UK is a signatory state, eg Universal Declaration of Human Rights.

17.2.2 HUMAN RIGHTS 'BOLSTERING' PROPERTY LAW

We focus on two sources: the common law (and its 'constitutional' values), and the European Convention on Human Rights as modulated through the Human Rights Act 1998 (HRA). Commencing with the former, as most will know, the UK does not have a written constitution, nor does it have a domestic Bill of Rights. There have been calls for such, and the Conservative government under David Cameron did suggest that it might introduce such a Bill. The likelihood of this happening whilst Brexit negotiations continue and the UK's position within wider Europe remains uncertain, is negligible. We have to look, therefore, to the subtle shapings of 'human rights' within the common law and the unwritten constitution. The starting point for this, is, as mentioned earlier, *Entick v Carrington*,[2] which in upholding the principles of rule of law, of liberty without prohibition, and of the importance of property, represents many of the same values as does the ECHR.

> **Key case: *Entick v Carrington* (1765) 2 Wilson**
>
> In this case, Entick, a clerk, was accused of having printed pamphlets defamatory to the King. His house was raided by messengers of the King. These messengers had broken into the house. Entick argued that they had no authority to do so, and that his private property was sacrosanct such that explicit authority was needed for such a raid. Amongst other arguments, the messengers argued that, as representatives of the Secretary of State, they had an inherent jurisdiction to enter and search the premises.
>
> This is how the court (according to the more tempered court report) responded to that argument:
>
> > 'if this is law it would be found in our books, but no such law ever existed in this country; our law holds the property of every man so sacred, that no man can set his foot upon his neighbour's close without his leave; if he does he is a trespasser, though he does no damage at all; if he will tread upon his neighbour's ground, he must justify it by law. The defendants have no right to avail themselves of the usage of these warrants since the Revolution'.[3]
>
> There is also a more 'florid' report of the judgment, which may well be embellished, attributing these words to the court:
>
> > 'Such is the power, and therefore one should naturally expect that the law to warrant it should be clear in proportion as the power is exorbitant.'

---

[2] *Entick v Carrington* (1765) 2 Wilson, KB 275, 95 ER 807.
[3] *Entick v Carrington* (1765) 2 Wilson, KB 275, 95 ER 807, 817.

> If it is law, it will be found in our books. If it is not to be found there, it is not law.
>
> The great end, for which men entered into society, was to secure their property. That right is preserved sacred and incommunicable in all instances, where it has not been taken away or abridged by some public law for the good of the whole. The cases where this right of property is set aside by private law, are various. Distresses, executions, forfeitures, taxes etc are all of this description; wherein every man by common consent gives up that right, for the sake of justice and the general good. By the laws of England, every invasion of private property, be it ever so minute, is a trespass. No man can set his foot upon my ground without my license, but he is liable to an action, though the damage be nothing; which is proved by every declaration in trespass, where the defendant is called upon to answer for bruising the grass and even treading upon the soil. If he admits the fact, he is bound to show by way of justification, that some positive law has empowered or excused him. The justification is submitted to the judges, who are to look into the books; and if such a justification can be maintained by the text of the statute law, or by the principles of common law. If no excuse can be found or produced, the silence of the books is an authority against the defendant, and the plaintiff must have judgment'.[4]
>
> Whatever one's views as to the purpose for which men entered society—and for more on the idea that part of the foundation of this is for the protection of property, see Thomas Hobbes' work[5]—the general legal principle which the case establishes is that an individual has the freedom to do whatever he wishes as long as it is not prohibited by law: and that the state cannot do anything which is not authorised by law. This is a statement of rule of law, but it is made in the particular context of property. In this way, it establishes the general 'right to property', and the freedom associated therewith, which is the foundation stone of private property law in England and Wales. If we take this as a starting point for the interaction between human rights very broadly defined and property law, then we can say that rights to liberty and freedom in the first instance support claims to property.

The same can be said for the right to property contained in article 1 of the first protocol to the ECHR. This right states:

'Protection of property

(1) Every natural or legal person is entitled to the peaceful enjoyment of his possessions. No one shall be deprived of his possessions except in the public interest and subject to the conditions provided for by law and by the general principles of international law.

(2) The preceding provisions shall not, however, in any way impair the right of a State to enforce such laws as it deems necessary to control the use of property in accordance with the general interest or to secure the payment of taxes or other contributions or penalties'.

This provision, equally as important as the rights contained in the main document of the ECHR, establishes the human right to property within the signatory states. Not only does this provision guard against unjustified expropriations in the sense of forced takings by the state (except as the

---

[4] 19 Howell's State Trials 1029 (1765).
[5] T Hobbes, *Leviathan*, available free to access through the Guternberg project at https://www.gutenberg.org/files/3207/3207-h/3207-h.htm, accessed 6 Feb 2018.

second paragraph provides in relation to taxes and the like), it also sets down general conditions within which lawful and justified expropriations can be carried out by the state. The Strasbourg Court (the European Court of Human Rights—ECtHR) has developed additional guidance in explaining how this provision works in *Sporring and Lönnroth v Sweden*,[6] where the ECtHR explained that this provision contains three different aspects:

> 'Article 1 comprises three distinct rules: the first rule, set out in the first sentence of the first paragraph, is general and enunciates the principle of the peaceful enjoyment of property; the second rule, contained in the second sentence of the first paragraph, covers deprivation of possessions and subjects it to certain conditions; the third rule, stated in the second paragraph, recognises that the Contracting States are entitled, amongst other things, to control the use of property in accordance with the general interest'.[7]

Thus, we can see that article 1 protocol 1 protects rights to property in general terms, in respect of deprivations (or expropriations and compulsory purchases) and control of use. Control of use provisions are, in the way same of the takings clause in the US, potentially controversial in that they suggest that regulations which limit liberty to use property can be contrary to human rights. In the US this takings jurisprudence has led to difficulties in enacting zoning laws (the US equivalent of planning controls), environmental provisions and the like. This sort of problem has not occurred in the UK context, and it is clear that either these are not categorised as controls of use, in that they are a generalised provision which bound the scope of the property right from the outset (the so-called inherent limitation argument to which we return later at 17.3.2.2); or they are so manifestly justified in the public interest and proportionate to the need to have some oversight as to the way in which developments take place, that they have never attracted interest from human rights advocates. This is not to say that article 1 protocol 1 has not had an influence in English property law however, and we shall explore this interaction more shortly. It is nevertheless important to realise that English law has, in effect, two sources of 'human rights' (broadly understood) which can be used to 'bolster' or support pre-existing proprietary entitlements: article 1 protocol 1, and the common law rule that property is to be respected unless the law provides otherwise.

Additional protection for property rights may also be provided by article 8 of the ECHR, and it is here that we start to see why the precise mechanics of the interaction matter. Article 8, as we discuss later in detail, protects rights to a private life, and within that, rights to a home. From a land law perspective, rights to a home can be proprietary in the form of a leasehold or freehold estate, or they may be personal, in the form of an occupational licence. Thus, when article 8 protects the right that a person has to their home, from a national law perspective, that may either *support* the leasehold or freehold estate that such a person has, or it may *support* a licence, or a trespasser in their continued occupation in a property where they had not permission and no possession (or they would have acquired a possessory freehold estate—see chapter 6).

However, where article 8 is used as a means to bolster any of these pre-existing rights, be they proprietary or personal, or to prevent an action against a trespasser, the article 8 'argument' will also come into conflict with the property right of another, except in cases where the property in question is in the freehold (or leasehold where relevant) ownership of a public authority. We discuss these conflicts later. The consequence of the conflict, however, is that the strength of the

---

[6] *Sporring and Lönnroth v Sweden* [1983] 5 EHRR 35, [1982] ECHR 5, 7151/75.
[7] *Sporring and Lönnroth v Sweden* [1983] 5 EHRR 35, [1982] ECHR 5, 7151/75, [61].

support which article 8 lends to property rights in such situations is inevitably constrained by the support which article 1 protocol 1 will give to the other party's own proprietary interest. Thus, in such cases, land law has struck a balance between the proprietary rights of two individuals—let us say here, the landlord and the tenant—in a particular way, and the human rights of both 'strive' to adjust the balance. The ECHR is explicit that all rights contained therein rank equal, and this leaves a very difficult situation when it comes to questions of horizontal effect, as we shall see.

> **Summary: Rights which can 'strengthen' proprietary entitlements**
>
> 1. Common law principle that a property owner can do as they wish with their property unless prohibited by law acts as an interpretive guide.
> 2. Article 1 of the First Protocol stipulates that a person (a) must be allowed to enjoy peaceful enjoyment of their possessions; (b) cannot be deprived of their property without due compensation; and (c) that any controls of use of land must be in the public interest. All three of these are limited by any constraint on property which is a proportionate response to a legitimate aim in a democratic society and permitted according to national law.
> 3. Article 8 will protect an occupier's right to their home, which may in turn provide support to any property or personal right which entitles such occupation, or indeed occupation in the absence of such a right, as in the case of a trespasser.

17.2.3 HUMAN RIGHTS AND PROPERTY LAW—CONFLICTS

For the most part, however, the case law which has emerged in relation to the interaction between human rights and property has done so in cases of conflict. Thus, most commonly, there is conflict between rights to property *as defined by national law*, on the one hand, and right of others to their home (as distinct from their property per se), rights of freedom of expression and rights of association, on the other. Structurally, this conflict is simple in cases where the proprietary interest is held by a public authority, since in such cases the public authority does not themselves receive any protection from the ECHR. As such, article 1 protocol 1 is not relevant (see earlier). In other cases, those involving any species of horizontal effect, the interaction is highly complex. We therefore devote a section later to the nature and operation of horizontal effect (see 17.2.5).

When considering the conflicts that exist between property rules and human rights, unsurprisingly, the source of the conflict comes from the ECHR. The relevant rights which may come into conflict with property rights are, most significantly, article 8, article 10, and article 11. Article 8, the right to a private life, as explained earlier, states:

'Article 8 – Right to respect for private and family life

1. Everyone has the right to respect for his private and family life, his home and his correspondence.

2. There shall be no interference by a public authority with the exercise of this right except such as is in accordance with the law and is necessary in a democratic society in the interests of national security, public safety or the economic well-being of the country, for the prevention of disorder or crime, for the protection of health or morals, or for the protection of the rights and freedoms of others'.

This provision has been interpreted so as to include rights to an existing home (amongst much else). The protection of rights to a home (as distinct from a right to have a house), can result in conflicts with other property rights, including, but not limited to, the right of a landlord to seek possession against his tenant, and the right of a mortgagee to enforce a debt against the mortgagor by seeking possession and sale of the home. In both of these cases, the human right of the occupier of the home comes into direct conflict with the property rights of those who seek to dispossess her. We consider the meaning and operation of this provision in more detail later, since the precise meaning of 'home' and the ways in which this article 8 right operates will vary according to the context within which it is invoked (which again explains why a 'context free' explanation of the interaction between these rights is not possible).

It is not only article 8 which presents a potential conflict with the property rights as defined by national law. Freedom of expression (article 10) and freedom of association rights (article 11) also pose a potential conflict, particularly in the context of protests and trespass. In fact, it is in relation to this sort of case that the most interesting interactions between property law and human rights law have been encountered. We go into this in more detail later, but for completeness here it is useful to replicate these two articles.

'Article 10

1. Everyone has the right to freedom of expression. This right shall include freedom to hold opinions and to receive and impart information and ideas without interference by public authority and regardless of frontiers . . .

2. The exercise of these freedoms, since it carries with it duties and responsibilities, may be subject to such . . . restrictions . . . as are prescribed by law and are necessary in a democratic society, in the interests of . . . the protection of the reputation or the rights of others . . .'

'Article 11

1. Everyone has the right to freedom of peaceful assembly and to freedom of association with others . . .

2. No restrictions shall be placed on the exercise of these rights other than such as are prescribed by law and are necessary in a democratic society . . . or for the protection of the rights and freedoms of others . . .'.

> ### Summary: Human rights and property law
>
> There are two potential sources of human rights in English land law as far as is relevant to land law—common law articulations of rights, and the European Convention on Human Rights. In relation to the former this is most likely to be an additional *protection* for existing proprietary interests, and establishes the fundamental principle that unless a use of property is prohibited by law, the right-holder is at liberty to do as they wish with and on their land and that public authorities cannot interfere with this without due cause. In relation to the latter, the picture is more complex. On the one hand, the European

> Convention on Human Rights has its own protection of property rights as explained in article 1 of the first protocol. On the other hand, the Convention establishes rights which (most commonly) come into conflict with the property rights of others—the right to a private life in the form of a right to a home; the right to freedom of expression, and the right of freedom of association, but which can also be used to support a proprietary claim, in conflict potentially with the proprietary rights of others.

17.2.4 MECHANICS

To understand the ways in which these protections interact with the property law concepts explained in the rest of this book, it is important not only to understand the sources of the rights in question, but also the *mechanisms* by which these rights either come into conflict or act in a complementary way. This is not simply a question of how and when rights can be raised before a national court, but a more substantive issue since, in some cases, the mechanisms are dictating the power and scope of the various rights to shape property law.

In respect of the common law, the position is relatively simple. However, the precise operation of inherent assumptions made by the courts as to their appropriate role in policing property law can be hard to discover and unearth. The courts' inherent jurisdiction as defenders of rights conferred on those subject to the law of England and Wales is inferior to the most important constitutional principle, that of the sovereignty of Parliament. This means that Parliament can enact any legislation it wishes, whether or not that thereby undermines or completely removes the previously assumed proprietary rights of those subject to the new law. However, the courts' interpretive function means that, in cases where there is an ambiguity as to the meaning or scope of any particular provision, the courts will interpret the provision so as best to give effect not only to the intention of Parliament as expressed in its legislative enactments, but also so as to protect those common law rights as far as possible. This interpretive function is subtle, but extremely important, and we shall see the store put in the interpretive skills of the judiciary in the way in which the Human Rights Act 1998 has been enacted into English law.

In respect of the European Convention on Human Rights, this was brought directly into UK law by the Human Rights Act 1998. However, this is not a straightforward incorporation of the text of the ECHR and the jurisprudence of the ECtHR into national law. The Human Rights Act 1998 does not, in effect, render the ECHR directly effective into national law. Rather, it establishes three 'routes' by which human rights concerns can impact upon national law.

17.2.4.1 Section 3 Human Rights Act 1998

First, in section 3 of the HRA, the judiciary (and indeed all other public authorities) are obligated to interpret legislation as far as possible in line with the ECHR, 'taking account of' the jurisprudence of the ECtHR. The obligation, contained in section 3(1), requires that:

'Interpretation of legislation.

(1) So far as it is possible to do so, primary legislation and subordinate legislation must be read and given effect in a way which is compatible with the Convention rights.'

As mentioned earlier, this interpretive obligation utilises the judicial skills honed over centuries of legislative interpretation to give effect to the protections within the ECHR. It is not, however, a guarantee of compliance with human rights since the obligation only extends, 'as far as possible'. As we shall see later when considering *McDonald v McDonald*,[8] such interpretive creativity cannot stand up in the face of clear and wholly unambiguous language. The potential power that the section 3(1) obligation confers is nevertheless clear in the case of *Ghaidan v Godin-Mendoza*.[9]

> **Key case:** *Ghaidan v Godin-Mendoza* [2004] UKHL 30
>
> In this case, the courts were asked to examine whether the word 'spouse' in the Rent Act 1977 could be interpreted so as to include homosexual partners for the purposes of exploring statutory succession to security of tenure, following the death of a secure tenant. Para 2(2) of Schedule 1 of that Act, defined 'spouse' for the purposes of the Act as anyone living with the original tenant 'as his or her wife or husband'.
>
> The court held that section 3, in line with article 8 and article 14 (non-discrimination) of the ECHR, meant that these words should be read as to include any person living with the original tenant as if they were their husband or wife, and could therefore include homosexual partners.
>
> There is no doubt whatsoever that this goes beyond what was intended by Parliament in enacting the Rent Act 1977. Furthermore, in reaching the conclusion that they did, the House of Lords also overturned their previous jurisprudence in *Fitzpatrick*.[10] In this respect the decision in *Godin-Mendoza* has two effects. First, it interprets the statutory provision at the very edge of its linguistic possibilities. Second it recognises that even though this was a case involving two private parties, the court would also fall under a direct obligation in relation to its own decisions, to ensure that they too were compatible with the ECHR. The key word, as Lord Nicholls recognised in his judgment, then became how far the word 'possible' should extend.
>
> The following citation from the judgment shows how far the section 3 obligation extends, and therefore how the courts should operate.
>
>> 'Unfortunately ... section 3 itself is not free from ambiguity ... The difficulty lies in the word "possible" ...
>>
>> One tenable interpretation of the word "possible" would be that section 3 is confined to requiring courts to resolve ambiguities. Where the words under consideration fairly admit of more than one meaning the Convention-compliant meaning is to prevail. Words should be given the meaning which best accords with the Convention rights.
>>
>> This interpretation of section 3 would give the section a comparatively narrow scope. This is not the view which has prevailed. It is now generally accepted that the application of section 3 does not depend upon the presence of ambiguity in the legislation being interpreted ...
>>
>> From this it follows that the interpretative obligation decreed by section 3 is of an unusual and far-reaching character. Section 3 may require a court to depart from the unambiguous meaning the legislation would otherwise bear ... The question of difficulty is how far, and in what circumstances, section 3 requires a court to depart from the intention of the enacting Parliament'.[11]

---

[8] *McDonald v McDonald* [2016] UKSC 28, [2017] AC 273.
[9] *Ghaidan v Godin-Mendoza* [2004] UKHL 30, [2004] 2 AC 557.
[10] *Fitzpatrick v Sterling Housing Association Ltd* [2001] 1 AC 27.
[11] *Ghaidan v Godin-*Mendoza [2004] UKHL 30, [2004] 2 AC 557, [27]ff.

Lord Steyn agreed with Lord Nicholls' approach:

> 'My impression is that two factors are contributing to a misunderstanding of the remedial scheme of the 1998 Act. First, there is the constant refrain that a judicial reading down, or reading in, under section 3 would flout the will of Parliament as expressed in the statute under examination. This question cannot sensibly be considered without giving full weight to the countervailing will of Parliament as expressed in the 1998 Act.
>
> The second factor may be an excessive concentration on linguistic features of the particular statute. Nowhere in our legal system is a literalistic approach more inappropriate than when considering whether a breach of a Convention right may be removed by interpretation under section 3. Section 3 requires a broad approach concentrating, amongst other things, in a purposive way on the importance of the fundamental right involved'.[12]

These statements by the highest court show how significant the interpretive obligation in section 3 can be.

17.2.4.2 Section 4, Human Rights Act 1998

The second 'route' by which the Human Rights Act 1998 integrates the ECHR into national law is through the section 4, 'declaration of incompatibility' process. This section states that:

'4 Declaration of incompatibility.

(1) Subsection (2) applies in any proceedings in which a court determines whether a provision of primary legislation is compatible with a Convention right.

(2) If the court is satisfied that the provision is incompatible with a Convention right, it may make a declaration of that incompatibility ...

(6) A declaration under this section ("a declaration of incompatibility")—

   (a) does not affect the validity, continuing operation or enforcement of the provision in respect of which it is given; and

   (b) is not binding on the parties to the proceedings in which it is made'.

This provision allows the court to formally notify Parliament of an irresolvable inconsistency between the legislative provision in question and human rights enshrined in the ECHR. It does *not* allow the court to either displace the legislation in the instant case, or to strike it down in general. It is therefore, in terms of the courts' duty to resolve a dispute between two parties before it, less potent than is the section 3 interpretive approach since in the latter situation the court can ensure that in the instant case, justice is done in such a way as ensures compliance with the ECHR. Nevertheless, the power of a statement of incompatibility exists and bolsters the court's 'arsenal' in this respect.

---

[12] *Ghaidan v Godin*-Mendoza [2004] UKHL 30, [2004] 2 AC 557, [41].

17.2.4.3 Section 6, Human Rights Act 1998

Finally, and most critically in practice for property law, there is section 6. Section 6 provides that:

'6 Acts of public authorities.

(1) It is unlawful for a public authority to act in a way which is incompatible with a Convention right.

(2) Subsection (1) does not apply to an act if—

  (a) as the result of one or more provisions of primary legislation, the authority could not have acted differently; or

  (b) in the case of one or more provisions of, or made under, primary legislation which cannot be read or given effect in a way which is compatible with the Convention rights, the authority was acting so as to give effect to or enforce those provisions.

(3) In this section "public authority" includes—

  (a) a court or tribunal, and

  (b) any person certain of whose functions are functions of a public nature, but does not include either House of Parliament or a person exercising functions in connection with proceedings in Parliament.'

This means that a court is able to quash any decision made by a public authority (except Parliament itself) if that decision does not comply with the ECHR. Furthermore, the court *itself* is bound by section 6 as sub-section (3)(a) makes very clear. This provision, whilst seemingly relatively simple, has made for a very complex position concerning the question of 'horizontal' effect. We revisit this later.

Summary: The Human Rights Act 1998

The Human Rights Act 1998 integrates the ECHR into national law in three distinct ways:

1. Section 3—interpretation obligation requires the court to interpret legislation to be compatible with the ECHR as far as is possible.

2. Section 4—allows the court to make a declaration of incompatibility if legislation is irresolvable in conflict with the ECHR.

3. Section 6—allows the court to quash a decision of a public authority (including the court itself) if that authority breaches the provisions of the ECHR, and acts as a legal duty on such authorities to so-comply.

This means that human rights will filter into the law in a number of different ways and it is not possible to explain the effect of human rights in property law in a homogenous or context-free way.

What all this means is that it can sometimes be difficult to spot the influence that human rights law is having. When considering the wide range of apparently contradictory case law, it can be very difficult to disentangle a variety of strands of influence to produce a coherent structure. Why, for example, does the courts ask whether the ability of a mortgage lender to go into possession is a breach of human rights if the mortgage lender himself is not a public body in cases of bankruptcy, but feel unable to do even ask the question in cases of failure to pay rent in the case of a private landlord and tenant relationship? Not only is the position apparently contradictory, however, the development of many of these rules has occurred, as is normal in a common law system, in quite a piecemeal and fragmentary fashion. The law in this area is all new. Unlike the Land Registration Act 2002 for example, it has not been deliberately created. No one has decided how property law and human rights law *should* fit together. For that reason, and for many other reasons, they do not really fit together or work harmoniously side by side. Rather, different courts have taken different structural approaches to answering the question of the mutual influence of property and human rights leaving it hard not only to provide a simple—and short!—explanation of this, but more fundamentally, making it impossible to provide a coherent explanation.

One of the other consequences of the lack of deliberate action in this area is that there are some areas where the impact of human rights law has not yet been felt—in relation to land registration, and perhaps more surprisingly co-ownership, there have been no concerted attempts to rely on human rights to alter the existing rules or create new ones notwithstanding the occasional judicial recognition that there might be potential conflicts in these areas. But there are some areas where human rights have begun to emerge as form a distinct part of the rules. These are in relation to: (to a very limited extent) adverse possession; possession actions against leasees and licensees by public authorities; in relation to possession actions against trespassers; and finally in relation to mortgages. Before we examine these, however, it is important at this point to examine the very challenging question of horizontal effect.

17.2.5 UNDERSTANDING HORIZONTAL EFFECT

In very simple terms, the problem of horizontal effect is this. The Human Rights Act 1998 highlights that *direct* actions under its provisions can only be brought against organs of the state. This is what section 6 provides for. In this sense, the HRA does not make provision specifically for one private party to bring an action against another private party in which the cause of action is explicitly a breach of the human rights rules. However, that does not *necessarily* mean that the rights expressed in the Convention are not relevant in disputes between private parties thanks to the HRA. This is for two key reasons: first, the court itself, which will hear any dispute between private parties is itself a public authority. Second, the HRA does insist that legislation be interpreted in a human rights-compliant way. What neither of these provisions directly answer, however, is the question as to whether the interpretation obligation applies where the alleged perpetrator of the breach is a private individual, and second, whether the court is obliged to amend its own case law in order to make a private individual comply with human rights. The position is unclear.

Furthermore, we noted earlier that the picture relating to human rights varies according to the area of law in which the question has been addressed. In some—notably mortgages and actions for possession against trespassers, as we shall see—the courts seem comfortable to address the issue as to whether possession orders in such cases would constitute a breach of an occupier's human rights (even if they seem consistently to conclude that the answer is *no*) notwithstanding the fact that the landowner is a private party. In other places, they are clear that such a question goes outwith that which is required by the Human Rights Act 1998 and the European Convention on Human Rights case law. This disparity of treatment and attitude is a consequence of the failures within the case law to appreciate the mechanics of how the HRA 1998 integrates human rights into national law, and the different forms of so-called 'horizontal effect' which thereby arise.

The understand these different forms of vertical (citizen versus public authority) and horizontal effect, it is important to break the issue down somewhat as in this we can see how the different mechanisms of the HRA can influence disputes between private parties.

1. Direct vertical effect—direct enforcement of a human right against a public authority relying on section 6.
2. Indirect vertical effect—statutory interpretation to comply with ECHR rights in cases involving a public authority but where the court acts through section 3, not section 6. In cases of this type, if compliance cannot be found through section 3, then a section 4 declaration of incompatibility would be essential.
3. Direct horizontal effect—direct enforcement of a human right against a private individual. This is not possible, since individuals are not bound by the rights enshrined in the ECHR as integrated through the HRA 1998. However, it could be argued in such cases that whenever the *court* makes a decision, it must either do so on the basis of statutory provisions, in which case it will become an indirect horizontal effect question (can the relevant statute be re-interpreted?); or on the basis of common law, in which case the courts' own section 6 obligations come into play.
4. Indirect horizontal effect—using human rights to interpret statutory provisions in a compliant way in cases involving two private parties, as in *Ghaidan v Godin-Mendoza*,[13] and the cases involving section 335A Insolvency Act 1986 (see 17.3.5 later).
5. Common law horizontal effect—a shift in common law case law to meet with human rights in cases involving two private parties on the basis of the court's obligations under section 6.

Of these, only the third option appears not be mandated by the HRA. Indeed, it is difficult to see how a case of the third type could actually arise, since it is hard to imagine a dispute arising which his not in some way already covered by either statute or the common law. Given this, it seems that contrary to the Supreme Court's approach in *McDonald* which we considerlater,[14] it is possible to have horizontal effect. This in turn raises another question—that of balance. It will require the courts to look at the respective human rights of both parties (public authorities cannot be the beneficiaries of human rights). For example, in a case involving a landlord and a tenant, the landlord's article 1 protocol 1 rights will be just as important as the tenant's article 8 rights. This will put the courts into a difficult position since they will be required to add this balancing act into the proportionality assessment.

---

[13] *Ghaidan v Godin*-Mendoza [2004] UKHL 30, [2004] 2 AC 557.
[14] *McDonald v McDonald* [2016] UKSC 28, [2017] AC 273.

17.3 AREAS OF INFLUENCE

17.3.1 ADVERSE POSSESSION

One of the earliest areas of contention was in relation to adverse possession. It is easy to see why. The Limitation Act 1980 allows for an individual to be deprived of their property rights simply due to their own inaction and without any recourse or compensation. This clearly poses a potential conflict with the principle expressed in article 1 protocol 1 that a person is entitled to peaceful enjoyment of their possessions and that they should not be deprived of their possessions without appropriate compensation and so long as that expropriation is in accordance with the legitimate aims of a democratic society, and it is proportionate to those aims. The adverse possession rules were, unquestionably, on thin ice as far as the ECtHR was concerned. However, what happens in an adverse possession situation is that an individual loses out to another individual. The state is not taking away their property in the sense that the state becomes the new owner. And, as we said earlier it is the state in the form of public authorities, that is bound by human rights, not individuals. The *mechanisms* by which a complaint could be brought against the adverse possession regime in unregistered land, therefore, were two-fold—advocating that the Limitation Act 1980 be interpreted differently so as to better comply with the principle expressed in article 1 protocol 1; or an action against a court for enforcing the provisions of the Limitation Act 1980 since no other public authority would be involved in the proprietor's loss of their possessions. The difficulty with either of these actions was the nature of the Limitation Act 1980 itself. Its provisions are not ambiguous and so are not susceptible to re-interpretation. The section 6 obligation does not apply where, as we saw earlier, the action of the public authority is unavoidable by statute. In other words, where that public authority has no discretion, as is the case with the courts in relation to adverse possession, the court itself cannot be in breach of the provisions of the HRA. Did this lack of recourse on the basis of article 1 protocol 1 mean that the rules relating to adverse possession were in an irresolvable conflict with the ECHR? This question was considered in a series of cases concerning a conflict between a landowner and his former tenant, *Pye v Graham*.[15]

Key case: *Pye v Graham* [2002] UKHL 30 and *Pye v UK* Application no. 44302/02

The *Pye v Graham*[16] series of litigation involved hearings in both the House of Lords and the European Court of Human Rights. In the House of Lords, their Lordships concluded that Mr and Mrs Graham were entitled to the land by virtue of their adverse possession of it. In submissions before the Court of Appeal it had been argued that the HRA 1998 should have retrospectively been applied to the instant case (which was heard just after the coming into force of the Act), so that the Limitation Act 1980 should have been reinterpreted to protect Pye's human right to their property under article 1 of the first protocol. Their Lordships gave this argument very short shrift thanks to concessions from counsel.

---

[15] *JA Pye (Oxford) Ltd v Graham* [2002] UKHL 30, [2003] 1 AC 419.
[16] *JA Pye (Oxford) Ltd v Graham* [2002] UKHL 30, [2003] 1 AC 419 and Application no. 44302/02.

> They also gave short shrift to the argument that the common law would also have encouraged a narrow reading of the Limitation Act. Lord Browne-Wilkinson held that:
>
>> 'Before your Lordships' House, it was conceded that the Human Rights Act did not have a retrospective effect. But Pye submitted that, even under the common law principles of construction applicable before the Human Rights Act came into effect, the court should seek to apply the law so as to make it consistent with the European Convention for the Protection of Human Rights. Any such old principle of construction only applied where there was an ambiguity in the language of a statute. No such ambiguity in the Act of 1980 was demonstrated to your Lordships'.[17]
>
> Pye therefore brought a claim before the European Court of Human Rights. The question was whether the Limitation Act 1980 was human rights-compliant. If it was not, and the national court felt unable to interpret the legislation so as to bring it into line with human rights considerations, a declaration of incompatibility would be made. The Grand Chamber concluded, narrowly, that the Limitation Act 1980 was human rights compliant, but only just. The 2002 land registration reforms much better accorded with both the letter and the spirit of the ECHR by ensuring that inaction alone would not lead to a deprivation of property without any kind of reasonable warning that such was a possibility.
>
> The consequence was to allow the Limitation Act 1980 rules to continue undisturbed, although as explained in chapter 6, these rules have now been replaced in respect of registered land. Strictly speaking, the decision in *Pye v UK* was not actually binding on an English court. However, the Court of Appeal in *Ofulue v Bossert*[18] confirmed that as a matter of English law, the coming into force of the HRA 1998 did not alter the operation of the law relating to adverse possession.

In relation to the adverse possession rules, despite what can only be described as unhappiness at the pre-reform rules, the fact that reform had now taken place, and that it was easy to get oneself within the protection of the registration system, there was no breach of human rights here.

17.3.2 POSSESSION ACTIONS AGAINST PUBLIC AUTHORITY TENANTS AND LICENSEES

The next area of land law to receive intense scrutiny from a human rights perspective is the question as to whether a public authority landlord who seeks an order for possession against a tenant or residential licensee is in breach of the tenant/licensee's article 8 rights. This question can arise in two ways. First, it can be argued that the legislation constraining the powers of a public authority to bring an action for possession in such cases is itself incompatible with the HRA 1998 rights, at least on its current interpretation. This argument would involve the court either exercising its powers to comply with the section 3 interpretation obligation, or would involve a declaration of incompatibility in line with section 4. Under both of these approaches, the challenge is to the

---

[17] *JA Pye (Oxford) Ltd v Graham* [2002] UKHL 30, [2003] 1 AC 419, [18].
[18] *Ofulue v Bossert* [2008] EWCA Civ 7, [2009] Ch 1.

legislation itself (either in general, or in how the legislation applied in the instant case). The second option would be for an individual to bring an action based on section 6 HRA 1998, alleging that although the legislation *itself* is compatible, the operation of the public authority discretion *within the framework* of that legislation, was a breach of the human rights of the individual concerned. This sort of argument can look only at the facts of the instant case.

The difficulty with the second kind of approach is that the public authority is, by definition, acting *in compliance with existing statutory provisions* (otherwise an action could simply be brought under national law). The argument therefore runs that the public authority is 'further' bound by human rights concerns *on top of* the statutory controls already in place. To fully understand the question being asked in these cases, it may be useful to look to chapter 10 concerned with leases and consider the security of tenure (at 10.5.5). To summarise very briefly here for the purposes of clarity—in circumstances where the tenant is an individual and they use the property as their principal or only home, the local authority cannot evict that tenant except for certain prescribed reasons unless exceptional circumstances apply meaning that the individual has been deprived of this security of tenure for some (statutorily justified) reason. Thus, in cases where an additional human rights challenge is being brought the tenant is alleging that, notwithstanding the fact that the local authority can prove that a prescribed reason applies, or the tenant has been deprived of their security of tenure because either they have behaved in such a way as to have had their tenancy 'demoted', or, at the outset of their tenancy, they were given a tenancy without security of tenure by the local authority (eg an introductory or flexible tenancy), the deprivation was nevertheless a breach of their human rights.

17.3.2.1 Traditional approach—judicial review proceedings

The traditional approach to resolving these questions was to see local authority actions as being subject to two existing controls: statutory control and the overarching supervisory jurisdiction of the courts in the form of judicial review. Whilst the former would provide for security of tenure, the latter ensured that the local authority's decision would be made not only in accordance with the law, but also in compliance with the principles of natural justice, equality, and reasonableness. If, the courts originally reasoned, the local authority not only complied with the statutory provisions (which, by definition were themselves convention-compliant or the section 3 and 4 HRA 1998 powers would have come into play), but *also* complied with the procedural and other requirements embodied in judicial review, then it would not be possible for any additional protection for the tenant to be found in the ECHR itself. If any additional protection was required in order to ensure compliance with the ECHR, then it would be the statute itself which was at fault. Therefore, either a new interpretation would have to be given to the statute as a result of section 3, or a declaration of incompatibility would be required under section 4. This position was essentially one based on logic: if the statute complied with the ECHR, then any action justified by that statute was also compliant. This logic was best embodied in the decision of the House of Lords in *Qazi v Harrow LBC*.[19]

---

[19] *Qazi v Harrow LBC* [2003] UKHL 43, [2004] 1 AC 983.

Key case: *Qazi v Harrow LBC* [2003] UKHL 43

The case involved the operation of the rule in *Hammersmith & Fulham v Monk*[20] which we consider later and which was also addressed in chapter 10, at 10.4.1. Essentially, Qazi and his wife were joint tenants of a tenancy. Mrs Qazi then gave notice to quit, bringing to an end Mr Qazi's rights in respect of the property. Qazi argued that this deprivation of his rights to his home breached his article 8 rights.

The House of Lords' approach was to rely on the principles of judicial review, and the general structure of property law, to ensure compliance with article 8. There was to be no individual assessment of compliance by a local authority with article 8. Rather, once the general scheme was considered to be compliant with human rights, any decision made under that scheme would also be human rights compliant.

Lord Hope explained the issue at the heart of this case:

'The question which lies at the heart of the case is whether, having regard to the provisions of article 8(1) of the Convention, it is unlawful for a public authority to recover possession from a former tenant by a procedure which leads to possession being granted automatically, or whether the court must always be given an opportunity to consider whether the making of an order for possession would be proportionate'.[21]

In other words, the essential question was whether an individual proportionality assessment was required in every case, or whether it could be assumed that the statutory and common law framework in place already constituted a balancing exercise so as to produce a proportionate outcome. Lord Millett gives the clearest guidance on how the majority understood this issue: 'article 8 is not ordinarily infringed by enforcing the terms on which the applicant occupies premises as his home'.[22] Thus, the right to respect of one's home includes respect for the contractual and statutory provisions surrounding the right to occupy that home. As long as the statute itself did not represent a disproportionate interference with an article 8 right, neither too would local authority actions within the parameters of that statute.

The approach in *Qazi* was heavily criticised in the European Court of Human Rights in their decision in *Kay v UK*.[23] In that case, once again, the ECtHR highlighted that the national court's approach needed to change, so as to be open to the possibility of a proportionality assessment in individual cases.

Further analysis: Structural versus case specific questions

The jurisprudence in *Qazi*, although now superseded in this particular context by the later cases, still has an appealing logic, and that logic is apparent elsewhere in this chapter (for example, when we consider the case law on section 335A Insolvency Act 1986 at 17.3.5). It is therefore useful to consider this issue of the structural question of statutory compliance in general, versus the specific question as to whether an individual's rights are adequately protected in a particular case.

---

[20] *Hammersmith & Fulham v Monk* [1992] 1 AC 478, 24 HLR 206 HL.
[21] *Qazi v Harrow LBC* [2003] UKHL 43, [2004] 1 AC 983, [36].
[22] *Qazi v Harrow LBC* [2003] UKHL 43, [2004] 1 AC 983, [100].
[23] *Kay v UK* [2010] ECHR 1322, 37341/06.

> This distinction has been examined by Wilson Stark who explains that contrary to how it may appear, courts are actually reluctant to answer the 'structural' question in general. Rather, they will look to the instant case to ensure compliance on the facts before them, but not beyond. She argues that: 'the courts largely use a case-specific approach to ss.3 and 4 as well as ss.6 –8'.[24] This means that whilst the division between the structural and the specific question works well in theory, the actual practice of the courts is to undermine the appealing logic of ascertaining whether statutory provisions are *in general*, compliant. The ECtHR may therefore be right to require the national courts to examine each case afresh, precisely because a thorough structural examination has not actually taken place.

17.3.2.2 The new approach

Following criticism by the ECtHR, the Supreme Court changed its jurisprudence in *Manchester City Council v Pinnock*.[25] In this case, the court held, albeit clearly reluctantly, that they were duty-bound to conclude that whilst a local authority's action might comply with an ECHR-compliant statute, that did not necessarily mean that as far as that individual was concerned, their human rights had been sufficiently protected. This is because, in the words of the court, in certain exceptional circumstances, the precise requirements relating to that individual might mean that the statute, although in general compliant with human rights, did not provide sufficient protection. The 'exceptional' nature of such a potential conflict must, however, be emphasised. More detail is given on this in *Hounslow LBC v Powell*.[26]

> **Key case:** *Manchester City Council v Pinnock* [2011] UKSC 6
>
> Here, a housing authority brought possession proceedings against a secure tenant on the basis of a series of anti-social incidents by the tenant's children. The anti-social acts of residents of a property, even where those residents are not themselves tenants, was sufficient grounds under the relevant legislation to justify the landlord seeking possession. However, it also meant that the tenant was being evicted through no fault of their own. The court was therefore required to assess whether the action for possession in this case was proportionate.
>
> Following from the jurisprudence in the ECtHR, the Supreme Court acknowledged that a proportionality defence was indeed possible.
>
> In the judgment of the court:
>
> 'Where . . . there is a clear and constant line of decisions whose effect is not inconsistent with some fundamental substantive or procedural aspect of our law, and whose reasoning does not appear to overlook or misunderstand some argument or point or principle, we consider that it would be wrong for this court not to follow the line'.[27]
>
> The power of this proportionality defence, and its availability to claimants, has however been curtailed by the subsequent decision in *Powell*.

---

[24] S Wilson Stark, 'Facing facts: judicial approaches to section 4 of the Human Rights Act 1998' (2017) 133 LQR 631, 650.
[25] *Manchester City Council v Pinnock* [2011] UKSC 6, [2011] 2 WLR 220.
[26] *Hounslow LBC v Powell* [2011] UKSC 8, [2011] 2 AC 186.
[27] *Manchester City Council v Pinnock* [2011] UKSC 6, [2011] 2 WLR 220, [48].

Key case: *Hounslow LBC v Powell* [2011] UKSC 8

This case concerned five conjoined appeals concerned with human rights review of possession actions by local authorities against introductory, or otherwise non-secure tenants. In this case, because the tenants were introductory tenants or had been deprived of their security of tenure for some other reason, the statutory provisions allowed the local authority to seek an order for possession against that tenant without having to prove any particular reason for so-doing.

In confirming the basic position outlined in *Pinnock*, *Powell* gives detail on the circumstances in which the court has to consider separately the human rights protections given to the tenant (emphasis added in the following quotation).

> 'The basic rules are not now in doubt. The court will only have to consider whether the making of a possession order is proportionate <u>if the issue has been raised by the occupier</u> and it has crossed the high threshold of being <u>seriously arguable</u>. The question will then be whether making an order for the occupier's eviction is a <u>proportionate means of achieving a legitimate aim</u>. But it will, of course, be necessary in each case for the court first to consider whether the property in question constitutes the defendant's "<u>home</u>" for the purposes of article 8. This is because it is only where a person's "home" is under threat that article 8 comes into play ... It is well established in the jurisprudence of the Strasbourg court that an individual has to show *sufficient and continuing links* with a place to show that it is his home for the purposes of article 8'.[28]

Summary: Post-*Powell* rules

From the guidance in *Powell* we can therefore see that the court must answer a number of questions before in can be concluded that there has been a breach of article 8. We shall see that some of these have been fleshed out or added to in subsequent case law.

1. Has the issue been raised by the occupier?
2. Is article 8 engaged? Is the property the defendant's (in possession proceedings, the tenant's) home such that they have 'sufficient and continuing links' with the property?
3. Is the case seriously arguable? In other words, is the case exceptional in the sense expressed in *Powell* so as to be disproportionate?
4. Is the order a proportionate means of achieving a legitimate aim?

We will now discuss these issues in order.

Has the issue been raised by the occupier?

This may seem like a very small issue and indeed it is not a substantive question. It is however hugely significant. The reason why this is so important is that the most vulnerable tenants, ie those with exceptional circumstances which may mean that they require a higher degree of protection, are the very same tenants who may be unaware of the need to put this on the claim form issued

---

[28] *Hounslow LBC v Powell* [2011] UKSC 8, [2011] 2 AC 186, [33].

before the commencement of proceedings. Such tenants are highly unlikely to have legal advice, and the vast majority would not do so at least until they arrive at court where they may receive the advice of a legal friend.

Is article 8 engaged?

As Lord Hope in *Powell* explained, in order for article 8 to be engaged, the claimant must show that the property is their home. This requires them to demonstrate sufficient and continuing links. In most cases it could be taken for granted that a claim by a person who was in lawful occupation to remain in possession would attract the protection of article 8. However, this approach to what constitutes a person's 'home' is also significant in telling us what interests the courts think this article seeks to protect. Furthermore, it can be criticised on the grounds that it is potentially discriminatory and therefore may need to be read in conjunction with article 14 of the ECHR.

> **Further analysis: The definition of home**
>
> To understand the scope of this provision, however, it is necessary first to get to grips with what is meant by a 'home' in this context. The courts have held that by home here is meant somewhere with which the clamant has sufficient and continuing links.
> In *Paulic v Croatia* the court said:
>
>> '"Home" is an autonomous concept which does not depend on classification under domestic law. Whether or not a particular premises constitutes a 'home' which attracts the protection of article 8(1) will depend on the factual circumstances, namely, the existence of sufficient and continuous links with a specific place'.[29]
>
> This definition was followed in *Pinnock* and *Powell*, and indeed was adopted with no difficulty in *Qazi*. This definition is generally quite straightforward, but it has caused some problems in relation to transient and travelling communities (as can be seen in *Kay*). For this reason, article 8 can be read alongside article 14 which prohibits discriminatory treatment on the basis of race or other affiliation and is therefore applicable to the definition of home, implying stability as it does, which appears to discriminate against traveller communities.
>
> Arguably, this approach to defining home is, as has been suggested by Hohmann and Essert amongst others, a misrepresentation of why having a home is valuable, and therefore does not represent the true 'human' value of property rights. Rather, according to Hohmann, the value in a home lies in the triple advantage which it provides: security, privacy and identity.[30] To Essert, the great value of the home lies in its being a private and individualised space within which the only decision-maker is the privileged (in the sense of having rights to occupy) occupier.[31] If this approach is taken to the definition of home, then it can be seen that focus on the permanence or continuity of links to a particular property undermines the value of the human rights protection conferred. Reasoning about article 8 rights to a home, especially given the context of that right being more broadly, a right to a 'private life', is really reasoning about why homes are important in this sense, and what they provide to individuals. If the essence of what they provide is indeed a safe and private space, then perhaps our definition of home should flex to encapsulate that?

---

[29] *Paulic v Croatia* 3572/06, [2009] ECHR 1614, [33].
[30] J Hohmann, *The Right to Housing: Law, Concepts, Possibilities* (Hart, Oxford, 2013).
[31] C Essert, 'Property and homelessness' 44 Philosophy and Public Affairs 266.

Is it seriously arguable that article 8 was 'breached' such that exceptional circumstances are present?

Lord Hope also made clear in *Powell* that the case must be seriously arguable before the courts are required to engaged in a specific assessment as to the proportionality between the article 8 protections, and the local authority's need to manage its housing stock by obtaining an order for possession. Subsequent case law has shown that the courts will take this exceptional circumstances test very seriously, and it has been strictly interpreted. We can see this if we look at the three most significant post-*Powell* cases: *Birmingham City Council v Lloyd*;[32] *Scott v Corby BC*;[33] and *Thurrock BC v West*.[34] In each of these, as we will see, the courts demonstrate that whilst in theory they are open to examination of a tenant's specific circumstances before they conclude that article 8 has not been breached, the intensity of this examination may leave something to be desired.

Key case: *Birmingham CC v Lloyd* [2012] EWCA Civ 969

In this case, Lloyd was a secure tenant of a property owned by the local authority. His brother was also a secure tenant, of a different flat. On his brother's death, L moved into his brother's flat because he preferred it. The local authority told him that they would not grant him a tenancy of the brother's flat, but rather that he should move back to his own flat. He did not do this. This meant that his tenancy of his own flat was no longer secure (because the status of secure tenant requires occupation), and he was a trespasser in his brother's flat. He was therefore evicted from both.

He claimed that his eviction was disproportionate because (1) he had a history of depression; (2) his financial circumstances would make it difficult for him to obtain alternative accommodation; (3) his effort in starting up his web-design business would be wasted if he were evicted; (4) there was confusion; and (5) D was not guilty of any anti-social behaviour.

The court held that a trespasser will have to show even more exceptional circumstances to rely on human rights arguments in possession proceedings (we consider the position of trespassers later). Just because the claimant here was at one point a secure tenant, that did not mean that he could argue that he was in a special position regarding his status as trespasser. Furthermore, the court was clear that any time a person seeks to rely on their medical history as part of an article 8 defence to possession proceedings, they will need to bring evidence of that medical history, rather than merely claiming it. Thus, the court was very unsympathetic to Lloyd's cause in this case.

Key case: *Scott v Corby BC & West Kent Housing Association v Haycraft* [2012] EWCA Civ 276

This case involved two joined appeals. In *Scott*, Ms Scott attempted to rely on article 8 on the grounds that the order for possession against her was disproportionate. In part she relied on the fact that a short time earlier she had been the victim of a violent assault.

The court held that this was not disproportionate and that there were no exceptional circumstances here. The court acknowledged that the assault had been a very violent one, but reasoned that this had nothing to do with the proportionality of her eviction. There was no injury, either mental

---

[32] *Birmingham City Council v Lloyd* [2012] EWCA Civ 969, [2012] HLR 44.
[33] *Scott v Corby BC* [2012] EWCA Civ 276, [2012] HLR 23.
[34] *Thurrock BC v West* [2012] EWCA Civ 1435, [2013] HLR 5.

or physical, arising from the assault which would have made it particularly problematic for her to move house. This somewhat unsympathetic attitude is perhaps indicative that the courts' focus is not on whether the individual in general is in the midst of exceptional circumstances which are causing them hardship, but rather on whether there would be a causal link between their eviction, and the exceptional circumstances said to arise from it. As Lord Neuberger explains: 'exceptionality is a measure of outcome'.[35]

In *Haycraft*, an assured shorthold tenancy was granted. A neighbour complained that the tenant had indecently exposed himself, and there were other allegations of anti-social behaviour. There had been no proof of the exposure however, and there had been no allegations of bad behaviour for a year. The tenant contended that evicting him was disproportionate on the grounds that he was not guilty of indecent exposure; that he had health problems; and that he had recently married and now had a child, as well as there being no new complaints.

Again, the court held that this was not exceptional enough for article 8 to be successfully relied upon. Furthermore, the court considered the ill-health of the tenant, and emphasised, in line with their view in *Scott*, that whilst he was indeed in poor health, that would be unaffected by his being evicted. The focus again was on the exceptionality of the outcome following eviction, not the nature of the claimant's circumstances prior to eviction. Finally, and very significantly, the court also considered it irrelevant whether or not the tenant was going to have to be re-housed by the local authority in any case. Lord Neuberger explained:

> 'First, art.8 is primarily concerned with respect for his particular home, as opposed to a general right to be provided with a home. Secondly, the right to be re-housed appears to me to be a factor weighing against the art.8 claim prevailing, rather than the absence of such a right being a factor in favour of such a claim prevailing'.[36]

Key case: *Thurrock BC v West* [2012] EWCA Civ 1435

D's grandparents were tenants of a house. D was not entitled to succeed to the tenancy and so the local authority brought an action for possession against him. He contended that he could rely on article 8 because he was not in arrears and that his family would suffer from severe disruption from having to move.

The court held that there is nothing exceptional in a family having to move house. This much is unsurprising given the approach we have already seen in the other cases. However, the general comments by the Etherton LJ in this case provide a very good guide to the general operation of these principles:

> 'First, it is a defence to a claim by a local authority for possession of a defendant's home that the possession is not necessary in a democratic society within art.8(2), that is to say it would be disproportionate in all the circumstances...
>
> Secondly, the test is whether the eviction is a proportionate means of achieving a legitimate aim...
>
> Thirdly, it is nevertheless clear that the threshold for establishing an arguable case that a local authority is acting disproportionately and so in breach of art.8 where repossession would otherwise be lawful is a high one and will be met in only a small proportion of cases...

---

[35] *Scott v Corby BC* [2012] EWCA Civ 276, [2012] HLR 23, [27].
[36] *Scott v Corby BC* [2012] EWCA Civ 276, [2012] HLR 23, [30].

> Fourthly, the reasons why the threshold is so high lie in the public policy and public benefit inherent in the functions of the housing authority in dealing with its housing stock, a precious and limited public resource. Local authorities, like other social landlords, hold their housing stock for the benefit of the whole community and they are best equipped, certainly better equipped than the courts, to make management decisions about the way such stock should be administered . . .
>
> Fifthly, that is why the fact that a local authority has a legal right to possession . . . will be a strong factor in support of the proportionality of making an order for possession without the need for explanation or justification by the local authority . . . It will, of course, always be open to a local authority to adduce evidence of particularly strong or unusual reasons for wanting possession . . .
>
> Sixthly, an art.8 defence on the grounds of lack of proportionality must be pleaded and sufficiently particularised to show that it reaches the high threshold of being seriously arguably . . .
>
> Seventhly, unless there is some good reason not to do so, the court must at the earliest opportunity summarily consider whether the art.8 defence, as pleaded . . . If the pleaded defence does not reach that threshold, it must be struck out or dismissed... The resources of the court and of the parties should not be further expended on it.
>
> Eighthly, even where an art.8 defence is established, in a case where the defendant would otherwise have no legal right to remain in the property, it is difficult to imagine circumstances in which the defence could operate to give the defendant an unlimited and unconditional right to remain'.[37]

This general guidance from the court is welcome, but in reality, the situation involving local authority actions against their tenant is not particularly difficult for the precise reason that the tenant almost never succeeds in overturning the housing authority's decision on human rights grounds (they may well succeed on the broader judicial review principles). This is because the statutory provisions in place are so specific and detailed that it is somewhat difficult to imagine circumstances where the statute has not already effectively dictated the balance between the parties, even though those statutory provisions make no reference to the individual circumstances of tenants in terms of hardship.

Further analysis: Should the courts be more generous with article 8 claims?

The comments by Etherton LJ in *Thurrock* are indicative as to the policy concerns at play here:

> 'Sympathy for the predicament of the respondent and his family, which is entirely understandable, cannot obscure the remarkable effect of the district judge's decision. That decision precludes the Council from recovering possession of the Property from persons who have never been granted by the Council any right to occupy it, and whose housing needs are less than the accommodation provided by the Property, and confers on those persons a right to remain without any limitation of time or other conditionality, in conflict with the lawful legislative policy limiting succession rights to secure tenancies. It deprives the Council of its public right and duty to make management decisions about the Property as part of its housing stock. In effect, the court has assumed for itself the power Parliament has conferred on the Council to select the most suitable property for the numerous and various persons who have a legal right to social housing. This has been done without any knowledge on the court's part as to who are those other people who have an

---

[37] *Thurrock BC v West* [2012] EWCA Civ 1435, [2013] HLR 5, [22]ff.

> equal, or possibly better, claim to be housed and for whom the Property would be as suitable or possibly more suitable that the respondent and his family. On the basis that it would be wrong for the Council to permit the respondent to remain in the Property without payment of rent and other conditions, the effect of the order is to compel the Council to grant the respondent a new tenancy of the Property to which he has no legal right'.[38]
>
> Comments like this raise the question as to whether the law would be improved were the courts to be more generous in respect of article 8. The arguments in favour of such generosity are, essentially, that individual circumstances can never fully be captured in the broad and generally applicable terms of legislation. As a result, even where a statute has been carefully and sensitively drafted to try to strike a balance between the individual needs of occupiers, and the collective public need for local housing providers to be able to managing their (limited) housing stock and resources effectively, the drafters of the statute cannot envisage the very wide range of personal circumstances in which an occupier may find themselves, both before and theoretically subsequent to any eviction. Allowing the courts to take 'an extra look' at such unusual cases is therefore warranted in this sense.
>
> However, any litigation of this sort is likely to take up both court and local authority resources. Both are in limited supply. Furthermore, the certainty and predictability which the relatively clear statutory security of tenure regimes provide would be significantly undermined if each case was further subject to the courts' supervision (without a clear list of factors which would shape their discretion in so supervising). In this sense we come back to the questions raised elsewhere in this book, regarding the importance of individual fairness when balanced against a more systemic kind of fairness. It is in respect of very challenging human rights-based cases that we see this contrast at its most stark.

When is such a breach justified as a proportionate response to a legitimate societal aim?

Unsurprisingly, perhaps, given that that the courts are so reluctant to find that an article 8 case is seriously arguable, they have given very little guidance on exactly what constitutes a proportionate order for possession in such cases. The particular facts of the majority of the cases considered simply do not require the courts to answer this question. However, there is some academic discussion as to the meaning both of proportionality in this context, and as to what will constitute a legitimate societal aim.

1. Proportionate

The proportionality test is one which is utilised in a number of different contexts in English law, being relevant both under EU law and in human rights cases. It is also a legal concept with a long history, being the guiding standard in many administrative law systems around the world. It is therefore a concept which carries with it a lot of 'baggage'. It is unsurprising that there is some uncertainty as to how proportionality interacts with the more specific balance struck in a leasehold/public authority context, by the various statutory provisions. In essence, proportionality means that the measure is, 'appropriate and necessary to achieve a legitimate aim, strikes a proper

---

[38] *Thurrock BC v West* [2012] EWCA Civ 1435, [2013] HLR 5, [36].

balance and avoids imposing excessive burdens'.[39] However, as Loveland explains, in the context of human rights and property law, whilst the idea that the statutory rules in these cases will be subject to a proportionality assessment has been accepted in the abstract:

> '*Pinnock* and *Powell* really do not tell us what proportionality actually means, and that establishing the applicability of the principle will not count for very much if what proportionality means is no or little more than that a decision to grant a possession order would not be *Wednesbury* irrational in the core substantive sense'.[40]

However, even if the particular standard of proportionality does not appear to be likely to change the particular outcome in any case, it should be acknowledged that thinking in terms of *rights to a home*, rather than rights as pre-defined by property law, does provide a new framework within which the question of the appropriate strength of security of tenure can be answered.

One question which does not appear to have been answered in the existing case law is what precisely the interaction is between the proportionality test and the exceptional circumstances test, and whether the two are asking the same questions. This is important, since the courts have reasoned that it is only in seriously arguable, and therefore exceptional cases, that a full-blown proportionality assessment must actually be carried out. It is important, as a result, to consider whether the factors taken into account at the 'seriously arguable' stage are the same as those considered at the proportionality stage. We know from the case law earlier that the seriously arguable/exceptionality question seems to require an assessment as to the position in which the claimant will find themselves *after* the eviction. It may well be, however, that the proportionality test, in seeking to balance the claimant's right to their home with a legitimate societal goal, may take into account features of the claimant's life, whilst not specifically worsened by their pending eviction, but which may nevertheless shape how we consider the 'fairness' or otherwise of the proposed possession order, and which may, therefore, feed into the proportionality assessment stage.

2. Legitimate Aim

It is important to emphasise that the proportionality assessment does not take place in a vacuum. The proportionality assessment assumes that the balance in question is being struck between the claimant's right to their home, and other considerations related to the public interest. These latter concerns must be 'legitimate' in the sense that they constitute a proper aim for a local authority to be pursuing. Is the management of housing stock always a legitimate aim in this sense? And if so, does that mean that all a local authority must ever argue is that the eviction of the tenant will secure such effective management? If that is right, then it will not even be necessary for the local authority to point to some particular feature of the tenant's individual situation, beyond the fact that either they have lost their security of tenure; they were never provided with

---

[39] M Fordham, *Judicial Review Handbook* (6th ed) (Hart, Oxford, 2012), 427.
[40] I Loveland, 'The holy grail as an empty chalice? Proportionality review in possession proceedings after *Pinnock* and *Powell*' [2013] Journal of Planning and Environmental Law 622, 622.

security of tenure; or one of the grounds for possession is met (so that any order for possession is grounded in national law). It seems likely that the need to manage housing stock will constitute such a legitimate aim. As Loveland explains, '[b]oth *Pinnock* and *Powell* indicate that courts should accept as "a given" that a public authority landlord is pursuing a legitimate aim in an art.8 sense; the presumed legitimate aim being simply a desire to regain control of the premises in order to let them to someone else'.[41] Furthermore, it is important to note that in this context, the legitimacy of a local authority's aim will be enhanced by the fact that the courts generally give public authorities a degree of deference in deciding questions outwith the expertise of the courts (such as the availability of public housing). At European level, the ECtHR achieves a similar outcome through the use of margin of appreciation, which recognises that circumstances regarding resources will vary from signatory state to signatory state, making the court more reluctant to intervene in such circumstances. This means that neither the national nor the Strasbourg jurisprudence is likely to too closely scrutinise the local authority's aim.

Is article 1, protocol 1 engaged?

It is not just article 8 rights that a claimant will seek to protect in attempting to defend themselves in an action for an order for possession brought by a local authority landlord. They may also seek to rely on their article 1 protocol 1 rights, by claiming that their proprietary right, ie their lease, is in a sense separately protected, as well as their residential status as occupier of their home. This argument raises the question, however, as to precisely when article 1, protocol 1 will be engaged, and what that actually means this article protects. This is a very difficult question, and the so-called inherent limitation argument poses a significant challenge not only for working out when article 1 protocol 1 will be relevant in cases of this type, but also for how property rights and human rights ought to interact in general.

Before we consider the inherent limitation argument, however, it is useful to examine some of the case law explaining when A1P1 may be relevant. This issue has arisen most prominently in respect of the 'rule' from *Hammersmith & Fulham v Monk*.[42] This rule states that where a person holds a tenancy from a local authority as a periodic tenant (until recently this was by far the most common way in which tenancies were granted to local authority tenants), and they do so as *joint* tenants of the lease, then if one of the joint tenants serves notice to quit, then the periodic tenancy will not be renewed for any other tenants (see chapter 10 at 10.4.1). If this is the case, since the termination of the lease came from the tenant, not the landlord, no security of tenure provisions apply, and the 'non-terminating co-tenant' would be required to give up possession without any protection. The question has arisen as to whether this not only engages article 8 (they undoubtedly lose their home), but whether it also engages A1P1 because they lose their leasehold title (albeit that in theory, on the renewal of a periodic tenancy, they in fact get a *new* lease each time). This was addressed in *Sims v Dacorum BC*.[43] This case also appears in chapter 10.

---

[41] I Loveland, 'Proportionality review in possession proceedings' [2012] Conv 512, 519.
[42] *Hammersmith & Fulham v Monk* [1992] 1 AC 478, 24 HLR 206 HL.
[43] *Sims v Dacorum BC* [2014] UKSC 63, [2015] AC 1336.

Key case: *Sims v Dacorum BC* [2014] UKSC 63

In this case, Mr and Mrs Sims were joint tenants of a tenancy from Dacorum BC. Mrs Sims requested that the local authority re-house her, following the breakdown of the couple's relationship, and allegations of acts of domestic violence. The council responded that they would not do so unless she served a notice to quit in respect of her original tenancy, thus allowing the council to obtain possession against Mr Sims. Mrs Sims did serve such a notice. Mr Sims then alleged that this loss of his property right was a deprivation of property under article 1 protocol 1, and that a proportionality assessment was therefore required.

The Supreme Court was very unimpressed with these arguments, and concluded that Mr Sims never had a right to occupy alone, such that he was not deprived of a property right here. Furthermore, the statutory and contractual elements present in the landlord and tenant relationship could not be simply overridden by human rights concerns. However, the judgment given by Lord Neuberger is very short, and some of the potential intricacies of the law in respect of this rule were not discussed. This is what the court says in terms of the A1P1 argument:

> 'Given that Mr Sims was deprived of his property in circumstances, and in a way, which was specifically provided for in the agreement which created it, his A1P1 claim is plainly very hard to sustain'.[44]

Further analysis: Inherent limitation

Whilst the decision in *Sims* itself is not particularly elucidating, it does hint at a very important issue in terms of how A1P1 works. A1P1 is parasitic upon some conception of 'property'. 'Property' is a legal construct, and even though the ECtHR has held consistently that this notion is autonomous, it still does depend to a greater or lesser extent on the definition given to property under national law. The consequence of this is that in cases where a person loses their proprietary interest *in line with* national law and the national law definition of the scope of that right, it is difficult to see how A1P1 can add anything to the debate. It is easiest to understand this with an example.

Imagine a 10-year leasehold interest. When that leasehold comes to an end, simply by the running of time, would we say that the tenant has 'been deprived' of their property, or is it better to say that they were never entitled to anything beyond the 10-year period? To use another example, where a tenant contractually agrees not to carry out a business in the rented property, are they being deprived of their property rights when the landlord enforces that covenant and forfeits the lease when the tenant refuses to comply with their contractual obligations?

In both cases, we can see that there is a tension between the concerns of the ECHR—which are to 'strike a balance' between the private interest in keeping a home, and the public interest in ensuring that contracts are complied with and that landlords and tenants are not tied indefinitely to their agreement—and of national law, which are to ensure that national rules relating to the scope of property are maintained. We can add to this mix the landlord's own property rights, protected both through national law and through the ECHR. As a matter of logic, it is clear that the tenants in these cases are not really being deprived of their 'property' here—they never had the right to do what they claim. If this argument is true, however, any time that a deprivation is in line with national law, A1P1 cannot add anything. For this reason, the ECtHR seems to seek an autonomous definition not only of what property is, but also of what certain categories of property right, eg leasehold estates, should entail.

---

[44] *Sims v Dacorum BC* [2014] UKSC 63, [2015] AC 1336, [15].

17.3.2.3 Quasi-public authorities

Finally, in respect of the influence which human rights arguments are having in the context of local authority housing, it is also useful to consider how these rules are affecting the operation of private housing providers acting as substitutes for local authorities in this sense, including housing associations and the like. Whilst local authority housing providers will always be public bodies, what is less clear is the status of a private housing association when providing social housing, whether they are public bodies or quasi-public bodies engaged in a public function. If they are quasi-public bodies, then any time that they engage in a public function, their actions will be caught by the prohibition on actions in breach of ECHR rights in section 6 HRA 1998. Handy and Alder consider this tension:

> 'The underlying principle here might be that of arm's-length commercial dealings. The distinction might also turn on the kind of governmental intervention that is involved in the particular act. Governmental regulation intended to ensure that a body does not behave badly does not in itself point to the body being public. Otherwise most enterprises would be potentially public. The kind of intervention that attracts a stamp of "publicness" is where government directs the nature and purpose of the act in question. Admittedly it is often difficult to draw a clear line between these two aspects of governmental intervention'.[45]

17.3.3 ACTIONS FOR POSSESSION BY PRIVATE LANDOWNERS IN THE CONTEXT OF LEASES AND LICENCES

It might have been thought that in the aftermath of *Pinnock*, there would be increasing pressure for human rights controls to rest not only on public authority landlords, but also on private landlords. In order for this to emerge, two hurdles would need to be overcome: first, in cases where the lease was freely negotiated, and the tenant received additional protection from statutory provisions, it would need to be shown that one of the following alternatives was correct: (a) the landlord was herself directly bound by article 8; (b) that the landlord herself was not bound, but that the court was bound to limit the rights of the landlord in any action before them (thus raising the landlord's own article 1 protocol 1 rights); or (c) that the statutory provisions which bounded the contractual freedom of the parties was incompatible with both parties' human rights so that a re-interpretation was required. The response so far from the courts has been to reject such arguments. However, it is not entirely clear precisely why they have reached the conclusion that article 8 should not affect the power of a private landlord to bring proceedings against a tenant. In this particular context, therefore, the possibility of horizontal effect has been rejected, as can be seen in *McDonald v McDonald*.[46]

---

[45] C Handy and J Alder, 'Housing associations: "sufficient public flavour"' (2009) 12 Journal of Housing Law 101, 104.
[46] *McDonald v McDonald* [2016] UKSC 28, [2017] AC 273.

> **Key case:** *McDonald v McDonald* [2016] UKSC 28
>
> The case concerned an action for possession against a tenant by receivers (appointed by a lender). The tenant, Ms M, had psychological problems such that it would be disruptive to her well-being for her to lose her home. Her parents acquired the freehold to the property with the help of a mortgage and fell into arrears. The question for the court was whether they could assess any breach of article 8 in the action between Ms M and the receivers, notwithstanding the fact that both were private parties.
>
> The court held that article 8 could not come into play here, but it did so for reasons which are not entirely clear. The first issue which the court addressed was whether article 8 was even relevant, given that the action was between two private parties. The court held that it was not required to assess whether there was a breach in this case. This meant that the question of the compliance of the statutory provisions with the rights guaranteed under article 8, and the proportionality of the particular action for possession simply did not arise.
>
> This reasoning is not convincing, however, for the simple reason that although the parties were two private parties, as in *Ghaidan v Godin Mendoza*,[47] for example, the real issue was one of statutory interpretation and consideration. It was the mandatory wording of the relevant provisions which meant that the court's discretion, often present in possession actions, could not be brought into play (so that section 6 would then become relevant where appropriate). The Supreme Court in this case, rather than examining the mechanics of the case, to examine where the protections in article 8 were to 'bite', instead looked at the identity of the parties and reasoned from there.

17.3.4 ACTIONS FOR POSSESSION AGAINST TRESPASSERS

The conclusions in relation to the effect of article 8 on private landlords has not, however, been replicated in all areas of potential application. Rather, in the context of actions for possession against trespassers, the courts seem to have been relatively comfortable with consideration of trespassers' article 8, 10 and 11 rights, and balancing these against the landowner's article 1 protocol 1 rights. However, it is clear from cases such as *Birmingham City Council v Lloyd*[48] that in cases of trespassers in public authority housing, the courts are going to look for 'exceptionally exceptional' cases before they will find that an eviction is disproportionate. Per Lord Neuberger in that case:

> 'It would, I accept, be wrong to say that it could never be right for the court to permit a person, who had never been more than a trespasser, to invoke art.8 as a defence against an order for possession. But such a person seeking to raise an art.8 argument would face a very uphill task indeed, and, while exceptionality is rarely a helpful test, it seems to me that it would be require the most extraordinarily exceptional circumstances'.[49]

The possibility of such constraints applying to private landowners was discussed in *Malik v Fassenfelt*.[50]

---

[47] *Ghaidan v Godin*-Mendoza [2004] UKHL 30, [2004] 2 AC 557.
[48] *Birmingham City Council v Lloyd* [2012] EWCA Civ 969, [2012] HLR 44.
[49] *Birmingham City Council v Lloyd* [2012] EWCA Civ 969, [2012] HLR 44, [18].
[50] *Malik v Fassenfelt* [2013] EWCA Civ 798, [2013] 3 EGLR 99.

> **Key case:** *Malik v Fassenfelt* [2013] EWCA Civ 798
>
> In this case, the Court of Appeal was asking whether and how, if squatters have established homes, in the context of political protest and expression, without the permission of the landowner, when the landowner brings an action for possession against those squatters, article 8 ECHR is relevant. In other words, does article 8 have horizontal effect in this context? The comments in this case in respect of article 8 have, to a certain extent, been superseded by *McDonald*,[51] but it is nevertheless useful to consider the tone of the judgments. Furthermore, in this case Ward LJ goes significantly further than the other judges in the case, and so many of these comments do not receive the support of the majority of the court.
>
> The facts of the case were that M bought the land with a view to developing in later. Before M could make any further use of the land, a group of unknown persons entered without his permission. These were part of the 'Grow Heathrow' movement. Their aim was to clear up the land and use it in a way beneficial both to them and to the community. They cleared the land and made it their home.
>
> As to whether this meant that the court should assess the proportionality of any order for possession, Ward LJ reasoned:
>
> > 'the court must approach the claim made by a private landowner against a trespasser in a similar way to that adopted to claims of various sorts made by a local authority . . . Thus the test is whether the eviction is a proportionate means of achieving a legitimate aim. The fact that the landowner has a legal right to possession is a very strong factor in support of proportionality: it speaks for itself and needs no further explanation or justification. Thus, even if the defendants have established a home on the land but where they have otherwise no legal right to remain there, it is difficult to imagine circumstances which would give the defendant an unlimited and unconditional right to remain. The circumstances would have to be exceptional'.[52]
>
> This is an entirely orthodox explanation of the test employed in the public authority cases explained previously, but was nevertheless surprising since it suggests that the proportionality of a private landowner's seeking possession can be assessed in this way. Ward LJ explained that in cases such as these, whilst the action was indeed a matter between two private parties, in exercising its judicial function, the court itself was bound by section 6.
>
> However, Toulson LJ was much more cautious. He reasoned that:
>
> > 'It would be a considerable expansion of the law to hold that article 8 imposes a positive obligation on the state, through the courts, to prevent or delay a private citizen from recovering possession of land belonging to him which has been unlawfully occupied by another. There would also be a weighty argument that for the state to interfere in that way with a private owner's right to possession of his property would be contrary to a long standing principle of the common law, which finds echo in article 1 to protocol 1'.[53]

17.3.5 MORTGAGEE'S REMEDIES

Finally, we consider how the rules relating to protection of an individual's home relate to the remedies of a mortgagee. We consider the operation of these remedies in chapter 11. However, it is useful to recap here. In cases where a legal mortgage has been duly created with the

---

[51] *McDonald v McDonald* [2016] UKSC 28, [2017] AC 273.
[52] *Malik v Fassenfelt* [2013] EWCA Civ 798, [2013] 3 EGLR 99, [28].
[53] *Malik v Fassenfelt* [2013] EWCA Civ 798, [2013] 3 EGLR 99, [45].

proper formalities, as long as the mortgagee has priority over any interests under a trust or leasehold estate, the mortgagee can sell title to the property; can go into possession; can (in a very narrow range of cases) foreclose; can appoint a receiver; or can sue on the contractual promise for sums due. The most popular of these are going into possession followed by a sale of the mortgaged property. The consequence of an exercise of such remedies is that the mortgagor, and any co-owners or occupiers of residential property without priority over the lender, will lose their home and the legal title to their property. As such, article 8 and article 1 protocol 1 are engaged. However, the courts have been most reluctant to conclude that the operation of these rules is a breach of the protections provided by the ECHR. This has been demonstrated both in respect of 'normal' proceedings, and in cases where the mortgagor as co-owner of property in equity has gone bankrupt and a possession order is being sought against a co-owner with priority. We can see this in relation to the normal proceedings in *Horsham Properties v Beech*.[54]

Key case: *Horsham Properties v Beech* [2008] EWHC 2327

The question in this case was whether the mortgagee's out of court sale of the mortgaged property was a breach of the mortgagor's article 8 and article 1 protocol 1 rights. This arose because unlike in the normal situation where the mortgagee will usually seek a court order for possession before selling the property, the mortgagee here decided to sell without ever going into possession of the land. This allowed them to by-pass the limited protections given to mortgagors by, amongst others, section 36 Administration of Justice Act 1970 (see chapter 11 at 11.4.3.2). The operation of that section required that the court set a balance between the individual's desire to remain in their home and willingness and ability to repay the sums in arrears, and the lender's desire to realise their security. Thus, it was argued that the court's discretion under section 36 was typically responsive (albeit before the event) to the requirement imposed by article 1 for a proportionate balance to be struck as between private property and public interest. Where no court action took place, no such balance could be ensured, and therefore the article 1 protocol 1 rights had been breached.

The court held that there was no such breach here. The comments of Briggs J are noteworthy here, not least because they clearly mirror the approach in *Qazi*.

'In my judgment, any deprivation of possession constituted by the exercise by a mortgagee of its powers under section 101 of the LPA after a relevant default by the mortgagor is justified in the public interest, and requires no case-by-case exercise of a proportionality discretion by the court, for the following reasons. First, it reflects the bargain habitually drawn between mortgagors and mortgagees for nearly 200 years, in which the ability of a mortgagee to sell the property offered as a security without having to go to court has been identified as a central and essential aspect of the security necessarily to be provided if substantial property based secured lending is to be available at affordable rates of interest. That it is in the public interest that property buyers and owners should be able to obtain lending for that purpose can hardly be open to doubt, even if the loan-to-value ratios at which it has recently become possible have now become a matter of controversy'.[55]

---

[54] *Horsham Properties v Beech* [2008] EWHC 2327 (Ch), [2009] 1 WLR 1255.
[55] *Horsham Properties v Beech* [2008] EWHC 2327 (Ch), [2009] 1 WLR 1255, [44].

A similarly dismissive approach is taken in the courts in respect of lenders obtaining orders for sale under section 14 Trusts of Land and Appointment of Trusts Act 1996, and section 335A Insolvency Act 1986, albeit that in such cases the court recognises the importance of its interpretation obligations. This can be seen if we consider the approaches in *Barca v Mears*[56] and *Nicholls v Lan*.[57]

> **Key case:** *Barca v Mears* [2004] EWHC 2170
>
> In *Barca v Mears*, the question arose as to whether the special needs of the bankrupt's son constituted exceptional circumstances for the purposes of section 335A Insolvency Act 1986. The court concluded that they did not do so. They concluded this because the child was able to reside with his mother during the week so that he did not need to move schools, and because the possession order in relation to the home would not prevent the father from continuing to provide his son with significant help in respect of his education.
>
> Barca therefore argued that this interpretation of section 335A would be inconsistent with his and his son's article 8 and article 1 protocol 1 rights. The judge held that whilst in the instant case there may have been no breach of these articles, the 'blanket' approach which had been taken to section 335A, which was to in effect provide very little consideration to individual cases, might well lead to a breach of these rights in some cases. Therefore, in order to ensure compliance with the rights in the ECHR, it would be necessary for a court to genuinely and openly examine whether exceptional circumstances were actually present.
>
> In respect of this argument, Dixon comments:
>
> > 'In this, it is respectfully submitted, he is entirely right. As the judge says, the "almost universal rule" which prefers the interests of the creditors at the expense of the personal or property rights of third parties--members of the family--who owe the creditors nothing at all at best looks cavalier in the light of the Convention. This is made no more acceptable by an "exceptional circumstance" rule which effectively rules out a postponement unless the circumstances are highly unusual--like terminal illness --and which take no account of the severity of the consequences for the family even when the creditors " suffering" might be less or even negligible if a sale is refused'.[58]
>
> Thus, the approach of the court in this case suggests that whilst the ECHR has not formally altered the rule, or even the interpretation of the rule, it may well warrant a change in judicial attitude to the interpretation of section 335A.

This slightly more 'generous' approach to the exceptional circumstances test, was not however followed in *Nicholls v Lan*,[59] which seems to take the view that the exceptional circumstances test *is* the balance between the rights of the creditor and those of any third parties in the house, rather than that balance being sought by a potential wide interpretation of those provisions should the case require it.

---

[56] *Barca v Mears* [2004] EWHC 2170 (Ch), [2005] 2 FLR 1.
[57] *Nicholls v Lan* [2006] EWHC 1255 (Ch), [2007] 1 FLR 744.
[58] M Dixon, 'Trusts of land, bankruptcy and human rights' [2005] Conv 161, 166.
[59] *Nicholls v Lan* [2006] EWHC 1255 (Ch), [2007] 1 FLR 744.

> **Key case:** *Nicholls v Lan* [2006] EWHC 1255
>
> In this case, the wife owned the matrimonial home jointly with her husband, who had been declared bankrupt. On his bankruptcy, the husband's half share in the property vested in his trustee in bankruptcy who then sought an order for the sale of the house under s.14 of TOLATA 1996. One of the issues raised at first instance before the district judge was whether the case was one where the circumstances were 'exceptional'. The wife, who continued to live at the house, suffered from long-term schizophrenia and argued that this constituted an exceptional circumstance which would justify delaying the sale beyond the usual 'year' cut-off in cases involving bankruptcy.
>
> In support of this contention, it was argued that the wife's right to respect for her home under Art.8 should have been fully considered by the courts, rather than assumed to be irrelevant according to the very narrow approach usually taken to the exceptional circumstances test. The judge here concluded that section 335A was compatible with the rights contained in article 8. By definition, those rights were bounded by public purpose. Thus, the purpose of the exceptional circumstances test was in fact the means by which the need to respect the fact that the property was a home. As such, the law already provided for protection of article 8 rights as far as the public interest required it in cases of bankruptcy, by the exceptional circumstances test itself.

In this way, whilst the courts have been perfectly willing to address the question of the compliance of mortgage law with human rights provisions (even, it should be noted, in cases between private parties), they have not found that the provisions in fact do breach human rights. This is unsurprising if we look at the local authority and tenant cases, which demonstrate that the courts are certainly unwilling to upset a careful set of balances that have been articulated through statute and common law in regulating these kinds of disputes. We saw in chapters 10 and 11 that the balance is not always struck in the right place, but the courts are certainly of the view that it is not their role to refine that balance except in cases where it is manifestly unjust to evict an individual from their home in the circumstances which have befallen them.

> **Summary: Impact of human rights on property law**
>
> The impact of human rights in property law has been felt differently in different contexts.
>
> 1. Adverse possession. The courts were willing to consider whether the Limitation Act 1980 breached an individual's human rights, even in a case involving another private party, but concluded that no breach had occurred.
> 2. Actions for possession brought by local authorities against tenants, licensees or trespassers. Human rights will apply in such cases, but where the statutory provisions themselves comply with these provisions, then an individual can only claim additional protection where exceptional circumstances exist, where they have raised the issue of breach of their own accord, and where the local authority's actions are disproportionate.
> 3. Actions for possession brought by private individuals against tenants, licensees or trespassers. The courts have not been willing to consider human rights controls in private actions against tenants.

> They have considered the question in relation to actions against trespassers, but generally conclude no breach taking account of the landowner's own property rights, and human rights under article 1 protocol 1.
> 4. Actions for possession by mortgagees. The court have considered the degree to which certain elements of mortgage law comply with human rights, but have not found breach.

17.4 CONCLUSION

The interaction between human rights and property law is an unusual topic when compared with the other chapters in this book. It is unusual in two ways. First, the law in this area is heavily directed by public law rules: those concerned with statutory interpretation, with judicial power vis-à-vis the executive and Parliament, and with judicial review. This makes description of many of the precise subtleties of the interaction between human rights and property dependent upon a certain degree of knowledge of public/constitutional law more generally. Second, these rules have not been designed and have developed entirely unconsciously and completely piecemeal in response to unconnected litigation across different areas of land law. Whilst many of the rules studied in this book did have their origins in such a process, they are no longer still in their infancy in this sense. For that reason, it is not possible, for example, to usefully analyse the way in which property right is affected by human rights by reference to the *aim* of such rules, as it is not clear what the aim of these rules would be. This makes the presentation here as much in the nature of an attempt to tidy up what is without doubt messy and unclear as it is an attempt to think about the policies driving such developments. Nevertheless, we can still examine the effects of these rules on the wider property law landscape.

PRINCIPLES

How does this mean that human rights shape the balance of the principles operating in relation to land law? To recap, these principles were:

1. Certainty
2. Sensitivity to context
3. Transactability
4. Systemic and individual effects
5. Recognition of the social role of the land law system.

One might assume that human rights would have a hugely significant effect in this regard. Indeed, the whole essence of human rights protections is that they allow for sensitivity to context above all else, as they require an open and genuine consideration of the vast range of circumstances which can befall individuals as they attempt to navigate their way through those structures instituted by property law, be it mortgages or leaseholds. However, the courts have been reluctant to allow this individual, case-by-case approach to assessment precisely because they recognise that sensitivity to context is problematic in the wider system. The whole question of how far human rights should impact upon the shapes of property law is, therefore, essentially a question of how far land law should become responsive to individual circumstances.

This presents us with a good opportunity to explore this particular question. There are a number of reasons for why the courts have resisted pressure to examine individual circumstances. The first, as we can see in the reasoning in *Sims* amongst other cases, is that the courts generally recognise that where Parliament has either deliberately created a series of rules, or has deliberately chosen not to intervene in relation to a particular common law rule, then we must assume that the democratically elected legislature wishes the balance to be maintained as it is, rather than altered by human rights. Whilst this is a strong argument, it is not all-powerful since of course part of Parliament's intention was indeed the enactment of the HRA itself. Second, however, the courts, on the flipside, do not want to unduly meddle in private relationships, freely negotiated on the grounds that this undermines the sanctity and freedom of contract. Again, whilst this approach is appealing, it actually fails to reflect the reality of many transactions involving land where both the bargaining power between parties is often very unequal, and where the 'terms' of the contract and rules of that contract are set out in advance through standard terms and conditions or more powerfully through statutory provisions. The idea that individual circumstances are appropriately catered for through the contract negotiation process is therefore unpersuasive. Finally, courts are reluctant to allow too much examination of individual circumstances because in addition to being very time consuming (and therefore costly), such a process hugely undermines certainty for all involved. In cases where a breach of human rights is found, of course we may say that the uncertainty, cost and delay were warranted by the protection of fundamental standards. Where no breach is found, the whole process will have been hugely damaging to the interests of the individuals concerned. Thus not examining human rights in relation to property law except in the most exceptional of cases is at once potentially sweeping a series of problems under the carpet, and yet also preventing a series of alternative problems emerging.

This is not to argue that the balance is currently struck in the right place, but that here the principle of sensitivity to context is shown in particularly sharp relief, allowing us to examine the precise effects of un-thinking total compliance with this principle. Furthermore, it cannot be said either that the current approach does wonders for the degree of certainty present in the law. It is true that a lawyer advising client could give a relatively clear statement that any human rights challenge, whether against a public authority or a private individual is likely to fail, it is not entirely satisfactory that they are unable to point to why it will fail, be that because the courts simply will not engage with it, because the structural question of horizontal effect has not been resolved, or because the balance being sought has already been assessed and found compliant. In this sense, in failing to be truly sensitive to context, we cannot truly say that the current approach has achieved certainty either.

Finally, it goes without saying that recognition of the social role of land law involves a recognition of the ways in which fundamental rights should interact with what is a relatively 'closed' system. When one examines the facts of many of the cases studied in this chapter, one can see a number of repeated themes. In many of the cases, human rights challenges are brought by very vulnerable individuals—those with mental health problems, disabilities, or home lives blighted by violence or domestic abuse. In these cases, the degree of leeway given by land law for their individual cases is minimal, and they are seeking to be treated differently than most because of these problems in their lives. We must recognise that as a social institution, land law is currently deliberately unable to confer such differential treatment and we must ask whether this is satisfactory in a system which, after all, has been consciously designed to achieve a certain set of social purposes.

From a doctrinal perspective, the main challenge in the relationship between human rights and property law lies in the lack of clarity and lack of understanding about the various mechanisms in play. From a wider analytical frame, however, we can see that there is much to be done in this area but that the starting point has to be recognising that there is an interaction and that we should decide how we want this interaction to be managed, rather than pretending that the interaction is not there.

TABLE OF DEFINITIONS

Vertical effect	The impact of human rights in an action between citizen and a public authority alleging public authority breach.
Horizontal effect	The impact of human rights in an action between private citizens.
Article 8	Right to a private life, of relevance to property law as the right to one's home.
Article 10	Right to freedom of expression.
Article 11	Right to freedom of association.
Article 1 of the first protocol	Right to property.
Interpretation obligation	The obligation resting on a court to interpret legislation in compliance with human rights as far as possible.
Declaration of incompatibility	The power of a court to declare that a statutory provision is in irresolvable conflict with human rights provisions.

FURTHER READING

There is a lot of writing on the interaction between human rights and private law generally, and property law specifically. For a starting point, see:

GOYMOUR, A., 'Property and Housing' in HOFFMAN, D. (ed), *The Impact of the UK Human Rights Act on Private Law* (CUP, 2011).

LEES, E., 'Article 8, proportionality and horizontal effect' (2017) 133 LQR 31.

NIELD, S., 'Shutting the door on horizontal effect: McDonald v McDonald' [2017] Conv 60.

WALSH, R., 'Stability and predictability in English property law—the impact of article 8 of the European Convention on Human Rights reassessed' (2015) LQR 131, 585.

18

TORTS

18.1 Introduction	582	18.5 Conclusion	604
18.2 Trespass	583	Principles	605
18.3 Nuisance	587	Table of Definitions	606
18.4 *Rylands v Fletcher*	604	Further Reading	606

> **CHAPTER GOALS**
>
> By the end of this chapter you should understand:
>
> - The basic components of the torts of trespass and nuisance (and the additional rules arising under *Rylands v Fletcher*);
> - The relationship between these torts and rights in land; and
> - The remedies which are available in response to such tortious actions.

18.1 INTRODUCTION

For much of this book we have been concerned with how proprietary interests in land are created, negotiated, and rank between each other. None of this tells us how they are protected against the outside world. This is where tort law comes in, for it is in actions on the basis of tort that individuals are able to protect their proprietary entitlements in relation to land. This book considers two torts relevant to the operation of rights in land: trespass and nuisance. Of course, other torts may tangentially affect and protect property rights. Actions can be brought in negligence, for example, against those who carelessly damage property by their actions, causing loss, and that could cover damage to land. However, trespass and nuisance are the torts against land, or at least, against rights in land, and in that sense are of special concern in this book.

18.2 TRESPASS

Trespass to land is the unlawful interference with or incursion on another's possession of land. It is not a tort which protects *ownership* (indeed, as we have noted throughout this book, there is no such concept in English law). Its operation is relative. Thus, a trespasser can themselves sue a subsequent trespasser on the basis of this tort, if the first trespasser has gone into possession of the land. Trespass in this sense is a tort against *possession of land*.

18.2.1 WHAT CONSTITUTES A TRESPASS?

Unlike many torts, this tort is committed merely by physical presence within the zone of possession of another. It does not require a particular state of mind in terms of intention, nor any knowledge or carelessness. Furthermore, trespass can be committed through the unlawful interference with some aspect of the land without a need for the physical presence of the tortfeasor on the land—eg the overhanging of trees, and the leaning of things against another's wall.[1] Indeed, the committing of trespass is remarkably easy. Furthermore, there is no defence to trespass if the trespasser had no knowledge of the trespass, even if they genuinely and reasonably believed that the relevant land actually belonged to them. In comparison to a lot of tort actions, trespass is therefore very easy to prove in terms of the defendant's acts. The more difficult questions are who is able to sue in trespass, and what the appropriate remedy should be.

> **Summary: Trespass**
>
> Trespass consists of physical presence (either personal, or of belongings) within the zone of possession of another.

18.2.2 WHO CAN SUE IN TRESPASS?

Given the intimacy of connection between the tort of trespass and possession of land, it is no surprise that the ability to sue in trespass falls to a person in possession of land, at least in the majority of cases. We saw in chapter 2 at 2.2.3 how the line can be occasionally blurred in this respect in the discussion of *Manchester Airport v Dutton*[2] and related cases. It does not matter whether or not the person in possession is themselves a trespasser. This is thanks to the English law reliance on the concept of relativity of possession (again, see chapters 2 and 9). Of course, a trespasser cannot however maintain an action against a person with a superior title to them, either because they themselves had been in possession earlier as a trespasser (subject to limitation rules as discussed in chapter 6), or because they are in fact the paper title-holder. As a consequence of this, it is also impossible for a trespasser to defend themselves on the basis that the person suing them

---

[1] Eg *Gregory v Piper* (1929) 8 BC 591.
[2] *Manchester Airport v Dutton* [2000] QB 133 (CA).

for trespass is not the paper title-holder. It is not a defence to a claim in trespass that the person bringing the action is also a trespasser.

Given the importance of possession to the operation of this tort, it is essential to be able to ascertain who is in possession of land. For an understanding of this concept, consider chapter 6 on adverse possession and chapter 10 concerning leases.

> **Summary: Who can sue in trespass?**
>
> Except in very rare cases, an action in trespass lies at the suit of a person in possession of land.

18.2.3 DEFENCES TO AN ACTION IN TRESPASS

Trespasses will not be actionable if the person entering the land of another can show that their entry onto the land was 'justifiable', eg because they have the benefit of an easement or profit, or a licence to be on land. Indeed, a licence, in proprietary terms, is merely a permission to be on land and thus operates as a defence to trespass by definition. It is important to note, in this respect, the discussion in chapter 2, section 2.2.1, concerning the nature of property rights and the nature of licences, and the effect that licences can have on third parties in terms of binding that third party to a permission given by a previous owner of land. It is also possible to avoid liability in trespass where, for example, entry onto the land was necessary to save a life.[3] This is, of course, relatively rare.

18.2.4 REMEDIES

The remedies available for trespass are damages and orders for possession where appropriate.

18.2.4.1 Damages

A claimant who suffers trespass will be able to recover damages. If he has suffered substantial loss as a result of the trespass, then of course the measure of damages will reflect that. But in many cases trespass does not cause such identifiable economic loss. In such cases, it is unlikely that a person with only a very transitory interest in the land would be able to recover any damages at all. A squatter of only one day's occupation has no right in the land beyond his possessory freehold title of one day's duration, nor a right to remain, and so any person coming onto the land deprives him of something of very limited value. However, there will be cases where mere deprivation of a right to possession through the trespass of another is remedied with an action in damages to the value of the land. If substantial damage has been caused, there are three types of such damage: advantage to the trespasser received from the claimant without compensation; physical damage to the land; and removal of items which were previously part of the land—'severance' of objects.

In the first case, the 'loss' is essentially a loss of ability to control access to land, even if no damage was done. It is in this sense an objection to entry based on principle. In order to reflect this, the courts use a fictitious negotiation approach to ascertain how much the landowner would reasonably be able to charge for the access that the defendant has gained through their trespass.

---

[3] *Maleverer v Spinke* (1583) Dyer 53b.

Further analysis: Negotiated damages in trespass and *Eaton Mansions (Westminster) Ltd v Stinger Compania De Inversion SA* **[2013] EWCA Civ 1308**

The confirmation of the negotiated damages approach in the recent Court of Appeal decision in *Eaton Mansions (Westminster) Ltd v Stinger Compania De Inversion SA*[4] has highlighted the unusual nature of this remedy, and there has been extensive consideration in the literature about how this approach to damages does and should work. For example, Chew highlights that the court was required to consider the information that they should take into account when assessing hypothetical agreements:

'The judge went on to consider how hypothetical the hypothetical parties were. This is a tension at the heart of the negotiating damages concept. By definition, the parties will not have successfully negotiated for the infringement of the right that did in fact occur. They may not have negotiated at all, or if they did negotiate, those negotiations will have failed. If the negotiations had succeeded, there would have been no wrong and so no need to quantify damages by reference to negotiations. Therefore, there is an element of abstraction in the quantification as the court necessarily moves away from the real parties. The judge identifies acting reasonably as "an integral feature" of the hypothetical parties. This is consistently the case in negotiating fee damages, and also in non-legal definitions of valuation… As the judge noted at [59], this reasonableness requirement divorces the exercise from the actual position of that of the real parties. This is often the case, and makes the negotiations hypothetical in a very important sense. The more difficult issue is how far other characteristics of the actual parties are incorporated into the hypothetical negotiations. The judge noted that the "focus of more recent authorities appears to be on the actual parties, albeit ignoring their personal characteristics". This raises a paradox: how does one focus on the actual parties whilst ignoring their characteristics?'.[5]

One feature of this approach to remedies, therefore, is that assumptions have to be made that the personalities in the case do not, more often than not, have the personalities that they do! The assumption of reasonableness and willingness to negotiate, in cases of on-going and deliberate trespass in particular, is a fictitious one. This is not to say that the idea of negotiated damages is entirely divorced from common sense, but rather that it is certainly artificial.

Furthermore, the decision in *Eaton Mansions* also prompted consideration of whether the court will consider the effect of the trespass beyond, as it were, the actual dates of that trespass, when considering the negotiated damages. In other words, the court was required to consider whether, in the fictitious negotiation, they should take account of the fact that the person in possession would never have allowed access for such a short period of time (or, in this case, where the trespass was by a tenant, whether this should be for the duration of the lease, or the duration of the actual trespass). The court rejected an approach which allowed recovery beyond the actual period of trespass. Per Patten LJ:

'Although the hypothetical negotiations for a licence fee have been adopted as a convenient means of valuing the benefit to the trespasser (and, in that sense, the loss to the claimant) which results from the defendant's tortious conduct, its accuracy depends upon the negotiations centering on the period and extent of the trespass which actually occurred. The nature and duration of the trespass is not a valuation event in the sense in which that term was used in *Lunn Poly* but rather it is what dictates and shapes the nature of the valuation exercise. It is therefore wrong to say that the parties would not have known at the commencement of the trespass how long it would last. The valuation construct is that the parties must be treated as having negotiated for a licence which covered the acts of trespass that actually occurred. The defendant is not required to pay damages for anything else.'[6]

---

[4] *Eaton Mansions (Westminster) Ltd v Stinger Compania De Inversion SA* [2013] EWCA Civ 1308, [2014] HLR 4.
[5] J Chew, 'What price trespass? *Eaton Mansions v Stinger*' [2013] Conv 439, 445.
[6] *Eaton Mansions (Westminster) Ltd v Stinger Compania De Inversion SA* [2013] EWCA Civ 1308, [2014] HLR 4, [21].

> This position must be correct. As Hill and Morton explain, 'the conclusion that the trespasser must only pay by reference to the period of trespass and the value of the benefit of the trespass must be right'[7] since otherwise the person in possession of the land would have been able to recover their losses twice.
>
> Finally, this, and other cases in trespass, contribute to the wider discussion concerning the question of whether it ought to be possible to focus not on the harm done to the landowner by the trespass, but rather to strip the trespasser of any profit they may have made as a result of their trespass, profits which may well be substantial. This issue has been considered by Edelman when considering an American case:[8]
>
>> 'In the same manner as cases of unjust enrichment, English courts have made profits awards for the wrong of trespass where the profit represents the traceable proceeds of value transferred from the plaintiff, such as cases of removal of coal from a plaintiff's land... However, cases which operate to award a plaintiff the true profit, independently of any value transferred (where those profits would never have accrued to the plaintiff and are not traceable to any property transferred from the plaintiff), are less common. In cases where the trespass is wilful, some courts in the United States have been prepared to strip a defendant of such profits... In England, such a deliberate trespass would probably also result in profits being stripped from the defendant with an award of exemplary damages, for wrongful conduct designed to make a profit.'[9]
>
> As is clear from Edleman's comments, however, this approach is certainly not the norm.
>
> Finally, it is worth noting that this approach to remedies in trespass does not appear to have been significantly affected by the Supreme Court decision in *Morris-Garner v One Step*[10] which has limited the availability of negotiated damages in other contexts, where the actual loss suffered may be more easily identified.

Where there is physical damage to the land—through damage to doors, locks etc—then the courts will usually assess how much of a loss in value the land has suffered (rather than how much it costs to repair). This is essentially a reflection of the fact that this is a tort against the value inherent in the privatisation of proprietary interests in land. Sometimes the courts will look at repair costs, as long as they are reasonable, on the 'principle of putting the claimant he had been in prior to the infliction of harm'.[11] Finally, where items have been taken from the land, then the claimant can cover the value of those things.

18.2.4.2 Order for possession

We considered the role of actions for recovery of possession of land in chapter 2 when considering *Dutton* (see 2.2.3). This action allows a claimant who has been dispossessed by a trespasser to recover possession to the land. To do this he has to show that he has some claim to the land, in line with the general principle earlier that there is effectively a presumption of title in favour of a person currently in possession.

---

[7] C Hill and T Morton, 'Assessment of damages for trespass - the hypothetical negotiation model' (2014) 18 Landlord and Tenant Law Review 26, 29.
[8] J Edelman, 'Restitutionary damages for torts' (2000) 116 LQR 542.
[9] J Edelman, 'Restitutionary damages for torts' (2000) 116 LQR 542, 544.
[10] *Morris-Garner v One Step (Support) Ltd* [2018] UKSC 20.
[11] J Murphy, in M A Jones (general editor), *Clerk and Lindsell on Torts* (Thompson & Reuters, London, 2010), [19–66].

> **Summary: Remedies**
>
> Remedies for trespass lie in damages, and in an order for possession. An order for possession allows the claimant to recover possession of the relevant land. An award of damages will be calculated according to the nature of the loss suffered. Where the loss is simply the unlawful incursion, then a negotiated damages approach will be taken. Where the loss is an identifiable diminution in the value of land or property, the damages will reflect that loss.

18.3 NUISANCE

Unlike trespass, which is in many ways a straightforward tort claim, the law relating to nuisance is complex and even incoherent. Furthermore, given the complexity of the rules, and their place at the boundary between property and tort law, some have argued that whilst a general understanding of what nuisance does is useful, a fully coherent conceptual picture is not possible. This makes it difficult, if not impossible, to provide a reasonably concise but still accurate presentation of the tort, which captures the enormous range of circumstances in which liability in nuisance can be found. From claims relating to noxious smells arising from landfill,[12] to noisy neighbours,[13] nuisance covers a wide range of cases and its principles, although centred around certain core elements, do not explain all the case law as it currently stands.

In its absolute basic terms, nuisance is the tort of interference with another's reasonable use or enjoyment of their land, usually as a result of an unreasonable use of neighbouring land. In this part, we consider first what the role of nuisance is in relation to property, before examining what acts can constitute a nuisance, who can sue and be sued in nuisance, defences, and finally, remedies. We then explore the related issue of liability under *Rylands v Fletcher*.[14] This explanation should not be read as comprehensive, especially in relation to the types of acts which can constitute a nuisance. There is an enormous amount of case law, and it is possible only to give a flavour of the *sorts of acts* which can give rise to a nuisance here.

In reading this chapter, it is also important to realise that, in respect of the modern law, we can say that the difficulties caused by nuisance extend beyond this issue of categorisation and coherence—significant though that issue is—into a more subtle and perhaps more invidious prioritisation of the rights and interests of certain kinds of persons within the purview of the legal system, a prioritisation that maintains privilege and hinders environmental and social justice. In this sense, the dusty parameters of 19th century tort law can be seen as maintaining a 19th century approach to different strata of society in terms of wealth and influence.

18.3.1 THE ROLE OF NUISANCE

We noted earlier that nuisance is a remarkably incoherent tort. Its boundaries are blurred; its justification and purpose, unclear. Indeed, this incoherence may be a result of the very role which

---

[12] *Barr v Biffa Waste Services Ltd* [2012] EWCA Civ 312, [2013] QB 455.
[13] Eg *Halsey v Esso Petroleum Co Ltd* [1961] 1 WLR 683 (QB).
[14] *Rylands v Fletcher* (1868) LR 3 HL 330.

we expect this tort to play. Nevertheless, as Essert explains, it may be possible to, at the very least, provide a coherent explanation of how the tort of nuisance sits in relation to our understanding of property rights and that finding such an explanation is extremely important to our understanding of property in land:

> 'A moment's reflection on these formulas [defining nuisance]—Just what is it to use and enjoy land or to have that use and enjoyment interfered with? What is it to have a right to use and enjoy real property?—shows that the tort of nuisance sits close to the heat of a justification of property rights, a topic of perennial and crucial concern. A complete theory of property would help explain what counts and what does not count as nuisance, since if we knew what the right to use and enjoy property was, we would be closer to knowing what counts as interfering with it. And conversely, a complete theory of nuisance would help explain the rights definitive of ownership of real property, since the scope of what does or does not count as an infringement of that right would help us see the scope of the right itself. So anyone concerned—as we should all be—with the nature and justification of private ownership should be concerned with nuisance law'.[15]

The tort of nuisance is, in effect, an unreasonable interference with another's reasonable use and enjoyment of their property right. It is a tort which has at its heart the idea of balance and is the means by which the liberty of one landowner to act in a particular way on their own land is weighed against the liberty of another to be free from the inconvenience or disturbance which such nuisances cause. Nuisance is also a tort which can be seen most prominently as a product of its history, of the history behind the shape and scale of our cities, and the types of property which we inhabit. Similar to easements, there are a number of valid nuisance claims which seem very odd in modern law: actions against neighbours where persons with small pox were present on neighbouring land;[16] actions against a shop for selling pornographic material;[17] and using a property for prostitution[18] have all constituted valid actions in nuisance. Some of these may seem now to be rather more the preserve of public law than of private actions in tort; others a question of free speech over neighbourly sensibilities.

However, it must be kept in mind when considering the scope of the tort, that it developed very quickly in the 19th and early 20th centuries in response to rapid industrialisation, changing patterns of occupation from rural to urban dwelling, and to societal changes in terms of how land was owned and occupied, change accelerated by the first and second world wars. In this way, nuisance has had to act as early anti-pollution and air quality control;[19] as defender of public health against infectious disease;[20] and as protector against harassment and intimidation.[21] It is perhaps unsurprising when this history is kept in mind that the boundaries of the tort are relatively incoherent. The following section is therefore split into two halves: the first considers whether it is possible to develop a *single* explanation as to the sorts of acts which can constitute nuisance; the second considers some of the established categories of nuisance.

---

[15] C Essert, 'Nuisance and the normative boundaries of ownership' (2016) 52 Tulsa Law Review 85, 86.
[16] *Metropolitan Asylum District Managers v Hill (No.2)* (1881) 6 App Cas 193 (HL).
[17] *Laws v Florinplace Ltd* [1981] 1 All ER 659.
[18] *Thompson-Schwab v Costaki* [1956] 1 WLR 335 (CA).
[19] See B Pontin, *Nuisance Law in Context: A Study of Injunctions in Practice* (Lawtext Publishing, London, 2013).
[20] *Metropolitan Asylum District Managers v Hill (No.2)* (1881) 6 App Cas 193 (HL).
[21] *Church of Jesus Christ of the Latter-Day Saints v Price* [2004] EWHC 3245 (QB).

18.3.1.1 A unified explanation?

One of the leading tort law textbooks defines nuisance as, 'unlawful interference with a person's use or enjoyment of land, or some right over, or in connection with it'.[22] A very broad definition, this does not really provide a very clear explanation of what can and cannot be an act forming the basis of an action in nuisance. However, what it does do is highlight the importance of interference with *use* of land—not, for example, focussing on the presence of a foreign substance or person on the claimant's land. It is this focus on the usability of land which is said to help distinguish the tort of nuisance from that of trespass. However, as we shall see, not all academics agree that this is the best way to characterise nuisance. Other jurisdictions do nevertheless seem to take a similar approach to nuisance, as shown by the US restatement of torts which provides that, 'a private nuisance is a non-trespassory invasion of another's interest in the private use and enjoyment of land'. We can see again here the focus on the use and enjoyment of land, rather than on the direct interference with that land. Scots law takes a similar approach,[23] as Nolan has explained.[24]

This is certainly a relatively convincing account of what nuisance does—and indeed, as we shall see later—has the advantage over other, perhaps more precise and predictable theories—of best reflecting the totality of the case law, rather than struggling to account for some of the more unusual (particularly historical) cases. The downside of this theory is that it does not really explain when a nuisance is actionable and is, in this sense, somewhat circular. It requires that we establish what 'enjoyment' a person is entitled to in relation to their land, and that depends upon the boundaries—both physical and normative—in relation to their property. However, establishing those boundaries is as much a matter of looking at the nuisance case law, as it is consideration of some external rules. Thus, an act interferes with the (justified) usability of land where it is a nuisance, and is a nuisance where it interferes with such (justified) usability.

This focus on the use (or in the words of Nolan[25] and Newman,[26] usability) of land, is challenged by others who seek to show that the essence of the tort is in fact a physical invasion of land which somehow does not constitute a trespass. This alternative approach is explained by Epstein, who argued that nuisance arises in case of 'invasions of the plaintiff's property that fall short of trespasses' but which still constitute interference into the use and enjoyment of land.[27] Merrill has taken this further, removing the 'use and enjoyment' aspects of Epstein's approach, and arguing that nuisance is properly understood as the tort which protects the right to exclude interference by others, rather than protecting use.[28] This essentially highlights the other side of the coin to the use theory: it is not about what I can do on my land, but rather about what you cannot do in relation to my land. Thus, on this approach, trespass is the tort which protects the right to exclude a *person* crossing the physical boundary onto your land, whereas nuisance becomes the tort which

---

[22] W E Peel and J Goudkamp, *Winfield & Jolowicz on Tort* (19th ed) (Sweet & Maxwell, London, 2014) [15–008].
[23] *The Laws of Scotland: Stair Memorial Encyclopaedia* (Lexis Nexis, London, updates on-going), [2017].
[24] *Forthcoming*, D Nolan, 'The essence of private nuisance'.
[25] *Forthcoming*, D Nolan, 'The essence of private nuisance'.
[26] C Newman, 'Using things, defining property' in J Penner and M Otsuka (eds), Property Theory (Cambridge, Cambridge University Press, forthcoming) 23, cited in *Forthcoming*, D Nolan, 'The essence of private nuisance'.
[27] R Epstein, (1979) 8 Journal of Legal Studies 49, 53.
[28] T Merrill, 'Trespass, nuisance, and the costs of determining property rights' (1985) 14 Journal of Legal Studies 13, 27–30.

protects your right to keep up a more metaphorical boundary. The tort then no longer protects your activities within that space, but rather protects your right to not have others interfere within that space. This assessment of nuisance is, in a sense, much more focussed on the economic value of land (which comes essentially from its exclusivity), than it is on the more 'human-centred' notions of use and enjoyment.

Arguments which focus on the interference with land tend to do so from a number of different perspectives, including this economic function. However, McFarlane and Douglas come at this from a different perspective and they argue that it is not possible to see nuisance as being about protection of enjoyment and use because the common law does not give such a right to enjoy and use in the first place.[29] There is, on their thesis, no aspect of property law which confers this right, and so tort law cannot be said to be concerned with protecting it. Per Douglas, 'the gist of liability in nuisance is not the impairment of the utility of the freeholder's land, but the physical interference with this'.[30]

These approaches, challenging the more orthodox 'use' view as they do, however, have now been the subject of a 'counter-challenge'. Essert for example has explained in detail why the view which Douglas and McFarlane propose, despite its appealing simplicity, is wrong. He gives a number of reasons for this. First, he shows by referring to a number of cases, that it is quite simply untrue as a matter of case law that nuisance only involves direct interference. Of the cases he cites we have already mentioned some—the fear of contagious disease, the displeasure at seeing a shop selling pornography in the vicinity. These do not involve the transfer of something onto, or the direct interference with, the claimant's land. As Essert notes, 'the case books are rife with cases in which liability for nuisance does not rest on any kind of emanation by defendant onto plaintiffs' land'.[31]

Accounts such as those of Douglas and McFarlane do not deny, however, that the interferences in such cases may be difficult to find. Rather, they say that despite the difficulty in some cases, this should still be considered to be the driving paradigm of nuisance. Essert explores the arguments made by Douglas and MacFarlane as to why we should *nevertheless* see these cases as interferences, despite the conceptual difficulties in so-doing. Douglas and MacFarlane attempt to explain the prostitution case earlier, for example, as being an invasion in the sense that those viewing the prostitutes, and being offended by them, were in fact offended as a result of the invasion of light rays.[32] This, as Essert suggests, is not a particularly convincing argument because it means that everyday millions of nuisances are committed against (almost) every single landowner because everyday the sight of someone else's property must be visible from at least one point on that person's land (save perhaps the very rare if not impossible instance of a person owning an entire island with only international waters beyond the boundaries of their proprietary rights).[33]

---

[29] S Douglas and B McFarlane, 'Defining property rights' in J Penner and H Smith, *Philosophical Foundations of Private Law* (OUP, Oxford, 2013).

[30] S Douglas, 'The content of a freehold: a "right to use" Land?' (2013) 7 Modern Studies in Property Law (N Hopkins, ed).

[31] C Essert, 'Nuisance and the normative boundaries of ownership' (2016) 52 Tulsa Law Review 85, 96.

[32] S Douglas and B McFarlane, 'Defining property rights' in J Penner and H Smith, *Philosophical Foundations of Private Law* (OUP, Oxford, 2013), 232.

[33] C Essert, 'Nuisance and the normative boundaries of ownership' (2016) 52 Tulsa Law Review 85, 97.

The result of this is that despite the strength of the arguments that nuisance is not about protecting use—either because such a characterisation does not reflect the economic function of the tort of nuisance, or because it suggests that property rights in land confer on a person the right to enjoy and use land whereas in fact this is *not* what property rights allow a person to do—the 'usability' approach nevertheless seems to be the more convincing explanation. However, the fact that this explanation also has its flaws, suggests that in reality there is no single explanation of nuisance, and that the various competing academic approaches are really concerned with what nuisance *should* protect, rather than being wholly accurate explanations as to what it already does protect.

18.3.2 CATEGORIES OF NUISANCE

It is said in the orthodox academic commentary on nuisance that there are three kinds of nuisances (a characterisation challenged by the unifying theories explored earlier): nuisance by encroachment, which involves a physical incursion of some substance or items onto the claimant's land; nuisance by physical damage; and nuisance by interference with enjoyment and comfort.[34] Whatever the merits of these arguments, however, from a descriptive perspective it makes sense to at least keep in mind these three categories in order to provide a point of access into the relevant case law.

18.3.2.1 Encroachment

Nuisance by direct encroachment or damage is usually easy to detect. It involves cases where, thanks to the design of a property or similar, some substance crosses the physical boundary between two plots of land so as to interfere with the claimant's rights. Examples in the case law include the growth of tree roots into another's land causing problems on that land;[35] and of trees overhanging land (which could also be considered a direct trespass).[36] Unlike in relation to some other forms of nuisance, when dealing with direct invasions of this sort, there is no need to consider reasonableness in the sense that no balancing act is done to take into account the nature of the overall environment in the locality to establish whether the interference is unreasonable. Of course, it may be that the user of the defendant's land is reasonable, but there is no balancing act required to show that *prima facie* the encroachment is not a reasonable step to take in relation to another's land. The different way in which such encroachment cases are treated in relation to this question of location can be seen from the comments of Lord Westbury LC in *St Helen's Smelting Co v Tipping*:[37]

> 'it is a very desirable thing to mark the difference between an action brought for a nuisance upon the ground that the alleged nuisance produces material injury to the property, and an action brought for a nuisance on the ground that the thing alleged to be a nuisance is productive of sensible personal discomfort. With regard to the latter, namely, the personal inconvenience and interference with one's enjoyment, one's quiet, one's personal freedom, anything that discomposes or injuriously affects the senses or the nerves, whether that may or may not be denominated a nuisance, must undoubtedly depend greatly on the circumstances of the place where the thing complained of actually occurs. If a man lives in a town, it is necessary that he should subject himself to the consequences of those operations of trade which may be carried on in his immediate locality, which are actually necessary

---

[34] J Murphy, in M A Jones (general editor), *Clerk and Lindsell on Torts* (Thompson & Reuters, London, 2010).
[35] *Butler v Standard Telephones & Cables Ltd* [1940] 1 KB 399 (KB).
[36] *Smith v Giddy* [1904] 2 KB 448 (KB).
[37] *St Helens Smelting Co v Tipping* 11 ER 1483, (1865) 11 HL Cas 642 (HL).

for trade and commerce, and also for the enjoyment of property, and for the benefit of the inhabitants of the town and of the public at large. If a man lives in a street where there are numerous shops, and a shop is opened next door to him, which is carried on in a fair and reasonable way, he has no ground for complaint, because to himself individually there may arise much discomfort from the trade carried on in that shop. But when an occupation is carried on by one person in the neighbourhood of another, and the result of that trade, or occupation, or business, is a material injury to property, then there unquestionably arises a very different consideration.'[38]

We consider the flip side of this discussion, ie that some nuisances do depend upon the character of the location, ('the locality principle') later.

18.3.2.2 Direct damage

Similar comments can be made about those nuisances which appear to involve direct physical damage to property (without the encroachment of a substance per se), eg as a result of vibrations on land damaging neighbouring property (of course, in a sense, this does involve the 'travel' of a substance, ie the vibration wave)[39] but it can be sensibly distinguished from the passage of a harmful chemical, or the damage caused by flood water. However, there is an increasingly popular view that in modern law, physical damage cases may be better understood as cases of negligence rather than nuisance. As Lee notes:

> '[a]s negligence has become dominant in tort, there has been a definite and unhelpful confusion between negligence and nuisance. There is some controversy as to whether the confusion is due to the type of harm the claimant suffers, and so whether there is still a place for physical damage to property in private nuisance.'[40]

This is not an issue which can sensibly be resolved here, but it is useful to note the 'shaky ground' which physical damage cases maintain in relation to their continuing status within the category of nuisance. We consider the relationship between nuisance and negligence further later.

18.3.2.3 Interference with comfort and enjoyment

Nuisances which are said to be constituted by interference with enjoyment can be harder to spot, and require a more delicate balancing exercise, but are, in this way, the more 'classic' explanations of what constitutes an interference with the usability of another's land. Examples of the kinds of behaviour which are said to result in such an interference include the production of noxious smells;[41] spreading coal dust;[42] the using of property as a hospital for infectious disease, such as smallpox;[43] and loud noises—such as from musical instruments, machinery, vehicles, or animals, amongst much else.[44]

However, it will not always be the case that any action of this kind will be enough to constitute a nuisance, even if there are loud noises, coal dust, or smells etc. This is because in cases involving interference with comfort in relation to the relevant land, there is always a balance to be struck.

---

[38] *St Helens Smelting Co v Tipping* 11 ER 1483, (1865) 11 HL Cas 642 (HL), Lord Westbury, taken from Bailii.
[39] *Shelfer v City of London Electric Lighting Co (No.1)* [1895] 1 Ch 287 (CA).
[40] M Lee, 'What is private nuisance?' (2003) 119 LQR 298, 300.
[41] *St Helens Smelting Co v Tipping* 11 ER 1483, (1865) 11 HL Cas 642 (HL).
[42] *Pwllbach Colliery Co Ltd v Woodman* [1915] AC 634 (HL).
[43] *Metropolitan Asylum District Managers v Hill (No.2)* (1881) 6 App Cas 193 (HL).
[44] Eg *Halsey v Esso Petroleum Co Ltd* [1961] 1 WLR 683 (QB).

This balance is determined by two factors: the degree of interference with the expected standard of comfort, and the degree to which this interference is created by some sort of unreasonable behaviour on the part of the defendant. The courts therefore consider whether the act is enough to constitute a nuisance from these two perspectives.

Interference with claimant's comfort

Considering first the nature of the claimant's comfort, in all nuisance cases there will be questions as to the degree of interference a claimant is expected to put up with. As Clerk and Lindsell explain, 'in organised society everyone must put up with a certain amount of discomfort and annoyance caused by the legitimate activities of his neighbours'.[45] For example, it would be wholly unreasonable for a landowner to spend all day drilling holes in a wall just for the sheer joy of making the noise, knowing that this was extremely loud for their neighbour. By contrast, it cannot be considered too much to ask to expect a neighbour to put up with the noise of the occasional comings and goings of visitors, and voices in the street. The difficulty comes in finding the tipping point, and in articulating for future cases what factors should be taken into account in finding the line. To articulate this balance, the courts, as we have noted, rely on the idea of 'unreasonable interference with reasonable user'—putting limitations on both what the claimant can expect to avoid, and what the defendant can expect to be able to do. In this section we consider those factors which make up the court's assessment as to whether any interference is too extensive. In the following section, we explore the question from the perspective of the defendant.

The analysis in determining the question of the claimant's entitlement in terms of their own comfort is very fact and circumstances sensitive, as noted in *Stone v Bolton*:[46]

> 'Whether such an act does constitute a nuisance must be determined not merely by an abstract consideration of the act itself, but by reference to all the circumstances of the particular case, including, for example, the time of the commission of the act complained of; the place of its commission; the manner of committing it, that is, whether it is done wantonly or in the reasonable exercise of right; and the effect of its commission, that is, whether those effects are transitory or permanent, occasional or continuous; so that the question of nuisance or no nuisance is one of fact'.[47]

The courts therefore will look at these factors: timings, the manner of the act, the repeated nature of any act, the effect of the interferences, etc, to determine whether the act is not one which, keeping in mind the principles of give and take and (importantly) the locality principle (which we consider later—in brief it is the idea that the extent of the claimant's entitlement to enjoy their land is in part determined by the nature of the locality in which their land is situated).

Extra-sensitive claimant

What happens in cases where for some reason the claimant is unusually sensitive to the kind of activity being carried out on the defendant's land? This issue has been considered in a number of cases and it is clear that the claimant's unusual use of their land will not be taken into account.[48]

---

[45] J Murphy, in M A Jones (general editor), *Clerk and Lindsell on Torts* (Thompson & Reuters, London, 2010), [20–10].
[46] *Stone v Bolton* [1949] 1 All ER 237 (HC).
[47] *Stone v Bolton* [1949] 1 All ER 237, 238–9 (HC).
[48] *Robinson v Kilvert* (1889) 41 ChD 88 (CA).

Although this principle may seem somewhat harsh, it is a reflection of the fact that where a person decides to put their land to an unusually sensitive use, they cannot thereby unilaterally alter the balance between themselves and their neighbours by making it impossible for those neighbours to continue to carry out what had otherwise been a lawful activity. This is not to say that an activity which is currently lawful cannot later become a nuisance, but rather the claimant cannot render it so where their use falls outside the normal range of uses and instead becomes something hyper-sensitive. Where, however, the claimant's use of their land is not particularly unusual, but which means that an activity which was previously affecting no one's comfort is now significant, that will be relevant to the establishment of the nuisance. We can show this with an example.

Imagine that Rosemary has recently purchased freehold title to a large barn deep in the countryside. It is situated next to a farm. The farmer, Tony, has developed a system of working which involves packaging and processing of produce in the middle of the night. This is a noisy process, not least because of the coming and goings of lorries. However, given that there are no other nearby residents, no one has been disturbed by this process. Rosemary then decides to apply for planning permission to convert the barn into a modern oasis in the countryside. After having completed many months of works, on moving in she discovers the farmer's night time activities. She is very upset and brings an action for nuisance.

On the one hand, we could say that it is Rosemary's own use of the land which has turned what was not a nuisance into a nuisance. It is, in that sense, the sensitivities of this user which have made the activities of the farmer problematic. But, crucially, there is nothing unusual about Rosemary's use of the land which is shaping how Tony's working methods affect her. To put this another way, any time there had been a person resident on this land, Tony's user would have been a *prima facie* nuisance. Prior to the arrival of Rosemary, it was simply that there was no one there to complain. Rosemary would therefore be able to claim in nuisance. Similarly, it is no defence for Tony to say that Rosemary 'came to' the nuisance in the sense that she voluntarily decided to purchase the property when his use was already established. This is not a defence to a nuisance, as was confirmed in the recent decision in *Coventry v Lawrence*,[49] which we discuss later. This principle of the irrelevance of 'coming to the nuisance' is shown by the famous decision in *Miller v Jackson*.[50]

> **Key case: *Miller v Jackson* [1977] QB 966**
>
> This decision is significant not particularly because of the eventual decision, but rather because of the mode of language used in the judgment given by Lord Denning MR. It is best to explain the facts by citing directly this very famous passage:
>
> 'In summertime village cricket is the delight of everyone. Nearly every village has its own cricket field where the young men play and the old men watch. In the village of Lintz in County Durham they have their own ground, where they have played these last 70 years… Yet now after these 70 years a judge of the High Court has ordered that they must not play there any more. He has issued an injunction to stop them.

---

[49] *Coventry (t/a RDC Promotions) v Lawrence* [2014] UKSC 13, [2014] AC 822.
[50] *Miller v Jackson* [1977] QB 966 (CA).

> He has done it at the instance of a newcomer who is no lover of cricket. This newcomer has built, or has had built for him, a house on the edge of the cricket ground which four years ago was a field where cattle grazed. The animals did not mind the cricket. But now this adjoining field has been turned into a housing estate. The newcomer bought one of the houses on the edge of the cricket ground. No doubt the open space was a selling point. Now he complains that when a batsman hits a six the ball has been known to land in his garden or on or near his house… They say that this is intolerable. So they asked the judge to stop the cricket being played. And the judge, much against his will, has felt that he must order the cricket to be stopped: with the consequence, I suppose, that the Lintz Cricket Club will disappear. The cricket ground will be turned to some other use. I expect for more houses or a factory. The young men will turn to other things instead of cricket. The whole village will be much the poorer'.[51]
>
> Perhaps unsurprisingly, Denning MR decided that the claimant could not bring a claim in nuisance here, arguing that they had voluntarily bought this house. This was not the approach of the rest of the Court of Appeal however, who confirmed that there could be liability in nuisance here, it being no defence that the claimants were aware of the cricket ground prior to their arrival. Even in reaching the decision which the court did, however, they nevertheless seem to have taken account of the public interest factors to which the court refers in terms of assessing the appropriate remedy. We return to the question of remedies, and the relationship with public interest, later.

The courts have also been clear that they are unconcerned with 'fussiness' when establishing the existence or otherwise of a nuisance. Thus, per the court in *Walter v Selfe*: 'an inconvenience materially interfering with the ordinary comfort physically of human existence, not merely according to elegant or dainty modes and habits of living, but according to plain and sober and simple notions among the English people',[52] would suffice to establish a nuisance, but the law of tort could not be invoked to protect 'dainty modes of living'.[53]

> ### Summary: Reasonableness of interference
>
> In assessing the levels of interference which a claimant is expected to endure, therefore, we can discern three key principles:
>
> 1. The nature of the interference will be assessed by reference to a multiplicity of factors, all of which go into judging, on the principle of give and take, whether the interference is more than the claimant should reasonably be expected to endure;
> 2. In making this assessment, whilst the court will take account of the nature of the use to which the claimant puts the land, albeit that the fact that their use creates an extra sensitivity to the defendant's activities will not influence the court's assessment of the degree of interference; and
> 3. The fact that the claimant was or could have been aware of the defendant's use of the land prior to their purchase of the land is not relevant to the assessment as to whether they should be expected to endure that use, albeit that it may be relevant to the question of appropriate remedy.

---

[51] *Miller v Jackson* [1977] QB 966 (CA), 976.
[52] *Walter v Selfe* 64 ER 849, (1851) 4 De G & Sm 315, 322.
[53] *Walter v Selfe* 64 ER 849, (1851) 4 De G & Sm 315, 322.

18.3.2.4 Defendant's actions—unreasonableness and foreseeability

Just as it is necessary to take both the degree and nature of the interference with the claimant's enjoyment into account, the courts also consider the degree to which the defendant can be said to have acted unreasonably regardless of how impactful the use is for the claimant. This assessment takes account of factors such as the deliberateness of the harm, the knowledge of the defendant in terms of the likelihood of their activities causing harm, and the foreseeability of harm. The fault of the defendant is also bounded by the principle of 'give and take' in the sense that even where harm is foreseeable, this will not necessarily mean that there is an actionable nuisance if, all things considered, the courts conclude that the use of the defendant's land is nevertheless justifiable. The flipside of this is that there may be liability in nuisance even where damage was *not* foreseeable. Since the tort does not depend upon negligence per se, the degree to which the defendant could have predicted harm is not determinative of that outcome. Again, there is no fixed test, but a fluid and context-dependent assessment of the balance between the parties.

Furthermore, since liability in nuisance depends upon the degree of interference, as well as any question of fault, it is possible for liability to arise in nuisance even where the defendant has tried all that they can to avoid causing a nuisance. This is clear from *Eastern Counties Leather*,[54] where Lord Goff highlighted that, 'the fact that the defendant has taken all reasonable care will not itself exonerate from liability, the relevant control mechanism being found within the principle of reasonable user'[55] (reasonable user is being used as an explanation for the acceptability of the defendant's activities). The courts will not, however, impose liability where harm was not foreseeable in some sense since in such cases it is hard to justify a finding that the use was in any way unreasonable.

> **Further analysis: Nuisance and negligence**
>
> Discussion of factors such as reasonableness and foreseeability bring to mind the tort of negligence. As was mentioned earlier in relation to damage to property in nuisance cases, there is considerable consternation in the literature as to where the boundary line sits between nuisance and negligence. This is a result, in part, of the relatively late development of the independent tort of negligence, and partly a result of a lack of case law clarity as to where the duties owed in tort can be distinguished, and in this respect the relevant principles appear to be converging. For example, the modern law of nuisance takes a much greater account of foreseeability of harm as did the older case law. It is not the place of this textbook, concerned as it is more with the property aspects of nuisance, than the overlap with negligence, to consider these issues in great detail, but it can be helpful to keep in mind when reading the relevant literature on nuisance, as well as when drawing links between different core law subjects.
>
> The difficulty has come about, therefore, because of the relationship and meaning between the concepts of 'reasonable user' which defines liability in nuisance, and the duty of reasonableness which underpins the whole of the law of nuisance. Furthermore, as we have seen earlier, there is considerable difficulty in defining not only the 'edges' of private nuisance, but even its core, and this means that there are a few cases which academics attempt to explain 'out of' nuisance by arguing that they are more

---

[54] *Cambridge Water Co Ltd v Eastern Counties Leather Plc* [1994] 2 AC 264 (HL).
[55] *Cambridge Water Co Ltd v Eastern Counties Leather Plc* [1994] 2 AC 264 (HL), 300.

appropriately seen as a negligence cases and would be decided as such today were it not for the relatively recent development of the law of negligence, particularly as regards pure economic losses.

The approach of the courts has not been particularly helpful in this regard. For example, in *Goldman v Hargrave*,[56] Lord Wilberforce reasoned that: 'the tort of nuisance, uncertain in its boundary, may comprise a wide variety of situations, in some of which negligence plays no part, in others of which it is decisive'.[57] However, the blurring of the boundary line between the two torts should not be seen as undermining the core of nuisance, and it may simply be best to accept that at the edges, there is inevitable difficulty in distinguishing these concepts, particularly since both are concerned to assess how we should treat those who cause harm to others, where their behaviour seems more or less reasonable, as part of living together within a broader society.

18.3.3 LOCALITY PRINCIPLE AND PLANNING PERMISSION

Finally, in respect of the kinds of actions which constitute unlawful interference with enjoyment, it must be kept in mind that for (only) this branch of the tort of nuisance, the balancing act between claimant and defendant will be shaped by the nature of the locality—other uses in the area etc—in which the actions take place. Much debate has been generated in recent years by what is referred to as the locality principle, and also the interaction between nuisance law and the law relating to planning permission. In essence, these debates are about the extent to which the wider community as a whole and the nature of the location should be taken into account in judging what is a nuisance as between two neighbouring private parties. The locality principle was first established in the famous case of *Sturges v Bridgman*,[58] where Theisger LJ stated that:

> 'It may be answered that whether anything is a nuisance or not is a question to be determined, not merely by an abstract consideration of the thing itself, but in reference to its circumstances; what would be a nuisance in Belgrave Square would not necessarily be so in Bermondsey; and where a locality is devoted to a particular trade or manufacture carried on by the traders or manufacturers in a particular and established manner not constituting a public nuisance, Judges and juries would be justified in finding… that the trade or manufacture so carried on in that locality is not a private or actionable wrong… It would be on the one hand in a very high degree unreasonable and undesirable that there should be a right of action for acts which are not in the present condition of the adjoining land, and possibly never will be any annoyance or inconvenience to either its owner or occupier; and it would be on the other hand in an equally degree unjust, and, from a public point of view, inexpedient that the use and value of the adjoining land should, for all time and under all circumstances, be restricted and diminished by reason of the continuance of acts incapable of physical interruption, and which the law gives no power to prevent'.[59]

This principle has been affirmed many times since, but it has also been made clear, as we mentioned earlier, that the locality principle will not apply to all cases of nuisance. Rather, it only applies in so-called amenity cases. Thus, if McFarlane and Douglas amongst others are right about

---

[56] *Goldman v Hargrave* [1967] 1 AC 645 (PC).
[57] *Goldman v Hargrave* [1967] 1 AC 645 (PC), 657.
[58] *Sturges v Bridgman* (1879) 11 ChD 852 (CA).
[59] *Sturges v Bridgman* (1879) 11 ChD 852 (CA), 865.

all nuisances involving invasion, then the locality principle would no longer has a role to play in modern law.[60] The future of the locality principle however seems safe, having recently been affirmed in the Supreme Court decision in *Coventry v Lawrence*.[61]

> **Further analysis: Should we retain the locality principle?**
>
> The locality principle has been criticised in the literature due to its potentially discriminatory nature. In essence, the nature of the principle is to say that if someone lives in a noisy, dirty, polluted area, then more pollution or noise is merely something they should be expected to put up with because they have chosen to live in such an area. Were this choice a real choice, then perhaps that reasoning would be valid, but choice in this context is choice constrained by financial resources and land values. It is as a result of this that there is a valid argument that nuisance breaches the principle that persons in society should be treated equally by law, as it seems, in effect, to prioritise the interests of the wealthy who can afford to buy somewhere peaceful and quiet in the first place, and to leave those with fewer financial resources to suffer environmental harms.[62] This appears particularly unsettling in the context of modern scientific understandings of the effects that constant noise, light, and air pollution can have on health—both physical and mental.

Related to, but separate from, the locality principle, is the question of planning permission. Just as it is not a defence to an action in nuisance to allege that the claimant 'came to' the nuisance, nor is it a defence that the action has planning permission. This reflects the fact that planning permissions are effectively a public assessment of relative need and benefit within a local area, but they are not determinative of the scope of private property rights, acquired as part of title to land. Until recently, there was a rule in the case law that where a planning permission was sufficiently 'strategic' that it effectively changed the character of a locality (for example, the creation of a large dock and harbour complex would fundamentally alter a rural coastal location)—thus bringing the locality principle into play—then that would constitute a sufficient defence in nuisance. However, the Supreme Court in *Coventry v Lawrence*[63] recently rejected this argument, and confirmed that planning permissions of any sort will never alter the balance of factors applied by the courts in determining the existence of a nuisance. Again, as earlier, planning permissions may however influence the remedy which the courts will grant.

> **Key case: *Coventry v Lawrence* [2014] UKSC 13**
>
> The importance of both the locality principle and of the irrelevance of planning permissions to the establishment of a nuisance, can be seen here. This case involved a dispute between neighbouring owners of land in Suffolk. The claimant lived about half a mile away from a stadium at which were held regular motor races. These produced a significant amount of noise, and the claimant complained on the basis of

---

[60] S Douglas and B McFarlane, 'Defining Property Rights' in J Penner and H Smith, *Philosophical Foundations of Private Law* (OUP, Oxford, 2013).
[61] *Coventry (t/a RDC Promotions) v Lawrence* [2014] UKSC 13, [2014] AC 822.
[62] S Porter, 'Do the rules of private nuisance breach the principles of environmental justice?' (2019) 21 Env LR.
[63] *Coventry (t/a RDC Promotions) v Lawrence* [2014] UKSC 13, [2014] AC 822.

nuisance. The defendant argued that they had planning permission for the operation of the stadium, and so should not be prevented from using it in this way on the basis of private law. Furthermore, they alleged that the locality principle meant that the nature of the local environment was sufficiently changed that there was no nuisance here.

In assessing, first, the role of planning permission in relation to nuisance, the Supreme Court highlighted that planning permission cannot act as a defence to an action in nuisance, as we explained previously.[64] Furthermore, they overturned the previous indication in the case law that where there is a 'strategic' decision in terms of planning permission, that new nuisances created to put that strategic permission into place would not be actionable.[65] Instead, the planning permission was wholly irrelevant to the existence of a nuisance or not. As explained elsewhere, this approach is largely welcome, but the court made some concessions to the role of public law in relation to nuisance, explaining, for example, that a planning permission may be relevant in terms of assessing remedies, and in determining the relevant characteristics of a local area. This means that, whilst 'the courts have reached a sensible, practical solution to a difficult problem of legal policy' they have not yet fully resolved the issues, thus 'leav[ing] open the door for future problems in the interaction between private and regulatory law'.[66]

The second issue which the court considered was what the appropriate remedy would be in cases where a nuisance had been established (we explain the position for remedies later). This case is revolutionary in this respect in that it represents a move away from what had been assumed—that in the majority of cases an injunction would be the most appropriate remedy—to an assumption that damages will suffice. There are a number of possible explanations for the court's change of attitude here. According to Howarth, this may be that 'Lord Neuberger was filling the gap he himself identified in the planning system, which is that it offers no compensation to those adversely affected by grants of planning permission'.[67] However, if that is the explanation, as Howarth goes on to reason, 'the overall effect of his [Lord Neuberger's] approach in practice will be that where nuisances flow from planning consents, the view of the planning system will prevail and the nuisances will continue but the beneficiaries of the consents will have to pay compensation to those whose private rights are violated'.[68]

However, the shift from injunction to damages is not necessarily as 'equitable' as this approach may suggest. Whilst it is true that trying to balance the relationship between tort and the public interest in this way may well strike a middle ground by providing compensation, it may only provide compensation to one claimant, whereas in fact a whole area has been affected by the creation of the nuisance. As I have argued elsewhere:

> 'If D carries on a very noisy activity on his or her land, which is acknowledge to be a nuisance, and remedied by an injunction, if D were to carry on with this, another neighbour could claim in nuisance... If, however, the court sanctions D's actions and D's act now becomes part of the character of the locality... then a subsequent claimant would not be able to complain. Thus one claimant's failure to obtain an injunction in a nuisance action would fundamentally impact upon a subsequent, different claimant's ability to bring a successful nuisance action at all. The bad defendants, in these cases, can then only buy his or her way out of breaching one claimant's property rights through the payment of damages, but can in fact buy his or her way out of breaching all of his or her neighbour's rights., And the defendant achieves this by paying only one of them'.[69]

---

[64] *Coventry (t/a RDC Promotions) v Lawrence* [2014] UKSC 13, [2014] AC 822, [156].
[65] *Coventry (t/a RDC Promotions) v Lawrence* [2014] UKSC 13, [2014] AC 822, [82].
[66] E Lees, 'Lawrence v Fen Tigers: where now for nuisance?' [2014] Conv 449, 455.
[67] D Howarth, 'Noise and nuisance' (2014) 73 CLJ 247, 249.
[68] D Howarth, 'Noise and nuisance' (2014) 73 CLJ 247, 249.
[69] E Lees, 'Lawrence v Fen Tigers: where now for nuisance?' [2014] Conv 449, 456.

> This case, then, is not without its critics. But it must be acknowledged that this area is one where, as Lee has argued, the policy arguments in all directions are so finely balanced that it is not possible to respond satisfactorily with a single, all or nothing, response to the relationship between planning permission and private law rights.[70] Rather, this question in relation to nuisance really goes to the heart of the debate which we have encountered numerous times in this book: to what extent are private law rights subject to the requirement of civil society and public interest, and to what extent is the public interest beholden to private rights? Nuisance, to a large extent, polices this interaction, and we can see from this case law and earlier case law how much it struggles so to do.
>
> Lee's comments in this respect are extremely instructive, and provide a good conclusion to this discussion: 'taking public interests into account in private nuisance is not straightforward... But the ubiquity of public interests in tort already shapes our rights and duties, including in respect of property, and the argument here is that we need to think hard about how we identify and evaluate public interests in private law... It [this debate] also reiterates the close and dynamic connections between property and the public interest, and the absence of any isolated or absolute approach to property'.[71]

18.3.4 WHO CAN SUE?

The issue of standing in relation to nuisance is one with simple rules, but where the rules reveal much about the nature of nuisance as a tort and confirm the impression gleaned from the way the locality principle works earlier, that the tort of nuisance may privilege the wealthy. In essence, in order to have standing in nuisance it is necessary to have a proprietary interest in the land 'harmed' by the nuisance. This means that those in possession of land can certainly sue, as can those with a relevant right in the land where that right is itself harmed by the nuisance. Mere occupiers, however, without a property right, cannot sue. This was established in *Hunter v Canary Wharf*.[72]

> **Key case: *Hunter v Canary Wharf* [1997] AC 655**
>
> This case was brought by individuals who alleged that they was going to suffer harm in respect of their home by the construction of Canary Wharf tower, following the redevelopment of the London docklands area. The case, which made it to the House of Lords, was particularly focused on the potential for an alleged nuisance thanks to the height of the Canary Wharf buildings blocking television reception and the creation of excessive amounts of dust during the construction phase. However, the court was required to assess also a more general question, which related to the ability of those without property rights to bring a claim in nuisance.
>
> The court's starting point was, per Lord Goff, that nuisance is a 'tort to land'.[73] After reviewing the relevant authorities, Lord Goff concluded that the consequence of this was that:
>
>> 'On the authorities as they stand, an action in private nuisance will only lie at the suit of a person who has a right to the land affected. Ordinarily, such a person can only sue if he has the right to exclusive possession of that land, such as a freeholder or a tenant in possession, or even a licensee with exclusive possession.

---

[70] M Lee, 'The public interest in private nuisance: collectives and communities in tort' (2015) 74 CLJ 329.
[71] M Lee, 'The public interest in private nuisance: collectives and communities in tort' (2015) 74 CLJ 329, 357.
[72] *Hunter v Canary Wharf* [1997] AC 655 (HL).
[73] Newark, 'The Boundaries of Nuisance' (1949) 65 LQR 480.

> Exceptionally however… this category may include a person in actual possession who has no right to be there; and in any event a reversioner can sue in so far as his reversionary interest is affected. But a mere licensee on the land has no right to sue.[74]

This was not the end of the question, however, since of course the House of Lords was in a position to change this fundamental principle if they so wished, expanding the capacity of individuals without rights in land to sue and thereby changing the nature of the tort in nuisance. The court declined this opportunity. This was based on three key reasons. First, since the primary remedy was, at the time of the judgment, an injunction, it was considered to be more expedient for all parties to negotiate and reach a settlement, to allow a modified continuation of the behaviour, for example, rather than litigation which would produce an all or nothing result. But, as Lord Goff highlighted, 'the efficacy of arrangements such as these depends upon the existence of an identifiable person with whom the creator of the nuisance can deal for this purpose. If anybody who lived in the relevant property as a home had the right to sue, sensible arrangements such as these might in some cases no longer be practicable'.[75]

Second, any change to the law here would require the creation of a new test to establish who did have a sufficient link to the land in question in order to sue. It would not be possible to shore nuisance free from the need for a link to land precisely because it is a tort concerned with harm to land. The problems with so-doing were explained by the court: 'but is the category also to include the lodger upstairs, or the au pair girl or resident nurse caring for an invalid who makes her homes in the house while she lives there? If the latter, it seems strange that the category should not extent to include places where people work as well as places where they live, where nuisances such as noise can be just as unpleasant and distracting'.[76] If such an extension were made, then it is difficult to see where the boundaries of nuisance would lie.

Third, any person who does occupy is of course able to encourage, and in some cases require, a person with rights in land to sue in connection with the nuisance. It is therefore not the case that a licensee is without recourse, rather than recourse must be to and through a person with a proprietary interest.

One notable feature of this decision by the House of Lords is the degree to which their lordships engaged with the academic discussion of the nature of nuisance in reaching their decision. Lord Goff cited extensively from Newark's article,[77] and Lord Cooke also made use of a variety of academic approaches in his dissenting judgment in respect of the standing to sue. The role of academics in relation to the development of law is the subject of interesting comment on this case by Cane.[78] However, Cane also goes into detail about the substance of the decision, and analyses what the standing rules tell us about the nature of nuisance as a tort.

> 'Central to *Hunter* was the question of when the law should compensate for loss of enjoyment of life. Should it only provide such compensation to victims of personal injury and to persons in exclusive occupation of land; or should the class of potential beneficiaries of such compensation be expanded? And should any liability to pay such compensation be strict or based on negligence or intention? Answers to such questions found by consideration of whether nuisance is a property tort or whether claims to such compensation should be framed in nuisance or negligence are likely to be at best oblique and at worst insensitive to the social importance of the issues at stake. The traditional division of the law into "torts" is, at most, of expository value. To allow the preservation of the supposed conceptual integrity of this structure to influence the law's approach to social problems is to allow the tail to wag the dog. Whatever one thinks

---

[74] *Hunter v Canary Wharf* [1997] AC 655 (HL), 692.
[75] *Hunter v Canary Wharf* [1997] AC 655 (HL), 693.
[76] *Hunter v Canary Wharf* [1997] AC 655 (HL), 693.
[77] Newark, 'The Boundaries of Nuisance' (1949) 65 LQR 480.
[78] P Cane, 'What a nuisance!' (1997) 113 LQR 515.

of the decision in *Hunter*, to justify it by saying that the impact of Canary Wharf Tower on residents of the Isle of Dogs who did not enjoy exclusive possession of their dwellings was "just not nuisance" would be to fall into the very trap of substituting assertion for analysis about which Lord Goff so rightly warned us.'[79]

A salutary lesson in the importance of open-minded analysis of the effect of doctrine, this approach to *Hunter* also highlights the 'hidden' effects of standing requirements.

18.3.5 WHO CAN BE SUED IN NUISANCE?

Although nuisance is clearly a tort *against* land, and it is normal for the tort to be committed by a neighbour, it is not actually necessary for a neighbour to have committed the relevant interference. Rather, the person who carries out the interference, regardless of their relationship with any land, will be liable. However, it is clear that where a nuisance is carried out from neighbouring land, it may also be that the landowner of such land is liable for permitting the nuisance, even if the actual acts are carried out by a third party. This is shown clearly in the decision in *Lippiatt v South Gloucester*,[80] where a person was liable in nuisance because they allowed travellers onto their land, and neighbours suffered noise disruption, amongst other interferences, as a result. Recent case law in *Cocking v Eacott*[81] has confirmed that licensors may also be liable for the act of their licensees. Of this decision, Hickey comments that:

> 'This is a clear and principled decision, which... coheres with a more general understanding of nuisance as a property tort, and with the underlying ideas of possession and control entailed by an orthodox understanding of ownership... The decision does not mean that one needs to be in possession and control of land to be liable for nuisance; rather it means that where one is in possession and control of land, liability may follow where one is aware of activity on the premises that may amount to a nuisance, unless steps are taken to abate the nuisance'.[82]

Thus, whilst liability in nuisance is primarily a question of causation of the relevant harm, there can also be liability for a landowner who knowingly allows activities on her land which result in nuisances being caused to a neighbour. Such liability is not extended to situations where the nuisance is caused by a trespasser however.

18.3.6 DEFENCES TO NUISANCE

There are a number of defences to private nuisance actions. In line with the discussion regarding the relationship between public and private law earlier, whilst it is not a defence to rely on a planning permission to authorise a nuisance, in cases where there is specific statutory authority for the action, then it will not constitute a nuisance, thanks to the principle of Parliamentary sovereignty. It is also a defence if it can be shown that the defendant has acquired, through prescription, a right to use her land in the way which has been said to give rise to the nuisance. This is in a sense

---

[79] P Cane, 'What a nuisance!' (1997) 113 LQR 515, 520–1.
[80] *Lippiatt v South Gloucestershire Council* [2000] QB 51 (CA).
[81] *Cocking v Eacott* [2016] EWCA Civ 140, [2016] QB 1080.
[82] R Hickey 'Possession, control and a licensor's liability for nuisance' [2016] Conv 303, 303.

a competing proprietary entitlement to use the land in a way which oversteps the normal balance struck between neighbouring landowners.

18.3.7 REMEDIES

The remedies available for nuisance are damages and an injunction. Until very recently, following the decision in *Coventry v Lawrence*,[83] the primary remedy was an injunction as a result of the decision in *Shelfer*.[84] This case established that there was a 'strong presumption' in favour of an injunction in nuisance cases, and that damages should only be awarded in exceptional cases. In *Coventry v Lawrence*,[85] the court concluded that this was not the right way to go about trying to find a mutual accommodation between the principles of private law in the tort of nuisance, and the public interest and public benefit encapsulated in planning law in particular. Lord Sumption was particularly critical of the preference for injunctions, stating:

> 'In my view, the decision in *Shelfer* is out of date, and it is unfortunate that it has been followed so recently and so slavishly. It was devised for a time in which England was much less crowded, when comparatively few people owned property, when conservation was only beginning to be a public issue, and when there was no general system of statutory development control. The whole jurisprudence in this area will need one day to be reviewed in this court. There is much to be said for the view that damages are ordinarily an adequate remedy for nuisance and that an injunction should not usually be granted in a case where it is likely that conflicting interests are engaged other than the parties' interests. In particular, it may well be that an injunction should as a matter of principle not be granted in a case where a use of land to which objection is taken requires and has received planning permission.'[86]

The other justices also expressed such views, albeit not always so strongly, and they recognised the force in the arguments of the clash between public and private law in particular. As a result, the jurisprudence shifted so that damages would now become a more usual remedy. This is hugely significant in telling us what nuisance is for. It also has the consequence that, as with trespass earlier, there will be a need to value some losses which are not obviously economic in their nature. This was a point on which there was not extensive discussion in this case itself. Rather the point was remitted for reconsideration. The value of the loss could be assessed by the consequential diminution, if any, in the value of the land. Such an approach would obviously penalise much more severely those nuisances which were of an on-going nature—such as in *Coventry v Lawrence* itself—since one-off nuisances are less likely to result in a seriously detrimental effect on the value of the land, except of course where they are in the nature of a contamination of soil or other form of pollution. In such cases, however, it is likely that public law environmental controls would also operate to attempt to ensure that the landowner did not suffer on-going losses and a result of such pollution.

Such an approach to remedies is not however welcomed by all. Indeed, some argue, in line with the discussion earlier regarding the role of nuisance as defining the parameters of ownership of land, that the approach to prefer an injunction has the effect of significantly reducing the value

---

[83] *Coventry (t/a RDC Promotions) v Lawrence* [2014] UKSC 13, [2014] AC 822.
[84] *Shelfer v City of London Electric Lighting Co (No.1)* [1895] 1 Ch 287 (CA).
[85] *Coventry (t/a RDC Promotions) v Lawrence* [2014] UKSC 13, [2014] AC 822.
[86] *Coventry (t/a RDC Promotions) v Lawrence* [2014] UKSC 13, [2014] AC 822, [161].

of rights in land to their transactable price, rather than the more intangible value which privacy, security, and enjoyment of use of land can bring. Thus, per Dixon:

> 'For an unrepentant property lawyer, this is hard to swallow: the whole point of proprietary rights, be they of ownership or more limited, is that they are about land use, not land value. They are not mere expressions of a contractual bargain which can be avoided by paying a suitable price. No doubt, changing patterns of land use and land value should always be borne in mind—after all, land law is organic with the law following use and not vice versa. But, if I have an easement I want to use it; if I have the benefit of a restrictive covenant I want to enforce it by stopping the prohibited use, and if my estate is affected by a nuisance, I want it to stop. I have a proprietary right'.[87]

It if of course possible, however, that injunctions will still be given in particularly acute cases.

18.4 RYLANDS V FLETCHER

When considering nuisance, it is necessarily, very briefly, to explore the 'sub-set' of nuisance known as *Rylands v Fletcher*.[88] This rule is not discussed in detail here, thanks to its place within the modern law as, effectively, part of the wider law of nuisance. This case established the parameters for liability for damage caused to a neighbour by the 'escape' of a substance stored on the defendant's land. It should now be seen as being simply part of nuisance, albeit explained in reference to a particular form of facts. In *Rylands* itself, the court outlined the following principle, per Blackburn J:

> 'the true rule of law is, that the person who for his own purposes brings on his lands and collects and keeps there anything likely to do mischief if it escapes must keep it in at his peril, and, if he does not do so, is prima facie answerable for all the damage which is the natural consequence of its escape'.[89]

The breadth of this rule is limited by the fact that it only applies where the use of the land is 'non-natural' (in the words of the court in *Rylands*), which is now better seen as simply a different conceptualisation of the principle of reasonable use on behalf of the defendant. It should also be noted, that the elements of this tort (such as the definition of 'likely to do mischief' have been interpreted narrowly by the courts). This tort is also an example of strict liability, in that there is no need to prove fault (beyond the keeping of the dangerous substance) on the part of the defendant.

18.5 CONCLUSION

Nuisance is, therefore, as Essert and others have argued, the tort which defines how far property rights entitle one to use land. Trespass is the tort which protects the physical scope and integrity of that land. Both, however, relying as they do on property rights creating standing to sue, privilege certain persons, ie those with a 'property stake' in land. This is particularly noticeable in relation

---

[87] M Dixon, 'The sound of silence' [2014] Conv 79, 84.
[88] *Rylands v Fletcher* (1868) LR 3 HL 330.
[89] *Rylands v Fletcher* (1865–66) LR 1 Ex 265, 279–80.

to nuisance, where occupiers are unable to sue even for repeated and hugely detrimental effects on their occupation of land, if they do not have the protection of a proprietary right. This skewing in favour of certain types of claimant is emphasised all the more in nuisance by the locality principle on the one hand, and the approach to planning permissions and, to an extent, remedies on the other. The way in which the character of a location is taken into account in nuisance effectively gives extra protection to those who were able to afford to purchase property in a clean, safe and quiet environment, whilst disadvantaging those whose economic situation meant that they were already subject to significant interferences with their land. Furthermore, the fact that the courts do not see planning permissions as a defence to tort emphasises that the public interest is relegated behind the importance and exclusivity of property rights. The approach to remedies in *Coventry v Lawrence* may have diminished this somewhat, but it will still be the case that the only person entitled to the remedy in damages will be the person who is in an economic position to be able to afford the costs of litigation. For other potential neighbouring landowners, the risk of the cost of litigation may be too high for them to pursue a remedy against a tortfeasor, in which case since injunctions are no longer presumed, they will have to continue to suffer interference without even the recompense of damages to make them feel better.

PRINCIPLES

How does this discussion shape our understanding of the principles explained in chapter 1? To recap, these principles were:

1. Certainty
2. Sensitivity to context
3. Transactability
4. Systemic and individual effects
5. Recognition of the social role of the land law system.

When considering the questions raised elsewhere in this book, about the social impacts of our assumed approaches to analysing property law, it would be a folly to ignore nuisance in this assessment. We have already explained earlier how the rules of nuisance may subtly protect certain kinds of relationships with land over others, thereby prioritising a 'class' of claimants, sometimes referred to as the property owning class. Thus, those individuals who may most suffer from the effects of pollution and the like—that is, individuals with fewer resources who are unable to afford accommodation in more expensive areas—will suffer from nuisance actions without any recourse.

Furthermore, whilst the uncertainty relating to nuisance (unlike in most of the rest of this book) is unlikely to have a hindering effect on the marketability and transactibility of land, it does have an effect in respect of the ability of individuals to plan their use of land. We considered this aspect of certainty in chapter 1, where it was explained that there is a merit in reaching clarity because that enhances autonomy. In being unable to clearly define what will constitute a nuisance in advance, the law hinders rather than facilitates autonomy. However, we can put this directly at the door of a pursuance of another of the principles—that of sensitivity to context. By emphasising the 'give and take' nature of the nuisance rules, and by highlighting that the search is always to find balance, the law gives itself the flexibility and responsiveness needed to apply 'fairly' in a very wide range of circumstances.

In this summary of the relationship between land law and the principles we have not yet referred to the law relating to trespass. This is because the trespass rules are essentially parasitic upon the existence of property rights in others: trespass protects what the rest of this book defines. If there are tensions and problems in the law elsewhere in this book (and there most certainly are), then trespass merely serves to back up the law giving rise to such problems. Indeed, it is only really at the very fringes of its operation that there are problems with the law of trespass itself, and this is experience in relation to cases such as *Dutton* where the problem lies more conceptually in our articulation of the boundary between property and personal rights than it does in relation to the elements of trespass per se.

TABLE OF DEFINITIONS

Trespass to land	Trespass to land is the unlawful interference with or incursion on another's possession of land.
Possession	The right to, or the fact of, control of land characterised by the ability to exclude others.
Negotiated damages	An approach to assessment of damage which relies on a fictional negotiation between the parties, assuming reasonableness and a willingness to engage.
Nuisance	An unreasonable interference with the reasonable use of another's land.
Locality principle	The rule that any assessment of nuisance, where the allegation involves a claim of interference with comfort and enjoyment of land, must take account of the nature of the wider locality in considering the overall balance to be struck between competing uses of land.

FURTHER READING

There is an enormous amount of further reading on torts in relation to land, especially nuisance. For a flavour of this, some of the works already mentioned in the chapter provide an ideal starting point:

Douglas, S. and McFarlane, B., 'Defining Property Rights' in Penner, J. and Smith, H., *Philosophical Foundations of Private Law* (OUP, 2013).
Essert, C., 'Nuisance and the Normative Boundaries of Ownership' (2016) 52 Tulsa Law Review 85.
Lee, M., 'What is private nuisance?' (2003) 119 LQR 298.
Murphy, J., in Jones, M. A., (ed), *Clerk and Lindsell on Torts* (Thompson Reuters, 2010).

INDEX

Note: References are to page numbers and where appropriate are prefixed as a table (*t.*) or figure (*f.*)

A
Absolute titles 118–19
Acquisition mortgages
   waiver of priority 482–6
Actions for possession
   see also **Possession of land**
   impact of human rights
      actions against
         trespassers 574–5
      repossession actions by private landowners 573–4
      repossession actions by public authorities 560–73
   mortgagee's remedy
      court powers of deferral 340–8
      impact of human rights 348–9, 575–9
      soft law restraints 348
      use of violence 340
Actual notice 74–5
Actual occupation
   factual test of actual occupation 469–74
   knowledge, inquiries, and discoverability 477–8
   priority rules 468
   relevant date 475–7
   relevant property rights *t.*468
Adverse possession
   continuity of possession 170
   criminal sanctions 184–5
   effect on general principles of land law 189–90
   enclosure 169–70
   factual possession 165–7
   impact of human rights 559–60
   intention to possess 168–9
   leasehold estates
      against a tenant 182
      by tenant against landlord 182–3
      by tenant against third party 183

   multiple squatters 172–4
   'possession' 163–4
   problems of proof with unregistered land 78
   registered land
      'exceptions' in relation to the notification and counter-notice process 177–81
      Land Registry procedure 176–7
      multiple squatters 181
      new statutory rules 174–6
   underlying rationales 185–8
   unregistered land
      consequences for title-holder 172
      multiple squatters 172–4
Alteration of the register
   outline of system 127–9
   statutory provisions 131–4
Ambulatory constructive trusts 218, 220
Animus possedendi 168–9
Annexation of freehold covenants
   enforceability by successors in title 428–31
Assurance-based estoppel
   'assurance' 238–41
   detrimental reliance 244–52
   domestic and commercial distinction 242–4
   importance of context 242–4
   unconscionability 252–7
Auctions
   formality rules 98–9
   mortgagee sales 339, 348–9, 353

B
Bare licences
   meaning and scope of rights 34–6
Bona vacantia 285–7

Boundaries
   adverse possession of registered land 180–1
   corporeal dimension of land 46–7
   demarcating agreement *f.*99
   disposing agreement *f.*100
   formality rules for agreements 99–102
   registered titles 126–7
'Bruton' leases 308–11
Building schemes 432–4

C
Cautions against first registration 119
Certainty
   general principle of land law 6–9
   relevance in shaping decisions 54–5
   relevance to specific aspects of land law
      adverse possession 189–90
      co-ownership 541–4
      easements 415–16
      estoppel 271
      formality rules 112–14
      freehold covenants 444–5
      freehold estates 288–9
      human rights 579–81
      implied trusts 231–2
      land registration 160–1
      leasehold estates 328–9
      mortgages 373–5
      nuisance 605–6
      options to purchase 460–1
      priority rules 493–4
      registered land 79–80
      trespass 606
Charges *see* **Mortgages**
Clogs on the equity of redemption of mortgages 359–60
Cohabitation
   implied trusts
      joint names cases 211–12

Cohabitation (*cont.*)
  Kernott and the uncertainties of *Stack* 207
  key cases 200–3
  reform proposals 228
  societal changes 196, 200
  shared accommodation 296
  undue influence 367
Collateral contracts 95, 104–5
Commonholds
  meaning and scope 284–5
Common intention constructive trusts
  see also **Constructive trusts**
Compulsory registration of title
  first registration of title
    cautions against first registration 119
    effect of registration 118–19
    trigger events 117–18
  new first mortgages 334
  registrable dispositions
    categories of notice 122–3
    effect of registration - estates and charges 120–1
    effect of registration - interests protected by notice 120–1
    interests cannot be entered as the subject of a notice 121–2
    relevant dispositions 120–1
  statutory goals 117
Consideration
  general requirements 88, 94
Constructive notice 75–7
Constructive trusts
  history and development 195–200
  leading cases
    Jones v Kernott 204–7
    Stack v Dowden 200–4
  new 'rules'
    ambulatory constructive trusts 218, 220
    criticism of imputed intentions 219
    finality of express trusts 215
    presumption that equity follows the law 216

quantification of shares 217–18
rebuttal of general presumption 216–17
relationship with resulting trusts and estoppel 219–20
resulting trust more appropriate 215–16
two levels of uncertainty 218–19
post-*Stack* case law
  joint names cases 211–12
  sole names cases 208–10
reform proposals 228–30
relationship with estoppel 266–70
resulting trust more appropriate 212–14
sensitivity to context 11
uncertain area of law 195
Context *see* **Sensitivity to context**
Contracts
  formality rules
    categories of agreement f.88
    consequences of compliance 106
    consequences of failure to comply 105–6
    exceptions 94–105
    general rule 87–94
    guide to statutory provisions 93, 94
Contractual licences
  effect against third parties 37–41
  effect between parties 37–41
  property rights for some purposes 36
Co-ownership
  constructive trusts
    history and development of law 195–200
    post-*Stack* case law 211–12
    presumption that equity follows the law 216
    resulting trust more appropriate 212–14
  dispute resolution
    applications under s14 TOLATA 1996 517–31

priority disputes with third parties 531–41
effect on general principles of land law 541–4
forms of ownership
  joint tenancies 503–5
joint tenancies
  creation 192–3
  requirement for four unities 504–5
  'sharing' of legal title 503–4
  underlying concept 504–5
number and nature of legal owners 504
sensitivity to context 11
severance 507–16
statutory trusts 194–5
tenancies in common
  creation 192–3
  effect of severing joint tenancies 507
  equitable rights and interests 506
Corporeal dimension of land
  fixtures and fittings
    decorative features 50
    house boats 48
    mobile homes and caravans 48–50
  horizontal and vertical scope
    questions of boundaries 46–7
Costs *see* **Transactability**
Covenants *see* **Freehold covenants**; **Leasehold covenants**
Creation of rights and interests *see* **Formality rules and the creation of rights and interests**
Criminal sanctions
  adverse possession 184–5
  mortgages taking possession 340
  need for certainty 7
  recognition of the social effects of rules 15
Critical to the operation of priority disputes
  actual notice 74–5
Curtain principle
  overreaching 68–70
  'Torrens' system of land registration 63

Index

D

Deeds
- formality rules
  - consequences of having used a deed 109–11
  - relevant transfers t.110
  - requirements of a valid deed 107–9
  - when required 109
- implied easements under s.62 LPA 1925 400

Detrimental reliance
- assurance-based estoppel
  - detriment 249–52
  - reliance 244–9
- constructive trusts
  - *Agarwala v Agarwala* 210
  - *Lloyds Bank v Rosset* 199

Dispositions *see* **Transfer of rights and interests**

Doctrine of clogs and fetters 359–60

Doctrine of notice
- constructive notice 75–7
- imputed notice 77–8
- priority disputes 74

Dominant tenement
- easements
  - changes of use 405–9
  - easement must 'accommodate' the dominant tenement 380–3
  - essential requirement 379
  - separate ownership 379–80
- freehold covenants 418–20
- running of burden of restrictive covenants
  - dominant land is benefited by covenant 436
  - requirement for servient and dominant tenement 435

E

Easements
- changes of use 405–9
- creation of rights
  - express easements 394–5
  - implied easements 394–404
  - by prescription 404–5
- dominant tenement
  - easement must 'accommodate' the dominant tenement 380–3
  - essential requirement 379
  - separate ownership 379–80
- effect of dispositions on the benefit and burden of easements
  - express equitable easements 412–13
  - express legal easements 410
  - implied equitable easements 414
  - implied legal easements 411–12
- effect on general principles of land law 415–16
- estate contracts 447–8
- extinction 410
- implied easements
  - easements of common intention 398–9
  - easements of necessity 398
  - grants and reservations 396
  - methods of grant and reservation f.397
  - reservation and grant distinguished 397–8
  - rule in *Wheeldon v Burrows* 403–4
  - s.62 LPA 1925 399–403
- possession and control test 392
- reform proposals 414–15
- registrable dispositions 121
- relevant 'rights' 377–8
- right must be capable of being subject matter of a grant
  - easement must be clear, defined, and capable of certain expression 384
  - list of rights t.385–t.7
  - not 'too extensive' 388–92
  - relationship with nuisance 387–8
  - similar to existing forms of easement 384–8
- servient tenement
  - easement must 'accommodate' the dominant tenement 380–3
  - essential requirement 379
  - separate ownership 379–80
- social function of easements 415
- use of land
  - changes of use 405–9
  - reasonable user 392–4

E-conveyancing
- advantages and disadvantages 62–3
- imminence 158–9
- signatures 93–4
- transactability 12–13

Environmental issues
- limitations on freehold use 275, 288
- nuisance 587, 591, 598, 603, 605
- recognition of the social effects of rules 15
- right to property (art 1, protocol 1) 550
- sensitivity to context 9
- third party effects of licences 45

Equitable rights and interests
- creation and transfer 5
- easements
  - estate contracts 447–8
- estate contracts *see* **Estate contracts**
- legal rights distinguished
  - essence of distinction 18–19
  - terminology 17–18
- overreaching 305
- redemption of mortgages
  - definitions 375
  - doctrine of clogs and fetters 359–62
- registration as land charges 72
- unregistered land - purchasers for value without notice
  - doctrine of notice 74–8
  - freedom from equitable rights and interests 73

Errors on the register
- alteration and rectification 127–9
- analysis—title by registration or registration of title 154–5
- availability of indemnities 155–7
- categorisation of errors 129–31
- history and development of law in practice 134–54

Errors on the register (*cont.*)
  reform of rectification and
      indemnities 157–9
  statutory provisions 131–4
Escheat 285–7
Estate contracts
  conveyance involving transfer
      of a lease
    completed transfer *f*.452
    estate contract and interest
        under trust merge *f*.454
    estate contract and trust
        separate *f*.453
    persistent estate
        contract *f*.455
  meaning and scope of
      rights 32
  nature of rights
    existence of only one
        interest 452
    practical approaches to the
        various options 452–5
  vendor-purchaser
      constructive trusts
      distinguished 448–52
  registration as land
      charges 72
  rule in *Walsh v Lonsdale* 447
Estates in land 23
  freehold estates
    commonholds 284–5
    definitions 289
    effect on general principles
        of land law 288–9
    flying freeholds 283–4
    priority of rights and
        interests 279–80
    relativity of title 280–2
    'return' of title to the
        crown 285–7
    transfer and registration
        282–3
  interests distinguished 26
  leasehold estates
    adverse possession *see*
        Adverse possession
    'Bruton' leases 308–11
    concurrent leases 327
    conflict with mortgage
        rights 372–3
    creation of rights and
        interests 303–5
    effect on general principles
        of land law 288–9
    exclusive possession 292–9

first registration of
    title 117–18
forfeiture 319–21
freeholder's reversionary
    interest 327–8
intention to create legal
    relationship 302–3
leasehold covenants *see*
    Leasehold covenants
meaning and scope of
    rights 30
periodic tenancies 305–7
problems of mislabeling
    292–2
registered titles 118–19
registrable dispositions
    120–1
rent 302
security of tenure 322–7
sub-leases 327
surrender 321–2
tenancies at will 307–8
tenant's fixtures 327
termination by effluxion of
    time 318–19
termination by notice 321
term of limited dura-
    tion 299–302
Estoppel
  by acquiescence 235–6
  assurance-based estoppel
    'assurance' 238–41
    detrimental reliance
        244–52
    domestic and commercial
        distinction 242–4
    importance of context
        242–4
    unconscionability 252–7
  different 'requirements' 233–4
  effect on general principles of
      land law 271
  effect on third parties
    benefit of estoppel 264–5
    burden of an estop-
        pel 262–4
  equitable remedies 258–62
  equities arising by estop-
      pel 258–62
  defined 23, 56
  meaning and scope of
      rights 32
  licences
    meaning and scope of
        rights 41–2

proprietary estoppel
    equitable remedies 258–62
    equities arising by
        estoppel 257–8
    three separate forms
        234–7
    underlying doctrine 233–4
    relationship with constructive
        trusts 266–70
    relationship with formality
        rules 265–6
    by representation 236–7
    three separate forms 234–7
Exclusive possession
  importance 292–4
  keeping of keys 294–5
  provision of services 294
  sham transactions 297–9
  shared accommodation
      295–7
Express trusts
  conclusiveness 193, 215
  creation 192–4
**Extinction of rights and inter-
    ests** *see* **Termination of
    rights and interests**

F
Factual possession
  adverse possession of unregis-
      tered land
    open and undeveloped
        land 166–7
    riverbeds 167
    sufficient control 165–6
Family homes
  constructive notice 76–7
  constructive trusts 105
  co-ownership *see*
      Co-ownership
  general principles of land law
    recognition of the social
        effects of rules 15
    sensitivity to context
        10–11
  implied trusts *see* **Implied
      trusts**
  interaction of rights 6
**Fetters on the equity of
    redemption** 359–60
First refusal *see* **Rights of
    pre-emption**
First registration of title
  cautions against first
      registration 119

effect of registration 118–19
overriding interests 479–80
trigger events 117–18
Fixtures and fittings
decorative features 50
house boats 48
mobile homes and caravans 48–50
tenant's fixtures at termination of lease 327
Flying freeholds
underlying problems 283–4
Foreclosure of mortgages
equitable mortgages 357
legal mortgages 337–8
Forfeiture of leases
procedure 319–21
relief from forfeiture 321
'Formal certainty' 7
Formality rules and the creation of rights and interests
deeds
consequences of having used a deed 109–11
requirements of a valid deed 107–9, 110
when required 109
easements
express easements 394–5
implied easements 394–404
by prescription 404–5
effect on general principles of land law 112–14
express trusts 192–3, 192–4
freehold covenants 421
importance 81–2, 112
leasehold estates 303–5
mortgages
equitable mortgages 334–5
legal mortgages 333–4
unregistered land 334
purposes
assessment of risk 84–6
cautionary function 83
channelling function 83
evidentiary function 82
protection of the vulnerable 83–4
relationship with estoppel 265–6
relevant transactions
contracts 87–107
transactions and statutory provisions t.87

trusts
dispositions of equitable interests 112
failed trust resulting trusts 228
trusts of land 500–1
Freedom of association (art.11)
source of conflicts 552–3
Freedom of expression (art.10)
source of conflicts 551–3
Freehold covenants
complexity and 'piecemeal' nature of rules 444
effect on general principles of land law 444–5
enforceability between original parties
effect of s.56 LPA 1925 423–6
general rule 422–3
statutory extension of privity rules 426–7
enforceability by successors in title
annexation of the benefit 428–31
assignment of the benefit of the covenant 427–8
building schemes 432–4
formality rules and the creation of rights 421
interpretation 421–2
modification 441–2
negative covenants
fundamental requirements 419–20
passing of benefit where covenantor has different geographical estate 433
passing of the benefit in equity 434
positive covenants
circumvention of benefit and burden principle 438–41
restrictive covenants distinguished 418–19
'private' mechanism for controlling use of land 417–18
reform proposals 442–4
restrictive covenants
positive covenants distinguished 418–19
running of burden 435–8

Freehold estates
ability to use land 275–6
commonholds 284–5
effect on general principles of land law 288–9
essential content
ability to use land 275–6
geographical scope 276–8
importance 274–5
rights of reversion and re-entry 278–9
flying freeholds 283–4
geographical scope 276–8
mandatory first registration of title 117–18
meaning and scope of rights 29–30
priority of rights and interests 279–80
registered titles 118–19
registrable dispositions 120–1
relativity of title 280–2
'return' of title to the crown 285–7
rights of reversion and re-entry 278–9
transfer and registration 282–3

G

General principles of land law
certainty 6–9
recognition of the social effects of rules 14–16
relevance in shaping decisions 54–5
relevance to specific aspects of land law
adverse possession 189–90
co-ownership 541–4
easements 415–16
estoppel 271
formality rules 112–14
freehold covenants 444–5
freehold estates 288–9
human rights 579–81
implied trusts 231–2
land registration 160–1
leasehold estates 328–9
mortgages 373–5
nuisance 605–6
options to purchase 460–1
priority rules 493–4
registered land 79–80
trespass 606

General principles of land law (*cont.*)
sensitivity to context 9–11
systematic and individual effects 13–14
transactability 11–13
Gifts
constructive trusts 267
estoppel 262–3
priority of interests 492
resulting trusts *see* **Resulting trusts**
rights of pre-emption 459
setting aside of transactions 469
Good leasehold titles 118–19

H
Human rights
adverse possession 187–8
areas of influence
actions against trespassers 574–5
adverse possession 559–60
mortgage repossessions 575–9
repossession actions by private landowners 573–4
repossession actions by public authorities 560–73
effect on general principles of land law 579–81
interaction with property rights
'bolstering' of right to property 548–51
mechanisms by which rights operate 553–7
problem of horizontal effect 557–8
rights which can 'strengthen' proprietary entitlements 551
sources of conflict 551–3
as sources of law 547–8
mortgagee repossessions 348–9
recognition of the social effects of rules 15

I
Implied easements
easements of common intention 398–9
easements of necessity 398
effect of dispositions on the benefit and burden of easements
equitable easements 414
legal easements 411–12
grants and reservations 396
methods of grant and reservation f.397
overriding interests 478
reservation and grant distinguished 397–8
rule in *Wheeldon v Burrows* 403–4
s.62 LPA 1925 399–403
Implied trusts
constructive trusts
history and development 195–200
leading cases - *Stack* and *Jones* 200–7
new 'rules' 214–20
post-*Stack* case law 208–12
reform proposals 228–30
resulting trust more appropriate 212–14
uncertain area of law 195
effect on general principles of land law 231–2
focus on market rather than people 230
resulting trusts
key issues 220–1
underlying rationale 221–2
when they arise 223–8
severance of joint tenancies 515–16
Imputed notice 77–8
Incorporeal dimension of land 51–2
Indemnities
errors on the register 157–9
rectification of register
availability of indemnities 155–7
statutory provisions 133–4
Insurance principle
reliance on register and compensation for loss 66–7
'Torrens' system of land registration 63
Intention
adverse possession 168–9
constructive trusts
ambulatory constructive trusts 218, 220
conduct of the parties 199–200
criticism of imputed intentions 219
detrimental reliance 195
express, implied or imputed intentions 197
imputation of intention 199–200
leading cases - *Stack* and *Jones* 200–7
delivery of deeds 108–9
easements of common intention 399
e-signatures 94
fixtures and fittings 49
freehold covenants 418–20
leasehold estates
to create legal relationship 302–3
exclusive possession 298–9
relativity of title 52
resulting trusts 222
purchase money resulting trusts 223–6
voluntary conveyance resulting trusts 227
running of burden of restrictive covenants 437
signatures 94
Interests in land
property rights
easements 30–1
equities arising by estoppel 32
estate contracts 32
estates and interests distinguished 26
freehold estates 29–30
leasehold estates 30
mortgages 30
nature of rights 26–9
options to purchase 31
rectification 32
restrictive covenants 31
rights of pre-emption 32
third party effects 42–6
trusts of land 32–3
Investment contracts 98–9

J
Joint tenancies
creation 192–3
requirement for four unities 504–5

severance
- by creation of an implied trust 515-16
- by mutual agreement 511-13
- by mutual conduct 514-15
- by unilateral action in relation to a 'share' 510-11
- by written notice 507-10

'sharing' of legal title 503-4
underlying concept 504-5

K
Key cases
adverse possession
- boundaries 180-1
- criminal sanctions 185
- human rights 188
- 'possession' 165
- registered land 176-7

assurance-based estoppel
- 'assurance' 238-41
- detriment 250
- reliance 247-9
- unconscionability 253-4

constructive trusts
- conduct of the parties 199-200
- imputation of intention 198-9
- *Jones v Kernott* 204-7
- objective reasonableness 197-8
- resulting trust more appropriate 212-14
- sole names cases 208-10
- *Stack v Dowden* 200-4

dispute resolution over co-ownership applications under s14 TOLATA 1996 518-20
overreaching 533-8
easements
- easement must 'accommodate' the dominant tenement 381-3
- easements of common intention 399
- effect of dispositions on the benefit and burden of easements 413
- implied easements under s.62 LPA 1925 402
- relationship with nuisance 387-8
- relevant 'rights' 376-7

right must be capable of being subject matter of a grant 389-91
- separate ownership of dominant and servient land 380

equitable remedies 259-60
estate contracts 449-50
formality rules
- boundary agreements 100-2
- contracts 90

freehold covenants
- annexation of the benefit 430-1
- building schemes 432
- enforceability between original parties 424-5
- passing of the benefit 434
- positive covenants 439-40
- running of burden of restrictive covenants 436

freehold estates
- flying freeholds 283-4
- geographical scope 277-8
- relativity of title 281-2

human rights
- adverse possession 559-60
- 'bolstering' of right to property 548-9
- mechanisms by which rights operate 554-5
- mortgage repossessions 576-8
- repossession actions by private landowners 574-5
- repossession actions by public authorities 562, 563-4, 566-8, 572

leasehold estates
- 'Bruton' leases 309-11
- keeping of keys 295
- periodic tenancies 306-7
- problems of mislabeling 292
- shared accommodation 295-6
- tenancies at will 308
- term of limited duration 299-301

licences
- bare licences 35
- contractual licences 36-41

mortgagee remedies
- action on debt 336-7
- equitable mortgages 357

power of sale 352-4
repossession 339, 342-6
mortgagor protection
- interest rates 363-4
- premiums on redemption 361-2
- rights of redemption 359-60
- undue influence 366-7, 367-8

nature of property rights 27-9
nuisance
- interference with comfort and enjoyment 594-5
- locality principle 598-600
- standing to sue 600-2

options to purchase 456-7
overreaching 487-8
priority of rights and interests
- effect of loss of priority 490-1
- persons in actual occupation 471-2, 474, 475-6
- waiver of priority 480-1

rectification of register 134-54
relationship between estoppel and constructive trusts 268-9
rights of pre-emption 459
severance of joint tenancies
- by mutual agreement 512-13
- by mutual conduct 514
- by written notice 508-9

L
Land
corporeal dimension
- fixtures and fittings 47-50
- horizontal and vertical scope 46-7

incorporeal dimension 51-2
Land charges
- effects of registration 73
- mandatory registration 71-2
- rights to be registered 72-3

Land law
- five general concerns 21
- general principles
  - certainty 6-9
  - recognition of the social effects of rules 14-16
  - sensitivity to context 9-11

Land law (*cont.*)
  systematic and individual effects 13–14
  transactability 11–13
  history and development of current system 59–60
  importance of registered land 57–9
  interaction with human rights
    'bolstering' of right to property 548–51
    mechanisms by which rights operate 553–7
    problem of horizontal effect 557–8
    rights which can 'strengthen' proprietary entitlements 551
    sources of conflict 551–3
    as sources of law 547–8
  legal rights
    creation and transfer 4–5
    meaning and scope 3–4
    priority of rights and interests 5–6
  logic of the system
    case law disputes 21
    estates in land 20
    legal and equitable rights distinguished 17–19
  relativity of title 52–3
  three fundamental questions 21

Land registration
  see also **Registered land**
  analysis—title by registration or registration of title 126, 154–5
  boundaries 126–7
  consequences of registration 127
  effect on general principles of land law 160–1
  errors on the register
    alteration and rectification 127–9
    analysis—title by registration or registration of title 154–5
    availability of indemnities 155–7
    categorisation of errors 129–31
    history and development of law in practice 134–54

  reform of rectification and indemnities 157–9
  statutory provisions 131–4
  freehold covenants 438
  freehold estates 282–3
  interests which must be registered
    first registration 117–20
    registrable dispositions 120–3
    restrictions 123–4
  owners powers and guarantee of title 124–6
  priority rules 465–6

Leasehold covenants
  see also **Freehold covenants**
  enforceability
    importance 311
    original landlord and tenant 311–12
    subsequent landlord and/or tenant—pre-1996 leases 312
    subsequent landlord and tenant—post-1996 leases 312–18
  remedies for breach
    forfeiture 319–21

Leasehold estates
  see also **Leasehold covenants**
  adverse possession
    against a tenant 182
    by tenant against landlord 182–3
    by tenant against third party 183
  concurrent leases 327
  conflict with mortgage rights 372–3
  creation of rights and interests 303–5
  effect on general principles of land law 288–9
  essential elements
    exclusive possession 292–9
    intention to create legal relationship 302–3
    problems of mislabeling 292–2
    rent 302
    term of limited duration 299–302
  forms of leases
    'Bruton' leases 308–11

  equitable leases and trusts of leases *f.*304
  periodic tenancies 305–7
  tenancies at will 307–8
  freeholder's reversionary interest 327–8
  impact of human rights on repossessions 573–4
  mandatory first registration of title 117–18
  meaning and scope of rights 30
  priority rules
    short leases 466–7
    social housing leases 467–8
  registered titles 118–19
  registrable dispositions 120–1
  security of tenure
    business tenancies 323–4
    residential tenancies 325–7
    underlying concept 322–3
  sub-leases 327
  termination
    by effluxion of time 318–19
    forfeiture 319–21
    by notice 321
    by surrender 321–2
  tenant's fixtures 327

Legal rights
  equitable rights distinguished
    essence of distinction 18–19
    terminology 17–18
  need for certainty 7
  unregistered land
    binding legal interests 70–1

Licences
  bare licences 34–6
  contractual licences 36–41
    effect against third parties 37–41
    effect between parties 36–7
    property rights for some purposes 36
  coupled with an interest 42
  estoppel licences 41–2
  impact of human rights on repossessions 573–4
  third party effects
    defining characteristic 42–5

Limited owner's charges 72
Locality principle
  nuisance 597–8

M
Mandatory registration
  see **Compulsory registration of title**
Mirror principle
  notion of guaranteed title 65–6
  overriding interests 65
  register as accurate reflection of title 64
  'Torrens' system of land registration 63
Mistake see **Errors on the register**
Mixed contracts 95, 103–4, 113
Mortgages
  conflict with third party rights
    multiple mortgages 368–9
    priority disputes between mortgagees and purchasers 373
    priority disputes between mortgagees and tenants 372–3
    subrogation 369–70
    trust interests 370–2
  consequences of creating a legal mortgage 332–3
  effect on general principles of land law 373–5
  equitable mortgages
    classification 333
    key analysis 358
    mortgagee remedies 356–8
  formalities for creation
    equitable mortgages 334–5
    legal mortgages 333–4
    unregistered land 334
  general principles of land law
    need for certainty 7
    sensitivity to context 10
    systematic and individual effects 13
  importance 331
  mandatory first registration of title 117–18
  meaning and scope of rights 30
  mortgagee remedies
    action on debt 336–7
  appointment of receiver 355–6
  equitable mortgages 356–8
  foreclosure 337–8
  human rights protection for mortgagors 575–9
  power of sale 350–5
  right to possession 338–50
  mortgagor protection
    interest rates 363–4
    rights of redemption 359–62
    statutory provisions 364
    undue influence 364–8
  new first mortgage 112
  priority of rights and interests
    acquisition mortgages 482–6
    registered charges 480
    subrogation 488
  registrable dispositions 121
  registration as land charges 72
  relationship between freedom of contract and proprietary entitlements 373
  required elements 332
  'return' of title to the crown 287
  terminology 332
  undue influence
    affect on lender 367–8
    two-strand test for the presence of undue influence 365–6
Multiple mortgages 368–9

N
Negative covenants see **Restrictive freehold covenants**
Notice
  doctrine of notice
    actual notice 74–5
    constructive notice 75–7
    critical to the operation of priority disputes 74
    defined 80
    imputed notice 77–8
Notices on the register
  categories of notice 122–3
  interests cannot be entered as the subject of a notice 121–2
  interests protected 121

Nuisance
  categorisation
    direct damage 592
    encroachment 591–2
    interference with comfort and enjoyment 592–5
    unreasonableness and foreseeability 596–7
  defences 602–3
  easements to create a nuisance 387–8
  effect on general principles of land law 605–6
  irrelevance of planning permissions 598–600
  locality principle 597–8
  recognition of the social effects of rules 15
  remedies 603–4
  Rylands v Fletcher 604
  standing to sue 600–2
  underlying role
    importance 588
    need for unified explanation 589–91
  use of land 51
  who can be sued 602
Numerus clausus **('closed lists')**
  contractual licences 39
  easements 392
  mortgages 332
  nature of leases 291, 311, 329
  property rights generally 26–7, 45–6
  purpose of formality rules 83
  relativity of title 54

O
Occupation of land
  dispute resolution under s14 TOLATA 1996 529–31
  implied easements under s.62 LPA 1925 400–1
  incorporeal dimension of land 51–2
  priority of persons in actual occupation
    factual test of actual occupation 469–74
    knowledge, inquiries, and discoverability 477–8
    relevant date 475–7
    relevant property rights t.468

616 Index

Official searches 480
Options to purchase
  effect 457
  effect on general principles of land law 460–1
  essential features for validity 456
  meaning and scope of rights 31
  nature of rights 455–6
  priority of rights and interests 457–8
Overreaching
  curtain principle 68–70
  equitable leases 305
  equitable leases and trusts of leases *f.*305
  equities arising by estoppel 264
  nature of rights 487–8
  regulation of disputes between co-owners and third parties
  consequences of no overreaching 538–41
  requirements of overreaching 532–8
Overriding interests
  cases involving first registrations 479–80
  implied legal easements and profits 478
  leases
    short leases 466–7
    social housing leases 467–8
  mirror principle 65
  persons in actual occupation
    factual test of actual occupation 469–74
    knowledge, inquiries, and discoverability 477–8
    relevant date 475–7
    relevant property rights *t.*468
  unregistered interests covered by statute 478–9
Ownership of land 20

P

Personal rights
  property rights distinguished 3
Persons in actual occupation
  see Actual occupation
Planning *see* Town and country planning

Positive freehold covenants
  circumvention of benefit and burden principle 438–41
  restrictive covenants distinguished 418–19
Possession of land
  see also Actions for possession
  adverse possession
    criminal sanctions 184–5
    leasehold estates 181–3
    registered land 174–81
    underlying rationales 185–8
    unregistered land 163–74
  easements 392
  exclusive leasehold possession
    defined 328
    importance 292–4
    keeping of keys 294–5
    provision of services 294
    sham transactions 297–9
    shared accommodation 295–7
  incorporeal dimension of land 51–2
  short leases and their formality requirements 96–7
Possessory titles 118–19
Pre-emption *see* Rights of pre-emption
Prescriptive rights
  defence to nuisance 602
  importance 404
  statutory provisions 405
  three 'methods' of prescription 404–5
Priority of rights and interests
  cases involving first registrations 479–80
  conflicts with mortgage rights
    multiple mortgages 368–9
    priority disputes between mortgagees and purchasers 373
    priority disputes between mortgagees and tenants 372–3
    subrogation 369–70
    trust interests 370–2
  co-ownership disputes
    overreaching 532–41
    two sets of rules 531

effect of dispositions on the benefit and burden of easements
  express equitable easements 412–13
  express legal easements 410
  implied equitable easements 414
  implied legal easements 411–12
effect of loss of priority 488–91
effect of official searches 480
effect on general principles of land law 493–4
equitable leases 304
freehold covenants 438
freehold estates 279–80
mortgages
  acquisition mortgages 482–6
  registered charges 480
  subrogation 488
options to purchase 457–8
overreaching 487–8
persons in actual occupation
  factual test of actual occupation 469–74
  knowledge, inquiries, and discoverability 477–8
  relevant date 475–7
  relevant property rights *t.*468
priority rules
  basic rule - first in time 464
  formulaic application 491
  implied legal easements and profits 478
  persons in actual occupation 468–78
  short leases 466–7
  social housing leases 467–8
  special priority rule - registered land 465–6
  summary of statutory provisions 492–3
rights of pre-emption 459
unregistered interests covered by statute 478–9
waiver and consent
  acquisition mortgages 482–6
  general rule 480–1

Index   617

Profits à prendre
  miscellaneous category of rights 376–7
  overriding interests 478
  reasonable user 393–4
  registrable dispositions 121
  rights capable of constituting profits 392–3
Property rights
  contractual licences 36
  easements 30–1
  equities arising by estoppel 32
  estate contracts 32
  freehold estates 29–30
  interaction with human rights
    'bolstering' of right to property 548–51
    mechanisms by which rights operate 553–7
    problem of horizontal effect 557–8
    rights which can 'strengthen' proprietary entitlements 551
    sources of conflict 551–3
    as sources of law 547–8
  leasehold estates 30
  meaning and scope 3–4
  mortgages 30
  nature of rights 26–9
  options to purchase 31
  rectification 32
  restrictive covenants 31
  rights of pre-emption 32
  third party effects
    defining characteristic 42–5
  trusts of land 32–3
Proprietary estoppel
  see also **Assurance-based estoppel**
  equitable remedies
    remedial approach 258–60
    types of remedy 261–2
  equities arising by estoppel 257–8
  relationship with constructive trusts 219–20
  three separate forms 234–5
  underlying doctrine 233–4
Proprietors of registered land
  first registration of title 120
  owners powers and guarantee of title 124–6

Public authority housing *see* **Social housing**
Purchase money resulting trusts
  meaning and scope 223–6
Purchasers for value without notice
  doctrine of notice
    actual notice 74–5
    constructive notice 75–7
    critical to the operation of priority disputes 74
    imputed notice 77–8
    freedom from equitable rights and interests 73

Q
Qualified titles 118–19

R
Receivership
  mortgagee's remedy 355–6
  private actions for possession 574
Recognition of the social effects of rules
  general principle of land law 14–16
  relevance in shaping decisions 54–5
  relevance to specific aspects of land law
    adverse possession 189–90
    co-ownership 541–4
    easements 415–16
    estoppel 271
    formality rules 112–14
    freehold covenants 444–5
    freehold estates 288–9
    human rights 579–81
    implied trusts 231–2
    land registration 160–1
    leasehold estates 328–9
    mortgages 373–5
    nuisance 605–6
    options to purchase 460–1
    priority rules 493–4
    registered land 79–80
    trespass 606
Rectification
  meaning and scope of rights 32
  of register
    analysis—title by registration or registration of title 126, 154–5

  availability of indemnities 155–7
  history and development of law in practice 134–54
  outline of system 127–9
  reform proposals 157–9
  statutory provisions 131–4
Redemption of mortgages
  doctrine of clogs and fetters 359–60
Re-entry *see* **Rights of re-entry**
Registered land
  see also **Land registration**
  adverse possession
    'exceptions' in relation to the notification and counter-notice process 177–81
    Land Registry procedure 176–7
    multiple squatters 181
    new statutory rules 174–6
  curtain principle
    curtain drawn against trusts 67–8
    overreaching 68–70
  effect of official searches 480
  effect on general principles of land law 79–80
  history and development of current system 59–60
  insurance principle
    reliance on register and compensation for loss 66–7
  key component of land law 57–9
  Land Registration Act 2002
    modernising agenda 60–1
    underlying purpose 61–4
  mirror principle
    notion of guaranteed title 65–6
    overriding interests 65
    register as accurate reflection of title 64
  priority rules 465–6
  unregistered land compared 79
Registration
  first registration of title *see* **First registration of title**
  land charges
    effects of registration 73
    mandatory registration 71–2
    rights to be registered 72–3

Registration (*cont.*)
  land registration *see* **Land registration**
  mandatory registration *see* **Compulsory registration of title**
  of title *see* **Land registration**
Relativity of title
  freehold estates 280–2
  meaning and scope 52
  underlying rationale 53
Reliance *see* **Detrimental reliance**
Remedies
  contractual licences 37–8
  mortgagee remedies
    action on debt 336–7
    appointment of receiver 355–6
    equitable mortgages 356–8
    foreclosure 337–8
    human rights protection for mortgagors 575–9
    power of sale 350–5
    right to possession 338–50
  nuisance 603–4
  proprietary estoppel
    remedial approach 258–60
    types of remedy 261–2
  trespass
    damages 584–6
    orders for possession 586
Rent
  forfeiture for non-payment procedure 319–21
  relief from forfeiture 321
  not strictly required for valid lease 302
  short leases and their formality requirements 96–7
Rentcharges
  registrable dispositions 121
Repairs
  adverse possession 170
  damages for trespass 586
  flying freeholds 283–4
  freehold covenants 419, 424
  leasehold covenants
    assignment of the benefit of the covenant 312
    'grounds' for possession 324
    personal covenants 316
    residential tenancies 326
    rights of entry 295

mortgagee's remedy 343, 351
rights of entry
  easements 386, 388, 391
  leasehold covenants 295
Restrictions on the register
  limiting trustee powers 503
  prevention of invalid or unlawful dispositions 123–4
Restrictive freehold covenants
  meaning and scope of rights 31
  positive covenants distinguished 418–19
  property rights 31
  recognition of the social effects of rules 15
  registration as land charges 72
  running of burden
    dominant land is benefited by covenant 436
    intended that covenant run with land 437
    requirement for servient and dominant tenement 435
    rule in *Tulk v Moxhay* 435
Resulting trusts
  key issues 220–1
  relationship with constructive trusts 219–20
  underlying rationale 221–2
  when they arise
    failed trusts 228
    purchase money resulting trusts 223–6
    voluntary conveyance resulting trusts 227
    where preferred to constructive trust 212–14, 215–16
Reversionary interests
  essential right of freeholder 278–9
  position of freeholder in practice 327–8
Rights of pre-emption
  meaning and scope of rights 32
  nature of rights 458–9
Rights of re-entry
  forfeiture of leases procedure 319–21
  relief from forfeiture 321

freehold estates 278–9
registrable dispositions 121
Right to private life (art.8)
  'bolstering' of right to property 550–1
  co-ownership 529
  mortgages 348
  periodic tenancies 307
  repossession actions
    by mortgagees 575–9
    by private landowners 573–4
    by public authorities 560–73
    against trespassers 574–5
Right to property (art 1, protocol 1)
  adverse possession 187
  'bolstering' of right to property 549–50
  periodic tenancies 307
  repossession actions
    by mortgagees 575–9
    by private landowners 573–4
    by public authorities 560–73
    against trespassers 574–5
  source of conflict 551
Rylands v Fletcher 604
  see also **Nuisance**

S

Sales *see* **Transfer of rights and interests**
Sensitivity to context
  conflict with certainty 11
  general principle of land law 9–11
  relevance in shaping decisions 54–5
  relevance to specific aspects of land law
    adverse possession 189–90
    co-ownership 541–4
    easements 415–16
    estoppel 271
    formality rules 112–14
    freehold covenants 444–5
    freehold estates 288–9
    human rights 579–81
    implied trusts 231–2
    land registration 160–1
    leasehold estates 328–9
    mortgages 373–5

nuisance 605–6
options to purchase 460–1
priority rules 493–4
registered land 79–80
trespass 606
Servient tenement
easements
changes of use 405–9
easement must 'accommodate' the dominant tenement 380–3
essential requirement 379
separate ownership 379–80
freehold covenants 418–20
running of burden of restrictive covenants
requirement for servient and dominant tenement 435
Setting aside of transactions 23, 55
Severance of joint tenancies
by creation of an implied trust 515–16
by mutual agreement 511–13
by mutual conduct 514–15
by unilateral action in relation to a 'share' 510–11
by written notice
Short leases
formality rules 95–8
priority rules 466–7
Signatures
contracts 93
deeds 108
Social housing
impact of human rights on repossessions
new approach 563–72
quasi-public authorities 573
traditional approach 561–3
priority rules for leases 467–8
Statutory charges 72
Sub-leases 327
Subrogation of mortgages 369–70
Surrender of leases 321–2
Systematic and individual effects
general principle of land law 13–14
relevance in shaping decisions 54–5

relevance to specific aspects of land law
adverse possession 189–90
co-ownership 541–4
easements 415–16
estoppel 271
formality rules 112–14
freehold covenants 444–5
freehold estates 288–9
human rights 579–81
implied trusts 231–2
land registration 160–1
leasehold estates 328–9
mortgages 373–5
nuisance 605–6
options to purchase 460–1
priority rules 493–4
registered land 79–80
trespass 606

T
Tenancies
passing of the benefit of freehold covenants 433
periodic tenancies 305–7
at will 307–8
Tenancies in common
creation 192–3
effect of severing joint tenancies 507
equitable rights and interests 506
Termination of rights and interests
easements
extinction 410
loss of priority 410
leasehold estates
by effluxion of time 318–19
forfeiture 319–21
by notice 321
by surrender 321–2
Term of lease
essential elements 299–301
termination by effluxion of time 318–19
Third parties
adverse possession by tenant against 183
conflict with mortgage rights
multiple mortgages 368–9
priority disputes between mortgagees and purchasers 373

priority disputes between mortgagees and tenants 372–3
subrogation 369–70
trust interests 370–2
co-ownership disputes
overreaching 532–41
two sets of rules 531
effect of contractual licences 37–41
effect of estoppel
burden of an estoppel 262–4
effect of option to purchase 457
effect of property rights
defining characteristic 42–5
effect of rights of pre-emption 459
equities arising by estoppel
benefit of estoppel 264–5
nature of property rights 26–9
unregistered land - purchasers for value without notice
doctrine of notice 74–8
freedom from equitable rights and interests 73
'Torrens' system of land registration 63–4, 80
Torts
care in making land registry applications 158
interference with contract 43
nuisance
categorisation 591–7
defences 602–3
easements to create a nuisance 387–8
irrelevance of planning permissions 598–600
locality principle 597–8
recognition of the social effects of rules 15
remedies 603–4
standing to sue 600–2
underlying role 587–91
use of land 51
who can be sued 602
Rylands v Fletcher 604
trespass
bare licences as defence 34–6
criminal sanctions against adverse possession 184–5

Torts (*cont.*)
- defences 584
- defined 583
- geographical scope of land 276–7
- impact of human rights 548–52, 557–8, 566, 574–5
- licences coupled with an interest 42–4
- mere physical presence 583
- remedies 584–7
- standing to sue 583–4

Touching and concerning land
- freehold covenants 419, 428–32, 436, 444
- leasehold covenants 312, 316

Town and country planning
- binding effect of conditions 71
- irrelevance to nuisance 598–600, 602, 603
- limitations on freehold use 275, 288
- mortgagee sales 353
- proprietary estoppel 238–40
- recognition of the social effects of rules 15
- relevance of general principles 55

Transactability
- general principle of land law 11–13
- relevance in shaping decisions 54–5
- relevance to specific aspects of land law
  - adverse possession 189–90
  - co-ownership 541–4
  - easements 415–16
  - estoppel 271
  - formality rules 112–14
  - freehold covenants 444–5
  - freehold estates 288–9
  - human rights 579–81
  - implied trusts 231–2
  - land registration 160–1
  - leasehold estates 328–9
  - mortgages 373–5
  - nuisance 605–6
  - options to purchase 460–1
  - priority rules 493–4
  - registered land 79–80
  - trespass 606

Transfer of rights and interests
see also **Contracts**
- effect of dispositions on the benefit and burden of easements
  - express equitable easements 412–13
  - express legal easements 410
  - implied equitable easements 414
  - implied legal easements 411–12
- estate contracts *see* **Estate contracts**
- formality rules
  - dispositions of equitable interests 112
  - requirements for a deed 109
  - sales or dispositions 89–90
- freehold covenants
  - enforceability between original parties 422–7
  - enforceability by successors in title 427–32
- freehold estates 282–3
- implied easements under s.62 LPA 1925 400–1, 402
  - 'continuous and apparent' requirement 401–3
  - prior diversity of occupation 400–1
  - underlying rationale 399–400
- mandatory first registration of title 117–18
- mortgagee's power of sale
  - advantages 350
  - equitable mortgages 356–7
  - mortgagee's duties 351–4
  - mortgagor's remedies for breach of mortgagee's duty 354–5
  - statutory provisions 350–1
- options to purchase *see* **Options to purchase**
- purchase of land subject to existing mortgages 372–3
- registrable dispositions
  - categories of notice 122–3
  - effect of registration - estates and charges 120–1
  - effect of registration - interests protected by notice 120–1
  - interests cannot be entered as the subject of a notice 121–2
  - relevant dispositions 120–1
- rights of pre-emption *see* **Rights of pre-emption**
- transactability 12

Trespass
- bare licences as defence 34–6
- criminal sanctions against adverse possession 184–5
- defences 584
- effect on general principles of land law 606
- geographical scope of land 276–7
- impact of human rights
  - 'bolstering' of right to property 548–51
  - mechanisms by which rights operate 557
  - problem of horizontal effect 557
  - repossession actions by public authorities 566
  - simple possession actions 574–5
  - source of conflict 552
- licences coupled with an interest 42–4
- mere physical presence 583
- remedies
  - damages 584–6
  - orders for possession 586
- standing to sue 583–4

Trusts
- conflict with mortgage rights 370–2
- curtain principle 67–8
- formality rules
  - dispositions of equitable interests 112
- express trusts 192–3
- implied trusts
  - constructive trusts 195–221
  - definitions 232
  - focus on market rather than people 230

reform proposals 228–30
resulting trusts 220–8
severance of joint tenancies 515–16
statutory trusts 194–5
types of trust *f.*193
Trusts of land
creation 500–1
dispute resolution under s14 TOLATA 1996
 circumstances involving bankruptcy 528–9
 discretionary powers of court 517–20
 disputes regarding occupation 529–31
 relevant factors 521–8
 standing to make application 520–1
 statutory provisions 517
meaning and scope of rights 32–3
nature of interests arising 497–500
restrictions on the register 503
rights and powers of trustees 501–3

U

Unconscionability
assurance-based estoppel 252–7
'double assurance' 254–6
defined 272
Undue influence
co-ownership 524, 539, 541

mortgages
 affect on lender 367–8
 two-strand test for the presence of undue influence 365–6
 setting aside of transactions 469
trusts 193, 215
void and voidable transactions 150
Unregistered land
adverse possession
 'adverse' 170–1
 consequences for title-holder 172
 continuity of possession 170
 enclosure 169–70
 factual possession 165–7
 intention to possess 168–9
 multiple squatters 172–4
 'possession' 163–4
 four fundamental elements 70–1
land charges
 effects of registration 73
 mandatory registration 71–2
 rights to be registered 72–3
legal rights
 binding legal interests 70–1
new first mortgages 334
problems of proof
 adverse possession 78
 requirement for 15-year title 78

purchasers for value without notice
 doctrine of notice 74–8
 freedom from equitable rights and interests 73
 registered land compared 79
Use of land
easements
 changes of use 405–9
 reasonable user 392–4
freehold estates 275–6
incorporeal dimension of land 51–2
nuisance
 direct damage 592
 encroachment 591–2
 interference with comfort and enjoyment 592–5
 unreasonableness and foreseeability 596–7
reasonable user
 easements 392–4
 profits à prendre 393–4
 role of freehold covenants 417–18

V

Variation of contracts 104–5
Voluntary conveyance resulting trusts
meaning and scope 227

W

***Walsh v Lonsdale*, rule in** 447
***Wheeldon v Burrows*, rule in** 403–4
Written requirements
contracts 91
deeds 107–8